D1826153

DICTIONARY *of*
LUTHER
and the Lutheran Traditions

DICTIONARY *of*
LUTHER
and the Lutheran Traditions

Timothy J. Wengert
GENERAL EDITOR

Mark A. Granquist, Mary Jane Haemig,
Robert Kolb, Mark C. Mattes, and Jonathan Strom
ASSOCIATE EDITORS

Baker Academic
a division of Baker Publishing Group
Grand Rapids, Michigan

© 2017 by Baker Publishing Group

Published by Baker Academic
a division of Baker Publishing Group
P.O. Box 6287, Grand Rapids, MI 49516-6287
www.bakeracademic.com

Printed in the United States of America

All rights reserved. No part of this publication may be reproduced, stored in a retrieval system, or transmitted in any form or by any means—for example, electronic, photocopy, recording—without the prior written permission of the publisher. The only exception is brief quotations in printed reviews.

Library of Congress Cataloging-in-Publication Data
Names: Wengert, Timothy J., editor.
Title: Dictionary of Luther and the Lutheran traditions / Timothy J. Wengert, general editor ; Mark A. Granquist, Mary Jane Haemig, Robert Kolb, Mark C. Mattes, and Jonathan Strom, associate editors.
Description: Grand Rapids, MI : Baker Academic, 2017. | Includes bibliographical references and indexes.
Identifiers: LCCN 2016058819 | ISBN 9780801049699 (cloth)
Subjects: LCSH: Lutheran Church—Dictionaries. | Luther, Martin, 1483–1546—Dictionaries.
Classification: LCC BX8007 .D53 2017 | DDC 284.103—dc23
LC record available at https://lccn.loc.gov/2016058819

Cover Art: Philip Melanchthon, Martin Luther, Johannes Bugenhagen, and Caspar Cruciger Sr. translating the Bible in 1532. English lithograph by Willian Henry Simmons (1811–82) after a painting by Pierre Antoine Labouchere (1807–73). See Gerhard Schwinge, *Melanchthon in der Druckgraphik* (Ubstadt-Weiher: Verlag Regionalkultur, 2000), 108.

Unless otherwise indicated, Scripture quotations are from the New Revised Standard Version of the Bible, copyright © 1989, by the Division of Christian Education of the National Council of the Churches of Christ in the United States of America. Used by permission. All rights reserved.

Scripture quotations labeled NIV are from the Holy Bible, New International Version®. NIV®. Copyright © 1973, 1978, 1984, 2011 by Biblica, Inc.™ Used by permission of Zondervan. All rights reserved worldwide. www.zondervan.com

17 18 19 20 21 22 23   7 6 5 4 3 2 1

In keeping with biblical principles of creation stewardship, Baker Publishing Group advocates the responsible use of our natural resources. As a member of the Green Press Initiative, our company uses recycled paper when possible. The text paper of this book is composed in part of post-consumer waste.

green press INITIATIVE

Contents

Contributors

Albers, James W. ThD, Concordia Seminary, St. Louis. Professor Emeritus of Theology, Valparaiso University. **American Lutheranism Controversy; Fritschel, Sigmund and Gottfried; Lutheran Social Services; Sieveking, Amalie Wilhelmina**

Albertsen, Andrés Roberto. PhD candidate, Luther Seminary, St. Paul. **Argentina; Bolivia; Chile; Colombia; Ecuador; Peru**

Albrecht, Ruth. DHabil, University of Hamburg. Professor, University of Hamburg. **Petersen, Johanna Eleonora; Petersen, Johann Wilhelm**

Alfsvåg, Knut. DTheol, Asian Graduate School of Theology, Kobe, Japan. Professor, School of Missions and Theology, Stavanger, Norway. **God and Trinity**

Anderson, Mary E. PhD, Luther Seminary, St. Paul. Integrated Learning Librarian, Central College. **Lundensian School**

Appold, Kenneth G. PhD, Yale University. Professor, Princeton Theological Seminary. **Lutheran Orthodoxy**

Arand, Charles P. ThD, Concordia Seminary, St. Louis. Professor, Concordia Seminary, St. Louis. **Creeds, Ecumenical; Ecology**

Atwood, Craig D. PhD, Princeton Theological Seminary. Associate Professor, Moravian Theological Seminary. **Moravian Church (Unitas Fratrum); Spangenberg, August Gottlieb; Zinzendorf, Nikolaus Ludwig von**

Austad, Torleiv. DTheol, University of Oslo. Professor, Norwegian School of Theology. **Norway**

Bacon, Paul M. PhD, University of Wisconsin, Madison. Lecturer, Dominican University. **Art; Cranach, Lucas, the Elder; Cranach, Lucas, the Younger; Holbein, Hans (the Younger)**

Baer, H. David. PhD, University of Notre Dame. Professor, Texas Lutheran University. **Just-War Theory; Ordass, Lajos**

Baglyos, Paul A. PhD, University of Chicago. Coordinator for Missional Leadership, Region 3, ELCA. **American Lutheran Church (1930–60); Reu, Johann Michael**

Barnett, Victoria J. PhD, George Mason University. Director, Program on Ethics, Religion, and the Holocaust, United States Holocaust Museum. **Altona Confession; Ansbach Memorandum (Ansbacher Ratschlag); Barmen Confession; Confessing Church; German Christians (Deutsche Christen)**

Becker, Matthew L. PhD, University of Chicago. Associate Professor, Valparaiso University. **Bonhoeffer, Dietrich; Elert, Werner; Erlangen; Harnack, Theodosius Andreas; Hoffmann, Johannes Christian Konrad von; Pelikan, Jaroslav; Piepkorn, Arthur Carl; Preus, Jacob; Schlink, Edmund; Troeltsch, Ernst**

Benne, Robert. PhD, University of Chicago. Professor Emeritus, Roanoke College. **Economic Issues: Capitalism and Socialism; Economic Life and Lutheranism; Priesthood of All Believers; State**

Bielfeldt, Dennis. PhD, University of Iowa. President, Institute for Lutheran Theology. **Theological Prolegomena**

Blank, Rudolph. Missionary to Venezuela, retired. **Venezuela**

Bode, Gerhard. PhD, Concordia Seminary, St. Louis. Associate Professor, Concordia Seminary, St. Louis. **Chytraeus, David; Eber, Paul; Mörlin, Joachim; Pfeffinger, Johann; Selnecker, Nikolaus; Strigel, Viktorin; Synergistic Controversy; Westphal, Joachim; Wigand, Johann**

Braaten, Carl E. ThD, Harvard University. Professor Emeritus, Lutheran School of Theology at Chicago. **Tillich, Paul J.**

Braun, Mark E. PhD, Concordia Seminary, St. Louis. Professor, Wisconsin Lutheran College. **Wisconsin Evangelical Lutheran Synod**

Brosseder, Claudia R. DHabil, Munich University. Professor, Heidelberg University. **Astrology**

Brown, Christopher Boyd. PhD, Harvard University. Professor, Boston University School of Theology. **Gerhardt, Paul; Household, Children, Parents**

Buggeln, Gretchen T. PhD, Yale University. Associate Professor, Valparaiso University. **Architecture**

Burnett, Amy Nelson. PhD, University of Wisconsin, Madison. Professor, University of Nebraska, Lincoln. **Bucer, Martin; Karlstadt, Andreas Bodenstein von; Oecolampadius, Johannes; Strasbourg; Switzerland; Wittenberg Unrest; Zwingli, Ulrich**

Burnett, Stephen G. PhD, University of Wisconsin, Madison. Professor, University of Nebraska, Lincoln. **Jews; Reuchlin, Johannes**

Burreson, Kent J. PhD, University of Notre Dame. Associate Professor, Concordia Seminary, St. Louis. **Lectionary**

Buss, Paulo Wille. ThD, Concordia Seminary, St. Louis. Professor, Seminário Concórdia/Universidade Luterana Do Brasil. **Brakemeier, Gottfried; Brazil; Dohms, Hermann Gottlieb; Igreja Evangélica de Confissão Luterana no Brasil (IECLB) (Evangelical Church of the Lutheran Confession in Brazil); Igreja Evangélica Luterana do Brasil (IELB) (Evangelical Lutheran Church of Brazil); Kuhr, Karl Otto; Mahler, Carl Wilhelm Gustav; Rotermund, Wilhelm; Schlieper, Ernesto Theophilo; Universidade Luterana do Brasil (ULBRA)**

Carlsson, Eric. PhD, University of Wisconsin, Madison. Lecturer, University of Wisconsin, Madison. **Eighteenth Century; Enlightenment; Mosheim, Johann Lorenz von; Rationalism; Semler, Johann Salomo**

Christman, Robert J. PhD, University of Arizona. Associate Professor, Luther College, Decorah, Iowa. **Papacy**

Christudas, Damodher. PhD, Gurukul Lutheran Theological College, Chennai. Professor, Concordia Theological Seminary, Nagercoil, India. **Kumari Samuel, Prasanna**

Cook, Timios. PhD candidate, Concordia Seminary. **Mecklenburg**

Cummings, Orin W. PhD, Luther Seminary, St. Paul. Pastor, Blue Ridge Trinity Evangelical Lutheran Church, Raytown, Missouri. **El Salvador; Guatemala; Honduras; Mexico; Nicaragua**

Daniel, David P. PhD, Pennsylvania State University. Dozent of Church History Emeritus, Jan Comenius University, Bratislava. **Hurban, Jozef Miloslav; Krman, Daniel, Jr.; Kuzmány, Karol; Slovak Confessions of the Faith; Slovakia; Stöckel, Leonard**

Daniels, Paul A. MA, Luther Seminary, St. Paul. Head of Arts and Archives, Luther Seminary, St. Paul. **Kurds**

Daugirdas, Kęstutis. DTheol habil, University of Tübingen. Privat Dozent, University of Tübingen; Research Fellow, Leibnitz–Institute for European History, Mainz. **Antitrinitarians; Campanus, Johannes; Servetus, Michael**

Deffenbaugh, Ralston. JD, Harvard Law School. Assistant General Secretary for International Affairs and Human Rights, Lutheran World Federation. **Refugees**

DeMeuse, Eric J. PhD candidate, Marquette University. **Cajetan (Thomaso de Vio); Cochlaeus, Johannes; Eck, John; Emser, Jerome; Luther's Roman Catholic Opponents; Prierias, Sylvester; Tetzel, Johann**

Eom, Jin-Seop. ThD, Luther Seminary, St. Paul. Associate Professor, Luther University/Seminary, Korea. **Ji Brothers; Korea**

Erling, Maria. ThD, Harvard University. Professor, Lutheran Theological Seminary, Gettysburg. **Aulén, Gustaf; Knubel, Frederick Hermann; Nygren, Anders; Pentecostal/Charismatic Christianity; Söderblom, Nathan; Wingren, Gustaf**

Erwin, R. Guy. PhD, Yale University. Bishop, Southwest California Synod, ELCA. **Wittenberg, City of**

Estes, James M. PhD, Ohio State University. Professor Emeritus, University of Toronto. **Brenz, Johannes; Erasmus of Rotterdam (Desiderius Erasmus Roterodamus); Württemberg**

Gehrt, Daniel. DPhil, Friedrich-Schiller University, Jena. Gotha Research Library. **Electors of Saxony; Georg, Duke of Saxony; Saxonies**

Gordon, Bruce. PhD, University of St. Andrews. Professor, Yale University. **Bullinger, Heinrich; Zurich**

Granquist, Mark A. PhD, University of Chicago. Associate Professor, Luther Seminary, St. Paul. **Augustana Synod; Evangelical Lutheran Church in America; Finnish-American Lutheranism; Giertz, Bo Harald; Kingo, Thomas Hansen; Laestadius, Lars Levi; Lutheran Denominations in America, Minor; Marty, Martin Emil; Migration; Passavant, William Alfred; Paulssen, Bertha; Petri (Nericus), Laurentius; Petri, Olavus; Predestination (Election) Controversy; Rudbeckius, Johannes; Seminex and the Association of Evangelical Lutheran Churches; Sunday and Sabbatarianism; Sweden; Temperance and Prohibition; Theological Education; Tolstadius, Erik; United States of America; Walther, Carl Ferdinand Wilhelm**

Grindal, Gracia. MFA, University of Arkansas. Professor Emeritus, Luther Seminary, St. Paul. **Hauge, Hans Nielson; Hymnody; Literature; Rosenius, Carl Olof; Sandell-Berg, Karolina Wilhelmina (Lina); Wallin, Johan Olof**

Grundmann, Christoffer H. DHabil, University of Hamburg. Professor, Valparaiso University. **Bultmann, Rudolf (Karl)**

Haemig, Mary Jane. ThD, Harvard University. Professor, Luther Seminary, St. Paul. **Catechisms; Corvinus, Antonius; Cruciger, Elisabeth; Franconia; Prayer**

Hafermann, Herbert J. STM, Wartburg Seminary. Pastor and Missionary, retired. **Greiner, Johann Jakob; Morogoro, Lutheran Junior Seminary; Moshi, Stefano Ruben; Reusch, Richard Gustavovich; Tanzania**

Haga, Joar. PhD, Norwegian Lutheran School of Theology. Assistant Professor, NLA University College. **Natural Theology**

Hall, H. Ashley. PhD, Fordham University. Associate Professor, Creighton University. **Catholicism**

Halvorson, Michael J. PhD, University of Washington. Associate Professor, Pacific Lutheran University. **Charles V; Georg, Margrave of Brandenburg-Asbach; Hesshus, Tilemann (Heshusens, Heshusius); Holy Roman Empire; Icono-**clasm; **Joachim II Hector; Peace of Augsburg; Philip of Hesse; Smalcald War; Thirty Years' War; Vasa, Gustav**

Harrisville, Roy A. ThD, Princeton Seminary. Professor Emeritus, Luther Seminary, St. Paul. **Adiaphora; Apocrypha and Pseudepigrapha; Baur, Ferdinand Christian; Bible Interpretation; Gospels; Harnack, Adolf von; Hell; Wellhausen, Julius**

Heen, Erik M. PhD, Columbia University. Professor, Lutheran Theological Seminary, Philadelphia. **Canon; Paul; Scripture; Word of God**

Heininen, Simo. DTheol, University of Helsinki. Professor Emeritus, University of Helsinki. **Finland; Seamen's Missions**

Heise, Matthew. PhD candidate, Concordia Seminary. Executive Director, Lutheran Heritage Foundation. **Dieckhoff, Heinrich Wilhelm; Gregorius, Johann Gottfried; Kalnins, Harald; Kretschmar, Georg; Meier, Theophil; Muss, Kurt; Russia**

Hequet, Suzanne S. PhD, Luther Seminary, St. Paul. Term Professor, Concordia University, St. Paul. **Regensburg Colloquy**

Herrmann, Erik. PhD, Concordia Seminary, St. Louis. Associate Professor, Concordia Seminary, St. Louis. **Augustine of Hippo; Humanism and the Reformation; Lord's Supper**

Hiebsch, Sabine. DPhil, University of Amsterdam. Professor, VU University Amsterdam. **Netherlands, The**

Hinlicky, Paul R. PhD, Union Seminary, New York. Professor, Roanoke College. **Anthropology; Exorcism; Kant, Immanuel; Leibniz, Gottfried Wilhelm; Prophecy**

Hoffmeyer, John F. PhD, Boston College. Associate Professor, Lutheran Theological Seminary, Philadelphia. **Hegel, Georg Wilhelm Friedrich**

Holm, Bo Kristian. PhD, Aarhus University. Associate Professor, Aarhus University. **Beck, Vilhelm; Grundtvig, Nikolai Frederik Severin; Munk, Kaj**

Hopman, Nicholas. MDiv, Luther Seminary, St. Paul. Pastor, Peace Lutheran Church, Nevis, Minnesota. **Atonement; Free Will**

Huggins, Marvin A. MDiv, Concordia Seminary, St. Louis. Associate Director (retired), Concordia Historical Institute. **Lutheran Church–Missouri Synod; Pieper, Francis**

Humann, Joel. PhD, University of Durham. Preceptor, Westfield House, Cambridge. **England**

Hunsinger, George. PhD, Yale University. Professor, Princeton Seminary. **Barth, Karl**

Ilić, Luka. PhD, Lutheran Theological Seminary, Philadelphia. Pastor, Evangelical-Lutheran Church in Württemberg. **Balkan Lands; Flacius, Matthias Illyricus, and the Flacians; Schwenckfeld, Caspar von**

Jacobson, Kevin L. MDiv, Luther Seminary, St. Paul. Pastor and Missionary, Evangelical Lutheran Church in Suriname. **Suriname**

Jaynes, Jeffrey. PhD, Ohio State University. Professor, Methodist Theological School in Ohio. **Church Law; *Kirchenordnungen*; Palatinate, The**

Jensen, Gordon A. PhD, University of St. Michael's College, Toronto. Professor, Lutheran Theological Seminary, Saskatoon. **Augsburg Confession; Baptism; Colloquy; Marburg Colloquy; Wittenberg Concord**

Jetter-Staib, Christina. PhD, University of Tübingen. Catholic Deanery of Göppingen-Geislingen. **Ziegenhagen, Friedrich Michael**

Jeyaraj, Daniel. DHabil, University of Halle. Professor, Liverpool Hope University. **Ziegenbalg, Bartholomäus**

Jodock, Darrell. PhD, Yale University. Professor Emeritus, Gustavus Adolphus College. **Holocaust; Imperialism; Ritchl, Albrecht; Tumsa, Gudina**

Johnson, Anna Marie. PhD, Princeton Seminary. Assistant Professor, Garrett-Evangelical Theological Seminary. **Jonas, Justus; Myconius, Friedrich; Rhegius, Urbanus; Spalatin, Georg**

Johnson, Kathryn L. PhD, Yale University. Director of Ecumenical and Inter-Religious Relations, Evangelical Lutheran Church of America. **Lutheran World Federation**

Johnson, Richard O. PhD, Graduate Theological Union. Affiliated Associate Professor, Fuller Theological Seminary. **American Lutheran Church** (1960–88); **Berggrav, Eivind; Boe, Paul A.; Fliedner, Theodore; General Council of the Evangelical Lutheran Church in North America; Krauth, Charles Porterfield; Lenski, Gerhard Emmanuel; Lenski, Richard Charles Henry; Lutheran Council in the United States of America; Ohio/Buffalo/Iowa Synods; Schmucker, Samuel Simon; Tappert, Theodore Gerhardt; United Lutheran Church in America; World Wars I and II; Youth Work**

Jones, Ken Sundet. PhD, Luther Seminary, St. Paul. Professor, Grand View University. **Death and Dying**

Jürgens, Henning P. PhD, University of Göttingen. Senior Research Fellow, Leibniz–Institute for European History, Mainz. **Printing in Sixteenth-Century Lutheranism**

Kääriäinen, Jukka A. PhD, Fordham University. Professor, China Lutheran Seminary, Taiwan. **Taiwan; Yu, Thomas (Yu Qi-bing)**

Kalme, Guntis. PhD, Concordia Seminary, St. Louis. Instructor, Luther Academy, Riga. **Courland (Kurland); Feldmanis, Roberts Emīls; Grīnbergs, Teodors; Irbe, Kārlis; Latvia; Livonia; Rumba, Edgars; Turss, Gustavs (Tūrs)**

Kilcrease, Jack D. PhD, Marquette University. Adjunct Professor, Institute of Lutheran Theology. **Mystical Union**

Kjeldgaard-Pedersen, Steffen. DTheol, University of Copenhagen. Professor, University of Copenhagen. **Luther Congresses**

Klän, Werner. DTheol habil, University of Münster. Professor of Systematic Theology, Lutherische Theologische Hochschule, Oberursel. **Apartheid**

Kleckley, Russell C. DTheol, University of Munich. Associate Professor, Augsburg College. **Boltzius, Johann Martin; Ebenezer Community**

Klotz, D. Jerome. MDiv, Luther Seminary, St. Paul, Minnesota. Pastor, St. Timothy Lutheran Church, Charleston, West Virginia. **Predestination**

Koch, Paul. MDiv, Luther Seminary, St. Paul, Minnesota. Pastor, St. John's Lutheran Church, Howard Lake, Minnesota. **Sanctification**

Kolb, Robert. PhD, University of Wisconsin, Madison. Professor Emeritus, Concordia Seminary,

St. Louis. **Albrecht of Mainz; Amsdorf, Niko-laus von; Andreae, Jakob; Augsburg Interim; Augustinianism; Austria; Book of Concord; Chemnitz, Martin; Cologne; Confessionaliza-tion, Confessional Age; Confession of Faith; Dannhauer, Johann Konrad; Estonia; Exile; For-mula of Concord; Hermann, Nikolaus; Leipzig Proposal (Interim); Luther Interpretation and Reception; Luther's Works; Magdeburg; Mathe-sius, Johannes; Mau, Carl Henning, Jr.; Mission and Evangelism; Mömpelgaard/Montbéliard Colloquy; Musculus, Andreas; Namibia; Noko, Ishmael; Peucer, Caspar; Quenstedt, Johann An-dreas; Reformation and Luther Jubilees, Anni-versaries; Spangenberg, Johann and Cyriacus; Staupitz, Johann von;** *Treatise on the Power and Primacy of the Pope;* **Twofold Righteousness; Two Realms; Wittenberg Circle; Wittenberg Circle, Parties within**

Korcok, Thomas. PhD, Free University, Amsterdam. Associate Professor, Concordia University, Chi-cago. **Lutheran Education**

Krentz, Michael E. DMusic, Northwestern Uni-versity. Director of Music Ministries, Lutheran Theological Seminary, Philadelphia. **Crüger, Johann; Praetorius, Michael; Rinckart, Martin**

Krēsliņš, Jānis. DD, University of Stockholm. Se-nior Academic Librarian for Research Affairs, National Library of Sweden, Stockholm, Sweden. **Glück, Johann Ernst; Mancelius, Georgius**

Krey, Philip D. PhD, University of Chicago. Profes-sor Emeritus, Lutheran Theological Seminary, Philadelphia. **Nicholas of Lyra**

Krueger, Karl. PhD, University of Michigan. Profes-sor and Library Director, Lutheran Theological Seminary, Philadelphia. **Bible Translations; Müh-lenberg, Heinrich (Henry) Melchior**

Kühnel, Martin. PhD, University of Halle. Lecturer, University of Halle. **Pufendorf, Samuel; Thoma-sius, Christian**

Lagerquist, L. DeAne. PhD, University of Chicago. Professor, St. Olaf College. **Danish-American Lutheranism; Fedde, Elizabeth Tonette; Kugler, Anna Sarah; Norwegian-American Lutheranism; Women's Movement**

Lange, Dirk G. PhD, Emory University. Associate Professor, Luther Seminary, St. Paul. **Liturgy and Worship; Monasteries, Evangelical**

Leroux, Neil. PhD, University of Illinois, Cham-paign-Urbana. Professor Emeritus, University of Minnesota, Morris. **Rhetoric**

Limthongviratn, Pongsak. Program Director, Asian and Pacific Islander Ministries for the ELCA. **Thailand**

Lindberg, Carter. PhD, University of Iowa. Profes-sor Emeritus, Boston University. **Luther, Martin; Luther's Breakthrough; Orphanages; Salvation; Social Ministry, Community Chest, Poor Relief**

Lohrmann, Martin J. PhD, Lutheran Theological Seminary, Philadelphia. Assistant Professor, Wartburg Seminary. **Bugenhagen, Johannes; Prussian Union**

Ludwig, Frieder. DHabil, Ludwig-Maximilians Universität–Munich. Professor, Fachhochschule for Intercultural Theology, Hermannsburg. **An-gola; Botswana; Congo, Democratic Republic of the; Desta, Kentiba Gebru (Gobaw); Dlamini, Paulina; Eritrea; Ethiopia; Fathme, Pauline; Ghana; Jammo, Daffa; Liberia; Malawi; Mission Societies and Academies; Mozambique; Nesib, Onesimos; Nigeria; Sewushane, Martinus; Sierra Leone; Slavery and Colonialism; South Africa; Tikhuie, Vehettge Lena; Zambia; Zimbabwe**

Lund, Eric. PhD, Yale University. Professor Emeri-tus, St. Olaf College. **Arndt, Johann; Calov, Abraham; Denmark; Devotional Literature; Hemmingsen, Niels; Iceland; Nicolai, Philipp; Tausen, Hans**

Maag, Karin. PhD, University of St. Andrews. Pro-fessor, Calvin College. **Geneva**

Maas, Korey D. DPhil, University of Oxford. As-sistant Professor, Hillsdale College. **Alesius, Alexander; Barnes, Robert; Cranmer, Thomas; Elizabeth I; England; Hamilton, Patrick; Henry VIII; Tyndale, William; Wyclif, John**

MacDonald, Gerald. ThD, University of Marburg. Independent scholar. **Walch, Johann Georg**

Mäkinen, Virpi. DTheol, University of Helsinki. Professor, University of Helsinki. **Jurisprudence**

Malcolm, Lois. PhD, University of Chicago. Professor, Luther Seminary, St. Paul. **Holy Spirit**

Manetsch, Scott M. PhD, University of Arizona. Professor, Trinity Evangelical Divinity School. **Beza, Theodore; Calvin, John; Musculus, Wolfgang**

Martinson, Paul Varo. PhD, University of Chicago. Professor Emeritus, Luther Seminary, St. Paul. **China**

Masaki, Makito. PhD, Concordia Seminary, St. Louis. President, Kobe Lutheran Seminary, Kobe. **Japan; Kitamori, Kazoh; Nabetani, Gyoji; Tokuzen, Kazuyoshi**

Maschke, Timothy. PhD, Marquette University. Professor, Concordia University, Wisconsin. **Luther's Bible**

Mattes, Mark C. PhD, University of Chicago. Professor, Grand View University. **Bayer, Oswald; Braaten, Carl; Forde, Gerhard; Hamann, Johann Georg; Justification; Lindbeck, George; Philosophy; Theology of the Cross**

Matthews, Rex D. ThD, Harvard University. Professor, Emory University. **Methodism; Wesley, John and Charles**

Maxfield, John A. PhD, Princeton Seminary. Associate Professor, Concordia University, College of Alberta. **Good Works; History; University of Wittenberg in the Sixteenth Century**

Mayes, Benjamin T. G. PhD, Calvin Seminary. Associate Professor of Church History, Concordia Theological Seminary, Fort Wayne. **Calixt, Georg; Gerhard, Johann; Patristics**

McArver, Susan Wilds. PhD, Duke University. Professor, Lutheran Theological Southern Seminary. **American Civil War; General Synod South; Jacobs, Henry Eyster**

McMullen, Dianne M. PhD, University of Michigan. Professor, Union College. **Freylinghausen, Johann Anastasius; Telemann, Georg Philipp**

Mejrup, Kristian. DPhil, University of Copenhagen. Postdoctoral Fellow, University of Copenhagen. **Holberg, Ludvig; Pontoppidan, Erik Ludvigsen**

Menacher, Mark D. PhD, University of Manchester. Senior Pastor, St. Luke's Lutheran Church, Costa Mesa, California. **Ebeling, Gerhard; Independent Lutheran Organizations; Inner-Lutheran Ecumenism; Ministry**

Meshack, Samuel W. PhD, University of Leicester. Director, Hindustan Bible Institute and College. **Aaron, S.; Manikam, Rajah Bushanam; Rajaratnam, Kunchala**

Miller, Gregory. PhD, Boston University. Professor, Malone University. **Islam**

Morton, Peter A. PhD, University of Western Ontario. Professor, Mount Royal University. **Witchcraft and Magic**

Müller-Bahlke, Thomas. DPhil, Georg-August-University, Göttingen. Director, Francke Foundations, Halle. **Francke Foundations**

Nafzger, Samuel H. ThD, Harvard University. Director Emeritus, Commission on Theology and Church Relations, LCMS. **International Lutheran Council**

Nelson, R. David. PhD, University of Aberdeen. Acquisitions Editor, Baker Academic and Brazos Press. **Jenson, Robert W.; Jüngel, Eberhard; Pannenberg, Wolfhart**

Nygard, Mark. PhD, Luther Seminary. Pastor, Bowman Lutheran Church, Bowman, North Dakota. **Cameroon; Darman, Paul; Gunderson, Adolphus; Middle East; Sudan Mission**

Olson, Jeannine. PhD, Stanford University. Professor, Rhode Island College. **France**

Omolo, Joseph T. PhD, Concordia Seminary, St. Louis. Professor, Neema Lutheran College, Matongo. **Kenya**

Orde, Klaus vom. DTheol, Phillips-University of Marburg. Senior Researcher, Spener-Forschungsstelle, Leipzig. **Spener, Philipp Jakob**

Panchu, Olav. PhD candidate, Concordia Seminary, St. Louis. Pastor in Saratov and assistant to the bishop, Evangelical Lutheran Church of Ingria. **Kugappi, Aari; Volga Germans**

Paulson, Steven D. PhD, Lutheran School of Theology at Chicago. Professor, Luther Seminary, St. Paul. **Atonement; Christology; Free Will; Law and Gospel; Predestination; Sanctification**

Persaud, Winston D. PhD, University of St. Andrews. Professor, Wartburg Seminary. **Guyana**

Peters, Ted. PhD, University of Chicago. Professor Emeritus, Pacific Lutheran Theological Seminary. **Evolution; Natural Science**

Peterson, Cheryl M. PhD, Marquette University. Associate Professor, Trinity Lutheran Seminary. **Church**

Pettke, Sabine. DHabil, University of Rostock. Professor Emeritus, University of Rostock. **Oldendorp, Johannes**

Pless, John T. MDiv, Trinity Lutheran Seminary. Assistant Professor, Concordia Seminary, Fort Wayne. **Althaus, Paul; Apologetics; Bodelschwingh, Friedrich (the Elder) and Friedrich (the Younger) von; Lilje, Hanns; Loehe, Wilhelm Konrad; Niemoeller, Martin; Repristination Theology; Sacraments; Sasse, Hermann; Spitta, Karl Johann Philipp; Ten Commandments; Thielicke, Helmut; Three Estates**

Plummer, Marjorie Elizabeth. PhD, University of Virginia. Associate Professor, Western Kentucky University. **Augsburg; Convents; Marriage and Divorce**

Ptaszyński, Maciej. PhD, University of Warsaw. Professor, University of Warsaw. **Poland; Pomerania; Prussia**

Rajashekar, J. Paul. PhD, University of Iowa. Professor, Lutheran Theological Seminary, Philadelphia. **India**

Říčan, Marek. ThD, Charles University, Prague. Assistant to the bishop, Silesian Evangelical Church of the Augsburg Confession. **Czech Republic**

Riches, Daniel. PhD, University of Chicago. Associate Professor, University of Alabama. **Gustavus Adolphus; Thomas Aquinas**

Rittgers, Ronald K. PhD, Harvard University. Professor, Valparaiso University. **Confession (Private) and the Confessional; Dietrich, Veit; Nuremberg; Penance, Penitence, Repentance; Sachs, Hans**

Rivera, Nelson. PhD, Temple University. Associate Professor, Lutheran Theological Seminary, Philadelphia. **Liberation Theology and Marxism**

Robinson, Paul W. PhD, University of Chicago. Professor, Concordia Seminary, St. Louis. **Bernard, Abbot of Clairvaux; Biel, Gabriel; German Mysticism; Hus, Jan; Ockham, William of;**
Scholasticism, Late Medieval; Thomas Aquinas; Valla, Lorenzo

Roth, John D. PhD, University of Chicago. Professor, Goshen College. **Anabaptists/Spiritualists; Hoffmann, Melchior**

Russell, William R. PhD, University of Iowa. Pastor, Augustana Lutheran Church, Minneapolis. **Smalcald Articles**

Salvadori, Stefania. DPhil, University of Venice and University of Zürich. Research Scholar, Academy of Sciences, Göttingen. **Andreae, Johann Valentin**

Schmit, Clayton J. PhD, Graduate Theological Union. Provost, Lutheran Theological Southern Seminary. **Preaching**

Schnurr, Jan Carsten. DPhil, University of Tübingen. Lecturer, Freie Theologische Hochschule, Gießen. **Revivals, *Erweckungsbewegung***

Schuler, Rhoda Grever. ThD, Luther Seminary, St. Paul. Professor, Concordia University. **Confirmation**

Schulz, Klaus D. PhD, Concordia Seminary, St. Louis. Professor of Missiology, Concordia Theological Seminary, Fort Wayne. **Gossner, Johannes Evangelista**

Schuurman, Douglas J. PhD, University of Chicago. Professor, St. Olaf College. **Vocation**

Schwarz, Hans. DTheol, University of Erlangen. Professor, University of Regensburg. **Creation; Eschatology (Apocalypticism, Chiliasm, Millennialism, Millenarianism); Heim, Karl**

Serina, Richard J. PhD, Concordia Seminary, St. Louis. Guest Lecturer, Concordia Seminary, St. Louis. **Conciliarism**

Shantz, Douglas H. PhD, University of Waterloo. Professor, University of Calgary. **Arnold, Gottfried; Bengel, Johann Albrecht; Oetinger, Friedrich Christoph**

Stayer, James M. PhD, Cornell University. Professor Emeritus, Queens University. **Luther Renaissance; Müntzer, Thomas; Peasants' War**

Stewart, Richard N. DMin, Lutheran Theological Seminary, Philadelphia. Associate Professor, Lutheran Theological Seminary, Philadelphia. **Race/Minorities**

Stjerna, Kirsi. PhD, Boston University. Professor, Pacific Lutheran Theological Seminary. **Agricola, Mikael; Bora, Katharina von; Finnish Interpretation of Luther; Gender: Men and Women; Mannermaa, Tuomo; Sexuality**

Strandquist, Jason L. PhD, Pennsylvania State University. Independent scholar. **Bremen; Hamburg; Lübeck**

Strauch, Solveig. DPhil, University of Cologne. Instructor, Anna Herrmann Schule, Kerpen, Germany. **Seckendorff, Veit Ludwig von**

Strom, Jonathan. PhD, University of Chicago. Professor, Emory University. **Boehm, Anthony William; Conventicles; Conversion and Regeneration; Deaconesses; Pietism; Scriver, Christian; Welz, Justinian von**

Sundberg, Walter. PhD, Princeton Seminary. Professor Emeritus, Luther Seminary, St. Paul. **Harms, Claus; Harms, Ludwig; Hengstenberg, Ernst Wilhelm; Vilmar, August Friedrich Christian**

Threinen, Norman J. DTheol, Concordia Seminary, St. Louis. Professor Emeritus, Concordia Seminary, Edmonton. **Canada**

Tinambunan, Victor. DTheol, Trinity Theological College, Singapore. Professor, HKBP Theological Seminary. **Batak Church; Batak Confession; Nommensen, Ludwig Ingwer**

Trueman, Carl. PhD, University of Aberdeen. Professor of Church History, Westminster Theological Seminary, Philadelphia. **Calvinism as a Second Reformation**

Valčo, Michal. DHabil, University of Prešov, Slovakia. Associate Professor, University of Žilina. **Kierkegaard, Søren Aabye**

Venables, Mary Noll. PhD, Yale University. Independent scholar. **Ernst the Pious of Saxe-Gotha, Duke**

Vethanayagamony, Peter. PhD, Lutheran School of Theology at Chicago. Associate Professor, Lutheran School of Theology at Chicago. **Fabricius, Johann Philipp; Fry, Franklin Clark; General Synod; Heyer, Johann Friedrich Christian; Lutheran Church in America; Petersen, Anne Marie; Schultze, Benjamin; Schwartz, Christian Friedrich**

Vigen, James B. PhD, Lutheran School of Theology at Chicago. Pastor, Orangeburg Lutheran Church. *Fifohazana* **Movement; Madagascar**

Walter, Gregory. PhD, Princeton Seminary. Associate Professor, St. Olaf College. **Existentialism; Holl, Karl; Iwand, Hans Joachim; Liberalism**

Wendebourg, Dorothea. DHabil, Ludwig-Maximilians University, Munich. Professor, Humboldt University, Berlin. **Eastern Orthodoxy; Germany since 1870**

Wengert, Timothy J. PhD, Duke University. Professor Emeritus, Lutheran Theological Seminary, Philadelphia. **Agricola, Johann; Antinomianism/Antinomian Controversies; Apology of the Augsburg Confession; Cruciger, Caspar, Sr.; Major, Georg; Melanchthon, Philip; Ninety-Five Theses; Ninety-Five Theses, Posting of the; Osiander, Andreas**

Westermeyer, Paul. PhD, University of Chicago. Professor Emeritus, Luther Seminary, St. Paul. **Bach, Johann Sebastian; Buxtehude, Dietrich; Music; Schütz, Heinrich**

Westhelle, Vitor. PhD, Lutheran School of Theology at Chicago. Professor, Lutheran School of Theology at Chicago. **Gómez, Medardo Ernesto; Nihilism and Postmodernism**

Whitmer, Kelly J. PhD, University of British Columbia. Associate Professor, University of the South. **Brahe, Tycho; Kepler, Johannes; Rheticus, Georg Joachim**

Wiersma, Hans. PhD, Luther Seminary, St. Paul. Associate Professor, Augsburg College. **Law, Uses of the; Martyrdom and Persecution**

Williams, Kim-Eric. DMin, Graduate Theological Foundation. Lecturer, University of Pennsylvania. **Campanius, Johan; Falckner, Justus; Ministerium of Pennsylvania; New Sweden**

Williams, Louise. DD, Wartburg Seminary. Executive Director Emeritus, Lutheran Deaconess Association. **Deaconesses**

Wilson, Andrew L. PhD, Princeton Seminary. Independent scholar. **Spain**

Wilson, Sarah Hinlicky. PhD, Princeton University. Researcher, Institute for Ecumenical Research, Strasbourg. **Authority; Ecumenical Dialogues;**

Grumbach, Argula von; Hammarskjöld, Dag; Honterus, Johannes; Original Sin; Revelation; Tradition

Wu, Albert. PhD, University of California, Berkeley. Assistant Professor, American University of Paris. **Inner Mission; Wichern, Johann Hinrich**

Yoder, Peter James. PhD, University of Iowa. Assistant Professor, Berry College. **Böhme, Jacob; Francke, August Hermann; Francke, Gotthilf August; Hildebrand, Carl (Baron von Canstein);** **Löscher, Valentin Ernst; Meyfart, Johann Matthäus**

Zászkaliczky, Márton. PhD, Central European University. Faculty member of the Hungarian Academy of Sciences, Institute for Literary Studies. **Hungary**

Zweck, Dean. ThD, Lutheran School of Theology at Chicago. Professor, Australian Lutheran College. **Australia; Australian Aboriginal People; Flierl, Johann; Fritzsche, Gotthard Daniel; Kavel, August Ludwig Christian; Papua New Guinea**

Abbreviations

Note: Some abbreviations have more than one referent. To avoid confusion, the appropriate referent is clarified where necessary in the articles.

AALC	American Association of Lutheran Churches (1987–)
ACMMRN	Association for Christian-Muslim Mutual Relations in Nigeria
AELC	American Evangelical Lutheran Church (1872–1962) *or* Association of Evangelical Lutheran Churches (1976–87)
AIM	African Inland Mission *or* American Indian Movement
ALC	American Lutheran Church (1930–60) *or* American Lutheran Church (1960–88)
ALLIA	Association of Liberian Lutherans in the Americas
ALM	Australian Lutheran Mission
ANC	African National Congress
Ap	Apology of the Augsburg Confession
ARG	*Archiv für Reformationsgeschichte.* Verein für Reformationsgeschichte. 1906–
art.	article
ASV	American Standard Version
b.	born
BBKL	*Biographisch-bibliographisches Kirchenlexikon.* Bautz, 1970–
BC	*Book of Concord.* Fortress, 2000
BCE	before the Common Era
BfdW	Brot für die Welt
BMS	Berlin Mission Society
BWV	*Bach-Werke-Verzeichnis.* Ed. A. Dürr and Y. Kobayashi. Breitkopf & Härtel, 1998
ca.	circa, around
CA	Augsburg Confession (Confessio Augustana)
CB	*Correspondance de Théodore de Bèze*
CCath	Corpus Catholicorum
CCLF	Council of Churches on Lutheran Foundation in South Africa
CCM	Called to Common Mission
CCT	Christian Council of Tanzania
CD	*Church Dogmatics*, by Karl Barth. 4 vols. in 14 parts. T&T Clark, 1936–88
CE	Common Era
CELC	China Evangelical Lutheran Church *or* Confessional Evangelical Lutheran Conference *or* Czech Evangelical Lutheran Church
CETA	Centro de Estudios Teológicos Augsburgo
cf.	*confer*, compare
CLB	American Church of the Lutheran Brethren
CLBC	Chinese Lutheran Brethren Church
CLC	Church of the Lutheran Confession
CLGC	China Lutheran Gospel Church
CLM	Cooperating Lutheran Mission
CLS	China Lutheran Seminary
CMS	Church Missionary Society (Anglican)
CNLC	Commission for the New Lutheran Church
CO	*Ioannis Calvini opera omnia quae supersunt*
CONCAP	Council of Central America and Panama
CPCE	Community of Protestant Churches in Europe
CR	*Corpus Reformatorum*
CRALOG	Council of Relief Agencies Licensed to Operate in Germany
CSI	Church of South India
CTQ	*Concordia Theological Quarterly*
d.	died
DDR	Deutsche Demokratische Republik (East Germany, 1949–90)
diss.	dissertation
DMS	Danish Missionary Society
DRC	Democratic Republic of the Congo *or* Dutch Reformed Church (Nederduits Gereformeerde Kerk)
ECAC	Evangelical Church of the Augsburg Confession
ed(s).	editor(s), edited by
EDS	Evangelical Development Service

EECMY	Ethiopian Evangelical Church Mekene Yesus	ELFCN	Evangelical Lutheran Free Church in Norway
EELC	Église Evangélique Luthérienne du Cameroun	ELIM	Evangelical Lutherans in Mission
EFLC	Église Fraternelle Luthérienne du Cameroun	ELKS	Evangelical Lutheran Church in Suriname
EFS	Evangeliska Fosterlandsstiftelsen (= SEM)	ELS	Evangelical Lutheran Synod
		ELSA	Evangelical Lutheran Synod of Australia
e.g.	*exempli gratia*, for example	*ELW*	*Evangelical Lutheran Worship*. Augsburg Fortress, 2006
EKD	Evangelische Kirche in Deutschland		
EKU	Evangelische Kirche der Union	EOC	Ethiopian Orthodox Church
ELC	Evangelical Lutheran Church (1917–60)	Ep	Epitome of the Formula of Concord
		ER	*Encyclopedia of Religion*. 2nd ed. 15 vols. Macmillan, 2005
ELCA	Evangelical Lutheran Church in America (1988–)	esp.	especially
ELCB	Evangelical Lutheran Church in Bavaria *or* Evangelical Lutheran Church in Botswana	ET	English translation
		et al.	and others
		FC	Formula of Concord
ELCC	Evangelical Lutheran Church of Canada (1960–85) *or* Evangelical Lutheran Church in Congo	FELCI	Federation of Evangelical Lutheran Churches in India
		FELM	Finnish Evangelical Lutheran Mission
ELCE	Evangelical Lutheran Church of Eritrea	FELSiSA	Free Evangelical Lutheran Synod in South Africa
ELCG	Evangelical Lutheran Church of Ghana *or* Evangelical Lutheran Church in Guyana	FIEL	Federación de Iglesias Evangélicas Luteranas
ELCIC	Evangelical Lutheran Church in Canada (1985–)	FLM	Fiangonana Loterana Malagasy *or* Finnish Lutheran Mission
ELCIN	Evangelical Lutheran Church in Namibia	FMLN	Frente Farabundo Martí para la Liberación Nacional
ELCJHL	Evangelical Lutheran Church in Jordan and the Holy Land	FMS	Finnish Missionary Society
ELCK	Evangelical Lutheran Church in Kenya	GLC	Gutnius Lutheran Church
		GNP	gross national product
ELCLS	Evangelical Lutheran Church in Liberia Synod	HKBP	Huria Kristen Batak Protestan (Indonesia)
ELCM	Evangelical Lutheran Church in Malawi *or* Evangelical Lutheran Church in Mozambique	HRE	Holy Roman Empire of the German Nation (Heiliges Römisches Reich Deutscher Nation)
ELCONG	Evangelical Lutheran Church of New Guinea	ICLH	Iglesia Cristiana Luterana de Honduras
ELC-PNG	Evangelical Lutheran Church of Papua New Guinea	ICMA	International Christian Maritime Association
ELCROS	Evangelical Lutheran Church of Russia and Other States	i.e.	*id est*, that is
		IECLB	Igreja Evangélica de Confissão Luterana no Brasil
ELCSA	Evangelical Lutheran Church of Southern Africa	IELA	Iglesia Evangélica Luterana Argentina
ELCSL	Evangelical Lutheran Church of Sierra Leone	IELB	Iglesia Evangélica Luterana Boliviana *or* Igreja Evangélica Luterana do Brasil
ELCT	Evangelical Lutheran Church in Tanzania *or* Evangelical Lutheran Church in Thailand		
		IELC	Iglesia Evangélica Luterana Confesional (in Mexico) *or* India Evangelical Lutheran Church
ELCZ	Evangelical Lutheran Church in Zimbabwe		

IELCH	Iglesia Evangélica Luterana de Chiclayo *or* Iglesia Evangélica Luterana en Chile	LCNT	Lutheran Church of Northern Tanganyika
IELP	Iglesia Evangélica Luterana en el Perú	LCROC	Lutheran Church of the Republic of China
IEL-P	Iglesia Evangélica Luterana-Perú	LCSA	Lutheran Church in Southern Africa
IELU	Iglesia Evangélica Luterana Unida	LCT	Lutheran Church of Taiwan
IERP	Iglesia Evangélica del Río de la Plata	LCUSA	Lutheran Council in the United States of America (1967–88)
ILAG	Iglesia Luterana Agustina de Guatemala	LEAF	Lutheran Evangelical Association in Finland
ILC	International Lutheran Council (1993–)	LECAC	Lutheran Evangelical Church of the Augsburg Confession
ILCH	Iglesia Luterana en Chile	LECT	Lutheran Evangelical Church in Thailand
ILCW	Inter-Lutheran Commission on Worship	LFC	Lutheran Free Church (1897–1963)
ILS	Iglesia Luterana Salvadorena	LIRS	Lutheran Immigrant and Refugee Service
ILSN	Iglesia Luterana Sinodo de Nicaragua		
ILV	Iglesia Luterana de Venezuela	LJS	Lutheran Junior Seminary
ISEDET	Instituto Superior Evangélico de Estudios Teológicos	LLL	Lutheran Laymen's League
		LMNG	Lutheran Mission New Guinea
JCMWA	Joint Christian Ministry in West Africa	LMS	London Missionary Society
		LMT	Lutheran Mission in Thailand
JDDJ	Joint Declaration on the Doctrine of Justification	*LQ*	*Lutheran Quarterly*
		LSA	Lutheran Services in America
JELC	Japan Evangelical Lutheran Church	LTSP	Lutheran Theological Seminary at Philadelphia
KELC	Kenya Evangelical Lutheran Church		
KKKT	Kanisa la Kiinjili la Kilutheri Tanzania	LTU	Luther Theological University
		LUCCEA	Lutheran Commission in Central and Eastern Africa
KLM	Korean Lutheran Mission		
LAM	Latin American (Lutheran) Mission	LUCSA	Lutheran Communion in Southern Africa
LAMP	Lutheran Association of Missionaries and Pilots	LW	Luther's Works. St. Louis and Philadelphia, 1955–
LBI	Lutheran Bible Institute		
LBT	Lutheran Bible Translators	LWC	Lutheran World Conventions (1923–35)
LBW	*Lutheran Book of Worship*. Augsburg, 1978	LWF	Lutheran World Federation (1947–)
LC	Large Catechism	LWR	Lutheran World Relief (1945–)
LCA	Lutheran Church in America (1962–88)	*MBW T*	*Melanchthons Briefwechsel: Kritische und kommentierte Gesamtausgabe. Texte*. Frommann-Holzboog, 1991–
LCAs	Lutheran Church in Australia		
LCC	Library of Christian Classics *or* Lutheran Church Canada *or* Lutheran Church of China		
		MEC	Methodist Episcopal Church
		MELM	Middle East Lutheran Ministry
LCCA	Lutheran Church of Central Africa	MLC	Mexican Lutheran Church
LCCN	Lutheran Church of Christ in Nigeria	MTC	Marangu Teachers College
		NALC	North American Lutheran Church (2010–)
LCK	Lutheran Church in Korea		
LCL	Lutheran Church in Liberia	NEF	National Evangelical Foundation (Evangelisk Fosterlands Stiftelsen)
LCMC	Lutheran Congregations in Mission for Christ (2001–)		
		NELC	Norwegian Evangelical Lutheran Church
LCMS	Lutheran Church–Missouri Synod (1847–)		
		NELFC	Norwegian Evangelical Lutheran Free Church
LCN	Lutheran Church of Nigeria		

NGO	nongovernmental organization	SLM	Sínodo Luterano de México (Lutheran Synod of Mexico) *or* Swedish Lutheran Mission
NIV	New International Version of the Bible		
		SM	Sudan Mission
NLC	National Lutheran Council (1918–66)	SMO	social ministry organization
		SPCK	Society for Promoting Christian Knowledge
NLK	Japan Lutheran Church		
NLM	Norsk Luthersk Misjonssamband (Norwegian Lutheran Mission)	SPG	Society for the Propagation of the Gospel
NMS	Norwegian Mission Society	SUM	Sudan United Mission
no(s).	number(s)	s.v.	*sub verbo*, under the word
n.p.	no publisher identified	TALC	The American Lutheran Church
NP	National Party (in South Africa)	TELC	Tamil Evangelical Lutheran Church
NRK	Nihon Ruteru Kyodan (Japan Lutheran Church)	THRP	Trauma Healing and Reconciliation Program
		TLC	Taiwan Lutheran Church
NRSV	New Revised Standard Version of the Bible	TLH	*The Lutheran Hymnal.* Concordia, 1941
NS	new series	trans.	translated by
NT	New Testament	TRE	*Theologische Realenzyklopädie.* Ed. G. Krause and G. Müller. De Gruyter, 1977–
OT	Old Testament		
par.	paragraph		
PEL	Pastors Emergency League	UEK	Union evangelischer Kirchen
r.	reigned/ruled	UELC	United Evangelical Lutheran Church (1896–1960)
RAC	*Reallexikon für Antike und Christentum.* Edited by T. Kluser et al. Stuttgart, 1950–		
		UELCAs	United Evangelical Lutheran Church in Australia
RGG	*Religion in Geschichte und Gegenwart.* Ed. H. D. Betz. 4th ed. Mohr Siebeck, 1998–2007	UELCI	United Evangelical Lutheran Churches in India
		UELCSA	United Evangelical Lutheran Church in Southern Africa
RPP	*Religion Past and Present: Encyclopedia of Theology and Religion.* Ed. H. D. Betz et al. 14 vols. Brill, 2007–13	ULBRA	Universidade Luterana do Brasil
		ULCA	United Lutheran Church in America (1918–62)
RQ	*Renaissance Quarterly*	UMC	United Methodist Church
RS	Riograndian Synod	UNESCO	United Nations Educational, Scientific, and Cultural Organization
SA	Smalcald Articles		
SACC	South African Council of Churches	UNHCR	United Nations High Commissioner for Refugees
SC	Small Catechism		
SD	Solid Declaration of the Formula of Concord	UNLC	United Norwegian Lutheran Church
		UNLCA	United Norwegian Lutheran Church of America (1890–1917)
SECAC	Silesian Evangelical Church of the Augsburg Confession	USA	United States of America
SELC	Synod of (Slovak) Evangelical Lutheran Churches	USSR	Union of Soviet Socialist Republics
		VELKD	Vereinigte Evangelisch-Lutherische Kirche Deutschland
SEM	Swedish Evangelical Mission		
SEMLA	Seminario Luterano Augsburgo	vol(s).	volume(s)
SETELA	Seminario Teológico Luterano Andino (Andean Lutheran Theological Seminary)	WA	Weimarer Ausgabe: Luther's Works, Writings, Weimar edition
		WA BR	Luther's Works—Correspondence, Weimar edition
SIM	Sudan Interior Mission		
SLEY	Suomen Luterilainen Evankeliumiyhdistys. *See* LEAF	WARC	World Alliance of Reformed Churches

WA TR	Luther's Works—Table Talk, Weimar edition	WMPL	World Mission Prayer League (1937–)
WCC	World Council of Churches (1948–)	YAGM	Young Adults in Global Mission
WELS	Wisconsin Evangelical Lutheran Synod (1892–)	YMCA	Young Men's Christian Association
WJELC	West Japan Evangelical Lutheran Church	YWCA	Young Women's Christian Association

Introduction

Today Lutherans form a worldwide movement within the church catholic. This dictionary demonstrates that thesis at every turn. Not only did Martin Luther and his colleagues in Wittenberg and beyond insist on their continuity with the witness of the early church and even of certain medieval thinkers, but also from the very inception of the Reformation the Reformers influenced church life and proclamation for a much wider audience than simply German-speaking Christians within the Holy Roman Empire. Students from all over Europe came to study in Wittenberg. German writings of Luther and others and those already available in the academic lingua franca of Latin were quickly translated into a variety of languages. Reformers indebted to Luther and what grew to be the Lutheran traditions spread many of these ideas throughout Western Europe, Scandinavia, Finland, parts of the kingdoms of Poland and Hungary, and beyond.

But the movement that grew out of the Reformation did not stop in the sixteenth century. As important as the persons and events of that time were for shaping the Lutheran traditions, the new social, political, and theological contexts of the ensuing centuries provided Lutheran churches with opportunities for continued growth and development. The evolution of Lutheran orthodoxy in the seventeenth century, with its creative approaches to theological debate and lively church life—during which many cherished Lutheran hymns and chorales were written—enlivened the second century of the Lutheran traditions at the same time that the Thirty Years' War (1618–48) nearly destroyed central Europe.

If the periods often labeled Pietism and the Enlightenment shaped the broader church and intellectual life in the eighteenth century, they also did not hinder the continued growth of Lutheran traditions. One of the most important aspects of that development was the training of pastors and missionaries for other lands—especially characteristic of the Franckean form of Lutheran piety centered in Halle, which sponsored, among others, the work of Ziegenbalg in India and Henry Melchior Mühlenberg in the British colonies of North America.

The nineteenth century saw an explosion of mission work, as new churches were founded in the wake of European expansion throughout Asia and Africa, and immigrant churches served new European arrivals settling especially in North and South America and Australia. At the same time, a variety of theological movements—ranging from the very different pieties of Grundvig in Denmark and Hauge in Norway to the repristination theology championed at the University of Erlangen and, in a different way, the liberalism of Albrecht Ritschl—continued to enrich the Lutheran conversation.

In 1883, at the four-hundredth anniversary of Martin Luther's birth, a monumental project to publish his complete works began in Weimar and resulted, over the next century, in producing over one hundred volumes of the Reformer's works. It fed into the so-called Luther Renaissance, sparked above all by the work of church historian Karl Holl, a movement that sought to understand Luther from his own writings and in his own context. But the twentieth century also saw the development of several important new movements. The deep commitment of Lutherans to the social welfare of the neighbor, already a hallmark of the Reformation and continued by such venerable institutions as the Franckean Foundations in Halle and the "Inner Mission" of nineteenth-century Germany and parts of Scandinavia (especially Denmark), came to special fruition after World War II in the Lutheran Immigration and Refugee Service and in Lutheran World Relief. The interest in concord among Lutherans, which in the sixteenth century gave rise to the Formula of Concord, now came to new expression in the Lutheran World Federation and, in a different way, in the International Lutheran Council. At the same time, what had sometimes been viewed as mission outposts of North American and European churches quickly evolved into churches in their own right, with indigenous pastors and leaders, while continuing to maintain relationships with their founding churches.

It would be easy to say that it all simply began with Martin Luther, but this would be incorrect on two levels. For one thing, Luther himself was dependent on the witness of past Christians (for example, Augustine, Bernard of Clairvaux, and Johann von Staupitz). For another, his special brand of theology arose out of the renewed interest in history and biblical studies in the Renaissance. This interest in returning to the sources (*ad fontes*) drove Luther to reassess canon law and later medieval theology and, more important, to learn anew the central biblical message of justification by faith alone. Thus, other witnesses in the church's history have also found a place in this dictionary.

Of course, Martin Luther himself plays a special role in this work. By his careful reading of the Psalms and Paul's Letters (often aided by the very latest interpretive tools, such as Erasmus's Greek text of and annotations on the New Testament), Luther came to a renewed appreciation for God's mercy and unmerited gifts in Christ. He also discovered a way of approaching God's Word that carefully distinguished God's condemning word, which terrifies the sinner, from God's justifying word, which comforts the terrified. In part due to his Ockhamist training and to his absorption of certain elements of the monastic piety fostered by Johannes Tauler and his circle, Luther also came to emphasize the scandal of the cross and the way it overturned human reason, leading the way to trust in God as revealed in Christ.

With the publication of the Latin Ninety-Five Theses in 1517 and the German *Sermon on Indulgences and Grace* in early 1518, Luther suddenly became a household name and was at the same time suspected of heresy by his archbishop, Albrecht of Mainz, to whom Luther had sent his theses on October 31, 1517. Thus began Luther's legal case with Rome, culminating in his being declared a heretic of the church by Pope Leo X in early 1521 and an outlaw of the Holy Roman Empire in April of the same year. By this time, Luther's theological development led him to question the seven sacraments by reducing the number to two or three (baptism, the Lord's Supper, and, sometimes, absolution), to appeal to the empire's princes for help in reforming church life, and to explain the nature of faith and good works (in the *Treatise on Good Works* and *Freedom of a Christian*). Whisked off to protective custody in the Wartburg, Luther continued his literary output with his *Judgment on Monastic Vows*, his exposition of the Sunday texts for Advent and Christmas, and, above all, his translation of the New Testament into German from the original Greek. Returning to Wittenberg in 1522, Luther faced down colleagues who in his opinion insisted that the reform of practice could best precede the proclamation of Wittenberg's gospel. In the face of uncertainty about the Christian's place in the world, he wrote *On Temporal Authority: The Extent to Which It Should Be Obeyed*. But practical reform did come: for liturgy (1523/1526), for catechesis (1522/1529), for the university (1524/1527), and, finally, for forms of ecclesial oversight, launched through an official visitation of Saxony's churches in 1527. Throughout this period, Luther's and Wittenberg's polemical output continued, now aimed not only at his Roman opponents but also at Reformers who denied Christ's real presence in the Eucharist (1524–29) or the efficacy of infant baptism (1528) and at Erasmus over free will (1524–29). In contrast, this period also saw Luther's production of the less explicitly polemical catechisms of 1529—works that, alongside his commentary on the texts from the standard one-year lectionary (the *Kirchenpostil*), had some of the greatest impact on succeeding generations.

In 1530 the imperial diet held in Augsburg and presided over by Emperor Charles V himself marked a turning point in the history of the Lutheran movement with the presentation to the diet on June 25 of what became known as the Augsburg Confession, which was subsequently rejected by the opponents in their Confutation. With Luther unable to attend the diet, the drafting of the document fell to his colleague in Wittenberg, Philip Melanchthon, who was aided by other Evangelical theologians (including Justus Jonas, Andreas Osiander, and Johannes Brenz). The Confession's twenty-eight articles confessed the signers' fidelity to the catholic faith grounded in justification "by grace through faith on account of Christ" (Augsburg Confession, IV) in the first twenty-one articles and provided grounds for changes in practice in the final seven.

After 1530 the pace of the Reformation movement did not slacken, as more cities and territories joined forces with the Saxon theologians, adding to the original signers of the Augsburg Confession (Saxony, Hessen, Brandenburg-Ansbach, Braunschweig-Lüneberg, Anhalt, Nuremberg, and Reutlingen) a host of others, including Denmark, Mecklenburg, Württemberg, Pomerania, and cities like Braunschweig, Lübeck, and Hamburg. Desire for unity among Protestants issued in the Wittenberg Concord between Martin Bucer's party (representing southern German cities such as Augsburg and Strasbourg) and the Wittenberg theologians, including Luther and Melanchthon. Even conversations with the Roman party continued with colloquies in Worms (1540) and Regensburg (1541, 1546). With the death of Luther's sworn enemy George of Saxony, the nearby duchy of Saxony also became Evangelical. Universities also joined the movement, including institutions in Frankfurt/Oder, Leipzig, Rostock, and Tübingen. In this same era, the University of Wittenberg began ordaining pastors for a host of churches and awarding doctorates in theology for their leaders. The papal call for a general council in 1536 (which eventually led to the Council of Trent [1545–63]) led Luther's prince, Elector John Frederick, to ask of Luther a confession (the Smalcald Articles, 1536–37 [published in 1538]) and led both Luther and Melanchthon to write tracts on ecclesiology in 1539.

Luther's death in 1546 did not end the Lutheran movement, but, coupled with the disastrous defeat of Evangelical princes in the Smalcald War and the accompanying harsh measures effected in the 1547–48 Diet of Augsburg, it did cause severe difficulties in leadership, theology, and practice. While Charles V's attempts to assert direct control over the religious life of the empire finally failed, leading to the Peace of Augsburg (1555), theological struggles erupted among Lutherans over questions related among other things to adiaphora, original sin, free will, justification by faith, the role of good works in salvation, and the relation of law and gospel (antinomianism). At the same time, the period experienced what many viewed as the defection of some theologians and territories from the Wittenberg Concord, renewing struggles over the Lord's Supper. By 1580, twenty years after the death of Philip Melanchthon, the Formula of Concord and its accompanying body of Lutheran confessional documents (the ecumenical creeds, the Augsburg Confession and its Apology, the Smalcald Articles, Treatise on the Power and Primacy of the Pope, and Luther's catechisms) were published, bringing approximately two-thirds of the empire's Lutherans into its fold. Meanwhile, the Lutheran movement continued to spread into the Nordic and Baltic lands and into parts of Poland and the Slovakian parts of the kingdom of Hungary, while Reformed churches came to dominate England, France, and the Netherlands. The Roman Catholic Church, revitalized especially by the Council of Trent and the new order of the Society of Jesus (Jesuits), began to reclaim Evangelical territories in Austria, Poland, and Germany.

The entries in this dictionary trace the remarkable growth and development of the Lutheran traditions, focusing on Luther and including not simply well-known, influential names and movements from Germany and Scandinavia but also lesser-known but nonetheless crucial figures who founded and preserved a Lutheran witness to the gospel throughout the world. Brief sketches of Lutheran churches throughout Africa, Asia, the Americas, and Australia provide the reader with a view into the rich diversity of cultures in which the Lutheran witness to the gospel has flourished over the centuries. What better way to commemorate the five-hundredth anniversary of the Reformation than to document its historical, theological, and cultural impact around the world!

This dictionary also stands in the shadow of several earlier English-language reference works, which paved the way for this present, more modest effort. Henry Eyster Jacobs and John A. W. Haas, in cooperation with Otto Zöckler of the University of Greifswald, published *The Lutheran Cyclopedia* (Scribner's Sons, 1899), providing the English-speaking world with a one-volume overview of many major figures and topics in Lutheran history and its ongoing life. Another book with almost the same name (*Lutheran Cyclopedia*)—but arising out of an earlier *Concordia Cyclopedia* (Concordia, 1927) and edited this time by Erwin L. Lueker—appeared in 1954, published by Concordia Publishing House, St. Louis. Scarcely a decade later, Augsburg Publishing House, Minneapolis, and Fortress Press, Philadelphia, published in 1965 an even more ambitious three-volume work, *The Encyclopedia of the Lutheran Church*, edited for the Lutheran World Federation by Julius Bodensieck and counting over seven hundred contributors among its authors. (Since then, smaller works have appeared, including *Historical Dictionary of Lutheranism* [Scarecrow, 2001; 2nd ed., 2011], edited by Günther Gassmann, Duane H. Larson, and Mark W. Oldenburg.) This current volume presents the scholarship of Lutherans from around the world and especially the United States, and once again attempts to capture the lively movement that began with Martin Luther and continues unabated in a variety of traditions today, thus offering the reader a wide variety of articles on the theology, practice, and history of Luther and Lutheranism worldwide.

In the first decade of the twenty-first century, several editors of this volume had already begun serious discussions about the possibilities of a reference work on Lutheran history, theology, and practice. In the fall of 2012, Dave Nelson, acquisitions editor at Baker Academic, approached us about just such a project. In anticipation of the 2017 anniversary year, the publisher had envisioned a single-volume reference work on Martin Luther and the traditions of Lutheran thought and practice. We are pleased to present this volume as a contribution to Baker Academic's list of theological dictionaries, which also includes the award-winning volumes *Dictionary for Theological Interpretation of the Bible* (2005) and *Dictionary of Scripture and Ethics* (2011). The editors wish to express their deepest appreciation to the entire editorial staff at Baker Academic and most especially to Dave Nelson, whose indefatigable efforts and overall vision have made this longtime dream a reality. But thanks are also due to Rachel Klompmaker, Brandy Scritchfield, and Brian Bolger for their painstaking work of turning over six hundred submitted articles into a readable, usable reference work.

The editors and authors represent a broad sweep of scholarship on different aspects of the Lutheran traditions. Timothy J. Wengert is the general editor for this project. He is Ministerium of Pennsylvania emeritus professor of church history at The Lutheran Theological Seminary at Philadelphia, having received his PhD at Duke University. He is well known for his work on Philip Melanchthon (for which he received the Melanchthon Prize from the city of Bretten, Germany, in 2000), on several of the Lutheran confessional documents (the Formula of Concord and Martin Luther's catechisms), and on Martin Luther, and for his collaboration, with Robert Kolb, on editing the English translation of *The Book of Concord* (Fortress, 2000). He also edited two volumes of the translation of Henry Melchior Mühlenberg's correspondence and is associate editor of *Lutheran Quarterly*.

Mark A. Granquist, the managing editor of this project, is associate professor of the history of Christianity at Luther Seminary, specializing in the history of Lutherans in America. He serves as editor of *Word & World* and of the *Journal of the Lutheran Historical Conference*. His publications include *Lutherans in America: A New History* (Fortress, 2014); *Scandinavian Pietists: Spiritual Writings from 19th-century Norway, Denmark, Sweden, and Finland* (Paulist, 2015); and with Maria Erling, *The Augustana Story: Shaping Lutheran Identity in North America* (Fortress, 2008).

The associate editors are Mark Mattes, Robert Kolb, Mary Jane Haemig, and Jonathan Strom. Mark Mattes serves as chair of the department of theology at Grand View University in Des Moines, Iowa. He holds a PhD from the University of Chicago and has authored several books, including *Martin Luther's Theology of Beauty* (Baker Academic, 2017) and *The Role of Justification in Contemporary Theology* (Eerdmans, 2004). He has also coedited Gerhard Forde's theological essays, *A More Radical Gospel* and *The Preached God*, and has cotranslated works of Oswald Bayer and Klaus Schwarzwäller. Additionally, he serves as an associate editor for *Lutheran Quarterly*.

Robert Kolb is emeritus missions professor of systematic theology at Concordia Seminary, St. Louis. He was granted a PhD from the University of Wisconsin and did early work on Jakob Andreae and Nicholas von Amsdorf. Among his recent books are *Martin Luther, Confessor of the Faith* (Oxford, 2009), *Martin Luther and the Enduring Word of God* (Baker Academic, 2016), and *Luther and the Stories of God* (Baker Academic, 2012). He coauthored with Charles Arand *The Genius of Luther's Theology* (Baker Academic, 2008) and is co-editor of *The Oxford Handbook of Martin Luther's Theology* (Oxford, 2014) and of the *Book of Concord* (Fortress, 2000).

Mary Jane Haemig is professor of church history at Luther Seminary in St. Paul, Minnesota, where she is also director of the Reformation Research Program. She joined the faculty in 1999 after teaching five years at Pacific Lutheran University. She received her ThD from Harvard University, writing on Lutheran catechetical preaching. Her scholarly articles have appeared, among other places, in *Lutheran Quarterly*, *Sixteenth Century Journal*, *Church History*, and *Word & World*. She has been associate editor and book review editor of the *Lutheran Quarterly* and is, with Robert Kolb and Mark Mattes, a member of the continuation committee for the International Luther Research Congress.

Jonathan Strom is associate professor of church history and associate dean at the Candler School of Theology, Emory University, in Atlanta, Georgia. He received his PhD from the University of Chicago. He is author of *Orthodoxy and Reform: The Clergy of Seventeenth-Century Rostock* (Mohr Siebeck, 1999), editor of *Pietism and Community in Europe and North America* (Brill, 2010), and coeditor of *Pietism in Germany and North America: 1680–1820* (Ashgate, 2009).

In his introduction to the *Lutheran Cyclopedia*, dated February 1, 1954, Erwin Lueker outlined his editorial principles as follows: (1) Unless otherwise required, treating topics factually and/or historically, and (2) avoid statements that "could be regarded as polemical and propagandic" (p. vii). The same has been asked of our contributors, namely, a fair-mindedness that tries accurately to present the many topics in this book. It is our fervent hope that this work measures up favorably to Lueker's lofty goals and well serves twenty-first-century readers.

Timothy J. Wengert, general editor
Riverton, New Jersey
February 18, 2016, Commemoration
of Martin Luther,
renewer of the church (1546)

A

Aaron, S.

The first Protestant Indian ordained pastor, S. Aaron (1698–1745), was born into a Shivite family at Cuddalore, Tamilnadu, and named C. Arumugam (meaning "six-faces," representing the Hindu god Murugan). He was baptized in Tranquebar in 1718 by Bartholomäus Ziegenbalg, who christened him S. Aaron. He served as a catechist from 1719 to 1733. As a catechist, Aaron performed the duties of communicating the gospel of Jesus Christ, instructing the catechumens and preparing them for baptism, and other pastoral tasks. The request of the people for an indigenous pastor led the Danish mission board in Copenhagen to authorize its missionaries in Tranquebar "to ordain an able person of Indian nation for the office of a pastor." Aaron was chosen and was ordained as the first Indian pastor on December 28, 1733. He married Rachel and, after her early death, Anandaj. He himself died in 1745 of a pneumatocele, leaving behind his third wife when she was pregnant.

See also India; Ziegenbalg, Bartholomäus

Bibliography

Jeyaraj, D. *Ordination of the First Protestant Indian Pastor Aaron*. Lutheran Heritage Archives, 1998; Koschorke, K., F. Ludwig, and M. Delgado. *A History of Christianity in Asia, Africa, and Latin America, 1450–1990: A Documentary Sourcebook*. Eerdmans, 2007.

SAMUEL W. MESHACK

Adiaphora

The term "adiaphora" is a transliteration of the Greek term (Latin: *indifferentia*; undifferentiated matters) meaning "indifferent things." Historically, the Stoics were first to inquire after things that existed outside moral law, which were thus morally neutral as such but became morally relevant by their use.

The New Testament knows of nothing outside God's purpose, will, and activity and so has no concept of adiaphora. The Pauline passages cited in support of such a view (1 Cor. 6:12; 8:8–9; cf. Col. 3:17) make clear that freedom in the use of things or in action does not allow for arbitrariness or license, but is a freedom birthed by love. Within this freedom the Christian acts without determining by way of a legal, external norm *how* to act. In this sense there are no "indifferent things." Only when freedom sprung from love is replaced with orientation to external norms does the concept of adiaphora emerge.

In general, early Christian authors rejected the concept of adiaphora, insofar as all created things were good by nature and only in their use were good or evil. In particular, they rejected adiaphora when opposing philosophical opinion, or allowed them in opposition to ceremonial rules and local liturgical customs. Thomas Aquinas also argued that adiaphora was possible only theoretically but not in practice, where the church's authority holds sway.

Martin Luther regarded all the phenomena of life and its norms as human activities, to be evaluated respecting their utility in light of faith and its exercise of freedom oriented to God's will. His position was similar to that of Augustine, who allowed for adiaphora *within* the state of grace. From faith oriented to God's will, such things or acts were to be tested for their usefulness, thus leaving no room for adiaphora conceived as external, or morally undifferentiated. Luther accordingly rejected and condemned human ordinances when regarded as a service to God, when forced on congregations, or when conceded to enemies in time of persecution. Article 7 of the Augsburg Confession of 1530 reads that "It is not

1

necessary for the true unity of the Christian church that uniform ceremonies, instituted by human beings, be observed everywhere."

Twice in the history of the Evangelical church disputes arose over adiaphora. The first occurred in 1548, when Charles V attempted to unite Catholics and Protestants under the so-called Augsburg Interim. For either side the point at issue was whether, under the duress of the emperor's edict following the Smalcald War, elements that were neither commanded nor forbidden by God's Word could be retained or taken up again. Melanchthon rejected the Interim, though he later worked on an alternative, nicknamed the Leipzig Interim, which defined practices unrelated to justification as adiaphora. Matthias Flacius and others attacked this Leipzig Interim, expanding Luther's position to read that "in the matter of confession or offense nothing is an adiaphoron" (*nihil est adiaphoron in casu confessionis et scandali*).

In the second dispute Lutheran and Reformed churches came into conflict. The issue was whether types of behavior per se are neither good nor evil, but become so in the individual instance. Luther had maintained the right to a temperate enjoyment of secular amusements, but Calvin enforced the so-called Genevan code outlawing the notion of adiaphora. In the eighteenth century, when some Pietists contended that the pursuit of corporal, social, and aesthetic goods was sinful, while some Orthodox Lutheran theologians insisted that there was no explicit divine prohibition against their pursuit, the biblical and Reformation understanding often faded into the background.

By 1576 both extremes were rejected in the Formula of Concord. In article 10 of the Solid Declaration, the Formula noted the controversy among theologians of the Augsburg Confession respecting ceremonies and rites neither commanded nor forbidden; it declared that when, under the pretext of external adiaphora, such rites were proposed as were in principle contrary to God's Word, they were not indifferent. Nor were those rites to be reckoned as adiaphora that were designed to indicate that the religion of the theologians of the Augsburg Confession did not differ greatly from that of the papists. On the other hand, the Christian community had the right to change, diminish, or increase "genuine" adiaphora if unrelated to the worship of God. The Formula went on to state that in time of confession, there was to be no yielding to adversaries who tried to force adiaphora on the community of God. The renowned freedom of the Formula—summarized in the sentence *in statu confessionis nihil adiaphoron* (in the instance of confession nothing is an adiaphoron), that is, wherever the gospel is endangered, freedom is suspended, and wherever it is not at risk, freedom may be exercised—cannot be applied in a legalistic way; yet the theological issue denoted by the sentence stands and is echoed in other persuasions, as in the familiar line of Moravians: "In necessary things unity, in doubtful things liberty, in all things charity."

In the centuries following, the concept of adiaphora came into discredit, principally in philosophical circles. The following dictum of Immanuel Kant may have contributed to its demise: "The doctrine of morals is chiefly concerned with allowing no room for morally indifferent things, neither in acts (*adiaphora*), nor in human characters, so long as it is possible; for with regard to such ambiguity all maxims run the danger of losing their determinacy and solidity." Following Kant, Friedrich Schleiermacher contended that no sphere of existence per se could occur outside life under the ethical alternative. Many later Evangelical authorities have been in substantial agreement with this position.

See also Andreae, Jakob; Augsburg Interim; Iconoclasm; Kant, Immanuel; Leipzig Interim; Wittenberg Circle, Parties within

Bibliography

"Adiaphora." *RAC* 1:85–86. Hiersemann, 1950; "Adiaphora." *RGG* 1:94–96, 119. Mohr, 1957; "Adiaphora." *RGG*. 1:116–19. Mohr Siebeck, 1998; "Adiaphora." *RPP* 1:54–56. Brill, 2007; Article 10. In Ep/SD; Kant, I. *Die Religion innerhalb der Grenzen der blossen Vernunft*. Ed.

K. Vorländer. Para. 9, p. 21. Felix Meiner, 1956; Schleiermacher, F. "Grundlinien einer Kritik der bisherigen Sittenlehre." In *Sämmtliche Werke: Dritte Abtheilung, zur Philosophie*, vol. 1. G. Reimer, 1846.

ROY A. HARRISVILLE

Agricola, Johann

Johann Agricola (1494–1566) was a reformer, teacher in Eisleben, professor in Wittenberg, and court preacher and general superintendent in Berlin. Born Johann Schneider in Eisleben as the son of a master carver and hence often referred to as "Eisleben," Agricola received his bachelor's degree at the University of Leipzig, came to Wittenberg as a student in 1516, heard Luther's lectures on Romans, and received his master of arts degree there in 1518 and a bachelor of Bible degree alongside Melanchthon in 1519. He married Else Mohauer in 1520 and, after brief study in medicine, returned to theology; in 1525 he moved to his hometown of Eisleben, where he became rector of the Latin school and preacher at St. Nicholas Church. In the 1520s he published commentaries on Luke and Colossians and several catechisms. Agricola was involved in several controversies, the first arising in 1527, when he and Philip Melanchthon fought over the nature of repentance and whether it originated in the law and fear (Melanchthon) or the gospel and love (Agricola), in what is sometimes labeled the prelude to the antinomian controversy.

He was preacher for Elector John of Saxony at the imperial diets in Speyer (1526 and 1529) and in Augsburg (1530). After a quarrel with Count Albrecht of Mansfeld, he left Eisleben and started teaching and preaching in Wittenberg by 1538. It was then that he became embroiled in a controversy with Martin Luther over the role of the law in theology, which resulted in unrest in Wittenberg over preaching the law (under the slogan: "The law belongs in city hall") and in Luther's penning *Against the Antinomians* (LW 47:99–119). After several attempts had been made at reconciliation between the two men, Agricola fled to Berlin in 1540 under the threat of house arrest. In Berlin he immediately became the court preacher for Elector Joachim II

of Brandenburg and in 1543 the general superintendent. As Joachim's theological representative at the 1547–48 imperial diet in Augsburg, he assisted in the drafting of the Augsburg Interim. His collaboration on this document resulted in attacks from several quarters, including Philip Melanchthon (who broke off all correspondence with him), his good friend Caspar Aquila (pastor in Saalfeld), and his Berlin colleague Georg Buchholzer. Despite these attacks, his support for the so-called Leipzig Interim, and subsequent fights over the law with Buchholzer and other "Philippists" in 1563, he remained in Berlin until his death from the plague in 1566. Apart from his theological work, Agricola was also known for his collection of German adages, first published in 1529. Andreas Musculus, his brother-in-law and professor at the University of Frankfurt/Oder, was instrumental in inserting something of Agricola's lively sense of Christian freedom from the law into the final drafts of the Formula of Concord.

See also Antinomianism/Antinomian Controversies; Augsburg Interim; Formula of Concord; Leipzig Proposal (Interim); Melanchthon, Philip; Musculus, Andreas

Bibliography
Rogge, J. *Johann Agricolas Lutherverständnis: Unter besonderer Berücksichtigung des Antinomismus*. Evangelische Verlagsanstalt, 1960; Wengert, T. J. *Law and Gospel: Philip Melanchthon's Debate with John Agricola of Eisleben over "Poenitentia."* Baker, 1997.

TIMOTHY J. WENGERT

Agricola, Mikael

Architect of the Reformation in Finland and father of the Finnish language, Mikael Agricola (ca. 1507–57) was a peasant's son and was educated in Vyborg (Viipuri) in the 1520s, where he was exposed to humanist and Reformation influences. He attended Wittenberg University in 1536–39 and earned his master's degree under the tutelage of Luther and Melanchthon. In Finland he became a pioneering educator, administrator, church leader, translator, diplomat, and prolific writer.

Agricola created written Finnish. Before producing the first Finnish translation of the

New Testament (Se Wsi Testamenti) in 1548, Agricola's ABC-book (*ABC-kiria*) from 1543 offered basic catechetical teaching influenced by Luther's, Melanchthon's, and Andreas Osiander's catechetical texts—with instruction on Finnish spelling, pronouncing the Finnish alphabet, and numbers. After serving in 1539–48 as schoolmaster at the Cathedral School in Turku (Åbo), Agricola was installed as the first Lutheran bishop of Turku (1554). He supplied the principal manuals for the new Lutheran worship life and pastoral office (Käsikiria, Messu, and Piina) by 1549, followed by translations of parts of the Old Testament, including the Psalms (*Dauidin Psalttari*, 1551), Hymns and Prophecies (*Weisut ia Ennustoxet*, 1551), and the Prophets (*Ne Prophetat*, 1552). Agricola's original Prayer Book (*Rucouskiria*) from 1544 included forty psalms, over five hundred prayers, and other materials; it was widely used in church life and private devotion.

He was married to Birgitta Olav's daughter; their only son, Christian, became the bishop of Tallinn. While in Russia as one of Gustav Vasa's peace negotiators, Agricola died suddenly on September 4, 1557, and was buried in Vyborg. Agricola made lasting contributions to Finnish language, identity, culture, and church life.

See also Catechisms; Finland; Petri, Olavus; Sweden

Bibliography

Agricola, M. *Se Usi Testamenti*. 1548. Facsimile at http://www.doria.fi/handle/10024/43367; Gummerus, J. *Michael Agricola, der Reformator Finnlands: Sein Leben und sein Werk*. Luther-Agricola Seura, 1941; Heininen, S. *Mikael Agricola: Elämä ja Teokset*. Edita, 2007.

KIRSI STJERNA

Albrecht of Mainz

This archbishop of Mainz was a younger brother of Elector Joachim I of Brandenburg. As scion of the Hohenzollern family, Albrecht of Mainz (1490–1545) strove with success to advance Hohenzollern interests against those of the Wettin family of Elector Frederick the Wise, as he became archbishop of Magdeburg (1513) and then of Mainz (1514), assuming two important offices formerly held by two of Frederick's brothers. He had also become administrator of the bishopric of Halberstadt (1513). The archbishopric of Mainz brought him the positions of "primate of Germany" and "arch-chancellor of the German empire," but his young age and acceptance of plural ecclesiastical offices required substantial payments to the papacy. Pope Leo X (1475–1521) granted him the right to sell indulgences for the building of St. Peter's cathedral in Rome to help alleviate the debt. This sale provoked Luther's Ninety-Five Theses on Indulgences in October 1517. Albrecht did not react to Luther's letter accompanying the theses when it reached him in December but, suspecting heresy, referred the matter to his university theologians and jurists and to Rome.

In contrast to his strong-willed brother, Albrecht is described as gentle, indecisive, and interested in the arts and learning. His patronage supported a spectrum of scholars and artists, and he counts as one of the founders (with his brother) of the University of Frankfurt/Oder. His piety led him to practice his priestly office with some rigor. He attempted some reform measures in the archdiocese of Mainz, though he could not implement his plans because of the opposition of his clergy.

Albrecht's relationship with Luther was ambiguous. Luther's initial deference and respectful tone in late 1517 turned to fervent appeals for reform in Albrecht's lands; criticism of his failure to reform; accusations of involvement in the 1527 assassination of Georg Winckler, a citizen of Halle, under Albrecht's jurisdiction; and rebuke for the archbishop's role in the execution of one of his courtiers, the Evangelical Hans von Schnitz, in 1535. Hopes for Albrecht's playing a decisive mediating role at the Diet of Augsburg in 1530, voiced particularly by Melanchthon, proved groundless. On the other hand, communication between Albrecht and the Wittenberg theologians continued; Albrecht gave Luther and his wife a generous wedding gift in 1525. Luther urged Albrecht to go through with thoughts of marrying and secularizing his lands. But toward the end of his life, the Jesuit Peter Faber encouraged him in persecuting adherents of the Wittenberg Reformation.

Though he occupied very powerful positions, Albrecht ended up playing a relatively minor role in his time and in the Reformation.

See also Ninety-Five Theses; Ninety-Five Theses, Posting of the

Bibliography

Hendrix, S. H. "Martin Luther und Albrecht von Mainz: Aspekte von Luthers reformatorischem Selbstbewußtsein." *Lutherjahrbuch* 49 (1982): 96–114; Jürgensmeier, F., ed. *Erzbischof Albrecht von Brandenburg (1490–1545): Ein Kirchen- und Reichsfürst der Frühen Neuzeit.* Knecht, 1991; Krodel, G. G. "Wider den Abgott zu Halle." *Lutherjahrbuch* 33 (1966): 9–87.

ROBERT KOLB

Alesius, Alexander

Born Alexander Allane (or Alan) in Edinburgh and educated at St. Andrews (BA, 1515), the Scottish Lutheran theologian and polemicist Alexander Alesius (1500–1565) publicly opposed Luther's theology in the mid-1520s. In 1528 his views began to change when he was called on to confute suspected Lutheran Patrick Hamilton. After Hamilton's execution, Alesius fled Scotland. Matriculating at Wittenberg in 1532, he began lecturing there in the following year while continuing to encourage reform in Britain. In 1533 he published an appeal to James V to allow vernacular Scripture in Scotland; in 1535 he delivered copies of Melanchthon's *Loci Communes* to Henry VIII (to whom it was dedicated) and Thomas Cranmer, remaining in England both to teach at Cambridge and to participate in ongoing Anglo-Smalcaldic negotiations. When parliament's passage of the Act of Six Articles in 1539 prevented further advocacy of Lutheran theology in England, he returned to Germany and received, upon Melanchthon's recommendation, a Frankfurt professorship. In 1542 he moved again to Leipzig University, where before his death on March 17, 1565, he published widely in exegetical, dogmatic, and polemical theology.

See also Cranmer, Thomas; England; Hamilton, Patrick; Henry VIII

Bibliography

McNeill, J. T. "Alexander Alesius: Scottish Lutheran (1500–1565)." *ARG* 55 (1964): 161–91; Wiedermann, G. "Martin Luther versus John Fisher: Some Ideas concerning the Debate on Lutheran Theology at the University of St. Andrews, 1525–30." *Records of the Scottish Church History Society* 22 (1984–86): 13–34; Wiedermann, G. "Der Reformator Alexander Alesius als Ausleger der Psalmen." PhD diss., Erlangen University, 1988.

KOREY D. MAAS

Althaus, Paul

The German systematic theologian and Lutheran scholar Paul Althaus (1888–1966) was born into a family of theologians. His interest in Luther and the Lutheran confessions was influenced by his father, Paul Althaus Sr. (1861–1925). At Tübingen he learned from New Testament scholar Adolf Schlatter (1852–1938) to hold exegesis and dogmatics together. Althaus also studied with Karl Holl (1866–1926), whose pioneering Luther research opened the way for his own scholarship. He completed his university studies at Göttingen, where the work of Carl Stange (1870–1959), Martin Kähler (1835–1912), and Karl Heim (1874–1958) further defined his approach to the theological task. Althaus was the defining figure for Erlangen theology in the mid-twentieth century.

After serving as a chaplain in World War I, Althaus returned to teach at Göttingen before accepting a call to Rostock in 1919. In 1925 Althaus moved to Erlangen, where he remained for the rest of his life and established himself as a careful scholar, articulate teacher, and eloquent preacher. He signed the Ansbacher Ratschlag (Ansbach Memorandum, 1934), a document that theologically endorsed the so-called Aryan clause in the German church constitution claiming that due to the orders of creation, nations are assigned distinct callings by their Creator.

Even though Althaus would distance himself from the anti-Semitic ideology of National Socialism, never speaking positively of the party after 1938, his earlier endorsement of the party caused him to be viewed with suspicion and criticism.

Like other Erlangen theologians such as Werner Elert (1885–1954) and Hermann Sasse (1895–1976), Althaus rejected the Barmen Declaration as a confusion of law and gospel, resulting in a "Christomonism" that dismissed general revelation. In 1952 Althaus published a monograph titled *The Divine Command*. Seeking to avoid a "third use" of the law and yet critical of Barth's collapse of the law into the gospel, Althaus asserted that God's commandments, heard by the Christian, are not legal demands but words of personal address received in faith, revealing God's will for the new life.

While Althaus is best remembered for his Luther scholarship, his theological career was multidimensional, embracing systematic theology and New Testament studies. While at Rostock, Althaus completed a book on eschatology. This book, *Die letzten Dinge* (The last things), is perhaps the most comprehensive Lutheran treatment of the topic in the twentieth century. Eschatology grounded in the resurrection of Jesus, with hope directed toward the fulfillment of all things yet experienced now in time by faith, characterizes Althaus's approach. During this period he and Carl Strange founded the *Zeitschrift für systematische Theologie* in 1923. His massive book on dogmatics, *Die christliche Wahrheit*, was published in 1947. His approach to systematic theology bears some similarity to Paul Tillich's notion of a method of correlation in that Althaus seeks to engage culture and science theologically. There is knowledge of God apart from Christ (Rom. 1), but salvation is only in Christ. The doctrine of the Trinity is not a foreword to Christian theology but its doxological conclusion. Althaus was at home in New Testament studies, writing commentaries on Galatians, Romans, and 1 and 2 Corinthians. His work on Jesus challenged Bultmann's divorce of history and faith as Althaus affirmed the necessity of the resurrection for Christian faith. In this sense, Althaus demonstrated apologetic acumen in both academy and church, influencing one of his most well-known students, Helmut Thielicke (1908–86). His work on the doctrine of God became important for Paul Knitter and others working with questions raised by world religions and interfaith dialogues.

Althaus's best-known Luther studies are his two volumes on Luther's theology and ethics. Convinced that Luther's theology continued to be relevant for the church, Althaus sought to provide a vivid and accurate description of Luther's thought, distinguishing Luther from Lutheran orthodoxy but also from liberal Protestantism.

See also Ansbach Memorandum (Ansbacher Ratschlag); Barmen Confession; Barth, Karl; Bultmann, Rudolf (Karl); Elert, Werner; Erlangen; Eschatology (Apocalypticism, Chiliasm, Millennialism, Millenarianism); Heim, Karl; Holl, Karl; Law, Uses of the; Luther Interpretation and Reception; Thielicke, Helmut; Tillich, Paul J.

Bibliography
Althaus, P. *The Ethics of Martin Luther*. Trans. R. Schultz. Fortress, 1972; Althaus, P. *Fact and Faith in the Kerygma of Today*. German, 1957. Trans. D. Cairns. Muhlenberg, 1959; Althaus, P. *The Theology of Martin Luther*. Trans. R. Schultz. Fortress, 1966; Green, L. "Paul Althaus: The Meditator." In *The Erlangen School of Theology*, 265–87. Lutheran Legacy, 2010; Jasper, G. *Paul Althaus (1888–1966): Professor, Prediger und Patriot in seiner Zeit*. Vandenhoeck & Ruprecht, 2013.

JOHN T. PLESS

Altona Confession

The Altona Confession was written by a group of Lutheran pastors in the Evangelical Lutheran Church of Hamburg; the document was named for the Hamburg district of Altona, where the group had convened. Titled The Dangers and Disruptions of Public Life, it was issued on January 11, 1933, shortly before Adolf Hitler was named chancellor and the Nazis came to power. As its title indicates, the focus of the Altona Confession is the widespread political extremism, uncertainty, and turbulence of the time. It was an attempt to express a Christian response to the political atmosphere that could guide church members and leaders. While much of the document focuses on the church-state relationship and the responsibilities of Christians as citizens, its central message is that Christians should focus on the teachings of the Gospels and their own consciences in determining how to respond to the challenges that faced them. The authors of the Altona Confession carefully avoided aligning the church with any political movement, but the message is clear, particularly with respect to the ethno-nationalism that was already being expressed by the pro-Nazi German Christians. The Altona Confession was widely distributed throughout Germany; in the winter semester of 1933, Dietrich Bonhoeffer discussed it with his students and contrasted the document with pro-nationalist tracts such as Wilhelm Stapel's *The Christian Statesman: A Theology of Nationalism*. As the earliest such statement, the Altona Confession subsequently became a point of reference for confessional statements by the Confessing Church, including the Bethel Confession (September 1933), and the Barmen and Dahlem statements (1934).

See also Barmen Confession; Bonhoeffer, Dietrich

Bibliography

Bethge, E. *Dietrich Bonhoeffer: A Biography*. Rev. ed. Fortress, 2000; Helmreich, E. C. *The German Churches under Hitler*. Wayne State University Press, 1979.

VICTORIA J. BARNETT

American Civil War

The major conflict between the Northern and Southern states in the United States of America in 1861–65, the American Civil War, culminated a lengthy period of tension emerging between states in the North and the South from the time of the founding of the nation until the middle of the nineteenth century. The complex and varied causes of the war included unresolved issues related to the relative rights of the federal government versus the rights of individual states, the emergence of different cultures and economies in different regions of the country, and the strong desire of some to preserve the Union at all costs standing against

the equally strong desire of others to form their own independent governments. Yet the specific cause of the war, underlying all these factors, was the institution of slavery.

As Lutherans came to the New World during the seventeenth and eighteenth centuries, they found slavery already established throughout the Western Hemisphere. Danish Lutherans imported slaves into the Danish West Indies (now the US Virgin Islands), as early as the mid-seventeenth century. However, in the early days of settlement on the mainland, many Lutherans opposed slavery, even in the Southern colonies. Over time, however, Lutherans increasingly began to adopt a position on slavery that reflected the surrounding cultural context of which they became a part. While slavery began to decline in the northern states, slavery increased dramatically in both economic and cultural importance in the South, and it became contested in the newer states forming in the West.

The General Synod, composed of individual member synods in both Northern and Southern states, wrestled most directly with the issue. The most well-known leader of the General Synod, Samuel Simon Schmucker, stood as an outspoken abolitionist. Another prominent leader of the General Synod, however, the Rev. John Bachman of Charleston, defended the institution. Some Northern constituent synods of the General Synod, such as Wittenberg and Pittsburgh, published antislavery sentiments, and in 1837 a group of abolitionist Lutherans in upstate New York formed an explicitly abolitionist body, the Franckean Synod. Such actions led to bitter responses from the Southern synods; as tensions and rhetoric mounted, the General Synod struggled to avoid division at all costs by agreeing to consider slavery a political issue, with no place in ecclesiastical discussions.

The midwestern synods proved less directly affected by the issue, but C. F. W. Walther of the Missouri Synod ignited controversy when he refused to condemn slavery as a sin, since slavery could be found in the Bible. He enjoined slave owners to treat their slaves humanely, but other midwestern Lutherans, including many Germans and the majority of Norwegians, believed that slavery itself could not be defended, and a rift developed between the conservative Norwegians and Germans over the issue.

As in other Southern denominations, slaves regularly attended the Lutheran churches of their masters, although white Lutherans debated over their exact membership status and confined them to separate galleries, the rear pews of the church, or separate services. By 1860, slaves and "free persons of color" constituted almost one-quarter of the South Carolina Synod's entire membership.

Once war came in April 1861, Lutherans, like other mainline Protestants before them, separated along regional lines. While the Texas Synod remained aligned with the General Synod throughout the war, Lutherans in North Carolina, South Carolina, Virginia, Western Virginia, and Georgia withdrew, beginning in the fall of 1861, to form the General Synod of the Evangelical Lutheran Church in the Confederate States of America (the General Synod South). Both Northern and Southern synods went on record supporting their individual regions and causes with zeal and passion, creating bitter wounds that would not be healed for many years.

Driven by a strong desire to secede both ecclesiastically and politically, the General Synod South strove to remove all previous reliance on Northern Lutheran institutions and forms and called for the creation of its own separate hymnal, liturgy, and literature. To counter the strong pro-Union and antislavery stance of the General Synod's *Lutheran Observer*, published in Baltimore, in August 1861 Southern Lutherans also began publication of a rival paper, *The Southern Lutheran*, which was published until invasion by Northern forces and economic collapse ended it in January 1865.

Both sides interpreted the war in theological terms. Each believed that God fought on their side, and they scrutinized the ebb and flow of victories and losses as signs of either God's favor or God's judgment. Pastors on both sides enlisted in military service, and attendance at local synodical gatherings often depended on the military situation in the area. Church bodies tried to care for their soldiers through chaplaincy and the distribution of religious tracts and newspapers. Lutheran women in both regions served in hospitals, supported their troops with letters and supplies, and increasingly constituted the majority of the church population as the war progressed.

In July 1863, Gettysburg Lutheran Seminary stood squarely in the middle of the three-day Battle of Gettysburg, and its buildings became both headquarters and hospital as townspeople struggled to care for the thousands of Union and Confederate casualties. Skirmishes in and around St. Louis, and rumors that Concordia Seminary there had flown the Confederate flag from its main building, reflected the tensions and dangers experienced in the border states. Union cavalry ranged throughout the Shenandoah Valley throughout the war, causing extensive damage to homes, churches, colleges, farms, and livelihood. Constant bombardment reduced Charleston to rubble, and General William T. Sherman's march through Georgia and the Carolinas destroyed not only the matériel of war but homes and major churches as well. Economic ruin, physical destruction, and the heavy losses sustained by a generation would cripple Southern Lutherans, and the entire South, for decades.

At the conclusion of hostilities in April 1865, Southern Lutherans did not return to the General Synod and voted instead to maintain the regional separation of their church bodies. White Southern Lutheran churches did little to welcome or retain the now-freed African American members of their congregations. While North Carolina did create a separate "Alpha Synod" for African American Lutheran pastors and congregations in 1889 at their request, it did not support it, and after 1891, African American Lutherans sought and received help from the midwestern Missouri Synod instead.

Gradually over time, joint ministry efforts brought Northern and Southern Lutherans together again, particularly through their respective laywomen's and laymen's auxiliaries and their work together on common hymnals and worship books. In 1918 the Northern Lutherans of the General Synod and the General Council eventually reunited with the Southern Lutherans of the renamed United Synod in the South to form the United Lutheran Church in America (ULCA).

See also Boltzius, Johann Martin; General Council of the Evangelical Lutheran Church in North America; General Synod; General Synod South; Mühlenberg, Heinrich (Henry) Melchior; Schmucker, Samuel Simon; United Lutheran Church in America

Bibliography
Anderson, H. G. *Lutheranism in the Southeastern States, 1860–1886*. Mouton, 1969; Johnson, J. *Black Christians: The Untold Lutheran Story*. Concordia, 1991; Nelson, E. C. *The Lutherans in North America*. Fortress, 1975; Records of the Northern and Southern synods, including official minutes of the general church bodies, are located in the respective regional archives of the ELCA.

SUSAN WILDS MCARVER

American Lutheran Church (1930–60)

The ecumenical movement of the twentieth century included numerous achievements of unity among Lutheran church bodies in the United States, of which the formation of the American Lutheran Church (ALC, 1930–60) in 1930 was among the most significant, both for what it accomplished and for what it portended. Two milestone mergers had occurred earlier: in 1917 three Norwegian Lutheran bodies in the United States came together to form the Norwegian Lutheran Church of America, and in 1918 three bodies sharing roots in the colonial period of American history formed the United Lutheran Church in America (ULCA). For all their importance, however, those earlier mergers represented narrower achievements than the formation of the ALC. The Norwegian merger united a majority of Lutherans who had emigrated to the United States from Norway within the previous century, and the ULCA reunited Lutherans who

had shared a common history in the United States until sectional conflict and theological disagreement in the 1860s led to divergent organizations among them. The ALC merger united Lutheran bodies that had not previously shared a common history and, although predominantly German in background, did not identify themselves primarily by ethnic kinship.

The two bodies principally responsible for the formation of the ALC were the Ohio Synod, organized in 1818 among Lutherans with historic ties to colonial Pennsylvania, and the Iowa Synod, founded in 1854 among more recent Lutheran immigrants from Germany. The Ohio and Iowa Synods had become aware of each other through various mutual contacts, especially with the Missouri Synod, founded in 1847. Virulent controversy in the late nineteenth century over the theological doctrine of predestination, in which the Missouri Synod played a major role, spurred the Ohio and Iowa Synods to discern a degree of common interest and understanding that distinguished them both from the attitudes of the Missouri Synod and from the attitudes of the three bodies that would later form the ULCA. A long series of colloquies intended to explore the possibilities of mutual agreement eventually led the Ohio and Iowa Synods to prepare for merger. Once the plans for merger were under way, they included the participation also of two other bodies: the Buffalo Synod, founded in 1845, and the Texas Synod, founded in 1851. Thus in 1930 the ALC united four previously independent bodies in a new Lutheran church body in the United States.

The ALC identified itself as a middle way between the conservatism of the Missouri Synod and the more liberal attitude of the ULCA. From this position, the ALC attended vigorously to the challenges of Lutheran unity in and beyond the United States and to the ecumenical movement globally. The ALC engaged in interchurch relationships under three categories of intention and practice, which may be termed in accordance with ALC usage as cooperation, fellowship, and union. "Cooperation" referred to collaborative ventures that neither required doctrinal agreement nor involved doctrinal contradictions. As examples of such cooperation, the ALC became an active member of the National Lutheran Council, the Lutheran World Federation, and the World Council of Churches. In ALC understanding and practice, "fellowship" indicated the interchange of ministries among church bodies that had formally acknowledged doctrinal agreement while remaining independent organizations. Under the umbrella of the American Lutheran Conference, the ALC secured such fellowship arrangements with other Lutheran bodies in the United States. The third category of interchurch relationships, "union," meant the full merger of church bodies under new ecclesiastical organization. Just as the ALC itself came into being through the union of its own predecessor bodies, so it also became a strong promoter of further union within the American Lutheran Conference, leading in 1960 to the formation of a new Lutheran body, named The American Lutheran Church (with capitalization of "the" as the only difference in name), which united the ALC with Norwegian-background and Danish-background church bodies in the United States.

Throughout its thirty-year history, the ALC continued to engage in dialogue with the Missouri Synod and the ULCA. Although its relation to the former tended to grow cooler, its relation to the latter gradually warmed, encouraged by positive experiences of cooperation in the National Lutheran Council. The ALC's approval of "selective fellowship" with both bodies in the 1940s arose from its enduring intention to chart a middle way between them. While the ALC and the ULCA never reached a point of union in their relationship, both of them helped to secure the subsequent church mergers that became party to the formation of the Evangelical Lutheran Church in America in 1988.

See also American Lutheran Church (1960–88); Evangelical Lutheran Church in America; Inner-Lutheran Ecumenism; Lutheran Church–Missouri Synod; Lutheran World Federation; Ohio/Buffalo/Iowa Synods; Reu, Johann Michael; United Lutheran Church in America

Bibliography
American Lutheran Church. *Official Reports and Minutes* of the biennial conventions, 1930–58. Columbus, Ohio; Meuser, F. W. *The Formation of the American Lutheran Church: A Case Study in Christian Unity.* Wartburg, 1958; Nelson, E. C. *Lutheranism in North America, 1914–1970.* With foreword by K. S. Knutson. Augsburg, 1972.

PAUL A. BAGLYOS

American Lutheran Church (1960–88)

The American Lutheran Church (1960–88) was formed in 1960 by the merger of the American Lutheran Church (ALC), the Evangelical Lutheran Church (ELC), and the United Evangelical Lutheran Church (UELC); officially called The American Lutheran Church (TALC); and became part of the merger that produced the Evangelical Lutheran Church in America (ELCA) in 1988. It was the first large US Lutheran merger between churches of different ethnic heritages (German, Norwegian, and Danish). Conversations toward union began among the five member churches of the American Lutheran Conference in the 1940s. As plans progressed, two of the five withdrew from the conversations—the Augustana Synod, because it sought a broader union among members of the National Lutheran Council; and the Lutheran Free Church, whose congregations rejected the proposal (but which subsequently united with The American Lutheran Church in 1963). The three remaining bodies united at the constituting convention in Minneapolis in 1960, forming a new church with some 2.3 million members in 4,941 congregations, demographically centered in the upper Midwest, but with strong pockets in upstate New York and Ohio. The convention elected Fredrik A. Schiotz, who had led the ELC since 1954, as TALC's first president. TALC began its existence with twelve colleges and four seminaries (in Columbus, Ohio; St. Paul, Minnesota; Dubuque, Iowa; and Berkeley, California) and with overseas mission work in some eighteen nations. It established its headquarters in Minneapolis, naming Augsburg Publishing House as its publisher and *The Lutheran Standard* as its official magazine. TALC maintained membership in the National Lutheran Council and the Lutheran World Federation, as well as the World Council of Churches. President Schiotz served until 1970, when Kent S. Knutson was elected to succeed him. Knutson, a respected younger theologian and churchman, gave promise of bringing new energy to the church, but his service was cut short by his untimely death in 1973. He was succeeded by TALC's vice president, David W. Preus, a Minneapolis pastor, who led TALC until it became part of the ELCA in 1988. Throughout its life TALC generally regarded itself as "centrist" among the three largest American Lutheran Church bodies, more liberal theologically than the Lutheran Church–Missouri Synod (LCMS) but more conservative than the Lutheran Church in America (LCA), and more congregational in polity, especially among some of its Norwegian American constituents, yet with a fairly strong denominational identity. Seeing itself rather consciously in the role of "bridge church," in 1968 TALC declared itself to be in fellowship with both the LCA and the LCMS. In 1969 the latter church approved altar and pulpit fellowship with TALC. This relationship lasted, though often with some tension, until 1981, when LCMS severed it; the issues precipitating that decision included TALC's approval of the ordination of women in 1970, its active involvement in ecumenical organizations, and a continuing disagreement over the meaning of the inspiration and inerrancy of the Scriptures. With the severing of fellowship with LCMS, TALC aligned itself more closely with the LCA; these two churches, along with the Association of Evangelical Churches (a break-off group from the LCMS), formed the ELCA in 1988. At the time of this merger, TALC comprised 2.3 million members in 4,974 congregations.

See also American Lutheran Church (1930–60); Evangelical Lutheran Church in America; Inner-Lutheran Ecumenism; Lutheran Church–Missouri Synod; Lutheran World Federation; United Lutheran Church in America

Bibliography
Nelson, E. C. *Lutheranism in North America, 1914–1970*. Augsburg, 1970; Nichol, T. W. "The American Lutheran Church: An Historical Study of Its Confession of Faith according to Its Constituting Documents." PhD diss., Graduate Theological Union, 1988; Rogness, A. N. *The Story of the American Lutheran Church*. Augsburg, 1980.

RICHARD O. JOHNSON

American Lutheranism Controversy

"American Lutheranism" refers to a nineteenth-century attempt to create a uniquely American form of Lutheranism. While it included broad, nondoctrinal issues, such as language, ethnicity, worship styles, and conversion techniques, its primary controversy was an attempt to revise the Augsburg Confession. American Lutheranism began in the 1820s, when its leading advocate, Samuel S. Schmucker, determined to make Lutheranism in America both a national denomination with formally educated and self-consciously Lutheran pastors and a major contributor in shaping American Protestant culture.

After helping preserve the General Synod, Schmucker became the first professor at Gettysburg Lutheran Seminary in 1826. Composing his own professorial installation vow, he pledged to teach in accordance with the "inspired Word of God . . . , the Augsburg Confession, and Catechisms of Luther," which were "a summary and just exhibition of the fundamental doctrines of the Word of God." By "fundamental doctrines," Schmucker meant those basic Christian teachings that separated Lutherans (and other Christians) from non-Christians, such as deists, atheists, and Unitarians. In 1828 he drafted an ordination vow for use in the General Synod: it affirmed that the "fundamental doctrines of the Word of God are taught in a manner substantially correct in the doctrinal articles of the Augsburg Confession."

While the expressions "substantially correct" and "doctrinal articles" afforded interpretative latitude, Schmucker viewed the new vow as a confessional advancement over earlier vows, which lacked reference to the Augsburg Confession. While emphasizing Lutheranism, the 1828 vow also afforded flexibility in working with other evangelicals in promoting Bible and tract societies, Sunday schools, obligatory Sunday observance, abolition, prison reform, temperance, and other social causes. Although commitment to the Bible as the sole source of authority was a common denominator among American evangelical Protestants, Schmucker rejected anticreedalism but also distrusted long and complex belief statements.

Schmucker viewed the uniqueness of American religious freedom as both human progress and an opportunity to fashion a uniquely American Lutheranism. While Lutheran territorial and national churches in Europe were legally constituted and at least loosely defined by their confessions, American Lutherans had no governmental restraints in revising both practices and theological expressions.

Already in the first edition of his seminary text *Popular Theology* in 1834, Schmucker used the Augsburg Confession as a basic outline but included sections of his detailed disagreement with several of its articles. He understood these views to represent the vast majority of contemporary American Lutheran clergy.

Dissenters from American Lutheranism, however, gradually appeared. Some were new arrivals from Europe, influenced by the confessional awakening there. Immigrating also were university-educated clergy who were acquainted with recent Reformation studies. In the late 1830s Lutherans known already in Germany as "Old Lutherans," because they embraced the entire Book of Concord, began arriving and formed the Missouri, Buffalo, and Iowa synods. By the mid-1840s the Missouri Lutherans publicly criticized Schmucker and American Lutheranism.

Ohio emerged as a border state between predominantly English-speaking, eastern American Lutherans and newly arriving Germans, many of whom leaned toward Old Lutheranism. The Ohio Synod (1818) began a seminary in Columbus in 1830 and provided a more conservative alternative to the Gettysburg Seminary; its *Lutheran Standard* provided perspectives different from the *Lutheran Observer*, edited by Benjamin Kurtz, an ardent advocate of American Lutheranism.

Although American Lutheranism was supported by prominent General Synod leaders, by 1840 its presumed near-universal support was questionable, prompting Schmucker to support American Lutheranism with *Portraiture of Lutheranism*. Nevertheless, opposition to American Lutheranism strengthened during the decade. In 1848 the Eastern District of the Joint Synod of Ohio adopted the entire Book of Concord. In 1849 William Reynolds, Schmucker's former student, publicly renounced American Lutheranism and with Charles Philip Krauth cofounded *The Evangelical Review*, a conservative theological journal. General support for American Lutheranism among English-speaking Lutherans was also challenged with the 1851 publication of the Book of Concord in English by Henkel Press in New Market, Virginia.

Indefatigable and convinced that the restatement of his beliefs with greater clarity and logic might still prevail, Schmucker published *The American Lutheran Church* in 1851. Yet personnel changes at both college and seminary at Gettysburg had shifted faculties in a more conservative direction. In 1853 the Ministerium of Pennsylvania both adopted the entire Book of Concord and rejoined the General Synod, while Samuel Sprecher, president of Wittenberg College in Ohio, urged a clearer definition of American Lutheranism. The particularly poor reception accorded Schmucker's 1855 *Lutheran Manual* signaled an imminent inflection point. Supporters of American Lutheranism gathered during the General Synod meeting in 1855 and concluded that a more definitive statement of American Lutheranism would be useful, especially for new synods being formed in Ohio, Indiana, and Illinois. With special support from Kurtz and Sprecher, Schmucker wrote the forty-two-page *Definite Platform*, which, without attribution of authorship, was mailed in early fall of 1855 to pastors within the General Synod.

Reactions to the *Platform* were immediate, vociferous, and overwhelmingly negative. The document's request either to pay for the unsolicited mail or to return it was irksome, as was its anonymity—though authorship was quickly ascertained. Individual synods that wished to adopt the *Platform* were instructed not to modify it, a condition that appeared presumptive, undemocratic, and not without irony, in that this was itself a major adaptation. Yet the most serious criticism lay in its modifications of the Augsburg Confession.

The *Platform*'s preface noted that five errors had been removed: approval of the ceremonies of the Mass, use of private confession and absolution, denial of the divine obligation of the Christian Sabbath, baptismal regeneration, and the real presence of Christ in the Eucharist. The *Platform* began by affirming the normative role of the Old and New Testaments, followed by the Apostles' and Niceno-Constantinopolitan Creeds, omitting the Athanasian Creed. Next came the "American Recension of the Augsburg Confession," which included only the first twenty-one so-called doctrinal articles. Statements condemning specific sixteenth-century groups were deleted. Probably the most controversial change was in article 10, on the Lord's Supper, where the Recension substituted "Christ is present with the communicants in the Lord's Supper . . . under the emblems of bread and wine," for the original "the body and blood of Christ are truly present and distributed," thereby supporting a Reformed interpretation of the Supper and rejecting the traditional "real presence." Article 11, private confession, was entirely omitted. Part 2 was a twenty-three-page discussion of the previous five alleged errors as well as four others it identified in the Book of Concord: exorcism, the form of baptism, the

personal or hypostatic union of the divine and human natures in Christ, and the "special sin-forgiving power of the Lord's Supper." Part 2 was not intended as a constitutional document but simply as a fuller explanation of American Lutheranism.

The proposed platform was adopted by only three small synods in Ohio. Other synods either denounced or ignored it. Within a year, heated public exchanges were halted by mutual agreement, and the General Synod reaffirmed its existing confessional subscription to the unaltered Augsburg Confession.

Matters simmered unresolved until 1864, when the Franckean Synod joined the General Synod with confessional statements less specific than those of the General Synod. The conservative Ministerium of Pennsylvania delegates withdrew in protest. Subsequently the Franckean Synod stated that its application assumed agreement with the confessional position of the General Synod. Furthermore, the General Synod removed the phrase "substantially correct" from its own commitment to the Augsburg Confession, effectively rejecting American Lutheranism. That same year Schmucker retired, but when the Ministerium of Pennsylvania candidate was not chosen to succeed him, the ministerium started a confessional, bilingual (German and English) seminary in Philadelphia.

An aftershock occurred in 1866. When the somewhat reassured Ministerium of Pennsylvania arrived for the General Synod meeting, its 1864 departure was ruled a formal severance requiring formal readmission. Rebuffed, the ministerium explored options that led to the 1867 formation of the more confessional General Council, which the Old Lutherans, however, declined to join, forming instead the Synodical Conference in 1872.

Throughout his career Schmucker remained consistent in his understandings of Lutheranism, while Lutheranism in America became increasingly confessionally oriented. Clearly the publication of the *Definite Platform* was the catalyst for defining Lutheranism in America.

Although Schmucker's version of "American Lutheranism" ended, many of the broader issues remained, as did aspects of the meaning of confessional subscription and use of the Augsburg Confession for cooperation, communion fellowship, and even mergers with other groups. There has been no subsequent attempt to alter the Augsburg Confession.

See also Augsburg Confession; General Synod; Lutheran Church–Missouri Synod; Ministerium of Pennsylvania; Ohio/Buffalo/Iowa Synods; Schmucker, Samuel Simon

Bibliography

Ferm, V. A. *The Crisis in American Lutheran Theology*. With appendix B, the *Definite Platform*. Century, 1927; Gustafson, D. A. *Lutherans in Crisis: The Question of Identity in the American Republic*. Fortress, 1993; Schmucker, S. S. *Elements of Popular Theology with Occasional Reference to the Doctrines of the Reformation, as Avowed before the Diet at Augsburg, in 1530*. Smith, English, 1834; Suelflow, A. R., and E. C. Nelson. "Following the Frontier, 1840–1875." In *The Lutherans in North America*, 147–251. Rev. ed. Fortress, 1980; Wentz, A. R. *Pioneer in Christian Unity: Samuel Simon Schmucker*. Fortress, 1967.

JAMES W. ALBERS

Amsdorf, Nikolaus von

Amsdorf (1483–1565) was professor at the University of Wittenberg, first Evangelical bishop, and Luther's friend and interpreter. From the lesser nobility, Amsdorf, a nephew of Johannes von Staupitz, became an instructor at the infant university of Wittenberg (1502). Among the first to support Luther's ideas for reform, he accompanied Luther to Leipzig (1518) and Worms (1521) and stood alongside Philip Melanchthon in developing Wittenberg reform, although the two began to disagree over the interpretation of Luther's teaching at some points in the 1530s. Amsdorf left Wittenberg to lead the reformation of Magdeburg (1524–42) against fierce opposition from local Roman Catholic clergy but with the city council's full backing. Luther ordained him as first Evangelical bishop of Naumburg-Zeitz (1542). Deprived of that position in the course of the Smalcald War, he spent his final years leading the church in the lands of the former elector, Duke Johann Friedrich of Saxony, during and after the time the prince was a prisoner of Emperor Charles V. Following his sharp critique of the Augsburg Interim (1548), Amsdorf became embroiled in controversy over the proper definition of Luther's teaching, condemning the Leipzig Proposal (1548) of Elector Moritz of Saxony and his theological advisers, led by Melanchthon. This controversy issued into disputes within the Wittenberg circle over Georg Major's defense of the Leipzig Proposal's proposition that "good works are necessary for salvation" (Majoristic controversy) and Johann Pfeffinger's defense of the activity of the human will in conversion (synergistic controversy). Amsdorf helped organize the Jena edition of Luther's Works and played a vital role in encouraging the Gnesio-Lutheran party as it developed. His ninety publications, all brief, mainly defend his understanding of Luther's theology against opponents from within Lutheran ranks as well as Roman Catholics, Sacramentarians, and Anabaptists.

See also Luther's Works; Major, Georg; Pfeffinger, Johann; Synergistic Controversy; Wittenberg Circle, Parties within

Bibliography

Dingel, I., ed. *Nikolaus von Amsdorf (1483–1565): Zwischen Reformation und Politik*. Evangelische Verlagsanstalt, 2008; Kolb, R. *Nikolaus von Amsdorf (1483–1565): Popular Polemics in the Preservation of Luther's Legacy*. De Graaf, 1978.

ROBERT KOLB

Anabaptists/Spiritualists

Including "Anabaptists" and "spiritualists" as a single entry reflects an interpretation of the two groups, no longer supported by most Reformation scholarship today, that goes back to the polemical writing of the sixteenth century, especially that of Luther and Melanchthon. The term "Anabaptist" denotes those groups emerging in the early Reformation who practiced baptism upon confession of faith (thereby rejecting pedobaptism), held to a "Sacramentarian" view of the Lord's Supper (designating the position of those allied with Ulrich Zwingli and Johannes Oecolampadius), regarded sanctification as an inevitable corollary of the divine gift of grace, and practiced some form of church discipline consistent with their commitment to a visible church. "Spiritualists," by contrast, rejected external forms of the sacraments, elevated the Inner Word over the written word of Scripture, and regarded the true church as necessarily invisible.

In the context of the early Reformation, the distinction between these two emerging traditions—like the lines separating supporters of Luther from the followers of Zwingli or Calvin—were often blurred. Faced with the challenge of defending the orthodoxy of the Evangelical Reformation against attacks from the Catholic Church, the early Lutheran reformers tended to regard all radical groups as an undifferentiated threat, generally under the heading of "Schwärmerei" (fanaticism). In their eyes, these movements were dangerously subjective and thus a threat to the Reformation cause and to public order. With a few significant exceptions (e.g., the debate late in Luther's life with the spiritualist Caspar Schwenckfeld), Lutheran reformers focused most of their concerns on the Anabaptist movement.

Following a pattern established by Luther and Melanchthon, Lutheran historiography has traditionally identified the beginnings of the Anabaptist movement with the Zwickau Prophets, the iconoclasm of Andreas Karlstadt, and the apocalyptic teachings of Thomas Müntzer; and it regarded the Peasants' War of 1524–26 and the so-called Anabaptist Kingdom of Münster in 1534–35 as the inevitable outcome of Anabaptist doctrines. For nearly four centuries, through the time of the Luther Renaissance of the early twentieth century, standard readings of the Reformation generally dismissed the Anabaptists as heretics and seditious revolutionaries. They were, in the wording of a standard church history text, the "deformation of the Reformation" (Kurtz).

By the middle of the twentieth century, however, confessionalist polemics had moderated considerably, leading to more nuanced understandings of the Anabaptists and their descendant groups, the Hutterites, Mennonites, and Amish. This new view found its clearest contemporary expression in a series of ecumenical conversations between Lutherans and Mennonites that culminated in an international Study Commission (2005–9) of representatives from the Lutheran World Federation and the Mennonite World Conference. In early 2010 the Study Commission issued a jointly written account of Lutheran-Anabaptist beginnings, *Healing Memories, Reconciling in Christ: Report of the Lutheran-Mennonite International Study Commission*, which became the basis for a service of reconciliation at the Eighth General Assembly of the Lutheran World Federation at Stuttgart in July 2010.

Although Luther referred to the Anabaptists (*Wiedertäufer* = rebaptizers) in one way or another in at least fifty letters, sermons, or table conversations, he had very limited actual contact with Anabaptist leaders. In 1528, responding to a request for assistance in refuting the arguments of the Anabaptists, Luther published *Von der Widertauffe: An zwen Pfarherrn ein Brief* (*A letter to two pastors about rebaptism*; LW 40:229–62), his only major work on the Anabaptists. His primary concern in the tract was to refute their teachings regarding adult, or believer's, baptism. The Anabaptists, he insisted, turned faith into a subjective experience, making baptism dependent on human will and the inner certainty of one's own convictions. In response, Luther vigorously defended infant baptism by drawing on arguments from tradition (the practice dated back to the time of the apostles) and Scripture (the infant John responded to Christ by leaping in Elizabeth's womb even before he was born). Like Zwingli, he insisted that infant baptism was a continuation of the Old Testament ritual of circumcision. He closed by highlighting the inherent association of Anabaptism with social unrest.

In the same year, two other significant Lutheran texts appeared regarding the Anabaptists. Philip Melanchthon, in his *Adversus*

Anabaptistas Iudicium (*Judgment against Anabaptists*), also focused on the theme of baptism. Drawing extensively on the writings of the church fathers, Melanchthon offered a vigorous theological defense of infant baptism and charged the Anabaptists with rejecting the divine power of God's grace conveyed by the sacrament. At the end of the treatise, he denounced Anabaptist teachings on community of goods as fanatical and seditious.

On January 4, 1528, almost simultaneous with the appearance of Melanchthon's tract, Emperor Charles V issued an imperial rescript (based on declarations from the late Roman Empire) that made the practice of "rebaptism" a capital offense. In response to a request from the city of Nuremberg for a theological opinion on capital punishment for Anabaptists, the Württemberg reformer Johannes Brenz counseled moderation. In his *An Magistratus Iure Possit Occidere Anabaptistas* (*Whether the government can legally put Anabaptists to death*), Brenz drew a sharp distinction between spiritual and secular offenses. Spiritual offenses, he insisted, should be attacked only with the spiritual sword of Scripture. Insofar as the Anabaptists did not force their beliefs on anyone, their only crime was misunderstanding Scripture. To impose any punishment harsher than exile, he argued, "would be tyranny and oppression and unjust."

In the end, however, Luther and Melanchthon's views prevailed. In April 1529 the Diet of Speyer strengthened the law against Anabaptists—extending capital punishment to all who harbored an Anabaptist or refused to baptize their children—while also demanding that the decree against Luther and his teachings be strictly enforced. Eager to disassociate the Evangelical movement from the radical teachings of the Anabaptists, Melanchthon hardened his position, referring to the Anabaptists as "angels of the devil."

At the imperial diet of Augsburg in 1530, Melanchthon and other authors of the Augsburg Confession again vigorously distanced the Evangelical cause from the radicals by explicitly condemning the Anabaptists in six articles. Several of the condemnations make clear that the authors were either misinformed about Anabaptist teachings or assumed that the teaching of a single individual represented the Anabaptist movement as a whole. But in at least two articles, CA 9 (on baptism) and CA 16 (on secular government), the descriptions of condemned Anabaptist teachings appear to be reasonably accurate.

In the aftermath of the Augsburg Confession, Lutheran suspicions regarding Anabaptist teachings were seemingly confirmed by an uprising in the North German city of Münster in 1534–35 by people who had rejected infant baptism and were therefore understood to be Anabaptists. The "Anabaptist Kingdom of Münster" triggered a wave of renewed persecution of Anabaptist groups throughout the Holy Roman Empire, including groups resolutely committed to nonviolence.

In February 1536 Melanchthon published *Verlegung etlicher unchristlicher Artikel, welche die Widerteuffer furgeben* (*Refutation of some unchristian articles that the Anabaptists hold*) that escalated the argument to a new level. In the treatise Melanchthon provided familiar arguments defending infant baptism. But his primary intention was to denounce Anabaptist social teachings—particularly their rejection of secular government, the sword, oaths, and private property—that he thought undermined public order. In strong language, he urged government authorities to impose the death sentence on Anabaptists not only for sedition but also for blasphemy against God's Word. In so doing, Melanchthon seemingly contradicted earlier Lutheran positions, put forward by Luther as well as Brenz, that warned against punishing people for false belief.

This same position was endorsed in a memorandum to Landgrave Philip of Hesse written by Luther and Melanchthon and signed by them and Johannes Bugenhagen and Caspar Cruciger Sr. The statement, published in August 1536, offered a formal response to Philip's request for theological counsel regarding capital punishment of several Anabaptists who had been arrested in Hesse. Arguing that secular authorities needed to guard against blasphemy as well as sedition, the writers enumerated Anabaptist heresies, underscored their threat to the civil order, and identified them with the work of the devil. The use of coercive force against the Anabaptists, including capital punishment, they concluded, was appropriate.

Despite these arguments, Lutheran princes were generally reluctant to carry out executions of Anabaptists arrested in their territories. Philip of Hesse, for example, notably rejected the counsel of his theologians, preferring a milder course of fines, imprisonment, or exile rather than capital punishment. Of the estimated three thousand Anabaptists executed in the course of the sixteenth century, more than 80 percent were killed in Catholic lands rather than Reformed or Lutheran territories.

Relations between Lutherans and groups descending from the Anabaptists and spiritualists generally moderated in the following centuries. In the Lutheran tradition, conversations with spiritualist groups occurred in encounters with various expressions of radical Pietism—that is, forms of church renewal that stressed the Inner Word while rejecting or assigning less value to the sacraments and the visible church. Descendants of the Anabaptists took great pains to distance themselves from the Münsterites by emphasizing their pacifism, sober-minded commitment to Christian morality, and political "harmlessness." Many also consciously rejected the label "Anabaptist," preferring to identify themselves as Mennonites, Hutterites, Amish, or Baptism-Minded (*Doopsgezinden, Taufgesinnten*). Although Lutheran clergy occasionally complained when magistrates tolerated the presence of Anabaptist-related minorities, at a local level relations were generally cordial. In the middle of the eighteenth century Lutheran refugees, who were forcibly resettled by Empress Maria Theresa to Transylvania, encountered

a remnant group of Hutterites who had abandoned community of goods. When the Lutherans read the printed sermons and confessions of the Hutterites, however, they were inspired to revive the practice of communal living. Thus the most common names among the Hutterites today (e.g., Waldner, Hofer, Kleinsasser, Glanzer) are all of Lutheran origin. In the early nineteenth century, several Mennonite pastors in southern Germany turned to their Lutheran peers for counsel when devising a new confession of faith. And Lutheran and Mennonite immigrants to colonial Pennsylvania frequently settled in close proximity to each other, sharing a German dialect and folkways that became known colloquially as "Pennsylvania Dutch."

The path to reconciliation was slower among historians and theologians. In the early twentieth century, the influential church historian Karl Holl could still describe the Anabaptists as "fanatics" (*Schwärmer*). But in the 1930s the Verein für Reformationsgeschichte sponsored the publication of several massive source collections on the Anabaptist movement of the sixteenth century, and a growing number of Lutheran historians began to adopt more nuanced understandings of the Radical Reformation.

In 1980 the celebration of the 450th anniversary of the Augsburg Confession led to new conversations between Lutherans and Mennonites regarding the meaning and status of the "condemnations" of the Anabaptists. In July 1980 the executive committee of the Lutheran World Federation adopted a "Statement on the Confessio Augustana," acknowledging that "the specific condemnations of the Confession against certain opinions that were held at the time of the Reformation have caused pain and suffering for some." The statement continued, "We realize that some of these opinions are no longer held in the same way in those churches, and we express our hope that the remaining differences might be overcome." The event prompted a series of official dialogues between Lutherans and Mennonites at the national level in France (1981–84), Germany (1989–92), and the United States (2001–4), which culminated in an international dialogue between the Lutheran World Federation and the Mennonite World Conference. At an international service of reconciliation in July 2010, the Lutheran World Assembly formally endorsed the "Action on the Legacy of Lutheran Persecution of Anabaptists" as an act of repentance for "past wrongdoings and the ways in which Lutherans subsequently forgot or ignored this persecution and have continued to describe Anabaptists in misleading and damaging ways," and the assembly expressed commitments to interpreting Lutheran confessions in light of this history of persecution and to ongoing dialogue and cooperative action between Lutherans and Anabaptists.

See also Baptism; Ecumenical Dialogues; Hoffmann, Melchior; Lutheran World Federation; Switzerland; Zwingli, Ulrich

Bibliography

Brecht, M. "A Statement by Johannes Brenz on the Anabaptists." *Mennonite Quarterly Review* 44 (April 1970): 192–98; Furmanski, W. "Accuracy of the Condemnations of Anabaptists in the Lutheran Confessional Writings." MA thesis, Graduate Theological Union, 2006; *Healing Memories: Reconciling in Christ.* Report of the Lutheran-Mennonite Study Commission. Lutheran World Federation. Mennonite World Conference, 2010; Kurtz, J., *Lehrbuch der Kirchengeschichte für Studierende*. 9th ed. Neumann, 1885; Lienhard, M. "Von der Konfrontation zum Dialog: Die lutherischen Kirchen und die Täufer im 16. Jr. und Heute." In *Einheit der Kirche: Neue Entwicklungen und Perspektiven*, ed. G. Gassmann and P. Norgaard-Hojen, 25–38. Lembeck, 1988; Oyer, John S. *Lutheran Reformers against Anabaptists: Luther, Melanchthon and Menius and the Anabaptists of Central Germany*. Martinus Nijhoff, 1964; Roth, J. D. "A Historical and Theological Context for Mennonite-Lutheran Dialogue." *Mennonite Quarterly Review* 76 (July 2002): 263–76; Seebaß, G. "Luthers Stellung zur Verfolgung der Täufer und ihre Bedeutung für den deutschen Protestantismus." In *Die Reformation und ihre Aussenseiter*, ed. I. Dingel and C. Kress, 271–82. Vandenhoeck & Ruprecht, 1997.

JOHN D. ROTH

Andreae, Jakob

Jakob Andreae (1528–90) was a professor at the University of Tübingen and a primary drafter of the Formula of Concord. Born in Waiblingen, in the duchy of Württemberg, this son of a blacksmith received a ducal scholarship for secondary school in Stuttgart and university studies. Ordained as a deacon in 1546, like most clergy in the duchy he forfeited his position in 1548 when imperial occupying forces imposed the Augsburg Interim. With support from Duke Christoph, he worked in Tübingen against the interim and earned his doctorate before being called to the ecclesiastical superintendency in Göppingen (1553), by which time the interim was no longer in effect. His attempts to promote a decentralized church polity and a rapprochement with Genevan positions on the Lord's Supper (through negotiations with Theodore Beza, 1557) did not lead to a breach with Württemberg's leading churchman, Johannes Brenz, but rather ended with Andreae's being won over to Brenz's positions and to ducal service as an ecclesiastical diplomat outside the duchy. His acceptance of the Württemberg Confession of 1559 against Calvinist views of the Lord's Supper and Christology typified his public defense of specific Lutheran doctrines the rest of his life.

In 1557 his diplomatic missions brought him to the Colloquy at Worms, where he earned Gnesio-Lutheran animosity for his and Brenz's mediating position on Osiander's doctrine of justification. As Christoph's court preacher at the Diet of Augsburg in 1559, Andreae preached two sermons that attempted to establish his faithfulness to Luther's theology on justification and the Lord's Supper. In 1561 he traveled to Erfurt for negotiations on a common German Evangelical front at the Council of Trent; to the Colloquy of Poissy, where his delegation arrived too late to participate in the confrontation of Roman Catholic and Calvinist parties; and to Ducal Saxony, where he offended Gnesio-Lutherans through his formulation of a compromise over Victorin Strigel's position on the freedom of the human will. In 1563 he led a successful mediation in the dispute over the Lord's Supper and the doctrine of election in Strasbourg. At the Maulbronn Colloquy with theologians from the electorate of the Palatinate (1564), he, Brenz, and colleagues from Württemberg defended their "Swabian" position on the communication of the attributes of the divine and human natures in Christ's person and the true presence of Christ's body and blood in the Lord's Supper. During this period his sharp critiques of Roman Catholics, Zwinglians, Anabaptists, and Schwenckfelders, as in a series of thirty-three sermons preached in Esslingen in 1568, did not fully erase his earlier reputation as a theological lightweight and compromiser.

Duke Christoph called Andreae to the University of Tübingen in 1561 in an effort to strengthen its theological faculty. Andreae continued to advise the duke and support his efforts at achieving agreement among disputing parties within the Lutheran churches. When Christoph's cousin Julius, Duke of Braunschweig-Wolfenbüttel, requested Andreae's services in introducing the Reformation to his lands in 1568, Christoph dispatched Andreae, with the additional assignment of launching a new effort to establish concord. He did so with "Five Articles," on justification, good works, freedom of the will, adiaphora, and the Lord's Supper—brief, general, and positive summaries, expressing Wittenberg teaching in very broad terms. As he journeyed from one princely court or town to another, he accepted suggestions for improving his expressions, which convinced Gnesio-Lutheran critics that he was changing his position under pressure. At a meeting Duke Julius and other princes sponsored under Andreae's aegis in 1570, representatives of several Evangelical governments expressed approval of the final form of these articles but resolved not to subscribe to them officially. Andreae's delight over this meeting quickly turned to disappointment when Electoral Saxon theologians, who had accepted his articles, rejected his Christology during discussions held in Wittenberg.

In 1573 Andreae again offered a proposal for settling differences among Lutheran theologians with his *Six Christian Sermons on the Divisions That Have Continued to Surface*

among the Theologians of the Augsburg Confession. Written in the homiletical form he had used earlier to acquaint laity with significant theological issues on the basis of the text of Luther's Catechism (so that even illiterate laypeople could defend their beliefs), it set forth solutions to six areas of dispute: justification, good works, original sin and freedom of the will, law and gospel, adiaphora, and Christology. His method changed. It now included much more detailed discussion of the issues, with explicit condemnations of false teachings and false teachers (by name), and it sought agreement among theologians apart from princely supervision. Colleagues whom he approached, especially Martin Chemnitz and David Chytraeus, believed that a more substantial argument than one based on the Catechism was necessary. They suggested that the Tübingen faculty compose such a proposal. Andreae persisted, writing the Swabian Concord in 1574, which Chemnitz and Chytraeus revised into the Swabian-Saxon Concord of 1575. With the independently compiled Maulbronn Formula of 1576, this document served as the basis for the Formula of Concord's Solid Declaration.

Even this effort might have gone nowhere had not Elector August of Saxony, confronted by the betrayal of his religious policies by trusted crypto-Philippist advisers, called Andreae to aid in the renewal of Luther's insights within his domains in 1576. Together they decided to promote a larger Evangelical settlement of disputes. August enlisted a committee of his own theological advisers headed by Andreae and Nikolaus Selnecker, to which he added Chemnitz, Chytraeus, and two representatives of the Elector of Brandenburg, Andreas Musculus and Christoph Körner. They hammered out the agreement reached in the Formula of Concord. At the same time, Andreae was enlisted to write a digest of the now-lengthy Solid Declaration, which became the Epitome. Andreae tirelessly promoted acceptance of the Formula and won adherence from two-thirds of the Evangelical ministeria in Germany by

1580. He fashioned the preface of the Book of Concord, which combined other Lutheran confessions with the Formula.

In 1586 Andreae represented his duke, now Ulrich, and Lutheran theology at a colloquy in Mömpelgard (Montbéliard) with Theodore Beza and a team of Calvinists. His last decade he spent in teaching and defending the theology of the Formula of Concord against Roman Catholic and Reformed critiques.

See also Augsburg Interim; Book of Concord; Brenz, Johannes; Formula of Concord; Inner-Lutheran Ecumenism; Württemberg

Bibliography

Dingel, I. *Concordia controversa*. Gütersloher Verlagshaus, 1996; Kolb, R. *Andreae and the Formula of Concord: Six Sermons on the Way to Lutheran Unity*. Concordia, 1973; Müller-Streisand, R. "Theologie und Kirchenpolitik bei Jacob Andreae bis zum Jahr 1568." *Blätter für württembergische Kirchengeschichte* 60–61 (1960–61): 2294–395.

ROBERT KOLB

Andreae, Johann Valentin

The theologian and minister Johann Valentin Andreae (1586–1654) was founder of Christian brotherhoods and promoter of church reform. Andreae was born in Herrenberg, grandson of the Lutheran theologian Jakob Andreae. After his father's death, he moved to Tübingen, where he studied wide-ranging disciplines, including astronomy and mathematics (1601–7); after five years abroad he turned to theological studies (1612–14). During this period he came into contact with many teachers and thinkers, among whom were Kepler and Maestlin. With the Paracelsian physician Tobias Hess and the professor of law Christoph Besold, Andreae was involved in the compilation of the first Rosicrucian manifestos (1610–14). He also wrote alchemical and utopian works, such as *Chymische Hochzeit* (1616) and *Christianopolis* (1619).

From 1614 Andreae served as deacon in Vaihingen and from 1620 to 1638 as chief pastor in Calw. This second period of his life is characterized by both a lively literary production and pastoral activities. Dissociating himself from the Rosicrucian turmoil, Andreae was involved in several attempts to create a Christian brotherhood within Lutheranism, which in his opinion had neglected church discipline and catechetical instruction. Drawing on Johann Arndt's mystical teaching, he aimed to gather a group of learned Lutheran believers under the patronage of a "pious prince" in order to promote a spiritual, political, and educational improvement of society, a vision represented in blueprints for the constitution of a Christian union he drafted between 1619 and 1628. Andreae's original literary output decreased in the last decades of his life, due to the difficulties of the time (e.g., the Thirty Years' War) and his increasing pastoral responsibilities.

In 1639 he was appointed court preacher and councillor in Stuttgart, where he devoted himself to the reorganization of the church in Württemberg. Then he withdrew to Bebenhausen, where he served as bishop of the local abbey from 1650 till his death. His correspondence with other theologians and fellows, which reached its climax during these years, vividly discloses Andreae's intellectual world in connection with seventeenth-century church and society as well as his contribution as a writer of devotional literature, preacher, Christian utopian, art collector, naturalist, and member of the Fruchtbringende Gesellschaft. Of particular relevance in this period is the correspondence with August the Younger Duke of Braunschweig-Lüneburg (1579–1666). Andreae's practical- and piety-oriented theology belongs to a European movement for the renewal of intellectual culture, spiritual literature, and modern science. He saw himself as a genuine Lutheran, shared Arndt's emphasis on developing an inner Christian life, and stressed that spiritual regeneration necessarily entails a practical commitment. His teaching, which often combines theological principles with hermetical and utopian elements, had a deep influence on the Lutheranism in Württemberg and later on Pietism.

See also Andreae, Jakob; Arndt, Johann; Formula of Concord

Bibliography

Bibliotheca Philosophica Hermetica, ed. *Rosenkreuz als europäisches Phänomen im 17. Jahrhundert*. In de

Pelikaan, 2002; Brecht, M. *Johann Valentin Andreae, 1586–1654: Eine Biographie*. Vandenhoeck & Ruprecht, 2008; Dickson, D. R. *The Tessera of Antilla: Utopian Brotherhoods and Secret Societies in the Early Seventeenth Century*. Brill, 1998.

STEFANIA SALVADORI

Angola

The fast-growing Lutheran Church in Angola (Portuguese: Igreja Evangélica Luterana de Angola, IELA) numbered nearly fifty thousand members in 2013 and is a member of the LWF and of LUCSA (Lutheran Communion in Southern Africa).

The Rhenish Mission was active in the former kingdom of Kwanyama (in southern Angola) since 1871; the first converts were baptized in Omuponda in 1895. The number of Christians increased to twelve hundred in 1915. However, when the political situation became difficult in 1915, Lutherans left Angola for northern Namibia. In 1933 some of them returned to do missionary work for the Evangelical Lutheran Church in Namibia. Thus African leadership was instrumental from the beginning. The Lutheran Mission of Oshitata/Namayaka was founded in 1955 by Pastor Simson Ndatibo, while the mission of Shangalada was established in 1965 by Rev. Noah Ndeutapa. Another group of Lutherans penetrated from the North. In 1994 they united in the IELA. Since the end of the civil war, IELA has focused on reconstruction as well as on proclamation.

The Confessional Lutheran Church of Angola began in Cabinda in 1991, under the auspices of the German Bleckmar Mission, and in 1997 entered into a cooperative relationship with the Brazilian church, the IELB. The IELB seminaries have provided theological formation through Theological Education by Extension since 1999. The church has five congregations, with seven hundred members.

Bibliography
Ndawanapo, T. "As influências religiosas e educativas da igreja evangélica luterana de Angola no seu contexto ontem e hoje." Diss., Sao Leopoldo, 2010.

FRIEDER LUDWIG

Ansbach Memorandum (Ansbacher Ratschlag)

The Ansbach Memorandum was a Lutheran critique of the Barmen Confession, issued two weeks after the Barmen Synod concluded in May 1934. Written by Werner Elert, a professor of historical and systematic theology at Erlangen University, it was signed by eight Lutheran theologians, including Paul Althaus. The memorandum claimed to represent "the genuine Lutheran voice" in addressing the issues that were dividing German Protestantism at the time, particularly with respect to the church-state relationship and its consequences for the church's self-understanding of its historical role. The eight theses of the Ansbach Memorandum (countering the six theses of Barmen) emphasized its signers' loyalty to the Führer and the new Nazi state, as well as the necessity for theological openness to the demands of history, *Volk*, and race. While Elert and Althaus were not members of the German Christian movement, the two theologians had written the 1933 Erlangen opinion on the "Aryan paragraph," defending the exclusion of "non-Aryan" Christians from congregations. The Ansbach Memorandum was immediately attacked by the supporters of the Barmen Confession as a document that blatantly supported the German Christians. Althaus in particular came under fire from colleagues and subsequently attempted to distance himself from the memorandum, claiming it was intended to be a theological response to what Althaus viewed as theological problems in the Barmen Confession, particularly its interpretation of revelation.

See also Althaus, Paul; Barmen Confession; Elert, Werner; Erlangen

Bibliography
Ericksen, R. P. *Theologians under Hitler*. Yale University Press, 1985; Helmreich, E. C. *The German Churches under Hitler*. Wayne State University Press, 1979.

VICTORIA J. BARNETT

Anthropology

Theological anthropology tells of "the justifying and saving God and sinful and lost humanity" (LW 12:311). In this definition, not only did Luther intend to accent the existential character of the knowledge of God (Lohse 40–41) but he was at the same time delimiting the place of theology among the faculties of the university, where medicine, law, and philosophy had other ideas about human nature and destiny. Theological anthropology does not say all that can be said, but rather interprets the human phenomena in its relation to God from the perspective of the gospel of Jesus Christ.

If this distinction between regions of inquiry is not respected, theological anthropology becomes vulnerable to category mistakes. It will think that it must contradict the human sciences when science appears to contradict theology, or it will think that it can only speak credibly when it follows the lead of the human sciences, even when they appear to contradict theology. Theology surely hopes in the unity of truth. In the interim, however, theology denies that anyone yet sees as if from heaven. Believers see through a glass but dimly, even as they look to the day when they shall know, even as they have been known (1 Cor. 13:12). The sound reason for this humility in theological anthropology is that in relation to the God of the gospel, humanity is not a single thing; speaking rightly about it is ever a matter of careful discernment.

In theology, humanity is taken as a historical event passing *in a series through states*, as in Israel's journey from Egypt to the promised land, in a cosmic drama larger than itself. Lutheran Orthodoxy, following a pattern set in the Formula of Concord, accordingly codified theological anthropology in a fourfold scheme of humanity, specifying the states of created integrity, corruption by sin, justification in Christ, and final perfection in the Spirit (Schmid 217–68). Within this scheme, the motif of the image of God from Gen. 1:26–28 was given central play. Created in the image of God, the image was lost by Adam's sin, restored in the new Adam, Jesus Christ, and is to be perfected on the last day in the praises of redeemed humanity, mirroring back to God the glories of his love.

Tidy as the scheme is, it was the product of profound controversy with confessional opponents and within early Lutheranism itself. While post-Tridentine Catholicism could move in the Pelagian direction of Molinism with Rome's decision against Jansenism, Lutheranism itself came to oscillate between the poles of Pelagianism and Manichaeism, the Scylla and Charybdis laid out in the would-be settlement of intra-Lutheran quarrels over theological anthropology and codified in the first two articles of the 1576 Formula of Concord (Hinlicky, *Paths*, 142–76).

The root of the difficulty lies in the ambiguity of the claim, going back to Luther himself but resting on certain medieval and ancient understandings, that the image of God was "lost" in Adam's fall (LW 1:62–65). The biblical text explicitly affirms, however, that in spite of human fallenness (Gen. 8:21), the abiding status of humanity as image of God remains. Indeed, it makes this divine regard for fallen humanity the theological basis for human dignity and earthly justice (Gen. 9:7; cf. LW 2:141–42) without regard, then, to the lost worthiness. The same text from Genesis reiterates the mandates of creation from Gen. 1:26–28 and enunciates anew God's resolve to bless, which in turn becomes the divine motive in the election of Abraham and the initiation of the history of salvation (Gen. 12:1–3), as Luther also sees (LW 2:142–43, 257–60). Thus Luther explicitly affirms that despite the loss, human nature remains "restorable," with a "capacity for immortality" or with a "passive disposition" to be converted (cf. SD 2.89 in *BC* 561). For the very purpose of creation, theological anthropology also speaks of a *freed* will that cooperates *willingly* with the Spirit (SD 2.88 in *BC* 561).

The springboard of Luther's Reformation theology had been his sharp break from the optimistic anthropology concerning natural powers upheld in the late medieval nominalism in which he had been schooled (Gassmann and

Hendrix 149–63), particularly the claim that if the human beings "do what [power] is in them" (*facere quod in se est*), God is obligated to do the rest (Oberman 84–103). Luther found sublime sin masked in this. Not only does it presume a sovereign self, obligating God, "as if God were in our service and debt and we were his liege lords" (LC, Ten Commandments 22, in *BC* 389), but it makes nugatory the costly grace of Christ to save and redeem lost and sinful humanity.

When Luther claimed that the image was lost, then, his specific target was such sublime religiosity that "wants to be God and does not want God to be God" (LW 31:10), that makes "God into an idol . . . and set[s] ourselves up as God" (LC, Ten Commandments 23, in *BC* 389). In place of the living human image of God the Giver, there now appears this human *caricature* of God, reflecting the serpent's false promise, "You shall be as God. . . ." Accordingly, in commenting on Gen. 5:1–3, Luther made note of a possible distinction between image and similitude (likeness), so that, *unlike* the *caricature* but according to the similitude, a human being living as image of God would "understand God and . . . desire what God desires" (LW 1:337). If we take up this suggestion, we could explicate Luther's undifferentiated claim about the loss of the image by saying that the *image* (that is, the command, calling, and promised blessing of Gen. 1:26–28) is filled by the caricature of God with *unlikeness* to God the Giver (in its response of disobedience and unfaith). Just this *unlikeness* to God the Giver in the *image* of God is the *corruption* of the human's creaturely nature, the wages of which are curse and death.

Supporting such an explication of Luther's meaning is the observation that Luther exposits the loss of the image in Adam's fall as his loss of the Spirit, who had filled him with the filial trust in God. This filial trust was true likeness to God, the "original righteousness" (which Karl Barth called the "analogy of faith" in distinction from the Thomist "analogy of being"; cf. *CD* I/1:236–45). Just this *loss of*

the Spirit brings *spiritual* death. If we follow out this line of thought, we do not get trapped in the static categories of substance and accident that tripped up early Lutheranism in the so-called synergistic controversies (Mildenberger 154–62) that arose after Luther's death (though in the Genesis lectures, Luther may already have been responding to the first soundings of those later controversies; cf. Kolb).

If we take human "nature" as an abiding substance that persists unchanged through time, then we have to regard acquired properties as accidents, as nonessential additions (in the case of sin, nonessential privations) to its being. The substance-accident scheme forces us to say one of two unseemly things. Either we must say that sin is a nonessential, merely accidental deprivation that can do no substantial damage, or we must say that sin transubstantiates human beings into offspring of the devil, that is, either Pelagianism or Manichaeism—neither a good choice. The 1576 Formula of Concord excludes either extreme (so Gassmann and Hendrix). But by retaining the Aristotelian categories, Mildenberger claims, the Formula hardly settles the questions of theological anthropology in a satisfactory way.

Another approach is, however, already indicated in Luther's use of his Augustinian legacy in theological anthropology. That approach focuses on the role of desire, in Luther's vocabulary, *voluntas*, willingness that is bound (*unfree* to do otherwise than) to desire its good and turn away from its evil. Willingness is Luther's anthropological concept for the "passive disposition" that remains with the image of God even after likeness to God has been lost (Hinlicky, *Luther*, 139–78). Willingness is what the Spirit must capture if the justifying and saving God is to grasp and set free the lost and sinful creature. *What* good and *what* evil do human beings willingly will? That is the true question of theological anthropology, as may be seen in Luther's exposition of what it means to "have a god."

First, the category of desire explicates the ecstatic character of the human's creaturely "nature"; what makes a creature by nature a creature is a peculiar kind of "having, as having not" (cf. 1 Cor. 7:29–31), namely, a having that is not the possessing of another but willing trust in another. Creatures desire. They desire because they are needy, not having life in themselves but only from other lives physically and with other lives socially. If human beings do not know that they are such needy creatures, they become "blind" to their true state. They are blinded to their being as creatures when they want to be God and do not want God to be God.

Second, then, the predicament of wanting the impossible overtakes human beings, since no one can simply have others, physically or socially, in the sense of taking them into possession, like the rich fool in Jesus's parable. One who would take possession of others physically exploits them and subverts the physical ecology of things; one who takes possession of others socially dominates them and so distorts the social economy. Augustine explicated sin in terms of these disordered desires of *greed* and *the lust to dominate*, concepts that Luther readily appropriated.

But "to have a god" is not properly possession—"to grasp him with your fingers, or to put him in your purse, or to shut him up in a box"—but rather to have "something in which the heart trusts completely," a joyful surrender into the keeping of another. In this light, "that to which your heart clings in every time of trouble . . . is really your god" (LC, Ten Commandments 13–15, in *BC* 387–88), whether properly so or idolatrously. So the critical questions of human life become clear: *Who* is trustworthy? *What* is our good and *what* is our evil?

In this connection Luther observes that "there has never been a nation so wicked that it did not establish and maintain some sort of worship. All people have set up their own god, to whom they looked for blessings, help, and comfort." One could say that in sinfulness, humans manufacture idols by which to secure blessing because to do so is and remains "natural," in the sense that human beings are and remain creatures of desire, ecstatic becomings and not persisting substances, looking as they must for blessing, however corruptly. Gross or refined, idolatry thus bears a covert witness to an ineradicable thirst for God, the Giver of life.

In that light, the always concrete question in preaching the gospel is not whether human beings love, as creatures must, but what they love, whether it is worthy of all our trust. That is humanity's "point of contact"—its crumbling idols, its demonic possessions—in preaching the justifying and saving God. Such preaching accomplishes *prophetic* critique: "false worship" of refined idolatry is the "greatest" of all that would "wrest heaven from God" just because it is "unwilling to receive anything as a gift from God" in joyful thanksgiving but instead is "desiring to earn everything by itself or to merit everything by works" (LC, Ten Commandments 22, in *BC* 388–89). Corrupted natural desire leads to death, not life, because it worships what is by nature not God. It is therefore satisfied by extinguishing it (LW 31:54), that is, by baptismal dying with Christ.

Being done through the cross with that sublime idolatry of human religiosity (not to mention the grosser ones), the redemption and fulfillment of the human creature's desire would be "the sort of heart that expects from [God] nothing but good, especially in distress and need, and renounces and forsakes all that is not God," for "then you have the one, true God" (LC, Ten Commandments 28, in *BC* 390) and his "good law . . . in which one lives." Thus he cites Augustine's favorite Bible verse, Rom. 5:5, "God's love has been poured into our hearts through the Holy Spirit" (LW 31:15).

See also Augustine of Hippo; Creation; Justification

Bibliography

Barth, K. *Church Dogmatics*. Trans. G. W. Bromiley and T. F. Torrance. T&T Clark, 1975; Gassman, G., and S. Hendrix. *Introduction to the Lutheran Confessions*.

Fortress, 1999; Hinlicky, P. R. *Luther and the Beloved Community: A Path for Christian Theology after Christendom.* Eerdmans, 2010; Hinlicky, P. R. *Paths Not Taken: Fates of Theology from Luther through Leibniz.* Eerdmans, 2009; Kolb, R. *Bound Choice, Election, and Wittenberg Theological Method: From Martin Luther to the Formula of Concord.* Eerdmans, 2005; Kolb, R., and T. J. Wengert, eds. *The Book of Concord: The Confessions of the Evangelical Lutheran Church.* Fortress, 2000; Lohse, B. *Martin Luther's Theology: Its Historical and Systematic Development.* Trans. R. A. Harrisville. Fortress, 1999; Mildenberger, F. *The Theology of the Lutheran Confessions.* Trans. E. Luker. Fortress, 1986; Oberman, H. A. *The Dawn of the Reformation: Essays in Late Medieval and Early Reformation Thought.* T&T Clark, 1986; Schmid, H. *The Doctrinal Theology of the Evangelical Lutheran Church.* 3rd ed. Lutheran Publication Society, 1899.

PAUL R. HINLICKY

Antinomianism/Antinomian Controversies

Antinomianism is a theological perspective, especially debated among Lutherans, that minimizes or eliminates the role of the law in Christian experience. From its origins, Christianity has had to deal with an ambiguous relation to the category of "law." In the New Testament Gospels, Jesus is often depicted as breaking, ignoring, or superseding the law (e.g., Matt. 7:28–29; 9:3; Mark 2:18–28; 3:1–6; Luke 19:1–10; John 9). In Acts, the apostles do the same thing (Acts 10). In Rom. 6, the apostle Paul anticipates the objection that his teaching about justification by faith is a recipe for licentiousness (v. 1, "Should we continue in sin in order that grace may abound?" cf. Gal. 2:17), while in Rom. 10:4 he insists that "Christ is the end of the law."

One solution to the ambivalent relation to the law, especially in Paul, which came to dominate medieval interpretations, was proposed by Jerome, who insisted that the "law" did not pertain to moral law but only to ceremonial and political laws in Israel. In addition, he insisted that the moral law was within human capacity to fulfill—although not without the Holy Spirit's aid. Augustine, on the contrary, insisted in *On the Spirit and the Letter* that Paul uses the word "law" to include all commandments and especially moral law. Moreover, by quoting the rules of Tychonius in *On Christian Doctrine* (3.33.46), as well as in *On the Letter and Spirit*, Augustine provides a secondary interpretation of 2 Cor. 3:6 ("the letter kills"), as distinguishing law from promises. His comment in the *Confessions* (10.29), "Give what you command, and command what you will," met with strong objection from Pelagius, who attacked it for promoting licentiousness (and thus for being antinomian).

Martin Luther's arguments in favor of justification by faith alone, coupled with his distinction between law and gospel as God's word that alternatively terrifies and comforts, opened him early on to charges of promoting licentiousness. Thus his Palm Sunday sermon of 1519, published that year as *The Two Kinds of Righteousness* (LW 31:293–306), and *Freedom of a Christian* (LW 31:327–77), published in late 1520 with a preface to Leo X, both address the accusation. This persistent charge, included in John Eck's *404 Articles* published in Augsburg in 1530, received a direct answer in the Augsburg Confession, article 20, which begins: "Our people have been falsely accused of forbidding good works." This article, most likely drafted by Philip Melanchthon, points to the Reformers' works on the Ten Commandments, while dismissing as "childish" many works of late medieval piety (e.g., pilgrimages, monasticism, rosaries). It continues, however, to insist on justification by faith alone, on the effects of the gospel (as comfort for the terrified), and on faith as trust and assurance. Good works, then, are the Holy Spirit's fruit in the justified life, not its basis.

Nevertheless, several intra-Lutheran struggles centered on the role of the law in Christian life and were especially sparked by the theology of Johann Agricola. In 1527, in what some call the prelude to the antinomian controversy, Johann Agricola (then rector of the Latin school in Eisleben) complained to the Saxon court about the *Visitation Articles*, published in Latin in the fall of that year, and its primary author, Philip Melanchthon. To Agricola, Melanchthon made knowledge of sin dependent on preaching the law and as arising out of servile fear rather than being dependent on the gospel and filial fear (i.e., faith), where servile and filial fear were familiar categories of late medieval Scholastic theology. Agricola even cited Luther's use of a German adage: "Not to do a thing again is the highest form of penitence." The law could only terrify, as the examples of King Saul and Judas proved, whereas only the gospel brought about true repentance, as in the cases of King David and Peter. Meeting at the Torgau Castle in late November, Martin Luther provided compromise language, to which Agricola agreed and which made its way into the official German *Instructions by the Visitors for Parish Pastors in Electoral Saxony* (LW 40:263–320, here 275–78), published in 1528. While the *Instructions* acknowledged that faith in the God who threatens and commands precedes repentance, yet for the sake of the simple believers especially, it was necessary to teach that the law reveals sin and thus must be preached and that the gospel and justifying faith remove sin. Despite this agreement, Agricola's three catechisms, published around this time, continued to treat the law as useful but secondary to the Christian life, to be employed by the Christian like Ciceronian rules for rhetoric.

Ten years later, with the arrival of Agricola in Wittenberg and his entry into the theological faculty there, the antinomian controversy proper erupted between Agricola and Martin Luther. It began in January 1537 with Agricola's preaching that only the gospel brought about true penitence and was heightened when anonymous theses circulated in Wittenberg, arguing that the law belonged only in city hall (and not in the pulpit). Arising at the same time as the Cordatus controversy (when Conrad Cordatus attacked Caspar Cruciger Sr. and Philip Melanchthon for teaching that good works were a *conditio sine qua non* for salvation), Agricola's complaints now seemed to hold that the law had no role to play in the Christian life. Later in the spring, several of Agricola's sermons appeared in print, and when Luther refused to allow the publication of another of Agricola's writings, Agricola responded by letter, claiming that his teaching was apostolic and matched Luther's own earlier position. In a summary of his teaching, Agricola affirmed the law's usefulness for civil order but not for repentance. In turn, Luther preached and published several sermons on law and gospel, beginning in a sermon delivered on September 30, 1537. When an armistice of sorts was reached in October, Elector John Frederick sent his chancellor to oversee Agricola's adherence to it, and Luther blocked the publication of Agricola's *Summaries* of the Gospels, already under way in Wittenberg— summaries that consistently excluded the law from justification. Following another dustup in November, Luther published the anonymous theses (for which he held Agricola responsible) and his own countertheses, which he defended (on December 18) in a disputation that Agricola did not attend. For Luther, the law's work on the sinner preceded the work of grace; moreover, believers' existence as simultaneously righteous and sinner meant that the law had continuing significance for them. In deriving repentance from the gospel, the anonymous theses erroneously separated defaming Christ from breaking the first commandment. Combating past legalism in the church by eliminating the law simply led to false security.

In the following weeks, Luther published three more sets of theses on the subject. As the controversy threatened to upset the unity of Wittenberg's theological faculty, Melanchthon, Katharina Luther, and Justus Jonas tried to act as mediators. Luther, exercising his authority as dean of the theological faculty, first relented and allowed Agricola license to teach before rescinding that permission and turning the matter over to the university senate on January 6, 1538. Instead of a trial, a second disputation was held on January 12, 1538, in which Agricola participated and because of which reconciliation again was temporarily achieved.

By late summer, due to suspicions about Agricola from Luther and the court preacher in Mansfeld, Michael Coelius, the controversy again boiled over, leading to another antinomian disputation (WA 39/1:354–57) held by Luther on September 6 of that year. Among other things, he likens imagining that the law need not be preached to "putting on a play in an empty theater" (WA 39/1:355, lines 39–40), since the law and its accusation cannot be wished out of existence by a theological sleight of hand but can only be ended by faith in Christ's redemption. Again, attempts at reconciliation, mediated by Melanchthon, fell short, and by January 1539, Luther's attack, *Against Antinomianism*, dedicated to Agricola's opponent in Eisleben, Caspar Güttel, appeared (LW 47:99–119). In it Luther attacked Agricola by name, contrasting Agricola's approach to the law and its place only in city hall to the Augsburg Confession and Apology and claiming that he (Luther) had never rejected the commandments. Because the law reveals sin, "If there is not sin, Christ is nothing" (LW 47:110). Moreover, there is no such thing as a pure Christian without sin. He appealed to Agricola (111): "Preach that sinners must be roused to repentance not only by the sweet grace and suffering of Christ . . . but also by the terrors of the law." If Luther were to refrain from preaching the law, it not only would contradict his own confession of faith (and that of Bernard of Clairvaux) but also would make the law's accusation worse, since the law is written in the human heart. He then specifically attacked the antinomians' claim "whereby one is to preach grace first and then the revelation of wrath." This contradicts the movement of Paul's own arguments in Rom. 1:18–3:20. Luther recounts all of his opponents, beginning with the papacy, Müntzer, Karlstadt, the Anabaptists, the antitrinitarians, and compares his situation with that of the early church, attributing it to the devil's work, and commending the church to God's care.

At this point, Agricola's teaching also seemed to be gaining traction with several disciples in Saalfeld (Caspar Aquila) and in the duchy of Crossen (Heinrich Hamm), as well as in Wittenberg and Eisleben. Agricola himself first attempted a kind of defense in a disputation held in the arts faculty in February 1539 but then went on the offensive, lodging a formal complaint against Luther with the rector of the university and with Johannes Bugenhagen (as the superintendent of Saxony) in August, then with the Mansfeld clergy in January 1540, and finally with the Saxon elector in March 1540. At this point the die was cast, and when it became clear that not only were his demands for Luther's apology falling on deaf ears but also that he would not be exonerated but rather subject to further attacks from Luther (see the public disputation in September 1540 by Joachim Mörlin) and perhaps arrested, Agricola secretly escaped to Berlin and was appointed court preacher for the Brandenburg elector Joachim II. Luther and Agricola were never fully reconciled, although Melanchthon and the two electoral courts arranged a cease-fire in 1541 that involved an apology and recantation by Agricola, in which he blamed his Roman opponent in Eisleben (Georg Witzel) for inciting such radical statements from him. In 1548 Agricola's isolation became even greater in the wake of the Augsburg Interim, in the writing of which he participated, when both Melanchthon and Aquila broke off relations with him.

Agricola's chief concern—that the Wittenberg theologians were reverting to a kind of Christian moralism and that true repentance stems from the gospel—continued to play itself out after Luther's death in a series of disputes, sometimes called the second antinomian controversy, involving the role of the law in the Christian life and sparked by the Majoristic controversy. From 1563 to 1571, pastors in Nordhausen (Anton Otto) and in Erfurt (Andreas Poach) fought with Mörlin and Matthias Flacius over the use of the law in the Christian life (i.e., the third use), as defined in Melanchthon's 1534 commentary on Colossians and in his *Loci communes* from 1535 and 1543. While admitting that the law kept order and restrained evil in the world (first or civil use) and revealed sin and drove to Christ (second or theological use), Otto and Poach denied that it functioned in the Christian life itself, since faith in Christ, not law, generated good works. A similar debate arose at the University of Frankfurt an der Oder, where Andreas Musculus (Agricola's brother-in-law) and Abdias Praetorius fought specifically over the existence of a "third use" of the law for the Christian life, and Musculus insisted on the spontaneity of good works in the life of believers, as Luther had taught in *Freedom of a Christian*. Although incorrectly labeled "antinomian," these debates were included in the Formula of Concord, where article 5 addressed the distinction between law and gospel (and the varying definitions of gospel) and article 6 dealt specifically with the third use of the law. In the latter article, Musculus (one of the Formula's authors) contributed directly to formulations that admitted to a third use of the law but insisted that for the new creature, qua new creature, good works came spontaneously from a "free and merry spirit."

These debates continued to echo throughout the later history of the Lutheran Church. Thus Stephan Praetorius (1536–1603), sometimes seen as a precursor to Pietism, was accused of antinomianism and perfectionism in the period after publication of the Book of Concord (1580). Similarly, Johann Arndt's theology also tried to define more precisely the role of law in the life of the regenerate. This same interest was also found in the Rostock theologian Theophil Großgebauer (1627–61). For his part, Philip Jacob (Philipp Jakob) Spener, while influenced by Arndt's so-called mystical theology, opposed Praetorius and Großgebauer and insisted on the role of the law in the life of the regenerate. At the same time, other Orthodox Lutheran theologians continued to investigate the distinction between law and gospel and the third use of the law—for example, Philip Nicolai and John Gerhard.

In more recent times, a twentieth-century debate over law and gospel among Lutheran theologians arose out of the nineteenth-century controversy over the nature of the atonement. Such scholars as Werner Elert and Gerhard Forde argued that the distinction between law and gospel formed the very center of Lutheran theology. When Karl Barth wrote an article in the 1920s titled "Gospel and Law," insisting that only the gospel could truly lead to repentance, Lutheran theologians, including Elert, responded with articles on law and gospel, insisting that the sinner first encountered the law, which drove to repentance and the forgiveness of the gospel. By contrast, the stern moralism of Søren Kierkegaard and the attacks by Dietrich Bonhoeffer on "cheap grace," while clearly reflecting earlier concerns of Pietism, continued to stimulate debate over the law's place in Lutheran theology. Especially in the wake of World War II and the Holocaust, some (including Paul Tillich) traced Lutheranism's perceived political quietism to its weak understanding of the law as contrasted to the more robust admiration of law among the Reformed. With the rise of individualism in contemporary European and North American cultures, which values self-expression (provided no harm is done to others) as crucial for human fulfillment, some, counter to the Lutheran tradition, even claim the gospel as giving license to sin. Such a stance is incompatible with Luther's thinking since Luther, with Paul, acknowledged that Christians have "died to sin" (Rom. 6:2). Current debates among Lutherans over specific moral issues often bring with them charges of antinomianism on the one side or moralism and legalism on the other. For the most part, however, these debates have more to do with how to understand and apply specific moral injunctions of Scripture than with the elimination of the law in all aspects of the Christian life.

See also Agricola, Johann; Flacius, Matthias Illyricus, and the Flacians; Law, Uses of the; Major, Georg; Mörlin, Joachim; Musculus, Andreas

Bibliography

Arand, C. P., R. Kolb, and J. A. Nestingen. *The Lutheran Confessions: History and Theology of The Book of Concord*. Esp. 194–99. Fortress, 2012; Brecht, M. *Martin Luther: The Preservation of the Church, 1532–1546*. Trans. J. Schaaf. Esp. 156–71. Fortress, 1993; Forde, G. *The Law-Gospel Debate: An Interpretation of Its Historical Development*. Augsburg, 1969; Mann, J. K. *Shall We Sin? Responding to the Antinomian Question in Lutheran Theology*. Lang, 2003; Richter, M. *Gesetz und Heil: Eine Untersuchung zur Vorgeschichte und zum Verlauf des sogenannten Zweiten Antinomistischen Streits*. Vandenhoeck & Ruprecht, 1996; Wengert, T. *Law and Gospel: Philip Melanchthon's Debate with John Agricola of Eisleben over "Poenitentia."* Baker, 1997.

TIMOTHY J. WENGERT

Antitrinitarians

Thinkers of the sixteenth and seventeenth centuries who rejected the doctrines of the Trinity and the two natures of Christ as expounded since the dogmatic decisions of the early Christian councils at Nicaea (325), Constantinople (381), and Chalcedon (451) have come to be collectively known as antitrinitarians. This negation was often all that the various strands of antitrinitarianism had in common. In terms of their positive christological concepts and their understanding of God, they represented a whole spectrum of views. Even the answers of antitrinitarians varied considerably in explaining how God the Father, God the Son, and God the Holy Spirit relate to one another and how the person of Christ is to be understood. The Spanish antitrinitarian Michael Servetus propounded a modalistic concept of God in his early works *De Trinitatis erroribus libri septem* (Seven books on the errors of the trinity, 1531) and *Dialogorum de Trinitate libri duo* (Two books of dialogues on the trinity, 1532). He argued in favor of the incarnation (understood literally) of the preexisting Son of God, which was combined with Neoplatonic speculation about the *Logos* in his later work *Restitutio christianismi* (The restoration of Christianity, 1553). While the Italian antitrinitarians Matteo Gribaldi and Valentino Gentile, who had been influenced by Servetus's early works, adopted his Christology, they believed that the Son of God, who had been begotten before the

world was created, and the Holy Spirit were subordinate to God the Father, who was unbegotten, and they distanced themselves from Servetus's modalistic view. This tritheistic perspective was then revised by Lelio and Fausto Sozzini, the founders of the most important branch of antitrinitarianism, Socinianism. The Sozzinis rejected all ideas of the preexistence of Christ and propounded the Unitarian principle that Jesus Christ was a unique human being in historical terms, unto whom divine power was only transferred by God the Father through his resurrection and ascension.

As civil law in the Holy Roman Empire of the German Nation made antitrinitarian ideas illegal, they did not lead to the formation of new churches there. However, they did lead to the formation of new churches in eastern central Europe. In this process, the Unitarian or Socinian strand of the antitrinitarian Reformation came after the tritheistic strand. Developed by the Padua legal scholar Matteo Gribaldi around 1554, tritheistic ideas were circulated in Poland-Lithuania by his Lithuanian follower Petrus Gonesius as early as 1556. After the Italian physician Giorgio Biandrata succeeded in communicating these ideas to a number of influential nobles such as Nikolaus Radziwiłł (The Black), an antitrinitarian church, the so-called Ecclesia reformata minor (Minor Reformed Church), emerged in the early 1560s. Tritheistic works written by Italian and Polish-Lithuanian authors during this phase of the antitrinitarian Reformation gave rise, around 1565, to a Europe-wide debate in which the prominent Lutheran theologians Johann Wigand and Jakob Andreae and the Tübingen philosopher Jakob Schegk participated. Some of their arguments then became part of article 12 of the Formula of Concord (1576) via Jakob Andreae.

The Unitarian phase of the antitrinitarian Reformation began with the commentaries on the prologue to the Gospel of John written by Lelio Sozzini in Zurich, the *Brevis explicatio* (Short explication, ca. 1561), and by Fausto Sozzini in Basel, the *Explicatio* (Explication,

1563). The manuscripts were brought to Transylvania by migrating Italians. There Biandrata, who was court physician to King Johann Sigismund Zápolya, and Franz Dávid had them printed. The *Brevis explicatio* was published in 1568 in Alba Iulia (German: Weißenburg; Hungarian: Gyulafehérvár) as chapter 11 of volume 2 of *De falsa et vera unius Dei patris, filii et spiritus sancti cognitione* (On the false and true knowledge of one God the Father, the Son, and the Holy Spirit), and the *Explicatio* was published anonymously as a separate publication in the same year and in the same place. Around the same time, the two commentaries came to the attention of leading Polish-Lithuanian antitrinitarians such as Simon Budny and Gregor Paweł, who under their influence rejected the preexistence of Christ. In spite of the resistance of Peter Gonesius and other adherents of tritheism, the unitarian Christology developed by the Sozzinis was largely adopted by the Polish-Lithuanian Ecclesia reformata minor during the course of the 1570s. In the antitrinitarian church in Transylvania, it was the dominant doctrine from the start.

With the arrival of Fausto Sozzini in Poland-Lithuania in the winter of 1579–80, the formation of the doctrine of the antitrinitarian Ecclesia reformata minor entered its final phase. After internal unitarian debates, in some cases very heated, Sozzini succeeded in communicating to the younger generation of unitarians his concept of salvation and his anthropology, which he had developed in the manuscripts *De Jesu Christo Servatore* (On Jesus Christ the Savior, 1578, printed 1594) and *De statu hominis ante lapsum* (On the condition of man before the fall, 1578, printed 1610) as a logical consequence of unitarian beliefs regarding Christ. The idea that Jesus Christ is only relevant to salvation by virtue of his historically unique moral teachings, which he demonstrated in an exemplary way through his life, and that humans, who are mortal by nature, can and must follow the example he set in order to attain eternal life—that became the official doctrine of the Ecclesia reformata

minor during the 1590s. In this form, Socinian unitarianism—as systematically described in *Unterrichtung von den vornehmsten Hauptpunkten der christlichen Religion* (Instruction on the most important chief points of the Christian religion, 1604) by Christoph Ostorodt and in the Racovian Catechism (Polish: 1605; German: 1608; Latin: 1609) prepared by Hieronymus Moskorzowski, Valentin Schmalz, and Johannes Völkel—received attention throughout Europe. Since the German version of the Racovian Catechism was dedicated to Wittenberg University, Lutheran theologians, who until then had only intermittently polemicized against unitarian Christology, began to engage the central ideas of Socinianism intensively. The Wittenberg theology professor Wolfgang Franz started the long series of anti-Socinian disputations in 1608, with colleagues such as Nikolaus Hunnius, Balthasar Meisner, and Albert Grauer in Jena soon following his lead.

See also Andreae, Jakob; Servetus, Michael

Bibliography

Balázs, M. *Early Transylvanian Antitrinitarianism (1566–1571): From Servet to Palaelogus.* Éditions V. Koerner, 1996; Daugirdas, K. *Antitrinitarier.* In *Mainz*, European History Online (EGO), published by the Institute of European History (IEG), August 9, 2011. http://www.ieg-ego.eu/daugirdask-2011-de URN: urn:nbn:de:0159-201108; Dingel, I., ed. *Controversia et Confessio.* Vol. 9, *Antitrinitarische Streitigkeiten: Die tritheistische Phase (1560–1568).* Prepared by K. Daugirdas. Vandenhoeck & Ruprecht, 2013; Wilbur, E. M. *A History of Unitarianism: Socinianism and Its Antecedents.* Harvard University Press, 1946; Wilbur, E. M. *A History of Unitarianism in Transylvania, England, and America.* Harvard University Press, 1952; Williams, G. H. *The Radical Reformation.* 3rd ed. Sixteenth Century Journal Publishers, 1992.

KĘSTUTIS DAUGIRDAS

Apartheid

The concept of "apartheid" most likely appeared in printed form for the first time in 1929 in South Africa. Rev. J. C. du Plessis expressed the conviction that the "spirit of apartheid" had always determined the theology of the Dutch Reformed Church and the mind-sets of its members. Indeed, in 1857 the Dutch

Reformed Church (DRC, *Nederduits Gere-formeerde Kerk*) had already decided that nonwhites should hold their own worship services in separate rooms or buildings; previously, shared worship services and celebrations of the Lord's Supper had been customary. Lutheran missionary work, which mainly had been initiated by Hermannsburg, likewise separated "white" immigrant congregations from "black" mission congregations relatively early. In Reformed theology this separation was religiously based on references from Deut. 23:3 or Josh. 23:9–13. In Lutheran theology it was argued mainly on the basis of the "orders of creation," since people, language, "race," and societal organization were understood as God-ordained "orders of creation." The white church remained unaware that the (at least tacit) agreement with the political system of apartheid concurrently destroyed the orders of marriage and family for the majority of peoples.

Additionally there were political, economic, and ideological reasons that led to the transformation of apartheid mentality, especially in South Africa, into a definite political system. After the Boer Wars at the end of the nineteenth century and the beginning of the twentieth, there arose a new pattern for the state. During British rule, the South African Native Affairs Commission was founded, which suggested that a "segregation" should be established between territories so that some would be inhabited by whites and others by blacks. Indeed, black voters should be registered with their own voting list and white-only representatives could be chosen. Finally, in 1910 the South African Union was founded out of the previous four colonies (Cape Colony, Natal, Transvaal, Orange Free State). From the beginning it was governed by the white population, which at most consisted of 20 percent of the total population. Tensions nevertheless between those of British and those of Boer backgrounds remained. Even so, a continuing politics of segregation was pursued against the blacks and so-called coloreds (other nonwhite

groups apart from black South Africans). In 1911 unequal treatment between blacks and whites in the arena of the economy was cemented by the Mines and Work Act. In 1913 the Natives Land Act limited the black population to their own designated "locations," which consisted of about 7.3 percent of the whole land. The longer this jurisdiction lasted, the more black workers were disenfranchised and through the code of the "Civilized Labor Policy" were excluded from employment in government offices. Further restrictions followed in the 1930s.

But with the surprising victory of the National Party (NP) in 1948, the erection of a state-sanctioned apartheid regime systematically transformed South Africa. This party was ideologically defined by the mind-set of the Boer (Afrikaner) groupthink. The consciousness of being a "chosen people" was religiously and historically determined. Afrikaans was cultivated and propagated as an elite language; the story of the Great Trek, which was publicly called to remembrance in a highly profiled manner in 1938, galvanized an Afrikaner nationalism. Anti-British sentiment was added to it. At the same time the Boer sense of group identity was threatened by the beginning of the politics of decolonialization: India declared independence in 1947.

In the 1950s the voice and influence of the NP steadily increased. But with Henrik Verwoerd—first professor of sociology at the University of Stellenbosch, minister of native affairs beginning in 1950, and prime minister from 1958 until his murder by a worker in Parliament in 1966—the ideological character of apartheid first gained traction. With a growing parliamentary majority, the NP was in position to enact more restrictive laws and thereby secure white rule. Accordingly political power was restricted to the white segment of the population; a "racial" point of view was enforced in all areas of life, which led to classification as white, Indian, colored, and black; a law forbade mixed-race relations between men and women, allocated racially separated areas of settlement, separated educational systems for elementary and advanced education, and strictly controlled residential permits for blacks in the cities (Native Laws Amendment, 1952). The plans for the establishment of "homelands" for the black population go back to Verwoerd. Soon the blacks were forced from mixed areas of settlement, which especially had been established in the suburbs (Group Areas Act, 1950). Only 13 percent of the land was at their disposal for settlement. The black migrant workers were forced to live separately from their families for months, which to a great extent led to the destruction of familial relations. Added to that was the increasing expulsion of all nonwhites from political representation.

In the years after World War II until the early 1970s, South Africa profited strongly from the economic boom in the Western world, but it was mainly to the advantage of the governing stratum of whites. In the time of the Cold War, South Africa's strict anticommunist disposition hindered the Western countries from criticizing South Africa. Gradually economic sanctions began. The South African government saw the progressive decolonizing of Africa as threatening. After the independence of Angola from Portugal, South African troops intervened in occupied Namibia.

In contrast, within South Africa the discriminated populations increasingly fomented resistance and opposition. The African National Congress (ANC), founded by 1912, in the 1950s grew into a mass movement. It upheld the Charter of Freedom adopted in 1955, which advocated for the equality of all population groups, and organized demonstrations, such as against the passport laws. In 1960 this kind of demonstration in Sharpeville led to a massacre in which sixty-nine blacks died at the hands of the police. In the same year the ANC was "banned" by the government, forbidding any such activities (Unlawful Organizations Act, 1969). One consequence of this measure of enforcement was that the ANC felt forced to take up weapons against

the hated regime. This shift in strategy was implemented by Nelson Mandela, who, with seven other compatriots, was given a life sentence in the Rivonia Trial (1963).

In the following years the government's oppressive measures became ever more stringent. The brutality of the police increased. Black workers' strikes and the creation of independent unions added to a heightened level of organization. As Afrikaans was made the mandatory language of teaching in all schools in 1976, a student revolt arose in Soweto, a southwestern black township of Johannesburg; the police fired into the crowd without warning. The protests spread from a base in Soweto across the entire country; in total up to seven hundred people were killed.

In these years, the division of races continued in most South African Christian churches whose origins were as European missions. The practice of altar fellowship between black and white Christians of the same confession was negligible. This was true for Reformed churches as well as Lutherans, not least for the confessionally grounded churches in South Africa. Engaging in the struggle against apartheid was Christian Frederick Beyers Naudé, originally a pastor of the DRC and a charter member of the strongly racist-nationalistic Afrikaner Broederbond, who founded the Christian Institute of Southern Africa in 1961, not least as a reaction to the Sharpeville massacre. Consequently the institute was closed by the state in 1977, and Beyers Naudé, as the first white person so treated, was placed under house arrest until 1984.

In 1971 the World Council of Churches (WCC) adopted its Anti-racist Program, which especially condemned "institutional" racism. In conjunction with this, an endowment was established from which funds for the support of liberation movements were placed at the disposal especially for those in southern Africa yet also for those in Asia and South America. Armed groups in Mozambique, Angola, Guinea-Bissau, Namibia, and South Africa also received monies from this endowment.

Representatives of the Evangelical Church in Germany protested against the praxis of a widespread uncontrolled allocation of church monies. In 1982 the DRC was excluded from the World Alliance of Reformed Churches (WARC) because of its affirmation of apartheid. The Roman Catholic Church began to take an ongoing critical stance against apartheid from the middle of the 1970s.

The Lutheran World Federation at its Sixth General Assembly, in Dar es Salaam (1977), demanded that the white member churches in South Africa recognize the situation as one of *Status Confessionis* and required that the churches reject the apartheid system. An "Appeal to Lutheran Christians in Southern Africa concerning the Unity and Witness of Lutheran Churches and Their Members" in 1975 had already criticized the so-called natural laws grounded in creation in order to realize a comprehensive "pulpit and altar fellowship among the Lutheran churches." Seven years later the Seventh General Assembly of the LWF in Budapest (1984) decided to suspend the membership of the Evangelical-Lutheran Church in South Africa (Cape Church) and the German Evangelical-Lutheran Church in Southwest Africa (Namibia) because they had not sought to implement the Dar es Salaam resolution. This resolution was only lifted by the LWF in 1991.

In South Africa, the South African Council of Churches (SACC), which represented about half of the South African churches, tried to develop a statement about the white government's apartheid system. This resulted in a massive intervention on the part of the government, with the specific consequence of the 1988 destruction of the Khotso House, the seat of the SACC, which was ordered by the erstwhile state president Pieter Wilhelm Botha. From 1978 to 1984, the future Archbishop Desmond Tutu functioned as the SACC General Secretary. His successor was Beyers Naudé, who repeatedly demanded the release of political prisoners, including Nelson Mandela, and advocated for negotiations with the ANC. In 1976 Wolfram Kistner transferred from service in the Evangelical Lutheran Church to the Department for Justice and Reconciliation in the SACC, which he led until 1988, and where he developed a strategy for overcoming the apartheid regime. The 1985 Kairos Document, drafted by a group of black theologians, criticized not only the subjugation laws and measures of the South African regime because of their "moral illegitimacy" but also the more cautious criticism from the majority of churches, and it challenged Christians to contribute to the "fight for liberation and a just society."

From the side of the confessional Lutheran Church in Germany, Friedrich Wilhelm Hopf, director of the Lutheran Church Mission (Bleckmarer Mission), was particularly tireless in protesting on theological grounds against the apartheid regime and its effects. He could thus refer to a letter of Hermann Sasse, already written in 1956: "No Lutheran missionary may ever represent or defend Apartheid." In this sense Hopf brought to bear "the just, immutable will of God" on the relationships of this time and world. Later some of the Lutheran Churches in South Africa arrived at a rejection of the apartheid politics of the government.

With increasing foreign and domestic political pressure, a gradual convergence between the government and opposition groups arose after 1986. One after another, many of the discriminatory race laws were abolished. With the inauguration of F. W. de Klerk as prime minister (February 1989), however hesitantly, a shift in the official political line began: Mandela was freed at the beginning of 1990; in January 1992 he and de Klerk were awarded the Nobel Peace Prize. In May 1994 the first free elections for all South African citizens were held; winners were mostly of the ANC. Mandela was elected the first president of all South Africa.

In South Africa, the Truth and Reconciliation Commission was constituted to reappraise the history of apartheid. The victims and perpetrators testified about their experiences in public hearings. In this connection the DRC apologized for its wrongdoings during the apartheid era. But not all Lutheran churches took part in this process. One of the recognized difficulties was that the concept of reconciliation is marked in strong Christian and church terms, yet the commission had a quasi-governmental brief. In addition, Christians were not only addressed as victims but also as perpetrators. This meant that for the political arena in South Africa, reconciliation would not be possible without "truth" and "acknowledgment," for reconciliation aims at a comprehensive invitation to take part in societal life. But clear distinctions needed to be made between a legal/moral understanding of "reconciliation" and a theological one. For example, this distinction could be defended by using Dietrich Bonhoeffer's distinction between the "penultimate" (political reconciliation) and the "ultimate" (reconciliation in a spiritual sense).

As it concerns the Lutheran Church, not only in South Africa, many questions remain to be answered: What is the relation between the teaching of the Scriptures and the actual interpretation in the various churches? How does the confessional grounding of Lutherans relate to their advocacy and witness to God's Word and the Lutheran confessions? How can defining the relationship between the concept of the "orders of creation" and of salvation be understood? Can the concepts "orders of creation" and the two kingdoms still be used, or are Lutherans instead more at home in a Calvinist sphere? How do (or did) religious leaders and boards react to apartheid legislation (e.g., standards of legislation that finally led to establishing the apartheid regime)? What relationships should exist between caring for souls, defending the oppressed, theological objection (Acts 5:29), and political adaption to the apartheid system? How is the relationship between the scriptural principle and the so-called zeitgeist to be understood? Was the gift of "distinguishing the spirits" in those years present and/or alive in the church? How was the two-kingdoms doctrine misused to ignore

obvious injustices? By what principles were decisions based, to intervene with the South African state and/or its security apparatus? How would the political use of the law (in the Lutheran sense) be brought to bear in the preaching and teaching of the confessional Lutheran churches? Would pastors, judicatories, congregational members, and church governing officials be in a position to understand and admit personal misdeeds, inequities, and false and mistaken decisions?

See also Lutheran World Federation; Namibia; Race/Minorities; Slavery and Colonialism; South Africa; State

Bibliography

Beinart, W., and S. Dubow, eds. *Segregation and Apartheid in Twentieth-Century South-Africa.* Routledge, 1995; Bonner, P., P. Delius, and D. Posel. *Apartheid's Genesis, 1935–1962.* Ravan/Witwatersrand University Press, 1993; Klän, W., and G. Da Silva. *Mission und Apartheid: Ein unentrinnbares Erbe und seine Aufarbeitung durch lutherische Kirchen im südlichen Afrika.* Edition Ruprecht, 2013; Morris, M. *Apartheid: An Illustrated History.* Jonathan Ball Publishers, 2012; Nordholt, H. *Apartheid und Reformierte Kirche: Dokumente eines Konflikts.* Neukirchener Theologie, 1983; Renwick, R. *The End of Apartheid: Diary of a Revolution.* Biteback Publishing, 2015.

Werner Klän

(Trans. Ken Sundet Jones and Mark C. Mattes)

Apocrypha and Pseudepigrapha

The term "apocrypha," meaning "hidden," or "secret," denotes writings from the period of the Second Temple (350 BCE–CE 70). Used of the Old Testament (OT), the term refers to a corpus that expands or revises biblical texts, continues literary genres found in the Hebrew Bible, and exhibits close connection with figures in the canonical writings. Currently, writings from the same period as the Old Testament Apocrypha but not associated with Western tradition are termed "Pseudepigrapha." Composed under the aliases of OT patriarchs, they were rejected by the synagogue but preserved by the Christian church. Due to fluidity of boundaries, some writings such as the *Letter of Aristeas* or *4 Ezra* are labeled "pseudepigraphical" while others are labeled "apocryphal." The following constitute the kernel of OT Apocrypha: Tobit, Judith, the Wisdom of Solomon, Sirach, Baruch, Additions to Esther and Daniel, 1 and 2 Maccabees, and the Epistle of Jeremiah. Greek tradition likewise preserves 3 Ezra, the Prayer of Manasseh, Ps. 151, and 3 Maccabees. The OT Pseudepigrapha comprise five groups, with *4 Maccabees* in the first group, the *Odes of Solomon* in the second, Ethiopic and Slavonic *Enoch* in the third, the *Testaments of the Twelve Patriarchs* in the fourth, and in the fifth a series of narrative types such as *Jubilees*.

The term "New Testament Apocrypha" refers to writings similar to those in the New Testament (NT) but that are almost universally rejected from being included in the New Testament canon. Attempts to list the NT Apocrypha might include the *Gospel of Thomas*, *Gospel of the Ebionites*, *Gospel of Peter*, *Gospel of the Hebrews*, *Gospel of the Egyptians*, *Gospel of the Nazarenes*, *Protevangelium of James*, and *Apocryphon of John*, all from the second century. Attempts to list the NT Pseudepigrapha might include the *Gospel of Truth*, *Gospel of Philip*, *Acts of Peter*, *Acts of Paul*, *Kerygma Petrou*, and *Apocalypse of Peter*. Coptic texts discovered at Nag Hammadi in 1945 have added to the number of the Apocrypha or Pseudepigrapha and, in addition to the *Gospel of Thomas* with its seventy-five parallels to the Synoptic Gospels, contain dialogues with the Savior and literature dealing with the deeds of the apostles.

From 1529 to 1534, Luther wrote prefaces to eight of the OT Apocrypha. Several he described as "fine," "good," "useful," or even "sacred." He went so far as to write of 1 Maccabees that it deserved to be numbered with Holy Scripture. Since Judith did not rhyme with the biblical histories, he described it as "poetic," identifying Judith as Judea, Holofernes as the godless prince, Bethulia as the virgin, and suggesting that the piece may have been performed. Tobit and the additions to Esther and Daniel were treated in similar fashion, although the story of Susanna was often used to illustrate the eighth commandment in catechisms. Luther thought least of Baruch and 2 Maccabees, writing of Baruch that Aesop or lesser books contained just as good material, and of 2 Maccabees that it had fittingly been "thrown out." Measured by the length of his prefaces, Luther gave first place to the Wisdom of Solomon, then to Sirach, and 1 Maccabees. He set Wisdom within the context of the legation to Rome of Philo of Alexandria, on behalf of Jews in that city (ca. CE 40), a mission that the emperor Caligula spurned, thus moving the writer to threaten heathen, godless rulers with the judgment of God. He described Sirach as a book that had been torn, trampled on, and scattered, but which he had now managed to piece together, and of 1 Maccabees that we learn from it to recognize the antichrist. Evidence that Luther was aware of the NT Apocrypha, or ventured any opinion of them, is lacking. Of the Pseudepigrapha, Luther did show a fondness for the Prayer of Manasseh.

Lutheran Orthodoxy shared with Luther the opinion that the Apocrypha contributed to the edification of believers. It could even acknowledge that the NT Apocrypha merited more favor and approbation than that of the Old Testament. Unlike their Reformed and Roman Catholic contemporaries, some orthodox theologians even allowed some edifying use to the pseudo-Pauline *Letter to the Laodiceans*. The point at which Lutheran Orthodoxy differed from Luther was that its ironclad ascription of canonical authority to the current number of NT books from the outset excluded the Apocrypha. The canon was closed, and the reasons given varied but in large measure were formal in nature: The origins of the canonical books had been clearly ascertained; they were approved by the apostles; they were written by those whose names they bear; they were read publicly in the churches. Ultimately, however, their authority was guaranteed by the Spirit, or, as the dogmatician David Hollatz (1648–1713) put it: "By the internal testimony of the Holy Spirit illuminating the minds of men."

See also Bible Interpretation; Canon; Scripture

Bibliography
"Apocrypha." *RPP* 1:308. Brill, 2007; "Apokrypha." *RAC* 1:517–19. Hiersemann, 1950; "Apokrypha." *RGG* 1:600–604. Mohr Siebeck, 1998; Charles, R. H. *The Apocrypha and Pseudepigrapha of the Old Testament.* 2 vols. Clarendon, 1913; James, M. R. *The Apocryphal New Testament.* Clarendon, 1924; Hennecke, E., W. Schneemelcher, and R. M. Wilson. *The New Testament Apocrypha.* 2 vols. Westminster, 1963–66; *Luthers Vorreden zur Bibel.* Ed. H. Bornkamm. Furche, 1967; Schmid, H. *The Doctrinal Theology of the Evangelical Lutheran Church.* Trans. C. A. Hay and H. E. Jacobs. Augsburg, 1961; Stuhlmacher, P. "Die Bedeutung der Apokryphen und Pseudepigraphen des Alten Testaments für das Verständnis Jesu und der Christologie." In *Die Apokryphenfrage im ökumenischen Horizont,* ed. S. Meuer, 13–26. Deutsche Bibelgesellschaft, 1989.

ROY A. HARRISVILLE

Apologetics

The term "apologetics" is from *apologia*, meaning to make a defense. Apologetics is the theological task of making a defense for the Christian faith in the face of those who challenge its legitimacy on historical, scientific, or philosophical grounds. There are three aspects to this task. First, apologetics aims at dismantling and dismissing misconceptions of the faith. Second, apologetics seeks to demonstrate the weaknesses in arguments offered by opponents of Christianity. Third, apologetics endeavors to set forth the credibility of Christian truth claims.

Contemporary literature on apologetics suggests that there are five types or methods of apologetics (Dulles 353–59). There is the classical type, which seeks to demonstrate the existence of God and then demonstrate that Christianity is the highest expression of theism. The evidential approach relies on historical evidence to arrive at a truth claim. The cumulative-case method seeks to state a hypothesis that will account for the available data. Presuppositional apologetics begins with particular assumptions about the existence of God or the veracity of the Scriptures and then moves to assert claims for the coherence of Christian faith in light of these presuppositions. A fifth category, Reformed epistemology, maintains that there is a way of knowing devoid of external evidences, rooted in John Calvin's notion of internal testimony of the Spirit (*testimonium Sancti Spiritus internum*).

The apologetic effort is taken up in the New Testament itself. This can be seen in 1 Pet. 3:15, where Christians are exhorted to be ready to give a defense for the hope that is within them, and in 1 John 1:1, where the apostle testifies to his own contact with the crucified and risen Lord. Peter's preaching in Acts 2:22 invites his hearers to notice the signs and wonders which they are said to know that God did in their midst through Jesus. Apologetics is carried forward in the patristic period as Christianity is challenged by both Judaism and paganism. Arguments for the existence of God, such as that of Anselm and Thomas Aquinas, characterize apologetics in the Middle Ages. Luther and his immediate successors, strictly speaking, were more engaged in polemics—that is, defending the truth of the gospel against distortions—than apologetics as such. In this sense, it is only with the advent of the Enlightenment that Lutheran theologians were pressed to give attention to apologetics. This is not to say that Luther and his immediate successors have nothing to contribute to contemporary apologetics.

Luther recognized a "natural" but not salvific knowledge of God. The creation and the human conscience bear testimony to the existence and power of God, but the Creator's mercy and grace are accessible only in Jesus Christ. Luther was not so much interested in offering proofs for God's existence as he was in arguing from the existence of God that human beings are to fear, love, and trust in the Creator alone.

In the twentieth century, in the wake of the Luther Renaissance, many scholars focused on Luther's negative evaluation of the place of reason, often ignoring that reformer's appreciation for reason as a divine gift both necessary and serviceable within its own sphere. Thus it was often concluded that Luther had little or no interest in apologetic approaches that would seek to make a persuasive case for the Christian faith. More recent scholarship, such as that of Siegbert Becker and Mark Mattes, has rightly challenged such a reading. Luther affirmed reason as a divine endowment in his explanation of the first article of the creed in the Small Catechism while asserting in article 3 that human beings cannot come to saving faith by their own reason or strength. For Luther, reason is never the source of doctrine, but it is a necessary tool in articulating the Christian faith. To use the language of later Lutheran theology, Luther rejects a magisterial use of reason while affirming reason's ministerial necessity. In his *Confession concerning Christ's Supper* of 1528, he wrote, "We must use our reason or else give way to the fanatics" (LW 37:224). Without an appropriation of reason, theology would fall prey to the very enthusiasm that this reformer rejected.

While apologetics in the modern sense stems from the Enlightenment, theologians in the period of Lutheran Orthodoxy provide examples of the endeavor to make a defense for the coherence of Christian doctrine and the uniqueness of Christian faith in contrast to pagan religions. In the theologians of the age of Orthodoxy, apologetics is most often done as part of the prolegomena.

The Reformed theologian Friedrich Schleiermacher (1768–1834) understood his own work as an apologetic undertaking that sought to make Christian religion accessible to its "cultured despisers." Schleiermacher appealed to the spiritual sterility of the Enlightenment, inviting his audience to make space for religious sentiment unencumbered by antiquated dogmas, asserting that it was possible to be both rational and religious. Substituting principles of religious philosophy for traditional prolegomena, Schleiermacher aimed to provide an experiential rather than a historical or rational basis for Christianity. For him, apologetics is an aspect of philosophical theology rather than practical theology, which concerns itself with evangelization. F. A. Tholuck (1799–1877) and C. E. Luthardt (1823–1902), with

his two-volume work *Apologie des Christentums*, were leading Lutheran apologists in the nineteenth century. In varying degrees both stood in the shadow of Schleiermacher in trying to base the certainty of faith on the basis of spiritual experience.

Several Lutheran theologians in the twentieth century also engaged apologetics. The historian of early Christianity Kurt Aland (1915–94) made an "apologetic for apologetics" in his 1948 book, *Apologie der Apologetik*, in light of the aversion to apologetics by the prevailing Barthian theology of the day. The Tübingen theologian Karl Heim (1874–1958) related Christian faith to natural sciences, arguing the case that Einstein's theory of relativity renders the notion of a universe closed to transcendence untenable. According to Heim, this gives space for a biblical understanding of creation and the miraculous. Heim commends the lordship of Jesus as the only credible answer to the destructive results of human autonomy seen in the despair of skepticism. Science cannot provide answers to the ultimate questions of life and must be shown its own limitations.

For a time a colleague of Heim at Tübingen, Helmut Thielicke (1908–86), later at the University of Hamburg, demonstrated the significance of apologetics in his systematic theology, ethics, popular writings, and sermons. After World War II, Thielicke worked to address nihilism. Later in his career, a significant contribution was the Faith Information Project, which Thielicke initiated in 1971 in collaboration with former students. In the context of informal meetings, Thielicke would engage religious and theological questions raised by young people while at the same time helping pastors prepare for meaningful preaching. In this context Thielicke saw himself as an evangelist and apologist, seeking to explain the Scriptures and make credible the claims of Christianity to a generation influenced by skepticism and uncertainty. Thielicke believed that many in this generation rejected the Christian message because either they had little knowledge of its content or they harbored erroneous misconceptions of the biblical faith. He sought to persuade the intellectually serious to give Christianity another hearing based on a more adequate understanding of what actually constitutes the faith. The fruit of Thielicke's dialogical-catechetical apologetics was compiled in 1976 under the title *The Faith Letters: The Answer of Faith for Today's Questions*.

Paul Tillich (1886–1965) developed a "method of correlation" whereby he sought to use theological language to address contemporary humanity's existentialist questions under the conditions of modernity. Tillich's student Carl Braaten, using more classical Lutheran categories than his teacher, took up the apologetic task in relation to the historicity of Jesus and the uniqueness of the Christian message in the world of religions. Braaten's work was also influenced by Wolfhart Pannenberg (1928–2014), who maintained that the resurrection of Jesus happened historically and that in this event the significance of universal history is made known.

John Warwick Montgomery is a conservative Lutheran theologian who has worked in both North America and Europe, often in conversation and collaboration with apologists from the Reformed tradition. Trained in both theology and law, Montgomery's approach might be characterized as evidentialist, with a strong juridical component. Montgomery's apologetic works range widely, from the existence of God and the historicity of the New Testament to a variety of contemporary ideologies and ethical issues. His historical work includes a defense of the place of apologetics in the Lutheran confessions on the basis of an appeal to Luther, the confessions, and theologians of Lutheran Orthodoxy. Montgomery has created a particular Lutheran approach to apologetics, and his work has influenced a circle of Lutheran apologists, including Rod Rosenblatt, Adam Francisco, Craig Parton, and Korey Maas.

Apologetics will remain a necessary theological task for Lutherans in the twenty-first century as challenges raised by world religious pluralism, relativism, and privatized spirituality confront the central claims made by the Lutheran confessions. An apologetic approach consistent with these confessions will avoid both a rationalistic synergism, which assumes that the human will can be overcome by persuasion, and a retreat into an "enthusiasm," which sees religious truth claims as private and therefore beyond verification. Asserting the primacy of the first commandment and the proclamation that the wisdom of the cross of Christ is the only way of salvation, Lutherans will use apologetics. Apologetics functions to clear away misplaced or unnecessary objections to the faith so that the cross of Christ can stand as the scandal that it is. In this way apologetics can serve both the missionary outreach of the Lutheran Church and as a means to provide the faithful with a coherent rendering of the credibility of the doctrine confessed by this church.

See also Heim, Karl; Lutheran Orthodoxy; Pannenberg, Wolfhart; Philosophy; Theological Education; Thielicke, Helmut; Tillich, Paul J.

Bibliography

Becker, S. *The Foolishness of God: The Place of Reason in the Theology of Martin Luther.* Northwestern, 1982; Braaten, C. *Who Is Jesus? Disputed Questions and Answers.* Eerdmans, 2011; Dulles, A. *A History of Apologetics.* Ignatius, 2005; Francisco, A., and K. Maas, eds. *Making the Case for Christianity: Responding to Modern Objections.* Concordia, 2014; Francisco, A., K. Maas, and S. Mueller, eds. *Theologia et Apologia.* Wipf & Stock, 2007; Mattes, M. "A Contemporary View of Faith and Reason in Luther," In *Propter Christum: Christ at the Center; Essays in Honor of Daniel Preus*, ed. Scott Murray et al., 145–68. Luther Academy, 2013; Montgomery, J. W. *Christ as Centre and Circumference: Essays Theological, Cultural, and Polemic.* Wipf & Stock, 2012; Schwarz, H. *Vying for the Truth: Theology and the Natural Sciences.* Vandenhoeck & Ruprecht, 2012.

JOHN T. PLESS

Apology of the Augsburg Confession

A defense of the Augsburg Confession by Philip Melanchthon, the Apology was first published in 1531. With the presentation of the Augsburg Confession on June 25, 1530, by the Evangelical (Lutheran) princes and cities to the imperial diet meeting in Augsburg, a process began that issued in the publication of its defense (Greek and Latin: *apologia*) the following year. In July 1530 opponents of the Evangelicals, under the aegis of the imperial court and the papal legate, Cardinal Campeggio, worked on a rebuttal or Confutation of the Augsburg Confession. After the emperor dismissed a harsh response that rejected all articles of the Augsburg Confession, a more moderate draft was presented on August 3, 1530. Not allowed access to an official copy of the text, stenographers on the Evangelical side, including Philip Melanchthon's close friend Joachim Camerarius, transcribed what they heard. Even as various (failed) attempts at negotiations were taking place throughout August 1530, work on a defense of the Augsburg Confession began. During the diet's official recess of September 22, the Evangelical princes and cities were confronted by Emperor Charles V's insistence on the unequivocal acceptance of the Confutation (and hence the rejection of the Augsburg Confession) and attempted in vain to present their defense, drafted in large part by Philip Melanchthon but with the input of others (Justus Jonas, Johann Agricola, Georg Spalatin, and Johannes Brenz). Instead, the Evangelical estates were given six months to conform to the imperial decree.

Already on the return trip to Wittenberg, Melanchthon had begun to edit and expand this original version of the Apology, in one instance (in Altenburg) even working on it on Sunday until rebuked by Luther himself for breaking the Sabbath. By the end of October or early November, Melanchthon had come into possession of a bona fide written copy of the Confutation. With the threat (from Landgrave Philip of Hesse) of possible armed conflict and with what Melanchthon judged to be the insidious nature of the Confutation, it became clear that simply adding to the text of the Augsburg Confession itself would not suffice and that a much more thoroughgoing refutation and defense was needed.

From November 1530 until April 1531, Melanchthon worked on the text of the Apology, concentrating especially on article 4 (on justification by faith). Other lengthy sections included articles 12 (on penance) and 24 (on the sacrifice of the Mass). By the end of April 1531 the first Latin edition of the Augsburg Confession and its Apology rolled off Georg Rhaw's presses in Wittenberg in quarto format. To take into account suggestions (in particular from Martin Luther, whose marginal notes on the first edition are extant) and to answer reservations (in particular of Johannes Brenz), Melanchthon produced a second edition in September 1531, now printed in octavo format. His reworking of article 4, on justification, further distinguished between Wittenberg's understanding of being declared righteous and Augustine's (and Brenz's) insistence that the Holy Spirit reckoned people righteous in anticipation of their becoming righteous by doing righteous deeds. At nearly the same time, Justus Jonas was working on a German translation, initially basing his work on the first Latin edition but in the later articles using the (unpublished) text of the second. By the appearance of the second German edition in January 1533, however, Melanchthon introduced changes, especially in article 4, to bring the text even more in line with the second Latin edition. Until Melanchthon's death, the second Latin and German editions were generally considered to be the standard forms of the text.

The 1580 German version of the Book of Concord used the first German edition of Jonas's 1531 translation. When Nicholas Selnecker published an unauthorized Latin edition that same year, he employed the octavo (second) Latin edition, in which Melanchthon had abbreviated the explanation of the presence of Christ in the Lord's Supper. As a result of objections by some who felt that a clearer refutation of those who denied Christ's real presence in the Lord's Supper was needed, the official Latin version of 1584 used the first Latin edition of the Apology, even though the official German text was based on the second Latin edition.

The Apology of the Augsburg Confession provides not only a useful commentary for understanding the Augsburg Confession but also a rejection of the Confutation by providing alternate interpretations of biblical texts used by the opponents and by clarifying the Evangelicals' own arguments. Melanchthon relied not only on Scripture passages to make his case but also on important arguments from the ancient church fathers, canon law, and even (esp. in art. 2, on original sin) medieval Scholastic theologians, as he attempted to demonstrate the catholicity of Evangelical theology. The Apology's arguments centered on a defense of justification by faith alone without works (articles 2, 4, 12, and 20) and underscored the importance of the comfort of the gospel for terrified souls (articles 4, 20, and 24). Article 24 also included an extensive discussion of sacrifice and a rejection of a sacrament's effectiveness *ex opere operato* (by the mere performance of the rite). It also reiterated Luther's basic understanding of the church, its marks, and its pastors' authority (articles 7, 14, and 28). Written in Melanchthon's characteristically clear Latin and often structured according to the rules of rhetoric, these articles helped shape Evangelical self-understanding in the aftermath of the diet in Augsburg. While not as all-encompassing as Melanchthon's second and third editions of the *Loci communes*, the Apology provided an important defense of the central Evangelical teachings. Melanchthon thus included it in his 1560 *Corpus doctrinae*, a collection of his writings that quickly became a standard of doctrine in Electoral Saxony. Competing bodies of doctrine published in the ensuing years in Ducal Saxony and Braunschweig also invariably included it, so that its place in the Book of Concord was also assured.

See also Augsburg Confession; Melanchthon, Philip

Bibliography

Arand, C., trans. "The Apology of the Augsburg Confession." In *The Book of Concord*, ed. R. Kolb and T. J. Wengert, 107–294. Fortress, 2000; Peters, C. *Apologia Confessionis Augustanae: Untersuchungen zur Textgeschichte einer lutherischen Bekenntnisschrift (1530–1584)*. Calwer, 1997.

Timothy J. Wengert

Architecture

Lutheran houses of worship, places "where people can come together, pray, and give thanks to God," appear across the globe in great variety. Luther emphasized that all truth flowed from the Word. Architecture and the arts, as long as their expression did not hinder faith or Christian freedom, fell into the nondogmatic category of adiaphora. Architectural style and ornament thus naturally differ according to time and place. Lutheran worship space, however, is consistently organized around three liturgical centers: a font for the sacrament of baptism (typically at the front near the altar, but for symbolic and theological reasons may also be placed at the sanctuary entrance), an altar or table for the sacrament of Holy Communion, and a pulpit for proclaiming the Word. The need for the congregation to see, hear, and participate is facilitated by this centrally placed pulpit and open access to the liturgical centers, with no spatial barrier between clergy and laity. There may be a separate lectern, and crucifixes (more often crosses in the United States) are common.

Early European Lutheran churches were largely adaptations of former Roman Catholic buildings, typically longitudinal in orientation, with an altar at the east end, transformed primarily by centralizing a dominant pulpit. The practice of standing or bringing one's own seating was later superseded by arranging seating so the congregation could hear the preacher unimpeded. Much Catholic decoration remained, including images and even statues, and Lutherans added their own visual art. Over time the organ, already in many late medieval churches, became a hallmark of Lutheran churches.

The church that is often called the first purpose-built Lutheran worship space is the Castle Church at Torgau, where Luther preached a dedication sermon in 1544. This muted and plain space has two levels of galleries, with the table (behind which the pastor presided, facing the congregation) and font at one end, and a central, carved pulpit attached to a column that faces the main entrance on one of the long sides. While the overall austerity and functionality of the space reflect Luther's guidance, this was not a parish church and must thus be considered apart from common practice. From the sixteenth through the eighteenth centuries, the chief predictor of Lutheran worship space was the local context. Highly decorative Baroque Lutheran churches in Bavaria, for instance, contrast with more restrained, neoclassical buildings in the Netherlands and Scandinavia. The late Baroque floridity of the magnificent, multigalleried Frauenkirche in Dresden (1726–43) shows Lutheran architecture at its most exuberant, a feast for the senses. Within this variety of church types, regional and national Lutheran buildings are often consistent and distinctive: Baroque churches of southern Germany, stave churches of Norway, neoclassical temples of the Netherlands and England.

Nineteenth-century Lutheran churches adapted eclectic revival styles widely popular with other Christian denominations, including the Gothic, Romanesque, and Renaissance. The nineteenth-century brick or frame neo-Gothic Lutheran church was a particularly common sight in the American Midwest. From the nineteenth century through the early twentieth, Lutheran church plans were either traditionally rectangular/axial and formal, or, especially in parts of the United States, auditoriums arranged with a large stage and circular seats, more like a theater and generally signifying a type of worship centered on preaching. In the nineteenth century, Lutheran immigrants to the United States and elsewhere carried their architectural traditions with them, often including a semicircular altar rail with a copy of the *Welcoming Christ* statue from the Copenhagen cathedral or a painting depicting Christ above the altar.

In the 1920s in Europe, modernism began to affect Lutheran church design. Otto Bartning's Stahl Kirche (Steel Church) in Essen, Germany (1928, destroyed 1943), was an early influential example of what could be done by using new materials, in this case a structural steel frame that allowed for extensive use of glass-curtain walls in the nave. Following World War II, these tentative modern beginnings blossomed into a full-blown architectural and liturgical movement. The ideas behind the change in architecture were urgent and serious. The tragedy of war called for a church newly tuned to the needs of the day, one that could speak the language of the people, hence the turn toward modernism, the artistic idiom of the twentieth century. With an emphasis on the gathered church, the longitudinal plan increasingly fell out of favor. In northern Europe and North America, Lutherans were leaders in the modern church movement, creating innovative buildings that experimented with new material, such as folded concrete and faceted glass-block windows, new shapes, and an austerity that focused attention on the people and the liturgical centers. Albert Christ-Janer wrote in 1962, "Lutheran congregations have led the way in the contemporary approach to religious design, often electrifying conservative communities with their modern churches." Eliel Saarinen's Christ Lutheran Church in Minneapolis (1949), an elegant, simple, flat-roofed church with a rectilinear bell tower, was an influential expression of European trends in America. Today new Lutheran buildings range from functional worship halls modeled after evangelical preaching spaces to the revival of traditional forms.

A great variety of buildings may be called Lutheran architecture, including parish houses for congregational life and also schools and hospitals. Lutherans have left a mark on the landscape far larger than the footprint of their churches.

Bibliography
Buggeln, G. *The Suburban Church: Modernism and Community in Postwar America*. University of Minnesota Press,

2015; Hamberg, P. G. *Temples for Protestants: Studies in the Architectural Milieu of the Early Reformed Church and the Lutheran Church.* 1955. Reprint, Acta Universitatis Gothoburgensis, 2002; Luther, M. "Sermon at the Dedication of Castle Church, Torgau, 1544." Ed. and trans. J. W. Doberstein. LW 51:333–54. Concordia, 1959; Spicer, A., ed. *Lutheran Churches in Early Modern Europe.* Ashgate, 2012.

GRETCHEN T. BUGGELN

Argentina

The first Lutherans in Argentina were among the German Evangelicals who began coming to Buenos Aires in the early nineteenth century, formed a congregation in 1843, and called a pastor from the United Prussian Church. This model of not forming exclusively Lutheran congregations was imitated by other German-speaking Lutherans who immigrated to Argentina. In 1899 the German Evangelical congregations organized in Argentina (and in Paraguay and Uruguay) and created the German Evangelical Synod of the River Plate, which became officially affiliated with the German church in 1934. In 1965 the synod became autonomous as the Evangelical Church of the River Plate (Iglesia Evangélica del Río de la Plata [IERP]), although it maintains a privileged partnership with the Evangelical Church in Germany. As a united church, it recognizes the confessions of the Lutheran and the Reformed traditions and also is a member of the Lutheran World Federation (LWF) and of the World Communion of Reformed Churches.

Lutheran mission work in the Spanish language was started in Argentina in 1908 by a missionary from the General Synod of the Evangelical Lutheran Church of the USA and was suspended after the 1910 Edinburgh World Conference on Missions. In 1919, after the 1916 Panama Conference, missionaries of the United Lutheran Church in America (ULCA) resumed work and founded congregations, established schools, trained lay leaders, produced literature in Spanish, and benefitted from funds that became available especially after its missions to China were closed down in the 1930s. In 1924 the missionaries built the first church for a Spanish-speaking Lutheran congregation in South America in Buenos Aires. The nascent congregations constituted themselves in 1948 as the United Evangelical Lutheran Church (Iglesia Evangélica Luterana Unida [IELU]), which was received as an associate synod by the ULCA and soon became a member of the LWF. In the 1950s Hungarian, Latvian, and Estonian refugees formed their own congregations and affiliated with the IELU. The IELU maintains a partnership with the ELCA.

The LCMS started its work in Argentina in 1905, reaching out to German and German-Russian immigrants and their descendants, and using the Spanish language from the 1920s. It assumed the name Evangelical Lutheran Church of Argentina (Iglesia Evangélica Luterana Argentina [IELA]) in 1947, and became autonomous in 1986 while maintaining a partnership with the LCMS. The IELA founded its seminary in 1942 and is a member of the International Lutheran Council.

The first of four congregations associated with the Danish Church Abroad/Danish Seamen's Church was formed by Danes in 1866 in Tandil. The Swedes founded their congregation in Buenos Aires in 1918 and built their church in 1945, where today services are offered by traveling pastors from Sweden, Norway, and Finland.

A Lutheran Seminary serving IELU and IERP and other Spanish-speaking churches affiliated with LWF was founded in Buenos Aires in 1955. In 1969 it merged with another Protestant seminary to form ISEDET, of which the Danes also became members in 1997. ISEDET was liquidated in 2015.

IERP and IELU are committed to fight poverty, exclusion, and environmental destruction and to respect the growing pluralism of Argentine society while developing a new model of pastoral ministry.

Bibliography

Bachmann, T. E., and M. B. Bachmann. *Lutheran Churches in the World: A Handbook.* Esp. 532–40. Augsburg, 1989; Cruz, J. M. *The Histories of the Latin American Church:*

A Handbook. Esp. 101–32. Fortress, 2014; http://www
.dsuk.dk/vores-kirker/sydamerika/; http://www.iela.org
.ar/; http://ielu.org/wordpress/; http://ierp.org.ar/; http://
ilc-online.org/members/latin-america/argentina/; https://
www.lutheranworld.org/country/argentina; https://www
.oikoumene.org/en/member-churches/evangelical-church
-of-the-river-plate; https://www.oikoumene.org/es/member
-churches/united-evangelical-lutheran-church; http://sjo
mannskirken.no/soramerika/; https://www.svenskakyr
kan.se/ambulerande-praster.

ANDRÉS ROBERTO ALBERTSEN

Arndt, Johann

The most influential writer of devotional literature within the Lutheran tradition, Johann Arndt (1555–1621), was born in the principality of Anhalt, where his father was the Lutheran pastor in Edderitz and Ballenstedt. From 1575 to 1581 he studied medicine and theology at the universities of Helmstedt, Wittenberg, Strasbourg, and Basel. He was ordained in 1583 and began a pastorate in Badeborn in the next year. There he defended use of the traditional Lutheran exorcism rite at baptisms in response to Calvinist liturgical changes proposed by the prince of Anhalt. Forced out of his position, Arndt became pastor in Quedlinburg in 1590. He was called to St. Martin's Church in Braunschweig in 1599, where he faced difficulties for taking sides in a power struggle between the duke and the citizenry. Concerned over the decline of moral and spiritual life caused by this lengthy civil conflict, he began to write a practical guide to the Christian life in which he argued that justification through faith should lead to evident personal regeneration. This book was first published in 1605 and expanded over several years until it was reissued in 1610 as *Four Books of True Christianity*. Arndt ministered in Eisleben from 1609 to 1611 and then became general superintendent of the duchy of Braunschweig-Lüneberg. Based in Celle for the last ten years of his life, he conducted a major territorial visitation, prepared a new church ordinance, and published a number of devotional works, which were both widely popular and controversial. These included a prayer book (*Paradise Garden*, 1612) and sermons on lectionary texts (postils), the catechism (1616), and the Psalms (1617).

Although loosely organized, *True Christianity* as a whole was designed to overcome spiritual complacency, inspire contrition, console with the promise of union with Christ, and prepare readers for a long struggle against sinful impulses. From the very beginning the book had its critics. In Braunschweig some of Arndt's pastoral colleagues claimed that his theology was synergistic and perfectionistic. Near the end of his life the clergy of Danzig faulted him for paraphrasing medieval writers such as Angela da Foligno and Johannes Tauler and for borrowing (selectively) from Spiritualists such as Valentin Weigel and Paracelsus. In response, Arndt modified parts of book 1 and wrote an extensive rebuttal, added in 1620 as books 5–6. After his death theologians in Tübingen launched a new attack on his writings, and down to the present there have continued to be interpreters who see Arndt more as a spiritualist than as a Lutheran.

Nevertheless, *True Christianity* became one of the major influences on trends in Lutheran popular piety. More than 240 German editions were printed before 1800, and it was translated into at least eighteen other languages. Arndt inspired numerous seventeenth-century devotional writers and was widely read for several centuries by many types of Lutherans. His most significant impact was on the development of Pietism. Philipp Jacob Spener's Pietist manifesto, *Pia Desideria* (1675), was first issued as a preface to a new edition of Arndt's sermons.

See also Devotional Literature; Pietism; Spener, Philipp Jakob

Bibliography

Arndt, J. *True Christianity (Selections).* Ed. and trans. P. Erb. Paulist Press, 1979; Braw, C. *Bücher in Staube: Die Theologie Johann Arndts in ihrem Verhältnis zur Mystik.* Brill, 1986; Geyer, H. *Verborgene Weisheit: Johann Arndts "Vier Bücher vom Wahren Christentum" als Programm einer spiritualistisch-hermetischen Theologie.* Vols. 1–2 in 1. De Gruyter, 2001; Illg, T. *Ein anderer Mensch werden: Johann Arndts Verständnis der "Imitatio Dei" als Anleitung zu einem wahren Christentum.* V&R Unipress, 2011;

Lexutt, A. "Johann Arndt und das lutherische Bekenntnis." In *Frömmigkeit oder Theologie*, ed. H. Schneider and H. Otte. V&R Unipress, 2007; Lund, E. "'Sensus docendi mysticus': The Interpretation of the Bible in Johann Arndt's Postilla." In *Hermeneutica Sacra: Studien zur Auslegung der Heiligen Schrift im 16. und 17. Jahrhundert*, ed. T. Johansson, R. Kolb, and J. A. Steiger, 223–45. De Gruyter, 2010; Schneider, H. *Der fremde Arndt: Studien zu Leben, Werk und Wirkung Johann Arndts.* Vandenhoeck & Ruprecht, 2006; Wallmann, J. "Johann Arndt." In *The Pietist Theologians*, ed. C. Lindberg, 21–37. Blackwell, 2005.

Eric Lund

Arnold, Gottfried

As a Pietist, theologian, and historian, Gottfried Arnold (1666–1714) was the key literary figure among radical German Pietists and author of the *Impartial History of Churches and Heretics* (1699–1700). He sets the "young Luther," with his message of liberating faith, over against the "older Luther," with his promotion of the godly prince, catechism, sacraments, and hence Lutheran Orthodoxy and its chief proponent (in Arnold's eyes), Philip Melanchthon. Arnold was born and raised in Annaberg, Saxony, where his father was a teacher in the town's Latin school. In 1688, near the end of theology studies in Wittenberg, Arnold began a lifelong correspondence with Philipp Jakob Spener, court preacher in Dresden. Thanks to Spener, Arnold found tutoring positions in Dresden (1689) and Quedlinburg (1693). From 1693 to 1701 Arnold made his home in Quedlinburg, the center of a mystical-spiritualist piety led by Pastor Johann Heinrich Sprögel. In 1701 he married Sprögel's daughter and became court preacher in Allstedt; later he became pastor in Perleberg. Author of seventy books, Arnold is best known for the *Impartial History* and for a history of the early church, *Die erste Liebe* (The first love, that is, a true portrait of the first Christians according to their living faith and holy life, 1696). Arnold portrayed the first Christians as a community without clergy, hierarchy, dogmas, confessions of faith, formal liturgy, or church buildings, and observed a falling away from these ideals under Constantine. His portrayal was influential among Pietist separatists but also found academic supporters in more recent times among those who continue to pit the younger and older Luther against each other.

See also History; Pietism; Spener, Philipp Jakob

Bibliography
Arnold, G. *Die Erste Liebe*. Ed. H. Schneider. Evangelische Verlagsanstalt, 2002; Erb, P. "Gottfried Arnold." In *The Pietist Theologians*, ed. C. Lindberg, 175–89. Blackwell, 2005.

Douglas H. Shantz

Art

Christian art has a long and complex history. Its earliest forms and functions were appropriated and adapted from those found in the visual cultures of the Jewish and Greco-Roman societies from which the first Christians emerged. As these forms and functions continued to develop and evolve over the centuries, they became essential bearers of meaning and likewise assisted in the establishment and promotion of distinct Christian identities and practices. In both the West and the East, struggles over images and icons were settled in favor of their use in worship and for religious devotion.

By Martin Luther's time the Christian cult of images, which encompassed a wide variety of art forms, was thoroughly intertwined with its sister institutions, the cults of saints and relics, as complementary aspects of the Roman Catholic penitential system. It was generally taught and understood that Christians who provided endowments for the decoration of chapels and churches, or who otherwise commissioned works of art that supported sanctioned rituals and promoted the faith, were performing good works that could help earn them a reduction in their penalty for sin or assist in the freeing of loved ones from purgatory.

Luther's earliest statements on religious art appear in his academic lectures on St. Paul's Epistles to the Galatians (1516–17) and the Hebrews (1517–18), sermons on the Ten Commandments (1516–17), and in his church sermons on usury (1519–20) and good works (1520–21). Here he was particularly critical of adorning churches with images and endowing them with costly liturgical equipment when the money that went into the production of these material objects might be better spent on the needy. As he developed his doctrine of justification by faith alone, Luther would also come to reject the established belief that art patronage was a good work that could aid in one's salvation. This was strongly stated in his *Sermon on Good Works*. While Luther cautioned his followers against engaging in rituals that involved the veneration of holy images and relics, he did not necessarily think that images automatically moved viewers to idolatrous worship.

The same could not be said of his more radical Evangelical contemporaries. In December 1521 and January 1522, when Luther was at Wartburg Castle, his Wittenberg colleagues Gabriel Zwilling and Andreas Karlstadt directed the removal and destruction of religious images from the Augustinian cloister and the city church. While Luther may have seemed to support these acts of iconoclasm, his own position soon took shape—supported by Elector Frederick the Wise and his close friend and Saxon court artist Lucas Cranach the Elder—and he rose to the defense of images. The exiled reformer returned to Wittenberg in March 1522 and delivered eight Lenten sermons in the city church (the "Invocavit" sermons). A subchapter of the third and fourth sermons, titled "On Images," informed his listeners that religious art could be considered a nonessential aspect of the Christian faith, but permissible nonetheless. Furthermore, while religious images would always be subordinate to preaching the gospel in the true church, they could serve an important function as mediators of the Word of God, in particular when used as part of the Christian education of children and the "simple folk." Thus Luther essentially repeated an argument made centuries earlier by the Latin church father and pope Gregory the Great (ca. 540–604), who had promoted Christian images during his own time as "books for the unlearned."

Similar statements in defense of religious art were reiterated and expanded on in a later polemical tract titled *Against the Heavenly Prophets: Concerning Images and the Sacraments* (1524–25). Issued partly in response to further acts of iconoclasm that transpired outside of Wittenberg under the direction of Karlstadt and others, *Against the Heavenly Prophets* devoted seventeen pages to the question of images and their proper Christian uses, going so far as to describe a program for an illustrated Bible. As appropriate decorations for places of worship, Luther proposed scenes of Christ's passion, foremost among them the crucifixion and resurrection, and other themes based on events from Jesus's life and ministry described in the Bible. In Luther's opinion, those who called for the systematic removal of religious images from Christian society were placing limits on the freedom of individual Christians to express their faith and share it with others. Additional statements concerning images are scattered among Luther's later writings and those of his followers, the latter mainly found in the so-called Table Talk. However, Luther's 1522 "On Images" and the discussion of art contained within *Against the Heavenly Prophets* are his most comprehensive and clearly expressed treatment of these matters. The Lutheran confessional writings do not directly address the theology of Christian art.

By 1525 Luther was a confirmed defender of religious art, especially its usefulness as a complement to the Word of God. Paintings and printed images made visible what was otherwise invisible. His translation of the Bible and catechisms always included pictures. He relied heavily on his friend Lucas Cranach the Elder to advise him on art-related matters, and Lutheran churches in Europe retained visual art, created before, during, and after the Reformation. During the final twenty years of his life, Luther worked closely with Cranach and others in the Cranach workshop in Wittenberg on the selection and representation of Bible-based themes that effectively conveyed the reformer's doctrine of justification by faith and theology of the cross and identified the visible signs of the church.

Some have argued that Luther's demystification of religious images subsequently contributed to the decline and death of Christian art within modern Western culture. This claim is debatable and requires one to make certain aesthetic value judgments. Certainly, Luther's primary emphasis on preaching the gospel, personal interest in composing hymns, and some indifference toward the visual arts as aspects of faith and worship have continued to shape his legacy to the present day. Whereas devotional art (i.e., images intended to promote and support rituals associated with prayer and veneration) has little or no official standing within the Lutheran Church, those who identify themselves as Lutherans freely exercise their Christian liberty through the production and display of religious art and images serving a wide variety of functions, from the didactic and decorative to the liturgical and confessional.

See also Cranach, Lucas, the Elder; Cranach, Lucas, the Younger; Electors of Saxony; Good Works; Justification; Karlstadt, Andreas Bodenstein von; Law, Uses of the; Sacraments; Theology of the Cross; Wittenberg Unrest

Bibliography

Christensen, C. C. *Art and the Reformation in Germany.* Ohio University Press, 1979; Hofmann, W., ed. *Luther und die Folgen für die Kunst.* Prestel, 1983; Koerner, J. L. *The Reformation of the Image.* University of Chicago Press, 2004; Michalski, S. *The Reformation of the Visual Arts.* Trans. C. Kisiel. Routledge, 1993; Scribner, R. *For the Sake of Simple Folk.* Cambridge University Press, 1981.

PAUL M. BACON

Association of Evangelical Lutheran Churches. *See* Seminex and the Association of Evangelical Lutheran Churches

Astrology

Astrology was a highly debated subject in the Lutheran tradition. Expanding on Martin Luther's own position, some Lutherans considered astrology a diabolical art. Others, such as Philip Melanchthon and many of his students, however, considered astrology to be the most up-to-date science in sixteenth-century Wittenberg. Both advocates and critics in sixteenth-century German-speaking countries looked back on a long tradition of arguments for and against astrology. The most controversially discussed art was judicial astrology, the art of casting horoscopes. Since Thomas Aquinas, in contrast, natural astrology, as based on the observation of influences of the stars on nature, was usually considered a lawful pursuit. Luther's own reservation against judicial astrology, which he considered a game with the devil, stemmed from his interpretation of Gen. 1:14 and other Bible passages, adopting positions from the majority of church fathers. In his *Commentary on Genesis*, Luther interpreted Gen. 1:14 ("And God said, 'Let there be lights in the vault of the sky to separate the day from the night, and let them serve as signs to mark sacred times, and days and years'" [NIV]) in view of Luke 21:7–19 as signs for God's apocalypse. Among those following Luther in this matter were Flacius Illyricus, Thomas Erastus, Augustin Lerchheimer, Andreas Musculus, and the author of Luther's Table Talk, Johann Aurifaber. They all viewed astrology as a pagan pursuit, which illicitly enabled human beings to enter a dialogue with demons and the devil.

Melanchthon and his followers, however, interpreted the stars mentioned in Gen. 1:14 as God-given signs that called for an interpretative art and enabled human beings to gain insight into God's providence. Melanchthon put much energy into justifying the legitimacy of judicial (and natural) astrology through his interpretation of the Bible. He proved that astrology was not an art of communicating with the demons, since planets were not demons or places where demons resided. According to Melanchthon, drawing on Pietro Pomponazzi and Girolamo Cardano and in line with the Thomistic tradition, planets were natural forces that indicated natural inclinations. They did not determine the fate of human beings. Even under the influences of the stars, human beings continued to possess a free will.

According to Melanchthon, horoscopes laid open physical and psychological dispositions of human beings. Natural forces as perceived through a horoscope all enabled human beings to glimpse God's intentions and behave accordingly. But astrology needed reform. It had to be harmonized with Luther's theological convictions, and especially with the ideal of human free will in matters of this earth.

On the basis of this interest and under Melanchthon's influence, Wittenberg became a center for learning astrology and for its reform. Teachers at Wittenberg taught astrology in mathematics, physics, and medicine. They consolidated their instruction on Ptolemy's *Tetrabiblos* (Latin: *Quadripartitum*) and *Almagest*, Sacrobosco's *Sphaera*, Pliny the Elder's *Naturalis historia*, and Melanchthon's commentary on Ptolemy's *Quadripartitum* (1553), which remained the standard European handbook of astrology throughout early modern times. Wittenberg's reform efforts mirrored themselves in various publications from Melanchthon, his colleagues, and students. He laid down his standard thoughts on astrology in his *Initia doctrinae physicae* (Wittenberg, 1550). It was complemented by Jakob Milich's *Oratio de dignitate astrologiae*, written by Melanchthon and delivered by Milich in 1535; Johannes Garcaeus's *Astrologiae methodus* (1570), a comprehensive collection of horoscopes that was popular among German astrologers; and especially Caspar Peucer's *Commentarius de praecipuis generibus divinationum* (first ed., 1553). Peucer was Melanchthon's son-in-law and his most prolific disciple and colleague who shaped the astrological convictions in the Lutheran tradition during the second half of the sixteenth century. In Peucer's popular handbook of prognostic arts, he meticulously separated the unlawful from the lawful arts of divination. Peucer presented astrology as the most reliable system of elements that allowed for foreseeing the future—provided that it was exercised in the right spirit, with the right conviction, as well as in the right manner. Peucer also supported Copernicus, however, since the latter's theory aided in accurately predicting the movement of the heavenly bodies.

Lutherans who followed Melanchthon's opinions were not the only ones in sixteenth-century Germany who intensively discussed the advantages of astrology as a science and who tried to rescue astrological prognostications from the many critics who survived. Several Catholic astrologers in Ingolstadt and Cologne communicated with astrologers in the Lutheran tradition. Yet unlike the latter, and especially after the Tridentine Council, Catholic astrologers encountered more difficulties in exercising their skills. Catholic astrologers came into conflict with the Index congregation as well as with official proclamations of Popes Sixtus V and Urban VIII, who forbade astrological prognostications via horoscopes in 1586 and in 1631.

Despite its many advocates during the second half of the sixteenth century, astrology in the Lutheran tradition lost its appeal during the early seventeenth century. Global intellectual trends ultimately undermined the conceptual foundations on which Wittenberg astrology rested. Aristotelian natural philosophy, the geocentric vision of the cosmos, and Galen's humoral pathology—all were soon to be replaced. Compared with the criticism of astrology from intellectuals like Pierre Gassendi, Robert Boyle, and Isaac Newton, to name but a few, the criticism that theologians like Martin Luther had voiced against astrology weighed weak. In the long run of the intellectual history of early modern Europe, however, even Luther's critique of astrology outweighed the manifold efforts of Melanchthon and his disciples and colleagues. Their hopes to establish astrology as a reliable, God-intended natural science that would open up many new insights into God's intention on earth did not survive.

See also Melanchthon, Philip; Natural Science; Peucer, Caspar

Bibliography

Luther's Works: *Kurtze Erclerung uber den Propheten Danielem.* Frankfurt am Main, 1543; "Predigt am

Pfingstdienstag nachmittags, 18. Mai 1529." WA 29:376–79; Tischreden, nos. 855, 589, 5573. WA TR 1:275, 418–21, and 5:254; **Other Primary Sources:** Melanchthon, P. *Initia doctrinae physicaem.* Lufft, 1549; Melanchthon, P. *Oratio de dignitate astrologiae* (1535). In *CR* 13:261–66; Peucer, C. *Commentarius de praecipuis divinationum generibus.* Crato, 1553; **General Works:** Bauer, B. "Naturphilosophie, Astronomie, Astrologie." In *Melanchthon und die Marburger Professoren (1527–1627)*, ed. B. Bauer, 345–439. Universitätsbibliothek Marburg, 1999; Bauer, B. "Philipp Melanchthons Gedichte astronomischen Inhalts im Kontext der natur- und himmelskundlichen Lehrbücher." In *Melanchthon und die Naturwissenschaften*, ed. G. Frank and S. Rhein, 137–81. Thorbecke, 1998; Brosseder, C. *Im Bann der Sterne: Caspar Peucer, Philipp Melanchthon und andere Wittenberger Astrologen.* Akademie-Verlag, 2004; Grafton, A. *Cardano's Cosmos: The Worlds and Works of a Renaissance Astrologer.* Harvard University Press, 1999; Haustein, J. *Martin Luthers Stellung zum Zauber- und Hexenwesen.* Kohlhammer, 1988; Kusukawa, S. *The Transformation of Natural Philosophy: The Case of Philip Melanchthon.* Cambridge University Press, 1995; Warburg, A. "Heidnisch-antike Weissagung in Wort und Bild zu Luthers Zeiten (1920)." In *Aby Warburg: Die Erneuerung der heidnischen Antike*, ed. H. Bredekamp et al., 487–558. Reprint, Akademie-Verlag, 1998; Zambelli, P., ed. *"Astrologi Hallucinati": Stars and the End of the World in Luther's Time.* De Gruyter, 1986.

CLAUDIA R. BROSSEDER

Atonement

The doctrine of the atonement, central to all Christian confessions and none more than the Evangelical-Lutheran confession, describes how Jesus Christ's death on the cross redeems human beings and reconciles them with their Creator. God's law segregates God in his holiness from sinners, but Martin Luther's radical understanding of Christ's atonement claims that God in Christ came into the world to destroy this segregation and create something truly new (2 Cor. 5:17), and beyond the law (Rom. 10:4). Luther claims that Christ came into the world precisely to take the sin of the world into himself on the cross.

The Formula of Concord identifies Luther's *Lectures on Galatians* (1531) as the *locus classicus* of his doctrine of Christ's atonement by directing readers to this "wonderful, magnificent" commentary for an explanation of the article of justification, "upon which the salvation of our souls depends" (SD 3.67 in *BC*,

573). As academic lectures they are removed from any confining polemical circumstance, at least by Luther's standards. Luther's comments on Gal. 3:13 describe what is traditionally referred to as Christ's atonement: "Christ redeemed us from the curse of the law, having become a curse for us—for it is written: 'Cursed is everyone who hangs on a tree.'" Luther claims that Christ became "the greatest thief, murderer, adulterer, robber, desecrator, blasphemer, etc.," that "Christ took all our sins upon Himself, and for them He died on the cross" (LW 26:277), and that Christ became a curse and sin itself "substantially," as in 2 Cor. 5:21.

How and why did this happen? No *lex aeterna* (eternal law) or unstoppable desire to pour out wrath compelled the Father to sacrifice his Son to fulfill legal righteousness or wrath. God did not send his Son to die because his honor was offended by human sin, nor did he fear that "cheap grace" would lead to immorality.

Instead, God "the merciful Father saw that we were being oppressed through the Law" and decided to liberate sinners from the law and wrath by taking their sins away from them. He "heaped all the sins of all men upon [Christ]" (280). The Father said to the Son, "Be Peter the denier; Paul the persecutor, blasphemer, and assaulter. . . . In short be the person of all men, the one who committed the sins of all men. And see to it that You pay and make satisfaction for them" (280). Christ obeyed his Father, took the sins of the world "in His body" (277), and died for them. He did this "not by compulsion but of His own free will [*sponte . . . voluntate*]." No law within God (*lex aeterna*) compelled Christ to do this. His completely free will, bound only by his love for sinners and his love for his Father, obeyed his Father.

The central question of the atonement then is, What role did the law play in these events? The law played a secondary, alien role. It could only react to the events rather than determine them. The Father and Son did not conduct a legal transaction between themselves in which the Son gained a legal righteousness through accepting the results of the Father's supposed need to pour out his wrath. Instead, the Father and Son, in mercy, worked together outside the law, stealing sinners' most precious possessions, their sins. The law then reacted and legally condemned Christ for his sin.

Now the law comes and says: "I find Him a sinner, who takes upon Himself the sins of all men. I do not see any other sins than those in Him. Therefore let Him die on the cross!" And so it attacks and kills him (280).

The Father and Son, working together outside the law, force the law to do a strange work. The law's proper work is to reveal sinners' sin, bind them to the sinner, and kill and damn the sinner. However, when the law performs this proper work in Christ's case, "the sins of the entire world . . . do in fact damn Him" (281). God is forcing law to do the alien work of testifying that these sins no longer belong to the sinner, but to Christ the Savior: "For unless [Christ] had taken upon Himself my sins, your sins, and the sins of the entire world, the Law would have had no right over Him, since it condemns only sinners and holds them under a curse" (284). Because the law killed and damned Christ, sinners can trust that he really took their sins away.

In passively suffering the law's righteous assault, Christ pays for sins, suffers punishment, and makes satisfaction. However, this satisfaction is not the goal or driving force behind his dying. The primary force is the Father's merciful will that Christ come to take away the sins in order to prevent the sins from damning sinners. Therefore, Christ suffers and pays the price of sin, which is death (Rom. 6:23). However, for Luther this punishment is the result of God's merciful loving desire to take away sinners' sins, the law, and his wrath (not vice versa): "But what does it mean to 'bear' [sin]? *The sophists* [i.e., medieval Scholastic theologians] reply: 'To be punished.' Good. But why is Christ punished? Is it not because He has sin and bears sin?" (279). God wanted his

Son to take away the sin of sinners. Therefore, Christ suffered everything involved in bearing sin. Luther reasons backward from God's "love born of the cross" (Heidelberg Disputation [1518], LW 31:57), rather than forward from an idealistic order of law and righteousness (*lex aeterna*).

Among second-generation Lutherans, few were as important in preserving Luther's teaching as Matthias Flacius and Martin Chemnitz, joining other Lutherans in rejecting the approach of Andreas Osiander. Although Chemnitz was the primary author of the Formula of Concord, which rejected elements of Flacius's teaching, their teaching on the atonement was very similar. This teaching blossomed into the modified Anselmian (Anselm of Canterbury, ca. 1033–1109) atonement doctrine of Lutheran Orthodoxy (1580–1730).

For Flacius the "essential" (*wesentliche*) righteousness of God is the driving force behind Christ's death. It is this essential righteousness, even of the inner Trinity, that demands Christ must pay the penalty for humans' sin in order for sinners to be justified. For Flacius the essential righteousness of God is the law. Chemnitz too claims, "The norm of righteousness which is revealed in the Law is the eternal, immovable, and unchangeable will of God. For sins this norm requires fullest satisfaction" (quoted in Kolb, "Human Performance," 133–34).

For both men the righteousness of the law requires God to send his Son and make satisfaction and so controls events in Christ's life and death. Therefore, Christ's obedience is to the law and in opposition to Luther's claim that Christ's obedience is to his Father. For Flacius and Chemnitz, this obedience to the law is not only to suffer its punishment passively, as in Luther, but atonement also depends on Christ's active obedience to the law.

For three centuries after Luther's death, the Orthodox Lutheran understanding of the atonement was the consensus among Lutherans. J. C. K. von Hoffmann (1810–77) began the modern Lutheran debate concerning the atonement by observing that Christ's death cannot be objectively separated from Christians in the present. The resulting debate between and among Erlangen and Repristination theologians (e.g., Ernst Hengstenberg [1802–69], Gottfried Thomasius [1802–75], Theodosius Harnack [1817–89]) led to the Luther Renaissance in Germany that continues to the present.

Hoffmann's insistence on the present experience of Christians understands a key aspect of Luther's discussion of the atonement. The genre of Luther's *Lectures on Galatians* (academic lectures presented to students at the University of Wittenberg) is preaching. The commentary on Gal. 3:13 is filled with first- and second-person pronouns. Christ took "our" sins, "your" sins, and "we" must see him wrapped in them. Luther's driving goal in analyzing Christ's death is pastoral care (*Seelsorge*). He repeatedly returns to the claim that everything the Father and Son are doing in the atonement is for the sake of providing comfort to sinners, specifically in the present. The aim of Luther's commentary/preaching is faith (*fiducia* = trust) in the hearer. "Hence it is evident that faith alone justifies" (287). The proclamation that Christ has taken away sins is ultimately true "for you," the hearer, alone. "Therefore wherever there is faith in Christ, there sin has in fact been abolished, put to death, and buried. But where there is no faith in Christ, there sin remains" (286).

Vilmos Vajta (1918–98) concluded that one cannot accurately describe the work of Christ without reference to the people for whom he died. Christ's death and resurrection are objective historical facts, but Luther often stated that even the devil knows this and tolerates it. What the devil cannot tolerate is when Christ is applied to sinners in their present need.

Albrecht Ritschl (1822–89) saw that no theological theory could bridge the historical gap between Christ's past death on the cross and God's reconciliation with sinners in the present, and that this unity must simply be experienced in the Christian community in the present. However, he failed to see that this "experience" is faith itself and is created precisely by the word of the cross, preached in the church. This word is the very presence of Christ, the crucified and resurrected head of the church.

Gustaf Aulén (1879–1977) in his modern classic, *Christus Victor* (1931), showed that the atonement should be understood as Christ's victory over the devil and his evil powers of sin and death. Aulén claimed that this was the true atonement motif for the ancient church, Luther, and the New Testament itself.

In the orthodox system, the resurrection of Christ and the salvation of sinners follows logically from Christ's fulfillment of the law. Because the law is the "eternal, immovable, and unchangeable will of God," once Christ satisfies the law on the cross, God's will is fulfilled. Therefore the Father owes Christ his resurrection and owes salvation to the sinners who apply Christ's fulfillment of the law to themselves through faith—that is, *notitia, assensus, fiducia* (knowledge, assent, trust)—to Christ's fulfillment of the law.

Instead, for Luther, Christ fulfills the law by passively suffering its holy condemnation of the sin of the world, which he bore on the cross. However, this fulfillment of the law is not in and of itself Christ's victory and eternal salvation for sinners. The fulfillment of the law in Christ's death instead becomes the occasion for a real, wonderful, and terrible duel (*duellum mirabile*). On one side are the forces of sin and death, on the other righteousness and life. The victory of righteousness over sin is the same victory of life over death. Therefore, righteousness does not win the victory over sin in Christ's obedient death on the cross by making a payment for sin to the law (as in the orthodox system). Instead, righteousness defeats sin in Christ's resurrection. Aulén was correct that in Luther's teaching the resurrection plays an important, real, and dynamic role in Christ's atonement. The resurrection as Christ's victory over sin, death, hell, the devil, and even God hidden in wrath (*Deus absconditus*) is something truly new.

Because of the role of the resurrection in Luther's teaching, the atonement is not an objective fact accomplished on Calvary. Rather, the history of Christ's fulfillment of the law on Calvary in obedience to the loving, merciful will of his Father and Christ's resurrection victory over the powers of sin and destruction—both authorize atonement in the present between Christ and his beloved sinners. Faith is in Christ's blood (Rom. 3:25) rather than in an atonement theory or in history alone. Christ with his blood is present in the world in word and sacrament. Like the resurrected Christ present with his scars in the story of doubting Thomas, the word and sacraments bear and preach Christ's scars. Christ is present in this proclamation because he is risen from the dead. Atonement is not a legal transaction between the Father and the Son. Instead, the Father, Son, and Holy Spirit (who preaches and believes the good news) work together outside the law in mercy.

What does the word of the cross do to sinners in the present? It kills them and raises them from the dead. Aulén admits that Luther understood and taught Christ's atonement with greater depth than the church fathers. The fathers did not understand that Christ must not only first lose on the cross before becoming *Christus victor*, but also that the sinners he saves must die in him in order to rise in him. Why did Christ have to die? Luther understood that there must be a divine death into which the sinner is baptized and dies. This also explains Luther's strongest statements about satisfaction. Until the law is satisfied—that is, until the sinner dies—there simply will be no atonement and reconciliation with God.

However, in sending his Son to die, God was not subject to the law, but instead he used the law as a disposable tool to accomplish his ultimate, eternal, and proper evangelical purpose and will. Where the satisfaction of the law is seen not as derivative of God's immutable will to have mercy, and as God's penultimate and alien work, but is held to be the primary, motivating, eternal, or final force in understanding Christ's death, then "satisfaction" is too weak, according to Luther. It says too little about the grace of Christ and does not sufficiently honor Christ's suffering. Lutheran Orthodoxy failed to understand Luther's teaching about Christ's death and the relationship between law and gospel in this crucial locus, greatly harming Lutheranism throughout the world and helping to deliver it into the legalistic arms of Pietism, antisacramental Protestantism, and modern secularism.

See also Aulén, Gustaf; Chemnitz, Martin; Erlangen; Flacius, Matthias Illyricus, and the Flacians; Hoffmann, Johannes Christian Konrad von; Justification; Law, Uses of the; Luther Interpretation and Reception; Repristination Theology; Ritschl, Albrecht; Theology of the Cross

Bibliography

Luther's Works: "Ein ander Predigt: Evangelium am Osterdienstage, Luk. 24, 36–47" (April 1531). WA 21:242–64; Heidelberg Disputation (1518). LW 31:35–70; *Lectures on Galatians* (1535). LW 26; "2. Galatervorlesung (cap. 1–4)" (1531). WA 40/1; **Confessional Documents:** Kolb, R., and T. Wengert, eds. *The Book of Concord: The Confessions of the Evangelical Lutheran Church.* Fortress, 2000; **General Works:** Aulén, G. *Christus Victor: An Historical Study of the Three Main Types of the Idea of Atonement.* Trans. A. Herbert. Macmillan, 1961; Forde, G. "The Work of Christ." In *Christian Dogmatics,* ed. C. Braaten and R. Jenson, 2:5–99. Fortress, 1984; Hagen, K. "Luther on Atonement-Reconfigured." *CTQ* 61 (1997): 251–76; Haikola, L. *Gesetz und Evangelium bei Matthias Flacius Illyricus.* Gleerup, 1952; Haikola, L. *Studien zu Luther und zum Luthertum.* A.-B. Lundequistska Bokhandeln, 1958; Haikola, L. *Usus Legis.* A.-B. Lundequistska Bokhandeln, 1958; Kolb, R. "Human Performance and the Righteousness of Faith: Martin Chemnitz's Anti-Roman Polemic in Formula of Concord III." In *By Faith Alone: Essays in Honor of Gerhard O. Forde,* ed. J. Burgess and M. Kolden, 125–39. Eerdmans, 2004; Kolb, R. "'Not without the Satisfaction of God's Righteousness': The Atonement and the Generation Gap between Luther and His Students." In *ARG, Sonderband: Die Reformation in Deutschland und Europa: Interpretationen und Debatten,* ed. H. Guggisberg and G. Krodel, 136–56. Gütersloher, 1993; Kolb, R. "Resurrection and Justification: Luther's Use of Romans 4,25." *Lutherjahrbuch* 78 (2011): 39–60; Paulson, S. D. *Lutheran Theology.* T&T Clark, 2011; Vatja, V. *Luther on Worship: An Interpretation.* Muhlenberg, 1958.

STEVEN D. PAULSON AND NICHOLAS HOPMAN

Augsburg

A biconfessional free imperial city located in Swabia on the Lech River, south of the Danube. A thriving financial and cultural center during the late fifteenth and sixteenth centuries, Augsburg also served as an important regional ecclesiastical center. Although the Prince-Bishop of Augsburg had his main residence in nearby Dillingen, the city was home to the administrative centers of the bishop, the cathedral, and seventeen monasteries and convents. Throughout the 1520s and 1530s, Augsburg emerged as a significant location of imperial, clerical, and popular activity for and against the Lutheran reform movement.

Augsburg was one of the earliest regions outside of Saxony to experience significant reform activity. Martin Luther's meeting with the papal legate Thomas Cajetan (1469?–1534) at the Fugger Palace during the imperial diet of 1518 was soon followed by active reform support by local publishers, clergy, and citizens. From 1521 onward, Augsburg printers, publishing houses, and booksellers defied local and imperial prohibitions by publishing and distributing the works of Luther and his supporters, making Augsburg a major source of Lutheran tracts throughout the Holy Roman Empire. In 1522, Bishop Christoph von Stadion (1478–1543) complained to the city council that local clergy were spreading Luther's teachings. By 1523 the city witnessed its first public defiance of imperial and local prohibitions against supporting Luther's teachings, including the marriage of a priest in a local tavern. In 1524 the popular Schilling Uprising occurred after the city council threatened to banish Johann Schilling, a well-liked evangelical preacher. By 1525 evangelical clergy, most notably Urbanus Rhegius (1489–1541), gained significant public acceptance of Lutheran teachings in Augsburg.

From 1525 until 1534, the Augsburg city council followed a cautious middle way of neither fully condemning nor fully accepting the Lutheran reform movement in order to avoid imperial condemnation. This policy allowed the diversification of the local reform movement. From the late 1520s through the 1530s, Lutheran reformers, such as Urbanus Rhegius, along with Reformed-leaning theologians like Wolfgang Musculus (1497–1563), competed with the growing local support for Zwinglian and Anabaptist clergy such as Michael Keller (ca. 1500–1548) and Balthasar Hubmaier (1485–1528). As one of the signers of the Confessio Tetrapolitana, alongside Strasbourg, the city tended toward a Reformed understanding of the Lord's Supper; beginning in 1534, Augsburg's city council introduced a Zwinglian-styled reformation; it was completed in 1537, but now within the aegis of the Wittenberg Concord (signed by Musculus) and the Smalcaldic League. A more or less Reformed church order lasted until 1548, when the victorious Charles V tried to impose the Augsburg Interim. In the aftermath of the Revolt of the Princes (1552) and the subsequent Peace of Augsburg (1555), Lutheranism was reintroduced as the principal Protestant belief in Augsburg.

Throughout the Reformation era, Augsburg served as the setting for meetings leading to significant changes in political and religious policy. During the sixteenth century, the imperial diet met nine times in Augsburg, most notably in 1518, 1530, 1547/1548, and 1555. The Diet of Augsburg (1530) brought together political leaders and theologians in a failed attempt at reconciling doctrinal debates introduced by Luther. One of the enduring legacies of this meeting was the Augsburg Confession. In 1547/48, Emperor Charles V entered the city after defeating the Smalcaldic League to declare the Augsburg Interim. Catholicism was reintroduced into the city, and the rights and privileges of the predominately Protestant guilds were revoked. After a brief period of shifting power, the Religious Peace of Augsburg (1555) established Augsburg as one of a few fully biconfessional cities where Catholic and Lutherans were granted religious protection. This religious identity was to be codified into political and legal protection after the

Thirty Years' War in a document that granted parity in the Augsburg city council between Catholics and Lutherans. Nonetheless, confessional relations between Lutherans and Catholics remained complicated throughout the seventeenth and eighteenth centuries.

The commemoration of the Peace of Augsburg continues in a local holiday on August 8 [*Friedenstag*], observed since the seventeenth century. On October 31, 1999, the Lutheran World Federation and the Roman Catholic Church signed the Joint Declaration on the Doctrine of Justification in St. Anna's Church in Augsburg as a form of reconciliation.

See also Anabaptists/Spiritualists; Augsburg Confession; Augsburg Interim; Cajetan (Thomaso de Vio); Justification; Musculus, Wolfgang; Peace of Augsburg; Printing in Sixteenth-Century Lutheranism; Rhegius, Urbanus; Smalcald War

Bibliography

Creasman, A. *Censorship and Civic Order in Reformation German, 1517–1648.* Ashgate, 2012; Künast, H.-J. *"Getruckt zu Augspurg": Buchdruck und Buchhandel in Augsburg zwischen 1468 und 1555.* Niemeyer, 1997; Roeck, B. *Eine Stadt in Krieg und Frieden: Studien zur Geschichte der Reichsstadt Augsburg zwischen Kalenderstreit und Parität.* 2 vols. Vandenhoeck & Ruprecht, 1989; Roper, L. *The Holy Household: Women and Morals in Reformation Augsburg.* Clarendon, 1984; Roth, F. *Augsburgs Reformationsgeschichte.* Ackermann, 1901–11. Reprint 1974; Tlusty, B. A. *Augsburg during the Reformation Era: An Anthology of Sources.* Hackett, 2012.

MARJORIE ELIZABETH PLUMMER

Augsburg Confession

The primary Evangelical confession of faith, also in the Book of Concord, that defines Lutheranism within the church catholic. Presented to Emperor Charles V on June 25, 1530, the Augsburg Confession (CA) responded to his request that the Evangelical parties justify changes they had made in their territories, especially due to the Saxon visitations of 1527–28. These changes threatened the Roman church's commitment to uniform liturgical practices and its ecclesial authority. At the Second Diet of Speyer (1529), when Evangelical rulers protested the lifting of the moratorium on enforcing the Edict of Worms

(1521), enacted at the First Diet of Speyer (1526) and when Pope Clement VII remained unwilling to call a free council to settle the theological disputes, the emperor attempted to settle matters by calling the estates of the Holy Roman Empire to a diet in Augsburg.

Elector John of Saxony received the invitation in early March (1530) and asked the Wittenberg theologians to prepare a defense (*apologia*) explaining the correction of abuses in his territories. The Wittenberg delegation took draft statements on changes in practice, prepared in Torgau (and hence later called the Torgau Articles), to Augsburg. As an outlaw of the empire, Luther remained in Coburg Castle for his safety but stayed in touch with his colleagues. Arriving in Augsburg, the Saxons found that the Catholic theologian John Eck had published 404 Articles, delineating hundreds of heretical statements taught by the Evangelical party, among others, and culled from their works. The Saxons quickly realized that they needed more than a defense of their reforms. To show that their theology was truly catholic, Melanchthon and his colleagues borrowed material from Luther's confession of faith in his *Confession concerning Christ's Supper* (1528) and the Schwabach Articles (1529). The rhetoric of the Schwabach Articles was softened, however, to reflect the October 1529 agreement reached in the Marburg Articles (except for "real presence") and to make it more acceptable to Philip of Hesse and cities such as Nuremburg. Statements on purgatory and the pope as antichrist were omitted, and the bodily presence of Christ in the Supper was confessed but not elaborated upon. In late May and early June, Melanchthon and his colleagues joined together the edited versions of the so-called Torgau Articles, the revised seventeen articles of the Schwabach Articles, and additional articles (esp. art. XX, a refutation of some of Eck's charges) as both a confession of faith and a defense of corrected practices. Melanchthon with others' help translated the German into Latin. It was read aloud to the diet in German by the Saxon Chancellor,

Christian Beyer; those outside the episcopal palace could hear the confession through the open windows. The Latin version, prepared in the church's official language, was handed over at the same time and eventually given to the archbishop of Mainz. The original signers included Elector John, his son and future elector Duke John Frederick, Margrave Georg of Branenburg-Ansbach, Duke Ernst of Lüneburg and his son Duke Francis, Landgrave Philip of Hesse, Prince Wolfgang of Anhalt, and the cities of Nuremberg and Reutlingen.

The first twenty-one articles deal with doctrinal statements. Articles I–III address the Trinity, original sin, and Christology. Articles IV–VI form a unity, tying justification of sinners through faith to the means of grace and new obedience. The subsequent fifteen articles treat the church, sacraments and ecclesial practices (VII–XV), the role and limits of governmental authority (XVI), and disputed issues (the return of Christ [XVII], free will and the cause of sin [XVIII–XIX], the relation of faith and works [XX], and the commemoration of the saints [XXI]). Articles XXII–XXVIII treat the corrected abuses (regarding communion in both bread and wine, married priests, the sacrifice of the mass, confession, fasting, monastic vows, and ecclesiastical authority, respectively).

After Roman Catholic theologians rejected the entire CA out of hand, Charles V forced them to judge each article separately, resulting in the rejection of many but not all of the doctrinal articles and all of the practical ones, read out as the Confutation a month later. Melanchthon wrote a defense of the CA, which the emperor refused to accept or have read and which he expanded into first the May and then the September/October edition of the *Apology* [defense] *of the Augsburg Confession*, published, despite an imperial ban, alongside the CA (itself in a slightly revised version [the editio princeps]).

The authority of the CA comprises three aspects. First, the very act of confessing was considered central, as Martin Luther's 1532 sermon at Elector John's funeral makes clear. Second, it became the basis for confession of faith by others who agreed with its doctrine. Thus membership in the Smalcaldic League in 1537 included the Augsburg Confession. In 1533, substantial additions were made to the Latin and German versions. Melanchthon's later altered version of the CA (the Variata, 1540/1542), commissioned by the Evangelicals for use in negotiations with Roman Catholics at the Colloquies in Worms and Regensburg, became the subject of debate in the 1550s and beyond because of changes in the language regarding the Lord's Supper (originally added to reflect language of the Wittenberg Concord). In agreement with text of the Book of Concord (which reverted to the editio princeps), it is generally not used by Lutherans today for its potential "Calvinist" interpretation in the article on the Lord's Supper. By this time it was used, in the third place, as a doctrinal standard. The so-called unaltered CA is still the primary defining document for Lutherans today.

The confessional revival arising in German-speaking lands in the early 1800s, in part a reaction to the Reformed-Lutheran union imposed by the King of Prussia in 1817, led some groups loyal to the CA and the Book of Concord to immigrate to the Americas or Australia. In the United States, they encountered other Lutherans, some of whom did not share their strong attachments to the CA, creating new tensions. When Samuel Simon Schmucker published the *Definite Synodical Platform* (1855), revising the CA's articles on baptism, the Lord's Supper, the Mass, private confession, and absolution, and also inserting the obligation of the Christian Sabbath, these tensions led to fractures in the American Lutheran church bodies (esp. between the General Synod and the General Council) that were somewhat overcome in the early twentieth century (with the formation of the United Lutheran Church in America, the constitution of which included adherence to the CA) but in other forms still exist today.

Today the Lutheran World Federation and the International Lutheran Council recognize the CA as a defining document in their constitutions. Ordained and consecrated leaders in various Lutheran churches often must vow to teach and preach not only according to the Scripture and the ecumenical creeds, but also according to the Augsburg Confession and some or all of the other Lutheran confessions.

See also Apology of the Augsburg Confession; Augsburg; Charles V; Melanchthon, Philip

Bibliography

Arand, C. P., R. Kolb, and J. A. Nestingen. *The Lutheran Confessions.* Fortress, 2012; Gassmann, G., and S. Hendrix. *Fortress Introduction to the Lutheran Confessions.* Fortress, 1999; Grane, L. *The Augsburg Confession.* Augsburg, 1987; Kolb, R. *Confessing the Faith.* Concordia, 1991; Maurer, W. *Historical Commentary on the Augsburg Confession.* Fortress, 1986.

GORDON A. JENSEN

Augsburg Interim

The Augsburg Interim is the decree of German imperial policy aimed at eradicating the Wittenberg Reformation. Following the defeat of the Evangelical princes and cities in the Smalcald War, Holy Roman Emperor Charles V called the imperial estates together for a diet in September 1547 in Augsburg. He commissioned a group of theologians to draft a religious policy for the empire to serve as an interim solution to religious division until the Council of Trent reached its final decisions. This committee consisted of two theologians from Charles's Iberian lands, his brother Ferdinand's court preachers, and two Erasmian humanists—the suffragan bishop of Mainz, Michael Helding, and the bishop of Naumburg-Zeitz, Julius Pflug—along with one Evangelical representative, Johann Agricola. With a draft composed by another reform-minded Erasmian Roman Catholic, Johann Gropper, the group forged its interim solution for imperial religious policy, which Evangelical opponents promptly dubbed "the Augsburg Interim."

The document held firm to medieval Catholic doctrine but strove to set aside superstitious practices widespread in the Middle Ages. It acknowledged the authority of the pope and the bishops, who alone could interpret Scripture. The sacrificial nature of the Mass and transubstantiation lay at the heart of its understanding of the Lord's Supper. The traditional seven sacraments conveyed sacramental grace and thus formed the heart of the Christian existence. Use of many medieval ceremonies, festivals, sacramentals, and other ritual practices was required. The Interim made two concessions to the Evangelicals: communion of the laity in both kinds (bread and cup) and clerical marriage.

Charles may have intended that the Augsburg Interim serve as a program for religious life throughout his German lands, but in fact it was imposed only on Evangelical territories where imperial troops could enforce it. No Roman Catholic government accepted it. One month after its formal promulgation, on May 15, 1548, Charles also published a Formula for Reformation, prescribing reform of congregational and monastic life.

Philip Melanchthon initiated a series of critiques rejecting the Interim, first written for his new prince and elector, Moritz, but then published in the summer of 1548. Other Evangelical theologians also attacked the document. Some Evangelical rulers and cities tried to work out compromise solutions. One of these, the Leipzig Proposal in Electoral Saxony, while never officially enacted, provoked intense controversy within Lutheran lands.

See also Charles V; Exile; Leipzig Proposal (Interim); Smalcald War

Bibliography

Arand, C. P., et al. *The Lutheran Confessions.* Fortress, 2012; Dingel, I. *Controversia et Confessio: Theologische Kontroversen 1548–1577/80.* Vol. 1, *Reaktionen auf das Augsburger Interim. Kritische Auswahled.* Vandenhoeck & Ruprecht, 2010; Kolb, R., and J. A. Nestingen, eds. *Sources and Contexts of the Book of Concord.* Esp. 144–82. Fortress, 2001; Mehlhausen, J. *Das Augsburger Interim von 1548, deutsch und lateinisch.* Neukirchener Verlag, 1970; Rabe, H. *Reichsbund und Interim: Die Verfassungs- und Religionspolitik Karls V. und der Reichstag von Augsburg 1547/1548.* Böhlau, 1971; Schorn-Schütte, L., ed. *Das*

Interim 1548/50: Herrschaftskrise und Glaubenskonflikt. Gütersloher Verlag, 2005.

ROBERT KOLB

Augustana Synod

The American Lutheran denomination founded by Swedish immigrants is called the Augustana Synod (1860–1962). Scattered Scandinavian-American congregations were formed in the upper Mississippi River region in the 1840s and 1850s and were gathered into a conference within the Synod of Northern Illinois in 1851 by early leaders L. P. Esbjörn, Erland Carlsson, and T. N. Hasselquist. Unhappy with the theological position of this synod, these congregations separated from it in 1860, taking the name Augustana to show their loyalty to the Augsburg Confession. The Augustana Synod consisted of Swedish and Norwegian congregations until 1870, when the Norwegians separated to form their own organizations. A surge in Swedish immigration after the Civil War challenged the new denomination to provide enough pastors and congregations for the new arrivals. Augustana founded a seminary and college in 1860, eventually located in Rock Island, Illinois, which became the center of synodical life. Joining as a synodical member of the General Council in 1867, Augustana remained a member until 1918 but did not follow the rest of the synods into the newly formed United Lutheran Church in America. The leaders of the Augustana Synod were strongly influenced by the nineteenth-century Pietist revival in Sweden and were not interested in trying to replicate the institutions and ethos of the Church of Sweden in the United States. But as the synod grew, there were internal tensions about how self-consciously Lutheran it should be. When controversy erupted in Sweden in the 1870s over the theological positions of Pietist leader P. P. Waldenström, especially in confessional matters, this dispute spread to the congregations of the Augustana Synod. A period of strife ensued, during which many congregations were divided, with the more free-church element withdrawing to form the Swedish Covenant (1885) and Swedish Evangelical Free (1884) denominations. Augustana also had to compete for the immigrants with Swedish-American Baptist and Methodist congregations, and a number of American denominations, including the Congregationalists and Episcopalians. As Swedish immigrants spread out across America, Augustana eventually formed new regional conferences in Minnesota, Iowa, the Great Plains states, and in the East, especially in Pennsylvania and Massachusetts. These regional conferences gained strength in relation to the national entity until a constitutional revision in 1894, but even after this there was little structured national organization until the 1930s. Regional conferences formed their own colleges, including Gustavus Adolphus in St. Peter, Minnesota (1862); Bethany in Lindsborg, Kansas (1881); Luther in Wahoo, Nebraska (1883); and Upsala in East Orange, New Jersey (1893). Augustana was also well known for its social-service institutions, including numerous hospitals, orphanages, nursing homes, and other specialized care centers. While its main focus in the nineteenth century was on forming congregations within the United States for Swedish Americans, the synod was also keenly interested in foreign missions. Lacking the funds to establish its own missions overseas, Augustana cooperated with General Council missions in India and with Swedish missions in Africa and China. In the twentieth century the synod would form its own missions in China, Tanzania, Japan, and Colombia. A major factor in the support of these missions was the Women's Missionary Society, founded in 1893. Led by Emmy Carlsson Evald, this group quickly became a powerful presence within the synod. In the twentieth century the synod expanded further, establishing regional conferences in the Pacific Northwest, California, Texas, Canada, and Florida and becoming a national denomination. Until World War I the synod was overwhelmingly Swedish speaking, but internal generational pressures and the collapse of immigration rapidly pushed the synod into using the English language in the 1920s. The synod joined with other America Lutheran denominations to form the National Lutheran Council (1918) and the American Lutheran Conference (1930), and it sought to work cooperatively through these organizations. Augustana also played an important role in world Lutheranism through the Lutheran World Federation (1947) and beyond, as a member of the National Council of Churches (1950) and the World Council of Churches (1948). As American Lutheran denominations considered further consolidation through the 1940s and 1950s, Augustana played a leading role in these efforts. Augustana wanted merger negotiations to be open to all American Lutheran groups, but some other denominations were wary of the United Lutheran Church in America, and this impasse resulted in two separate mergers in the 1960s, with Augustana joining with the ULCA, the Finnish Suomi Synod, and the Danish American Evangelical Lutheran Church to form the Lutheran Church in America in 1962. At the time of merger, Augustana had 1,255 congregations and 618,000 members.

See also Finnish-American Lutheranism; Lutheran Church in America; Lutheran World Federation; Norwegian-American Lutheranism; Pietism; Sweden

Bibliography

Arden, G. E. *Augustana Heritage: History of the Augustana Lutheran Church*. Augustana Press, 1963; Bergendoff, C. *The Augustana Ministerium*. Augustana Historical Society, 1980; Erling, M., and M. Granquist. *The Augustana Story: Shaping Lutheran Identity in North America*. Fortress, 2008; Söderström, H. *Confession and Cooperation: The Policy of the Augustana Synod in Confessional Matters*. CWK Gleerup, 1973; Stephenson, G. *Religious Aspects of Swedish Immigration*. University of Minnesota Press, 1932.

MARK A. GRANQUIST

Augustine of Hippo

Augustine of Hippo (354–430) was the most important and influential church father for Luther's thought and for the Lutheran Reformation in general. Augustine's high esteem for the authority of the Scriptures, his interpretation of and approach to Pauline theology, his

reflection on sin and free will and on the centrality of divine grace—these all continue to find deep resonance within Lutheran theology today.

In one sense, the entire Western church can be understood to be "Augustinian," for no theologian had a greater impact on the form and substance of Latin theology. But Luther's association with Augustine was far from generic. Joining the Augustinian friary in Erfurt in 1505, Luther received Augustine as the great progenitor of his order and his own spiritual formation. In his initial training, Luther would have heard Augustine's writings read often as a source and guide for devotion and communal life. There is some evidence that a more careful and systematic study of Augustine's writings was fostered among some in the Augustinian order—perhaps even an Augustinian "school" within the order—but as Luther himself stated in an early letter (LW 48:24), devotion to the order did not necessarily translate into being a scholar of the church father. Luther's own study of Augustine appears to be from his own initiative to return to the sources of Christian theology, beginning at least by 1509, as his marginal annotations indicate in a copy of *Opuscula plurima*, a small collection of Augustine's works. But Luther's interest in the church father quickly turned to Augustine's insights into biblical interpretation.

In particular it was Augustine's writings against Pelagius that occupied Luther. As he lectured on Paul (Romans, 1515–16; Galatians, 1516–17), Luther utilized the new complete edition of Augustine's works published by the Basil printer Johann Amerbach (ca. 1440–1513), in 1506, citing the anti-Pelagian writings frequently (and *On the Spirit and the Letter*, for the most part a commentary on Romans, in particular) for their interpretation of the apostle's doctrine of the law and grace. In the convergence of Paul and the anti-Pelagian Augustine, Luther first began to see with clarity the deep rift that stood between what he believed to be the correct understanding of the Scriptures and the Scholastic theology in which he was trained. Scholasticism was steeped in Aristotle and interpreted the Scriptures accordingly, but Augustine seemed to be free from such constraints and adhered more closely with Paul's language and argument. It was this conflict between theological and exegetical authorities that shaped the course of Luther's initial reform efforts at Wittenberg. In 1516 Luther's student Bartholmäus Bernhardi set forth his teacher's new appropriation of Augustine in a disputation on grace and free will for the entire theological faculty to hear. Though initially greeted with reservations, Luther's position was gradually adopted by faculty colleagues as they read Augustine for themselves. This was followed by a series of programmatic theses arguing for a return to Augustine's Pauline theology. Luther's colleague Andreas von Karlstadt published 151 theses on Augustine's *On the Spirit and the Letter*, followed by a commentary on the same work. Luther himself made his case in his 97 theses *Against Scholastic Theology* (1517) and in the Heidelberg Disputation (1518), which was cast as an exposition of Paul's theology and that of Augustine, "his most faithful interpreter." Thus the early stages of Luther's reforms in the university were intentionally set on a return to the mature Augustine's writings over against the writings of the Scholastic theologians. In May 1517 Luther wrote to his former colleague Johannes Lang: "Our theology and Saint Augustine are advancing as hoped and reign in our university by God's help. Aristotle declines gradually and is heading toward complete ruin in short order. It is remarkable how the lectures on the *Sentences* [of Peter Lombard] are disdained; there is no one that can expect to have any students, unless they profess this theology, that is, the Bible or Saint Augustine, or some other teacher of ecclesiastical authority" (WA BR 1:99, lines 8–13; cf. LW 48:42). In 1533, *On the Spirit and the Letter* became a required course in Wittenberg's revised theological curriculum.

The theological themes in Augustine's later writings, distinctly important for the Wittenberg school, were his view of original sin and concupiscence, his interpretation of the Pauline doctrine of the law, and his understanding of grace with respect to the will and justification. On sin, Luther combined Augustine's understanding of original sin and concupiscence into a single, overarching concept. Just as Augustine described the nature of fallen human beings as a disordered love of self (*amor sui*) or love for one's own benefit, so also Luther portrayed sin as radically inward and egocentric, that is, *incurvatus in se est*, "to be curved in on oneself": "Our nature, by the corruption of the first sin, is so deeply curved in on itself that it not only bends the best gifts of God towards itself and enjoys them, . . . but it also fails to realize that it so wickedly, curvedly, and viciously seeks all things, even God, for its own sake" (LW 25:313).

Regarding Paul's doctrine of the law, Luther sided with Augustine over against the majority of the exegetical tradition to stress that the apostle's negative appraisal of the law's contribution to justification was not limited to the Old Testament ceremonial laws but entailed the moral law as well. As Augustine articulates most clearly in his treatise *On the Spirit and the Letter*, the law cannot bring life because without the love of the Spirit its moral injunctions can only produce a reluctant, superficial obedience, exacerbating one's pride on the one hand or desperation on the other. Thus the law is a prelude to grace, but as its opposite it opens sinners' eyes to their own bondage that they might flee to Christ, their only help.

Grace, which Augustine maintained as the absolute sine qua non for justification, was expanded by Luther to be coextensive with the whole of the gospel. Thus salvation in its entirety does not just require grace but is, in fact, the very gift of grace itself, namely, the possession of Christ and his Spirit in the heart of the one who has faith. Here Luther agreed with the Augustinian notion of "uncreated grace," that the gift of grace is the self-giving of God himself rather than the later Scholastic doctrine that defined grace as a created effect and quality given to the soul (cf. Peter Lombard [ca. 1095–1160], *Sentences* 1.d.17).

Like Augustine, Luther also argued that the human will was, with respect to spiritual things, constrained by the inward curve of its nature and the external demands of the law (i.e., to be *sub lege*, "under the law") so that only sin was possible. One could only speak meaningfully about the freedom of the will in the context of the regenerate who, having received the Holy Spirit, can begin to love God for his own sake.

But Augustine did not speak to every matter that concerned the reformers in accord with their own thinking. Luther and his colleagues used Augustine eclectically and strategically while at the same time recognizing the differences between his thought and their own formulations. Many reformers (including Luther, Melanchthon, and Johannes Brenz) had to find new ways to interpret Augustine's statement that he would not have believed the gospel if the authority of the church had not moved him, a favorite passage in Augustine cited by their Roman opponents. In his preface to his collected Latin writings (1545), Luther famously mentioned that Augustine taught the imputation of righteousness "imperfectly" (LW 34:327–38). Melanchthon was especially sensitive to this difference. For example, in a 1531 letter to the Württemberg reformer Johannes Brenz (1499–1570), Melanchthon clarified the difference between Augustine and what the Wittenberg school taught about justification: "[Augustine] gets to the point of denying that the righteousness of reason is reckoned for righteousness before God—and he thinks rightly. Next he imagines that we are counted righteous on account of that fulfillment of the Law which the Holy Spirit works in us. . . . Augustine does not fully accord with Paul's pronouncement, even though he gets closer to it than the Scholastics. And I cite Augustine as fully agreeing with us on account of the public conviction about him, even though he does not explain the righteousness of faith well enough. . . . For faith justifies, not because it is a new

work of the Holy Spirit in us, but because it lays hold of Christ, on account of whom we are accepted, not on account of the gifts of the Holy Spirit in us" (*MBW T* 5, no. 1151; *CR* 2, cols. 501–3).

In spite of these differences, Lutherans continued to appeal to Augustine's writings in their confessional documents, citing him over thirty times in the Book of Concord and always positively. Martin Chemnitz, a student of Melanchthon, was particularly influenced by his appropriation of Augustine and the fathers and took great pains to establish the relative continuity of the Lutheran faith with that of the early church. His detailed *Examination of the Council of Trent* repeatedly cites Augustine in support of the Lutheran doctrine over against Rome, though like Melanchthon he takes a more cautious and critical approach in his academic lectures on Melanchthon's *Loci theologici*. For the subsequent generations of Lutherans, Augustine became one of many patristic sources utilized in the ongoing reflection and systemization of Lutheran theological thought. Even so, his authority remained contingent on the quality and utility of his biblical interpretation, with Lutherans continuing in the vein of Luther's sentiment: "Let me not put my trust in Augustine; let us listen to the Scriptures" (WA 7:142.30–31).

See also Augustinianism; Bible Interpretation; Patristics

Bibliography

Delius, H.-U. *Augustin als Quelle Luthers: Eine Materialsammlung.* Evangelische Verlagsanstalt, 1984; Grane, L. *Modus Loquendi Theologicus: Luthers Kampf um die Erneuerung der Theologie (1515–1518).* Brill, 1975; Herrmann, E. "Luther's Absorption of Medieval Biblical Interpretation and His Use of the Church Fathers." In *The Oxford Handbook to the Theology of Martin Luther*, ed. R. Kolb, I. Dingel, and L. Batka, 71–90. Oxford University Press, 2014; Oberman, H. A. *Masters of the Reformation: The Emergence of a New Intellectual Climate in Europe.* Trans. D. Martin. Cambridge University Press, 1981; Saak, E. L. "The Reception of Augustine in the Later Middle Ages." In *The Reception of the Church Fathers in the West*, ed. I. Backus, 1:367–404. Brill, 2001; Schulze, M. "Martin Luther and the Church Fathers." In *The Reception of the Church Fathers in the West*, ed. I. Backus, 2:573–626. Brill, 1997; Steinmetz, D. C. "Luther and the

Late Medieval Augustinians: Another Look." *Concordia Theological Monthly* 44 (1973): 245–60; Wengert, T. J. "Philip Melanchthon and Augustine of Hippo." *LQ* 22 (2008): 249–67.

Erik Herrmann

Augustinianism

No theologian of the ancient church influenced the development of Western medieval theology more than Augustine of Hippo (354–430). All schools of thought in monastic and Scholastic streams of teaching adopted and adapted elements of his work, particularly his exegetical and catechetical treatises and those on issues of sin and grace and on the relationship of church and world or society. Yet even those who strove to represent his thought correctly often introduced changes via their account of his way of thinking. That was especially true in regard to his view of predestination and the human ability to contribute some merit to salvation and to his understanding of the relationship between the "two cities" of church and world.

Augustine's name became attached to a monastic rule composed during his lifetime. This rule underwent adaptations at various times, particularly after its revival in the eleventh century. The Augustinian Canons (cathedral priests) were organized by groups pledging themselves to poverty, celibacy, and obedience in the reform movement of the late eleventh century. In 1243 Pope Innocent IV brought together several groups of Italian "hermits" and submitted them to the Rule of Saint Augustine. This Augustinian Eremite order followed the form of other recently organized groups of friars, such as the Dominicans and Franciscans. In 1256 Pope Alexander IV expanded the order by placing other eremitic groups under the order. By the sixteenth century stricter and less austere houses (called Observants and Conventuals, respectively) had acquired separate governance within the order.

The Augustinian Eremites cultivated a monastic piety and practiced an approach to exegesis that emphasized the literal meaning of the text. In the fourteenth century Brother Hermann of Schildesche (ca. 1290–1357), who spent time briefly in the Augustinian monastery in Erfurt, where Luther later became a brother, composed rules for this exegetical approach. Another inhabitant of this cloister was Johannes von Paltz (ca. 1445–1511), who strove to make the fulfillment of demands of God's law necessary to merit God's grace more possible for more people. Luther's mentor and head of the Augustinians in German-speaking lands, Johannes von Staupitz, represented a much more faithful use of Augustine's views on sin and grace among his contemporary Augustinians.

Members of the Augustinian order, such as Gregory of Rimini (ca. 1300–1358), departed from the line of thinking among its members that deviated from Augustine's definition of God's grace as unconditionally given. Gregory, who taught in Italy after studying in Paris, held to a strict predestination view of salvation. Augustine's theology of sin and grace also shaped the teaching of the secular priest, Oxford professor, and archbishop of Canterbury Thomas Bradwardine (ca. 1290–1349). Few others among their contemporaries, however, had found such interpretations of Augustine's positions acceptable.

The fifteenth-century Augustinians read Augustine's works along with those of many Scholastic theologians. However, three trends among them may have influenced Luther even before he plunged into Augustine's writings around 1509: their practice of a practical monastic mystical devotion, their dedication to studying Paul's Letters, and their early acceptance of humanist learning. This provided the setting in which Luther learned and then began to teach theology.

See also Augustine of Hippo; Staupitz, Johann von

Bibliography

Oberman, H. A. *Archbishop Thomas Bradwardine, a Fourteenth Century Augustinian*. Kenink & Zoon, 1957; Oberman, H. A., ed. *Gregor von Rimini: Werk und Wirkung*. De Gruyter, 1981; Ocker, C. *Biblical Poetics before Humanism and Reformation*. Cambridge University Press, 2002; Saak, E. L. "The Reception of Augustine in the Late Middle

Ages." In *The Reception of the Church Fathers in the West*, ed. I. Backus, 1:367–404. Brill, 2001.

ROBERT KOLB

Aulén, Gustaf

Writing lucidly through seventy years as professor and bishop in Sweden, Gustaf Aulén (1879–1977) influenced Swedish Lutheran theology and church life, insisting that the ongoing dynamic power of God's love in and through Christ was a living reality in the Christian's life and the church's message. In his autobiography, *Från mina 96 år* (From my 96 years), Aulén wrote that his early questions as a youth, answered by what he perceived as rigid and formulaic textbook orthodoxy, vaccinated him against any such recourse in his own work. His first book replaced the old textbook on the history of dogma. It came out in 1917, providing several decades of Swedish students a useful guide, along with a companion volume, *The Faith of the Christian Church*. Its translation into English by Swedish American theologian Eric Wahlstrom in 1923 provided the introduction to theology for American students even into the 1970s and thus is testament to the author's knack for understanding beginning theological students and keeping them interested. In this work and in his study of the atonement, *Christus Victor* (1931), Aulén showed how Christ's passion could be understood as struggle and triumph. This more dynamic way of understanding the atonement brought new life into the study of dogmatics.

In 1933 Aulén became bishop of Strängnäs, a diocese southwest of Stockholm. With a major work translated into English, Aulén had entrée into a phase of ecumenical work among Scandinavian, American, Continental, and British churches, just as World War II shoved their relationships underground. Aulén and other Swedish theologians nevertheless put energy into this work, self-consciously carrying forward the ecumenical legacy bequeathed to the Church of Sweden by Nathan Söderblom. Interrupting both vision and momentum, however, the traumatic war years held countries as well as Christian unity hostage. The Nazi occupation of Denmark, Finland, and Norway isolated church leaders from ecumenical and international colleagues, even while the ecumenical movement served to provide visibility that in some measure protected them. Aulén's connections in Norway because of his wife's family also made for interesting avenues for subversion. His short 1944 book, *The Church and National Socialism*, was issued by the publisher as *Prayer Book for Home and School*. Nazi censors apparently did not bother to look inside such a book cover to see the intense critique in its pages.

Aulén's contribution to the church life of Sweden included his founding of the Swedish theological journal *Svenskt Teologisk Kvartalskrift* in 1925. Less visible to English readers were Aulén's musical gifts, including the 1909 setting to the banner hymn of Sweden's university-centered Young Church Movement, "Fädernas Kyrkan" (The church of our fathers), as well as a setting of Grundtvig's "O liv, som blev tänt" (Oh life, that is sparked), and late in life a tune for the popular text writer Anders Frostenson's "Guds kärlek är som stranden" (God's love is wide as the shore) in 1968.

A career that spanned so many decades as theological professor, pastor, and bishop did not atrophy, as Aulén continually responded to new theological challenges facing an urban, secular, technological, industrial, and democratic society. The great care that Aulén took in being a Swedish theologian, for the Church of Sweden, helped his work hit home in that land, but his attention to the pertinent questions of that particular cultural context made his theological work reach far beyond a limited geography precisely because of his ability to accurately and truthfully describe and delineate the essential questions of people, ones that proved to be broadly applicable to the situation of pastors and students in many other lands. The model of active engagement with actual problems did attract attention from an international audience, even while the full depth and scope of Aulén's work can be appreciated best by those who read Swedish.

See also Atonement; Lundensian School; Sweden

Bibliography

Aulén, G. *Christus Victor.* Macmillan, 1951; Aulén, G. *The Faith of the Christian Church.* Muhlenberg, 1948; Aulén, G. *Från mina 96 år.* Verbum, 1975; Ferré, N. F. S. *Swedish Contributions to Modern Theology.* Harper & Row, 1967; "Gustaf Aulén." *Svenskt Biografiskt Lexikon.* 33 vols. Riksarkivet, 1917–.

MARIA ERLING

Australia

The founding narrative of the Lutheran Church in Australia is the story of "the Old Lutherans" (*die Alt-Lutheraner*) who emigrated from Prussia and arrived in Adelaide as religious refugees in November 1838. Prussian king Friedrich Wilhelm III hoped that a union of the Lutheran majority and the Reformed minority in Prussia could be effected by introducing a common worship book for his lands. Convinced that to follow the king's decree and use the new *Agende* (order for worship) would be to compromise Lutheran belief in the real presence of Christ's body and blood in the Lord's Supper (and for other reasons as well), the Old Lutherans protested and resisted for several years. The persecution was severe enough to motivate some groups to emigrate. While many found their way to North America, Pastor August Kavel and his people made the long voyage to the new colony of South Australia, whose founders were looking for suitable free settlers.

Kavel's people and those who followed them soon prospered, not least because of their farming skills and strong work ethic. Wherever they settled, they formed close-knit communities centered on church and school. Though the persecution in Prussia soon ended, Lutherans continued to emigrate to Australia, often encouraged by good reports from relatives and friends in the new country.

A serious rift in 1846 between the first two pastors, Kavel and Fritzsche, and their respective groups seriously affected Australian Lutheranism's early history, a rift that took 120 years to heal. Three issues caused division: how the church in Australia should be constituted and organized; how the Lutheran confessional writings are to be interpreted at certain places; and what is to happen when Christ appears in glory (the question of chiliasm). Further divisions took place, mostly because of disagreements about which training institutions overseas could provide suitable pastors. Graduates from two confessional Lutheran mission seminaries in Germany, Hermannsburg and Neuendettelsau, were accepted as orthodox, but there was opposition to accepting graduates and former missionaries who had trained in nondenominational seminaries, such as that at Basel. Furthermore, new synods sprang up as Lutheran groups in the eastern colonies of Victoria and Queensland organized themselves and worked out their relationship with the two major groups emerging in South Australia.

Early German Lutheran emigrants were initially well received in the Australian colonies. However, when war broke out in 1914, the situation altered rapidly. Church buildings were vandalized or burned down, some people of German descent (including pastors) were interned in camps, and church schools were shut down. Anti-German feeling lingered postwar, but by the late 1920s the situation was returning to normal. The reprieve was short-lived, however, because the rise of Nazism in Germany set the stage for another difficult period for Lutheranism in Australia, although persecution and injustices were not as severe as during World War I. The stigma of being known as "the German church" meant that for almost half a century Lutherans in Australia felt isolated from the rest of the population.

Having experienced isolation and vulnerability, Australian Lutherans began to realize that it was time to mend differences and become one church. In the period between the wars, a number of synods joined to form the United Evangelical Lutheran Church in

Australia (UELCAs). A major unifying factor for this church was the influence of Wilhelm Loehe (Löhe) and the Neuendettelsau tradition in theology, liturgy, and mission. The other major group was the Evangelical Lutheran Synod of Australia (ELSA, later ELCA), which from the 1890s had been strongly influenced by the Lutheran Church–Missouri Synod (LCMS), especially through the provision of teachers for the seminary and many parish pastors. Theologically this church stood steadfastly in the Walther–Missourian tradition, as is attested by the fact that the English edition of Walther's *Law and Gospel* was dedicated to the seminary in Adelaide in recognition of the doctor of divinity degree that it had conferred on him.

Despite the fact that both churches stood firmly in confessional Lutheran traditions, the path to Lutheran union in Australia was long and difficult. There was little progress until 1948, when the ELCA revised its stance on joint prayer. The fact that the two sides could now pray together was a major breakthrough. So also was the 1949 arrival of the former Erlangen theologian Hermann Sasse, who contributed significantly to intersynodical dialogue. The doctrinal agreements that were hammered out along the long road to union came to be known as "The Theses of Agreement." The last sticking point was the practical issue of relating to other churches or churchly organizations, such as the Lutheran World Federation, sister churches overseas, and missions in New Guinea. After many delays, in 1965 it was agreed that for the sake of unity in Australia, both sides would suspend their current overseas ties, except for the work in New Guinea, with the intention of addressing overseas issues subsequently. A document of union was adopted, pulpit-and-altar fellowship was declared, and in October 1966 a great service of thanksgiving was held to celebrate Lutheran union in Australia and the founding of the Lutheran Church of Australia (LCAs). At its beginning the LCAs was a church of about 115,000 baptized people (including 3,000 in New Zealand) in 634 congregations, served by 341 pastors, and led by its first president, Dr. Max Loehe (Löhe). As its founding documents testify, the LCAs is a confessional and Evangelical Lutheran Church.

In the almost fifty years of its existence, the LCAs has kept "the unity of the Spirit in the bond of peace" (Eph. 4:3), although not without tensions. Theological tensions over the doctrine of Scripture continue, and, as voting at pastors' conferences and synods shows, the church has for a long time been deeply divided over the issue of the ordination of women (a slight majority in favor). Like most churches in Australia, the membership of the LCAs is aging and declining. Like other Lutheran churches, the LCAs is struggling to find the right balance between faithfulness to its Lutheran liturgical tradition and hymnody and the need to communicate to Australians of the twenty-first century in language, music, and style that are intelligible, appealing, and appropriate. On the positive side, the LCAs is well respected in the ecumenical scene. Fruitful theological dialogues continue with Roman Catholics, Anglicans, and the Uniting Church. One former president has served as chair of the National Council of Churches in Australia, and another currently holds the position. At its synod in April 2013 the LCAs decided to change the title for its leaders from "president" to "bishop," a change that seems to have been readily accepted. Involvement in mission, both to Aboriginal people and overseas, especially in New Guinea, has been a significant and enduring part of the Lutheran story in Australia, as has outreach to new arrivals from many countries. At the present time the LCAs holds associate membership both in the Lutheran World Federation and in the International Lutheran Council.

The first Lutherans came to Australia "for faith and freedom," and their hope was not disappointed. Lutherans in Australia today would overwhelmingly agree that, above all else, it is for faith and freedom that they are still here.

See also Australian Aboriginal People; Fritzsche, Gotthard Daniel; Kavel, August Ludwig Christian; Prussian Union

Bibliography

Brauer, A. *Under the Southern Cross: History of Evangelical Lutheran Church of Australia.* Ed. P. G. Strelan. Lutheran Publishing House, 1956. Reprint, 1985; Hebart, T. *The United Evangelical Lutheran Church in Australia (U.E.L.C.A.): Its History, Activities and Characteristics, 1838–1938.* English version ed. J. J. Stolz. Lutheran Book Depot, 1938. Reprint, Lutheran Publishing House, 1985; Koch, J. *When the Murray Meets the Mississippi: A Survey of Australian and American Lutheran Contacts, 1838–1974.* Lutheran Publishing House, 1975; Leske, E. *For Faith and Freedom: The Story of Lutherans and Lutheranism in Australia, 1836–1996.* Rev. ed. Friends of Lutheran Archives, 2009; Schild, M., and P. Hughes. *The Lutherans in Australia.* Australian Government Publishing Service, 1996; Schubert, D. *Kavel's People.* Lutheran Publishing House, 1985.

DEAN ZWECK

Australian Aboriginal People

The Lutherans who went to Australia were imbued with a strong sense of mission. The first two Lutheran pastors to arrive in South Australia, C. Schürmann and C. Teichelmann, were missionaries sent by the Dresden Mission in 1838 to evangelize the Kaurna people of the Adelaide region. Slightly earlier in the same year, Gossner missionaries had arrived in Queensland and established a mission called Zion Hill. Neither of these early attempts resulted in any baptisms. When European explorers "discovered" different groups of Aboriginal people in the Outback, Lutherans heard this as a call from God. Hermannsburg missionaries arrived in 1866 and journeyed over a thousand kilometers into the interior to begin work among the Dieri people. In 1878 missionaries W. F. Schwarz and A. H. Kempe made it all the way to the center of Australia after an epic two-thousand-kilometer, twenty-month journey and began work among the Aranda people at a place they called Hermannsburg. The work of the Finke River Mission, as it came to be called, survived and even prospered because of the faithful and heroic missionary service of the early missionaries and those who followed them, both European and Aboriginal—in particular, Neuendettelsau-trained Carl Strehlow, evangelist Tjalkabota (Blind Moses), and Hermannsburger F. W. Albrecht. Due to their faithful labors a majority of central Australian Aborigines regard themselves as Lutheran Christians. Other missions were begun at Hope Vale in North Queensland (1889) and on the West Coast of South Australia (1901). As a relatively small church, the Lutheran contribution to the evangelization and Christian care of Aboriginal people in Australia is notable.

See also Australia

Bibliography

Albrecht, P. *From Mission to Church, 1877–2002: Finke River Mission.* Finke River Mission, 2002; Leske, E. *For Faith and Freedom: The Story of Lutherans and Lutheranism in Australia, 1836–1996.* Rev. ed. Friends of Lutheran Archives, 2009.

DEAN ZWECK

Austria

Luther's message spread throughout the Hapsburg lands of Austria, adjacent territories, and neighboring ecclesiastical principalities in the 1520s and quickly commanded the allegiance of a majority of the population, despite persecution by both Hapsburg officials and the abbots, bishops, and archbishops of church territories. Anabaptist preachers also attracted followings. Kaspar Tauber, a citizen of Vienna, and Leonhard Kaiser, a pastor in western Austria, were two of the early martyrs among Luther's adherents. Local nobles encouraged preaching and reforms along Wittenberg lines within Hapsburg and ecclesiastical domains throughout the sixteenth century, despite sometimes severe governmental pressure to return to Roman obedience. Emperor Maximilian II, who showed some sympathy for Wittenberg reform, supported the request of the estates of Lower Austria for the help of David Chytraeus in creating—along with Christoph Reuter (1520–81), a pastor active in Austria—a church order that structured the Lutheran church and regulated its practice (1569–72). Austrian Lutherans supported efforts by Primus Truber, Matthias Flacius, and others to bring Wittenberg theology to Slovenians and Croats. Followers of Flacius and his concept of original sin as the substance of the fallen human creature found refuge in Austrian congregations in the final third of the sixteenth century. In 1566 under Flacian influence, the Lutherans in Carinthia and in Lower Austria produced confessions of faith.

Emperor Rudolf II initiated intensified pressure on Lutherans in the Hapsburg domains in the 1570s and 1580s; these efforts came to completion in the first decade of the Thirty Years' War. By 1628 the Counter-Reformation had driven those remaining faithful to Lutheran teaching into the underground. Not until 1781, with Joseph II's Patent of Toleration, was the restoration of congregational life possible. Protestants were tolerated in the archbishopric of Salzburg until 1731, when thousands were forced into exile and settled in other German territories and even the colony of Georgia.

The restoration of limited congregational life, with church buildings forbidden to have steeples and bells, permitted the tolerated Evangelicals both of the Augsburg Confession and of the Helvetic Confession to organize formal church structures. However, under the Hapsburg monarchy, until its end in 1918, the situation of these churches remained somewhat tenuous. The National Socialist government severely restricted and oppressed the Protestant churches from 1938 to 1945. An organizational union brought the churches of the Augsburg Confession and the Helvetic Confession together in 1988, while each retained its confessional position and administration. The University of Vienna has a Protestant theological faculty.

See also Chytraus, David; Flacius, Matthias Illyricus, and the Flacians

Bibliography

Böhl, E. *Beiträge zur Geschichte der Reformation in Österreich.* Fischer, 1902; Leeb, R., et al. *Geheimprotestantismus und die evangelische Kirche in der Habsburger Monarchie und in der Erzstift Salzburg.* Böhlau, 2009; Leeb, R. *Geschichte des Christentums in Österreich.* Überreuter, 2005; Leeb, R., et al. *Staatsmacht und Seelenheil: Gegenreformation und Geheimprotestantismus in der Habsburgermonarchie.* Oldenbourg, 2007; Mecenseffy, G. *Geschichte des Protestantismus in Österreich.* Böhlau, 1956; Reingrabner, G. *Protestanten in Österreich.* Böhlau, 1981; Wiedemann, T. *Geschichte der Reformation und Gegenreformation im Lande unter der Enns.* Tempsky, 1879.

ROBERT KOLB

Authority

Martin Luther's ideas about authority in the church developed within and because of crisis: the church leaders were persecuting the gospel, which meant that something had gone terribly awry in the church's exercise of its authority.

In terms of content, Luther argued from the beginning that there was no other or greater authority in the church than Holy Scripture. By its measure alone were all of the church's doctrines, practices, and morals to be judged. Scripture alone did not mean only Scripture: Luther commended the creeds, the decisions of the first four ecumenical councils, and various theologians in the church's history as insightful interpreters of Scripture and thus authoritative. But it was always normative Scripture that they were interpreting and by which their interpretations were to be judged.

When Luther raised questions in the Ninety-Five Theses about the limits of papal authority to issue indulgences for divine penalties for sin, the point of controversy almost immediately shifted to the authority of church offices, primarily the papal but also the episcopal. To the reformer's great frustration, his opponents (Cajetan, Eck, Emser) consistently refused to discuss the issue at hand on the basis of Scripture, appealing instead to papal authority and canon law, even exalting these authorities over Scripture. Insofar as Luther was willing to meet them on their own ground, he argued that the early church and the churches of the East were true Christians yet not under papal authority, and furthermore—joining a long-running battle in medieval Western Christendom—that a general council ought to have greater authority than the pope. In any event, under no circumstances was a heretical pope to be obeyed. Melanchthon would later reassert these points in his *Treatise on the Power and Primacy of the Pope* in 1537.

Still, Luther's preference was to refer the dispute to the Scripture, where he could find no grounds for Roman supremacy over Scripture, for the sharp distinction between pastors and bishops, for authority over temporal powers accorded to clergy (esp. the pope), or even for calling the clergy "priests" (*sacerdotes*). His words at the Diet of Worms in 1521 are a justly famous summary of his position on indulgences, papal authority, and indeed everything else: "Unless I am convinced by the testimony of the Scriptures or by clear reason (for I do not trust either in the pope or in councils alone, since it is well known that they have often erred and contradicted themselves), I am bound by the Scriptures I have quoted and my conscience is captive to the Word of God" (LW 32:112).

Alongside the controversies that enveloped him, Luther developed two lines of thought about authority as exercised by persons within the church, organically related to one another. On the one hand, in the true church all authority rests in Christ. According to 1 Pet. 2:9, all Christians are priests in common. No one person can ever claim any authority over another, for all are equally under Christ. All participate in Christ's kingship and priesthood by faith, which means that all may "appear before God to pray for others and to teach one another divine things" (*The Freedom of a Christian* [1520], LW 31:355). He reiterated the point in *Temporal Authority* (1523): "Among Christians there shall and can be no authority; rather all are alike subject to one another," citing Rom. 12:10; 1 Pet. 5:5; and Luke 14:10. "Among Christians there is no superior but Christ himself, and him alone. What kind of authority can there be where all are equal and have the same right, power, possession, and honor, and where no one desires to be the other's superior, but each other's subordinate? Where there are such people, one could not

establish authority even if he wanted to. . . . Where there are no such people, however, there are no real Christians, either" (LW 45:117).

On the other hand, Luther acknowledged that "although we are all equally priests, we cannot all publicly minister and teach" (*The Freedom of a Christian*, LW 31:356). Yet it is only by the common consent of the community (the call) that anyone accepts a call to administer word and sacrament, "for what is the common property of all, no individual may arrogate to himself, unless he is called" (*Babylonian Captivity* [1520], LW 36:116). External things do not make priests. "Rather, priesthood and power have to be there first, brought from baptism and common to all Christians through the faith which builds them upon Christ the true high priest" (*Dr. Luther's Retraction of the Error . . .* [1521], LW 39:237). The nature of the authority conferred by ordination is one of service, not power or privilege. There is absolutely no place for the sword or force among Christians, because Christ rules them by the Spirit alone. "Heresy is a spiritual matter which you cannot hack to pieces with iron, consume with fire, or drown in water. God's word alone avails here" (*On Temporal Authority*, LW 45:114). Later, Luther changed his opinion in the controversies with the Anabaptists, recommending their execution not only for secular crimes (rebellion) but also for blasphemy.

Consistent across Luther's writings is the contention that the ordained ministry has been given the authority to preach the gospel, administer the sacraments, forgive sins, judge doctrine, and discipline the ungodly. Melanchthon succinctly crystallized Luther's points in the Augsburg Confession (1530), where article 4 on justification is immediately followed by the assertion of article 5: "To obtain such faith God instituted the office of preaching, giving the gospel and the sacraments." Subsequent articles argue that, to ensure "the gospel is purely preached and the holy sacraments are administered according to the gospel" (CA 7), "no one should publicly teach, preach, or administer the sacraments without a proper [public] call" (CA 14 in *BC* 40, 42, 46, German Text). CA 28 addresses even more sharply the abuse of power by the bishops who had arrogated to themselves the power of the secular sword in addition to various spiritual abuses. The sole authority of the keys, or of bishops, is "to preach the gospel, to forgive sin, to judge doctrine and reject doctrine that is contrary to the gospel, and to exclude from the Christian community the ungodly whose ungodly life is manifest—not with human power but with God's word alone." Accordingly, "one should not obey bishops, even if they have been regularly elected, when they err or teach and command something contrary to the holy, divine Scriptures" (CA 28 in *BC* 94, German Text).

Early on, and clearly shaped by his struggle against Rome and its failure of leadership, Luther rather optimistically asserted the "right and power" of a Christian congregation to judge doctrine and call or dismiss its own leaders, as he asserted in a famous treatise of 1523. By the time of the Saxon visitation in late 1528 and early 1529, he had developed a different approach. "Dear God, what misery I beheld!" he remarked after meeting the ignorant laity and incompetent pastors (*BC* 347). The Small Catechism was the immediate fruit of this discovery, but overall Reformation efforts toward the education of both pastors and laypeople were intended to enable the real ministry of the gospel to take place.

In terms of broader church structures beyond the congregation, Luther in the Smalcald Articles (1536) asserted that "the church cannot be better ruled and preserved than if we all live under one head, Christ, and all the bishops—equal according to the office (although they may be unequal in their gifts)—keep diligently together in unity of teaching, faith, sacraments, prayers, and works of love" (*BC* 308). He commended the binding and loosing of sin by the office of the keys but not the "great" excommunication (excommunicating entire lands), and he asserted the right of the Evangelical party to ordain its own pastors

since the bishops were unwilling to do the true work assigned to them. In his 1539 treatise *On the Councils and the Church*, he identified the general council of the church as a court to judge current practice and teaching according to Scripture—though schools and parishes also would need to do this on a regular basis and not wait for the convening of a council. He concluded: "One should now be able to understand what a council is, its rights, power, office, and task; also, which councils are genuine and which false: namely, that they should confess and defend the ancient faith, and not institute new articles of faith against the ancient faith, nor institute new good works against the old good works, but defend the old good works against the new good works" (LW 41:135–36). Nevertheless, this was purely an exercise in theory since by now Luther had all but abandoned hope of a genuinely free council of the church. The prospective council to be convened in Mantua in 1537 was repeatedly postponed for political reasons, and when it finally met in Trent in 1545, the Protestants, contrary to the express wishes of the Smalcaldic League, were definitely not invited as full and equal participants.

Practically speaking, the Lutheran movement had to create new structures and offices to deal with the education and appointment of pastors, judgment of doctrine, and discipline. In the course of his lifetime, Luther himself exercised the office of oversight to a great if somewhat unofficial degree (but always as a doctor of theology). Theology faculties in universities became de facto part of the magisteria for Lutheran churches in the countries where the Reformation took hold, though in equal measure the princes took Luther's invitation in the *Address to the Christian Nobility* (1520) at his word and exercised a great deal of oversight in the churches of their territories, sometimes with results directly at odds with Luther's own standards. At the same time, pastors, preachers, consistories, superintendents, general superintendents, and even occasionally Evangelical bishops (esp. in Nordic lands) also exercised authority. The confessional writings of the sixteenth century and the writings of Luther and (less often) other reformers also gained prominence as authoritative interpreters of Scripture and confessors of the faith.

Luther's ultimate appeal was to the clarity of Scripture in presenting the gospel of Jesus Christ, and his means of fostering a proper understanding of Scripture were intensive linguistic and theological education. All authority in the church, whether of teaching, practice, or officeholders, was to be held accountable to Scripture. An ecclesiastical process or institution could certainly be criticized for structural corruption or inadequacy, leading to false and unscriptural decisions. However, the converse would not hold: no decision could be justified only on the grounds that the process or institution had been legitimately conducted. All decisions must be judged and justified by their content alone. For this reason, a situation of *status confessionis* may arise in which the faith itself demands a clear confession of the gospel over against false teaching or corrupt practice, even if endorsed by church authorities—including those of Lutheran churches.

The fact that Christians continue to disagree over the meaning of Scripture can be taken as the Achilles' heel of Luther's position: there is no possible conclusive end to debate in the church. On the other hand, history has demonstrated that absolute solutions executed by human hands invariably lead to treachery. Authority must remain, in the Lutheran understanding, an eschatological confession (cf. Matt. 28:18–20; 1 Cor. 15:24; Rev. 12:10).

See also Papacy; Priesthood of All Believers; Scripture; Tradition

Bibliography

Luther's Works: *The Babylonian Captivity of the Church* (1520). LW 36:3–126; The Book of Concord (1580): Small Catechism (1529). Smalcald Articles (1537). *Treatise on the Power and Primacy of the Pope* (1537); *Dr. Luther's Retraction of the Error Forced upon Him by the Most Highly Learned Priest of God, Sir Jerome Emser, Vicar in Meissen* (1521). LW 39:225–38; *The Freedom of the Christian* (1520). LW 31:327–77; *Luther at the Diet of Worms* (1521). LW 32:101–31; *On the Councils and the Church* (1539). LW 41:3–178; *Temporal Authority: To What Extent It Should Be Obeyed* (1523). LW 45:75–129; *That a Christian Assembly or Congregation Has the Right and Power to Judge All Teaching and to Call, Appoint, and Dismiss Teachers, Established and Proven by Scripture* (1523). LW 39:301–14; **Another Work:** Melanchthon, Philip, ed. Augsburg Confession.

SARAH HINLICKY WILSON

B

Bach, Johann Sebastian

The famous church musician and composer Johann Sebastian Bach (1685–1750) was born in Eisenach, the eighth and youngest child of the town musician Johann Ambrosius Bach and Maria Elisabeth Lämmerhirt Bach, part of a large and extended family of German musicians. From 1693 to 1695 he attended the Latin school in Eisenach. In 1694 his mother died, and a year later his father died, both at the age of fifty. From 1695 to 1700 he and his brother Johann Jacob lived with their oldest brother, Johann Christoph, in Ohrdruf, where he attended the *Gymnasium* (secondary school).

From 1700 until 1702 Bach was a choirboy in the Michaelis school in Lüneberg. In 1703 he became the organist of the Neue Kirche in Arnstadt, where he wrote the *D Minor Toccata and Fugue*. In 1705 he went to Lübeck to hear Dieterich Buxtehude and the *Abendmusik* concerts there. His request of four weeks from the Arnstadt officials for this trip turned into four months. From 1707 until 1708 he was the organist at the Blasiuskirche in Mühlhausen, where he wrote some early cantatas, including *Christ lag in todesbanden* (Christ lay in death's strong bands). In 1707 he married his second cousin Maria Barbara Bach.

His next move was to Weimar, where from 1708 until 1717 he was chamber musician and court organist for the codukes Wilhelm Ernst and Ernst August of Saxe-Weimar. The first six of his twenty children were born there. He wrote the *Orgelbüchlein* (Organ booklet), preludes and fugues for organ, the *English Suites*, and the beginnings of *The Well-Tempered Clavier*. In 1717 he signed an agreement to become *Kapellmeister* and director of chamber music at the court of Prince Leopold of Anhalt-Cöthen, but Duke Wilhelm Ernst did not want to release him and slapped him in jail from November 6 to December 2. He stayed in Anhalt-Cöthen from 1717 until 1723, when a seventh child was born. There he wrote the *Brandenberg Concertos*, the *French Suites*, *The Well-Tempered Clavier*, the sonatas and partitas for solo violin, and the suites for solo cello.

When he was on a trip with Prince Leopold to Karlsbad from May to July in 1720, his wife Maria Barbara died unexpectedly. She was buried in July. Together they had seven children. Bach married Anna Magdalena Wilcke in December of the next year. From 1723 until 1742 they had thirteen children, all born in Leipzig, where from 1723 until his death in 1750 Bach was Cantor at the St. Thomas Church and School, with responsibilities at the St. Nicholas Church and other churches there.

In Leipzig he wrote four or possibly five cycles of cantatas for the church year. Cantatas were the centerpiece of his composing. They were conceived as proclamatory expositions of the gospel—for which Bach has been called the "fifth evangelist"—in connection with the biblical readings from the lectionary and the hymn of the day for each Sunday and feast day. Since the penitential Sundays of Lent and the three Sundays before Christmas excluded this music, about sixty cantatas were required for each cycle. Twenty minutes or so in length, each cantata was linked with the hour-long sermon, sometimes divided on either side of it. The Sunday service began at 7:00 AM and took three to four hours, depending on how long Communion lasted. Bach did the bulk of this composing by 1729, during the first years of his tenure in Leipzig.

According to Christoph Wolff, the most productive period of Bach's cantata writing occurred between June 1724 and March 1725, when he composed about forty cantatas in a period of forty weeks. Wolff describes his workweek like this: with the texts selected by the clergy in booklets, on Monday or possibly earlier Bach began to compose the music, then organized and supervised the copying, reviewed the copies, rehearsed in one run-through on Saturday, and performed the cantata the next day in the service. The rest of Bach's workweek included teaching in the St. Thomas School, a prayer service every Friday, weddings and funerals after three in the afternoon so as not to interfere with instruction in the school, and family life.

Bach's vocation was related to the choral music of the church. It was built on the bedrock of congregational hymnody that used the chorales of Martin Luther and those who followed him. With his remarkable harmonizations for the choir, he built these chorales into the cantatas. Bach composed and improvised organ preludes to introduce them for the congregation, which sang them in unison and without accompaniment.

In addition to cantatas, Bach wrote motets at Leipzig: the *Magnificat*, the *St. John Passion*, the *St. Matthew Passion*, six cantatas called the *Christmas Oratorio*, the *Clavier-Übung*, the second part of *The Well-Tempered Clavier*, the *Canonic Variations*, the *Musical Offering*, the *Art of Fugue*, and the *B Minor Mass*.

Bach ranks as the finest Lutheran composer. Robert Shaw suggested that he may "be the single greatest creative genius of the Western World" and that the *B Minor Mass* may be "his greatest achievement." Although this piece employed the texts of the Ordinary Mass, it is, unlike others of the time, too massive for any actual worship service. Bach never heard it as a whole. It is a musical, liturgical, and theological celebration of the life and worship of the whole church catholic, thus a gift to the world.

Behind the skillful sounds of Bach's music lie rhetorical symbolism that can be heard with careful listening and numerical symbolism that cannot. While commentators can engage in fanciful excursions about these, they are hard to deny. They, the formal structures, and mostly the music itself reflect an uncanny sense of proportion. Cadences are where they should be, order is linked with freedom, and an unusually gracious ebb and flow are part of Bach's music. Eliot Gardiner says it chips away at toxicity, chastens, elates, and cleanses.

See also Buxtehude, Dietrich; Music; Schütz, Heinrich

Bibliography

David, H., A. Mendel, and C. Wolff. *The New Bach Reader: A Life of Johann Sebastian Bach in Letters and Documents*. Norton, 1998; Gardiner, J. E. *Bach: Music in the Castle of Heaven*. Knopf, 2013; Geck, M. *Johann Sebastian Bach: Life and Work*. Trans. J. Hargraves. Harcourt, 2000; Leaver, R., ed. *J. S. Bach and Scripture*. Concordia, 1985; Schweitzer, A. *J. S. Bach*. Trans. E. Newman. Bruce Humphries, 1911; Spitta, P. *Johann Sebastian Bach*. Trans. C. Bell and J. S. Fuller-Maitland. Dover, 1951; Stiller, G. *Johann Sebastian Bach and Liturgical Life in Leipzig*. Trans. H. Bouman. Concordia, 1970; Wolff, C. *Johann Sebastian Bach: The Learned Musician*. Norton, 2000.

PAUL WESTERMEYER

Balkan Lands

In the sixteenth century two empires were fighting for control over southeastern Europe. The Ottoman Turkish Empire had been steadily expanding toward the northwest since the end of the fourteenth century. Following key battles in Kosovo (1389) and Nicopolis (1396), the sultan's army conquered present-day Bulgaria and Serbia, making headway westward into Bosnia and Croatia and expanding northward into Hungary after the decisive battles of Belgrade (1521) and Mohács (1526), and the fall of the Hungarian capital, Buda, in 1541.

The small kingdoms and principalities on the Balkan Peninsula either fell into Ottoman hands and ceased to exist (e.g., Bosnia), were dramatically reduced (e.g., Hungary), or became tribute-paying Ottoman vassals (e.g., Transylvania). With Constantinople (present-day Istanbul) as their capital since 1453, the Ottomans had ambitious plans, and nothing made the Turkish threat in Europe more real than the sieges of Vienna, the capital of

Austria and later of the Hapsburg Empire, in 1529 and 1683. The sultan hoped that conquering this strategic city would open the way to conquering western Europe as well.

Parallel to the invasions from the east, the Hapsburgs were looking to increase their influence in the region from the west and to secure their borders from the expanding Ottoman Empire. Ruled by a staunchly Roman Catholic dynasty, they did not view the developments in the German lands resulting from the Lutheran Reformation favorably.

Because far fewer students from southeastern Europe than from central Europe studied in Wittenberg, Luther's ideas reached these lands more slowly. The tenets of the Reformation spread more through already existing transnational connections and networks among noble families, learned scholars, and members of the church hierarchy. Lutheranism did not always arrive directly from Germany: in the case of the Adriatic coastline, another major political power, Venice, acted as the transmitter, with seamen, merchants, and travelers as the messengers.

In the lands that make up Slovenia today, several influential persons embraced the Lutheran Reformation. Among them were two brothers from the Venetian-controlled portion of Istria, Pietro Paolo Vergerio the Younger (1498–1565) and Giovanni Battista Vergerio (1497–1548), both Roman Catholic bishops. Giovanni Battista, bishop of Pula, was poisoned, and Pietro Paolo, bishop of Capodistria (Koper), eventually fled his homeland, fearing persecution, and found refuge in the Swiss canton of Graubünden. After working there as a Protestant pastor, he was invited to be an adviser to Duke Christopher of Württemberg (1515–68) and remained in Tübingen until his death.

The single most influential Slovenian representative of Lutheranism in the sixteenth century was Primus Truber (Primož Trubar, 1508–86). Born in the Austrian-controlled region of Carniola, Truber studied in Rijeka, Salzburg, Trieste, and Vienna. Upon returning

to his homeland, he worked as a priest. As he was becoming increasingly Protestant-leaning, for example preaching in Slovenian at St. Nicholas Cathedral in Ljubljana, he was expelled in 1547. He fled to Rothenburg ob der Tauber and later lived in Kempten. In 1550 he published *Catechismus in der windischen Sprach*, the first book printed in Slovenian. In addition to the catechism Truber issued further books, translating the New Testament into Slovenian, making contributions to the establishment of a literary Slovenian language (*Abecedarium*, 1550), and writing a first Slovenian Protestant church order (*Cerkovna Ordninga*, 1564). In light of his accomplishments he is referred to as the "Slovenian Luther" and as the "Father of the Slovenian Language." Following a brief return to Ljubljana, where he became superintendent, Truber was exiled again in 1565, and he spent the rest of his life in Germany, pastoring congregations in Württemberg.

Sebastian Krelj (1538–67), who followed Truber as Lutheran superintendent in Ljubljana, was also active as a translator and author of theological texts. His most significant legacy, however, is as a linguistic innovator, for having created a systematic Slovenian orthography, which was in turn implemented by Georg Dalmatin (1547–89), who produced the first complete Bible translation into Slovenian, printed in Wittenberg in 1584. Adam Bohorič (1520–98), a school principal, likewise depended on Krelj's system in writing the first Slovenian grammar book, which he fashioned after Philip Melanchthon's Latin grammar guide.

In 1560–61 a printing press for producing biblical and Protestant literature in South Slavic languages was set up in Urach near Tübingen by Baron Hans Ungnad von Sonnegg (1493–1564). He gathered a group of translators and theologians, who published thirty-seven titles in around thirty-one thousand copies in Croatian and Slovenian, using three different alphabets (Latin, Cyrillic, and the now defunct Glagolithic) until the printing press closed in 1565, after Ungnad's death.

It was here that the first complete Croatian translation of the New Testament was issued by Stephan Consul (1521–79) and Anton Dalmatin (d. 1579), who also translated and edited numerous Protestant theological works.

In the Croatian lands under the control of Venice or the kingdom of Hungary, a few influential individuals accepted the Lutheran faith. Lutheranism even gathered groups of followers in Istria and in several Dalmatian towns. Most prominent among the Lutherans from present-day Croatia was theologian and church historian Matthias Flacius Illyricus (1520–75), who spent most of his adult life in Germany. He was also Krelj's professor at the University in Jena.

Lutheranism could not have gained a hold in southeastern Europe if it had not been supported by influential members of the nobility, such as the Croatian-Hungarian Zrinski (Zrínyi) and Frankopan (Frangepán) families, who between them controlled large parts of northern Croatia and the Island of Krk, Hans von Ungnad, or the Nádasdy and Bánffy families in the Prekmurje region. Although some of the noble patrons did not personally convert to Lutheranism, they were nonetheless favorable to it and either passively tolerated or actively supported Protestant worship and the publication of Protestant literature in their realms of influence.

Due to the complex political and social situation in the region, Lutheranism did not take root among the masses but remained within the confines of a relatively privileged group. It also did not last long, on the one hand due to the strong Roman Catholic orientation of the Venetian Republic and on the other as a result of the Hapsburg Counter-Reformation, which reached this area by the end of the sixteenth century. This undertaking was aimed at cleansing the land of Protestant teaching and bringing Catholic renewal through inviting Pauline Fathers and Jesuits, who developed increasing influence over the educational system and within the church hierarchy. Nonetheless, the short-lived and socially limited impact of the Lutheran Reformation in the sixteenth century is still traceable today, in large part through the linguistic and literary innovations of the vernaculars that it introduced into mainstream culture.

See also Flacius, Matthias Illyricus, and the Flacians; Hungary

Bibliography

Ilić, L. "Primus Truber (1508–1586), the Slovenian Luther." *LQ* 22 (2008): 268–77; Lorenz, S., A. Schindling, and W. Setzler, eds. *Primus Truber (1508–1586): Der slowenische Reformator und Württemberg.* Kohlhammer, 2011; Louthan, H., and G. Murdock, eds. *A Companion to the Reformation in Central Europe.* Brill, 2015; Pierce, R. A. *Pier Paolo Vergerio the Propagandist.* Edizion di Storia e Letteratura, 2003; Pörtner, R. "Confessionalization and Ethnicity: The Slovenian Reformation and Counter-Reformation in the 16th and 17th Centuries." *ARG* 93 (2002): 239–77; Rajšp, V., K. W. Schwarz, B. Dybaś, and C. Gastgeber, eds. *Die Reformation in Mitteleuropa.* Založba ZRC, 2011; Zigerius, E., and M. Flacius Illyricus. *Ein schrifft / eines fromen Predigers aus der Türckey an Illyricum geschrieben / Darinnen angezeiget wird / wie es dort mit der Kirche und dem Evangelio zugeht.* Lotter, 1550.

LUKA ILIĆ

Baptism

Baptism, whether accomplished through sprinkling or immersion, is one of the two sacraments of the Lutheran church. As a means of grace, baptism both promises forgiveness of sins, (new) life, and salvation and makes them an ongoing, present reality in the one who is baptized. Further, through the work of the Holy Spirit, the baptized is made a part of the church, God's gathered community, and is united to Christ. Unlike the Lord's Supper, however, baptism is considered an unrepeatable sacrament.

Luther viewed the sacraments as a means by which God's grace and forgiveness is imparted to the recipient. The focus of attention, then, is on God's actions. The sacraments are thus theocentric or, as the Large Catechism says, it is "God's own act" (LC Baptism 10 in *BC* 457). As Luther states, "What human work can possibly be greater than God's work?" (LC Baptism 10 in *BC* 458). Thus, in response to the development of believer's baptism with its focus on a person's commitments made,

Luther highlighted instead the actions and declaration of God. When the focus is placed on a human response, even if it is one's confession of faith, then it ceases to be a sacrament or means of grace. Baptism is a proclamation of the gospel to, and is realized in, the baptized. This proclamation does what it promises, so that through baptism God justifies that person. A declaration of one's faith, on the other hand, common in believer's baptism, cannot be a sacrament or a means of grace because such declarations are based on what a person promises to God and the community. In that sense, a declaration of faith becomes from a Lutheran viewpoint a self-justification or a justification before others, rather than justification by God's grace.

Baptism is also an entrance rite into the church, made possible by God's actions. In Luther's explanation of the third article of the Apostles' Creed in the Small Catechism (SC Creed 6 in *BC* 355), a person is made a member of the body of Christ because of the calling and gathering activities of the Holy Spirit, and not by a human being's "own understanding or strength." This focus on God's actions allowed Luther to affirm infant baptism, for nowhere was it more obvious that baptism was an action of God. Baptism unites a person to the crucified and risen Christ and to the church, Christ's body, as the person is submerged in the water and then raised from the water (Rom. 6:3–11).

Understanding baptism as an entrance rite has not been without its difficulties, however. In the late medieval Roman church, for example, the grace in baptism was lost after commission of a mortal sin and considered insufficient for salvation. Participation in the other penitential sacraments, especially penance, was required for salvation, again moving someone from a state of sin to a state of grace. This approach allowed the Roman church to recognize as valid baptisms that were done by laity or non-Roman Catholics. Luther insisted, however, that since baptism gives what it proclaims, the forgiveness of sins, life, and salvation, baptism was a "complete" sacrament and

accessible to the sinner throughout life. He thus saw public and private confession and absolution as a return to baptism not separate from it.

Luther observed that difficulties with baptism arose when the Word was separated from the earthly element. For example, the "spiritualists" felt that only the Word was needed, thus ignoring the water, while the Roman church focus on the mere doing of the action (*ex opere operato*) was enough to constitute a sacrament, while the Word was forgotten. But Luther insisted that "without the Word of God the water is plain water and not a baptism" (SC Baptism 9–10 in *BC* 359).

When the focus is placed on God's activities, it becomes easy to describe what benefits God gives in baptism. Besides being justified, welcomed into community, and united with God in Christ through the work of the Word and Spirit, baptism also "brings about the forgiveness of sins, redeems from death and the devil, and gives eternal salvation" (SC Baptism 5–6 in *BC* 359).

Luther often described the gospel as the forgiveness of sins. However, Luther's opponents were concerned that if baptism grants forgiveness, then Christ's forgiveness obtained on the cross could be ignored. If this were so, baptism could become nothing more than an "eternal fire insurance policy," guaranteeing passage into heaven when one dies. But this would be possible only if the Word (Christ) is separated from the water. Moreover, in his *Confession concerning Christ's Supper* (LW 37:192), Luther argued that the forgiveness granted at the cross is "distributed" in the Lord's Supper, rather than separate from it. So it is with baptism, he argued. Baptism simply distributes the forgiveness proclaimed and won through Christ's death and resurrection. Baptism cannot be separate from the living Word. Further, since article 4 of the Augsburg Confession defines justification as receiving the forgiveness of sin, justification and the water are united by the breathing, living Word. They are not contradictory.

The question about how baptism removes original sin was raised by the Roman church in response to the article on original sin in the Augsburg Confession (CA 2). Melanchthon acknowledged that baptism removes the guilt of original sin, but not its "material element" (Ap 2.35). This element of original sin is completely removed only in the death and resurrection of the baptized. Thus baptism's waters must not only "wash" away one's sinful actions but also "put to death" the old creature trying to be a god in God's place. Only when a person dies will they no longer try to usurp God. This captures Luther's insistence that baptism is more a lifelong, ongoing process than a onetime event. One is to live in their baptism, rather than point to when they were baptized. In eschatological language, the baptized are now—but not yet—fully forgiven, even as they live as simultaneously sinner and justified (*simul iustus et peccator*). Baptism is completed only when a person is drowned in Christ's death and resurrection.

Life and salvation are also a gift of baptism. There is a tendency, however, to see both of these only in futuristic terms: that baptism gives one eternal life and salvation when a person dies. Yet the promises that God makes in baptism are also meant for the present, for in baptism the baptized are reborn (regeneration) to a new life in which God is actively at work destroying sin, death, and the devil in them daily, while also giving them life and healing (one aspect of salvation) in the present. (Thus, Luther retained exorcism in his German baptismal liturgy.) The Holy Spirit works through baptism as the person is called and gathered into a new community, a community of life, in which one is set free from the need for spiritual self-justification, so that they can now be fully engaged in being helpful to their neighbor. Only after focusing on the present, "now" nature of baptism in terms of life and salvation can its future, "not yet" aspect be understood. The promises and gifts given in baptism are not only for life in the present; they are also promises for life after death.

One of the early debates about baptism in the Reformation era came out of the phrase in the Latin text of CA 9 that "baptism is necessary for salvation." This echoed the argument about whether baptism actually forgives sin or merely points to the One who forgives sin. If baptism gives salvation on its own, then Christ is not needed. Lutheran Orthodoxy responded by insisting that the starting point was God's gracious, forgiving nature, a God who wants all to be saved. Thus, while baptism is "ordinarily" necessary for salvation, it is not "absolutely" necessary. While helpful in situations where a child died before being baptized, allowing the church to deny automatic damnation for the child, this approach missed an opportunity to highlight Luther's emphasis on what God does in baptism and the connection with the Word. Thus baptism is necessary for salvation because in baptism God promises graciously to encounter people and give life and salvation. It is only apart from this promise of salvation given in baptism with God and God's proclaiming Word of life that one cannot be saved.

Most of the controversy over baptism in the Reformation era and today revolves around infant baptism and the role of faith within the sacrament. At heart is this question: Does baptism require faith to be valid, or does it create faith? Many traditions require, or assume, a confession of faith in baptism. However, Luther argued that baptism's validity did not depend on the faith of the baptized person. Baptism was valid because it is bound to the Word, rather than to a person's faith. Thus faith does not make baptism, but it receives baptism (LC 4.53). Further, the faith that receives baptism is given in baptism through the Word by the Holy Spirit. This connection of baptism to the Word, rather than faith, meant that Luther basically sidestepped the argument of whether it was the infant's faith, the faith of the gathered community, or the faith of the parents and godparents that validated baptism. The focus on "whose faith" detracted from "what God gives" in the sacrament. On the other hand, Luther did acknowledge that making full use of the benefits of baptism did require faith, but this faith was given and created in the person in baptism.

Luther's approach has not been consistently followed in Lutheranism. Late sixteenth-century Lutherans were sometimes pressured to give up the exorcism in the baptismal service. In the age of rationalism, for example, the focus shifted back onto the faith of the baptized, rather than the creating Word that is proclaimed in baptism. (Similar shifts can be observed among some Lutheran Pietists.) Further, faith was understood as a function of reason. That meant that infant baptism was problematic because infants did not have such rational abilities. Infant baptism was retained, however, but was not viewed as a means of grace. This also meant that baptism was no longer seen as a rebirth or regeneration. Rather, it was now simply an entrance rite into the community, which could be safely omitted. This position was compatible with some Reformed and Roman Catholic traditions in North America. Thus, when American Lutheran Samuel Simon Schmucker introduced his revised version of the Augsburg Confession in 1855, baptismal regeneration was rejected in favor of making it simply an entrance rite to the church. Later on, Karl Barth, among others, also struggled with infant baptism because he felt that infants could not possess faith. While Lutherans caught up in the confessional renewal movement of this time criticized such an approach to baptism, to a large degree they were in the minority.

In 1982 the World Council of Churches Commission on Faith and Order released the document Baptism, Eucharist and Ministry. In the section on baptism, this paper tried to bring together and summarize teachings on baptism that were prevalent in the Christian community. This document noted that the various families of the church generally accepted baptism done in another tradition, as long as it was done in the name of the Triune God or Christ. The document also acknowledged significant differences between those who practiced a "believer's baptism" and those who uphold "infant baptism." These tensions, which existed at the time of the Reformation, are still present in the Christian family. The ecumenical conversations of the last century, however, have been helpful in reminding denominations that baptism is into the body of Christ, not to a particular denomination.

See also Confirmation; Conversion and Regeneration; Liturgy and Worship; Original Sin; Sacraments; Salvation; Word of God

Bibliography

Jetter, W. *Die Taufe beim jungen Luther: Eine Untersuchung über das Werden der reformatorischen Sakraments- und Taufanschauung.* Mohr, 1954; Peters, A. *Commentary on Luther's Catechisms: Baptism and the Lord's Supper.* Concordia, 2012; Scaer, D. *Baptism.* Luther Academy, 1999; Scaer, D. *Infant Baptism.* Concordia, 2011; Spinks, B. *Reformation and Modern Rituals and Theologies of Baptism: From Luther to Contemporary Practices.* Ashgate, 2006; Stjerna, K. *No Greater Jewel: Thinking about Baptism with Luther.* Augsburg, 2009; Triggs, J. *Baptism in the Theology of Martin Luther.* Brill, 1994; Wengert, T., *Martin Luther's Catechisms: Forming the Faith.* Fortress, 2009.

GORDON A. JENSEN

Barmen Confession

The Barmen Confession of Faith (sometimes called the Barmen Declaration) was issued by a national synod of the German Evangelical Church, held on May 30, 1934, in the Wuppertal district of Barmen. As a succinct statement of doctrine affirmed unanimously by representatives of all the United, Reformed, and Lutheran regional churches throughout Germany, its significance for Lutheran history cannot be underestimated, particularly since it was issued at the height of one of the most contentious internal church battles since the Reformation. In the sixteen months since the Nazi regime had come to power, the German Evangelical Church had been torn between the pro-Nazi German Christians, the groups that emerged in opposition to them (including the Pastors Emergency League and the Young Reformation Movement), and "neutral" church leaders who hoped to avoid a complete schism of the churches.

These internal church debates as well as growing fears of a complete state takeover of church governance were the impetus for a national synod. The day before the Barmen Synod, leaders from the Old Prussian Union churches met in Barmen to establish the Confessing Church, a self-governing body that would remain within the church but take a clear stand in opposition to the German Christians.

The next day these leaders joined other delegates from every regional and provincial church to discuss the draft of the Barmen Confession, which had been written by theologian Karl Barth. Barth's draft consisted of six theses, each of which was introduced by a scriptural passage, followed by a theological affirmation of the scriptural text and a rejection of the German Christians' misinterpretation and misuse of the text. Each thesis drew a clear distinction between the demands of God's Word and those of the state, rejecting any kind of special commission or claim that the state could make on the church. The unanimous approval of the document by leaders of all the Reformation theological traditions was a rare moment of unity and a clear rejection of the German Christian agenda, and ultimately it helped avert a state takeover of the churches.

The Barmen Confession, however, focused only on matters directly related to the church issues and said nothing about the persecution of the Jews or other Nazi measures. Despite the unity of the delegates at Barmen, the document itself was interpreted differently in the months that followed. More conservative church leaders viewed it purely as an internal church document; the more radical members of the Confessing Church saw it as the foundation for opposition against the Nazi state. At the Dahlem Synod, only five months after Barmen, delegates split sharply over these issues, and the more radical leaders of the Confessing Church decided to establish their own governance structures and theological seminaries.

Because of its text and historical significance, the Barmen Confession is widely recognized as a historical confession and has been adopted as a creedal confession by the Presbyterian Church (USA) and the Evangelical Church in America.

See also Ansbach Memorandum (Ansbacher Ratschlag); Barth, Karl; Confessing Church; German Christians (Deutsche Christen); State

Bibliography

Barnett, V. *For the Soul of the People: Protestant Protest against Hitler*. Oxford University Press, 1992; Bethge, E. *Dietrich Bonhoeffer: A Biography*. Rev. ed. Fortress, 2000; Helmreich, E. C. *The German Churches under Hitler*. Wayne State University Press, 1979.

VICTORIA J. BARNETT

Barnes, Robert

The English Lutheran theologian Robert Barnes (1495–1540) was a sometimes Anglo-Lutheran ambassador and then Henrician martyr. Born in Norfolk and educated at Cambridge and Leuven, Barnes became prior of his Cambridge Augustinian friary in 1523. Though not explicitly Evangelical, his criticisms of English church life, and especially of Cardinal Thomas Wolsey, made public in a sermon of Christmas Eve 1525, prompted his swift arrest, trial, and imprisonment. Still under house arrest in 1526, he participated in the prohibited circulation of Tyndale's New Testament. When this was discovered in 1528, he escaped and fled to the Continent, where he traveled under the pseudonym Antonius Anglus. By 1530 he was lodging with the Wittenberg pastor Johannes Bugenhagen, who provided the preface for Barnes's first publication, the *Sentenciae ex doctoribus collectae*, a compilation of biblical, patristic, and medieval quotations arranged in support of Lutheran doctrinal loci. The first of two editions of his *Supplication* to Henry VIII was published the following year, gaining him the favor of Henry's chief minister, Thomas Cromwell, and subsequent sporadic employment in the Crown's theological negotiations with the Lutheran rulers of Germany and Denmark.

Barnes was known in England especially for his preaching, and it was, as in 1525, a sermon that precipitated his second arrest and eventual execution. Though the 1539 Act Abolishing Diversity in Opinions (the "Act of Six Articles") signaled Henry VIII's refusal to countenance further doctrinal debate, in early 1540 Barnes preached in defense of justification by faith alone from London's most prominent pulpit, Paul's Cross. Explicitly countering the theology proclaimed there two weeks earlier by the bishop of Winchester Stephen Gardiner, Barnes's sermon, and his intentionally unconvincing recantation, put him out of the always tenuous favor he had with the king. With the arrest of Cromwell in June, Barnes was left without political protection. Condemned by attainder, he was burned in London on July 30, 1540.

The manner of Barnes's death and the frequently reprinted record of his last words at the stake assured the preservation of his memory in Protestant martyrologies for a century after his death. Although not a genuinely original thinker, his *Supplication* has been described as the nearest the early English reformers came to producing a systematic theology; similarly, his 1536 *Vitae Romanorum Pontificum* (Lives of the Roman pontiffs), for which Luther wrote the preface, is often credited with being the first Protestant history of the papacy.

See also England; Henry VIII

Bibliography

Beiergrößein, K. *Robert Barnes: England und der Schmalkaldische Bund (1530–1540)*. Gütersloher Verlagshaus, 2011; Maas, K. *The Reformation and Robert Barnes: History, Theology and Polemic in Early Modern England*. Boydell, 2010; Parker, D., ed. *A Critical Edition of Robert Barnes's "A Supplication Vnto the Most Gracyous Prince Kynge Henry the VIII," 1534*. University of Toronto Press, 2008; Trueman, C. *Luther's Legacy: Salvation and English Reformers, 1525–1556*. Oxford University Press, 1994.

KOREY D. MAAS

Barth, Karl

More than most theologians in the Reformed tradition, Karl Barth (1886–1968) was deeply influenced by Luther. The index volume to Barth's *Church Dogmatics* contains more references to Luther than to any other theologian. Barth's famous Christocentrism was greatly indebted to Luther even though he claimed he had to think it through more radically than was done in the sixteenth century. The "Alexandrian" side to Barth's Christology, though not its only feature, was perhaps finally the dominant one, and this christological sensibility placed him closer to Luther in many matters than to Calvin. Like Luther (but unlike Calvin), Barth affirmed a single-subject Christology that made room for the suffering of God. Like Luther (but also like Calvin), he insisted vigorously that Christ was the sole Saving Agent in our redemption even though there was also an indispensable but decidedly noncausal role for the church and for individual Christians as acting subjects. Christ alone, by grace alone, through faith alone—these were the watchwords of the Reformation as inspired by Luther, mediated by Calvin, and championed in the twentieth century by Barth.

Barth also picked up Luther's phrase *simul iustus et peccator* (at the same time righteous and sinner). He affirmed it in all of its distinctive aspects: *simul*, *sola*, and *totus* (at the same time, alone, and wholly). In Christ the believer is simultaneously "righteous" and "sinful," and these predicates have to be understood qualitatively rather than quantitatively. They have to be seen categorically and not as a matter of degree. Although Luther himself tended to slide back and forth between the language of *partim/partim* (i.e., partly sinner and partly righteous) and the language of *totus/totus* (wholly both), Barth took the more difficult path by ditching the *partim/partim* idea while highlighting the much more counterintuitive *totus/totus*. More than Luther, therefore, and contrary to Calvin, Barth would allow no place for any sort of soteriological gradualism. Like Luther yet only more so, he advanced an essentially baptismal soteriology. The Christian life was not a matter of growing in grace more and more over time. It was rather a matter of dying and rising with Christ as a whole person, first and once for all by faith, and then again and again each day. Barth constantly tried to take the best from Luther and Calvin even as he went his own way.

Barth claimed that Luther and Calvin are constantly concerned about two great themes at heart. Luther teaches the freedom of the Christian as someone who believes in God's Word. Calvin teaches the majesty of God, who gives the gift of faith and obedience. These are the two poles, so to speak, of the Reformation. Luther is more oriented toward humanity, and Calvin more toward God (Barth, *Gespräche 1964–1968*, 193). Barth wanted to incorporate Luther's understanding of Christian freedom into a Calvinistic theology emphasizing the majesty of God.

Two of Barth's main departures from Luther have to do with sanctification and with how law and gospel are related. Justification without sanctification, he felt, could lead to quietism, weak resignation, and cultural capitulation. Barth believed that he had witnessed too much of these maladies among German Lutherans, even those aligned with the Confessing Church, called to resist Hitler. In his frustration he eventually hung down a large Asian rug from his bookshelf, blocking his view of Luther's works. In an effort to reinvigorate moral and social responsibility in the church, Barth reversed the familiar Lutheran order of law/gospel so that instead it ran gospel/law. Although some Lutherans would never forgive him for this move, one careful reading of what Luther himself says about the Ten Commandments in his Large Catechism is arguably not all that far removed from what Philip Melanchthon, followed by Calvinists and Barth, would identify as the "third use" of the law, by which they meant that the law functioned not just to convict us of sin and to maintain civil order, but also to provide guidance for the Christian life.

See also Calvin, John; Christology; Justification; Law, Uses of the; Luther Interpretation and Reception; Sanctification

Select Bibliography

Barth, K. *Gespräche, 1964–1968*. Ed. E. Busch. Theologischer Verlag, 1997; Börsch, E. *Geber, Gabe, Aufgabe: Luthers Prophetie in den Entscheidungsjahren seiner Reformation, 1520–1525*. Kaiser, 1958; Forde, G. O. *The Law-Gospel Debate: An Interpretation of Its Historical Development*. Augsburg, 1969; Marga, A. E. "Jesus Christ and the Modern Sinner: Karl Barth's Retrieval of Luther's Substantive Christology." *Currents in Theology and Mission* 34 (2007): 260–70; Stroud, D. G., ed. *Preaching in Hitler's Shadow: Sermons of Resistance in the Third Reich*. Eerdmans, 2013; Zachman, R. *The Assurance of Faith: Conscience in the Theology of Martin Luther and John Calvin*. Fortress, 1993.

GEORGE HUNSINGER

Batak Church

The Batak Church is a large Lutheran church in the Southeast Asian country of Indonesia. The name Batak refers to an ethnological grouping of peoples who share some differing and yet mainly similar cultures and whose languages are closely related. Anthropologists usually refer to six Batak groups: Mandailing and Angkola Batak in South Tapanuli, Toba and Dairi Batak in North Tapanuli, and Simalungun and Karo Batak to the east and northeast of North Tapanuli, Sumatra, Indonesia. In modern times many have migrated into neighboring areas or to other regions of Indonesia. The Toba Batak is the largest of the Batak ethnic groups that has traditionally lived in North Sumatra, Indonesia. The Batak homeland, which forms the larger part of the Indonesian province of North Sumatra, lies between Aceh in the north and the province of West Sumatra and Riau in the south, approximately fifty thousand square kilometers, or one-ninth of the land area of Sumatra.

In the nineteenth century the first attempt to proclaim the gospel in Sumatra was made during the time of British occupation. In 1819 British missionaries Richard Burton and Nathaniel Ward landed on the west coast of Sumatra and eventually reached Silindung, a region of the Bataklands. Though no Batak converted to Christianity, the presence of the two missionaries opened the Bataks' eyes and in one way or another created a kind of obsession to be like Westerners.

The more successful Protestant mission among the Bataks was associated with the Rhenish Mission, mostly German by nationality, which started in 1861. The Huria Kristen Batak Protestan (HKBP) is the fruit of the Rhenish Mission in the Batakland. One of the most prominent missionaries who worked in the Batakland was Ludwig Ingwer Nommensen (1834–1918), who arrived in Sumatra in 1862 and resided in Silindung from 1864.

HKBP is the largest Protestant church in Southeast Asia, based on the number of congregations and members. By 2015 it had 3,238 congregations, 1,800 pastors, and around four million members.

The HKBP is a member of World Council of Churches, the Lutheran World Federation (which it joined in the 1950s on the basis of its own confession of faith and *not* the Augsburg Confession), Christian Conference of Asia, and Indonesian Community of Churches.

See also Batak Confession; Nommensen, Ludwig Ingwer

Bibliography

Aritonang, J. S., and K. Steenbrink, eds. *A History of Christianity in Indonesia*. Brill, 2008; Hasselgren, J. *Rural Batak, Kings in Medan: The Development of Toba Batak Ethno-religious Identity in Medan, Indonesia, 1912–1965*. Elanders Gotab, 2000; Lehmann, M. E. *A Biographical Study of Ingwer Ludwig Nommensen, 1834–1918: Pioneer Missionary to the Bataks of Sumatra*. Mellen, 1996.

VICTOR TINAMBUNAN

Batak Confession

Konfessi Huria Kristen Batak Protestan (The confession of the Batak Protestant Christian Church [HKBP], 1951) is the first confession of faith of this Indonesian church body. From its beginning in the nineteenth century, the Batak Church was not confessionally bound but was strongly influenced by Lutheran theology and Pietism. Moreover, from the beginning Luther's Small Catechism was used exclusively in catechetical instruction in the mission schools. The Batak Church became a member of the Lutheran World Federation (LWF) at the general assembly in Hannover (1952). The Confession of Faith of the HKBP was formulated in 1951 as one of the requirements to become a member of the LWF. At that time various spiritual menaces threatened the church. These came from other Christian groups (Roman Catholic, Adventist, and Pentecostal, in particular), from other religions (Islam and traditional Batak religions such as an ancestral spirits cult), from syncretism and secular teachings (such as theosophy, communism, and capitalism), as well as from troublemakers within the church. Because the confession rejected all those dangerous teachings, the influence of the confession became clearly evident in the spiritual life of the church.

The confession names both the true teachings to be followed and false doctrines that must be rejected or resisted. The articles concern (1) God, (2) The Word of God, (3) The Human Being, (4) Society, (5) Culture and Environment, (6) Salvation, (7) The Church, (8) The Holy Sacrament, (9) Those Who Minister in the Church, (10) Church Order, (11) Sunday, (12) Good Works and Faith, (13) Government, (14) Food, (15) Remembrance of the Dead, (16) The Lord's Second Coming, and (17) The Angels.

Many parts of the Batak Confession are consistent with the Augsburg Confession (CA), especially in articles 1, 2, 6, 8, and 12. Some parts add to the CA. For example, in Batak Confession 7, the signs of the true church are that (a) the gospel is purely preached and taught, (b) the two sacraments are rightly administered (Matt. 28:19; Mark 16:15–16), and (c) the order of pastoral care and discipline is rightly exercised. Signs a and b are adopted from CA, article 7. Sign c is adopted from the Heidelberg Catechism, although it can also be found in some of Philip Melanchthon's later works.

At the Great Synod of the HKBP in 1996, the Batak Confession was expanded so it would speak more clearly to contemporary people. It was not a matter of renewing, changing, or extending the Batak Confession of 1951, but rather adjusting the form to the context of the time as well as providing a response to challenges not included in the Batak Confession of 1951 concerning humankind (art. 3), society (art. 4), and culture and the environment (art. 5).

The meaning of the Batak Confession remains unchanged. It encompasses the entire content of faith based on Holy Scripture. The intent of the Batak Confession is (1) to be part of the lives of church members, (2) to be proclaimed in the world, (3) to be relied on in facing all temptations and enemies of faith, and (4) to be inherited by the coming generations in the church, so they may pursue the unity of faith together with those who came before us.

See also Batak Church; Nommensen, Ludwig Ingwer

Bibliography

Lumbantobing, A. M. "The Confession of the Batak Church: An Introduction and Explanation." In *The Church and the Confessions: The Role of the Confessions in the Life and Doctrine of the Lutheran Churches*, ed. V. Vajta and H. Weissgerber, 121–35. Fortress, 1963.

VICTOR TINAMBUNAN

Baur, Ferdinand Christian

Ferdinand Christian Baur (1792–1860) studied at the Lutheran preparatory school, the Maulbronn Cloister between 1807 and 1809, then at Tübingen University, where he spent five years in the Evangelische Stift, the seminary. On completion of theological studies in 1814, he served as vicar in two parishes and as assistant in a lower theological seminary. In 1816 he returned to Tübingen as tutor at the Stift. From 1817 to 1826, he served as professor at the Blaubeuren seminary, and then was appointed *ordinarius*, or full professor, at Tübingen, with special responsibility for historical studies.

Not until Baur had produced volumes on symbolism and mythology, Manichaeism and Gnosticism, the divide between Catholicism and Protestantism, the atonement, the Trinity, and the incarnation—not till then did he turn in earnest to critical investigation of the New Testament. In 1831 he had elaborated on Johann Salomo Semler's (1725–91) observations respecting the divisions in earliest Christianity,

an essay that would prove to be key to his ultimately assigning earliest Christianity two contrasting poles. Not until the debate over David Friedrich Strauss's 1835 *Life of Jesus*, however, did he devote all his energies to the New Testament and earliest Christianity. From this period emerged two of his most celebrated works, *Das Christentum und die christliche Kirche der drei ersten Jahrhunderte* (1860), and *Paulus, der Apostel Jesu Christi* (1867).

In prefaces to those works, Baur answered the charge that historical-critical research tended only to negate and destroy. The question, he wrote, had to do with what was negated and destroyed, by what right, and whether such research was in fact conservative, since it operated on the principle of allowing each its own. His viewpoint, he continued, was purely historical, its sole concern to view what was historically given in its "pure objectivity," a viewpoint that did not spell aloofness on the part of the interpreter. In the preface to the volume on symbolism and mythology, Baur wrote that without personal reflection, historical data was lifeless and dumb. "Without philosophy," he wrote, "history always remains dead and mute."

Baur detected two poles in earliest Christianity, a Petrine-Jewish party and a Pauline-gentile party. The Petrine group was Ebionitic (holding to a low Christology), taking a law-oriented view, accenting the Jewish national Messiah, and insisting that gentiles could become Christians only by way of Judaism. The Pauline group was universal, law-free, accenting the divinely exalted Christ, and insisting that gentiles could be saved without observing the Mosaic law. Accordingly, writings that clearly reflected the opposition were to be taken as original. In Galatians, Baur wrote, the conflict between Jewish and gentile Christianity first appeared. What the one party regarded as true and original Christianity the other regarded as servitude resistant to freedom. Apart from what he regarded as the genuine Pauline Letters to the Galatians, Corinthians, and Romans, Baur defined the remainder of the New Testament documents according to their position in the move toward compromise or accommodation. Of the Gospels, Baur described Matthew as displaying the least "tendency" toward the one or other pole, thus as the best source for a life of Jesus. Mark he described as derived from Matthew and Luke. Originally Pauline, it was later reworked to accommodate the two contrasting poles. Since the contrast between the two parties could not continue if any unity was to emerge, one or the other party had to concede. Accordingly, Acts reflects a concession of the Paulinists through assigning equal worth to Peter and Paul.

The extent of Schleiermacher's and Hegel's influence on Baur and his method has been exaggerated. Before Baur read Schleiermacher, he was already outside the orthodoxy of the old Tübingen School, and before he encountered Hegel, he had already detected the antitheses within earliest Christianity. If he agreed with Schleiermacher that miracles should be psychologically explained, and if Hegel's idea of the Spirit as God setting himself against the world he made and then taking it back into himself in order to unite it with himself seemed compatible with his own view, Baur finally charged both with docetism, with endangering the historical foundation of Christianity.

According to Baur, critical understanding of the starting point was crucial to understanding any historical process. Respecting Christian faith, this meant beginning with Jesus. To understand the gospel history, nothing was more important than addressing the question as to how two different but coherent elements—the universal and divinely exalted, which gave Jesus's person its absolute significance, and the narrow and limited national messiah idea, which he had to embrace—combined into the unity of his self-consciousness and became the moving principle of his life. The contrast of these two elements within the personal unity of Jesus's self-consciousness was the motivational force in the historical development that began

with him. It explained the division struggling toward unity in the New Testament witness to him.

See also Bible Interpretation; Gospels; Hegel, Georg Wilhelm Friedrich; Liberalism; Paul; Scripture

Bibliography
"Baur." *RGG* 1:935–38. Mohr, 1957; "Baur." *RGG* 1:1183–85. Mohr Siebeck, 1998; "Baur." *RPP* 1:647–49. Brill, 2007; Baur, F. C. *Das Christenthum und die christliche Kirche der drei ersten Jahrhunderte.* 2nd ed. 1860; Baur, F. C. "Die Christuspartei in der korinthischen Gemeinde, der Gegensatz des petrinischen und paulinischen Christenthums in der ältesten Kirche, der Apostel Petrus in Rom." *Tübinger Zeitschrift für Theologie* 4 (1831): 61–206; Baur, F. C. *Paulus, der Apostel Jesu Christi, Sein Leben und Wirken, seine Briefe und seine Lehre: Ein Beitrag zu einer kritischen Geschichte des Urchristenthums.* Ed. E. Zeller. First Section. 2nd ed. Fues, 1866. Second Section. 2nd ed. Fues, 1867; Hodgson, P. *A Study of Ferdinand Christian Baur: The Formation of Historical Theology.* Harper & Row, 1966; Hopper, M. T. "Historical Theology as the Crossroads of Faith and Reason: The Contribution of Ferdinand Christian Baur." MA thesis, University of Georgia, 2008.

ROY A. HARRISVILLE

Bayer, Oswald

As a systematic theologian and an expert on Martin Luther and Johann Georg Hamann, Oswald Bayer (b. 1939) is a professor emeritus at Tübingen. Bayer's chief contribution to Luther Studies has been to bring into focus the implications of the doctrine of justification by grace alone through faith alone for the doctrines of creation, ecclesiology, eschatology, and ethics. His work grows out of Luther's view of *promissio*, which Bayer interprets as a performative word, one that does what it says and says what it does, and not primarily a descriptor of reality, let alone a directive for ethical agenda. Instead, it creates reality anew. As such, the gospel is an action word on a continuum with the same action words by which God from moment to moment sustains and addresses humanity along with all creatures. God only speaks through an external word such as the absolution. For Bayer, God's saving action and his action of supporting the world are both expressions of God's generous address. Bayer rules out any attempt to interpret the gospel as ethics, theory, or psychology. The gospel frees people by opening them to creation as gift and can lead humans to appreciate and not merely consume the world. Bayer retrieves Luther's "three estates" (church, household, state) to affirm that humans are embedded in communities of reciprocal agency and responsibility and that it is in such thick relationships that God shapes humans. Unlike the modern tendency to separate theology and spirituality, Bayer affirms that devotion to God and academic work in theology are inseparably linked through Luther's association of prayer, meditation, and spiritual trial (*oratio*, *meditatio*, *tentatio*). Hence he brings to the fore Luther's emphasis on spiritual trial (*tentatio*, *Anfechtung*) and complaint.

See also Forde, Gerhard; Three Estates

Bibliography

Bayer, O. *Living by Faith: Justification and Sanctification.* Trans. G. Bromiley. Eerdmans, 2003; Bayer, O. *Martin Luther's Theology: A Contemporary Interpretation.* Trans. T. Trapp. Eerdmans, 2008; Bayer, O. *Theology the Lutheran Way.* Trans. J. Silcock and M. Mattes. Eerdmans, 2007.

MARK C. MATTES

Beck, Vilhelm

Danish Lutheran pastor, cofounder of *Kirkelig Forening for Indre Mission i Danmark* (Churchly Association of the Inner Mission in Denmark), Vilhelm Beck (1829–1901) was a late child of nineteenth-century Pietism. Since the start of the pietistic movement in 1861, Beck was part of its management, and from 1881 to 1901 he was its chairman. Under Beck the Inner Mission prospered, making Beck a leading figure in Danish church life. He emphasized the churchly character of the movement, and so the Inner Mission stayed within the Danish Lutheran Church. Like Nikolai Grundtvig, Beck emphasized the sacraments and the confession of faith. Unlike Grundtvig, however, he drew a sharp line between Christian and worldly life, which in North America caused a split within the Danish Church in 1894. Beck wanted to be a true disciple of the Lutheran tradition but caused heated discussion over his understanding of the sacraments.

Unlike many awakening movements, he emphasized the gift of baptism, where conversion was necessary only for those fallen away from it.

See also Grundtvig, Nikolai Frederik Severin; Pietism

Bibliography

Beck, V. *Memoirs: A Story of Renewal in the Denmark of Kierkegaard and Grundtvig.* Trans. C. A. Stub. Fortress, 1965; Larsen, K. E. *Vilhelm Beck: Missionspræsten.* Lohse, 2001; Sorensen, J. "Kierkegaard, Grundtvig, and Danish Literature in the Plains." PhD Diss., University of Nebraska, 1984. Esp. 42–56.

BO KRISTIAN HOLM

Bengel, Johann Albrecht

As biblical scholar and leading figure of Württemberg Pietism, Johann Albrecht Bengel's legacy (1687–1752) includes establishing the field of New Testament textual criticism, producing works on biblical interpretation, and providing pastoral care for a generation of Württemberg theologians and pastors—his former pupils. He was born on June 24, 1687, in Winnenden, near Stuttgart, where his father was a Lutheran pastor. Orphaned at six, Bengel went to live with a friend of his father, the separatist-minded schoolteacher David Spindler. In 1704 Bengel completed his master of arts degree at the University of Tübingen; he spent three more years studying theology. From 1713 to 1741 he served as preceptor in the Lutheran cloister school in Denkendorf, a preparatory school for Tübingen. For Bengel, as for Spener, it was through study and edifying application of the Bible that Christians experienced spiritual renewal. The emphasis on conversion by some Halle Pietists was foreign to Bengel. His study of Revelation led to a distinctive understanding of dual millennial ages. Generations of Lutheran pastors turned to Bengel's *Gnomon Novi Testamenti* (1742) as a helpful guide in biblical interpretation, the book was the main source for John Wesley's work on the New Testament. His motto was "Apply yourself completely to the text; apply the matter [of the text] completely to yourself."

Bibliography

Burk, J. C. F. *A Memoir of the Life and Writings of Johan Albert Bengel.* Trans. R. F. Walker. William Ball, 1837; Ehmer, H. "Johann Albrecht Bengel." In *The Pietist Theologians,* ed. Carter Lindberg, 224–38. Blackwell, 2005; *John Albert Bengel's Gnomon of the New Testament.* 2 vols. Perkinpine & Higgins, 1862.

DOUGLAS H. SHANTZ

Berggrav, Eivind

The Norwegian pastor and bishop Eivind Berggrav (1884–1957) was a leader in both the Church of Norway and the ecumenical movement. Born in Stavanger to a schoolteacher who would become a prominent church official, Berggrav struggled through his young adulthood with his faith and vocation. Working as a journalist, he met ecumenical leaders such as John R. Mott and Nathan Söderblom, ultimately discerning a call to the ministry. His liberal theology was challenged by his experiences as a parish pastor and prison chaplain, as well as his study of psychology, bringing him ultimately to a theological position hard to classify. Appointed bishop of the Arctic diocese of Halogaland in 1928, Berggrav quickly became one of the most respected and articulate of Norwegian churchmen; he was named bishop of Oslo in 1937. Through his ecumenical contacts, he worked tirelessly for peace, but following the German invasion of Norway, he became a leader of the Norwegian resistance and moved the Church of Norway to renounce the Quisling regime. He was arrested in 1942 and held under house arrest for the duration of the war. Resuming his office in 1945, he became an early leader in the World Council of Churches and United Bible Societies.

See also Norway

Bibliography

Berggrav, E. *With God in the Darkness, and Other Papers Illustrating the Norwegian Church Conflict.* Ed. G. K. A. Bell and H. M. Waddams. Hodder & Stoughton, 1943; Robertson, E. H. *Bishop of the Resistance: The Life of Eivind Berggrav.* Concordia, 2000.

RICHARD O. JOHNSON

Bernard, Abbot of Clairvaux

As a Cistercian abbot, mystical theologian, and figure of profound authority in twelfth-century Europe, Bernard (1090/91–1153) has been called a "paradox" and "the difficult saint" because of his diverse activities, his inherent contradictions, and the difficulty of penetrating his thought. In one letter he referred to himself as "the chimera of my age." Bernard was born in Burgundy to noble parents in 1090 or 1091. The third son, he was destined by his mother for an ecclesiastical career. When Bernard was converted to the monastic life, he appeared at the gate of the new monastery at Cîteaux. This foundation represented an experiment in a return to the original rule of Benedict and, as such, stood near the beginning of the so-called Twelfth-Century Reformation. Bernard became a seminal figure in this movement. At Cîteaux he headed a group that included his brothers and other relatives and has been credited with invigorating, perhaps even reviving, the Cistercian experiment. In 1115 Bernard was named abbot of the Cistercian monastery at Clairvaux. Not only did Bernard face the difficulties typically faced by an abbot, but also his health deteriorated to a dangerous degree as a result of his ascetic life. His friend William of Champeaux, who had taught at Paris and had become bishop of Châlons, intervened so that Bernard was ordered to spend a year living outside the cloister and convalescing. During this time, Bernard first encountered William of St. Thierry, who would become his biographer.

Bernard as abbot inspired the expansion of the Cistercian order. He also defended the Cistercian observance against its detractors, most notably in his *Apologia to Abbot William* (of St. Thierry). It contains Bernard's famous criticism of the unreformed monasticism associated with the abbey of Cluny. Bernard's own efforts toward monastic reform included a profound mysticism developed in conversation with other monastic theologians, particularly William of St. Thierry. Though this mysticism was rooted in monastic contemplation, Bernard's own monks often failed to grasp it. Despite the difficulties they might pose, his mystical writings, such as *On Loving God* and *Sermons on the Song of Songs*, proved quite popular.

In the course of his abbacy, Bernard came to be increasingly active outside the Cistercian order. The power of his personality and preaching made him a sought-after adviser, advocate, and arbitrator. Bernard lived in a time of profound tension between the papacy and European governments as the Investiture Controversy was only beginning to be settled. When the papal election of 1130 resulted in schism, Bernard emerged as a supporter of Innocent II, whom he thought most likely to continue the reform begun by popes in the previous century, against Anacletus II. Although Bernard persuaded the kings of England, France, and Germany to support Innocent, the pope was unable to occupy Rome permanently until after Ancletus's death in 1138. Subsequent conflict with rulers such as Roger II of Sicily meant that Bernard continued to function as an important adviser to the pope. Bernard himself viewed this political activity as fundamentally opposed to his monastic vows and his duty as an abbot.

Bernard had also become champion of a new military and monastic order, the Knights Templar. His *In Praise of the New Knighthood* extolled the order's service in the Holy Land following the First Crusade. It is not surprising, then, that Bernard was employed to preach in support of a Second Crusade after the fall of Edessa to the Turks in 1145. Although we have no record of Bernard's actual words, his preaching proved persuasive. When he preached the crusade at Vezelay, the story goes, so many responded that the supply of cloth crosses used to mark those who took the crusade vow was exhausted, and Bernard supplied the lack by tearing strips from his habit. Some sources report the numerous miracles Bernard is said to have performed during this preaching trip. Despite Bernard's efforts in recruiting and planning, the Second Crusade failed miserably and tarnished the abbot's reputation. Yet Bernard continued to promote the cause of the crusades.

Bernard's involvement in matters of heresy also had mixed results. In particular, his relentless pursuit of Peter Abelard was not universally admired. Often portrayed as a great contest between monasticism and Scholasticism, their conflict was more complicated than such a summary suggests. Bernard entered the fray only reluctantly as a result of the prodding of William of St. Thierry, but once engaged he attacked Abelard tenaciously, charging him with trinitarian heresy. In reality, Bernard failed to understand what Abelard was arguing. Nevertheless, the Council of Sens condemned Abelard without a hearing in 1141. He found refuge at the abbey of Cluny, where he died in 1142. Several years later, Bernard became involved in proceedings against Gilbert de la Porrée, bishop of Poitiers, again on charges of heresy regarding the Trinity. This time, Bernard failed to win a condemnation; Gilbert, who had powerful friends, was exonerated. Some contemporaries accused Bernard of using his considerable personal authority in a questionable case.

Bernard died at Clairvaux on August 20, 1153. According to a later source, when the abbot of Cîteaux arrived for the funeral, he commanded the deceased Bernard to stop performing miracles to ease the crush of pilgrims to Clairvaux.

Luther expressed great appreciation for Bernard, often quoting him and citing him as an example. He credited a fellow friar in Erfurt for helping him through a spiritual crisis early in his monastic life by pointing him to passages in Bernard's sermon on the Annunciation. This appreciation, however, was sometimes mixed with criticism of Bernard's monasticism. Nevertheless, Luther cited Bernard's letter to Pope Eugene III to justify his open letter to Pope Leo X in 1520. Similarly, Luther praised Bernard's spiritual writings as examples of the Christian's relationship with Christ without embracing the abbot's mysticism. Luther valued Bernard as a genuine

Christian, who died relying on Christ for salvation, and sometimes even called him the last of the church fathers.

Bibliography

Bell, T. *Divus Bernhardus: Bernhard von Clairvaux in Martin Luthers Schriften.* Von Zabern, 1993; Bredero, A. H. *Bernard of Clairvaux: Between Cult and History.* Eerdmans, 1996; Evans, G. R. *Bernard of Clairvaux.* Oxford University Press, 2000; McGuire, B. P., ed. *A Companion to Bernard of Clairvaux.* Brill, 2011; McGuire, B. P. *The Difficult Saint: Bernard of Clairvaux and His Tradition.* Cistercian Publications, 1991; Posset, F. *Pater Bernhardus: Martin Luther and Bernard of Clairvaux.* Cistercian Publications, 1999.

PAUL W. ROBINSON

Beza, Theodore

Pastor, professor of theology, and moderator of Geneva's Reformed church, Theodore Beza (1519–1605) was born in Vézelay (Burgandy) on June 24, 1519, to parents of France's lower nobility. At age nine, Beza was sent to Orléans to study in the household of the renowned Hellenist (and secret Protestant) Melchior Wolmar, who instructed him in humanistic studies and exposed him to the writings of the reformer Heinrich Bullinger. When Wolmar retired to Germany in 1534, Beza matriculated at the University of Orléans, where he earned his license in civil law four years later. Beza's infatuation with the "Muses" thereafter drew him to Paris, where he spent the next decade associating with a sodality of young humanists, reading classical literature, studying Greek and Hebrew, and writing provocative love poetry, which bore fruit in the published collection *Poemata* (1548). During this period Beza was probably in contact with Evangelical-minded colleagues who were reading John Calvin's writings. In October 1548, after recovering from a life-threatening illness, Beza renounced the Catholic religion and fled Paris with his clandestine wife, Claudine Denosse, seeking refuge in Calvin's Geneva.

Calvin's personal friendship and theology were decisive for Beza. During 1549–58, Beza served as Greek professor at the Lausanne Academy, where he matured into a seasoned churchman committed to Calvin's version of Reformed theology. His writings during this period included a French tragedy titled *Abraham Sacrifiant* (1550), a defense of Calvin's doctrine of double predestination (*Tabula praedestinationis*, 1555), and a highly regarded Latin translation of the New Testament with theological and exegetical notes (*Annotationes*, 1555). On three occasions, Calvin sent Beza as theological emissary to the German princes, seeking support for persecuted Reformed Christians in France; on one such embassy to Worms, the reformer Beza encountered Lutheran theologians Philip Melanchthon, Johannes Brenz, and Jakob Andreae.

In 1558 religious tensions in Lausanne prompted Beza's departure for Geneva, which became his home-in-exile for the remainder of his life. Beza served as pastor and preacher in the city church, taught theology at Calvin's Academy, and defended Reformed Protestantism with his active pen. His summary of Reformed Christianity, titled *Confession of the Christian Faith* (1559), was reprinted in thirty editions during his lifetime. Even more popular was the Huguenot Psalter (1562), which Beza and the French poet Clément Marot produced for congregational worship. As an expatriate Frenchman, Beza watched closely and intervened regularly in the political and religious crisis in his homeland. In 1561 he led a delegation that defended Protestantism before the French royal court at the Colloquy of Poissy; ten years later he was elected moderator of the French Reformed national synod at La Rochelle.

Following Calvin's death in 1564, Beza became the chief theologian and polemicist for the French Reformed churches, a position he held until his death on October 13, 1605. In that capacity, Beza played a leading role in the confessional battles that divided the Lutheran and Reformed churches, engaging in acrimonious pamphlet disputes with Lutheran "ubiquitarians" (as he called them) such as Joachim Westphal, Tilemann Hesshus, Nicholas Selnecker, and Andreae, over the nature of Christ's presence in the sacramental meal and the communication of the properties of Christ's two natures. When the Formula of Concord appeared in 1577, Beza likened it to a Pandora's box that was unleashing division on the Protestant world. He and several colleagues responded by publishing the *Harmony of Confessions of Faith* in 1581 to demonstrate the fundamental doctrinal agreement of eleven Protestant confessions, including the Augsburg Confession (Variata). This effort came to nothing, however. The distance between the confessional parties was illustrated five years later at the Colloquy of Montbéliard, when Beza and Andreae engaged in a ten-day-long disputation in the presence of the Duke of Württemberg over the sacraments, Christology, religious images, and predestination. At the close of the colloquy, Andreae rejected Beza's extended hand of concord, offering instead the hand of friendship—which Beza refused.

Amid this confessional strife, Beza continued to hold Luther in high esteem—but with qualifications. In his correspondence, Beza praised the Wittenberg reformer as an "excellent instrument of God," whom he numbered among "those great heroes" whom God raised up to rescue the church from papal superstition. At the same time, he believed Luther to be "completely blind" in his explanation of the nature of the sacramental signs (*CB* 8.239; 16.93). Similarly, in his *Icones* (1580), Beza extolled the courage, piety, and zeal with which Luther proclaimed the Christian gospel and attacked false religion. Unfortunately, Luther's good judgment was sometimes marred by his human sinfulness and the "turbulent spirit" of his disciples (*Icones*, 27). For Beza, Martin Luther was a Christian hero to be emulated, even if his followers were diminishing the German reformer's illustrious legacy.

See also Calvin, John; Calvinism as a Second Reformation; Geneva; Mömpelgaard/Montbéliard Colloquy

Bibliography

Backus, I., ed. *Théodore de Bèze (1519–1605)*. Droz, 2007; Bèze, T. de. *Correspondance de Théodore de Bèze* [*CB*].

Vols. 1–38. Ed. H. Aubert, H. Meylan, A. Dufour, et al. Droz, 1960–2014; Bèze, T. *Les vrais portraits des hommes illustrés* [*Icones*]. Slatkine Reprints, 1986; Dufour, A. *Théodore de Bèze: Poèt et théologien*. Droz, 2006; Geisendorf, P.-F. *Théodore de Bèze*. Jullien, 1967; Manetsch, S. M. *Theodore Beza and the Quest for Peace in France*. Brill, 2000; Raitt, J. *The Colloquy of Montbéliard: Religion and Politics in the Sixteenth Century*. Oxford University Press, 1993; Steinmetz, D. "Theodor Beza (1519–1605)." In *Reformers in the Wings: From Geiler von Kaysersberg to Theodore Beza*, 114–20. Oxford University Press, 2001.

SCOTT M. MANETSCH

Bible Interpretation

Applied to the Bible, the science or art of interpreting life expressions in fixed written form reached its zenith in the nineteenth century. Obviously, earlier attempts had been made. From the fourth century to the Reformation period and beyond, the list of interpreters in the various precritical eras is long and varied. For example, Luther the reformer owed a great debt to Augustine (354–430), William of Ockham (1285–1349), Lefèvre d'Étaples (Faber Stapulensis, 1455–1536), and Erasmus of Rotterdam (1469–1536).

Initially, Luther's interpretation was comparable to twelfth-century attempts, to the so-called Quadriga, or fourfold, method of interpretation: *Littera gesta docet* (the letter tells of actual events); *quid credas allegoria* (allegory, what you believe); *moralis, quid agas* (the moral, how you are to behave), *sed quid speres, anagoge* (the anagogic, what you hope for). Convinced that the weakness of the Quadriga was its failure to relate everything to Christ and dependent on Augustine, Luther altered the Quadriga from a mechanical scheme by way of the tropological sense, according to which the biblical texts were interpreted in the light of the revelation in Christ and faith. He also made use of symbolic and typological exposition and only gradually reduced his use of allegory. But again, the christological principle was used as standard to keep the uncontrolled use of these methods in check.

Luther gave little space to outlining his interpretive method. In the 1520 defense of his articles against the papal bull, he wrote that he did not wish to put himself forward as more learned than any, but only that Scripture rule, that it be interpreted only by itself and its spirit. In his 1530 *Open Letter on Translating*, Luther responded to those who objected to his insertion of the term *sola* or *allein* (alone) in his translation of Rom. 3:21–22a. Conceding that the term did not appear in the Greek or Latin text, he argued that the German tongue required it to make the phrase clearer and more complete.

In his interpretation of various biblical books, this reformer repeatedly insisted on the text's autonomy, signaled in the so-called exclusive particle, *sola scriptura* (Scripture alone). The particle indicated reaction to the claim that any subjectivity, bias, or prejudice in interpretation could be transcended by a magisterium, by a papal office, or by the collective "spirit" of the like-minded. "Scripture alone" would guarantee it, but that particle needed supplementing in an understanding of Scripture as "its own interpreter," in Luther's words, as *sui ipsius interpres*. This assumed a radically different interpretive model, for now the roles of text and interpreter were reversed: The text, not the exegete, functioned as interpreter; the text interpreted the exegete. This did not mean Luther rejected other authorities (creeds, councils, ancient interpreters) but rather viewed them as witnesses to Scripture and under its authority.

Moreover, for the text to speak, to be heard, the subjectivity of the individual or collective, or as Luther put it, "one's own spirit," "one's own perception" (*spiritus proprius / sensus proprius*), had to be transcended. Neither pope nor spiritualist could avoid the danger of the *spiritus* or *sensus proprius*, nor could construing Scripture as a purely formal authority. The way needed to be cleared for the *scopus* (goal), for Christ himself, and thus the test by which to judge all books was whether they "bore" or "carried" him (Luther's term was *treiben*). From out of this christological center, Luther developed the bases for his exposition, and whatever multiple senses he used bent them in its service.

This *scopus* gave Scripture its authority, or better, since Scripture's intention was what is now called "orality"—that is, since it intended further to be heard—from that hearing it derived its authority. The text intended to speak, intended to be heard, for which reason hearing took precedence over cognition: through hearing, the word of Scripture did its work, that is, created faith. Herein lay the Scriptures' authority, and for this reason interpreters were not to transfer the spirit of the text into their own spirit, but rather to transfer their own spirit into that of the text. "The strength of Scripture," Luther wrote, "is that it is not changed into the one who studies it, but that it transforms its lover into itself and its strengths."

In sum, it was the *usus* (use) to which interpretation is put that engaged Luther's attention. Use was the category of the existential relation to the text. It is not enough, say, to know the story of the resurrection; instead, exegetes must also know its use and fruit, and unless the exegetes have first experienced the power of Scripture as the bearer of Christ, they cannot teach others. In this regard, Philip Melanchthon's interpretation of Scripture matched Luther's, with an emphasis on the christological *scopus*, the native meaning of a text, and its use in bringing comfort.

Pietists of the seventeenth and eighteenth centuries without exception echoed Luther's insistence on the necessity of faith for Bible interpretation. Johann Arndt (1555–1621), a forerunner, and Philip Jacob Spener (Philipp Jakob Spener, 1635–1705), "father" of Pietism, awaited moral results from a reading of the Bible. To Spener can be traced the founding of the *Collegia pietatis*, the house group that met for prayer, meditation, and edifying Bible study. With August Hermann Francke (1663–1727), insistence on faith for understanding led to giving the reborn exclusive right to interpretation, thus endangering the gospel's claim to universality, distancing wide circles from the Bible, and furnishing no response to emerging historical-critical method. Others were concerned with questions of context, with setting the biblical record within a salvation-historical scheme, and with philological matters. Johann Albrecht Bengel (1687–1752) produced a terse and concentrated explanation of the New Testament titled *Gnomon* (pointer of a sundial) alongside his critical edition of the New Testament text (a text heavily used by John Wesley). To Bengel also belongs the distinction of having arranged the Greek exemplars of the New Testament into families. Following early Pietism's almost universal rejection of the historical method, scholars of the nineteenth and early twentieth centuries such as Martin Kähler (1835–1912) and Adolf Schlatter (1852–1938) worked to give the doctrine of Scripture a form able to take historical research into account.

In 1560 as the "Second Martin," Chemnitz (1522–86), orthodox theologian and a primary author of the Formula of Concord, developed an interpretation of Scripture calculated to meet the Jesuit work in Germany. He wrote that just as at the time of Moses, so in his time the oral tradition of the apostles was in danger of being falsified. At the Apostolic Council (Acts 15) a divine intervention and commission occurred for setting the gospel in writing. This event, Chemnitz continued, was the beginning of the divinely inspired writings of the New Testament. Through the activity of the Spirit, these writings became the "canon," or rule, by which to protect the transmission of the divine doctrine, with their authentic interpretation guaranteed through the tradition of the church's symbols, so that faith was conceived at the outset as intellectual, cognitive. This theory, coupled with early Lutheran concerns to criticize papal claims to biblical interpretation, soon developed into a fuller theory of Scripture inspiration. For example, Johannes Andreas Quenstedt (1617–88) insisted that canonical Scripture does not contain the slightest error, not even respecting historical, chronological, or topographical data. With this conceptualizing, often using Aristotelian terms, the Lutheran

Orthodox as well as Pietists, who also held to a theory of "verbal inspiration," undermined the Reformation understanding, distancing themselves from Luther and Melanchthon, who had formulated no explicit doctrine of scriptural inspiration, and thus down to the present can be at odds with biblical-historical investigation.

Since the advent of modern historical-critical method, fathered by Baruch Spinoza (1632–77), reason has been assigned a place in Bible interpretation. Augustine (354–430) used reason to untangle ambiguous passages, harmonizing what appeared to contradict church authority, and taking as figurative whatever did not relate to morals or faith. And according to the "early" Schleiermacher (1768–1834), interpretation occurred by way of comparison and "divination." The argument between the Reformed theologian Karl Barth (1886–1968) and the Lutheran Rudolf Bultmann (1884–1976) over "preliminary understanding of the subject matter" of the biblical text was nothing if not a conflict over the place of reason apart from faith.

On the other hand, the view that only the exercise of the critical faculties suffices for interpretation has had few supporters. Schleiermacher's notion of interpretation, either early or late, as an "art" that assumed a humanity shared by author and interpreter—and thus a "life-relation"—was a blow aimed at interpretation as a mere cerebral function. In his 1926 lectures on theological encyclopedia (*What Is Theology?*), Bultmann argued that Christian interpretation involves acknowledging the biblical sources as a priori, admitting that what is to be known cannot be known beforehand since the self lives from the text that offers itself for reflection. It thus assumes a relation to its content, a *tua res agitur* (the matter has to do with you).

From a Lutheran perspective, on the other hand, modern subjectivity, with its identification of text and interpreter to the point where the text takes its life from interpretation, requires correcting. The interpretation of Scripture cannot be undertaken in solitary fashion, but only within the context of common statements of faith reflected in confessions received by the Christian church. Such is nothing but a consciousness of the history of the text's effects that existed prior to and independently of the interpreter. But since the text deserves priority, the Christian community cannot be the ultimate guarantor of the interpreter's discovery. The force of the "formal principle" of the Reformation (*sola scriptura*) lies in the acknowledgment that the church is under the constraint of Scripture as the guarantor of genuine interpretation.

Late in his career, Schleiermacher defined the task of interpretation as entering into the author's frame of mind, as understanding the author better than he understood himself. In his second preface to his commentary on Romans, Barth declared that "intelligent comment" allows the biblical author to speak in his own name and the commentator to speak in his; Barth obviously had authorial intent in mind. And if for Bultmann existential interpretation begins with inquiry into the matter of which the text speaks, and if genuine understanding presupposes a life-relation to the matter created by the text, behind that speaking or that matter created by the text stands an author. More recently, the requirement that interpretation concern itself with authorial intent has been challenged by the assertion that the primitive meaning of a text may not be its only valid meaning.

A century ago the question was reopened regarding Jesus's accommodation to the ideas and notions of his age. Augustine and Hilary of Poitiers (ca. 300–368) had embraced that view, and it was key to Calvin's (1509–64) understanding of God's self-revelation. Flaring up in the seventeenth century, debate over the position reached its zenith in the eighteenth century, condemned by the Lutheran Orthodox and hailed by rationalists. Biblical interpretation has experienced considerable stress over the years when it succumbs to the idea of the univocal equivalence of the biblical

text and the reality to which it refers. On the other hand, when adopted as a kind of epistemological axiom, accommodation can lead to the text's meaning anything at all.

Despite criticisms of the historical method of interpretation and opposition to it from a host of methods and perspectives, including structuralism, postmodernism, and some feminist interpretations, an alternative to historical-critical interpretation has not emerged. First, an author, real or implied, is not merely looking for dramatic results but for linking them to an independent reality. Second, faith or other interested interpretations need not remain aloof from critical testing. Sooner or later the advocate of a referentiality beyond the horizontal or synchronic must allow that referentiality to be challenged. For the Christian community, rejecting or avoiding historical interpretation forgoes its claim to scholarship and thus the gospel's claim to a public hearing. Third, what was learned from the last century's greatest interpreters is that it is possible to separate the method from the climate of opinion that once gave rise to it and to harness it to proclamation of the gospel. Finally, the Bible is a self-effervescing source that does not take its credibility from anything or anyone. Its integrity is not derived. It is its own interpreter. On its own it yields understanding. On its own it gives the Spirit through whom it is understood. On its own it possesses the quality of certainty that neither feeling nor experience can equal. What produces this effervescence, this independence and nonderivability, is its witness to Jesus Christ. He is its content and rules the method of its understanding.

See also Bengel, Johann Albrecht; Bultmann, Rudolf (Karl); Scripture; Word of God

Bibliography

Barth, K. *The Epistle to the Romans.* Trans. E. C. Hoskyns. Oxford University Press, 1933; Baur, J. *Luther und seine klassischen Erben.* Mohr, 1993; "Bibelwissenschaft." *RGG* 1:1517–34. Mohr Siebeck, 1998; Brecht, M., ed. *Geschichte des Pietismus.* Vandenhoeck & Ruprecht, 1993; Bultmann, R. "Das Problem der Hermeneutik" (1950). In *Glauben und Verstehen: Gesammelte Aufsätze,* vol. 2. Mohr, 1952; Luther, M. "Preface to James and Jude, in LW 35:395–98; Oftestad, B. T. "Traditio und Norma-Haupzüge der Schriftauffassung bei Martin Chemnitz." In *Der zweite Martin der Lutherischen Kirche*. Ev.-luth. Stadtkirchenverband und Propstei Braunschweig, 1986; Schleiermacher, F. *Hermeneutik*. Carl Winter Universitäts-verlag, 1959; Schleiermacher. F. *Hermeneutik und Kritik*. Suhrkamp, 1977.

ROY A. HARRISVILLE

Bible Translations

Luther's edition of the New Testament (1522) was the nineteenth to be printed in German but the first to be translated directly from Greek. The earlier editions, fourteen in High German, four in Low, were translations from the Latin Vulgate. Melchior Lotter Jr. published Luther's shortly before September 25, 1522, for sale at the Leipzig Fair (September 29–October 6) complete with Cranach woodcuts for Revelation. The three thousand copies sold quickly, and a second edition was printed in December 1522. A copy cost half a guilder, the weekly wage of a traveling carpenter. By 1523 Luther had translated the Pentateuch from Hebrew. The historical books, Job, Psalms, and the Song of Songs were completed in 1524. The remaining poetic books, the Prophets, and the Apocrypha arose out of Wittenberg's *collegium biblicum*, which Luther and his colleagues (Philip Melanchthon, Matthäus Aurogallus, Johannes Bugenhagen, Justus Jonas, and Caspar Cruciger Sr.) dedicated to translating the Scriptures into German. The entire Bible was printed in Low German in 1533–34 by Ludwig Dietz (d. 1559) in Lübeck and featured seventy-nine woodcuts by Erhard Altdorfer (ca. 1480–ca. 1561). The woodcut on the title page depicted a law/gospel motif inspired by a panel painting (*Tafelbild*) by Lucas Cranach Sr. The High German edition was released in Wittenberg by Hans Lufft in 1534 and featured 117 woodcuts from the shop of the Cranach family, including a depiction of law and gospel inserted before the prophets.

Luther worked very closely with Wittenberg's printers throughout his life and came to respect the skill of Hans Lufft. That cannot be said for the printers Johann Gronenberg (d. ca. 1525), Hans Herrgott (d. 1527), or the volatile Melchior Lotter Jr. (d. ca. 1542). In terms of page layout, Luther inherited two traditions: the medieval style, with prefaces at the beginning of each book and biblical text in the center of each page surrounded by the *Glossa Ordinaria* (the commentary of the church fathers and medieval theologians); and the Renaissance *ad fontes* format, which translated from the original languages and—while still providing prefaces—printed only the biblical text on each page. In these editions commentary appeared in the back of the book or in a separate volume. Luther harvested the best of both traditions, introducing each biblical book with a preface, placing exegetical notes in the margins when it was deemed necessary, and providing the reader with the best German translation from contemporary Hebrew and Greek editions. The 1541 and 1545 editions of the German Bible were the last two that Luther worked on during his lifetime and demonstrate his lifelong dedication to translating.

In opposition to the iconoclast Andreas Karlstadt (ca. 1477–1541), Luther accepted images as a means of proclaiming the gospel and included them, along with the diagrams from Nicholas of Lyra's medieval commentaries, in his editions of the Bible. Testimony from Christian Walther (ca. 1515–74), a corrector in Hans Lufft's printshop (1535–36), confirms Luther's collaboration with artists and printers concerning the design and placement of woodcuts in his editions. Committed to proclaiming the gospel with text and image, Luther and like-minded artists developed a graphic theology to portray Evangelical themes. The title page of the 1541 edition, designed by Lucas Cranach Jr., consisted of the classic visual presentation of law/gospel and justification by grace.

Luther utilized the pioneering Greek and Latin translations of noted scholars like Erasmus of Rotterdam (1466–1536) and Santes Pagnino (1470–1541), as well as the German translation of the Radical Reformers Ludwig Hätzer (1500–1529) and Hans Denck

(1495–1527). Never satisfied with the "word for word" (*verbum e verbo*) translations of earlier German editions, Luther employed a German heard at home, on the street, and at market. Luther defended his approach in *On Translating: An Open Letter* (1530), which responded to the criticism of Jerome Emser (1478–1527), and in *Defense of the Translation of the Psalms* (1531), which addressed the ongoing critique of opponents like Johannes Dietenberger (1475–1537) and John Eck (1486–1543). At the same time, Luther, like his humanist contemporaries, was sensitive to the Hebraisms and Hellenisms in the biblical text and at times preserved such word usage when he thought that it conveyed the actual meaning of the text more accurately.

Luther's editions were printed throughout the Holy Roman Empire and influenced the English translations of William Tyndale (ca. 1494–1536) and Miles Coverdale (ca. 1488–1569). Luther Bibles became affordable in the eighteenth century when Carl Hildebrand, the baron von Canstein (1667–1719), paid eleven thousand talers for casting the five million pieces of moveable type needed to set the forms for printing the entire Bible. Instead of returning type to the compositor's box, the forms were shelved and reused at the Franckean Anstalt. By eliminating the labor-intensive cost of setting type, the Luther Bible could sell for six groschen. By 1719 eighty thousand Bibles and a hundred thousand New Testaments had been sold in German-speaking territories. Emigrants brought their Luther Bibles with them to the United States and other English-speaking destinations, but these were replaced with popular English editions as the second and subsequent generations acculturated. Only with the publication of the *Concordia Self-Study Bible* (1986) and the *Lutheran Study Bible* (2009) was the heritage and insight of Luther as an editor of the Scriptures reclaimed for English-speaking audiences.

See also Bible Interpretation; Canon; Cranach, Lucas, the Elder; Cranach, Lucas, the Younger; Emser, Jerome; Erasmus of Rotterdam (Desiderius Erasmus Roterodamus); Hildebrand, Carl (Baron von Canstein); Humanism and the Reformation; Iconoclasm; Jonas, Justus; Karlstadt, Andreas Bodenstein von; Luther's Bible; Melanchthon, Philip; Nicholas of Lyra; Scripture

Bibliography
Bluhm, H. *Martin Luther, Creative Translator.* Concordia, 1965; Christensen, C. *Art and the Reformation in Germany.* Ohio University Press, 1979; Füssel, S. *The Book of Books: The Luther Bible of 1534; A Cultural-Historical Introduction.* Taschen, 2003; Luther, M. *Defense of the Translation of the Psalms* (1531). LW 35:205–23; Luther, M. *On Translating: An Open Letter* (1530). LW 35:177–202; Pelikan, J. *The Reformation of the Bible: The Bible of the Reformation.* Yale University Press, 1966; Reu, J. *Luther's German Bible.* Lutheran Book Concern, 1934; Stolt, B. "Luther's Translation of the Bible." *LQ* 28 (2014): 373–400.

KARL KRUEGER

Biel, Gabriel

The Scholastic theologian Gabriel Biel (ca. 1412–95) was born in Speyer and ordained a priest in or before 1432, at which time he entered the University of Heidelberg. Biel received the master of arts degree in 1438 and taught at Heidelberg for three years. He briefly attended the University of Erfurt in 1442 or 1443 and returned to the university in 1457 to study theology. When and where Biel took his degree is not clear, but at some point he received the licentiate in theology, perhaps from Erfurt. By the early 1460s Biel was serving as cathedral preacher and vicar general in Mainz. During this time he was caught up in a dispute over the appointment of an archbishop for the city. Diether von Isenburg had been elected by the cathedral chapter but failed to fulfill the conditions for confirmation by the pope. When he was placed under the lesser ban as a result, he appealed to the antipapal parties in the empire for support. A papal emissary came to Mainz with a bull deposing Diether and confirming his rival for the position, Adolph von Nassau. Because Biel supported Adolph, he was forced to flee Mainz and went to preach in the Rheingau (Rhine district). He defended Adolph's cause in his sermons and wrote *Defensorium obedientiae apostolicae* (A defense of apostolic obedience). The

Defensorium upheld the papal plenitude of power but also asserted that papal power was to be used only for the edification of the church and that church authority depended on the unity of the church. Warfare led to Adolph's possession of the archbishopric after his forces brutally assaulted Mainz.

In 1468 Biel joined the house of the Brethren of the Common Life in Marienthal near Mainz. He had known the Brethren for some time, since he had taken an active role in founding this particular house while he was cathedral preacher. A year later Biel became the rector of the new Brethren house in Butzbach, where he may also have reformed the school. When Count Eberhard I of Württemberg wished to establish a Brethren house in his territory, Biel was one of two rectors dispatched to transform the city church of Urach into a Brethren house. He continued to be involved in subsequent foundations in the duchy.

Biel's Scholastic contributions appeared late in his life, such as his *Exposition of the Canon of the Mass* and his commentary on Lombard's *Sentences*, both given as lectures at the University of Tübingen, where Biel began to teach in 1484. Retired from teaching, Biel served as provost in the Brethren House at Einsiedel, where he died on December 7, 1495. He has been called the last of the Scholastics.

Biel had studied both the *via antiqua* and the *via moderna*, but the theological system he created was, especially on the question of justification, a practical working out of Ockham's nominalism. Like Ockham, Biel understood human cognition to be knowledge of individual things that resulted in the formation of concepts and, as a result, that true human knowledge was based on sense perception. Biel also accepted the idea, common in the Franciscan tradition, that the will was the primary faculty in both human beings and God. Biel's contribution was that he built on these theoretical foundations to explore issues that Ockham had not addressed—for example, salvation. Biel began with God's freedom to do anything with regard to his absolute power (*potentia absoluta*), which also meant that creation and even the church were contingent rather than necessary. Rather than result in uncertainty, this situation, according to Biel, required an understanding of God's ordained power (*potentia ordinata*). In order to save human beings from sin, God had made a covenant to accept their best efforts as sufficient to earn the reward of grace: "To those who do what is in them, God will not deny grace" (*facientibus quod in se est deus non denigat gratiam*). Those who persisted in grace and good works would receive eternal life. Human works were not in themselves sufficient to earn these rewards, but within the covenant God had committed to give grace as if human works were meritorious. Biel's position attempted to take seriously human sinfulness without negating the religious impulses and efforts of human beings by denying their capacity to cooperate with salvation.

Luther encountered Biel's theology through his teachers at the University of Erfurt—Bartholomeus Arnoldi, Jodocus Truttvetter, and John Nathin—and he was familiar with Biel's commentary on the *Sentences*. Luther also read Biel's *Exposition of the Canon of the Mass* as part of his preparation for ordination to the priesthood. Although in some ways profoundly influenced by nominalist theology, Luther parted ways with Biel himself early in his intellectual development, and he subsequently mentioned Biel most often as representative of a Pelagianizing understanding of salvation.

See also Ockham, William; Scholasticism, Late Medieval; Theology of the Cross

Bibliography

Biel, G. *Defensorium obedientiae apostolicae et alia documenta*. Ed. and trans. H. A. Oberman, D. E. Zerfoss, and W. J. Courtenay. Belknap, 1968; Biel, G. *Gabrielis Biel Canonis Misse Expositio*. Ed. H. A. Oberman and W. J. Courtenay. 4 vols. Steiner, 1963–67; Grane, L. *Contra Gabrielem: Luthers Auseinandersetzung mit Gabriel Biel in der Disputatio Contra Scholasticam Theologiam 1517*. Gyldendal, 1962; Landeen, W. N. "Gabriel Biel and the Brethren of the Common Life." *Church History* 20 (1951): 23–26; Landeen, W. N. "Gabriel Biel and the *Devotio Moderna* in Germany." *Research Studies of Washington State University* 27 (1959): 135–214, and 28 (1960): 21–45, 61–79;

Oberman, H. A. *"Facientibus Quod in Se Est Deus Non Denegat Gratiam*: Robert Holcot, O.P., and the Beginnings of Luther's Theology." In *The Dawn of the Reformation*, 84–103. T&T Clark, 1986; Oberman, H. A. *The Harvest of Medieval Theology: Gabriel Biel and Late Medieval Nominalism*. Harvard University Press, 1963.

PAUL W. ROBINSON

Bodelschwingh, Friedrich (the Elder) and Friedrich (the Younger) von

The father (1831–1910) was a German pastor and social ministry leader, and the son (1877–1946) was a German pastor and churchman active in opposition to National Socialism. The elder Bodelschwingh was born into a devout Berlin family. After reading a missionary tract, he was moved to prepare himself for missions, studying at Basel, Erlangen, and Berlin. His first call was to serve destitute Germans in Paris in 1858–64. He returned to Germany to serve a parish near Dortmund, where he also published a weekly magazine offering his views of spiritual and social issues. In 1872 he was called to Bethel in Bielefeld, where he would direct this institution of mercy for those who suffered in body and mind. Rejecting liberal theology, Bodelschwingh recognized that industrialization was a catalyst for impoverishment, but that ultimately these distressing conditions were a symptom of the moral and spiritual poverty of humanity with God. In his work at Bethel, he sought to embody mercy for the sick, disabled, mentally ill, homeless, and unemployed; in doing so he utilized the work of deaconesses. He became a pioneer in the care of epileptics. A theological school was added in 1905, and in the same year the East Africa Mission Society would be headquartered in Bethel. Bodelschwingh sought to create an ordered Christian environment for life and work where those suffering from disability might live in dignity. Believing in the therapeutic power of work, Bethel provided shops where residents would be employed at the level of their capacity, to contribute to the good of the community. His approach to diaconal service was based on his understanding of the sacrificial love of Christ. Bodelschwingh's work stood in the tradition of Theodore Fliedner (1800–1864), Johann Wichern (1808–81), and Wilhelm Loehe (Löhe, 1808–72). A prominent and respected figure in the deaconess movement and the Inner Mission, he was affectionately revered as Father Bodelschwingh.

After the elder Bodelschwingh's death, the work at Bethel was carried forward by his son, who built on and expanded his father's efforts as a home for orphans, a vocational school for boys, and a girls' high school; programs to minister to Russian refugees and emigrants to South America were now included at Bethel. Along with Dietrich Bonhoeffer (1906–45), Georg Merz (1892–1959), Hermann Sasse (1895–1976), and Wilhelm Vischer (1895–1988), Bodelschwingh was instrumental in producing the Bethel Confession in 1933. On May 27, 1933, the younger Bodelschwingh was elected Reichsbishop of the old Evangelical Church of the Prussian Union. The following month, through the political machinations of the Nazis, he was unseated and replaced by Ludwig Müller (1883–1945), who was the German Christians' candidate defeated by Bodelschwingh. Throughout the war, Bodelschwingh vocally and courageously opposed efforts to euthanize those suffering from physical or mental incapacity; yet his position on enforced sterilization was ambivalent. In the years since his death in 1946, his legacy of work on behalf of the disabled has been commemorated on three German postage stamps.

Bibliography

"Friedrich von Bodelschwingh." In *The Spirituality of the German Awakening*, ed. D. Crowner and G. Christianson, 333–408. Paulist Press, 2003; Gerhardt, M., and A. Adam. *Friedrich von Bodelschwingh: Ein Lebensbild aus der deutschen Kirchengeschichte*. 2 vols. Bethel, 1950–58; Hong, E. *Bright Valley of Love*. Augsburg, 1976; Nelson, E. C. *The Rise of World Lutheranism: An American Perspective*. Fortress, 1982.

JOHN T. PLESS

Boe, Paul A.

The American Lutheran pastor, church executive, and social activist Paul A. Boe (1915–90) was a graduate of St. Olaf College

(Northfield, Minnesota) and Luther Seminary (St. Paul, Minnesota). He studied social work at the University of Chicago and later earned an MSW degree at Seattle's Washington University. After serving two parishes, he became executive director of Lutheran Welfare Society of Iowa, then was named the first executive director of The American Lutheran Church's Division of Social Service. In that capacity, Boe became involved with the American Indian Movement (AIM). In 1973, at the request of AIM leaders, he went to Wounded Knee, South Dakota, where a group of Oglala Lakota were protesting the government's failure to fulfill treaties with Native American people and were engaged in a confrontation with federal officials. Boe later refused, on grounds of clergy confidentiality, to answer questions before a federal grand jury about his knowledge of the participants. Sentenced to jail for contempt of court, an appellate judge vacated the judgment just as Boe was preparing to surrender himself to federal authorities. He retired from his ALC position in 1974, then received a special call from a Minnesota congregation to do ministry with Native Americans.

Bibliography

Boe, P. A. Biographical File. ELCA Archives; Boe, P. A. Interview by G. S. Thompson, December 1, 1984. Oral History Collection of the ALC, AELC, and LCA. Archives of Cooperative Lutheranism, LCUSA.

RICHARD O. JOHNSON

Boehm, Anthony William

The court chaplain, ecumenical leader, translator, and author Anthony William Boehm (also Böhme) (1673–1722) was born in Oesdorf and attended schools in Lemgo and Hameln. He began his university studies in Halle in 1693, where he was influenced by August Hermann Francke and the Pietist movement. In 1698 he became a house tutor in Waldeck, but his Pietist convictions and criticisms of the church led to his dismissal by the consistory. He returned to Halle in 1700, and shortly thereafter he was sent to London, where he founded a school. In 1705 he became a preacher in the German Lutheran Royal Chapel at St. James for Prince George, consort of Queen Anne. Boehm's Pietism was well received by Prince George, and after the prince's death in 1708 Boehm continued to have good rapport with Queen Anne. He remained court preacher under the Hanoverian George I, who otherwise had little affinity for Pietism. Boehm became the leading figure connecting the work of the Society for Promoting Christian Knowledge (SPCK) to German Protestantism, especially Halle Pietists. Boehm, for instance, was instrumental in securing funding from the SPCK to support the mission to Tranquebar. He was also an avid translator of Pietist works into English, especially those by Francke and about the work of Pietist missions.

See also England; Francke, August Hermann; Pietism

Bibliography

Brunner, D. *Halle Pietists in England: Anthony William Boehm and the Society for Promoting Christian Knowledge.* Vandenhoeck & Ruprecht, 1993; Sames, A. *Anton Wilhelm Böhme (1673–1722): Studien zum ökumenischen Denken und Handeln eines halleschen Pietisten.* Vandenhoeck & Ruprecht, 1990.

JONATHAN STROM

Böhme, Jacob

The mystic and devotional writer Jacob Böhme (1575–1624) was one of the most influential lay Protestant mystics. He was born to a farmer in the Silesian town of Alt-Seidenberg and became a shoemaker in nearby Görlitz, where he died in 1624. At the age of twenty-five he received his first spiritual illumination, which he described in his work *Aurora* (1612). The controversial nature of *Aurora* led the Görlitz magistrate to ban Böhme from further publishing his ideas. Böhme's silence lasted until 1618, after which he resumed producing devotional and theologically innovative works that were influenced by alchemy, Kabbalah, and the ideas of Paracelsus. His theosophic system, most clearly seen in *De tribus principiis* (1618), does not entirely conflate the being of God with creation but depicts the latter as the visible emanation of the invisible God, who lay hidden in the abyss (*Ungrund*). Böhme applied concepts of birth and generation to illustrate the creation process and the ability of nature, especially in the individual human, to reveal the being of God. He adopted antinomies (e.g., good and evil, love and wrath, light and darkness) to describe the cosmos and God. Echoing gnostic tendencies, Böhme believed that Adam was created for spiritual life with the divine Sophia, but fell, along with his posterity, from this spiritual state; humanity would find redemption through a rebirth in Christ. Böhme's ideas concerning God, creation, and humanity were taken up in the thought of Pietist Friedrich Christoph Oetinger (1702–82), and later in the works of Georg Wilhelm Friedrich Hegel (1770–1831) and Friedrich Wilhelm Joseph Schelling (1775–1854).

See also Arndt, Johann; German Mysticism; Hegel, Georg Wilhelm Friedrich; Mystical Union; Oetinger, Friedrich Christoph

Bibliography

Erb, P., ed. *Jacob Boehme: The Way to Christ*. Paulist Press, 1977; Ingen, F. van *Jacob Böhme in seiner Zeit*. Frommann-Holzboog, 2015; Wehr, G. *Jakob Böhme: Ursprung, Wirkung, Textauswahl*. Marixverlag, 2010.

PETER JAMES YODER

Bolivia

The South American Mission Prayer League, founded by Lutherans in Minneapolis in 1937 and direct predecessor of the World Mission Prayer League (WMPL), sent its first missionaries that same year to Bolivia. Two autonomous synods resulted from the work initiated by the WMPL: the Bolivian Evangelical Lutheran Church (Iglesia Evangélica Luterana Boliviana, IELB), formed in 1972, and the Federation of Evangelical Lutheran Churches of Bolivia (Federación de Iglesias Evangélicas Luteranas, FIEL), formed in 1974.

IELB is the largest Quechua and Aymara indigenous Lutheran church in Latin America. It promotes a holistic approach to evangelism and service, in partnership with the ELCA, the Finnish Evangelical Lutheran Mission, and the LWF, of which it is a member. FIEL works with the mestizo population in Spanish and with Quechua natives in Quechua and Spanish, mostly in the area of Apolo, and focuses on disciple formation, in partnership with the WMPL. FIEL and WMPL have headquarters in Redeemer Church in La Paz, built in 1966.

The Norwegian Norsk Lutersk Misjonssamband began a mission in Cochabamba and Sucre in 1978, which resulted in the founding of the Christian Evangelical Lutheran Church of Bolivia in 1997. This church is a member of the International Lutheran Council.

A German-speaking Lutheran congregation founded in La Paz by German immigrants in the 1920s continues to exist.

Bibliography

Cruz, J. M. *The Histories of the Latin American Church: A Handbook*. Esp. 133–52. Fortress, 2014; http://ilc-online .org/members/latin-america/bolivia/; https://www.luther anworld.org/country/bolivia; http://www.nlm.no/nlm /internasjonalt/soer-amerika/nlm-i-soer-amerika; https:// www.oikoumene.org/en/member-churches/bolivian-evan gelical-lutheran-church; https://wmpl.org/our-work /bolivia/; Theodore, E., and M. B. Bachmann. *Lutheran Churches in the World: A Handbook*. Esp. 513–16. Augsburg, 1989.

ANDRÉS ROBERTO ALBERTSEN

Boltzius, Johann Martin

Eventually serving as the founding and lead pastor of the immigrant Ebenezer community near Savannah, Georgia, from the time of the community's founding in 1734 until his death, Johann Martin Boltzius (1703–65) was born in the town of Forst in Lower Lusatia (Niederlausitz). He was educated at the University of Halle and the institutions of August Hermann Francke's Orphan House, where he became steeped in the theology and spirituality of Halle Pietism. In 1733 Boltzius was appointed, along with Israel Christian Gronau, to lead a small contingent of Lutheran religious refugees, expelled from the Catholic territory of Salzburg, to settle in the newly established British colony of Georgia in North America. Arriving in March 1734, Boltzius and the Salzburger exiles settled next to the Savannah River, where they named their settlement Ebenezer (soon renamed New Ebenezer, following a relocation to a nearby site), about twenty-five miles northwest of the town of Savannah. For the next three decades, Boltzius supervised the economic and social as well as spiritual life of the community as it grew through the arrival of additional immigrants, mainly from southwest Germany. Boltzius maintained contact with Henry Melchior Mühlenberg in Pennsylvania after Mühlenberg landed in Savannah in 1742. He also was acquainted with John Wesley during Wesley's brief time in Savannah (1736–37) and established close ties with George Whitefield. Though personally opposed to slavery, Boltzius relented to the demands of the community and allowed slaves into Ebenezer after the practice became legal in Georgia in 1751. Illness, particularly recurring bouts of fever from malaria, plagued Boltzius throughout his time in Ebenezer. Though the community enjoyed some success and significant growth under Boltzius's leadership, his vision of an enduring community founded on the ideals of Halle Pietism and serving, in part, as a base for missionary work among Native Americans had already begun to give way by the time of his death to the realities of a geographically spreading population adapting to the American context. Jerusalem Church, dedicated by Boltzius on November 20, 1741, remains an active Lutheran congregation and serves as a visible sign of his legacy. The current building, envisioned by Boltzius, was completed in 1770, five years after Boltzius's death.

See also Ebenezer Community; Pietism

Bibliography

Jones, G. F. *The Salzburger Saga*. University of Georgia Press, 1984; Kleckley, R., ed. and trans. *The Letters of Johann Martin Boltzius*. Mellen, 2009; Urlsperger, S., G. F. Jones, and R. Wilson, ed. and trans. *Detailed Reports on the Salzburger Emigrants Who Settled in America*. 18 vols. in 16. University of Georgia Press, 1968–95; Winde, H. "Die Frühgeschichte der Lutherischen Kirche in Georgia." PhD diss., Martin-Luther-Universität Halle-Wittenberg, 1960.

RUSSELL C. KLECKLEY

Bonhoeffer, Dietrich

The Lutheran theologian, pastor, and ecumenist Dietrich Bonhoeffer (1906–45) was born in Breslau (then part of Germany) and raised in Berlin, where his father was the leading university professor of psychiatry and neurology. Both sides of the large family were populated with highly educated, well-regarded pastors, doctors, lawyers, professors, mayors, and military officers. Three years after his oldest brother died in World War I, Bonhoeffer undertook the study of theology at Tübingen and then at Berlin. Although he was educated by liberal Protestants (such as Harnack, Lietzmann, Holl, and Reinhold Seeberg [his thesis adviser]), the figure who had the most significant impact on his theological development was Karl Barth.

Bonhoeffer's initial dissertation, *Sanctorum Communio* (1927), analyzes the church both theologically and sociologically. For him, the church is "Christ existing as community," a concept that he would develop further in subsequent writings. After serving as an assistant pastor in Barcelona, he returned to Berlin to complete his second dissertation, *Act and Being* (1930), which makes use of Luther's 1535 *Lectures on Galatians* to articulate a theological epistemology grounded in divine revelation. During a yearlong postdoctoral fellowship at Union Seminary, New York, he studied social ethics with Reinhold Niebuhr, encountered Christian pacifism as a serious theological position, deepened his understanding of Barth and dialectical theology, and experienced the black church in Harlem. Back in Berlin, he periodically offered lecture courses in systematic theology at the university. A high point of his academic work at that time were his lectures on Christology, creation, and sin. In this period he also embraced a form of pacifism, which distinguished his theology from other Lutherans. Following his ordination (1931), he continued to serve as an adjunct lecturer, but he also worked as a chaplain at a technical university, taught a confirmation class in a struggling part of the city, frequently preached, and participated in a variety of international ecumenical conferences.

During the difficult years of 1933–34, he voiced a theology of peace and worked with those who resisted the inroads of Nazism into the German Protestant Church. He was one of the few among the clergy to speak out against the persecution of German Jews. A cofounder of the Pastors Emergency League (1933), he later became frustrated with efforts in the Confessing Church to weaken the Bethel Confession, which he and Hermann Sasse had crafted as a way of identifying the heresy of the racist German Christians (Deutsche Christen). He thus left Germany to serve two German-speaking congregations in London (1933–35). There he became friends with Bishop George Bell, an important figure in his circle of ecumenical partners. Called back to Germany by the Confessing Church, Bonhoeffer served as the director of an illegal "preachers' seminary" in Zingst, later in Finkenwalde (1935–37). There he completed his book *Discipleship* (1937), which addresses the basic question: What does it mean to be a follower of Jesus Christ today? In this work he stresses the deep connection between "faith" and "obedience to Christ," and he utilizes the Kierkegaardian notion of "cheap grace" to criticize Christian complacency and the false theology of the German Christians. His most important theological influence here was Luther, whose 1532 sermons on the Sermon on the Mount he applied to his own situation. He also wrote *Life Together*, drawn from reflections on life in the Finkenwalde seminary.

After the Gestapo closed the Finkenwalde seminary, Bonhoeffer was later enlisted by his brother-in-law, Hans von Dohnanyi, a military lawyer, to serve in the German Office of Military Intelligence (1940). Through von Dohnanyi, Bonhoeffer was brought into a circle of conspirators who tried to assassinate Hitler. Bonhoeffer served as a courier between the conspirators and his ecumenical contacts in other countries, especially Bell. Along with von Dohnanyi, Bonhoeffer was arrested in 1943, placed in a Berlin prison, and eventually sent to Buchenwald. He was hanged by the Gestapo at Flossenburg (April 1945). After the war, his closest friend, Eberhard Bethge, published the letters and papers that Bonhoeffer had sent him and others during his imprisonment. He also helped to edit Bonhoeffer's unfinished magnum opus, his *Ethics*. In these writings Bonhoeffer struggled, often quite tentatively, with many complex theological and ethical issues, including the problem of secularization and the church's need to reform itself in the changed situation of a "world come of age." In the decades since his death, Bonhoeffer has become one of the most discussed theologians of the twentieth century. His legacy has been embraced and discussed by secularists, liberal social activists, confessional Lutherans, and conservative American evangelicals. More recently, scholars have debated his beliefs and actions toward the Jews and his role in the political resistance against the Nazi dictatorship.

See also Confessing Church; German Christians (Deutsche Christen); Germany since 1870

Bibliography

Bethge, E. *Dietrich Bonhoeffer*. Rev. ed. Fortress, 2000; Bonhoeffer, D. *Dietrich Bonhoeffer Works*. 17 vols. Fortress, 2002–14; de Gruchy, J., ed. *The Cambridge Companion to Dietrich Bonhoeffer*. Cambridge University Press, 1999; Green, C. *Bonhoeffer: A Theology of Sociology*. Rev. ed. Eerdmans, 1999; Haynes, S. R. *The Bonhoeffer Phenomenon*. Fortress, 2004; Schlingensiepen, F. *Dietrich Bonhoeffer*. T&T Clark, 2010; Sifton, E., and F. Stern. *No Ordinary Men: Dietrich Bonhoeffer and Hans von Dohnanyi*. New York Review Books, 2013.

MATTHEW L. BECKER

Book of Concord

The collection of confessional documents first published in 1580 and accepted by many Lutheran churches as the standard of teaching and practice is called the Book of Concord. By the 1530s Wittenberg theologians were labeling their own "rule of faith" a *corpus doctrinae* (body of doctrine), a summary guide for public teaching of the biblical message. By the 1550s they were listing documents that defined that corpus, and in 1559/60 Philip Melanchthon published a collection of his own writings, including the Augsburg Confession and its Apology, the Saxon Confession of 1551, his "Examination of Those Awaiting Ordination," and his *Loci communes*, later called the *Corpus Doctrinae Philippicum [Misnicum]*. Accepted as the public standard for teaching in Electoral Saxony and a few other German lands, it elicited similar works collecting defining documents for public teaching in Reformed principalities. When the proposed Formula of Concord (1577/78) found widespread approval in German Evangelical lands, Jakob Andreae, supported by Elector August of Saxony and other Lutheran princes, spearheaded an effort to bring together the most frequently and widely used documents as an overarching standard and replacement for local "bodies of doctrine." To preclude the charge that this effort detracted from Melanchthon and his collection, Andreae avoided the title *Corpus doctrinae*. Andreae wrote a preface, setting the Formula of Concord within the development of Lutheran confessions of the faith and introducing the texts of the ancient creeds (Apostles', Nicene, and Athanasian), the Augsburg Confession, the Apology of the Augsburg Confession, Luther's Small and Large Catechisms, his Smalcald Articles, Melanchthon's *Treatise on the Power and Primacy of the Pope*, and the Formula of Concord. As appendixes, many early editions included a list of signatories and a collection of christological statements of the church fathers, the Catalogue of Testimonies. Following Melanchthon's example in his *Corpus doctrinae*, the book included indexes guiding readers to pertinent doctrinal topics. Titled the Book of Concord, the collection quickly became the doctrinal standard of the German-speaking churches that had accepted the Formula of Concord. Published in German on the fiftieth anniversary of the presentation of the Augsburg Confession in 1580, the Book of Concord was accepted by the church of Sweden (1686) and by many immigrant and mission churches in the Lutheran tradition. After a first attempt at a Latin translation in 1580 aroused severe criticism, Nikolaus Selnecker oversaw a revised translation, published in 1584, which served as a textbook at German universities for several centuries.

See also Apology of the Augsburg Confession; Augsburg Confession; Catechisms; Creeds, Ecumenical; Formula of Concord; Selnecker, Nikolaus; Smalcald Articles; *Treatise on the Power and Primacy of the Pope*

Bibliography

Arand, C., R. Kolb, and J. Nestingen, eds. *The Lutheran Confessions: History and Theology of the Book of Concord.* Fortress, 2012; Gassmann, G., and S. Hendrix. *Fortress Introduction to the Lutheran Confessions.* Fortress, 1999; Jacobs, H. E. *The Book of Concord.* Vol. 2, *Historical Introduction, Appendixes, and Indexes.* G. W. Frederick, 1882; Kolb, R., and J. Nestingen, eds. *Sources and Contexts of the Book of Concord.* Fortress, 2001.

ROBERT KOLB

Bora, Katharina von

Beloved wife of Martin Luther, Katharina von Bora (1499–1552) was mother of six biological and several foster children, efficient manager of Luther's household affairs and finances, and matriarch of the German Reformation. She embodied the Protestants' elevation of the domestic and marital vocation for women and of the household as the cradle of faith.

Katharina was born on January 29, 1499, as a daughter of the impoverished Saxon nobility Hans von Bora and Katharina von Hauswig, from Libbendorf (near Leipzig). After her mother died and her father remarried, Katharina's home was in convents: from age five till nine or ten, she lived at a Benedictine convent in Brehna; at sixteen, in 1515, she took a Cistercian veil as a cloistered nun in Marienthorn, Nimbschenn. After reading Luther's writings, particularly against monastic vows and celibacy, Katharina joined eleven other nuns who escaped the convent on the eve of Easter 1523. At the risk of punishment by death, Leonard Koppe (merchant and city council member) transported the women in his wagon, with Martin Luther's involvement.

In Wittenberg, Katharina learned household management and other domestic skills while boarding in different households, most notably with Lucas and Barbara Cranach. She hoped to marry Hieronymus Baumgartner, a student at Wittenberg University from Nuremberg, who under family pressure chose a wealthier and younger woman, Sibylle von Dichtel. Frustrated with Luther's well-meaning matchmaking efforts, Katharina reportedly quipped that only Nicholas von Amsdorf or Luther himself would do; otherwise she would be supporting herself. On June 13, 1525, Katharina (26) was wedded to Luther (42), who was happy to do so "to spite the pope and the devil." We know little about the private ceremony at the Augustinian friary (the "Black Cloister") because only a handful of friends witnessed it (the Cranachs, Johannes Bugenhagen, Justus Jonas, and Johan Apel). The public celebration two weeks later evoked cheers from friends but sneers from critics of ex-monastics getting married.

The couple soon found themselves deeply in love with one another, as Luther's letters and anecdotal information from the Table Talks convey. "The Herzliebe" and "carissima" Käthe whom Luther would not exchange for Venice or France was the formidable lady of the Black Cloister, the former Augustinian monastery that the Luthers received from the Elector of Saxony. In addition to the flow of family and visitors, as well as persons needing a place for a temporary stay (e.g., Duchess Elisabeth of Brandenburg and her daughter, and the Bugenhagens), the house served as a hostel for many a student whose boarding fees Katharina gladly collected. Supervising the finances with creativity and organizational genius, Katharina secured the family's wealth by purchasing orchards and a farm, thereby also making their household self-sustaining with their own fruit, vegetables, fish and game, bread and cheese—even beer. Having received rare permission to have a private water well, Katharina's microbrewery became famous.

Katharina suffered two miscarriages and gave birth to six live children—Hans in 1526, Elisabeth in 1527, Magdalena in 1529, Martin in 1531, Paul in 1533, and Margaretha in 1534. Elisabeth died in 1528 and Magdalena in 1542. Katharina survived Luther by six difficult years, punctuated by recurring plague, the Smalcald War (when she fled Wittenberg with the Melanchthons), and financial struggle. Even though Luther had, in his will, made her the sole beneficiary—unheard of at the time when women were strictly under male legal guardianship—the income stopped with Luther's death, and Katharina was placed under the guardianship of Philip Melanchthon and Justus Jonas. She secured her children's future by dividing their possessions between the boys and girls and by soliciting help in letters. Eight letters dictated by Katharina are extant, such as three addressed to King Christian III of Denmark, a relative of a previous Danish King Christian II who had given the yet-unmarried Katharina a ring as a sign of friendship.

"The most holy lady doctor," as Luther called her affectionately, had sufficient education from her cloister days to follow Latin and German conversations at her dinner table and to converse with her spouse on matters of interest. Luther's correspondence reveals his views on the equality of the spouses as well as their different callings and spheres of authority. By Luther's own admission, "Lord" Katharina ruled his affairs, second only to the Holy Spirit. Luther's bribing Katharina to reread the Bible was less appealing to her than living her faith. She wished to stick to Christ like a "burr to a coat." She embraced Lutheran theology as her own. As one of the first and the most famous pastor-professor's wives, she helped create the parsonage as a religious and cultural institution. As a wife and a mother, a calling on a par to that of bishops and professors, Katharina exemplified Evangelical *vita activa*.

Katharina died in Torgau on December 20, 1552, after injuries incurred in a wagon accident while fleeing plague-stricken Wittenberg. She is buried in St. Mary's Church in Torgau.

See also Bugenhagen, Johannes; Vocation

Bibliography

Kroker, E. *Katharina von Bora, Martin Luthers Frau: Ein Lebens-und Charakterbild.* Herrmann, 1906; Markwald,

R. K., and M. M. Markwald. *Katharina von Bora: A Reformation Life*. Concordia, 2002; Smith, J. "Katharina von Bora through Five Centuries: A Historiography." *Sixteenth Century Journal* 30 (1999): 745–74; Stjerna, K. *Women and the Reformation*. Wiley-Blackwell, 2008; Thoma, A. *Katharina von Bora*. Georg Reimer, 1900; Treu, M. *Katharina von Bora. Biographien zur Reformation*. Drei Kastanien, 1995; Treu, M., ed. *Katharina von Bora, die Lutherin: Aufsätze anläßlich ihres 500. Geburtstages*. Martin Treu im Auftrag der Stiftung Luthergedenkstätten in Sachsen-Anhalt. Elbe-Druckerei, 1999; Treu, M. "Katharina von Bora, the Woman at Luther's Side." *LQ* 13 (1999): 157–78.

KIRSI STJERNA

Botswana

The Evangelical Lutheran Church in Botswana (ELCB) records 18,800 members. The ELCB has been affiliated with the LWF since 1986.

The first Lutheran mission station was founded in Dithubaruba in 1857 by Hermannsburg missionaries. Soshong soon followed. Notables such as Khama III were baptized. However, conflicts led to the end of the work among the Baharuthse, and the Hermannsburgers focused on the Balete and other ethnicities. The Berlin Mission Society and the Rhenish Missionary Society were also active in Botswana, especially in the Kgalagadi region. Later these Lutheran congregations operated under the auspices of ELCSA. When ELCB was established in 1978, the ELCSA leadership in South Africa did not accept it easily, and there was a split. In 2006 the ELCSA had about eight thousand members in Botswana. Slowly progress toward unity is being made.

The predecessor bodies of the Lutheran Church in Southern Africa (LCSA) entered Botswana from South Africa in 1969. In 2014 the LCSA recorded six thousand members in Botswana.

See also South Africa

Bibliography
Mignon, A. *Nineteenth Century Lutheran Mission in Botswana*. Botswana Society, 1997; Pöntinen, M. *African Theology as Liberating Wisdom: Celebrating Life and Harmony in the Evangelical Lutheran Church in Botswana*. Brill, 2013.

FRIEDER LUDWIG

Braaten, Carl

As professor of systematic theology at Lutheran School of Theology at Chicago for decades and as a prolific author, Carl Braaten (1929–) has distinguished himself as a major American Lutheran dogmatician, missiologist, ecumenist, and apologist. Early in his career he was influenced by the renewal of the law-and-gospel distinction, which had gained prominence in Luther studies. However, Braaten has also worked for stronger ecumenical ties between Roman Catholics and Lutherans. He argued that due to papal tyranny at the time, Protestants were exiled from their original Catholic home. Accordingly, he has recently promoted the work of Tuomo Mannermaa, who favors union with Christ over forensic justification as a more ecumenically viable approach to justification. Late in his career, he was troubled by the lack of confessional identity among Evangelical Lutheran Church in America leaders and advocated that the gospel needs to be secured by an episcopal order as a teaching office, responsible both to and for the Word. Braaten has tended to be critical of mainline Protestant accommodation to "progressive" social causes when they eclipse what he views as the apostolic message. His signature contribution has been not only a passion for Evangelical outreach to the secular world but also a defense of the essential historical accuracy of the Gospels in light of negative criticism.

See also Ecumenical Dialogues; Jenson, Robert W.

Bibliography
Braaten, C. *Justification: The Article by Which the Church Stands or Falls*. Fortress, 1990; Braaten, C. *Mother Church: Ecclesiology and Ecumenism*. Fortress, 1998; Braaten, C. *Principles of Lutheran Theology*. Fortress, 1983.

MARK C. MATTES

Brahe, Tycho

The Danish nobleman and astronomer Tycho Brahe (1546–1601) fostered a uniquely Lutheran approach to the study of astronomy, closely associated with Philip Melanchthon (1497–1560) and the University of Wittenberg, and he made efforts to reform institutions of higher education after the Reformation. Brahe studied at the Universities of Denmark and Leipzig, where his professors sought to make the study of astronomy more practical—in keeping with Melanchthon's advice—and to revise existing ways of imagining the organization of the heavens by using Copernicus's very compelling heliocentric planetary models. Like many of his colleagues, Brahe was not entirely comfortable with the implications of the earth being in constant motion around the sun, so he created his own planetary model, or "Tychonic" system. In his model, the earth remained stationary as the sun moved around it, with the other planets moving around the sun. Because of his status, Brahe acquired political and financial backing from the Danish Crown to build a modern observatory called Uraniborg, on the island of Hven. Brahe spent roughly twenty years there conducting a series of observations that he hoped would help him better demonstrate the reality of his system. Even though he was eventually unsuccessful at this and left to take up a position as "Imperial Mathematician" in Prague, his efforts helped generate support for new state-sponsored observatories and the development of new astronomical instruments.

See also Astrology; Kepler, Johannes; Melanchthon, Philip; Natural Science

Bibliography
Christianson, J. R. *On Tycho's Island: Tycho Brahe and His Assistants, 1570–1601*. Cambridge University Press, 2000; Mosley, A. *Bearing the Heavens: Tycho Brahe and the Astronomical Community of the Late Sixteenth Century*. Cambridge University Press, 2007; Thoren, V. *The Lord of Uraniborg: A Biography of Tycho Brahe*. Cambridge University Press, 2000.

KELLY J. WHITMER

Brakemeier, Gottfried

The Brazilian Lutheran pastor, professor, and theologian Gottfried Brakemeier (1937–) studied theology in São Leopoldo, Brazil, and earned a doctorate in New Testament theology in Göttingen. He lectured in the field of New Testament and later in systematic and ecumenical theology at the School of Theology in São Leopoldo. Brakemeier served as president of the Evangelical Church of the Lutheran Confession in Brazil (1985–94), president of the National Council of Christian Churches (1986–90), and president of the Lutheran World Federation (1990–97). He retired from his teaching activities in 2003. Brakemeier emphasizes the mission of his church in the Brazilian context, which in his view includes social responsibility, the promotion of justice and ecumenical involvement, linked with the preservation of Lutheran identity.

See also Brazil; Igreja Evangélica de Confissão Luterana no Brasil (IECLB) (Evangelical Church of the Lutheran Confession in Brazil)

Bibliography
Brakemeier, G., ed. *Presença Luterana 1990*. São Leopoldo, 1989; Brakemeier, G. *Preservando a unidade do espírito no vínculo da paz*. São Paulo, 2004.

PAULO WILLE BUSS

Brazil

Lutheranism is numerically small in Brazil, with about one million members in a total population of over two hundred million. For more than three centuries after Europeans discovered Brazil in 1500, Roman Catholicism was the only religion allowed in the country. The Portuguese Crown had practically absolute control over the church in Brazil through the exercise of the patronage granted by the pope. Only a few individual Lutherans came to Brazil in this colonial period. After the Brazilian independence from Portugal in 1822, a new constitution maintained Roman Catholicism as the official religion of the Brazilian Empire but also granted some limited religious toleration to all other religions.

The need for laborers in Brazil, however, made it necessary to attract European immigrants regardless of their religious faith. Approximately three hundred thousand Germans emigrated to Brazil, about 60 percent of whom were Protestants. Although the reason for their emigration had been mainly economic and not religious, the people did not abandon their

Evangelical faith when they came to Brazil. They soon established some church communities. A few pastors had accompanied the immigrants to Brazil; they were engaged and paid by the Brazilian government to serve the communities. Three of these pastors went to the province of Rio Grande do Sul and one to the province of Rio de Janeiro. Four more theologically trained pastors came to Brazil before 1848. Some years later, the Supreme Council of the Union Church of Prussia began sending pastors to central Brazil. In 1861 the Basel Mission Society also began sending pastors to congregations in central Brazil and to the province of Santa Catarina.

But during the first forty years after the beginning of the immigration, no pastors were sent by any German ecclesiastical organization to the province of Rio Grande do Sul, where most of the immigrants and their descendants lived. The absence of ordained clergy led the Protestants there to organize community life on their own. They erected buildings that served as both schools and churches and engaged laypersons to teach their children and also to serve them as preachers. The congregations originally had no clear confessional identity, accommodating members who were either Lutheran, Reformed, or Union church members. After 1864, some German organizations began to show interest in the Germans in Rio Grande do Sul. The Prussian Union Church, the Basel Mission Society, and the Committee for the German Protestants in the South of Brazil sent several pastors to that province. One of the pastors sent to Brazil by the Supreme Church Council of Berlin was Hermann Borchard, who made the first effort to gather the German Protestant congregations of Rio Grande do Sul into a synod in 1868. This synod, the German Evangelical Synod of the Province of Rio Grande do Sul, dissolved in 1875. An attempt to affiliate this synod with the Prussian Territorial Church failed.

In May 1886 Wilhelm Rotermund, pastor in São Leopoldo, founded the Riograndian Synod (RS) together with twelve pastors, nine laypeople, two teachers, and the German Consul of Porto Alegre. The founders rejected a reference to the Augsburg Confession as well as the designation "united-Protestant"; the synod thus remained without a clear confessional orientation. In 1901 it changed its name to German Evangelical Church of Rio Grande do Sul (RS). In 1922 a reference to the Augsburg Confession and Luther's Small Catechism was included in its constitution. Societies of the Lutheran Lord's Treasuries (Gotteskasten) in Germany expressed concern about the spiritual situation of the Lutherans in South America since the 1880s. The founding of the RS, which they viewed as an attempt to extend the influence of the German Union Church abroad, led them to look for opportunities to begin work in Brazil. Pastor Johann F. Brutschin, who had left the RS, was asked by the Lord's Treasury to identify possible places where their work might be welcomed, especially among the newly immigrated Germans from Russia. The Riograndian Synod reacted against this attempt to introduce confessional Lutheranism in the province. Even so, the Lord's Treasury societies decided to send Pastor Karl Otto Kuhr as an itinerant preacher in southern Brazil. Kuhr arrived in the province of Santa Catarina in 1897 and was soon followed by other Gotteskasten pastors. On October 9, 1905, under Kuhr's leadership, eight pastors and four laypeople formed the Evangelisch-lutherische Synode von Santa Catarina, Paraná und anderen Staaten von Südamerika (the Evangelical-Lutheran Synod of Santa Catarina, Paraná, and Other States of South America), known also as the Gotteskasten-Synode. In its constitution, the synod declared acceptance of Holy Scripture as the only rule and norm of faith and life and of the Lutheran confessions as the pure and clear exposition of the Word and will of God. Several pastors working in Santa Catarina and Paraná, earlier sent by the Prussian church and by other German Protestant mission societies, did not join the Gotteskasten-Synode but, along with their congregations, organized a new synod in 1911. This synod, known as the Association of Evangelical Communities of Santa Catarina and Paraná, worked in the same geographical region as the Gotteskasten-Synode. This resulted in considerable tension and rivalry between the two synods. A fourth Protestant synod was formed in central Brazil in 1912 by pastors and congregations who had not joined the Gotteskasten-Synode in that region. This synod, called the Synod of Central Brazil, was formed by small congregations scattered over a wide geographical area.

Beginning in 1900, a growing attachment of Brazilian Protestant communities and pastors to Germany was noticeable. A Prussian church law made it possible for Protestant communities abroad to affiliate with the Prussian church. The affiliated communities were promised financial help from Prussia, and the pastors would benefit from better wages and a lifelong pension. Several communities of the three Brazilian Protestant synods, but not of the Gotteskasten-Synode, then affiliated with the Prussian church. In 1911 the Supreme Church Council of Berlin sent a permanent representative to Brazil. In the same year, the Prussian church also founded a seminary to train pastors for the Brazilian communities.

World Wars I and II interrupted all connections with Germany and forced the synods into a closer cooperation among themselves, especially for training future pastors in Brazil. In 1921 the Riograndian Synod established a preseminary school, and in 1946 a school of theology. The Lutheran Synod affiliated with the Federation of the German Evangelical Churches in 1933. But after World War II the cultivation of German language and culture in Brazil gave way to a theological and confessional reorientation. The need for cooperation led to several meetings between the presidents of the four synods, with the resulting creation of a Synodical Federation in 1949 and the founding of the Igreja Evangélica de Confissão Luterana no Brasil (IECLB), through the merger of the synods, in 1968.

The Synodical Federation and the new church identified themselves as Lutheran although their leadership made it clear that they did not endorse a strict confessionalism.

Lutheranism was also brought to Brazil through the efforts of the Lutheran Church–Missouri Synod. During the 1890s a growing concern about the spiritual situation of the German Lutherans and their descendants in Brazil came to the attention of the Missouri Synod. A resolution of its 1899 national convention led to the sending of Pastor Christian J. Broders to Brazil in 1900 in order to survey the missionary possibilities in the country. Meanwhile, Pastor Johann Brutschin sent a letter to the Missouri Synod, asking the synod to send a pastor to his congregation in southern Brazil since he was planning to return to Germany. This direct call from Brazil strengthened the conviction in the synod that the time had come to begin work there. Broders found a group of Russian-Germans and Pomeranians without church assistance in the south of Rio Grande do Sul and was able to organize a Lutheran congregation in São Pedro, Pelotas, on July 1, 1900. Several other congregations in that area and in other regions of the state sent out calls for Missouri Synod pastors. The first group of pastors coming from the United States established an institute for training local pastors and teachers in 1903. In June 1904, eight pastors, eight lay delegates, and one teacher organized the work in Brazil as the fifteenth district of the Missouri Synod. The district changed its name to Synodo Evangélico Lutherano do Brasil in 1920 and to Igreja Evangélica Luterana do Brasil (IELB) in 1953. However, officially it remained a district until 1980, when it became a partner church of the Missouri Synod. The IELB identifies itself as a confessional Lutheran Church and accepts the Holy Scriptures as the inspired and infallible Word of God and the Lutheran confessions contained in the Book of Concord of 1580 as the true exposition of the Word of God.

There has been dialogue and cooperation between the two larger churches in Brazil, but differences between them remain mainly in the way the Bible and the Lutheran confessions are viewed and interpreted by each church and in the view about the involvement of the church in issues of the society at large. These fundamental distinctions entail several other theological and practical differences that pose significant challenges and difficulties in the way of a closer cooperation and approximation between the churches. Besides the two larger churches, there are also some other small Lutheran groups in Brazil.

See also Igreja Evangélica de Confissão Luterana no Brasil (IECLB) (Evangelical Church of the Lutheran Confession in Brazil); Igreja Evangélica Luterana de Brasil (IELB) (Evangelical Lutheran Church of Brazil); Kuhr, Karl Otto; Mahler, Carl Wilhelm Gustav; Universidade Luterana do Brasil (ULBRA)

Bibliography

Buss, P. W. *Um Grão de Mostarda*. Vol. 2. Concordia / Porto Alegre, 2006; Dreher, M. N. *Kirche und Deutschtum in der Entwicklung der Evangelischen Kirche Lutherischen Bekenntnisses in Brasilien*. Vandenhoeck & Ruprecht, 1978; Fischer, J., and C. Jahn, eds. *Es begann am Rio dos Sinos*. Evangelisch-Lutherischen Mission, 1970; Prien, H.-J. *Evangelische Kirchwerdung in Brasilien*. G. Mohn, 1989; Rehfeldt, M. *Um Grão de Mostarda*. Vol. 1. Concordia / Porto Alegre, 2003.

PAULO WILLE BUSS

Bremen

As a Hanseatic city in northwestern Germany, Bremen was strongly influenced by both Lutheran and Reformed theology during the sixteenth century. In the century following Martin Luther's break with Rome, the decline of the Hanseatic League did less to strain relationships between the core Hansa cities of Lübeck, Hamburg, and Bremen (the westernmost of the three) than did growing differences over religion. Reform-minded preaching commenced in Bremen—an archbishop's seat since the thirteenth century—with a sermon delivered by Augustinian friar Heinrich von Zütphen (1488–1524) in St. Ansgar's Church in 1522. Zütphen had absorbed Christian humanist ideas in Augustinian houses in the Netherlands and had studied at Wittenberg before his sojourn in Bremen; fellow Augustinian Jakob

Propst (1486–1562), originally from Ypres in Belgium, did much to popularize his predecessor's early calls for reform. Anticlericalism among the townspeople prompted the city council to dissolve Bremen's monasteries and cloisters between 1523 and 1528, and the introduction of Evangelical preaching into the Bremen Cathedral, the city's principal church, marked a victory for the Reformation in 1532. Protracted social unrest known as the "104-Man Revolt" underlay this success; this began in 1530 as a citizen protest over access to the city's pasturelands, which escalated into a dispute between citizens' representatives, the city council, and their elite allies in the cathedral chapter. By 1532 growing violence prompted the council to exile several antireform magistrates and to permanently remove the cathedral chapter from the city. Today, this 104-member protest committee is commemorated as the city's first permanent representative institution. In 1534 the council and citizens adopted a new church order authored by a third former Augustinian, Johann Timann (ca. 1500–1557), with the approval of Luther and Johannes Bugenhagen, and Bremen officially became a Lutheran city.

Bremen's "Second Reformation"—part of a broader phenomenon in which some Lutheran cities and principalities remade their Protestant churches on the model of Calvin's Geneva—owed much to its status as a North Sea port, which facilitated an influx of Reformed preaching and printing from France, the Rhineland, and the Netherlands. Here the dispute growing out of the theological controversy over Christ's presence in the Lord's Supper led to a bitter conflict between Johann Timann and cathedral pastor Albert Hardenberg, a correspondent of Philip Melanchthon, beginning in 1555. Derided by his opponents for "crypto-Calvinism," Hardenberg's sympathy for Swiss-style reform led to his exile from the city in 1561, from which point the embattled cathedral was shuttered indefinitely. Many ordinary citizens shared Hardenberg's desire for preaching and discipline on Calvin's model, however, and the influence of Reformed confessions grew rapidly in Bremen; by 1568 all of the city's churches (apart from the cathedral) had been restructured on the Geneva model. To the chagrin of Lutheran allies and trading partners, Bremen's refusal to endorse the Formula of Concord and its participation in the Synod of Dordrecht in 1618–19 confirmed the city's adherence to the Reformed confession, although the protracted strife of the Thirty Years' War did persuade the council to reopen the cathedral for Lutheran worship in 1638. This remained the sole Lutheran house of worship until the nineteenth century, but Reformed Bremen's tolerance for its Lutheran minority made the city lastingly biconfessional.

See also Hamburg; Lübeck

Bibliography

Hägermann, D., U. Weidinger, et al., eds. *Bremische Kirchengeschichte im Mittelalter*. Hauschild, 2012; Lohse, B. "Humanismus und Reformation in norddeutschen Städten." In *Die dänische Reformation vor ihrem internationalen Hintergrund*, ed. L. Grane and K. Hørby, 13–16. Vandenhoeck & Ruprecht, 1990; Nischan, B. *Prince, People, and Confession: The Second Reformation in Brandenburg*. University of Pennsylvania Press, 1994.

JASON L. STRANDQUIST

Brenz, Johannes

The reformer of the imperial city of Schwäbisch-Hall (1522–48), Johannes Brenz (1499–1570) also reorganized the church in the duchy of Württemberg (1551–70). While a student at the University of Heidelberg, Brenz belonged to a circle of Erasmian humanists whose leader was Johannes Oecolampadius, but his personal encounter with Luther at the Heidelberg Disputation (1518) turned him into a lifelong advocate of Luther's cause. In 1522 the council of the imperial city Schwäbisch-Hall in Franconia appointed Brenz as city preacher at St. Michael's Church, in which capacity he gradually introduced Lutheran doctrines and ceremonies. By the end of 1526 the main city churches had been thoroughly reformed, but the difficult process of reforming the parishes in the city's rural territory was not completed until the 1543 publication of a church order for the entire territory.

Meanwhile, though still based in Schwäbisch-Hall, Brenz had become an influential figure beyond its borders. In the summer of 1525 he published a pamphlet urging the princes who had been victorious over the rebellious peasants to show leniency toward them, arguing that the rebellion would not have occurred if the princes had provided their subjects with decent government and true preaching. Later that same year his publication, in conjunction with a number of other pastors in Swabia and Franconia, of the so-called *Syngramma Suevicum*, a spirited defense of Luther's view of the real presence of Christ in the Lord's Supper against the contrary view of Zwingli and his followers, established him as the leading champion of Wittenberg's reformation in southwestern Germany. In 1528 he published a treatise (subsequently much republished and widely heeded) urging governments not to impose the death penalty on Anabaptists. By 1529 he had established himself as the principal theological adviser to Margrave George of Brandenburg-Ansbach, at whose instigation he was invited to the Marburg Colloquy, in whose entourage he attended the Diet of Augsburg in 1530, and at whose invitation he joined Andreas Osiander in the preparation of the church order that Brandenburg-Ansbach and Nuremberg issued in common in 1533. Similarly, in 1535, when Duke Ulrich of Württemberg needed someone to help with the introduction of the Reformation into his principality, Brenz journeyed to Stuttgart to help prepare a church order (published in 1536) and to Tübingen to reorganize the university (1537–38), thus contributing significantly to the victory of Lutheranism in an area where Zwinglian and Lutheran influences had been struggling for dominance.

In 1548 Brenz was forced to flee Schwäbisch-Hall to escape arrest and imprisonment because of his opposition to the Augsburg Interim; he found refuge with Duke Ulrich in Württemberg, where the Interim had also been imposed but where he could be hidden away safely. Following the abrogation of the Interim (1552), Brenz was appointed provost of the Stuttgart Collegiate Church (the highest ecclesiastical post in the duchy) by Ulrich's successor, Duke Christopher. By this time the reorganization of the church in Württemberg, begun in secret while the Interim was still in effect, was already far advanced, and under Brenz's leadership it reached its culmination with the publication of the Great Church Order of 1559. This was the full realization of ideas about church organization that Brenz had advocated in the 1520s and 1530s but had only partially achieved in practice. Routine control of ecclesiastical matters was in the hands of a committee of theologians and secular councillors in the ducal chancellery known as the *Kirchenrat* (consistory), with a division of labor between the theologians (appointment and dismissal of clergymen, enforcement of uniformity of doctrine and ceremonies) and the secular councillors (management of church property and income). The authority to make church law and impose excommunication was reserved to a *Synodus* (essentially the *Kirchenrat* in special session). Supervision of the pastors and local congregations was in the hands of clergymen known as superintendents, who conducted regular visitations and submitted detailed reports that were the basis for the deliberations of the *Kirchenrat* and the *Synodus*. This system of territorial church government was widely imitated in Protestant Germany and survived (with modifications) until 1918–19.

Unlike Luther and Melanchthon, Brenz was never (except for the brief interlude in Tübingen) an academic theologian, but he was an amazingly prolific one nonetheless (517 imprints of his works during his lifetime). He wrote pamphlets, treatises, and memoranda that addressed every issue facing the first generation of reformers, as well as biblical commentaries (based largely on his sermons) that won Luther's praise, and catechisms that were second only to those of Luther in popularity

and were in continuous use in Württemberg from Brenz's day to today. The bulk of this output, highly esteemed at the time, still awaits investigation by modern scholars.

See also Württemberg

Bibliography

Estes, J. M. *Christian Magistrate and Territorial Church: Johannes Brenz and the German Reformation.* Centre for Reformation and Renaissance Studies, 2007; Estes, J. M., trans. and ed. *Godly Magistrates and Church Order: Johannes Brenz and the Establishment of the Lutheran Territorial Church in Germany, 1524–1559.* Centre for Reformation and Renaissance Studies, 2001; Estes, J. M. "Johannes Brenz and the German Reformation." *LQ* 16 (2002): 373–413.

JAMES M. ESTES

Bucer, Martin

Theologian and pastor in Strasbourg, Martin Bucer (1491–1551) was active as a teacher, church organizer, and advocate of church unity. Born in Schlettstadt (Sélestat, Alsace), Bucer entered the Dominican order as a teenager and was trained in the realist theology of Thomas Aquinas in his order's school in Heidelberg. There he also became involved in a humanist circle strongly influenced by Erasmus. Bucer became an enthusiastic supporter of Luther after attending the Heidelberg Disputation in April 1518, although his account of the disputation shows that at the time he understood Luther's theology within an Erasmian framework. Growing opposition from his fellow Dominicans caused Bucer to obtain a dispensation from his monastic vows in 1521. Through the patronage of Franz von Sickingen he became a pastor first in Landstuhl and then in Wissembourg. In 1522 he married Elizabeth Silbereisen, a former nun. Forced out of his parish by the turmoil of the Knights' Revolt, Bucer moved to Strasbourg in 1523. To support his family, he translated Luther's German commentaries and postils into Latin for readers outside of Germany. He also produced a German commentary on the Psalms whose title identified it as a translation of Johannes Bugenhagen's Latin commentary, although it was only loosely related to Bugenhagen's work (*Psalter wol verteutscht auß der heyligen Sprach* [Psalter well translated from the holy language]). Bucer also began lecturing publicly on the Bible for both clergy and laypeople. Over the next decade he published commentaries on Ephesians (1527), the Gospels (1527/28, revised 1530 and 1536), Zephaniah (1528), the Psalms (1529), and Romans (1536) that grew out of these lectures.

In 1524 Bucer became pastor of the church of St. Aurelia in Strasbourg, and over the next year he joined with his colleagues Wolfgang Capito, Matthaeus Zell, and Caspar Hedio in pushing for the introduction of Evangelical reforms. He and his colleagues are credited with retaining confirmation (a sacrament Luther had rejected in 1520) as a rite of the church associated with catechesis, a practice that quickly spread to other Evangelical churches. When controversy over the Lord's Supper broke out in late 1524, Strasbourg's pastors supported the Swiss reformers against Luther. Bucer was originally an ardent partisan of the Swiss, but he differed from them in being more willing to associate Christ's spiritual presence with the elements. In 1528 he published *Vergleichung D. Luthers vnnd seins gegenteyls vom Abentmal Christ* (Agreement of Dr. Luther and his opponents on Christ's Supper), which emphasized the common ground held by both sides. Luther mistrusted Bucer, however, because of the Zwinglian understanding of the Lord's Supper contained in Bucer's German Psalms commentary published under Bugenhagen's name. Luther rebuffed Bucer's offer of fellowship at the Marburg Colloquy in 1529, but Bucer's meetings with both Luther and Melanchthon at the time of the Diet of Augsburg (1530) were the first positive step toward concord. Over the next few years Bucer worked tirelessly to formulate an understanding of the Lord's Supper acceptable to all parties. His chief contact in Wittenberg was Philip Melanchthon, and the result was the Wittenberg Concord (1536), which was endorsed by the churches of Saxony and Hessen and most of the churches in southern Germany but rejected by Zurich. Acceptance of the Wittenberg Concord made it possible for the German cities to be included in the Smallcald League and the Peace of Augsburg (1555) and paved the way for the eventual victory of Lutheranism in Strasbourg.

Bucer was instrumental in founding the Strasbourg Academy in 1539, and in 1542 he became dean of the St. Thomas chapter, whose benefices supported that academy. He was a strong proponent of pastoral oversight of the laity, publishing a major work of pastoral theology, *Von der waren Seelsorge* (On true pastoral care) in 1538. His views on both church discipline and the Lord's Supper influenced John Calvin while the latter served as professor and pastor to the French refugee church in Strasbourg from 1538 to 1541.

Bucer was the architect of the Strasbourg synod held in 1533 to counter the growing number of Anabaptists in the city, and he drafted the church ordinance that was adopted the following year. He also served as consultant on issues concerning the practical outworking of Evangelical reform for many smaller imperial cities in southern Germany. Through the 1530s he was invited to help reform the churches of Ulm, Augsburg, and Hessen, and the ordinances he wrote for these churches were influential models for other territories. Like Melanchthon, he provided advice for the possible reform of the French church in 1534. Landgrave Philip of Hesse increasingly relied on Bucer's advice, and in 1539 he sent Bucer to Wittenberg to persuade Luther and Melanchthon to endorse Philip's bigamous marriage. Beginning with the religious colloquy of Hagenau in 1540, Bucer became involved in negotiations with Catholic theologians to reunite the church within the Holy Roman Empire. Together with the Roman Catholic Johannes Gropper, he composed the Regensburg Book, which served as the basis for negotiations at the Regensburg Colloquy in 1541. In 1542 Bucer and Melanchthon were invited to help reform the secular territories of the archbishop of Cologne. Their efforts ultimately failed due to the intervention of Emperor

Charles V, but the church ordinance that the two reformers wrote for the archbishop's territories later influenced the English Reformation. In several publications from this period, Bucer justified the colloquies and addressed the practical problems of reuniting and reforming the German church independent of Rome.

Bucer was present at the Diet of Augsburg (1548) and signed the Augsburg Interim under duress, but after his return to Strasbourg he repudiated its provisions and led the resistance to its imposition on the city. In the spring of 1549 he was banished from Strasbourg and went to England, at the invitation of the archbishop of Canterbury Thomas Cranmer. Upon his arrival, Bucer provided input on the Edwardian revision of the Book of Common Prayer and wrote a blueprint for the reform of the English church, *De regno Christi* (On the kingdom of Christ). He was appointed Regius Professor of Divinity at Cambridge, but his lectures were interrupted by his poor health, and he died on February 28, 1551. Several of his lectures and treatises written in England were published posthumously in the *Scripta Anglicana* (1577).

See also Augsburg Interim; Marburg Colloquy; Regensburg Colloquy; Strasbourg; Switzerland; Wittenberg Concord; Zwingli, Ulrich

Bibliography

Amos, N. S. *Bucer, Ephesians and Biblical Humanism: The Exegete as Theologian.* Springer, 2015; Bucer, M. *Concerning the True Care of Souls.* Trans. P. Beale. Banner of Truth, 2009; Greschat, M. *Martin Bucer: A Reformer and His Times.* Westminster John Knox, 2004; Krieger, C., and M. Lienhard, eds. *Martin Bucer and Sixteenth Century Europe.* Brill, 1993; Pauck, W., ed. *Melanchthon and Bucer.* Westminster, 1969; Stupperich, R., et al., eds. *Martini Buceri Opera Omnia*: Series 1, *Deutsche Schriften.* Series 2, *Opera Latina.* Series 3, *Correspondance.* Brill, 1955–; Wendel, F., et al., eds. *Martini Buceri Opera Latina.* Brill, 1954–; Wright, D. F., ed. *Common Places of Martin Bucer.* Sutton Courtenay, 1972; Wright, D. F., ed. *Martin Bucer: Reforming Church and Community.* Cambridge University Press, 1994.

AMY NELSON BURNETT

Bugenhagen, Johannes

As pastor, superintendent, and professor in Wittenberg, Johannes Bugenhagen (1485–1558) was author of pastoral writings, biblical commentaries, and Evangelical church orders. Sometimes called the "organizer of the Reformation" or the "apostle to the north," Bugenhagen was born in Wollin in Pomerania. After receiving a humanist education at the University of Greifswald, he became rector of a Latin school at the age of nineteen. Ordained in 1509, he later taught at a Premonstratensian monastic school in Pomerania, though it is unclear whether he ever took monastic vows himself.

Inspired by Luther's writings, Bugenhagen moved to Wittenberg in 1521 and took a room at Melanchthon's house. His talents as a teacher and a scholar were quickly recognized, and he became a lecturer at the University of Wittenberg. His status as a Wittenberg reformer was cemented when he was elected to be pastor of Wittenberg's city church (St. Mary's) in October 1523. This appointment set important Reformation precedents since he was elected with the input of the city council and was already a married priest, having married Walpurga (nee Rörer?) the previous year.

Often called Dr. Pomeranus, he was skilled at connecting justification by faith alone with practical reform. His 1526 *Letter to Hamburg*, for instance, is a pastoral letter that combines Evangelical faith with matters of church organization. This combination of faith and practice became the basis for his church orders or agendas; between 1528 and 1544 he composed or oversaw church orders for Braunschweig, Hamburg, Lübeck, Pomerania, Denmark, Schleswig-Holstein, Braunschweig-Wolfenbüttel, and Hildesheim. These church orders began with statements of faith, provided the outline of a common liturgy and worship life, and gave instructions for the establishment and maintenance of churches, schools, and social welfare programs.

In addition to published works like the church orders, a Gospel harmony, and biblical commentaries on books of the Old and New Testaments, Bugenhagen took part in many ecclesiastical discussions. He was involved in preparing the Instructions for the Visitors in

Electoral Saxony (1527/28), the Torgau Articles (1529), the Wittenberg Articles (1536), the Wittenberg Concord (1536), and the Smalcald Articles (1537). After the imposition of the Augsburg Interim (1548), Bugenhagen helped craft an alternative Lutheran proposal with Melanchthon and others. These theologians received heavy criticism from Lutherans outside of Electoral Saxony, though their efforts contributed to the Augsburg Interim's demise in 1552 and to the Peace of Augsburg (1555), which legalized the faith of the Augsburg Confession in the Holy Roman Empire.

Bugenhagen stepped down from his pastorate in 1556 due to declining health. By that time he had served as a full faculty member and sometimes dean of the University of Wittenberg's theology department and as general superintendent of the Wittenberg-area churches. He enjoyed a long relationship with Martin Luther, marrying and burying Luther (in 1525 and 1546, respectively), assisting in Luther's translation of the Bible, serving as his pastor and confessor, and frequently participating in the table talks held in Luther's home. His career is marked by his collegial and clear teaching, preaching, and implementation of the Evangelical faith.

See also Augsburg Interim; Smalcald Articles; Wittenberg, City of; Wittenberg Circle; Wittenberg Concord

Bibliography

Bugenhagen, J. *Werke: Reformatorische Schriften*. 4 vols. Ed. A. Bieber-Wallmann. Vandenhoeck & Ruprecht, 2013–; Dingel, I., and S. Rhein, eds. *Der späte Bugenhagen*. Evangelische Verlaganstalt, 2011; Hendel, K. "Johannes Bugenhagen, Organizer of the Lutheran Reformation." *LQ*, NS 18 (2004): 43–75; Lohrmann, M. *Bugenhagen's Jonah: Biblical Interpretation as Public Theology*. Lutheran University Press, 2012; Vogt, K. A. T. *Johannes Bugenhagen Pomeranus: Leben und ausgewählte Schriften*. Friederichs, 1867.

MARTIN J. LOHRMANN

Bullinger, Heinrich

As leader of the Zurich church after Ulrich Zwingli died, Heinrich Bullinger (1504–75) was one of the most important figures in sixteenth-century Protestantism. The Swiss reformer, a native of Bremgarten near Zurich, was an early admirer of Martin Luther and Philip Melanchthon. While Bullinger was studying in Cologne during the early 1520s, he witnessed firsthand the tumult of the Luther affair. Such was the impact on the young man that he abandoned his theological studies to embrace the reform movement and adopt the humanist educational program. When he returned to his native Zurich, he served as a schoolmaster at Kappel and was ordained a pastor. Zwingli took the young man under his wing, encouraging him in both his scholarly and pedagogical work. During the 1520s Bullinger was a prolific writer, producing works of history and biblical commentary. Although Bullinger was personally and intellectually close to Zwingli, he did not surrender his admiration for Luther, whom he regarded as the founder of the Reformation. Nevertheless, in the sacramental dispute that arose in 1524, Bullinger strongly sided with the Zurich position.

In 1531, when Zwingli died at the Battle of Kappel, Heinrich Bullinger was selected by the Zurich Council as his successor. He was only twenty-seven years old, but his learning and pastoral manner recommended him to political leaders who needed stability. At first Bullinger was optimistic that the rift with Wittenberg could be healed, but the atmosphere soon soured, with the Zurich clergy rebuffing the efforts of Martin Bucer. By 1536, as negotiations were taking place that would lead to the Wittenberg Concord, Bullinger published Zwingli's final work, *A Short and Clear Exposition of the Faith*, with a preface in which he praised his predecessor. Luther was adamant that the Swiss were in error on the Lord's Supper, and Bullinger's act caused considerable alienation among the southern German cities. The Wittenberg Concord marked a lessening of Zurich's influence among these cities, leaving Bullinger an isolated figure.

In 1543 another incident marked the downward spiral of relations between Bullinger and Luther. The Zurich church produced a Latin translation of the Bible, known as the *Biblia sacrosancta*, and the publisher, Froschauer, sent a copy to Luther. In a brutal letter, the German reformer thanked the printer for the gift but stated that the two parties were not of the same spirit. He requested, therefore, that no such further gifts should be sent. Bullinger was deeply insulted, and Martin Bucer and Philip Melanchthon worked to assuage his anger. Matters only worsened in the same year when Luther published his Short Confession on the Lord's Supper, in which he once more attacked the Swiss and other "fanatics," making it clear that he had nothing to do with their teaching.

In 1545 Bullinger published the most complete rebuttal to Luther from the Zurichers. In the *True Confession*, Bullinger presented the Zurich account of what had taken place at the Colloquy of Marburg in 1529, a catalog of Luther's attacks on the Zurich church, and a defense of the Zurich sacramental theology. Bullinger also offered a sustained critique of the manner in which Luther had conducted himself with regard to the Zurichers. One by one, Bullinger moved through the charges Luther had made against the Swiss church, including that they were liars who awaited his death to attack him. Bullinger repeated what he had often stated: the Zurichers had the greatest respect for Luther, but they would not remain silent in the face of false accusations. When Luther died in 1546, Bullinger wrote to his friend Ambrosius Blarer that the German reformer had "passed to the Lord." In a series of exchanges, culminating in an official letter of condolence to Philip Melanchthon, Bullinger repeatedly separated Luther the prophet from the man who had divided the church with his conduct.

In the thirty years after Luther's death, Bullinger remained a staunch supporter of the Reformed cause in the face of Lutheran and Catholic hostility. His major work, *The Decades*, was a defense of the apostolic nature of the Reformed churches and doctrine. When he and John Calvin signed the Consensus Tigurinus (Zurich Consensus) on the Lord's Supper, occasion was given to Lutherans, notably Joachim Westphal, to attack the document and especially Calvin. Together with John Calvin, Bullinger served as an adviser and mentor to many of the nascent Reformed groups and churches that emerged across Europe.

See also Bucer, Martin; Calvin, John; Lord's Supper; Zurich; Zwingli, Ulrich

Bibliography

Edwards, M. U., Jr. *Luther and the False Brethren*. Stanford University Press, 1975; Gordon, B. "Holy and Problematic Deaths: Heinrich Bullinger on Zwingli and Luther." In *Tod und Jenseits in der Schriftkultur der Frühen Neuzeit*, ed. M. Kobelt-Groch and C. Nickus-Moore, 47–62. Harrassowitz, 2008; Gordon, B. *The Swiss Reformation*. Manchester University Press, 2002; Gordon, B., and E. Campi, eds. *Architect of Reformation: An Introduction to Heinrich Bullinger, 1504–1575*. Baker Academic, 2004.

BRUCE GORDON

Bultmann, Rudolf (Karl)

The German Lutheran theologian Rudolf (Karl) Bultmann (1884–1976) was one of the most influential, albeit controversial, biblical scholars of the twentieth century. Son of a Lutheran pastor, the maternal grandson of a pietistic Lutheran minister, and the paternal grandson of a missionary to Africa, he was raised in the Lutheran faith, lived and practiced, which left a lasting mark on his academic pursuits. Studying theology at Tübingen, Berlin, and Marburg, Bultmann in 1921 became professor for New Testament at the University of Marburg, Germany, a position he held for thirty years until his retirement in 1951.

Trained in liberal theology, which perceived Jesus as one noble example of morality worth imitating and God as an object to reflect about reverently, Bultmann—like contemporary theologians Karl Barth (1886–1968), Emil Brunner (1889–1966), and Friedrich Gogarten (1887–1967)—turned against that liberal theology by arguing that the biblical God is a "Wholly Other," never a neutrally given object. Knowledge of God comes about solely by God's gracefully granted revelation (*sola gratia*), that is, in the actual proclamation of the Word of God, which Bultmann termed *kerygma*. In hearing this proclamation as Word of God, realizing and accepting it as such in faith, humans encounter the self-revealing God as the one who calls them into authentic existence irrespective of their virtues and accomplishments (justification by faith). The *kerygma* confronts self-contained, self-centered people with the cross and resurrection of Jesus Christ as an alternative way of being (*solus Christus*), as rooted in God, a state of being attainable not by idealistic, pious reflection (works) but only by believing the Word (*sola scriptura*). Convinced that to make the Word of God known to the world in this way is the singular ministry of the church, Bultmann devoted his scholarly efforts, which he always regarded as a service for the church, to the erudite study of biblical texts, the New Testament in particular, so to enable responsible preaching of *kerygma* under the conditions of modernity.

Gifted with an exceptional intellectual capacity, Bultmann not only published several seminal books about the Synoptic Gospels, Jesus, the Gospel of John, and Pauline and New Testament theology that for generations shaped the field of biblical studies in Protestant and Roman Catholic circles across the globe, but also seriously engaged in dialogue with the philosopher Martin Heidegger (1889–1976), his colleague at Marburg from 1923 to 1928. Heidegger analyzed human existence as anxious awareness of finitude as a being-toward-death while at the same time always being bound to decide for authentic living; this analysis not only helped Bultmann to fathom the situation of modern individuals without God but also became for him the key to unlocking the summons to faith of biblical texts. Instead of objective realities, which the pious are asked to believe, biblical texts speak in contingent terminology about experiences of what the living God has done to humans in history. While existential categories—consciousness, anxiety, decision, finitude, authenticity—became typical for Bultmann's style of theological

discourse, it was the existential reading of Scripture that caused serious unrest among Christian circles and churches.

The intensity of the controversy hinged on a tragic misunderstanding of the interpretative methodology, called "demythologizing," which Bultmann employed to characterize the biblical texts as a summons to faith starting in 1941. His choice of terms was somewhat problematic because many understood "myth" to be synonymous with "invented, fictitious story," void of any factuality. His critics quickly concluded that to demythologize New Testament accounts like the virgin birth, Jesus's miracles, and the resurrection means to eliminate these from Scripture, whereas all Bultmann wanted to achieve was to interpret these "myths" in such a way that they become *kerygma* again, that is, that they can be grasped as expressions of genuine Christian faith here and now summoning people to take a conscious decision to surrender the self to God.

Another contentious issue was Bultmann's thorough application of historical criticism to the Bible. His often brilliant analyses, which sometimes certainly took him beyond the reasonable, were nothing but the consequence of his serious and true Lutheran concern for not letting faith become a "work" by turning it into blind acceptance of contingent propositions, because faith is faith only when it does not depend on warranties, historical or otherwise (*sola fide*). Many, however, regarded such radical criticism as an expression of profound disrespect for Holy Scripture, not accepting the argument that it emerged from honest reverence for the Word of God as a summons to faith.

See also Barth, Karl; Bible Interpretation; Existentialism; Liberalism; Scripture

Bibliography

Bultmann, R. *Faith and Understanding.* Fortress, 1987; Bultmann, R. *The Gospel of John.* Westminster John Knox, 1971; Bultmann, R. *History and Eschatology: The Presence of Eternity.* Harper, 1962; Bultmann, R. *New Testament and Mythology.* Fortress, 1984; Bultmann, R. *Theology of the New Testament.* Baylor University Press, 2010; Johnson, R., ed. *Rudolf Bultmann: Interpreting*

Faith for the Modern Era. Fortress, 1991; Longenecker, B. W., and M. C. Parsons, eds. *Beyond Bultmann: Reckoning a New Testament Theology*. Baylor University Press, 2014; Schmithals, W. *An Introduction to the Theology of Rudolf Bultmann*. SCM, 2013.

CHRISTOFFER H. GRUNDMANN

Buxtehude, Dietrich

The place and date of birth for the composer and musician Dietrich (Dieterich) Buxtehude (ca. 1637–1707) are uncertain, likely from Helsingborg, Sweden. His father, Johannes Buxtehude (1602–74), was an organist and teacher from whom Buxtehude learned his craft. By 1658 he had become organist in the church his father had served in Helsingborg; in 1660 he became organist at the Marienkirche in Helsingør; and in 1668, after Franz Tunder died, he took the post of organist at the Marienkirche in Lübeck, Germany, until his death.

Buxtehude was the finest German church musician and composer between Heinrich Schütz and J. S. Bach. Bach visited him in 1705 to hear him play the organ and to be present for the *Abendmusik* concerts that Buxtehude had renewed and placed on Sunday afternoons at the end of the church year and in Advent. Though best known for his chorale preludes, other preludes and fugues, and a passacaglia for organ, Buxtehude also wrote a variety of music with German and Latin texts for choral forces, solo voices, and instruments, useful throughout the church year.

See also Bach, Johann Sebastian; Music; Schütz, Heinrich

Bibliography

Snyder, K. J. *Dieterich Buxtehude*. University of Rochester Press, 2007; Webber, G. *North German Church Music in the Age of Buxtehude*. Oxford, 1996.

PAUL WESTERMEYER

C

Cajetan (Thomaso de Vio)

As professor of sacred theology, Italian cardinal, and Dominican, Thomaso de Vio Cajetan (1469–1534) was the first Roman authority commissioned to interrogate Luther, in October 1518. Born to nobility in Naples, Cajetan joined the Dominican order in 1484. Studying at Naples, Bologna, and Padua, he eventually became a professor at the latter, commenting and lecturing on the metaphysical works of Thomas Aquinas. In 1494, after a public disputation against Pico della Mirandola, Cajetan became master of sacred theology; three years later he accepted the chair of Thomistic theology at Pavia before being sent to Milan and eventually to Rome. In these years Cajetan produced the first complete commentary on the *Summa theologiae* of Thomas Aquinas, published incrementally between 1508 and 1523. Cajetan's fidelity to Thomas's thought remains a disputed question today, though the incredible influence of his commentary on future generations of theologians cannot be ignored. From 1508 until 1518, Cajetan served as the master general of the Dominican order, during which time Pope Leo X made him a cardinal. As master general, Cajetan focused his efforts on reform both within the Dominican order and within the church at large. In 1517 he composed a treatise on the use of indulgences, seeking to curb abuses while nonetheless affirming the validity of the practice. He was not yet aware of Luther's writings on the topic. Fearing the imminent threat of the Turkish armies, Pope Leo X sent Cajetan as the papal legate to the imperial Diet of Augsburg in 1518, to rouse German financial support for the Italian campaign. During this time Rome grew increasingly vexed by "the Luther affair" and commissioned Cajetan to interrogate Luther and bring him to Rome for trial. Ingrained rivalries between Germans and Italians did not well predispose either side to impute the sincerity of the other. Before the meeting, Cajetan met with Prince Frederick the Wise of Saxony and agreed to engage Luther *paterne, non judicialiter* (as a father, not as a judge). While awaiting Luther's arrival in Augsburg, Cajetan closely studied the *Explanations of the Ninety-Five Theses.* Therein Cajetan singled out only two points of contestation: thesis 58, on the treasury of merits, and the explanation of thesis 7, on the necessity of certain faith for the efficacy of sacramental absolution. After little progress in the proceedings, Cajetan dropped the second, asking only that Luther recant thesis 58. Luther refused. Unsuccessful in his engagement both with the imperial diet and with Luther, Cajetan returned to Rome in 1519, where he served on the consistories assembled to deal with the Luther affair and wrote further treatises against Luther, Zwingli, and Henry VIII. With the help of Jewish Hebraists and Greek scholars, Cajetan devoted the final decade of his life to producing literal commentaries on the Psalter, Gospels and Epistles, Pentateuch, and other books of the Old Testament. Due to his interpretive principles as well as other theological opinions on marriage, the authority of the Vulgate, and the canonicity of certain books (including James), Cajetan drew suspicion from the theological faculty at Paris, on account of which Luther famously said that in his later days Cajetan had practically "become a Lutheran" (WA TR 2:596.14, no. 2668).

See also Catholicism; Luther's Roman Catholic Opponents; Ninety-Five Theses

Bibliography

Fabisch, P., and E. Iserloh, eds. *Dokumente zur Causa Lutheri (1517–1521).* Vol. 2. CCath 42. Aschendorff, 1991;

Janz, D. *Luther and Late Medieval Thomism: A Study in Theological Anthropology*. Wilfrid Laurier University Press, 1983; O'Connor, M. "A Neglected Facet of Cardinal Cajetan: Biblical Reform in High Renaissance Rome." In *The Bible in the Renaissance*, ed. R. Griffiths, 71–94. Ashgate, 2001; Wicks, J., ed. and trans. *Cajetan Responds: A Reader in Reformation Controversy*. Wipf & Stock, 2011; Wicks, J. *Cajetan und die Anfänge der Reformation*. Aschendorff, 1983.

Eric J. DeMeuse

Calixt, Georg

The German Lutheran theologian and irenicist Georg Calixt (1586–1656) was labeled "syncretist" by opponents. In 1614 he was called to the University of Helmstedt, where he taught his entire career. At a religious colloquy in Thorn, Poland (1645), his plans for mutual toleration in Poland and East Prussia were thwarted by Abraham Calov. Calixt promoted a moderate Lutheran theology, avoiding some Lutheran distinctives. To settle religious controversies, he proposed the consensus of the ancient church as an infallible criterion of truth alongside Scripture, limited fundamental doctrines to the Apostles' Creed, and viewed Lutheran confessions as unnecessary. His ecumenical proposals were rejected by Catholics but were used by the Reformed elector Frederick William of Brandenburg to challenge Lutheran distinctions in his lands. Calixt also detached moral theology from positive (dogmatic) theology and used the analytical method. Under Calov's leadership, Lutheran opponents sought to check his influence with a new confession, the Repeated Consensus of the Truly Lutheran Faith (1664).

See also Calov, Abraham; Lutheran Orthodoxy

Bibliography

Mager, I. "Einführung." In *Einleitung in die Theologie*, ed. G. Calixt, 9–28. Vandenhoeck & Ruprecht, 1978; Schmeling, T. R. "Lutheran Orthodoxy under Fire." *Lutheran Synod Quarterly* 47 (2007): 316–55; Wallmann, J. "Union, Reunion, Toleranz." In *Union—Konversion—Toleranz*, ed. H. Duchhardt, 21–37. Von Zabern, 2000.

Benjamin T. G. Mayes

Calov, Abraham

One of the most forceful theologians and controversialists of the age of Lutheran Orthodoxy, Abraham Calov (1612–86), was born in Mohrungen (East Prussia). Calov (Kalau) matriculated at the University of Königsberg at the age of fourteen and graduated in 1632. Subsequently he studied at the University of Rostock, receiving a theological doctorate in 1637. The philosophical and theological works he began to produce while in Rostock earned him an invitation to join the theological faculty at Königsberg in 1637. He moved to Danzig in 1643 to become rector of the city's Evangelical gymnasium and pastor of Trinity Church. In 1650 he was called to a professorship at the University of Wittenberg, where he taught theology for the next thirty-six years. His lectures were attended by as many as five hundred students at a time. In addition he served as preacher at the city church and as general superintendent of Electoral Saxony from 1652 until his death.

During his lifetime Calov published more than five hundred writings. His twelve-volume systematic theology (1655–77) ranks with Johann Gerhard's *Loci theologici* as one of the most thorough and influential presentations of Lutheran theology written during the seventeenth century. He is particularly remembered for his contributions to theological method in his *Systema locorum theologicorum* as well as in earlier works such as *Methodologia* (1632) and *Gnostologia* (1633). For example, he sorted out the relationship of faith to theological reasoning, clarified the practical purpose of a theologian's work, and helped introduce a new analytical approach to the sequencing of doctrinal loci, which focused on the goal of God's plan for humanity and how attainment of eternal blessedness has been made possible. In his handling of the doctrine of justification, Calov laid out a detailed order of salvation (*ordo salutis*), progressing from God's initial calling (*vocatio*) to final glorification and the believer's mystical union with Christ. Along with his contemporary, P. H. Friedlieb (1603–63), he also introduced the term "eschatology" to describe theological discussion of "the last things."

Calov, who called himself a vigorous athlete for Christ (*strenuus Christi athleta*), supplemented his systematic writings with numerous polemical tracts against rival movements of his day. He was most notably a critic of syncretism, the effort to bring about unity or at least toleration among the different confessional traditions. At the Colloquy of Thorn, called by the king of Poland in 1645 to promote reconciliation between Catholics and Protestants, Calov upheld a strict Lutheran position. Confronting Georg Calixt, the leader of the irenic party, he argued that the Lutheran Church was the only true church and that acceptance of the Apostles' Creed was not a sufficient basis for reunification because it did not articulate all fundamental articles of faith. In 1655 Calov proposed a more detailed antisyncretistic enhancement to the Formula of Concord, the *Consensus repetitus*, but it did not gain sufficient support to become a binding confession. His confrontation with Calixt revived in 1661 at the Conference of Kassel. Altogether he wrote twenty-eight works against syncretism; in addition he published seventy writings against Socinianism and further polemics against Catholic, Reformed, and Remonstrant theologies.

Calov also made notable contributions to biblical scholarship. He was an ardent defender of biblical inerrancy and composed a four-volume Latin commentary on the Old and New Testaments, the *Biblia illustrata* (1672–76), in part to counter the more liberal interpretations of the Dutch scholar Hugo Grotius. His most lasting legacy was probably the publication of a popular three-volume commentary on the Bible, consisting of Luther's German translation plus copious annotations by Luther and himself.

See also Calixt, Georg; Gerhard, Johann; Lutheran Orthodoxy

Bibliography

Appold, K. *Abraham Calov's Doctrine of Vocatio in Its Systematic Context*. Mohr Siebeck, 1998; Jung, V. *Das Ganze der Heiligen Schrift: Hermeneutik und Schriftauslegung bei Abraham Calov*. Calwer, 1999; Preus, R. *The Theology of Post-Reformation Lutheranism*. Vol. 1. Concordia, 1970; Schmeling, T. "*Strenuus Christi Athleta*—Abraham Calov (1612–1686): Sainted Doctor and Defender of the Church." *Lutheran Synod Quarterly* 44 (2004): 357–99; Wallmann, J. "Calov, Abraham." *TRE* 7:563–68. De Gruyter, 1981.

ERIC LUND

Calvin, John

The French Reformed theologian John Calvin (1509–64) was pastor and moderator of Geneva's church from 1536. Calvin was born on July 10, 1509, in the cathedral city of Noyon, in the region of Picardy in northern France. His father, Gérard Calvin, a notary for the cathedral chapter, procured two church benefices that provided necessary support for his son to pursue his education in Paris beginning in 1523. After studying briefly at the Collège de la Marche, Calvin transferred to the more prestigious Collège de Montaigu, where he completed the arts curriculum in preparation for the study of theology and the priesthood. In 1528, however, this career path was dramatically altered when Gérard, embroiled in a conflict with the cathedral chapter, determined that his talented son should pursue a more lucrative career in law. Consequently, over the next three years, Calvin studied law at the Universities of Orléans (with the humanist law professor Andreas Alciati) and Bourges, where he became a partisan of French humanist culture, with its focus on achieving cultural renewal through the recovery of classical languages and texts, and the promotion of liberal learning and refined eloquence. Following his father's death in 1531, Calvin returned to Paris with his law license in hand and devoted himself to humanistic studies. He broadened his knowledge of classical literature and early Christian authors, studied the biblical languages of Greek and (probably) Hebrew, and published his first writing, a commentary on the Stoic philosopher Seneca's *Concerning Clemency* (1532). Also, he rubbed shoulders with reform-minded intellectuals in Paris, such as Nicolas Cop, who were reading and discussing the writings of Desiderius Erasmus and

Martin Luther. On November 1, 1533, Cop delivered an inflammatory speech as newly elected rector of the University of Paris, defending Evangelical teachings, including justification by faith "without the works of the law." In response, Catholic authorities tried to arrest not only Cop but also Calvin: both were forced to flee Paris.

Calvin provides few clues as to the precise date of his "sudden conversion" to the Evangelical faith, but it appears that by the summer of 1534 he was committed to the main teachings of the Protestant reformers. Calvin later reported that he was reading the writings of Luther at the time he began to extricate himself from the "darkness of the papacy" (CO 9:51). Calvin's new confessional loyalties placed him in a most dangerous position in the Catholic kingdom of France. In 1535 he found refuge in the Reformed city of Basel, where he completed the first edition of his *Institutes of the Christian Religion* (1536). Though Calvin did not mention Luther by name in this influential compendium of Reformation doctrine, the work borrowed extensively from Luther's theological writings, including his Small and Large Catechisms, *Babylonian Captivity of the Church*, *On Christian Liberty*, and *Two Sermons on the Supper*. To some extent, Calvin's *Institutes* also bore the imprint of the Protestant theologians Philip Melanchthon, Martin Bucer, and Ulrich (Huldrych) Zwingli.

In the summer of 1536, during a brief stopover in Geneva, Calvin was confronted by the fiery preacher Guillaume Farel, who demanded that the twenty-seven-year-old theologian remain in the city and serve the struggling church, which had embraced the Reformation only two months earlier. Calvin complied and soon was the city's chief pastor and theologian, responsible for constructing a new church order and writing a preliminary catechism. Calvin quickly forged ties with other Reformed leaders, such as Bucer in Strasbourg and Heinrich Bullinger in Zurich, with whom he shared letters and theological opinions. In a letter to Bucer in 1538, Calvin expressed his earliest recorded sentiments regarding Luther: though the German reformer was a godly man, he was too obstinate and abusive in defending his theological viewpoints; on several debated doctrines he was guilty of ignorance and gross delusion (CO 10.2:138–39).

Calvin's first tenure in Geneva was cut short when the city magistrates expelled the reformer in April 1538 for resisting their efforts to dictate religious policy in the church. At the invitation of Bucer, Calvin spent the next three years in "exile" in Strasbourg, serving as the pastor of the French refugee congregation. At the same time, he taught biblical exegesis at the city's academy; he set up a household with his new bride, Idelette de Bure; and he completed several important book projects, including expanded Latin and French editions of the *Institutes* (1539; 1541), a biblical commentary on Romans (1539), and a defense of the Genevan Reformation against the attacks of Cardinal Jacopo Sadoleto (1539). Also during this period the French reformer's attitude toward Luther significantly shifted. Calvin responded with almost childlike enthusiasm when, in 1539, he received word from Wittenberg that Luther held him in "great favor" and approved of his treatise against Sadoleto. Moreover, as Calvin participated in religious colloquies held at Frankfurt, Hagenau, Worms, and Ratisbon-Regensburg, where he met Melanchthon and other Lutheran theologians, he gained a more favorable opinion of the Wittenberg reformers and their theology. Hence, in the decades that followed, though Calvin sometimes criticized Luther's overbearing personality and his harsh attacks on the Swiss churches and their views on the Lord's Supper, he nevertheless considered Luther a "most respected father" and presented himself as Luther's faithful yet critical disciple (CO 12:8). Luther was "a gifted man," an "illustrious servant of God," a "faithful doctor of the church," and even "a remarkable apostle of Christ, through whose work and ministry . . . the purity of the gospel has been restored in our time" (CO 10.2:432; 11:774–75; 15:212–13; 6:250).

As the political and religious winds changed in Geneva, Calvin's talents were once again in demand. In September 1541 the French reformer returned to Geneva to resume pastoral ministry. Within several months, he had drafted a constitution and liturgy for the church and had started work on a new catechism. These documents accented such distinctive Reformed doctrines as the fourfold ministerial office (pastors, elders, deacons, professors), church discipline, the so-called third use of the law, God's sovereign predestination in salvation, and unadorned, Word-centered worship. In the decades that followed, Calvin continued to revise and expand his *Institutes* (the definitive Latin edition appeared in 1559), wrote more than thirty biblical commentaries, founded the Genevan Academy (1559), and engaged religious opponents at every turn. One of the reformer's central concerns was to pacify the theological conflict between the German Lutherans and the Swiss Reformed over the Lord's Supper by proposing a mediating view known as "real spiritual presence": through the ministry of the Holy Spirit, believers partaking of the sacrament are nourished on the real substance of Christ's body, which is located in heaven. Although Calvin insisted that his overall theological position was in agreement with Luther's (he had signed the Augsburg Confession Variata [Altered] at the Colloquy of Ratisbon in 1541 and agreed to the Wittenberg Concord of 1536), and although he maintained an extensive and friendly correspondence with Melanchthon during the 1540s and 1550s, nevertheless Luther and his followers continued to harbor suspicions that Calvin's position on the Lord's Supper did not differ significantly from Zwingli's memorial view. Consequently, when the Genevan reformer sent a packet of letters to Melanchthon in 1544 that contained Calvin's first and only letter addressed to Luther, Melanchthon pocketed the letter so as to avoid what he feared would be Luther's explosive reaction. Even so, Luther's sharp attacks on Swiss "Sacramentarians" did not lessen Calvin's respect for the German reformer: "I

often say," Calvin commented, "that even if [Luther] should call me a devil, I should still pay him the honor of acknowledging him as an illustrious servant of God, who yet, as he is rich in virtues, so also labors under serious faults" (CO 11:774–75).

Calvin's relationship with some Lutherans deteriorated further following Luther's death in 1546. The Consensus Tigurinus (1549), an accord between the churches of Zurich and Geneva on the doctrine of the Lord's Supper, appeared to justify Lutheran criticisms of Calvin's sacramental doctrine. Beginning in 1552, the Gnesio-Lutheran minister Joachim Westphal initiated a protracted pamphlet war against Calvin and the Consensus that not only reignited smoldering hostility between Lutherans and the Swiss Reformed, but also sharpened the divide between Melanchthon's allies and other Lutherans back in Germany. If this bitter conflict did nothing to promote unity between confessional groups, it did highlight Calvin's strong aversion to Lutheran views regarding the ubiquity of Christ and the sacramental eating of unbelievers (*manducatio indignorum*). From Calvin's perspective, Lutheran "monkeys" like Westphal, who mimicked Luther's vehemence, had departed from their founder's more moderate theological positions. In the midst of the crisis, Calvin moaned: "Oh, if only Luther was still alive!" (CO 15:501–2). Calvin's death on May 27, 1564, did nothing to diminish the climate of hostility created by the sacramental controversy, which continued to rage during the next decade. The doctrine of the Supper defended by Calvin and similar to the position of some of Melanchthon's students (the so-called crypto-Calvinists or crypto-Philippists) in Saxony was explicitly rejected in articles 7 and 8 of the Formula of Concord (1577). Though Calvin admired Luther as an illustrious teacher in Christ's church, Lutheran views of Calvin have been mixed.

See also Bucer, Martin; Bullinger, Heinrich; Calvinism as a Second Reformation; Geneva; Lord's Supper; Switzerland; Westphal, Joachim; Wittenberg Concord; Zwingli, Ulrich

Bibliography

Calvin, J. *Ioannis Calvini opera omnia quae supersunt* [CO]. Ed. G. Baum, E. Cunitz, and E. Reuss. 59 vols. C. A. Schwetschke, 1863–1900; Ganoczy, A. *The Young Calvin.* Trans. D. Foxgrover and W. Provo. Westminster, 1987; Gerrish, B. *The Old Protestantism and the New: Essays on the Reformation Heritage.* University of Chicago Press, 1982; Gordon, B. *Calvin.* Yale University Press, 2009; Linder, R. "The Early Calvinists and Martin Luther: A Study in Evangelical Solidarity." In *Regnum, Religio et Ratio,* ed. J. Friedman, 103–16. Sixteenth Century Journal, 1987; Neuser, W. H. "Calvin and Luther: Their Personal and Theological Relationship." *Hervormde teologiese studies* 38 (1982): 89–103; Selderhuis, H. *The Calvin Handbook.* Eerdmans, 2009; van't Spijker, W. *Luther en Calvijn: De invloed van Luther op Calvijn blijkens de Institutie.* Kok, 1985; Wendel, F. *Calvin: Origins and Development of His Religious Thought.* Trans. P. Mairet. Baker, 1997; Zeeden, W. "Das Bild Martin Luthers in den Briefen Calvins." *ARG* 49 (1958): 177–95.

Scott M. Manetsch

Calvinism as a Second Reformation

The Reformed faith never had a single individual who dominated the nature of theological and ecclesiastical discussion in the way in which Luther did for Lutherans. Even so, the term "Calvinism" was soon established in the mid- to late sixteenth century as a virtual synonym for Reformed theology and thereby created the impression that John Calvin was the dominant figure in the movement.

In fact, while Calvin was no doubt one of the most influential Reformed theologians both for his own and for subsequent generations, he was at best the first among equals, and "Calvinism" therefore needs to be understood as having broader, more eclectic origins. The fundamental break between Lutherans and Reformed occurred at Marburg in 1529, over the issue of Christ's presence in the Lord's Supper and the various christological issues that raised. Zwingli's denial of the direct communication of attributes between Christ's divine and human nature remained a hallmark of Reformed theology and was adopted by Calvin. Yet Calvin was never Zwinglian and argued for a view of the Lord's Supper that stressed a real though spiritual feeding on Christ in the sacrament and eschewed the language of mere memorialism, thus placing him closer to

Martin Bucer than to Zwingli or Oecolampadius. Nevertheless, while "Calvinism" and its cognates emerged as terms for the Reformed in the sixteenth century, it elided differences among the Reformed on the Lord's Supper by placing all under the Calvin label.

The 1560s were a particularly fertile period for the Reformed as they sought to define themselves confessionally against the background of a resurgent Roman Catholicism at the Council of Trent and the remaking of Europe after 1555. The Scots Confession (1560), the Thirty-Nine Articles (1563), the Heidelberg Catechism (1563), the Belgic Confession (1562), and the Second Helvetic Confession (1566)—these were the key documents that defined the major contours of confessional Reformed theology, and thus Calvinism, in the late sixteenth century.

Toward the end of the century, the Calvinist consensus on predestination and on the perseverance of the saints came under increasing pressure. In the Netherlands, Jacob Arminius rejected the supralapsarianism of his teacher, Theodore Beza, but disillusionment with classical Reformed predestinarianism was no Dutch monopoly. In England, Archbishop John Whitgift attempted to clarify and supplement the Thirty-Nine Articles with the Lambeth Articles of 1595. These made clear the teaching of predestination and perseverance but failed to meet with favor from Queen Elizabeth I and thus never attained confessional status. The complete text of the Lambeth Articles was then included in Archbishop Ussher's Irish Articles of 1615. This confession was a function both of the need to elaborate the doctrinal framework of Calvinist theology and of the Irish episcopal church's desire to assert some independence from its English counterpart.

As the Reformation was established across Europe, its very nature changed from a movement of protest and reform to a more stable form, something that affected both Lutherans and Calvinists. The term "Second Reformation" is sometimes used to designate significant developments based on the work of earlier

Protestant reformers or at other times to define attempts by Reformed (Calvinist) princes to move their territories from Lutheranism to Calvinism.

In Lutheran territories the Second Reformation received its most famous instantiation in Brandenburg. The Lutheran Reformation was initially established there by Elector Joachim II (1535–71) in a moderate form. Under his successor, John George (1571–98), and in the wake of the Formula of Concord, a more strictly confessional Lutheranism took hold. This began to slacken under his son, Joachim Frederick (1598–1608), when church services were simplified and shorn of certain perceived "Roman" elements, such as the elevation of the host. Under John Sigismund (who ruled from 1608–19) (and secretly converted to Calvinism in 1606), the process was completed when the elector took Communion according to the Reformed pattern on Christmas Day, 1613. The elector did not impose his new faith on his subjects but instead allowed for the peaceful coexistence of both Lutherans and Reformed.

In 1614 the elector published a confession of faith, the *Confessio Sigismundi*, which presented the turn to Calvinism as the logical conclusion of Lutheranism. Indeed, the Second Reformation in Brandenburg tended to minimize differences between Lutheran and Reformed on all issues but the communication of attributes, the Lord's Supper, and the precise significance of baptism. Thus the debates surrounding the Brandenburg Second Reformation tended to focus on the theology and liturgical actions involved in the sacraments. In addition, Reformed concerns about feast days, images, and crucifixes played into the interconfessional arguments.

The Brandenburg Second Reformation was both a reaction to the earlier, strict Lutheranism of John George and, in the issues on which it centered, reflective of the basic differences between Lutheran and Reformed theology and practice. The end result was the continuation of a more-or-less strict Lutheran territorial church under a Reformed princely family.

Reformation Protestantism in its Calvinist form shaped two other important and related historical phenomena: Puritanism and the Dutch Nadere Reformatie. Each is sometimes referred to as the Second Reformation. Early Reformed theology transformed the nature of church life and pastoral care. The working out of its theological and practical implications took place over many decades, and thus the work of later Reformed theologians marks a significant contribution to the Protestant understanding of theology, pastoral care, practical Christian living, and the relationship between each.

Puritanism was an English movement. Most Puritans were Reformed and Calvinistic in their theology. Two particular concerns shaped the movement. First, it desired to see a more thorough Reformation of the Church of England in accordance with the patterns established in Geneva and Zurich. This originated in the 1540s and 1550s when various exiles returned to England from the continent, bringing with them visions of reform shaped by time spent among the Reformed in Switzerland. The aesthetically moderate reformation of Thomas Cranmer was seen by such to be somewhat halfhearted.

The basic idea underlying Puritan worship was the Regulative Principle, adumbrated in the work of people such as John Hooper (ca. 1495–1555) and John Knox (ca. 1513–72), whereby that which was not prescribed in Scripture for worship was to be forbidden. This led to fierce debates over the legitimacy of kneeling at Communion and the wearing of clerical vestments in England in the 1560s. It also led to permanent suspicion between the Scottish kirk, which was Presbyterian and committed to the Regulative Principle, and the Church of England. This culminated in military conflict in the late 1630s, when the Crown tried to impose the English Prayer Book on the Scots. If debates over adiaphora in the Brandenburg Second Reformation had proved relatively peaceful, that was not the case in the English context.

Second, Calvinistic Puritanism gave birth to a strand of piety that stressed the practical and experiential aspects of Christianity in relation to such matters as the nature of Christian obedience to the law and assurance of salvation. These issues found their origins theologically in the Reformation teaching of justification by grace through faith and practically in the emphasis on the Word, read and preached, as the foundational element of the Christian life.

Confessionally, the Calvinistic Puritans' finest hour was the Westminster Assembly (1643–53). In the preceding century Calvinism had been significantly elaborated under the impact of broad theological polemics (with Roman Catholics, Lutherans, and then Socinians) and the exigencies of the university context. Westminster theology represented a synthesis of this Reformed Orthodoxy with the ecclesiological, pedagogical, and pastoral elements that typified the wider Puritan movement. The Westminster Assembly produced several documents intended to replace the Anglican settlement as embodied in the Book of Common Prayer, the Thirty-Nine Articles, and the First and Second Books of Homilies. The Assembly's Confession (1647), Larger and Shorter Catechisms (1647, 1648), and Directory of Public Worship (1645) offered a Calvinistic theology and a more rigorously Reformed and simplified aesthetic of worship.

While these documents laid the foundation for Scottish Presbyterianism, the Restoration of the English monarchy in 1660 paved the way for a reestablishment of Prayer Book Anglicanism and the radical exclusion of those of Calvinistic Puritan convictions from both the Anglican Church and the cultural and intellectual establishment. In the long term, this meant that Calvinism as a force in Britain was restricted almost entirely to English and Welsh nonconformity and Scottish Presbyterians.

The Second Reformation in the Low Countries took a path analogous to, but at points somewhat distinct from, Puritanism. The impact of the revisionist Reformed theology of Jacob Arminius and his followers, and the way in which this played into politics in the Dutch Republic, culminated in the work of the Synod of Dordrecht in 1618. The synod refuted Arminianism and proposed five doctrinal points in opposition to it, the so-called five points of Calvinism: total depravity, unconditional election, limited atonement, irresistible grace, and perseverance of the saints. Of these, limited atonement has proved typically the most contentious and indeed the most difficult to define with any precision.

The church life of the Dutch Nadere Reformatie after Dordrecht had many points of similarity with English Puritanism, in large part due to the substantial overlap of theology as indicated by the vibrant Anglo-Dutch book trade, of which a significant part was theological. The Dutch combined Reformed dogmatics with the same experiential concerns found among the English Puritans. Indeed, the works of such English writers as William Perkins and William Ames (1576–1633), who was himself a professor at Franeker, had a formative impact on Dutch church life and theology. Pastoral practice was also very similar: a focus on the preached Word, a form of public worship that was aesthetically very simple, and an emphasis on catechesis and family worship—all these marked the Dutch Nadere Reformatie.

Key figures in this Dutch movement included Gisbert Voetius (1589–1676) and Wilhelmus à Brakel (1635–1711), as well as the Scottish émigré Alexander Comrie (1708–74). In particular à Brakel captures the essence of much of the Nadere Reformatie: his *Redelijke Godsdienst* (The Christian's reasonable service) is a classic synthesis of doctrinal and practical theology that epitomizes the basic concerns of the Second Reformation.

Both Puritanism and the Dutch Nadere Reformatie ultimately collapsed in the wake of new philosophical paradigms emerging in the seventeenth century and the rise of critical biblical studies, both of which put strains on the formulations of classical orthodoxy. By the mid-eighteenth century, both streams had fallen into forms of rationalism tending to either Unitarianism or Pietism, which tended to eschew dogmatic concerns while continuing to accent the practical and experiential in a manner now detached from doctrine.

See also Adiaphora; Beza, Theodore; Calvin, John; England; Prussian Union; Zwingli, Ulrich

Bibliography

Beeke, J. R. *Assurance of Faith: Calvin, English Puritanism, and the Dutch Second Reformation*. Lang, 1991; Brienen, T., ed. *De Nadere Reformatie en het gereformeerd piëtisme*. Boekencentrum, 1989; Coffey, J., and P. H. C. Lim, eds. *The Cambridge Companion to Puritanism*. Cambridge University Press, 2008; Collinson, P. *The Elizabethan Puritan Movement*. Oxford University Press, 1967; Nischan, B. *Prince, People, and Confession: The Second Reformation in Brandenburg*. University of Pennsylvania Press, 1994.

CARL TRUEMAN

Cameroon

A nation on the west coast of Africa, Cameroon has been independent since 1960 after a colonial history that has included trading influence by the Portuguese and other Europeans from 1472, northern domination by the Fulani from 1809, and occupation by the Germans from 1884 and the French and English from 1919. In 1886 the German colonial authorities invited the Basel Mission to begin operations there. They took over work begun by English Baptists in 1845, which has matured into what today is the 700,000-member Presbyterian Church in Cameroon.

Cameroon is also currently home to three Lutheran churches. The largest of these is the Église Evangélique Luthérienne du Cameroun (EELC) with some 350,000 members nationwide. Its headquarters in north-central Ngaoundéré betokens the church's origins and historic strength in Adamaoua, North, and East provinces. Here the EELC began through the work of two mission societies, the American-based Sudan Mission (SM) from 1923, and the Norwegian Mission Society (NMS) from 1925. The SM began work in Mboula among the Gbaya-speaking people and soon extended this work to Meiganga and Mbéré to the east; Garoua Boulai, Bétaré Oya, and Abba

to the south; and Poli and eventually Tchollire to the north, where the market language was Fulfulde (Fulani). The NMS settled in Ngaoundéré, focusing initially on the Mboum-speaking people there and toward Tibati to the southwest, but soon diversifying to reach the Dii people around Mbé to the north, the Tikar toward Bankim and Banyo farther west and southwest, and the Wuté as far south as Yoko. The two missions cooperated as sisters in faith almost from the beginning, and a trajectory of steps toward independence through the 1950s led to one united church being formed in 1960 and to the continuing integration of institutions since then. These institutions include a seminary in Meiganga, a high school in Ngaoundéré, 4 Bible schools, 41 primary schools, 4 kindergartens, 3 hospitals, 4 health centers, 7 dispensaries, a leprosarium, 13 literature centers, a broadcasting studio, and a number of other projects. The church is served by 146 pastors ministering to 1,300 congregations in 10 regions and 46 districts. The first Cameroonian president of the church was Paul Darman (1963–66 and 1977–85), and presidents since then include Joseph Mekoudan (1966–77), Songsare Pierre (1975–97), Philémon Barya (1997–2000), Nyiwé Thomas (2000–2013), and Rubin Ngozo (2013–). It has been a Lutheran World Federation member since 1971.

The second of the three churches, the Église Fraternelle Luthérienne du Cameroun (EFLC), numbering 157,276 members, has its strength farther to the north, with headquarters in Garoua. The EFLC grew out of the work of missionaries of the Lutheran Brethren Church in the United States. Berge and Herborg Revne left the United States in 1918 but did not receive permission from their home church to begin work in Yagoua until 1923. That same year J. I. and Sophie Kaardal began work among the Mundang people across the Chad border in Lere. A first baptism occurred in 1927. Continued growth of the church led to independence from the mission in the early 1960s, and the departure of the last American Lutheran Brethren missionary in 1997. The two sister churches continue to cooperate in preparing pastors, missionaries, teachers, and leaders, notably in the area of outreach to Muslims. The EFLC maintains a hospital at Yagoua, a dispensary at Pouss, and a leprosarium at Kaélé. A teaching ministry includes six schools, a high school, and an agricultural school. A seminary at Kaélé is supplemented by four Bible schools and a special school focused on furthering Christian-Muslim relations, run in cooperation with the church service of the Netherlands. The EFLC has been a member of the Lutheran World Federation since 1992.

The most recently formed of the three is the Lutheran Church of Cameroon, which grew out of the Biafran War, when Lutheran Christians fled across the border from Nigeria. Appeals to the Wisconsin Evangelical Lutheran Synod (WELS) for help in education and organization eventually led to training seminars for church leaders during the 1980s and the formation of a seminary in Kumba, with a graduating class in 1999 of 16 pastors. These serve 4,358 baptized members in 34 LCC congregations and 7 preaching points stretching through the southwest and northwest provinces.

See also Darman, Paul; Gunderson, Adolphus; Sudan Mission

Bibliography

Dronen, T. *Communication and Conversion in Northern Cameroon: The Dii People and Norwegian Missionaries, 1934–1960.* Studies in Christian Mission. Brill, 2009; Lode, K. Appelés à la Liberté. IMPROCEP, 1990; Messina, J., and J. van Slageren. *Histoire du christianisme au Cameroun: Des origines à nos jours; Approache oecuménique.* Esp. 105–18. Clé, 2005.

MARK NYGARD

Campanius, Johan

The most famous of the six pastors who served the New Sweden Colony on the Delaware River (1638–55), Johan Campanius (1601–83) was born in Stockholm and is sometimes given the surname Holm in reference to his birthplace. He was ordained in 1633, accompanied a delegation to Russia, and was chaplain to the Stockholm Orphanage before being called to America. He arrived with Governor Johan Printz in 1643 and was placed at the new capital on Tinicum Island (Essington, Pennsylvania). He consecrated the first Lutheran church building in America there on September 4, 1646. When he returned to Sweden in 1648 and was senior pastor at Frösthult in Uppland, he completed a translation of Luther's Small Catechism into the Algonquian language. This was the first book published in an Indian language by any Protestant missionary and shows the close relationship that the Swedes and Finns enjoyed with the Lenape. It is notable for its understanding of Indian cultural norms and uses the Delaware trade jargon that was the common mode of speaking between Europeans and the Lenape. When the Church of Sweden renewed its mission on the Delaware, that translation of the Small Catechism was printed (1696) and sent over, where it had only limited usage.

Bibliography

Craig, P. S., and K.-E. Williams, eds. *Colonial Records of Swedish Churches in Pennsylvania.* Vol. 1, *The Log Churches at Tinicum Island and Wicaco, 1646–1696.* Swedish Colonial Society, 2006; Johnson, A. *The Swedish Settlements on the Delaware, 1638–1664.* Vol. 1. Lippincott, 1911; Norberg, O. *Svenska Kyrkans Mission vid Delaware i Nord-Amerika.* A. V. Carlson, 1893.

KIM-ERIC WILLIAMS

Campanus, Johannes

An early antitrinitarian in central Europe, Johannes Campanus (ca. 1500–after 1574) was born in Maaseik near Maastricht, attended school in Düsseldorf, and began his university studies in 1517 in Cologne. For reasons unknown, he was expelled from the university in 1520. He later worked in the duchy of Jülich. Having become a supporter of the Reformation in the mid-1520s, Campanus enrolled at Wittenberg University in 1528. As his understanding of the Eucharist was only unofficially given consideration by Luther during the Marburg Colloquy (1529) and he was not admitted to negotiations, he came into conflict with the theologians in Wittenberg. The final breakdown in relations occurred in 1530/31, when Campanus wrote several Latin tracts, which only survive in fragmentary form, critically discussing the divine personality of the Holy Spirit and the Augustinian concept of original sin; he sent these tracts to Philip Melanchthon and others. Consequently, Melanchthon encouraged Konrad Heresbach, a councillor at the court of Duke Johann III of Jülich-Cleves-Berg, to have Campanus arrested. In 1532 the duke issued an order for the arrest of Campanus, which was not carried out for several years.

After leaving Electoral Saxony, it seems that Campanus spent some time in Strasbourg before he returned to the Lower Rhine. His main work, *Göttlicher und heiliger Schrifft Restitution (Restitution of the Divine and Holy Scripture)*, was published in Strasbourg in 1532 and caused much controversy. In this publication, intended for interested laity, he argued in favor of the restoration of the original Christian faith untainted by subsequent dogmas. He introduced his concept of a ditheistic God, according to which there are only two persons in the eternal Godhead, God the Father and God the Son, the latter being subordinate to the former and having been begotten an eternity ago. In the early 1540s, Campanus corresponded with the southern German spiritualist Sebastian Franck. However, he also exchanged views with the Roman Catholic mediating theologian Johannes Gropper and with Hermann von Wied, the archbishop of Cologne and a supporter of the Reformation. Having been thrown into prison sometime between 1547 and 1555 by Duke Wilhelm of Cleves, Campanus spent the rest of his life in custody.

See also Antitrinitarians

Bibliography

McCormick, C. "The *Restitution göttlicher Schrifft* of John Campanus: An Interpretation and the Text." PhD diss., Harvard University, 1959; Trechsel, F. *Die protestantischen Antitrinitarier vor Faustus Socin*. Vol. 1, *Michael Servet und seine Vorgänger*. Winter, 1839; Weigelt, H. *Campanus, Johannes*. TRE 7 (1981): 601–4.

KĘSTUTIS DAUGIRDAS

Canada

Lutherans from Denmark and Norway first set foot on Canadian soil as early as 1619, when they undertook an exploratory voyage to find a northwest passage to facilitate trade with India. A decade later, a Lutheran chaplain accompanied a British military expedition as it took temporary possession of French Canada. When England established Halifax as a base for colonizing Nova Scotia in 1749, German Lutherans from London were among the early founders; with support from the British authorities, they built the first Lutheran church in Halifax in 1755. Soon thereafter Germans from the Continent, enlisted as colonists by the British (whose king, George II, was also the Duke of Braunschweig-Lüneburg [Hannover]), established the first enduring Lutheran congregation in the nearby colony of Lunenburg. To provide pastoral support for them, the Lutherans in Nova Scotia appealed unsuccessfully for help to the German court chaplain in London, Friedrich Ziegenhagen, who was part of the Pietists network in Halle, as well as to the British authorities. When the authorities could not find a German Lutheran pastor for Nova Scotia, they erroneously assumed that they would accept an Anglican pastor. Without a Lutheran pastor, the congregation in Halifax became Anglican. Meanwhile, the Society for the Propagation of the Gospel located Swedish-born Paul Bryzelius to serve the Lunenburg Lutherans. He had been a Moravian, then a Lutheran; before moving to Nova Scotia, he had gone to London to become ordained an Anglican. Although he had been endorsed both by Ziegenhagen in London and Mühlenberg in Pennsylvania, the Lunenburg Lutherans rejected him. Ultimately Friedrich Schultze, one of the Halle Pietists who had earlier moved to New York, became the first resident Lutheran pastor in the Lunenburg settlement. When the American Revolution occurred, Loyalists, who preferred to remain under the British monarchy, and German troops, who had fought for the British in the conflict, arrived in Canada. Some of the Loyalists had been Lutherans in New York. In Nova Scotia and in Upper Canada (Ontario), where they were settled in sufficient numbers, they organized congregations that survived for a time in spite of mission efforts from the Anglicans and frontier Methodism. A major struggle for the Lutheran Loyalists was the question of whether being loyal to the British Crown included becoming part of the established Anglican state church. As a result, most of these congregations eventually became Anglican.

Pastoral supply was a perpetual problem for Lutherans on the Canadian frontier, and the Lutheran pastors were often attracted by the more adequate salary from the Society for the Propagation of the Gospel if they changed allegiance to the Anglican Church. Since Pietism and rationalism had significantly blurred confessional boundaries and a network of revivalist preachers was able to reach most frontier communities, there was also a tendency for them to drift into Methodism. Subsequent immigration of Lutherans from Germany and from the United States occurred as new areas were opened up for settlements and as new land was made available in Canada. This movement of the western frontier into Canada further increased the Lutheran population. In Waterloo County, some Lutherans were initially attracted by Mennonite preachers and were rebaptized into that faith. By the mid-nineteenth century, however, several Lutheran synods from the United States, especially the Pittsburgh and New York Synods, began to send missionary pastors to German Lutheran communities in Ontario. This resulted in the birth of the Canada Synod in 1861. By this time competing missionaries from the Lutheran synods of Buffalo and Missouri had also begun to arrive to serve German Lutheran communities in Ontario. This resulted in competition for the mission field and theological conflict, which mirrored the scene in the United States. In 1879, the Missouri Synod created a Canada District with Adam Ernst, an initial signatory of the Missouri Synod, as president.

In terms of language, most Lutherans in Canada at the time were initially Germans. However, some Lutherans of the Canada Synod had begun to use English by this time, and this invariably involved them in movements, such as temperance and revivalism, which were affecting other Protestant denominations. Small settlements of Icelandic, Danish, and Norwegian Lutherans were also in evidence by 1867. With the transfer of the western prairie region to Canada in 1870, the number of Lutherans increased, and the ethnic nature of the Lutheran scene broadened as Icelanders, Norwegians, Swedes, Danes, and Finns arrived in large numbers both from the Midwest of the United States and from the various Scandinavian countries. Germans also came to western Canada from Ontario and the United States, although most of them originated in Austrian territories of eastern Europe and in Russia, to which Germans had emigrated in the eighteenth century. The Lutheran conflicts in the United States were also perpetuated in western Canada with intense rivalry for mission fields, especially between missionaries of the three German synods of Missouri, Ohio, and Canada. When World War I occurred, Lutherans in Canada were all integral parts of ethnic Lutheran bodies that had their headquarters and the bulk of their membership in the United States; a notable exception was the Icelandic Synod, which had its head office in Winnipeg. The differing attitudes toward the war in Canada and the United States before 1918 and the fact that Canada was at war three years before the United States raised the issue of a unique Canadian identity for Lutherans in Canada. Their ethnic identity made especially the German Lutherans suspect in the face of a pro-British, pro-English bias in Canada and led to Lutherans asserting their loyalty to their country and the British Crown. It also led Canadian Lutherans to distance themselves from positions taken by some of their American leaders. When the United States finally entered the war in 1917, the North American Lutheran bodies recognized the need to have a separate Canadian

Lutheran Commission for Soldiers' and Sailors' Welfare to give cooperative attention to war service in Canada. The strong dependence on leadership and financial support from the American part of the Lutheran church bodies continued after the war, notwithstanding that by the 1920s there were other signs of an incipient Canadian identity among Lutherans in Canada. General Council seminaries had come into being in Waterloo (1911) and Edmonton/Saskatoon (1913); Ohio and Missouri preparatory schools in Melville/Regina (1914) and Edmonton (1921); Norwegian and Swedish colleges in Camrose (1911), Outlook (1911), and Percival (1912). Following the war, new church structures emerged in Canada, largely reflecting similar developments in the United States. Yet, significantly, the Canada District of the Norwegian Lutheran Church of America incorporated as the Norwegian Lutheran Church of Canada with a number of unique powers. With the cessation of hostilities and the resumption of immigration, efforts were also made in Canada to have joint Lutheran responses to the needs of immigrants. Since this involved relationships with government and the railways, much of the leadership had to be Canadian. The Depression of the 1930s prompted the formation of a Bible school in Camrose (1932) and a further call by church leadership in Canada for greater cooperation in missions and theological education. In World War II, Lutherans in Canada were again involved in the war before the United States. Wartime regulations again required Canadian leadership and inter-Lutheran cooperation in serving military persons through the Canadian Lutheran Commission for War Service. The Missouri Synod had only an arm's-length relationship with the joint commissions during the two world wars, but following World War II, Canadian Lutheran World Relief was formed in 1946 with the full participation of Missouri Synod leaders in the United States. After the war non-Missouri Canadian Lutherans also had a voice in the activities of world Lutheranism through a national committee

of the Lutheran World Federation. Councils were eventually formed to promote a broader range of joint Lutheran activities: Canadian Lutheran Council (1952), without Missouri participation; and Lutheran Council in Canada (1967), including Missouri participation. By the 1960s most Canadian Lutherans were in three umbrella church bodies in Canada, with varied relationships and degrees of autonomy from their American mother churches: Lutheran Church–Canada; the Evangelical Lutheran Church of Canada; and the Lutheran Church in America–Canada Section. In view of the strong sentiment among many Canadian Lutherans that they could and should be united, the Evangelical Lutheran Church of Canada issued a formal invitation to the other two bodies in 1972 to enter into negotiations to form one indigenous Lutheran Church in Canada. Set into the context of a major theological conflict in the Missouri Synod, the three-way merger talks faltered on two related issues: the nature of the Holy Scriptures and the ordination of women to the pastoral office. Two-way talks, which followed without the formal participation of the Missouri Synod, brought together the other two bodies to form the Evangelical Lutheran Church in Canada in 1985. The Canadian contingent of the Missouri Synod also formed as an indigenous church body in Canada in 1989, using the name Lutheran Church–Canada. A number of smaller church bodies continued to exist or have come into being while the above major bodies have held the limelight: the Wisconsin Synod, the Canadian Association of Lutheran Congregations, the Lutheran Brethren, and most recently, the North American Lutheran Church.

See also American Lutheran Church (1930–60); American Lutheran Church (1960–88); Lutheran Church in America; Lutheran Church–Missouri Synod; United Lutheran Church in America

NORMAN J. THREINEN

Canon

The term "canon" (Greek: *kanōn*, "measuring rod," "rule," or "list") of the church refers to

Holy Scripture in two senses. The first refers to the determination or "list" of texts (in their original languages or in translations) that are inspired and therefore authoritative in the life of the church. This notion of canon is reflected in the most common translation of 2 Tim. 3:16, as in the NRSV (with emphasis added): "*All scripture is inspired* by God and is useful for teaching, for reproof, for correction, and for training in righteousness." A second sense of "rule" sometimes falls under the rubric of "canon within a canon," which refers to particular biblical texts that are privileged in one's theological community as well as the hermeneutical lens through which they are viewed. This understanding of canon is supported by the alternative translation tradition of 2 Tim. 3:16, as in the ASV: "*Every scripture inspired of God is also profitable* for teaching, for reproof, for correction, for instruction which is in righteousness." Both understandings of canon can be found in the Reformation discussions of the extent of the Bible's content as well as and role of Holy Scripture understood as the efficacious Word of God.

While much of contemporary Western Protestant Christendom has a de facto (if not de jure) canon of sixty-six books (thirty-nine in the Old Testament; twenty-seven in the New Testament), the extent of the canon has been much disputed in the history of Christianity. The canon of Jesus and the earliest followers of Christ was, of course, the Hebrew Scriptures (or Aramaic Targums). As the church moved into Greek-speaking environs, Scripture was the Septuagint, the Greek translation of the Hebrew texts to which some apocryphal books were added. The "Bible" of the Greek-speaking apostle Paul from Tarsus in Cilicia, therefore, as well as for most if not all of the New Testament theologians, was the Septuagint. Initially the scriptural texts of the followers of Jesus as well as wider Judaism were formatted in scrolls (e.g., as in the famous Dead Sea Scrolls). Once the newly innovated technology of the codex (a book with cut leaves) became known, the "book" became the preferred technology of

Scripture production in the early church as epitomized, for example, in the great fourth-century handwritten uncial manuscripts such as Sinaiticus and Vaticanus. This innovation in textual reproduction reified the notion of "canon." "Canon" became a "book" rather than a negotiated "list."

The composition dates of the books included in most modern editions of the New Testament published in the West—texts that biblical scholars came to identify in terms of the New Testament genres of Gospels, Acts of the Apostles, Epistles, and Apocalypse—range from about 48 CE (the earliest letters of Paul) to the end of the first century. The first listing of the twenty-seven books of the present New Testament (Greek) canon, however, was made in a festal letter of Athanasius, bishop of Alexandria, in 367 CE. Additional centuries would pass before the church settled on the "canon" suggested by Athanasius. Athanasius's articulation in the fourth century indicates that the canon was becoming formalized at the same point in time that the rule of faith emerged in the Apostles' and Nicene Creeds. This suggests that the process of canonization and that of the articulation of the "symbols" of the faith were related historical processes. In fact, the distinction between "biblical canon" and "creedal formulation" is not particularly helpful since the biblical canon enfolds confessions of various kinds. In the New Testament the earliest confession of belief may be *kyrios Iēsous*, "Jesus is Lord" (as in 1 Cor. 12:3), and the creed Paul inherited, recounted at 1 Cor. 15:1–3, emerged very soon after the church's experience of the cross and resurrection of Christ.

The early Reformation participated in the humanist *ad fontes* (back to the sources) movement of the wider Renaissance. In this cultural context the patristic discussions concerning the canonical status of individual books of the Bible were discovered and reevaluated. Two Greek terms from that earlier conversation became important with regard to New Testament texts—*homolegoumena* (universally accepted) and *antilegomena* (spoken against, disputed). Books of the early church fell into the category of "disputed" for their theological content (e.g., the Letter to the Hebrews' claim of the impossibility of a second repentance in 6:4–6; 10:26–31; 12:17), noncanonical intertextuality (e.g., Jude's and 2 Peter's reference to the *Enoch* literature and the *Assumption of Moses*), or questionable authorship. Among these were James, Jude, Hebrews, and the book of Revelation. When Luther published the German New Testament in 1522, these books were set apart at the end of the corpus and not indexed, a practice also followed in printings of the complete Bible. Also in the German Bible, the books of the Apocrypha (books found in the Septuagint but not in the Hebrew Masoretic Text) are included, though the Reformers did not count them as having the same authority as the other books of the Bible. While the Roman Catholic Church officially canonized the Jerome's Latin translation (Vulgate) and the Apocrypha at the Council of Trent (1546), no such official action was taken by Lutherans with respect to the delineation of the biblical canon. The humanist impetus also was reflected in the early Reformers' excitement over the rediscovery of Hebrew and Greek and their rapid growth to sophisticated understandings of the ancient languages. Luther and his Wittenberg colleagues worked from the original Hebrew and Greek as he translated the biblical texts for the German-speaking people. Melanchthon also was known for his philological skill in both languages (esp. Greek), skill even surpassing Luther's. Knowledge of Hebrew and Greek became a desideratum for those were charged with the exegesis and interpretation of biblical texts. In time, training in the original biblical languages became a requirement for word and sacrament ministries within many Lutheran Church bodies.

The publication of the German Bible, with its inclusion of the Apocrypha as well as the marginalization of the *antilegomena*, suggests that the early Reformers made various discriminations among the books within the "canon" as it was later accepted by Rome at Trent. Luther's understanding that "Christ" is the chief content of the inscripturated Word of God provides the theological apologetic for the hierarchy discerned in the canon. As Luther stated in his preface to the Epistles of James and Jude (1546), "All the genuine sacred books agree in this, that all of them preach and promote [*treiben*] Christ. And that is the true test by which to judge all books, when we see whether they promote Christ" (LW 35:396). Similarly, Melanchthon in the first systematic theology of the Reformation (*Loci communes*, 1521), which was derived from his lectures on Romans, declared, "To know Christ is to know his benefits." That is, the authority of the canon is tied to the effectiveness of the Word to create faith in the mercy of God. Using this criterion, Luther noted in his preface to the New Testament, "St. John's Gospel and his first epistle, St. Paul's Epistles, especially Romans, Galatians, and Ephesians, and St. Peter's First Epistle are the books that show you Christ and teach you all that is necessary and salvatory for you to know" (LW 35:362). Luther's understanding that the Word of God encounters the hearer as law and gospel suggests that the biblical "canon" is not only a "rule" by which to measure one's faith or the church's doctrine but is also the instrument God uses in a complex dialectic that includes the death of the sinner (law) and the creation of new life and faith (gospel).

In the seventeenth century, the Lutheran Orthodoxy that followed the time of Luther and Melanchthon continued to discuss the relation of the Old Testament Apocrypha to the "canon" of Scripture, as well as the status of the *antilegomena* in the New Testament (Schmid 80–91). The Old Testament Apocrypha, at best, was held to be of a certain theological value, though its text could not provide the foundation for any doctrine of the church. Distinctions similar to those noted by Luther among the New Testament's twenty-seven books were also acknowledged, though the "higher" principle of their inspiration trumped the early Luther's reservations about the theological reliability of some books of the New Testament (e.g., James). Quenstedt (1617–88) reflects this subtle but significant adjustment in saying, "We call those books of the New Testament protocanonical, or of the first rank, concerning whose authority and secondary [i.e., human] authors there never was any doubt in the Church; and those deuterocanonical or of the second rank, concerning whose secondary authors (not their authority, however) there were at times doubts entertained by some. . . . And these doubts had not reference so much to their divine authority or primary author, the Holy Spirit, as to their secondary authors" (Schmid 91). In time, this reasoning would effectively remove the intracanonical discriminations observed by the early Reformers so that the notions of verbal inspiration and, in particular, the inerrancy of all biblical texts (including for some even the vowel pointing of the Masoretic Text) came to dominate the theological ethos of Lutheran Scholasticism. With this epistemological shift, biblical texts came to function not only as the "canon" of texts through which the Word of God, experienced as law and gospel, "promoted Christ," but also as authoritative in all its claims. Quenstadt, again, speaks for this position: "The canonical Holy Scriptures in the original text are the infallible truth and free from every error, or in other words, in the canonical Holy Scriptures there is found no lie, no falsity, no error, whether in the things or in the words; but all things, and each single one, that are handed down in them are the most true whether they pertain to doctrine or morals or history, chronology, topography, or nomenclature; no ignorance, no thoughtlessness or forgetfulness, no lapse of memory, can or dare be ascribed to the amanuenses of the Holy Ghost in their penning of the sacred writing" (Pieper 223). With the rise of modern science and the increasing application of historical criticism on the biblical texts, this commitment to the inerrancy of the biblical canon in all matters of fact became increasingly problematic for some Lutherans. One response, often legitimated by a return to the statements of the early Luther, was to suggest that the Bible is infallible only with regard to issues related to salvation. In this revision of the dominant view in Lutheran Orthodoxy's understanding of inerrancy, the language of the Epitome of the Formula of Concord (Ep/SD 1.7) is understood to pertain only to matters of salvation: "Holy Scripture alone remains the only judge, rule, and guiding principle, according to which, as the only touchstone, all teachings should and must be recognized and judged, whether they are good or evil, correct or incorrect." Henry Eyster Jacobs, for instance, using an analogy based in Chalcedonian confession of the full humanity as well as the full divinity of Christ, would say in 1898:

> The human element in Scripture reminds us of the human nature of Christ during the State of Humiliation. As Christ, in His humanity, refrained from the full use of the attributes communicated through its union with the divine nature, and thus shared in all the sinless weaknesses of humanity; so the Holy Spirit, in making the sacred writers infallible recorders of the hitherto unknown will of God towards men, in no way inspired them to be teachers of astronomy, or geology, or physics. These spheres do not belong to revelation. It is enough for us to know that, on these subjects, they had in the fullest extent the ordinary assistance granted believers even now, when, praying for the Spirit's guidance, they use earthly things in the service of the truth as it is in Jesus. No number of contradictions, that could be gathered within this sphere, would in the least degree shake our confidence in the absolute authority of Holy Scripture as the infallible test of theological truth, an inerrant guide in all matters of faith and practice. If it be fallible, then the very end for which a record of revelation has been provided, is defeated. (Jacobs 28–29)

See also Apocrypha and Pseudepigrapha; Bible Interpretation; Scripture; Word of God

Bibliography

Jacobs, H. E. *Elements of Religion*. General Council of the Evangelical Lutheran Church in North America, 1898; Krodel, G. "New Testament Canon." In *Encyclopedia of the Lutheran Church*, ed. J. Bodensieck, 3:1732–43. Augsburg, 1965; Pelikan, J. *The Reformation of the Bible: The Bible of the Reformation*. Catalog of the Exhibition, by V. R. Hotchkill and D. Price. Yale University Press, 1996; Pieper, F. *Christian Dogmatics*. Vol. 1. Concordia, 1950; Rasmussen, T. "The Biblical Canon of the Lutheran Reformation." In *Canon and Canonicity: The Formation and Use of Scripture*, ed. E. Thomassen, 141–58. Museum Tusculanum, 2010; Schmid, H. *The Doctrinal Theology of the Evangelical Lutheran Church*. Ed. C. A Hay and H. E. Jacobs. 3rd ed. 1899. Augsburg, 1961.

ERIK M. HEEN

Catechisms

A catechism is a short summary of the Christian faith, designed for basic instruction. Luther's Small Catechism has definitively shaped Lutherans for centuries. Luther adapted the catechetical form to the needs of his movement and provided simple and clear explanations of Evangelical insights in his Small Catechism.

"Catechism" traditionally had several meanings: a course of instruction in the Christian faith, the content of that instruction, and a written text that contains that content. In the early church, instruction in the basics of the faith (catechesis) and knowledge of those basics were prerequisites for baptism. Later, catechisms were used to instruct those baptized as children and prepare them for confirmation and/or reception of the Lord's Supper. The Apostles' Creed and the Lord's Prayer were used since the early centuries in such instruction. In the high and late Middle Ages, catechisms expanded in content and use. Considered an aid to the sacrament of penance, they came to include the Ten Commandments and other devices to help identify sins.

Martin Luther (1483–1545), beholden to late-medieval models, began preaching on parts of the catechism early; he published sermons on the Ten Commandments, the Apostles' Creed, the Lord's Prayer, penance, baptism, and the Lord's Supper, all before 1520. Some regard his *Betbuchlein* (*Little Prayer Book*, 1522) as an early catechism. Luther hoped that someone would supply his movement with a catechism. In the introduction to the *Deutsche Messe* (German Mass, 1526), Luther mentions his *Little Prayer Book* and notes the need for a good catechism. Some of his followers tried to write catechisms during the 1520s; none achieved wide resonance and lasting effect. Luther was finally prompted to write his catechisms by a series of events in the mid- to late 1520s. His participation in the visitations of parishes around Wittenberg in rural Saxony, 1527–28, convinced him that laypeople and pastors were ignorant of the basics of the Christian faith. A dispute among Wittenberg theologians posed questions concerning law and repentance that recurred among Luther's followers. Luther had to preach on the catechism three times in 1528. In Wittenberg the custom was to preach through the catechism four times annually. In 1528 Johannes Bugenhagen, who usually did such preaching, was away and the task fell to Luther. He used materials from his sermons in his Small Catechism and his Large Catechism, both published in early 1529. The Small Catechism was intended to provide basic instruction. The Large Catechism was for all Christians, and particularly for clergy, who wished to explore such topics in greater depth.

Luther used a simple question-and-answer format, arranging and explaining traditional catechetical elements in new ways. His catechisms organized the parts in this order: the Ten Commandments, the Apostles' Creed, the Lord's Prayer, baptism, and the Lord's Supper. Shortly after initial publication, he inserted a section on confession between baptism and the Lord's Supper. His ordering of the chief parts differed from that of medieval catechisms. The Ten Commandments summarized God's law and were God's gift and demand for all people. Thus Luther placed them first. Luther made clear that the commandments mandated what to do as well as what to avoid. Luther thought that God's work as expressed in the Apostles' Creed encompassed God's three basic moves—creation, redemption, and sanctification—rather than the twelve parts used in medieval catechisms. Creedal explanations became a personal statement of faith—what God has done "for me"—rather than a general statement of facts about God. Luther saw prayer as response to what God has done for us and placed the Lord's Prayer after the Apostles' Creed. We pray for faith and the fulfillment of the Ten Commandments. Luther had no catechetical section titled "sacraments" but rather sections on baptism and the Lord's Supper, in which he emphasized the benefits of each. The section on confession provided a simple rite and emphasized the work of absolution rather than the work of confession. Luther also included morning, evening, and table prayers, and a *Haustafel* (table of duties, or household chart of Bible passages) that used biblical passages to define callings in government, church, and household. Many editions of the Small Catechism also included his marriage booklet (*Traubüchlein*) and his baptismal booklet (*Taufbüchlein*).

Luther's Small Catechism appeared as a poster and as a pamphlet. Hymnals, prayer books, and even Bibles included it. A variety of forms furthered catechetical instruction, including catechetical hymns and sermons and prayers focused around parts of the catechism. The catechism was taught in several settings, including worship services, schools, homes, and the pastor's study. In Luther's time, a significant number of those learning the catechism were illiterate. Therefore instruction was oral and used frequent repetition to impress the text on the learner. Memorization was required, with the expectation that it would produce a deep, active engagement with the Christian faith rather than surface, parrot-like recitation of catechetical content. Pictures of Bible stories were used to illustrate the various parts of each section of the catechism and to aid instruction.

Luther's Small Catechism was a great publishing success. After declining in popularity after Luther's death (1546), the Small Catechism again became important for Lutheran practice in the 1570s and was included, along with the Large Catechism, in the Book of Concord. Many church and school ordinances mandated its use. Translations accompanied and/or spurred the spread of Luther's reform in Scandinavia and Eastern Europe. As it was reprinted and/or translated for different contexts, Luther's Small Catechism was often supplemented and expanded, most often with Bible verses and additional questions and explanations.

The success of Luther's catechisms did not discourage other followers of Luther from writing catechisms. Dozens were produced in the sixteenth century; they evidence that the search for appropriate catechetical materials continued. Johannes Brenz, the reformer of Schwäbisch-Hall and later of Württemberg, produced an often-reprinted catechism. Catechetical sermons were popular and frequently printed in sixteenth-century Germany.

For several reasons Lutheran reformers thought both laity and clergy should study and learn the catechism, which was a summary of and introduction to Scripture. Luther believed that the "total content of Scripture and preaching and everything a Christian needs to know is quite fully and adequately comprehended in [the Ten Commandments, Apostles' Creed, and Lord's Prayer]" (LW 43:13). By focusing on the central salvific message, the catechism provides a guide for reading Scripture. Luther thought that the catechism was the identifying mark of the Christian. He compared Christians who do not know the catechism to artisans who do not know their craft (LC, Preface, 2 in *BC* 383). Just as a craftsperson's knowledge defines their existence, so too the catechism defines and shapes the life of Christians. The catechism was also a weapon in the ongoing fight against sin, the devil, and heretics. It was a useful summary of doctrine and a measure for judging other teachings. Knowing the catechism empowered people to distinguish between true and false teaching, to judge what was being preached and taught to them. By enabling laity to judge preaching and teaching, it gave them the tools to perform a task traditionally assigned only to hierarchical church structures.

Luther's catechism and the Lutheran emphasis on catechesis had profound resonances in Europe. His catechism influenced both the form and content of subsequent catechisms. While his use of the question-and-answer format was not revolutionary or unique, it set a pattern for later catechisms. Lutheran emphasis on systematic instruction of laity helped produce a similar emphasis in other confessions. The Heidelberg Catechism, first published in 1563, became important in German, Hungarian, and Dutch Reformed churches. Of lasting significance in England was the catechism included in the Book of Common Prayer (1549). For Reformed Christians in the English-speaking world, the Westminster Shorter Catechism (1648) was most significant. It defined the Presbyterian tradition and was influential in North America. Peter Canisius (1521–97), a Dutch Jesuit working in Bavaria, produced three catechisms designed to counter the influence of Luther's catechisms.

Some scholars have claimed, largely on the basis of reports by official visitors of Lutheran churches, that German Lutheran catechetical efforts in the Reformation era, though extensive and well organized, were failures, with both knowledge of the faith and conduct of life falling far short of what the catechisms intended for the laity. Others have argued that laypeople did learn their catechism and were able to explain, defend, and be consoled by that faith. Much depends on how "success" and "failure" are measured. While most agree that catechisms did not measurably improve moral behavior, they continue to disagree on whether catechisms actually produced a knowledgeable and faithful laity.

Luther's catechisms were recognized as formal doctrinal standards for Lutheran churches. During the period known as Lutheran Orthodoxy, Lutherans produced many expanded catechisms, some featuring more detailed discussion of doctrinal topics and some adding topics not treated by Luther. Sometimes Luther's catechism was modified in response to Reformed and Roman Catholic alternatives. Pietists used catechisms in their efforts to produce a warm, lay-oriented Christianity. Particularly the work of Conrad Dietrich (1575–1639), professor in Giessen and superintendent in Ulm, shaped later instruction in both Germany and North America. His textbook for catechesis at the university level and his primers for learning the catechism at the primary and secondary level applied Luther's texts to his day. Philipp Jakob Spener (1635–1705) published his *Einfältige Erklärung der christlichen Lehr: Nach der Ordnung des kleinen Catechismi des theuren Manns Gottes Lutheri* (Simple explanation of the Christian faith: According to the order of the Small Catechism of the worthy man of God Luther) in 1677. At 1,283 questions and answers, this was not a simplification of Luther. To aid its use, Spener produced catechetical tables (in 1683) that divided the material into ninety-five parts. Erik Pontoppidan (1698–1764), Danish Pietist leader, modeled his catechism on Spener's. First published in Copenhagen in 1737 as *Sandhed til Gudfrygtighed* (Truth unto godliness), it contained 759 questions, was popular in Denmark and Norway, and came to North America with Scandinavian immigrants in the mid-nineteenth century.

The European Enlightenment produced catechisms reflecting its theological directions. These catechisms had little lasting impact: Christians tended to return to catechisms from the sixteenth and seventeenth centuries. The nineteenth and twentieth centuries did not see the emergence of major new influential catechisms in Western Christianity but rather a revival of earlier catechisms. Among Lutherans, Luther's Small Catechism continued to be used, often in edited and expanded forms.

Catechization was an important part of European mission to other parts of the world. European catechisms were translated into non-European languages. Sometimes new catechisms were composed to meet the challenges of a particular context. From 1642 to 1646 the Swedish pastor Johann Campanius (1601–83) worked in New Sweden, the Swedish colony in the Delaware River valley of North America. He translated Luther's Small Catechism into the Algonquian language of the Delaware tribe. (This was the first European attempt to put a Native North American language into writing.) Bartholomäus Ziegenbalg (1683–1719) patterned the Tamil catechism after Luther's Small Catechism, and in mission churches throughout the world translations have served instruction in the faith.

Luther's Small Catechism conveyed the basics of the faith in a simple and easily understandable fashion. It avoided bitter polemics and overt attacks found in some types of religious literature. It has shaped the lives and memories of Lutherans and has had influence beyond the religious realm. It continues to provide a summary of Lutheran beliefs, suitable to use for instructing newcomers in the faith, whether young or old. By offering a simple yet profound introduction to the Christian faith, it encourages thoughtful engagement in that faith.

See also Lutheran Education

Bibliography

Arand, C. P. *That I May Be His Own: An Overview of Luther's Catechisms.* Concordia, 2000; Bode, G. "Conrad Dietrich (1575–1639) and the Instruction of Luther's Small Catechism." PhD diss., Concordia Seminary, St. Louis, 2005; Bode, G. "Instruction of the Christian Faith by Lutherans after Luther." In *Lutheran Ecclesiastical Culture, 1550–1675,* ed. R. Kolb, 159–204. Brill, 2008; Brecht, M. "Philipp Jakob Spener, sein Programm und dessen Auswirkungen." In *Geschichte des Pietismus,* vol. 1, *Das 17. und frühe 18. Jahrhundert,* ed. M. Brecht. Vandenhoeck & Ruprecht, 1993; Brown, C. B. "Devotional Life in Hymns, Music, Liturgy, and Prayer." In *Lutheran Ecclesiastical Culture, 1550–1675,* ed. R. Kolb, 205–58. Brill, 2008; Cohrs, F. *Die evangelischen Katechismusversuche vor Luthers Enchiridion.* 4 vols. Hofmann, 1900–1902; Collijn, I. "The Swedish-Indian Catechism: Some Notes." *LQ,* NS 2 (1988): 89–98; Haemig, M. J. "Laypeople as Overseers of the Faith: A Reformation Proposal." *Trinity Seminary Review* 27 (2006): 21–27; Haemig, M. J. "The Living Voice of the Catechism: German Lutheran Catechetical Preaching 1530–1580." ThD diss., Harvard University, 1996; Kittelson, J. M. "Successes and Failure in the German Reformation: The Report from Strasbourg." *ARG* 73 (1982): 153–75; Kolb, R., and T. Wengert, eds. *The Book of Concord: The Confessions of the Evangelical Lutheran Church.* Fortress, 2000; Peters, A. *Kommentar zu Luthers Katechismen.* 5 vols. Vandenhoeck & Ruprecht, 1990–94. ET, *Commentary on Luther's Catechisms.* 5 vols. Concordia, 2009–13; Reu, J. M. *Quellen zur Geschichte des kirchlichen Unterrichts in der evangelischen Kirche Deutschlands zwischen 1530 und 1600.* 9 vols. G. Mohn, 1904–35. Reprint, Olms, 1976; Weismann, C. *Die Katechismen des Johannes Brenz.* Vol. 1, *Die Entstehungs-, Text- und Wirkungsgeschichte.* De Gruyter, 1990; Wengert, T. J. *Martin Luther's Catechisms: Forming the Faith.* Fortress, 2009.

MARY JANE HAEMIG

Catholicism

With 1.25 billion members, the Roman Catholic Church is the largest Christian denomination in the world. Roman Catholics consider the bishop of Rome to be the leader of the universal church and claim that their church is the true universal (i.e., catholic, from the Greek *katholikos*) church of Jesus Christ, even though they acknowledge that other churches, such as the Orthodox, have apostolic origins and so have the universal doctrines and practices established by Jesus. Vatican II Council's references to "separated brothers and sisters" (rather than errant children) indicate a renewed openness to conversations with Protestants as well.

The relationship between Lutherans and Roman Catholics is complex and subject to developing theological concerns. Since Luther's reform, Lutherans have often claimed to hold the purest elements of the Western catholic tradition. Hence the evaluation of Roman Catholicism from a Lutheran perspective is best told not as a rejection of Catholicism per se. Rather, the Lutheran confessions endeavor to show that Lutherans neither depart from the essential elements of the Catholic faith nor introduce anything new to their doctrines and practice. Thus Lutheranism defines itself in continuity with the one, holy, catholic, and apostolic church (see, e.g., CA 20 and the "Conclusion to Part One" of the CA in *BC* 52–60) and has argued to retain the doctrines and practices of this tradition that affirm the person and work of Jesus Christ. Attempts to reform Lutheranism (e.g., Friedrich Schleiermacher, Samuel Simon Schmucker, and Albrecht Ritschl) by removing its more explicitly Catholic doctrines and practices (e.g., baptismal regeneration, sacramental realism, understanding of the ordained office and the visible nature of the church, the authority of those with oversight to judge doctrine, use of the liturgical calendar and traditional vestments, etc.) have met with strong (though not universal) opposition.

Thus, theologically speaking, Lutheranism has not been anti-Catholic so much as anti-Roman. The polemical edge of Lutheranism has been to charge Roman Catholicism with deviation from this shared catholic tradition. In subsequent centuries, however, Lutherans also participated in a wider, social, and political anti-Catholicism (e.g., nineteenth-century Germany's *Kulturkampf* or the anti-immigrant sentiment in the United States of the same century). Yet, more recently, with the revival of interest in early Christian sources, liturgical renewal, the Luther Renaissance, and ecumenical perspectives, an awareness of how much is shared in doctrine and practice by Lutherans and Roman Catholics has given birth to a renewed appreciation between them. In the midst of these significant acknowledgments, however, doctrines unique to the Roman Catholic Church remain problematic for Lutherans; likewise, certain realities within Lutheranism (such as the ordination of women, latent congregationalism, and lack of a universal magisterial authority) cause deep concern for the Roman Catholic Church.

The Council of Trent. In response to the Protestant Reformation, the Council of Trent met over four periods between 1545 and 1563 and provided a definitive reaffirmation of Roman Catholic doctrine. It was held in part to placate Lutheran appeals (since the Leipzig Disputation of 1519 and often repeated) for a free and general council to address necessary reforms in the church.

Responsive to Protestant challenges, such as prohibition against the sale of indulgences,

Trent was a reform council in its own right; it can be characterized as a phenomenon of the Reform Catholic movement as much as a Counter-Reformation response. Decrees most pertinent to Lutheran concerns come from sessions 4 (Scripture and tradition, 1546), 5 (original sin, 1546), 6 (justification, 1547), 13 (the Eucharist, 1551), 21 (the reception of the Eucharist, 1562), and 22 (the sacrifice of the Mass, 1562). Some of these decrees, notably on justification, condemned positions (esp. of medieval nominalists) to which the reformers also had objected. In addition to the clarity of the canons related to doctrine and practice, the council's work ushered in several significant realities of Roman Catholic life, including an official catechism (1566), the Roman Breviary (1568), and the Roman Missal (1572), as well as sodalities and seminaries for the moral support and education of the clergy and new religious orders, such as the Society of Jesus/Jesuits, the Congregation of Clerics Regular of the Divine Providence/Theatines, and Ursulines.

In preparation for the Council of Trent (which Lutherans were initially ready to attend), Lutherans crafted two confessional documents, the Smalcald Articles and the *Treatise on the Power and Primacy of the Pope.* Likewise, when the third meeting was called in 1551 and it again seemed as though Lutherans might be present, two other significant theological works were prepared to reflect consensus: Melanchthon wrote the Saxon Confession, and Johannes Brenz wrote the Württemberg Confession. Although Lutheran theologians were not present at the Council of Trent, thinkers such as Martin Chemnitz continued the earlier critique that Rome had deviated from the catholic tradition.

In the twentieth century, work on comparing the decrees of Trent to actual Lutheran doctrines raised questions about how well the fathers of the council understood Lutheran thought (as opposed to caricatures). The result was an ecumenical discussion about whether the condemnations of the sixteenth century (esp. on the doctrine of justification) from both sides were indeed correctly framed and relevant. That discussion eventuated in producing the Joint Declaration on the Doctrine of Justification.

The First Vatican Council and Papal Infallibility; Marian Dogmas. The next major development in doctrine unique to Roman Catholicism occurred at the First Vatican Council (1869–70). The first dogmatic constitution (i.e., official, binding church teaching) was *Dei Filius* (1870), which discussed God, creation, revelation, and reason. The other dogmatic constitution was *Pastor Aeternus* (1870), which established the doctrine of papal infallibility. This document builds on previous assertions (i.e., the primacy of Peter, the continuation of Peter's primacy in the bishops of Rome, and the primacy of the bishop of Rome over all other bishops) to conclude that the pope, as bishop of Rome, may exercise supreme and infallible teaching authority (*magisterium*) on matters of faith and morals for the good of the whole church.

Although the document asserts emphatically that such teaching authority has always existed in the church and has been universally (if not explicitly) recognized, a few bishops only hesitantly accepted the doctrine, mainly because they believed it was an inopportune time for its promulgation (e.g., John Henry Newman). Proponents of the doctrine see papal infallibility as a gift to the whole church and as a necessary affirmation of faith in the promise of Christ fulfilled in and through the Holy Spirit. The doctrine is also generally misunderstood as giving the pope power to create doctrine or speak authoritatively on any matter. Rather, the conclusion of *Pastor Aeternus* makes clear that the bishop of Rome is able to speak infallibly only when he speaks *ex cathedra* (that is, in his official capacity as shepherd and teacher) on matters of faith and morals. Moreover, he exercises this authority in relation to the college of bishops, which he is neither subject to nor separate from, and out of the tradition of his predecessors.

To date, however, papal infallibility has been definitively invoked twice: once for the immaculate conception of Mary (that, through grace, Mary was preserved from the stain of original sin at the moment of her conception; *Ineffabilis Deus*, 1854) and again for the assumption of Mary (that Mary was assumed bodily into heaven at the end of her earthly life; *Munificentissimus Deus*, 1950). The Lutheran confessions maintain the traditional christological titles for Mary (e.g., Theotokos) and do not dispute the question of her perpetual virginity. Likewise, Lutherans retained the (biblical) Marian feast days of the Annunciation, the Purification of Mary, and the Visitation. However, since both Marian dogmas reflect specifically post-Reformation Roman Catholic piety and are affirmed by a unique Roman Catholic understanding of the papal office, they have no significance in Lutheranism.

The Second Vatican Council. The Second Vatican Council met in 1962–65, with Orthodox and Protestant observers present throughout the proceedings. The constitutions of the council are nuanced and complex documents that should be read in relation to each other and to previous councils. The first constitution was *Sacrosanctum Concilium* (*Constitution on the Sacred Liturgy*, December 4, 1963); it encouraged more active participation from the laity in the Mass, emphasized the role of Scripture in worship, and encouraged more use of the vernacular without abandoning the Latin language. The second was *Lumen Gentium* (*Dogmatic Constitution on the Church*, November 21, 1964); it defines the church as the "people of God," emphasizes the "priesthood of the faithful" without demoting the unique and particular ordained priesthood, and discusses the Virgin Mary within the context of the church as the first and model Christian. The third was *Dei Verbum* (*Dogmatic Constitution on Divine Revelation*, November 18, 1965); it affirms that sacred Scripture is the inspired Word of God, that the church affirms the role of tradition in guiding the interpretation of Scripture, that Scripture is both transcendent and rooted in historical time, and that Christians should dedicate themselves to the reading and study of Scripture. This solidified the Roman Catholic openness to historical-critical approaches to Scripture. The fourth was *Gaudium et Spes* (*Pastoral Constitution on the Church in the Modern World*, December 7, 1965); it both reasserts and reimagines the role of the church in the modern world, that the church (hierarchy and laity) must be engaged with the realities and crises of the world and in dialogue with all aspects of human knowledge in the pursuit of solutions to these problems.

The two remaining decrees address the Roman Catholic Church's relationship to other churches, *Unitatis Redintegratio* (*Decree on Ecumenism*, 1964) and *Orientalium Ecclesiarum* (*Decree on the Catholic Eastern Churches*, 1965). The latter clarifies the relationship between the Eastern rite Catholic churches in union with Rome, affirming unity without requiring uniformity. *Unitatis Redintegratio* outlines the principles of Roman Catholic efforts toward Christian unity. The document acknowledges that the division among Christians is a scandal that contradicts the will of Christ. It ranks various Christians according to the seriousness of division from the hierarchy of truths affirmed by the Catholic Church but who, nonetheless, share a "real but imperfect union" through the sacrament of baptism. The "separated church and communities" and "separated brethren" are deficient in some respects but "have been by no means deprived of significance and importance in the mystery of salvation."

The council concluded with three declarations: *Dignitatis Humanae* (*Declaration on Religious Liberty*), *Nostra Aetate* (*Declaration on the Relation of the Church to Non-Christian Religions*), and *Gravissimum Educationis* (*Decree on Christian Education*). The first two are particularly noteworthy. *Dignitatis Humanae* reframes the Roman Catholic Church's affirmation of religious liberty in light of the modern world (with the rise of secular and pluralistic societies as the norm) while retaining the fundamental claim that the Roman Catholic Church is the true church

and true protector of religious freedom and individual conscience (which are grounded in God's grace). Nonetheless, the document forbids coercion in religious matters. *Nostra Aetate* outlines the church's relationship to other religions. Without reducing the significant divisions between Christianity and other religions, the council states, "The Catholic Church rejects nothing that is true and holy in these religions," and then names positive elements in major religious traditions.

Ecumenical Dialogue and Joint Declaration on the Doctrine of Justification. Overcoming the centuries-long division with the Orthodox was (and remains) the primary ecumenical concern of the Roman Catholic Church. Even so, Lutheran ecumenical dialogue with Roman Catholics began in earnest after the Second Vatican Council, although the council was not the exclusive cause. Even before the council, the previously mentioned liturgical renewal movement and Luther Renaissance (with significant contributions from Roman Catholic scholars such as Joseph Lortz, Peter Manns, and Erwin Iserloh) helped create a confluence of interest and mutual appreciation. Moreover, intra-Lutheran dialogue and consolidation sparked an interest in the possibility of dialogue to reach reconciled diversity and institutional unity. The first official dialogue in the United States began in 1965 between the US Conference of Catholic Bishops and the National Lutheran Council. The US dialogue (which included the predecessor bodies of the ELCA and, up until round 11, the LCMS) has produced eleven volumes of reports on various topics. On the international level, a Joint Lutheran–Roman Catholic Study Commission was established in 1967 by the Lutheran World Federation and the Pontifical Council for Promoting Christian Unity. Likewise, this working group has produced eleven volumes outlining consensus and divergence.

A monumental movement in redefining Lutheran–Roman Catholic relations occurred in 1999 with the signing of the Joint Declaration on the Doctrine of Justification

(JDDJ) by representatives of the LWF and the Roman Catholic Church. The JDDJ stands as a monument in ecumenical dialogue. The general conclusions of the document—that Roman Catholic and Lutheran teachings about justification are not mutually exclusive—were formed in a long process of ecumenical dialogue and scholarship and were then received and affirmed by the members of the LWF and the Vatican's Pontifical Council for Promoting Christian Unity. Though not universally celebrated (critics argue either that neither side changed its position or that the JDDJ represents an abandonment of Lutheran doctrine), the document is a model of reconciled diversity, especially with subsequent acceptance by other communions of churches. Both sides mutually affirm core theological principles while also offering cautions about the real or perceived extremes on either side. The JDDJ became both the means and the pattern for subsequent ecumenical agreements.

See also Cajetan (Thomaso de Vio); Ecumenical Dialogues; Smalcald Articles; *Treatise on the Power and Primacy of the Pope*

Bibliography

Cunningham, L. S. *An Introduction to Catholicism*. Cambridge University Press, 2009; Hahnenberg, E. P. *A Concise Guide to the Documents of Vatican II*. St. Anthony Messenger Press, 2007; Kelly, J. F. *The Ecumenical Councils of the Catholic Church: A History*. Liturgical Press, 2009; Lutheran World Federation and the Roman Catholic Church. *Joint Declaration on the Doctrine of Justification*. Eerdmans, 1999; O'Malley, J. W. *Trent and All That: Renaming Catholicism in the Early Modern Era*. Harvard University Press, 2002; O'Malley, J. W. *What Happened at Vatican II*. Harvard University Press, 2008; Steimer, B., and M. G. Parker, eds. *Dictionary of Popes and the Papacy*. Trans. B. McNeil and P. Heinigg. Crossroad, 2001; Tanner, N. *Vatican II: The Essential Texts*. Image, 2012.

H. ASHLEY HALL

Charles V

Charles (1500–1558) was king of Spain (Charles I, 1516–56) and Holy Roman emperor (Charles V, 1519–56). As a teenager, he received one of the largest territorial inheritances in the history of Europe: the Netherlands, Luxembourg, and Franche Comté from his father, Philip I of Castile (1478–1506); Aragon, Castile, Navarre, Sicily, Naples, and the New World territories from his maternal grandparents, Ferdinand II (1452–1516) and Isabella I (1451–1504); and the Austrian Hapsburg possessions of his paternal grandfather, Emperor Maximilian I (1459–1519), including Bohemia and Hungary. After Maximilian I's death, Charles was elected Holy Roman emperor. Charles's younger brother, Ferdinand I (1503–64), was named Archduke of Austria in 1521 and governed the hereditary Hapsburg lands in Charles's name. Throughout his long rule, Charles defended the Roman Catholic faith, resisted Ottoman expansion, and clashed repeatedly with France in the Hapsburg-Valois Wars (1521–59). Charles was raised to age sixteen in Brussels, where he learned French and received a traditional religious education. In later years he learned Spanish, Latin, Italian, and some Dutch, but was weakest in the High German dialect of the Holy Roman Empire, where he was charged with maintaining the peace and presiding over the imperial diet (*Reichstag*).

At the Diet of Worms (1521) Charles V encountered Martin Luther for the first and only time. After a short hearing with Luther and a consultation with the empire's leading electors and princes, Charles declared Luther an outlaw of the empire and in the Edict of Worms stipulated that loyal subjects of the empire could not print, sell, or read Luther's writings. However, due to the federated structure of the empire, Charles was unable to fully enforce the edict against Luther or suppress his publications in the German lands. War against the Ottomans and the French eventually took precedence over the task of coming to terms with Luther and the Protestants. In 1530, he called an imperial diet to meet in Augsburg to resolve religious differences, where the failed result gave rise to the Augsburg Confession. Colloquies called in 1540–41 also ended in stalemate. Although Charles took to the field and soundly defeated the Protestant Smalcaldic League in 1546–47 and attempted thereafter to impose an interim solution to the religious divisions (the Augsburg Interim), the Evangelical movement was too deeply entrenched in the empire to be stamped out. In September 1556, in part due to losses inflicted by the Princes' Revolt, Charles V abdicated his title as Holy Roman emperor, ceding the position to his brother and heir, Ferdinand I (r. 1558–64). Charles's son Philip II (1527–98) took over his father's kingdoms in Spain, Naples, and the New World. After Charles V and Ferdinand I died, the Hapsburg dynasty continued to dominate imperial politics for the next two hundred years, sharing power and decision making with the Holy Roman Empire's electors, bishops, princes, and representatives of the imperial cities.

See also Holy Roman Empire; Peace of Augsburg; Smalcald War

Bibliography

Brady, T. A., Jr. *German Histories in the Age of Reformations, 1400–1650.* Cambridge University Press, 2009; Maltby, W. S. *The Reign of Charles V.* Palgrave, 2002; Whaley, J. *Germany and the Holy Roman Empire.* Vol. 1. Oxford University Press, 2012.

MICHAEL J. HALVORSON

Chemnitz, Martin

As ecclesiastical superintendent in the city of Braunschweig, Martin Chemnitz (1522–86) was a primary drafter of the Formula of Concord. Born in Treuenbrietzen, Saxony, the son of a cloth maker, he was orphaned at an early age and destined for the same trade by his brother. Chemnitz struggled to complete university studies, interspersing his study at Wittenberg and Frankfurt an der Oder with teaching assignments. To a large extent he taught himself theology through extensive, intensive reading of the church fathers, Peter Lombard's *Sententiae*, Philip Melanchthon, and Martin Luther. At Melanchthon's recommendation he became librarian for Duke Albrecht of Prussia, also casting horoscopes for the duke. While in Königsberg (1547–53) he formed a close friendship with Joachim Mörlin amid the dispute over the doctrine of

justification being set forth by Mörlin's colleague in the Prussian Ministerium and professor at the University of Königsberg, Andreas Osiander. This dispute finally drove Chemnitz back to Wittenberg for further study after Duke Albrecht exiled Mörlin for his public condemnation of Osiander's doctrine, which Chemnitz also found false.

Melanchthon favored Chemnitz, who held required lectures on Melanchthon's *Loci communes*, a basic course on biblical teaching in Wittenberg's curriculum. In 1554 Mörlin had the municipal council of Braunschweig, where he himself had begun to serve as superintendent the previous year, call Chemnitz to be his coadjutor, with duties that included providing continuing education for pastors and deacons of the city's ministerium. The two worked closely together for thirteen years, until Mörlin returned to Königsberg. In 1557 they led (unsuccessful) efforts to reconcile Matthias Flacius and his Gnesio-Lutheran colleagues with Melanchthon in the so-called Colloquy of Coswig. In 1561 they headed negotiations with the Bremen clergy over the doctrine of the Lord's Supper being promoted by a local pastor, Albert Hardenberg, who opposed Luther's understanding of the true presence of Christ's body and blood in the Lord's Supper. Mörlin's Lüneberg Articles unified the Lower Saxon towns against Hardenberg, who was removed from office. This discussion elicited from Chemnitz a significant treatise, *Repetition of Sound Teaching on the True Presence of the Lord's Body and Blood in the Lord's Supper* (1561), which marshaled biblical and patristic support for this teaching. In *On the Two Natures in Christ* (1570; revised and expanded, 1578), Chemnitz displayed his abilities as biblical and patristic scholar in his treatment of related issues in Christology. There he argued that on the basis of the ancient doctrine of the "communication of attributes" between Christ's divine and human natures, it is possible for Christ's human nature to be present in whatever form God wills whenever and wherever he wishes (multivolipresence), thus providing an important avenue of defense for Luther's teaching on the true presence of Christ's body and blood in the Lord's Supper.

In old age, Duke Albrecht came to regret the course of his ecclesiastical policy initiated to defend Osiander and in 1567 called Mörlin and Chemnitz back to Königsberg to reform his church. Both came, with Mörlin remaining but Chemnitz returning to Braunschweig, where he assumed the ecclesiastical superintendent's office. While still in Prussia, however, the two composed a *Corpus Doctrinae*, collecting several defining documents and a new formulation of public teaching for the duchy. Chemnitz created the same kind of collection for the duchies of Braunschweig-Wolfenbüttel and Braunschweig-Lüneburg in 1568 and 1569, all forerunners of the Formula and Book of Concord. In 1568–70 he actively participated, along with Jakob Andreae and Nikolaus Selnecker, in introducing the Reformation to the duchy of Braunschweig-Wolfenbüttel; some evidence indicates that during this team effort Chemnitz influenced his colleagues' thinking significantly.

The advance of the Jesuits in Germany elicited Chemnitz's *Chief Chapters of the Theology of the Jesuits* in 1562. A critique of this work by the Jesuit Diego Payva d'Andrada provoked his four-volume *Examination of the Council of Trent* (1565–73), which shaped Roman Catholic–Lutheran polemical exchanges well into the seventeenth century.

Andreae requested responses to his *Six Christian Sermons* and "Swabian Concord" and drew Chemnitz into attempts to reach accord among the disputing parties within the Wittenberg circle. With David Chytraeus, Chemnitz solicited reactions to the latter document in 1574–75 from ministeria in northern Germany. Invited by Elector August of Saxony to participate in the effort to create the Formula of Concord in 1576, his ability to formulate recognition of the valid concerns of conflicting sides while rejecting their errors and misleading formulations contributed to the reaching of agreement within Lutheran circles to a significant degree.

Chemnitz's criticism of Duke Julius's having two sons consecrated and tonsured according to Roman Catholic rites in order to win ecclesiastical offices with secular jurisdictions soured his relationship with the duke, leading to Julius's reversal of support for the Formula of Concord. Chemnitz joined co-signers of the Formula Selnecker and Timotheus Kirchner in authoring the Apology of the Book of Concord (1583). He continued to work for acceptance of the Book of Concord well into the 1580s even as his health began to fail. A Roman Catholic critic first formulated the observation that "if this second Martin had not come, the work of the first Martin would not have endured," a remark undoubtedly false but nonetheless a suitable acknowledgment of the vital role that Chemnitz played in shaping seventeenth-century Lutheran theology. His posthumously edited *Postil* and his lectures on Melanchthon's *Loci communes* helped shape the next generation of Lutheran teaching.

See also Andreae, Jakob; Book of Concord; Formula of Concord; Melanchthon, Philip; Mörlin, Joachim; Osiander, Andreas

Bibliography

Chemnitz, M. *Examination of the Council of Trent*. Trans. F. Kramer. 4 vols. Concordia, 1971–86; Chemnitz, M. *Loci Theologici*. Trans. J. A. O. Preus. 2 vols. Concordia, 1989; Chemnitz, M. *The Lord's Supper*. Trans. J. A. O. Preus. Concordia, 1979; Chemnitz, M. *The Two Natures in Christ*. Trans. J. A. O. Preus. Concordia, 1971; Dingel, I. *Concordia controversa*. Gütersloher Verlagshaus, 1996; Johansson, T. *Reformationens huvudfrågor och arvet från Augustinus: En studie i Martin Chemnitz' Augustinus reception*. Församlingsförlaget, 1999; Kolb, R. "The Braunschweig Resolution: The Corpus Doctrinae Prutenicum of Joachim Mörlin and Martin Chemnitz as an Interpretation of Wittenberg Theology." In *Confessionalization in Europe, 1555–1700: Essays in Honor of Bodo Nischan*, ed. J. M. Headley et al., 67–89. Ashgate, 2004; Preus, J. A. O. *The Second Martin: The Life and Theology of Martin Chemnitz*. Concordia, 1994.

ROBERT KOLB

Chile

Most of the Germans who immigrated to Chile in the nineteenth century were Evangelical. They were received by a hostile society and obliged to have all their activities exclusively in

German until 1925, when the Roman Catholic Church was separated from the state and freedom of religion was introduced. More Evangelical Germans went to Chile after the World Wars.

In the areas where they settled, they established schools, clubs, and congregations, generally in that order. The first congregation was founded in 1863 in Osorno, and its first pastor arrived from the United Prussian Church in 1865. Despite the distances, the congregations helped each other and received help from Germany in calling pastors and building churches. Not until 1906 was the German Evangelical Synod of Chile formed, with a very loose organization. In 1937 the synod became officially affiliated with the German Evangelical Church and agreed to use the liturgy of the United Prussian Church.

After World War II the congregations united under the leadership of the pastor Friedrich Karle (who was the provost of the church from 1937 to 64) and contributed financially and materially toward the reconstruction of Germany. At the same time, members were becoming more integrated into Chilean society; the use of Spanish was increasingly required. This "Chileanization" of the church was evident when the synod became autonomous in 1959, adopted the name Evangelical Lutheran Church in Chile (Iglesia Evangélica Luterana en Chile, IELCH), and approved the calling of non-German pastors. In the 1960s pastors from the Lutheran Church in America were received to help with reaching out in mission and service to Chileans in general, especially the poor.

In 1975 eight congregations seceded from IELCH because they felt underrepresented and were critical of Bishop Helmut Frenz, who had been elected in 1970. They reproached him for not having spoken out on behalf of the church members who had suffered economic losses during the presidency of Salvador Allende (1970–73) with the same emphasis as he was defending those persecuted under the military dictatorship of Augusto Pinochet, who took

power in 1973. Most of the pastors, however, stayed in the IELCH. Six of the withdrawn congregations immediately founded the Lutheran Church in Chile (Iglesia Luterana en Chile, ILCH), which the other two joined in the 1990s.

ILCH is a lay-centered denomination focusing on building up its communities and providing diaconal service without any politicization. IELCH focuses on doing its mission by participating in the struggles of the neighborhoods where its congregations are located and speaking out for those whose voices need to be heard. Both IELCH and ILCH are members of the LWF, and since 1981, through the Council of Lutheran Churches in Chile, they have been trying to reunify.

The LCMS came to Chile through Argentina in 1954. In 1992 its congregations constituted themselves as the Confessional Lutheran Church of Chile, which is a member of the ILC. The Evangelical Lutheran Synod has been engaged in mission work in Chile since 1993.

Bibliography

Bachmann, E. T., and M. B. Bachmann. *Lutheran Churches in the World: A Handbook*. Esp. 540–46. Augsburg, 1989; Cruz, J. M. *The Histories of the Latin American Church: A Handbook*. Esp. 191–220. Fortress, 2014; http://els.org/worldoutreach/world-outreach-chile/; http://ielch.cl/; http://ilc-online.org/members/latin-america/chile/; http://www.iglesialuterana.cl/; https://www.lutheranworld.org/country/chile; https://www.oikoumene.org/es/member-churches/evangelical-lutheran-church-in-chile.

ANDRÉS ROBERTO ALBERTSEN

China

China is the major cultural and political power of East Asia. Nestorian Christians arrived in China in the seventh century. Several Roman Catholic missions, including that of Matteo Ricci (1552–1610), reached China in the medieval and early modern periods. Protestant missions began in 1807; the first Lutheran missionary was Pomeranian Karl Friedrich August Gutzlaff (1803–51), pietistically influenced and educated at the Janicke Mission Institute in Berlin, who after some years in Southeast Asia arrived in China in the 1830s as an independent missionary. Inspired by his work, the mission societies of Berlin, Barmen, and Basel sent missionaries in the nineteenth century to southern China. Both European and American Lutherans sent missionaries to central and northern China in the late 1890s and early 1900s. Primary destinations included these: Norwegians and Americans went to Henan and Hubei; Norwegians, Swedes, and some Americans to Hunan; Danes and others to Manchuria; and Germans to Guangdong and Shandong. Mission activity consisted of evangelism, the establishment of primary and secondary schools, the establishment of Bible schools, and medical work in dispensaries and hospitals. Cooperative efforts among the missions, beginning in 1904, included the production of literature, a church paper, and the foundation of a theological seminary. The goal was to form one Chinese church as the result of several missions. In 1920 the congregations associated with five missions—the Lutheran United Mission, the Norwegian Mission Society, the Finnish Missionary Society, the Augustana Synod Mission, and the Church of Sweden Mission—chose to join the Lutheran Church of China (LCC). Others joined later. Political upheavals in China, particularly Communist-inspired nationalism, forced many missionaries to leave in the 1920s, but church work continued under indigenous leadership, and missionaries eventually returned. Significant revivals took place in the 1930s. After the Japanese incursion into China (Manchuria, 1931) and American entrance into the war (1941), American missionaries left China.

Prominent missionaries included Daniel Nelson (1853–1926), a Norwegian-American, previously a sailor and farmer, who arrived in China in 1890 and sought to evangelize in inland China, in areas yet unreached by missionaries. He eventually settled in southern Henan. Karl Reichelt (1877–1952), a graduate of the Mission School in Stavanger, Norway, first came to China in 1903, initially worked in Hunan province, and later taught at the Lutheran theological seminary at Shekou in Hubei province. He engaged in significant study of Buddhism and dialogue with Buddhist scholars. He initiated the founding of the Nordic Christian Buddhist mission in the 1920s. Dr. Casper Skinsnes (1886–1960), a Norwegian medical doctor who with his wife had just received US citizenship, arrived in 1915 and served in several places.

Rev. O. S. Nestegaard Sr., from Norway, had in the 1890s inspired interest in China in the midwestern United States. Rev. Halvor N. and Hannah (Rorem) Ronning, Sigvald Netland, Thea Ronning, Olava Hodnefield, and Rev. Carl W. and Alice (Holmberg) Landahl were among the early missionaries. The first Christian convert in Fancheng was baptized in 1896. Rev. G. M. Trygstad, who arrived in 1905, was put in charge of the work in Fancheng, a city in the northeastern part of Hubei province. Other American missionaries included Rev. Andrew and Anna (Hauge) Martinson (arrived in 1902), who went to Henan, where Kikungshan (Rooster Mountain; now Jigongshan) in Xinyang became "the Lutheran mountain" in China.

By the 1930s the children of the missionaries began returning to China after completing their education overseas. The first of these, Rev. Daniel (Jr.) and Esther (Idso) Nelson, arrived in 1930, as did Rev. Harold H. and Charlotte (Rosendahl) Martinson. Rev. Talbert and Ella (Gryting) Ronning arrived in 1931. In the same year Miss Lillian Landahl returned to China and became a part of the American School of Kikungshan on the mountain. Mission was building a sense of long-term relationship.

Revival took hold in many parts of China in the 1930s, not least in Lutheran areas of ministry, helping to build a deep sense of an indigenous and Bible-rooted piety. The most important leader of this renewal, Sung Shang Dzieh (Song Shangjie), was not a Lutheran but preached in most Lutheran areas with a profound impact. A leading Lutheran missionary theologian—Dr. Gustav Carlberg, who taught at the Lutheran Seminary established in Shekou, Hubei province, and later was president of the seminary in Hong Kong—wrote a book on this revival. The dominant missionary figure influencing the revival was the Norwegian missionary Marie Monson.

This revival empowered the indigenization of the church. For over two decades the building of a united Chinese Lutheran Church had been under way. Congregations had been established, boys' and girls' schools begun, a large community of women Bible teachers established, many evangelists trained, medical work developed, a publicity bureau established with Chinese leadership, and a seminary of both missionary and Chinese faculty established and trained the Chinese pastoral leadership of the church. A united church had been formed, the Xinyi Hui (the Faith-Righteousness Church) with 31,661 in baptized membership, 5,159 catechumens, and 335 congregations.

In 1931 Rev. Chu Hao-jan from Sinyang, Henan, was elected president of this church. The revival enriched the life of the churches and the seminary. Chinese pastors, including Wu Ying, Li Chi-wu, Li Heng-pei, Kan Yu-jen, Kuo Ch'ing, Li Kwang-pang, Lin Ch'ien, Lu I-hsuen, and many others, provided the congregational leadership throughout the provinces. The editor in chief of the *Sin I-pao* (*The Lutheran weekly*) was the Chinese theologian Yang Tao-jung. Rev. Peng Fu became the second Chinese president of the Faith-Righteousness Church, serving from 1937 to 1949, till official Communism took over China.

The results were severe for the church. Missionaries were forced from the country, denominations were eliminated, and many pastors were imprisoned, sent to forced labor, tortured, or in some cases executed. In 1948 the Lutheran seminary was relocated to Hong Kong. In the 1950s and 1960s church membership decreased dramatically. With the Cultural Revolution (1966–76) all organized religious activity was shut down. Church property was taken over by government agents or simply closed. New Communist leadership took power in 1978, and churches began reopening in 1979. Soon, together with the house-church

movement that had secretly begun in the latter years of the Cultural Revolution, the church began growing at an astonishing rate. The Bible women of the earlier period played an important role in restoring these Christian gatherings. Ordained leaders were severely restrained, and denominations remained forbidden. In 1949 there were almost one million Protestants. Currently the Protestant church in China consists of sixty million or more believers. The only churches officially recognized are the registered churches belonging to the non-denominational China Christian Council. To begin denominational churches is forbidden.

See also Taiwan

Bibliography

Biographical Dictionary of Chinese Christianity. http://www.bdcconline.net. 2005–14; Burgess, A. S. *Peng Fu from Junan: A Biography.* Augsburg, 1948; Carlberg, G. *The Changing China Scene: The Story of the Lutheran Theological Seminary in Its Church and Political Setting over a Period of Forty-Five Years, 1913–1958.* Lutheran Literature Society, 1958; Carlberg, G. *China in Revival.* Augustana Book Concern, 1936; Carlberg, G. *The Story of Our China Mission.* Board of Foreign Missions of the Augustana Synod, 1938; Carlberg, G., ed. *Thirty Years in China, 1905–1935: The Story of the Augustana Synod Mission in the Province of Honan.* Board of Foreign Missions of the Augustana Synod, 1937; Crouch, A. R., et al., eds. *Christianity in China: A Scholars' Guide to Resources in the Libraries and Archives of the United States.* M. E. Sharpe, 1989; Kilen, J. R. *Forty Years in China: A Brief History of the Church of the Lutheran Bretheren Mission Work in China, 1902–1942.* Broderbaandet, 1943(?); Lutz, J. *Opening China: Karl F. A. Gützlaff and Sino-Western Relations, 1827–1852.* Eerdmans, 2008; Martinson, H. H. *Red Dragon over China.* Augsburg, 1956; Monsen, M. *The Awakening: Revival in China, a Work of the Holy Spirit, 1927–1937.* China Inland Mission, Overseas Missionary Fellowship, 1961; Nelson, D., Jr. *The Apostle to the Chinese Communists.* Board of Foreign Missions of the Norwegian Lutheran Church of America, 1935; Nelson, M. L. *Daniel Nelson, His Life and Work.* Mercury, [1933/34]; Ose, R. K. "A History of the Evangelical Lutheran Church of America's Mission Policy in China, 1890–1949." PhD diss., New York University, 1970; Skinsnes, C. C. *Scalpel and Cross in Honan.* Augsburg, 1952; Syrdal, R. A. "American Lutheran Mission Work in China." 2 vols. PhD diss., Drew University, 1942; Syrdal, R. A. *White unto Harvest in China: A Survey of the Lutheran United Mission, the China Mission of the NLCA, 1890–1934.* Board of Foreign Missions / Augsburg, 1934.

PAUL VARO MARTINSON

Christology

For Luther, Jesus is the Redeemer, "crucified for our trespasses and raised for our justification" (Rom. 4): *Crux sola est nostra theologia* (the cross alone is our theology). Despite the claims of Karl Holl, Christ is not secondary in Luther's theology but is the article on which faith entirely rests: "Jesus Christ is, in his nature, both very God and very man" (LW 22:74). Christ is one person (hypostatic union) with two natures, divine and human. Otherwise, Christ would have neither the power to save nor the thing in need of being saved. This is for Luther not reason's logic but faith's: if it were not true, human beings would be dead in their sins. Therefore, Luther argues, faith begins not from above in deity, nor from below in humanity, but in the manger with its God at his mother Mary's breasts.

Yet the Chalcedonian (451) doctrine that these two natures were unconfused, immutable, undivided, and inseparable was seen to be incomplete and liable to misuse at the two crucial points of the proclamation: the crucifixion and resurrection of Christ. Church doctrine first balked at the crucifixion to say that when the man Jesus died, God died. Second, it balked at the resurrection to say that when God rose from the dead, so was the man Jesus raised. Thus the church's theology often failed to exploit the power of the incarnation at its piercing point of the *logos sarx egeneto*: God is a human being (John 1:14), who takes away the sins of the world (John 1:29, 36). When Luther recovered the full distinction of law and gospel, he also opened a new understanding of the *communicatio idiomatum* (the communication of attributes).

Christ is simply God, and God is this man, so that Christology means justification by faith alone. Epistemologically, this means not to know, but to be known (Gal. 4). Theologically, it means that Christ does not wait to be found. He is not idle but most active (*actuosissimus*) who both *is*, with God as God (Father and Son in complete unity) and *becomes* flesh—since only the Son suffered, not the Father, unlike modern or ancient Patripassianism (the Father suffering by imbibing humanity through the Son). Paradoxically, Christ's proper activity is to hide. On the one hand, Christ hides his true nature from those who seek him "naked," outside the incarnation. On the other hand, he hides from those who encounter him in preaching under the sign or appearance of his opposite: in the cross and as risen Lord of a new kingdom. God is to be found nowhere but in this Person in whom "the whole fullness of deity dwells bodily" (Col. 2:9). Thus that Person is found in the mouth of the preacher. His kingdom has come in faith in the word of forgiveness, not yet in sight.

Luther's basis for Christology is the distinction between God preached and not preached, crystallized in his debate with Erasmus (1525). Erasmus viewed Scripture as moral imperatives, implying human free will, because, according to Luther, Erasmus did not distinguish God hidden in naked majesty (so as not to be found apart from Christ) from the God hidden in the cross (in order to be found). Thus God is met either with Christ and his words, or without Christ. Erasmus's confrontation with Luther was not simply anthropological (debating the powers of the human will), but theological, specifically how God could be outside Christ. Modern trinitarian theology requires correspondence between the immanent and economic Trinity (e.g., "Rahner's Rule") so that God cannot be encountered without Christ. But the power of Luther's confession, "I have no other God than this man Jesus," is grasped only with the *Anfechtung* (attack on faith), where God is met with no preacher and no Christ.

Luther recognized that Christology was typically ordered according to the law alone. The effect was to seek a way around the gospel whenever it challenged God's essential justice, or to invoke the law of love for Christians. The mechanism for escape was to separate Christ's two natures, using what Luther—in the debate with Ulrich Zwingli over the presence of Christ in the Lord's Supper—called "the damned alloeosis," which absented the offending (human) nature from the sacrament and made Christ only halfway present. Among Protestants, this penchant for absence appeared in Zwingli's teaching on the sacraments (1527). At first, Luther was surprised. Why would a person seek to remove Christ's real presence from the Lord's Supper? He found the underlying problem was over the *communicatio idiomatum*, just as it had appeared in the fifth-century struggle between Cyril of Alexandria and Nestorius of Constantinople.

The arch-heretic of Christology, Arius, had denied both Christ's true divinity and his true humanity. Cyril of Alexandria held to the mystery (431) in a letter to the council in Ephesus, "that the Word . . . has become man in an inexpressible and incomprehensible way." When Nestorius denied calling Mary *Theotokos* (God-bearer), he did not adopt Arius's coarse denial of attributes, but used a subtle variation that denied the *communication* of the attributes. You could say Mary bore the man, but not the God. *Alloeosis* (a rhetorical term for speaking of one entity in terms of another) substituted Christ's humanity for something considered blasphemous for God, and his divinity for whatever it considered impossible for the human. The first protected the dignity of God from sin and death. The second preserved free will—a continually existing subject who had the capacity to become righteous according to the law.

Luther concluded that the story of Jesus Christ must be published without any sleight of hand: "Here you must take your stand, and . . . if you can say, 'Here is God,' then you must also say, 'Christ the human being is present too.' And if you could show me one place where God is and not the human being, then the person is already divided and I could at once say truthfully, 'Here is God who is not a human being and has never become a human being.' But no God like that for me! For it would follow from this that space and place had separated the two natures from one another and thus had divided the person, even

though death and all the devils had been unable to separate and tear them apart" (LW 37:218–19).

For Luther, space and time are not determined by a legal continuity of being, either in God or in the Christian. God died, and so does the Christian. Christ, who knew no sin, became sin (2 Cor. 5:21), and upon being raised in a great struggle in God, is the conquering Lord of a new kingdom that does not merely transform the old, but creates anew (*ex nihilo*). The double fear was exposed: that the law would come to an end and that the person with a free will would end. Luther made the distinction between an old reality and a new proclamation: as a fact of nature (the law) "Mary bore God" is wrong; but as preaching "for you," it is exactly right, because it creates a new being through the gospel, apart from the law.

The presence of Christ for sinners, wholly and completely, was challenged not only by Protestant "Sacramentarians," but also the antinomian Johann Agricola (1537). He misunderstood Luther's teaching as something "christocentric" that assumed everything under Christ ontologically, including teaching God's wrath and the repentance of a sinner. But for Luther both the full, bodily presence of Jesus Christ and "Christ is the end of the law" (Rom. 10:4) precisely fit together: "Thus the demand and the accusation of the law, because of what it demands, ends among the pious when Christ is present who says: 'Look at me who does for them what you demand—so stop it!'" But outside the preaching office's two words of law and gospel, there remains the law and God hidden without Christ (The First Antinomian Disputation in WA 39/1:390–91).

From this it is true, as Tuomo Mannermaa (1989) argued against the Kantian influence of the nineteenth century (e.g., Albrecht Ritschl), that it is not an ethical cause or transcendental effect in a Christian, but the presence of Christ himself that makes Christians righteous—indwelling as gift. Christ is the form of faith, so unity is no longer reduced to will. But it must also be said that faith is a "sort of knowledge of darkness that nothing can see, . . . and the mode of the presence cannot be thought," not least because the one in whom Christ dwells is *reductio in nihilum* (reduced to nothing). This means more, not less, than total annihilation of the moral subject (no work, no law, no love, no image, no free will). It is both complete death and a whole "new world above and beyond the Law" (LW 26:129–30).

That is why Luther did not look for a real, ontological indwelling of Christ in Andreas Osiander's sense, who created the controversy addressed in the third article of the Formula of Concord (1576). Osiander simply duplicated the "damned alloeosis" among the Lutherans both in questioning the effectiveness of public absolution and in proposing a theory of indwelling that preferred defining justification by participation in the divine nature of Christ alone. After all, who could occupy the human nature of Christ, or who would want to? But unlike Osiander, Luther and his students taught a real death and new creation, first for Christ, then for the Christians. Christians live by the forensic, external declaration of the word of forgiveness because God's divine word is more effective than sinners know. This is more than Christ being both subject and object of faith. It makes a new world above and beyond the law. "For Christ or faith is neither the Law nor the work of the Law" (LW 26:129–30).

Then how is it that Christ and the sinner belong together without any law in between? The Concordists' answer in articles 7 and 8 was to reject the *extra Calvinisticum* (the divine nature was neither added to nor subtracted from as incarnate and then unincarnate). They settled on a litmus test in the Formula of Concord 7 and 8 (1576) to expose "the damned alloeosis." First, they held that the *est* (This *is* my body), or real presence of Christ in the bread and wine in which Christ himself (both natures) is received, is actual forgiveness of sins and not only a reminder of it. This led to the *manducatio oralis* (oral eating) that rejects spiritualizing this *est*. The test case is the *manducatio impiorum*: even the unfaithful take the blood and body of Christ in their teeth. Thus the real presence depends on the *communicatio idiomatum*: wherever Christ is, there is his body and divinity. Finally, this assumes the ubiquity of Christ not only in "spirit" but also in body, a teaching that indirectly launched the orthodox "kenotic" controversies beginning with Johannes Brenz in the sixteenth century, and continuing into the seventeenth at the universities in Giessen and Tübingen, concerning whether Christ entirely abstained from using divine attributes in his "state of humiliation" (Greek: *kenōsis*) or used them secretly (*krypsis*). Kenosis returned with Ludwig, count von Zinzendorf (1700–1760), and became radicalized as an abandonment of divine attributes by the type of communication called *tapeinoticum*. Ritschl (1872) used this approach to discard metaphysics and equate the person of Christ with whatever grows from the moral experience of the Christian community.

But Martin Chemnitz and Nicholas Selnecker turned to Luther's *Confession concerning Christ's Supper* (1528) as the profound way to grasp the communication of attributes. Three phrases were central: "apart from this man Jesus there is no God"; Christ comes to us "deep in the flesh"; and "He is not halfway present, nor is just half of him present." They called this the "intimate linking" (*invicem communicans*; cf. FC, Ep 8.2 in *BC* 509) of the two natures in the person of Christ and explored the *communicatio idiomatum*, using not only types like *genus idiomaticum* (ascribing attributes of both natures to the whole person of Christ) and *genus apotelesmaticum* (the use of attributes of each or both natures in manners appropriate to certain actions), as Biel and the nominalists had done, but insisting that Luther's arguments pointed to a *genus maiestaticum*, an "exalted third" (or gospel) mode of Christ's presence "where they cannot measure or circumscribe him but where they are present to him so that he measures and circumscribes them" (FC, SD 7.101 in *BC* 610). Here subject and object reverse so that we ask not how God is present to us, but how we are present to God.

In sum, it means that Christ is not a "new Moses" (lawgiver) but a savior who makes sinners righteous apart from law in faith itself: "What the law, weakened by the flesh, could not do, God has done, sending his own Son in the likeness of sinful flesh" (cf. Rom. 8:3). Only *Deus incarnatus*, Christ incarnate as *sacramentum* (gift) and not merely *exemplum* (moral example), can free from death and sin by taking humanity's sins on himself and in return can give faith that is the certainty of salvation. This means that God's will is not properly the law but is his Son, Jesus Christ.

Thus Christians grasp two facts: "that Christ is in us, and that we are in Him. The one points upward; the other, downward." The first is the joyous exchange that we are forgiven, and thus we ascend "above ourselves and beyond ourselves to Him," where death and sin vanish. Then there is a dying descent, where he also manifests himself in us and we become "Christ's" to whom he says: "Go forth, preach, . . . serve your neighbor. . . . I will be in you and will do all this" (LW 24:143). The communication extends through our own demise from Christ through his chosen ones to the whole world in love.

In Christ, Creator and creature truly belong together—with no law in between. Jesus has the power to save; what he saves is you, the sinner, with all your "parts" (spirit, soul, body). This is not a reclamation project; it is a new creation (a new "is") through the preaching office. Thus, Luther concluded, Christ is "my Lord. He has redeemed me, a lost and condemned person, saved me at great cost. . . . All this he has done that I may be his own" (Small Catechism, 1529).

See also Formula of Concord; God and Trinity; Holl, Karl; Lord's Supper; Mannermaa, Tuomo

Bibliography

Luther's Works: *Confessions concerning Christ's Supper* (1527–28). LW 37; *De servo arbitrio* (1525). LW 33; *Lectures on Galatians* (1535). LW 26; *On the Councils and the Church* (1539). LW 41; *On the Divinity and Humanity of Christ* (1540). WA 39/2:93–96; *Sermons on the Gospel of St. John* (ca. 1537). LW 22; *Small Catechism* (1529); *Solus Decalogus est Aeternus: Martin Luther's Complete Antinomian Theses and Disputations.* Ed. and trans. H. Sonntag. Lutheran Press, 2008. **General Works:** Bayer, O. *Martin Luther's Theology.* Eerdmans, 2008; Brenz, J. *De personali unione duarum naturarum in Christo.* Tübingen, 1561; Chemnitz, M. *The Two Natures in Christ.* Trans. J. A. O. Preus. Concordia, 1971; Elert, W. *The Structure of Lutheranism.* Concordia, 1962; Forde, G. *Theology Is for Proclamation.* Fortress, 1990; Holl, K. *Gesammelte Aufsätze.* Vol. I.6. Mohr Siebeck, 1932; Lienhard, M. *Martin Luther's Witness to Jesus Christ.* Augsburg, 1982; Mannermaa, T. *Christ Present in Faith.* Trans. K. Stjerna. Fortress, 2005; Nilsson, K. *Simul.* Vandenhoeck & Ruprecht, 1999; Paulson, S. *Lutheran Theology.* T&T Clark, 2011; Ritschl, A. *The Christian Doctrine of Justification and Reconciliation.* T&T Clark, 1902; Siggins, I. *Martin Luther's Doctrine of Christ.* Yale University Press, 1970; Wengert, T. *Defending Faith: Lutheran Responses to Andreas Osiander's Doctrine of Justification, 1551–1559.* Mohr Siebeck, 2012.

STEVEN D. PAULSON

Church

In late medieval Christendom, the context for Luther's ecclesiology, the institutional church, played a central role, ordering society through laws and mediating salvation through the sacramental system. Even before the indulgence controversy, Luther expressed the pastoral concern that the church was not comforting Christians with the promise of the gospel in the midst of economic, social, and spiritual crises they faced.

Late medieval ecclesiology was concerned with the question, "Ultimately what or who can assure me that I am in God's grace?" Luther departed from the late medieval tradition by pointing solely to the promise of the gospel; he defined the church in reference to that same Word, rather than to offices, structures, or some form of pure ecclesial "remnant." For Luther, the true church existed wherever the Word was truly proclaimed and nourishing the faithful, an idea he initiated in his response to Augustine Alveld (1480–ca. 1535) in 1520 and fully developed in *Concerning the Ministry* (1523). As a "creature of the Word," the church owes not only its birth to the Word but also its very being and life.

Two difficulties confront those seeking to understand Luther's ecclesiology beyond this central insight. Although he wrote a treatise on the church in 1539, he seemed to hold differing and even contradictory views of the church, particularly with regard to the church's visibility. These can in part be explained by appeals to genre (polemical versus catechetical) or historical development based on the different controversies and opponents he faced ("early Luther" emphasizing the invisible church versus "later Luther" highlighting the church's visible aspects).

These differences may best be understood hermeneutically. Luther's understanding of the church as a "spiritual community" is based on a definition of "spiritual" that first emerges in his Psalms lectures (1513–15), where he defines the church as "the faithful," a people in whom Christ is present through faith (rather than love [caritas]). Faith as grounded in spiritual, divine things does not rely on a particular, external church structure. The faithful can exist in any community as long as faith is nurtured there through the Word of God's promise.

Luther articulates these insights in hermeneutical terms in his debate with Jerome Emser, among others, sparked by his 1520 treatise An Open Letter to the Christian Nobility, where he challenges the idea that there is a "spiritual estate" and a "temporal estate," showing how Scripture teaches that all Christians are spiritual and priests on account of baptism, gospel, and faith (1 Pet. 2:9). In response to Emser, who used 2 Cor. 3:6 to argue that each scriptural passage has a literal and a spiritual (allegorical) sense, Luther asserted that there is one grammatical-historical meaning of Scripture and that Paul is referring to two kinds of preaching: law and gospel.

Many historians note that Luther's ecclesiology shifts in 1522, in part because his ideas were appropriated and adapted by more-radical reformers and in part because his Roman opponents point to the uncertainty of knowing where the church actually exists if based on an invisible faith. This led Luther to emphasize the external means by which the Spirit works. Luther, however, does not replace an "invisible church" concept with a "visible church," but continues to stress the church's spiritual orientation. In Against the Heavenly Prophets (1525), Luther treats the twofold manner in which God deals with believers: outwardly through the oral word of the gospel and the sacraments and inwardly through the Holy Spirit and faith. In contrast to Andreas Karlstadt, who subordinates the word and sacraments to an inner spiritual reality, Luther emphasizes the mutual relationship between the Spirit and Word and the basic decision of the Spirit to work through the external Word. Luther's understanding of the spiritual nature of the church as a holy community does not imply a noncorporeal experience or existence but a hiddenness within experience. Christ and his kingdom are not bound to any physical place or external thing; yet the gospel is nonetheless experienced through bodily means.

The explanation of the third article of the Apostles' Creed in the Large Catechism (1529) defines the "spiritual community" not as a priestly estate set apart by ordination (as Emser and others argued), nor an "invisible church" of hearts united in faith (as is often taken to be his position), or the Spirit speaking apart from the Word (as he charged the "enthusiasts" [Schwärmer] with teaching), but as the "mother" who begets and bears each Christian through the Word, which they grasp and cling to by faith. Brought into his body, they receive forgiveness of sins, new life, and a community in which members "forgive, bear with, and aid one another" (LC, Creed 42 in BC 436). The Holy Spirit gathers this "holy little flock" in one faith, mind, and understanding, under Christ's headship, and will continue granting forgiveness of sins through the church until the last day.

In his later years Luther does not abandon this concept of the church as spiritual community, even as he finds himself increasingly defending order and structure in the church against the spiritualists' attacks. On the

Councils and the Church (1539) reiterates Luther's understanding of the church as a "Christian holy people" because of its possession of the first and principal mark of the church, the holy Word of God, and it maintains his hermeneutical distinction between letter and Spirit. The spiritualists attacked all externalities (water, bread, human speech), arguing that these cannot save; only the Spirit can. Luther retorts that the holy Christian people do not have mere externalities, but God's very promise is to work through these means of grace.

In 1539 Luther lists seven "marks" of the church: the Word; baptism; the sacrament of the altar; the office of the keys; the office of the ministry; prayer, public praise, and thanksgiving to God; and the cross (suffering for the sake of the gospel). He returns to the "marks of the church" in one of his most polemical works, *Against Hanswurst* (1541), addressing Roman Catholic claims that theirs is the only true church. Luther responds that the true church is identified, not by its name, but by the marks through which the Holy Spirit has promised to work. He compares nine marks that Reformation churches share with the ancient church to those "externalities" such as the Roman Church's holy pilgrimages, traditions invented without God's Word.

Luther's gospel-focused ecclesiology is reflected in articles 7 and 8 of the Augsburg Confession (CA, 1530) and in Philip Melanchthon's Apology (1531), which have become normative for Lutheran ecclesiology. Thus CA 7 defines the church as the assembly of believers among whom the gospel is purely preached and the sacraments are administered according to Scripture. These two conditions are "enough" for the unity of the Christian church, which, CA 7 affirms, will remain forever. Sinners and other hypocrites are members of the true church in name but not in fact, since the church is principally a fellowship of hearts united in faith, not just an association of external rites. While this assembly of believers or communion of saints is most clearly manifested at the level of congregation, the Lutheran confessions acknowledge the breadth of the universal church in their embrace of the Nicene Creed, which characterizes the church as one, holy, catholic, and apostolic.

Most of Melanchthon's Orthodox Lutheran successors in the seventeenth century, such as Johannes Andreas Quenstedt, preferred to emphasize the spiritual aspect of the church's nature, using the language of the CA, "the church properly speaking," to designate the "invisible" church. "The assembly of the elect," the narrower, invisible church, thus was said to exist within the wider, visible church, "the assembly of the called" who outwardly gather around word and sacrament. It was also common for these seventeenth-century theologians to speak of the "true" and the "false" church; however, in this case the distinction applied primarily to the visible church and had to do with correctness of doctrine. This distinction would lead later confessional theologians, such as the American theologian Francis Pieper, to reject any identification of the invisible church with any visible church (even the Lutheran Church) on the basis that the "true church" cannot have any hypocrites or unbelievers within its ranks. The church is the invisible community of the elect, the sum total of those in whom the Holy Spirit has created faith.

While Lutheran Pietists of the eighteenth and nineteenth centuries would agree that only God knows the faith of the heart, some emphasized the church's visibility and the congregation as the church's true locus. The empirical reality of the church is apparent in word and sacrament, yet also in spiritual renewal, ethical conduct, the ministry of the laity (now redefined as the "priesthood of all believers"), and the church's missionary activity. Often drawing from organic images like the vine and the branches in John 15, they emphasized that the common life and shared love of reborn Christians is not hidden, but manifest to all.

Twentieth-century developments in Lutheran ecclesiology include two significant trajectories that are often at odds with each other ecumenically: a reclamation of the church not only as "creature of the Word" but also as a "Word-event" itself, and the adaptation of the koinonia (Greek: *koinōnia*), or communion, paradigm for a more ecumenical vision for Lutheran ecclesiology. The idea of the church as a Word-event developed from the trajectory started by Luther and Melanchthon. Thus CA 7 is read through the lens of Karl Barth's actualist view of the church as continually being re-created by the event of revelation. The view of the church as an event that happens in the proclamation of the word and the administration of the sacraments became popularized in classic Lutheran writings of the twentieth century. Existentialists such as Rudolf Bultmann and Gerhard Ebeling emphasized the present impact of God's address on the individual believer's standing before God, making the church less a sphere of faith (as for Luther) and more a summons to faith. For Gerhard Forde, the focus of Word-event was on the slaying and the making alive of the sinner, accomplished in the hearing of the law and gospel, which had the effect of narrowing ecclesiology to the preaching office. His views would influence generations of Lutheran pastors as well as affect debates in American Lutheranism over ecclesiology, ecumenical agreements, and the doctrine of the ministry.

Twentieth-century Lutheran ecumenists proposed the flexible criteria of the CA as the basis of Christian unity (e.g., Edmund Schlink) and the Pauline metaphor of the body of Christ (e.g., Anders Nygren), but in the mid-twentieth century a shift toward a more trinitarian basis for Christian unity, and koinonia, or communion, ecclesiology emerged as a promising new paradigm. Communion ecclesiology builds on the twofold meaning of koinonia as both "fellowship" and "a common participation or partaking," thus offering an understanding of the church as a body into which believers are incorporated sacramentally and through which they experience communion with the Triune God and one another. This paradigm has been engaged by individual Lutheran theologians such as Robert W. Jenson and in bilateral ecumenical dialogues at the national and international level, as well as by the Lutheran World Federation (LWF), which in 1990 voted to change its constitution to define the LWF as a "communion of churches which confess the Triune God, agree in the proclamation of the Word, and are united in pulpit and altar fellowship." The 1997 statement "Toward a Lutheran Understanding of Communion" and background papers sought to bring this concept into dialogue with the Lutheran confessional tradition and the centrality of the Word for Lutheran ecclesiology. The statement affirmed that the foundation of communion in the church is the Triune God's own self-giving nature and action through the word and sacrament. Little is said about the forms and structures of ecclesial communion, such as episcopacy, except to stress that these are not foundational to a Lutheran view of the church.

More recently Lutheran ecclesiologists have engaged the question of the church missiologically. They seek to define the nature or identity of the church not only in the classic Lutheran understanding of an assembly that is gathered around word and sacrament, but also as a people who are sent out by these same means of grace into the world, to bear the gospel in word and *diakonia* to a broken world. The role of the Holy Spirit is highlighted in both movements of the church: gathering and sending.

See also Baptism; God and Trinity; Sacraments; Word of God

Bibliography

Hendrix, S. H. *Ecclesia in Via: Ecclesiological Developments in the Medieval Psalm Exegesis and the "Dictata Super Psalterium" (1513–1515) of Martin Luther*. Brill, 1974; Holze, H., ed. *The Church as Communion: Lutheran Contributions to Ecclesiology*. LWF Documentation 42. Lutheran World Federation, 1997; Knutson, K. S. "The Community of Faith and the Word: An Inquiry into the Concept of the Church in Contemporary Lutheranism." PhD diss., Union Theological Seminary, 1961; Lathrop, G., and T. J. Wengert. *Christian Assembly: The Marks of the Church in a Pluralistic Age*. Fortress, 2004; Luther, M. *Against Hanswurst* (1541). Trans. E. W. Gritsch and W. P. Stephens. LW 41:179–256; Luther, M. *Against the Heavenly Prophets in the Matter of Images and Sacraments*.

Trans. B. Erling and C. Bergendoff. LW 40:73–223; Luther, M. *Answer to the Hyperchristian, Hyperspiritual, and Hyperlearned Book by Goat Emser in Leipzig— Including Some Thoughts regarding His Companion, the Fool Murner* (1521). Trans. E. W. and R. C. Gritsch. LW 39:137–224; Luther, M. *Concerning the Ministry* (1523). Trans. C. Bergendoff. LW 40:3–44; Luther, M. *On the Councils and the Church* (1539). Trans. C. M. Jacobs. Rev. E. W. Gritsch. LW 41:3–178; Luther, M. *An Open Letter to the Christian Nobility.* Trans. C. M. Jacob. In *Three Treatises of Martin Luther.* Fortress, 1960; Peterson, C. M. *Who Is the Church? An Ecclesiology for the Twenty-First Century.* Fortress, 2013.

CHERYL M. PETERSON

Church Law

Initial notions of church law date to the post-apostolic era, when collections like the *Didache*, the *Apostolic Tradition*, and the *Apostolic Constitutions* shaped the early practice and liturgy of the church. The canons or decrees of the first ecumenical councils of the fourth and fifth centuries after Emperor Constantine (d. 337) claimed universal stature for these traditions, although regional differences and the singular claims of the Roman church restricted their application to "all times and in all places." The unique authority of the bishop of Rome, the pope, fostered the development of the Western canon law tradition, eventually harmonized by Gratian (ca. 1140) in his *Concordia discordantium canonum*, or *Decretum*. The legal status of the Roman church, partially centralized in the law faculty at the University of Bologna, evolved over the next several centuries, securing the jurisdiction of the church over a broad arena of political, social, and religious concerns. By the fifteenth century a series of official writings, which included the *Decretum*, several subsequent papal collections (*Decretals*), and their commentaries circulated as the *Corpus iuris canonici*. Together with secular legislation, notably the Roman legal tradition contained in Justinian's *Corpus iuris civilis*, the principles of canon law shaped a *ius commune*, a common reservoir of law governing both church and state.

Prior to the sixteenth-century reformations, secular authorities increasingly sought to erode the jurisdiction of the church. In December 1520 Martin Luther's decision to burn a copy of one of the church's legal codes, the *Liber extra*, illustrated his rejection of the legal status of the Roman church. Instead, Luther appealed to secular authorities for their assistance as princes in implementing reforms in the church over against a recalcitrant clergy. Numerous Lutheran cities and territories adopted legislation known as *Kirchenordnungen*, which regulated worship, education, ecclesiastical administration, and community welfare. Marriage remained a complicated arena of jurisdiction, and Lutheran reformers and jurists drew heavily from the canon law tradition as they sought to construct marriage courts or consistories.

Although most Protestant territories officially abandoned adherence to Roman canon law, the mixed legislative character of the *ius commune*, which featured both secular and church law, continued in most of Europe until the nineteenth century. Swedish universities founded in the seventeenth century emphasized law faculties with expertise in church law, and Dutch academies continued to produce significant numbers of graduates with degrees in both civil and church law: *Doctor utriusque iuris*. In England, initial attempts to rewrite a code of ecclesiastical legislation (known as the *Reformatio legum ecclesiasticarum*) failed. However, many Anglican bishops continued to exercise some limited diocesan legislative authority following the precepts of canon law. By the nineteenth century, the separate legal stature of the church gradually disappeared from European states, both Protestant and Roman Catholic, as it had been rejected from the outset in the founding of the United States.

See also Household, Children, Parents; Marriage and Divorce

Bibliography

Brundage, J. *Medieval Canon Law.* Longman, 1995; Heckel, J. *Lex charitatis: A Juristic Disquisition on Law in the Theology of Martin Luther.* Trans. G. Krodel. Eerdmans, 2010; Helmholz, R., ed. *Canon Law in Protestant Lands.* Duncker & Humblot, 1992. Mäkinen, V., ed. *Lutheran Reformation and the Law.* Brill, 2006; Prodi,

P. *Eine Geschichte der Gerechtigkeit: Vom Recht Gottes zum modernen Rechtsstaat.* Beck, 2003; Witte, J. *Law and Protestantism: The Legal Teachings of the Lutheran Reformation.* Cambridge University Press, 2002.

JEFFREY JAYNES

Chytraeus, David

The German Lutheran theologian David Chytraeus (1531–1600) was one of the drafters of the Formula of Concord. Chytraeus (German: Kochhafe) was born at Ingelfingen, Württemberg, on February 26, 1531, the son of a Lutheran pastor. A gifted child, Chytraeus began studies at the University of Tübingen at age eight. There he was influenced by Joachim Camerarius, Erhard Schnepf, and Jakob Heerbrand. He received the MA degree at fourteen. In 1544 he went to Wittenberg, lived in Melanchthon's house, and studied under Luther, Melanchthon, and Eber. In 1546, when the Smalcald War disrupted his studies, he left for Heidelberg and then Tübingen. In 1548 he returned to Wittenberg, where he began giving lectures on astronomy, rhetoric, and Melanchthon's *Loci communes*. After a tour of Italy, he was called to lecture in the arts faculty at the University of Rostock in 1551. He also taught theological subjects at the Rostock Paedagogium, or academy. His Latin catechism, the *Catechesis*, first published in 1554, was intended for students in the academy and was largely an epitome of Melanchthon's *Loci communes*. His *Regula vitae* (1555) expanded on the catechetical material to present instruction in Christian ethics following Melanchthon's conceptions.

After 1553 Chytraeus taught courses at the university, chiefly in theology and history, receiving his doctorate in theology in 1561. He also lectured on biblical exegesis, producing commentaries on nineteen biblical books. His *De morte et vita aeterna* (1581) was the first book on the Lutheran doctrine of eschatology. His historical works include a history of his homeland, the Kraichgau, and the *Historia der Augspurgischen Confession* (1571), one of the earliest critical examinations of Reformation historiography, especially important for its analysis of the textual history of the Augsburg Confession.

Chytraeus participated in the Diet of Augsburg in 1555 and the Colloquy of Worms in 1557. At the convention of Evangelical princes in Naumburg in 1561, he strongly advocated the 1530 Unaltered Augsburg Confession as the lawful Lutheran confession in the empire. At the 1566 Diet of Augsburg he became aware of the extent to which the Philippists had developed Melanchthon's understanding of the Lord's Supper in a Calvinistic direction. He drafted the response of the University of Rostock to the Weimar Confutation of 1559.

In 1569 Chytraeus traveled to Austria to help organize the Lutheran churches there. He helped them prepare an agenda, an order for the consistory and superintendents, a commentary on the Augsburg Confession, and an *examen ordinandorum*, a guide for candidates of theology preparing for their examination before ordination. In 1572 he wrote a catechism for the Lutheran estates of Lower and Upper Austria, and he was instrumental in establishing the Lutheran churches in Styria in 1574.

Chytraeus was one of six theologians responsible for drafting the Formula of Concord. He was especially responsible for the articles on free will (2) and the Lord's Supper (7). He assisted in the preparation of the Torgau Book, 1576, and worked alongside his colleagues to produce the Bergic Book in 1577, which became the Formula of Concord's Solid Declaration. He died at Rostock on June 25, 1600, the seventieth anniversary of the presentation of the Augsburg Confession.

See also Book of Concord; Formula of Concord

Bibliography

Czaika, O. *David Chytraeus und die Universität Rostock in ihren Beziehungen zum schwedischen Reich.* Luther-Agricola-Gesellschaft, 2002; Green, L. C. "The Three Causes of Conversion in Philipp Melanchthon, Martin Chemnitz, David Chytraeus, and 'the Formula of Concord.'" *Lutherjahrbuch* 47 (1980): 89–114; Jungkuntz, T. R. "David Chytraeus—Alter Philippus?" In *Formulators of the Formula of Concord: Four Architects of Lutheran Unity*, 69–88. Concordia, 1977; Keller, R. *Die Confessio*

Augustana im theologischen Wirken des Rostocker Professors David Chyträus. Vandenhoeck & Ruprecht, 1994; Keller, R. "David Chytraeus (1530–1600): Melanchthon's Geist im Luthertum." In *Melanchthon in seinen Schülern*, ed. Heinz Scheible, 361–71. Harrassowitz, 1997; Montgomery, J. W. *Chytraeus on Sacrifice.* Concordia, 1962.

GERHARD BODE

Cochlaeus, Johannes

The German humanist and Catholic controversialist Johannes Cochlaeus (1479–1552) was a lifelong opponent of Luther. Born of peasants in Wendelstein as Johannes Dobneck, he studied at Nuremberg before matriculating at the University of Cologne in 1504, where he received his bachelor of arts (1505) and his master of arts (1507) and adopted the moniker Cochlaeus (Greek for "spiral" after his hometown of Wendelstein [spiral stone]). During 1510–15 Cochlaeus served as the rector of the Latin school of St. Lorenz in Nuremberg. There, among other and diverse publications, he wrote the first historical geography of Germany (*Brevis Germaniae descriptio*), aligning himself with contemporary interest in the German nation. Cochlaeus then proceeded to Italy, where he received his doctorate in theology at Ferrara (1517), followed by a two-year residence in Rome. In 1518 Cochlaeus was ordained a priest; in 1520 he was sent back to Germany as dean of St. Mary's in Frankfurt am Main. At this time Cochlaeus encountered Luther's *Address to the Christian Nobility* and *Babylonian Captivity of the Church*, against which he took up the pen. After initial difficulty in attaining publication, Cochlaeus soon became the most prolific Catholic controversialist of the 1520s. In 1521 he attended the Diet of Worms; then between 1522 and 1525 he wrote over seventeen pamphlets and books—most directed against Luther—and edited or translated fourteen works by other authors, including a translation of Cyprian's *De unitate ecclesiae* (*On the Unity of the Church*). Cochlaeus's style, though certainly influenced by the German humanism of the period, also betrayed a Scholastic bent. During 1524 and 1525 Cochlaeus wrote two treatises to the German people (*Paraclesis* and *Pia exhortatio*) arguing that support for the Holy Roman Empire and support for the Roman church went hand in hand, and thus Luther's attack on the papacy was not only heresy but also treason. With the outbreak of the German Peasants' War, Cochlaeus fled to Cologne in 1525 and the following year accepted a position at St. Victor's in Mainz. In 1528 Cochlaeus succeeded fellow Catholic controversialist Jerome Emser (1477–1527) as secretary and chaplain to Duke George of Saxony. In the following years Cochlaeus continued to involve himself in the confessional controversies of the time. One year after comparing Luther to the sevenheaded dragon of the Apocalypse, Cochlaeus attended the Diet of Augsburg in 1530 and wrote against the Augsburg Confession and Philip Melanchthon thereafter. In the ensuing decade, Cochlaeus would compose a polemical biography of Luther, eventually published in 1549, three years after Luther's death. In 1539 the Duke of Saxony died, and Cochlaeus became canon at Breslau, Poland, where, after a brief sojourn in Eichstätt, he died in 1552. Cochlaeus continued to write polemic against Luther, Melanchthon, and other reformers until the end, producing over two hundred works in his prolific career.

See also Emser, Jerome; Luther's Roman Catholic Opponents

Bibliography
Bagchi, D. V. N. *Luther's Earliest Opponents: Catholic Controversialists, 1518–1525.* Fortress, 1991; Bäumer, R. *Johannes Cochlaeus (1429–1552): Leben und Werk im Dienst der katholischen Reform.* Aschendorff, 1980; Samuel-Scheyder, M. *Johannes Cochlaeus: Humaniste et adversaire de Luther.* Presses Universitaires de Nancy, 1993; Vandiver, E., R. Keen, and T. D. Frazel, ed. and trans. *Luther's Lives: Two Contemporary Accounts of Martin Luther.* Manchester University Press, 2003.

ERIC J. DEMEUSE

Colloquy

As a gathering of interested or appointed individuals, a colloquy facilitates conversation and dialogue on specific matters under dispute. Within the Lutheran Church, colloquies were often called to discuss specific theological issues and to resolve the controversies that kept dialogue partners apart. In this way, they functioned much the same as ecumenical dialogues of the last hundred years.

Many crucial colloquies took place in the sixteenth century. Philip of Hesse hosted the first "Protestant" colloquy in Marburg in October 1529. Lutherans and other reformers from Switzerland and Germany were invited. Its goal was to forge a common front among the Evangelical territories and theologians involved, following the Diet of Speyer (1529), and in preparation for the Diet of Augsburg (1530). Agreement (in the Marburg Articles) was reached on fourteen of fifteen issues, but not on the chief matter under dispute: the nature of the real presence of Christ in the Lord's Supper. As a result, participants in the Marburg Colloquy brought separate confessions of faith to Augsburg.

In 1540 Emperor Charles V invited Protestants and Roman Catholics to hold a colloquy on disputed issues first in Worms and then in Regensburg (1541), where the leading theologians were Philip Melanchthon and John Eck. A tentative agreement was reached on justification, but other matters related to the Lord's Supper and papal authority kept them apart. The tentative agreement on justification was later rejected by the Roman curia. Luther, who could not attend the colloquy, and Johannes Bugenhagen also turned down the agreement.

The third major colloquy took place in Altenburg in 1568–69. The Lutheran rulers were dismayed over the factions among Lutherans that had arisen after Luther's death (1546). In an effort to bring together the supporters of Melanchthon and those claiming to uphold Luther's pure teachings, a colloquy was held. The main issue was the role of good works in relation to justification. While agreement was not reached, from that failure arose impetus for unity leading to the Formula of Concord (1577).

In later centuries, colloquies were held whenever theological controversies arose or when evangelically minded political leaders needed to present a common front against Roman Catholic forces. The 1631 colloquy at Leipzig, for example, was prompted by the threat posed by Roman Catholic military forces during the Thirty Years' War (1618–48). Lutheran and Reformed rulers met in colloquy to forge a Protestant defensive alliance, while the theologians were asked to settle their theological differences. Many of the animosities among them arose over the 1555 Peace of Augsburg, which granted Lutherans, but not the Reformed, religious recognition in the Holy Roman Empire. The development of strict Reformed and Lutheran Orthodoxies at the turn of the seventeenth century divided them further. While the two sides agreed to cooperate in a defensive alliance against the Roman Catholic forces and accepted twenty-six of the twenty-eight articles of the Augsburg Confession, they could not agree on the Lord's Supper, thus repeating the failure of the Marburg Colloquy. Nor could they agree on predestination, which had also been unsuccessfully discussed at the 1586 Colloquy of Montbéliard (Mömpelgard) between Reformed and Lutheran theologians. The later success of the Protestant military forces led Lutheran and Reformed leaders to ignore the agreements reached at Leipzig.

In the nineteenth century many nonbinding colloquies, or free and independent conferences, were held in North America in an attempt to resolve controversies between various Lutheran church bodies. At these colloquies, the parties could discuss theological issues without being forced to vote on them. For example, the controversy over predestination arose, once again, in the late 1870s, leading to the split between the Missouri and Norwegian synods after unsuccessful conversations at the Milwaukee Colloquium (1881). Colloquies, now more commonly known as "Dialogues," were also instrumental in bringing about many mergers between Lutheran bodies at the end of the nineteenth century and throughout the twentieth century. This pattern of conversation or dialogue on theological controversies is often carried out in bilateral and multilateral ecumenical dialogues today.

The term "colloquy" was also used by the Lutheran Pietist movement. The *Colloquia philobiblica* (Colloquies for lovers of the Bible) were a series of significant conferences for the development of Pietism, held in Leipzig (1686) and supported by the leading figures of Lutheran Pietism, August Francke and Philipp Jakob Spener. Rather than meetings to overcome division, these colloquies were meant to stimulate the study of God's Word.

Today the term "colloquy" may also be used to denote the formal examination of a ministerial candidate by a panel of theologians and church representatives, in order to determine whether the church body will approve the candidate for a call for public ministry.

See also American Lutheranism Controversy; Ecumenical Dialogues; Formula of Concord; Inner-Lutheran Ecumenism; Marburg Colloquy; Mömpelgaard/Montbéliard Colloquy; Predestination (Election) Controversy; Regensburg Colloquy; Wittenberg Concord

Bibliography

Empie, P., and J. McCord, eds. *Marburg Revisited: A Re-examination of Lutheran and Reformed Traditions.* Augsburg, 1966; Gritsch, E. *A History of Lutheranism.* 2nd ed. Fortress, 2010; Hequet, S. *The 1541 Colloquy at Regensburg: In Pursuit of Church Unity.* VDM Verlag Dr. Müller, 2009; Sasse, H. *This Is My Body: Luther's Contention for the Real Presence in the Sacrament of the Altar.* Augsburg, 1959; Wolf, R. *Documents of Lutheran Unity in America.* Fortress, 1966.

GORDON A. JENSEN

Cologne

With forty thousand inhabitants in 1500, Cologne was the largest city in Germany at the time of the Reformation and one of the few more populous German cities to have largely resisted any significant infiltration from Evangelical reform sentiments. An imperial city but also the seat of the elector archbishop of Cologne, the city and its university theological faculty had an ambiguous relationship to its archbishops, prizing their independence while remaining loyal to the papacy and the old faith. Although a center of printing, Cologne's printers only rarely ventured to publish treatises by reformers. The attempt to publish William Tyndale's English translation of the New Testament in the city was aborted by the authorities. In 1528 two followers of Luther, Adolf von Clarenbach and Peter Fliedesten, were burned at the stake for their beliefs.

Archbishop Hermann von Wied (1477–1552), who had served as the elector archbishop of Cologne since 1515, initiated reforms from 1527 onward and began serious Evangelical reform in 1542, enlisting the aid of Martin Bucer and Philip Melanchthon. They composed a church order that won the approval of the provincial diet but was rejected by the cathedral chapter. Excommunicated in 1546, Archbishop Hermann was forced by military threats to abdicate. In 1582 Archbishop Gerbhard, Truchsess von Waldburg (1547–1601), renounced his allegiance to Tridentine reform and papal obedience, married his mistress Agnes von Mansfeld, and initiated Evangelical reforms. Excommunicated in 1583, he succumbed to military action by Bavarian and Spanish forces and fled the archbishopric; a second attempt at introducing the Reformation in Cologne had failed. The city and its university remained a stronghold of Tridentine Catholicism.

See also Bucer, Martin; Holy Roman Empire; Melanchthon, Philip

Bibliography

Scribner, R. W. "Why Was There No Reformation in Cologne?" In *Popular Culture and Popular Movements in Reformation Germany*, 217–41. Hambledon, 1987.

ROBERT KOLB

Colombia

In the 1930s a group of Lutheran men and women in Minnesota, led by John Carlsen and Ernest Weinhardt (who in 1937 would be sent as missionaries to Bolivia by the South American Prayer League), started to meet periodically to pray for the mission of bringing the gospel to all the world. Two women of this prayer league, Myrtle Nordin and Marie Thompson, felt that God was calling them to do more than pray; although their peers refused at that time to organize themselves as an agency, the two women went to Colombia at their own risk, constituting themselves as the Colombia Evangelical Mission of South America. This was the beginning of what in 1958 became the Evangelical Lutheran Church of Colombia. A member of the Lutheran World Federation (LWF) and in partnership with the Evangelical Lutheran Church in America, it is committed to proclaim the gospel in words and service for the salvation of human beings and the creation.

There are also two independent congregations recognized by the LWF: St. Matthew's in Bogotá (still speaking German) and St. Martin's in Cali, both connected with the Evangelical Church in Germany.

The LCMS and the WELS are also currently undertaking missions in Colombia.

Bibliography

Cruz, J. M. *The Histories of the Latin American Church: A Handbook*. Esp. 221–44. Fortress, 2014; http://www.ielco .org/; https://www.lutheranworld.org/country/colombia; http://wels.net/serving-others/missions/south-america/co lombia/history/; Theodore, E., and M. B. Bachmann. *Lutheran Churches in the World: A Handbook*. Esp. 516–20. Augsburg, 1989.

ANDRÉS ROBERTO ALBERTSEN

Conciliarism

There was a growing medieval proposal that final decision-making authority in the church rests with councils rather than with popes. A conciliar polity involves a representative assembly of church leaders, ordinarily bishops, who reach theological and administrative resolutions through vote (usually of a supermajority). Councils first came into widespread use in the ancient church and grew in popularity during the fourteenth and fifteenth centuries, but arguments for their supreme authority had become a minority opinion by the time of the Reformation. Though neither Luther nor later Lutheran churches adopted a strictly conciliar theory of church governance, Lutheran ecclesiology incorporated many of its elements, including the synodal form of church polity still prevalent among Lutheran churches internationally.

The Jerusalem council (Acts 15) provided biblical precedent for conciliarism. The early church resolved numerous doctrinal disputes through the use of councils composed of bishops. In the fourth century, a variety of councils met to settle the trinitarian and christological controversies that wracked the church. In time, seven ecumenical councils of the church, which dealt with conflicts over these doctrines and others, were generally regarded as authoritative in both the Latin and Greek churches throughout the first millennium. In the Latin Middle Ages, councils lost their role as assemblies of bishops and became instruments for papal-sponsored reform, especially the first four Lateran councils (1123, 1139, 1179, 1215). In the fourteenth century, the relocation of the papacy and Roman curia to Avignon (1305–78)—the first so-called "Babylonian Captivity of the Church"—eventually led to the Great Western Schism (1378–1417), when two popes arose with separate courts in Rome and Avignon. As a means for resolving the schism, theologians and canon lawyers began making recourse to a provision in medieval canon law that accorded councils the right to remove popes who were in error and resistant to correction.

The fifteenth-century conciliar movement arose out of this attempt to rectify the schism through appeals to conciliar authority. The Council of Pisa (1409) deposed the two rival claimants, Gregory XII and Benedict XIII, and replaced them with Alexander V. This resulted in three rival popes, all unwilling to abdicate. The Council of Constance (1414–18) ended the schism by excommunicating both Benedict XIII and Alexander's successor, John XXIII, acquiring the resignation of Gregory XII, and electing Martin V to replace him as unquestioned pope. The council also issued two important decrees: *Haec Sancta*, which asserted the superiority of a general council to the papacy; and *Frequens*, which stipulated the periodic convocation of councils to reform the church. Both Martin V and his successor, Eugenius IV, resisted the reform efforts of councils at Pavia-Sienna (1424) and Basel (1431–49), provoking an extended contest over authority in the church. Eugenius transferred the latter council to Ferrara for dialogue with the Greeks (1437), while the remaining council at Basel deposed him and elected a rival pope. Only through a series of pacts with secular authorities, in particular the 1448 Concordat of Vienna struck with Emperor Frederick III, did the papacy earn support for its cause against the council in exchange for specific administrative and fiscal liberties granted to Western European territorial churches.

In 1460, Pope Pius II issued the bull *Execrabilis* prohibiting, under threat of excommunication, the practice of appealing papal decisions to future councils. Despite this decree, the question of conciliarism remained open into the sixteenth century. In 1511 a group of dissident bishops convoked a council in Pisa, at the instigation of the French government, but Rome quickly decried it as a *conciliabulum*, or "pseudo-council," and called its own alternative, the Fifth Lateran Council (1512–17). Several prominent Parisian theologians, including the Scot John Mair and Parisian master Jacques Almain, continued defending conciliar authority at the time of the council. Lateran V reaffirmed the prohibition of *Execrabilis*, but cries for a council continued because few efforts at church reform had come to fruition.

Luther's view of conciliarism emerged progressively in the course of the indulgence controversy that began on the heels of Lateran V. His earliest opponents, Cardinal Cajetan (Thomas de Vio) and Sylvester Prieras, mistook Luther for a conciliarist. Luther did make official appeals to a "pope better informed" and subsequently to a "future council," both of which were common practices of late medieval conciliarists, but it was only in the course of the Leipzig Debate that he came to express his position on councils more fully. In preparation for the June 1519 debate with John Eck, Luther drafted a controversial set of theses stating that papal decrees were not superior to Scripture, tradition, or church councils. Consequently, the Leipzig Debate revolved around the question of church authority. During the disputation, when Luther maintained that the Council of Constance had erred in its condemnation of Bohemian reformer Jan Hus, Eck pressed him on the authority of councils and forced Luther to admit that councils, like popes and church fathers, were fallible and always subordinate to the infallible authority of Scripture. The view Luther enunciated at Leipzig would prove pivotal in his radical subsuming of papal authority and conciliar authority alike under Scripture.

The final statement from Luther on conciliarism came in response to Rome's convocation of a council for Mantua in 1536. As early as 1520, Luther and the German princes had repeatedly called for a "Free Christian Council on German Lands" to address the ongoing religious division within the church. Popes resisted such calls, despite the demands of Charles V to convoke a council, until the election of Paul III in 1534. He established a reform commission to make recommendations to the council and published a bull of convocation. In response to the bull and on the basis of an extensive historical study of church councils, Luther drafted his 1539 *On Councils and the Church*. (For the same reason and in the same year, Philip Melanchthon published his tract on the church, originally titled *Book on the Authority of the Church and the Writings of the Ancient [Fathers]*.) Luther argued that only the first four councils were authoritative, not intrinsically, but because they adhered to Scripture in their teachings on the Trinity and the person of Christ. This became the central statement of Lutheran teaching on church councils, in that it affirmed—as Luther had at Leipzig—the primacy of Scripture over church authority.

In the period after Luther's death, Lutherans convoked a variety of colloquies to deal with intra-Lutheran debates. Attended by theologians and superintendents, these were seldom successful in ending such disputes and never claimed to have broader, conciliar authority for the church. In contrast, the development of bodies of doctrine (*corpora doctrinae*) by various territorial churches in German-speaking lands led to the writing of the Formula of Concord by a small number of theologians, its inclusion in the Book of Concord, and the use of widespread subscription, by political entities and their pastoral leaders, thus providing a different means of reaching doctrinal agreement.

See also Marburg Colloquy; Regensburg Colloquy

Bibliography

Avis, P. *Beyond the Reformation? Authority, Primacy, and Unity in the Conciliar Tradition.* T&T Clark, 2006; Bäumer, R. *Nachwirkungen des konziliaren Gedankens in der Theologie und Kanonistik des frühen 16. Jahrhunderts.* Aschendorff, 1971; Black, A. *Council and Commune.* Burnes & Oates, 1979; Hendrix, S. *Luther and the Papacy.* Fortress, 1981; Oakley, F. *The Conciliarist Tradition.* Oxford, 2003; Spehr, C. *Luther und das Konzil.* Mohr Siebeck, 2010; Tierney, B. *Foundations of the Conciliar Theory.* Cambridge University Press, 1955.

RICHARD J. SERINA

Confessing Church

The Confessing Church was a faction within the German Evangelical Church that sought theologically and institutionally to prevent the nazification of that church between 1933 and 1945. Its name derives from its founders' conviction that a true church had to be grounded in faithfulness to God's Word as found in the confessions and the act of confessing them, not through the church's relevance for or conformity to a particular historical moment. Theologically, it challenged the notion, advocated by some German theologians and church leaders, that the rise of National Socialism and additional orders of creation such as race and *Volk* (nation) represented a form of revelation in history. The theologians primarily associated with the Confessing Church were Karl Barth and Dietrich Bonhoeffer, yet the movement included a wide range of theologians, including Rudolf Bultmann, Martin Niemoeller, and Helmut Thielicke.

Institutionally, the Confessing Church emerged out of the opposition to the German Christians, a nationalist and anti-Semitic group within the German Evangelical Church that theologically embraced the rise of Nazism and sought to align the church with the Nazi state, particularly by trying to introduce an "Aryan paragraph" into church law. Over the course of 1933 the German Christians gained control of most regional church governments and threatened to create a *Reichskirche* (National Church) that would conform to Nazi ideology. In September 1933 Pastor Martin Niemoeller organized the Pastors Emergency League (PEL) to defend clergy considered to be "non-Aryan" and to oppose the theological extremism of the German Christians.

By November 1933 the German Evangelical Church was sharply divided; about a third of its pastors were members of the German Christians, a third were members of the PEL, and the remaining third were somewhere in the middle. With German Christians now in influential church governance posts, many church leaders feared that the state might completely seize control of the churches. They also feared a church schism, however, and thus sought compromise with the German Christians.

These developments launched the Church Struggle (*Kirchenkampf*), an internal battle for control over the theological and political course of the German Evangelical Church, culminating in May 1934 in the national Barmen Synod, which was attended by representatives from every regional and provincial church. One day before the national synod, representatives from the Old Prussian Union churches met in Barmen and established the Confessing Church. The following day the national synod unanimously approved the Barmen Confession of Faith, which repudiated the theological extremism of the German Christians and clearly stated that any church's ultimate obedience must be to God and the Scriptures, not to worldly authorities. Written primarily by Karl Barth, the Barmen Confession became the founding document of the Confessing Church. At the Dahlem Synod five months after Barmen, Confessing Church delegates broke with more moderate church leaders and decided to establish their own church governance structures and ordination process, as well as five independent theological faculties.

Despite the outcome of the Dahlem Synod, the Confessing Church was never a completely separate entity from the German Evangelical Church, and its members and leaders encompassed a wide spectrum of theological and political viewpoints, even including some pastors who were Nazi Party members. The Confessing Church existed primarily in the Old Prussian Union church provinces, but there were individual Confessing parishes throughout Germany. It is difficult to determine the size of the Confessing Church membership; its numbers dropped as divisions within the movement grew. Confessing Church leaders were united only in their opposition to the extremism of the German Christian movement and to state interference in church affairs; relatively few of them became engaged in active political resistance against the Nazi regime.

Despite this ambiguous record, the Confessing Church and its resistance to the German Christians after 1945 were viewed as a theological and institutional turning point in the history of the German Evangelical Church. Theologically, its clear delineation between faithfulness to Scripture and obedience to state authority, in conjunction with the record of the churches' failures under Nazism, laid the foundation for a more critical Protestant approach on church-state issues in postwar Germany, and its legacy was particularly claimed by political theologians. Institutionally, the Confessing Church's decentralized form of governance and its independence of state support were adopted as a model in the German Democratic Republic from 1948 to 1989, although not in the postwar western Evangelical Church of Germany.

See also Barmen Confession; Barth, Karl; Bonhoeffer, Dietrich; Bultmann, Rudolf (Karl); German Christians (Deutsche Christen); Niemoeller, Martin; Thielicke, Helmut

Bibliography

Barnett, V. *For the Soul of the People: Protestant Protest against Hitler*. Oxford University Press, 1992; Bethge, E. *Dietrich Bonhoeffer: A Biography*. Rev. ed. Fortress, 2000; Gerlach, W. *And the Witnesses Were Silent: The Confessing Church and the Jews*. University of Nebraska Press, 2000; Helmreich, E. C. *The German Churches under Hitler*. Wayne State University Press, 1979.

VICTORIA J. BARNETT

Confession (Private) and the Confessional

Despite Martin Luther's sharp criticism of the late medieval sacrament of penance in the early years of the Reformation, he was consistently a strong proponent of a revised version of private confession and absolution. Luther believed that the sacrament of penance promoted works-righteousness and anxious consciences because of its requirement that penitents confess every mortal sin in order to be forgiven and the requirement that penitents perform works of satisfaction in order for the priestly absolution to be efficacious. Luther's Evangelical soteriology held that human beings' fallen condition made it impossible to discern all their sins and that Christ's atonement precluded the need for human works of satisfaction. Forgiveness was a gift of sheer grace that was received by faith. Luther furthermore opposed the clerical jurisdiction over lay consciences that was assumed in the traditional sacrament, arguing that it amounted to an abuse of the power of the keys, which he believed belonged to all Christians. But Luther still insisted that private confession and absolution were a necessary and even central rite in Evangelical pastoral care.

Luther sought to reform private confession, not to abolish it. He thought the private encounter between confessant and confessor (whether lay or clerical) provided the best opportunity for the gospel to be applied to the individual troubled conscience. When Andreas Bodenstein von Karlstadt sought to abolish private confession in Wittenberg, Luther returned from the Wartburg and preached in his Invocavit sermons (1522), "I will allow no man to take private confession away from me, and I would not give it up for all the treasures in the world, since I know what comfort and strength it has given me. No one knows what it can do for him except one who has struggled often and long with the devil. Yea, the devil would have slain me long ago, if confession had not sustained me" (LW 51:99). Luther would force no one to private confession, but neither would he allow anyone to deny him access to it. He had suffered much in the confessional, to be sure, but he had also received wonderful consolation, and he refused to deprive others of the same comfort.

Owing in large part to Luther's strong support for the practice, Lutherans developed a reformed version of private confession that was alluded to in the Augsburg Confession (art. 11), with a prescribed form found in the Small Catechism of 1531. Thus, nearly every Evangelical church order of the early modern period included one. Lutheran private confession consisted of the following parts: an examination of faith (*Glaubensverhör*), an acknowledgment of one's depravity, a voluntary confession of specific sins bothering the one confessing, and absolution. Gone was the traditional examination of conscience, the insistence on making a full confession (i.e., one in which every mortal sin committed since the last confession was listed), the attempt to assess degrees of sorrow, the assigning of penances to satisfy or reduce time in purgatory, the belief in purgatory itself, the distinction between the guilt for sin (*culpa*) and the penalty for sin (*poena*), and the formula of absolution: *ego absolvo te* (I absolve you). The confessor was no longer judge in the courtroom of conscience: he was now a servant of the Word who tested knowledge of the catechism and then ministered the gospel to troubled souls. This Evangelical version of private confession typically took place in a Saturday-evening vesper service. Those who wished to participate in the Lord's Supper on the following Sunday were required to register (*anzaigen*) and to attend the confession vesper service. Lay confession and absolution were still encouraged, but confession to a pastor soon became the norm.

The new rite took some time to become an accepted part of Lutheranism. Luther's own equivocation in *The Babylonian Captivity of the Church* (1520) about the sacramental status of private confession helps to account for this delay. He began the treatise with three sacraments but concluded with just two, reasoning that confession was a return to baptism and therefore was not a sacrament in its own right. There was no agreement on the sacramental status of confession among Lutherans during this time, in part due to debates about the relationship between private confession and general confession, most notably in Nuremberg in the 1530s and 1540s. Andreas Osiander, a pastor in Nuremberg, argued that general confession and absolution were an abuse of the power of the keys, because the pastor who pronounced such absolution had no way of knowing whether members of the congregation were penitent, and therefore he risked losing people who should be bound. Osiander also argued that in most people's minds general confession precluded the need for private confession. Luther and Melanchthon weighed in on the issue, and while they were sympathetic to Osiander's concern to promote private confession, they argued that general confession was still a valid use of the keys since only those who received such absolution with faith would be forgiven. Osiander lost the debate. The delay in implementation of Lutheran private confession also has do with the fact that many Lutherans viewed the new rite with suspicion, fearing it meant a return to "popish" Christianity. But in time Evangelical private confession gained acceptance and went on to become a popular theme in Lutheran devotion during the late sixteenth and early seventeenth centuries, especially over against the Reformed churches' rejection of it. It was practiced well into the seventeenth and eighteenth centuries.

Two factors led to the decline of Lutheran private confession: the religious fervor of German Pietism and the rationalism of the German Enlightenment. Already in the early 1620s devout Lutherans began complaining that many people were participating in private confession in a purely perfunctory manner. Particularly scandalous was the reintroduction of *Beichtgeld* (confession money), which suggested to confessants that forgiveness could be purchased. By the end of the seventeenth century, Philipp Jakob Spener and August Hermann Francke, the two most prominent leaders of German Pietism, had each published pamphlets urging the laity to a more sober observance of confession and Communion. Pietism led to the decline of private confession not because it devalued the practice but because it could not tolerate abuses of it, something that is especially evident in the case of Johann Caspar Schade, a Pietist deacon in Berlin's Nikolaus Church, who successfully lobbied for the abolition of mandatory private confession owing to improper observance of it. Private confession was still available but only on a voluntary basis.

Though important for the eventual decline of Evangelical private confession, pietistic critique was not nearly as significant as the calculated assault of German *Aufklärer* (enlightened thinkers). As part of their effort to promote a more rational and ethical religion, apostles of the Enlightenment sought to liberate their fellow Germans from their "self-incurred tutelage" to puerile forms of piety, private confession being a notorious example. Using Luther's early arguments against the sacrament of penance to attack the version of private confession for which Luther advocated, proponents of "enlightened" religion maintained that Lutheran private confession was a "popish" rite that had no place in a purified Christianity. These efforts met with considerable success, and private confession was abolished in many Lutheran lands.

After World War II there were efforts to resurrect Evangelical private confession, in part owing to the efforts of Dietrich Bonhoeffer, who was a strong proponent of the practice, but in the modern period it has largely remained a forgotten sacrament, or half-sacrament, of the Lutheran Church. Official guides for belief and worship still contain liturgies for private confession, and at least some pastors are still trained to use such liturgies, but few Lutherans participate in them. However, there remains a small but vocal group of Lutheran pastors and theologians who continue to advocate for the importance of the rite that Luther first developed.

See also Osiander, Andreas; Penance, Penitence, Repentance; Sacraments

Bibliography

Aland, K. "Die Privatbeichte im Lutherthum von ihrem Anfängen bis zu ihrer Auflösung." In *Kirchengeschichtliche Entwürfe: Alte Kirche, Reformation und Luthertum, Pietismus und Erweckungsbewegung*, 452–519. G. Mohn, 1960; Bezzel, E. *Frei zum Eingeständnis: Geschichte und Praxis der evangelischen Einzelbeichte*. Calwer, 1982; Bonhoeffer, D. *Life Together*. Trans. J. W. Doberstein. Esp. chap. 5, "Confession and Communion." HarperCollins, 1954; Henze, E., ed. *Die Beichte*. Vandenhoeck & Ruprecht, 1991; Klein, L. *Evangelisch-Lutherische Beichte: Lehre und Praxis*. Bonifacius, 1961; Lohse, B. "Die Privatbeichte bei Luther." *Kerygma und Dogma* 14 (1968): 207–28; Luther, M. *De captivitate Babylonica ecclesiae* (1520). WA 6:497–573. ET, *The Babylonian Captivity of the Church*. LW 36:3–126, esp. 81–91, 124; Luther, M. "Kurze Unterweisung wie man beichten soll" (1519). WA 2:57–65; Luther, M. "Ein Sermon vom Sakrament der Busse" (1518). WA 2:709–23; Luther, M. "Ein Sermon von der Beichte" (1524). WA 15:481–97; Luther, M. "Von den Schlüsseln" (1530). WA 30.2:465–507. ET, "The Keys." LW 40:321–77; Luther, M. "Von der Beicht, ob die der Bapst macht habe zu gepieten" (1521). WA 8:129–85; Obst, H. *Der Berliner Beichtstuhlstreit: Die Kritik des Pietismus an der Beichtpraxis der lutherischen Orthodoxie*. Luther-Verlag, 1972; Precht, F. "Confession and Absolution: Sin and Forgiveness." In *Lutheran Worship*, ed. F. Precht, 322–86. Concordia, 1993; Rittgers, R. K. "Luther's Reformation of Private Confession." *LQ* 19 (2005): 312–31. Reprint, in *The Pastoral Luther: Essays on Luther's Practical Theology*, ed. T. J. Wengert, 211–30. Eerdmans, 2009; Rittgers, R. K. *The Reformation of the Keys: Confession, Conscience, and Authority in Sixteenth-Century Germany*. Harvard University Press, 2004; Uhsadel, W. *Evangelische Beichte in Vergangenheit und Gegenwart*. G. Mohn, 1961.

RONALD K. RITTGERS

Confessionalization, Confessional Age

The terms "confessionalization" and "confessional age" have emerged in late-twentieth-century scholarship of sixteenth-century Europe to describe the period in which the Reformation made an extensive impact on and was absorbed into specific political entities and societies. The period is defined chronologically in many ways but may be said to begin in Lutheran lands theologically with the Formula and Book of Concord (1577/80) or politically with the Religious Peace of Augsburg (1555). Its end may be dated anywhere between 1675, with the beginnings of Pietism, and around 1750, with the deaths of the last prominent "Orthodox" theologians, such as Valentin Ernst Loescher.

Attempts to analyze the relationships of the several theological streams of the German Reformation (and Tridentine Roman Catholicism) to their governments, societies, and cultures find their roots in the studies of Tübingen professor Ernst Walter Zeeden, who in 1964 proposed an explanation for the "formation of the confessions" (*Konfessionsbildung*), which spoke of the confessions not as theological documents defining the faith but rather in the German usage of "confession" as an ecclesiastical tradition, the institutions of the Roman Catholic, Lutheran, and Reformed churches. Zeeden did not ignore the theological elements of this formation process yet did not focus on the period's development of confessional documents and theological frameworks for viewing reality, as have others, including Ernst Koch and Irene Dingel.

In 1981 the Giessen (later Berlin) professor Heinz Schilling set forth his theory of "confessionalization" (*Konfessionalisierung*) in a study designed to deconstruct the often-repeated equation of Lutheranism with princely absolutism and Calvinism with progressive tendencies toward modern democratic views of society. Schilling argued that the similarities of the programs of the three "confessions" or ecclesiastical traditions for culture and society were more similar than different, as Luther also argued with his contention that in the realm of reason, reasonable people should perceive such matters in similar ways. Schilling defined "confessionalization" as "a fundamental process in society, which plowed up the public and private life of Europe in thoroughgoing fashion," redefining society in terms of political, social,

economic, and cultural attitudes and structures along with the theological or ecclesiastical elements involved (Schilling, *Religion*, 219).

In 1981 the Augsburg professor Wolfgang Reinhard also advanced his theory of confessionalization, focusing on the phenomenon within Roman Catholicism. He traced the development of coherence within the cultures of the three great German confessional groups, emphasizing their basis in clear theoretical conceptions of the truth, the spread and enforcement of new norms for public behavior, the use of propaganda and polemic against other confessional ideologies, the internalization of the new order through education, the disciplining of adherents, the use of ritual, and the shaping of language. Through the reinforcement of their identity, externally and internally, modern territorial states thus developed control over the church, whether Roman Catholic or Protestant, and managed to discipline their subjects.

Many other scholars have published their extensions, qualifications, and critiques of the works of Schilling and Reinhard. The focus of the thesis on territorial states rather than local communities, its ignoring the pluralism existent even in so-called absolutist political-social structures, its failure to take seriously the coincidence of biblical norms with the ideals for public behavior in the period, the significance of religious factors in the worldview and thinking of the common people—these as well as other issues have earned criticism. The chronological definition of the period of "confessionalization" has also been fiercely debated, with some scholars seeing its beginning in the earliest forms of institutionalization of reform measures in the 1520s and 1530s, while others have argued that true "confessionalization" was completed only in the nineteenth century.

Ernst Koch's definition of the "confessional age" takes seriously the involvement of the church and its theologians in political and social changes in the early modern period but also highlights the changes wrought by the

Reformation in ecclesiastical life and popular piety as well as formal theology.

While many treatments of the theology and church life since the early nineteenth century have labeled the period between Luther's death and the advent of Pietism and the Enlightenment around 1700 as "sterile," "rigid," and "unfruitful," at least two factors belie this. First, Kenneth Appold has demonstrated the dynamic nature of theological discussion within the framework of commitment to the Lutheran confessions at Lutheran university faculties in this period. Second, the production of devotional literature and hymnody from Philip Nicolai to Johann Sebastian Bach reveals a very lively and intense piety that, through a variety of printed works and oral use, spread broadly among the population of Lutheran lands. Fresh research is just beginning to uncover the vibrant, vigorous ecclesiastical life behind the dogmatic tomes produced to summarize the teaching of the faith and to bring it into the larger ecumenical exchange with Roman Catholic, Reformed, and also Socinian ideas.

See also Catholicism; Lutheran Orthodoxy; Peace of Augsburg

Bibliography

Brady, T. A., Jr. "Confessionalization: The Career of a Concept." In *Confessionalization in Europe, 1555–1700: Essays in Honor and Memory of Bodo Nischan*, ed. J. M. Headley et al., 1–20. Ashgate, 2004; Dingel, I. *Concordia controversa*. Gütersloher Verlagshaus, 1996; Dingel, I. "The Function and Historical Development of Reformation Confessions." *LQ* 26 (2012): 295–321; Kaufmann, T. "Die Konfessionalisierung von Kirche und Gesellschaft: Sammelbericht." *Theologische Literaturzeitung* 121 (1996): 1008–25, esp. 1112–21; Koch, E. *Das konfessionelle Zeitalter—Katholizismus, Luthertum, Calvinismus (1563–1675)*. Evangelische Verlagsanstalt, 2000; Reinhard, W., and H. Schilling, eds. *Die katholische Konfessionalisierung: Wissenschaftliches Symposion der Gesellschaft zur Herausgabe des Corpus Catholicorum und des Vereins fur Reformationsgeschichte*. Gütersloher Verlagshaus, 1995; Rublack, H.-C., ed. *Die lutherische Konfessionalisierung in Deutschland*. Mohn, 1992; Schilling, H., ed. *Die reformierte Konfessionalisierung in Deutschland—Das Problem der "Zweiten Reformation."* Mohn, 1986; Schilling, H. *Religion, Political Culture, and the Emergence of Early Modern Society*. Brill, 1992; Zeeden, E. W. *Die Entstehung der Konfessionen: Grundlagen und Formen der Konfessionsbildung im Zeitalter der Glaubenskämpfe*. Oldenbourg, 1964.

ROBERT KOLB

Confession of Faith

Confessing that Jesus Christ is Lord and confessing the content of the creedal summary of biblical teaching belongs to the fundamental acts of Christians throughout history. The early church understood that God was addressing humankind with a message of salvation from sin and restoration of human identity through Christ's death and resurrection. It spread on the basis of winning others to accept and confess this message. This confession expressed the personal identity of the one confessing and also was intended to create and strengthen faith in those who heard it.

Medieval usage of the term "confession" did not ignore this aspect of the concept of confession but emphasized, first, the confession of sins in confession and absolution, as practiced eventually in the sacrament of penance, and second, the confession of God's glory in praise and worship. Relatively few official doctrinal pronouncements of bishops and councils used the term "confess" as a synonym for "teach" or "decree" in asserting proper teaching or practice. "Confession" became a synonym for "creed," "canon," or "decree" as the designation of a definition of faithful belief and practice. In this way, Philip Melanchthon used it as the title for the statement of faith and proper ecclesiastical life in the Augsburg Confession of 1530, and when it was subsequently published, its printed form served as an interpretive authority within the church.

Elector John of Saxony and his Evangelical colleagues in the imperial diet assigned Melanchthon the task of composing the explanation of their reform measures for Holy Roman Emperor Charles V, who demanded a justification of these reforms introduced in the 1520s in accord with Luther's call for reform. Melanchthon prefaced his explanations of specific changes in practice with twenty-one doctrinal articles affirming the catholicity and biblical faithfulness of Luther's followers. At first he titled this text for an oral presentation to the emperor a "defense" (*apologia*) but altered the title, making the speech that was to be read to the emperor and the diet a "confession." This reflected the Wittenberg theology of the primacy of God's Word in addressing his people.

Because of the nature of this oral statement as a formal presentation within the diet and because the Wittenberg reformers had learned to use the printing press to best advantage, it was inevitable, despite the imperial prohibition of such publication, that the document would be printed. From the 1530s onward its printed version served as an identifying definition of what it means to embrace Wittenberg reform. Since it was a brief document and was opposed by the Roman party's "Confutation," it required commentary, which Melanchthon provided in his Defense, or Apology, of the Augsburg Confession. Throughout the sixteenth century regional statements of doctrine were composed by others, within and beyond the Wittenberg circle, with the same purpose of defining the church by its teaching. Without exception those within the Wittenberg circle viewed themselves as extensions or reiterations of or even commentaries on the Augsburg Confession. The final point in this development was reached in the Formula of Concord (1577).

The Wittenberg reformers understood "confession," referring to the document, as a kind of "verbal noun," in which content could not be separated from the action of presenting the content to the world. For them, holding a confession of the faith meant to be speaking it in public, living according to it, and being prepared to die for it.

Other documents became classified as confessions. Among Luther's followers his Smalcald Articles, an agenda for negotiations with the Roman Catholic party presented in 1536 and printed in 1538, and his catechisms of 1529 became formal definitions of the church, its teaching, and its practice. In 1551 Melanchthon penned a "Repetition" of the Augsburg Confession (the Saxon Confession), which was to serve as the Saxon position at the Council of Trent. In the same year Johannes Brenz composed the Württemberg Confession. Other churches also chose to define themselves with documents regarded as confessions, particularly within Reformed circles, where also the Heidelberg Catechism served as an important defining document. In Roman Catholic, Anglican, and Anabaptist circles the term "confession" is also applied to documents, some of which formally bear the title "Articles," such as the Anglican Thirty-Nine Articles and the Anabaptist Schleitheim Articles. In each Christian church tradition these confessional statements hold different weight. Lutherans have always regarded them in some sense as secondary authorities and adjudicators of disagreements over specific biblical teachings.

See also Apology of the Augsburg Confession; Augsburg Confession; Smalcald Articles

Bibliography

Dingel, I. "The Function and Historical Development of Reformation Confessions." *LQ* 26 (2012): 295–321; Dingel, I. "Philip Melanchthon and the Establishment of Confessional Norms." *LQ* 20 (2006): 164–69; Kolb, R. *Confessing the Faith: Reformers Define the Church, 1530–1580*. Concordia, 1991.

ROBERT KOLB

Confirmation

In common Lutheran usage today "confirmation" means (1) instruction in the Christian faith, usually of children and adolescents; and (2) a public rite upon completion of the instruction. One of the seven sacraments of the Roman Catholic Church, the rite's sacramental status was rejected by all Lutheran sixteenth-century reformers because Jesus did not institute confirmation and no divine promise was associated with it. Nevertheless, the rite of confirmation was seen by some reformers, especially Martin Bucer and (later) Martin Chemnitz, as an ancient custom of the church worth retaining. Sixteenth-century reforms of the rite replaced the anointing of chrism by the bishop with the laying on of hands by the pastor, a ritual practice of the apostles described in the New Testament (Acts 6:6; 8:17; 19:6) and in early church fathers. Other significant innovations by the reformers—although they perceived these as a return to ancient customs of the church—included catechetical instruction prior to the rite of confirmation and the addition of a public confession of faith by the candidate within the rite.

During the sixteenth century, a variety of practices developed. In some areas, especially those under the Augsburg and the so-called Leipzig Interims (1548), opponents of the interims resisted any ritual called confirmation. Church orders from these areas illustrate this model. Given various titles, such as *Catechismus*, *Beichtverhör*, or *Communiciren Kinder*, these church orders outlined programs for catechetical instruction based on Luther's Small Catechism and an examination (either public or private) prior to first Communion without any public rite of confirmation or use of the term. Such practices emphasized preparation for and proper reception of the Lord's Supper with little or no reference to baptism. Other geographic areas adopted an Evangelical form of confirmation at the end of formal catechetical instruction. These rites typically included public examination of the candidates in the articles of the faith, public confession of faith similar to that in the rite of baptism, and prayer invoking the Holy Spirit with the laying on of hands. It was thus considered a necessary rite prior to first Communion, although it may also have had a ritual link to baptism. Bucer, an advocate for the public confession of faith in the rite of confirmation, may have been influenced by contacts with Anabaptists in Strasbourg and by his later mediating efforts between the Anabaptists and Lutherans in Hesse (1538). Martin Chemnitz, another advocate for the rite, was less influential at introducing a "purified" rite, but Philipp Jakob Spener invoked Chemnitz when he promoted its adoption with great success in Germany in the seventeenth century; Scandinavia followed in the eighteenth century.

Spener promoted confirmation as a way to make one's faith a matter of "heart" as well as "head." The goal of instruction in the faith was the personal conversion of the individual, then professed in public through the rite. Hence the rite gave new emphasis to the vows or promises of confirmands and stressed the "renewal" or "ratification of the baptismal covenant." Similar rites and emphases for catechetical instruction were brought across the Atlantic by Lutheran immigrants. The core text for confirmation instruction, carried out primarily by the pastor, was Luther's Small Catechism. As rationalism and the Enlightenment led to secularization in Europe, confirmation took on new meanings: it became a coming-of-age ritual, a bestowal of membership rights, and a rite in which one made a commitment to a particular denomination. The latter meaning also held true in the denominational pluralism in places such as the United States. The pietistic tone of the rites would come under greater scrutiny in nineteenth-century Europe by leaders in the confessional movement, who felt this language implied that baptism is a bilateral covenant requiring human assent for its completion. Through these centuries, confirmation continued to be the gateway to reception of the Lord's Supper.

In the twentieth century, Lutherans first addressed the question of confirmation practices shortly after the formation of the Lutheran World Federation (LWF). The Commission on Education of the LWF undertook an international study of the history, theology, and practice of confirmation instruction and its culminating ritual from 1957 to 1963. The situation in the divided Germany illustrates some issues discussed. As a ritual in the churches of West Germany, confirmation was viewed by most as a folk-church ceremony marking the completion of school and through which participants were granted full membership rights in the church; for many scholars, this ritual and its popular understanding undermined Lutheran baptismal theology. For East German Lutherans, the rite of confirmation requiring a personal pledge to the church was a voice of resistance over against the atheist youth dedication ceremony.

North American Lutherans in the twentieth century established joint commissions and studies to address variations in the practice and theology of confirmation and related topics. Predecessor bodies of the American Lutheran Church and Lutheran Church in America jointly studied confirmation prior to merging, and these two bodies joined with the Lutheran Church–Missouri Synod in the 1960s to study further the theology and practice of confirmation. This commission "redefined confirmation as a ministry (or process) and advocated the separation of confirmation and first Communion" (Truscott 143). In 1969 the major Lutheran bodies in North America (ALC, LCA, LCMS, and the Evangelical Lutheran Church of Canada) established the Inter-Lutheran Commission on Worship (ILCW) with the goal of producing a common service book and hymnal for North American Lutherans; those serving on the ILCW committees, influenced by the liturgical movement, sought to have liturgical rites that reflected recent liturgical scholarship and that addressed some of the theological issues raised in the recent studies. The result was the publication of the *Lutheran Book of Worship* (*LBW*) in 1978. The *LBW* rite of confirmation followed the recommendation of the early commission on confirmation, separating the rite of confirmation and first Communion and tying confirmation more closely to Baptism.

Variety characterizes current practices and theological understanding of the rite worldwide. In North America the ELCA uses a repeatable rite called "Affirmation of Baptism," while the LCMS retains a specific rite of confirmation popularly understood as a onetime ritual. In contrast to the decoupling of confirmation from first Communion in North America, nearly all African churches, many Asian churches, and all churches in Central and Eastern Europe link the rite of confirmation to first Communion. Instruction in the faith leading to the rite of confirmation is shaped by the local context, yet there is consensus among church leaders that its intent is to form the Christian identity of youth and to encourage a lifelong journey of faith. Commonalities include instruction in the faith (based on the Bible and Luther's Small Catechism) prior to the rite, which includes a confession of faith, questions about the confirmands' intentions, and the laying on of hands with a blessing. However, the popular understanding of the ritual as a rite of passage to adulthood together with the pattern of instruction followed by a public rite conspire to convey a meaning that confirmation is the end of the journey, not a milestone along the way.

See also Baptism; Lord's Supper; Sacraments

Bibliography

Chemnitz, M. E*xamination of the Council of Trent*. Part 2. Trans. F. Kramer. Concordia, 1978; Frör, K., ed. *Confirmatio: Forschungen zur Geschichte und Praxis der Konfirmation*. Evang. Presseverband für Bayern, 1959; Frör, K., ed. *Zur Geschichte und Ordnung der Konfirmation in den lutherischen Kirchen*. Claudius, 1962; Jagger, P. *Christian Initiation 1552–1969: Rites of Baptism and Confirmation since the Reformation Period*. SPCK, 1970; Lutheran World Federation. *Confirmation Ministry Study: Global Report*. LWF, 1995; Repp, A. *Confirmation in the Lutheran Church*. Concordia, 1964; Sehling, E., ed. *Die evangelischen Kirchenordnungen des XVI. Jahrhunderts*. 15 vols. Mohr, 1902–55; Truscott, J. *The Reform of Baptism and Confirmation in American Lutheranism*. Scarecrow, 2003.

RHODA GREVER SCHULER

Congo, Democratic Republic of the

The first congregations of the Evangelical Lutheran Church in Congo (formerly Evangelical Lutheran Church of Zaïre) were founded after a group of laypeople had followed Bible studies of the *Radio Voice of the Gospel*. This international Lutheran radio station began operations in the Ethiopian capital, Addis Ababa, in 1963. The first leaders of the group studied theology at Makumira Theological College in Tanzania. In 1976 the association of Lutheran churches was received into the Church of Christ in Zaire (now in the Congo), the state-recognized organization for all Protestant churches. The Lutheran Church received official government recognition in 1981. It is difficult to gather correct statistics of church members because of the political situation. Many people were killed or uprooted during the civil war. The situation is still unstable. The ELCC reported about 136,000 members in 2013.

Bibliography

Balz, H. *Weggenossen am Fluss und am Berg: Von Kimbanguisten und Lutheranern in Afrika*. Erlanger Verlag für Mission und Ökumene, 2005; Melton, J. "Evangelical Lutheran Church in Congo." In *Religions of the World: A Comprehensive Encyclopedia of Beliefs and Practices*, ed. M. Baumann and J. G. Melton, 2:1048–49. ABC-CLIO, 2010.

FRIEDER LUDWIG

Conventicles

In the context of early modern Protestantism, where territories and countries generally had no legal guarantee of freedom of assembly, conventicles referred to devotional gatherings outside of appointed worship, under clerical or lay leadership. In the first century after the Reformation, conventicles played little role in Lutheranism. Luther briefly discussed the possibility of such gatherings in his 1526 preface to the German Mass, in which he proposed that earnest Christians might "meet alone in a house somewhere to pray, to read, to baptize, to receive the sacrament, and to do other Christian works" (LW 53:64). Luther never thought the time ripe for such gatherings, however. At Strasbourg in 1547, Martin Bucer and others proposed that smaller groups of select Christians would meet within the large parishes for devotion and discipline, but the imposition of the Augsburg Interim stifled their plans. In general, the challenge posed by radical religious groups rendered any kind of conventicle-type gatherings suspect among Lutheran clerical and civil authorities.

During the seventeenth century, proposals for small-group gatherings occasionally surfaced among Lutherans, as did ephemeral conventicles in places like Hamburg and Lübeck, but the most significant conventicle movement of seventeenth-century Lutheranism began in Frankfurt am Main under the auspices of Philipp Jakob Spener in 1670. The decisive impetus came from two laymen who encouraged him to hold devotional gatherings in his home. The *collegia pietatis*, as the groups became known, were intended to deepen scriptural knowledge, devotion, and Christian practice. By gathering pious Christians, Spener envisioned them as an adjunct to regular worship and preaching that would renew the church, as *ecclesiola in ecclesia* (a small church within the church). He defended these gatherings in his famous 1675 *Pia Desideria* by comparing them to the ancient apostolic church meetings in 1 Cor. 14 and by drawing on Luther's understanding of the common priesthood. The *collegia pietatis* flourished, but soon Spener had to contend with dissenting conventicle meetings in Frankfurt, and he sought to regulate their practice closely. After he moved to Dresden in 1686, he no longer organized *collegia pietatis*. Gatherings like these became one of the most controversial aspects of the early Pietist movement, but Spener's proposals were not universally rejected by Lutheran theologians.

The Pietist controversies in Leipzig of the late 1680s and the proliferation of lay-led conventicles there sharpened the controversy surrounding conventicles. Orthodox Lutheran opponents of Pietism saw them as a challenge to clerical authority and a seedbed of heterodoxy. Even moderate Pietists were wary of excesses that occurred in these meetings. Alarmed, civil authorities in many cities and territories in Germany released prohibitions against conventicles in the early 1690s. Even at Halle, the center of church Pietism in the early eighteenth century, conventicles, or *collegia pietatis*, did not become a major feature of August Hermann Francke's reform ideas. Nevertheless Pietist ideas and practices often spread through conventicle meetings in Germany, Scandinavia, and the Baltic, which in turn were met by legal proscriptions in Sweden (1726) and Denmark (1741). Radical and dissenting Pietists utilized small groups outside the authority of ordained clergy to propagate heterodox ideas. Prohibitions of conventicles were often employed to blunt the growth of radical streams of Pietism. But in many cases the persecution of individuals in conventicles proved counterproductive and often helped further radicalize participants. In some cases new religious associations emerged out of separatist conventicles such as the Dunker Brethren, the notorious Mother Eve Society founded by Eva von Buttlar (1670–1721), or the Harmony Society of Georg Rapp (1757–1847).

The 1743 *Pietistenreskript* made Württemberg the first territorial church in Lutheranism to endorse conventicle gatherings explicitly, albeit under the control of the local minister. Conventicles, especially those not led by ordained ministers, remained prohibited in many areas, but by the later eighteenth century the conventicle-type gatherings had lost much of their notoriety as the religious framework of the old Holy Roman Empire weakened, and places like North America afforded greater liberty for religious dissenters. Nevertheless, in Europe laws against conventicles still on the books could be used against religious dissenters. In the early nineteenth century, Hans Nielsen Hauge was prosecuted and imprisoned for violating the 1741 Anti-Conventicle Act of Denmark and Norway. Norway only repealed the Anti-Conventicle Act in 1842; Sweden repealed its 1726 prohibition of conventicles in 1858. Conventicles and private religious gatherings still played a formative role well into the nineteenth century. Zersen argues that many of those who emigrated to the United States and later established the Missouri Synod, including C. F. W. Walther, were profoundly influenced by private gatherings in Leipzig that were consciously modeled on earlier Pietist conventicles. Later, however, Walther and the Missouri tradition decisively rejected the formation of conventicles.

The word "conventicle" retains pejorative connotations to the present day. Yet the small-group gatherings commonplace among Lutherans and other major denominations in the twentieth and twenty-first centuries in Europe and North America do share many practices of Pietist conventicles, but without the divisive overtones that attended the earlier gatherings. Conventicle-type practices live on in areas where Christianity faces opposition, including among the house churches in China.

See also Pietism; Spener, Philipp Jakob

Bibliography

Bellardi, W. *Die Vorstufen der Collegia pietatis bei Philipp Jakob*. Brunnen, 1994; Strom, J. "Early Conventicles in Lübeck." *Pietismus und Neuzeit* 27 (2001): 19–52; Strom, J. "The Problem of Conventicles in early German Pietism." *Covenant Quarterly* 61 (2003): 3–16; Zersen, D. "C. F. W. Walther and the Heritage of Pietist Conventicles." *Concordia Historical Institute Quarterly* 62 (1989): 10–29.

JONATHAN STROM

Convents

By the early sixteenth century at least a thousand convents and female religious houses cloistered over ten thousand nuns, novices, and lay sisters throughout the German-speaking part of the Holy Roman Empire. These institutions had played a significant cultural role in art, music, and literature in many communities throughout the Middle Ages, providing a spiritual and devotional role for unmarried women. The subsequent closure of many convents during the Protestant Reformation and the Lutheran redefinition of marriage as the chief normative vocation open for women over the next decades challenged, but ultimately did not end, female monastic life. The emergence of Lutheran and Reformed female monasticism in the late sixteenth and early seventeenth centuries changed how convents and nuns functioned in Protestant communities.

When Martin Luther first rejected the efficacy of good works in salvation in 1520, he also questioned the purpose of monasticism and monastic vows, although explicitly only for monks. In his first two extensive works on monastic vows, *Themes concerning Vows* (1521) and *The Judgment of Martin Luther on Monastic Vows* (1521), Luther mentioned the vows of nuns in passing. After 1522, nuns began fleeing their monastic houses in increasing numbers, leading Luther and his followers to address female monasticism in a series of pamphlets, such as by Luther, *Answer on Why Nuns May Leave the Convent in a Godly Way* (1523); Bernhard Rem, *A Letter to Several Nuns in St. Katharina and St. Nicolas in Augsburg* (1523); and Matthias Wurm, *Consolation to Those Imprisoned in Convents* (1523). Both theologians and secular authors characterized convents as sites of immorality, where women's souls were actively jeopardized by their mistaken perpetual vows and their own inability to remain chaste. In condemning convents and calling for their closure, Luther argued that the only true vocation open for all women was as a wife, mother, and head of the household (*Hausfrau*) with her husband.

Like many others during the early reform movement, nuns were divided in their responses to such calls for the closure of convents. Throughout the 1520s nuns fled monastic life after reading published pamphlets or learning about the new reform movement from family or local clergy. A few nuns, such as Ursula von Münsterberg and Florentine von Oberweimar, published works defending this decision. A significant number of former nuns, such as Elisabeth Cruciger (née von Meseritz) and Katharina von Bora, eventually married former priests and monks, and they played an important role in the building of the first Lutheran parishes. Other nuns remained in their convents despite pressure to leave (although in Saxony convents were never forcibly closed during the official visitations beginning in 1527). Some nuns, such as Caritas Pirckheimer, adamantly defended female monastic life in print or in person, resisting attempts to close their houses. By the late 1520s continued resistance from Catholic nuns and the need to house Lutheran nuns unable to return to families or marry reopened debate on the role of convents and female religious life.

Although 20 percent of convents closed during the sixteenth century, the majority of them continued with fewer nuns, either as traditional Catholic convents, Lutheran religious houses, or multiconfessional religious foundations. Initially imagined as a temporary phase in a woman's life, Lutheran convents, religious houses, and foundations developed as the insistence on marriage as the only calling for women shifted slightly. Such institutions flourished especially in the duchy of Braunschweig, the county of Mark in Westphalia, and in Electoral Brandenburg beginning in the late sixteenth century. Lutheran theologians in these regions, such as Antonius Corvinus, Martin Chemnitz, and Jakob Andreae in the duchy of Braunschweig, argued in pamphlets, church orders, and convent ordinances that female monasticism was possible, and even necessary, for Lutheran women in specific circumstances. Together with local territorial princes, they modeled their convent regulations on the *Damenstift*, or female religious communities housing canonesses, to establish female religious institutions without solemn monastic vows.

Lutheran orders of nuns still exist throughout the world. In these institutions, Lutheran women give temporary vows of poverty, chastity, and obedience, and many wear a modified habit during formal celebrations. The greatest concentration of Lutheran nuns in Germany is in Lower Saxony, including six convents in the Lüneburg region (Isenhagen, Ebstorf, Lüne, Medingen, Walsrode, and Wienhausen) and five in Calenberg (Mariensee, Marienwerder, Barsinghausen, Wennigsen, and Wülfinghausen). Congregations of nuns outside of Germany, such as the Lutheran deaconesses in the United States and the Evangelical Sisterhood of Mary in Israel, Germany, and the United States, continue to flourish, although the official relationship of these groups with the Lutheran Church varies by location and institution.

See also Bora, Katharina von; Bugenhagen, Johannes; Corvinus, Antonius; Cruciger, Elisabeth; Marriage and Divorce; Monasteries, Evangelical; Rhegius, Urbanus; Vocation

Bibliography

Klueting, E. "Damenstifte im nordwestdeutschen Raum am Vorabend der Reformation." In *Studien zum*

Kanonissenstift, ed. I. Crusius, 317–48. Vandenhoeck & Ruprecht, 2001; Leonard, A. *Nails in the Wall: Catholic Nuns in Reformation Germany*. University of Chicago Press, 2005; Otte, H., ed. *Evangelisches Klosterleben: Studien zur Geschichte der evangelischen Klöster und Stifte Niedersachsen*. Vandenhoeck & Ruprecht, 2013; Wiesner, M. "Ideology Meets the Empire: Reformed Convents and the Reformation." In *Gender, Church, and State in Early Modern Germany*, 47–62. Longman, 1998; Wolf, M. "Konfessionell gemischte Stifte." In *Westfälisches Klosterbuch: Lexikon der vor 1815 errichteten Stifte und Klöster von ihrer Gründung bis zur Aufhebung*, ed. Karl Hengst, 3:246–93. Aschendorff, 2003.

MARJORIE ELIZABETH PLUMMER

Conversion and Regeneration

"Conversion" and "regeneration" are terms referring to fundamental alteration in faith and relationship to God. "Conversion" employs metaphors of movement and turning to express a new religious orientation to the world and God, whereas "regeneration" draws on the biological language of rebirth to portray the new relationship to God and to the Christian community. Both are rooted in Christian Scripture and tradition. The definition of conversion, however, was not fixed in the Reformation and post-Reformation era and could refer to a range of theological meanings and religious phenomena. For example, conversion appears in Philip Melanchthon's 1559 *Response to the Bavarian Inquisition Articles* as an equivalent to justification. In the seventeenth century and especially in Pietism, conversion gained new prominence and controversy within the Lutheran tradition, often referring to a specific moment or period in an individual's life that led to an assurance of salvation. The meaning of regeneration or rebirth varied less, especially given the consistent Lutheran emphasis on baptism as the beginning of regeneration.

Luther inherited medieval notions of conversion (esp. conversion from secular life to a monastic one), but as Harran argues, the fundamental meaning of conversion for Luther referred to God becoming human through the incarnation. Conversion could also refer to the onetime entrance into Christian life through baptism as well as the repeatable events of repentance and contrition. Much more rarely did Luther speak of conversion as a dramatic change in an individual's life along the model of Paul or Augustine (Harran 22–23).

Two events in Luther's life were later identified as "conversions," primarily in popular accounts. One is his 1505 decision to enter the Augustinian order in Erfurt following a dramatic thunderstorm in Stotternheim. Some contemporaries compared this to Paul's experience on the road to Damascus, but Luther did not characterize it in these terms either then or later. Another is Luther's so-called tower experience, which has some basis in his autobiographical reflections that formed the preface to the first volume of his Latin works, where he describes himself as "altogether born again" following his Evangelical discovery (LW 34:337). Interpreting this as a conversion remains controversial.

Beginning with the Small Catechism, regeneration remained closely tied to baptism, especially in connection with the "water of rebirth" in Titus 3:5, but as the Formula of Concord notes, regeneration could also represent, at times, justification, vivification, renewal, and sanctification, though always with the understanding that the "justified and reborn are and remain sinners to the grave" (FC 2.58–60). A distinct experience of conversion never became part of the Lutheran tradition in the sixteenth century. Luther and his colleagues remained skeptical of any preparation for grace that conversion in this sense might imply. Instead, conversion remained tied to baptism, and in the ongoing life of a believer, it referred to a process of repentance and continual turning toward God. In the German edition of the *Apology*, repentance and conversion functioned in places synonymously (Ap 12.28, 44). In the Formula of Concord, conversion began to represent a discrete step in the order of salvation, but it still remained tied fundamentally to the regenerating work of the Holy Spirit through word and sacrament, especially through baptism (FC 2.48–90). As Althaus put it for the sixteenth-century Lutheran tradition, "Conversion or daily repentance is nothing other than the event of baptism realized continually in life" (13).

In the early modern world, conversion could also refer to changes in religious identification. One mode, with a long history in Christianity, is conversion from another religious tradition, when, for instance, a Jew is baptized and joins a Christian community. Luther often employed language of converting and conversion in relation to Jews becoming Christians (e.g., LW 45:201) as well as non-Jewish "gentile" conversion (LW 13:378). Despite hopes for Jewish conversion, few Jews became Protestant in the sixteenth century, although there were some prominent instances, such as Immanuel Tremellius (1510–80).

The confessional divisions that followed the Reformation made a new form of conversion possible later in the sixteenth century: the conversion from one Christian confession to another. In this instance, a Christian would reject a previous form of confessional identity and affiliate with another, such as when a Lutheran becomes Roman Catholic, or a Catholic becomes Lutheran. This form of conversion almost never referred to changes among the major Protestant confessions such as alternation between the Lutheran and Reformed. Rather "conversion" in this context signified more fundamental changes in affiliation, which contemporaries understood as incompatible. Political, economic, and social forces could be at work in all forms of conversion, but it is important to recognize that, for Christians, true conversion in any form is divine in origin, though one individual's convert is often another's apostate.

Because regeneration remained so closely connected to baptism in the Lutheran tradition, language of conversion, in an inner-Christian sense, typically referred, well into the seventeenth century, to ongoing, profound repentance and a turn to faith, not a temporal moment in an individual's spiritual development. Devotional writers often linked repentance and conversion (*Busse und Bekehrung*) to describe the New Testament notion of *metanoia*.

Two changes spurred new understandings of conversion in the Lutheran tradition. First, the dogmatic tradition defined conversion with greater precision, giving it a specific place in the order of salvation (*ordo salutis*). Abraham Calov, for instance, made it part of his understanding of effective calling (*vocatio*). For Calov it remained only analytical and not temporal or psychological (Appold 129). Later Orthodox Lutherans such as Quenstedt articulated conversion further. Quenstedt identified two forms of conversion, transitive and intransitive. Transitive conversion referred to the work of the Spirit, which converts an individual, who remains passive. This is, in fact, the true form of conversion, since all conversion flows from the renovating work of the Spirit. In intransitive conversion, an individual may be said to convert oneself, but this is the effect and result of the first form, a conversion that necessarily expresses itself in the life of a Christian but that could be interpreted as having temporal and not just analytical implications.

Second, alongside the articulation of conversion within the *ordo salutis*, some theologians began to question the durability of baptismal regeneration. Conversion thus came to be seen as temporal moment or process in the life of a convert, especially though not exclusively among Pietists. Theophil Großgebauer (1627–61) rejected baptismal regeneration altogether and advocated a datable moment of conversion. This Puritan-inflected position did not take hold among most Lutheran Pietists; much more common was Spener's view that regeneration in baptism could be lost but then regained. This in turn opened the possibility of a temporal conversion experience as an expression of this spiritual rebirth. Spener never emphasized conversion experiences, but his disciple August Hermann Francke made conversion central to the life of the Christian.

Language of conversion and rebirth became prevalent in the devotional and theological works of Francke and those in the Halle Pietist tradition. Francke interpreted his own powerful conversion experience from 1687 as a dividing point between his "atheistic" prior life of doubt and the certainty of his new life in faith. Francke differed from Spener and much of the Lutheran tradition in conceiving doubt as a sign of unbelief. In principle, then, a conversion experience could function as warrant that one has moved from unbelief and sin to an assurance of one's salvation. But where conversion became a goal for many Pietist devotional writers, there remained considerable ambivalence about the certainty of conversion experiences and the role of conversion narratives. Some Pietists built on Francke's ideas to construct schematic patterns of conversion that centered on a *Busskampf* (repentance struggle) before an explicit *Durchbruch* (breakthrough) to grace, but even at Halle such rigid understandings of conversion were less common than often assumed in the literature.

The Orthodox opponents of Pietism did not reject all aspects of a temporal understanding of conversion or conversion experiences. However, they were highly critical of any perfectionist implications of conversion, a position that some radical Pietists espoused but most church Pietists rejected. The Orthodox especially criticized the Pietist call for a converted ministry, which they argued denigrated the office of ministry and verged on Donatism. In the so-called Terminist controversy of the late 1690s, the Orthodox also criticized some Pietists for arguing that God had set a "period of grace" for each individual, after which conversion could no longer take place, but most Pietists came to espouse the universality of divine grace against the Terminists' position. The frequent exhortations to conversion sometimes lent the impression that the will could play an effective role in conversion, yet Pietists continued to insist that only God through the Word and Spirit had the power to convert.

The emotional conversion experiences advocated by many Pietists fell out of favor among many Enlightenment theologians, who later in the eighteenth century increasingly saw conversion in primarily moral terms. However, conversion experiences remained important for many Lutherans in the *Erweckungsbewegung* and other descendants of Pietist movements well into the twentieth century. In the theological controversies over predestination in nineteenth-century American Lutheranism, the human contribution to conversion would play a role, but in much modern Lutheran theology, the highly articulated *ordo salutis* and notions of personal conversion have retreated in favor of positions more consonant with those of the sixteenth century.

See also Baptism; Francke, August Hermann; Justification; Lutheran Orthodoxy; Pietism; Salvation; Sanctification

Bibliography

Althaus, P. "Die Bekehrung in reformatorischer und pietistischer Sicht." *Neue Zeitschrift für systematische Theologie* 1 (1959): 3–23; Appold, K. *Abraham Calov's Doctrine of Vocatio in Its Systematic Context*. Mohr Siebeck, 1998; Corpis, D. *Crossing the Boundaries of Belief: Geographies of Religious Conversion in Southern Germany, 1648–1800*. University of Virginia Press, 2014; Harran, M. *Luther on Conversion: The Early Years*. Cornell University Press, 1983; Schmid, H. *Doctrinal Theology of the Evangelical Lutheran Church*. Trans. C. Hay and H. Jacobs. Lutheran Publication Society, 1876; Steinmetz, D. "Reformation and Conversion." *Theology Today* 35 (1978): 25–32; Strom, J. *German Pietism and the Problem of Conversion*. Penn State University Press, forthcoming in 2017; Strom, J. "Pietist Experiences and Narratives of Conversion." In *A Companion to German Pietism (1600–1800)*, ed. D. Shantz, 293–318. Brill, 2014.

JONATHAN STROM

Corvinus, Antonius

The northern German theologian and reformer Antonius Corvinus (1501–53) entered the monastery at Loccum in 1519, was sent to study in Leipzig, and was then expelled from the Cistercian monastery at Riddagshausen for his alleged "Lutheran" views. Introduced before 1523 to reforming views through the humanists and Erasmus's writings, Corvinus gained much of his education through self-study. Installed as a preacher in Goslar in 1528, Corvinus met the Wittenberg reformers when he was a part of Goslar's delegation to Wittenberg. Convinced of their views, thereafter he maintained steady contact with them. In 1529 he became a pastor in Witzenhausen in Hesse. He received his master's degree in Marburg (1536). Corvinus participated in a number of important meetings, including a discussion between Philip Melanchthon and Martin Bucer in Kassel in 1535, the meeting of the Smalcaldic League in 1537 (he was a signatory of the Smalcald Articles), and colloquies in Nuremberg, Hagenau, Worms, and Regensburg in 1539–41. Philip of Hesse sent him to Münster in 1536 to try to convert several imprisoned Anabaptist leaders.

Corvinus was influential as a church administrator, preacher, and writer. He produced important postils (collections of sermons on lectionary texts for each Sunday of the church year). Luther wrote the introductions for his Gospel postil (first published in 1535) and Epistle postil (first published in 1537). His postils, frequently reprinted, were among the best-selling postils of the sixteenth century and were translated into several languages, including English (1550). He composed several important northern German church orders, including those for Northeim (1539), the Braunschweig duchies of Calenberg (1542) and Wolfenbüttel (1543), and the episcopal city of Hildesheim (1544, with Johannes Bugenhagen). Corvinus opposed the Augsburg Interim; for this reason Duke Erich of Braunschweig imprisoned him in 1549. Imprisonment damaged his health: though released in October 1552, he died a few months later.

Bibliography

Frymire, J. *The Primacy of the Postils: Catholics, Protestants, and the Dissemination of Ideas in Early Modern Germany*. Brill, 2010; Luther, M. Prefaces for the *Postils* of Antonius Corvinus (1535, 1537). Trans. J. D. Lane. Ed. A. M. Johnson. LW 60:103–11; Uhlhorn, G. "Antonius Corvinus, ein Märtyrer des evangelisch-lutherischen Bekenntnisses." *Schriften des Vereins für Reformations-Geschichte* 9, no. 37 (1892): 1–38.

MARY JANE HAEMIG

Courland (Kurland)

The Baltic territory Courland is situated in what is today western Latvia. After the partition of Livonia in 1561, Courland and Semigallia went with the last master of the Livonian order, Gotthard Kettler (1517–87), who abolished the order in 1561, converted to Lutheranism, and became the duke of Courland and Semigallia (1559–63), a vassal of the Polish king. A 1565 review of churches and schools mentions conditions of physical and spiritual misery among the people of Courland and Semigallia. Kettler rebuilt and restored dozens of churches, parsonages, schools, and poorhouses. Pastors were taught Latvian, but Latvians themselves were kept away from the ministry. Only eight Latvian pastors are known in the sixteenth century.

Courland's *Kirchenordnung* (1570) organized the church on the German model. The superintendent resided in Mitau (today Jelgava). The consistory represented mainly the interests of nobility. Before 1565 only nineteen Lutheran pastors resided in the duchy; by 1600 their number had increased by one hundred. Over half were graduates of the Universities of Rostock, Königsberg, and Wittenberg. Through the influence of the Universities of Rostock and Königsberg in later centuries, Pietism and rationalism both affected Courland.

Duke Gotthard made possible the printing of the *Latvian Enchiridion* (a catechism, in 1586), the hymnal *Undeutsh Psalmen* (1587), and the lectionary *Gospels and Epistles* (1587).

Georgius Mancelius (1593–1654) served in Latvian parishes. He was a pastor in Dorpat in 1625–38, professor at the University of Dorpat beginning in 1632, and later rector. He wrote and translated a number of books in Latvian. In 1654 his mastery of Latvian allowed him to complete the first Latvian postil (1,180 pages), a collection of sermons that was the major source on Latvian history and beliefs. It was also the first major prose work in Latvian, beginning a new phase of Latvian as a literary language. Mancelius reformed Latvian orthography; wrote the first

German-Latvian dictionary, *Lettus* (Latvian; in 1638), containing translations of six thousand words, examples, and phraseology; and published *Phraseologia lettica* (1638).

Christophor Fürecker (ca. 1615–ca. 1685) translated and composed hymns. He collected more than three hundred in a hymnal (1685), which are retained even in the present (2015) hymnal. Fürecker started to translate the Bible into Latvian from the original languages but, after a stroke, was unable to complete it. His collection of Latvian-language materials was used by others, such as Heinrich Adolphi (1622–86), superintendent of Courland, who printed an introduction to Latvian grammar (1685), translated hymns, edited Luther's Small Catechism (1685), and organized the printing of prayer books and hymnals. Fürecker's work influenced dean Ernst Glück (1652–1705), the first to translate the complete Bible into Latvian from the original languages (NT in 1685, OT in 1689). Latvian pastor Jānis Reiters (1632–95) had translated the Gospel of Matthew into Latvian in 1664.

Courland had small, short-lived overseas colonies in the seventeenth century. Pastor Gottschal Ebeling (d. ca. 1654) was sent as a missionary to what is now Gambia in 1651. Pastor Peter Engelbrecht (d. 1695) was sent to the island of Tobago in the Caribbean, and a Lutheran church was built in 1654, possibly the first Lutheran church in or near South America.

Other notable figures include Superintendent Paul Einhorn (d. 1655), who fought against popular superstition. His major works were *Paraphrasis orationis Dominicae* in 1625, *Reformatio gentis Letticae in ducata Curlandiae* in 1636, and the famous *Historia lettica* in 1649.

Latvian pastor Vilis Šteineks (1681–1735) served in Tukums and addressed a poem to Duke Ferdinand in 1730 describing the poor conditions of the peasants and asking him to restrict the prerogatives of the nobility.

Pastor Gotthard Stender (1714–96; called the Old Stender) was a notable representative

of the Enlightenment. His literary works include didactic tales and poems. Stender was an outstanding Latvian grammarian and lexicographer. He collected and analyzed Latvian folk songs, riddles, proverbs, and sayings. Stender compiled grammar books, dictionaries, and a popular encyclopedia; he also wrote catechisms and hymns.

After the third partition of Poland, in 1795, Courland became part of the Russian Empire.

See also Latvia; Livonia; Mancelius, Georgius

Bibliography

Arbusow, L. *Grundriß der Geschichte Liv-, Est- und Kurlands*. Behre, 1890; Arbusow, L. *Liv-, Est- und Kurländisches Urkundenbuch*. Part 1, vols. 1–3 (1494–1510). Deubner, 1900–1914; Kreslins, J. *Dominus narrabit in scriptura populorum: A Study of Early Seventeenth-Century Lutheran Teaching on Preaching and the Lettische langgewünschte Postill of Georgius Mancelius*. Harrassowitz, 1992; Wittram, R. *Baltische Geschichte: Die Ostseelande Livland, Estland, Kurland 1180–1918*. Oldenbourg, 1973.

GUNTIS KALME

Cranach, Lucas, the Elder

The German artist Lucas Cranach the Elder (1472–1553) was primarily active in Wittenberg at the court of the Ernestine electors of Saxony from 1505 to around 1547. After collaborating on a Ten Commandments panel (1516) for the Wittenberg town hall, Cranach and Martin Luther developed a close friendship. The artist would later serve as best man and surrogate father of the bride at Luther's 1525 marriage to Katharina von Bora; both men acted as godparent to one of the other's children. Such intimate ties demonstrate that Cranach enjoyed a privileged status among Luther's advisers and that his art would play a definitive role in shaping the Wittenberg reformer's public image and the early development of Lutheran art.

Prior to the Diet of Worms (1521), Frederick the Wise gave his court secretary, Georg Spalatin, the task of working with Cranach to produce an official portrait of Luther. Cranach's bust-length portraits of *Luther as an Augustinian Monk* (1520) and *Martin Luther as Doctor of Theology* (1520) promoted the reformer as an obedient son of the church and a learned interpreter of the Bible. Later Cranach portraits, such as the frequently reproduced portrayal of Luther disguised as Junker Jörg (1521–22), continued to explore various aspects of the reformer's persona and, in so doing, fed the growing demand for images of the reformer. The early 1520s also witnessed Cranach's first foray into the realm of polemical imagery. While Luther was sequestered at the Wartburg, Philip Melanchthon and Johann Schwertfeger worked with Cranach to publish the illustrated *Passion of Christ and Antichrist* (1521), a scathing indictment of the Renaissance papacy. He also produced woodcuts on the book of Revelation for Luther's translation of the New Testament in 1522.

In the later 1520s, as Luther was further challenged by Evangelical and Catholic contemporaries to develop more thoroughly his ideas concerning the ritual and doctrinal elements of the emerging Lutheran confession, Cranach's expertise and advice on artistic matters was more valuable than ever. Around 1529 Cranach, Luther, and Melanchthon collaborated on the earliest versions of what would become the trademark exemplar of Lutheran art, the so-called allegory of *The Law and the Gospel* (painting by Lucas Cranach the Elder, 1529). Here viewers were presented with visual aids to understanding Luther's doctrine of justification by faith through grace. All later painted and printed versions of the theme derived their form and essential iconography from Cranach's two original prototypes, which now belong to art collections in Gotha and Prague.

By the 1530s Cranach's Wittenberg workshop had perfected an efficient assembly-line process for meeting the constant demand for Luther portraits and Luther-approved religious imagery. Examples of the latter were generally modest in scale, portable, and available in a variety of media. Single-panel paintings, woodcut prints, and book and Bible illustrations were the most common.

Large-scale church art, in the form of multi-paneled altarpieces or depictions of Jesus blessing the children (for baptismal fonts), was less common but likewise engaged Cranach and his assistants, including his son Lucas the Younger, in producing works that functioned primarily as public statements of Lutheran identity while providing visual representations of Luther's theology of the cross and conception of true religion. The three most noteworthy examples were created for Lutheran churches in Schneeberg (1539), Wittenberg (1547), and Weimar (1553–55). With the defeat of Duke John Frederick in the Smalcald War, Cranach left Wittenberg for the duke's court in Weimar.

See also Art; Bora, Katharina von; Cranach, Lucas, the Younger; Electors of Saxony; Holbein, Hans (the Younger); Justification; Melanchthon, Philip; Spalatin, Georg; Theology of the Cross

Bibliography

Koerner, J. L. *The Reformation of the Image*. University of Chicago Press, 2004; Noble, B. *Lucas Cranach the Elder: Art and Devotion of the German Reformation*. University Press of America, 2009; Ozment, S. *The Serpent and the Lamb: Cranach, Luther, and the Making of the Reformation*. Yale University Press, 2011.

PAUL M. BACON

Cranach, Lucas, the Younger

The German artist Lucas Cranach the Younger (1515–86) was primarily active in Wittenberg from 1535 to 1586. Trained by his father, Saxon court artist Lucas Cranach the Elder (1472–1553), Cranach the Younger's earliest known contributions to Lutheran art and visual culture date to the late 1530s. A leading figure within the Cranach family workshop, he oversaw an army of assistants trained to execute works quickly and in a clearly recognizable style that mimicked the appearance of his father's signature works. In so doing, he bore responsibility for meeting the constant demand for religious art depicting biblical and allegorical themes favored by Martin Luther and, most notably, portraits of the Wittenberg reformer. The latter were often paired with portraits of Katharina von Bora or Philip Melanchthon. Hung on the walls of homes, churches, and schools, these portraits (paintings and prints) functioned in part as symbols of Lutheran pride and identity.

Following typical sixteenth-century workshop practice, Cranach the Elder's paintings, prints, and designs for such themes as law and gospel, charity, Christ blessing the children, and Christ and the woman taken in adultery also functioned as models copied or adapted by Lucas the Younger and reproduced in great numbers by other assistants. Evidencing the mercy and grace of God witnessed in the lives of the faithful and drawing on the biblical record of Christ's life and redeeming sacrifice, the repertoire of Lutheran images produced by the Cranachs promoted the Wittenberg reformer's doctrine of justification by faith alone and reflected Luther's understanding of faith.

Cranach the Younger also collaborated with his father on a number of altarpiece projects in the 1540s. Completed the year after Luther's death, the *Wittenberg Altarpiece* (1547) in Wittenberg's City Church is a prime example. The central panel of this retable depicts Cranach the Younger in the guise of a table servant at the Last Supper, receiving the cup from a bearded Luther as Junker Jörg. Here both artist-servant and reformer-apostle bear witness to the doctrine of Christ's real presence in the Lord's Supper and the practice of lay reception of the cup, introduced in Wittenberg in 1521, while Luther was at the Wartburg, disguised as Junker Jörg.

Also in 1547, following the imperial defeat of the Protestant armies in the Smalcald War and Emperor Charles V's publication of the Augsburg Interim, the Cranach workshop produced two polemical woodcut broadsheets illustrating *The Difference between True and False Religion* (ca. 1547–50). At that time, Cranach the Elder was semiretired and in the process of joining his defeated patron, Duke John Frederick of Saxony, in Weimar exile. The antithetical format of these prints, whose design and publication have been attributed to Cranach the Younger, is similar to earlier Lutheran polemical imagery, such as the elder Cranach's *Passion of Christ and Antichrist* (1521).

Cranach the Younger also made significant contributions to the emerging genre of Lutheran memorial art, the most noteworthy examples include the *Weimar Altarpiece* (1553–55) and the single-panel memorials for Michael Meyenburg (1558) and Prince Joachim of Anhalt (1565), as well as many epitaphs in the Wittenberg City Church. Each portrays the deceased patrons in the company of Luther and other members of the Wittenberg reform movement. While Luther had eliminated the practice of endowing memorial Masses, his wealthy followers carried on the tradition of providing altarpieces and memorial panels as tomb markers and visual testaments of faith.

See also Art; Augsburg Interim; Baptism; Bora, Katharina von; Cranach, Lucas, the Elder; Electors of Saxony; Justification; Melanchthon, Philip; Sacraments; Smalcald War

Bibliography

Brinkmann, B., ed. *Cranach*. [London's] Royal Academy of Arts, 2008; Koerner, J. L. *The Reformation of the Image.* University of Chicago Press, 2004; Schade, W. *Cranach: A Family of Master Painters*. Trans. H. Sebba. Putnam, 1980.

Paul M. Bacon

Cranmer, Thomas

As English reformer, liturgist, and archbishop of Canterbury under Kings Henry VIII and Edward VI, Thomas Cranmer (1489–1556) greatly influenced the shape of the nascent Church of England. Born in Nottinghamshire and educated at Cambridge (BA, 1511; MA, 1515; DD, 1526), he was ordained by 1520. Though in Cambridge during the years in which Luther's writings began circulating with some influence in the university, Cranmer appears initially not to have been supportive of the Evangelical cause, taking offense at Luther's critique of papal and conciliar authority. In 1529, however, as Henry began vigorously to pursue the case for annulling his marriage to Katherine of Aragon, Cranmer was recruited to assist in the Crown's endeavors, and by 1531 the Basel reformer Simon Grynaeus was confidently reporting on Cranmer's Evangelical sympathies. Some explicit evidence of these sympathies became clear in the following year, when, while on a legation to Nuremberg, he broke his ordination vows by entering into marriage with the niece of the prominent Lutheran reformer Andreas Osiander. Upon the 1532 death of Archbishop William Warham, Cranmer was recalled by the king (from whom the marriage was kept secret) and consecrated as archbishop of Canterbury in March of 1533.

From this unexpected position at the pinnacle of the English church, for more than a decade Cranmer, in concert with Vicegerent in Spirituals Thomas Cromwell, increasingly tried to steer the king and his subjects toward a settlement of religion reflecting that of continental Lutheranism. He acted as patron to British natives with Wittenberg ties, such as Robert Barnes and Alexander Alesius; throughout the second half of the 1530s he participated in theological negotiations aimed at bringing England into the Smalcaldic League; and as late as 1548 he brought into English translation Justus Jonas's Latin version of Andreas Osiander's Nuremberg catechism. Brief articulations of his own Evangelical theology are evident in his model sermons on Scripture, salvation, faith, and good works, composed for the official Book of Homilies (1547). By this time, however, his theology of the Eucharist had begun to depart from that of the Lutherans and to align more with that of some Swiss reformers. With the death of Henry VIII, whose own confession of transubstantiation had been promulgated as official doctrine in the 1539 Act of Six Articles, Cranmer became increasingly open in defending a "spiritual" account of Christ's presence in the sacrament, most fully articulated in *A Defense of the True and Catholic Doctrine of the Sacrament* (1550). Though the first edition (1549) of the Book of Common Prayer, Cranmer's most lasting legacy, retained language permitting a corporeal presence (a concession, almost certainly, to those conservative bishops still loyal to Henrician theology), his 1552 revision, especially via its so-called black rubric, clearly prevented such a reading. Further indicative of the Reformed direction in which Cranmer guided the Church of England under Edward VI was his successful courting of prominent Continental exiles such as Martin Bucer and Peter Martyr Vermigli. (In an unsuccessful attempt, he also tried to persuade Philip Melanchthon to take up a professorship at Cambridge.) As in his liturgical formulations, Cranmer's imprint would also endure in the Edwardian doctrinal formula, the Forty-Two Articles (1553), revived and revised under Elizabeth I as the Thirty-Nine Articles (1571).

Cranmer's influence, substantial under Henry and greater under Edward, waned immediately upon the latter's death in 1553, not least because of his implication in the failed attempt to prevent the Catholic Mary Tudor's succession to the throne. Protesting the Marian restoration of the Mass, he was arrested and in November 1553 convicted of treason. Imprisoned in Oxford and tried again for heresy in September 1555, he was formally condemned in December of the same year. Though signing no fewer than six recantations in early 1556, he attempted publicly to renounce them when allowed to speak before his execution in Oxford on March 21, 1556. Pulled from the pulpit, he was led to his death by burning, there completing the disavowal of his recantations by holding to the flames the hand with which they were signed.

See also Alesius, Alexander; Barnes, Robert; England; Henry VIII

Bibliography

Ayris, P., and D. Selwyn, eds. *Thomas Cranmer: Churchman and Scholar.* Boydell, 1993; Brooks, P. N. *Thomas Cranmer's Doctrine of the Eucharist.* 2nd ed. Palgrave, 1992; Cox, J. E., ed. *Miscellaneous Writings and Letters of Thomas Cranmer.* Parker Society, 1846; Cox, J. E., ed. *Writings and Disputations of Thomas Cranmer.* Parker Society, 1844; Ketley, J., ed. *The Two Liturgies, A.D. 1549 and A.D. 1552.* Parker Society, 1844; MacCulloch, D. *Thomas Cranmer.* Yale University Press, 1996; Null, A. *Thomas Cranmer's Doctrine of Repentance.* Oxford University Press, 2000; Surtz, E. J., and V. Murphy, eds. *The Divorce Tracts of Henry VIII.* Moreana, 1987.

KOREY D. MAAS

Creation

Luther did not neglect the subject of creation in his work at all. He lectured on Genesis from 1535 to 1545 and preached on the same book for over a year, 1523–24. In his exegesis of John 1–4 and in his exposition of the first article of the Apostles' Creed in his catechisms, he also dealt with the topic. For Luther, God's creative activity is of prime importance. When Luther states, "The creature comes into being from nothing. Hence all things of which the creature is capable are nothing" (LW 4:61), he affirms the traditional church teaching of *creatio ex nihilo* (the creation out of nothingness), which for him is characteristic of all of God's activity. Without any presuppositions God always creates out of nothingness. According to Luther, plants and animals, prior to their creation, do not rest in the earth and then emerge from it, but they rest in God's will and are simply nothing until God calls them forth (see LW 1:48–49). God does not need anything in order to create. "God's nature is to create everything out of nothing. And his most proper nature is to call into being that which is not" (WA 40/3:154.11). It is always creation from God's word. God says it, and it is so. This also holds true for justification: "God rejoices in making light out of darkness out of nothing, etc. So he created everything, So he helps the forgotten, justifies the sinners, brings the dead to life, saves the condemned" (WA 40/3:154.15). The very way God creates (out of nothing through the Word) is the way God also justifies and saves. From John 1:1–2 Luther gathers that God created everything through his word, which he sees as pointing to Christ as the mediator of creation (cf. LW 22:14).

Since creation is not static, it needs continuous preservation. Luther writes: "Whatever God creates he also sustains; this is simply true and must be admitted. Nevertheless it does not follow, that nature is unspoiled. Daily it becomes [more] corrupt because God has created the creatures as changeable" (WA 39/1:107, 117–20). The relationship between God and the world is different from the relationship between human beings and the products they produce. When a human-made product is finished, it gains a certain independence from its producer, for it can continue to exist apart from the one who produced it. The world, however, including humans, could not exist for one moment apart from God's sustaining activity. Luther explained: "[God] did not therefore create the world, like a carpenter builds a house, and then go away, leaving it stand as it is. Rather, he remains and sustains everything as he made it; otherwise it would neither be able to stand nor continue" (WA 21:521, 21–25). This continuous divine work of preservation is at the same time an ongoing new act of creating. God is not yet finished with the work of creation but continues the creation process.

Through God's active preservation and ongoing creation, God is present in all reality. Luther can even maintain that God is present in a tree leaf since God preserves and keeps all things through his presence. "For he dispatches no officials or angels when he creates or preserves something, but all is the work of his divine power itself. If he is to create or preserve it, however, he must be present and must make and preserve his creation both in its innermost and outermost aspects" (LW 37:58). But God's all-present power is not identical with the course of world history, for the power of God transcends the world. With this distinction Luther is able to avoid every form of pantheism.

God is totally independent of and superior to everything created. "He is alone and alone he makes everything out of nothing" (WA 39/2:340.20). Insisting on a literal use of Scripture "unless an article of faith demands otherwise," Luther affirms a six-day creation (WA 24:19.28–34) and rejects all speculation as to how the six days are to be understood or how God did the creating. Most important for him is that God has created everything for his creatures, as he states especially well in his explanation of the first article of the Apostles' Creed. The affirmation of God as Creator of heaven and earth is immediately explained in its existential significance for the individual person, in all the details pertaining to one's own being and also to the aspects of daily life. Since God has created everything "for me," God also expects human cooperation within the created order, without thinking too highly of that cooperation. Human beings are chosen to be God's "cooperators but not cocreators" (WA 47:857.35), because they cannot produce life, neither in the limited earthly sense nor in terms of eternal life. Though God could do everything without such cooperation, God usually works through secondary means. "All creatures are God's masks and costumes which God wants to work with him [God] to help create all manner of things, yet he can and does also work without them" (WA 17/2:192.28–30). Luther graphically writes that God "could produce children without using men and women. But he does not want to do this. Instead, he joins man and woman so that it appears to be the work of man and woman, and yet he [God] does it under the cover of such masks" (LW 14:114).

Therefore human beings should not view themselves as the proper authors of the fruits of their labors and rely on these since God produces them. In his Small Catechism, Luther explains this in the fourth petition of the Lord's Prayer, "Give us today our daily bread." Luther writes: "In fact, God gives daily bread without our prayer, even to all evil people, but we ask in this prayer that God cause us to recognize what our daily bread is and to receive it" (SC, Lord's Prayer 13 in BC 347). Ultimately all human success or human results come from God's gracious action, and it only appears as if there were a causal connection between human effort and success. Through God's command and promise, work and blessing are connected and related to one another. Because the honor of "authorship" belongs to God alone, human beings can rely on God in their labor. "Creatures are only the hands, channels, and means through which God bestows all blessings" (LC, Creed 26 in BC 389). God's creative will not only provides human effort with meaning but

also sets its boundaries. God gives creatures nothing without the active readiness for cooperation, but that cooperation alone does not bring about the result. Ultimately everything is God's own doing. In an exemplary way this is shown in Luther's Small Catechism where he attributes everything to God's "goodness and mercy, without any merit or worthiness of" our own (SC, Creed 2 in BC 354).

Being convinced of God's sovereign involvement in the affairs of the world, Luther assumed that creation was filled with God's signs yet rejected astrology's attempt to forecast the future accurately. Philip Melanchthon, by contrast, viewed astrology as a science and understood the stars and their supposed warnings as part of God's providence. This also furthered his understanding that vestiges of creation could be ascertained through the investigation of nature. Melanchthon therefore furthered the advancement of natural science in Wittenberg and, for his time, was even considered an authority in science as well as in many other areas. John Calvin also perceived the world as "the theater of God's glory" (Schreiner 2001) since the order and splendor of the world mirrors God's invisible being. Through an investigation of nature, one must be able to perceive something of God's creative power and might. Creation was not a point of controversy among Lutherans, Calvinists, and Roman Catholics, since all three affirmed that God's mighty works can be known by studying the book of nature, while *the Book*, the Bible, reveals God's saving will.

Paul Gerhardt (1706–76) expressed this well in his hymn: "Evening and morning, sunset and dawning, wealth, peace, and gladness, comfort and sadness: these were your works, rich in glory divine!" (*Evangelical Lutheran Worship*, no. 761). For the Lutheran astronomer (and theologian) Johannes Kepler (1571–1630), too, "the heavens are telling the glory of God" (Ps. 19:1) and the greatness of his works. Eventually there developed a physico-theology through which one wanted to show that by exploring creation one could prove God's wisdom and power. Exemplary for this trend is Isaac Newton (1642–1727), who concluded his *Mathematical Principles* (1687) thus: "If the fixed stars are the centers of other like systems, these, being formed by the likewise counsel, must be all subject to [the] dominion of One. . . . This Being governs all things, not as the soul of [the] world, but as Lord over all. . . . It is allowed by all that the Supreme God exists necessarily; and by the same necessity he exists *always* and *everywhere*" (2:544–45). It was assumed that God as the Creator and Sustainer of everything can be proved by the investigation of nature. But this optimism soon vanished.

In his famous reply to Napoleon's inquiry regarding the proper place for God, the French mathematician and astronomer Pierre Laplace (1749–1827) stated in his five-volume work *Mécanique céleste* (Celestial mechanics, 1799–1825): "Sir, I do not need this hypothesis." For Laplace, God was no longer necessary within a scientific worldview. The world made sense without any reference to a creator. A naturalistic view of the world evolved for which theology was unprepared. Theology withdrew from the created world to the interior person and declared the world to be the domain of science. Friedrich Schleiermacher (1768–1834), for instance, asserted the "feeling of absolute dependence" on God, and affirmed the creation out of nothingness through the "Word." Creation covers barely six pages in the more than seven hundred pages of his book *Christian Faith*. Albrecht Ritschl (1822–89) wrote in *The Christian Doctrine of Sanctification and Reconciliation* that "theology has to do, not with natural objects, but with states and movements of man's spiritual life" (20). In his *Instruction in the Christian Religion*, in which one would expect a survey of the Christian faith, again the topic of creation is completely missing. Only in a short sentence does Ritschl explain that God is the Creator of the universe, whose will determines everything toward God. In a footnote he declares, "The conception of the creation of the world by God [is] entirely

outside of all observation and ordinary experience, and therefore outside of the realm of scientific knowledge, which is limited by these" (§11). Therefore one cannot use the analogy to natural causes to speak of God creating the world. The abandonment of the natural world was in some ways continued by Karl Barth (1886–1968). In his *Church Dogmatics* (CD) he unfolded the doctrine of creation in more than 2,200 pages, but right at the beginning he claimed: "There is free scope for the natural science beyond what theology describes as the work of the Creator" (CD III/1:x). No interaction with the natural sciences was deemed necessary concerning God's relation to the world. The only noteworthy exceptions in the late nineteenth and early twentieth centuries in German Lutheran theology were Otto Zöckler (1833–1906) in Greifswald and Karl Heim (1874–1958) in Tübingen, who argued that the findings of science did not threaten the Christian belief in God as the Creator and Preserver of everything that is. The situation was somewhat different in British and American Protestantism, where some scientists were not as antagonistic toward the Christian faith as in Germany. Nevertheless, the publication of Darwin's *Origin of Species* (1859) sparked deep reactions among some Christians against what was viewed as an attack on God as Creator and the reliability of Christian Scripture.

Yet scientists increasingly asked questions about the relationship between God and the world. According to the systematician and Luther scholar Paul Althaus (1892–1965), leading scientists testify that their research confronts them with the reality of God, but with few exceptions theologians ignore this and claim that "nature has no relevance for our knowledge of God" (82–83). While the affirmation of the world as creation is not a hypothesis to explain the world but a personal existential recognition, "a theoretical view of the cosmos points in the direction of the idea of a creation" (301). But the verdict of Barth against a dialogue was still often heeded in the mid-twentieth century. In the 1960s it began to be recognized again that nature is God's creation and therefore that theology must enter into dialogue with the natural sciences. This was most notable with Wolfhart Pannenberg (1928–2014), who asserted in his *Anthropology in Theological Perspective* (1983; ET, 1985) that the secular description of humanity must be deepened through another "theologically relevant dimension" (20). Secular knowledge therefore is only partial and incomplete unless it also considers a religious or theological dimension. Philip Hefner (1932–) with his book *The Human Factor* deserves mention here since he attracted considerable attention when he named the human being "created cocreator." As longtime editor of the journal *Zygon*, he advanced the dialogue concerning the created order, especially from the side of scientists. Thus an intellectually credible doctrine of creation may best be promulgated in interaction with the natural sciences.

See also Anthropology; God and Trinity

Bibliography

Althaus, P. *Die christliche Wahrheit.* 5th ed. Bertelsmann, 1959; Bayer, O. *Schöpfung als Anrede.* 2nd ed. Mohr Siebeck, 1990; Elert, W. *Morphologie des Luthertums.* Vol. 1. Beck, 1931; Hefner, P. *The Human Factor: Evolution, Culture, and Religion.* Fortress, 1993; Link, C. *Schöpfung: Schöpfungstheologie in reformatorischer Tradition.* G. Mohn, 1991; Löfgren, D. *Die Theologie der Schöpfung bei Luther.* Vandenhoeck & Ruprecht, 1960; Pannenberg, W. *Anthropology in Theological Perspective.* Westminster, 1985; Schreiner, S., *The Theater of His Glory: Nature and the Natural Order in the Thought of John Calvin.* Baker, 2001; Schwarz, H. *Creation.* Eerdmans, 2002; Schwarz, H. *Vying for Truth—Theology and the Natural Sciences: From the 17th Century to the Present.* Vandenhoeck & Ruprecht, 2014; Wingren, G. *The Flight from Creation.* Augsburg, 1971.

HANS SCHWARZ

Creeds, Ecumenical

The Apostles' Creed, Nicene Creed, and Athanasian Creed have historically been referred to as ecumenical creeds inasmuch as they enjoyed acceptance/approval by the entire Western church. Of these three, only the Nicene Creed (in its 381 form) has enjoyed the approval of both the Eastern and Western churches. The Apostles' Creed and Athanasian Creed are technically Western creeds in terms of their origin and their use. In the Middle Ages and throughout the Reformation, they were regarded as ecumenical, having been accepted by the entire Western church. The text of the Nicene Creed developed out of work at the Council of Nicaea in 325 and, after the Council of Constantinople (381), reached its final form by the end of the fourth century. The text of the Apostles' Creed evolved from earlier baptismal creeds in the late second and early third centuries, reaching its final form by the eighth century. The Athanasian Creed or "Quiqunque vult" was composed in the fifth century and only later attributed to Athanasius (c. 293–373) because of its fierce defense of the Trinity.

In general, the creeds were occasioned by two needs of the church. First, they arose out of the need to summarize succinctly the church's message for the baptized in an age when most people could not read and texts were not readily available. The creeds distilled the message and narrative of the gospel by answering the questions: Who is this God? What has he done? In this regard, Scripture has a number of summary narratives that serve as precedents for the creeds (e.g., Neh. 9:6 and 1 Cor. 15:1–4). Second, the creeds arose out of a need to deal with distortions to that message. As either misreadings of Scripture arose or misrepresentations of the gospel were proclaimed, churches often found it necessary to insert clauses into the creeds that dealt with those specific issues. The most obvious example in the early church was the need to counter the error of Arius, who maintained that the Son of God was a creature and not the Creator. Here the creed borrowed from 1 Cor. 8:6–8 and inserted a number of phrases to make it clear that the Son of God was God in every way that the Father was God.

Theologically, the creeds focus on two central themes. Both of these themes can be seen as a response to the question, who is Jesus? They answer that question by speaking of his relationship to the Father and the Spirit. Hence all three creeds focus on the person and work of Christ within a trinitarian structure that reflects the larger narrative of God and his creation and re-creation. The Apostles' and Nicene Creeds have clear trinitarian structures in that they were frequently organized into three articles. The Athanasian Creed reflects these two themes by dealing with the Trinity in the first half and Christology in the second half.

The creeds served as useful teaching tools of the faith in catechesis and baptism. And so in the East the Nicene Creed is used in the baptismal liturgy, while in the West the Apostles' Creed (and its predecessor, the Old Roman Creed) served that function for most of the church's history. As summaries of the faith, the creeds provided the catechumen a hermeneutic for reading and hearing Scripture (as Irenaeus emphasized with the rule of faith while arguing against the gnostics in the second century). Already in early published sermons, in his *Personal Prayer Book* of 1522 and in his 1529 catechisms, Martin Luther included interpretations of the Apostles' Creed. Thus the Augsburg Confession (art. 1), dealing with the doctrine of God, mentions that the Nicene Creed "taught in one accord"; and article 3, on the person of Christ, paraphrases the Apostles' Creed. The 1533 statutes for the University of Wittenberg include regular lectures on the Nicene Creed, resulting in commentaries from the 1540s and 1550s by Caspar Cruciger Sr. and Philip Melanchthon.

See also Confession of Faith

Bibliography

Arand, C. P., et al. *The Lutheran Confessions*. Fortress, 2012; Behr, J. *The Nicene Faith*. 2 vols. St. Vladimir's Seminary Press, 2004; Behr, J. *The Way to Nicaea*. St. Vladimir's Seminary Press, 2001; Bray, G. *Creeds, Councils, and Christ: Did the Early Christians Misrepresent Jesus?* Mentor, 1997; Kelly, J. N. D. *The Athanasian Creed*. Harper & Row, 1964; Kelly, J. N. D. *Early Christian Creeds*. 3rd ed. Longman, 1972; Westra, L. H. *The Apostles' Creed: Origin, History, and Some Early Commentaries*. Brepols, 2002; Young, F. *The Making of the Creeds*. Trinity Press International, 1992.

CHARLES P. ARAND

Cruciger, Caspar, Sr.

After studying under Martin Luther and Philip Melanchthon, Caspar Cruciger (Kreutziger) Sr. (1504–48) became professor of theology at the University of Wittenberg. Born in Leipzig, where his father was a citizen, Cruciger began his studies there, witnessed the Leipzig Debate between Luther and John Eck in 1519, but came to Wittenberg in 1521 to escape the plague. He quickly became a supporter of Luther. He married the former nun Elisabeth von Meseritz in 1524, and the next year he was sent to Magdeburg to assist Nikolaus von Amsdorf in the reform of the city as rector of the Latin school there and to improve his speaking abilities. He returned to Wittenberg in 1528, where he taught in the arts and theology faculties and was preacher at the Castle Church. He was one of the first three (with Johannes Bugenhagen and Johannes Aepinus) to receive a doctorate in theology under the revised statutes of the theology faculty. His abilities in Hebrew made him an important part of the team (under Luther's leadership) to translate the Bible into German. In addition to orations, he edited and published lectures on 1 Timothy (1540), on various psalms, on the Gospel of John (1546), and on a portion of the Nicene Creed (1548); the latter was expanded after his death by Philip Melanchthon (1550). In 1536, while lecturing on 1 Timothy, he (along with Melanchthon, who had provided him with an outline of the lectures) faced accusations by Conrad Cordatus, pastor in Niemegk, of teaching that good works were a *conditio sine qua non* for salvation. Cleared by Luther, the offending passage was translated into German by Georg Spalatin and published the same year. He was perhaps best known as editor of Luther's *Kirchenpostil* (sermons and expositions on the appointed Sunday texts), first published in 1544 and often in the centuries following. Luther even called him his Elisha. He remained in Wittenberg throughout the Smalcald War and, as rector, was instrumental in reopening the university. While bedridden with a fatal illness, he completed the Latin translation of

Luther's commentary on David's last words (1 Sam. 23), which was published after his death in 1550. His son, Caspar Cruciger Jr. (1525–97), also a theologian, was involved in the Lord's Supper controversies in the 1570s, and was imprisoned and banished from Saxony because of his "Philippist" understanding.

See also Cruciger, Elisabeth

Bibliography

Wengert, T. J. "Caspar Cruciger (1504–1548): The Case of the Disappearing Reformer." *Sixteenth Century Journal* 20 (1989): 417–41; Wengert, T. J. "Caspar Cruciger Sr.'s 1546 'Enarratio' on John's Gospel: An Experiment in Ecclesiological Exegesis." *Church History* 61 (1992): 60–74.

TIMOTHY J. WENGERT

Cruciger, Elisabeth

The first female Evangelical hymn writer, Elisabeth Cruciger (ca. 1500–1535) was born Elisabeth von Meseritz; became a nun in Treptow, Pomerania; and fled from the convent to Wittenberg in the early 1520s. She married Caspar Cruciger (1504–48) in 1524. Her hymn "Herr Christ der einig Gottes Sohn" ("Lord Christ, the only Son of God") was published in the very first Evangelical hymnals, including the Erfurt *Enchiridion* (1524). Olavus Petri (1493?–1552) translated the hymn into Swedish in the 1520s; it came to Denmark-Norway in Claus Mortensøn's *Salmebog* (1528). Translated into English, it was included in Miles Coverdale's hymnal *Goostly psalmes* (ca. 1535). The hymn has a long history in Lutheran hymnals in Europe and North America and still appears in many of these today.

See also Cruciger, Caspar, Sr.; Hymnody; Music

Bibliography

Ellrich, H. *Die Frauen der Reformatoren*. Imhof, 2012; Haemig, M. J. "Elisabeth Cruciger (1500?–1535): The Case of the Disappearing Hymn Writer." *Sixteenth Century Journal* 32 (2001): 21–44; Stjerna, K. *Women and the Reformation*. Wiley-Blackwell, 2008.

MARY JANE HAEMIG

Crüger, Johann

The cantor, composer, and hymnal editor Johann Crüger (1598–1662) was born in Prussia as the son of an innkeeper. In 1620 he began the study of theology at Wittenberg University, but in 1622 left to become cantor at St. Nicholai Church in Berlin, where he worked until he died. He was also director of music in the gymnasium of the Grey Cloister. Crüger became a friend of Paul Gerhardt in Berlin and printed many of his hymns, some with Crüger's own tunes. Crüger edited and published books of chorales—texts and tunes— from 1640 onward. His *Newes vollkömliches Gesangbuch* (1640) had 248 texts and 135 tunes, including twenty by Crüger himself. The tunes were printed over a figured bass, a first step toward the printing of harmonized chorale melodies, and also toward the use of the organ in accompanying chorales. In 1644 Crüger published *Praxis Pietatis Melica*. The tenth edition of that book (1661) was the last edited by Crüger; it contained 550 chorales (18 by Paul Gerhardt). Others continued to publish editions well into the eighteenth century. In all, Crüger wrote between seventy-one and eighty chorale tunes; he also wrote more extended chorale settings for choir and instruments, and other larger choral works. His *Geistliche Kirchen-Melodien* (1649) contains settings of single stanzas of 161 chorales for four singing voices and two instruments; these are a step toward the chorale movements in the cantatas of J. S. Bach. Crüger's chorale melodies are widely sung to this day, both in Germany and in English-speaking countries. They include "Herzliebster Jesu" (Ah, dearest Jesus); "Auf, auf mein Herz" (Awake, my heart, with gladness); "Schmücke dich" (Soul, adorn thyself); "Jesu, meine Freude" (Jesus, priceless treasure); and "Nun danket alle Gott" (Now thank we all our God).

See also Bach, Johann Sebastian; Gerhardt, Paul; Hymnody; Music

Bibliography

Asper, U. "Johann Crüger." Trans. E. Hornby. In *The Canterbury Dictionary of Hymnology*, ed. J. R. Watson and E. Hornby, http://www.hymnology.co.uk/j/johann-crueger. Canterbury Press, 2013–; Julian, J. "Crüger, Johann." *A Dictionary of Hymnology*. Esp. 271–72. Dover, 1957;

Westermeyer, P. *Hymnal Companion to Evangelical Lutheran Worship*. Esp. 4–6. Augsburg Fortress, 2010.

MICHAEL E. KRENTZ

Czech Republic

In the Czech Republic the Lutheran church is a minority in three ways: in relationship to the secularist majority of the population, to the Roman Catholic religious majority, and to the Reformed-molded Protestant majority. In the 2001 census 59 percent of the population self-identified as having no religion, 26.8 percent as Roman Catholic, and 1.5 percent as Reformed-minded. The census of 2011 did not require that the rubric "religion" be filled out.

In the Czech Republic, Lutheranism is represented by the Silesian Evangelical Church of the Augsburg Confession (SECAC, with 8,162 members in the 2011 census; in its own records, 15,538 in 2011) and the Lutheran Evangelical Church of the Augsburg Confession (LECAC, with 2,591 members in the 2011 census; in its own records 18,500). Both of these churches operate in the northeastern part of the country around Těšín, Silesia. Their membership is also Polish, so these churches are bilingual, Czech and Polish, in their worship life, although in some congregations of the Silesian Evangelical Church the Polish element is becoming weaker due to assimilation. This denomination, while partially Pietist in its character, also strives to uphold its Lutheran identity. The Evangelical Church of the Augsburg Confession (ECAC, with 6,645 members in 2011) formed in 1993 as originally a Slovak Lutheran congregation in Prague, yet now a denomination with Czech and American membership and congregations in two other large cities of Brno and Plzeň. In Prague it cooperates with the LCMS. There are also three congregations in Plzeň and its area belonging to the Czech Evangelical Lutheran Church (CELC, with 238 baptized members, and 94 confirmed), founded and supported by the mission of the ELS after 1990. The CELC does not enter into the ecumenical life and structures of the country. Ecumenically more active are the SECAC and ECAC. They both belong to the Ecumenical Council of Churches in the Czech Republic, while the former is a member of the Synod of Leuenberg Churches too. The ECAC does not tend ecumenically in a Reformed direction and endeavors to profile itself confessionally by showing certain high-church tendencies (in liturgy). LECAC is not represented in the national ecumenical bodies, for the time being.

The Church of the Bohemian Brethren, the largest Protestant denomination (51,936 members in the 2011 census), professes a Lutheran heritage too. On one hand, as a union church, it acknowledges the Augsburg Confession (1530) as one of the four doctrinal declarations to which it subscribes. (In addition, it also accepts the Second Helvetic Confession [1566], the Brethren Confession [1535], and the Bohemian Confession [1565].) However, it has developed and preserved a Reformed identity since its inception in 1918. On the other hand, it has been a member of the Lutheran World Federation since 2004.

See also Hus, Jan; Slovakia

Bibliography

Just, J., Z. R. Nešpor, O. Matějka, et al. *Luteráni v českých zemích v proměnách staletí*. Lutherova společnost, 2009; http://www.celc.info/site/cpage.asp?sec_id=180010197&cpage_id=180031336; http://www.luterani.cz/index.php?option=com_content&task=section&id=4&Itemid=30.

MAREK ŘÍČAN

D

Danish-American Lutheranism

A Dane, Rasmus Jensen, conducted the first Lutheran worship in the Western Hemisphere in 1619 aboard a ship, and Danish Lutherans established a congregation on the Caribbean island of St. Croix in 1666; however, the few Danes who settled in the New World prior to the 1800s were seldom visible as a group. Immigration to the United States reached its peak between 1860 and 1914. Compared to other Nordic groups, a smaller proportion of the 366,000 Danes who arrived between 1820 and 1970 affiliated with Lutheran congregations. Estimates range from less than 10 percent to a third. Along with Baptists and Methodists, there were several thousand Danish Mormons. They were among the earliest arrivers and account for the fact that in the 1870s, 1880s, and 1890s, Utah had the largest number of Danish-born residents. Although Danes in the Midwest often scattered, others formed colonies, including those in Askov, Minnesota; Dannebrog, Nebraska; and Solvang, California. Danish missions in the Virgin Islands, begun in the 1750s, brought African descendants into Lutheran congregations.

Denmark experienced considerable political and some religious change during these years. Having lost significant land and population to Sweden in the 1600s, in 1814 Denmark ceded Norway to Sweden and in the 1860s relinquished Schleswig-Holstein, a territory of the Danish crown, to Germany. A desire not to become German motivated some immigration to the United States. Others were attracted by recruitment efforts mounted by railroads, steamship companies, and some state commissions. Religious motives were more significant among members of minority religions than Lutherans. The constitution of 1849 shifted sovereignty away from the monarch and toward the people themselves, providing a new degree of religious freedom. This allowed Mormon evangelization and Baptist growth but left in place the structure of the Lutheran state church, or folk church. Within the official church were three distinct groups: the more high-church Centrum group, the Pietistic Indre Mission led by Vilhelm Beck, and the Grundtvigians. Each influenced the development of Danish-American Lutheranism.

Initially Danish Lutherans in the United States hoped that a single church body could, like the church in Denmark, contain all three groups. In 1872 five pastors withdrew from cooperation with the Norwegians to found the Kikelig Missions Forening. Divergent theology and cultural attitudes led to a series of organizations and reorganizations, which resulted in two bodies: the Grundtvigian Danish Evangelical Lutheran Church in America (eventually named the American Evangelical Lutheran Church—AELC) centered in Des Moines, Iowa (1878), and the more Pietistic United Danish Evangelical Lutheran Church (eventually United Evangelical Lutheran Church—UELC) centered in Blair, Nebraska (1896). The latter group merged into the American Lutheran Church (1960), the former into the Lutheran Church in America (1962). Each body also established the usual array of educational and social-service institutions, including a Deaconess Motherhouse and Sanatorium in Brush, Colorado, now the Eben Ezer Care Center. Grand View College, located in Des Moines, continues operation; Dana College, in Blair, is now closed. The two churches did cooperate to produce the *Hymnal for Church and Home* in 1927. Since 1917 congregations in the Virgin Islands, established by Danes and including African American members, have been affiliated with Lutheran church bodies in the United States.

The UELC, sometimes identified as the Sad or Holy Danes, continued the Indre Mission emphasis on repentance, moral life, and evangelism. Their strict view of biblical authority was a point of disagreement with the AELC, which held that the Bible contains rather than is the Word of God. This position was consistent with that of N. F. S. Grundtvig (1783–1872). A significant yet controversial figure in Denmark, Scandinavia, and the United States, Grundtvig gave greater weight to tradition as the carrier of faith. His expectation that Christian life should be characterized by joy rather than penitence informed the AELC (known as the Happy Danes). The influence of his educational ideals and promotion of Danish culture was evident in the establishment of several folk schools including Danebod in Tyler, Minnesota, which opened in 1888, operated until the 1930s, and now offers summer programs. These ideals also informed groups beyond Danish and Lutheran circles, such as the John C. Campbell Folk School in Brasstown, North Carolina.

See also Denmark; Grundtvig, Nikolai Frederik Severin

Bibliography

Hansen, T. *Church Divided: Lutheranism among the Danish Immigrants*. Grand View College, 1992; Jensen, J. *The United Evangelical Lutheran Church: An Interpretation*. Augsburg, 1964; Kildegaard, A. C. "Danish Grundtvigians in the United States: Challenges Past and Present." In *Grundtvig in International Perspective*, ed. A. M. Allchin et al., 59–74. Aarhus University Press, 2000; Mortensen, E. *The Danish Lutheran Church in America: The History and Heritage of the American Evangelical Lutheran Church*. Board of Publication, Lutheran Church in America, 1967; Nyholm, P. C. *The Americanization of the Danish Lutheran Churches in America: A Study in Immigrant History*. Institute for Danish Church History, 1963.

L. DeAne Lagerquist

Dannhauer, Johann Konrad

The Lutheran theologian Johann Konrad Dannhauer (1603–66), professor in Strasbourg, was a prolific author of dogmatic texts and other theological materials. After studying in Strasbourg, Marburg, Altdorf, and Jena (where he also lectured on Ephesians), Dannhauer first assumed a professorship of rhetoric (1628) and then a theological professorship in Strasbourg in 1633, serving in that position until his death. He also became pastor of the Strasbourg Münster (Cathedral) and presiding chair of the ecclesiastical administration in the city. His defense of Lutheran teaching brought him into sometimes sharp conflict with Roman Catholics, Calvinists, and "syncretistic" programs for pan-Christian reunion proposed by Georg Calixt and the Englishman John Durie, who was active in Germany. His dogmatic works not only contained polemical passages but also promoted a fervent piety that influenced his student Philipp Jakob Spener. His catechetical work also aimed at the pious life. Among his most important works were the christological treatise *Christosophia* (1638), a presentation of sacramental theology titled *Mysteriosophia* (1646), and *Hodosophia christiana* (1649), which has been compared to Bunyan's *Pilgrim's Progress* although it also has dogmatic elements.

See also Lutheran Orthodoxy; Pietism; Spener, Philipp Jakob

Bibliography

Preus, R. D. *The Theology of Post-Reformation Lutheranism*. 2 vols. Concordia, 1970–72.

Robert Kolb

Darman, Paul

One of the first Cameroonian pastors and Cameroonian president of the Evangelical Lutheran Church of Cameroon, Paul Darman (ca. 1925–2001) was born in Mboula, Cameroon, the village in which the Sudan Mission had begun its work just years before. He attended mission schools and was identified early on as a gifted child. He soon proved himself an expressive writer, a capable administrator, a good translator, and master of several languages, including his native Gbaya plus Mboum, Fulfulde, Boulou, Sango, French, and eventually English. He attended Bible school in 1949 and became a catechist of the growing church. In 1952 he was chosen for studies leading to ordained ministry in 1958. He served assignments in Norwegian as well as American mission areas, developing cross-cultural trust critical to the transition to Cameroonian control and the uniting of the two missions into one church in 1960. Darman did further theological studies at the theological faculty in Yaoundé, 1966–69, and taught Sango at the University of Wisconsin in 1969–70. He served as missionary to the Dowayo people in 1970–72, translator for the Gbaya Translation Center in Meiganga in 1972–77, and president of his church in 1962–66 and 1977–85. He traveled on behalf of his church to France, Norway, and the United States and led delegations to the LWF assemblies in Tanzania and Hungary, serving as a member of its Committee of Social Development. He was a founding member of the Joint Christian Ministry in West Africa (JCMWA), an outreach to the Fulani people, and served as its president until 1996. In 1989 his nation honored him with the medal Le Mérite Camerounais.

See also Cameroon; Sudan Mission

Bibliography

Christiansen, R. *For the Heart of Africa*. Augsburg, 1956; Pindzié, R. "Darman, Paul." In *Dictionary of African Christian Biography*, http://www.dacb.org/stories/cameroon/f-darman_paul.html. Overseas Ministries Study Center, 2008.

MARK NYGARD

Deaconesses

In several places Martin Luther writes about the importance of the diaconate in the church's life, especially for care of the poor, but the Reformers did not establish a formal diaconate for men or women. Among Lutherans, the idea of the diaconate was revived by Johannes Wichern and Theodor Fleidner (1800–1864) in the nineteenth century as a response to the upheavals early in that century. Lutheran deaconesses can trace their origins to the work of Fleidner and his wife, Frederike, who opened a halfway house for women prisoners in 1833. In part inspired by Mennonite deaconesses in

the Netherlands, Fleidner sought to restore the apostolic office of the deaconess. He and his wife established a hospital in Kaiserswerth in 1836, where the first deaconess, Gertrud Reichardt, took up her work. The Kaiserswerth institutions quickly grew beyond a motherhouse and hospital to include a training facility, a number of schools, an orphanage, and a mental health facility. Within very few years, deaconesses from Kaiserswerth served in hospitals and other institutions around the world. Deaconess houses following the Kaiserswerth model sprang up throughout Germany and other European countries where Protestant (esp. Lutheran) Christians were found.

William Alfred Passavant (1821–94) brought the deaconess model to North America. After he visited Kaiserswerth in 1846, he encouraged the Fleidners to send deaconesses to Pennsylvania. Four deaconesses arrived in 1849 and began work at the Pittsburgh Infirmary under Passavant's supervision. The Institution of Protestant Deaconesses was chartered in 1850, and the same year the first American deaconess, Sister Louisa Marthens, was consecrated. New hospitals were established in Milwaukee (1863) and Chicago (1865), and orphanages in Germantown (1859) and Jacksonville, Illinois (1870). Modeled after German counterparts, the establishment of the Philadelphia motherhouse in the late 1880s and the Baltimore motherhouse in 1895 marked important expansions of the work of deaconesses in North America. In establishing the Board of Deaconess Work in 1895, Weiser argues, the General Synod now explicitly recognized the diaconate as "an office of the church," the first church body in Lutheranism to do so (430). In addition, motherhouses were established in Brooklyn; Omaha; Milwaukee; Minneapolis; Chicago; Brush, Colorado; Axtell, Nebraska; and Fort Wayne.

Most deaconesses worked in nursing, health care, and education, but many also contributed to parish work and missions abroad. In the second half of the twentieth century, the Lutheran deaconess communities in North

America moved in new directions. Deaconesses were allowed to marry, and the residential motherhouses consolidated; by the end of the century all had closed. The vocation of deaconess as service to the church continues in North American Lutheranism, supported by the Deaconess Community of the ELCA/ELCIC in Chicago, the Lutheran Deaconess Association in Valparaiso, Indiana, and the Concordia Deaconess Conference (LCMS) in Union, Illinois. Internationally, Lutheran deaconess communities can be found beyond Europe and North America, in Brazil, Indonesia, Kenya, Tanzania, and India; the Kaiserswerth General Conference continues to this day, including deaconess houses, diaconal institutions, and other service communities in many parts of the world.

See also Fedde, Elizabeth Tonette; Fliedner, Theodore; Inner Mission; Mission Societies and Academies; Passavant, William Alfred

Bibliography

Naumann, C. *In the Footsteps of Phoebe: A Complete History of the Deaconess Movement in the LCMS.* Concordia, 2009; Olson, J. *Deacons and Deaconesses through the Centuries.* Concordia, 2005; Weiser, F. *Love's Response: A Story of Lutheran Deaconesses in America.* Board of Publication, ULCA, 1962; Weiser, F. "The Origins of Lutheran Deaconesses in America." *LQ* 13 (1999): 423–34.

JONATHAN STROM AND LOUISE WILLIAMS

Death and Dying

In his 1524 hymn "In the Midst of Life We Are," based on a Latin antiphon, Martin Luther recognized the fact of death's presence throughout life as well as the ultimate question death poses: "Who will from such dire distress / Free and scathless [unharmed] set us?" His hymn serves as a concise description of death's presence early in the sixteenth century and during the Reformation. Both the nobility and the common folk were intimately acquainted with death via famines, epidemics, and infant mortality; in particular, wave after wave of the plague dropped life expectancy and brought the people of Europe to a vivid realization of death's power and presence. In Wittenberg, it was common practice to flee the city if one knew the plague was approaching. If one could escape death from other threats, there always lay the possibility of an occurrence of the plague, which in epidemics brought death in some areas to half the population.

The Roman church's theological emphases combined with death's unavoidability to bring forth specific ways of contending with this final human enemy. Death was regarded as the end of all possibilities to fulfill the dictum "Do what is within you to do" or to satisfy the requirements of faithful Christian life to die within a state of grace and thus achieve a "blessed death." When a death occurred, one could also contribute toward a funeral Mass on behalf of the one who died or gain an indulgence by performing a pious act, either of which could help assure the person a gracious place in eternity. A genre of death literature and illustrations, which included the *memento mori* and *Totentanzen* (dances of the dead) arose to remind readers and viewers of the nearness and arbitrariness of their own death by depicting scenes where death appeared in instances of daily life, thus urging them to make amends for their sins and turn to the church's beneficent storehouse of grace. The *ars moriendi*, treatises on the art of dying such as those by Jean Gerson and Thomas Peuntner, also served as preparation for death and judgment by schooling a person in the process of dying and the achievement of a blessed death. They exhorted a person to make an accounting of one's life and deeds, pray to the saints, and look to Christ as an example for how to approach one's death.

Martin Luther approached death and dying as a matter of pastoral care and the delivery of the gospel to those experiencing *Anfechtung* (attack) and a troubled conscience at death's approach. His practice, based on his Evangelical theology, served as a corrective. Because the human will is so captive to itself that it can and will not do what is required for salvation, the gospel only takes root when a person despairs of being able to act counter to that captivity or achieve an active righteousness. At the point where a person is "stretched out with Christ," God exercises the office of ministry in the gospel and sacraments, in which the Holy Spirit creates saving faith. The task and gift of salvation are Christ's to bear and bestow, and the certain advent of death becomes the occasion not for action to achieve a blessed death, but a place to declare Christ's action promised to godless mortals. In the divine promise Luther found a new way of thinking about God and of experiencing God's graciousness, a way that was free of demands on those who, like the reformer himself, knew themselves to be dead in sin and unable to create the good works necessary for salvation. While Luther used some of the language of earlier approaches to death, he shifted their underpinnings so his practice was just as radical a shift as it was in other contentious issues, always with the goal of liberating troubled consciences.

In contrast to the recommendations of the medieval *ars moriendi*, Luther's *Sermon on Preparing to Die* (printed in 1519, reprinted ten times over the next six years) is more concerned with providing the reader or listener with a saving faith in the face of death and grief. Where the *ars* urged the dying person to contemplate a crucifix in order to align one's attitude to Christ's on the cross, Luther saw the cross as the focus for meditation on the great and gracious gift offered there, a theme reiterated in his "Sermon on Contemplation of Christ's Holy Suffering" (1519). Instead of praying to the saints and angels for admission to their ranks, Luther preached the dying person's place in the company of saints. Instead of trying to preserve a state of salvation for the dying person, Luther sought to announce to the sinner God's promise of salvation and eternal life, along with the forgiveness of sins, and thus provide the faith that both saves and gives comfort. This same commitment to comfort is expressed in his tract addressed to women who had suffered stillbirths or miscarriages (1542).

Such shifts were in keeping with Luther's dictum to become familiar with death during life, reflected in his 1527 tract *Whether One*

May Flee from a Deadly Plague. In essence, Evangelical preaching and practice were aimed at preparation for death prior to the deathbed so that a person can approach it with the confidence of faith. Luther had already struck at the roots of late medieval sacramental piety in the Mass and offered changes that shifted the focus to a clearer proclamation of the gospel, so the 1532 funeral for his prince, Elector John, was no Mass for the dead. Instead, Luther proffered a sermon aimed at the faith of those in attendance. He gave neither eulogy nor moral exhortation, but voiced the promise of the resurrection in the face of and in anticipation of death so his hearers would be steeled against the onslaught of death's *Anfechtungen*. The Evangelical funeral thus included no encomiums about the dead person's goodness or worthiness, although, as in the elector's funeral sermon, it could include mention of the faith visible in the person's witness to Christ's goodness and worthiness. This practice was continued in the work of contemporaries such as Johann Spangenberg and later reformers such as Nikolaus Selnecker and Siegfried Sack.

The Evangelical funeral sermon thus had the same goal as Luther's hopes expressed in a 1531 letter to his mother, who faced a fatal illness, that God had provided her "preachers and comforters" who would bring Christ as the "cornerstone" for all those "who face tribulation and death." Indeed, more than other traditions, Lutherans cultivated funeral preaching as central to the funeral liturgy. The catechisms of the late 1520s can be seen as serving the same task of hardwiring the language of faith proclaimed in the Gospels to a person's heart, allowing the person a way to battle the terror of death apart from Christ. Similarly, Luther's hymns, such as "Death Held Our Lord in Prison" (1524) and "From Trouble Deep I Cry to Thee" (1523), used music to cement the proclamation of Christ's saving death and resurrection. Luther's approach can be summarized in his 1530 letter to his dying father: "Let your heart be strong and at ease in your trouble, for we have yonder a true mediator with God, Jesus Christ, who has overcome death and sin for us. . . . He has such great power over sin and death that they cannot harm us, and he is so heartily true and kind that he cannot and will not forsake us."

With faith in such a promise, a person could face not only the troubled conscience and accusations of the law that were sure to come with death's arrival, but also the promise would stand a person in good stead throughout life's troubles, even when "life be wrenched away" ("A Mighty Fortress Is Our God"). Because Christ's death had swallowed death, death itself would "become a laughter" ("Death Held Our Lord in Prison"). If, as in Luther's hymn "In the Midst of Life We Are," a person were to ask where to turn when facing death, the reformer's answer would consistently be "To thee, Lord Christ, to thee."

During the period of Lutheran Orthodoxy, Johann Gerhard's *Handbook on Consolations for the Fears and Trials That Oppress Us in the Struggle with Death* (1611) proved popular, appearing in ten European languages. The hymn writers of this period also addressed preparation for death, as did Nikolaus Hermann, "When My Last Hour Is Close at Hand" (1562). Lutheran prayer books continued to contain prayers for the dying. Johann Habermann's prayer book, popular among Lutherans for centuries, contained a prayer for a blessed end. In the nineteenth century, Wilhelm Loehe's *Seed-Grains of Prayer* contained a prayer for a blessed death as well as "evening prayers, for a daily readiness to die." Other strands of post-Reformation thought have influenced approaches to death and dying so that pastors following Luther's practice today sometimes face customs far afield from the Reformer's proclamation of an external word of promise and the assurance of faith.

See also Catechisms; Devotional Literature; Hymnody; Prayer; Preaching

Bibliography

Luther's Works: "Death Held Our Lord in Prison" (1524). LW 53:255; "A Mighty Fortress Is Our God" (ca. 1528). In *Evangelical Lutheran Worship*, no. 503–5. Augsburg, 2006; "From Trouble Deep I Cry to Thee" (1523). LW 53:221; "In the Midst of Life We Are" (1524). LW 53:274; Large Catechism (1529). In *The Book of Concord: The Confessions of the Evangelical Lutheran Church*, ed. R. Kolb and T. J. Wengert, 377–480. Fortress, 2000; "Letter to Hans Luther, Wittenberg, February 15, 1530." LW 49:267; "Letter to Mrs. Margarethe Luther, [Wittenberg,] May 20, 1531." LW 50:17; *Sermon on Preparing to Die*. LW 42:95; Small Catechism (1529). In *The Book of Concord: The Confessions of the Evangelical Lutheran Church*, ed. R. Kolb and T. J. Wengert, 345–75. Fortress, 2000; *Two Funeral Sermons* (1532). LW 51:231; **Other Primary Sources:** Geiler von Kaysersberg, J. *Wie man sich halten sol by eym sterbenden menschen*. In *Sämtliche Werke*, ed. G. Bauer, 1:3–13. De Gruyter, 1989; Gerhard, J. *Handbook of Consolations for the Fears and Trials That Oppress Us in the Struggle with Death* (1611). Wipf & Stock, 2009; Staupitz, J. *Ein Buchlein von der Nachfolge des willigen Sterbens Christi*. Lottherus, 1515; **General Works:** Ariès, P. *Western Attitudes toward Death: From the Middle Ages to the Present*. Johns Hopkins University Press, 1974; Dingel, I. "'True Faith, Christian Living, and a Blessed Death': Sixteenth-Century Funeral Sermons as Evangelical Proclamation." *LQ* 27 (2013): 399–420; Kolb, R. "'Life Is King and Lord over Death': Martin Luther's View of Death and Dying." In *Tod und Jenseits in der Schriftkultur der Frühen Neuzeit*, ed. M. Kobelt-Groch and C. N. Moore, 23–44. Harrassowitz, 2008; Moore, C. N. *Patterned Lives: The Lutheran Funeral Biography in Early Modern Germany*. Harrassowitz, 2006; O'Connor, M. C. *The Art of Dying Well: The Development of the "Ars Moriendi."* Columbia University Press, 1942; Reinis, A. *Reforming the Art of Dying: The "Ars Moriendi" in the German Reformation (1519–1528)*. Routledge, 2007.

KEN SUNDET JONES

Denmark

The reception of Lutheran teaching in Denmark was prepared by reform-minded biblical humanists in several cities and most notably by the Carmelite scholar Poul Helgesen (Paulus Helie, 1485–1535) in Copenhagen. Christian II, who became king in 1513, was also sympathetic toward church reform but lost his throne in 1523 after provoking a revolt in Sweden and alienating the nobles and conservative bishops on the national Council (Rigsrådet) of Denmark. He was succeeded by his uncle Frederik I, who attempted at first to minimize religious conflict in the kingdom but eventually gave support to a number of Lutheran sympathizers among the clergy in Jutland. Foremost among them was Hans Tausen of

Viborg (1494–1561), who had studied under Luther in Wittenberg. Frederik made him a royal chaplain in order to protect him from his Catholic critics and eventually called him to a pastorate in Copenhagen. Malmö, in Danish-controlled southern Sweden, also became a center of the new Evangelical movement during his reign. In 1526, at a meeting of the Council in Odense, the king decreed that the pope would no longer control the appointment of Danish bishops. He also gave permission for the creation of a Lutheran seminary in Viborg. These changes were opposed by some of the humanist reformers, such as Helgesen, who, like Erasmus, could not bring themselves to leave the Catholic Church.

When Frederik died in 1534, he was succeeded by his son, Christian III, who had been *stadtholder* (governor) of the duchies of Schleswig and Holstein, where support for Lutheran teaching was also growing. After emerging victorious from a two-year civil war between Protestant and Catholic sympathizers, Christian III took the decisive final steps to make the Danish church Lutheran. At a meeting of the Council in Copenhagen in 1536, he blamed the bishops for fomenting the civil war, confiscated their properties, and imprisoned all of them. He invited Johannes Bugenhagen, Luther's coworker in Wittenberg, to Denmark to create the ordinances for an independent state church. Bugenhagen presided at the coronation of the king and appointed seven Lutherans as "superintendents" in place of the bishops whom the king had dismissed. The most distinguished of the new superintendents was Peder Palladius (1503–60), who had also studied in Wittenberg. He carried out a visitation to all the parishes in Zealand and initiated many efforts to explicate Lutheran theology to clergy and laity. His altar book established a new pattern of worship, and he helped finalize the process of creating a Danish translation of the Bible (1550).

The influence of humanism is evident in the *Confessio Hafniensis* (1530), the earliest articles of faith proposed by Tausen and other pastors during the reign of Frederik I. Christian III endorsed a more clearly Lutheran theology, but the influence of Melanchthon was especially strong in Denmark. Niels Hemmingsen (1513–1600), who had studied with Melanchthon, was the most influential theologian of this period. At first, Denmark avoided the doctrinal disputes that divided Philippists and Gnesio-Lutherans in Germany in the late sixteenth century, but Hemmingsen's clear advocacy of a more Calvinistic understanding of the Lord's Supper in 1574 provoked a controversy. Frederik II, who had become king in 1559, nurtured close ties with the Lutheran princes in Germany and bowed to pressure from his brother-in-law, the Elector August of Saxony, who called for the dismissal of Hemmingsen from his university professorship. The king had Hemmingsen reassigned to the position of canon at the cathedral in Roskilde but continued to appoint his disciples to key positions in the church. King Frederik resisted the Formula of Concord because of its theological precision, and it never became an official confession for the Danish Lutheran Church.

When Christian IV was crowned king in 1596, after an eight-year regency, he expanded royal power in Denmark and required greater uniformity in religious life. During his reign, the most noted influences on church affairs were Hans Poulsen Resen (1561–1638) and Jesper Brochmand (1585–1652), who both manifested a deeper commitment to Lutheran orthodoxy. Resen prepared a new translation of the Bible in Danish (1607). He clashed with theologians in both Denmark and Norway who continued to defend Philippist views. Brochmand, who succeeded Resen first as theological professor at the University of Copenhagen and then as bishop of Zealand, worked to suppress a resurgence of Catholicism attempted by Jesuits. King Christian IV, who had ambitions to make Denmark more influential internationally, also came to the defense of Lutherans in Germany in the second phase of the Thirty Years' War but was soundly defeated in 1626.

Frederik III, who ruled from 1648 to 1678, continued his father's stress on religious uniformity. He managed to make the monarchy hereditary and forged a tighter union between church and state. Church leaders such as Brochmand supported the move toward more absolutist rule. Pietist influences made inroads into Denmark from Germany and gradually gained support in the royal court. In 1705 King Frederik IV provided financial support for the sending of German missionaries, trained by A. H. Francke at Halle, to Denmark's colony in southeast India and also established a missionary college in 1714. His son, Christian VI, called "the Pietist on the throne," made church attendance compulsory in 1735 and introduced obligatory confirmation in 1736. Count Nikolaus Ludwig von Zinzendorf participated in his coronation and was allowed to form Moravian societies in Denmark as long as they remained loyal to the state church. Southern Jutland became a Pietist stronghold, and among its most notable leaders was Hans Adolph Brorson (1694–1764), bishop of Ribe, who is most remembered for his hymns.

After the death of Christian VI, Pietism lost its official sponsorship. His successors, Frederik V and Christian VII, had much less interest in religion, and the influence of the Enlightenment advanced during the late eighteenth century. Leading cultural figures, such as the playwright Ludvig Holberg, were often freethinkers, and a morally focused rationalism spread among the clergy. This trend was countered in the early nineteenth century by popular revival movements. Efforts to revitalize religious life were combined with social welfare work in the Inner Mission movement, which maintained an association with the national church under the strong leadership of pastor Vilhelm Beck (1829–1901).

The two most influential and controversial religious thinkers of nineteenth-century Denmark were a pastor, N. F. S Grundtvig (1783–1872), and a layman, Søren Kierkegaard (1813–55). Early in his life Grundtvig experienced a conversion, which turned him away from the Enlightenment, but he was a strong advocate of religious freedom and called for an inclusive state church. He inspired a Grundtvigian movement within Danish Lutheranism, which endured long after his death. He also contributed to educational reform by founding folk high schools, designed to unleash human creativity and equip students to contribute positively to society. Many of his hymns are still sung in Danish churches. Kierkegaard, by contrast, has a much more critical perspective on Danish society and the church. A writer of complex philosophical works that contributed to the later development of existentialism, he also reflected profoundly on what it means to live a Christian life. Unlike Grundtvig, who sought to promote harmony between Christianity and human culture in general, Kierkegaard began an "attack upon Christendom" in 1854, which faulted church leaders for their comfortable relation to worldly culture and their compromising of the demand for the unconditional commitment articulated in New Testament Christianity.

Since the middle of the nineteenth century the place of the Lutheran Church in Danish society has undergone extensive changes. After the Constitution of 1849 established religious freedom, Danish citizens were no longer obliged to be members of the state church. Industrialization and urbanization eroded the traditional social bonds that attached people to the church. The rise of the modern welfare state also forced the church to reconsider its role in responding to societal needs. As in the other Scandinavian countries, secularization has diminished the church's influence. Nevertheless the Lutheran Church continues to function as a "folk church" (Danish: *Folkekirke*) with a privileged status compared to other religious organizations. A state tax is collected from church members to help pay for salaries and the upkeep on church properties, and the parliament maintains some legislative control over church affairs. The church continues to maintain the registry of births and deaths of all Danish citizens regardless of their religion.

In 2014 almost 80 percent of Danes were members of the national church, but less than 3 percent regularly attended weekly services.

See also Danish-American Lutheranism; Grundtvig, Nikolai Frederik Severin; Hemmingsen, Niels; Kierkegaard, Søren Aabye; Tausen, Hans

Bibliography

Dunkley, E. H. *The Reformation in Denmark*. SPCK, 1948; Grell, O., ed. *The Scandinavian Reformation*. Esp. chaps. 1 and 5. Cambridge University Press, 1995; Hope, N. *German and Scandinavian Protestantism, 1700–1918*. Clarendon, 1995; Koch, H., and B. Kornerup. *Den danske kirkes historie*. Vols. 3–8. Gyldendal, 1958–66; Lausten, M. S. *A Church History of Denmark*. Ashgate, 2002; Lockhart, P. D. *Frederik II and the Protestant Cause: Denmark's Role in the Wars of Religion, 1559–1596*. Brill, 2004; Lodberg, P. "The Evangelical Lutheran Church in Denmark, 1940–2000." In *Nordic Folk Churches—A Contemporary Church History*, ed. B. Ryman, 8–26. Eerdmans, 2005; Lund, E. "Nordic and Baltic Lutheranism." In *Lutheran Ecclesiastical Culture, 1550–1675*, ed. R. Kolb, 411–54. Brill, 2008.

ERIC LUND

Desta, Kentiba Gebru (Gobaw)

Born in 1845 in Alefa Takus Gazgie, not too far from Gondar, Ethiopia, Kentiba Gebru Desta (1845–1949) came to Debre Tabor and there was introduced to Theophilos Waldmeier, a Swiss missionary who cared for him and educated him. In 1868, when the missionaries were expelled from Ethiopia after the Battle of Meqdela, Waldmeier and Gobaw left the country and went to Jerusalem, where Gobaw continued his education at the Samuel Gobat Missionary School. In 1872 Gobaw went to St. Chrischona, near Basel, Switzerland, for four years of further education and graduated with a diploma in theology in 1876. In 1879 he returned to Ethiopia, where he worked with the Swedish Mission. He became the first evangelist to the Oromo. He was also politically active; in 1930, he became the vice president of the first parliament in Ethiopia. Soon after the Ethiopian liberation from the Italian occupation, he became president of the parliament.

See also Ethiopia

Bibliography

Menberu, D. "Kentiba Gebru (Gobaw) Desta, 1845 to 1949. Protestant. Ethiopia." In *Dictionary of African Christian Biography*, http://www.dacb.org/stories/ethiopia/gebru_desta.html. Overseas Ministries Study Center, 2005.

FRIEDER LUDWIG

Devotional Literature

Lutheran teaching sought not only to reshape the theological focus of Western Christianity but also to reorient the way Christians gave expression to their faith in their daily lives. For this reason, from the very beginning, the reform movement produced books and pamphlets designed to promote spiritual formation. Practical religious literature was intended not only to teach correct beliefs but also to console, edify, and motivate. Such works sought to touch the heart and influence the will as well as instruct the mind.

The medieval Catholic Church had produced abundant spiritual literature. Sometimes these resources were cautiously recirculated by Lutherans. For example, Martin Luther prepared an edition of the fourteenth-century mystical treatise *Theologia Germanica* in 1518. In the seventeenth century this process of reappropriation increased, most notably with the issuing by Johann Arndt of new editions of Thomas à Kempis's *Imitation of Christ* (1606) and the sermons of Johannes Tauler (1621). In general, however, Lutheran writers considered Catholic spiritual books to be in need of so much correction that they produced new works to provide appropriate guidance for the practice of piety.

Luther himself was attentive to pastoral theology and repeatedly responded to requests for practical guidance. One of his most important attempts to reshape the daily living patterns of laypeople was the issuance of the Small and Large Catechisms in 1529 after the Visitation in Saxony revealed a low level of religious knowledge and moral behavior. The catechisms summarized correct belief but also encouraged religious disciplines such as daily prayers in the morning and evening and at meals. Luther held up the Lord's Prayer as the preeminent model for prayer. The Small

Catechism also concluded with a table of duties for each estate. Dissatisfied with medieval prayers that focused on the saints and often made extravagant claims of rewards for recitation, Luther had already issued a new prayer book in 1522 (reedited in an expanded edition in 1529). In addition he wrote thirty-six hymns, which proclaimed the Evangelical message and expressed prayers of praise and supplication in poetic and musical form. These hymns were important for promoting lay involvement in worship through congregational singing and had a lasting impact on Lutheran devotion.

Luther wrote many letters of consolation, several of which also appeared in print, and several practical treatises addressing matters such as how to pray (1535). His sermons were doctrinal but also sought to cultivate the fruits of faith. In printed form, his sermons became a model for other pastors to follow and were also used by laypeople as devotional aids.

Many of Luther's coworkers and early successors produced additional contributions to these genres of religious writings. Johann Habermann's prayer book was reprinted dozens of times, and several hundred other prayer book editions were published before 1600. As many as fifteen hundred hymn collections were published by Lutherans between 1520 and 1600, and hymns increasingly became important for family devotions as well as communal worship. Luther's Small Catechism or more detailed explanations of it were central to devotional life in homes as well as schools.

Church life in the late sixteenth and early seventeenth centuries was stressed by both internal disputes (reflected in the Book of Concord of 1580) and external religious conflict (with Catholics and other Protestants). As a result, the defense of correct theology and sacramental practice was foremost in the minds of many church leaders. However, some pastors felt the need for a shift of attention away from doctrinal disputes and polemics and toward the nurturing of practical piety and a deeper personal appropriation of the faith. The leading theologian of this period, Johann Gerhard, also produced heartfelt books of edification, most notably *Sacred Meditations* (1606), but other writers such as Johann Arndt eschewed most discussion of subtle theological matters and concentrated on the encouragement of spiritual growth. Arndt produced some of the most enduringly significant Lutheran devotional works, especially *Four Books of True Christianity* (1605–10) and *Paradise Garden*, a prayer book (1612). In his writings, Arndt not only spoke of what Christ had done ("for us") to make salvation possible but also described how Christ united with the soul and worked ("in us") to effect sanctification. This mode of piety employed language commonly associated with christocentric mysticism and sometimes provoked controversy for doing so. Others from the same time period who participated in this trend were Martin Moller (*The Great Mystery*, 1595), Philip Nicolai (*Mirror of the Joys of Eternal Life*, 1599), and Stephan Praetorius (*Spiritual Treasure Chest*, 1622). Arndt, especially, had several disciples during the seventeenth century, whose books of meditations had a deep impact on popular piety. These included Joachim Lütkemann (*Foretaste of Divine Goodness*, 1653), Heinrich Müller (*Spiritual Hours of Refreshment*, 1664), and Christian Scriver (*The Treasure of the Soul*, 1675). All of these writers had more optimistic expectations about the possibility of personal regeneration than were common among Lutherans previously, and this theme continued to be important for the major writers associated with Lutheran Pietism, including Philipp Jakob Spener (1635–1705) and August Hermann Francke (1663–1727). Spener's *Pia Desideria* (1675), the initiating manifesto of Pietism, suggested various practices that would promote spiritual rebirth. Francke, like Spener, wrote many devotional treatises, including an account of his conversion, and started organizational initiatives that would influence the practice of piety in all the countries to which Lutheran teaching had spread.

The seventeenth century was also a prolific period for hymn writing. Among the most notable poet-composers were Philipp Nicolai, Johann Heermann, Martin Rinckart, and Paul Gerhardt. Their hymns praised God for many blessings, offered consolation in times of trouble, and testified to the transforming power of grace. Over the course of that century, hymns tended to become more emotionally expressive, sometimes employing more personal "I" language instead of the traditional communal "we." This trend continued in the hymns produced by Pietists.

To some extent the advance of the Enlightenment diminished the influence of the Lutheran churches in Germany during the eighteenth century, but an awakening began to take place in the early decades of the nineteenth century. Some notable devotional writings came out of this movement, authored by August Tholuck, Johann Wichern, Claus Harms, and Wilhelm Loehe (Löhe). The influence of the classic devotional writings of the past diminished during the twentieth century, but important new contributions included Dietrich Bonhoeffer's *Cost of Discipleship* (1937) and *Life Together* (1939).

German devotional literature was translated and circulated widely among Lutherans in Scandinavia and North America, but these regions also produced their own spiritual writers. The most influential devotional work in Iceland was Hallgrímur Pétursson's *Passion Hymns* (1659). Erik Pontopiddan's *Truth onto Godliness* (1737), an explanation of Luther's catechism, was widely used in both Denmark and Norway. Among the most notable Danish hymn writers were Thomas Kingo, Hans Adolph Brorson, and N. F. S. Grundtvig. Søren Kierkegaard wrote *Edifying Discourses* (1843) as a parallel religious track to his philosophical writings. Hans Nielsen Hauge (1771–1824), lay leader of the Pietist movement in Norway, developed a colportage system that circulated many practical religious writings, including his own. A similar role was played in Sweden by the layman Carl Olof Rosenius (1816–68).

In the twentieth century, Ole Hallesby (1879–1961) influenced many pietistically inclined Lutherans in Scandinavia and the United States. Devotional writings by American Lutherans have tended to have a more ephemeral impact, but the various denominations have continuously made available material for daily devotional practices.

See also Arndt, Johann; Catechisms; Hymnody; Prayer

Bibliography

Classics of Western Spirituality: Paulist Press, 1979–. Lutheran volumes: Arndt, J. *True Christianity*. 1979; Crowner, D., and G. Christianson, eds. *Spirituality of the German Awakening*. 2003; Erb, P. C., ed. *The Pietists*. 1983; Granquist, M. A., ed. *Scandinavian Pietism*. 2015; Kray, P. D. W., and P. D. S. Kray, eds. *Luther's Spirituality*. 2007; Lund, E., ed. *Seventeenth Century Lutheran Meditations and Hymns*. 2011. **Other Works:** Beck, H. *Die religiöse Volkslitteratur*. F. A. Perthes, 1891; Grosse, C. *Die Alten Tröster: Ein Wegweiser in Die Erbauungsliteratur*. Missionsbuchhandlung, 1900. Reprint, Nabu, 2010; Hanson, B. *Grace That Frees: The Lutheran Tradition*. Esp. 98–116, chap. 6. Orbis, 2004; Lindberg, C., ed. *The Pietist Theologians*. Blackwell, 2005; Lund, E. "Second Age of the Reformation: Lutheran and Reformed Spirituality, 1550–1700." In *Christian Spirituality*. Vol. 3, *Post-Reformation and Modern*, ed. L. Dupré and D. Saliers. Vol. 18 of *World Spirituality: An Encyclopedic History of the Religious Quest*. Esp. 213–39, chap. 8. Crossroad, 1989; Olsson, B. "Devotional Literature." In *Encyclopedia of Lutheranism*, ed. J. Bodensieck, 1:687–96. Augsburg, 1965; Senn, F., ed. *Protestant Spiritual Traditions*. Esp. 9–54, chap. 1. Paulist Press, 1986.

ERIC LUND

Dieckhoff, Heinrich Wilhelm

The founder of a school for the blind in Moscow, Heinrich Wilhelm Dieckhoff (1833–1911) was born in Poltava. He moved to Moscow in 1843, when his father became pastor of Sts. Peter and Paul Lutheran Church. He studied at Dorpat University and was ordained at Sts. Peter and Paul–Moscow in 1858. Dieckhoff helped found a school for the deaf in 1860. In 1871, he traveled to Europe to learn more about educating the blind. With assistance from Czarina Maria Fedorovna (wife of Czar Alexander III), he was able to gather support from financiers in Russia for the founding of a school for the blind, which opened in 1882 and still operates today. After receiving the Order of St. Ann in 1908 from Czar Nicholas II for his charitable work in Russia, the czar, as official head of the Lutheran church, bestowed upon him the title of bishop.

MATTHEW HEISE

Dietrich, Veit

Luther's amanuensis and reformer in Nuremberg, Veit Dietrich (1506–49) was a native of Nuremberg. In 1522 he moved to Wittenberg and, with Luther's strong encouragement, decided to study theology instead of medicine. After completing his master's studies in 1529, Dietrich taught in the university arts faculty and was named its dean in 1533. He had especially close ties to Luther, serving as the reformer's amanuensis. Dietrich lived in Luther's home, the former Augustinian Cloister, and provided early (and reasonably accurate) transcriptions of the *Tischreden* (Table talk). He accompanied Luther to the Marburg Colloquy (1529) and then to the Coburg Castle during the Diet of Augsburg (1530), overseeing Luther's correspondence with the reformers in Augsburg. In 1535 Dietrich was called to become the preacher in Nuremberg's St. Sebald Church, even though he, like his colleague Andreas Osiander, had never been ordained by a bishop. He had a tension-filled relationship with Osiander, in part because of the latter's opposition to general confession and absolution, which Dietrich, along with Luther and Melanchthon, held to be a valid exercise of the power of the keys, although both preferred private confession and absolution. Dietrich continued to edit Luther's and Melanchthon's works, especially the reformer's *Hauspostille* (House postils), which he authored in part. But Dietrich also produced many of his own works, including an influential chapter-by-chapter summary of the Old and New Testaments, along with the equally influential 1543 *Liturgy Booklet for Pastors in the Countryside*, which, as the name suggests, provided instruction on Lutheran worship and belief for rural pastors.

(It was in use until the late eighteenth century.) Dietrich also produced preaching aids, devotional works, catechetical literature, and an important collection of children's sermons. He signed the Smalcald Articles on behalf of Nuremberg and played a role in the Reformation of Hiltpoltstein and Regensburg. He was also present at the 1546 Regensburg Colloquy. His deep opposition to the Augsburg Interim caused him to be suspended from his preaching office, and yet he remained in Nuremberg until his death, arguing passionately for the superiority of Evangelical Christianity over its papal counterpart.

See also Nuremberg

Bibliography

Dietrich, V. *Agendbüchlein für die Pfarrherrn auf dem Land*. In *Die evangelischen Kirchenordnungen des XVI Jahrhunderts*, ed. E. Sehling, 11.1:487–553. Mohr Siebeck, 1961; Grimm, H. *Lazarus Spengler: A Lay Leader of the Reformation*. Ohio State University Press, 1978; Klaus, B. *Veit Dietrich: Leben und Werk*. Verein für Bayerische Kirchengeschichte, 1958; Kolb, R. "The 'Summaria' of Veit Dietrich as an Aid for Teaching the Faith." *ARG* 99 (2008): 97–119; Rittgers, R. K. *The Reformation of the Keys: Confession, Conscience, and Authority in Sixteenth-Century Germany*. Harvard University Press, 2004.

RONALD K. RITTGERS

Dlamini, Paulina

The South African Zulu Paulina Dlamini (1856–1942) was given to King Cetshwayo's household in 1872, where she spent her adolescent years. After the War of 1879 she converted to Christianity and preached and taught in Northern Zululand. Her memoirs were recorded much later by the Hermannsburg missionary Heinrich Filter, who described her as a female apostle of Northern Zululand.

See also South Africa

Bibliography

Borquin, S., ed. and trans. *Paulina Dlamini: Servant of two Kings*. Compiled by H. Filter. Pietermaritzburg, 1986; Rüther, K. *Conflict, Congregations and Community: African Christianity and the Idea of Chieftaincy in the Nineteenth-Century Eastern and Northern Transvaal*. Basler Afrika Bibliographien, 2002.

FRIEDER LUDWIG

Dohms, Hermann Gottlieb

The Brazilian Lutheran pastor and educator Hermann Gottlieb Dohms (1887–1956) was born in Brazil. At the age of eleven he went to study theology in Germany. Initially under the influence of pietistic circles, he later became attracted to the theology of Schleiermacher. Upon his return to Brazil in 1914, he became pastor of the Evangelical Church in Cachoeira do Sul, Riograndian Synod (RS). He exerted a pronounced influence over that synod through the publication of a periodical. In 1921, he began a pretheological institute in his own home and in 1946 founded a school of theology. At the time of his death he was director of the pretheological school, president of the theological school, professor of systematics, and president of the RS and of the Synodical Federation. From an early neo-Lutheran emphasis on ethnicity as a divine ordination, Dohms later moved to a theological position heavily influenced by Karl Barth.

See also Brazil; Igreja Evangélica de Confissão Luterana no Brasil (IECLB) (Evangelical Church of the Lutheran Confession in Brazil)

Bibliography

Prien, H.-J. *Evangelische Kirchwerdung in Brasilien*. G. Mohn, 1989; São Leopoldo-RS. *Simpósio de História da Igreja*. Editora Sinodal, 1986.

PAULO WILLE BUSS

E

Eastern Orthodoxy

The Reformation was an event within the Western church. Yet it claimed that its theological insights were not a regional or confessional matter: since they brought to light the gospel, these understandings were relevant to the whole of Christendom since the gospel itself is universally valid. And indeed the Reformers, especially those in Wittenberg, were well aware that Christendom was not limited to the western half of Europe, but also had taken root in the eastern part, and even beyond the continent. What they had in mind was first of all the Greek church. Humanism had focused attention not only on the Greek classics but also on the Greek church fathers and their later heirs. Among adherents of the Reformation, who themselves had to fear suppression of their faith, the Ottoman invasion of Christian lands created a sense of solidarity with its Orthodox victims. Yet most of all the Greek church—and to a limited extent also the other Eastern churches—played an important role in the Reformers' altercation with the Roman Catholic Church. The existence of the Eastern churches was living proof that the Roman church was only an *ecclesia particularis* (particular church), not the *tota ecclesia Christi* (the whole church of Christ), and that the church catholic transcended the church of the pope. For that reason alone specific traits of the Roman church like papacy, celibacy, private Mass, expiatory sacrifice, Communion for the laity in one kind (bread), and indulgences could not be considered essential for salvation. The Reformers rather invoked the Greek church—not always correctly—in favor of changes in church life and doctrine they introduced.

This positive attitude toward the Greek church did not mean that its doctrine and institutions were considered normative. Luther, as well as Melanchthon, could also criticize it harshly. As for every ecclesial tradition, so that of the Greeks was considered testimony to and expression of the gospel, and thus it could claim authority only as far as it was in agreement with the Word of God. Where such agreement was lacking, a tradition had to be criticized and rejected, even if it was the outcome of an ecumenical council. According to the Reformers, in the Roman church the true church was only held in captivity and had not ceased to exist because Christ had always raised and preserved true believers in spite of its many non-Christian doctrines, institutions, and representatives; so also the Reformers' awareness of the bonds with the Greek church was based less on supposedly similar phenomena than on the axiomatic conviction that Christ would prevail in the whole of Christendom. However, at least Philip Melanchthon, who was particularly interested in visible continuity as a testimony to the continuous effectiveness of the gospel, always considered the Reformation to be close to the Greek church, especially the ancient Greek church.

Beyond this theoretical relationship with the Greek church, Melanchthon had a few contacts with living Greeks of his time. Among them was the Moldavian fugitive Jakobos Basilikos Herakleides, who in the late 1550s spent some time in Wittenberg. Jakobos was won over for the Reformation, and when he gained power in his home territory a few years later, he tried to reshape the Moldavian church accordingly (1561), albeit with little success. Another Eastern Orthodox theologian who appeared in Wittenberg in those years was the Serbian deacon Demetrios Mysos (1559).

Presumably he had been sent by the ecumenical patriarch in order to gather information about the Reformation. Melanchthon used Mysos's presence to gain knowledge in turn about the Greek church. At Mysos's departure Melanchthon gave him a letter for the patriarch, to which was appended the *Confessio Augustana Graeca*, a Greek translation of the Augsburg Confession drawn up a few years earlier by a Lutheran schoolteacher as a didactical enterprise; Melanchthon revised it slightly in order to make technical terms of Western theology (e.g., *satisfactio*, *justificatio*, *meritum*) more understandable for Greek readers. In his letter to the patriarch he described the eschatological plight that afflicted the adherents of the Reformation as well as the Eastern Orthodox and expressed his hope that God would rally "the holy assemblies [*ekklēsiai* in the sense of congregations] all over the world." The patriarch was asked not to give credence to slanders that he might have heard about the Reformation, but rather to believe in the reports Mysos would bring him, that in Wittenberg the Holy Scripture, the dogmatic decisions of the ancient synods, as well as the doctrines of many church fathers were diligently upheld and heresies rejected. The *Confessio Augustana Graeca* was meant as a proof to these claims. As it seems, the package never reached Constantinople. At least there was never a reaction to it.

Melanchthon's former student David Chytraeus (1530–1600) shared his teacher's interest in the Greek church, and gathered information about it on a large scale. His *Über den heutigen Zustand der Kirchen in Griechenland, Asien, Afrika, Ungarn, Böhmen, etc.* (*On the present state of the churches in Greece, Asia, Africa, Hungary, Bohemia, etc.*), which first appeared in 1569 and was republished many times, presented the public with a rather detailed picture of the Eastern churches, their doctrines, and their practices. Chytraeus's interest, like Melanchthon's earlier, was driven by motives of humanistic learning as well as of theology. He belonged to a second generation of reformers.

Thus he possessed a clear confessional identity over against other confessional churches, including the Greek. On the other hand, this second generation of Lutherans still presupposed that there were basic common convictions, especially with the Greek tradition. So the "Catalogue of Testimonies" that accompanied many editions of the Book of Concord, which was the work of that generation, quoted a host of Greek theologians from the church fathers down to the fourteenth century.

On the Greek side the perspective was less positive. There was little knowledge about the Reformation, and if there was some, it was negative. Rumors had presented the religious changes and altercations in Germany, Switzerland, France, and other lands as yet another deterioration within the Latin church, a new stage of the mania for innovation (*neōterismos*), of which the West was accused anyway. Since most information came across the Venetian Aegean Sea, often the polemics of the Counter-Reformation presented an additional negative lens. Occasional writings by Greek authors (Nikandros Nukios, Pachomios Rhusanos) took up the subject. Their general image of the Reformation portrayed a movement that rejected images, monasteries, and the invocation of saints; despised traditions of the church and changed the liturgy; used *azyma* (unleavened bread) in the Eucharist; upheld the addition of the *Filioque* term to the Niceno-Constantinopolitan Creed (Holy Spirit proceeding from the Father "and the Son"), perhaps even questioned the Trinity; and simply led to atheism. This depiction indicated no awareness of the differences between the Lutheran and the Reformed strands of the Reformation. The antitrinitarian movement, which had one of its strongholds in the Balkans, further darkened the picture.

Thus each side had a quite different basis for the first theological exchange between representatives of the Lutheran and the Greek churches, which began in 1573. The reason why this exchange came about and grew into a serious correspondence over several years was the presence of a Lutheran theologian, Stephan Gerlach, in Constantinople. He succeeded in creating an atmosphere of trust. Gerlach, the chaplain of the ambassador of the Holy Roman Empire in Constantinople, had been a student of the leading Lutheran theological faculty of the time, Tübingen. His former professors seized the opportunity to enter into contact with Ecumenical Partriarch Jeremias II (1536–95). The driving force behind this move was the foremost Grecist of his time, Martin Crusius (1526–1607), who became the father of neo-Hellenic studies. He convinced the theologian Jakob Andreae, one of the authors of the Formula of Concord and a leading figure not only of the church of Württemberg but also of Lutheranism as a whole, to join him, and both wrote to Jeremias. Crusius, who presented himself as a "lover of all things Greek" (*philellēn*), hoped to gain knowledge about the Greeks of his time; Andreae supported his efforts. For the decisive step, taken in the following year, Andreae played the crucial role. In 1574 the *Confessio Augustana Graeca* was again sent to Constantinople. This time it did arrive and triggered an ecumenical dialogue in written form, which also involved other prominent Lutheran theologians of the time (e.g., Jakob Heerbrand) and lasted until 1581, when Jeremias broke it off. The following six topics were discussed: the procession of the Holy Spirit (*Filioque*); free will, faith, grace, and good works; saints and icons; monasticism; sacraments; and tradition. One basic difference finally made Patriarch Jeremias conclude that the dialogue led nowhere: different theological methods and their ecclesiological implications. The patriarch simply offered long quotations from the church fathers and other texts of tradition. The Lutheran theologians presented systematic arguments developed on the basis of Holy Scripture.

The correspondence between Tübingen and Constantinople was the first and only theological exchange between Lutherans and Eastern Orthodox on a larger scale for centuries. Crusius tried to launch similar contacts with the Ethiopian church, but failed. In Russia, Czar Ivan IV held a public debate with a Lutheran theologian, yet without positive results, as was to be expected (1570). Only in Romania did the proximity of the Romanian Orthodox and the Siebenburgian Lutheran churches allow regular communication. The first book printed in Romanian was a translation of Luther's Small Catechism, followed by translations of biblical books on the basis of Protestant translations in other languages; the Small Catechism was widely used by Romanian Orthodox theologians. In the eyes of those Orthodox hierarchs, however, the Lutherans remained Western heretics.

After the end of the exchange between Tübingen and Constantinople, the Calvinist churches were more engaged with the Greek Orthodox, who became an object for missionary competition with the Roman church. The effect was a general rejection of all Western churches from the Orthodox side in the seventeenth century. Jeremias II's answers to the Lutherans gained semiofficial status as a pan-Orthodox rejection of Lutheranism. Yet below the official level there continued to be a trickle of mutual interest and contact between Lutheranism and Eastern Orthodoxy, at least with Russian Orthodox Christians. Gottfried Wilhelm Leibniz asked Czar Peter the Great to call a general council for a union of all Christian Churches (1712–13), and Nikolaus von Zinzendorf tried to build closer ties with the Eastern Orthodox Church (1739–40). The Lutheran Pietist August Hermann Francke (1663–1727) founded a *Collegium Orientale* for Eastern Orthodox students and a printing office for Russian publications in his school complex in Halle. He also sent missionaries to Turkey and Russia. They met with little success, but Russian translations of Lutheran books printed in Halle were widely read in Russia; devotional works were used even in monasteries (e.g., Johann Gerhard's *Meditationes* and Johann Arndt's *True Christianity*); and theological intellectuals consulted more systematic works, in Russian or in the Latin original (e.g., Johann Gerhard's *Loci theologici*). Some even incorporated elements from these books into their own theological works (Feofan Prokopovicz/Prokopovich).

Another theological exchange between representatives of Lutheran and Eastern Orthodox churches, however, did not take place until the second half of the twentieth century. Prepared by the participation of both confessional families in the multilateral ecumenical institutions initiated in the first half of that century (Commissions of Faith and Order and Life and Work, World Council of Churches), individual Lutheran and Eastern Orthodox churches began dialogues (Germany, Finland, United States). Finally the Lutheran World Federation and the Pan-Orthodox Conference followed suit (1981). The themes at the center of these dialogues are still the same as those discussed between Tübingen and Constantinople four centuries earlier.

See also Chytraeus, David; Ecumenical Dialogues; Finnish Interpretation of Luther; Melanchthon, Philip; Russia

Bibliography

Hering, G. "Orthodoxie und Protestantismus." In *XVI. Internationaler Byzantinistenkongreß*, Akten 1, no. 2:823–74. Verlag der österreichischen Akademie der Wissenschaften, 1981 (= *Jahrbuch der österreichischen Byzantinistik* 31, no. 2 [1981]: 823–74); Kretschmar, G. "Die Confessio Augustana Graeca." *Kirche im Osten* 20 (1977): 11–39; Saarinen, R., S. H. Wilson, and E. F. Fortino. "Dialogue: Eastern Orthodox Church—Lutheran Church." In Farrugia, E., ed., *Encyclopedic Dictionary of the Christian East*, 635–40. Pontifical Oriental Institute, 2015; Wallmann, J., and U. Sträter, eds. *Halle und Osteuropa: Zur europäischen Ausstrahlung des Pietismus*. Verlag der Franckeschen Anstalten, 1998; Wendebourg, D. *Reformation und Orthodoxie: Der ökumenische Briefwechsel zwischen der Leitung der Württembergischen Kirche und Patrarich Jeremias II. von Konstantinopel in den Jahren 1573–1581*. Vandenhoeck & Ruprecht, 1986.

Dorothea Wendebourg

Ebeling, Gerhard

As Lutheran pastor, Luther scholar, and professor of church history and later of systematic theology, Gerhard Ebeling (1912–2001) specialized in hermeneutics and the bases for Christian theology. Born in Berlin-Steglitz into an extended family of teachers and seeking initially to avoid an educational vocation, Ebeling began his theological studies in 1930 at the University of Marburg, Germany. Lectures by Rudolf Bultmann on Romans and Galatians and seminar work with Wilhelm Maurer on Luther set the tone for his theological development. After a semester's philosophical study with Nicolai Hartmann in Berlin, Ebeling ventured to Zurich, Switzerland (1932/33), where Emil Brunner engaged him in extensive study of Luther's works. While there, Ebeling met Kometa Richner, his future wife. Returning to Berlin during the *Kirchenkampf* (church struggle), Ebeling completed his first theological exams in the Confessing Church (1935) and served his vicarage in two parishes, Crossen-on-the-Oder und Fehrbellin (1935/36). In 1936 he attended the preaching seminary in Finkenwalde led by Dietrich Bonhoeffer, who facilitated Ebeling's doctoral studies in Zurich on Luther's interpretation of the Gospels in his sermons (1937–38, published in 1942). Completing his second theological examinations in 1939, Ebeling was ordained an "illegal" pastor in the Confessing Church to the "emergency parishes" of Berlin-Hermsdorf und -Frohnau. He married Kometa Richner later that year. Concurrent with pastoral duties, Ebeling also served in the military medical corps from 1940 to the end of World War II.

In 1945 after the war, Ebeling came to the University of Tübingen to become an assistant professor in church history and in 1946 a full professor. In 1954, shortly after publishing his seminal essay on the beginnings of Luther's hermeneutics, Ebeling moved into systematic theology and held professorships at Tübingen (1954–56, 1965–68) and in Zurich (1956–65, 1968–79), leading institutes of hermeneutics and religious studies at both universities. From 1950 to 1978, Ebeling edited the prestigious theological journal *Zeitschrift für Theologie und Kirche* and the series Beiträge zur historischen Theologie (Mohr Siebeck). In 1955 he became a member of the Commission for the Publication of the Weimar Edition of *Luthers*

Werke (WA, Weimarer Ausgabe) and in 1969–89 served as its president. At the request of Lutheran bishop Joachim Heubach, Ebeling chaired the board of trustees of the Luther Academy Ratzeburg (1985–97).

Following Luther's dictum that "only experience makes a theologian" (WA 5:163.28–29) and influenced by certain strains of existentialist philosophy, Ebeling's service during the *Kirchenkampf* and the depth of his Luther scholarship provided the impetus and theological means to give account of the Christian faith against adversaries inside and outside the church, all who detract from or interfere with the pure proclamation of the gospel of Jesus Christ, understood as the justification of sinners alone through word and faith (see his *Wort und Glaube* [Word and Faith]). In this spirit, Ebeling (then in his 80s) oversaw the final editing of the first protest petition against the Joint Declaration on the Doctrine of Justification signed by more than 160 German university theology professors in 1998. A prolific writer, Ebeling continued to publish seminal works explicating Luther's theology well into retirement. Ebeling's influence in the English-speaking theological world has been limited somewhat by the translation of only some of his vast oeuvre, *Luther: An Introduction to His Thought* and *Word and Faith*.

See also Bonhoeffer, Dietrich; Bultmann, Rudolf (Karl); Confessing Church; Existentialism; Luther's Works

Bibliography

Beutel, A. *Gerhard Ebeling—Eine Biographie*. Mohr Siebeck, 2012; "Gerhard Ebeling." In *Hermeneutische Blätter* (Sonderheft July 2003). Institut für Hermeneutik & Religionsphilosophie, Theologische Fakultät, Universität Zürich; Menacher, M. D. "Gerhard Ebeling (1912–2001)." In *Twentieth-Century Lutheran Theologians*, ed. M. C. Mattes, 307–34. Vandenhoeck & Ruprecht, 2013; Menacher, M. D. "Gerhard Ebeling's Lifelong *Kirchenkampf* as Theological Method." *LQ* 18 (Spring 2004): 1–27.

MARK D. MENACHER

Ebenezer Community

A community of religious exiles who settled near Savannah, Georgia, in 1734 was called the Ebenezer Community. In 1731, the Catholic archbishop-prince of the territory of Salzburg, Leopold von Firmian, imposed religious conformity, resulting in the departure of approximately twenty thousand Lutherans, the majority of whom resettled in Prussia while others relocated in the Netherlands. Through a cooperative endeavor that included the institutions of the Franckean Orphan House in Halle and the Society for the Propagation of Christian Knowledge in London, a small contingent of about forty-one Salzburger exiles were designated for settlement in the newly established colony of Georgia in America, where they arrived on March 12, 1734. Led by their Halle-supplied pastors, Johann Martin Boltzius and Israel Christian Gronau, the group established their settlement, Ebenezer, approximately twenty-five miles northwest of Savannah, moving two years later to a nearby location, "New" Ebenezer, next to the Savannah River.

Ebenezer's population grew rapidly through the arrival of later "transports," including three additional groups of Salzburger exiles, but was increasingly composed of "redemptioners," or indentured servants from Swabia and the Palatinate. The settlement steadily developed into a significant town in early Georgia that included the colony's first self-standing church building and orphanage. In addition to farming, Ebenezer's economic efforts focused on silk production, which ultimately failed, and lumber. Despite Boltzius's initial misgivings, slave labor began to appear in the community after its legalization in Georgia in 1751. The establishment of farms, or "plantations," spread the community beyond the confines of Ebenezer and into closer contact with other German-speaking settlers. Pastoral leadership continued to come from Halle through the first quarter of the nineteenth century. Following Gronau's early death in 1745, Hermann Heinrich Lemke arrived to provide assistance to Boltzius. The appointment of a third pastor, Christian Rabenhorst, provided needed support to the numerically and geographically expanding community but also created tensions over leadership roles and arrangements for the material support of the three pastors. After Boltzius died in 1765 and Lemke in 1768, Christian Triebner arrived from Halle to serve with Rabenhorst. Lack of clarity over leadership and seniority, along with a pronounced personality clash between the two pastors, divided the community into factions for a time, with separate worship services held in Ebenezer's Jerusalem Church. Mediation by Henry Melchior Mühlenberg, who traveled to Ebenezer from Philadelphia in 1774 to adjudicate the dispute, gave at least the appearance of reconciliation sufficient to keep peace until Rabenhorst's death in 1776 and Triebner's departure due to accusations of misconduct and his support of the British in the Revolutionary War. The 1786 arrival of Johann Ernst Bergmann, the last of the German-born pastors to serve Ebenezer, restored regular pastoral leadership to the community, which was also dealing with the lingering impact of the war. The majority of Ebenezer's population had supported the patriot cause, an indication of Ebenezer's shifting identity from that of an immigrant community to a settled American one. Johann Adam Treutlen, who had arrived in 1746 with the fourth Palatine transport (and eleventh overall), was elected as the state of Georgia's first governor in 1777, but served less than one year and was later hacked to death in South Carolina in 1781, allegedly by British Loyalists. During the Revolutionary War, Ebenezer itself endured periods of occupation and significant damage under the British.

Bergmann's assessment of both the spiritual and material circumstances of this later period in Ebenezer's life, measured against his perception of the community in its heyday during Boltzius's time, was unrelentingly negative. The growing presence and influence of Baptist and Methodist congregations had drawn a notable portion of Ebenezer's Lutheran members. Under Bergmann's son and successor, Christopher F. Bergmann, worship services in Jerusalem Church (established in 1741) were conducted for the first time in English. By this time, little remained of the actual town of Ebenezer, whose population had largely dispersed, though Jerusalem Church continues as a Lutheran congregation to this day, worshiping in the second building constructed on the site, completed in 1770. The location of New Ebenezer preserves several buildings, a museum, and the cemetery from the early community, and also hosts a retreat center. The legacy of the Salzburgers and other settlers of New Ebenezer is maintained through the Georgia Salzburger Society.

See also Boltzius, Johann Martin

Bibliography

Jones, G. F. *The Georgia Dutch: From the Rhine and Danube to the Savannah, 1733–1783.* University of Georgia Press, 1992; Jones, G. F. *The Salzburger Saga.* University of Georgia Press, 1984; Urlsperger, S., G. F. Jones, and R. Wilson, ed. and trans. *Detailed Reports on the Salzburger Emigrants Who Settled in America.* 18 vols. in 16. University of Georgia Press, 1968–95; Winde, H. "Die Frühgeschichte der Lutherischen Kirche in Georgia." PhD diss., Martin-Luther-Universität Halle-Wittenberg, 1960.

RUSSELL C. KLECKLEY

Eber, Paul

In the second generation of the Reformation, the German Lutheran theologian and churchman Paul Eber (1511–69) held a mediating position in the disputes between Philippists and Gnesio-Lutherans, especially after Philip Melanchthon's death (1560). Born in Kitzingen, Franconia, on November 8, 1511, Eber was injured in an accident as a youth, leaving him deformed and weakened. Yet his intellectual abilities were strong and quickly drew the attention of his teachers. After initial studies in Nuremberg with Joachim Camerarius and Eobanus Hessus, he matriculated at the University of Wittenberg in 1532, where he was mentored by Melanchthon. In 1536 he received his MA degree and the following year joined the arts faculty at the university. By 1541 he was named professor of Latin, and afterward also of physics. Eber taught broadly in the liberal arts and published works on history, astrology, physics, and natural history. His marriage in 1541 produced thirteen children.

In 1552 he lectured on dialectic and catechesis. In 1557 he was named professor of Old Testament and was appointed preacher at the Castle Church. Eber and Melanchthon took part in the Colloquy of Worms (1557) with Roman Catholic theologians, a colloquy that collapsed due to intra-Lutheran dissension. In 1558 he succeeded Johannes Bugenhagen, becoming preacher in the city church and general superintendent of Electoral Saxony. He received his doctorate in 1559.

In the controversies of the time, Eber maintained a moderating position. He sided with his Wittenberg colleagues in the controversies over adiaphora and synergism. Eber wrote several theological treatises, including works addressing the Lord's Supper controversy. Like Melanchthon, he understood the elements of the Supper alongside the Word as signs, emphasizing that the assurances of forgiveness of sins and life are given. After Melanchthon's death in 1560, Eber clarified his views, affirming that those receiving bread and wine in the Supper receive with it the true, essential body and blood of Christ, yet he did not present his views to the satisfaction of some Gnesio-Lutherans. His position remained a mediating one. At the Altenburg Colloquy of 1567 he continued to attempt to salvage some of Melanchthon's distinctions, which he thought necessary, on the proper definition of justification and its relationship to good works.

At the request of Duke August of Saxony, in 1565 Eber and his university colleague Georg Major published a Bible containing both Luther's German translation and a Latin revision of the Vulgate. He wrote a number of poems and hymns. Collections of his sermons were published after his death. The sermons reflect his concern not only for sound biblical teaching but also for equipping his hearers to confess the Evangelical faith and to live it out in their lives. Eber died at Wittenberg on December 10, 1569.

See also Colloquy; Wittenberg Circle

Bibliography

Gehrt, D., and V. Leppin, eds. *Paul Eber (1511–1569): Humanist und Theologe.* Evangelische Verlagsanstalt, 2014; Thüringer, W. "Paul Eber (1511–1569): Melanchthons Physik und seine Stellung zu Copernicus." In *Melanchthon in seinen Schülern*, ed. H. Scheible, 285–321. Harrassowitz, 1997.

GERHARD BODE

Eck, John

The preacher and exegete John Eck (1486–1543) was chair of theology at the University of Ingolstadt. He was also an opponent of Luther at the Leipzig Disputation of 1519 and promulgator of the papal bull *Exsurge Domine* (June 15, 1520) in Saxony. Born in the German region of Swabia, Eck entered the University of Heidelberg at the age of eleven. After Heidelberg, Eck received an eclectic education under various influential schools of the time: Nominalists and Scotists at Tübingen, Albertists and Thomists at Cologne, and humanist influences at Freiburg, where he was ordained a secular priest in 1508 and received his doctorate in theology in 1510. That same year, Eck accepted the chair of theology at the University of Ingolstadt, where he remained until his death. There Eck developed a reputation for his theological opinions and pugnacious personal style. His early works, such as the *Chrysopassus praedestinationis* (1514) and *Disputatio Viennae Pannoniae habita* (1517), clearly reveal his Scholastic training and thorough method of argumentation. Eck's opponents, such as Erasmus of Rotterdam and Andreas Bodenstein (Karlstadt), revered his skills at disputation even if they did not necessarily like or agree with him. In early 1517 Eck's relationship to Luther was initially cordial. After receiving a copy of the Ninety-Five Theses, however, Eck retorted in early 1518 with his unpublished Obelisci, wherein he branded Luther a "Hussite" and condemned his positions as heretical. In August of that year Luther responded with his *Asterisci*, which he published with Eck's *Obelisci*. Eventually their opposition came to a head at Leipzig in the summer of 1519. Karlstadt provoked this debate to square off with Eck on grace and freedom. However, with Luther's invitation to the stage, the new focus became his fidelity to the authority of the church and the pope. Eck quickly pushed Luther into the position of an accused, provoking reluctant responses that later would warrant Luther's condemnation as a heretic. After Leipzig, Eck was called to Rome in 1520 to serve on a committee with Cardinal Cajetan and two others to draw up grounds for Luther's condemnation. The result was the papal bull *Exsurge Domine*, threatening Luther's excommunication, which Eck promulgated throughout the Holy Roman Empire. The credibility of the bull was questioned by many, however, especially after Eck independently added other German names he deemed suspect (Willibald Pirckheimer and Bernhard Adelmann, among others) to the document. In 1520 Eck's *De primatu Petri*, a defense of the papacy against Luther, was published, and in 1525 his popular *Enchiridion locorum communium adversus Lutteranos* was released, going through forty-six editions over the next fifty years. In 1526, Eck deposed Oecolompadius at Baden, and in later years he composed works against Erasmus, Melanchthon, Zwingli, and Bucer, among others. Eck was involved in the colloquies of Worms and Regensburg, where he debated with Philip Melanchthon. He died in Ingolstadt in 1543.

See also Cajetan (Thomaso de Vio); Luther's Roman Catholic Opponents

Bibliography

Battles, F. L., trans. *Enchiridion of Commonplaces against Luther and Other Enemies of the Church* (1525). Baker, 1979; Fraenkel, P., ed. *Johannes Eck: Enchiridion locorum communium adversus Lutherum et alios hostes ecclesiae (1525–1543)*. Aschendorff, 1979; Iserloh, E. *Johannes Eck, 1486–1543: Scholastiker, Humanist, Kontroverstheologe*. 2nd ed. Aschendorff, 1985; Janz, D. "Johann Maier of Eck." In *Contemporaries of Erasmus: A Biographical Register of the Renaissance and Reformation*, ed. P. Bietenholz and T. Deutscher, 1:416–19. University of Toronto Press, 1985; Minnich, N. "On the Origins of Eck's 'Enchiridion.'" In *Johannes Eck (1486–1543) im Streit der Jahrhunderte*, ed. E. Iserloh, 37–73. Aschendorff, 1988; Wiedemann, T. *Dr. Johann Eck, Professor der Theologie an der Universität Ingolstadt*. Pustet, 1865.

ERIC J. DEMEUSE

Ecology

The term "ecology" was coined by Ernst Haeckel (1834–1919) in 1866. It is taken from the Greek word *oikos*, "household," and provided a way to describe the interdependence of living organisms on each other and on the inorganic world. In the twentieth century the insights of ecology gave rise to calls for a corresponding ethic. Aldo Leopold was one of the first to call for such an environmental ethic with his famous "Land Ethic" in *The Sand County Almanac*. It reads, in part, "A thing is right when it tends to preserve the integrity, stability, and beauty of the biotic community. It is wrong when it tends otherwise" (224–25). The concept of ecology entered the consciousness of most Americans when the environmental movement took off in the 1960s, following the publication of Rachel Carson's book *Silent Spring*, which drew attention to the deadly dangers of DDT and other chemicals making their way up the food chain.

In 1967 Lynn White, a medievalist at UCLA, issued a challenge to Christian thinkers with a seminal article in *Science*, "The Historical Roots of Our Ecologic Crisis," which laid the blame for ecological crisis at the doorstep of Christianity, whose teaching on the image of God and dominion seemed to give Christians license to do whatever they wished with creation. The central question raised by environmental ethics can be framed thus: How do we see ourselves and our relation to the creation? Does creation have any intrinsic value apart from human use? Are we a part of nature, or do we stand apart from it?

In the mid-twentieth century, the Lutheran theologian Joseph Sittler was not only one of the first Lutheran theologians to address ecology and the environment in a serious way, but also one of the first Christian theologians to do so. Of particular significance is his 1961 speech to the General Assembly of World Council of Churches in New Delhi, India, in which he developed the theme of a cosmic Christology on the basis of Col. 1. Since then, many Lutheran theologians have taken up the cause, from Paul Santmire to David Rhoads to Oswald Bayer.

See also Creation

Bibliography
Carson, R. L. *Silent Spring*. 1962. Reprint, Mariner Books, 2002; Leopold, A. *A Sand County Almanac: And Sketches Here and There*. 1949. Reprint, Oxford University Press, 1968; Sittler, J. *Evocations of Grace: Writings on Ecology, Theology, and Ethics*, ed. S. Bouma-Prediger and P. Bakken. Eerdmans, 2000; Westhelle, V. "The Weeping Mask: Ecological Crisis and the View of Nature." *Word & World* 11 (1991): 137–46; White, L., Jr. "The Historic Roots of Our Ecologic Crisis." *Science* 155 (March 10, 1967): 1203–7; Wingren, G. "The Doctrine of Creation: Not an Appendix but the First Article." *Word & World* 4 (1984): 353–71.

CHARLES P. ARAND

Economic Issues: Capitalism and Socialism

Luther's discussion of economic issues belongs to teachings regarding the earthly regime. According to his theory of the two regimes or realms (*Reiche/Regimente*), the economy (*oeconomia*) is one of the only three divinely instituted orders or estates (*Stände*), along with politics (*politia*) and the church or religion (*ecclesia*). With its origins in the medieval tradition, this tripartite division gave to it an anthropological significance as descriptive of basic human faculties in the earthly regime in which humans are called to cooperate with God (*cooperatio homine cum Deo*, as described in *Bondage of the Will* [1525], LW 33:242–43). This distinction of orders that make up for the earthly regime is elaborated most extensively in Luther's *Commentary on Genesis* (cf. LW 1) but also emphasized in his (*Great*) *Confession concerning Christ's Supper* of 1528 (see LW 37:364–65) in addition to several other places. Most importantly, this distinction sharpens the unique peculiarities attributed to the economic and the political arenas. They are equivalent to Aristotelian distinction between the "faculty" (*dianoia*) of *poiēsis* (work or labor) and of *praxis* (human interaction) that had been lost in the West since Latin took over Greek as the lingua franca. However, the precise Aristotelian distinction,

kept in the tripartite distinction of these institutions, led Luther to recognize two distinct forms of human trials. One was the *poena oeconomica* coming down on Adam and his descendants (labor as productive, but toil after the fall) and upon Eve and her descendants (childbearing as reproductive, but full of pangs after the fall); and the other was the *poena politica* falling on Cain and societies he instituted (see Cain as the founder of the first city; Gen. 4:17).

Luther lived in a time when financial capitalism was developing, and its most distinguishing characteristic was the practice of usury, in which money itself became a kind of merchandise, and the lending of it turned into a means of producing more value. The first consequence was the further impoverishment of those in need of sustenance for life that their labor alone should provide, but from which through usury they were now alienated. Some of Luther's sharpest criticism of social and economic issues is evident in several of his writings on usury, as in the "Sermon on Usury" from 1520, on "Trade and Usury" from 1524 (both in LW 45), and particularly in his treatise *Admonition to Pastors to Preach against Usury* of 1540 (WA 51:325–424). This last text from 1540 (not yet translated into English) made quite an impression on Karl Marx, who called Luther the "first economist of the German nation" (*der erste Nationalökonom*) and has several pages of *Das Capital* (vol. 1) dedicated to this particular text. The other consequence that the sin usury generates is to blur the distinction between economy and politics (WA 44:440.25). Due to this infringement, the produce of labor was alienated and used to amass political power, turning bankers into mighty political brokers.

As a child of his time, Luther certainly should not be understood as a proto-socialist or communist. In spite of the importance of the doctrine of vocation for "inner-worldly asceticism," as Max Weber argued, the sociologist and his Lutheran theological friend Ernst Troeltsch contended that Luther, contrary to

Calvin and his legacy, was a precapitalist and premodern thinker. But whether these characterizations apply or not, it is still true that Luther's social ethics implied a severe criticism of the emerging mercantile capitalism of his days, as Luther provided remedial programs to attend the needy and proposed universal education.

See also Creation; Economic Life and Lutheranism

Bibliography
Duchrow, U. *Christenheit und Weltverantwortung: Traditionsgeschichte und systematische Struktur der Zweireichelehre.* Klett, 1970; Fabiunke, G. *Martin Luther als Nationalökonom.* Akademie-Verlag, 1963; Küppers, J. "Luthers Dreihierarchienlehre als Kritik und der mittelalterlichen Gesellschaftsauffassung." *Evangelische Theologie* 8 (1959): 361–74; Rieth, R. *"Habsucht" bei Martin Luther: Ökonomisches und theologisches Denken, Tradition und soziale Wirklichkeit im Zeitalter der Reformation.* Universität Leipzig, 1992; Troeltsch, E. *Protestantism and Progress.* Trans. W. Montgomery. Beacon, 1958; Weber, M. *The Protestant Ethic and the Spirit of Capitalism.* Trans. T. Parsons. Allen & Unwin, 1930.

ROBERT BENNE

Economic Life and Lutheranism

The general view of Luther's teaching on economic life is that it was mired in late medieval thought and practice. He roundly condemned the practice of usury while Calvin did not, thus making economic life in the Lutheran territories less dynamic. He believed money was "sterile" and that lending it ought to have no economic dividends (*Admonition to Pastors to Preach against Usury* [1540]; Lindberg 191–92). Perhaps as a vestige of his life as a monk, he tended to see commercial activity as inherently selfish, and therefore he was suspicious of it. Private gain was inherently tainted. He believed in the static hierarchical order of kings, nobility, and peasants and saw little room for giving the poor more power in economic affairs. Even if arrangements were unjust, he tended to prefer order over justice, though he criticized the nobility sharply for their mistreatment of the poor.

Yet there were important differences from late medieval economic practice that the Lutheran Reformation enacted. Since Luther argued for much less churchly power over worldly life in general, economic life came under the control of the political powers of the time rather than the religious. This pushed Germany toward mercantilism, an economic system that favored government regulation of economic life in order to augment national power over rival states. This had lasting effects in Germany, making it hostile to free-market thinking and practice and opening it up to central direction of economic production on behalf of the nation.

At the same time, Lutheranism went beyond the individualistic and churchly charity of Roman Catholicism. Luther, Johannes Bugenhagen, and others recommended community chests in the cities in the Lutheran territories. These were to be financed by taxation and would offer, besides charity for the indigent, interest-free loans to those who needed them (with the stipulation that they would repay the loans in due time), and even medical care. Further, Lutheran teaching on vocation enlisted the laity in performing economic activity as service to the neighbor. Lutherans became known as excellent workers. Their work ethic is something of a product of the Lutheran teaching on vocation.

Traditionalist Lutheran thought and practice were buffeted on the right by rising capitalist powers (Netherlands, Britain, the United States) and on the left by socialist and communist regimes (Scandinavian socialism and Russian and later Soviet Communism). In attempting to find a middle way in Germany, the Lutheran chancellor Otto von Bismarck (1815–98) achieved a notable paternalistic welfare state.

However, the combination of free-market capitalism and constitutional democracy on the one hand, and democratic socialism on the other, were not to be denied. Lutheran thought has accommodated to those modern formulations, usually preferring the latter over the former.

See also Economic Issues: Capitalism and Socialism; Vocation

Bibliography

Lindberg, C. *Beyond Charity*. Fortress, 1993; Rieth, R. "Luther's Treatment of Economic Life." In *The Oxford Handbook of Martin Luther's Theology*, ed. R. Kolb, I. Dingel, and L. Batka, 383–96. Oxford University Press, 2014; Spiegel, H. "Martin Luther." In *The Growth of Economic Thought*. Duke University Press, 1971. 3rd ed., 1991; Torvend, S. *Luther and the Hungry Poor*. Fortress, 2008.

ROBERT BENNE

Ecuador

The World Mission Prayer League (WMPL), a direct heir of the American Board of the Santal Mission, arrived in Cuenca, Ecuador, with its first missionaries in 1951. In 1968 it invited the Norwegian Santal Mission (today Normisjon) to collaborate in mission work. The congregations formed as a result of the work of WMPL and Normisjon united in the Federation of Evangelical Lutheran Churches in Ecuador in 1974, but the differences between mestizo Spanish-speaking congregations and Quichua (Quechua) congregations, along with the desire in some congregations for a more hierarchical church polity, led to the end of the federation and the creation of the Spanish-speaking Evangelical Church of Lutheran Confession of Ecuador and the Quichua-speaking Evangelical Lutheran Indigenous Church of Ecuador in 2009.

The Evangelical Lutheran Church of Ecuador, recognized by the LWF, was formed by German immigrants in Quito in 1958, with German-speaking, English-speaking, and Spanish-speaking congregations in the same building. There are some independent Lutheran congregations in Ecuador. One is Peace of God in Cuenca, born in the living room of a WMPL missionary in the 1980s, and today sending missionaries out of Ecuador.

Normisjon helped create the Lutheran Bible Institute of Ecuador in Guayaquil, which receives students from all the Lutheran churches in the country.

See also Mission and Evangelism

Bibliography

Cruz, J. M. *The Histories of the Latin American Church: A Handbook*. Esp. 297–317. Fortress, 2014; http://www.iglesialuterana.ec/; http://www.normisjon.no/internasjonalt/ecuador; http://pazdedios.org/; Theodore, E., and M. B. Bachmann. *Lutheran Churches in the World: A Handbook*. Esp. 520–22. Augsburg, 1989; https://wmpl.org/our-work/ecuador/.

ANDRÉS ROBERTO ALBERTSEN

Ecumenical Dialogues

Lutherans' participation in ecumenical dialogues has been coterminous with their growing awareness as a global movement. Swedish archbishop Nathan Söderblom is said to have made the first concrete proposal for an "ecumenical council" in 1919 at a meeting of the World Alliance for Promoting International Friendship through Churches. As head of Life and Work, he spearheaded intense Lutheran involvement in the two precursors to the World Council of Churches (WCC), the other being Faith and Order.

The first worldwide Lutheran organization, responding to the refugee crisis after World War I, was born under the leadership of an American Lutheran, John Morehead. The beginnings of this Lutheran World Convention (LWC) were ecclesially modest: at neither the 1923 Eisenach gathering nor the 1929 Copenhagen one was Holy Communion celebrated, so as to avoid the impression of creating a single global Lutheran church. Nevertheless, the LWC was cohesive enough to produce a statement in 1936, Lutherans and the Ecumenical Movements. It held that Lutheranism had always been an "ecumenical" undertaking; reference to Augsburg Confession, article 7, would become a standard of Lutheran ecumenism thereafter.

Negotiations toward the formation of the WCC wrestled over two models of membership, one regional and the other confessional. The Orthodox had already made their case for the latter, but it was not clear that Protestants would follow suit until, essentially, Lutherans insisted that they did. For a long period after the WCC's founding in 1948, there continued to be a great deal of doubt as to whether a strong confessional identity could coexist with strong ecumenical commitments.

Subsequent history placed these doubts in question. The Lutheran World Federation (LWF), founded in 1947, was an immediate and committed partner of the WCC. One of the LWF's constitutional principles was to "serve Christian unity throughout the world" and "foster Lutheran participation in ecumenical movements." Early work in the LWF's Commission on Theology came to the conclusion that it was possible to talk about doctrinal agreement without actually subscribing to the same historic confessions. One therefore ought to seek a communion among existing churches, or "church fellowship," rather than the establishment of a new, single organizational body that dispensed with the unique character of its predecessors.

The Second Vatican Council startled the ecumenical movement with the sudden interest of Roman Catholicism in joining the conversation. Explicitly rejecting the "home to Rome" model, the conciliar document *Unitatis Redintegratio* (1964) identified Protestants as "ecclesial communities" that "have been by no means deprived of significance and importance in the mystery of salvation." The result was a shift from the previous dominance of multilateral dialogue to a new model stressing bilateral dialogue.

This change in direction suited the Lutheran confessional orientation well. The 1963 assembly of the LWF in Helsinki voted to establish the legally and financially independent Institute for Ecumenical Research, which eventually found its home in Strasbourg, France, in 1965. From the institute have come key concepts and commitments in Lutheran ecumenism, such as the goal of "visible unity" among Christian churches and the methods of "unity in reconciled diversity" or "differentiated consensus." In keeping with the parallel developments in Lutheran global identity and Lutheran ecumenism, the institute also laid the groundwork for the evolution in the LWF's own self-understanding, especially the declaration of full altar and pulpit fellowship among LWF churches at the Budapest assembly (1984) and

the declaration of the LWF as a "communion of churches" at the Curitiba assembly (1990).

There has been wide variety in the results of the various ecumenical dialogues; thus it is sensible to treat each confessional set individually.

Roman Catholic. This dialogue, the forerunner of all other bilaterals, has been by far the most intensive and productive. Meetings in the mid-1960s established international commissions on the gospel and the church, the theology of marriage, and the problems of mixed marriages. Since then numerous official statements have been released, often enhanced by the work of national dialogues, especially the prolific American and German ones. These two produced Justification by Faith (1983) and The Condemnations of the Reformation Era: Do They Still Divide? (1986), respectively, which were critical stages on the way to the Joint Declaration on the Doctrine of Justification (JDDJ). The JDDJ was signed by the Catholic Church and the LWF in 1999, making it to date the only binding doctrinal statement with a Protestant body ever promulgated by Rome. The JDDJ articulated a common understanding of justification (while acknowledging the ongoing differences in terminology and emphasis between the two parties), such that the anathemas of the sixteenth century on this topic were no longer seen to condemn the contemporary partner. Fierce opposition to the JDDJ was raised in some quarters, particularly by a group of German Lutheran theologians. Nevertheless, it remains notable that the LWF was only able to articulate a contemporary understanding of justification in an ecumenical setting, since an earlier effort to do so for Lutherans at the Helsinki assembly in 1963 had failed. Subsequent work by the dialogue produced a long statement on the apostolicity of the church (2005), while the 2013 statement From Conflict to Communion offered an interpretation of the sixteenth century intended to facilitate joint commemoration in 2017.

Reformed. The first Lutheran-Reformed conversations took place under the aegis of

Faith and Order, but by the late 1960s the LWF and the World Alliance of Reformed Churches took charge of the dialogue. At the same time, conversations among the Lutheran, Reformed, and Union churches in Europe led to the Leuenberg Agreement (1973). This statement identified three traditional areas of dispute between the two parties—predestination, Christology, and Christ's presence at the Lord's Supper—and declared that contemporary understandings of these three loci allowed for a "common understanding of the Gospel" such that "they are no longer an obstacle to church fellowship." The Leuenberg Fellowship in time gave rise to the Community of Protestant Churches in Europe, which now includes other churches such as Methodists and Waldensians. Other local Lutheran-Reformed agreements exist elsewhere, among them the Formula of Agreement (1997) in the United States between the Evangelical Lutheran Church in America and the Presbyterian Church (USA), the Reformed Church in America and the United Church of Christ. Nevertheless, Lutheran-Reformed accord has not met with universal acceptance: the Evangelical Lutheran Church of Finland has never joined the CPCE, for example, due to sacramental issues.

Anglican. Anglican-Lutheran dialogue was also launched in the 1960s and has generally seen strong doctrinal consensus emerge with recommendations toward closer church relations, as seen in the Pullach Report (1972), the Cold Ash Report (1983), and the Niagara Report (1988). However, the historic episcopate has remained a sticking point and led to the anomalous situation of unequal regional agreements that do not translate into an international policy. For instance, the Porvoo Common Statement (1992) between the Anglican churches of Great Britain and Ireland and Scandinavian and Baltic Lutheran churches allows for full altar and pulpit fellowship, premised on the retention of the historic episcopate by Lutherans in the Nordic region. By contrast, Anglican agreements with German Lutherans (the Meissen agreement,

1988) and French Lutherans (the Reuilly agreement, 1999) allow for church communion but without a common exercise of episcopé. In the United States, Called to Common Mission (1999) required the introduction of ordaining Lutheran candidates by a bishop consecrated in historic succession, yet allowed for conscientious objectors to opt out. However, opposition within the Evangelical Lutheran Church in America was still strong enough that a large number of congregations formed Lutheran Congregations in Mission for Christ, which adopted a deliberately more congregationalist polity.

Orthodox. The first meetings between the ecumenical patriarchate and the LWF took place in the 1960s, and by the late 1970s a concrete invitation by the former to initiate bilateral dialogue led to the formation of the Lutheran-Orthodox Joint Commission. Its first official meeting took place in Espoo, Finland, in 1981. To date twelve joint statements have been released (with more anticipated). Despite its declared goal of full communion, this remains the most difficult of the LWF's dialogues, with the widest cultural gap. Regional Lutheran-Orthodox dialogues have been able to reach greater doctrinal accord; notable examples include those of the Protestant Church in Germany (EKD) with the Russian Orthodox and Romanian Orthodox Churches and the ecumenical patriarchate; and of the Evangelical Lutheran Church of Finland with the Russian Orthodox and the Orthodox Church of Finland. Efforts toward engagement with Oriental Orthodox at the international level have not come to fruition, though regional conversations take place in the one country where Lutherans and Oriental Orthodox live in large numbers together: Ethiopia.

Methodist. At the international level there has been only one round of dialogue, from 1979 to 1984, culminating in the document The Church: Community of Grace, which examined both consensus and differing emphases in doctrine. Full communion has been declared locally in Germany, Norway, Sweden, and the United States. The most significant development in recent years is the World Methodist Council's 2006 Statement of Association with the Joint Declaration on the Doctrine of Justification.

Baptist. Unlike most other LWF international dialogues, that with the Baptist World Alliance did not identify full communion as a goal for its dialogue from 1986 to 1989 but rather an improvement in "mutual knowledge, respect, and cooperation" between the respective churches. The goodwill and concerted effort are evident in the resulting statement, Baptists and Lutherans in Conversation: A Message to Our Churches; nevertheless, no solution to the stumbling block of infant versus believer's baptism could be found.

Adventist. After initial contacts had been made through the meetings of the secretaries of the Christian World Communions, bilateral dialogues took place between the LWF and the Seventh-Day Adventist Church from 1994 to 1998, resulting in the statement Adventists and Lutherans in Conversation. Here again the goal was not unity, visible or otherwise, but improved mutual understanding.

Mennonite. Not fully realizing that today's Mennonites are the heirs of sixteenth-century Anabaptists, Lutherans invited them to the 450th anniversary celebration of the Augsburg Confession in 1980, which condemns the Anabaptists in articles 5, 9, 16, and 17. This sparked national dialogues in France (1981–84), Germany (1989–92), and the United States (2001–4). The LWF and the Mennonite World Conference began talks in 2002, initially on doctrinal matters, but the focus shifted quickly to bad past relations. As a result, the commission composed a joint history of Lutheran persecution of Anabaptists in the sixteenth century, the first of its kind. Based on the rediscovery of its forebears' evildoing, the 2010 LWF assembly in Stuttgart voted unanimously to apologize publicly to the Mennonites, who at the same event offered their full forgiveness. Since then a task force has been established

to improve mutual relations and correct misapprehensions about the other. A trilateral conversation including Roman Catholics on baptism began in 2013.

Pentecostal. The institute in Strasbourg initiated work from a Lutheran perspective on Pentecostal and charismatic churches already in the 1970s, but it was not until 2004 that it undertook on behalf of the LWF a "proto-dialogue" with Pentecostal leaders and scholars. The result of the six-year encounter was the publication in 2010 of *Lutherans and Pentecostals in Dialogue*, intended as a handbook for further dialogue between the churches on both the regional and the international level. The LWF-Classical Pentecostal dialogue met for the first time in the fall of 2015 with plans in the works to conduct a five-year cycle of dialogues on the topics of experience, prosperity, and healing, among others. The existence of significant numbers of charismatics within North American, European, Latin American, and especially African Lutheranism makes this dialogue notably different from the others.

Lutherans worldwide have continued to be active in the multilateral movement, for instance in the formulation of and response to *Baptism, Eucharist and Ministry* (1983) and more recently in the Global Christian Forum. The reception of dialogue results within national churches and local congregations remains a challenge.

Lutherans affiliated with the Lutheran Church–Missouri Synod and the related International Lutheran Council have engaged in certain dialogue efforts; however, they tend to remain skeptical about the ecumenical process and extremely wary of fellowship agreements, which are often generally perceived negatively as "unionism."

See also Anabaptists/Spiritualists; Catholicism; Eastern Orthodoxy; Lutheran World Federation; Söderblom, Nathan

Bibliography
Agreement between Reformation Churches in Europe. Leuenberg Agreement. Trilingual ed. Evangelische Verlagsanstalt, 2013; *The Apostolicity of the Church: Study*

Document of the Lutheran–Roman Catholic Commission on Unity. Lutheran University Press, 2007; *The Condemnations of the Reformation Era: Do They Still Divide?* Ed. K. Lehmann and W. Pannenberg. Fortress, 1990; *From Conflict to Communion: Lutheran-Catholic Common Commemoration of the Reformation in 2017.* Report of the Lutheran–Roman Catholic Commission on Unity. Evangelische Verlagsanstalt / Bonifatius, 2013; *Growing Consensus: Church Dialogues in the United States, 1962–1991.* Ed. J. A. Burgess and J. Gros, FSC. Statements of American Lutheran dialogues with Baptist, United Methodist, Reformed, Evangelical, Episcopal, and Roman Catholic Churches. Paulist Press, 1995; *Growth in Agreement: Reports and Agreed Statements of Ecumenical Conversations on a World Level.* Ed. H. Meyer and L. Vischer. The Anglican-Lutheran "Pullach Report." The Lutheran–Roman Catholic "Malta Report," "The Eucharist," "Ways to Community," "All Under One Christ," and "The Ministry in the Church." The Lutheran-Reformed–Roman Catholic "The Theology of Marriage and the Problem of Mixed Marriages." WCC / Paulist Press, 1984; *Growth in Agreement II: Reports and Agreed Statements of Ecumenical Conversations on a World Level, 1982–1998.* Ed. J. Gros, FSC, H. Meyer, and W. G. Rusch. The Anglican-Lutheran "Cold Ash Report," "Episcopé," and "The Diaconate as Ecumenical Opportunity." The Baptist-Lutheran "A Message to Our Churches." The Lutheran-Methodist "The Church: Community of Grace." The Lutheran-Orthodox "Divine Revelation," "Scripture and Tradition," and "The Canon and the Inspiration of Holy Scripture." The Lutheran-Reformed "Towards Church Fellowship." "Adventists and Lutherans in Conversation." The Lutheran–Roman Catholic "Martin Luther—Witness to Jesus Christ," "Facing Unity," "Church and Justification," and "Joint Declaration on the Doctrine of Justification." WCC / Eerdmans, 2000; *Growth in Agreement III: International Dialogue Texts and Agreed Statements, 1998–2005.* Ed. J. Gros, FSC, T. F. Best, and L. F. Fuchs, SA. The Lutheran-Orthodox "The Ecumenical Councils," "Understanding of Salvation in the Light of the Ecumenical Councils," "Salvation: Grace, Justification and Synergy," "Word and Sacraments (*Mysteria*) in the Life of the Church," "*Mysteria*/Sacraments as Means of Salvation," and "Baptism and Chrismation as Sacraments of Initiation into the Church." The Anglican-Lutheran "Growth in Communion." The Lutheran-Reformed "Called to Communion and Common Witness." WCC / Eerdmans, 2007; Harding, M. "To Serve Christian Unity: Ecumenical Commitment in the LWF." In *From Federation to Communion: The History of the Lutheran World Federation*, ed. J. H. Schjørring, P. Kumari, and N. A. Hjelm, 248–83. Fortress, 1997; *Healing Memories: Reconciling in Christ.* Report of the Lutheran-Mennonite International Study Commission. LWF / Mennonite World Conference, 2010; *Justification by Faith: Lutherans and Catholics in Dialogue VII.* Ed. H. G. Anderson, T. A. Murphy, and J. A. Burgess. Augsburg, 1983; *Lutherans and Pentecostals in Dialogue.* Institute for Ecumenical Research / David du Plessis Center for Christian Spirituality / European Pentecostal Charismatic Research Association, 2010; *The Porvoo Common Statement: Conversations between the British and Irish Anglican Churches and the Nordic and Baltic Lutheran Churches.* Council for Christian Unity of the General Synod of the Church of England, 1993.

Sarah Hinlicky Wilson

Eighteenth Century

Since the period itself, what historians now label the "long eighteenth century" (typically dated from the end of the European Wars of Religion [1648] to the end of the French Revolution [1799]) has been seen as a watershed in the history of Western Christianity. A viable secular alternative to a religious worldview arose for the first time, and Europe's churches faced intellectual and political challenges unmatched since antiquity. Still, the era was not primarily a time of ecclesiastical and theological retrenchment. Popular renewal movements—most notably Pietism, that part of the Protestant Evangelical Awakening that arose on Lutheran soil—expanded religious life among the laity and spurred global missions, while theologians seized on new lines of thinking to revise and rearticulate Christian teaching. Lutheranism played an integral role in these trends and was in turn transformed by them.

In telling the story of eighteenth-century theology, both contemporary and later interpreters have invoked the language of rupture and revolution. Ernst Troeltsch, for example, influentially depicted the rise of a neo-Protestantism that rejected medieval assumptions about a unified culture under clerical authority in favor of a theology grounded in experience, private judgment, and contemporary thought. Karl Barth charted a process of "humanization" in which Protestant teaching, under the twin banners of Pietism and the Enlightenment, was molded to fit the needs of bourgeois morality and the absolutist state. While such readings see a sharp break with earlier Protestantism, eighteenth-century Lutherans of all stripes appealed to Luther and Reformation precedent for their various reform programs, whether in doctrine, biblical orientation, lay participation, or freedom of conscience. Recent scholarship has rooted new departures in earlier developments, while underscoring that the hegemonic shift from Orthodoxy to liberalism indeed constitutes a crucial change within the Lutheran tradition.

The 1700s saw Lutheran theology branch into several distinct movements. They often defined themselves against each other but shared certain concerns, owing to a common situation formed by the preceding century's religious wars and their aftermath, confessionalization projects, and intellectual trends. Efforts to revive spiritual life produced a stream of devotional literature from Orthodox, Pietist, and Enlightenment writers alike. Weariness with confessional strife fueled (largely unsuccessful) ecumenical attempts and, with the partial exception of Orthodoxy, a tendency to focus on core teachings and practical piety at the expense of dogmatic distinctives. The seventeenth century's philosophical and scientific revolutions dramatically raised the status of autonomous reason and empirical observation, and for the first time theologians of every confession faced formidable rationalist and deist attacks on Scripture and dogma. Also key for Lutheran theology was a body of Western European philological, biblical, and historical scholarship, which was frequently tied to an Erasmian humanist stance that valorized a nondogmatic and ethical construal of Christianity.

Lutheran Orthodoxy still reigned in most university theological faculties in Germany and Scandinavia in 1700. Its last major exponent was V. E. Löscher (1673–1749), who polemicized against Calvinism and Catholicism as well as Pietism and rationalism. The latter censured Orthodoxy for its perceived aridity and obscurantism, but many Orthodox writers paid ample attention to the practice of piety and gave increasing scope to natural reason. Though adamant that the fall had damaged human rational faculties, they affirmed in principle the compatibility of reason and biblical revelation and reserved space for a natural theology that demonstrated the existence and providence of God from the order, purposefulness, and beauty of nature. From 1650 onward, the project of "physicotheology" took on independent life, finding a popular audience and adherents outside the church.

By the 1730s Orthodoxy had largely been overtaken by Pietism and Enlightenment theology. Pietism gained official backing in Prussia and an institutional center at the University of Halle. Its clout waned in the 1740s, but it continued to have profound influence on theology and intellectual and artistic life in Lutheran lands. Practically oriented, Pietism grounded true Christianity in the subjective certainty of experience. Taking the individual's salvation and sanctification as the focal point of theology, Pietism blunted the sharp edges of confessionalism. It elevated the Bible over metaphysics and dogmatics, giving impetus to a mass of text-critical and exegetical work, epitomized in Tübingen scholar J. A. Bengel's 1734 edition of the Greek New Testament. Inspired by P. J. Spener's "hope for better times," Pietism's meliorist eschatology fueled large-scale programs of social reform and international missions as well as Enlightenment notions of progress. Pietism's cultivation of inner spirituality could foster separatist tendencies, and it molded both the liberal theology of the Enlightenment and the Romantic reaction against it.

Enlightenment theology was fed by other streams, as well. The rationalism of Christian Wolff (1679–1754), a professor of philosophy at Halle reinstated by the Prussian King Frederick the Great in 1740, governed German philosophy and university curricula until Kant and produced a school of theological Wolffians who drew on the master's "scientific" method to demonstrate the rationality of Christian belief, while reserving a category of revealed "truths above reason." Wolffian confidence in natural reason was taken up by neology, which retained the category of special revelation, and by deism, which rejected it. Another version of early *Aufklärung* (Enlightenment) theology was eclecticism, or "transitional theology," a movement rooted in orthodox dogma that sought to engage new intellectual currents in an unprejudiced manner. J. F. Buddeus and J. L. von Mosheim, among others, developed a "pragmatic" historiography that put dogmatic developments into historical context and promoted irenicism. S. J. Baumgarten (1706–57) united Pietism, Wolffianism, and critical historiography at Halle, where he taught a large corps of future theological enlighteners.

In the 1770s the term "neology" came to designate the mature phase of *Aufklärung* theology. Neology dominated Lutheran theological faculties after midcentury and reached a broad educated public. Anthropocentric and optimistic about human moral potential, neology reframed doctrine so as to promote an active piety. Berlin minister J. J. Spalding's *Reflection on the Determination of Man* (1748), one of the century's most widely read works, offered an argument for Christianity that started with the aesthetic and moral experience of the self-reflective individual. Antideist apologetics motivated in part the neologians' vast historical and biblical scholarship, as did the still more pressing aim of revising or excising unwanted features of the biblical and dogmatic traditions, including original sin, spirit belief, and apocalypticism. J. S. Semler, J. D. Michaelis, J. G. Eichhorn, J. J. Griesbach, and J. P. Gabler made seminal contributions to modern biblical criticism premised on a distinction between the diverse, historically conditioned texts that made up the biblical canon and the eternal Word of God, which they imperfectly conveyed. Neology also sponsored a version of progressive revelation, treating Christianity as a perfectible religion that would eventually dissolve denominational divisions and become a universal religion of humanity. This vision would nourish the secular millenarianism of Kant and nineteenth-century idealist philosophies of history.

Enlightenment theology provoked a reaction from the *Sturm und Drang* and Romantic movements. A formidable attack came from J. G. Hamann (1730–88). His dramatic conversion in a Pietist mode led him to reject exalted ideas of human autonomy and rationalism and to insist on the primacy of faith as a means of immediate, intuitive knowledge of God, who revealed himself through nature, history, and supremely in Jesus Christ. Mystical and antirationalist approaches to faith never disappeared at the popular level. While the Protestant Evangelical Awakening's center of gravity shifted to Great Britain and North America after the 1730s, revivals continued to take place in Lutheran lands, and as late as the 1770s a popular Catholic exorcist, J. J. Gassner, could provoke the *Aufklärung*'s theological establishment.

Published in 1799, Friedrich Schleiermacher's *On Religion: Speeches to Its Cultured Despisers* is often treated as a seminal text of German liberal Protestantism. But in its apologetic cast, anthropocentrism, and prioritizing of experience, feeling, and intuition over creeds and intellectual systems, it can also be read as a culmination of the preceding century's theological developments. While future theologizing would harbor diverse and often deeply critical stances toward the inheritance of the eighteenth century, in manifold ways this transformative period of Western history created the conditions for all modern thinking about religion.

See also Bengel, Johann Albrecht; Bible Interpretation; Enlightenment; Francke, August Hermann; Hamann, Johann Georg; Kant, Immanuel; Lutheran Orthodoxy; Natural Science; Natural Theology; Philosophy; Pietism; Rationalism; Semler, Johann Salamo; Spener, Philipp Jakob

Bibliography

Barth, K. *Protestant Theology in the Nineteenth Century*. German, 1948. ET, 1972. New ed., Eerdmans, 2002; Bayer, O. *A Contemporary in Dissent: Johann Georg Hamann as a Radical Enlightener*. Trans. R. A. Harrisville and M. C. Mattes. Eerdmans, 2012; Beetz, M., and G. Cacciatore, eds. *Hermeneutik im Zeitalter der Aufklärung*. Böhlau, 2000; Beutel, A. *Kirchengeschichte im Zeitalter der Aufklärung*. Vandenhoeck & Ruprecht, 2009; Hirsch, E. *Geschichte der neuern evangelischen Theologie*. Vols. 4–5. 1964. Reprint, Spenner, 2000; Hornig, G. "Lehre und Bekenntnis im Protestantismus." In *Handbuch der Dogmen- und Theologiegeschichte*, ed. C. Andresen and A. M. Ritter, 3:71–146. Vandenhoeck & Ruprecht, 1998; Lindberg, C. *The Pietist Theologians: An Introduction* to Theology in the Seventeenth and Eighteenth Centuries. Blackwell, 2005; Midelfort, H. C. E. *Exorcism and Enlightenment: Johann Joseph Gassner and the Demons of Eighteenth-Century Germany.* Yale University Press, 2005; Reventlow, H. G. *History of Biblical Interpretation.* Vol. 4, *From the Enlightenment to the Twentieth Century.* Trans. L. G. Perdue. Society of Biblical Literature, 2010; Taylor, C. *A Secular Age.* Harvard University Press, 2007; Ward, W. R. *Early Evangelicalism: A Global Intellectual History.* Cambridge University Press, 2006.

ERIC CARLSSON

Electors of Saxony

The electors of Saxony, including John Frederick and Augustus, were high-ranking German princes. In 1423 members of the Wettin dynasty, were invested with the Saxon electoral dignity and the title of Arch-Marshal of the Holy Roman Empire as lords of the duchy of Saxe-Wittenberg. In 1485 the Wettin dominions (concentrated in Saxony, Thuringia, Osterland, Vogtland, and the Franconian area surrounding Coburg) were divided. Ernest (1441–86), founder of the Ernestine line (as opposed to his brother Albert's Albertine line), was allotted Wittenberg and the electoral dignity. In consultation with their advisers and the estates of the land, these electors of Saxony promoted the Lutheran Reformation, pioneered alongside Landgrave Philip of Hesse (1504–67) the establishment of the Evangelical confession at a territorial level, and championed the Protestant cause in the German Empire.

Elector Frederick III ("the Wise," 1463–1525) pursued an ambivalent political course at the outbreak of the Wittenberg Reformation, neither actively promoting it nor preventing traditional church structures from collapsing. He was, however, vital in providing conditions that allowed the new movement to unfold and rapidly spread. The intellectual climate at the University of Wittenberg, founded by Frederick in 1502, offered favorable grounds for humanistic ideals and reform-oriented theology. In addition, the elector granted Luther the freedom to campaign against the indulgence trade, which was financing the rise to power of his political rival Cardinal Elector Albrecht of

Brandenburg (1490–1545; brother of Margrave Joachim II, Elector of Brandenburg), and to print controversial writings under lenient censorship provisions. What is more important, Frederick protected Luther after the Roman papacy had declared him a heretic and after he was subsequently outlawed by the emperor via the Edict of Worms (1521).

Unlike his brother, Elector John ("the Steadfast" or "Constant," 1468–1532) openly embraced the Wittenberg Reformation. Under his rule Lutheran teaching and liturgy were introduced through administrative acts, and the foundations were laid for a centrally controlled territorial church. Instrumental in this process was the institution of visitations conducted to examine the clergy and the local conditions of churches and schools, assuming the economic administration of monasteries, restructuring church finances, and establishing regional ecclesiastical supervisors called superintendents. The Speyer Recess (1526) provided the legal justification for these changes. In a further step, John, at the behest of Emperor Charles V, submitted a comprehensive confession, drafted in large part by Philip Melanchthon, to the emperor at the Diet of Augsburg in 1530. This Augsburg Confession, also subscribed by other princes and cities at Augsburg, quickly became the generally accepted confession of faith in Protestant areas. Together with Philip of Hesse, John founded the Smalcaldic League in 1531, a defensive military alliance to secure Protestant interests in the empire.

Succeeding his father, Elector John Frederick I ("the Magnanimous," 1503–54) continued to institutionalize branches of episcopal responsibility into the territorial church by establishing the rite of ordination in 1535 and a consistory in 1539 as church and marital court. The emperor imposed the imperial ban on the elector and Landgrave Philip after they had attacked the Duke of Brunswick in 1542. In the ensuing war the Smalcaldic League was defeated in 1547, and John Frederick was arrested and for a time placed under a death sentence. He lost Wittenberg, with its electoral dignity and large portions of his territory, to Duke Moritz of Saxony, member of the Albertine line of the Wettins.

The new elector Moritz (1521–53) proceeded with the Lutheran reforms in Albertine Saxony that his father, Duke Henry (1473–1541), had initiated during his short rule from 1539 to 1541. Moritz founded elite schools in Meissen and Pforta in 1543 and continued reform of the University of Leipzig. Although allied with the emperor in the Smalcald War, Moritz opposed the emperor's religious settlement called the Augsburg Interim (1548) and countered his extensive gain of power over the princes by allying himself to the king of France. The successful revolt of the princes headed by Moritz ended in the Treaty of Passau (1552), nullifying the Interim and forming the basis for the Peace of Augsburg (1555), which legally secured adherents to the Augsburg Confession a place in the empire. Moritz died from wounds incurred in battle against a rogue prince in 1553.

His brother, Elector Augustus (1526–86), played a dominant role in the efforts to establish a consensus in the wake of the inner-Protestant controversies following the death of Luther (1546). Negotiations at the Colloquy of Worms (1557), the articles of the Frankfurt Recess (1559), and the assembly in Naumburg (1561) to re-sign the Augsburg Confession all failed to unify a larger majority of the Protestant princes. After a theological crisis over the Lord's Supper within Saxony in 1574 Augustus increasingly promoted the diplomatic efforts of Jakob Andreae (1528–90) and others that culminated in the Formula of Concord (1577) and the Book of Concord (1580), a compilation of confessional documents still authoritative today among many Lutherans worldwide. The ordinance that he issued in 1580 regulated church and school life in Saxony in part into the nineteenth century.

See also Augsburg Interim; Charles V; Georg, Duke of Saxony; Peace of Augsburg; Saxonies; Smalcald War

Bibliography

Brandenburg, E., J. Herrmann, and G. Wartenberg, eds. *Politische Korrespondenz des Herzogs und Kurfürsten Moritz von Sachsen.* 6 vols. Teubner / Akademie-Verlag, 1900–2006; Herrmann, R. *Thüringische Kirchengeschichte.* Vol. 2. Böhlau, 1947; Junghans, H., ed. *Das Jahrhundert der Reformation in Sachsen.* 2nd ed. Evangelische Verlagsanstalt, 2005; Leppin, V., G. Schmidt, and S. Wefers, eds. *Johann Friedrich I.—der lutherische Kurfürst.* Gütersloher Verlagshaus, 2006; Ludolphy, I. *Friedrich der Weise: Kurfürst von Sachsen, 1463–1525.* Vandenhoeck & Ruprecht, 1984; Wellman, S. *Frederick the Wise.* Concordia, 2015.

DANIEL GEHRT

Elert, Werner

Born in Saxony, Werner Elert (1885–1954), Lutheran professor of theology at Erlangen, was raised in Schleswig-Holstein, where he was active in the Evangelical-Lutheran Church in Prussia, the "old Lutheran" church that had been formed by confessional Lutherans who had resisted the 1830 decree of Friedrich Wilhelm III to unite the Reformed and Lutheran churches in Prussia. Elert studied at Breslau, Erlangen, and Leipzig. His philosophical dissertation (Erlangen, 1910) examined Rudolf Rocholl's speculative philosophy of history in relation to the thought of Böhme, Schelling, and Hegel. His theological dissertation (Erlangen, 1911) analyzed the tension between the Christian's personal certainty of existence and the fulfillment of humanity in the person of Jesus Christ, who is believed by Christians to be "the center" of history. This certainty, given in the experience of baptismal rebirth and faith, is the basic presupposition of Christian theology. From within this perspective the theological task is to explicate the Christian worldview and to place Christian doctrine into a critical position over against contemporary non-Christian and anti-Christian worldviews.

After serving as a parish pastor (1912–19) and military chaplain during World War I, he became the director of the Lutheran seminary in Breslau (1919–23). Then he taught church history, the history of dogma, systematic theology, and ethics at Erlangen. Alongside his colleague Paul Althaus, he became one of the world's leading proponents of a lively, critical Lutheran confessional theology. His classic two-volume study, *The Structure of*

Lutheranism, treats its subject as a vital religious and cultural totality and not as a static corpus of pure doctrine. The heartbeat of Lutheran vitality resides in what he called the *evangelischer Ansatz*, the Evangelical "point of departure" that grounds all of Christian doctrine and life in the gospel. This "grounding in the gospel," the Evangelical "constant," is, however, distinct from the "structure" (Greek: *morphē*) of Lutheranism, that is, its various historical developments and cultural instances. According to Elert, Luther's original Evangelical *Ansatz*, the proper distinction between the law and the gospel, was genuinely developed in the early confessional writings of the sixteenth century, partly sharpened and partly distorted by Melanchthon, partly renewed and partly distorted in the Formula of Concord, and significantly distorted in Lutheran Orthodoxy, Pietism, and rationalism.

In his *Dogmatics* (1940) Elert attempted to establish, for the church of his day, "the mandatory content of the church's preaching," that which must be present in it for it to be *Christian*. The organizing principle of the entire work is the sharp contrast between the law and the gospel, which entails the ultimate triumph of the gospel—through faith alone in Christ alone—over against the accusing judgment of the law. This same organizing principle also informs Elert's presentation of Christian ethics (1949). Here the question is not, What should I do? but rather, What is the "ethos" or quality of the individual Christian under the law and under the gospel?

Along with Althaus, Elert opposed what he perceived to be the theological errors in the Barmen Declaration, such as its apparent contradictions regarding the two kingdoms and its confusions regarding the law and the gospel, errors that he attributed to the influence of Karl Barth, Elert's central theological opponent. Although Elert was never a member of the Nazi Party—he was a constitutional monarchist, at least until 1945—he publicly supported the regime of Hitler through the middle 1930s, especially in the Ansbach Mem-orandum and against those whom he thought were calling for political disobedience. Because of these actions, he was sharply criticized after the war, despite his own earlier, public criticism of those Germans who had tried to harmonize Nazism and Christianity.

See also Althaus, Paul; Ansbach Memorandum (Ansbacher Ratschlag); Barmen Confession; Barth, Karl; Erlangen; German Christians (Deutsche Christen); Luther Interpretation and Reception

Bibliography

Becker, M. "Werner Elert (1885–1954)." In *Twentieth-Century Lutheran Theologians*, ed. M. Mattes, 93–135. Vandenhoeck & Ruprecht, 2013; Beyschlag, K. *Die Erlanger Theologie*. Martin-Luther-Verlag, 1993; Elert, W. *Law and Gospel*. Fortress, 1972; Elert, W. *The Structure of Lutheranism*. Concordia, 1962; Eyjolfsson, S. A. *Rechtfertigung und Schöpfung in der Theologie Werner Elerts*. Lutherisches Verlagshaus, 1994; Slenczka, N. *Selbstkonstitution und Gotteserfahrung: Werner Elerts Deutung der neuzeitlichen Subjektivität*. Vandenhoeck & Ruprecht,1999; Sparn, W. "Werner Elert." In *Profile des Luthertums*, ed. W. Hauschild, 159–83. Güterslohverlagshaus, 1998.

MATTHEW L. BECKER

Elizabeth I

As Queen of England, Elizabeth I (1533–1603) restored Protestantism after Mary I had returned the realm to the Catholic fold, and she oversaw the settlement of religion defining the Church of England's middle way between Calvinism and Roman Catholicism. Born at Greenwich to Henry VIII's second wife, Anne Boleyn, Elizabeth's education at court included the study of Melanchthon's *Loci communes*. During the reign of her half sister Mary, Elizabeth conformed to reestablished Catholicism, but her suspected complicity in a failed uprising of 1554 prompted her temporary imprisonment. As Mary's death approached in 1558, however, she acknowledged Elizabeth as her rightful heir. She was crowned on January 5, 1559, and the first parliament of her reign commenced ten days later. Here was laid the foundation of Elizabethan religious policy: Rome was again sidelined, the Act of Supremacy was revived (though with Elizabeth named supreme "governor" rather than, as her father, "head" of the church), and the Act of Uniformity imposed the Book of Common Prayer (slightly revising the 1552 edition) on English parishes. (The Thirty-Nine Articles, a revision of the Edwardian Forty-Two Articles, would be promulgated in 1571.)

Those who feared such policy would satisfy neither her Catholic subjects nor many of the realm's Protestants were soon proved correct. The "vestiarian crisis" of the mid-1560s flared up when those coming at this time to be called Puritans objected to the requirement of what they deemed "popish" vestments. Late in the same decade a rebellion by northern nobles also gave the queen reason to doubt the loyalty of her Catholic subjects, as did the 1570 papal bull of excommunication, which enjoined English Catholics to withdraw obedience from her. Such controversies strained Elizabeth's toleration of dissenting opinion, famously summarized in Francis Bacon's remark that she preferred not to make windows into men's souls. Yet she continued to restrain what she deemed extreme parliamentary proposals, vetoing, for example, a bill that would have required annual reception of the sacrament, and amending another that would have made conversion to Catholicism a treasonable offense.

If the nature of the church defined by Elizabethan policy remained somewhat ambiguous, so also did the queen's personal faith. Though she would, in 1538, leave Mass to avoid witnessing the elevation of the host, she seems to have maintained a belief in Christ's bodily presence in the sacrament. She provided support to beleaguered Protestants in France and the Netherlands yet dismayed many English Protestants by retaining a crucifix in her private chapel and restoring many saints' days to the liturgical calendar. The suggestion that Elizabeth was personally sympathetic to Lutheranism is partially predicated on such evidence, but also, for example, on that of her famously cagey marriage negotiations. Not only did she entertain overtures by the Lutheran Eric XIV of Sweden, but in negotiations concerning a match with the Catholic Archduke Charles of Austria, she took pains to emphasize that her religious settlement was consistent with the Augsburg Confession. Though never adopting a Lutheran confession, by her death on March 24, 1603, Elizabeth's England had become firmly Protestant.

See also England; Henry VIII

Bibliography

Collinson, P. *The Religion of Protestants: The Church in English Society, 1559–1625.* Clarendon, 1982; Doran, S. *Elizabeth I and Religion, 1558–1603.* Routledge, 1994; Haigh, C., ed. *The Reign of Elizabeth I.* Macmillan, 1984; Haugaard, W. *Elizabeth and the English Reformation.* Cambridge, 1968; McGrath, P. *Papists and Puritans under Elizabeth I.* Walker, 1967.

KOREY D. MAAS

El Salvador

German and Scandinavian Lutherans did not take advantage of religious freedom in this predominantly Roman Catholic country until 1956, when Swedish pastor Ake Kastlund established a congregation in San Salvador. Lutheran influence spread through La Hora Luterana (the Spanish-language "Lutheran Hour" radio broadcast). In 1950 Aldrich Forbes became interested in Lutheranism after listening to a radio broadcast, was introduced by Robert Gussick to mission work of the Lutheran Church–Missouri Synod, and instructed in Luther's catechisms. Forbes encouraged a group of dissenting Assembly of God members in Pasaquina to become Lutheran. Ciro Mejia, a pastor of Central American Mission, invited the Lutheran Church to take over its work in May 1952.

In 1953 Mejia was installed as a Lutheran lay pastor. He built a self-reliant congregation, appointed congregational leaders and evangelists, and with LCMS vicars expanded the work to San Miguel. Mejia completed his theological education under Robert Hoeferkamp at the Bible Seminary in Guatemala while still at Pasaquina, was examined by LCMS professors, and on November 23, 1961, was ordained as the first Lutheran pastor of Central America.

From 1960 onward the LWF sought cooperation with the LCMS in cultivating Christian social responsibility as second-generation pastors practiced ecumenical openness by joining Diaconia (a nongovernmental service organization), working together with Roman Catholics, Episcopalians, and other Protestants to alleviate suffering and address displacement and urban squalor due to years of civil war.

Differences between national pastors and missionaries were obvious, especially with regard to social engagement. In the early 1970s LCMS withdrawal affected the Council of Central America and Panama (CONCAP), resulting in a decline of seminary candidates. In 1981 Seminario Luterano Augsburgo (SEMLA)—which began in 1964 as Centro de Estudios Teológicos Augsburgo (CETA), where most Salvadoran pastors had been educated—closed its doors. In September 1970 Sinodo de las Iglesias de Confesion y Ritos Luteranos was established, and Mauro Recinos became president of Iglesia Luterana Salvadorena (ILS).

In 1983 Dr. Angel Ibarra was arrested while conducting medical clinics and subsequently fled the country. Pastor David Ernesto Fernandez Espino was not as fortunate. He was arrested, tortured, and murdered. A defining moment for the ILS occurred in the 1980s when the government determined that the ILS was supportive of Frente Farabundo Martí para la Liberación Nacional (FMLN). Medardo Gomez, a Lutheran heir to the mantle of the murdered Roman Catholic bishop Óscar Romero, insisted that the spiritual and physical needs of humanity could not be separated and maintained close ties to FMLN on humanitarian grounds. This led the German-speaking Evangelical Lutheran Church and ILS to part ways. Yet ILS grew to national and international prominence; in 1986 Gomez became its bishop.

Shaped by Lutheran mission support and strategy, ILS national pastors who were trained in the region and lay leaders practice ecumenism with the vision of Bishop Gomez to build a more just and life-giving society. ILS takes some small credit for peace accords signed on January 16, 1992, between the government and FMLN. It publishes *El Heraldo Lutherano*, covering events in the church and country, and is in partnership with the ELCA and other Lutheran churches as well as the LWF.

See also Honduras

Bibliography

Gomez, M. E. *Fire against Fire: Christian Ministry Face-to-Face with Persecution.* Augsburg, 1990; Jahnel, C. *The Lutheran Church in El Salvador.* Servicio Educativo Cristiano-LBCM, 2009; http://www.lcms.org/elsalvador; http://www.lutherancentral.com; Penvak, L. M., and W. J. Petry. *Religion in Latin America: A Documentary History.* Orbis, 2006.

ORIN W. CUMMINGS

Emser, Jerome

The German humanist and professor of theology Jerome Emser (1477–1527) was a Catholic controversialist and early opponent of Luther. Born of a prominent family near Ulm, Emser pursued studies in Tübingen in 1493, there acquiring knowledge of Latin and Greek. In 1497 Emser studied law and theology at the University of Basel before departing in 1502, receiving holy orders, and eventually matriculating at Erfurt in 1504. At Erfurt, Luther may even have attended Emser's lectures. Later that year Emser moved to Leipzig, where he continued teaching theology and in 1505 was employed as secretary and chaplain to Duke George of Saxony, a post he retained until his death. In the early stages of the indulgence controversy, Emser viewed Luther rather favorably and shared the latter's desire for ecclesial reform. In 1519, however, Emser accompanied John Eck to the Leipzig Disputation and there suffered insult from Luther, both personally and theologically. Yet in Emser's account of the Leipzig Disputation, he staunchly opposes Luther only on the question of the divine institution of the papacy, interpreting him generously on a number of other points. This, however, did not affect Luther's sentiments; he burned Emser's works along with those of Eck and the papal bull in December 1520.

The following year the polemic increased as Emser and Luther engaged in a heated and quite extensive pamphlet war (cf. LW 39:105–238). Luther's *Answer to the Hyper-Christian Book* (LW 39:137–224) includes an extensive examinations of Lutheran hermeneutics. At one point Luther wrote to "the Goat at Leipzig" (Emser's crest was a goat's head), to which Emser responded with an address to "the Bull at Wittenberg." In addition to criticizing Luther's opinion of papal primacy, Emser took special issue with Luther's suggestion that religious vows could be broken for the sake of conscience (*Vorlegung*, 1521), and further criticized Luther's translation of the New Testament. In 1527 Emser produced his own German New Testament, in which the translation (ironically) relied heavily on Luther's but the introductions and marginal notes did not. Emser died in Dresden that same year. To the end he remained an advocate of ecclesial reform, though he always bemoaned what he deemed the impatience of Luther to see it carried out.

See also Cajetan (Thomaso de Vio); Eck, John; Luther's Roman Catholic Opponents

Bibliography

Bagchi, D. V. N. *Luther's Earliest Opponents: Catholic Controversialists, 1518–1525*. Fortress, 1991; Emser, H. *Schriften zur Verteidigung der Messe*. Ed. T. Freudenberger. CCath 28. Aschendorff, 1959; Smolinsky, H. *Augustin von Alveldt und Hieronymus Emser: Eine Untersuchung zur Kontroverstheologie der frühen Reformationszeit im Herzogtum Sachsen*. Reformationsgeschichtliche Studien und Texte 122. Aschendorff, 1983; Strand, K. A. *Reformation Bibles in the Crossfire: The Story of Jerome Emser, His Anti-Lutheran Critique and His Catholic Bible Version*. Ann Arbor Publishers, 1961.

ERIC J. DEMEUSE

England

Through the early decades of the sixteenth century, England appeared an unlikely candidate for the reception of Evangelical reform, especially in its Lutheran mode. In contrast to previous generations of scholarship, recent studies emphasize that English parishioners remained overwhelmingly content with the ecclesiastical status quo. The native Lollard heresy had been successfully suppressed, if not entirely eradicated. The realm was allied by marriage to intensely Catholic Spain, and the king remained supportive of the papacy. Moreover, as an island nation with its few printing presses almost wholly concentrated in London, England was uniquely situated effectively to police the production or importation of potentially disruptive literature.

Especially by means of London's Hanseatic merchants, however, Luther's writings quickly entered the country, where they were often received with some interest. Already early in 1519 they were being exported in bulk from Switzerland, and in 1520 they appeared in an Oxford bookseller's inventory. During this same period Erasmus would inform Luther that important Englishmen held his writings in esteem. Royal and ecclesiastical authorities, however, were decidedly not among these. In 1521 alone, fears were expressed about Oxford being infected with Lutheranism; Cardinal Thomas Wolsey convened the Cambridge and Oxford theological faculties to request that they write against the Lutheran heresy; Luther's works were burned in London; and King Henry VIII himself responded to Luther's *Babylonian Captivity of the Church* with the *Assertio Septem Sacramentorum* (Assertion of the seven sacraments). Given such clear indications that a "popular" reformation would not be countenanced, a number of native Evangelicals began in the 1520s to exit the realm, matriculating with some regularity at Wittenberg.

The dissemination of Luther's ideas did not cease in England, especially in London and the university cities. The first public declaration of Reformation sympathies might be credited to the Augustinian friar Robert Barnes, whose Cambridge sermon of 1525 was cribbed in part from one of Luther's own published sermons. Through the 1520s similar unattributed borrowing is evident in printed works intended for English consumption. John Frith's 1529 *Revelation of Antichrist*, for example, combined select translations of Luther and Melanchthon, while William Tyndale reproduced Luther in English in his own treatises and, most famously, in his New Testament prefaces.

While remaining hostile to Luther himself, at the turn of the decade King Henry did make overtures to the Wittenberg faculty as he sought theological justification to annul his marriage to Catherine of Aragon. Wittenberg consistently refused to sanction the annulment, but when the king broke with Rome to secure it, he recognized the potential advantage of alliances with Continental Protestants. Throughout the second half of the 1530s a political and theological alliance with the Lutheran Smalcaldic League seemed a real possibility. Not only did the Crown's repudiation of Catholicism appear obvious with the 1534 rejection of the papacy and subsequent dissolution of the monasteries (1536–40), but a growing sympathy for the Lutheran confession also appeared equally evident. Regular, if never conclusive, negotiations with representatives of the Smalcaldic League were undertaken through the decade's end; in 1535 Henry handsomely rewarded Philip Melanchthon for having dedicated his 1535 *Loci communes* to him; his chief minister and vicegerent in spirituals Thomas Cromwell commissioned English translations of the Augsburg Confession and its Apology; and archbishop of Canterbury Thomas Cranmer, since 1532 secretly married to the niece of Nuremberg reformer Andreas Osiander, brought into English the Lutheran catechism of Justus Jonas's Latin version of Osiander's work.

Despite appearances, however, Henry had consistently made clear that he did not intend a wholesale adoption of Lutheranism. How conservative he remained theologically was finally made evident when parliament was induced in 1539 to pass the Act of Six Articles, enshrining in law the traditional teachings on transubstantiation, clerical celibacy, and more. The Six Articles (nicknamed by Protestants "a whip with six cords") effectively precluded any further Anglo-Lutheran rapprochement under Henry. Even more dramatically signaling the

end of any Crown support for a settlement of religion favorable to Lutheranism were the executions of Cromwell and Barnes in July of the following year. Cromwell, primary architect of the separation from Rome and the Anglo-Smalcaldic dialogues, was beheaded on charges of working contrary to the king's own ecclesiastical interests. Barnes, who had regularly participated in the Smalcaldic dialogues, was burned in the aftermath of a protracted public dispute in defense of justification by faith alone, a doctrine consistently rejected by the king. The conservative reaction signaled by the events of 1539 and 1540 continued in the new decade. In 1543 restrictions on vernacular Scripture reading, which had been lifted in the previous decade, were again imposed on women and laborers. The same year the doctrinally Evangelical "Bishops' Book" (The Institution of the Christian Man) of 1537 was supplanted by the more traditionalist "King's Book."

Despite such public policy, however, the education of Prince Edward, heir to the throne, remained entrusted to Evangelical tutors. Further, upon Henry's death in 1547, Edward, still a minor, came under the guardianship of Evangelical councilors Edward Seymour and John Dudley. Accordingly, with the accession of Edward VI, later Henrician statutes were rescinded and more vigorous expressions of Protestantism were allowed, even encouraged. One source of such encouragement was Cranmer, whose earlier Lutheran sympathies became increasingly Reformed, especially with respect to the Eucharist. As archbishop he invited like-minded Continental exiles such as Martin Bucer and Peter Martyr Vermigli to settle in England. At the same time, many of the natives who had fled the realm in Henry's last years returned, often with the theology of former host cities in Switzerland. Thus, while the Edwardian liturgies of the Book of Common Prayer (1549 and 1552) and the doctrinal formula of the Forty-Two Articles (1553) still evidence a debt to Lutheran documents, they are no less revealing of more recent Reformed influence, again, most obviously with respect to the Eucharist.

Even the little engagement with Continental Lutherans under Edward, such as Cranmer's attempts to woo Melanchthon to Cambridge, came to an abrupt end with the king's death in 1553. The accession of Catholic Mary I, Henry's eldest daughter by Catherine of Aragon, brought with it not only the undoing of the more explicitly Evangelical Edwardian policies but also a restoration of the papal relations severed by her father. The subsequent martyrdoms of first-generation English reformers who had been onetime Lutheran sympathizers, such as Cranmer and Hugh Latimer, further broadened the gulf between English and German Protestants. Similarly, as they had in the last years of Henry's reign, the Evangelicals able to escape into exile most often found refuge in cities adhering to the Reformed faith, including increasingly prominent Geneva. The result, again, was that when Mary's short reign ended with her death in 1558, the exiles returning under Elizabeth I further strengthened the Reformed character that English Protestantism had begun to assume, especially under Edward.

Like her father, Henry, however, Elizabeth was determined not to let a popular reformation simply take its course. Thus, while working with parliament to reverse Marian religious policy, she at the same time acted to restrain the radical forms of Puritanism that had begun to take hold during her reign. The "middle way" pursued by Elizabeth combined broadly Reformed doctrine with the maintenance of an episcopal polity and much traditional piety, including mandated clerical vestments and the restoration of many feast days abolished under Edward. Coming to exemplify Elizabethan policy was the again-imposed Book of Common Prayer (slightly revised from its 1552 iteration), as well as the revived and revised Edwardian doctrinal formula, now pared down as the Thirty-Nine Articles.

There is, though, good reason to believe that the queen herself, who had studied Melanch-thon's *Loci communes* as a youth, leaned more toward Lutheranism than her public policy reveals. Upon her accession, the Germans were heartened by rumors that Elizabeth preferred the Augsburg Confession over all other formulas—rumors that the queen would verbally confirm on more than one occasion. Even though never officially adopting the Augsburg Confession, she continued to insist that the English ecclesiastical settlement was consistent with it. At least one of her bishops, Richard Cheyney of Gloucester, also continued publicly to maintain an explicitly Lutheran confession of the Eucharist.

By the second half of the sixteenth century, however, Cheyney had become an anomaly. England's "Lutheran moment" had long passed, and Elizabeth was clear-sighted enough to recognize as much. Though insisting on outward conformity to the Prayer Book and religious injunctions, the queen did remain relatively tolerant of privately held dissenting beliefs. Throughout her reign, however, these beliefs were primarily those of the growing radical Puritan community and a still-sizeable Catholic minority. Arminianism would also grow in prominence under Elizabeth's successors, the Stuarts James I and Charles I, but Lutheranism would never regain its influence. Foreigners, including the Hanse merchants who had played a role in introducing Luther's writings in the 1520s, were granted some small exception to the 1559 Act of Uniformity, being allowed to worship at the Dutch "Stranger Church," which had been granted a royal charter in 1550. Thus Lutheran merchants of the Steelyard in London, the main trading base of the Hanseatic League, worshiped at the parish church of All Hallows the Great. Finally in June 1669, following the influx of Germans recruited to help rebuild London after the Great Fire of 1666, Charles II issued a warrant authorizing explicitly Lutheran worship for London's foreign Lutherans. Contributions from Hanseatic towns and imperial cities and the kings of Denmark-Norway, Sweden, and other Lutheran princes financed the construction.

Full license for Lutheran worship at Holy Trinity (later renamed Hamburg Lutheran Church) was granted in 1672. Four other London Lutheran congregations were established in the wake of the 1689 Toleration Act. In 1700 the Lutheran Court Chapel of Saint James was endowed by Prince George of Denmark, consort to Queen Anne. With the accession of George I, a German Lutheran prince Elector of Hannover became king and had a Lutheran pastor as chaplain. Thus, when Henry Melchior Mühlenberg was sent from Halle to the American colonies, his immediate supervisor was the court chaplain Friedrich Michael Ziegenhagen (1694–1776). Nevertheless, the Hannoverian kings were supreme governors of the English church and certainly by George IV had become completely Anglicized.

In the nineteenth century, Lutheran seamen's missions were established in port cities, including Liverpool and Grimsby. The Association of German Lutheran Congregations in Great Britain and Ireland formed in 1904. The influx of forty thousand displaced European Lutherans from Poland and the Baltic states after World War II led to the formation of numerous preaching stations and the Lutheran Council of Great Britain (1948). Today there are two small indigenous Lutheran synods. The Evangelical Lutheran Church of England was founded in 1954 from two congregations, initially composed of German immigrants: Kentish Town (established 1896) and Tottenham (1903). The Lutheran Church in Great Britain, a member of the Porvoo Communion since 2014, was founded in 1961.

See also Barnes, Robert; Cranmer, Thomas; Elizabeth I; Henry VIII; Tyndale, William

Bibliography

Bray, G., ed. *Documents of the English Reformation.* James Clarke, 2004; Dickens, A. G. *The English Reformation.* 2nd ed. Pennsylvania State University Press, 1989; Haigh, C. *English Reformations: Religion, Politics, and Society under the Tudors.* Oxford University Press, 1993; Hall, B. "The Early Rise and Gradual Decline of Lutheranism in England." In *Reform and Reformation: England and the Continent, c. 1500–c. 1750,* ed. D. Baker, 103–31. Blackwell, 1979; O'Day, R. *The Debate on the English Reformation.* 2nd ed. Manchester University Press, 2014; Ryrie, A. "The Strange Death of Lutheran England." *Journal of Ecclesiastical History* 53 (2002): 64–92; Scarisbrick, J. J. *The Reformation and the English People.* Blackwell, 1984; Schofield, J. *Philip Melanchthon and the English Reformation.* Ashgate, 2006; Wendebourg, D., ed. *Sister Reformations: The Reformation in Germany and in England.* Mohr Siebeck, 2010; Whiting, M. *Luther in English: The Influence of His Theology of Law and Gospel on Early English Evangelicals (1525–1535).* Wipf & Stock, 2010.

JOEL HUMANN AND KOREY D. MAAS

Enlightenment

While the concept of enlightenment was widespread in eighteenth-century Europe, the notion of a more or less unitary secular Enlightenment that ushered in modern intellectual culture was created only retrospectively and finds little support in recent historiography. A relatively small cadre of freethinkers did pit autonomous reason against all traditional sources of authority, revealed religion included. But the more common Enlightenment project was to co-opt the era's advances in knowledge to reform and revitalize Europe's confessional traditions and to set forth versions of Christianity and Judaism that met the perceived intellectual, moral, and political demands of the age.

In the German-speaking lands, unlike France or England, Lutheranism and Enlightenment had a deeply symbiotic relationship. Clergy and theologians brought *Aufklärung* (Enlightenment) to a broader public, particularly where, as in Brandenburg-Prussia, the movement gained semiofficial sponsorship. Enlighteners tapped new learning to construct an alternative to what they censured as Orthodox dogmatism, Pietist enthusiasm, and naturalistic unbelief. In the process Lutheranism itself was transformed. In 1794 the biblical scholar J. G. Eichhorn looked back on a "new revolution in theology" that had occurred in recent decades. Later scholars have spoken of the emergence of theological liberalism, neo-Protestantism (Ernst Troeltsch), and historical-critical theology, and also of Christianity's humanization in the eighteenth century (Karl Barth). Central to this transformation was a shift in the locus of religious authority, from Scripture, creeds, and dogma (*fides quae creditur*, "faith that is believed") to the faith and religious experience of the believing subject (*fides qua creditur*, "the faith by which it is believed"). Viewed through a wider lens, Enlightenment theology extended the Christian humanist tradition—which since the Renaissance had combined historical and philological scholarship with an individualistic, nonsacramental, and moral construal of religion—into the modern era.

The Lutheran Enlightenment was led by prominent clergy, such as J. F. W. Jerusalem, A. F. W Sack, and J. J. Spalding—and by university theologians and scholars, including J. L. von Mosheim, S. J. Baumgarten, J. A. Ernesti, J. S. Semler, J. D. Michaelis, J. G. Toellner, W. A. Teller, G. S. Steinbart, J. J. Griesbach, and J. P. Gabler. The theological *Aufklärung* may be roughly divided into a more conservative and a more radical phase. Prior to 1750, reformers drew on eclectic historiography and the philosophy of Christian Wolff to rebut deist attacks on Scripture, show the compatibility of reason and revelation, and set out an irenic theology focused on moral transformation. After midcentury, enlighteners increasingly sought to revamp the Lutheran dogmatic tradition itself. Appealing to the spirit of Luther and freedom of conscience, neologians (as the theological *Aufklärer* came to be called in the 1770s) reframed Lutheranism as a practical, this-worldly faith that meshed with the self-reflective experience of the pious and reasonable believer.

The demand for a practical and ethically oriented religion led neologians to revise Lutheran dogma. They rejected Augustinian doctrines of original sin and bondage of the will in favor of an optimistic anthropology emphasizing human dignity, freedom, and moral perfectibility. The question of sin and salvation was turned into a pedagogical issue: how to grow toward ethical perfection in present social life. While not generally abandoning orthodox Christology per se, neologians focused on Jesus Christ's role as an inspired and enlightening teacher of inner, spiritual religion, whose death was the ultimate example of self-giving love.

The theological Enlightenment's reform agenda fueled its groundbreaking historical and biblical scholarship. Initially used mainly for apologetic purposes, after midcentury critical history became a chief tool for reshaping theology. The *Aufklärer* historicized creeds and dogmatic systems as time-bound attempts to express the presumed universal and moral essence of Christianity in the language of the day, and as capable of revision in the light of new knowledge. Reversing the myth of decline from an early golden age of the church, Semler and Teller saw an unfolding revelation of God in history and envisioned a future in which a perfected Christianity would become the universal religion of humankind. Ernesti, Michaelis, Semler, Eichhorn, Griesbach, and Gabler also pursued textual criticism and grammatico-historical exegesis that placed biblical books and their component sources in their diverse original contexts and that separated the time-bound Bible, which reflected ancient worldviews and was open to historical criticism, from the Word of God, which was universal and eternal and had nothing to fear from such criticism.

The Enlightenment marks a sea change in the history of Lutheran theology and of modern religious thought more generally. Liberal Protestant interpreters have depicted the *Aufklärung* as freeing theology from the shackles of dogmatic tradition, while others have accused the enlighteners of relativizing and secularizing Christianity from within. Idealist, Romantic, and atheistic thinkers did indeed draw on Enlightenment theology's anthropocentrism, critique of dogma and metaphysics, and historical progressivism. But it was the liberal Protestant tradition that was the direct heir to the aspiration to ground theology in religious experience and to fundamentally reconstruct theology in the light of modern knowledge. Despite trenchant critiques of the answers given by Enlightenment thinkers, the questions they raised have continued to animate theology and biblical scholarship since the eighteenth century.

See also Bible Interpretation; Eighteenth Century; Hamann, Johann Georg; Kant, Immanuel; Liberalism; Lutheran Orthodoxy; Natural Science; Natural Theology; Philosophy; Pietism; Rationalism; Semler, Johann Salomo; Thomasius, Christian

Bibliography

Aner, K. *Die Theologie der Lessingzeit*. Reprint, Georg Olms, 1964; Beutel, A., et al., eds. *Aufgeklärtes Christentum: Beiträge zur Kirchen- und Theologiegeschichte des 18. Jahrhunderts*. Evangelische Verlagsanstalt, 2010; Beutel, A., et al., eds. *Glaube und Vernunft: Studien zur Kirchen- und Theologiegeschichte des späten 18; Jahrhunderts*. Evangelische Verlagsanstalt, 2014; Hornig, G. "Lehre und Bekenntnis im Protestantismus." In *Handbuch der Dogmen- und Theologiegeschichte*, ed. G. A. Benrath and C. Andresen, 3:71–287. 2nd ed. Vandenhoeck & Ruprecht, 1998; Reventlow, H. G. *History of Biblical Interpretation*. Vol. 4, *From the Enlightenment to the Twentieth Century*. Trans. L. G. Perdue. Society of Biblical Literature, 2010; Sheehan, J. *The Enlightenment Bible: Translation, Scholarship, Culture*. Princeton University Press, 2005; Sorkin, D. *The Religious Enlightenment: Protestants, Jews, and Catholics from London to Vienna*. Princeton University Press, 2008; Sparn, W. *Frömmigkeit, Bildung, Kultur: Theologische Aufsätze*. Vol. 1, *Lutherische Orthodoxie und christliche Aufklärung in der Frühen Neuzeit*. Evangelische Verlagsanstalt, 2012; Sparn, W. "Vernünftiges Christentum: Über die geschichtliche Aufgabe der theologischen Wissenschaften im 18. Jahrhundert in Deutschland." In *Wissenschaften im Zeitalter der Aufklärung*, ed. R. Vierhaus, 18–57. Vandenhoeck & Ruprecht, 1985.

Eric Carlsson

Erasmus of Rotterdam
(Desiderius Erasmus Roterodamus)

The Dutch humanist Erasmus (ca. 1467–1536) was a forerunner of the Reformation and reluctant antagonist of Martin Luther. After many, scantily documented years of study, research, and travel in his native Holland, as well as in Paris, England, and Italy, Erasmus emerged in midlife as the greatest classical scholar of the northern Renaissance and the foremost advocate of reform on the eve of the Reformation. He was the heir of the Italian humanists in his championing of the wisdom of ancient Greece and Rome as the basis for an educational curriculum and a literary culture suited to the needs of the commercial and governing elites of early modern Europe. Yet he was also the heir of the Modern Devotion (*devotio moderna*), a late medieval reform movement that sought, in the Bible and in simple manuals of devotion, a piety suitable to ordinary people who were not ordained and had not entered the religious life as monks or nuns. So for Erasmus, classical scholarship was never an end in itself; it was intended to serve the cause of Christian piety and religious reform. In a series of influential writings (including *The Praise of Folly*, the work by which he is still best known, and *Handbook of the Christian Soldier*), he applied his classical erudition and his mordant wit to lamenting and lampooning the human foibles of worldly popes and bishops, arrogant theologians, greedy monks, ignorant preachers, superstitious laypeople, empty ceremonies, warlike princes, sycophantic courtiers, and more besides.

To remedy these ills of church and society and produce a Christendom worthy of the name, he called on theologians to turn away from their preoccupation with the textbooks and compendiums of the medieval theologians and return to the approach of the ancient church fathers, including Jerome and Augustine; this involved reflecting directly on the text of the Bible itself and clearly expounding its meaning in commentaries and sermons adorned with the fruits of classical scholarship. In his pursuit of this goal of reorientation, Erasmus became the principal inventor and chief practitioner of "biblical humanism," which would set the standard for biblical scholarship until the appearance of the "higher criticism" in the nineteenth century. It consisted of the application to the text of the Bible the techniques of historical-grammatical criticism that the Italian humanists had perfected for establishing the content and meaning of the pagan classics.

With respect to the New Testament, the focus of Erasmus's attention, this involved (1) mastering Greek, still a rare achievement in Western Europe; (2) acquiring a detailed knowledge of the history, culture, and literature of ancient Greece and Rome, the only context in which it was possible to determine the real meaning of what the New Testament authors and the church fathers had said; and (3) finding and collating the surviving manuscripts in order to establish the most accurate text possible. In 1516, having pursued these related goals for a decade and a half, Erasmus published the first of his five editions of the Greek text of the New Testament, which had never before appeared in print (the other four editions followed in 1519, 1522, 1527, and 1535). Accompanying the Greek text were Erasmus's own Latin translation (a revision of the Vulgate) and a separate volume of his extensive *Annotations*. Keyed to the Vulgate, the *Annotations* were an extensive commentary on its adequacy as a translation of the Greek, calling attention to errors in the translation itself as well as to mistaken inferences from it by theologians over the centuries. This was a potentially dangerous undertaking. In his annotation on Matt. 4:17, for example, Erasmus pointed out that where the Vulgate said, "Do penance, for the kingdom of heaven is at hand," the Greek original said, "Repent [change your way of life]," thus depriving the text of any value as a support for the sacrament of penance. (Martin Luther would base the first of his Ninety-Five Theses on this annotation.) Even more controversial was Erasmus's discovery that 1 John 5:7–8, the only direct reference to the Trinity in the Bible, was an interpolation not found in the Greek manuscripts (and thus omitted from Luther's German translation of 1522). This led to his being charged with Arianism. Erasmus in fact believed the church's teaching on both the sacrament of penance and the Trinity, but he did not accept that doctrine should be based on a faulty or misinterpreted version of the divine text: the text and the author's intended meaning came first.

While those of a humanistic turn of mind, including Pope Leo X and the monarchs of Western Europe, were delighted with Erasmus's achievement, conservative theologians were aghast. They knew no Greek, were inclined to attach canonical importance to the received Latin text, were not disposed to treat it as the object of historical-grammatical criticism, and were deeply resentful of the implication that a "mere grammarian" should claim to have the last word on the meaning of a text whose interpretation was their professional responsibility. They were thus quick to find evidence of impiety and heresy in Erasmus's *Annotations*, as well as in his other works, and to denounce humanist scholarship itself as a danger to orthodoxy. When, moreover, Luther appeared on the scene, they were quick to exploit real or imagined similarities of Erasmus's views to those of Luther as the basis for accusing Erasmus of being the source of the Wittenberger's heresies.

Erasmus's initial reaction to Luther was in fact positive, seeing in him someone who was attacking real abuses and issuing a biblically based call for genuine repentance and improvement of life. He used his influence to persuade Luther's prince, Frederick the Wise of Saxony, to protect his professor against "the fury of the theologians" who wanted him sent in chains to Rome, and who, as Erasmus believed, wanted to make Luther the pretext for an all-out assault on "good letters," meaning Erasmian biblical scholarship and all its adherents. By the autumn of 1520, however, the threat of excommunication from Rome and Luther's defiant reaction to it had produced a situation in which humanists increasingly found themselves under pressure to decide between remaining loyal to the papal church or joining Luther in rejecting it. Many humanists of the younger generation had already joined Luther's cause or would soon do so. Indeed, the roster of the first generation of Evangelical reformers consists almost entirely of the names of onetime Erasmians (Philip Melanchthon, Johannes Brenz, Martin Bucer, Johannes Oecolampadius, and many more) who had found the transfer of allegiance from Erasmus to Luther both easy and natural. Erasmus, however, stubbornly refused to join them. The most important reason was his conception of the church.

When called on to define the church, Erasmus invariably used some variation of the formula "the consensus of all the people of Christ." That was a definition that attached no importance to any particular external order (the one that existed was good enough, he thought), but it attached supreme importance to consensus, unity, and harmony. "The essence of our religion is peace and harmony," Erasmus wrote in 1523. To breach that unity, to foment discord, and thus to undermine the basis for the peaceful exercise of piety and moral virtue, was, to Erasmus, far more reprehensible than being wrong about this or that point of doctrine. As he saw it, adherence to the articles of faith summarized in the Apostles' Creed was sufficient to qualify one as an orthodox Christian. This meant that Luther was by definition not a heretic, and that Rome was thus seriously mistaken in hastily treating him as one because of his views on matters of secondary importance. But it also meant that Luther was gravely at fault for sundering Christian unity for no good reason. Difficult and disputed questions should be considered by qualified experts who, over time and under the guidance of the Holy Spirit, would determine what the "consensus of the church" on the questions should be. Correctly foreseeing that confessional conflict would eventually lead to armed conflict, Erasmus (famous for his opposition to war) became the tireless advocate of a negotiated settlement that could only come about by concession and accommodation from both sides. He knew perfectly well that, in an age obsessed with the search for dogmatic clarity on many issues not covered in the Apostles' Creed, this was not going to happen, at least not anytime soon. But in the firm belief that this was what *should* happen because it was what God expected of Christians, he resolutely continued to advocate it. (In modern times, particularly since the 1950s, Erasmus's insistence that Christians should celebrate what unites them rather than dwell

on what divides them has found more adherents than it ever did in his own day.)

Meanwhile, the course of events had brought Erasmus and Luther into direct confrontation. With gratitude Luther acknowledged the providential importance of Erasmus's having opened the door to the proper study of the Bible, and of his having focused attention on many of the abuses that clearly needed remedy. The second edition of Erasmus's New Testament, particularly the *Annotations*, was at Luther's side in 1522 as he translated the New Testament into German. But as early as 1516 Luther had seen evidence in the *Annotations* that Erasmus did not correctly understand Paul on grace and justification. Erasmus could read the words in Greek, but he did not get the message. He should therefore stick to literature and leave theology to those competent to do it. (Philip Melanchthon came to the same conclusion, relegating Erasmus to the status of competent teacher of civic virtue, with little of value to say as a theologian.) Having initially solicited Erasmus's support, Luther quickly decided to leave him in peace with his literary studies and avoid a public encounter with him. It was Erasmus who in 1524 picked a quarrel by yielding to the urgent demand of both his friends and his critics in the Catholic camp that he demonstrate his loyalty to the church by taking a public stand against Luther. Since he could not honestly charge Luther with heresy, he chose instead to invite Luther to consider that the question of free will, though interesting and important, was not one that justified a breach of concord and unity. The result was the carefully titled *Discussion of Free Will* (1524). Luther responded with *On the Servitude of the Will* (1525). Both argued from Scripture, with frequent references to the fathers, but nothing revealed more clearly how fundamentally different their approach to Scripture was. For Erasmus, Scripture was a difficult text, full of puzzles and contradictions. Where Scripture did not speak clearly, he relied on the "consensus of the church" for instruction. In obedience to that consensus,

Erasmus believed many things (e.g., the real presence) for which he could not find clear evidence in Scripture.

Surveying the biblical evidence for and against free will, he found abundant testimony on both sides, and he also found that theologians over the centuries had held different positions on the question without achieving a clear consensus. In such circumstances, with absolute certainty beyond reach, the job of a theologian was to seek the most probable solution, avoiding confident assertions until the church, slowly and under the guidance of the Holy Spirit, arrived at a consensus. He came close to agreeing with Luther that St. Paul attributed nothing to free will, and in later years he came even closer, but for him Paul was only one biblical witness to be considered alongside all the others and the church fathers. So he declared his personal preference for the moderate view that free will, though it counts for little compared to grace, still counts for something, and that God does not withhold his grace from those who do the best they can (the very view against which Luther had rebelled). Erasmus saw in this the advantage of giving Christians a motive for moral effort, whereas denying the freedom of the will could easily remove that motive.

In Luther's view, by contrast, the Bible was perfectly clear on the subject of free will, and the church had no authority to arrive at any "consensus" that contradicted what the Bible said. This was because, unlike Erasmus, Luther had a hermeneutic that provided a reliable key to the meaning of all Scripture, namely, the message of justification by faith alone found in Paul's Epistle to the Romans, where everything is attributed to grace and nothing to free will. He and Melanchthon were in agreement that no one who read Paul with an open mind and the proper application of the method of textual analysis similar to what Erasmus himself advocated could honestly come to any other conclusion. This being so, passages that seemed to teach otherwise had to be reinterpreted to bring them into harmony with Paul's

teaching. The matter was clear, unambiguous, and beyond dispute. Luther's response to Erasmus was, therefore, not to accept his invitation to discuss the pros and cons of a doubtful matter, but rather to mount a relentless assertion of what to him was the central truth of his theology, as well as a rhetorically brutal demolition of Erasmus's arguments to the contrary, dismissing him as an atheist, a skeptic, and no Christian at all. Stung, Erasmus responded with the long-winded, two-part *Hyperaspistes* (1526–27), in which he defended himself with greater theological acumen than has commonly been attributed to him. His defense of Catholic truth pleased and impressed his friends but did nothing to quiet his enemies among Catholic conservatives, who hounded him into his grave with their accusations that he was a clandestine Lutheran. After his death, the church from whose consensus he had so resolutely refused to depart rewarded him by placing all his works without exception on the Index of Forbidden Books (though the harshness of that judgment was soon moderated). As for Luther, he did not deign to reply to the *Hyperaspistes* directly and for the rest of his life treated Erasmus with derision and contempt. Melanchthon, who did respond in his 1528 commentary on Colossians (without naming names), was kinder. He did not alter his poor judgment of Erasmus as a theologian, which had been reinforced by Zwingli's claim that he had taken his denial of the real presence straight from Erasmus. Nonetheless, Melanchthon maintained civil relations with Erasmus, and after Luther's death paid tribute to him as someone who had played a vital role in preparing the ground for Luther's achievements.

Erasmus had more influence on the Lutheran Reformation, as well as the Protestant Reformation in general, than he realized or cared to admit. This was because (as already seen in the case of Zwingli) his views, liberated from the constraint of his loyalty to the consensus of the (papal) church, could be carried to conclusions at variance with his own intentions.

Thus the first generation of reformers, who had learned from Erasmus that Christian princes are responsible for the establishment and maintenance of true religion, could make use of Erasmus's arguments and evidence for the purpose of justifying the establishment of Evangelical churches by friendly rulers. Moreover, in the exercise of their responsibility for organizing their new churches, they manifested a typically Erasmian, humanist concern for the achievement of a Christian social order by means of the discipline of morals, the establishment of schools, measures for poor relief, and the proscription of doctrinal dissensions that threatened public peace and order.

See also Bible Translations; Free Will; Humanism and the Reformation; Luther's Roman Catholic Opponents; Melanchthon, Philip

Bibliography

Estes, J. M. "*Officium principis christiani*: Erasmus and the Origins of the Protestant State Church." *ARG* 83 (1992): 49–72; Hendrix, S. H. "Too Little Too Late: The Erasmus-Luther Debate." In *Collaboration, Conflict, and Continuity in the Reformation: Essays in Honour of James M. Estes on His Eightieth Birthday*, ed. K. Eisenbichler, 355–74. Toronto University Press, 2014; Kittelson, J. M. "Humanism and the Reformation in Germany." *Central European History* 9 (1976): 303–22; Kroeker, G. G. *Erasmus in the Footsteps of Paul.* Toronto University Press, 2011; McConica, J. *Erasmus.* Oxford University Press, 1991; Nauert, C. "Desiderius Erasmus." *Stanford Encyclopedia of Philosophy*, winter 2012 Edition, ed. E. N. Zalta, http://plato.stanford.edu/archives/win2012/entries/erasmus/; Thompson, C. R. Introduction to *Inquisitio de fide: A Colloquy by Desiderius Erasmus Roterodamus, 1524*, 1–51. Yale University Press, 1950; Trinkaus, C. Introduction to the translation of *De libero arbitrio* and *Hyperaspistes I.* In Collected Works of Erasmus, vol. 76, *Controversies*, xi–cvi. University of Toronto Press, 1999.

JAMES M. ESTES

Eritrea

The Evangelical Lutheran Church of Eritrea—alongside the Eritrean Orthodox Tewahedo Church, the Eritrean Catholic Church, and Islam—was one of four religious organizations to be officially recognized by the Eritrean government in 2002. It has eleven thousand members, but many vibrant congregations have been founded by Eritreans abroad.

The church has been called "the oldest autonomous Lutheran Church in Africa and the mother of the large EEC Mekane Yesus" (Bachmann and Bachmann 64). The roots go back to nineteenth-century Swedish missionary efforts: In 1866 three members of the Swedish Evangelical Mission (SEM) arrived in Massawa with the intention to commence work among the Oromo people in Ethiopia. Since this was not possible, they started a congregation in Massawa. Eritrean and Ethiopian Christians soon took over responsibilities, and in 1909 Tewolde-Medhin and Tekle Tesfa-Kristos (ca. 1879–1924) were ordained by the SEM director. In 1926 the church became self-governing. In 1963 it joined the LWF. The ELCE survived and expanded in spite of challenges and hardships such as foreign invasion, civil war, persecution, and periodic famine.

See also Ethiopia

Bibliography

Bachmann, E. T., and M. B. Bachmann. *Lutheran Churches in the World: A Handbook*, 64–67. Lutheran World Federation, 1989.

FRIEDER LUDWIG

Erlangen

Located just north of Nuremberg in the region of Franconia, in the predominantly Catholic state of Bavaria, the small town of Erlangen became a major center for neo-Lutheran confessional theology between the 1830s and 1970s. When the University of Erlangen was formed (1743), its theology faculty was required by law to teach in accord with the Lutheran confessions. For the next ninety years, most Erlangen theologians generally promulgated a mild form of rationalistic, anti-Pietist Lutheranism. That situation changed, however, when the Reformed preacher Johann Christian Krafft (1784–1845) and others brought the German Spiritual Awakening (*Erweckungsbewegung*) to Erlangen and paved the way for antirationalistic theologians to join the faculty (after 1833). The publication of the Erlangen edition of Luther's Works (1826) also contributed to this development.

The most important figure among the "older" Erlangers was Johannes (J. C. K.) von Hoffmann (1810–77; at Erlangen 1838–42, 1845–77). In addition to lecturing on hermeneutics, dogmatics, and ethics, he completed a two-volume study of biblical prophecy, a three-volume summary of biblical theology, and an unfinished eleven-volume commentary on the New Testament. For nearly three decades he edited the *Zeitschrift für Protestantismus und Kirche* (Journal for Protestantism and church), which was the major organ for disseminating Erlanger theology between 1838 and 1876. Along with several colleagues, he also helped to form an important missionary society. For them, theology serves the church and its mission, both at home (e.g., vis-à-vis the newly formed Bavarian Lutheran Church) and abroad.

Hoffmann wanted to avoid both unhistorical biblicism (which he thought undermined the historical character of the Scriptures) and rationalistic historicism (which rejected its theological subject matter). He thus developed an approach to the Scriptures that correlated a systematic analysis of the Christian's personal experience of faith in Christ, grounded in the risen Christ and mediated through the church, with a historical investigation of the ancient biblical texts. The goal of such correlation is to confirm and, if necessary, to correct one's personal faith. In his view, the entire Bible is the record of God's saving actions in history (*Heilsgeschichte*, salvation history), whose center and goal is Christ, the One who has reconciled God and humankind. The individual believer is incorporated into *Heilsgeschichte* by faith, which is produced and nourished through word and sacrament in the church.

Hoffmann's genius, his unique theological emphases—such as his criticism of traditional understandings of divine wrath and vicarious satisfaction, his reformulation of the atonement, and his use of Luther's theology against aspects of Lutheran Orthodoxy—plus his progressive political commitments place him in a category by himself. Nevertheless, features in his theology tie him to other Erlangen theologians at that time and later. Among the most important of these figures were Adolph von Harless (1806–79), J. W. F. Höfling (1802–53), Gottfried Thomasius (1802–75), Heinrich Schmid (1811–85), Franz Delitzsch (1813–90), Theodosius Harnack (1817–89), Karl A. G. Zezschwitz (1825–86), and Franz von Frank (1827–94). These theologians also rejected rationalism and idealism and stressed the importance of human and Christian "experience" in theology (*Erfahrungstheologie*)—thus showing their positive relationship to Schleiermacher—and the "certainty" of individual Christian faith in God, apart from all human reasoning. But unlike Pietists, they emphasized the Lutheran confessions as normative for the articulation of church doctrine, especially with respect to the church and the sacraments, and they rejected various proposals for church unity that were not based on doctrinal agreement. These theologians nonetheless differed from more conservative Lutherans in that they did not try to repeat older formulations of doctrine but developed novel ways of articulating classic Christian teaching in view of their contemporary situation (e.g., in Christology, with respect to the *kenōsis* of Christ). These theologians also then sought to maintain an organic-historical view of the development of the Bible, the church, and the Lutheran confessions. Such a view is especially evident in the systematic theology of von Frank, Hoffmann's principal disciple.

In the early twentieth century, the Erlangen tradition was furthered by several important Bible scholars and church historians who had studied under Hoffmann and von Frank: Theodor Zahn (1838–1933), Albert Hauck (1845–1918), H. F. T. Kolde (1850–1913), and Ludwig Ihmels (1858–1933). During this period (1890–1933) a new journal, *Neue kirchliche Zeitschrift*, furthered Erlanger perspectives on church, ministry, and mission.

The last great flowering of Erlangen theology occurred in the middle third of the twentieth century through the work of Werner Elert

(1885–1954), Paul Althaus (1888–1965), and Otto Procksch (1874–1947). Their respective concerns to articulate classic Lutheran teaching in relation to modern intellectual developments, to understand the realities of human experience apart from Christ and under the law of God, to define faith as an existential encounter with the living Christ through the church's *kerygma*, and to distinguish properly the divine law and gospel for the sake of faith alone in Christ alone—all of these foci connect them to the older Erlangers. Because of Elert's and Althaus's teaching about the so-called orders of creation, however, which they explicitly tied to "race" and "nation"—and their support for Hitler and his program of national, post-Versailles "renewal"—both theologians were criticized after World War II. With the retirements of their students, the Erlangen tradition has largely come to an end in Germany, if not entirely in the United States, where several writings by both theologians continue to be studied in translation.

See also Althaus, Paul; Elert, Werner; Hoffmann, Johannes Christian Konrad von; Repristination Theology

Bibliography

Becker, M. *The Self-Giving God and Salvation History: The Trinitarian Theology of Johannes von Hofmann.* T&T Clark, 2004; Beyschlag, K. *Die Erlanger Theologie.* Erlangen, 1993; Hein, M. *Lutherisches Bekenntnis und Erlanger Theologie im 19. Jahrhundert.* G. Mohn, 1984; Kantzenbach, F. *Die Erlanger Theologie.* Evangelisch Presseverband für Bayern, 1960; Slenczka, N. *Der Glaube und sein Grund: F. H. R. von Frank, seine Auseinandersetzung mit A. Ritschl und die Fortführung seines Programms durch L. Ihmels.* Studien zur Erlanger Theologie I. Vandenhoeck & Ruprecht, 1998.

MATTHEW L. BECKER

Ernst the Pious of Saxe-Gotha, Duke

As the German Lutheran ruler of a small Thuringian territory, Ernst the Pious (1601–75) was known as a religious reformer, astute administrator, and pedagogical innovator. The eighth son of Johann of Saxe-Weimar and Dorothea Maria of Anhalt, Ernst was descended from the Ernestine Saxon electors who supported Martin Luther in the sixteenth century. Ernst fought in the Thirty Years' War with Gustavus Adolphus and sponsored the production of the Weimar Bible (1641), a heavily annotated edition of Luther's German Bible. In 1636 he married Elisabeth Sophie of Saxe-Altenburg, and in 1640 he inherited Saxe-Gotha. His territory was enlarged in 1644, in 1660, and in 1672; after his death his heirs divided Saxe-Gotha into seven territories.

Convinced that the suffering of the war represented God's judgment, Ernst renewed churches and schools through ecclesiastical visitations, catechetical instruction for adults, and mandatory schooling for children. Luther's Small Catechism formed the basis of visitations and schooling. One of the first German political scientists, Veit Ludwig von Seckendorff, is thought to have based much of his *Teutscher Fürsten-Staat* (1656) on Ernst's rule in Gotha. Later Lutheran Pietists, including Philipp Jakob Spener, respected Ernst as an example of a godly ruler who shepherded the church.

See also Gustavus Adolphus; Thirty Years' War

Bibliography

Albrecht-Birkner, V. *Reformation des Lebens: Die Reformen Herzog Ernsts des Frommen von Sachsen-Gotha.* Evangelische Verlagsanstalt, 2001; Venables, M. N. "Pietist Fruits from Orthodox Seeds: The Case of Ernst the Pious of Saxe-Gotha-Altenburg." In *Confessionalism and Pietism: Religious Reform in Early Modern Europe,* ed. F. van Lieburg, 91–109. Von Zabern, 2006.

MARY NOLL VENABLES

Eschatology (Apocalypticism, Chiliasm, Millennialism, Millenarianism)

In the sacristy of St. Mary's in Wittenberg, the church in which Martin Luther usually preached, there is a stone relief depicting Christ issuing from his mouth "a sharp two-edged sword" (Rev. 1:16). As the worn condition of this relief shows, its original place was most likely outside the church reminding passersby of Christ's impending judgment. The late medieval era in which Luther lived was pregnant with the fear of death and of the impending last judgment. Luther's existential question, How to find a gracious God?

spoke to a general longing. How would God spare people from judgment and lead them to life eternal? One year before his death, he still admitted in retrospect: "I was terribly afraid of judgment day" (WA 54:179.32). But Luther discovered that God's righteousness does not mean that human beings must be righteous to be acceptable to God. God attributes unmerited righteousness to them out of unmerited grace. With that realization Luther no longer conceived of the last day as a day of wrath. He was looking forward to that as a day of redemption. "May God have mercy on us and accelerate the day of salvation" (WA BR 10:275.6–7, #3855).

Along with many of his contemporaries, Luther was convinced of the imminent coming of the end. He interpreted events in history and nature—such as the Turkish advance toward Vienna, severe floods, or even a calf born with two heads—as portents of the end. This was compounded by a vivid awareness of the antichrist as an end-time figure. Luther concluded: "The pope is the spirit of the antichrist, and the Turk is the flesh of the antichrist. Both help each other in killing, this one bodily with the sword, the other one through the doctrine and spiritual things" (WA TR 1:135.15–17, #330). While Luther shared with his own age the sense that he was living in the end times, this did not intensify his fears about the last days. To the contrary, he asked: "Why should believers be afraid and not rejoice to the utmost, since they trust Christ, the judge who will come for the sake of their salvation who is their portion?" (WA 10/1/2:110.31–33). Then he lashed out at those "awful preachers of dreams" who attempt to scare people into piety by fire-and-brimstone preaching and demanding that people make satisfaction for a sinful life through good works. According to Luther, nobody could survive if only presented with Christ as a stern judge. Since Christ, however, is the Savior, there can be hope and trust in the future.

Luther shares with tradition the conviction that at death the soul is separated from the body. While the whole church teaches that "it is yet another question whether body and soul are separate items" (WA 39/2:354.10–12), Luther was convinced that an intermediate state after death could not be a neutral state but would already presuppose our acceptance or rejection by God. Yet it would not be a final state, since this would preempt the fulfillment and perfection of the resurrection. Luther often "described" this state as a deep sleep without dreams, without any consciousness and feelings. He confessed that he had tried to observe himself when he fell asleep, but never succeeded. He remembered that he was awake, and then, suddenly, he woke up again. So it is with death: "In a similar way as one does not know how it happens that one falls asleep, and suddenly morning approaches when one awakes, so we will suddenly be resurrected at the last day, not knowing how we have come into death and through death" (WA 17/2:235.17–20). And on another occasion he says: "We shall sleep until he comes and knocks at the tomb and says: 'Dr. Martin, get up!' Then in one moment, I will get up and I will rejoice with him in eternity" (WA 37:151.8–10).

Actually, he confessed, human beings do not know much about this state between death and resurrection. Perhaps those who will be rejected will already suffer, and perhaps those who will be accepted will have a foretaste of the eternal joy they are waiting for and will listen to God's discourses with the angels. He realized that in staying as close as possible to God's self-disclosure as reflected by the biblical witnesses, there was not much that could be said about this state. Untenable for him was the idea of a purgatory since there was too much abuse connected with it (see SA 2.12). According to Luther, purgatory is an idea emerging from the uncertainty of whether God's justification makes us fully acceptable in God's eyes. At the end all will be resurrected and face judgment. Since our Savior is the judge, the faithful will live forever with Christ while the impious will face eternal death with the devil and his angels. Echoing this, CA 17 (*BC* 50) states: "Rejected, therefore, are the Anabaptists who teach that the devils and condemned human beings will not suffer eternal torture and torment." Luther and his followers lived on this earth but longed for the return of Christ and the consummation of the kingdom. But others had less patience. There were Thomas Müntzer (ca. 1490–1525), preaching the apocalyptic utopia during the Peasants' War, and many other enthusiasts, such as Melchior Hoffmann and the utopian experiment at Münster. Müntzer drew on the millennial ideas of Joachim of Fiore (ca. 1135–1200), who advanced a tripartite view of history—the ages of the Father, of the Son, and of the Holy Spirit—and claimed to stand at the threshold of this third and final age. Luther and his followers, however, categorically rejected any utopian ideas, as CA 17 also avows: "Likewise rejected are some Jewish teachings, which have also appeared in the present, that before the resurrection of the dead, saints and righteous people alone will possess a secular kingdom and will annihilate all the ungodly." Philip Melanchthon also assumed that the world's end was near, basing his position in part on a saying from the Kabalah, which he mistakenly attributed to the prophet Elisha.

In the seventeenth century the focus shifted to the salvation of the individual. While Philipp Nicolai's "Wake, Awake" ("Wachet auf"; *ELW* 436) still anticipated the return of Christ, Johann Heermann (1585–1647), for instance, wrote in a hymn: "O Christ, our light, O Radiance true, shine forth on those estranged from you, and bring them to your home again, where their delight shall never end" (*ELW* 675.1). In this instance the faithful want to be with Christ but express little about the coming of Christ and judgment day. This was also the direction taken by Lutheran Orthodoxy, which reduced "Last Things" to a single locus within their theological systems. The hymn writer Paul Gerhardt (1607–76) wrote: "Christ brings me to the portal that

leads to bliss untold" (*ELW* 378, 5). Reaching heaven is central, but forgotten is that this is possible only through judgment. Salvation and completion of the whole creation had by and large become far less important. In Pietism the narrow focus on the individual broadened once again. August Hermann Francke (1663–1727), for instance, reminded students who journeyed "to count each day as the last one" ("Vermahnung an zwölf nach Livland reisende Studenten," 1722). One expected the coming of Christ and engaged in working toward his kingdom. Johann Albrecht Bengel (1687–1752), who exerted considerable influence through his carefully executed New Testament studies, claimed in his preface to the book of Revelation (1740): "The time [of Christ's return] is close at hand" (preface to *Erklärte Offenbarung Johannis*, 2nd ed., 1746, §15). In an apocalyptic timetable he dated the beginning of the millennium at the year 1836.

Johann Christoph Blumhardt (1805–80) continued the biblical realism of Bengel. When he died, he was certain that at least his children would witness the visible commencement of the kingdom. His son Christoph Blumhardt (1842–1919) continued the preaching on the in-breaking of the kingdom of God through the victorious power of Jesus Christ and the waiting for a new outpouring of the Holy Spirit. Blumhardt had socialist leanings and had significant influence on the so-called Swiss Socialists, Leonhard Ragaz (1868–1945) and Hermann Kutter (1863–1931). Even Karl Barth (1886–1968) admitted: "Once I was a religious socialist. I discarded it because I believed I saw that religious socialism failed to take as serious and profound a view of man's misery and of the help for him, as do the Holy Scriptures" (*God in Action*, 125 [Round Table 1963]).

In the context of millennialism we must also mention the idea of the kingdom of God in America, a country that is not called the New World just because it was discovered relatively late. Many groups settled there because they believed in the imminent coming of the kingdom, such as the German George Rapp

(1757–1847), who got into trouble with his fellow Lutherans in Württemberg, Germany, and left for the "New World" together with his followers, the Harmonites, first settling in Harmony, Pennsylvania, then establishing New Harmony, Indiana, and finally founding Economy, Pennsylvania. Their preferred form of life was celibacy, to prepare themselves for the coming millennium. The nineteenth century was not just an age of progress but also one of intense expectations for the kingdom of God, as attested to by origin of such American denominations as the Mormons, the Millerites, the Seventh-Day Adventists, Jehovah's Witnesses, and many other millennial groups. It is with these groups that the terms "millennialism," "millenarianism," "chiliasm," and "apocalypticism" have their origin. In the late nineteenth century, the Missouri Synod and the Iowa Synod debated certain aspects of Christ's return as well.

While the intense expectation of Christ's return was rarely a central topic for Lutheran theology, the doctrine of the last things was never forgotten. This is indicated by the important publication by Paul Althaus (1888–1966), *Die letzten Dinge* (The last things). It was first published in 1922, with the tenth edition in 1970. Initially Althaus advocated an axiological eschatology in which life eternal is experienced as a present value. History and, above all, the ethical norms show the presence of the eternal. Christian hope is directed toward completion of the fullness of life, which is already given in faith. Althaus advocated both an immortality that does not preclude judgment and a twofold outcome of history. In 1933, however, Althaus began focusing on an eschatology in which the personal completion takes place in the resurrection on judgment day in conjunction with the completion of the world. For Althaus, there is no immortality of the soul such that a soul would live on forever, but immortality means that our personal relationship with God cannot be revoked. There is also no intermediate state after death. Althaus asserted: "The question concerning the future of the dead cannot be answered in any other way, but by pointing to death and judgment day. Not one word can be added! Whatever is in between is of evil!" (159). There is no intermediate state and no purgatory. Althaus also rejected a totally present-oriented eschatological theology as advocated by Barth and Bultmann. And he rejected a noneschatological theology as presented by Albert Schweitzer (1875–1965) and Fritz Buri (1907–95). His extensive treatment of the so-called last things had no equal in the German language until Jürgen Moltmann (a Reformed theologian, b. 1926) published in 1995 (ET 1996) *The Coming of God: Christian Eschatology*. Yet Moltmann approached the subject from a very different angle. Wolfhart Pannenberg (1928–2014) observed that, in the later editions of *Die letzten Dinge*, Althaus had already anticipated Moltmann's eschatological concept by basing eschatology on the divine promise (3:594–95).

In his seminal work *Theology of Hope* (1964; ET 1967), Moltmann showed that eschatology is not confined to the so-called last things but also embraces the hoped-for goal, as well as the history moving toward that goal. This has been especially important for liberation theology. With reference to the Old Testament prophets, its proponents claim that the eschatological promises should at least find their partial fulfillment in history, which moves toward the future and creates a continuously advancing dynamic. Wolfhart Pannenberg demonstrated that with Christ's resurrection the envisioned end has already occurred in a forward-reaching and individual way, and thereby attests to the future universal resurrection to new life. According to Pannenberg, humanity can expect, on a universal scale, that which occurred in and with the resurrection of Christ. Without the certainty of the resurrection of Jesus Christ, the Christian church could not have come into existence and then grown as quickly and vigorously as it did. Jesus's death and resurrection form the foundation for Christian trust in the future.

See also Althaus, Paul; Bengel, Johann Albrecht; Pannenberg, Wolfhart

Bibliography

Althaus, P. *Die letzten Dinge: Lehrbuch der Eschatologie.* 7th ed. C. Bertelsmann, 1957; Barth, K. *God in Action: Theological Addresses.* Round Table, 1936; Leroux, N. R. *Martin Luther as Comforter: Writings on Death.* Brill, 2007; Lohse, B. *Martin Luther's Theology: Its Historical and Systematic Development.* Fortress, 1999; Modalsli, O. "Luther über die Letzten Dinge." In *Leben und Werk Martin Luthers von 1526–1547,* ed. H. Junghans, 1:331–45, 2:834–39. Vandenhoeck & Ruprecht, 1983; Moltmann, J. *The Coming of God: Christian Eschatology.* Fortress, 1996; Pannenberg, W. *Systematic Theology.* Vol. 3. Eerdmans, 1998; Schwarz, H. *Eschatology.* Eerdmans, 2000; Stephenson, J. R. *Eschatology.* Luther Academy, 1993; Walls, J. L., ed. *The Oxford Handbook of Eschatology.* Oxford University Press, 2008.

HANS SCHWARZ

Estonia

The first Christian mission among the Estonians, at the end of the twelfth century, forged a popular religion that retained significant elements of pagan Estonian religious perceptions of reality. German, Danish, and Swedish nobles, merchants, and artisans provided civic leadership in the area under successive occupations, particularly by German crusading orders. The Reformation came to Estonians through the German elements, from which pastors were drawn into the nineteenth century, although many of them were able to preach and minister in Estonian.

Initial proclamation of Luther's message in the early 1520s resulted in the association of Tallinn (Reval), the largest Estonian town, first with the second largest, Tartu (Dorpat) and then with Riga (in Latvia) in 1524. Luther's Small Catechism appeared in Estonian in 1535; in 1551 a translation of the pericopes, Psalms, and Gospels in Estonian by Heinrich Susi was published. The first Estonian hymnal appeared in 1565; not until 1686 (in the southern dialect) and 1715 (in the northern dialect) was the New Testament available in Estonian, and the entire Bible in 1739.

The German nobility and bourgeois maintained the Lutheran faith despite pressure from Russian and Polish forces, who invaded and occupied parts of Estonia during the sixteenth and seventeenth centuries. Polish forces tried to introduce the Counter-Reformation with military force in the war years of 1558 to 1629. Lutheranism was strengthened under Swedish control, established in 1561. King Gustavus Adolphus II sent his trusted former court preacher, the bishop of Västeros Johannes Rudbeckius, who introduced reforms and expressed some limited critique of baronial oppression of peasants. Under Bishop Joachim Ihering and Superintendent Herman Samson came continued efforts to enliven church life. The *Handbook for the Home* of Heinrich Stahl in Estonian aided the cultivation of piety among the peasantry.

Gustavus Adolphus also established a university in Tartu (Dorpat), which trained Baltic Germans for ministry throughout the Baltic lands during its irregular history. Russian invasions interrupted the university's functioning after 1656. After the Russian assumption of power in Estonia (after 1710), the university remained closed until 1802. In the nineteenth century Dorpat served as an important theological center within the German ecclesiastical world, with several influential professors on the faculty, including Friedrich Adolf Philippi (1842–51) and Theodosius Harnack (1842–53, 1865–75). In 1860 the faculty began to train Estonians for the pastoral ministry.

Revivals of peasant piety took place with the arrival of the Moravian Brethren in 1729. Nikolaus Ludwig von Zinzendorf visited Estonia in 1736. The Brethren established prayerhouses in most parishes, sometimes working harmoniously with local pastors, sometimes not. Periodic separatist movements arose; through Swedish and other foreign influences in the nineteenth century, Baptist and Methodist churches were established.

Early in the nineteenth century the Russian government began a program of Russification, which gave the Lutheran church status only as a tolerated church. Active pressures, with offers of land and other instruments, were aimed at converting Lutherans to Russian

Orthodoxy, with very limited success. A Sunday school movement strengthened piety from the mid-nineteenth century onward. Beginning in 1841, Estonians served overseas, especially in Africa with the Leipzig Mission and later with Finnish mission societies.

With Estonian independence (1918–20) the German domination of the church diminished. In 1920 Jacob Kukk was elected the first Estonian bishop of the newly organized Estonian Lutheran Church. In the 1920s and 1930s at the University in Tartu, three streams of thought emerged: Pietist, confessional, and liberal. The establishment of Soviet domination in 1940 and then 1944 resulted in massive deportations and executions of Estonian leaders, including ecclesiastical leaders. Under Soviet control severe pressure limited congregational activities, ended university theological training, and significantly reduced the number of members of the Lutheran Church. During Soviet oppression important ecumenical contacts developed between the Lutheran Church and other churches.

With the declaration of the independence of the Estonian second republic in 1991, the church resumed a more active role in Estonian society. The church established its own theological institute in Tallinn, and the university restored its theological faculty as well. Programs supporting mission and evangelism took on an important role in Estonian church life.

See also Latvia; Livonia

Bibliography

Altnurme, R., ed. *Estnische Kirchengeschichte im vorigen Jahrtausend/Estonian Church History in the Past Millennium*. Wittig, 2001; Altnurme, R., ed. *History of Estonian Ecumenism*. Estonian Council of Churches, 2009; Vööbus, A. *The Martyrs of Estonia: The Suffering, Ordeal, and Annihilation of the Churches under the Russian Occupation*. ETSE, 1984.

ROBERT KOLB

Ethiopia

The Ethiopian Evangelical Church Mekane Yesus (EECMY) is the largest Lutheran church in Africa. It counts more than five million

baptized and about 2.5 million communicant members, mainly in western, central, and southern Ethiopia. The EECMY was the first church after the ancient Ethiopian Orthodox Church (EOC) to be recognized by the government. Constituted in 1959, it took the name of its first congregation, Mekane Yesus, "Jesus's dwelling place." Since 1970s the EECMY developed the theme "Serving the Whole Person," which includes proclamation as well as development and social service.

The earliest Protestant missionary initiatives date back to Peter Heyling (1607/1608–52), who traveled to Ethiopia in 1634. Here he became an influential minister, teacher, and doctor at the court of King Fasilides (1632–67) and attempted to bring about reform and renewal in the Ethiopian Orthodox Church. He was expelled from the country and died on his homeward journey, but there are traces of his work in the EECMY.

Ethiopian evangelists and laity have also contributed much to the EECMY. The presence of the former Oromo slave Pauline Fathme (ca. 1830–55) in Germany and Switzerland during the mid-nineteenth century inspired the Protestant Oromo mission. A small biography was published after her death, in which she was depicted as a role model.

In 1877 two converts of the Swedish Evangelical Mission (SEM), which had arrived in Eritrea in 1866, went south and established themselves in Jima, a Muslim town in the province of Kefa. A bit later, Gebre-Ewostateos Ze-Mikael (ca. 1865–1905), an expelled evangelical Orthodox priest, proceeded to Boji in Welega. Onesimos Nesib (ca. 1856–1931), a freed Oromo slave and the SEM's first convert, translated the New Testament (1893), Luther's Small Catechism, many hymns, and other Christian literature into the Oromo language. Greatly assisting him were two Oromo women, Aster Ganno (ca. 1874–1964) and Lidia Dimbo (ca. 1872–1933).

Missionaries of the SEM arrived in Addis Ababa in 1904 and in Neqemte in 1923. The Hermannsburg mission followed in 1928, with centers in Addis Ababa, Wälläga, and Illuba-bor. After Emperor Haile Selassie allowed missions to "open areas" (as distinguished from areas that remained under the control of the Ethiopian Orthodox Church) in 1944, the Norwegian Lutheran Mission, the American Lutheran Mission, the Danish Ethiopian Mission, the Finnish Evangelical Lutheran Mission, and the Norwegian Mission Society came to Ethiopia.

Meetings to establish the EECMY were held in April 1958, and on January 21, 1959, this national church was instituted. In the same year it joined the LWF. In 1960 the EECMY established the Mekane Yesu Seminary in Addis Ababa. In 1973 the EECMY became a member of the All African Conference of Churches and in 1979 of the World Council of Churches.

The 1974 Ethiopian Revolution that led to the overthrow of Emperor Haile Selassie was accompanied by great hopes. Gudina Tumsa, then general secretary of the EECMY, made it clear that he opposed the exploitation of farmers and spoke out in favor of fundamental land reform. However, Tumsa never ceased to proclaim the gospel and therefore was seen as an opponent by the socialist regime. He was murdered in 1979.

Despite these persecutions, the EECMY gained new members and grew, a trend that continued after the end of the radical socialist period in 1991. Since then, there have been splits and reconciliations within the EECMY. In February 2013 the EECMY decided to end its partnership with ELCSA and the Church of Sweden because of their acceptance of same-sex marriages. Since 1974 many Ethiopians migrated to Western countries, and transnational connections play an important role for the EECMY as well as for other Ethiopian churches.

See also Desta, Kentiba Gebru (Gobaw); Fathme, Pauline; Jammo, Daffa; Nesib, Onesimus; Tumsa, Gudina

Bibliography
Arén, G. *Evangelical Pioneers: Origins of the Evangelical Church Mekane Yesus.* Stockholm EFS, 1978; Eide,
O. *Revolution and Religion in Ethiopia: The Growth and Persecution of the Mekane Yesus Church, 1974–85.* J. Currey, 2000; Haustein, J. "Navigating Political Revolutions: Ethiopia's Churches during and after the Mengistu Regime." In *Falling Walls: The Year 1989/90 as a Turning Point in the History of World Christianity*, ed. K. Koschorke, 117–36. Harrassowitz, 2009; Kussa, F. G. *Evangelical Faith Movement in Ethiopia: The Origin and Establishment of the Ethiopian Orthodox Church Mekane Yesu.* Lutheran University Press, 2009; Launhardt, J. *Evangelicals in Addis Ababa (1919–1991): With Special Reference to the Ethiopian Evangelical Church Mekane Yesus.* Lit, 2004.

FRIEDER LUDWIG

Evangelical Lutheran Church in America

The largest Lutheran denomination in North America is the Evangelical Lutheran Church in America (ELCA), with 3.8 million members in 9,900 congregations, grouped in 65 synods around the United States. It is headquartered in Chicago and headed by a presiding bishop. For many American Lutherans in the twentieth century, the dream was of a single, united Lutheran denomination. The Lutheran mergers of the early 1960s were a step in this direction, along with certain developments in the Lutheran Church–Missouri Synod. But controversies within the LCMS, and the withdrawal of some of its moderates to form the Association of Evangelical Lutheran Churches in 1976, dashed these hopes. The AELC, along with the Lutheran Church in America and the American Lutheran Church, began merger negotiations in 1982, with the formation of the Commission for the New Lutheran Church. The CNLC was designed to produce a Lutheran denomination that was "new" in a number of ways, with a revised understanding of the authority of Scripture and the Lutheran confessions and with strict quotas for the representation of women, laypersons, and ethnic minorities in the process. The new denomination, the ELCA, came into existence on January 1, 1988. Over the years, the ELCA has worked to broaden its ecumenical ties, as well as developing interdependence among its local, synodical, and church-wide expressions. Its eight seminaries train pastors and teachers not only for the ELCA but also for partner churches around the world. In its engagement with society, the church, like its predecessors (the ALC, LCA and AELC), has produced important social statements and maintains support for addressing issues of hunger and poverty. Its commitment to liturgy, hymnody, and worship led to the production of *Evangelical Lutheran Worship* (2006).

The ELCA has also faced a number of significant, divisive issues in its first years. At a church-wide level, an initial 1988 budget of $112 million dollars had to be reduced to $70 million dollars by 1995, resulting in significant reductions in staff and programming. The merger of the three former denominations was difficult because they had significantly different systems and organizational cultures, and in order to bring about the merger in 1988, the CNLC had to leave certain difficult issues for the new denomination to address. An early study of theological education left the eight seminaries of the church intact. The nature of the ministry had long been an issue among American Lutherans, and the three former denominations had differing roster categories, especially for lay professional church workers. In 1993 a Task Force for the Study of the Ministry recommended separate ordinations of diaconal ministers and bishops alongside that of pastors (resulting in a threefold order of ministry), which was rejected by the Church-Wide Assembly. Another crisis erupted in 1988, when several gay and lesbian seminarians were "irregularly ordained" as pastors by several congregations in California. The controversy led to the formation of an ELCA Task Force on Sexuality, which was to bring a report to the Church-Wide Assembly in 1995. Its initial report, which suggested the ordination of gay and lesbian persons, was leaked to the press in 1993 and caused controversy, so the process was suspended. The adoption in 1991 of a Declaration on Ecumenism committed the church to work toward "full communion" with other Christian denominations wherever possible. There had been a number of long-running ecumenical dialogues between American Lutherans and others, and this decision pushed the ELCA toward agreements with other churches. Despite some theological reservations, full communion with American Reformed denominations and later with the United Methodist Church was accomplished fairly easily. Full communion with the Episcopal Church was much more controversial, because interchange of clergy ran into the issue (again) of the threefold ministry and ordination into the "historic episcopate," both of which were integral to the Episcopalian denominational structure. The first proposal, the Concordat of Agreement, was not approved by the ELCA in 1997. Opposition to this concordat was led by a group that became known as the Word Alone Network. A revised agreement with the Episcopal Church, known as Called to Common Mission (CCM), still required bishops in the historic episcopate, but it did not specifically call for the threefold ministry, though critics charged that it was still implied in the document. The CCM was approved in 1999 by a slim majority at the Church-Wide Assembly. In 2001 a portion of the opposition formed a separate denomination, the Lutheran Congregations in Mission for Christ, taking about 1,000 congregations and 350,000 members out of the ELCA. The issue of gay and lesbian clergy remained a question within the ELCA, with an advocacy group called Lutherans Concerned/North America continuing to push for change. The failure of the first statement on sexuality did not end discussion, and another study on sexuality was commissioned, leading to further controversy within the denomination. The 2009 Church-Wide Assembly considered the recommendations of this study, which recognized the differences of opinion but proposed that gay and lesbian persons in committed relationships could be rostered. When this action and a social statement on sexuality passed, in 2010 another new Lutheran denomination, the North American Lutheran Church, was founded. With the loss of members to the LCMC and NALC, the ELCA had suffered the largest Lutheran schism since the 1860s, losing over half a million members. In 1988 the ELCA began with 5.2 million members, but by 2013 the denomination had somewhat less than 4 million members. The controversies and subsequent losses also affected the denomination's finances on all levels, having a serious impact on its ability to finance its programs. As the most recent major Lutheran merger, the short history of the ELCA has been one of struggle, and it faces the challenge of refocusing its ministry for the twenty-first century.

See also American Lutheran Church (1960–88); Ecumenical Dialogues; Inner-Lutheran Ecumenism; Lutheran Church in America; Lutheran Denominations in America, Minor; Seminex and the Association of Evangelical Lutheran Churches

Bibliography

Chilstrom, H. *A Journey of Grace: The Formation of a Leader and a Church.* Kirk House, 2011; Granquist, M. A. *Lutherans in America: A New History.* Fortress, 2015; Trexler, E. R. *The Anatomy of a Merger: People, Dynamics, and Decisions That Shaped the ELCA.* Fortress, 1991; Trexler, E. R. *High Expectations: Understanding the ELCA's Early Years, 1988–2002.* Fortress, 2003.

MARK A. GRANQUIST

Evolution

Although Lutherans did not start this nineteenth- and twentieth-century controversy, a number of Lutheran theologians and churches have been engaged in the dispute about evolution and its compatibility with the biblical account of creation. Five positions are discernible, making this battle much more complicated than the image of a simple war between science and religion might connote.

The first position is that of evolutionary biology as science alone—that is, science without any attached ideological or theological commitments. The reigning theory is sometimes labeled "neo-Darwinism," which combines Charles Darwin's original nineteenth-century concept of natural selection with the twentieth-century concept of genetic mutation to explain the development of new species over billions of years of life on Earth. Defenders of quality science education in the public schools most frequently embrace this "science alone" approach.

The second position combines this view with what can be called scientism to formulate a materialist ideology. This materialist ideology includes direct repudiation of any divine influence on the course of evolutionary development. Some more aggressive atheists describe religious traditions as outdated, rigidly dogmatic, and antiscience. Such materialist ideology denies that believers are in tune with transcendent reality.

The third position is creationism, which denies the validity of Darwinian theory and complains that evolutionary thinking leads to moral degradation. Creationists recall the way social Darwinism and eugenics led to such things as laissez-faire capitalism, the involuntary sterilization of prisoners in America, and the pseudoscientific justifications for genocide perpetrated by German Nazis against physically disabled, mentally disabled, homosexuals, Gypsies, and Jews. This "Darwinian influence," creationists argue, is still at work today, subverting society by sponsoring divorce, homosexuality, and anarchy. Creationists strongly support racial equality, but they see support of the rights of homosexuals as a threat to the divine order for creation.

It is important to distinguish two types of creationists, the biblical and the scientific. Biblical creationists appeal directly to the authority of the Bible, especially to the Genesis account of creation, to combat the rising influence of Darwinism in public education and the wider culture. The attack strategy of biblical creationists is made clear by the Answers in Genesis website (https://answersingenesis.org/) and the Creation Museum in northern Kentucky, on the outskirts of Cincinnati.

Scientific creationists, in contrast, are waging a war against science with science. They contend that science supports the creationist description of the natural world. They argue, for example, that the fossil record will contradict standard appeals to natural selection over long periods of time. Those known as young earth creationists, such as the leaders at the Institute for Creation Research near San Diego, California, hold that the earth is less than ten thousand years old and, further, that all species of plants and animals were originally created by God in their present form. No speciation has occurred. Every species we see today was created according to its own "kind" at the beginning, a very recent beginning. They deny macroevolution, that is, they deny that one species has evolved from prior species; although they affirm microevolution, that is, evolutionary change within a species. Key here is that such creationists seek to justify their arguments on scientific grounds, not simply by an appeal to biblical authority.

The fourth position is intelligent design. Advocates of this view sharply attack neo-Darwinian theory for overstating the role of natural selection in species evolution and argue that slow, incremental changes due to genetic mutations are insufficient to explain the emergence of new and more complex biological systems. Many of the life forms that have evolved are irreducibly complex, and this counts as evidence that they have been intelligently designed. Advocates of intelligent design stop short of declaring God to exist and to be the cause of the universe, instead pleading agnosticism regarding the designer. Like the scientific creationists, these combatants attack Darwinian theory with science. Unlike the scientific creationists, they admit that speciation has taken place in evolution, but they add that species evolution is due to an intelligent designer rather than blind natural selection. Despite this difference, it is not unusual to find both creationists and advocates of intelligent design supporting similar theological positions.

The fifth position is theistic evolution, according to which God employs evolutionary processes over deep time to bring about the human race and perhaps even carry the natural world to a redemptive future. Theistic evolution includes a variety of supporters. The minimalist theistic evolutionist respects the science and employs some form of the concept of *concursus* (concurrence) to harmonize the theological understanding of creation with this science. The maximalist theistic evolutionist reconstructs our entire worldview in terms of a long evolutionary process, drenched in temporality, moving progressively toward an eschatological fulfillment in our cosmic future. Most of today's theistic evolutionists find themselves somewhere between the minimalist and maximalist camps.

Where are the Lutherans in this culture war over Darwinian evolution? European Lutherans do not see what all the fuss is about. Darwinian theory and evolutionary principles are so integrated into European thinking that this war appears as an anachronism, a puzzle. In North America, a number of Lutherans in the Missouri Synod and Wisconsin Synod contribute to the thinking of both biblical creationism and scientific creationism. To the extent that Chinese-speaking Lutherans in Hong Kong and Singapore along with English-speaking Australians engage this topic, they tend to side with the creationists.

In the twenty-first century, Lutheran theologians and scientists associated with the new movement Theology and Science tend to find support among theistic evolutionists. Key here is respect and even appreciation for solid science and its methods, and this includes Darwinian theory in its current expressions. Lutheran theistic evolutionists have employed sacramental language to communicate *concursus*; they describe God as working "in, with, and under" natural processes to bring about our chapter in the story of the human race. Even non-Lutherans among theistic evolutionists have adopted this Reformation language to describe divine providence at work within natural processes.

Most Lutherans in the theistic evolutionist encampment—Wolfhart Pannenberg, Antje Jackelén, Johanne Stubbe Teglbærg Kristensen, Noreen Herzfeld, Gregory Peterson, James Haag, Joshua Moritz, and others— could best be described as minimalists. They hold to divine providence working "in, with, and under" natural processes, but their worldview is constructed primarily on the basis of scriptural promises. No less committed to scriptural promises yet tending toward a maximalist integration of evolution with theology would be Philip Hefner, at the Lutheran School of Theology at Chicago, plus the new school of "Deep Incarnation" led by Niels Henrik Gregersen at the University of Copenhagen.

That Christians continue to struggle over this issue is clear. However, because the actual points at issue deal specifically with the explanatory adequacy of natural selection, it would be misleading to simply dub this a war between science and religion. Lutherans prefer to fight on behalf of science at its best along with theology at its best.

See also Bible Interpretation; Creation; Heim, Karl; Natural Science; Natural Theology; Philosophy; Rationalism

Bibliography

Bennett, G., M. J. Hewlett, T. Peters, and R. J. Russell, eds. *The Evolution of Evil*. Vandenhoeck & Ruprecht, 2008; Gregersen, N. H. *From Complexity to Life: On the Emergence of Life and Meaning*. Oxford University Press, 2003; Hefner, P. *The Human Factor: Evolution, Culture, and Religion*. Fortress, 1993; Pannenberg, W. *The Historicity of Nature: Essays on Science and Theology*. Ed. N. H. Gregersen. Templeton Foundation Press, 2008; Peters, T., and M. Hewlett. *Can You Believe in God and Evolution?* Abingdon, 2009; Peters, T., and M. Hewlett. *Evolution from Creation to New Creation: Conflict, Conversation, and Convergence*. Abingdon, 2003.

TED PETERS

Exile

Exile is the expulsion of persons by a political authority from one's native land or place of residence, either by direct ejection or by threat of persecution for continuation of advocacy of certain beliefs or of certain practices. Since the sixteenth century, exile has played a significant role in the history of the Lutheran churches throughout the world.

In the 1520s preachers who were spreading Luther's message were threatened with imprisonment as well as burning at the stake and were indeed placed in prison, as in the Hapsburg lands. The number of priests who fled to Evangelical territories to escape jailing, who escaped prison, or who after release from confinement fled their place of service, was considerable, including such leading figures as Johannes Pfeffinger, Conrad Cordatus, Johannes Apel, and Paul Speratus. Wittenberg did not become a destination for the massive numbers of refugees who gathered a generation later in Geneva, but in this early period many of these priests spent some time hearing the Wittenberg faculty lecture before receiving calls to parish service.

In the aftermath of the Smalcald War and with his expulsion from his bishopric of Naumburg-Zeitz by victorious Roman Catholic imperial forces, Nikolaus von Amsdorf took the title *Exul* (or *exsul*, Latin for "wanderer, exile") to describe himself on the title pages of published critiques of the Augsburg Interim and other treatises. He was but one of several hundred Lutheran clergy (including Johannes Brenz and Martin Bucer) who were expelled from their pastorates by Roman Catholic forces in their imposition of the Augsburg Interim. In the quarter century of controversy among elements of the Wittenberg circle following the Augsburg Interim, Evangelical political authorities used exile as a means of strengthening their control over their churches, banishing critical theologians who refused to agree to new religious policies. Most exiles in this period were Gnesio-Lutherans, some were Andreas Osiander's followers (who found refuge in Württemberg), yet even Viktorin Strigel, when banned from the lecture hall by his Philippist colleagues on the Leipzig faculty for spiritualizing views of the Lord's Supper, also claimed the title "exile," and so did others. The Gnesio-Lutheran Johannes Wigand treated the topic "exile" as a form of persecution in his *On Persecution* (1580).

Several causes led to the expulsion of these pastors and professors. Some criticized the moral conduct of leading citizens of a town or their prince and/or his courtiers. Others opposed governmental injustice toward peasants and common people. Criticism of governmental interference in the affairs of the church earned others exile. Finally, princely decisions in doctrinal controversies led to the banishment of those leaders who disagreed with the government.

The Religious Peace of Augsburg (1555) granted the right of emigration to those who did not wish to conform to the religious confession of their prince. The Hapsburg rulers were able to ignore its terms in lands of theirs lying outside the German Holy Roman Empire. Indeed, Roman Catholic persecution of Evangelical Christians continued, not only in Mediterranean lands, but also within the German Empire and in eastern kingdoms, including Poland and Hungary, sporadically into the seventeenth century. Forced exile was among the tools of the Counter-Reformation. In Hapsburg lands during the seventeenth century, harsh policies sent pastors to the galleys and drove laypeople into a kind of inner exile; they gathered in forests with Bibles, hymnals, and catechisms to continue to practice their faith. Among those whose resistance to Hapsburg suppression of Lutherans finally led them into exile was the literarily gifted Catharina Regina von Greiffenberg (1633–94), a noblewoman from Upper Austria who lived out her days in Nuremberg.

In the adjacent territory of the archbishop of Salzburg, Archbishop Maximilian Gandolf von Künburg ordered Lutherans in the Deferegger Valley to leave their homes and all children under fifteen years of age in the middle of a particularly harsh winter, 1685, contrary to imperial law, which guaranteed a three-year grace period after the announcement of such edicts for banishment. His successor, Archbishop Leopold Anton Freiherr von Firmian, expelled all remaining Lutherans, again in winter, 1731–32, and at loss of children under twelve. King Frederick William I of Prussia opened lands in his eastern domains for the Salzburgers. Between April and August 1732 over twenty thousand Protestants left Salzburg for Prussia; several hundred died on the way.

More than ten thousand others emigrated to other destinations, including the British colony in Georgia (North America), other German territories, and the Dutch Republic.

In the early nineteenth century the Prussian government under King Frederick William III, whose family had been Calvinist since the early seventeenth century, ordered a union of Lutheran and Reformed churches under a common liturgical agenda that obscured the Lutheran doctrine of Christ's presence in the Lord's Supper. Lutheran resisters, led by Breslau professor Johann Gottfried Scheibel, were imprisoned. Some groups of these "Old Lutherans" chose exile and emigrated to Australia under August Kavel or to the United States, such as those who formed the Buffalo Synod under Johann Andreas August Grabau or those of the Lutheran Church–Missouri Synod.

In the twentieth and twenty-first centuries, Lutherans in areas of Africa torn by civil war, often aggravated by Muslim troops serving both tribal and religious purposes, were forced into exile. Despite the extreme suffering of the resulting conditions, evangelistic work led to the conversion of others in refugee camps.

See also Amsdorf, Nicholas von; Augsburg Interim; Lutheran Church–Missouri Synod; Martyrdom and Persecution; Ohio/Buffalo/Iowa Synod; Peace of Augsburg; Smalcald War

Bibliography

Dingel, I. "Die Kultivierung des Exulantentums im Luthertum am Beispiel des Nikolaus von Amsdorf." In *Nikolaus von Amsdorf (1483–1565)*, ed. I. Dingel, 153–75. Evangelische Verlagsanstalt, 2008; Florey, G. *Geschichte der Saltzburger Protestanten und ihrer Emigration 1731/1732.* Böhlau, 1977; Jones, G. F. *The Salzburg Saga.* University of Georgia Press, 1984; Kampmann, J., and W. Klän, eds. *Preußische Union, lutherisches Bekenntnis und kirchliche Prägungen.* Edition Ruprecht, 2014.

ROBERT KOLB

Existentialism

A philosophical, religious, and cultural movement rooted in nineteenth-century European thought that emerged in Germany and France. Its theological importance extended throughout the twentieth century, driving biblical interpretation, the interpretation of historical figures, such as Martin Luther, and systematic theology. Even though Martin Heidegger (1889–1976) shunned the mantle, his *Being and Time* (1927) elevated into prominence the themes of alienation, authenticity, and additional matters that distinguished existentialism from other movements, whether that of phenomenology or philosophy of language, which dominated the same period. The variety of other works extending through Jean-Paul Sartre's (1905–80) *Being and Nothingness* and, more significantly, Sartre's and Albert Camus's (1913–60) novels, have had enduring influence beyond that which accompanies explorations of existentialism in film, fine art, and literature. Throughout the twentieth century, several writers have been retrospectively adopted as antecedents of existentialism, chief among them are Søren Kierkegaard (1813–55), Friedrich Nietzsche (1844–1900), and Fyodor Dostoyevsky (1821–81).

Existentialism has seemed, in Paul Tillich's (1886–1965) words, "the good luck of Christian theology," even as much of the wider movement has harbored an ambiguous relationship to religious life. When confronted with the challenges of modernity, historiographical research, political and cultural criticisms, the various analyses of alienation, authenticity, and hermeneutics promised to give Christian theology new life by creating both a language intelligible to contemporaries and a theoretical warrant to justify theological labor. Doctrines of sin, for instance, were reformulated in terms of alienation; salvation in Christ became the return to authentic existence. Doubtful and seemingly antiquated doctrines received a fresh breath with the analyses that existentialist writers provided, even though some thought the use existentialists made of these doctrines seemed to depart drastically from traditional senses or purposes that these doctrines once had.

The motives of alienation and authenticity have great significance in existentialist analysis and interpretation. Alienation for existentialists has much in common with alienation as used in the Romantic or idealist philosophical movements. Such alienation can refer to the kinds of disjunction that human beings feel in modern life, whether caused by industrial technology, the remove felt from nature in urban settings, the distance between visions of the past and the present, the anonymity coming from a mass society, the ubiquity of modern media, or the pain caused by economic and social injustice. Alienation prevents right understanding and proper action; just so, alienation can refer to a wide range of circumstances. Most importantly for many existentialist theologians, such alienation precludes right speech about God. While alienated, a person is in exile and cannot sing God's praises, nor can one name or offer a description of God at all.

Martin Luther's thought and life have proved attractive to existentialist interpretation, as has the theology of other figures such as Thomas Aquinas. Whether it is his *Turmerlebnis* (*tower experience*) or his articulation that a person must follow the path of prayer, meditation, and suffering in order to be accounted a theologian, many dimensions of Luther's life seem well suited to analysis in terms of alienation, authenticity, and individual existence, because it is not until Luther obtained a particular existence through his understanding of the Word of God that he could rightly do theology. Likewise, Luther's theology has been interpreted existentially by such scholars as Gerhard Ebeling (1912–2001). In its existentialist modes, the doctrine of justification by faith alone has been used by many writers to show the doctrine's continuing significance: where some contend that the doctrine depends on guilt and a sense of sin, existentialists hold that a reinterpretation of these doctrines can address the modern experience of alienation and detachment. Specifically, existentialist interpreters of Luther highlighted Luther's theme of the hidden God, the motif of death and resurrection, and the *pro nobis* (for us) dimension of the gospel in order to draw out the experiential aspects of Luther's theology, in contrast to a purely didactic approach.

241

Further, existentialist interpretation of Luther carries out, in a new way, the older liberal Protestant commitment to a Luther free of metaphysical commitments, such as that advocated by Albrecht Ritschl (1822–89). Though existentialists break with liberal Protestants over the significance of history, both movements share a commitment to interpreting Luther as departing from and critical of theological metaphysics.

Beyond the interpretation of Luther and other theological figures, existentialism has had a special significance for biblical hermeneutics. As a kind of hermeneutics or analysis, existentialism has shown some kinship to other cultural and philosophical movements of its time, whether they are the practice of psychoanalysis, absurdist art, or phenomenology. All of these movements offer a method of interpreting texts, experience, or other phenomena. Existentialism has shown itself especially useful to complement or even overcome historical-critical study of the Bible. Rudolf Bultmann (1884–1976) especially has shown the power of this kind of interpretation in his various studies, ranging from his use of demythologization, the purpose of which is to make biblical texts have significance today, to his wide-ranging reflection on the role of the historical Jesus and any historical project for the purposes of Christian faith. Interpretation on the basis of a particular existence does not contest historical interpretation but can consider it apersonal and requiring translation in order to make it relevant to contemporary persons; therefore Bultmann can conclude that the historical Jesus is only significant as the Christ made present through proclamation.

Hermeneutics received a decisive push from existentialism by providing its own variation on particular contexts of meaning that were already emphasized in the philosophy of language throughout the late nineteenth and early twentieth centuries and in the individual world that arises from one's own existence. Leading theological figures in this effort are Ernst Fuchs (1903–83), Gerhard Ebeling (1912–2001), and John Macquarrie (1919–2007). Though Hans-Georg Gadamer (1900–2002) would not identify with existentialism, his work *Truth and Method* illustrates the hermeneutical significance of one's own perspective, the difficulty of extracting oneself from one's prejudgments and situation, and the importance of one's situation in a tradition. Existentialists vary in the degree to which they stress the singularity of the individual or the individual in conjunction with a community; despite this range, they take interpretation of the other person to require attention to one's own whole person and respect the difference that the other may possess over and against. Thus, like Gadamer, existentialist hermeneutics stresses the need to bridge different worlds, to "fuse horizons" rather than to resolve textual accounts into facts or the barely historical, as positivists would demand.

The warrants that existentialist theologians employ to justify their hermeneutics or use of the categories of authenticity and alienation vary widely. Sometimes the grounds used to justify theological inquiry for existentialists are nothing more than the adequacy of these categories to the experience of modern persons, which yet again shows how existentialism and liberal Protestantism share a common way of privileging experience and serve as a kind of naturalist empiricism. However, other times existentialists also employ significant metaphysical reflections such as Alfred North Whitehead's (1861–1947) process philosophy, Continental writers such as Gilles Deleuze (1925–95), or other phenomenologists, privileging the single existing thing or individual over general metaphysical accounts of a thing's essence or nature, refusing to diminish the actuality of the individual by abstracting from it and stating it in universal or ahistorical terms. These results indicate the contribution that existentialists make to theology in two divergent directions. On the one hand, existentialists seem to continue the long process of displacing metaphysics from theology, begun at various points in the Middle Ages, by abolishing discussions of being in general in favor of concrete individual existence. On the other hand, existentialists stress the primacy of actuality; underscoring this actuality leads theologians to recover metaphysics in another mode, such as the kind of theological metaphysics articulated by Pseudo-Dionysius or Thomas Aquinas. Though existentialism no longer has a widespread cultural purchase, it has significantly influenced the course of modern theology.

See also Bultmann, Rudolf (Karl); Ebeling, Gerhard; Kierkegaard, Søren Aabye; Luther's Breakthrough; Tillich, Paul J.

Bibliography

Bultmann, R. *Faith and Understanding*. Trans. L. Smith. Fortress, 1987; Ebeling, G. *Luther: An Introduction to His Thought*. Trans. R. A. Wilson. Augsburg Fortress, 2007; Fuchs, E. *Marburger Hermeneutik*. Mohr Siebeck, 1968; Gadamer, H. *Truth and Method*. 2nd ed. Trans. J. Weinsheimer and D. G. Marshall. Crossroad, 1989; Heidegger, M. *Being and Time*. Trans. J. Macquarrie and E. Robinson. Harper Perennial, 2008; Kierkegaard, S. *Fear and Trembling*. Trans. A. Hanny. Penguin, 1986; Sartre, J. P. *Being and Nothingness*. Trans. H. Barnes. Washington Square, 1984.

GREGORY WALTER

Exorcism

By the time of the Enlightenment, the discovery of hypnosis (mesmerism) and the identification of mental illnesses seemed to provide natural explanations for cases of apparent demonic possession and reputed healing by the ecclesiastical rite of exorcism (Midelfort 17–22). From this alternative account of psychic suffering and its therapy, the modern discipline of psychoanalysis gradually arose. In this new atmosphere, Luther's retention of exorcism in the Small Catechism's instruction for baptism was regarded as an embarrassing remnant of medieval superstition. The instruction "The baptizer shall say, 'Depart, you unclean spirit, and make room for the Holy Spirit'" (SC, Baptismal Booklet 11 in *BC* 373) was neglected or even deleted in later editions of Lutheran baptismal services.

Important historical nuances of the Reformation's reform of the rite of exorcism are lost from view, however, as a result of painting with so broad a brushstroke. Broadly speaking, Luther's experiential faith in Christ as saving Lord, into whose keeping the sinful human being is delivered by the Spirit in baptism, is inextricably bound up with the apocalyptic battle against sin, death, and the power of the devil (Oberman 102–6). Today, horrific experiences with the forces of darkness in the twentieth century, the cultural sense of post-Christian nihilism in the West and thus doubt about the conceits of "the" Enlightenment, the dramatic fall of psychoanalysis as a scientific therapy in the course of the last century, the equally dramatic growth of Lutheran churches in the Global South fueled in part by the ministry of exorcists (Austnaberg), and the "apocalyptic" interpretation of the New Testament—all combine to raise fresh interest in the healing ministry, including exorcism.

Luther was critical of the ecclesiastical office of the exorcist and of the elaborate ceremonies of exorcism that had evolved (LW 34:73–75). He regarded the miraculous expulsion of demons by direct address in the name of Jesus, as depicted in the New Testament, as a charism given uniquely to that apostolic time for the confirmation of the gospel. In present times, the devil's apparent "possession" of a human person must be soberly tested for fraud and, if ascertained, battled with the prayer of the church, the claim of baptism, and nothing but contempt for the proud and stupid spirit, who would like nothing better than the spectacle occasioned by the trappings of the ecclesiastical rite (Luther 52) to deflect faith from Christ as saving Lord.

The prayer of the church indicates that demonic assaults were taken as social rather than merely as individual phenomena. The purpose of exorcism was not only to heal the afflicted individual but holistically to cleanse the neighborhood of the impure spirit and restore the afflicted to holy fellowship. A public ministry was required, with the congregation engaged in prayer and the pastor and elders ministering to the possessed. The claim of baptism asserting the saving lordship of Christ over the afflicted was reiterated, thus denying any right to the demonic usurper. Luther recommended simple recitation of the Apostles' Creed and the Lord's Prayer, and the prayer of faith that God would, according to his loving will and saving purpose, liberate the assaulted soul from its tormentor. No negotiation or even conversation with the unclean spirit was permitted; it was to be treated with utter disdain. Along with this Evangelical simplification of exorcism, Luther continually expressed worry about superstition and fraudulent claims. He required careful discernment according to the medical knowledge of his day (Luther 42–43).

Despite this sober approach to the matter, early Lutheran exorcism and the connection to the demonic are fraught with problems. Charitably read, Luther can be seen as moving beyond folkloric fears of poltergeists to following Christ in confrontation with a true enemy of superhuman proportions that is sheerly malevolent, of whom Christ alone can prevail in battle. But Luther also shared the medieval fear of witches, about which feminist studies have raised important critical questions. His habit of "demonizing" theological opponents, beginning with the decision to name the institution of the papacy as "antichrist," is not anything still to be admired or emulated (Hinlicky 379–85), and his later writings against the Jews and Judaism now demand repentance. Karl Barth's important but perhaps exaggerated critique in this connection must be taken seriously: he argues that Luther became *too* concerned and even obsessed with the devil (*CD* III/3:519) and not confident enough, consequently, in Christ's victory over the forces of darkness. Surely a holistic ministry of healing is required today in renewed confidence of Christ's victory over the powers and principalities.

See also Baptism

Bibliography

Austnaberg, H. *Shepherds and Demons: A Study of Exorcism as Practiced and Understood by Shepherds in the Malagasy Lutheran Church.* Lang, 2008; Barth, K. *Church Dogmatics.* T&T Clark, 1975; Hinlicky, P. R. *Luther and the Beloved Community.* Eerdmans, 2010; Luther, M. *Letters of Spiritual Counsel.* Westminster, 1960; Midelfort, H. C. E. *Exorcism and Enlightenment: Johann Joseph Gassner and the Demons of Eighteenth Century Germany.* Yale University Press, 2005; Oberman, H. A. *Luther: Man between God and the Devil.* Trans. E. Walliser-Schwarzbart. Yale University Press, 1989.

PAUL R. HINLICKY

F

Fabricius, Johann Philipp

As a German Lutheran missionary to South India, Johann Philipp Fabricius (1711–91) served in Chennai (Madras) for forty-six years. Today he is remembered for the revision of the Tamil translation of the Bible (popularly known as the "Golden Version") and for his contribution to Tamil literature in the form of translation and production of a Tamil grammar and Tamil dictionaries.

Born in Frankfurt am Main, he studied law and theology at Giessen and Halle and was ordained at Copenhagen in 1739. He was sent in 1740 to work for the Danish-Halle Mission in Tranquebar. After two years of ministry there, he came to Chennai in 1742 to assist the "English Mission" (Madras Mission) commenced in 1728 by Benjamin Schultze. Shepherding the fledgling Protestant Christians in Chennai for four decades, he bore the privation caused by the French and English conflict. He had to seek shelter twice (1746 and 1758) in Pulicat, a Dutch territory, when the French occupied Chennai. In 1753 he solemnized the marriage of Robert Clive, one of the key figures in the creation of British India. He translated 335 German hymns into Tamil, enriching singing in the Lutheran congregations to this day. Fabricius also compiled and had published an English guide to Tamil grammar in 1778, a Tamil-English dictionary (1779), and an English-Tamil dictionary (1786). Of all his literary contributions his revision of the translation of the Bible is treasured and used by the Tamil Lutherans even today. In all these endeavors he was ably assisted by an Indian assistant named Mutthu and a fellow missionary, John Christian Breithaupt (d. 1782). He died in 1791 and was buried in Chennai.

See also India; Mission and Evangelism

Bibliography
Fenger, J. F. *History of the Tranquebar Mission*. Trans. E. Francke. M. E. Press, 1906; Lehmann, E. A. *It Began in Tranquebar*. Christian Literature Society, 1956.

PETER VETHANAYAGAMONY

Falckner, Justus

The first Lutheran ordained in the Western Hemisphere was Justus Falckner (1672–1723). He was born in Langenreinsdorf, in Saxony. He was in the first class at the new University of Halle (1692) and also studied at Leipzig and Rostock. Falckner immigrated to Pennsylvania in 1700 in order to help his older brother, Daniel Jr., with the administration of the new settlement of Germantown. He found himself attracted to the Swedish Lutheran Church of Gloria Dei at Wicacå (now South Philadelphia). Here the pastor, Andreas Rudman, could speak German but had to resign because of failing health. In 1702 Rudman agreed to take an interim assignment at the Dutch Lutheran parish in Manhattan and Albany, New York, and Hackensack, New Jersey. After a year of strenuous labor, he realized that he could not continue and wrote to Falckner, asking him to consider becoming ordained. Thus on November 24, 1703, Falckner was ordained at Gloria Dei by three Swedish priests. Andreas Rudman acted as superintendent, Andreas Sandell as pastor loci, and Erik Björk as pastor from Christina (now Wilmington, Delaware). Falckner served the three Dutch Lutheran congregations along the Hudson River plus a number of other German congregations that had been established by Palatine immigrants until his death.

See also Sweden

Bibliography
Clark, D. W. *The World of Justus Falckner*. Muhlenberg, 1946; Kessler, M. *Fundamental Instruction: Justus*

Falckner's Catechism. American Lutheran Publicity Bureau, 2003; Williams, K.-E. *The Journey of Justus Falckner.* ALPB, 2003.

KIM-ERIC WILLIAMS

Fathme, Pauline

Born in the Oromia Region of southern Ethiopia at the beginning of the 1830s, Pauline Fathme (ca. 1830–55) was kidnapped by Muslim slave traders and brought to Upper Egypt, where she finally became the personal property of the pasha of Egypt, Mehmet Ali. Mehmet Ali handed her over to John Baron von Müller, who brought her to Stuttgart in 1847. At the wish of the mother of the king of Württemberg, she was admitted to a girls' school in the Pietist settlement of Kornthal, where she was baptized on July 12, 1852. She died soon thereafter, but her enthusiasm for Protestant Christianity and her wish to do evangelistic work in her home country inspired later missionaries to Ethiopia.

See also Ethiopia

Bibliography
Ledderhose, K. D. *Aus dem Leben der Galla-Negerin Pauline Fathme.* C. F. Spittler, 1867; Smidt, W. "The Role of the Former Oromo Slave Pauline Fathme." In *Ethiopia and the Missions: Historical and Anthropological Insights*, ed. V. Böll, S. Kaplan, A. Martinez d'Alòs Moner, and E. Sokolinskaia, 77–98. Lit, 2005.

FRIEDER LUDWIG

Fedde, Elizabeth Tonette

The deaconess Elizabeth Tonette Fedde (1850–1921) was born on Christmas Day in rural Norway. She spent thirteen years ministering to her country's folk in Brooklyn, New York, and Minneapolis, Minnesota. She founded hospitals in both cities, helped to plan another in Chicago, and launched the deaconess movement among Norwegian-American Lutherans.

Informed by Haugean pietism, Fedde joined the Deaconess House in Kristiania (Oslo) in her twenties. There she studied nursing, Christian ethics, and social welfare. Following postings in Norway, in 1883 she went to Brooklyn. Immediately she organized a relief society to address Norwegians' various physical and spiritual needs. Eventually she was joined by other deaconesses, and together they provided home visits, employment aid, medical services, spiritual care, and other help. Her diary offers an intimate look at their activity and her own spiritual life. Fedde and the deaconesses led the way in expanding their church's ministry beyond its immigrant community. The nine-bed hospital and deaconess home she established provided the foundation for work that continues at Lutheran Health Care in Brooklyn. From 1888 to 1891 she worked with Minneapolis Norwegian-Americans to set up a deaconess home and hospital there. In 1896 she returned to Norway, where she married and lived until her death.

See also Deaconesses; Monasteries, Evangelical; Norway; Norwegian-American Lutheranism

Bibliography
Folkedahl, B., trans. and ed. "The Diary of Elizabeth Fedde, 1883–88." *Norwegian American Studies and Records* 20 (1959): 170–96; Grindal, G. *"To Do the Lord's Will": Elisabeth Fedde and the Deaconess Movement among the Norwegians in America.* Lutheran University Press, 2014; Rolfsrud, E. N. *Borrowed Sister: The Story of Elisabeth Fedde.* Augsburg, 1953.

L. DEANE LAGERQUIST

Feldmanis, Roberts Emīls

The Latvian confessor, pastor, theologian, and church historian Roberts Emīls Feldmanis (1910–2002) was influenced by Edgars Rumba, studied theology in Riga (1930–35), was ordained in 1935, and served several parishes. Rumba appointed him as secretary of foreign missions (1936–45), while Feldmanis assisted him as pastor of Riga's Jesus Church. Feldmanis edited the journal *Foreign Missions* (1937–40) and participated in the World Mission conference in Tambaram, India (1938). After earning his Licentiate of Theology degree in 1940, writing *The Development and Evaluation of the Idea of Unification of the South India Churches*, he ministered to Riga's Holy Trinity congregation (1940–44) and Jesus Church (1946–50), while also offering theological study courses.

Arrested in 1950 and deported to a concentration camp in the Arkhangelsk region, Feldmanis returned in 1954 to serve as pastor in three congregations, the last at Mežaparks (1969–98), fostering there a revival in the mid-1980s that attracted young men to pastoral ministry. From 1969, he lectured on church history in the church's theological education program and during perestroika restored several parishes, also serving as adviser of the church's consistory (1991–99). In 2010 Professor Roberts Feldmanis's Foundation was established to print his works (in Latvian): *Evangelical Lutheran Church and Service* (2009), *History of the Latvian Church* (2010), *Only Christ* (sermons, 2011), *The Creed* (2012), *The Fountains of Life* (theological articles, 2013), *Together with Christ* (sermons, 2014), and others.

See also Latvia; Rumba, Edgars

Bibliography
Rubenis, I. *Misionars Roberts Feldmanis*. Riga, 2007.

GUNTIS KALME

Fifohazana Movement

An indigenous revival movement called *Fifohazana* (awakening) in Madagascar is the main reason the Malagasy Lutheran Church is one of the fastest-growing Lutheran churches. Severe persecution of Christianity under Queen Ranovalona I in the nineteenth century caused the faith to be firmly rooted among the Merina people in the region around the capital, Antananarivo. However, this indigenization of the faith did not transfer well to other regions where the Merina were considered outsiders and even colonizers themselves. (The Merina are of pure Melanesia ancestry; most of the other groups are of African origin.)

Three major revivals have marked the history of Lutherans and other Christians in Madagascar. The first centered on the town of Soatanana in the Betsileo region. Led by a pastor named Rainisoalambo, his followers were called the *Mpianatry ny Tompo* (Disciples of the Lord). This revival dates from October 15, 1894, and continues today.

Rainisoalambo died on June 30, 1904. Beginning in August 1904, huge revival gatherings took place at Soatanana annually through 1911. However, when the movement split into a Lutheran and an independent, completely indigenous organization, the French colonial government refused to allow further meetings. After Madagascar's independence in 1960, annual meetings resumed.

The second revival was led by a teacher in the Norwegian Mission Society (NMS) school at Tsaratanana named Rakotozafy Daniel (1919–47). Very ill much of his life, Rakotozafy was healed and worked as a catechist in his district. The Norwegian Lutheran missionary Borgenvik urged Rakotozafy to attend seminary. Rakotozafy's catechetical work was in Farihimena, in the region of Vakinakaritra, the oldest field of the NMS work. Though a young pastor, Rakotozafy called for a district-wide revival on November 1, 1946. He died only a year later. The revival Rakotozafy called for and initially led had its greatest impact in the Vakinankaratra region but was also felt in other areas.

The most recent revival was led by a largely uneducated woman named Volahavana Germaine, known to her followers as Nenilava (tall mother). She was of the Antaimoro people group centered on the east coast of Madagascar. Her father was a petty king and a practitioner of indigenous religion. He was also an *ombiasa* (a diviner, castor of charms). Beginning at age twelve, Volahavana heard Jesus speak in visions. Many asked for her hand in marriage, but she always refused. Finally her parents forced her to marry an elderly catechist, Mosesy Tsirefo. At first she continued to live in her parents' home while she underwent instruction leading to baptism. After her baptism she went to live with her husband in Soatanana. According to Nenilava, Jesus called her to be instructed by him in heaven in May 1941. Jesus then ordered her to return to earth and preach the gospel, heal people in Jesus's name, and cast out demons. She became quite famous all over the island and even in the Comoros Islands. In addition to her other work, she also strove to heal rifts between Christians, especially when strife occurred between congregants and their pastor.

Today almost every person entering the seminary in preparation for the ministry of word and sacrament has first studied to be a *mpiandry* (shepherd) in the movement. There are *toby* (revival camps) in almost every major city as well as in many rural areas where the poor, the mentally ill, or those who feel oppressed by evil spirits can come and be cared for. All the top leadership of the Malagasy Lutheran Church are also *mpiandry*.

This movement bears many characteristics of the indigenous Christianity found among the African Independent Churches on the African continent; however, in Madagascar this movement is solidly embedded in the Lutheran Church. Its *mpiandry* undergo a lengthy period of instruction under the direction of the local Lutheran pastor. After being examined and found prepared, they are "set aside" or consecrated into a diaconal-like status, although the Malagasy Lutheran Church does not use that language. *Mpiandry* then wear white robes whenever doing their work, which takes place at special services held at times other than the regular Sunday gathering of the parish, although in some cases the revival service immediately follows the regular Sunday morning liturgy. Women *mpiandry* wear headgear similar to that of Roman Catholic nuns in earlier times. The *Fifohazana* celebrate a gathering at Soatanana each year. Even the president of the Malagasy Republic once visited.

Volahavana Germaine died on January 22, 1998. While the movement continues, it is no longer led by a single charismatic leader but by a directing committee.

See also Madagascar

Bibliography

Austnaberg, H. *Shepherds and Demons: A Study of Exorcism as Practiced and Understood by Shepherds in the Malagasy Lutheran Church*. Lang, 2008; Rich, C. *The*

Fifohazana: Madagascar's Indigenous Christian Movement. Cambria, 2008.

JAMES B. VIGEN

Finland

Finland is the easternmost Scandinavian country; its language and culture are distinctive, but historically its Christianity has been Western and, since the Reformation, Lutheran. Christianity came to Finland in the eleventh century from both east and west, but the Western church gained ground in most of the country. The boundary between the Western and Eastern churches, between Sweden and Novgorod, was drawn through Karelia in 1323. The English-born bishop Henry of Uppsala visited Finland in 1155 in order to organize the church. The following year he was martyred by a Finnish peasant, thus becoming the patron saint of Finland.

When Turku Cathedral was consecrated on June 17, 1300, its diocese was one of seven dioceses in the church province of Uppsala. It was led by a Finnish-born bishop; clergy received their education in the cathedral school of Turku. At the same time, the first Finns are found in the records of the University of Paris. At the end of the Middle Ages, Finland had one hundred parishes. Near Turku the distance between the churches could be only a couple of miles; in northern and eastern Finland, children were baptized only when they themselves were able to ski to the church.

The Reformation in Sweden, then in control of Finland, was led by the powerful, unscrupulous, and avaricious Gustav Vasa (r. 1523–60). Uninterested in theological questions, he realized that Lutheran beliefs gave him a pretext to confiscate church property and tax revenue and to challenge the church's political authority. Gustav broke ties with the (Catholic) Holy See in 1523. Subsequently he elevated himself to the highest ecclesiastical authority in his kingdom. He strove to avoid any abrupt changes in church ceremonies that could provoke opposition or rebellion. Leaving the church's episcopal structure intact helped ensure that the transformation of liturgy and church organization in Sweden was relatively uneventful and slow-paced.

The Reformation brought the New Testament (1526) and the entire Bible (1541), as well as liturgical books, in Swedish. Most Finns could not understand Swedish, and hence they had to be translated. Thus the Reformation gave Finns their written language. The Finnish reformer Mikael Agricola is the father of Finnish literature and written Finnish. Son of a Swedish-speaking peasant, Agricola attended Luther's and Melanchthon's lectures in Wittenberg in 1536–39; acted as headmaster of the cathedral school in Turku, Finland; and then became bishop. He wrote the ABC-book, the first book in the Finnish language (1543), a primer for reading that also contains a catechism, based mainly on Luther's Small Catechism. He translated the New Testament (1548), the Psalter, and a selection of the Old Testament Prophets, and published a Finnish church manual and a missal, translated from the works of the Swedish reformer Olavus Petri.

Sweden accepted the Augsburg Confession in 1593, the Formula of Concord in 1663. The Lutheran Church was a state church. During the age of confessionalism, Sweden was one of the great powers in Europe; Finns took part in the Swedish defense of Lutherans during the Thirty Years' War. In the seventeenth century Sweden expanded its territory south and east. In the area conquered from Russia, Ingermanland and Kexholms län, Lutheran ministers tried to convert Finnish-speaking Orthodox people to Lutheranism. But religion proved stronger than the common language; thousands of Orthodox fled to Russia.

The first Finnish University, in Turku, was founded in 1640. The university's theological faculty offered opportunities for the education of the clergy. The bishop of Turku was vice-chancellor of the university, and the three professors of theology were members of the Cathedral Chapter. The complete Bible, translated by two professors and two parish priests, appeared in Finnish in 1642. The church taught the Finns to read. To know the main articles of Luther's Small Catechism by heart was a precondition for confirmation and thus also for marriage. In western parts of Finland, most people at the end of the seventeenth century had a very basic literacy. Devotional books (many of English Puritan origin) were translated into Finnish and printed.

Lutheran Orthodoxy, Pietism, and the Enlightenment influenced the Finnish Church during the eighteenth century. Johannes Gezelius the Younger, who became bishop of Turku in 1690, as a student visited Philipp Jakob Spener in Frankfurt and translated *Pia Desideria* into Swedish. The manuscript was, however, left unprinted. Pietism appeared in Sweden and also in Turku first in radical form; as a result, the so-called Conventicle-Placat of 1726 prohibited devotional meetings led by the laity.

The eighteenth century in Sweden was also an age of Nordic Enlightenment, a golden era of natural sciences and economics. Most bishops of Turku then were natural scientists. A priest was a recognized leader in his parish. He was consulted not only on ecclesiastical matters but also in secular matters such as the draining of marshlands, the introduction of new plants, and the use of medication.

In 1809 Finland became a part of the Russian Empire. Although Czar Alexander I was head of the Orthodox Church in Russia, he promised to preserve Finland's Lutheran Church order. The union of throne and altar was still in force, even though the throne had moved from Stockholm to St. Petersburg. The bishop of Turku, who had proved his loyalty to the new ruler, was rewarded with a title of archbishop during the Reformation celebrations in 1817. The Finnish dioceses of Turku and Porvoo were no longer under the archepiscopal see of Uppsala, but part of an independent Lutheran Church under the protection of the czar.

The church was loyal to the emperor. The bishops (the third diocese for Northern Finland was founded in 1850) kept the pietistic revival movements that began early in the century under close surveillance: they could be seen nurturing nationalism and mutiny against the legitimate sovereign. The central figure in these revivals was a peasant, Paavo Ruotsalainen (1777–1852), who established himself as organizer and spiritual counselor. Another leader was Henrik Renqvist (d. 1866), a clergyman active in translating and publishing devotional literature and a member of the Finnish Bible Society (established 1812). Other leaders included clergymen Fredrik Gabriel Hedberg (1811–93) and Lars Levi Laestadius (1800–1861), a Sami of northern Sweden and founder of the Laestadian movement that spread to Norway, Finland, and North America. These revival movements remained within the church and did not establish themselves as free churches, as they did in Sweden. The Laestadian movement became rather exclusive in character, but did not separate from the state church and had many clergy among its supporters.

The Finnish Missionary Society (present name: The Finnish Evangelical Lutheran Mission, FELM), a product of the revival movements, was founded in 1859 and began its work in 1870 in Ovamboland, German Southwest Africa (now northern Namibia). The missionary work resulted in an independent church, the Evangelical Lutheran Church in Namibia (ELCIN), founded in 1954. Today FELM cooperates also with other young Lutheran churches, as in Senegal, Tanzania, Ethiopia, and China. A half dozen small Finnish missionary societies work in Japan, the Far East, and Africa.

Alexander II ascended the throne in 1855 and agreed to some liberal reforms in Finland. The new Ecclesiastical Act (1869) established a synod with a majority of lay members and the authority to adopt and amend church law. The government had the right to reject proposals, but not to amend them. Thus the relationship between church and state was more liberal than that of its Nordic sister churches in Sweden, Denmark, and Norway. In 1889 Lutherans were allowed to leave their church and to join other Protestant denominations, which in practice meant Baptists and Methodists.

Finland gained its independence from Russia in 1917. In 1918 a civil war broke out between "reds" and "whites," ending with the victory of the whites. The clergy had sided with the whites. This guaranteed a strong position for the church in the 1920s and 1930s, but the connection with the working class remained cold. Church suspicion of the labor movement was not lessened by the persecutions endured by the Orthodox and Ingrian Lutheran Churches in the Soviet Union.

The Freedom of Religion Act of 1923 gave Finns the right to belong to any religious community or none. Yet no mass exodus from the church occurred: only 2 percent had left by 1930. Religious freedom thus secured the position of the church; it remained a people's church, with membership voluntary.

The ecumenical movement reached Finland at the end of the nineteenth century through Christian student and youth movements. Finns were represented in the Life and Work Conference in Stockholm in 1925. The Evangelical Lutheran Church of Finland was one of the founding members of the Lutheran World Federation and the World Council of Churches, and it has conducted doctrinal dialogues with the Russian Orthodox Church. The dialogue with the Anglican Church was initiated in the 1930s, and the Porvoo Agreement was signed in 1995.

The Winter War of 1939–40, defending against the invading troops of the Soviet Union, united the Finnish people and healed the wounds of the 1918 civil war. The war was waged as a struggle for "home, faith, and fatherland." It reinforced the role of the church. Military chaplains on the front line discovered that soldiers were more religious than had been imagined, and the church's commitment in times of crisis overcame prejudice against it.

In the uncertain atmosphere after World War II, the church was seen as a protector of national identity. Family counseling, youth, and social work expanded rapidly. In 1946 the Social Democratic Party removed from its program the traditional goal of separating state and church and ending religious education in school. In the Paris Peace Treaties (1947), Finland lost 12 percent of its territory to the Soviet Union. The population of the lost territory (ca. 420,000 persons) was evacuated to the rest of Finland.

In the 1960s the church was accused of being undemocratic and conservative, but in the 1980s such criticism faded. With the collapse of Communism and the rise of Islam as an influential world force, interest in religion has increased. The church is consulted on ethical issues, and people turn to it in times of crisis. The first women priests were ordained in 1988—a sign of the church's commitment to equality.

Finland remains a religiously homogeneous country; about 75 percent of the population belong to the Evangelical Lutheran Church of Finland. The church's ties to the state are loose: it is best described as a folk church, seeking to exert an influence on the whole population regardless of membership, and embracing a range of revival movements and spiritual trends.

See also Agricola, Mikael; Laestadius, Lars Levi; Sweden

Bibliography

Arden, G. E. *Four Northern Lights: Men Who Shaped Scandinavian Churches.* Augsburg, 1964; Heininen, S., and M. Heikkilä. *Kirchengeschichte Finnlands.* Vandenhoeck & Ruprecht, 2002; Seppo, J. "Church and State in Finland in 1997." *European Journal for Church and State Research* 5 (1998): 121–27.

SIMO HEININEN

Finnish-American Lutheranism

In the eighteenth century, although some Finns were in the colony of New Sweden on the Delaware, the bulk of the 230,000 Finns who immigrated to North America came toward the end of the nineteenth century, settling in the upper Midwest, the Pacific Northwest, and Canada. Most of these immigrants spoke Finnish, but a smaller number were ethnic Swedes from western Finland; the latter generally joined Augustana Synod congregations. The nineteenth century brought several distinct revival movements within Finnish Lutheranism, each led by a different spiritual leader. The Laestadians, or Apostolic Lutherans, followers of Swedish revivalist Lar Levi Laestadius, were usually found in the northern part of Finland. Other revival movements were headed by Finnish pastor Frederick Gabriel Hedberg, and by lay leader Paavo Ruotsalainen. Though all these revival movements sought to revive Finnish Lutheranism, they also challenged the state church in Finland and fought among themselves, leading to a complicated situation, especially among the Laestadians. There was also a significant Finnish socialist movement in Finland and among Finnish-Americans, which often led to further conflict within the immigrant communities. The first Finnish-American congregations were established by 1876, but it was not until 1890 that the leaders of some of these congregations formed a national organization, the Finnish Evangelical Lutheran Church, most commonly known as the Suomi Synod. This synod eventually established a school and seminary in Hancock, Michigan, and this became the center of the denomination. The Suomi Synod was the largest of the Finnish religious groups in North America and the one most closely related to the Church of Finland, although it also contained elements of the revival movement headed by Ruotsalainen. The Suomi Synod maintained its independence through the first half of the twentieth century, but in 1962 it merged with the Augustana Synod, the United Lutheran Church in America, and the American Evangelical Lutheran Church to form the Lutheran Church in America (LCA). Because a number of Suomi congregations continued to use Finnish in worship well into the twentieth century, they formed a Finnish interest conference within the LCA to maintain their distinct heritage. In 1961 the Suomi Synod consisted of thirty-six thousand baptized members in seventy-seven congregations. In 1898 another group of Finnish pastors, mainly from the revival tradition of Hedberg, formed a competing denomination called the Finnish Evangelical Lutheran National Church in America, centered in Ironwood, Michigan. One of the original features of this group was its commitment to lay preaching. Since this group was smaller than the Suomi Synod, it struggled to find a place to educate its own pastors until the 1920s, when it reached an agreement with the Lutheran Church–Missouri Synod to train Finnish-speaking pastors. Increasingly influenced theologically by the LCMS, the National Finns moved into fellowship with that synod, and in 1964 merged into it. At the time of the merger, this group consisted of sixty-one congregations and twelve thousand baptized members. The Laestadian movement was also present from the 1870s within the Finnish-American communities, although this movement has splintered into many small, distinct groups, divisions often caused by conflict between prominent leaders. This distinctly Finnish religious movement stresses emotional, revivalistic lay preaching toward repentance and conversion, along with public individual absolution. The largest group, the Apostolic Lutheran Church of America, is perhaps most closely related to conservative evangelical Protestantism. Other groups include Heidemanians and Pollarites, as well as the "Firstborn," or Old Apostolic Lutheran Church. Since there is so much variation among the Laestadian congregations, it is difficult to make generalizations about the movement as a whole. They do tend toward a very conservative personal and social morality, however, and some of the smaller congregations adopted a strict separation of their members from the world, much along the lines of the Amish. It is difficult to know for certain, but some estimates suggest that the Laestadians in America number around twenty-five to thirty thousand. Recent immigration from Finland has resulted in the formation of a few new Finnish-language ministries scattered around the United States.

See also Finland; Laestadius, Lars Levi; Lutheran Church in America

Bibliography

Heikkinen, J. *The Story of the Suomi Synod: The Finnish Evangelical Lutheran Church of America, 1890–1962.* [J. W. Heikkinen] / Parta Printers, 1985; Jalkanen, R. J., ed. *The Faith of the Finns: Historical Perspectives on the Finnish Evangelical Lutheran Church in America.* Michigan State University Press, 1972; Kortekangas, P., and A. Lepisto, eds. *The Faith of the Finns on a New Continent.* [LCA, Suomi Conference] 2000; Kulla, C. *The Journey of an Immigrant Awakening Movement in America and A Brief History of Laestadianism and the Apostolic Lutheran Church.* Carl A. Kulla, 2004.

MARK A. GRANQUIST

Finnish Interpretation of Luther

In the last several decades, Tuomo Mannermaa, professor of ecumenical theology at Helsinki, and his students have proposed a paradigm shift in reading Luther's theology of salvation and justification. Criticizing German Luther research, such as that of Adolf von Harnack and Albrecht Ritschl, which dominated the theological landscape in the nineteenth and twentieth centuries, and with a desire to honor recent ecumenical dialogues, Finnish scholars have renewed the study of Luther's doctrine of justification by accentuating the effective dimension of righteousness as Christ's indwelling in believers, in opposition to an extrinsic or forensic approach and as a promising ecumenical lead.

Since the 1970s and 1980s, Finnish Luther scholars have further tested and developed the original arguments made by Tuomo Mannermaa. In his study of Luther's *Lectures on Galatians* (1535), Mannermaa argued that previous interpretations overemphasized the declarative or forensic aspect of justification at the expense of the renewal of one's being (as "real-ontic") that occurs when, through faith, Christ is present in the believer. In the "happy exchange," which Mannermaa sees as the basis of justification, the believer is united with Christ in all his fullness, receiving all that is Christ's, and in contrast, Christ becomes the "greatest sinner" (*maximus peccator*), absorbing the believer's sin and guilt. The fullness of this gift of justification, in which Christ is both the believer's favor and gift, includes not only a declaration of forgiveness but also an effective dimension of being made holy with Christ's righteousness. Because the oneness between Christ and the believer is ontic, affecting the being of the believer, Luther's view of justification can be understood as "deification" or "divination," similar to how salvation was understood by some early Greek church fathers.

The concepts "ontological" and "reality" have been at the center of Mannermaa's critical investigations and arguments. The decisive questions arising from Mannermaa's thesis include specific theological and spiritual dimensions: (1) What does it mean in real life that Christ justifies by faith? (2) What does "salvation" entail both before God (*coram Deo*) and before humanity (*coram hominibus*)? Mannermaa's thesis has likewise sparked discussion about how Lutheran theology connects with patristic and Eastern Orthodox traditions, specifically about how believers are being made like God due to their oneness with Christ.

Mannermaa's work arose from a specific context: the 1973–74 Ecumenical Council of Churches Conference in Bangkok, Thailand, whose theme was "Salvation Today," and the ensuing bilateral discussions between the Russian Orthodox Church and the Evangelical Lutheran Church of Finland (1974 and 1977, Kiev). Mannermaa was charged with the task of reexamining Luther's and the Lutheran confessions' position on salvation. With his Eastern Orthodox conversation partners in mind, Mannermaa began to explore the curious relationship between the Lutheran doctrine of justification as oneness with Christ in faith and the patristic doctrine of divinization (*theōsis*) as human beings' participation in God. In his 1978 book *In ipsa fide Christus adest*, a study of Luther's 1535 *Lectures on Galatians*, Mannermaa asserted that Luther's understanding of the doctrine of justification differed essentially from both Melanchthon and the Formula of Concord, which favored a forensic and judicial aspect of justification at the expense of the equally essential indwelling of Christ "in us." In the aftermath of the Osiandrian controversy and with the dominant Melanchthonian view, the authors of the Lutheran confessions had forgotten the centrality that Luther affirmed for the indwelling of Christ in faith. Mannermaa continued his argument with *Two Kinds of Love: Martin Luther's Religious World*, which defended Luther's interpretation of the faith-love connection in opposition to the Scholastic notion of "faith formed by love" (*fides caritate formata*) and love as a "unitive power" (*vis unitiva*). Commenting on the Heidelberg Disputation (1518), Mannermaa examined Luther's theology of the cross and God's creative love that makes what is "nothing" (cf. 1 Cor. 1:28) to be beautiful and pleasing to God.

Mannermaa's work is the centerpiece among the plethora of studies published from the Department of Theological Studies at the University of Helsinki, by its sister faculties at the Eastern University of Finland (Joensuu) and Turku University, and by individuals around the world. In addition to the historical connections between the Finnish Luther scholars and the Institut für Europäische Geschichte at Mainz and the Luther-Akademie at Ratzeburg, new global connections have evolved, especially among North Americans. Much of the work so far has been in systematic and historical analysis and in philosophical theology and ethics. In the Finnish approach, doctrinal, systematic, ecumenical, and historical theologies are typically interwoven. Feminist scholarship and reconstructive theological work with Luther are areas of expansion for the next phase, with the contribution of international scholars and increased involvement of women.

In addition to Mannermaa's foundational works, several others have contributed in fundamental ways in building the Finnish Luther research. Of greatest import is Juhani Forsberg, who in 1984 published a foundational study on Luther's theology that highlighted Abraham as the central Old Testament figure and the paradigm for the gospel. In his *Das Abrahambild in der Theologie Luthers: Pater fidei sanctissimus*, Forsberg argued that Luther considered justification as the new creation in righteousness-making and that the forensic approach has only marginal significance. The doctrine of justification that emerges in Luther's late *Lectures on Genesis* matches that of his Galatians commentary: both underscore the gift of justification as bringing the sinner into a new reality of being (*Seinswirklichkeit*), which can only be received via God's self-revelation under the form of the opposite (*sub contaria specie*).

The next collaborative work for the Mannermaa thesis comes from Eero Huovinen, formerly professor of dogmatics in Helsinki. *Wirklichkeitsrealismus* (reality realism), characteristic of Mannermaa's work, is evident in Huovinen's analysis of Luther's understanding of the original state of humankind in creation and after the fall in Luther's *Lectures on Genesis*. In his study of Luther's theology of death as a central ecumenical problem (*Kuolemattomuudesta osallinen: Martti Lutherin kuoleman teologian ekumeeninen perusongelma*, 1987), Huovinen concluded that for Luther, human beings as images of God enjoyed immortality as participation in the divine life and in a "real-ontic" relationship between God and human beings. Through Christ, human beings would participate in godly life even with original sin. In his *Fides infantium: Martin Luthers Lehre vom Kinderglauben* (1997), Huovinen wrote about Luther's radical idea of infant's faith, *fides infantium*, with the doctrine of *duplex iustitia* and the idea of *fides infusa*: an infant's faith effects an ontic participation in God and begins the "second kind of righteousness," in addition to receiving a *character indelebilis* effected by baptism.

Risto Saarinen, Mannermaa's successor in Helsinki, further developed Mannermaa's criticism of German Luther research (Ritschl, von Harnack, Wilhelm Herrmann), with its artificial divisions between being and nature or between religion and ethics. Specifying the nature of the "real-ontological" for Luther, Saarinen positioned the God-human relation in mainly ethical terms, affirming the will's necessary reorientation in accordance to the divine will. With Barth, Luther's theology was misunderstood as "actual" or "existential-theological," with the word "ontological" characterizing the "relations" between persons. Countering neo-Protestant tendencies, Saarinen made a case for Luther's "substance thinking" (*Substanzdenken*) and "effect thinking" (*Wirkungsdenken*). Saarinen's *Gottes Wirken auf uns: Die transzendentale Deutung des Gegenwart-Christi-Motivs in der Lutherforschung* (1989) and ensuing research has been ecumenically important in clarifying where the actual differences between Protestant and Roman Catholic views exist in Luther's theology.

Simo Peura, a long-term collaborator and assistant with Mannermaa, wrote the most provocative thesis on Luther's concept of divinization (German: *Vergöttlichung*; Greek: *theōsis*; Latin: *deificatio*): *Mehr als ein Mensch? Die Vergöttlichung als Thema der Theologie Martin Luthers von 1513 bis 1519* (1994). Peura analyzed the use of "divinization" in Luther's texts from 1513 to 1519 in three parts: (1) divinization as a spiritual birth in us (texts from 1513–16); (2) divinization in the context of justification and God's love (the Romans commentary); and (3) a synthesis-analysis of the different instances of Luther's use of the term "divinization" (1517–19 texts). On the basis of *theologia crucis* (theology of the cross) and the idea of "participation," Peura proposes divination and *unio* as the cohesive principles for interpreting Luther's entire theology, which, akin to Mannermaa, he also approaches in "real-ontic" terms.

Sammeli Juntunen's dissertation *Der Begriff des Nichts bei Luther in den Jahren von 1510 bis 1523* (1996) surveys the earliest writings of Luther—in 1515–18 and 1519–23, particularly the Psalms lectures and the Heidelberg Disputation—and demonstrates that by *nihil* Luther meant that human beings existentially and ontologically depend on God. Indeed, humans receive new being by participating in Christ, who like them became "nothing." In a radical ontological change, where human beings become "Christ" in faith, their human nothingness is destroyed through the alien work of God (*opus alienum dei*), and with both spiritual and natural *esse*, the new creature (*nova creatura*) lives in a new reality of grace, which manifests also in external relations.

With respect to Luther's ethics, Antti Raunio, in his (University of Helsinki, 1993) dissertation *Summe des christlichen Lebens: Die "Goldene Regel" als Gesetz der Liebe in der Theologie Martin Luthers von 1510–1527* (2001), argues that for Luther the Golden Rule is more than an ethical or social-ethical maxim: it is pivotal for ordering and completing human beings' relation to God and other creatures.

Olli-Pekka Vainio's dissertation *Luterilaisen vanhurskauttamisopin kehitys Lutherista yksimielisyyden ohjeeseen* (The development of the Lutheran doctrine of justification from Luther to Formula of Concord) (University of Helsinki, 2004) targets the development of the justification doctrine from Luther to the Formula of Concord and marks a new stage in Finnish Luther research, which expands Mannermaa research beyond the figure of Luther. He verifies Mannermaa's original thesis by showing agreement among the sixteenth-century reformers on the effectiveness of faith in justification; indeed, the "reality of faith" (*Wirklichkeit des Glaubens* or *forma fidei*) is arguably the most distinctive Lutheran teaching of justification. Likewise, the late Eeva Martikainen wrote on Luther's understanding of doctrine, *Oppi—metafysiikkaa vai teologiaa? Lutherin käsitys opista* (Doctrine—metaphysics or theology? Luther's notion of doctrine) (University of Helsinki, 1987; in German, 1992), and Anja Ghiselli studied the Virgin Mary, *Sanan kantaja: Martti Lutherin käsitys Neitsyt Mariasta* (Bearer of the Word: Martin Luther's understanding of the Virgin Mary) (University of Helsinki, 2005).

Any description of the uniqueness of Finnish Luther scholarship must recognize the contribution of the sixteenth-century reformer Mikael Agricola, a student of Luther and Melanchthon, a schoolmaster, bishop, and scholar who led the Reformation in Finland during the reign of the Swedish king Gustav Wasa and labored to translate Luther's works into written Finnish, newly crafted by Agricola. Since Agricola's days, Luther has prevailed as the focus of Finnish theological study, while study of the Lutheran confessional writings or the other reformers has been secondary. This investment in Luther shows in the theology curriculum in Helsinki, where Luther continues to play a central role. It is not a coincidence that Finland produces a significant, steady number of new Luther scholars.

See also Finland; Jenson, Robert W.; Justification; Luther Interpretation and Reception; Mannermaa, Tuomo; Osiander, Andreas

Bibliography

Forsberg, J. *Das Abrahambild in der Theologie Luthers: Pater fidei sanctissimus*. Steiner, 1984; Huovinen, E. *Fides infantium: Martin Luthers Lehre vom Kinderglauben*. Von Zabern, 1997; Juntunen, S. *Der Begriff des Nichts bei Luther in den Jahren von 1510 bis 1523*. Luther-Agricola-Gesellschaft, 1996; Mannermaa, T. Finnish: *In Ipsa Fide Christus Adest*. Missiologian ja Ekumeniikan Seura, 1979. German: *Der im Glauben gegenwärtige Christus: Rechtfertigung und Vergottung*. Lutherisches Verlagshaus, 1989; ET: *Christ Present in Faith: Luther's View of Justification*. Trans. K. Stjerna. Fortress, 2005; Mannermaa, T. Finnish: *Kaksi Rakkautta: Johdatus Martin Lutherin Uskonmaailmaan*. Söderström, 1983; ET: *Two Kinds of Love: Martin Luther's Religious World*. Trans. K. Stjerna. Fortress, 2010; Martikainen, E. *Doctrina: Studien zu Luthers Begriff der Lehre*. Luther-Agricola-Gesellschaft, 1992; Peura, S. *Mehr als ein Mensch? Die Vergöttlichung als Thema der Theologie Martin Luthers von 1513 bis 1519*. Von Zabern, 1994; Raunio, A. *Summe des christlichen Lebens: Die "Goldene Regel" als Gesetz der Liebe in der Theologie Martin Luthers von 1510 bis 1527*. Von Zabern, 2001; Saarinen, R. *Gottes Wirken auf uns: Die transzendentale Deutung des Gegenwart-Christi-Motivs in der Lutherforschung*. Steiner, 1989; Vainio, O.-P. *Justification and Participation in Christ: The Development of the Lutheran Doctrine of Justification from Luther to the Formula of Concord (1580)*. Brill, 2008.

KIRSI STJERNA

Flacius, Matthias Illyricus, and the Flacians

As a second-generation Lutheran reformer, church historian, and Hebraist, Matthias

Illyricus Flacius (1520–75) was a prolific author of theological texts. Born in Albona (Labin) on the Venetian-controlled portion of the Istrian Peninsula, Flacius began his educational journey in Venice, where he was trained in Renaissance humanism and classical languages. During his three-year stay in the city of canals, he developed an interest in theology. Upon the recommendation of his relative the Franciscan friar Baldo Lupetina, who was later tried and executed in 1556 for his Protestant beliefs, Flacius decided to pursue further studies north of the Alps. He first went to Augsburg, then to Basel in 1539, where he enrolled at the university, and to Tübingen the following year.

Flacius came to study at the University of Wittenberg in 1541, where among his professors were Martin Luther and Philip Melanchthon. At first he experienced an existential crisis in the epicenter of Lutheranism, plagued by doubt and homesickness, but after Luther reached out to him in a personal meeting, young Flacius had a breakthrough and credited the reformer with helping him rediscover his faith and find hope. In 1544 Flacius received a position teaching Hebrew at the university. The next year he married a pastor's daughter from the vicinity of Wittenberg. In 1546 he graduated with a master of arts degree as the best in his class of thirty-nine students. During the Smalcald War he left the city and fled first to Braunschweig. His first child, Matthias Jr., was born there and later became a professor at the University in Rostock.

After a brief return to Wittenberg, the family eventually moved to Magdeburg in 1549, where Flacius emerged as a vocal leader of the opposition to the Augsburg Interim and a decisive critic of the Leipzig Proposal of 1548 (the so-called Leizpig Interim) and its stance on adiaphora. He also became the unofficial leader of the so-called Gnesio-Lutheran group of theologians and pastors who disagreed with the post-Luther Wittenberg leadership of the Evangelical church. Flacius's seven-year stay in the city marked a professionally very productive period. He published numerous leaflets and pamphlets against both "Interims" and wrote several works on a wide range of theological issues. Most of these stemmed from his involvement in intra-Protestant polemics with Andreas Osiander on justification; with Caspar von Schwenckfeld concerning biblical interpretation, anthropology, and the sacraments; and with Georg Major regarding the role of good works in salvation, among other issues. Additionally Flacius worked on two major projects in church history. The *Catalogus testium veritatis* listed witnesses to the truth (individuals and groups of Christians, who in Flacius's view stayed true to biblical Christianity and independent of Rome) throughout the ages. The so-called *Magdeburg Centuries* was a groundbreaking undertaking at Flacius's initiative. The thirteen thick folio volumes, implemented by a group of Lutheran scholars, aimed to provide a Protestant perspective for a detailed history of the Christian church from its birth onward.

In early 1557 Flacius accepted a professorial position in New Testament at the University of Jena, along with a high-ranking role in the hierarchy of the church on the Ernestinian territories. As a result of a theological disagreement with his faculty colleague Viktorin Strigel on the role of free will in a person's conversion, Flacius had to articulate his positions publicly at the Weimar Disputation in 1560. In connection to the debate, he spoke about original sin and made the controversial statement that sin is the substance of the human being (although it is questionable whether he meant this to have the ontological consequences his opponents accused him of). Eventually he was dismissed from the university in December 1561. He left Jena for Regensburg, where his friend Nikolaus Gallus was superintendent of the church.

In 1564 his wife Elisabeth née Faust died. Flacius, who was also experiencing serious health problems, married Magdalena Ilbeck that same year. While in Regensburg, Flacius composed his most significant hermeneutical publication, *Clavis Scripturae Sacrae* (Key to the sacred Scripture), a systematic reference work for interpreting the Bible. At the same time, he was trying to clear his name of accusations coming from Jena and even petitioned Emperor Maximilian II to call a general synod together, where Flacius could explain his theological positions and thus—he was hoping—be rehabilitated. As it was, even the city of Regensburg placed restrictions on his activities, such as a prohibition on holding public speeches or printing anything in the city.

An invitation to Antwerp in 1566 allowed Flacius to escape his increasingly threatened existence. At Antwerp, however, he advised the Lutheran Church in theological and organizational matters and was principal author of the church order and confession, and so his stay was short: he was forced to leave the city in the spring of 1567 due to the encroaching Spanish (Catholic) forces. The city of Strasbourg offered refuge to Flacius and his family on condition that he stay out of theological controversies, but Flacius still became involved in new disputes, among them with Jakob Andreae of nearby Württemberg. This resulted in the city council revoking his permit of residence in 1573. Flacius spent much of the remainder of his life without the security of a place he could call home. His last refuge was in a cloister in Frankfurt am Main, where he died in March 1575.

Although much of modern scholarship has focused on Flacius's controversial position concerning original sin and on his polemics, his theological legacy is significantly broader and must be considered within the political and ecclesiastical developments of his day and in the increasingly confessionalized landscape of post-Luther Protestantism in the mid-sixteenth century. Flacius was influenced by both Luther and Melanchthon. On the one hand he was trying to preserve Luther's emphasis on human brokenness in his theological anthropology, which he feared was being threatened after the reformer's death. On the other hand, humanistic and specifically Melanchthonian principles and methods are observable in many of his writings.

Flacius published more than two hundred works during his lifetime as an author and editor. In addition to his contributions to church history (*Catalogus* and the *Centuries*) and biblical hermeneutics (*Clavis* and his master's thesis from Wittenberg, *De vocabulo fidei*, 1549; 2nd ed., 1555; 3rd ed., 1563), he also produced major exegetical and homiletic works that reflected his outstanding knowledge of Greek and Hebrew, among them *Glossa compendiaria* of the New Testament (1570). He also published more philosophical works, such as *Paralipomena dialectices* and *Gnōthi seauton* (*Know yourself!*). His vast correspondence with contemporaries of diverse walks of life reflects his broad range of scholarly interests and the widespread network of correspondents he had built up across the continent. Additionally, he authored countless dedications of his works to emperors, kings, territorial rulers, city mayors, and theologians. He did this in the hopes of gaining their favor or other forms of support, including financial provision.

Throughout his career Flacius considered it important to bring the ideas of the Lutheran Reformation to fellow speakers of south Slavic languages, who were facing the double threat of ecclesiastical control from Rome and the spread of the Ottoman Turkish Empire. For this purpose he maintained contact with other Lutherans from southeastern Europe and planned to establish academies in Regensburg and in Klagenfurt to provide theological training for students from the Balkan Peninsula.

Flacius's uncompromising stances earned him not only numerous enemies but also a group of followers. Among prominent Flacians were Cyriacus Spangenberg and Christoph Irenaeus. Flacians must be distinguished from other Gnesio-Lutherans, some of whom initially supported Flacius but later abandoned him, such as Tilemann Hesshus and Johann Wigand. In contrast, Flacians followed their leader's theological emphasis on original sin even after Flacius's death, and they refused to sign the Formula of Concord because of its rejection of Flacius's stance on human depravity in article 1, facing persecution as a result. Several Flacians found refuge in the Austrian territories as *exules Christi* (exiles of Christ), where they became increasingly radicalized and, as a result, more and more isolated, yet managed to survive into the early seventeenth century.

See also Atonement; Exile; Mörlin, Joachim; Schwenckfeld, Caspar von; Strigel, Viktorin; Wigand, Johann; Wittenberg Circle, Parties within

Bibliography

Bollbuck, H. *Wahrheitszeugnis, Gottes Auftrag und Zeitkritik: Die Kirchengeschichte der Magdeburger Zenturien und ihre Arbeitstechniken.* Harrassowitz, 2014; http://www.controversia-et-confessio.de; Dingel, I. *Concordia Controversa.* Gütersloher Verlagshaus, 1996; Gehrt, D. *Bekenntnisbildung, Herrschaftskonsolidierung und dynastische Identitätsstiftung vom Augsburger Interim 1548 bis zur Konkordienformel 1577.* Evangelische Verlagsanstalt, 2011; Hartmann, M. *Humanismus und Kirchenkritik: Matthias Flacius Illyricus als Erforscher des Mittelalters.* Thorbecke, 2001; Ilić, L. "Matthias Flacius Illyricus (1520–1575)." In *Das Reformatorenlexikon*, ed. I. Dingel and V. Leppin, 116–22. Wissenschaftliche Buchgesellschaft, 2014; Ilić, L. *Theologian of Sin and Grace: The Process of Radicalization in the Theology of Matthias Flacius Illyricus.* Vandenhoeck & Ruprecht, 2014; http://www.mat-flacius.com; Olson, O. K. *Matthias Flacius and the Survival of Luther's Reform.* Harrassowitz, 2002; Preger, W. *Matthias Flacius Illyricus und seine Zeit.* 2 vols. Bläsing, 1859–61. Reprint, Olms, 1964.

LUKA ILIĆ

Fliedner, Theodore

The German Lutheran pastor and father of the modern deaconess movement, Theodore Fliedner (1800–1864), was born in Eppstein, Germany, and was parish pastor at Kaiserwerth near Düsseldorf. On trips to Holland and England in search of financial support for his struggling parish, he encountered Moravian deaconesses and was impressed by their work. He began a prison ministry in Düsseldorf in 1825, and in 1833 opened a home for released women prisoners; two years later he began a nursing school. These various social ministries led him to believe that a reinstitution of the ancient office of deaconess would be a salutary thing; with the help of his wife, Frederike (née Münster), he opened a deaconess training institute in Kaiserswerth in 1836, with Frederike

serving as "mother superior." After her death in 1842, Fliedner married Karolina Bertheau, who stepped into the leadership role at the institute. Fliedner resigned from the parish in 1849 to devote full attention to the deaconess program. His promotion of the concept led to the establishment of deaconess work not just in Germany but also in many other countries. By the time of his death, there were some sixteen hundred deaconesses serving in more than four hundred locations in Europe, America, and the Middle East.

See also Deaconesses; Lutheran Social Services

Bibliography

Golder, C. *History of the Deaconess Movement.* Jennings & Pye, 1903; Wentz, A. R. *Fliedner the Faithful.* Board of Publication of the United Lutheran Church in America, 1936.

RICHARD O. JOHNSON

Flierl, Johann

In Papua New Guinea, Johann Flierl (1858–1947) is remembered and revered as "Senior Flierl" (or sometimes simply as "Senior") for his courageous and fruitful work as the pioneer Lutheran missionary. Flierl trained at the mission seminary in Neuendettelsau and as a twenty-year-old graduate volunteered when a call came for a missionary to serve among the Dieri people in the Outback of southern Australia. He was ordained at Tanunda and soon revitalized the mission by rapidly learning the language, rebuilding the mission, and faithfully catechizing the people. During this time he married Louise Auricht, a woman who then served with him for years. After seven years Flierl sought to go to New Guinea when he heard that Germany was becoming involved there. While waiting in northern Queensland for permission to enter the country, he began a new work among the Aboriginal people there, a work that has endured to the present under the name Hope Vale. Flierl arrived at Finschhafen on July 12, 1886, a day that Lutherans in New Guinea commemorate every year. Flierl and his colleague Tremmel were physically attacked when they erected their first camp at Simbang village. The mission was a labor of great patience—thirteen years before the first baptism—but it flourished in many important ways. Flierl was a missionary of the Loehe (Löhe)-Neuendettelsau tradition and saw to it that catechization was founded on the Bible and Luther's Small Catechism and that indigenous liturgy and church life were based on sound Lutheran practice.

See also Australian Aboriginal People; Mission and Evangelism; Papua New Guinea

Bibliography
Flierl, J. My Life and God's Mission. Open Book Publishers, 1999; Wagner, H., and H. Reiner, eds. The Lutheran Church in Papua New Guinea: The First Hundred Years, 1886–1986. Lutheran Publishing House, 1986.

DEAN ZWECK

Forde, Gerhard

As professor of systematic theology at Luther Seminary, St. Paul, Minnesota, Gerhard Forde's (1927–2005) early work dealt with the nineteenth-century rediscovery of how Luther made central the law-and-gospel distinction, the theology of the cross, and the bound will. Vital to Forde's teaching is the theology of the cross (theologia crucis), found in Luther's Heidelberg Disputation (1518), which Luther contrasts with the theology of glory (theologia gloriae). The theology of the cross recognizes that there is no program (a theology of glory) by which sinners can be improved. God's answer for sinners is to execute his wrath upon them, kill them as sinners (God's alien work), but only for the purpose of raising them to a new life of faith (God's proper work). The upshot of Forde's overall contribution to theology is to claim that theology's primary purpose is for proclamation of both the law, which accuses sinners to death, and also the gospel, which liberates them for new life; it is not for metaphysical speculation, the cultivation of piety, or the execution of ethical agendas. Only proclamation of the law and the gospel can free human wills, which are captivated by self-justification.

Outside of Christ, for Forde as for Luther, God remains hidden from us (the deus absconditus), and humans have no security with respect to their status with God. Proclamation alone secures humanity's place before God. The law "does God" to humans, crucifies old beings by rendering the verdict of guilt on them. In a close reading of the Gospels, Forde claims that it is human self-righteousness that condemns Jesus to death; it is a defense against Jesus, who mercifully offered forgiveness to sinners. Like the Pharisees, humans mask their self-righteousness through their good deeds. Human "goodness" thereby proves to be nothing other than an expression of such self-righteousness. Humans cannot presume that their good deeds secure their ranking with God. Only faith (and not works) honors God's divinity.

Proclamation of the gospel is crucial because apart from it we encounter God only as hidden and wrathful. God's accusing law exposes human self-righteousness as the desire to serve as one's own god for oneself, manage one's own life, and avoid one's creatureliness. Only the word of absolution, God's unconditional forgiveness, proclaimed to terrified consciences, can liberate people from the tyranny of self-righteousness. Hence, Forde—following Luther—diverges from the perspective that the Christian life is a transition from sin to virtue. Instead, it is a transition from virtue to grace. For Forde, unlike the Enlightenment, the fulcrum for understanding the human condition is not heteronomy versus autonomy but instead the captivated will distortedly bound to assert itself versus the will liberated from such self-centeredness and self-righteousness. As liberated, humans live in faith as forgiven creatures appreciative of God's good creation. Thereby humans are truly human and can be coworkers with God in God's good creation.

See also Free Will; Law, Uses of the; Luther Interpretation and Reception; Theology of the Cross

Bibliography
Forde, G. Justification by Faith—A Matter of Death and Life. Fortress, 1983; Forde, G. A More Radical Gospel:

Essays on Eschatology, Authority, Atonement, and Ecumenism. Ed. M. Mattes and S. Paulson. Eerdmans, 2004; Forde, G. *On Being a Theologian of the Cross.* Eerdmans, 1997; Forde, G. *The Preached God: Proclamation in Word and Sacrament.* Ed. M. Mattes and S. Paulson. Eerdmans, 2007; Forde, G. *Theology Is for Proclamation.* Augsburg Fortress, 1990.

MARK C. MATTES

Formula of Concord

The final Lutheran confession of the sixteenth century is called the Formula of Concord. After repeated unsuccessful attempts to settle disputes over the proper definition of various elements of Luther's teaching and related practices (1548–70), the effort launched in 1573 by Jakob Andreae at the behest of his prince, Duke Christoph of Württemberg, resulted in the Formula of Concord. The document brought together two-thirds of German Lutheran churches (1577) and today serves many Lutheran churches throughout the world as a standard of teaching. Andreae's "Six Christian Sermons on the Divisions among the Theologians of the Augsburg Confession" (1573) was revised first by Andreae himself (Swabian Concord, 1574), then by north German theologians, led by Martin Chemnitz and David Chytraeus (Swabian-Saxon Concord, 1575). These drafts were integrated with the Maulbronn Formula, composed by theologians from Württemberg, Baden, and Henneberg (1576), to produce the text of the *Torgau Book* (1576). This book was composed by a committee organized by the Electoral Saxon government of Elector August, led by Andreae (Württemberg), Chemnitz (Braunschweig), Chytraeus (Mecklenburg), Nikolaus Selnecker (Electoral Saxony), Andreas Musculus (Electoral Brandenburg), and Christoph Körner (Electoral Brandenburg). Sent to the ministeria of all German Evangelical lands and cities, this book elicited criticism from many, on the basis of which the committee further revised the *Torgau Book* into the *Bergen Book*, the Solid Declaration of the Formula of Concord (1577). It also contained an "Epitome" of the *Torgau Book*, authored by Andreae, summarizing the main points of the Solid Declaration. The Formula was first published in the Book of Concord (1580). The Formula contains treatments settling disputes on original sin, freedom of the human will, justification by faith, good works, the distinction of law and gospel, the third use of the law, the Lord's Supper, Christology, Christ's descent into hell, adiaphora, and election, as well as rejection of teachings of Anabaptists, Schwenkfelder, and antitrinitarians. Chemnitz, Chytraeus, and Andreae each contributed more than one-quarter of the final text of the Solid Declaration; material from the Maulbroon Formula and revisions at Bergen and Torgau constitute the rest. The Formula of Concord largely sided with Gnesio-Lutheran positions while striving to honor the concerns of the Philippists and others. Opposition within Evangelical ranks came chiefly from adherents of Matthias Flacius's doctrine of original sin and supporters of a spiritualizing interpretation of the Lord's Supper and a Christology similar or identical to Calvin's.

See also Andreae, Jakob; Book of Concord; Chemnitz, Martin; Chytraeus, David; Flacius, Matthias Illyricus, and the Flacians; Musculus, Andreas; Wittenberg Circle, Parties within; Württemberg

Bibliography
Arand, C., R. Kolb, and J. Nestingen, eds. *The Lutheran Confessions: History and Theology of The Book of Concord.* Fortress, 2012; Dingel, I., ed. *Die Bekenntnisschriften der evangelisch-lutherische Kirche.* Vandenhoeck & Ruprecht, 1998; Dingel, I., ed. *Controversia et Confessio: Theologische Kontroversen 1548–1577/80.* Kritische Auswahl ed. Vandenhoeck & Ruprecht, 2010; Gassmann, G., and S. Hendrix. *Fortress Introduction to the Lutheran Confessions.* Fortress, 1999; Jacobs, H. E. *The Book of Concord.* Vol. 2, *Historical Introduction, Appendixes, and Indexes.* G. W. Frederick, 1882; Kolb, R., and J. Nestingen, eds. *Sources and Contexts of the Book of Concord.* Fortress, 2001.

ROBERT KOLB

France

The origins of the French Reformation arouse controversy, particularly regarding how much influence Martin Luther and the German Reformations had on France. Few would claim that only Luther was the founder of the French Reformation, nor would they credit alone the Swiss reformer Ulrich Zwingli. Others point to international phenomena such as the humanism prevailing in many early modern universities or to Frenchmen who predated or overlapped with Luther, such as the humanist Jacques Lefèvre d'Étaples (Latin: Faber Stapulensis; ca. 1455–1536) or the reforming French bishop Guillaume Briçonnet (ca. 1470–1534).

Nevertheless, Luther clearly influenced France and the French Reformation. "Justification by faith" was central to the Reformation in France. French translations of Luther's writings were published and circulated. Luther was well-enough known in France by 1521 for the Catholic theologians of the Sorbonne (the University of Paris) to condemn him and order his books burned. Those whom Catholics considered heretical in the 1520s and later were often labeled "Lutheran" even if they had nothing to do with Luther or the Lutheran Reformation and were followers of non-Lutheran reformers such as Zwingli or of no one in particular. This fact and others—for example, (1) Lutheranism never became an established state church in France; (2) beliefs such as justification by faith could easily have been transmitted to France by non-Lutheran reformers such as John Calvin (1509–64), who accepted Luther's theology in the main; and (3) the first clearly Reformed congregations in France were not recognized as established until 1555—muddy any analysis of Luther's and Lutheran influence in France. In addition, Lutheran congregations were not established in France during the first half of the sixteenth century except in regions that were not yet a part of modern-day France, namely, Alsace and Montbéliard (of the German duchy of Württemberg).

Thus the French of the first half of the sixteenth century who were sympathetic to the Reformation were typically of undefined confessional status. The confessionalization of the latter sixteenth century would encourage them to identify as either Catholic or Reformed, but in the first half of the sixteenth century people from diverse levels of society, both clergy and lay, had reforming ideas although they had no organized movement to be a part of other than the Catholic Church. Some of the laypeople engaged in trade and commerce, in the crafts, or in what the French call the "liberal professions" (teachers, lawyers, and public servants). Some laborers and farmers met together in groups for prayer, Bible study, and eventually Psalm singing, especially where the Bible had been made available in the French language, such as in the diocese of Meaux (just east of Paris), where Guillaume Briçonnet had for a time promoted preaching in the vernacular and the translation and distribution of Bibles in the French language. At French universities, some professors were sympathetic to reform in the Catholic Church. Typically these men were teaching the humanities in some of the provincial universities (outside of Paris), such as at the University of Orléans, where Calvin and Theodore Beza (1519–1605) studied. King Francis I's sister, Marguerite of Angoulême (1492–1549), appreciated Luther and provided protection from persecution to some notable early French reformers and to preachers in exile from the diocese of Meaux after Briçonnet repressed their preaching (in 1523) under pressure from the Franciscans and the Catholic theologians of the Sorbonne, who did not condone his lay preachers and Bibles in the vernacular.

All this activity attests to France being fertile ground for an organized reformation in the first half of the sixteenth century, but the French had to wait for the second half of the century. When an organized French Reformation did come, it originated outside France, engineered by Frenchmen who had fled France in the face of persecution under French Kings Francis I (r. 1515–47) and Henry II (r. 1547–59). Premiere among these early French expatriate reformers was John Calvin, born in Noyon, France, and educated in universities in Paris and in the French provinces. Calvin experienced a conversion but gave it no date. He fled France after the Affair of the Placards of October 18, 1534, when posters criticizing the Catholic Mass infuriated Francis I, who subsequently increased persecution of those whom he considered heretical. Calvin landed in Basel and wrote his *Institutes of the Christian Religion* (1st ed., 1536, with a lengthy dedication to Francis I), which would propel him to the leadership of the French Reformation. Calvin's opinions of Luther and the Lutheran Reformation would greatly influence other French reformers. His opinions of Luther were favorable, especially in these early years.

Calvin viewed himself and his generation of French reformers as continuing along the same reforming path as Luther and influenced by other reformers, especially Philip Melanchthon. By 1535–36 Geneva was experiencing a political revolution and a religious reformation. Genevans overthrew their prince-bishop from the duchy of Savoy (to the south) and became Protestant under the preaching of Guillaume Farel, a former lay preacher of Briçonnet's diocese. In late summer 1536, Farel persuaded Calvin to stay in Geneva to help with the solidification of Reformed practices. Both Calvin and Farel lasted there only two years, however, for they antagonized the Genevan city magistrates, who fired them as pastors, scattering Farel to Neuchâtel and Calvin to Strasbourg.

When Calvin arrived, Strasbourg (then a German-speaking part of the Holy Roman Empire) had accepted the Reformation. Having abolished the Mass in February 1529, Strasbourg reformers were on their own reforming tack, and in 1536 had signed the Wittenberg Concord, entailing agreement on the Lord's Supper with the Wittenberg reformers. Strasbourg also subscribed to the Augsburg Confession. Calvin appeared comfortable with this and had the confidence of the Strasbourg reformers. He lectured at Johannes Sturm's secondary school and attended international colloquies at Hagenau, Worms (1540), and Regensburg (1541), where he met and was befriended by Philip Melanchthon. Perhaps the best testimony to Calvin's relationship with Melanchthon is the testimonial Calvin made in his *Clear Explanation of Sound Doctrine concerning the True Partaking of the Flesh and Blood of Christ in the Holy Supper to Dissipate the Mists of Tileman Heshusius* (1561).

Calvin's years in Strasbourg (1538–41) made a solid impression and exposed him to a city that cooperated with the Wittenberg reformers and in which Lutheranism would eventually become established with subscription to the Formula of Concord in 1598. In 1541 Calvin was called back to Geneva and spent the next fourteen years overcoming opposition and solidifying the Reformation there. In 1555, finally, Calvin and his fellow French expatriates could concentrate more fully on the evangelization of France by an overt campaign of sending pastors and books in French (Bibles, Psalters, catechisms) into France via colporteurs. After his return to Geneva, Calvin's efforts were focused on making common cause with the leaders of the Reformed Reformation that proceeded from Zurich. Although Calvin and Zwingli did not share the same interpretation of the Lord's Supper, Zwingli's successor, Heinrich Bullinger, was more pliable. In 1549 he and Calvin agreed on the Consensus Tigurinus, including their understanding of the Lord's Supper. This agreement had the effect of shifting Calvin toward the position of Zurich on the Lord's Supper, separating Calvin and Geneva from accord with the Lutherans and from any hope of formal acceptance of the Augsburg Confession.

As time went on, leaders in the Reformed tradition rejected individuals who favored the Augsburg Confession, such as the French legal scholar Charles Du Moulin (1500–1566), while nevertheless often using the language and outline of that confession in their own works. At international ecumenical gatherings, such as the Colloquy of Poissy (1561), representatives of the Reformed (French, Genevan, Swiss, and Italian) would not accept any compromise with the Catholic representatives that involved subscribing to the Augsburg Confession or any confession that included the Lutheran position on the Lord's Supper. When the French cardinal of Lorraine suggested what appeared to be the Lutheran solution to the presence of Christ in the sacrament as a way toward agreement, the Reformed representatives backed off, but gingerly, since tiny Geneva and the Swiss and French Reformed needed the ongoing backing of the Germans in negotiations with the French king, such as those over the fate of imprisoned Reformed after a Reformed worship meeting was discovered and broken up in Paris in 1557.

In summary, although Calvin and Reformed Christians of Geneva, France, and Reformed Swiss cities admired and voiced support for Luther, their position on the Lord's Supper precluded accord between Lutherans and Reformed in the sixteenth century. Other differences existed. Reformed churches tended to hold strongly to "discipline," which was viewed in France and elsewhere in two ways: (1) as the organizational formation of Reformed churches in a hierarchy of representative bodies and synods, the members of which all adhered to commonly accepted confessions of faith; and (2) as an insistence on strict adherence to the Ten Commandments and concord within families and among Christians as well as obedience to customs that precluded dancing, ostentatious dress, and absence from church services as enforced through local consistories (committees consisting of pastors, elders, and sometimes deacons from the local congregations who could excommunicate church members).

Reformed congregations spread in France, whereas Lutherans in what is modern-day France tended to live in Alsace or Montbéliard (then ruled by the Lutheran Duke of Württemberg) or were from Swedish or German-speaking regions of Europe. In 1621 Lutherans were able to conduct a Lutheran worship service in the Swedish embassy chapel in Paris and apparently experienced no persecution. In 1626 Lutherans established the first Lutheran congregation in Paris. Professor Jonas Hambré was pastor and preached in Swedish and in German. A Reformed National Synod of 1631, meeting in Charenton (suburban Paris), invited Lutherans to Communion without renouncing their "special doctrine" concerning the sacrament. After the revocation of the Edict of Nantes in 1685, many Reformed Christians fled France to escape persecution; the few Lutherans, who worshiped in an embassy, apparently experienced no persecution. Swedes and Danes helped Reformed Christians in need and conducted baptisms and marriages for them. In the mid-eighteenth century the Danes formed a congregation at the Danish embassy. Full emancipation for Reformed and Lutheran alike came under Napoleon I, who granted freedom of worship and assigned to Lutherans (1806) and Reformed congregations (1802) church buildings already in existence. Lutheran churches in France, like the Reformed churches of the nineteenth century, engaged in inner mission work, founded a deaconess home, orphanages, schools, a hospital, a home for the elderly, a training school for servants, a Free Loans Society, a Society for Befriending Apprentices and Young Workers, a home for apprentices, and other charitable and educational work.

The geographical expansion of France—with the addition of Alsace and Montbéliard to the French monarchies, empires, and republics—added more Lutherans to France. Alsace and Montbéliard became centers of Lutheranism in France, with a sympathetic university faculty at Strasbourg. Alsace was lost to Germany after the end of the Franco-Prussian War (1871), but the Treaty of Versailles (1919) brought Alsace back into France.

Reformed and Lutheran churches, after a series of high-level discussions, came together in the Église protestante unie de France (United Protestant Church of France, 2013), headquartered in Paris. Significant is the struggle for survival of Protestant churches in the modern secular world. Only about 4 percent of France is Protestant. The membership of the Église protestante unie de France is about 400,000, with about 500 pastors (one-third of whom are women), and about 450 congregations.

See also Beza, Theodore; Bucer, Martin; Calvin, John; Geneva; Lord's Supper; Mömpelgaard/Mont-béliard Colloquy; Strasbourg; Zwingli, Ulrich

Bibliography

Calvin, J. *Clear Explanation of Sound Doctrine concerning the True Partaking of the Flesh and Blood of Christ in the Holy Supper to Dissipate the Mists of Tileman Heshusius* (1561). In *Calvin: Theological Treatises*, ed. J. K. S. Reid, 257–324. LCC 22. Westminster, 1954; Driancourt-Girod, J. *L'insolite histoire des luthériens de Paris de Louis XIII à Napoléon*. Albin Michel, 1992; Église évangélique luthérienne de France. *The French Evangelical Lutheran Church*. A. Tournon, 1918; Febvre, L. "The Origins of the French Reformation, a Badly-Put Question." In *A New Kind of History and Other Essays from the Writings of Lucien Febvre*, ed. P. Burke, 44–107. Trans. K. Folca. Harper & Row, 1973; Jundt, A. *Histoire résumée de l'Église luthérienne en France*. Église évangélique luthérienne, 1935; Kittelson, J. *Towards an Established Church: Strasbourg from 1500 to the Dawn of the Seventeenth Century*. Von Zabern, 2000; Lods, A. *L'Église Luthérienne de Paris pendant la Révolution et le chapelain Gambs*. Fischbacher, 1892; Pelikan, J., ed. *Interpreters of Luther: Essays in Honor of Wilhelm Pauck*. Fortress, 1968; Wackernagel, W. *The Lutheran Church in Paris: An Historical and Descriptive Sketch*. General Council Publication House, 1918; World Council of Churches. "United Protestant Church of France." http://www.oikoumene.org/en/member-churches/united-protestant-church-of-france.

JEANNINE OLSON

Francke, August Hermann

The theologian and educator August Hermann Francke (1663–1727) was a leading German Pietist. Francke's Foundations in Halle (*Franckesche Stiftungen*) and the Pietism that it promoted grew to have worldwide influence. Born in 1663 at Lübeck to Johannes Francke (1625–70) and Anna Gloxin (1635–1709), Francke moved with his family to Gotha, where at a young age he was introduced to the devotional writings of theologians like Johann Arndt (1555–1621) and Lewis Bayly (1575–1631). His intelligence and facility with languages led him to philological studies in Erfurt, Kiel, and Hamburg, and in 1685 the University of Leipzig conferred on him the master of arts degree. The following year Francke and Paul Anton (1661–1730) founded the Collegium Philobiblicum, a gathering of students interested in the academic study of biblical texts in their original languages. These meetings formed the basis of Francke's later conventicle work. In 1687 Francke translated Miguel de Molinos's (1628–96) *Guida spirituale* for an academic disputation on Quietism. The Italian mystic's ideas, along with a body of German and English devotional writings, helped pave the way for Francke's conversion experience.

In the fall of 1687, Francke traveled to Lüneburg, where he was to study Hebrew under the supervision of Caspar Hermann Sandhagen (1639–97). During preparation for a sermon on John 20:31, Francke began to question the nature of his own faith. He fell into a period of great spiritual turmoil, which culminated in doubt over the authority of Scripture and the existence of a personal God. This great despair, *Busskampf* (struggle of repentance), represented an important moment during which individuals are confronted with their sin and overcome with uncertainty regarding the state of their soul. Francke believed it would be preceded by spiritual trials (*Anfechtungen*) and followed by a "breakthrough," from which individuals were "reborn" into the family of God. Various theological voices were synthesized in his existential experience in Lüneburg. Francke's famous account has become the best-known conversion narrative of Pietism, and many consider it essential to interpreting his theology of conversion.

In 1688 Francke traveled to Hamburg, where he became involved with a circle of radical Pietists. Francke's early radical tendencies and incipient perfectionism became a flash point for his opponents, who accused him of holding unorthodox views. After two months with Philipp Jakob Spener (1635–1705) in Dresden, Francke returned to Leipzig in 1689. From this point onward, Francke considered Spener a spiritual father and remained in regular correspondence with him until the latter's death. He returned to lecturing at the university, but the content turned from philological studies toward personal application of biblical texts. Alongside the traditional law/gospel division of Scripture, Francke taught that biblical passages contain a "husk" and "kernel." The former encompassed the historical context while the latter signified Francke's belief that the text held a christocentric, spiritual significance that could only be rightly understood by the regenerate. Along with his lectures, Francke began holding private conventicle meetings (*collegia pietatis*) in the German language, during which men and women from the town would study the Scriptures. His university lectures attracted such a great number of students that other lecture halls began to empty, and suspicions arose among both the theological faculty and the city council concerning Francke's religious ideas. In 1689 the authorities conducted an investigation of his activity and teachings, but before his work in Leipzig was banned, Francke left the city. Through the help of his friend and later colleague in Halle, Joachim Justus Breithaupt (1658–1732), Francke was installed in Augustinian Church in Erfurt, where he immediately undertook a rigorous program of catechization, but as in Leipzig, fears and suspicions of Francke's Pietist ideas forced him to leave his post.

With the assistance of Spener, in 1691 Francke took up the pastorate at St. George Church in Glaucha, a poor community on the outskirts of Halle. He received a professorship of "oriental languages" at the university in Halle. In Glaucha, he began catechizing children, holding conventicles, and enforcing an unusually strict form of church discipline centered on participation in the Eucharist. Francke's connections to the court in Berlin allowed him to withstand the accusations and investigations mounted by Lutheran Orthodoxy against his Pietist activities. According to his own account, Francke received a donation of four taler and sixteen groschen in 1695 that allowed him to establish a ministry to street children. Francke's work began with a school for local poor children and quickly grew into an institution that housed schools for a wide range of children from various socioeconomic backgrounds, an orphanage, a printing press, an apothecary, a hospital, the first Bible institute, and the first organized Protestant mission. The Francke Foundations became a center for pedagogy, shaping the German educational system.

Francke became a professor of theology at the university in 1698; sixteen years later he was selected head pastor of the prominent Ulrich Church in Halle; along with King Fredrick William I's (1688–1740) visit to the institutes in 1713, these three moments signify the growing acceptance that Pietism found during the first decades of the eighteenth century (Wallmann 116). Francke's ideas were transmitted primarily through the publication of his sermons, commentaries, and reform and promotional writings. After his death in the summer of 1727, Francke's son Gotthilf August (1696–1769) and his assistant Johann Anastasius Freylinghausen (1670–1739) became directors of the foundations. Francke's institutes as an agent of Pietist ideas continued to have an important role in shaping Continental Protestantism throughout the eighteenth century.

See also Francke, Gotthilf August; Francke Foundations; Freylinghausen, Johann Anastasius; Hildebrand, Carl (Baron von Canstein); Pietism; Spener, Philipp Jakob

Bibliography

Albrect-Birkner, V. *Francke in Glaucha: Kehrseiten eines Klischees (1692–1704)*. Niemeyer, 2004; Brecht, M. "August Hermann Francke und der Hallische Pietismus." In *Geschichte des Pietismus*, vol. 1, *Der Pietismus vom siebzehnten bis zum frühen achtzehnten Jahrhundert*, ed. V. Albrect-Birkner, 440–527. Vandenhoeck & Ruprecht, 1993; Kramer, G. *August Hermann Francke: Ein Lebensbild*. 2 vols. Waisenhaus, 1880–82; Matthias, M. "August Hermann Francke (1663–1727)." In *The Pietist Theologians*, ed. C. Lindberg, 100–115. Blackwell, 2005; Matthias, M., ed. *Lebensläufe August Hermann Franckes*. Evangelische Verlagsanstalt, 1999; Peschke, E. *Bekehrung und Reform: Ansatz und Wurzeln der Theologie August Hermann Franckes*. Luther-Verlag, 1977; Peschke, E. *Studien zur Theologie August Hermann Franckes*. 2 vols. Evangelische Verlagsanstalt, 1964–66; Sattler, G. *God's Glory, Neighbor's Good: A Brief Introduction to the Life and Writings of August Hermann Francke*. Covenant, 1982; Wallmann, J. *Der Pietismus*. Vandenhoeck & Ruprecht, 2005.

PETER JAMES YODER

Francke, Gotthilf August

Director of the Francke Foundations (*Franckesche Stiftungen*) and theologian, Gotthilf

August Francke (1696–1769) was son of August Hermann Francke (1663–1727) and Anna Magdalena von Wurm (1670–1734). He reportedly had a conversion experience under his father's preaching in the summer of 1714, shortly after beginning his theological education in Halle. Francke finished his studies in Jena before returning in 1720 to Halle, where he eventually took up positions in the Market Church of Our Dear Lady and in the theological faculty of the university. He advanced through the ecclesial ranks, finally becoming a councillor in the consistory of the Duchy of Magdeburg in 1767.

After the death of his father in 1727, Francke became codirector, along with Johann Anastasius Freylinghausen (1670–1739), of the Francke Foundations. Under his leadership, the institutes established a global presence. He helped maintain the Danish-Halle Mission in India and established relations with Lutherans in North America through the organizing activity of Heinrich Melchior Mühlenberg (1711–87). Francke's work in editing and publishing missionary reports furthered Pietist networks in German territories. His efforts to preserve a relationship between the foundations and Frederick William I of Prussia allowed the foundations to place pastors in prominent positions throughout Brandenburg-Prussian territories. Successful at advancing the cause of "heartfelt" reform, Gotthilf August stands as an exemplar of the Prussian official identified with Halle Pietism.

See also Francke, August Hermann; Francke Foundations; Freylinghausen Johann Anastasius; Pietism

Bibliography

Francke, G. A., *Hertzliebe Mama: Briefe aus Jenaer Studientagen 1719–1720*. Ed. T. Müller and C. Wessel. Niemeyer, 1997; Sträter, U. "Gotthilf August Francke, der Sohn und Erbe: Annäherung an einen Unbekannten." In *Reformation und Neuzeit: 300 Jahre Theologie in Halle*, ed. U. Schnelle, 211–32. De Gruyter, 1994.

PETER JAMES YODER

Francke Foundations

The preeminent social and educational institution of Pietism, established by Lutheran theologian and pedagogue August Hermann Francke (1663–1727), is called the Francke Foundations. Francke came to Halle in 1692 as professor at the newly founded university and pastor in the suburb of Glaucha. As a committed Lutheran Pietist, he strove to achieve a comprehensive improvement of society through active piety. In many respects he took up ideas of Martin Luther, developed them further, and brought central, practical impulses of the Reformation to completion. He placed wide-reaching educational reforms at the center of his efforts. With a contribution from a private individual of four taler and sixteen groschen, he began his project in 1695. At first he brought needy children from the streets and provided them with school instruction, along with food and clothing; within a few years Francke had founded, in connection with the orphanage, a multilevel school system for boys and girls from all social classes. Known as the *Hallesches Waisenhaus* (Halle orphanage) or *Glauchasche Anstalten* (Glaucha [the village outside Halle where they were located] institutions) until the end of the eighteenth century, the founding of the Francke Foundations (*Franckesche Stiftungen*) dates to the charter issued by Elector Friedrich III of Brandenburg on September 19, 1698. This document confirmed Francke's initiatives as a public institution and provided it with extensive privileges, including tax benefits and real estate options, as well as permission to establish an apothecary, printshop, publishing house, and other commercial activities. Together with generous donations, these endeavors formed the economic basis of the foundations. The orphanage was the first building constructed, in 1698–1700, and by the mid-eighteenth century an entire school complex developed, with numerous spacious and functional structures including a library, a hospital, and farm buildings.

The institute's schools put into practice innovative pedagogical ideas based on a strict Christian education and a concern for the natural world. A characteristic mark was the goal of comprehensive general education that combined a broad range of specialties and emphasized practicality and demonstration. The system of modern secondary schools (*Realschulen*) that developed from this remains a part of German schooling today. The pupils received training appropriate to their individual talents. Social status played a secondary role, so that children from impoverished backgrounds could receive excellent education. Children from wealthy families paid tuition. Among others, Nikolaus Ludwig von Zinzendorf, founder of the Moravians, was educated here and influenced by Francke's ideas. Francke employed students as teachers, who in return received free board. In 1696 he founded the first teacher's college in Germany and contributed decisively to the professionalization of teaching.

After only a few years, the Francke Foundations had obtained great renown and drew increasing numbers. Early on it also became a center of global connections. Across Protestant Europe and in the corridors of European power from London and Copenhagen to St. Petersburg and Vienna, Francke's advocates sought to disseminate Halle's ideals and provide the Francke Foundations with the latest news, which made it into one of the best-informed places in Europe and at the same time into an intellectual center with extraordinary reach. The Protestant nobility played a key role. The Danish Church's sending of Bartholomäus Ziegenbalg to South India from Halle in 1706 marked the beginnings of the first standing Protestant mission to non-Christians. At the end of the seventeenth century, Francke had already established contacts in North America and corresponded with both Cotton Mather (1663–1728) and Lutherans and Moravians in Pennsylvania.

Together with Carl Hildebrand von Canstein, Francke in 1710 established the world's first Bible society as part of the foundations in order to realize the Reformation ideal of distributing the Bible in great numbers and making them affordable for everyone. Up

to the twentieth century, the Canstein Bible printshop produced over ten million copies of the Bible in a variety of languages. Shortly after August Hermann Francke's death in 1727, his student Johann Heinrich Callenberg (1694–1760) founded the Institutum Judaicum et Muhammedicum as the first Protestant mission to the Jews. At this time around 2,500 pupils attended the schools of the Francke Foundations. In addition, there were around 500 teachers, educators, and staff. The institute flourished, enjoyed immense prestige, and was economically successful. Francke's successors in the institution continued his vision. Relations to North America intensified, and in 1734, pastors from Halle accompanied Salzburg refugees to Georgia, where they settled. In 1742 Heinrich Melchior Mühlenberg became the first of many associates of the Francke Foundations to be sent to Pennsylvania. Halle supported their ecclesial work under the aegis of the Ministerium of Pennsylvania well into the nineteenth century.

From its inception there was close interaction between the Francke Foundations and the Prussian court. As a result of an economic decline at the end of the eighteenth century, the foundations became financially dependent on the Prussian royal family. In 1832 the foundations were attached to the Prussian school authorities, and in consequence flourished again, constructing four new impressive buildings before the outbreak of World War I. Until the end of World War II, the foundations retained their Christian character. In 1946 the foundations lost recognition as a legal entity and did not formally exist during the German Democratic Republic. The historic ensemble of buildings was badly neglected but remained completely intact. After German reunification, the Francke Foundations were revived as a public foundation. Since then, the complex of buildings, located on sixteen hectares in the center of Halle, has been extensively restored. Following the Christian tradition of Francke, the buildings today serve four thousand people in support of cultural, academic, social, and educational aims. The Francke Foundations today have a historic library, a vast archive, and an intact Baroque collection of natural history and artifacts. The Francke Foundations maintain numerous international partners and have been nominated for inscription on the UNESCO World Heritage List.

See also Francke, August Hermann; Francke, Gotthilf August; Freylinghausen, Johann Anastasius; Hildebrand, Carl (Baron von Canstein); Pietism

Bibliography

Brecht, M. "August Hermann Francke und der Hallische Pietismus." In *Geschichte des Pietismus*, ed. M. Brecht, 1:473–527. Vandenhoek & Ruprecht, 1993; Müller-Bahlke, T., and E. Baron. *A Guided Walk through the Francke Foundations*. Verlag der Franckeschen Stiftungen, 2013; Obst, H. *August Hermann Francke und sein Werk*. Verlag der Franckeschen Stiftungen, 2013; Obst, H., and P. Raabe. *Die Franckeschen Stiftungen zu Halle (Saale): Geschichte und Gegenwart*. Fliegenkopf, 2000; Zaunstöck, H., ed. *Gebaute Utopien: Franckes Schulstadt in der Geschichte europäischer Stadtentwürfe*. Katalog zur Jahresausstellung der Franckeschen Stiftungen. Verlag der Franckeschen Stiftungen, 2010; Zaunstöck, H., et al., eds. *Die Welt verändern: August Hermann Francke—Ein Lebenswerk um 1700*. Katalog zur Jahresausstellung der Franckeschen Stiftungen. Verlag der Franckeschen Stiftungen, 2013.

THOMAS MÜLLER-BAHLKE

Franconia

Franconia is a region of Germany, most of which today is part of northern Bavaria, but parts of it are in Baden-Württemberg and Thuringia. It includes the cities of Nuremberg, Würzburg, Erlangen, and Coburg.

Though the Wittenberg Reformation influenced the imperial city of Nuremberg early, with many strands of influence running from Wittenberg to Nuremberg, Franconia was divided politically and so experienced the Reformation in several ways. Lutheran preachers appeared in towns and villages of upper Franconia (specifically, the territory of Brandenburg-Ansbach-Kulmbach ruled by a branch of the Hollenzollern family) between 1521 and 1523. Reform impulses sprang from several causes and had a number of consequences. Margrave Casimir (r. 1515–27) had some sympathies with the Reformation

but did little to promote it. In 1525 peasant armies achieved considerable but not lasting success in Franconia. Margrave George the Pious (1527–43), a signatory of the Augsburg Confession, was committed to bringing his lands fully into the Evangelical faith. The Brandenburg-Nuremberg Church Ordinance (1533), cowritten by Andreas Osiander and Johannes Brenz, was influential both within and outside of Hohenzollern territories. George Friedrich (1556–1603), son of George the Pious, consolidated the Reformation in Brandenburg-Ansbach-Kulmbach. Much of lower Franconia and the western half of upper Franconia (including the prince-bishopric Bamberg) remained Roman Catholic. Important small imperial cities of the area that accepted the Reformation included Rothenburg ob der Tauber and Dinkelsbühl.

In the nineteenth century the Erlangen school of theology, a revival of Lutheran confessional thinking centered at the University of Erlangen, came to have considerable influence. The mission academy and deaconess training institution founded by Wilhelm Loehe (Löhe, 1808–72) at Neuendettelsau were of great influence internationally.

See also Brenz, Johannes; Georg, Margrave of Brandenburg-Ansbach; Loehe, Wilhelm Konrad; Mission Societies and Academies; Nuremberg; Osiander, Andreas

Bibliography

Dixon, C. S. *The Reformation and Rural Society: The Parishes of Brandenburg-Ansbach-Kulmbach, 1528–1603*. Cambridge University Press, 1996; Smith, W. B. *Reformation and the German Territorial State: Upper Franconia, 1300–1630*. University of Rochester Press, 2008.

MARY JANE HAEMIG

Free Will

The concept of free will claims that human beings have the freedom and power to make choices. Lutheran discussions of free will began, historically and dogmatically, with Martin Luther's early lectures and disputations, in which he challenged late-medieval theologians concerning the power of the human will. Later debate with Roman theologians climaxed in Luther's reply to Erasmus of Rotterdam (1466–1536): *De servo arbitrio* (*The Bondage of the Will*, 1525). In this treatise Luther allows human "free choice" in matters "below" pertaining to human "faculties and possessions," while denying human freedom in matters "above" pertaining to God and eternal life. Even in making this distinction, Luther asserts that it would be better never to use the term "free choice" in relation to human beings. "Free choice [*liberum arbitrium*]" should be a proper term reserved for almighty God (LW 33:68, 70). Even in earthly matters, in which human beings are free, human choice is still "controlled [*regatur*]" by God's will. This control is not exceptional or occasional, but total. So Luther concluded that "everything we do, everything that happens, even if it seems to us to happen mutably and contingently, happens in fact nonetheless necessarily and immutably, if you have regard to the will of God. For the will of God is effectual and cannot be hindered, since it is the power of the divine nature itself" (37–38). This is simply a matter of what it means to be a creature who has a Creator, which is frightening without faith and yet is "something fundamentally necessary and salutary for a Christian, to know that God foreknows nothing contingently, but that he foresees and purposes and does all things by his immutable, eternal, and infallible will. Here is a thunderbolt by which free choice is completely prostrated and shattered" (37).

By saying this, Luther was not making so much a philosophical argument as a biblical-theological one. God is the omnipotent Creator (*deus ex lex*, "God limited by no law"). As such, God does not provide room for participation or cooperation with the Deity by means of human free choices of will. Luther does adopt Scholastic philosophical terminology such as "immutable" and "necessity," but he states his dissatisfaction with such terms because they imply that God coerces human beings, but this is not what actually happens. Whatever a will wills, it, by definition, wants to will it. Humans carry out God's immutable will for them quite willingly. In fact, free will is an abstraction because the will is always already willing. There is no neutral moment or space prior to this willing. No one chooses to change their own will because no one wants (wills) to change that will. This would require a second greater will abstracted from the reality of the actual will, or some sort of neutral position in the will, neither of which actually exists in the human creature. The will wills what it wills. The human will can in fact be changed by a greater will—namely, God's will—but not by the human (so-called free) will.

So freedom of the will really concerns what kind of deity God is, not what kind of power the will has in itself. Christians confess that they believe in "God the Father, almighty." God is not only immutable in himself or his divine nature, whether humans believe it or not, but his immutability is also a necessary presupposition for the preaching of his promises in Christ. So Luther also approached the bound will from another perspective concerning the gospel. Here he is no longer teaching God in himself or hidden in wrath (*deus absconditus*), which teaches the absolute immutability of God's hidden will unto the death of the sinner, nor is he making an observation about the present state of human beings in God's creation. Instead, he reasons backward from the eschatological gospel, meaning the word that comes back in time from the judgment day to sinners in the present. Because salvation comes in Christ alone, apart from the law, by faith alone, by grace alone, in the forgiveness of sins alone, in the present the human will must belong to the devil, idolize the law, hate God's Word (unbelief), be inherently works-righteous, and so is nothing but sin. Because Christ alone justifies, sanctifies, saves, gives eternal life, and sets free, human beings must not be free, but instead bound in sin and death.

The terrible logic of creation teaches us that God's unpreached and hidden will is immutable, and everything happens by necessity. So, "God hidden in his majesty neither deplores nor takes away, but works life, death, and all in all; nor has He set bounds to Himself by His Word, but has kept himself free over all things" (LW 33:140).

However, in the preached word of Christ, God reveals to sinners an immutable will to save us through his promises. The gospel word is categorical, meaning absolute, without condition so that nothing can stop it. Only in this way is faith absolutely certain: "When [God] promises anything, you ought to be certain that he knows and is able and willing to perform what he promises. . . . For if you doubt or disdain to know that God foreknows all things, not contingently, but necessarily and immutably, how can you believe his promises and place a sure trust and reliance on them? And we ought not only to be certain that God wills and will act necessarily and immutably, but also to glory in this fact." When God's will is bound to his Word as forgiveness, what had previously been most frightening about God's almighty power now becomes the greatest comfort: "For this is the one supreme consolation of Christians in all adversities, to know that God does not lie, but does all things immutably, and that his will can neither be resisted nor changed nor hindered" (LW 33:43). The good news of Christ, applied to the sinner in word and sacrament for faith, provides unstoppable freedom from sin, death, and the devil. God does not lie!

God's revealed will in the gospel of Christ does not somehow contradict or soften the fact that God foreknows all things, not contingently, but necessarily and immutably. After establishing divine necessity and its destruction of human free will, Luther responded to Erasmus's objection that it would be better to simply preach Christ crucified and remain silent about all the matters pertaining to the will: "We too preach nothing but Jesus crucified. But Christ crucified brings all these things with him" (70). Furthermore, the sinner's will still remains a "beast of burden" when Christ knocks the devil out of the saddle and takes the reins himself, but now the "servile donkey" has become a "royal donkey" in royal freedom. For

the sinner forgiven in Christ, divine necessity is established in joy.

The great surprise is that in the end, what God immutably insists on doing (out of divine necessity) is not the law, but Christ and his forgiveness. God wills immutably to be outside the law (*deus ex lex pro nobis*, God outside the law for us). When God's promises are preached, his hidden unpreached necessity, which works weal and woe, including through the devil, is unseated by his revealed necessity in Christ. God's eternal unpreached will to be the almighty Creator kills sinners, but in God's immutable will revealed in Christ's word and sacraments, God's will to re-create sinners from the dead is more eternal for faith alone than his eternal unpreached will.

In article 18 of the Augsburg Confession of 1530, Philip Melanchthon (1497–1560) repeated Luther's distinction between what is above the human will and what is below it, referring to a text from pseudo-Augustine as a way of defending Lutheran teaching from the charge of Manichaeism. In the Apology he polemically asserts that human beings can do nothing regarding their salvation, but God does everything.

The synergistic controversy tested Lutheran teachings on the human will when, in 1557, Matthias Flacius (1520–75) was appointed to the theological faculty in Jena; he quickly attacked his colleague Viktorin Strigel (1524–69), a Philippist theologian, who asserted that the human will played a small role in justification or the creation of faith. At nearly the same time, Flacius's friend, Nicholas Gallus, was attacking Philip Melanchthon's position, as reflected in changes to the third Latin edition of the *Loci communes*. The Formula of Concord (1580), while attacking some aspects of Flacius's language, sided with Flacius in insisting that the human will is purely passive in justification.

Although Pietism, rationalism, and liberalism have claimed a human role in justification, large confessional groups and movements within the Evangelical-Lutheran churches have held to Luther's teaching on the complete passivity of the human will in justification. However, Luther's advice that Christians should wholeheartedly "glory" in divine necessity and their corresponding powerlessness has rarely been heeded by Lutheran theologians (Kolb, *Bound Choice*). Even the Formula of Concord has an ambiguous relationship with Luther on these matters.

The first controverted thesis of the Formula's Epitome, article 2 (Free Will) certainly agrees with Luther in stating: "We reject and condemn . . . [the teaching] that people do everything that they do . . . under coercion and that they are coerced to do evil works and deeds" (BC 492). As Luther states in *The Bondage of the Will*, God works all in all, both good and evil, but he certainly does not create evil "from scratch" (LW 33:178; *de novo*, WA 18:710.32) or coerce or force human beings to sin. Instead, God's immutable will works evil because it does not suspend its working in evil sinners.

However, the first half of the Formula's thesis, by rejecting what they elsewhere labeled "Stoic necessity" ("the mad dream . . . that everything that happens has to happen just so and could not happen in any other way") also could be seen as rejecting what Luther unambiguously taught in *The Bondage of the Will*: "Everything we do, everything that happens, . . . happens . . . necessarily and immutably, with regard to the will of God."

In 1537, twelve years after writing *The Bondage of the Will*, Luther claimed that, along with the Small Catechism, it was his greatest piece of work. In 1542, when Luther reminded his students in the Genesis lectures that not only had he preached that God's hidden will makes "everything absolute and unavoidable," but he had also preached God's will revealed in Christ (LW 5:42–50), he was in no way contradicting or softening his claims in *The Bondage of the Will*. Luther introduced the topic by referencing claims that some were using the immutability of predestination to avoid responsibility for their actions. Luther

did not respond by preaching moral responsibility (thereby contradicting divine necessity) or by claiming that God is immutable in the gospel alone. Instead, Luther asserted that he had also preached God's revealed will in Christ and that this preaching makes faith certain, "For . . . you can be sure about your faith and salvation." This was precisely his concern when establishing divine necessity and the corresponding immutability of divine promises in *The Bondage of the Will*. Luther never denies "that everything is absolute and unavoidable." Divine immutability is the presupposition behind his preaching of the absolute certainty of God's promises and faith, just as it was in 1525.

Modern Lutheran teaching as compiled by Klaus Schwarzwäller largely demonstrates the departure from Luther due to following the Kantian assertion that freedom is not a quality of the will but is autonomy, whose character is reason to the extent that it prescribes the law of its own acts (categorical imperative). Roman Catholic ecumenical interest in Luther prompted Harry McSorely to publish a Thomistic reply to Luther's argument against Erasmus, *Luther: Right or Wrong?* (1969), that accepted bondage as slavery to sin, but rejected the central argument concerning preached and unpreached necessity. It was H. J. Iwand who argued that from Protestant Scholastic dogmatics to the present, neither unfree will nor God's almighty power were upheld. This teaching degenerated into a mere codicil, closer to Thomism than Lutheranism, of the incapacity of sinners to be justified by their own power before God. The rediscovery of God preached and not preached in *Bondage of the Will* allowed Gerhard Forde (1927–2005) to hold that the law does not prove freedom by inference, as in Erasmus and the modern world, but that it takes freedom away. Only preaching that assumes bondage of the will for its hearers arrives to free the bound.

See also Book of Concord; Calvin, John; Erasmus of Rotterdam (Desiderius Erasmus Roterodamus); Flacius, Matthias Illyricus, and the Flacians; Formula of

Concord; Justification; Melanchthon, Philip; Original Sin; Strigel, Victorin; Synergistic Controversy

Bibliography

Luther's Works: "The Bondage of the Will" (1525). LW 33; "Lectures on Genesis: Chapters 26–30" (1541–1543). LW 5; "Luther and Wolfgang Capito in Straßburg" ([Wittenberg] 9. Juli 1537). WA BR 8:99–100, #3162; **Confessional Documents:** Kolb, R., and T. Wengert, eds. *The Book of Concord: The Confessions of the Evangelical Lutheran Church*. Fortress, 2000; **General Works:** Bayer, O. "God's Hiddenness." *LQ* 28 (2014): 266–79; Forde, G. *The Captivation of the Will: Luther vs. Erasmus on Freedom and Bondage*. Ed. S. D. Paulson. Eerdmans, 2005; Forde, G. *Theology Is for Proclamation*. Fortress, 1990; Iwand, H. J. "Die Freiheit des Christen und die Unfreiheit des Willens." In *Um den rechten Glauben: Gesammelte Aufsätze*. Theologische Bücherei, 1959; Kolb, R. *Bound Choice, Election, and Wittenberg Theological Record: From Martin Luther to the Formula of Concord*. Eerdmans / Lutheran Quarterly Books, 2005; McSorley, H. J. *Luther: Right or Wrong?* Augsburg, 1969; Paulson, S. D. "Categorical Preaching." *LQ* 21 (2007): 268–93; Paulson, S. D. *Lutheran Theology*. T&T Clark, 2011; Schwarzwäller, K. *Sibboleth*. Kaiser, 1969; Watson, P. *Let God Be God! An Interpretation of the Theology of Martin Luther*. Muhlenberg, 1947.

NICHOLAS HOPMAN AND STEVEN D. PAULSON

Freylinghausen, Johann Anastasius

The German hymnal compiler, hymn writer, pastor, and theologian Johann Anastasius Freylinghausen (1670–1739) was the son-in-law of August Hermann Francke. Freylinghausen was born in Bad Gandersheim. While studying at Erfurt he became acquainted with August Hermann Francke, the eventual leader of Halle Pietism. He followed Francke to Halle in 1692, becoming Francke's assistant pastor and close associate in founding and developing the Waisenhaus (orphanage), an institution that, in time, housed and educated more than two thousand children of all social standings. In 1715 he married Francke's daughter, Johanna Sophie Anastasia. Upon Francke's death in 1727, Freylinghausen became codirector of the Waisenhaus with Francke's son Gotthilf August Francke. Today Freylinghausen is especially known for the two hymnals he compiled, *Geistreiches Gesangbuch* (Spiritually rich songbook, 20 editions, 1704–ca. 1771) and *Neues Geistreiches Gesangbuch* (4 editions, 1714–33). The first hymnal experienced more editions in the entire history of the Lutheran Church other than Johann Crüger's *Praxis pietatis melica* (1647). Both of Freylinghausen's hymnals include old and new hymns, and both have printed melodies and basso continuo lines for many of the hymns. After Freylinghausen's death, G. A. Francke compiled the two hymnals into one large hymnal, *Geistreiches Gesangbuch* (two editions, 1741 and 1771). While some people, notably the theology faculty of the University of Wittenberg, criticized some texts and melodies in Freylinghausen's first hymnal in a 1714 publication, others embraced the pieces. Missionaries introduced them to India and North America, and the Wesleys did the same in England. Schemelli's *Gesang-Buch* (1736), associated with Johann Sebastian Bach, has pieces from Freylinghausen. Among his most well-known hymn tunes are "Fling Wide the Door" and "Spread, Oh, Spread, Almighty Word." Freylinghausen wrote forty-four hymns and a number of theological tracts. His *Grundlegung der Theologie* (1703), reflecting the structure of Spener's *Evangelischer Glaubenslehre* (1688), gives insight into the theology of Halle Pietism.

See also Francke, August Hermann; Francke, Gotthilf August; Francke Foundations; Hymnody; Pietism

Bibliography

Busch, G., and W. Miersemann, eds. *"Geist-reicher" Gesang, Halle und das pietistische Lied*. Niemeyer, 1997; McMullen, D. M. "The Geistreiches Gesangbuch of Johann Anastasius Freylinghausen (1670–1739): A German Pietist Hymnal." 2 vols. PhD diss., University of Michigan, 1987. University Microfilms International, 1989; McMullen, D. M., and W. Miersemann. *Johann Anastasius Freylinghausen: Geistreiches Gesangbuch; Edition und Kommentar*. 7 vols. De Gruyter, 2004–; Miersemann, W., and G. Busch, eds. *Pietismus und Liedkultur*. Niemeyer, 2002; Miersemann, W., and G. Busch, eds. *"Singt dem Herrn nah und fern": 300 Jahre Freylinghausensches Gesangbuch*. Niemeyer, 2008; Paul, M. *Johann Anastasius Freylinghausen als Theologe des hallischen Pietismus*. Verlag der Franckeschen Stiftungen, 2014.

DIANNE M. MCMULLEN

Fritschel, Sigmund and Gottfried

Sigmund (1833–1900) and Gottfried (1836–89) Fritschel, of Nuremberg, Germany, were the leading educators and confessional theologians of the Iowa Synod. Influenced by the nineteenth-century German religious awakening, both brothers studied directly under Wilhelm Loehe. In 1854 Sigmund was ordained and immigrated with a small group to Iowa, joining followers of Loehe who had migrated from Michigan. The same year he helped found the Iowa Synod. Gottfried, who studied at Erlangen University for a year, immigrated in 1857 to teach at the synod's fledgling seminary. After brief pastorates, Sigmund in 1858 also came to the seminary, where the brothers collaborated closely both in teaching and in editing the *Kirchen-Blatt* and *Kirchliche-Zeitschrift*. Both represented the Iowa Synod at the 1867 colloquium with the Missouri Synod, where they disagreed with Walther on "open questions" (later called "theological problems"). "Open questions" involved different interpretations of biblical passages on issues not addressed in the Lutheran confessions, but which were sufficiently significant to prohibit church fellowship for Walther but not for the Fritschels. Later the Fritschels opposed Walther's interpretation of predestination. Sigmund made successful fund-raising trips to Europe and attended meetings of the General Council.

See also American Lutheran Church (1930–60); Ohio/Buffalo/Iowa Synods

Bibliography

Fritschel, H. L. *Biography of Professor Dr. Conrad Sigmund Fritschel . . . and of Professor Dr. Gottfried Leonhard Wilhelm Fritschel.* Privately printed, 1951; Fritschel, S. *The Distinctive Doctrines and Usages of the General Bodies of the Evangelical Lutheran Church in the United States.* Lutheran Publication Society, 1893; Spaeth, A., and S. Fritschel. *A Short Biography.* Wartburg, 1901.

JAMES W. ALBERS

Fritzsche, Gotthard Daniel

As pastor and leader, Gotthard Daniel Fritzsche (1797–1863) went to Australia with the second wave of Old Lutherans (*Alt-Lutheraner*) who fled persecution in Prussia and migrated to the colony of South Australia as refugees, seeking religious freedom and a new life. He had studied at Breslau, where he was influenced by the Lutheran confessional revival led by Johann Gottfried Scheibel. After serving as a teacher for some years, he resigned from the Union Church and became a pastor of the illegal Evangelical Lutheran Church. For five years he escaped capture, sometimes dressed as a Polish peasant. At the invitation of Pastor August Kavel, who led the first Old Lutherans "to the ends of the earth," Fritzsche led his congregation to Australia, where they arrived in 1841 after a terrible voyage in which 50 of 270 persons died. His congregation settled in three rural locations, which meant for him incessant travel. In 1845 he established a small college at Lobethal, which provided the fledgling church with its first pastors trained in the country. It was not long before Fritzsche fell out with Kavel, with whom he differed on three major issues: Kavel's claim that his Apostolic Constitution was the only proper one, Kavel's chiliastic notions, and Kavel's "protestations" against certain statements in the Lutheran confessions. Against the "Protestations," Fritzsche published a strong refutation. The church that Fritzsche led eventually became the Evangelical Lutheran Synod of Australia. Fritzsche was a humble and self-effacing pastor, a pioneer church leader, and a competent confessional theologian who single-handedly founded the first seminary of any kind in Australia.

See also Australia; Kavel, August Ludwig Christian

Bibliography

Brauer, A. *Under the Southern Cross: History of Evangelical Lutheran Church of Australia.* Ed. P. G. Strelan. Lutheran Publishing House, 1956. Reprint, 1985; Leske, E. *For Faith and Freedom: The Story of Lutherans and Lutheranism in Australia, 1836–1996.* Rev. ed. Friends of Lutheran Archives, 2009.

DEAN ZWECK

Fry, Franklin Clark

The North American Lutheran clergyperson and leader Franklin Clark Fry (1900–1968) was the first president of the Lutheran Church in America (LCA) and a key figure in the ecumenical movement; he became known as "Mr.

Protestant" or "Mr. Lutheran." Born in 1900 in Bethlehem, Pennsylvania, Fry was the third generation in his family to seek ordination in the Lutheran Church. He was educated at Hamilton College, New York, and the Lutheran Theological Seminary at Philadelphia. In 1945 he was one of the organizers of the Lutheran World Relief and served as its first president. Before taking leadership of the LCA, Fry led the United Lutheran Church in America for eighteen years, since 1944, serving as its second president. He also was a key player in the formation of the Lutheran World Federation (LWF) in 1947, where he served as treasurer (1948–52), vice president (1952–57), president (1957–63), and on the LWF's executive committee until his death, thus becoming one of the most influential Lutheran, if not Protestant, world leaders. He was furthermore instrumental in the 1948 formation of the World Council of Churches (WCC), serving as vice chairman of the policy-making Central Committee from 1948 until 1954, when he became chairman; he served in this capacity until 1968, as well as chairing the executive committee. Fry was instrumental in Eastern Orthodox churches joining the WCC. He was elected to leadership in the LCA in 1962, having been instrumental in inviting other Lutheran bodies (the American Evangelical Lutheran Church, the Augustana Evangelical Lutheran Church, and the Finnish Evangelical Lutheran Church of America) to participate in merger discussions as early as 1956. Fry also was instrumental in the formation of the National Council of Churches (USA) in 1950; he served on the General Board as well as chairing the Policy and Strategy Committee, but never held office, consistently declining presidency of the organization. Fry also concerned himself with the civil rights movement in the United States, encouraging other Lutherans to work toward a solution. In recognition of this commitment and at the urging of the Rev. (later bishop) Herluf Jenson, he was one of the Scripture readers at Dr. Martin Luther King Jr.'s funeral. Toward the end of his life, Fry worked toward fostering dialogue between Lutherans and Roman Catholics. Several honors were bestowed on him to recognize his services, including honorary degrees from thirty-four colleges, universities, and seminaries, both from the United States and abroad, besides honors and awards he received from Korea, West Germany, and Austria.

See also Ecumenical Dialogues; Inner-Lutheran Ecumenism; Lutheran Church in America; United Lutheran Church in America

Bibliography
Fischer, R. H., ed. *Franklin Clark Fry: A Palette for a Portrait*. LQ 24, supplementary number. Wittenberg University, 1972.

PETER VETHANAYAGAMONY

G

Gender: Men and Women

"What I have written to you is no woman's chit-chat, but the word of God," penned Argula von Grumbach from sixteenth-century Bavaria. Insisting on her rights as a Christian woman, she indicated that women had their own views and experiences to bring to theological conversations. "Yes, and whereas I have written on my own, a hundred women would emerge to write against them. For there are many who are able and better read than I am; as a result they might well come to be called 'a school for women.'"

Most women in the Reformation century were not as outspoken, and those who ventured into the predominantly male realm of public discourse typically faced serious gender-based attacks. Male-defined gender norms shaped the lives of both men and women as the Reformation arose within patriarchally ordered societal and family systems that kept women subjected to men, legally and ecclesiastically. At the same time, with Luther's personal input and consistent teaching on the spiritual equality of men and women as sinners and saints, the domestic vocations of mothers and fathers gained new recognition as holier than those of the "self-chosen" lives of monastics, and public education was arranged for both boys and girls, to prepare them for their respective vocations.

Luther did not promote women's participation in the public affairs of the church, perhaps in part due to his own wife's satisfaction with the newly commended domestic vocations. Katharina von Bora, an ex-nun, enjoyed an equal status in their marriage and became an example for the holy vocation Protestant preachers offered for women: marriage, motherhood, and oversight of the household. Through their homes, women raised and taught new Christians, thus having the prestige of the apostles and bishops. Luther had a deep respect for the female sex and women's important function as partners and mothers. Equality in difference was the principle with which Luther considered the gender relations, the nature of which changed with the fall and the coming of sin into the world: struggle for power, independence and authority, and proneness for wrong choices have colored the human gendered experience since the fall.

In his lectures on Gen. 1 and 3, delivered in the 1530s, Luther discussed Adam's and Eve's created differences as the images of God and their similitude with God (Gen. 3:1; LW 1:141), and their equality in righteousness (Gen. 3:1; WA 42:113–14; LW 1:151). Eve as the *imago Dei* was not quite equal in prestige (Gen. 1:27; WA 42:51–52; LW 1:690) but weaker in nature (Gen. 3:16; WA 42:150) and with a different body, which was vulnerable to the devil's attacks. Like the sun and the moon, men were more excellent and stronger, while women were equally righteous (Gen. 1:27; WA 42:51–52; Gen. 3:1; WA 42:113–15). Luther underscored God's plan to create for Adam a partner in procreation (Gen. 2:19–20; WA 42:90–91), the loveliest Eve (Gen. 1:26; WA 42:500), who with the entrance of sin would serve as the antidote against the sin of fornication (Gen. 2:18; WA 42:89). In other venues, however, such as in comments on the sixth commandment in the Large Catechism, Luther said nothing about gender inequality and made mutual love and respect, not the avoidance of fornication, the center of his comments.

What was preached from the pulpit "for" women and "about" women was not unilaterally accepted by women who had their own sense of self and vocational aspirations, and who often took considerable risks in expressing their faith (such as exile, domestic abuse, and losing their children and possessions). Women contributed in varied roles as prophets, teachers, authors, and hymn writers, such as Elisabeth Cruciger (née von Meseritz). Elisabeth von Braunschweig stands out as a ruler who secured the teaching of the Augsburg Confession in her land. Despite the emphasis on the married life, some women remained in their convents, with the models for religious vocation and education outside the household, and with living arrangements in all-female communities. In some cases these women had to leave Protestant cities.

Today Lutherans build on the sixteenth-century principles of spiritual equality, while the gendered realities differ significantly around the globe. Some concerns are shared. For example, not all Lutheran communities recognize women's ordination or pastoral leadership or support equality in employment and pay; gender-based violence and injustice against women continue unabated; poverty continues to hurt women and their children the most; women's active participation and leadership in the reconstruction and application of Lutheran theology are just beginning in some churches; diverse cultural and theological conceptions around sex/gender and sexuality in the blending of traditions of the past and contemporary experiences create a complex reality, in which growing up as men and women with a healthy sense of self and the other remains extremely complicated in a rapidly changing world. Important challenges with these issues for Lutherans today include the following: (1) considering the meanings, building blocks, and effects of both biological "sexuality" and culturally defined "gender" and how these categories shape the lives of men and women; (2) determining ways to draw from the experiences of males and females to reconcile sources in Christian tradition with scientific and personal knowledge; (3) studying human nature and experiences with all

the apparatus available. Luther's example can prompt ongoing critical study of the biblical tradition, Christian values, and the varied human experience on what it means to be created as female and male in the image of God.

See also Bora, Katharina von; Creation; Cruciger, Elisabeth; Grumbach, Argula von; Sexuality; Women's Movement

Bibliography

Hendrix, S. H., and S. C. Karant-Nunn, eds. *Masculinity in the Reformation Era*. Cambridge University Press, 2010; Karant-Nunn, S., and M. Wiesner-Hanks. *Luther on Women: A Sourcebook*. Cambridge University Press, 2003; Matheson, P., ed. *Argula von Grumbach: A Woman's Voice in the Reformation*. T&T Clark, 1995; Neuenfeldt, E., ed. *Lutheran World Federation Gender Justice Policy*. Lutheran World Federation, 2013. http://www.Lutheranworld.org/content/resource-lwf-gender-justice-policy; Stjerna, K. *Women and the Reformation*. Wiley, 2008; Wiesner-Hanks, M. *Women and Gender in Early Modern Europe*. Cambridge University Press, 1993. 3rd ed., 2008.

KIRSI STJERNA

General Council of the Evangelical Lutheran Church in North America

As an American Lutheran church body, the General Council of the Evangelical Lutheran Church in North America (1866–1918) was formed in 1866 by dissidents who left the General Synod of the Evangelical Lutheran Church in America. The 1850s and 1860s had seen increasing controversy among Lutherans in the Muhlenberg tradition—most of whom had joined together in the General Synod—over the meaning and authority of the Lutheran confessions. In 1864 the General Synod admitted to membership the Franckean Synod, a group that did not subscribe to the Augsburg Confession; the delegates from the Ministerium of Pennsylvania withdrew in protest because they viewed this as a violation of the General Synod's own constitution. At the 1866 convention of the General Synod, the Ministerium of Pennsylvania delegates were denied seating, on the grounds that their delegates' actions in 1864 had constituted withdrawal from membership. The issue was exacerbated by the fact that the Ministerium of Pennsylvania had recently founded a new seminary at

Philadelphia without consulting the General Synod; this action was viewed as hostile to the General Synod's seminary at Gettysburg. When the General Synod refused to seat the Ministerium of Pennsylvania in 1866, the latter withdrew once again and called for a new organization to be established as an alternative to the General Synod.

The organizational meeting was held in December 1866 at Reading, Pennsylvania, with thirteen synods (both members and nonmembers of the General Synod) sending representatives. They adopted the Fundamental Principles of Faith and Church Polity, a document drafted by Charles Porterfield Krauth, a professor at the Philadelphia Seminary who would become the primary theologian of the new body. It was hoped by many that the General Council would be able to bring several of the more conservative midwestern immigrant synods into relationship with those in the Muhlenberg tradition, but this was not to be; meanwhile, representatives from the Missouri Synod, the Joint Synod of Ohio, and the Norwegian Synod were present at the organizational meeting in 1866, but all three declined to join the General Council. The Wisconsin, Minnesota, and Illinois Synods all joined the General Council but withdrew within a few years; they became part of the more conservative Synodical Conference when it was organized in 1872. Another midwestern immigrant synod, the Swedish Augustana Synod, did join and participated throughout the General Council's existence. The first regular convention of the new body was held the following year. It officially constituted the General Council of the Evangelical Lutheran Church in North America, with eleven synods fully participating and two others participating in discussion but not voting—a kind of consultative membership permitted by the constitution as it was adopted.

The early years of the General Council were closely tied to discussions over the so-called Four Points, raised originally by the Joint Synod of Ohio, asking the council's position on chiliasm, altar fellowship, pulpit fellowship, and secret societies. The council's immediate response to these issues was not satisfactory to the Joint Synod, which refrained from further participation, but over the next years the General Council debated them, particularly the questions of pulpit and altar fellowship. The result was the so-called Akron Rule, adopted in 1872 and reaffirmed in 1875 in a slightly revised version called the Galesburg Rule: "Lutheran pulpits for Lutheran ministers only—Lutheran altars for Lutheran communicants only," but with a caveat of pastoral discretion objected to by the Missouri Synod. The first presidents of the General Council, G. Bassler, C. W. Schaeffer, and G. F. Krotel, served for only a year each; in 1870 Krauth became president and served for ten years. He was, for most of the council's early years, its dominant personality and guiding theological light.

The General Council conducted home missions in both English and German, as well as foreign missions, particularly in India. It also had an active ministry with German immigrants. Its "inner mission" program (what today might be called social welfare ministries), particularly in urban settings, was inspired and led by W. A. Passavant. The council produced significant liturgical materials, including the well-received *Church Book*. In its earliest years the council did not have an official publication, but in 1897 it began *The Lutheran*, the successor to two independently published papers that had been in circulation primarily among General Council Lutherans. Near the end of its existence, it added a German weekly, *Der Deutsche Lutheraner*. The council as such did not operate colleges or seminaries, though several institutions were run by its constituent synods. While the council conceived of itself as a kind of consultative body composed of independent synods, as time went on it became more centralized with regard to missions and some other matters. This centralization of authority grew particularly under the strong leadership of Theodore

Schmauk, who served as president from 1903 until the General Council's conclusion in 1918.

In the late nineteenth century, the General Council participated in a series of free conferences with other Lutherans in the Muhlenberg tradition. These increased contacts led eventually to the uniting of the General Council, the General Synod, and the General Synod South into the United Lutheran Church in America in 1918. As this merger approached, one of the General Council's members, the Augustana Synod, withdrew on friendly terms; Augustana believed that its unique identity as the "Swedish" Lutheran church could be best fostered by remaining independent. The most significant contribution the General Council made to American Lutheranism was its role in anchoring the Muhlenberg tradition to a moderate confessionalism that endured (if in somewhat weakened form) in the ULCA. At the time of the merger, the General Council consisted of thirteen synods; it brought into the ULCA nearly fourteen hundred congregations with more than half a million baptized members.

See also American Lutheranism Controversy; General Synod; Krauth, Charles Porterfield; Ministerium of Pennsylvania; United Lutheran Church in America

Bibliography

Good, W. A. "A History of the General Council of the Evangelical Lutheran Church in North America." PhD diss., Yale University, 1967; Ochsenford, S. E. *Documentary History of the General Council of the Evangelical Lutheran Church in North America*. General Council Publication House, 1912.

RICHARD O. JOHNSON

General Synod

The Evangelical Lutheran General Synod of the United States of North America, more commonly known as the General Synod, came into existence in 1820, uniting two-thirds of the Lutherans in the United States. The chief architect of the General Synod was Samuel Simon Schmucker (1799–1873), and the initiative for establishing the General Synod came from the Ministerium of Pennsylvania. The charter members of the General Synod were the synods of New York, North Carolina,

Maryland, and Virginia, as well as the Ministerium of Pennsylvania. Though desire for the unity of Lutherans was expressed as early as 1807, the definite proposal that led to the formation of the General Synod can be traced to the 1819 Ministerium of Pennsylvania gathering. The need came because American expansion westward was far outstripping church attempts to keep pace with the rising tide of movement. New immigrants were unwilling to stay in the established territories of Lutheran synods in the old colonial states, so some sort of organizational body was needed to incorporate the newer Lutheran synods into an overarching body for organizational purposes, and more importantly to prevent injurious and unnecessary divisions within the churches. The General Synod was a federative, consultative, and advisory body that did not trespass on the rights of member synods to appoint or ordain ministers, or to pass regulations or rules, within their own constituency. Local synods had a great degree of independence under the General Synod. On October 22, 1820, the General Synod met for the first time in Hagerstown, Maryland. The General Synod's first constitution did not mention the Augsburg Confession or any of the key confessional documents of the Lutheran Church, in spite of spirited remonstrations of the Tennessee Synod, which opposed the new body. The General Synod was in jeopardy when, three years into the union, the Ministerium of Pennsylvania withdrew to stem dissension within its jurisdiction over the new General Synod. However, the General Synod continued, and the Ministerium of Pennsylvania returned to the General Synod after a thirty-year absence. In order to provide well-educated Lutheran clergy, the General Synod founded Lutheran Theological Seminary at Gettysburg in 1826, the oldest surviving Lutheran seminary, as well as Gettysburg College in 1832. The issue of slavery and the American Civil War left its marks on the General Synod, with the withdrawal of its southern synods during and after the war. Further theological disputes over the authority of the Lutheran confessions occasioned more division, leading to the formation of the rival General Council in 1867. Beginning in 1841 the General Synod sent missionaries to India, Johann Christian Frederick Heyer being the first. The missionary work of "Father Heyer" eventually led to the establishment of Andhra Evangelical Lutheran Church. Later the General Synod sent missionaries to Liberia and also engaged in missionary work in the United States. In 1918 it joined with other Lutheran bodies to form the United Lutheran Church in America (ULCA).

See also General Council of the Evangelical Church in North America; General Synod South; Inner-Lutheran Ecumenism; Ministerium of Pennsylvania; Schmucker, Samuel Simon; United Lutheran Church in America

Bibliography

Ferm, V. *The Crisis in American Lutheran Theology: A Study of the Issue between American Lutheranism and Old Lutheranism.* Century, 1927; Gustafson, D. A. *Lutheranism in Crisis: The Question of Identity in the American Republic.* Fortress, 1993; Nelson, E. C., ed. *The Lutherans in North America.* Fortress, 1975; Neve, J. L. *The Formulation of the General Synod's Confessional Basis.* German Literary Board, 1911.

PETER VETHANAYAGAMONY

General Synod South

The church bodies comprising Lutherans in the southeastern United States in existence between 1863 and 1918 were called the United Synod of the Evangelical Lutheran Church in the South. General Synod South commonly delineates three separate organizations in existence between 1863 and 1886. The United Synod in the South refers to the larger organization of southern Lutherans that succeeded it during 1886–1918.

German Lutherans began arriving in significant numbers in the southeastern United States in the 1730s, either through the ports of Charleston, South Carolina, and Savannah, Georgia, or by travel down the Great Wagon Road from Pennsylvania through the Shenandoah Valley.

In 1820 most Lutherans in the South joined the Evangelical Lutheran General Synod of the United States (General Synod) at its founding, although its formation caused a severe division within southern Lutheranism over issues related to theology, polity, language, and personality. The disagreement led to the formation of the confessional Tennessee Synod, a non-geographical synod that resisted participation in larger church associations and eventually encompassed churches located throughout Virginia and both Carolinas.

As a result of the political divisions of the American Civil War, Lutherans in the synods of Virginia, North Carolina, South Carolina, Georgia, and western Virginia (later known as the Synod of Southwestern Virginia) began to withdraw from the General Synod in July 1861. Although formal organization was delayed because of logistical difficulties caused by the war, the southern synods formed their own church body, the General Synod of the Evangelical Lutheran Church in the Confederate States of America (the General Synod South), in May 1863.

Because of wartime conditions, the General Synod South met only twice during the war itself, yet a strong desire to establish distinctive southern Lutheran expressions free from reliance on northern Lutheranism led the synod to call for its own hymnal, liturgy, official newspaper, and military chaplaincy program. The official newspaper, *The Southern Lutheran*, was published from August 1861 until lack of funds, paper, and means of delivery ended it in January 1865. The General Synod South was more successful in working toward the publication of its own *Book of Worship*, which appeared shortly after war's end in 1867.

After the war, lingering bitterness and continuing postwar divisions fed a desire to continue as a separate regional expression, and in 1866 the body reorganized under the name Evangelical Lutheran General Synod in North America. In 1878 it changed its name once more to the General Synod of the Evangelical Lutheran Church in the South.

Constituent southern Lutheran synods moved in and out of the larger body during its history. The Holston Synod, an offshoot synod of Tennessee and consisting of churches in eastern Tennessee and southwestern Virginia, joined the General Synod South in 1867, but left in 1872, joining the General Council two years later. North Carolina withdrew in 1871 after perceived slights, but returned to the synod in 1881. The Mississippi Synod joined the General Synod South in 1872.

In 1867 the General Synod South assumed responsibility for Lutheran Theological Southern Seminary (founded in 1830 by the South Carolina Synod). Despite postwar economic pressures on both seminary and students, a full seminary education increasingly became the encouraged and expected norm.

African Americans, both slave and free, constituted a significant minority of membership in several of the southern synods until the end of the Civil War. After the war, only the North Carolina Synod addressed the issue directly. It developed a program of licensure for African American ministerial candidates as early as 1868, but the effort received little support.

The end of political Reconstruction in 1876 led to a gradual warming of relations with the North. The General Synod South played a pivotal role and provided significant leadership in the original development of the Common Service when it issued an invitation to the General Synod and General Council in 1876 to participate in the formation of a common liturgy.

In 1886 the Tennessee and Holston Synods joined with the existing synods of the General Synod South to form a new organization, the United Synod of the Evangelical Lutheran Church in the South. The formation of the United Synod marked the first time almost all Lutherans in the Southern states belonged to one general body.

The United Synod saw the *Book of Worship* through to publication in 1888 and became the first of the three bodies to put the work into print and widespread use, leading to a growing appreciation of historic Lutheran theology and liturgical worship across the southeast.

The United Synod continued to maintain the South's seminary, which, after existing in several sites, by 1911 settled permanently in Columbia, South Carolina. In 1895 the United Synod adopted the work of the Lutheran Orphan Home of the South in Salem, Virginia (founded in 1887), and in 1916 it assumed responsibility for the Lowman Home for the Aged and Helpless (founded in 1911). Individual synods rather than the general body, however, operated numerous junior colleges and three colleges on the territory of the United Synod: Newberry, Roanoke, and Lenoir (later Lenoir Rhyne).

A separate Alpha Synod for African American Lutherans was formed in 1889, but it received little encouragement from either the United Synod or the individual synods and disbanded in 1891. Eventually the African American pastors requested and received aid from the Missouri Synod and joined with that body.

Beginning in 1892, the United Synod sponsored foreign missionary work in Japan, where it built several schools. In 1911 it opened Kyushu Gakuin in Kumamoto, which included a small seminary to train leaders for indigenous ministry. By 1918 seven individuals, four men and three women, served as United Synod missionaries.

Active laywomen's and laymen's auxiliaries emerged to fund both this foreign missionary effort and the organization of new congregations in the emerging towns and cities of the post–Civil War South. Women's auxiliaries of the United Synod organized missionary societies for young people and children and increasingly published their own religious mission literature. The Laymen's Movement successfully promoted the increasing use of the "every-member canvass" and the duplex envelope system. A weekly church paper, *The Lutheran Church Visitor*, established in 1904 from the merger of two previous papers, and an active Lutheran Publishing House in Columbia served as important voices in promoting the ministries of the United Synod and in encouraging joint work with the two Northern church bodies.

As relationships with the North became more cordial, the moderate theological position of the United Synod increasingly allowed it to serve as a mediator between the positions of the General Synod and the General Council. In 1895 the United Synod proposed joining with the two Northern bodies for work on a new *Common Service Book with Hymnal*, eventually published in 1917. This effort, as well as an increasing recognition of their shared interests and ministries, spurred the formation of a joint committee made up of representatives from all three church bodies to guide the celebration of the quadricentennial of the Reformation in 1917. This in turn led to the 1918 merger of the General Synod, General Council, and United Synod into the United Lutheran Church in America (ULCA). At the time of merger, the United Synod held a membership of approximately fifty-three thousand members and five hundred congregations.

See also American Civil War; General Council of the Evangelical Lutheran Church in North America; General Synod; United Lutheran Church in America

Bibliography

Anderson, H. G. *Lutheranism in the Southeastern States, 1860–1886.* Mouton, 1969; McArver, S. W. "'A Spiritual Wayside Inn': Lutherans, the New South, and Cultural Change in South Carolina, 1886–1918." PhD diss., Duke University, 1995; Oldenburg, M. "Southern Lutherans and the Common Service." *Essays and Reports of the Lutheran Historical Conference* 16 (1995): 177–94; Voigt, G. P. *A History of the United [Lutheran] Synod [of the] South.* Beaufort, SC: n.p., 1955.

SUSAN WILDS MCARVER

Geneva

Geneva, located in southwestern Switzerland, is the city most closely associated with John Calvin and sixteenth-century Calvinism, just as Wittenberg is with Luther and Lutheranism. In the 1400s, Geneva was a chief city in the duchy of Savoy, a territory at the intersection of France, Italy, and the Swiss confederation. Geneva was governed by a prince-bishop (usually a relative of the Duke of Savoy), though increasingly the city's magistrates gained greater political rights. In the fifteenth century, its economy flourished thanks to its trade networks and annual fairs, but by the early 1500s the trade routes had shifted and Geneva (population about ten thousand in 1520) had declined.

Luther's early influence in Geneva spread primarily by traveling merchants and others who made his Reformation teachings known. By the early 1530s, the Reformation took root in Geneva through the preaching and teaching of Antoine Froment, Pierre Viret, and Guillaume Farel, encouraged by the powerful and newly Protestant Swiss canton of Berne. Political circumstances and the ferment of religious change combined by the mid-1530s, forcing out the prince-bishop and leading to an assembly of all Genevan voters in May 1536, swearing to live according to the Reformation. In doing so, the Genevans declared unilateral political independence from the Catholic Duke of Savoy, leading to repeated attempts by successive dukes to retake the city over the next eighty years.

John Calvin came to Geneva in August 1536, intending only to stay overnight. However, Farel pressed the young French religious refugee to remain and help consolidate the Genevan Reformation. Farel, Calvin, and their ministerial colleagues faced major challenges. Part of the problem was political: threatened by Savoy, Geneva turned to neighboring Swiss Protestant powers for protection. This protection came at a price, however: a financial cost saddled Geneva with significant debt to cover the costs of Swiss troops, and a religious cost was that the Swiss Protestant powers pressured the Genevans to set up their liturgy and church government along Swiss lines. At the same time, Genevans who had voted for the Reformation (many for political reasons) resented any attempts by pastors to reshape traditional worship practices, oversee stringent church discipline, and set up common doctrinal standards. Tensions grew so high that Farel and Calvin were banished from Geneva in 1538 after refusing to obey the magistrates' directives regarding church discipline and admission to the Lord's Supper.

However, the Genevan magistrates quickly discovered that they needed a man of Calvin's caliber as their leading pastor. Following his return in 1541, several key Genevan institutions took root, including the consistory: a body of elders and pastors that met weekly to oversee faith and behavior. This disciplinary body, which (after much controversy) operated semi-independently from the government, could reprimand wrongdoers and bar them from the Lord's Supper, usually on a temporary basis until they repented and were restored to full fellowship. The magistrates retained sole control over other punishments, up to and including death. Those who challenged the received doctrines in Geneva could be banished (Jerome Bolsec over his rejection of predestination in 1551) or executed (antitinitarian Michael Servetus in 1553).

Geneva's population swelled several times in the 1500s due to the arrival of religious refugees, mostly from France. While they contributed actively to the Genevan economy, including through printing and bookselling, some refugees also began to displace prominent Genevan families, leading to tensions that culminated in an abortive riot against the refugees in 1555. Subsequently, magistrates were elected who largely favored Calvin and his fellow pastors' perspective, leading to a more stable internal situation that continued beyond Calvin's death in 1564.

Geneva became a reference point for Reformed Christians from across Europe, thanks to the reputation of Calvin and Theodore Beza, his chief successor, but also because of the attraction of the Genevan Academy (established in 1555), which provided higher education for successive generations of future Reformed pastors and political leaders. Geneva's chief confessional ally was the Swiss city of Zurich. Together, Zurich and Geneva established the Consensus Tigurinus of 1549, coming to agreement on Christ's spiritual presence in the Lord's Supper, in contradistinction to the Lutheran view as expressed in the Wittenberg Concord. Meanwhile, the Dukes of Savoy continued to target Geneva, culminating in a failed attack on the city in December 1602. By Theodore Beza's death in 1605, Geneva was the recognized mother church of Reformed Protestantism, albeit under threat from its enemies and less prominent than it had been in Calvin's heyday.

In the twentieth century, Geneva, having become a center for international political and social institutions, also became the home of several ecumenical institutions, including the World Council of Churches and the Lutheran World Federation.

See also Beza, Theodore; Calvin, John

Bibliography

Binz, L. *A Brief History of Geneva*. Chancellerie d'Etat, 1985; Jussie, J. de. *The Short Chronicle*. Ed. and trans. C. Klaus. University of Chicago Press, 2006; Kingdon, R., with T. Lambert. *Reforming Geneva: Discipline, Faith and Anger in Calvin's Geneva*. Droz, 2012; Monter, W. "De l'Evêché à la Rome protestante." In *Histoire de Genève*, ed. P. Guichonnet, 129–83. Privat / Payot, 1974; Naphy, W. G. *Calvin and the Consolidation of the Genevan Reformation*. Manchester University Press, 1994.

KARIN MAAG

Georg, Duke of Saxony

As an initial sympathizer and later opponent of Luther, Georg "the Bearded" (1471–1539), the well-educated Duke of Saxony, pursued an ambitious policy of church renewal in Albertine Saxony, pushing for the reform of the monasteries and strengthening traditional forms of piety. He received positively Luther's critique of the indulgence trade, which was financing the rise to power of his political rival Cardinal Albrecht of Brandenburg (1490–1545). Providing a platform to discuss the indulgence issue, he hosted a debate at the University of Leipzig in 1519 between the Ingolstadt theologian John Eck (1486–1543) and the Wittenberg theologians Andreas Karlstadt (ca. 1486–1541) and Luther. The ecclesiastical views expressed by Luther undermined existing church authority by questioning the primacy of the pope and the infallibility of the councils. Luther also defended positions derived from Jan Hus (ca. 1369–1415) that had led to the execution of the Bohemian reformer as a heretic at the Council of Constance (1415). Because of these radical positions, the debate became the turning point in Duke Georg's relation to the emerging Reformation. In the last two decades of his life he staunchly opposed Luther and strove instead for reform within existing church structures. He called for the imprisonment of runaway monks and nuns (and even executed someone for smuggling them out of their convents), public supporters of Evangelical teaching, and communicants accepting both bread and wine, and he discouraged students from enrolling at the University of Wittenberg. He successfully campaigned for the canonization of Bishop Benno of Meissen (1524), a figure significant for the historical identity of the region, in an attempt to intensify the cult of the saints. In the duke's eyes the widespread Peasants' Revolts (of 1525) were a direct result of the Wittenberg Reformation. He attacked Luther in controversial writings, encouraged his court chaplains Jerome Emser (1478–1527) and Johannes Cochlaeus (1479–1552) to publish similar propaganda, and enforced the censorship of Luther's books. In reaction to Luther's translation of the New Testament (1522), he commissioned Emser to publish an alternative version (1527) that, while freely borrowing from Luther's work, underscored the traditional biblical interpretation of the Roman Catholic Church in its introductions and notes. These measures could not, however, inhibit the spread of the Evangelical movement. Immediately after Duke Georg's death, his son Henry (1473–1541) introduced the Reformation into Albertine Saxony with very little resistance from the population.

See also Cochlaeus, Johannes; Eck, John; Electors of Saxony; Saxonies

Bibliography

Gess, F., eds. *Akten und Briefe zur Kirchenpolitik Herzog Georgs von Sachsen.* 4 vols. Böhlau, 1905–2012; Junghans, H. "Georg von Sachsen (1471–1539)." In *TRE* 12 (1984): 385–89; Volkmar, C. *Reform statt Reformation: Die Kirchenpolitik Herzog Georgs von Sachsen, 1488–1525.* Mohr Siebeck, 2008.

DANIEL GEHRT

Georg, Margrave of Brandenburg-Ansbach

As margrave of Brandenburg-Ansbach in the Holy Roman Empire, Georg "the Pious" (1484–1543) first learned about Luther's ideas at the Diet of Worms (1521) and corresponded with Luther in 1523 to deepen his understanding of Evangelical theology. Georg's courts in Jägerndorf (Silesia) and Ansbach (Franconia) became centers of Evangelical activity in the 1520s. The margrave was among the original group of Evangelical princes who lodged an official protest against decisions of the Diet of Speyer (1529). He was also a signer of the Augsburg Confession (1530). Georg later encouraged the Elector of Brandenburg Joachim II to reform his territories according to the Lutheran faith. He also supported the use of church orders (*Kirchenordnungen*) to reform his territories. The margrave was a dedicated Lutheran prince during the first generation of Evangelical reforms in central Europe.

See also Augsburg Confession; Holy Roman Empire; Joachim II Hector

Bibliography

Müller, U. "Markgraf Georg der Fromme: Ein protestantischer Landesherr im 16. Jahrhundert." *Jahrbuch für fränkische Landesforschung* 45 (1985): 107–23; Vogler, G. "George of Brandenburg-Ansbach." In *The Oxford Encyclopedia of the Reformation*, ed. H. Hillerbrand, 2:166–67. Oxford University Press, 1996.

MICHAEL J. HALVORSON

Gerhard, Johann

Early in life Johann Gerhard (1582–1637) was advised by Johann Arndt to study theology. He became recognized as a German Lutheran theologian, receiving his doctor of theology in 1606; serving as superintendent at Heldburg (1606–15) and superintendent-general of Coburg (1615–16), where he compiled a new church order for the territory; and finally serving as professor of theology in Jena (1616–37). One of the best-known and most influential Lutheran theologians of the seventeenth century, Gerhard was recognized for his dogmatic writings (e.g., *Theological Commonplaces* and *Catholic Confession*) as well as devotional writings (e.g., *Sacred Meditations* and *School of Piety* [*Schola pietatis*]). Gerhard was also significant as an exegete, evidenced by his massive *Harmony of the Gospels* and by his editorship, until his death, of the *Weimar Bible* (*Kurfürstenbibel*). Of a gentle and earnest spirit, he avoided invective yet clearly rejected opposing viewpoints. Four groups of opponents recur in his writings: Roman Catholics (esp. Robert Bellarmine), Calvinists, Photinians (i.e., Socinian Unitarians), and spiritualists. Especially Gerhard's eschatology, moral theology, doctrine of Scripture, concept of theology, and devotional works have interested recent researchers.

See also Lutheran Orthodoxy

Bibliography

Fischer, E. R. *Vita Ioannis Gerhardi*. Coerner, 1723. ET, Repristination, 2001; Gerhard, J. *Theological Commonplaces*. ET of *Loci theologici*. Concordia, 2007–; Steiger, J. A., ed. *Bibliographia Gerhardina*. Frommann-Holzboog, 2003.

BENJAMIN T. G. MAYES

Gerhardt, Paul

The pastor, poet, and hymnodist Paul Gerhardt (1607–76) was, after Luther, the greatest hymn writer of the Lutheran tradition, authoring some 120 hymns. Dozens are still in regular use among Lutherans throughout the world. He was a notable German poet, an orthodox Lutheran pastor, and stood by the Formula of Concord in leading resistance to the Calvinizing religious policy of the electors of Brandenburg.

Gerhardt's early life, known from scant sources, was overshadowed by the Thirty Years' War. Born in 1607 in Gräfenhainichen, near Wittenberg, he was orphaned by 1621. He matriculated at the princes' school at Grimma in 1622 and then at the university in Wittenberg in 1628, studying poetry as well as theology. From 1643 to 1651, as a theological

candidate, Gerhardt worked as a private tutor in Berlin. In 1651 Gerhardt was ordained for his first parish in Mittenwalde. He married Anna Maria Berthold (1622–68) in 1655. Of five children, only one son survived his parents. In 1657 Gerhardt returned to Berlin as deacon at the Nicolaikirche, becoming a public voice for the Lutheran clergy seeking to maintain their adherence to the Formula of Concord. Gerhardt served for ten years amid religious strife with Elector Friedrich Wilhelm (himself Reformed). The elector removed Gerhardt from office in 1666 but after general outcry restored him in 1667. In the face of the elector's continued opposition, Gerhardt resigned his office in 1668, taking up his final pastorate, in Lübben, Saxony, in 1669.

Gerhardt began writing hymns during his time as a tutor, continuing through his ministry in Mittenwalde and Berlin. His musical collaborator and patron was the cantor Johann Crüger (1598–1662), whose 1647 *Praxis pietatis melica* contained eighteen hymns by Gerhardt; the 1661 edition had eighty-nine hymns. After Crüger's death, his successor at the Nikolaikirche, Johann Georg Ebeling (1637–76), continued to set Gerhardt's texts to music and published a complete collection of Gerhardt's hymns in his *Geistliche Andachten* of 1666.

Gerhardt's hymns drew from diverse sources, including scriptural texts, especially the Psalms, but also medieval hymns, such as "O Haupt voll Blut und Wunden [O sacred head]," ascribed to Bernard of Clairvaux, prayers from Johann Arndt's *Paradiesgärtlein*, and outlines from the dogmatics of Johann Gerhard or Leonhard Hutter.

Gerhardt's hymns joined doctrine with affective piety in the new poetic idiom of the seventeenth century. The central themes of the hymns included trust in God's care and his forgiveness for Christ's sake amid adversity, such as "Befiehl du deine Wege [Commit whatever grieves you]," "Warum sollt ich mich denn grämen [Why should cross and trial grieve me]," "Sollt ich meinem Gott nicht singen

[Shall I not his praise be singing]," and "Ist Gott für mich so trete [If God himself is for me]." Many celebrated the incarnation and passion of Christ, such as the Advent hymn "Wie soll ich dich empfangen [O how shall I receive thee]" and the Christmas hymns "O Jesu Christ, dein Kripplein ist [O Jesus Christ, thy manger is]," "Fröhlich soll mein Herze springen [All my heart with joy is springing]," and "Wir singen dir, Immanuel [We sing, Immanuel, thy praise]"; also the passion hymns "Ein Lämmlein geht . . . [A lamb goes uncomplaining forth]" and "O Welt, sieh hier dein Leben [Upon the cross extended]," in addition to "O Haupt" [O sacred head] and the Easter hymn "Auf, auf, mein Herz mit Freuden [Awake my heart with gladness]." Gerhardt's hymns supplied daily private devotion, including his morning hymn "Die güldne Sonne [The golden sunbeams]" and his beloved evening hymn "Nun ruhen alle Wälder [Now rest beneath night's shadow]," before becoming an enduring part of the public worship of Lutheran congregations.

See also Calvinism as a Second Reformation; Formula of Concord; Hymnody; Music

Bibliography

Axmacher, E. *Johann Arndt und Paul Gerhardt: Studien zur Theologie, Frömmigkeit und geistlichen Dichtung des 17. Jahrhunderts.* Francke, 2001; Bachmann, J. F., ed. *Paulus Gerhardts geistliche Lieder: Historisch-kritische Ausgabe.* Oehmigke, 1866; Bunners, C. *Paul Gerhardt: Weg—Werk—Wirkung.* Rev. ed. Vandenhoeck & Ruprecht, 2006; Kelly, J., trans. *Paul Gerhardt's Spiritual Songs.* A. Strahan, 1867; Ruschke, J. *Paul Gerhardt und der Berliner Kirchenstreit.* Mohr Siebeck, 2012; Steiger, J. A. *"Geh' aus, mein Herz, und suche Freud'": Paul Gerhardts Sommerlied und die Gelehrsamkeit der Barockzeit.* De Gruyter, 2007; Zager, D., ed. *Celebrating the Life and Hymns of Paul Gerhardt and Martin Franzmann.* Concordia Theological Seminary Press, 2008.

Christopher Boyd Brown

German Christians (Deutsche Christen)

The German Christians (Deutsche Christen) was a movement within German Protestantism that emerged from several ethno-nationalist and anti-Semitic Protestant groups in Germany that were active during the 1920s. With organized groups in all the regional churches, the movement officially constituted itself as a national movement in May 1932 and issued ten guidelines that embraced the Nazi concept of "positive Christianity," affirmed anti-Semitism and Nazi racial ideology, and claimed to express the spirit of Lutheranism (*Luther Geist*) in that historical moment.

After January 1933 the German Christians quickly gained a following among Protestants who saw the rise of National Socialism as a hopeful development that deserved church support. In national church elections held in July 1933, German Christian representatives were elected to governance bodies in all the regional churches and quickly gained control of most of the theological faculties. German Christian leader Ludwig Müller was elected Reich Bishop in a contentious process in the summer of 1933, with the goal of unifying the regional churches into a *Reichskirche* (nationalistic church) that would conform to the Nazi state.

The group's attempt to introduce an "Aryan paragraph" into church law that would replicate Nazi civil service laws sparked growing resistance from theologians and church leaders who viewed "racial" criteria for church baptism and membership as heresy; by May 1934 the groups opposing the German Christians had coalesced into the Confessing Church. Support for the German Christians had already begun to diminish as its more extremist theological views came to light. In November 1933 the German Christians held a mass rally at the Berlin Sport Palace, where leaders called for a fully Germanic church, the establishment of separate churches for Christians of Jewish descent, and the removal of the Old Testament from Christian Bibles. In the wake of the rally, many people resigned from the movement, the church opposition movement drew more supporters, and a full-fledged battle for control of the German Evangelical Church (the Church Struggle, or *Kirchenkampf*) began throughout the country. Although Nazi regime leaders had initially viewed the German Christians as allies in their goal of bringing the churches into conformity with the Nazi ideological agenda, the regime distanced itself from the German Christian movement as the internal Church Struggle intensified.

Nonetheless the German Christians retained control of most church administrations and theological faculties until 1945, and while their more extreme theological views were controversial among mainstream theologians, the nationalism and anti-Semitism of the group was widespread. Moderate leaders of the German Evangelical Church and of the regional churches wanted to avoid a church schism, and thus the church as a whole followed both a pattern of compromises with the German Christian leadership within the churches and a cautious accommodation with regard to all dealings with the Nazi state. The movement's influence was augmented by the support of some of the preeminent theologians of the era, including the systematic theologian Emanuel Hirsch, who edited the German Christian national journal during 1934–43, and the New Testament scholar Walter Grundmann. Gerhard and Helmuth Kittel, Friedrich Gogarten, and Heinrich Bornkamm were among the theologians who initially supported the German Christians but withdrew their support after the Sport Palace rally.

The German Christians were most influential in controlling theological education and ensuring Protestant church conformity to state measures, particularly those that affected Jews and Christians of Jewish descent. In April 1939 German Christian leaders published the Godesberg Declaration, declaring the unity of Christian and Nazi principles and emphasizing the fundamental anti-Judaism of Christianity, which led to founding the Institute for the Study and Eradication of Jewish Influence on German Religious Life in Eisenach. Separate congregations were established for "non-Aryan Christians" in the five regional churches that were most heavily German Christian.

Although the movement was repudiated after 1945, none of the German Christian leaders suffered lasting consequences for their actions. Even church leaders who had been critical of the German Christians before 1945 had made compromises with them and worked with them, and most postwar German Evangelical Church leaders were reluctant to pursue the issue. Siegfred Leffler, director of the Eisenach Institute and one of the most prominent national leaders of the movement, was reinstated to church service in 1949.

See also Barmen Confession; Confessing Church; Holocaust; Jews; World Wars I and II

Bibliography

Bergen, D. *Twisted Cross: The German Christian Movement in the Third Reich*. University of North Carolina Press, 1996; Ericksen, R. P. *Theologians under Hitler*. Yale University Press, 1985; Helmreich, E. C. *The German Churches under Hitler*. Wayne State University Press, 1979; Heschel, S. *The Aryan Jesus: Christian Theologians and the Bible in Nazi Germany*. Princeton University Press, 2008.

VICTORIA J. BARNETT

German Mysticism

German mysticism (ca. 1300–ca. 1500) as a mode of religious thought contributed significantly to the theology and reception of the Reformation, though scholars debate the precise nature of those contributions. Mystical theology or a mystical orientation had its roots in monastic practices of contemplation. The twelfth-century reformation of monasticism led, among other things, to developments in mystical thought and the language used to describe it. More precisely, mysticism became at the same time more scholastic and more practical as theologians tried to bring order to the whole idea of love for God and emphasized the affective elements in one's relation to God. In the following century what has been called a new mysticism emerged and was more democratic than the monastic forms of mysticism that preceded it. This new mysticism saw the emergence of women as important figures, along with written expressions in the vernacular languages of Europe. The excesses of this mysticism led to suspicion and repression, particularly of those accused at the time of the heresy of the Free Spirit, so called because they practiced a freedom that came from their consciousness of being completely one with God.

Beginning around 1300, mystics in the German-speaking lands distinguished themselves by their creativity and originality. Writing prolifically, they profoundly influenced the course of mysticism in the Late Middle Ages. Foremost among them is Meister Eckhart (ca. 1260–ca. 1328), a Dominican theologian and preacher. Eckhart's mysticism of the ground (*grunt*), to use Bernard McGinn's label, distinguished itself from other currents of mysticism in Germany, such as that of Mechtild of Magdeburg. Eckhart was concerned, above all, with how the human person could be united with God. After becoming a Dominican, Eckhart studied with Albert the Great at Cologne and at the University of Paris. His service in the order included teaching at Paris in addition to holding positions providing pastoral care to monks and nuns. As a result, Eckhart's mystical thought can be described as scholastic and speculative, but also with a democratizing impulse. Many of his treatises and sermons were probably intended for an even wider audience than monks and nuns. In preaching about the mystical union between God and human beings, Eckhart used the term "ground" as a way of describing union that occurs at the deepest level of being. He could say, for example, "God's ground is my ground." To explain how this union is achieved, Eckhart also appropriated the Neoplatonic idea of movement from the divine (*exitus*) and return to it (*reditus*). The return to the divine is facilitated not by specific methods or works but by abandoning all created things, to be left with God alone in a union that, because it is with God's own ground, transforms human beings into God in the sense of becoming completely identified with the divine being. The breakthrough to this union comes through the work of Christ—not necessarily the historic work of Christ but the birth of the Son in the soul of the individual. As a result

of such expressions and given the fear of the Free Spirit heresy, Eckhart was charged with heresy. In 1329 the papal bull *In agro dominico* condemned him even though he had probably died in the previous year.

This condemnation did little to inhibit the activities of Eckhart's faithful and talented disciples Henry Suso (ca. 1295–1366) and Johannes Tauler (ca. 1300–1361). Suso had become a Dominican in his birthplace, Constance, at age thirteen. When he was sent to study in Strasbourg and Cologne, he came into contact with Meister Eckhart. After returning to his home convent, Suso, as a result of criticism of his own teaching, defended Eckhart's teaching (after its condemnation) in the *Little Book of Truth*, which was also denounced as heretical. Suso avoided condemnation but was no longer allowed to teach although he eventually became prior of the convent. At this time he also had the experience of being mystically married to Divine Wisdom. This event influenced his book *Clock of Wisdom*. For the rest of his life, Suso cultivated the inner life and practiced spiritual direction, especially of women. Exiled from Constance during the conflict between the pope and the emperor, he was transferred to Ulm, where he spent the last two decades of his life. Although in his works Suso used images, including specially commissioned manuscript illuminations, he insisted that no images were possible in the highest states of ecstasy. Suso agreed with Eckhart that (relying on ancient tropes) "God became man so that man might become God," but he also embraced a contemplation and imitation of Christ's passion that was deeply emotional. The goal was a spiritual imitation that echoed Eckhart's emphasis on abandonment. Unlike Eckhart, however, Suso relied heavily on visions, both sleeping and waking, to describe the mystical experience. Suso's works show that he was the most literary of the German mystics and also, based on the number of surviving manuscripts, the most popular.

Johannes Tauler, too, was greatly influenced by Eckhart's thought. Having become a Dominican in his birthplace, Strasbourg, Tauler no doubt encountered Eckhart there. Eventually Tauler became a preacher in Strasbourg. Much of his preaching was for Dominican nuns. When the city was placed under interdict for supporting the emperor rather than the pope, he shared in the exile of his fellow Dominicans. Upon his return, Tauler experienced numerous horrors, including plague, all of which reinforced his rejection of the world. In the last years of his life Tauler traveled extensively. His influence came entirely through his preaching and the written records of his sermons that began to be assembled during his lifetime. Though indebted to Eckhart, Tauler had other influences as well. He mentions the Friends of God, a group dedicated to mystical piety that he had encountered while in exile; he read the traditional Latin mystics, as well as Mechtild of Magdeburg; he most likely met John Ruusbroec. As a result, Tauler's preaching cannot be seen merely as a simplified or popularized version of Eckhart's preaching. Yet the two do share many themes, including the need for spiritual poverty, or emptying oneself, as well as a focus on the inner life. With regard to the inner life, Tauler emphasizes that what he calls the highest part of the soul—*gemuete*, which is similar to though not the same as Eckhart's *grunt*—seeks union with God. Tauler's mysticism was eminently practical and biblical, as a result of his textual preaching, his critique of Scholastic theology, and his moralism. He focused on humility in following Christ, believing that union with God could result only from such an orientation.

Nicholas of Cusa (1401–64) represents the end of an era in German mysticism. As a young priest and canon lawyer in Trier, Nicholas gained prominence when he was sent as a representative to the Council of Basel in 1432. A year later he had produced *De concordantia catholica* (*The Catholic Concordance*), a defense of conciliarism based on the Dionysian notion of hierarchy that also included a program for the reform of the church and the empire. Eventually he joined the minority party

that sided with the pope against the council, leaving Basel to attend the papal council that was negotiating a reunion with the Greek Church. After the council, Nicholas labored mightily on the pope's behalf in an effort to return the empire to papal obedience. He was rewarded with a cardinal's hat in 1450 and undertook a major reform of the church in the Tyrol as bishop of Brixen. His reform efforts met stiff resistance, and he was eventually recalled to Rome. In Rome he quickly tired of the corruption of the curia and eventually asked to be released from his duties there. He died at Todi in 1464. An exceptional humanist scholar and prolific writer, Nicholas explored a wide range of topics. He is significant in the history of mysticism not because he himself was a mystic, though he did report that he had received the insight to complete *De docta ignorantia* (*On Learned Ignorance*) while at sea as a "heavenly gift" that enabled him to "embrace incomprehensible realities in an incomprehensible manner." This treatise was followed by companion pieces, *De coniecturis* (*On Conjectures*) and later *De visione dei* (*On the Vision of God*), among many others. Nicholas's approach to mysticism was academic and theoretical and rooted firmly in the Dionysian tradition. His importance lies in the fact that he addressed how contact between God and human beings transforms human existence.

Luther published two separate editions (1516 and 1518) of the anonymous *Theologia Deutsch* (*German Theology*), which he believed to be a summary of Tauler's work, as confirmation of his own theological orientation and expression. Yet the nature and impact of his encounter with the mystical tradition has been much debated since it is complicated by the twin problems of defining mysticism and of determining how Luther read his sources. For example, Luther's unqualified praise of Tauler seems to separate that author from other German mystics and thus makes it difficult to say that Luther's embrace of German mysticism as a whole was unqualified. Even in the case of Tauler, what Luther appropriated was not necessarily mysticism, but rather an understanding of God's work that embraced affect, which Luther understood as personal faith. Luther's exposition of the theology of the cross in 1518 also echoes some of Tauler's paradoxical language and thought.

Bibliography

Davies, O. *Meister Eckhart: Mystical Theologian*. SPCK, 1991; Eckhart, M. *The Essential Sermons, Commentaries, Treatises, and Defense*. Trans. E. Colledge and B. McGinn. Paulist Press, 1981; Hackett, J. M., ed. *A Companion to Meister Eckhart*. Brill, 2013; Hamm, B. *Religiosität im späten Mittelalter*. Mohr Siebeck, 2011; Leppin, V. "Luther's Roots in Monastic-Mystical Piety." In *The Oxford Handbook of Martin Luther's Theology*, ed. R. Kolb, I. Dingel, and L. Batka, 49–61. Oxford University Press, 2014; Lund, E. "Tauler the Mystic's Lutheran Admirers." In *Piety and Family in Early Modern Europe: Essays in Honour of Steven Ozment*, ed. M. R. Forster and B. J. Kaplan, 9–27. Ashgate, 2005; McGinn, B. *The Harvest of Mysticism in Medieval Germany*. Crossroad, 2005; McGinn, B. *The Mystical Thought of Meister Eckhart: The Man from Whom God Hid Nothing*. Crossroad, 2001; Nicholas of Cusa. *Selected Spiritual Writings*. Trans. H. L. Bond. Paulist Press, 1997; Oberman, H. "*Simul gemitus et raptus*: Luther and Mysticism." In *The Dawn of the Reformation: Essays in Late Medieval and Early Reformation Thought*, 126–54. Eerdmans, 1992; Tauler, J. *Sermons*. Trans. M. Shrady. Paulist Press, 1985; Vogelsang, E. "Luther und die Mystik." *Lutherjahrbuch* 19 (1937): 32–54.

PAUL W. ROBINSON

Germany since 1870

Since the first half of the nineteenth century, Protestantism exists in Germany in two organizational forms. The first is the *Landeskirchen* (territorial churches), whose members constitute all Protestant citizens of a given territorial unit. These units were originally coincident with the self-governing territories within the Deutsche Bund (German Federation), created in 1815 (after Napoléon's defeat) as successor institution to the Holy Roman Empire, but they largely continued to define the boundaries of the churches even beyond the political structure of 1815 throughout the Second Empire (1871–1918), the Weimar Republic (1919–33), the Third Reich (1933–45), the phase of political separation (East/West), and into the time of the reunited Federal Republic (1990–). The second form is the *Freikirchen* (free churches), whose members are defined by commitment only, not geography.

Within this setting Lutheranism took form in three kinds of ecclesial institutions: in confessional Lutheran *Landeskirchen*, territorial churches with an exclusively Lutheran membership; united *Landeskirchen*, embracing Lutheran and Reformed members in one body without dissolving the confessional distinctness of their parishes and pastors; and Lutheran *Freikirchen*. In 1870 there were twenty-eight *Landeskirchen*, the largest Lutheran ones in Saxony, Hannover, Württemberg, and Bavaria; the largest among the united *Landeskirchen* and indeed among all Protestant churches in Germany was the church of Prussia, which comprised nearly half of Germany's Protestants. Among the *Freikirchen*, all very small, the most important was the Old Lutheran Church in Prussia, founded in 1830 in protest against the Prussian Union. A few others emerged in other regions. Most of these free churches merged after World War II into the Selbständige Evangelisch-Lutherische Kirche (Independent Evangelical Lutheran Church).

As long as Germany was made up of monarchies, dukedoms, and similar nobility-ruled territories, their rulers were the temporal heads of the respective *Landeskirchen* (*Landesherrliches Kirchenregiment*). This did not mean that the *Landeskirchen* were state churches, as they had been in the late Holy Roman Empire. After the Napoleonic era most states of the German Federation were at least biconfessional, with both Protestant and Roman Catholic inhabitants, and the states were confessionally neutral, with the citizens enjoying legal parity. This did not preclude a special relationship between the Protestant churches (Lutheran as well as Reformed and United) and the rulers as persons, who continued to be their *summepiscopi* (highest bishops). The princes who held such positions did not need to belong to the church over which they presided; for example, the *summus episcopus* of the Lutheran Church of Bavaria was the Roman Catholic king of that state. Yet the actual government of the Protestant churches was in the hands of consistories, the holders of episcopal offices (superintendents, general superintendents), and of the synods that arose during the nineteenth century in nearly all churches.

Thus, with the collapse of the Prussian empire in 1918, princely oversight of church governments ended, and separation of church and state was enacted. The *Landeskirchen* already possessed stable governing bodies, which continued their work. They only had to substitute ordained pastors for the princely *summepiscopi*, creating an ecclesial episcopacy for governance. The plurality of many distinct Lutheran, Reformed, and United churches, some large, some small, remained the same. Already in the nineteenth century there had been advocates of a less fragmentary structure, ideally of one Protestant church for the whole of Germany (*Reichskirche*). Such ideas reemerged after World War I. They failed, but after Adolf Hitler had come to power and *Führertum* (authoritarian one-man leadership) became the ideal for all fields of life, Protestants who sided with the new regime, the Deutsche Christen (German Christians), renewed those older deliberations. Because they had gained majorities in the synods of all *Landeskirchen* except the Lutheran Church of Bavaria, they created a *Reichskirche* with one *Reichbischof*, causing the *Landeskirchen* to lose their independence (1933). Sharp protests, especially from several Lutheran churches that refused to be integrated in a *Reichskirche* (not least because that necessarily had to be a United Church), resulted in the official restitution of their independence (1934).

In the renewal of the churches after World War II, the ensemble of independent *Landeskirchen* was taken for granted. Any attempt toward creating a strong common structure met with the suspicion of the Lutheran churches that such a structure would be a vehicle for a United Church. They could voice their opposition all the more forcefully since union-minded Lutheranism within the huge United Church of Prussia had suffered a severe blow: Silesia, East Prussia, and Pomerania, whose Protestants had been practically all Lutheran, were ceded to Poland (a small part also to Russia), and their inhabitants had either fled or were driven out. Thus the Prussian church shrank enormously, and in the remaining parts the Lutheran element was greatly weakened; the western parts (Rhineland, Westphalia), where the Reformed tradition was strong, gained strength. Soon after the war the Prussian church was dissolved into several regional United *Landeskirchen*. However, although the Lutheran churches successfully resisted becoming part of one larger church, they agreed to set up a common institution to deal with common concerns, the Evangelische Kirche in Deutschland (EKD, Protestant Church in Germany), which comprises all Lutheran, Reformed, and United *Landeskirchen* (1945). Until the Leuenberg Agreement (1973) they were not in communion with each other. This was different from the start (1948) in the Vereinigte Evangelisch-Lutherische Kirche Deutschlands (VELKD) (United Evangelical-Lutheran Church of Germany), which unites most of the Lutheran *Landeskirchen*, and in the common body of the United churches (originally Evangelische Kirche der Union, EKU, now Union evangelischer Kirchen, UEK). During the decades of separation for the Federal Republic of Germany (West) and the German Democratic Republic (East), the eastern member churches of the EKD were forced to organize a body on their own, but they reversed this step after reunification. In the last years there has been a growing tendency to strengthen the EKD and abandon special bonds and prerogatives of the VELKD. Bishops were elected across confessional (Lutheran, Reformed, United) borders. In some cases Lutheran and United *Landeskirchen* merged. Occasional Lutheran confessional reservations have met with little response, but nowadays they seem to gain weight.

Most Protestant theologians in Germany were and are Lutheran. There was and is, however, a spectrum of theological viewpoints among them. In 1870, on the one hand, confessional Lutherans, not only but predominately in the Lutheran *Landeskirchen*, defined Lutheranism in confessional terms, as adherence to the Lutheran confessions (as defined by the theological faculties of Leipzig and, in a modernizing fashion, Erlangen). For other Lutheran theologians, what was decisive in the Wittenberg reformer, indeed in the Reformation as a whole, had been a new religious and cultural impulse. For the "conservative" or "positive" theologians this impulse meant a piety and ethics faithful to the New Testament understood in a more or less literalistic way, a view that brought them into fierce conflicts with the rising historical-critical exegesis. For the "liberal" theologians who admitted or even affirmed the distance between the New Testament and both the Reformation on the one hand and their own time on the other, the impulse initiated by Luther was the rediscovery of a balance between justification as the religious dimension of Christian existence and the ethical dimension realized in working faithfully toward the kingdom of God understood as communion-oriented social order (Albrecht Ritschl) or the rediscovery of the freedom of conscience before God and other human beings, with everything thereof implied culturally, socially, and so forth (Adolf von Harnack). Thus Lutheranism could claim to be at the forefront of modernity without denying the obvious premodern traits of Luther and the Reformation. The revolutionary religious impulse given by Luther was set against its ecclesial, social, cultural, and political implications realized only later, in Pietism and the Enlightenment—a differentiation that led to the distinction between old Protestantism and new Protestantism (Ernst Troeltsch). A movement of enormous momentum that came out of liberal Lutheranism, but led into its rejection, was the so-called Luther Renaissance during and after World War I (Karl Holl); on the basis of hitherto unknown sources of Luther's early years, the "young Luther"

appeared as a figure who had little to do with the Luther images of later times, particularly those of the late nineteenth century, but was before all else the exponent of redemption from tribulation through justification by faith alone. This Luther, put forward against the liberal zeitgeist, met the existential needs of the generation after World War I and, as its adherents claimed, the needs of all humankind before God. With its program the Luther Renaissance exercised widespread influence across theological camps and generations (e.g., all "dialectical theologians," Emanuel Hirsch, Dietrich Bonhoeffer, Gerhard Ebeling).

Alongside these theological movements, the decades after 1870 saw the rise of the "National Luther." The Wittenberg reformer appeared as the embodiment of the German nation, politically realized in the Second Empire under the (Reformed) Hohenzollern dynasty (1871). This vision was promoted by (though it did not dominate) the Luther jubilee of 1883. In World War I and the jubilee of 1917, the nationalistic use of Luther, despite serious warnings from different theological quarters (Holl, Hirsch, Troeltsch, Martin Rade), became all embracing. When, after Germany's defeat, racist views that had appeared already in the late nineteenth century in certain nationalistic circles intensified and became prominent in the ideology of the National Socialists, Luther was used for this ideology too; abridged folk versions of his anti-Jewish writings, which for centuries had been hardly read, were reprinted and promulgated by National Socialist propagandists and their Lutheran allies, the Deutsche Christen. On the other hand, the Confessing Church claimed to be the true heir of Luther and the Reformation (Karl Barth, Bonhoeffer). The creedal document of the *Kirchenkampf*, the Barmen Declaration (1934), was a reinstatement of the confessions of the Reformation.

After World War II the theological currents of the previous decades, except for the German Christian movement, continued, with the dialectical theology of the Barthian direction and the exegetical program of demytholo-gization (Rudolf Bultmann) dominating the academic scene. Confessional Lutheranism lived on in those churches (Hanover, Bavaria) and faculties (Erlangen) where it had earlier been strong, accompanied by efforts toward a positive reevaluation of the creeds as a result of the *Kirchenkampf* (Edmund Schlink). A hermeneutical theology in dialogue with the philosophical trends of the time attempted to open up Lutheran theology to new perspec-tives (Ebeling). Reflection on the failure of large parts of the German Protestantism in the Third Reich led to a break with theological nationalism as well as to a positive affirmation of the democratic order, expressed in a series of *Denkschriften*, ecclesiastical memoranda on acute socioethical and political problems. From the 1960s a new generation of Lutheran theologians who had not been shaped by the currents of prewar theology insisted that his-tory had to be taken more seriously as a theo-logical category than had been the case in a theology primarily molded by the concerns of the religious and ethical individual (Wolfhart Pannenberg). More recently the theological and socioethical perspectives of Schleier-macher reentered Lutheran theology.

After the Second Vatican Council (1962–65) the ecumenical dialogues with Roman Ca-tholicism became a matter of interest for academic theologians and churchmen alike. However, the documents that resulted from these dialogues, national or international (The Condemnations of the Reformation Era: Do They Still Divide?, 1986; the Joint Declara-tion on the Doctrine of Justification, 1997; the Joint Official Statement, 1999), met with widespread criticism by theologians and were received by the churches with explicit reserva-tions (Joint Declaration) or not at all (Con-demnations; Joint Official Statement). This did not prevent the *Landeskirchen* and the Roman Catholic Church in Germany and their parishes from common services and close col-laboration in many fields. The most success-ful ecumenical dialogue in which the German

Lutheran *Landeskirchen* participated was the dialogue between European Lutheran and Re-formed churches that led to the Leuenberg Agreement (1973), opening up full commu-nion among the signatory churches, later on also with the Methodist churches. The Meißen Agreement (1988) and further dialogues in its wake allowed many levels of communion below the episcopal level with the Church of England.

See also Althaus, Paul; Barmen Confession; Barth, Karl; Bonhoeffer, Dietrich; Bultmann, Rudolf (Karl); Catholicism; Confessing Church; Ebeling, Gerhard; Ecumenical Dialogues; German Christians (Deutsche Christen); Liberalism; Pannenberg, Wolfhart; Troeltsch, Ernst; World Wars I and II

Bibliography

Nowak, K. *Geschichte des Christentums in Deutschland: Religion, Politik und Gesellschaft vom Ende der Aufklä-rung bis zur Mitte des 20. Jahrhunderts*. Beck, 1995; Wall-mann, J. *Kirchengeschichte Deutschlands seit der Refor-mation*. 7th ed. Mohr Siebeck, 2012; Wendebourg, D. "Die Reformationsjubiläen des 19. Jahrhunderts." *Zeitschrift für Theologie und Kirche* 108 (2011): 270–335.

DOROTHEA WENDEBOURG

Ghana

Early Lutheran activities in Ghana can be traced back to the seventeenth century, when the Danish Lutheran chaplain Wilhelm Johan Müller worked at a trading post for the Dan-ish trading company. His ministry was mainly confined to the European employees of the company, but there were also some missionary efforts to the indigenous population. However, these activities were sporadic and short-lived.

The Evangelical Presbyterian Church in Ghana traces its roots to the missionary ac-tivities of the North German Mission Society, which was founded in 1836 by Lutheran and Reformed Mission Associations in Hamburg. Together with the Basel Mission, they started to work in today's Ghana in 1847.

In the middle of the twentieth century, the LCMS began work in Ghana. Since 1958 congregations and preaching stations in ten regions of Ghana were established. The Evan-gelical Lutheran Church of Ghana (ELCG) was formally registered as a new ecclesiastical institution in 1964. The ELCG has opened mission stations in Uganda, Benin, and Ivory Coast. In 1998 the Lutheran Clergy Study Programme was founded to further train local evangelists to become pastors.

The theology and practice is conservative Lutheran, and the ordination of women is rejected. The ELCG is also involved in social and educational services in the country, such as day care, plus primary and junior secondary schools in nine locations. Special programs have been established for the blind and the deaf in several regions. In 2014 membership of the ELCG stood at twenty-nine thousand.

Bibliography

Lenz, D., and E. Schöck-Quinteros. *150 Jahre Norddeutsche Mission, 1836–1986*. Norddeutsche Mission, 1986; Melton, J. G. "Evangelical Lutheran Church of Ghana." In *Religions of the World: A Comprehensive Encyclopedia of Beliefs and Practices*, ed. M. Baumann and J. G. Melton, 3:1062. ABC-CLIO, 2011; Müller, W. J. *Die Africanische auf der Guineischen Gold-Cust gelegene Landschafft Fetu*. Z. Härtel, 1676. ET in *German Sources for West African History, 1599–1669*, comp. A. Jones, 134–259. F. Steiner / Coronet Books, 1983.

FRIEDER LUDWIG

Giertz, Bo Harald

Early in life the Swedish Lutheran bishop, theologian, and author Bo Harald Giertz (August 31, 1905–July 12, 1998) became a Christian through involvement with a Christian student association at Uppsala University even though his parents were professionals who did not believe in God. Switching to study theology, he was ordained as a priest in 1934. The liberal theology at Uppsala did not attract him, but he became deeply influenced by the theology of the Swedish Pietist Henric Schartau. This deep, churchly Pietism marked the rest of his career, though he was also a strong advocate for formal church structures and the historic liturgy, unusual in Pietist circles. During his time in the parish, he traveled widely, visiting schools in an attempt to stem the tide of secularism among young people. He also wrote a number of influential books, most notably the novel *Stengrunden* (1941; ET, *The Hammer of God*, 1960), about the theological struggles of three pastors. Elected bishop of Gothenburg in 1949, he served there until his retirement in 1970. As a bishop he served widely, both in Sweden and within the Lutheran World Federation. He was an opponent of the decision by the Church of Sweden in 1958 to ordain women and served to rally theological conservatives in that church.

See also Sweden

Bibliography

Giertz, B. *The Hammer of God*. Trans. C. A. Nelson and H. O. Andræ. Augsburg Fortress, 2005.

MARK A. GRANQUIST

Glück, Johann Ernst

Born in the eastern regions of present-day Germany, Johann Ernst Glück (1654–1705) was educated at the secondary level at Altenburg (Thüringen) and pursued university study at Wittenberg. He journeyed to Swedish Livonia, where he, under the auspices of Swedish church authorities, devoted himself to developing a school network and preparing the first complete translation of the Bible into Latvian. Glück's career spanned vast expanses of territory in northeastern Europe; he pioneered in the field of language and literacy development in the Baltic states and Russia. As a translator into vernacular languages, educator, and church official, he radically transformed the cultural topography of regions whose inhabitants some 150 years after the advent of the Reformation were still only marginally infused with a consciousness of religious particularity.

As Russian troops moved into Swedish territory in 1702, Glück was taken prisoner and deported to Moscow. In 1703 he was tapped by Czar Peter I to participate in the educational reform of Russia. He is generally regarded as the introducer of Western, Latin-based educational values into Russia. Recognizing the multifariousness of the language used in existing texts, he compiled one of earliest grammars of the Russian language.

See also Russia; Sweden

Bibliography

Dunsdorfs, E. *Pirmās latviešu bībeles vēsture: Geschichte der ersten lettischen Bibel.* Latviesu ev.-lut. Baznica Amerika, 1979; Glück, H., and I. Polanska. *Johann Ernst Glück (1654–1705): Pastor, Philologe, Volksaufklärer im Baltikum und in Russland.* Harrassowitz, 2005; Glück, J. E. *Grammatik der russischen Sprache (1704).* Ed. H. Keipert and B. Uspenskij. Böhlau, 1994.

JĀNIS KRĒSLIŅŠ

Gnesio-Lutherans. *See* Wittenberg Circle, Parties within

God and Trinity

The Bible can describe God as far above the earth and eternal, and therefore inaccessible to human understanding, yet at the same time as the God revealed through creation and history, specifically through the election of Israel, by becoming human in the person of Jesus Christ and through the work of the Holy Spirit. The key problem in the Christian understanding of God is therefore the question of how to maintain both that God is beyond reason's grasp (unknowable) and that God is present especially in the incarnation without one of these emphases nullifying the other. According to the doctrine of the Trinity articulated in the Nicene and Apostles' Creeds, this can only be maintained by confessing one's faith in God both as the origin of, and thus different from, everything else, and at the same time acknowledging God's presence in the world as Creator, Savior, and Sanctifier.

Luther shared the view of the ancient church both concerning the unknowability of God and the indispensability of the doctrine of the Trinity. Concerning the first of these aspects, he was influenced both by mysticism and the Neoplatonic approach to the unknowable One as maintained by both ancient and medieval teachers of the church. Many of these authors he studied in depth, particularly through the formative years before he became a professor and then reformer, though he eventually came to the conclusion that some of them considered the human alienation from God more as a theoretical than a practical and existential problem. In Luther's view, God is always active to the effect that one is confronted by God in every aspect and every moment of one's existence, and some knowledge of this relationship is therefore to be expected of every human being. Yet this general knowledge of God has no help to offer with regard to the danger of finding oneself in an inadequate relationship with God, thus experiencing the world as the sphere of his wrath rather than his love.

Divine difference and hiddenness, however, do not lead Luther into any kind of skepticism toward the significance of biblical revelation; on the contrary, it grounds his appreciation of its importance. This is shown first in the Heidelberg Disputation of 1518 and most clearly in *The Bondage of the Will* (1525), where Luther distinguishes sharply between the hiddenness of God and the clarity and relevance of the Scripture as the definite word from the One who is the undefinable origin of the world. Through this word, God even creates faith among sinful humans, thus reestablishing the loving relationship between God and human beings that fulfills God's original purpose in creating the world. In this way, human freedom is seen as realized through a person's finding oneself utterly dependent on God in every aspect of one's existence. The relation between divine and human agency is, however, a problem that does not lend itself to a theoretical solution any more than does the question of how God's election of some and not of others relates to God as eternal love.

In his exposition of the content of the Christian faith, Luther is deeply informed by the doctrine of the Trinity, both because this is the traditional doctrine of the church, given to it by God, who does not change, and because it is the adequate way of summarizing the content of the biblical revelation. For Luther, the doctrine of the Trinity maintains the principle of divine difference by avoiding the error of seeing God as in any way dependent on the created world. Through the relationship between the persons of the Trinity, God is love from eternity and does not need either the world or human sinfulness in order to kindle mercy and compassion. Creation, redemption, and sanctification are thus ways of manifesting divine love, not its origin. At the same time, the doctrine of the Trinity allows for God's actions in the world to be seen as real, revelatory events, without God's eternity and unchangeability being compromised; God dies on the cross in his Son while the doctrine of divine impassibility is still upheld and through the work of the Holy Spirit makes the confession of this faith a reality. This is what makes it possible to proclaim and receive the gospel as the unalterable promise of the Savior who does not change. Thus in Luther's view, as reflected in the explanation of the Apostles' Creed in the Large Catechism (1529), there is a close relationship between the doctrine of the Trinity and the essence of the gospel both in the sense that it is only as Triune that God can be understood as the unchangeable guarantor of the promises founded on the death and resurrection of his Son, and in the sense that God is the Creator, and thus the sole origin, of the world, the atonement, and the fellowship of believers.

This approach to the doctrine of the Trinity was upheld by Lutheran Orthodoxy. It did not accept, however, all aspects of Luther's understanding of God's hiddenness and unknowability, returning instead to a more scholastic use of Aristotelian logic as a means for maintaining theology's transparency and theoretical stability. Luther's untroubled combination of divine sovereignty and human freedom was thereby replaced by solutions that explored the reborn human's capacity for a theoretically satisfying understanding of the relation between God and human beings, more or less synergistic approaches thus being reintroduced even within the tradition of Lutheran theology. When Pietism reacted against the intellectualization of theology and tried to bring it back on a more practical track, it tended, however, to replace Luther's trust in the Word of God with an emphasis on spiritual experience, which strengthened the tendency toward synergism.

During the Enlightenment, this attempt at establishing a rational theology was radicalized and lost its moorings within the Christian faith. One then tried to find answers to the questions Luther had considered unanswerable, such as the relation between divine sovereignty and human freedom, and the problem of evil. The outcome was an emphasis on the independence of the human intellect that issued in the idea of divine difference being lost; God was subsumed under a concept of being that was supposed to be commonly relevant both for the Creator and created reality as elements of the world equally accessible for human rationality. Both the world and the human being were then considered as entities that could be satisfactorily investigated independently of their relationship to God. The life of faith was then no longer oriented along the difference between Creator and creation transcended by incarnational revelation, but along the difference between the material and spiritual elements of the world, the latter being considered as the religiously interesting aspect. On this approach, God was found relevant only insofar as he appeared to be spiritually interesting.

Anticipating this development in some ways were already Luther's opponents Erasmus of Rotterdam (1466–1536), with his idea of human independence, and Ulrich Zwingli (1484–1531), with his understanding of the spiritual as the area of the encounter between God and the human. It becomes even clearer with René Descartes (1596–1650), for whom God is first and foremost interesting as the guarantor of the adequacy of the concepts humans use in exploring the world, and with Gottfried Leibniz (1646–1716), who wrote the first theodicy: a defense of the rationality of God's justice. With Immanuel Kant (1724–1804), the element of unknowability was reintroduced, but it was conceived according to the difference between reality and the human experience thereof, not according to the difference between Creator and creation. Georg W. F. Hegel (1770–1831) challenged even the Kantian approach to unknowability, maintaining that it was perfectly within the possibility of the thinking human being to grasp the inner essence of the absolute Spirit (God) as that Spirit was self-manifested through the development of world history.

Nineteenth-century liberal theology tried to develop theological approaches according to the demands of this new paradigm, emphasizing religion's significance for emotion (Friedrich Schleiermacher, 1768–1834) and morality (Albrecht Ritschl, 1822–89). Since theologians, especially Ritschl and his followers, had little interest in the problem of the relation between God's eternity and the reality of his revelation, the problem to which the doctrine of the Trinity was supposed to provide the answer, they did not consider this doctrine as important. Hegel had, however, incorporated an approach to the Trinity in his philosophy, maintaining that the relationship between Father, Son, and Holy Spirit was the ultimate manifestation of a development according to the pattern of thesis, antithesis, and synthesis. The irreducible difference of the eternal One is, however, lost also in Hegel's approach, which tends toward seeing the persons of the Trinity as temporally different manifestation of the one God (modalism), God thus being essentially determined by the history of revelation. The twentieth century saw a renaissance of trinitarian theology among theologians who in many respects found the liberal approach insufficient; Karl Barth (1886–1968) was the initial and in many ways the leading representative of this renewal of more classical ways of doing theology. Many of these attempts for renewal, both Protestant and Roman Catholic, however, made themselves dependent on Hegel in way that has led to the problem of modalism being central within contemporary discussions of the Trinity.

During the nineteenth century confessional Lutherans, such as Wilhelm Loehe (1808–72) and C. F. W. Walther (1811–87), tried to maintain their distance both from Pietism and liberal theology without being able to challenge their underlying philosophical assumptions.

This was done more effectively by atheists like Ludwig Feuerbach (1804–72), Karl Marx (1818–83), and Friedrich Nietzsche (1844–1900), who maintained that a God conceived as a part of the world and according to human criteria for relevance was among the less interesting constructions of the human mind and should therefore rather be dispensed with. Nietzsche in particular did this in a way that highlighted the existential implications of atheism and that has continued to attract the attention of theologians; the significance of faith in God can also be explored by investigating the consequences of its absence.

More consistent in thinking through the differences between Luther's and the church fathers' understandings of God on the one hand and the assumptions of modernity on the other hand, though largely neglected by their contemporaries, were Johann Georg Hamann (1730–88) and Søren Kierkegaard (1813–55). For Hamann, the world only makes sense as divine creation; for him, Kant's idea of pure reason therefore appears as anthropocentrism void of content. For Kierkegaard, the human being can only find oneself by reflecting on the God-given identity of oneself and on one's unwillingness to consider the unknowable One as one's origin, an error of which Kierkegaard finds Hegel guilty, an error at variance with reality in a way that has discernable psychological consequences. Both Hamann and Kierkegaard thus follow Luther in insisting on divine difference as the only starting point from which the world can be meaningfully explored. Among the twentieth-century Lutherans who have moved in the same direction are Hermann Sasse (1895–1976), Dietrich Bonhoeffer (1906–45), Gerhard Forde (1927–2005), and Oswald Bayer (1939–). A similar opposition to one-dimensional rationality and Hegelian modalism is also found in much Roman Catholic and in most Greek Orthodox theology today.

Bibliography

Luther's Works: "The Heidelberg Disputation" (1518). LW 31:39–70; "Dear Christians, Let Us Now Rejoice" (1523). LW 53:219–20; *The Bondage of the Will* (1525).

LW 33; Small and Large Catechisms (1529). In *The Book of Concord*, ed. R. Kolb and T. Wengert, 347–480. Fortress, 2000; Three Disputations (1543–45). In *The Substance of the Faith: Luther's Doctrinal Theology for Today*, by D. Bielfeldt, M. Mattox, and P. Hinlicky, 191–209. Fortress, 2008; **General Works:** Alfsvåg, K. "Impassibility and Revelation: On the Relation between Immanence and Economy in Orthodox and Lutheran Thought." *Studia theologica* 68, no. 2 (2014); Alfsvåg, K. *What No Mind Has Conceived: On the Significance of Christological Apophaticism.* Peeters, 2010; Bayer, O. *A Contemporary in Dissent: Johann Georg Hamann as Radical Enlightener.* Eerdmans, 2012; Bayer, O. "Poetological Doctrine of the Trinity." *Lutheran Quarterly* 15 (2001): 43–58; Helmer, C. *The Trinity and Martin Luther: A Study on the Relationship between Genre, Language and the Trinity in Luther's Works (1523–1546).* Von Zabern, 1999; Hyman, G. *A Short History of Atheism.* I. B. Tauris, 2010; Keating, J. F., and T. J. White, eds. *Divine Impassibility and the Mystery of Human Suffering.* Eerdmans, 2009; Lønning, I. "Gott VIII. Neuzeit/Systematisch-theologisch." *Theologische Realenzyklopädie.* Vol. 13. De Gruyter, 1984; Phan, P. C., ed. *The Cambridge Companion to the Trinity.* Cambridge University Press, 2011; Prenter, R. "Luther als Theologe." In *Luther und die Theologie der Gegenwart*, ed. L. Grane and B. Lohse, 112–24. Vandenhoeck & Ruprecht, 1980.

KNUT ALFSVÅG

Gómez, Medardo Ernesto

Born in San Miguel, El Salvador, on June 8, 1945, into a Roman Catholic family, Medardo Ernesto Gómez converted and was confirmed as Lutheran in 1964, in the local Lutheran Church created by missionaries of the Lutheran Church–Missouri Synod (LCMS). He studied theology at the Augsburg Lutheran Seminary in Mexico City, served his first congregation in Zacapa, Guatemala, in 1971–72, and in 1972 was sent by the LCMS mission to San Salvador, the capital of his native land, where he created a new Lutheran congregation, Resurrección. In 1983 he was kidnapped and tortured, after which he went into exile, returning with international support in 1985. This was the time of the rupture within the LCMS, and thus began a closer association of the El Savador Lutheran Church with the Lutheran World Federation and other Lutheran churches in the United States and Europe. The said rupture started with the ordination of "lay pastors" in 1979, including several women, using the Lutheran teaching of priesthood

of all believers as a justification, but crediting it also to old pre-Colombian indigenous traditions. On August 6, 1986, Gómez was consecrated bishop by the Swedish bishop Åke Kastlund, thus becoming a part of the historic episcopate tradition of Scandinavia. He received several international prizes and in 1992 was nominated for the Nobel Peace Prize for his work in defense of the poor and the persecuted. The priesthood of all believers was the formal principle of his ministry, and its theological content was defined by his "theology of life," his rendition of the theology of liberation.

See also El Salvador

Bibliography
Aaltonen, H. *Fe y Esperanza: Women's Road to Ministry in the Lutheran Church of El Salvador 1952–2009.* Åbo Akademi University, 2013; Gómez, M. *Fire against Fire.* Augsburg Fortress, 1990; Gómez, M. *Latinoamérica: Testimonio de Vida y Esperanza.* Prologues by Helmut Frenz and Manlio Argueta. Ed. S. Juárez. Iglesia Luterana Salvadoreña, 1993; Gómez, M. *Teología de la Vida.* Prologue and Selection by Immanuel Zerger. Nicarao, 1992.

VITOR WESTHELLE

Good Works

When Martin Luther's insights into justification by faith alone without works became the central message of the Reformation emanating from Wittenberg, the relationship between faith and works, and therefore the understanding of good works and their role in Christian life, also became a central concern of Evangelical reformers and their opponents. Luther's discovery, as he recalled it near the end of his life in the preface to the first volume of his collected Latin works, was that the gospel proclaimed a righteousness that God gives to the believer. Therefore from the standpoint of the believer it is a passive righteousness, received as a gift, without any fulfillment by the believer of the demands of God's own righteousness, which Luther had been taught to view as a formal or active righteousness because by it God is righteous and therefore must condemn the unrighteous sinner. Yet from the perspective of God's activity, this passive righteousness received through faith is still the power of God at work. Luther describes combing through Scripture by memory and finding analogies: "the work of God, that is, what God does in us, the power of God, with which he makes us strong, the wisdom of God, with which he makes us wise, [etc.]" (LW 34:337). For Luther, the comfort of forgiveness and the certainty of salvation brought by the gospel was pure gift, an activity of God, and any talk of human contribution or merit could only obscure or even blaspheme this gift. Justification is by faith *alone*.

This teaching challenged at their heart various medieval systems for understanding justification and salvation (soteriology). With their origins traceable to Augustine's understanding of God's grace bearing the fruit of love (*caritas*) that characterizes both the individual believer and the church as a community (e.g., *City of God* 14.28), these systems interpreted the justification of the sinner as an activity of God's grace, transforming the sinner through a faith that finds its end or goal in love, which must therefore be a faith formed by love (*fides caritate formata*), where this "form" is a disposition of love (*habitus caritatis*). Justification is by God's grace, but according to this understanding it is a grace that works with the human being who in some way prepares for grace or works together with grace to achieve salvation by meritorious works.

Already in the first of his major treatises of 1520, *On Good Works*, Luther turned on its head this Scholastic understanding of the relationship between faith and love, and therefore between faith and works. In Luther's understanding, love and works need to be perfected by faith rather than the other way around, and no work is good that is done without faith. Faith is "the first good work," done in obedience to the first and most important of the commandments (*Good Works*, 19; LW 44:25), and worked in human hearts by the Holy Spirit through the Word of God. The performance of good works, which were viewed as meriting salvation (for some late-medieval theologians through "doing what is in a person") or as satisfying the remaining penalty for sin (by the infused grace of justification, defined by medieval soteriology as a disposition of love), could not, in Luther's view, provide certainty that God was pleased with them. This led him to write: "All those good works are performed apart from faith; they amount to nothing and are completely dead, because the attitude of your conscience before God determines the goodness of the works that proceed from it" (*Good Works*, 19; LW 44:24). Throughout the treatise this theme of faith determining the "good" in good works serves as a refrain; Luther proceeds to define good works from the commands of God in the Decalogue and holds that the chief good work is faith. In sharp contrast Luther describes "our hypocrites" who behave as had the idolatrous Jews who were condemned by the prophets: "eager to perform every work but ignoring the chief work of faith" (*Good Works*, 31; LW 44:33).

When Luther later that year published *The Freedom of a Christian*, his concern was to describe this freedom as the experience of the power of faith, which is not the result of human cultivation of a virtue but is a divine power at work in the sinner through the gospel. "To preach Christ means to feed the soul, make it righteous, set it free, and save it, provided the preaching is believed. . . . The word of God cannot be received or honored by any works but must be grasped by faith alone. Therefore, it is clear that the soul needs only the word of God for life and righteousness; it is justified by faith alone and not by any works" (*Freedom*, 53–54; LW 31:346). For Luther this power of faith is threefold: (1) It sets the Christian free from the law's curse. (2) It "honors the one it trusts with the most reverent and highest regard. This is necessarily the case because faith sees the one it trusts as truthful and deserving of this esteem" (*Freedom*, 60; LW 31:350); here Luther's concept of faith as the first and most important good work is operative. And (3) it unites the soul of the believer with Christ and thus bestows Christ's own righteousness so that the sinner is justified before God without any works. This justification results in a new creature, a "good tree" that naturally, spontaneously, and inevitably produces the fruit of good works. In this way Luther displays the perfect congruity of the paradoxical concepts with which he opened his treatise on Christian freedom: "A Christian is a perfectly free lord of all, completely free of everything. A Christian is a servant, completely attentive to the needs of all" (*Freedom*, 50; LW 31:344).

Though for Luther this righteousness of faith is a passive righteousness received as a gift from God, faith itself never remains passive, for it is the power of God at work in the believer. Luther's richest descriptions come with his prefaces to the New Testament and to Romans (1522): "Truly, if faith is there, he [the believer] cannot hold back; he proves himself, breaks out into good works. . . . Everything that he lives and does is directed to his neighbor's profit, in order to help him" (LW 35:361). "O it is a living, busy, active, mighty thing, this faith. It is impossible for it not to be doing good works incessantly. It does not ask whether good works are to be done, but before the question is asked, it has already done them, and is constantly doing them. Whoever does not do such works, however, is an unbeliever" (LW 35:370). Thus justification and therefore salvation are received by faith alone; but without works, faith and its fruit of good works for Luther are inseparable: "It is impossible to separate works from faith, quite as impossible as to separate heat and light from fire" (LW 35:371). Similar descriptions of the relationship between faith and works as a necessary fruit of faith are found in Luther's later testament of his teaching from 1536, the Smalcald Articles (3.13.2–3). The avenue for good works are the three walks of life that God has instituted in the world as holy orders, in which God works to preserve and sanctify creation: *ecclesia*, the realm of the church; *oeconomia*, household and the economic realm; and *politia*, the civic realm and politics. "All who are saved in the faith

of Christ surely do these works and maintain these orders" (LW 37:364–65).

In the Augsburg Confession and its Apology, this careful separation of works from justification and salvation, and joining of faith and works in the Christian life, are expressed clearly in CA 4 (on justification) and in related articles on the new obedience and on faith and good works (CA 6 and 20), with extensive reply to the opponents in Ap 4 and 20. Works and all concepts of merit are totally excluded from forgiveness of sins and righteousness before God, which are received "by grace, for Christ's sake, through faith" (CA 4). This faith, however, "should yield good fruit and good works, and a person must do such good works as God has commanded for God's sake but not place trust in them as if thereby to earn grace before God" (CA 6). Article 20, on faith and good works, is by far the longest of the twenty-one doctrinal articles of the CA, and rejection of the opponents' traditions concerning good works dominates the remaining articles, which deal with abuses in the papal church.

After Luther's death and beginning with the controversy over the so-called Leipzig Proposal or Interim (an alternative to the Augsburg Interim decreed by Emperor Charles V in 1548), the relationship between good works and salvation became an intra-Lutheran dispute, in particular between Georg Major and Nikolaus von Amsdorf. Rejecting the Augsburg Interim but supporting the proposal dubbed by its opponents the Leipzig Interim, which had been developed in the Wittenberg circle led by Melanchthon, Major insisted, against von Amsdorf's attacks on that document, that "good works are necessary for salvation," meaning that they are the necessary fruit of a true, saving faith. But by coupling this concept of necessity with salvation, it appeared that Major was compromising justification by faith alone. Amsdorf countered by citing Luther's expressions that good works are harmful to salvation when confidence is placed in them for salvation rather than in Christ alone. Major thus had to defend himself against the charge that his opinion was a denial of justification. The Formula of Concord, citing both semantic and substantial aspects in the controversy, rejected both sides and maintained that the language used was in each case one-sided and denied some essential aspect of the Lutheran confession (Ep/SD 4). In the seventeenth and early eighteenth centuries, leaders within Pietism were sometimes accused of being "Majorists" because of their insistence on good works.

See also Amsdorf, Nikolaus von; Augsburg Confession; Formula of Concord; Justification; Law, Uses of the; Major, Georg; Musculus, Andreas; Ten Commandments; Vocation

Bibliography

Luther's Works: *The Freedom of a Christian.* Trans. M. Tranvik. Fortress, 2008. Also, LW 31:327–77; Preface to the Complete Edition of Luther's Latin Writings (1545). LW 34:327–38; Preface to the Epistle of St. Paul to the Romans (1522). LW 35:365–80; Preface to the New Testament (1522). LW 35:357–62; *Treatise on Good Works.* Trans. S. Hendrix. Fortress, 2012. Also, LW 44:15–114; **General Works:** Arand, C., J. Nestingen, and R. Kolb. *The Lutheran Confessions: History and Theology of The Book of Concord.* Fortress, 2012; Bayer, O. *Living by Faith: Justification and Sanctification.* Trans. G. Bromiley. Eerdmans, 2003; Gassmann, G., and S. Hendrix. *Fortress Introduction to the Lutheran Confessions.* Fortress, 1999; Grane, L. *The Augsburg Confession: A Commentary.* Trans. J. Rasmussen. Augsburg, 1987; Kolb, R., and T. Wengert, eds. *The Book of Concord: The Confessions of the Evangelical Lutheran Church.* Fortress, 2000.

JOHN A. MAXFIELD

Gospels

"Gospel," the term applied to the first four literary units of the New Testament (Greek: *euangelion*; Latin: *evangelium*), derives from Greco-Roman usage. Suitability of the term for Christian use lies in its dual significance, denoting good news and the reward for bringing it, thus involving its recipient. Superscriptions later attached to these units reflect earliest acknowledgment of the one, single Gospel, to which each of the four units attests, thus "The Gospel according to [Greek: *kata*] Matthew," "Mark," "Luke," or "John." The orientation of these units to the life and career of Jesus of Nazareth, confessed as Messiah and Lord, renders them sui generis. Other early Christian literature, such as "The Secret Words . . . [of] Jesus [Which] Didymus Judas Thomas Wrote," only later received the appellation "Gospel" (in this case "of Thomas"). The church preserved the four Gospels, supported by Athanasius's festal letter of 367, and associated them with the four creatures of Ezek. 1 and Rev. 4.

According to Martin Luther, following Paul's usage in Rom. 1:16, the term "gospel" denotes great jubilation, "good news," "good tidings hurled against the curse," about which one speaks or shouts. And just as there is only one Christ, so, he insisted, there is really only one Gospel (LW 30:3), for which reason there are scarcely any references to "the four Gospels" in his writings. The reformer's position thus reflects earliest Christian usage of one, single Gospel.

According to Luther the gospel was not so much a written but an oral word, since Christ himself did not call his teaching a writing but rather a good report or proclamation, not to be set forth with the pen but with the mouth. Moreover, it was a word intended to be further spoken. Centuries later, researchers would attempt to identify a saying or deed of Jesus within the period of its oral transmission, together with the life situation (*Sitz im Leben*) of the community that transmitted it. Further, Luther insisted that the power of the gospel lay in its nature as an oral word, a word which—when contrasted to the condemning word of law that puts the old creature to death—lifts condemnation and provides comfort and new life. Thus, hearing the gospel created in the hearer faith in God and God's mercy, the very thing demanded by the law. Luther's understanding of the gospel's orality was in its own way an anticipation of recent research with its accent on the oral over the textual. Luther would go so far as to state that the fixing of the gospel in writing was at bottom "improper," at the very least the result of an emergency. The writing of books, he wrote, was a "great loss and defect of spirit," incurred by necessity, "not the nature of the New Testament." The entire genre of literature, which arose with earliest Christianity, was a secondary phenomenon, merely a record of the proclamation that supported the church's witness.

In his translation of the Bible, Luther wrote no individual prefaces for the four Gospels, not even a preface to his favorite among the four, the "tender, really chief Gospel" of John, subsuming any comments under his preface to the New Testament (LW 35:357–62). Several reasons have been advanced for the omission (lack of time in 1522; Luther's commitment to the Old Testament), but the absence of prefaces could also be assigned to external circumstances. Of the New Testament writings, he lectured only on epistles, on Romans, Galatians, 1 Timothy, Titus, Philemon, 1 John, and Hebrews, whereas Gospel exposition was left to other Wittenbergers. However, he preached often on the appointed Sunday Gospels and, following Wittenberg's tradition, on Matthew on Wednesdays and John on Saturdays, especially during Johannes Bugenhagen's many absences from Wittenberg.

Luther wrote that just as his deeds, so also Christ's commandments and his exposition of the law were not yet the gospel. The gospel becomes clear only when a voice is heard to announce, "Christ is your own with his life, teaching, works, dying, and rising." Since much more is involved with the word than with the deeds of Christ, if one should ever lack the deeds or the word of Christ, it would be better to do without the deeds and the history than without the word and the preaching. "The deeds," Luther adds, "are of no help to me, but his words, they give life, as he himself says." For this reason, he states, those books are most highly to be praised that deal most with the words of Christ. In fact, if there were no marvelous deeds of Christ, and we knew nothing of them, we would still have enough in the word without which we cannot have the life.

At least in his preface to the New Testament, Luther assigned inferior status to the Synoptic Gospels. The Epistles, he wrote, especially those to the Romans, Galatians, and Ephesians, together with 1 Peter, are the books that show Christ and teach everything needed, even if one should never see or hear of any other book. These are the real core and marrow among all the writings of the New Testament. These are the best evangelists and deserve first place, since they set forth how faith in Christ alone makes righteous, and thus are more a gospel than Matthew, Mark, and Luke, who did little more than describe the history of the deeds or miracles of Christ.

On occasion, Luther would give a wholesale characterization of the four evangelists, assigning order to Luke, describing Matthew as collector of Christ's deeds and his audiences, Mark as zealous for brevity, and John as having written with authority. Or he would write of Matthew as portraying Christ the man, of Mark as describing Christ the king, of Luke as describing Christ the priest, and of John as portraying Christ the God. Of these four, Luther wrote, the first three were far behind Paul in their understanding of the Old Testament.

Again, when referring to each of the four evangelists, Luther would reiterate the ancient church's conviction respecting Matthew as the "churchly Gospel," concerned with the true humanity of Christ. He would state that Matthew and the others are industrious about describing the "histories," that such was greatly needed, but that they do not deal with the content (Latin: *res*), the words (Latin: *verba*), and the force or power (Latin: *vis*) behind the words of the Old Testament. On occasion Luther also noted Matthew's special material, an insight that modern research expanded on greatly in assuming two primary sources for the first three, the Synoptic Gospels (Mark and "Q"), and assigning oral or written materials peculiar to Matthew and Luke.

With respect to Mark's Gospel, Luther noted that it omits the childhood narratives of Jesus and begins with the Baptist, thus standing near John, Paul, and Peter. Later research would suggest a connection between

Mark and John, not with regard to their omissions, but in respect of their narratives of the passion.

According to Luther, just as Matthew does, so also Luke describes the *humanitas Christi* and sees in Christ the Savior of all the nations, for which reason the Gospel's genealogy is traced to Adam. On the basis of texts such as Luke 15 or 18, Luther sensed the "Pauline" character of the Gospel. On the other hand, the Gospel often gives the impression that righteousness comes by way of works (see Luke 16:9: "And I tell you, make friends for yourselves by means of dishonest wealth so that when it is gone, they may welcome you into the eternal homes"). The reason for this, wrote Luther, was that the situation in which Luke wrote was similar to Luther's own day. Preaching "grace alone" had rendered some indolent and slothful, so that they needed to hear of the necessity for the fruits of faith. Heresy, Luther wrote, furnished the occasion for the Gospel's composition. Written to combat falsification of the history of Jesus, it gave greater attention to historical order than the other evangelists. Thus Luther preferred the Lukan sequence of Jesus's three temptations over Matthew's account. This attribution of order to Luke would have later echo in a description of the Gospel's salvation-historical (*heilsgeschichtlich*) scheme, according to which the divine plan of salvation consists of a continuum, with successive stages marked by repeated attempts at thwarting the divine purpose but ultimately made to serve it.

Writing that John's Gospel reports much more of Christ's preaching and less of his deeds, whereas the other evangelists report more of Christ's deeds and less of his words, Luther held that it was "the one, tender, truly chief Gospel, and far, far to be preferred and higher to be held than the other three." Luther acknowledged that all four Gospels made clear the relation between faith and works and were therefore properly recognized by the church. He even conceded that in taking "the other part"—that is, in insisting on faith's becoming tangible in deeds—Matthew, Mark, and Luke stated their case so strongly that it was not forgotten, and in this respect were to be preferred to John. Nonetheless, he wrote, it was John's Gospel that most powerfully bore the chief article of faith and was thus the chief Gospel.

In contrast to now-current New Testament research, Luther thought in noncritical fashion regarding the historicity of the texts. He was not a life-of-Jesus researcher; his portrait of Christ did not reflect separation of the Synoptic Gospels from Paul or John. What is striking, however, is his emphasis on the humanity of Jesus. More than one Luther researcher has noticed this reformer's insistence on the total incarnation of God in Jesus Christ. For him, the Godhead could not be too totally drawn or lodged (the verb used was *ziehen*) into the flesh. Everywhere assuming the ancient church's dogma of the two natures, that dogma nevertheless allowed him to accent the humanity of Jesus without running the risk of losing the Godhead. The suggestion has been hazarded that such accent reflects a type of thinker who does not live from a priori principles, but from a perception hostile to speculation and construction, a type in love with the concrete. However inferior or subordinate the Synoptics were to the Pauline and Petrine literature, since Matthew, Mark, and Luke gave Luther a portrait of Jesus in all his humanity, they became for Luther an inexhaustible source of that penchant for perception and illustration.

In the majority of instances, it was in his sermons that Luther dealt with such matters as those mentioned above, matters currently termed "Introduction." Characterizing the Gospels and their authors, distinguishing their purposes and differences, drawing contrasts between them and the epistles of Paul or of Peter regarding their concentration on narrative or proclamation, and all throughout evaluating the individual work respecting its *res*, or theological perspective—for example, respecting the weight given law or gospel, faith or works—would hardly be heard in contemporary preaching. Luther's astonishing freedom toward historical questions and the conscious separation of them from matters of faith would wait long years before their like would appear again. In the post-Reformation period, identification of the Bible with the Word of God would lead to such extravagant definition of its production as in many respects excluding human agency or the drawing of distinctions. First, little contrast, such as Luther noted, would be drawn between the oral and the textual, the latter a "great loss and defect of spirit." Whether the Word of God was oral or committed to writing was often attributed to mere happenstance. Second, Orthodox Lutheran theologians, without ever abandoning the distinction between law and gospel, emphasized terms such as "dictation of the Holy Spirit." This perspective held that Holy Scripture originated by means of the Holy Spirit, who impelled the authors to write (Latin: *impulsus ad scribendum*) and communicated to them both the content (*suggestio rerum*) and the fitting word (*suggestio verbi*) of what was to be written. The result was that Luther's formal distinctions among the various literary units would be largely ignored until the emergence of a full-blown critical method borne by the Enlightenment. Finally, and most important, insistence on the value and the fate of a given writing as dependent on its orientation to the "gospel of Christ," given peculiar enunciation in the Epistles, would result in a suppression of Luther's "criticism" (esp. of James) by his descendants, and an attack on its one-sidedness on the part of contemporary scholarship.

See also Bible Interpretation; Law, Uses of the; Scripture; Word of God

Bibliography

Bornkamm, H., ed. *Luthers Vorreden zur Bibel*. Furche, 1967; Ebeling, G. *Luther: Einführung in sein Denken*. Mohr, 1965; "Evangelien." *RGG* 2:749–64; "Evangelium." In *Realenzyklopädie für Theologie und Antike*, 6:1107–55. Hiersemann, 1966; "Gospel." *RPP* 5:528–30. Brill, 2009; Löwenich, W. von. *Luther als Ausleger der Synoptiker*. Kaiser, 1954.

ROY A. HARRISVILLE

Gossner, Johannes Evangelista

The Roman Catholic priest Johannes Evangelista Gossner (1773–1858) converted to Protestantism on July 23, 1826, in Königshain, Silesia. Born in Hausen, Bavaria, and consecrated as priest on October 9, 1796, he served a number of congregations in that area before he was expelled from Bavaria over a dispute with Roman Catholic authorities for referring in his letters to justification by grace alone and Christ in us. Incentives for this theological orientation came from his association with the regional Roman Catholic Awakening, especially its two leaders Johann Michael Sailer and Martin Boos. In 1819, Gossner first moved to Düsseldorf, controlled at the time by the Kingdom of Prussia, then to St. Petersburg, Russia (1820–24). Banished from Russia, his unsettled life took him to Altona (1824), Leipzig (1824–26), and Königshain in Silesia (1836) before he finally settled in Berlin (1829–58), where until 1846 he was pastor of the Bohemian (Moravian) Bethlehem church.

Gossner's theological convictions are reflected in his translation of the Greek New Testament into German (1815), in exegetical and devotional literature such as his *Herzbüchlein* and his popular *Schatzkästchen*, and in his own mission journal, the *Biene auf dem Missionsfelde* (Bees in the mission field), published in 1834–68. His focus on Scripture as sole authority and on the cross as its center shows an affinity with Martin Luther's theology. Gossner kept ties to a pre-Reformation piety, such as the mysticism of Thomas à Kempis, which he corrected with a Lutheran focus on Christ's external righteousness revealed through the Word, while using the language and concepts of Nikolaus Ludwig von Zinzendorf. Though Luther's dialectic of law/gospel and of wrath/grace are not pronounced in Gossner's literature, he shows with Luther that penitence and faith are essential to Christian life. Gossner opposed an institutionalized understanding of church and a rigid dogmatism, arguing that true Christianity is found not in externals and in the mind but in the heart. In agreement with the reformer, Gossner supported the concept of the one, holy Christian church. However, where Luther's theology encourages a church confessing its faith, Gossner pointed to a church's faith expressed in practice, which lets the church be guided more by the Holy Spirit than by its organizational structures. Gossner is known for founding the Gossner Mission Society (chartered in 1842), asylums, and clinics.

Bibliography

Dalton, H. *Johannes Gossner: Ein Lebensbild aus der Kirche des neunzehnten Jahrhunderts*. 2nd rev. ed. Goßnerischen Missionsvereins, 1878; Gossner, J. *Das Herzbüchlein, oder, Das Herz des Menschen, ein Tempel Gottes, oder eine Werkstatt des Satans in zehn Figuren sinnbildlich dargestellt zur Beförderung des christlichen Sinnes*. Author (?), 1812. http://ebooks.fcdi.de/m1/fcdi-ebook 1004.pdf; Gossner, J. *Schatzkästchen, enthaltend biblische Betrachtungen mit erbaulichen Liedern auf alle Tage im Jahre zur Beförderung häuslicher Andacht und Gottseligkeit*. Tauchnitz, 1824; Holsten, W. *Johannes Evangelista Gossner: Glaube und Gemeinde*. Vandenhoek & Ruprech, 1949.

Klaus D. Schulz

Gregorius, Johann Gottfried

The founder of the Russian-German State Theater, Johann Gottfried Gregorius (1631–75) was born in Merseburg, Saxony, and then ordained in Dresden in 1662. Before ordination, he traveled to Russia in 1658 and served as a teacher at St. Michael's Lutheran in Moscow. In 1667 he became pastor of a Lutheran Church in Moscow, forming a school with the financial support of Ernst (or Ernest) the Pious, Duke of Saxe-Gotha. Gregorius wrote and directed a play, *The Acts of Artaxerxes*, based on the biblical book of Esther, in German (with Russian translation). It was performed in the Kremlin before Czar Alexey Romanov on October 17, 1672. Gregorius wrote and directed six additional plays that were secular in tone but based on biblical themes. He served as pastor of Sts. Peter and Paul in Moscow from 1670 until his death.

See also Russia

Matthew Heise

Greiner, Johann Jakob

An influential German missionary to East Africa (present-day Tanzania), Johann Jakob Greiner (1842–1905) was born May 16, 1842, in Brombach (Baden); he enrolled in the Chrischona Mission School in Basel in 1863. By 1865 he was chosen to proceed to a new mission station on the newly invented Apostles' Street, which was to stretch from Alexandria, Egypt, to Gondar, Ethiopia. He studied languages at the Schneller Institute in Jerusalem and was in Khartoum by 1867. He soon returned to Germany because of bad health but by 1872 returned to Shoa, Ethiopia. He hoped to reach the Galla people, but religiopolitical tensions forced him to leave in 1886.

Sent by the Evangelical Mission Society of Berlin, he with his wife and daughter passed through the Lutheran mission in Zanzibar on their way to Dar es Salaam, where they arrived on July 2, 1887. They found the town in disarray, with most buildings abandoned after the grandiose earlier settlement by the Omani sultan in the 1860s. He named his land on the cape overlooking the harbor "Immanelskop." There he built a residence and served those he had gathered, including a number of freed slave children, and established a school and a self-sustaining household.

The Bushiri revolt against the German colonial authority ended his role as house father and teacher on New Year's Eve 1888. His house was destroyed by the rebels, his cattle driven off, and his eighty-person community cut in half by death and reenslavement of many children. After a short interlude on Zanzibar, he returned to rebuild. However, in 1892 the Missionary Conference decided that it was safer to move the school up-country.

By 1888 Greiner had explored twenty miles inland to the Kisarawe area, where he was finally received by Zaramo Chief Sanze in 1892. In the next five years he built a mission house, established a school, and supervised a growing freed-slave community. He reached out to the Zaramo community (the major inhabitants of the area surrounding Dar es Salaam) from his headquarters Hoffnungshöhe (Hill of hope). He built the first church (1893) in the land of the Zaramo (later dynamited by the British during World War II). He worked with coworkers from Berlin in teaching and evangelistic outreach. In 1897 he retired to a government agricultural school at Minaki. He died there on June 21, 1905, and was buried near the church at Kisarawe, near the grave of Chief Sanze (d. 1898). He is still regarded as the pioneer of the faith among the Zaramo.

See also Tanzania

Bibliography

Maanga, G., ed. *Injili Kamili: History of KKKT*. Moshi Lutheran Press, 2013; Sahlberg, C.-E. *From Krapf to Rugambwa*. Evangel Publishing House, 1989; Von Sicard, S. *The Lutheran Church on the Coast of Tanzania, 1887–1914*. Almquist & Wiksell, 1970.

HERBERT J. HAFERMANN

Grīnbergs, Teodors

The first archbishop of the Latvian Evangelical-Lutheran Church, Teodors Grīnbergs (1870–1962) studied theology at Dorpat (Tartu), Estonia (1891–96), served as vicar in 1898–1899, and was ordained in 1899. He served as pastor, teacher, and finally as director of a secondary school (1899–1932) and edited two journals for youth and children, *Bitīte* (Little bee, 1913–15, 1925–40), *Bitītes kalendārs* (Calendar of the little bee, 1927–44), and *Evaņģeliuma Gaisma* (The light of the gospel, 1904–6). A member of the first Latvian parliament in 1921, he became director of the church's Theological Institute (1923–31), receiving an honorary doctorate in 1929 from the University of Riga, and teaching part-time at the Faculty of Theology (1932–42). He participated in preparation of the translation of the New Testament.

The church elected Grinsbergs its first archbishop in 1932. During World War II he saved Jews and Roma in Venstpils and Kandava who had converted to Christianity. As a result of his signing the anti-Nazi memorandum of the Latvian Central Council on March 17, 1944, the German security service *SD* (*Sicherheitsdienst*) deported him to Germany. From 1944,

as archbishop of Latvian Evangelical-Lutheran Church Abroad, he worked for its unification and revived *Bitīte* (1947–59) and *Bitītes kalendārs* (1947–59). In 1947, at its first meeting, the LWF elected Grinsbergs to its executive committee.

See also Latvia

GUNTIS KALME

Grumbach, Argula von

A best-selling pamphleteer of the Reformation, Argula von Grumbach (1492–1554/57) entered the fray in her native Bavaria when a student at the University of Ingolstadt was forced to recant his Reformation ideas. As a longtime reader of the Bible and more recently acquainted with Luther's writings, on September 20, 1523, she challenged the Ingolstadt professors to a debate, arguing that Matt. 10 and baptism demanded even a woman to confess Christ in a time of crisis. In the next two months the letter went through fourteen editions. She went on to write six more public letters in the next year, resulting in a total of thirty thousand copies in circulation, not a single one of which was ever answered. She also published a response to a vulgar anonymous poem tarnishing her character. The outrage of the Roman party against a female speaking on church matters was virulent; nevertheless, the Evangelical party interpreted her actions as a confirmation of Joel 2, quoted by Peter in Acts 2. She traveled to the Diet of Augsburg in 1530 and met Luther in person while he was sequestered at the Coburg Castle. She and two others also arranged a meeting between Philip Melanchthon and Martin Bucer, which eventually led to the Wittenberg Concord of 1536. In addition to Luther, she corresponded with Andreas Osiander, Paul Speratus, Georg Spalatin, Urbanus Rhegius, the early Anabaptist Balthasar Hubmaier, and even John Eck.

See also Gender: Men and Women

Bibliography

Matheson, P., ed. *Argula von Grumbach: A Woman's Voice in the Reformation*. T&T Clark, 1995; Matheson, P.

Argula von Grumbach (1492–1554/7): A Woman before Her Time. Wipf & Stock, 2013.

SARAH HINLICKY WILSON

Grundtvig, Nikolai Frederik Severin

The Danish poet, pastor, politician, and historian Nikolai Frederik Severin Grundtvig (1783–1872) was inspired by Romanticism and became the most influential person in Danish church life. He authored around one thousand hymns and songs and countless pedagogical, historical, theological, philological, and political writings. In his late twenties, Grundtvig experienced an "unparalleled discovery" and found himself with a call similar to Luther's: to speak against misconceptions of Christianity. The Reformation had to be continued. Through his writing career, lasting to his death, Luther remained his conversation partner, first admired, then criticized. Grundtvig was most critical of the Lutheran Orthodox insistence on "Scripture alone," arguing for freedom against any coercion in doctrine. His idea of the church's "spaciousness" had a huge impact on the Lutheran Church in Denmark, where 80 percent of the population are still members, yet in other respects Denmark is a secularized country. Instead of building only on the Bible and the Lutheran confessions, Grundtvig believed he had Luther on his side when he claimed the Apostles' Creed as the church's starting point for life and faith and thought that for historical reasons he could see this better than Luther. The church had to be built on the living faith of the congregation, not on rationalistic theologians and their interpretation of Scripture. Further, Grundtvig found Luther's understanding of human sinfulness to be too harsh. Fallen humanity was not totally alienated from the Creator. The image of God was not lost, although damaged to a degree that only Christ could restore it. Still, in every use of language, the divine Word of creation echoes. Sin was rather to be understood as something hindering human possibilities. In both cases, Grundtvig believed himself to be continuing what would be in accordance with Luther's intention yet against the ongoing Lutheran tradition. His understanding of the spaciousness of the church opened Grundtvig toward influence from other confessions, mainly the Greek and the Anglican traditions, as seen in his hymns. His understanding of worship centered on the sacraments (the bath and the table, where, according to Grundtvig, the Lord himself speaks to the congregation as in the Apostles' Creed) made him a liturgical renewer, emphasizing the Holy Spirit's work in the congregation's participation. His emphasis on the living Word, pedagogy, and history formed the basis for education of mainly rural citizens in folk high schools, but can be detected also in the history of the Danish public school. His positive evaluation of worldly life (human first, Christian then/so), rooted in his creation theology, has up until today had an immense impact on Scandinavian Lutheranism, balancing the influence of his contemporary Søren Kierkegaard.

See also Denmark; Kierkegaard, Søren Aabye

Bibliography

Allchin, A. M. *N. F. S. Grundtvig: An Introduction to His Life and Work.* Aarhus Universitetsforlag, 1997; Bradley, S. A-J., trans. *N. F. S. Grundtvig: A Life Recalled; An Anthology of Biographical Source-Texts.* Aarhus Universitetsforlag, 2008; Holm, A. "Kunsten at fortsætte reformationen: Grundtvig og Luther." In *Lutherbilleder i dansk teologi 1800–2000*, ed. N. H. Gregersen, 73–87. Anis, 2012; Jensen, N. L., ed. *A Grundtvig Anthology.* J. Clarke, 1984; Lathrop, G. "'The Bath and the Table, the Prayer and the Word': N. F. S. Grundtvig and the Lutheran Contribution to Ecumenical Liturgical Renewal." *Grundtvig Studier* 51 (2000): 104–17.

BO KRISTIAN HOLM

Guatemala

Three groups are credited for shaping Lutheran work in Guatemala. The first were German settlers who came under the spiritual care of the Lutheran Church–Missouri Synod. Missionaries were instrumental in educating and training locals to be pastors, catechists, and deacons; they developed Theological Education by Extension. The second were Quakers, in particular Alfredo Vasquez, a carpenter, who with Luther's Small Catechism and other Lutheran literature helped shape early Lutheran work among the natives. Third, Lutheran work was extended by English-speaking, Afro-Caribbean residents in Puerto Barrios. At various stages work was carried out in German, Spanish, and English.

The Lutheran presence in Guatemala predates World War II, with a German Evangelical congregation in Guatemala City under the care of pastors from Berlin. In 1947 the LCMS reached out to Lutherans in Guatemala with Christian literature in Spanish. Guatemala became the first Central American country to receive missionaries from the LCMS; the impact of La Hora Luterana (radio broadcast) prompted Vasquez to request mission work in Zacapa. Missionary efforts, including education and health care, succeeded in rural areas where Roman Catholic influence was minimal. In 1947 Robert Gussick implemented a trinitarian theological approach to mission, believing that people should be led from animistic or purely mystical images to belief in God as the father and keeper of his creation, shown in the redemptive work of Jesus Christ, through which God's love for his fallen creatures becomes historically tangible. Grateful for Christ's work, Gussick assumed, they would live in the Holy Spirit and bear fruit.

Gussick held the view that the American congregational model of a pastor living in a parsonage and paid by the congregation did not suit Central America. Influenced by theological concepts of Hudson Taylor and John Nevius, he trained and provided continuing theological education for national leaders in their home culture and urged leaders to provide for themselves and their family. The LCMS continued to pay indigenous candidates and pastors, which was an obstacle to building a holistic church that was self-governing, self-supporting, and self-propagating. Frustrated by this policy, Gussick accepted a position as US military chaplain in Panama and carried out mission work in Costa Rica.

Iglesia Luterana en Guatemala comprises nearly three thousand members in approximately sixteen congregations in Guatemala City and remote communities such as Quiché, Alta Verapaz, Peten, and Coban. Since 1962 it has pursued a philosophy focused on the holistic development of the human being, with the aim of providing support to people, administering pastoral care with an emphasis on human dignity and social justice, and promoting the development of leadership, education, and ministry among women and youth and children, plus health care.

In 1991 Bishop Horacio Castillo and Pastor Esther Eccheverra founded the Augustana Lutheran Church of Guatemala (Iglesia Luterana Agustina de Guatemala, ILAG). Baptized members number approximately four thousand. In February 2014 Bishop Castillo retired, and Pastor Karen Castillo was elected the president of the ILAG.

See also Honduras

Bibliography
"Guatemala." http://www.lcms.org/guatemala; "History of ILAG." http://iglesialuteranaagustina.org/about-us/history-of-ilag/; Jahnel, C. *The Lutheran Church in El Salvador*. Servicio Educativo Cristiano-LBCM, 2009.

ORIN W. CUMMINGS

Gunderson, Adolphus

The missionary to Cameroon Adolphus Gunderson (ca. 1890–1951) was founder of the Sudan Mission that birthed the Evangelical Lutheran Church of the Central African Republic and, together with the Norwegian Mission Society, cobirthed the Evangelical Lutheran Church of Cameroon. He was born near Stoughton, Wisconsin, the son of Norwegian immigrants. Gunderson studied carpentry and business before attending Moody Bible College and Luther Seminary. During early missionary work with the Sudan Interior Mission in northern Nigeria, from 1912–16, he was struck by the absence of gospel bearers across the West African savannah and returned to the United States to seek support for outreach there. He presented his plea to the 1918 organizing convention of the Norwegian Evangelical Lutheran Church. That nascent body found itself unable to respond to the challenge just then, so Gunderson founded the independent Sudan Mission, rooted in the Norwegian immigrant community, to address the task. By 1923 he, his wife (Marie), and two Lutheran deaconesses had completed French language study and, after seeking a place of work in Ngaoundere, finally settled in Mboula to the southeast the following year. Here the Gbaya people were predominant, and Gunderson gave himself to learning and eventually translating in the Yaayuwee dialect of the Gbaya language. By the 1930s he and a growing number of missionary colleagues in the Sudan Mission began medical work, started schools and an orphanage, and shepherded the rapid growth of the church. In 1935 Gunderson returned to the United States to serve as home director of the Sudan Mission, continuing to seek support for the work until his death in 1951.

See also Cameroon; Sudan Mission

Bibliography

Delisle, J., and J. Voodsworth, eds. *Translators through History.* Rev. ed. J. Benjamins, 2012; Hesterman, L. *Missionary Pioneers of the American Lutheran Church.* Augsburg, 1967.

MARK NYGARD

Gustavus Adolphus

King of Sweden from 1611 until his death, Gustavus Adolphus (1594–1632) was the famous military commander who led Sweden into the Thirty Years' War and gained the reputation as the savior of the Protestant cause. He was son of Duke Karl (later King Karl IX) of Sweden and Princess Kristina of Holstein-Gottorp. Karl was the youngest son of King Gustav I Vasa, the man who introduced the Lutheran Reformation into Sweden. In 1598 Karl led the revolt that drove his Catholic nephew Sigismund I, who was the son of Karl's late older brother Johan III and was also the reigning king of Poland, from the Swedish throne, assuring the permanent alignment of Sweden with the Lutheran faith. Upon Karl's death Gustav Adolph (the

Swedish form of his name), not yet seventeen years old, inherited from his father the questionable legitimacy of a usurped Crown as well as the enduring animosity of Sigismund in Poland and ongoing conflicts with both Russia and Denmark. Securing his precarious domestic position while dealing with Sweden's costly foreign entanglements dominated the early years of his reign. Recognizing the need to produce an heir to secure his line, while hoping also to gain a potentially valuable foreign ally, Gustav Adolph in 1620 married Maria Eleonora of Brandenburg, sister of the Calvinist elector of Brandenburg, though herself a Lutheran. The couple had one child who survived to adulthood, Christina, who reigned as queen of Sweden from 1632 until her abdication and conversion to Catholicism in 1654.

Gustav Adolph ruled in close cooperation with his chancellor Axel Oxenstierna, and the (largely published) correspondence between the two forms one of the best sources on the king's governance and thinking (see *Rikskanslern Axel Oxenstiernas skrifter och brevväxling*). He pursued a wide-ranging and ambitious program of governmental reforms, though his military reforms, which transformed the Swedish army into one of the most effective fighting forces in Europe, have attracted more scholarly attention. The Truce of Altmark with Poland (1629) freed his hands to use this army to intervene in the Thirty Years' War that had been raging in the Holy Roman Empire since 1618, and in the summer of 1630 he led his army into northern Germany. Gustav Adolph's motivations for bringing Sweden into the Thirty Years' War have been the subject of intense debate ever since: he combined the pursuit of Sweden's long-term objective of obtaining Baltic predominance—the *dominium maris Baltici* that held the promise of military security, economic prosperity, and domestic and national prestige—with legitimate concern for the fate of his Protestant coreligionists in the empire. Most German Protestant governments were initially cool to the king's intervention, but popular support ran high, fueled by the association that Gustav Adolph and those around him were keen to encourage the king with the legendary "Lion of the North." This image of an all-conquering mystical hero descending from the North to inflict God's wrath on his opponents had roots in Old Testament prophecy, with new life breathed into it in the sixteenth century via an apocalyptic vision attributed to Paracelsus that foresaw the northern hero laying low the eagle (coincidentally a symbol of the imperial Hapsburgs) and returning peace to the world after an era of unprecedented suffering, thus preparing the way for the second coming. Pressure from the king, the imperial sack of Lutheran Magdeburg (May 1631), and menacing moves from the emperor eventually moved Protestant governments, notably Saxony and Brandenburg, to ally with the Swedes, and in September 1631 Gustav Adolph enjoyed his signal victory at Breitenfeld over the previously undefeated General Tilly. Additional military successes followed, the first sustained series of Protestant victories since the war had begun, and Gustav Adolph began to be celebrated as the savior of the Protestant cause. In some Protestant circles talk even began of securing the imperial Crown for the Swedish king. Those hopes were dashed on November 6, 1632, when Gustav Adolph was killed in combat at the Battle of Lützen, though he continued to be revered for centuries in parts of Scandinavia, Germany, and the Baltic countries as a Lutheran hero.

See also Sweden; Thirty Years' War

Bibliography

Ahnlund, N. *Gustav Adolf den store*. Svenska kyrkans diakonistyrelse, 1932; Oredsson, S. *Gusatv II Adolf*. Atlantis, 2007; *Rikskanslern Axel Oxenstiernas skrifter och brevväxling*. 30+ vols. Vitterhetsakademien, 1888–; Roberts, M. *Gustavus Adolphus*. 2nd ed. Longman, 1992; Roberts, M. *Gustavus Adolphus: A History of Sweden, 1611–1632*. 2 vols. Longmans, Green, 1953–58; Styffe, C. G., ed. *Konung Gustaf II Adolfs Skrifter*. P. A. Norstedt & Söner, 1861.

DANIEL RICHES

Guyana

The history of Lutheranism in Guyana, extending over 270 years, is marked by confessional loyalty, racial-ethnic exclusiveness for the first 170 years, lay governance and support, and ecumenical openness on account of necessity. A gradual evangelical openness to and welcome of members from the diverse racial-ethnic mix of the population has marked the last century, as the church became a mission field for Lutherans in the United States, who provided a crucial supply of missionaries as well as financial support and control (ca. 1890–1980). Since 1980 the move toward and growth in indigenization are unmistakable.

Lutheranism in Guyana formally began on October 15, 1743, with a meeting of Dutch colonists in the Dutch colony of Berbice, part of modern-day Guyana. The Evangelical Lutheran Church in Guyana (ELCG), the second oldest Lutheran church in South America, was rooted in the Lutheran congregation in Amsterdam and held to an unequivocal commitment to the unaltered Augsburg Confession (1530). The ELCG's symbol includes a swan with the cross and a Bible to symbolize Luther. The initial gathering was an expression of the priesthood of all believers; however, it was a church for Dutch planters, with no evangelical outreach and openness to the African slaves or indigenous peoples (Amerindians). Rev. Johan Henrik Faerkenius, ordained in the Lutheran congregation in Amsterdam in 1752, was the first Lutheran pastor to serve the Berbice congregation, which was responsible for his financial support (Beatty 11–12). The pastors who served during 1743–79 had short tenures, and there was no Lutheran pastor from 1779 to 1818. An overriding concern with the survival of the Lutheran congregation led the Lutheran vestry on different occasions to call a Presbyterian and a Methodist to serve as pastor. While the Reformed congregation enjoyed favored status during Dutch rule, the Lutheran congregation was tolerated, provided it was self-supporting and Lutherans still paid the required tax to support the Reformed congregation.

Under British rule in the nineteenth century in a united British Guiana, the Portuguese, Chinese, and East Indian indentured emigrants increased the colony's religious diversity. The Portuguese were Roman Catholic. The Chinese quickly became Christianized. A majority of East Indians were Hindus, with a notable Muslim minority. Outreach beyond the European community meant that the Lutheran Church, like other churches and Christian mission societies, was challenged to share the gospel in the context of a complex religiocultural mix: different denominations of Christianity, Hinduism, Islam, African traditional religious beliefs and practices, and Amerindian beliefs and practices. Lutheran outreach to the diverse population increased under Rev. John Robert Mittelholzer, ordained by the London Missionary Society (1872), who served as pastor from 1875 to 1913.

Connections with American Lutherans shaped Guyanese Lutheranism in the twentieth century. The Evangelical Lutheran Synod of Pennsylvania (part of the General Synod) made the Evangelical Lutheran Church in Berbice a mission outreach in 1890. As a mission of the American Foreign Mission of the Lutheran Church (East Pennsylvania Synod, ULCA, and LCA), the expanding ELCG grew through the evangelical efforts of clergy, catechists, women missionaries, and laity involving the diverse population. Enormous financial support from the United States enabled construction of numerous churches, schools, parsonages, and other residences. Lutheranism was characterized by a widespread, high level of Christian education, with a strong biblical and Lutheran-confessional base that was intergenerational. Since the mid-1960s, candidates for ordination have been trained at the United Theological College of the West Indies, Jamaica. In 1984 a six-month program of studies began for ELCG pastors and ministerial candidates at Wartburg Theological Seminary in the United States. Since about 2009 local training through one- and two-day theological seminars is the primary means of preparing candidates for the diaconate and ordination and for lay preaching and leadership.

Bibliography

Beatty, P. B., Jr. *A History of the Lutheran Church in Guyana*. The Daily Chronicle, 1970; Cummings, O. W. "Shaping Influences of Lutheranism in Guyana: Implications for Self-Determination and Mission in the 21st Century Caribbean." PhD diss., Luther Seminary, 2014; Dayfoot, A. C. *The Shaping of the West Indian Church, 1492–1962*. University of the West Indies Press / University Press of Florida, 1999.

WINSTON D. PERSAUD

H

Hamann, Johann Georg

As a resident of Königsberg, East Prussia, Johann Georg Hamann (1730–88) was one of the first and most insightful critics of the Enlightenment. Primarily a journalist and writer, Hamann's writings remarkably combine detailed philological work with philosophical depth and breadth. Drawing on Luther's Christology, he criticized several Enlightenment perspectives incompatible with traditional Christian faith, including (1) subjectivity as the unity of self-consciousness, (2) freedom as the basic concept of anthropology and ethics, (3) nature as devoid of spirit, (4) reality construed as a metaphysical unity, and (5) faith in scientific and social progress. Such criticism does not mean that Hamann rejected all aspects of the Enlightenment; instead, he insisted that they must be nuanced so as to accommodate matters of contingency. As a young man, Hamann had unquestioningly embraced the Enlightenment, but after undergoing a conversion experience while on a business trip to London, he returned to a faith perspective informed by the Bible and Luther's Small Catechism.

As a critic of Immanuel Kant's (1724–1804) "purism" of reason, which sought truth independent of history, nature, and the senses, Hamann foreshadowed a postmodern critique of modern notions of abstract universality. Likewise, Hamann's criticism of "truth as system" was appropriated by Søren Kierkegaard as a powerful antidote to G. W. F. Hegel (1770–1831), who sought an encyclopedic metaphysic. And Hamann's views of the relationship between language and reason parallel those of Ludwig Wittgenstein (1889–1951), with his view of language as "language games" intertwined with various "forms of life."

Against the Enlightenment critique of traditional faith as irrational and enslaving of individual freedom, Hamann proposed a metacritique by which to evaluate the truth of Enlightenment suppositions. With his metacritique, Hamann insisted on the unity of public and private reason and on the unity of thought and language as the true element of reason. For Hamann, such metacritique was entailed by his Lutheran view of the "communication" between the "properties" of the two natures of Christ (*communicatio idiomatum*) and this Christology's corresponding view of the relation between the visible elements and the audible promise of grace in the sacrament. Hamann repeatedly asserted that this communication of the divine and human *idiomata* (properties) is fundamental, the key to all knowledge. He argued that philosophers such as Kant, Gottfried Wilhelm Leibniz (1646–1713), Gotthold Lessing (1729–81), or Moses Mendelssohn (1729–86) wanted to be independent of the sensuous and accidental, but their claim to the timelessness of truth was a chimera and a mysticism. For instance, the Cartesian separation of subject from object makes the subject to be without a world, and the world is reified as a pure object. As the medium through which God speaks to humankind, the world, or nature, was reduced to total silence. Moreover, all that interest of the Enlightenment in historical research was also for the purpose of gaining a distance from, and not communicating with, what was researched.

Ultimately, Hamann's message to the Enlightenment is that reason is rational only when it acknowledges that it does its work in a context or framework wider than itself, a framework that includes language, culture, and history. The Enlightenment sought a rational security for matters for which security cannot be had—the continuity and the consciousness of the knowing subject, the reality of the world of things and objects, the confidence that some things can be known clearly and distinctly, and the rational basis for governance. In Hamann's metacritique, all such matters are expressions of faith. Counter to Enlightenment theologians, he agreed that God's transcendence cannot be domesticated: God, world, and self cannot be subsumed under a rational "spiderweb" of a metaphysical system, of whatever kind of order, including any Kantian order. Hence, for Hamann the following are open to intense scrutiny: the dualisms of Enlightenment modernity (such as selves as subjects and things as objects, and the reduction of all experience into such subject/object schemata); the metaphysical matrix in which God, self, and world conform to a specific rational inquiry (since all share a place within the flattened scope of infinity); the quest for human freedom as autonomy independent of the social responsibilities that are pregiven; and government as artificially grounded in a hypothetical construct of the consent of the governed.

The importance of Hamann's thought can be seen in that it was the impetus for the questions raised by Herder, the *Sturm und Drang* movement, Romanticism, and Kierkegaard. The roots of some postmodern thinking can be traced to Hamann. It is hard to imagine the rise of confessional renewal among Lutherans in nineteenth-century Europe had Hamann not done this philosophical spadework.

See also Enlightenment; Hegel, Georg Wilhelm Friedrich; Kant, Immanuel; Kierkegaard, Søren Aabye; Nihilism and Postmodernism; Philosophy; Rationalism

Bibliography

Bayer, O. *A Contemporary in Dissent: Johann Georg Hamann as a Radical Enlightener*. Trans. R. Harrisville and M. Mattes. Eerdmans, 2012; Betz, J. *After Enlightenment: Hamann as a Post-secular Visionary*. Wiley-Blackwell, 2009; Dickson, G. *Johann Georg Hamann's Relational Metacriticism*. De Gruyter, 1995; Hamann, J. *Writings on Philosophy and Language*. Ed. K. Haynes. Cambridge, 2007.

MARK C. MATTES

Hamburg

As a Hanseatic port city on the Elbe River in northwestern Germany, Hamburg was one of the first in the region to adopt Wittenberg's model of church renewal. The shift from the Roman faith began with an influx of reform-minded preachers to northwestern Germany in the early 1520s. In contrast to the princely reformations that occurred in some German territories—a top-down model in which rulers legally imposed church renewal on subjects—the middle and lower ranks of Hamburg society were the first to embrace Luther's doctrine of justification by faith. As the ruling magistrates of an independent city-state, Hamburg's city council initially viewed reform with suspicion and collaborated with Lübeck, an ally and the capital of the Hanseatic trading league, in passing laws meant to limit Evangelical preaching, prohibit the sale of Luther's writings, and curb public criticism of the Roman faith. These regulations did not reverse the growing popularity of Lutheran teaching among the population, but their moderate tone did help to forestall the violence—often against clergy, iconography, and church property—that marked the early Reformation in Münster, Augsburg, and other cities of the Holy Roman Empire.

Popular pressure soon overcame magistrates' fears of reprisal by Emperor Charles V for violating the Edict of Worms; of particular significance was the demand to establish the new "common chests" (*Gotteskästen*), which in 1527 deprived the Roman Church of its traditional right to oversee relief for the poor and transferred that obligation to the city council. This marked a clear victory for the reform-minded craftsmen and artisans who made up the citizens' representative councils, the leaders of which now began to petition in earnest for reform on Luther's model. A public disputation between Roman and reform-minded clergymen held the following April (on the model of Luther and Eck's Leipzig debate) ended with a clear victory for the new teaching, and Hamburg's patrician governors now moved to implement Wittenberg-style reform. In 1528 Mayor Johann Wetken wrote to Wittenberg, asking Martin Luther to send his colleague Johannes Bugenhagen (1485–1558), who had recently drafted the new Lutheran Church order for the city of Braunschweig in Lower Saxony. Bugenhagen did the same for Hamburg in early 1529, and the city's new Evangelical status was officially accepted by the magistrates and citizens on May 23, 1529.

Hamburg's Reformation had a decisive impact on nearby Lübeck, which was then the more populous and more powerful urban center, owing to its status as chief city of the Hansa. Hamburg's experience of collaborative reform—in which popular agitation persuaded magistrates to embrace Wittenberg-style reform—provided a model that Lübeck's citizens and city council followed closely, including recruiting Bugenhagen to draft the new church constitution of 1531. In the 1550s, Hamburg was one of the centers of debate with more Reform-minded theologians over the Lord's Supper, with Joachim Westphal leading attacks on John Calvin. Later, Hamburg served as a haven for refugees displaced by religious strife of the subsequent "Confessional Age." The first Sephardic Jews arrived there from Iberia around 1600, and the outlying district of Altona became home to hundreds of Calvinists fleeing from the Eighty Years' War in the Netherlands (1568–1648) and from Catholic France following Louis XIV's revocation of the Edict of Nantes in 1685.

See also Bremen; Bugenhagen, Johannes; Lübeck

Bibliography

Postel, R. "Hamburg und Lübeck im Zeitalter der Reformation." *Zeitschrift des Vereins für Lübeckische Geschichte und Altertumskunde* 59 (1979): 63–81; Schilling, H. "The Reformation in the Hanseatic Cities." *Sixteenth Century Journal* 14 (1983): 443–56.

JASON L. STRANDQUIST

Hamilton, Patrick

The Scottish Lutheran theologian and martyr Patrick Hamilton (1504–28) was born of a noble family and was appointed abbot of Fearn Abbey in 1517. Within a year he had taken up studies at Paris, returning to Scotland to study theology at St. Andrews in 1523. Influenced by Luther's works, Hamilton fell under suspicion of heresy in 1527. Fleeing Scotland, he matriculated at the newly founded Lutheran university at Marburg, where he became the first student there to publish theses for debate. Emphasizing the bondage of the will, salvation by grace, and the appropriation of Christ's righteousness by faith, Hamilton's theses betray a reliance on Luther's *On the Freedom of a Christian* and Melanchthon's *Loci communes*. Returning to Scotland late in 1527, he began publicly preaching and was summoned to St. Andrews for examination. Charges brought against him included denials of free will, purgatory, and the intercession of saints. Condemned, he was burned to death on February 29, 1528, becoming the first "Lutheran" martyr in the British Isles. His Marburg theses, which came to be known in English as "Patrick's Places" (*Loci*), were published in multiple editions and translations, beginning in 1530.

See also Alesius, Alexander; England

Bibliography

Lorimer, P. *Patrick Hamilton, the First Preacher and Martyr of the Scottish Reformation.* T. Constable, 1857; Sanderson, M. *Cardinal of Scotland: David Beaton, c. 1494–1546.* J. Donald, 1986; Wiedermann, G. "Martin Luther versus John Fisher: Some Ideas concerning the Debate on Lutheran Theology at the University of St. Andrews, 1525–30." *Records of the Scottish Church History Society* 22 (1984–86): 13–34.

KOREY D. MAAS

Hammarskjöld, Dag

Swedish-born Dag Hammarskjöld (1905–61) was the second general secretary of the United Nations (1953–61) and a spiritual writer. Little in Hammarskjöld's public career gave any indication of his intensely religious inner life. Raised by devout Lutheran parents and directed from his early years toward a life of public service, he became the best-loved statesman of the twentieth century as an advocate of emerging postcolonial nations and a negotiator in extremely tense political situations. He is the only person to date to be awarded a Nobel Peace Prize posthumously. It was only after his death in a plane crash, likely due to terrorist interference, that his journal was discovered. Published in 1963 in Swedish and in 1964 in English as *Markings*, it revealed his relentless introspection, longing for God, and engagement with the Psalms and medieval mystics. His combination of knowledge and skill in the left-hand kingdom and devotional prayer in the right remains without peer in Lutheranism and, perhaps, in the entire church.

See also Sweden

Bibliography

Aulen, G. *Dag Hammarskjöld's White Book: The Meaning of "Markings."* Fortress, 1969; Hammarskjöld, D. *Markings.* Vintage, 2006; Lipsey, R. *Hammarskjöld: A Life.* University of Michigan Press, 2013.

SARAH HINLICKY WILSON

Harms, Claus

Theologian and opponent of the Prussian Union Claus Harms was born on May 25, 1778, at Fahrstedt and died at Kiel on February 1, 1855. A farmer's son, he studied at Kiel, where rationalist theology was dominant, and he was influenced by Schleiermacher's *Speeches* (1799). Harms underwent a dramatic awakening to the Lutheran faith. As archdeacon in Kiel, he wrote Ninety-Five Theses in honor of the three-hundredth anniversary of the beginning of the Reformation, publishing them alongside Luther's original Ninety-Five Theses. These sharp and biting theses were a dialectical tour de force meant to protest the creation of the Prussian Union under Friedrich Wilhelm III (1770–1840), declaring, for example, "The forgiveness of sins at least cost money in the sixteenth century; in the nineteenth one possesses it at no cost because one helps one's self to it" (thesis 21). The theses are considered foundational to the emergence of Neo-Lutheranism.

See also Germany since 1870; Harms, Ludwig; Prussian Union

WALTER SUNDBERG

Harms, Ludwig

Ludwig Harms (1808–65) converted from a rationalist position in theology by a dramatic awakening in 1830 to embrace the authority of Scripture, a pietistic reliance on personal faith, and allegiance to the Lutheran confessions. Harms followed his father as pastor in Hermannsburg. A remarkable preacher of the *Erweckungsbewegung* (Awakening movement), he made Hermannsburg a center of missionary outreach with the founding of the Hermannsburg Mission.

WALTER SUNDBERG

Harnack, Adolf von

After earning a research doctorate at Leipzig in 1873 and successfully defending a professorial thesis (*Habilitation*) in 1874, Adolf von Harnack (1851–1930) was appointed associate professor there in 1876. In 1879 he achieved full professorship at Giessen. After two years at Marburg and following vigorous debate *between* the Berlin Ministry and the Evangelical Senior Church Council (*Oberkirchenrat*), he was called to Berlin in 1888. Objections to Harnack's appointment were based chiefly on his *Lehrbuch der dogmengeschichte* (History of dogma), the first volume of which appeared in 1885. In it he questioned traditional views regarding the Fourth Gospel, Ephesians, and 1 Peter; refused to accept the conventional interpretation of the virgin birth, the resurrection, and the ascension of Christ; and denied that Jesus had instituted the sacrament of baptism. Ultimately Kaiser Wilhelm II ensured Harnack's place at the university. The Berlin period was marked by continually increasing scientific activity. Harnack joined the Prussian Academy of Sciences, edited the *Theologische Literaturzeitung* for twenty-nine years, served as rector of the University of Berlin and as director of the Royal Library, for which he was awarded the hereditary title (von) in 1914, and was the first president of the Kaiser-Wilhelm Foundation. Following World War I, he served as government commissioner in the 1919 consultations on the articles of the Weimar Constitution dealing with church and school.

In the winter semester of 1899–1900 at Berlin, Harnack offered a course of lectures delivered to over five hundred students of all faculties, later published under the title *Das Wesen des Christentums* (*What Is Christianity?*). More than any other of its type, the book represented the so-called liberal Protestant position and urged three questions: (1) What is the gospel of Jesus Christ? (2) What impact did Jesus and his gospel have on the first generation of his disciples? (3) What are the main types of the Christian religion that developed from Christianity's encounter with its environment? After first identifying the historian's task as distinguishing "kernel" from "husk," Harnack described the gospel of Jesus and its three elements: (1) the kingdom of God and its coming, (2) the fatherhood of God and the infinite worth of the human soul, and (3) the better righteousness and the commandment of love. Jesus, wrote Harnack, believed the kingdom to be a reign of God expected in the near future, but also as present and inward, the most original and essential aspect of his teaching. Whatever touched the eschatological or apocalyptic aspect was submerged. Of Jesus's own self-understanding, Harnack wrote that his consciousness of being the Son of God was nothing but the practical consequence of his knowledge of God as Father. Respecting the impact of Jesus and his gospel on his disciples, Harnack viewed the Synoptic Gospels as essentially faithful records of the first-century Palestinian tradition about Jesus, but had little regard for the Fourth Gospel or the Johannine community. As to what developed from Christianity's encounter with its environment, Harnack stated that the most fundamental type of Christianity appeared in the second century, when metaphysical significance was assigned to historical fact, and the Christian Church emerged as a continuation of Greek religion.

In 1892 conflict over Harnack's views emerged again during the so-called Apostolicum dispute. A cleric named Schrempf, who had rejected the virgin birth and bodily resurrection, refused to use the Apostles' Creed in the administration of baptism. He was deposed, but a battle ensued in which Harnack took the leading part. Harnack denied that the creed reflected true apostolic teaching or that the meaning presently attached to its clauses represented its true, original sense. Ten years later the "Bible-Babel" controversy erupted around Friedrich Delitzsch of Berlin, who argued that the Christian religion required a fundamental renewal and no longer needed the Old Testament. Delitzsch's position was identical to that of Harnack in his volume on Marcion. In 1911 a self-styled monist-pantheist named Jatho refused to use the Apostles' Creed during confirmation. Following the enactment of a new Prussian heresy law in 1910, he was removed from office. Though distancing himself from Jatho's views, Harnack publicly deplored his dismissal.

Respecting its substance, Harnack's work reflected allegiance to the approach of the Baur-Tübingen school. Like Baur, Harnack viewed the story of Christianity as a story of development. But whereas Baur perceived that development conceptually, Harnack perceived it psychologically, having on loan from Goethe the idea of personality as the vehicle of revelation. Respecting its methodology, Harnack's work reflected allegiance to the historical-critical approach of Albrecht Ritschl, who held that the understanding of Christianity demanded relating it to the culture in which it originated.

Harnack's work may have laid a foundation for the later form criticism and demythologizing program of the twentieth century, but as his book *Marcion* indicated, he was becoming a stranger to theology, and certainly to the changes occurring in it. For example, he attacked the Romans commentary of his former student, Karl Barth, as totally destitute of any historical-critical sense. The student, in turn, could only be appalled by his former teacher's signing the Manifesto of the Ninety-Three, the 1914 proclamation of German intellectuals endorsing Germany's military action in World War I.

Throughout his life, Harnack was denied all official recognition by the church. The Weimar government, however, thought sufficiently highly of him to offer him an ambassadorship to the United States, a post that he declined. He was twice invited to join the Harvard faculty.

Bibliography

Arnold, B. T., and D. B. Weisberg. "A Centennial Review of Friedrich Delitzsch's 'Babel und Bibel' Lectures." *Journal of Biblical Literature* 121, no. 3 (2002): 441–57; Harnack, A. *Das apostolische Glaubensbekenntnis: Ein geschichtlicher Bericht nebst einem Nachwort*. A. Haack, 1892; Harnack, A. *Lehrbuch der Dogmengeschichte*. Wissenschaftliche Buchgesellschaft, 1964; Harnack, A. *Marcion*. Wissenschaftliche Buchgesellschaft, 1960; Harnack, A. *Mission und Ausbreitung des Christentums in den ersten drei Jahrhunderten*. J. C. Hinrichs, 1924; Harnack, A. *Das Wesen des Christentums*. J. C. Hinrichs, 1900; "Harnack, Adolf." *RGG* 3 (1959): 78–79; "Harnack, Adolf." *RGG* 3 (2000): 1457–59.

ROY A. HARRISVILLE

Harnack, Theodosius Andreas

Lutheran professor of practical theology and university preacher Theodosius Andreas Harnack was born in St. Petersburg in 1817 and died in 1889. He was raised by pious, industrious parents who had moved from East Prussia to Russia. From them he learned to treasure the Scriptures and his parents' German-Baltic-Lutheran heritage in an area dominated by Russian Orthodoxy. The lay-oriented piety of the Herrnhut Brethren (Moravians), which had become popular among Protestants in the Baltic region, also had an influence on him. Orphaned at the age of fifteen (his mother died in a flood; his father died eight years later), he and his two sisters were dependent on aid from others. In 1834 the Russian Crown gave the gifted Harnack a scholarship to study theology at the University of Dorpat (now Tartu) in Estonia (1834–37). After serving as a private tutor for three years in the home of an aristocratic family, he continued his university studies at Berlin, Bonn, and Erlangen. In each of these settings he was drawn to conservative, antirationalist

Lutheran theologians (e.g., Hengstenberg in Berlin, Harless at Erlangen). Harnack taught practical theology at Dorpat (1848–52, 1866–75) and at Erlangen (1853–66). He and his first wife had five children, a daughter and four sons. His first wife died in childbirth, and he remarried seven years later. Each of the sons became university professors themselves, the most famous of which was the esteemed church historian Adolf (later known as *von* Harnack). In addition to writing a number of works on the nature and purpose of the church, the ministry, and the liturgy—writings in which he distanced himself from his earlier acceptance of Moravian piety and its indifference to liturgy and ministry—Theodosius Harnack wrote what Heinrich Bornkamm has called "the most significant, in fact, strikingly speaking, the only significant theological book on Luther in the nineteenth century." This work is not a historical-critical investigation of Luther's intellectual development but rather an extensive overall "systematic-dogmatic" summary of key motifs in his theology. Through numerous corroborating quotations (many of which are now deemed inaccurate, since they were cited from the Walch edition of the eighteenth century), Harnack hoped to explicate the heart of Luther's thought: the redemption and reconciliation accomplished by Christ that is received by faith. According to Harnack, Luther held that because of Jesus Christ and faith in him, God's relationship to the world is twofold: "outside of Christ" and "in Christ." Outside of Christ the world stands under God's judgment and wrath. In Christ, however, the gospel of God's love and forgiveness is revealed, which overcomes the wrath of God that is revealed to the world outside of Christ. This christocentric focus—God and the world "outside Christ" and "in Christ"—leads to fundamental distinctions in Luther's theology, such as between God's wrath and love, between *deus absconditus* and *deus revelatus*, between law and gospel, and so forth. In the second volume Harnack criticizes Albrecht Ritschl's appeal to Luther, especially regarding Ritschl's diminution of the significance of the concept of God's wrath, a criticism that also contributed to the theological conflict that developed between Theodosius and his son Adolf, and led to their eventual estrangement.

See also Erlangen; Harnack, Adolf von; Ritschl, Albrecht

Bibliography

Doerne, M., "Harnack, Theodosius Andreas." In *Neue Deutsche Biographie*, 7:690–91. Duncker & Humblot, 1966; Grundmann, C. "Theodosius Andreas Harnack." In *Nineteenth-Century Lutheran Theologians*, ed. M. Becker, 255–74. Vandenhoeck & Ruprecht, 2016; Harnack, T. *Luthers Theologie*. 2 vols. Blaesing, 1862. A. Deichert, 1886. Rev. ed., 1927; Harnack, T. *Praktische Theologie*. 2 vols. A. Deichert, 1877–78; Quill, T. "An Examination of the Contributions of Theodosius Harnack to the Renewal of the Lutheran Liturgy in the Nineteenth Century." PhD diss., Drew University, 2002; Wolff, O. *Die Haupttypen der neueren Lutherdeutung*. Kohlhammer, 1938.

MATTHEW L. BECKER

Hauge, Hans Nielsen

Born on a farm in Rolfsøy, near Fredrikstad in southeastern Norway, Hans Nielsen Hauge (1771–1824) was raised in a pious home. He suffered spiritual anxieties during his teenage years. On April 5, 1796, when he was twenty-five and plowing on his father's farm, Hauge had a spiritual experience that threw him unconscious to the ground. For some time he knew nothing. When he awoke, he knew he had the assurance of salvation (part of the *ordo salutis* of the Pietists) and was convinced that he had a call to bring the gospel to his people, to speak and preach salvation to his countrymen, and to love his neighbor. Quickly he wrote *Betragtning over Verdens Daarlighed* (Meditations on the folly of the world) and took it to Christiania (Oslo) to have it published. The printer, somewhat unimpressed by the manuscript, agreed to print it when he realized the young man had financial resources. After its publication, Hauge walked through Norway, selling his books, meeting with people in their homes, and encouraging them with extensive correspondence. Soon he ran afoul of the Conventicle Act of 1741, which forbade spiritual meetings held without the permission

of a pastor of the state church. He was thrown into jail several times for breaking this law and the vagrancy law. In 1804 he was imprisoned and languished in jail without a sentence until 1813, when he received a two-year sentence of hard labor and a fine of a thousand riksdaler. The government had let him out briefly in the middle of his term to build salt works, to produce the salt the country could not import because of the British blockade. On his return to prison, his living arrangements were improved, somewhat. On Christmas Day 1814, he was released.

Hauge bought a farm, Bakkehaugen, near Oslo, and married Andrea Andersdatter Nyhus. Their home became the center of the revival. Andrea died giving birth to their first son, Alfred. Hauge then married Ingeborg Marie Olsdatter and purchased another farm, Bredtvet. By this time his health was so compromised that he could do very little physical work. During his lifetime he wrote almost thirty books, the most important an autobiography, *Beskrivelse over Hans Nielsen Hauges reiser, vigtigste hændelser og tildragelser* (Hans Nielsen Hauge's journeys and most important adventures, 1816), founded several factories (such as paper mills, breweries, and salt works), became a merchant to sell his books, and bought a ship to expedite his publishing. He soon became one of Norway's wealthiest men, rich enough to be a benefactor of the new University in Christiania founded in 1811. He was a natural leader who recruited both men and women for his circle of leadership, even supporting women preaching if they had the gifts. In *Hans Nielsen Hauges Testament til sine venner* (Testament to his friends), he advised his followers, among other things, to remain faithful and not leave the state church.

As the most important religious leader in Norway after the Reformation, Hauge was an evangelist, not a theologian. His education was typical for his day and class: grammar school and confirmation, in which he studied the Bible, Martin Luther's Small Catechism (with Erik Pontoppidan's *Explanation* containing

710 more questions to memorize), and the hymnal, the common spiritual curriculum that Norwegians treasured as their Children Teaching (*Børnelærdom*). He preached conversion, the importance of a living faith that resulted in holy living and works of love for one's neighbor, and evangelism. His entrepreneurial skills are admired today as much as his spiritual gifts. Many of the Norwegian immigrants who came to America had been changed by Hauge's work and established lively and vigorous churches, colleges and seminaries, orphanages, hospitals, old people's homes, and missionary societies that flourished in America for the next century.

See also Norway; Norwegian-American Lutheranism; Pietism

Bibliography

Aarfolt, A. *Hans Nielsen Hauge: His Life and Message.* Augsburg, 1979; Granquist, M., ed. *Scandinavian Pietists: Spiritual Writings from 19th-Century Norway, Denmark, Sweden, and Finland.* Paulist Press, 2015; Shaw, J. *Pulpit under the Sky: A Life of Hans Nielsen Hauge.* Augsburg, 1955.

GRACIA GRINDAL

Hegel, Georg Wilhelm Friedrich

The philosopher Georg Wilhelm Friedrich Hegel (1770–1830) was author of *Phenomenology of Spirit* and *The Science of Logic* and professor at the University of Berlin. He was born into a family of civil servants and pastors, instructed in Latin by his mother before he was even five years old, and went on to study theology at the University of Tübingen, where he developed influential friendships with the poet Friedrich Hölderlin and the philosopher Friedrich Wilhelm Joseph Schelling. Disappointed with the theological scholarship offered at Tübingen, Hegel was glad not to pursue a pastoral career after completing his degree in 1793.

After spending most of the next decade as a private tutor for wealthy families, Hegel moved to Jena, home of the most exciting German university of the 1790s. There Hegel worked for a couple of years on the *Critical Journal of Philosophy* with his old seminary friend Schelling and sought to land a university teaching position. In 1801 he successfully defended a thesis written in Latin, giving him license to teach at the university level, but it would be another fifteen years before he would secure a professorial position with a regular salary. In the interim he worked as a nonstipendiary instructor in Jena, edited a newspaper in Bamberg, and served as principal of an academic high school in Nuremberg. Along the way he published his two masterworks: *Phenomenology of Spirit* (1807) and *Science of Logic* (vol. 1, 1812; vol. 2, 1813; vol. 3, 1816).

In his mid-forties, Hegel was finally appointed professor at the University of Heidelberg. The next year, 1817, he published the *Encyclopedia of the Philosophical Sciences*, intended for students to use as companion reading to his lectures. Hegel became professor at the new University of Berlin in 1818, where he published the final book from his own hand, *Elements of the Philosophy of Right*, in 1820. Many of the writings now read as Hegel's works are publications based on Hegel's lectures, drawing on both his lectures notes and the written records of his lectures taken by students. These lecture publications form the bulk of the written record of his years as a celebrated professor in Berlin. Most of Hegel's explicit references to Luther and Lutheranism are in these posthumously published lectures or in his letters.

His youthful aspiration was to be a popular educator, writing philosophy in a way that would speak to readers well beyond academic circles. His writings from his twenties—not published for over a century after their composition—show a distrust of abstract theory and a concentration on what will fire the popular imagination and move people's hearts. Theology, conceived as the business of abstract doctrines, left him cold. The distrust of abstract theory never left Hegel, although in his mature work he embraced academic philosophy as a means of criticizing and unmasking abstraction. He insisted that only that which is concrete can be true. His first book,

Phenomenology of Spirit, presents spirit as historical concrete or, alternatively, presents history as concretions of spirit.

Hegel's thought centers on his appropriation of the Christian doctrines of Trinity and incarnation. For Hegel the historical reality of the incarnation means that God is not distant, but historically embodied, acting and present in history. The trinitarian reality of the Spirit means that divine presence in history occurs not just in the particular life of Jesus of Nazareth. Instead, all finite beings are what they are because the infinite is present in them. Hegel insists that he is not thereby reducing the infinite to the finite. He is not unmasking the divine as a projection of finite human imagination. Hegel is a thinker of reconciliation—reconciliation not as a static result, but as a living process. His goal is to think unity in difference in a way that shortchanges neither, because each is constituted only in and through the other. The full Hegelian phrase for the reconciliation that he envisions is "the identity of identity and non-identity."

Hegel was a lifelong Lutheran and insisted that philosophy had only confirmed him in his Lutheranism. He prized the Protestant Reformation for its contribution to freedom. Hegel regarded Christianity as the leading religion of freedom, and he saw the Protestant Reformation as more fully doing justice to the centrality of freedom than Christianity's previous history. For Hegel the freedom that he saw at the center of Christianity entailed social and political freedom. He insisted that slavery stood in open contradiction to Christianity. It is highly probable that the successful revolt against slavery in Haiti at the dawn of the nineteenth century inspired Hegel's conviction that slaves had power to overcome slavery and a slavish consciousness. Hegel profoundly influenced two great nineteenth-century European thinkers of freedom, even while they strongly criticized him: Søren Kierkegaard and Karl Marx. Kierkegaard's legacy shaped dialectical theology and existentialism, while, besides its well-known political and economic influence, Marx's thought contributed to some elements of liberation theology.

Hegel saw Holy Communion at the heart of the life of the Christian church. He regarded the Lord's Supper as the appropriation of the very presence of God. He championed the Lutheran understanding of divine presence in the Supper because (1) it insists that God is indeed present in the sacrament, and (2) it insists on faith as the mediation of divine presence. In Hegel's view, the true consecration of the sacrament occurs in the act of receiving the sacramental elements in faith. He rejected the idea of consecration occurring in the action of a priest external to the believing recipient because he thought that this view robbed communicants of their proper freedom as spiritual agents, making them passively subservient to the external authority of the church. Hegel objected to what he diagnosed as a division between priests as spiritual insiders and laity as outsiders. In Hegel's view, Protestantism has no room for the idea of laity.

Hegel made much of the idea of the death of God, which he found in a seventeenth-century Lutheran chorale text by Johann Rist, which included the words: "O deepest dread, that God is dead." Hegel took this text as a witness to what he called the "speculative Good Friday": thus the life of spirit is a life that occurs not in immunity to death, or in avoidance of death, but in and through death. Although often misunderstood, by "speculative" Hegel does not mean "abstract" or "produced by arbitrary musing." In Hegel's use, "speculative" means "pertaining to the spiritual depth of things." Hegel's Good Friday emphasis has influenced later theologians such as Jürgen Moltmann, Eberhard Jüngel, and Hans Küng.

A central expression of Hegel's high regard for religion is his claim that religion knows the true content of spirit. What religion lacks is an appreciation of the form appropriate to that content. It is philosophy, in Hegel's view, that matches the true content of spirit with its true form. Formally, religion operates in the mode of *Vorstellung*—usually translated as "representation" or "representational think-ing." What Hegel means by *Vorstellung* is the inability to fully shake off the habit of seeing things in static juxtaposition or opposition. As long as there is a remnant of such thinking, one cannot grasp the simultaneous identity of identity and non-identity. In theological terms, this means that one cannot, for instance, prop-erly grasp the simultaneous transcendence and immanence of the infinite God in relation to finite creation. *Vorstellung* never works fully free of the alternative of seeing God as either beyond our finite life or identified with our finite life, but not fully both.

For Hegel, *Vorstellung* cannot do justice to the identification of the infinite with the finite that happens in the incarnation of God as a human being. In emphasizing that the infinite and the finite are fully identified in the incar-nation, even while remaining distinct, Hegel shows his kinship with Lutheran theology's readiness to interpret more radically than much of the Christian tradition the *communicatio idiomatum*, the communication of properties between the divine and the human natures in Jesus Christ. Hegel's language is particularly close to the sixteenth-century Lutheran claim, grounded in the Lutheran understanding of the *communicatio idiomatum*, that the finite has the capacity to bear the infinite (*finitum capax infiniti*). Hegel renders the point more precisely than the sixteenth-century slogan—although in keeping with the actual position of its Lutheran advocates—in arguing that the infinite is capable of being borne by the finite.

Despite Hegel's appeal to central elements of Lutheran theology and despite his explicit claims of Lutheran identity, later theologians have raised questions about his relation to Lutheran thought. Does Hegel's emphasis on the actuality of reconciliation lack a sufficient eschatological reserve, such that he surrenders too much of the gospel's capacity to criticize the status quo? Does Hegel fail to distinguish sufficiently between the intratrinitarian dif-ferentiation of the Second Person from the First Person of the Trinity, on the one hand, and the extratrinitarian differentiation of cre-ation from the divine Creator, on the other hand, such that divine freedom to be God without creation is called into question? Does Hegel shift Lutheranism's linguistic focus from the second-person "for you" of word and sacrament to third-person philosophical description?

See also Christology; God and Trinity; Jüngel, Eber-hard; Kierkegaard, Søren Aabye; Liberation Theology and Marxism; Lord's Supper; Pannenberg, Wolfhart; Philosophy; Theology of the Cross

Bibliography

Primary: Di Giovanni, G., trans. *The Science of Logic.* Cambridge University Press, 2015; Hodgson, P. C., ed. *Lectures on the Philosophy of Religion.* 3 vols. Oxford Uni-versity Press, 2008; Knox, T. M., trans. *Early Theological Writings.* University of Pennsylvania Press, 1971; Miller, A. V., trans. *Phenomenology of Spirit.* Oxford University Press, 1976; Wallace, W., A. V. Miller, and M. Inwood, trans. *Philosophy of Mind.* Part 3 of *Encyclopedia of the Philosophical Sciences in Outline.* Oxford University Press, 2007; **Secondary:** Burbidge, J. W. *Hegel on Logic and Religion: The Reasonableness of Christianity.* SUNY Press, 1992; Fackenheim, E. L. *The Religious Dimension in Hegel's Thought.* Indiana University Press, 1968; Hodgson, P. C. *Hegel and Christian Theology: A Reading of the "Lectures on the Philosophy of Religion."* Oxford Univer-sity Press, 2005; O'Regan, C. *The Heterodox Hegel.* SUNY Press, 1994; Pinkard, T. *Hegel: A Biography.* Cambridge University Press, 2000.

JOHN F. HOFFMEYER

Heim, Karl

Karl Heim (1874–1958) was a professor of systematic theology at the University of Tü-bingen (1920–48) and preacher at the Univer-sity Church (*Stiftskirche*) at Tübingen. Coming from a pietistic background, it was important for Heim to show that faith and reason are not opposed. To that end, he maintained vigorous dialogue with the natural sciences, atypical for German Protestant theology in the first half of the twentieth century. He showed that a scien-tifically trained person could be a sincere Chris-tian without compromising either faith or current scientific insights. He attracted many students from all disciplines, and his lecture room was overcrowded, as was the church when he preached. A whole generation of pastors from all over Germany was shaped by his intellectually informed piety. His first major work, *Das Weltbild der Zukunft* (The worldview of the future, 1904), caught students' attention so that student groups on many university campuses discussed its implications. Confronted by the rise of the Nazis, he consistently opposed their interference in the life of the church. He was a solitary thinker who neither founded a theological school nor joined one. His six-volume work, *Der evangelische Glaube und das Denken der Gegenwart: Grundzüge einer christlichen Lebensanschauung* (The Evangelical faith and present-day thinking: Foundations of a Christian worldview, 1931–37) is still available today. Many of his books have been translated into English.

See also Creation; Evolution

Bibliography

Heim, K. *God Transcendent: Foundation for a Christian Metaphysic.* Nisbet, 1935; Heim, K. *The Living Fountain: A Series of Sermons.* T&T Clark, 1936; Heim, K. *The Transformation of the Scientific World View.* Harper, 1953; Holmstrand, I. *Karl Heim on Philosophy, Science, and the Transcendence of God.* Almqvist & Wiksell, 1980.

HANS SCHWARZ

Hell

The English word "hell" is of Germanic origin (*Hölle*). The cultures of Mesopotamia reveal earliest evidence for the idea of a realm of the dead below heaven and earth and called (in Greek) Hades. The Old Testament describes that realm as Sheol, the "land of no return," which lies in the sphere of the chaotic powers of darkness and the sea but may also extend to this life. More important for the Old Testament, Sheol is the sphere of absolute distance from God. This does not mean it is removed from God's power. He may pursue his quarry as far as Sheol (see Ps. 139:8, "If I make my bed in Sheol, you are there"). In the Old Testament, but particularly in later Judaism, another term, *Gehinnom* or Gehenna, is used to denote a place of punishment. The threats in Jeremiah over *Hinnom*, where offerings were made to Moloch (Jer. 7:31–32; 19:2, 6; 32:35)

may have contributed to the later use of the term for the hell of fire to be opened after the final judgment. It is this stage which the NT reflects.

In the New Testament the terms used of hell are *Abyssos*, *Hades*, and *Gehenna*. *Abyssos* (the abyss) may be used of the abode of the dead or of the place of torment. Jesus is recorded as referring to Hades as a place of torment, as in the parable of Lazarus and the rich man (see Luke 16:23); as the diametric opposite of the heights, as in his judgment on Capernaum (Matt. 11:23); or as a nearly invincible power, as in his word to Peter at Caesarea Philippi (see Matt. 16:18). In Mark's Gospel, Jesus refers three times to Gehenna as the place of torment, in Matthew to Gehenna seven times, but in Luke only once. Hell can be viewed by the New Testament authors as a sphere of power. And, although that power has in principle been broken by the death of Christ, it continues to hold sway till the last judgment brings final deliverance from it or consignment to it.

The ancient church viewed the place of the dead and the hellfire of the end time as separate sites, existence in the hell of fire conceived either as finite, as did Origen (186–284), thus contributing to the later notion of purgatory; or as infinite, without end, as did Justin Martyr (100–165). Luther embraced the traditional idea, according to which the souls of the dead are kept in reserve till the day of resurrection, but on a number of occasions he confessed that he was not particularly certain regarding what happened to the wicked after their death. He wrote, "Some may feel punishments immediately after death, but others may be spared until that Day. . . . It is my opinion that these things are uncertain." What is more striking is that Luther could speak of the believer's inner conflict (*Anfechtung, tentatio*) as an experience of hell already in the *Explanation of the Ninety-Five Theses* (1518). To treat as a horror the God who gives salvation to one and cuts off all hope for the other was blasphemous. The thought had to be the fate of the damned in hell, and to suppress it had to be the apex of torture. Or again, to contemplate one's condition in face of the judgment of God meant to experience hell in the full and real sense: "God saves only the damned, not as some say, that they feel damned and yet are saved, but they are damned, and there's no pretending in that feeling." Solely to affirm God's will and to be totally free of self means to endure hell itself.

In marked contrast to the New Testament and Luther, the Orthodox Lutheran theologians were preoccupied to the point of obsession with depicting the tortures of hell after the fashion of apocalyptic literature. Johann Gerhard (1582–1637) refers to the ten types of torture experienced by the condemned at death, including pains such as criminals endure, anguish such as of those who endure the pains of childbirth, a sight of the elect in glory, remembrance of former good, and resistance to God. Matthew Hafenreffer (1561–1619) refers to the condemned as quaking among devils, and Johannes Andreas Quenstedt (1617–88) divides the mass of evils reserved for the damned into the "privative," including separation from the society of all the good, exclusion from heavenly light, denial of pity, and the "positive," of which some are internal, such as the damned experience within themselves. David Hollazius (1646–1713) writes that the damned are in a most foul dwelling place, feel association with devils, and burn without being consumed. While continuing to hold to the Orthodox position, Pietism's preachers and theologians emphasized rescue from sin, death, and hell more than they described it. Enlightenment theologians, by contrast, tended to minimize its importance or even its existence, a trend continued among more liberal theologians of the nineteenth and twentieth centuries.

Despite the popularity of universalism, or in face of attempts to treat Christ's references to eternal punishment as trajectories from a later generation, the biblical references cannot be wished away but require scholarly and serious attention.

See also Death and Dying; Eschatology (Apocalypticism, Chiliasm, Millennialism, Millennarianism)

Bibliography

"Gehenna." *Theologisches Wörterbuch zum Neuen Testament*, 1:655. Kohlhammer, 1953; Holl, K. *Gesammelte Aufsätze zur Kirchengeschichte*, 1:18, 27, 146, 151. J. C. B. Mohr, 1932; "Hölle." *RGG* 1:403–7. Mohr, 1959; "Hölle." *RGG* 3:1847–50. Mohr Siebeck, 2000; Luther, M. "Letter to Nicholas von Amsdorf." WA BR 2:422.4–6, 10–15; Luther, M. "Martin Luther's Torgau Sermon on Christ's Descent into Hell and the Resurrection." In R. Kolb and J. Nestingen, *Sources and Contexts of the Book of Concord*, 245–55. Fortress, 2001; Schmid, H. *The Doctrinal Theology of the Evangelical Lutheran Church*, 626–60. Trans. C. A. Hay and H. E. Jacobs. Lutheran Publication Society, 1899. Reprint, Augsburg, 1961.

ROY A. HARRISVILLE

Hemmingsen, Niels

The most internationally known Danish theologian of the sixteenth century, Niels Hemmingsen (1513–1600) was born on the island of Lolland. He studied in Roskilde and Lund before matriculating at Wittenberg in 1537, where he attended Luther's lectures and was strongly influenced by Philip Melanchthon. Returning to Denmark, he became professor of Greek (1543), dialectics (1545), and then theology (1553) at the University of Copenhagen, receiving a doctorate in theology in 1557. Hemmingsen was rector of the university four times and broadly influenced its curriculum, most noticeably through his books on systematic theology (*Enchiridion*, 1555), preaching (*Postilla*, 1561), and pastoral theology (*Pastor*, 1562). Because his books were first written in Latin, they were also read by many outside of Denmark. However, his view of the Lord's Supper espoused in his later treatises (*Demonstratio*, 1571; *Syntagma*, 1574) showed leanings toward John Calvin's understanding of spiritual presence and provoked controversy shortly after the approval of the Formula of Concord in Germany (in 1577). Widespread Philippist sympathies existed in the Danish Church, and when Hemmingsen's views became known in Germany, the Elector of Saxony pressured his brother-in-law, King Frederik II, into suspending Hemmingsen from his professorship. The king complied but made Hemmingsen canon at the cathedral in Roskilde, where he served for the final twenty-one years of his life, continuing his influence on the church and the king.

See also Denmark

Bibliography

Koch, H., and B. Kornerup, eds. *Den danske kirkes Historie.* Vol. 4. Gyllendal, 1959; Lund, E. "Nordic and Baltic Lutheranism." In *Lutheran Ecclesiastical Culture 1550–1675*, ed. R. Kolb, 411–54. Brill, 2008; Lyby, T., and O. Grell. "The Consolidation of Lutheranism in Denmark and Norway." In *The Scandinavian Reformation*, ed. O. Grell, 114–43. Cambridge University Press, 1995; Madsen, E. *Niels Hemmingsens Etik.* Gad, 1946; Schwarz-Lausten, M. *A Church History of Denmark.* Ashgate, 2002.

ERIC LUND

Hengstenberg, Ernst Wilhelm

Born in October 1802 in Fröndenberg, Ernst Wilhelm Hengstenberg was the son of a pastor. He was an important conservative Lutheran theologian and professor in Germany.

Hengstenberg studied classical and oriental philology in Bonn, along with philosophy and theology, receiving his doctorate there. He taught Arabic in Basel and completed his *Habilitationsschrift* (second dissertation) in philosophy in Berlin. His doctoral dissertation at Bonn (1823) argued that the science of philology rather than dogmatic theology discloses the meaning of the Scriptures. The following year, he reversed his position and thereafter dedicated his career both to the defense of orthodox Lutheran doctrine and the battle against historical-critical method.

Hengstenberg's dramatic change of position came about when he was "awakened" to "true faith" after joining the neo-Pietist circle of Baron Hans Ernst von Kottwitz (1757–1831). The purpose of this group of Prussian aristocrats and churchmen was to revitalize the Prussian people after the final defeat of Napoleon in 1813. For Kottwitz and his followers, including Crown Prince Friedrich Wilhelm (1795–1861), this meant that the Prussian state must restore its commitment to the Reformation teaching of sin and grace as the primary experience of Christian life and reject "the ideas of 1789."

Hengstenberg was one of von Kottwitz's most effective disciples. During his tenure at Berlin as professor of exegesis from 1828 to 1869, Hengstenberg encouraged the reintroduction of traditional dogmatic study of the Scriptures. As editor of the *Evangelische Kirchenzeitung* (1827–69), Hengstenberg was in the forefront of the struggle, representing the neo-Pietist governmental party line on ecclesiastical issues, and he regularly subjected Schleiermacher, Strauss, and Baur to fierce attack. Hengstenberg died in Berlin in 1869.

WALTER SUNDBERG

Henry VIII

As king of England, Henry VIII (1491–1547) ruled during the Reformation's introduction to England and separated the realm from Roman obedience while maintaining much doctrinal continuity with the medieval church. Born at Greenwich and educated at court, Henry ascended to the throne in 1509. The same year, with a papal dispensation, he married Catherine of Aragon, widow of his brother Arthur. Though already insisting early in his reign that England's kings had no earthly superiors, he maintained a high view of the papacy and its necessity. The *Assertion of the Seven Sacraments* (1521), published under the king's name and in response to Luther's *Babylonian Captivity of the Church* (1520), was rewarded with the pope's granting Henry the title "Defender of the Faith." Through the end of the decade, Henry did defend the old faith, enforcing heresy statutes, prohibiting the distribution and possession of Reformation literature, and commissioning scholars to publish against it. The failure of his marriage to produce a surviving male heir, however, precipitated open conflict with the papacy in the early 1530s.

Citing Lev. 20:21, Henry judged his marriage, and hence the dispensation permitting it, illegitimate. With the papacy's refusal to concur or to grant an annulment, parliament was induced to enact legislation curtailing papal power in England. Successive acts suspended annates paid to Rome (1532), prohibited legal appeals to Rome (1533), and finally declared the king "supreme head" of the church in England (1534). The execution of influential papal defenders Thomas More and John Fisher in 1535, the dissolution of monasteries begun in 1536, and the licensing of English Bibles in 1537 gave Evangelicals hope that Henry might complete the reform begun with his break from Rome, as did protracted negotiations respecting possible entrance into the Lutheran Smalcaldic League. In 1539, however, royal support of the Act of Six Articles placed decisive limits on reform initiatives by codifying, among other things, clerical celibacy and the doctrine of transubstantiation. The following year Thomas Cromwell—the royal minister who had spearheaded much reformist legislation, especially encouraging rapprochement with the Continental Lutherans, and even commissioning a translation of the Augsburg Confession—was executed on charges of working contrary to the king's ecclesiastical agenda. By 1543 even previous concessions, such as Bible reading by laborers and women, were being withdrawn, and the Evangelically catechetical Bishop's Book of 1537 was replaced by the more traditionalist King's Book.

Aside from his consistent rejection of justification by faith alone, Henry's personal beliefs remain ambiguous. Though always antipathetic to Luther, he greatly admired Melanchthon, whom he handsomely rewarded for dedicating his 1535 *Loci communes* to the king. He eschewed the traditional last rites at his death on January 28, 1547, but did provide in his will for perpetual Masses to be said for him. Despite the conservative direction of religious policy in the last years of his reign, he entrusted the education of Edward, his only surviving son and immediate successor, to known Evangelical tutors, paving the way for further reform upon his death.

See also Barnes, Robert; Cranmer, Thomas; England; Tyndale, William

Bibliography
Bernard, G. W. *The King's Reformation: Henry VIII and the Remaking of the English Church.* Yale University Press, 2007; McEntegart, R. *Henry VIII, the League of Schmalkalden, and the English Reformation.* Boydell, 2002; Rex, R. *Henry VIII and the English Reformation.* 2nd ed. Palgrave Macmillan, 2006; Scarisbrick, J. *Henry VIII.* Rev. ed. Yale University Press, 1997; Tjernagel, N. *Henry VIII and the Lutherans: A Study in Anglo-Lutheran Relations from 1521–1547.* Concordia, 1965.

KOREY D. MAAS

Hermann, Nikolaus

The cantor and hymn composer Nikolaus Hermann (ca. 1500–1561) came to Joachimsthal (Jáchymov) in Bohemia, a recently founded mining town, filled with miners who resettled there from Saxony and other points north. He soon became a follower of Luther, and after the arrival of Johann Mathesius as preacher in the town, Hermann worked closely with him to consolidate the town as an exemplary model of worship and life in the Wittenberg style. He wrote roughly one hundred hymns, among them "Let All Together Praise Our God" and "'As Surely as I Live,' God Said." His versification of Old Testament stories in *Stories of the Flood, Joseph, Moses, Elijah, Elisha and Susanna* (1562), and of New Testament accounts in his *Sunday Gospels* (1560), which rendered the appointed Gospel lessons of the year into song, all were intended to serve families as the basis for household devotional life. His musical gifts led him to promote polyphony and to adapt the medieval Latin traditions of hymnody and popular melodies of the day for Evangelical use.

See also Hymnody; Mathesius, Johannes; Music

Bibliography
Brown, C. B. *Singing the Gospel: Lutheran Hymns and the Success of the Reformation.* Harvard University Press, 2005.

ROBERT KOLB

Hesshus, Tilemann (Heshusens, Heshusius)

The Lutheran theologian, professor, superintendent, and bishop Tilemann Hesshus (1527–88)

was born in Wesel on the lower Rhine, in an area that voiced early support for Luther's Evangelical reforms. He attended school in Antwerp, Oxford, Paris, and arrived in Wittenberg a few months after Luther's death in 1546. Hesshus became a protégé of Melanchthon and earned a master of arts and a doctorate in theology in 1550 and 1553. He married Hanna von Bert and took his first clerical appointment as superintendent in Goslar. Hesshus later served as superintendent of Heidelberg, Bremen, and Magdeburg; bishop of Samland (Prussia); and professor of theology at Rostock, Heidelberg, Jena, Königsberg, and Helmstedt.

Hesshus wrote over a hundred works that vigorously defended Lutheran doctrine in the face of competing claims, treating the Lord's Supper, Christology, the office of public ministry, and other topics, and including biblical commentary, catechetical education, and model sermons. He participated in debates about original sin, "crypto-Calvinism," Osiander's doctrine of justification, and the Formula of Concord (which he ultimately rejected because of what he viewed as a flawed understanding of Christology). Hesshus was also a major patron in a regional network that supported Gnesio-Lutherans and their families, including Simon Musäus, Daniel Hoffmann, Johannes Olearius, and Hesshus's sons, Gottfried and Heinrich, who followed him into the ministry.

See also Flacius, Matthias Illyricus, and the Flacians; Formula of Concord; Osiander, Andreas; Wittenberg Circle, Parties within

Bibliography

Barton, P. F. *Um Luthers Erbe: Studien und Texte zur Spätreformation*. Luther-Verlag, 1972; Dingel, I. *Concordia Controversa*. Gütersloher Verlagshaus, 1996; Halvorson, M. *Heinrich Heshusius and Confessional Polemic in Early Lutheran Orthodoxy*. Ashgate, 2010; Krüger, T. *Empfangene Allmacht. Die Christologie Tilemann Heshusens (1527–1588)*. Vandenhoeck & Ruprecht, 2004.

MICHAEL J. HALVORSON

Heyer, Johann Friedrich Christian

The first Lutheran missionary sent abroad by the North American Lutheran churches (1842) was Johann Friedrich Christian Heyer (1793–1873). His labor laid the foundations for the Guntur and Rajamundry mission fields that evolved into Andhra Evangelical Lutheran Church (formed in 1927), the largest Lutheran church in India.

Born in Helmstedt, Germany, he migrated to the United States and studied theology at Philadelphia and later in Göttingen. In Pittsburgh he established First Lutheran Church and two German missions, one on each side of the Allegheny River. After serving as both a lay preacher and from 1820 an ordained minister of Home Mission of the Ministerium of Pennsylvania for twenty years, in Pennsylvania, Ohio, Kentucky, Indiana, and Missouri, he was sent to India in 1842 as a pioneer missionary of the Ministerium of Pennsylvania at the age of forty-eight. His first three years of ministry and the second assignment of seven years (1848–57, sent by the General Synod to work in Rajahmundry region) laid the foundation of the Lutheran church among the Telugu-speaking people in the Guntur and Rajahmundry regions of South India. The conversion and leadership of Malapati John of Pollepalli led to conversion en masse. One of the reasons for his success was the able leadership provided by native evangelists, including Tota Joseph, Nelaprolu Paulus, and Malapati John of Pollepalli. On his return to the United States on account of his failing health, Heyer served as a traveling missionary among Germans in Minnesota, where he organized the Minnesota Synod and served as its first president. He returned to India for the third time at the age of seventy-seven, when the Lutheran churches in the Rajahmundry regions were about to be handed over to the Anglican mission for want of Lutheran missionaries. During his last days he served as a chaplain at the Lutheran Theological Seminary at Philadelphia. His brief presence in a Lutheran theological seminary so influenced several students that they decided to go as missionaries to India. They called him "Father Heyer." He died in Philadelphia on November 7, 1873.

See also India

Bibliography

Bachmann, E. T. *They Called Him Father: The Life Story of John Christian Frederick Heyer.* Muhlenberg, 1942; Heyer, J. F. C. *Father Heyer's Own Story: Travel Letters of the Rev. C. F. Heyer.* Evangelical Lutheran Synod of Pennsylvania, 1861.

PETER VETHANAYAGAMONY

Hildebrand, Carl (Baron von Canstein)

Eventually a key figure in the expansion of Halle Pietism and founder of the Canstein Bible Institute in Halle, Carl Hildebrand (1667–1719) completed his studies in Frankfurt (Oder) in 1688, then briefly served the courts in Berlin and Potsdam before abruptly leaving his post and taking a military commission. In 1690 Canstein came across Pietist ideas in a booklet written by Philipp Jakob Spener (1635–1705). Shortly thereafter, while traveling, he became deathly ill and offered his life to the service of God should he survive. Upon recovery, Canstein immediately returned to Berlin, where he befriended Spener. In 1697 Spener introduced him to August Hermann Francke (1663–1727). Canstein became the middleman between Francke's Foundations in Halle and the court in Berlin, helping to expand Pietist patronage and fill vacant military chaplaincies with Halle-trained pastors. He is most famous for founding the first Bible institute in 1710, which had the goal of producing inexpensive Bibles. By Canstein's death only nine years later, the institute had produced approximately a hundred thousand New Testaments and eighty thousand complete Bibles.

See also Francke, August Hermann; Francke Foundations; Pietism; Spener, Jakob Philipp

Bibliography

Marschke, B. *Absolutely Pietist: Patronage, Factionalism, and State-Building in the Early Eighteenth-Century Prussian Army Chaplaincy.* Max Niemeyer, 2005; Schicketanz, P., ed. *Der Briefwechsel Carl Hildebrand von Cansteins mit August Hermann Francke.* De Gruyter, 1972; Schicketanz, P. *Carl Hildebrand Freiherr von Canstein: Leben und Denken in Quellendarstellungen.* Max Niemeyer, 2002.

PETER JAMES YODER

History

History, as one of the developing disciplines of the humanities (*studia humanitatis*) cultivated by Renaissance humanists, was, along with biblical studies, a significant link between Renaissance humanism and the Protestant Reformation and therefore with Lutheran traditions of scholarship. Luther engaged in intensive historical study amid the controversy over indulgences, in particular in writing the Ninety-Five Theses and in preparation for the Leipzig Debate (1519), as he grew increasingly skeptical of Roman ecclesiastical authority and disputed the claim that papal primacy in the church was ordained by God (*de iure divino*). From the beginning of the Reformation, therefore, historical analysis was a discipline practiced by Evangelical reformers. The Reformation not only participated in but also broadened and intensified the Renaissance humanist commitment to the discipline of history as a means for understanding and utilizing the past in the interest of present-day concerns regarding church and society. Central to the utility of history was historical narrative and analysis as a way of teaching moral philosophy (ethics), especially through examples of character and conduct to be either emulated or avoided.

Luther viewed Scripture as the revelation of God's activity and presence in human history; likewise he viewed other histories, when they (in his view) told the unvarnished truth, as "nothing else than a demonstration, recollection, and sign of divine action and judgment, how [God] upholds, rules, obstructs, prospers, and honors the world, and especially men, each according to his just desert, evil or good" (LW 34:275–76). Thus paradoxically joining human conduct and God's grace, Luther "displays the divided mind of Protestantism about the ecclesiastical past" (Kelley 162). Through his lectures on the Bible, in particular on Genesis, Luther interpreted universal history as the theater of conflict between God and the devil, with humankind divided between those who believe God's Word and those who persecute those believers, Cain and Abel representing two "churches," the (hypocritical) one asserting itself over and attacking the other. With this view of his own time and the future as well as the past, Luther reconstructed history, providing his followers with a new way of understanding the church and promoting his Evangelical reform, just as many a humanist historian used the discipline in political controversy and for national causes.

Other Lutherans likewise praised and practiced the study of history. Philip Melanchthon promoted history as an academic discipline and lauded its role in humanist studies at the University of Wittenberg and in his own writings, holding lectures in the 1550s and earlier on Johann Carion's chronicle of world history, which Melanchthon then published as his own *Chronicon Carionis* (through the time of Charlemagne, completed by his son-in-law, Caspar Peucer). He too insisted on viewing history as a struggle of the believing church of Abel, Elijah, Christ, and the apostles against the heretics led by Cain, the prophets of Baal, the Pharisees, and the opponents of Paul, a struggle that continued in Augustine's opposition to Pelagius and in Luther's challenge to "the monks." Matthias Flacius assembled a team of scholars to create a full-scale history of the church in the *Magdeburg Centuries*. Lutheran historian Johann Sleiden united the history of the Reformation with that of politics, regarding them as inseparable. Lutherans therefore played important roles in shaping history as a discipline, and important connections developed between Lutheran scholars of the Enlightenment era (e.g., J. G. Hamann and J. G. Herder) and the emergence of that modern historical consciousness called historicism.

See also Arnold, Gottfried; Flacius, Matthias Illyricus, and the Flacians; Humanism and the Reformation; Melanchthon, Philip; Mosheim, Johann Lorenz von; Seckendorff, Veit Ludwig von

Bibliography

Headley, J. *Luther's View of Church History*. Yale University Press, 1963; Kelley, D. *Faces of History: Historical Inquiry from Herodotus to Herder*. Yale University Press, 1998; Luther, M. "Preface to Galeatius Capella's History" (1538). LW 34:277–78; Maxfield, J. *Luther's Lectures on Genesis and the Formation of Evangelical Identity*. Truman State University Press, 2008; Smith, L. *Religion and the Rise of History: Martin Luther and the Cultural Revolution in Germany, 1760–1810*. James Clarke, 2010.

JOHN A. MAXFIELD

Hoffmann, Johannes Christian Konrad von

Born in Nuremberg and influenced by German Pietism, J. C. K. von Hoffmann (1810–77) studied history and theology at Erlangen and Berlin. Influenced less by Schleiermacher and Hegel than by von Ranke and Schelling, he earned degrees in both history and theology. Besides a short stint at Rostock (1842–45), he taught theology at the University of Erlangen for thirty-five years (1838–42, 1845–77). As the leading figure in the so-called Erlangen school, he emphasized baptismal regeneration, the certainty of faith in the risen Christ, and an organic-historical understanding of the Bible, the church, and the Lutheran confessions. His three main projects were the two-volume *Prophecy and Fulfillment in the Old and New Testaments*, the two-volume *Scriptural Proof* (a summary of biblical theology), and an unfinished eleven-volume commentary on the New Testament as canon. His posthumously published lectures on biblical hermeneutics highlight the crucial importance that personal faith and a properly theological "preunderstanding" of the Bible play in one's interpretation of Scripture. In his view, the Bible presents a basic narrative of *Heilsgeschichte* (salvation history) that reveals God's "self-giving" or "self-emptying" (*kenōsis*) in history. The "center" of this history is Jesus, the incarnate *Logos* of God, toward whom the history of Israel was moving and through whom all history is brought to its fulfillment. Hoffmann sought to understand this flow of history and his own place within it by correlating a systematic analysis of the Christian experience of baptismal regeneration with a historical investigation of the Christian Scriptures. He thought that by articulating the unity between experiential faith and historical investigation of the Scriptures, he could continue "to teach the old truth but in a new way." His particular form of "faith seeking understanding" led him to define theology as the discipline that is born out of theologians' own desires to understand and give expression to the "factual situation" that has made them to be the Christians they are. While many have benefited from Hoffmann's specific exegetical insights, his reinterpretation of Christ's atonement sparked a major controversy among German Lutheran theologians in the second half of the nineteenth century. Hoffmann rejected the traditional Lutheran, juridical understanding of the atonement, whereby God's wrath must first be appeased through the vicarious satisfaction of Christ on the cross before God can be merciful toward sinful humanity. Hoffmann held that the mission of Jesus is not grounded in such a legalistic framework. Rather, that mission is based in God's eternal will of love toward all of creation, a will that is actualized through the kenotic self-giving of the *Logos* in Jesus. This eternal divine love is more basic than the historical, temporal manifestation of God's wrath against sinners. By going to that point most separated from God—namely, the situation of sinful humanity under the wrath of God—the incarnate *Logos* has removed the opposition between God's eternal love and God's historical wrath in his own person. Attacked by several theologians (e.g., Philippi, Theodosius Harnack), Hoffmann responded with several "defensive writings," wherein he tried to show how Luther's theology supported his own. These writings helped to generate a new wave of interest in Luther's own understanding of the atonement.

See also Atonement; Erlangen; Harnack, Theodosius

Bibliography

Becker, M. *The Self-Giving God and Salvation History: The Trinitarian Theology of Johannes von Hofmann.* T&T Clark, 2004; Behr, W. *Politischer Liberalismus und kirchliches Christentum.* Calwer, 1995; Forde, G. *The Law-Gospel Debate.* Augsburg, 1969.

MATTHEW L. BECKER

Hoffmann, Melchior

As a furrier and lay theologian from Schwäbisch-Hall, Melchior Hoffmann (or Hoffman, ca. 1495–1543) was steeped in the writings of Johannes Tauler and the *Theologia Deutsch*. He was an ardent supporter of the Lutheran Reformation but was later expelled from the Lutheran Church and became an itinerant preacher in the Anabaptist tradition.

Hoffmann's association with the Reformation began formally in 1523, when he published a vehement attack on the Catholic Church while traveling in Livonia, a region along the eastern coast of the Baltic Sea, and began preaching against the use of images in Wolmar (Valmiera) and Dorpat (Tartu). In spring 1525 Andreas Knopken, a leading spokesman for the Lutheran Reformation in Riga, sought approval for Hoffmann's preaching before the local city council, and in 1526 the German Lutheran Church in Stockholm conferred on him the office of preacher. From there Hoffmann traveled to Wittenberg, where Luther initially received him warmly. He soon returned to Livonia with a tract by Luther and Bugenhagen, *Christliche Vermahnung von äusserlichem Gottesdienst und Eintracht* (*A Christian Admonition on External Worship and Unity* [WA 18:412–21]) and a written endorsement by Luther of his ministry.

However, Hoffmann's vehement anticlericalism—combined with convictions regarding the imminent return of Christ, a sacramentarian view of the Lord's Supper, and a strong emphasis on sanctification—soon created tensions with Lutheran pastors in Livonia. Hoffmann upheld Luther's doctrine of obedience to secular authority, but his renunciation of the use of armed force, defense of adult baptism, and view of the church as a gathering of the elect raised serious concerns. He was also associated with a view of the incarnation, borrowed from the spiritualist Caspar Schwenckfeld, that Jesus did not take his earthly flesh directly from Mary.

After further travels to Lübeck, Schleswig-Holstein, and East Frisia, Hoffmann enjoyed some success at the Danish court of King Frederik X. But at the Flensburg Disputation in 1529, Bugenhagen formally condemned Hoffmann's teachings, and the Lutheran Church in Denmark banished him. Hoffmann moved to Strasbourg. There he encountered Anabaptists and quickly became a leader in their circles before Strasbourg authorities expelled him in 1530. Hoffmann traveled to East Frisia, where his apocalyptic preaching—foretelling the second coming of Christ in 1533 and describing himself as Elijah foretold in Rev. 11—won a large number of artisans and urban refugees to his cause, while arousing concerns of secular authorities. Arrested in Strasbourg in spring 1533, Hoffmann spent the last ten years of his life imprisoned. His writings continued to be read. When his predictions regarding the return of Christ and the punishment of the godless failed to materialize, some of his followers were among those who gathered in the "Anabaptist Kingdom of Münster" in 1534–35. His association with the violent takeover of Münster and its apocalyptic theology helped to confirm Lutheran suspicions that Anabaptist teachings were inherently seditious.

See also Anabaptists/Spiritualists; Livonia

Bibliography

Deppermann, K. *Melchior Hoffman: Social Unrest and Apocalyptic Visions in the Age of Reformation.* T&T Clark, 1987; Klötzer, R. "The Melchiorites and Münster." In *A Companion to Anabaptism and Spiritualism, 1521–1700,* ed. J. D. Roth and J. M. Stayer, 217–56. Brill, 2007.

JOHN D. ROTH

Holbein, Hans (the Younger)

The German artist Hans Holbein the Younger (1497/98–1543) was primarily active in Basel and London from 1519 to 1543. His personal interest in Lutheran doctrine and the Wittenberg reform movement remains subject to speculation, but his artworks provide clear evidence of the roles visual culture played in shaping Luther's image and transmitting his ideas to others. Perhaps the most noteworthy example is a print depicting Martin Luther as the German Hercules (ca. 1523). Here text,

attributed to Erasmus of Rotterdam, and imagery, attributed to Holbein, combined to promote the cudgel-wielding Wittenberg monk as a fearsome enemy of the pope, Scholasticism, and the devil. Also around 1523, Holbein designed the title page and other illustrations for Adam Petri's Basel edition of Luther's German translation of the New Testament.

In 1526 the artist departed from Basel for England, with hopes of finding employment as court painter to King Henry VIII. These hopes were not realized until 1536, by which time Thomas Cromwell was Henry VIII's chief minister. Holbein's close ties to the reform-minded Cromwell resulted in commissions for religious art, such as the 1535/36 *Allegory of Law and Gospel*, based on a printed Cranach prototype (1529) of this popular Lutheran theme, and portraits of those sympathetic to Lutheran ideas in England.

See also Art; Cranach, Lucas, the Elder; Cranach, Lucas, the Younger; Erasmus of Rotterdam (Desiderius Erasmus Roterodamus); Henry VIII

Bibliography

Bätschmann, O., and P. Greiner. *Hans Holbein.* Princeton University Press, 1997; Foister, S. *Holbein and England.* Yale University Press, 2004; Wilson, D. *Hans Holbein: Portrait of an Unknown Man.* Weidenfeld & Nicolson, 1996.

PAUL M. BACON

Holberg, Ludvig

The historian, playwright, and satirist Ludvig Holberg (1684–1754) engaged in moral philosophy. "One corrects costumes by laughing at them," was one of his mottos. Before settling in Copenhagen as a university professor of logic, metaphysics (1717), and eloquence (1720), he had traveled Europe. Holberg has often been understood as a propagator of the Enlightenment against Pietism. He subscribed to the idea of steering the middle course, which placed him, as he said, right between Moravians and atheists (*Epistula* 17). His criticism of Pietism was subtle. In *Reservation concerning Conventicles* (1733), his criticism is couched as a defense of true piety—meaning sincere godliness in the church—and a radical attack against a rather indistinct group of opponents: the unschooled self-assigned prophets, hypocrites, hypochondriacs, misanthropes, separatists, and enthusiasts—those who prefer devotion in their living room rather than in church. In 1741 his international best-seller *Nicolai Klimii iter subterraneum* appeared and was soon translated into several European languages (e.g., *A Journey to the World Under-Ground*, 1742). The novel describes utopian spaces and uncustomary mind-sets. An important source of inspiration for his philosophical masterpiece *Moral Thoughts* (1744) was Pierre Bayle's *Historical and Critical Dictionary* (1697). Among his historical works, the *Ordinary Church History* (1738) is an important theological source.

See also Enlightenment; Pietism

Bibliography

Billeskov Jansen, F. J. "Efterskrift." In *Værker i tolv bind, digteren, historikeren, juristen, vismanden,* 10:355–84. Rosenkilde og Bagger, 1971; Mitchell, P. M., ed. *Ludvig Holberg's Moral Reflections and Epistles.* Norvik, 1991; Sejersted, J. M. "Bibel og protestantisme i Holbergs naturrett." In *Ludvig Holbergs naturrett,* ed. E. Vinje and J. M. Sejersted, 159–76. Gyldendal, 2012.

KRISTIAN MEJRUP

Holl, Karl

The historian, Luther scholar, and theologian Karl Holl (1866–1926) was born in Tübingen and educated at the University of Tübingen in 1884–89. After graduate work on early church history, he edited Greek patristic texts for the Berlin Kirchenväterkomission, under his teacher at the University of Berlin, Adolf von Harnack (1851–1930). Pastor Christoph Schrempf's (1860–1944) refusal to use the Apostles' Creed in a baptismal service coalesced into a wide-ranging, loose association of liberal Protestants that defended Schrempf, to which Holl bound himself. First in 1900 at Tübingen and then in 1906 at the University of Berlin, Holl acquired a teaching position. At this latter institution, Holl achieved his mature research program: historical investigation into the Reformation with a view toward its contemporary theological significance. Still later,

the discovery of Luther's Romans lectures (1515–16; first published in 1908) cemented Holl's work. With his significant 1910 study of Luther's doctrine of justification, Holl started his long preoccupation with Luther's exegesis in order to understand its theological significance. Together with others, he fostered continuation of the Luther Renaissance (which commenced with the 1883 critical edition of Luther's works, the Weimar Ausgabe). Counted as the pioneer in this investigation, Holl's many contributions shaped the contours of Luther studies for many generations. Holl drew attention to Luther's hermeneutics, the role of Luther's "tower experience" in theology, the theology of the cross, ecclesiology, and political philosophy. Owing to the recovery of Luther's early exegetical writings, Holl set in motion several judgments that privileged the early Luther throughout the twentieth century. His legacy extends not only to students, such as Erich Vogelsang (1904–44) and Emanuel Hirsch (1888–1972), who most directly continued Holl's research agenda, but also to Rudolf Hermann (1887–1962), Hans Joachim Iwand (1889–1960), and Dietrich Bonhoeffer (1906–45).

For Holl, Luther's doctrine of justification was of supreme importance. The doctrine not only allowed for the development of Christian ethics but was also crucial for a right understanding of God. Holl emphasized the concept of promise in order to unite the anthropological and theological dimensions of the doctrine of justification. Promise allowed him to state how it is that God justifies a human being and that, in faith, the human being likewise justifies God. Holl opposed forensic views of justification (blamed on Philip Melanchthon's influence), as had Albrecht Ritschl. Ultimately he shifted away from promise as a central category of theology and toward the human conscience. Famously, he stated that "Luther's religion is a religion of conscience." However, his students sought to explicate this religion of conscience by addressing its christological lacunae. Hermann, Iwand, and Bonhoeffer did so through attention to Christology, the category of promise, and ecclesiology. Vogelsang and Hirsch heightened Holl's understanding of conscience and reinterpreted Christology to fit it. Beyond his immediate students, Holl shaped a generation of Luther scholars and permanently cemented the "early Luther" as a figure with whom to reckon, both as a matter of historical interpretation and also as a vital source of theology.

See also Bonhoeffer, Dietrich; Christology; Justification; Luther Interpretation and Reception; Luther Renaissance; Ritschl, Albrecht

Bibliography

Assel, H. *Der andere Aufbruch: Die Lutherrenaissance—Ursprünge, Aporien und Wege: Karl Holl, Emanuel Hirsch, Rudolf Hermann (1910–1935)*. Vandenhoeck & Ruprecht, 1994; Holl, K. *Gesammelte Aufsatze zur Kirchengeschichte*. 3 vols. 3rd ed. J. C. B. Mohr (Paul Siebeck), 1932; Holl, K. *Kleine Schriften*. Ed. R Stupperich. J. C. B. Mohr (Paul Siebeck), 1966.

GREGORY WALTER

Holocaust

The Holocaust was the intentional, systematic, state-sponsored destruction of millions of noncombatants who were considered to be "subhuman" by the Nazi regime. The Nazis ruled in central Europe (esp. Germany) from 1933 to 1945, but most of the destruction occurred from 1941 to 1945. Slated for total annihilation were the Jews and the Roma people (Gypsies). Slated for slave labor, destruction, or displacement to the East were the Slavs. Because the Jews were the central target of Nazi propaganda, about twice as high a percentage of Jews were killed as were the Roma (ca. 65 percent vs. ca. 30 percent). Also targeted were political enemies, religious dissidents, and homosexuals, who, though victims no less, can be distinguished from the first three groups because some assessment of their behavior was involved (e.g., the Jehovah's Witnesses were targeted for refusing to salute). Since the word "holocaust" is used in the Bible for burnt offerings made to God, many prefer the title "Shoah," a destructive whirlwind with no connotation of an offering.

However, "the Holocaust" continues to be the usual designation.

The Nazis drew on social Darwinism, an anthropological theory that borrowed from biology the idea of a struggle for survival and applied it to the conflict among nations and peoples and was especially popular among not only German but also American scholars. And they drew on racial theories from the nineteenth century, in which race was determined by language. Some of those theories postulated a centuries-long conflict between Semitic and Aryan peoples. Whenever the two groups were allowed to mix, the advocates of this theory maintained, Aryan society was weakened. Nazi ideology yearned for a decisive battle in which the Aryans would triumph. This implied total war against the Semites, and the only Semites in Western Europe were the Jews. During the century prior to 1933, Jews had become increasingly integrated into Germany society. Between 1933 and 1939, the Nazis set about to reverse this trend and to isolate the Jews by removing them from public office, prohibiting intermarriage, excluding them from public schools, curtailing employment across the "racial" divide, confiscating Jewish businesses, and encouraging emigration. By 1939, two-thirds of the approximately 650,000 Jews in Germany had left. But many went to nearby countries and were swept up in the Holocaust as Germany overran its neighbors during the years 1938–40. In the summer of 1941, "special units" (*Einsatztruppen*) started rounding up and shooting Jews (and Gypsies and some Slavs) in Eastern Europe, and by December of that year the first death camp was opened. Train transports came from all over Europe, but the largest number of those killed were from Poland (about three million). No one knows exactly the total number who were murdered, but one credible estimate is roughly 5.5 million Jews and 5.5 million others.

Hitler took office in January 1933. Within two months he had ended parliamentary rule and won virtually unrestrained political power. The first protest from the Protestant church came in September 1933, when a Pastors' Emergency League, led by Martin Niemoeller and joined by approximately one-third of the Protestant pastors, objected to the inclusion of an "Aryan paragraph" in the national Protestant church's constitution. This paragraph prohibited persons of Jewish descent or those married to persons of Jewish descent from serving as pastors. The protest of Niemöller's group was not against Nazism per se but against governmental interference in the church. In May 1934 a group of Protestants under the leadership of Karl Barth, Hans Asmussen, and Thomas Breit wrote the Barmen Declaration, in protest against the elevation of Hitler to near-messianic status. Eventually two parties emerged in the church: the "Confessing Church," those opposed Nazi influence in the church, and the "German Christians," who welcomed it. Others remained in the middle. Only a few people, most notably Dietrich Bonhoeffer, spoke out against the treatment of the Jews.

Roughly two-thirds of Germans were Protestant and one-third Roman Catholic. In order to settle a long-simmering struggle about the political status of Catholicism in post-Bismarck Germany, the Vatican signed a Concordat with Hitler in July 1934. Hitler promised not to interfere in Catholic schools, hospitals, and religious orders, while the Catholic Church promised that its priests would not involve themselves in German politics. The terms of the Concordat were consistent with Hitler's overall policy, which was to neutralize the influence of the churches. Undeterred, Pope Pius XI in March 1937 issued a pastoral letter, *Mit Brennender Sorge*, protesting against the glorification of Hitler. He planned to issue another letter rejecting racism but died before it was finished. His successor, Pius XII, issued no public statements against the Nazis, though he did permit local rescue efforts. In 1941 Bishop Galen of Münster spoke out against the T4 euthanasia program that was systematically killing patients with mental disorders. The protest gained enough support to prompt the program's suspension.

In summary, one can say that the church held out against Nazi dominance more tenaciously than did many other institutions in Germany but did not do nearly enough to protest the treatment of Nazism's victims. With the exception of some courageous individuals who offered resistance or rescued victims, the church stood by as the "unfit" were rounded up and deported either for slave labor or for extermination. The situation was somewhat better in the Scandinavian countries that were occupied or otherwise controlled by the Nazis.

Beginning already in 1945, German Lutherans and other church groups confessed their complicity in Nazism, and over the years Lutherans in Europe and the United States have reconsidered the anti-Jewish teachings that for centuries created a climate in which Nazi anti-Semitism seemed credible. In response to the Holocaust and through extensive dialogue with Jews, Lutherans have come to endorse the ongoing validity of God's covenant with the Jews (based on statements found in Rom. 11) and have condemned anti-Semitism as an affront to the gospel. They, along with other Christians, have been led to examine the first century more extensively and have come to distinguish Jesus's attitude toward his fellow Jews from the positions reflected in the Gospel writers, who wrote amid the new tensions that developed after the destruction of the Jerusalem temple in 70 CE. What has become clear is that the portrait of the Pharisees in the Gospels is highly selective and that the Greek word translated as "the Jews" in the Gospel of John refers to the temple authorities and not to Jews as a whole. More internally, Lutherans have rethought the teaching of the two kingdoms. And they have rejected Luther's harsh statements against the Jews. Each of these last two developments deserves comment.

Luther taught that God relates to the world in two ways. One way is to show mercy and take the initiative in healing the God-human relationship that has been broken by sin.

Those who experience the grace of God are called to serve the neighbor. Through them, God cares for the well-being of the world in a completely noncoercive fashion. The other way is to work through the authorities and structures of the secular world to restrain evildoers and to promote order and justice. The authorities err if they are too lenient and err if they are too strict. But they sometimes need to use coercion or the threat of coercion to restrain those who harass or endanger or seek to kill their neighbors. Luther made this distinction to avoid coercion in matters of faith and to avoid utopian idealism or anarchism in society. In pre-Nazi Germany this teaching had often been interpreted to affirm two separate realms. In one realm, the church preached the gospel and showed mercy. In the other, the state maintained order. This separation implied that the church should not interfere with matters of the state. It encouraged some Christians in Germany to become bystanders, acquiescing to Nazi policies. But Luther used "kingdom" in the biblical sense of God's rule, rather than the territory over which that rule is exercised. Some German theologians also contended that, in addition to the traditional three areas of a believer's life (household, political life, and church), there was a fourth, nationhood. Since 1945, Lutherans have gone back to Luther, recognized that the idea of the two kingdoms is not about two realms but about two ways in which God works, and taken more seriously Luther's many exhortations for Christians to be involved in government, to challenge governmental actions that are unjust, to run programs that serve those without means, and to critique economic systems that disadvantage some citizens. This retrieval of Luther's more dynamic outlook has the effect of not walling politics off from Christian involvement and not endorsing passivity in the face of governmental misconduct.

Toward the end of Luther's life, he called for severe restrictions on the Jews. His recommendations had little influence in their own day and were known but often overlooked throughout the history of Lutheranism, but the Nazis retrieved his neglected teachings and claimed Luther as an authority for their anti-Semitism, blaming the church for having kept them from the German people.

Luther, of course, had no access to the racial theories of the nineteenth century and likely would not have endorsed them, because for him all humans are created in the image of God. In contrast to Nazi expectations, he certainly did not refrain from criticizing rulers or ridiculing their decisions, and he opposed any war that was not strictly defensive. In these ways and others he would have been out of step with Nazism. But Luther did subscribe to traditional Christian anti-Judaism—the teaching that Christianity had superseded Judaism and that Jewish interpretations of the Old Testament were wrong when they applied prophecies to historical developments in Israel rather than agreeing with Christians that they pointed to Jesus as the expected Messiah. Luther seems to have had little personal contact with Jews. And his attitude toward them varied. In 1523, when he wrote "That Jesus Christ Was Born a Jew," he lamented the church's treatment of the Jews and urged that kindness be shown to them. "We [Christians] are aliens and in-laws; they are blood relatives, cousins, and brothers of our Lord. Therefore, if one is to boast of flesh and blood, the Jews are actually nearer to Christ than we are" (LW 45:201). "We must receive them cordially, and permit them to trade and work with us" (LW 45:229). But in 1543 he wrote *On the Jews and Their Lies*, advocating harsh measures to restrict the practice of Judaism. He recommended that synagogues and Jewish homes be destroyed, prayer books and Talmudic writings confiscated, rabbis prohibited from teaching, safe conduct abolished, and usury prohibited (LW 47:268–70). More than one explanation for this shift in attitude is possible, but a chief factor was his response to reports that the Sabbatarians and the Jews were teaching in public and proselytizing. One such report about Sabbatarians (who apparently insisted that Christians interpret the Bible literally and practice the same Sabbath observance as the Jews) came from Bohemia and Moravia in 1538. Luther apparently assumed that they were being influenced by Jewish teachers. In 1542 a Moravian friend sent him a copy of a Jewish pamphlet that defended Judaism (the pamphlet has not been preserved), along with a request from his friend to refute it. This request seems to have occasioned his 1543 treatise. Though Luther favored religious freedom for individuals, he subscribed to the widely shared idea of his day that governments should prohibit any public teaching that contradicted basic Christian doctrines and were thus blasphemous. He called on the government to take up that responsibility. Unfortunately his recommendations, although not out of step with many others in his day, were chillingly harsh and eagerly reprinted by the Nazis in the 1930s, who even accused Lutherans of having suppressed Luther's position. As Luther also undertook to teach his readers about the evils of Judaism, he unfortunately relied on the distorted views propounded by writers who had converted to Christianity and portrayed the Judaism they had abandoned in the worst possible light. And even more significantly, as Eric Gritsch points out (70–77), when Luther presumed to know God's judgment about the Jews, he violated his own principle that such determinations belonged to the hidden God (whose decisions are unfathomable). In so doing, he also failed to heed the Scriptures where, at the end of Rom. 11, Paul leaves such matters to the mystery of God.

In the United States, both the Lutheran Church–Missouri Synod and the Evangelical Lutheran Church in America have rejected Luther's teachings against the Jews; these churches have officially declared that they carry no authority for Lutherans today. The Missouri Synod adopted a resolution in 1983 that says, "We deplore and disassociate ourselves from Luther's negative statements about the Jewish people." And "A Declaration of the Evangelical Lutheran Church in America to the Jewish Community" from 1994 says, regarding Luther's later writings against the Jews, "We reject this violent invective, and yet more do we express our deep and abiding sorrow over its tragic effects on subsequent generations. . . . We particularly deplore the appropriation of Luther's words by modern anti-Semites for the teaching of hatred toward Judaism or toward the Jewish people of our day, . . . [and] we express our urgent desire to live out our faith in Jesus Christ with love and respect for the Jewish people." Many Evangelical (Lutheran) churches in Germany have also rejected Luther's writings and teachings on this subject.

See also Barmen Confession; Barth, Karl; Bonhoeffer, Dietrich; Confessing Church; German Christians (Deutsche Christen); Jews; Niemoeller, Martin; State; World Wars I and II

Bibliography

Barnett, V. *For the Soul of the People: Protestant Protest against Hitler*. Oxford University Press, 1992; The Evangelical Lutheran Church in America's Declaration to the Jewish Community. http://download.elca.org/ELCA%20 Resource%20Repository/Declaration_of_the_ELCA_to_ the_Jewish_Community.pdf; Gritsch, E. *Martin Luther's Anti-Semitism: Against His Better Judgment*. Eerdmans, 2012; Haas, P. *Morality after Auschwitz: The Radical Challenge of the Nazi Ethic*. Fortress, 1988; Luther, M. *On the Jews and Their Lies*, 1543 (including introduction by F. Sherman). LW 47:121–306; Luther, M. "That Jesus Christ Was Born a Jew." LW 45:195–229; The Lutheran Church–Missouri Synod 1983 Resolution on Luther's anti-Semitic statements. http://www.lcms.org/faqs /lcmsviews#antisemitic; Probst, C. *Demonizing the Jews: Luther and the Protestant Church in Germany*. Indiana University Press, 2012; Redles, D. *Hitler's Millennial Reich: Apocalyptic Belief and the Search for Salvation*. New York University Press, 2005; Schramm, B., and K. Stjerna, eds. *Martin Luther, the Bible, and the Jewish People: A Reader*. Fortress, 2012; Sherman, F., ed. *Building Bridges: Documents of the Christian-Jewish Dialogue*. Vol. 1, *The Road to Reconciliation (1945–85)*. Paulist Press, 2011. Vol. 2, *Building a New Relationship (1986–2013)*. Paulist Press, 2014.

DARRELL JODOCK

Holy Roman Empire

As a political and geographic designation in central Europe, the Holy Roman Empire became the first setting for Martin Luther's Evangelical reforms and later political, religious, and military conflicts related to the European

Reformations. The Holy Roman Empire of the German Nation (HRE) originated in the expansion of Carolingian and Ottonian kingdoms in the Middle Ages and continued until its formal dissolution by Napoleon in 1806. The HRE was not a country or "state" in the early modern sense of the word but an amalgamation of independent territories, kingdoms, bishoprics, imperial cities, and other entities under the nominal control of (after 1356) an elected monarch known as the Holy Roman emperor. In 1500, the HRE contained some sixteen million people residing in the German lands, Burgundy, Alsace-Lorraine, Austria, Switzerland, Bohemia, parts of Poland, and the Netherlands. In addition to this core collection of territories and principalities, the HRE claimed jurisdiction over the so-called imperial lands (*Regnum Italicum*) of north and central Italy.

The challenges in defining the precise boundaries of the HRE arise out of its medieval roots in feudal relationships among regional kings, princes, and vassals. As dozens of competing noble dynasties intermarried, fragmented, and became extinct around and between the Rhine, the Alps, and the Danube, a patchwork of overlapping lordships, bishoprics, abbies, alliances, and jurisdictions took shape. Eventually some three hundred independent political entities emerged and resisted the pressures toward consolidation that had unified the kingdoms of England, Spain, and France during the later Middle Ages. In 1356 a legal agreement known as the Golden Bull stipulated that the Holy Roman emperor would be elected by seven imperial electors (*Kurfürsten*), including the archbishops of Mainz, Trier, and Cologne; and the Duke of Saxony, the count Palatine of the Rhine, the margrave of Brandenburg, and the king of Bohemia. Until the accession of Empress Maria Theresa in the eighteenth century, only males were allowed to rule. The Golden Bull also authorized the emperor to plan for joint defense and to call the immediate subjects of the emperor (princes, the representatives of

towns, and others entitled to vote) to assemble at the imperial diet (*Reichstag*). However, the emperor was not allowed to control ecclesiastical properties, appoint bishops, or put citizens on trial outside their home territories.

The term "Holy Roman Empire" is not a precise synonym for descriptive phrases such as "the German people," "the German lands," or "Germany." This is because the HRE included Italians, French-speaking Burgundians, Dutch- and Flemish-speaking residents of the Netherlands, Czech-speaking Bohemians, as well as Slavs, Poles, and other peoples. However, by 1500 some sense of what might today be viewed as national consciousness in the HRE was oriented around German identity, language, and culture. This gained momentum when Emperor Maximilian I (r. 1493–1519) and numerous humanists in his employ claimed that the German people possessed a distinctive language and history and that they were the heirs to the old Roman Empire in a continuous constitutional tradition. The association of the empire with "the German people" continued throughout the sixteenth century, especially during periods of war with France and the Ottoman Empire. By 1650 the removal of Burgundy, Lorraine (then still German-speaking), the Swiss Confederation, and the Dutch provinces contributed to some assumption of German national unity within the HRE.

Structure. In terms of structure, the empire was governed by a constitution that was refined and strengthened in the late fifteenth and early sixteenth centuries. This constitution gave a particular group of imperial subjects (the "Imperial estates," or *Reichsstände*) the right to assemble at the imperial diet and to vote on business relating to the empire. Over time, this group of territorial princes, bishops, and representatives of the independent cities began to push a program of reform. For example, at a diet in Worms (1495) and a diet in Augsburg (1500), the estates forced a restructuring agenda on Emperor Maximilian I, instituting a federal tax, halting private wars, establishing a court of justice (*Reichskammergericht*), and creating a governing council (*Reichsregiment*) that would make decisions and advise the emperor between meetings of the imperial diet. In 1512, a system of ten imperial circles (*Reichskreise*) was also created to help the emperor nominate judges, collect taxes, and defend the HRE against external threats. These constitutional reforms helped to maintain the peace, but they did little to curb the power of the territorial princes and the most powerful independent cities. As a result, governance remained distributed and local within the empire, with a multitude of overlapping rights and legal claims.

An important institutional development was the rise of strong regional dynasties that attempted to dominate the sprawling, multiethnic confederation. In the fourteenth and fifteenth centuries, the Luxemburg family tried to dominate the empire from their territorial bases in Luxemburg and Bohemia. This attempt ultimately failed with the death of Emperor Sigismund in 1437. In the later fifteenth and sixteenth centuries, the Hapsburg line more successfully controlled the administration of the empire from their networks in Austria, Spain, Bohemia, and the Netherlands. Several Hapsburg leaders became emperors during this period, including Maximilian I, Charles V (r. 1519–58), Ferdinand I (r. 1558–64), Maximilian II (r. 1564–76), and Rudolf II (r. 1576–1612). The crucial factor in their success was a strong territorial foundation, because an emperor could only be dominant when he was supported by a thriving home territory and a system of secure alliances. Over time the Hapsburgs developed specialized bureaucracies to manage trade, taxation, and governance; a skilled diplomatic corps; professional standing armies; and legal specialists— all the attributes of a successful early modern European state. The Hapsburgs also established the dominant pattern of consensual rule, in which the emperor shared power and decision-making authority with a narrow band of elite electors, princes, bishops, and the representatives of over eighty free and imperial cities. The Hapsburgs dominated the HRE, holding the imperial title from 1440 until the empire's dissolution in 1806 (with the exception of the reign of Charles VII in 1742–45).

Religious Reform. In 1500 most residents of the HRE were Catholics in communion with the pope in Rome. Exceptions included Hussites in Bohemia and small pockets of Jews in the empire, who were now protected only by the emperor's personal authority (as opposed to other legal authority, so that episodes of expulsion and forced conversion still took place). The church within the HRE was organized into a number of ecclesiastical provinces (collections of dioceses under an archbishop) including Mainz, Cologne, Trier, Salzburg, Besançon, Bremen, Magdeburg, and Prague. Maximilian I and Charles V took seriously their roles as defenders of Christendom and promoters of the church. However, the leaders of this church also enjoyed some independence from the emperor, since bishops and archbishops ruled ecclesiastical lands in the empire as prince-bishops (possessing their own lands and having standing at imperial or territorial diets); their appointments were controlled by papal procedures and not necessarily by the emperor or the imperial electors, whose families nevertheless controlled many of them. On the eve of the Reformation, thirty-eight bishoprics were ruled by thirty-three prince-bishops.

Luther's reforms spread from Wittenberg in the 1520s, aided by itinerant preaching, printing, and the vibrant intellectual life of the empire's great cities. In several early treatises, Luther appealed to the "German nation" and the "German people" as a way of rousing his audience in the empire. Luther's *Address to the Christian Nobility of the German Nation* (1520) set itself specifically in the tradition of pitting the German nation against papal interests. Luther attacked the secular power of the Roman papacy, arguing for the priesthood of all believers and proposing that reforms of the imperial church be carried out by local princes and civil magistrates. When Luther was put on trial at the Diet of Worms in 1521, he was treated as a German prophet and hero by many who shared his reforming sympathies. Although Luther was declared a heretic and an outlaw in the Edict of Worms (1521), the reformer was protected in Electoral Saxony by Frederick III "the Wise" (1463–1525), and many territorial rulers refused to publish the edict's condemnation of Luther in their lands. After the respite provided by the 1526 Diet of Speyer was rescinded at the second diet held there in 1529, a group of nineteen Evangelical princes and representatives of the free, imperial cities formally protested (by appealing to the imperial courts), signaling support at the highest level for those who wished to reform the church in the empire along Wittenberg's lines. At the 1530 diet, some of these "Protestants" presented what became known as the Augsburg Confession to the emperor and the imperial estates.

By the 1530s, the Lutheran Reformation had taken root in many important cities and territories. The changes made to the empire's constitution in the early sixteenth century paved the way for the success of these Evangelical movements by creating a durable federal system that allowed individual principalities to maintain their own traditions and laws. The Augsburg Confession (1530), Smalcald War (1546–47), Augsburg Interim (1548), and Peace of Augsburg (1555) can be seen as milestones in the working out of the Reformation within the political and religious contexts of the HRE. Although the process was fragmented and divisive, the structure of the HRE eventually provided mechanisms for resolving the conflict. In 1555 the estates finally won the legal right to reform their cities and principalities (*ius reformandi*). The end result was a functioning federal system that allowed individual rulers to determine the authorized religious confession (either Roman Catholic or Evangelical [Lutheran]) in their lands within certain limits. This principle was established in the imperial edict of 1555, later summarized as *cuius regio, eius religio*, "whose the rule,

his the religion." Using this mechanism, the HRE avoided the prolonged period of religious warfare and strife that plagued some European states during the era, such as France and the Netherlands.

By the end of the sixteenth century, the confessional makeup of the HRE included significant Lutheran and Reformed (Calvinist) communities as well as smaller minorities of Jews, Anabaptists, and other Protestant sects. Roman Catholicism continued to flourish in the southern and eastern territories, including Bavaria, Austria, and imperial cities such as Cologne and Trier. Both Lutheran and Catholic princes created new universities to encourage religious orthodoxy and to train new leaders in the arts, theology, law, and medicine. Confessional differences persisted and eventually entangled Lutheran, Reformed, and Roman Catholic factions (and the neighboring kingdoms of France and Sweden) in the disastrous Thirty Years' War (1618–48). After the Peace of Westphalia (1648), most Hapsburg emperors followed a policy of religious toleration, which allowed Catholicism and Protestantism to flourish. Some recent scholarship has emphasized that a key attribute of the later sixteenth and seventeenth centuries was the process of *confessionalization* in the empire, in which territorial governments worked with the Protestant and Roman Catholic churches to build effective bureaucracies, discipline the population, and regulate state power. The resulting clearly defined religious confessions indoctrinated the laity, prepared church orders, and enforced religious orthodoxy. Throughout this process, Lutherans continued to stress the importance of law and order within their communities and generally followed the dictates of the emperor and the civil magistrates. Secular leaders did not control the church in the Lutheran lands, but they were encouraged to use their divinely assigned roles to maintain order, construct hospitals and schools, provide for the poor, and perform other acts that nurtured the faithful and punished the wicked.

Recent scholarship has also emphasized the importance of creativity and flexibility within the structures and procedures of the empire. Rather than a weak and failed federation that delayed the progression of the German absolutist state, the HRE is now seen as a viable political entity that existed for a thousand years and was the largest and most important of the early modern European states. Such research has emphasized the importance of political institutions, religious innovation and diversity, and the history of daily life, gender, and people living on the margins of society.

See also Augsburg Interim; Charles V; Electors of Saxony; Peace of Augsburg; Smalcald War; Thirty Years' War

Bibliography

Brady, T. A., Jr. *German Histories in the Age of Reformations, 1400–1650*. Cambridge University Press, 2009; Evans, R. J. W., M. Schaich, and P. H. Wilson, eds. *The Holy Roman Empire, 1495–1806*. Oxford University Press, 2011; Friedeburg, R. von. "Church and State in Lutheran Lands, 1550–1675." In *Lutheran Ecclesiastical Culture, 1550–1675*, ed. R. Kolb, 361–410. Brill, 2008; Lotz-Heumann, U. "Confessionalization." In *Reformation and Early Modern Europe: A Guide to Research*, ed. D. M. Whitford, 136–57. Truman State University Press, 2008; Schmidt, G. *Geschichte des Alten Reiches: Staat und Nation in der Frühen Neuzeit, 1495–1806*. Beck, 1999; Strauss, G. *Law, Resistance, and the State: The Opposition to Roman Law in Reformation Germany*. Princeton University Press, 1986; Whaley, J. *Germany and the Holy Roman Empire*. Vols. 1–2. Oxford University Press, 2012; Wilson, P. H. *From Reich to Revolution: German History, 1558–1806*. Palgrave Macmillan, 2009; Wilson, P. H. *The Holy Roman Empire, 1495–1806*. 2nd ed. Palgrave Macmillan, 2011.

MICHAEL J. HALVORSON

Holy Spirit

Luther confessed the ancient church's trinitarian doctrine, affirming that the Holy Spirit—like the Son—is *homoousios* (of one substance) with the Father. Following Augustine, he assumed that the Holy Spirit proceeds from the Father and the Son, adopted the distinction between the Spirit as "person" (*persona*) and as "gift" (*donum*), and upheld the rule that God's actions in the world are indivisible and cannot be ascribed to specific persons within the Trinity. Yet the main thrust of Luther's pneumatology centered on who the Spirit is as Sanctifier and Comforter. If the Father gives self in the gifts of creation and the Son gives self by redeeming and reconciling to the Father in spite of sin, then the Spirit gives self by proclaiming and teaching what Christ has done for all—helping "receive and preserve it, use it to our advantage and impart it to others, increase and extend it" (Confession of 1528). Without the Holy Spirit, Christ's person and work would remain hidden to human beings. Indeed, what distinguishes the Holy Spirit from other spirits—human, heavenly, or evil—is that only God's Spirit can sanctify and make holy by bringing human beings to Christ to receive what they could not come to by themselves (Large Catechism).

The Spirit sanctifies human beings inwardly by means of faith and other spiritual gifts, and outwardly by means of the gospel, baptism, and the Lord's Supper—although Luther stressed, especially in his debates with the enthusiasts, that the external means come first and are the basis for the internal means. The Holy Spirit is free and sovereign, yet it is through the external Word that the Spirit speaks the Word, inculcating in the hearer Christ's sufferings for salvation—the "joyous exchange" whereby Christ shares in the human being's sins and death, and imparts his righteousness and life. Through the testimony of the Spirit and "what brings Christ" as the criterion for interpreting the canon of Scripture, Christ—who is the Word of God—is to be preached "for you and for me," that what is said about him may be "effectual in us" (Luther, *Freedom of a Christian* [1520]). Similarly, Luther did not regard the sacraments as magical rites; rather, by the Holy Spirit the signs of water, bread, and wine become for us Christ's crucified and raised body when God's Word, God's promise in Christ, is declared.

A signal contribution of Luther's pneumatology is his understanding of the Holy Spirit's work in the Word through law and gospel. Reworking Augustine's distinction between "person" and "gift," Luther asserted that the

Holy Spirit's alien work through the law takes place when the Spirit in "divine majesty" requires fulfillment of God's law and thus exposes sin and accuses the sinner (cf. John 16:8). By contrast, the Spirit's proper work through the gospel takes place when the Holy Spirit as "gift," "'swaddled' in tongues and spiritual gifts," sanctifies and makes alive (*First Disputation against the Antinomians* [1537]).

Through the means of word and sacrament, the Holy Spirit creates, calls, and gathers that unique community or assembly in the world, the one holy Christian church, "in one faith, mind, and understanding" and by it "creates and increases holiness, causing it daily to grow and become strong in the faith and in its fruits, which the Spirit produces." Possessing "a variety of gifts, and yet united in love without sect or schism," its members are participants and copartners in all its blessings, which the Spirit reveals and proclaims through the Word of God, illuminating and inflaming hearts "so that they grasp and accept it, cling to it, and persevere in it." At the heart of what the Spirit reveals and proclaims in this community "through the Word and signs" is the full forgiveness of sins—"both in that God forgives us and that we forgive, bear with, and aid another"—since although God's grace has already been acquired by Christ, forgiveness is constantly needed because no one is without sin in this life (Large Catechism).

Yet the Spirit sanctifies and makes holy not only by exposing and forgiving sin, but also by expelling it so that believers can carry the cross as Christ's disciples in daily life, serving the neighbor in love. Not open to empirical verification, believers' progress or growth in sanctification is marked by a deeper and deeper awareness of sin and a returning again and again to the promises of God in baptism. The Spirit's work of justifying and sanctifying is the same work that enables believers to cling to the promise of Christ's alien righteousness in their lives—living not in themselves but in Christ through faith and in the neighbor through love. In this way, the Spirit empowers believers to be "Christs" in the callings of daily life—active in love, obeying God's law, and doing good works that serve the neighbor while passively trusting in the promises of God's Word. Here "experience is the school of the Spirit," where believers daily prove, test, and feel for themselves God's promise that, in Christ, God is indeed one who looks into the depths of human need and misery, then creates "something" out of "nothing" by bringing down the mighty, the rich, and the proud and raising the lowly, the poor, and humble (sermon, "The Magnificat" [1522]).

As Regin Prenter observed in *Spiritus Creator*, pneumatology in later Lutheranism has tended to stress either a doctrine about justification resulting from Christ's work of satisfaction or, in reaction, a piety shaped by the law, spiritual experience, and a person's freedom to make choices. Both tendencies, however, can deemphasize Luther's focus on the crucified and living Christ made truly present by the Spirit. In turn, Luther's emphasis on the mediation of the Spirit's work through word and sacrament runs counter to much modern thought and experience, which tends to prioritize the inner experience of spirituality over external forms. The great exemplar of this is G. W. F. Hegel, who sought to reclaim the synthesis of the finite and infinite he found in Luther's thought, but nonetheless maintained that life in the Spirit could only truly be achieved when external religious forms disappear and our inner spirit is wholly united with the Absolute Spirit.

It is not surprising, then, that the first treatment of Luther's pneumatology drawing on historical research, Rudolf Otto's *Die Anschauung vom heiligen Geiste bei Luther*, focused primarily on the psychological impact of the Holy Spirit's work in Luther's thought. Erich Seeberg sought to correct this study by stressing the christological thrust of Luther's pneumatology, but he focused primarily on the Son's and the Holy Spirit's saving work and not on the person of the Spirit. Both studies were superseded by Prenter's *Spiritus Creator*, which remains to this day the most comprehensive exposition of Luther's pneumatology. In a treatment of Luther's disagreements with Rome and with the enthusiasts, Prenter brings to the fore the centrality of the Spirit in Luther's work, arguing that it is only the Spirit's real presence and creative work in law and gospel that keeps Luther's thoughts about Christ, justification, word and sacrament, and faith and love from being merely "a great ideology under the law."

Luther's pneumatology has had a profound influence on much twentieth-century trinitarian theology—as seen, for example, in such diverse theologians as Paul Tillich, Wolfhart Pannenberg, and Robert Jenson. This influence has extended even to such non-Lutherans as Karl Barth, who emphasizes the link between the Spirit and the Word of God, and Hans Urs von Balthasar and Jürgen Moltmann, who both locate the Spirit's work within a trinitarian theology of the cross. In turn, ecumenical dialogue with the Orthodox tradition has led the Maanerma school in Finland to rethink its interpretation of Luther's teaching on justification and theosis given Luther's emphasis on the real presence of God in Christ and the Holy Spirit in the believer. Further, the rise of Pentecostal and charismatic Christianity throughout the world has led to increased critical conversation regarding Luther's pneumatological emphases, which center on word and sacrament, and those of movements and traditions that highlight the Spirit's charismatic gifts.

As Luther's pneumatology engages twenty-first-century theology, one area to develop is his depiction of the Holy Spirit's ongoing work in creation, which also has relevance for relating theology to science, ecology, ethics, and politics. Moreover, Luther's pneumatology has much to engage recent developments in biblical scholarship, in Continental philosophy, and in contemporary pneumatologies emerging out of Africa, Asia, and Latin America, and testimonies to the Spirit's work among the poor and oppressed. Perhaps most poignantly, Luther's pneumatology has much to contribute to the public proclamation of the gospel in a post-Christendom era that is not only increasingly secular but also increasingly both interreligious and yet also spiritual but not religious.

Bibliography

Althaus, P. *The Theology of Martin Luther.* Trans. R. Schultz. Fortress, 1966; Bayer, O. *Martin Luther's Theology: A Contemporary Interpretation.* Trans. T. Trapp. Eerdmans, 2003; Jenson, R. *Systematic Theology.* 2 vols. Oxford University Press, 2001; Kärkkäinen, P. *Luthers trinitarische Theologie der Heiligen Geistes.* Zabern, 2005; Lohse, B. *Martin Luther's Theology: Its Historical and Systematic Development.* Trans. R. Harrisville. Fortress, 1999; Otto, R. *Die Anschauung vom heiligen Geiste bei Luther.* Vandenhoeck & Ruprecht, 1898; Pannenberg, W. *Systematic Theology.* 3 vols. Trans. G. Bromiley. Eerdmans, 1991–2009; Prenter, R. *Spiritus Creator.* Trans. J. Jenson. Fortress, 1953; Seeberg, E. *Grundzüge der Theologie Luthers.* Kohlhammer, 1940; Silcock, J. "Luther on the Holy Spirit and His Use of God's Word." In *The Handbook of Martin Luther's Theology,* ed. R. Kolb, I. Dingel, and L. Batka, 294–309. Oxford University Press, 2014; Tillich, P. *Systematic Theology.* 3 vols. University of Chicago Press, 1967; Zahl, S. *Pneumatology and Theology of the Cross in the Preaching of Christoph Friedrich Blumhardt: The Holy Spirit between Wittenberg and Azusa Street.* T&T Clark, 2010.

Lois Malcolm

Honduras

In 1953 the LWF Latin American Committee began providing pastoral services to a small German expatriate community. Lutheran outreach to native Hondurans began in 1961 and was linked to Guatemala because of the work of Robert Gussick, a Lutheran Church–Missouri Synod missionary, and refugees from El Salvador. It began with evangelizing efforts by Miguel Garcia from Puerto Barrios, Guatemala, and Aldrich Forbes, who was introduced to Lutheran doctrine and mission by Gussick. The most significant breakthrough came in 1964 when Ciro Mejia and LCMS missionary Gerhard Kempff worked among Salvadoran refugees. Kempff was sent to establish a church and worked in Tegucigalpa and Olancho. In 1969, when war broke out between Honduras and El Salvador, the church suffered because Salvadorans were expelled or had to flee the country. Kempff persevered but returned to the United States in 1971 and left Pastor Bonifacio Romero, who received his education at Seminario Luterano Augsburgo (SEMLA), in charge.

In the 1980s the Council of Central America and Panama (CONCAP) sent Eduardo Cabrera to Tegucigalpa and Guillermo Flores to San Pedro Sula. In 1981 they founded the Iglesia Cristiana Luterana de Honduras (ICLH), which was recognized by the state in 1984.

As in El Salvador, church leaders came under scrutiny because of their "preferential option for the poor," rooted in the biblical understanding of God's will for dignity, equality, and shalom for all people. The church continues its holist approach to mission, promoting the temporal and spiritual welfare of the people.

See also El Salvador

Bibliography

Jahnel, C. *The Lutheran Church in El Salvador*. Servicio Educativo Cristiano-LBCM, 2009. http://www.lutheran central.com; http://www.lutheranchurch.ca/missions.php ?s=nicaragua&p=3.

ORIN W. CUMMINGS

Honterus, Johannes

Johannes Honterus (1498–1549) was the reformer of Transylvania (Siebenbürgen), a region of Romania inhabited by ethnic Germans since the twelfth century, though the present-day German population has dwindled considerably. Honterus was born and raised in Kronstadt (Brașov). He was educated at the University of Vienna, where he embraced the humanist movement, and for a time worked in Krakow as a teacher, where he published his most famous works, a Latin grammar and a textbook on "cosmography" (astronomy and geography). During a stay in Basel in the 1530s he learned of the Reformation, whereupon he returned to Kronstadt to establish schools and a printing press based on Evangelical principles. He served as a teacher and city councilman, all the while publishing textbooks and works of linguistic, philosophical, and geographic scholarship, as well as editions

of church fathers such as Augustine. He exchanged letters with Luther, Melanchthon, Bugenhagen, and Bullinger. Due in part to his efforts, Kronstadt formally accepted the Wittenberg Reformation in 1542; its charter earned Melanchthon's high praise. At age fifty Honterus was elected and ordained city pastor, a post he held until his untimely death the next year.

See also Hungary

Bibliography

Hauptmann, P. "Honter, Johannes." *TRE* 15:578–80. De Gruyter, 1986; Pitters, H. "St. Johannes Honterus, Reformer of Transylvania." *Lutheran Forum* 48 (2014): 36–37.

SARAH HINLICKY WILSON

Household, Children, Parents

Luther elevated the household to a central place in his conception of human social and religious life. Alongside the political estate and the ecclesiastical estate, the household (*Hausstand, Ehestand*, or *ordo oeconomicus*) stood as one of the three estates, orders, or hierarchies (*Stände*, "walks of life") that God had appointed for human existence in this world. In place of the medieval third estate of peasants or *laboratores*, Luther set the estate of marriage, or the household, to which all people (except for the few with the extraordinary gift of celibacy) were called. Discourse about the "estate of marriage" is one of the enduring legacies of Luther's shift away from medieval terminology.

Though the word "family" in its modern sense is anachronistic in Luther, his definition of the household as based on marriage, on the relationship between parents and children, and finally on the productive activities of the household, including the participation of servants—all this is an essential part of the background of the modern idea of family. One implication of Luther's idea is to deny the independent basis of "economic" life in the modern sense, instead subordinating economic activity to the household.

Luther could speak of marriage and domestic life as an "external, worldly matter" (LW 36:92–93), over which the church as such (and its canon law) had no jurisdiction, and in which both Christians and non-Christians participated. Yet for Luther the household, like the secular government, was an order established by God in creation and also sanctified by God's Word. As such, marriage and the household were to be exalted above human-made estates like monasticism. Christians, discerning God's order in faith, could be sure that their works done in the household were pleasing to God. Family life was a "school of faith," replacing the cloister as the center of religious formation.

Luther affirmed the hierarchical structure of the household articulated in the New Testament Epistles, with wives subject to husbands and children to parents, summarizing this content in his order of marriage and in the Table of Duties (Household Chart) in the Small Catechism. His reform has been characterized as a bald reinforcement of patriarchy. Yet Lutheran application of these principles (e.g., in Luther's Genesis lectures) was usually quite flexible, and the Lutheran description of the household was characterized by mutuality and even playfulness as much as by rigid hierarchy.

Luther identified women, God's "building" ("Gott . . . baute," Gen. 2:22, Luther Bibel), as the center of the household, but in context, this placed women at the center of economic life—as in the case of Katharina Luther and her many enterprises—rather than marginalizing them from it. Parental authority, too, had limits, especially when parents sought to prevent their children from practicing the true faith, being educated, or establishing marriages and families of their own. Though the integral family of husband, wife, and children was central in Lutheran imagination, other family structures, especially in the case of widowhood, were also acknowledged sympathetically.

Luther set the family at the focus of religious pedagogy. The Small Catechism, though addressed to pastors as well, presents each of its sections under the heading "as the head of a household should teach his children." Luther also spoke of the ways in which children should teach their parents. Lutherans centered their private devotion in the household and produced a rich literature of domestic piety. The Thuringian reformer Justus Menius's *Oeconomia Christiana* (On the Christian household), published with Luther's preface, was a perennial favorite; Lutheran prayer books and hymnals were directed specifically to the domestic market even as they linked private devotion to public worship.

The fundamental religious task of the members of the household was to speak God's Word to one another in admonition and comfort and even absolution. In relation to the other estates, the household could, in time of crisis, stand on its own, resisting the persecution of the state or the apostasy of the church, with its own fidelity to God's Word, as Luther emphasized in his preface to Daniel.

Though seventeenth-century Pietist ecclesiology was directed explicitly against the sacramental worship of the church, to some extent the *ecclesiola* also challenged the place of the household in Lutheran religious life, replaced by the piety of the individual, who then sought out other similarly enlightened believers. The Lutheran tradition since has navigated between this religious individualism and Luther's ideal of the Christian household, as well as Luther's own tension between the household as independent of the two other estates yet the point at which the secular and the religious intersect.

See also Catechisms; Marriage and Divorce

Bibliography

Luther's Works: *The Estate of Marriage* [*Von ehelichem Leben*]. LW 45:11–49; Large Catechism, esp. on the fourth commandment; *Lectures on Genesis*. LW 1–8; Preface to Justus Menius, *Oeconomia Christiana*. LW 59:240–47; Small Catechism; **General Works:** Lazareth, W. H. *Luther on the Christian Home: An Application of the Social Ethics of the Reformation*. Muhlenberg, 1960; Mattox, M. *"Defender of the Most Holy Matriarchs": Martin Luther's Interpretation of the Women of Genesis in the*

Enarrationes in Genesin, 1535–45. Brill, 2003; Menius, J. *An die hochgeborne Furstin, fraw Sibilla Hertzogin zu Sachsen, Oeconomia Christiana, das ist, von Christlicher haushaltung.* Hans Luft, 1529; Ozment, S. "Luther on Family Life." In *Protestants: The Birth of a Revolution,* 151–68. Doubleday, 1992; Ozment, S. *When Fathers Ruled: Family Life in Reformation Europe.* Harvard University Press, 1983; Roeber, A. G. *Hopes for Better Spouses: Protestant Marriage and Church Renewal in Early Modern Europe, India, and North America.* Eerdmans, 2013; Roper, L. *The Holy Household: Religion, Morals, and Order in Reformation Europe.* Oxford University Press, 1989; Wunder, H. *He Is the Sun, She Is the Moon: Women in Early Modern Germany.* Trans. T. Dunlap. Harvard University Press, 1998.

CHRISTOPHER BOYD BROWN

Humanism and the Reformation

A complex and largely advantageous relationship linked northern humanism with Martin Luther and the Reformation movement. German humanism had its beginnings under Emperor Charles IV (1316–78) in Prague, tied especially to the Chancellor Johann von Neumarkt (r. ca. 1310–18) and his correspondence with the early humanist Francesco Petrarch (1304–74). Between 1456 and 1506 eight German universities were founded with influences from humanism, including the University of Wittenberg in 1502. During this time many intellectuals in northern Europe sought a renewal of Christian faith and piety through the rebirth of classical studies. These humanists sensed that the ancient sources of Christianity, esteemed along with other works of classical antiquity as *bonae litterae* (fine literature), could serve both their spiritual and their educational goals. In the North, where the *devotio moderna* and other lay movements exerted considerable influence on the religious climate, many humanists sought a simpler, more practical Christianity than that promulgated in the schools. For them, the scholastic approach to theology had turned the Christian faith into an arid, speculative discipline devoted to the exercise of academic acrobatics and pride, while the simple folk were left to pursue impiety and superstition. Thus one facet of the "religious renaissance" of northern humanism encouraged a simple, practical faith and piety

by returning to the Scriptures and the early church fathers, the pristine sources of Christianity purged of all Scholastic dross. This religious application of the humanist ideal, *ad fontes* (back to the sources), was in many ways exemplified in the work of Desiderius Erasmus (1466–1536) and his programmatic *philosophia Christi*. While Martin Luther's relationship to this movement was complex and not always clear, his early reforms did appeal to a confluence of ideals that brought humanism into felicitous connection with the Reformation movement.

Erfurt, where Luther began his university studies, had a tradition of humanist influences that, with the arrival of the philologian Nikolaus Marschalk (ca. 1460–1525) at the end of the fifteenth century, became increasingly antagonistic toward Scholasticism. Marschalk's influence extended to many of Luther's early colleagues and supporters, including Crotus Rubianus (1480–1539), Johannes Lang (ca. 1487–1548), Georg Spalatin (1484–1545), and even Andreas Bodenstein von Karlstadt (1486–1541), who studied in Erfurt from 1499 to 1503. When Elector Frederick III of Saxony founded his new university in Wittenberg in 1502, Marschalk went there for a time as professor of law, accompanied by Spalatin. Soon afterward, Spalatin became the librarian and the elector's secretary, bringing his humanist ideals to bear on the life of the university. Luther's friendship with Spalatin became an important partnership in his early reforms of Wittenberg's theological curriculum.

Yet even with these early connections, Luther's original impetus for reform stemmed from somewhat different concerns than the new learning of the *studia humanitatis*. For example, Luther's critique of Scholasticism was not an aversion to its method per se, but arose in the context of his attempts to understand the Scriptures while lecturing on the Bible. For this reason he valued the early church fathers; they were read for their exegetical insights, not simply their Latin eloquence. The typical humanist fulminations against the Scholastic's

343

barbarous Latin and abstruse dialectics were generally missing from Luther's polemic. In Luther's estimation the fundamental problem with Scholastic theology was its misreading of Scripture through the imposition of alien philosophical concepts, especially Aristotelian philosophy and ethics. Nevertheless humanists considered Luther's early efforts toward the reform of theology in accordance with their own. Humanists promulgated Luther's ideas, printed his pamphlets, and defended his cause. In the early days of Luther's conflict with Rome, he was regarded among the lettered as *Martinus noster*, "our Martin."

As for Luther, he placed great value on the educational and scholarly contributions of the humanists. Though not a humanist as such, Luther was widely read in the ancients, having a particular love for Virgil (the author of one of two books he took with him to the monastery). Later in life he constructed a version of Aesop's fables, regarding it as a treasure for teaching children virtue. Luther particularly valued and studied the new editions of the church fathers edited and published by humanists. But perhaps the most important contribution of humanism was the retrieval and study of the biblical languages. Luther's own facility with the languages was encouraged via the Hebrew grammars published by the humanist Johannes Reuchlin and the Greek New Testament produced by Erasmus in 1516. Securing instructors in Greek and Hebrew in order to strengthen the study of the Bible was one of the urgent goals of Luther's initial university reforms. For this reason one of humanism's brightest young stars, Philip Melanchthon, was brought to Wittenberg in 1518.

By 1520 Luther's association with the humanist movement had reached its high-water mark. Ulrich von Hutten (1488–1523), the imperial poet laureate, offered to take up Luther's cause and defend it with a sword. Others were less bellicose but turned their pens in support. But the threat of excommunication set before Luther's supporters a clear but difficult choice: the reform of religion would be

pursued either under the papacy or in spite of it. The future of the movement fell roughly along generational lines. The older humanists of Luther's generation tended to remain with Rome and parted ways with the Wittenberg Reformation. Erasmus was a representative of such conservatism. However, the younger generation of humanists saw Luther's efforts as the ideological home for their educational preparations and religious hopes. Thus, like the young Melanchthon, a broad group of younger humanists, including Martin Bucer (1491–1551), Johannes Sturm (1507–89), Justus Jonas (1493–1555), Johannes Brenz (1499–1520), Caspar Cruciger (1504–48), and Matthäus Aurogallus (1490–1543), would become collaborators and leaders in the new religious reformation sparked by Luther. By 1525 Luther's public split with the older humanist movement took place through his theological dispute with Erasmus on free will. In his work *The Bondage of the Will* (better translated *On Bound Choice*), Luther harnessed his own conversance with classical and patristic authors to attack Erasmus's position as well as his scholarly ambivalence to what Luther deemed were existential questions. While the substance of the debate centered on theological positions prevalent in late medieval Scholasticism rather than the methods of humanism per se, the conflict was emblematic of what had become a real parting of the ways.

After Luther's excommunication, humanism was now set on a path toward continuing service to the broader political and ecclesiastical movements in the sixteenth century. Its energies were particularly significant in education. Reforming the Wittenberg university curriculum (with revisions authored by Melanchthon for the arts faculty in 1524 and for theology in 1533) was only an initial step in efforts to broaden biblical literacy among the laity, the reformers' goal that all would be "taught by God" (John 6:45). To this end, schools were established to broaden literacy and inculcate Evangelical teaching and piety. Luther appealed to the need in several treatises:

To the Councilmen of All Cities in Germany That They Establish and Maintain Christian Schools (1524); and *A Sermon on Keeping Children in School* (1530). But the bulk of the work fell to Melanchthon, who led the effort by drafting school orders and writing instructional texts in rhetoric, logic, physics, and commentaries on Aristotle. For his enormous contributions he was deservedly dubbed the *Praeceptor Germaniae*, but there were others as well, most notably Johannes Bugenhagen (1485–1558) in northern Germany and Scandinavia, and Johannes Sturm in Strasbourg, whose gymnasium would become a pattern for many others, including Calvin's *académie* in Geneva.

In the latter half of the sixteenth century, the pedagogical goals of humanism continued to be realized among Lutheran educational institutions. At Wittenberg, Melanchthon had prepared a new generation of theologians and pastors, highly trained in the *tri-lingua* of Greek, Latin, and Hebrew and having a broad conversance with the sources of classical and Christian antiquity. Love of the humanities, theological reflection, and confession were steeped in these authors and shaped the Lutheran educational and dogmatic tradition well into the age of Lutheran Orthodoxy and beyond.

See also Brenz, Johannes; Bucer, Martin; Cruciger, Caspar, Sr.; Erasmus of Rotterdam (Desiderius Erasmus Roterodamus); Melanchthon, Philip; Reuchlin, Johannes; Wittenberg Circle

Bibliography

Grane, L. *Martinus noster: Luther in the German Reform Movement, 1518–1521*. Von Zabern, 1994; Grossmann, M. *Humanism in Wittenberg, 1485–1517*. De Graaf, 1975; Herrmann, E., and J. Prothro. "Philip Melanchthon's Poem to Martin Luther." *Concordia Journal* 36 (2010): 97–101; Junghans, H. *Der junge Luther und der Humanisten*. Vandenhoeck & Ruprecht, 1985; Moeller, B. "The German Humanists and the Beginnings of the Reformation." In *Imperial Cities and the Reformation: Three Essays*, ed. and trans. H. C. E. Midelfort and M. U. Edwards Jr., 19–38. Fortress, 1972; Rosin, R. "Humanism, Luther, and the Wittenberg Reformation." In *The Oxford Handbook of Martin Luther's Theology*, ed. R. Kolb, 91–104. Oxford University Press, 2014; Rummel, E. *The Confessionalization of Humanism in Reformation Germany*. Oxford University Press, 2000; Spitz, L. W., Jr. "Headwaters of the Reformation: Studia Humanitatis, Luther Senior, et Initia Reformationis." In *Luther and the Dawn of the Modern Era*, ed. H. A. Oberman, 89–116. Brill, 1974; Spitz, L. W., Jr. *The Religious Renaissance of the German Humanists*. Harvard University Press, 1963; Spitz, L. W., Jr. "The Third Generation of German Humanists." In *Aspects of the Renaissance*, 105–21. University of Texas Press, 1967; Springer, C. *Luther's Aesop*. Truman State University Press, 2011.

ERIK HERRMANN

Hungary

Even before the disastrous defeat of Hungarian forces by the invading Turkish army at the Battle of Mohács changed the political and religious landscape of the kingdom of Hungary in 1526, Wittenberg teaching had begun to spread its influence among German nobles and townspeople and among humanists at court and in educational institutions. The kingdom comprised what is today Slovakia, Hungary, and the Transylvanian (*Siebenbürgen*) area now in Romania. Though repeated diets enacted laws to extirpate the new "heresy," particularly in German-speaking urban populations, Luther's ideas took hold also among priests, especially Franciscans. In Transylvania, Johannes Honterus, a humanist who had not studied in Wittenberg, promoted reform of church and society. Between 1543 and 1547 the "Saxon" population of Transylvania received a church ordinance that created a framework for a newly emerging Lutheran community in the region.

The theological orientation of the Protestant churches was landmarked in the first series of confessional writings compiled and issued by various synods (Erdőd in 1545, Eperjes in 1546, Saxon in 1547, Pentapolitana in 1549/60, Montana in 1559, Szepesség in 1569). These confessional writings closely followed one of the versions of the Augsburg Confession and did not so much offer serious theological novelties as provide limited adaptations to the local circumstances. As Lutheran churches took hold and organized, some adherents moved toward the Reformed confession, and others became Unitarians. German speakers largely remained Lutheran, while a majority of Hungarian speakers became Reformed.

With more formal organization came reform of liturgical practice. The liturgy, following the lead of other Lutheran churches, maintained many elements of medieval practices. Thus there remained altars, pulpits, and images in the Lutheran churches as opposed to the Reformed ones, where the altars and sometimes even the organs were removed and the frescos were whitewashed over. The songbooks (graduals and cantionales) consisted of vernacular translations of medieval hymns and new Protestant songs as well as original Hungarian compilations, the most important writers of which were András Batizi and Mihály Sztárai. The first Bible translations were made under Erasmus's influence in the middle of the century (B. Komjáthy, G. Pest, J. Sylvester), but they covered only the Gospels and Paul's Letters until a full translation was published by the Reformed scholar Gáspár Károlyi in 1590.

Political tensions led to armed assaults on the Protestant communities around the turn of the seventeenth century. In the shadow of the Turkish threat, however, the 1606 Treaty of Vienna guaranteed the freedom of religion and formally recognized both Lutheran and Calvinist churches. The Palatine György Thurzó led the creation of a structure for Lutheran congregations at the synod of Zsolna in 1610, with three distinct areas led by bishops.

The seventeenth century witnessed a flourishing of the Lutheran churches and culture, including a publication boom. Books, printed in Hungarian, German, Latin, and ecclesiastical Czech, provided readings for schools, churches, and individuals, especially on religious topics. However, the new position of the Lutheran Church was regularly challenged by the Catholic prelates, so that the princes of Transylvania, Gábor Bethlen and György Rákóczi I, had to intervene for the protection of the Lutherans, thereby confirming their religious privileges in the peace treaties signed between the princes and the Hapsburg rulers. The Peace of Linz even extended the former freedom of religion to the peasantry and protected the ministers against the Catholic noble patrons.

In the 1670s, usually labeled by Protestants as the "Decade of Mourning," ministers were persecuted, sentenced to prison, or sent to exile or the slave galley while Protestant schools and churches were closed or confiscated. The memory of this period, especially of those who suffered in the galley or exile, contributed to new genres and narratives of church and literary history. Preachers, including Bishop Joachim Kalinka, were accused of plotting against the government and summoned to trials in Pozsony (now Bratislava) in 1671. The next year fifteen preachers were summoned to a special tribunal in Nagyszombat/Trnava and charged with resisting the confiscation of churches. They were offered three options: conversion with promised advancement, resignation from their church positions, or "voluntary" exile. Almost all opted for the third choice, and most left for Germany. Thirty-two Lutheran and Calvinist ministers from Upper Hungary were summoned in 1673 to attend the court of Primate György Szelepcsényi, the governor. The court ruled summary jurisdiction for the charges of crimes against the political authority and the church, incitement of sedition against the ruler, conspiracy with hostile countries, and torture of Catholic priests. In 1674 a mass trial was held in Pozsony involving all Protestant ministers and teachers from the seventeen counties in Hungary, all of whom had been summoned to court. Bishop György Szelepcsényi intended to destroy the Protestant heresies once and for all and to terminate the Protestant religion with the charge of rebellion. The ministers from the territories under Ottoman jurisdiction were banned by the Pasha of Buda from attending the trials. Finally, 336 Protestants, including 284 Lutheran persons, showed up to be threatened with execution, but two-thirds of them chose exile. The rest were sent to prison, where their harassment continued, but only eighteen Lutherans endured the torture, so they were sent together with twenty-four Calvinists to Spanish galleons in Naples. Those who survived were liberated, thanks to the diplomatic missions of European Protestants, but only a few could return home.

The diet of 1681 in Sopron allowed for the return of those who had been exiled, and it ruled that the confiscated churches be returned where it was possible (if built by Protestants and not consecrated by the Catholics). Where the return of the churches was not possible (as in many places it was not), as a compensation the law allowed for building new churches at the Protestants' own cost. Catholic opposition continued even after this, until some relief was provided by Emperor Joseph II's Patent of Toleration in 1781. In the nineteenth century, Protestantism experienced a cultural and spiritual blooming. (Catholics constituted 60 percent of the population, the Reformed 15 percent, the Orthodox 13 percent, the Lutherans 9 percent, and the Jews 2 percent.) Despite their minority status, Lutheran schools contributed to the educational and scientific progress of the Hungarian nation, including several pastors, such as the polymath Mátyás Bél, the lexicographer Dávid Czvittinger, and the school reformer Sámuel Tessedik, who offered education for peasants in sciences and agriculture. In the midst of the revolutionary movements of 1848, the Lutheran Lajos Kossuth led Hungarian forces in an attempt to establish independence from Hapsburg domination in Vienna, but his forces were defeated.

Lutherans adjusted to the many changes that swept over Hungary as a result of the defeat of 1918. Some church officials supported the revisionist governmental policies that created tensions between the nationalities within the church, while others criticized irredentism and the official policy of establishing a "Christian kingdom of Hungary" and advocated for good relations with the non-Hungarian ethnic groups and with neighboring countries, also opposing the official anti-Semitism of the government of the time. During World War II several Lutheran ministers, such as András Keken,

provided asylum for thousands of people during the German occupation (1944) and the Russian siege of Budapest (1945). Gábor Sztehlo's (1909–74) achievements were the most remarkable, as he also founded Pax Shelter for Children, saving more than a thousand children and five hundred adults. Some Protestant leaders also protested against the deportation of Jews, but the majority voted for the anti-Jewish legislation in the Upper House. Internal discord and financial dependence on the state paralyzed protest against these measures.

Under the Communist government, Bishop Lajos Ordass was jailed for criticism of the regime. He did address the LWF meeting in Minneapolis in 1957. His successor, Gyula Káldy, cooperated with the government, advocating a "theology of diaconia," which served governmental policies. Nonetheless a National Lutheran Museum was opened in 1979, and the LWF met in Budapest in 1984. Against protests from the Hungarian church, Káldy was elected LWF president as it tried to come to terms with Communist governance. Following the fall of Communism, the church again assumed a role in national life.

See also Balkan Lands; Exile; Honterus, Johannes; Hurban, Jozef Miloslav; Krman, Daniel, Jr.; Kuzmány, Karol; Slovakia; Stöckel, Leonard

Bibliography
Daniel, D. P. "Lutheranism in the Kingdom of Hungary." In *Lutheran Ecclesiastical Culture, 1550–1675*, ed. R. Kolb, 455–510. Brill, 2008; Fabiny, T. *A Short History of Lutheranism in Hungary*. Lutheran Press Department, 1997; Katalin, P. "Hungary." In *The Reformation in National Context*, ed. R. Scribner, R. Porter, and M. Teich, 155–67. Cambridge University Press, 1994.

MÁRTON ZÁSZKALICZKY

Hurban, Jozef Miloslav

The Slovak Lutheran theologian Jozef Miloslav Hurban (1817–88) was superintendent (bishop) of the Prešporok (Bratislava) district and a founder of Matica Slovenska (1863).

Active in the Slovak national revival, Hurban was a leader of the Slovak uprising in 1848–49 and agitated for greater rights for Slovaks in Hungary. His political and literary activities led to his arrest three times. In 1863, together with Ľudovít Štúr and Michal Miloslav Hodža, he participated in and promoted the codification of Slovak as a literary language. A supporter of Lutheran Orthodoxy as well as a Slovak nationalist, he opposed attempts to promote a unification of the Lutheran and Reformed churches in Hungary as promoted by Count Zay with the slogan "one nation, one king, one Protestant church." Hurban supported the imperial Protestant patent of September 1859, designed to reduce religious tension in the Austrian Empire. Hurban opposed liberal Protestant theology in his three major theological treatises (in Slovak): *A Statement of Lutherans of Unaltered Augsburg Confession, Union*, and his largely historical *The Evangelical Lutheran Church*. In 1863 he established the Slovak theological journal *Cirkewní listy*. In 1860 the theological faculty of the university in Leipzig awarded him an honorary doctorate.

See also Hungary; Slovakia

David P. Daniel

Hus, Jan

The surname for the Czech reformer Jan Hus (ca. 1370–1415) comes from his birthplace, Husinec, in southern Bohemia. He began his studies at the university in Prague in 1390, earning a bachelor of arts degree (1393) and a master of arts (1396). Ordained as a priest in 1400, he began to study theology and was appointed as preacher in the Bethlehem Chapel in 1402, a post that had been established for the purpose of preaching to the Czech people. By this time he had been influenced by the English reformer John Wyclif (Wycliffe). The university, like many at the time, was divided into nations for its governance, and the Bohemian nation to which Hus belonged was dominated by the other three nations (Bavarian, Polish, and Saxon). Many Bohemians at Prague had gravitated toward the realist thought of Wyclif, perhaps to assert their independence from the nominalist thought of the other nations.

Hus continued an indigenous tradition of reform-minded preaching. His sermons, doctrinally orthodox in their call for moral reforms, criticized aspects of piety, such as the pilgrimage to the bleeding hosts at Wilsnack. Above all, they censured the clergy. Hus became an enormously popular preacher because of these criticisms. Initially, Zbyněk von Hasenburg, the archbishop of Prague, leaned toward reform and appointed Hus to be synod preacher in 1405 and 1407, among other honors. By 1408, however, the German masters at the university had succeeded in bringing charges at the papal court against the "Czech Wycliffites." At this point Zbyněk turned against the reform movement.

The Great Schism and nascent Czech nationalism heightened the tensions between Hus and the church hierarchy. When the Council of Pisa exacerbated the schism by electing a third pope in 1409, King Wenceslas IV enthusiastically accepted the council's claimant, Alexander V, while the archbishop gave his allegiance somewhat reluctantly. Later that year the archbishop banned preaching in chapels in an attempt to silence Hus. The queen supported Hus, and he defied the ban with the approval of thousands of parishioners. The king gave control of the university, which up to that point had been a German institution, to the Czechs. The Germans left and went on to found the University of Leipzig. Hus was appointed university rector in Prague.

The reform movement suffered a setback in 1410, when the new Pope Alexander authorized the archbishop to proceed against Wycliffite heresy: Zbyněk condemned and burned Wyclif's books. When Hus protested this act, he was excommunicated by the archbishop, an action that he appealed to the pope. Hus was excommunicated a second time in 1411 for his failure to appear before the papal court for trial. This conflict only heightened Hus's attacks on the higher clergy. He appealed his excommunication from the papal court to Christ himself. At the same time King

Wenceslas had forced the archbishop to retreat from his opposition to the reform movement.

When John XXIII succeeded Alexander as the Pisan pope, it seemed that Hus's trial might have a more advantageous outcome. In 1412, however, John authorized a sale of indulgences. Hus preached against these indulgences, urging people not to buy them. King Wenceslas had supported the indulgence sale, and Hus's opposition led to his loss of the king's support. The reform movement itself was divided over the issue. Crowds gathered to protest indulgences, leading to the first three Hussite martyrdoms. Finally Prague was placed under interdict in 1412, and Hus voluntarily went into exile.

From southern Bohemia, Hus continued to preach and began to write. He composed no fewer than fifteen books in the next two years, among them his best known and perhaps most important work *De ecclesia* (On the Church). In this work and others, Hus continued his attack on the immorality of the clergy. He defined the true church in terms of the predestined. Thus clergy living immoral lives, including bishops and popes, could not be considered part of the true church. As a result they could not legitimately exercise authority in the church. He also supported giving the laity both bread and wine in the Eucharist.

In 1414 Hus agreed to appear before the Council of Constance to defend his views. The council had been called by John XXIII, and Hus had been offered safe conduct by the emperor-elect Sigismund. Despite that promise, Hus was imprisoned upon arriving in Constance. Some of the leading churchmen at Constance, including Jean Gerson, conducted Hus's trial, in which he was accused of thirty Wycliffite errors extracted from his works. Hus was asked to recant without further discussion. Hus refused, not because he defended the list of errors but because he did not believe it accurately reflected his teaching. His accusers persisted. On July 6, 1415, Hus was condemned to be burned as a heretic. He is said to have gone to the stake singing hymns.

Understanding Hus as, in some sense, a forerunner of Luther has a long history that goes back to the very beginnings of the Reformation. At first Luther protested when Eck identified him with Hus during the Leipzig Debates but also admitted that Hus had been unjustly condemned. In a 1520 letter to Georg Spalatin, Luther observed, after having read some of Hus's work, "We are all Hussites without realizing it," including Staupitz, Paul, and Augustine as "we." Lucas Cranach produced a woodcut showing Luther and Hus distributing Communion in both kinds. Luther himself repeated the legendary words of Hus about a successor to his reform: "Now they roast a goose [*hus* in Czech], but in a hundred years they shall hear a swan singing, which they shall not be able to do away with." The parallels between the two reformers are significant, but their theological foundations and impulses were quite different. Hus's moral approach to reform was typical of the Middle Ages and would indeed bear fruit in the sixteenth century, but despite the Lutheran reformers' own rhetoric, that fruit would be found primarily in the Catholic Reformation of the sixteenth century.

See also Czech Republic; Wyclif, John

Bibliography

Batka, L. "Jan Hus' Theology in a Lutheran Context." *LQ* 28 (2009): 1–28; Fudge, T. A. *Jan Hus: Religious Reform and Social Revolution in Bohemia.* Tauris, 2010; Fudge, T. A. *The Memory and Motivation of Jan Hus, Medieval Priest and Martyr.* Brepols, 2013; Hendrix, S. "'We Are All Hussites': Hus and Luther Revisited." *ARG* 65 (1974):134–61; Hus, J. *De Ecclesia: The Church.* Trans. D. S. Schaff. Scribner, 1915; Kaminsky, H. *A History of the Hussite Revolution.* University of California Press, 1967; Šmahel, F., and O. Pavlíček, eds. *A Companion to Jan Hus.* Brill, 2015; Spinka, M. *John Hus. A Biography.* Princeton University Press, 1968; Spinka, M. *John Hus' Concept of the Church.* Princeton University Press, 1966; Wernisch, M. "Luther and Medieval Reform Movements, Particularly the Hussites." In *The Oxford Handbook of Martin Luther's Theology,* ed. R. Kolb, I. Dingel, and L. Batka, 62–70. Oxford University Press, 2014.

PAUL W. ROBINSON

Hymnody

A hymn (Greek: *hymnos*) means a song of praise, perhaps for another human or more often for a deity. It entered the Christian vocabulary in the Pauline Letters: "psalms, hymns, and spiritual songs" (Eph. 5:19; Col. 3:16). It is understood by the New Testament writers to mean praise of God. Martin Luther translated *hymnos* as *Lobgesängen*, which also means a song of praise.

Luther was heir to the rich tradition of church song. He knew the Psalter in Latin, Hebrew, and then in his own German, plus the Greek and Latin hymns and canticles of the daily offices. He knew well the Pauline list of "psalms, hymns, and spiritual songs," which he interpreted to mean the Psalter, other biblical hymns, and the later songs and hymns of the church, respectively. Another secular form that Luther appropriated for his hymns was the ballad, a simple rhyming form popular throughout Europe. He realized early how important resources in the vernacular were. He confided to Spalatin that in "following the example of the prophets and fathers of the church, I intend to make German Psalms for the people, i.e., spiritual songs so that the Word of God even by means of song may live among the people" (LW 53:221). Luther clearly thought that the new Evangelical hymn was in fact the Word of God, capable of kindling faith in the heart of the hearer. He assumed that the purpose of his hymns was evangelical. Their rhetoric was to be directed to the congregation. All singers were, to some extent, preachers of the Word.

As he began writing hymns, he appropriated the ballad form. Luther's first song, "A New Song Here Shall Be Begun [Eyn newes lyed wyr heben an]," uses the convention of the balladeer (German: *Meistersinger*) and tells about some Augustinian brothers in Brussels martyred for holding to their Lutheran faith. Luther wrote a ballad to contradict the rumor that they had renounced their Lutheran faith as they were dying. Luther's next hymn, "Dear Christians, Let Us Now Rejoice [Nun freut euch, lieben Christen g'meyn]," among his greatest, uses the conventions of the balladeer to tell the good news brought to us from far away. Addressed to the congregation, the hymn tells the story of the author's situation in life. Upon hearing of the sinner's need, God, in his mercy, sends his Son, exhorting him to go down and kill Death. Jesus accepts the charge, preaching a sermon to the singers at the end. Luther's most famous hymn, "A Mighty Fortress Is Our God [Ein feste burg ist unser Gott]," is a sermon on the conflict between Christ and Satan. There is little praise directed to God, only rejoicing at the fact that God's kingdom lasts forever.

Luther also paraphrased psalms and rewrote some Latin hymns: "Kyrie Gott Vater," "All Praise to Thee, O Jesus Christ [*Grates nunc omnes* = Gelobet seystu Jhesu Christ]." He wrote hymns for the Ordinary of the Mass, translating them from Latin, to become part of his *Deutsche messe* (German Mass). He wrote hymns for the various parts of the Small Catechism, knowing that students would memorize more easily if they could sing the meanings to a tune with rhyming words. He also wrote hymns as prayers addressed directly to God, such as "Lord, Keep Us Steadfast in Your Word [Erhalt uns Herr]." Reformed churches, led by Ulrich Zwingli and John Calvin, among others, often rejected Luther's notion of hymns as sermons and ruled that the only hymns suitable for worship were the Psalms, paraphrased closely into the vernacular. The Psalms were best because that is where God taught us how to praise him, Calvin's followers believed.

Luther's work spawned a movement of hymn writers that defined Lutheran piety through the next five hundred years. Hymns written by those who came after Luther, such as Philip Nicolai's (1556–1608) "Wake, Awake [Wachet Auf]" and "How Lovely Shines the Morning Star [Wie schön leuchtet der Morgenstern]," became central to Lutheran worship. The Orthodox period of Lutheranism produced thousands of hymns. Most treasured are those by Paul Gerhardt (1607–74).

Gerhardt's hymns, meditations on biblical texts or Christian themes, developed from Luther's model. Gerhardt's hymns remain well loved today. "Commit Thou All That Grieves Thee [Befiehl du deine Wege]" was sung at the founding of congregations, dedications of church buildings, baptisms, weddings, deathbeds, funerals, and during any time of stress for the faithful. Others in the same period include Johann Heermann's (1585–1647) "Ah Holy Jesus [Herzliebster Jesu]," Martin Rinckart's (1586–1649) "Now Thank We All Our God [Nun danket alle Gott]," and Georg Neumarck's (1621–81) "If You but Trust in God to Guide You [Wer nur den lieben Gott lässt walten]."

Many international students were studying in Wittenberg when Luther began writing hymns and liturgies. They were also exposed to the lively humanist tradition of Latin poetry, fostered by Philip Melanchthon. They returned to their own countries to do what they had been taught. By 1526 Olaus Petri (1493–1552) of Sweden had translated Luther's hymns into Swedish and written several of his own. Finland had Mikael Agricola (1510–57). The Slovaks later would have their own Luther in Jiří Třanovský (1592–1637). All of these paid homage to Luther by translating his work into their own vernacular. In addition they were eager to use their own folk music, as Luther had for his hymns. By the end of the seventeenth century in Sweden, Bishop Jesper Svedberg (1653–1735) had compiled a collection of hymns by Luther and many other German and Swedish writers. Johan Olof Wallin (1779–1839) in 1819 prepared a hymnal stamped by Wallin's Enlightenment piety. His contemporaries, Franz Michael Franzén (1772–1847) and others, created a significant corpus of work included in Wallin's hymnal.

In Denmark, Claus Mortensen completed the first hymnal and service book (1528), followed by Hans Thomissøn's (1532–73) *The Danish Hymnal* (1569). Denmark and Norway received an authorized hymnal when Thomas Hansen Kingo (1634–1703) finally got his hymnal approved in 1699. Kingo's book remained in use throughout most of the eighteenth century. The work of Hans Adolph Brorson (1694–1764) was popularized by Erik Pontoppidan (1698–1764), the bishop of Bergen, and later professor in Copenhagen. Later Nicolai Frederick Severin Grundtvig (1783–1872) filled the Danish hymnal with his many hymns on every part of the church year and occasion.

Norway had its own Luther in the poet-pastor Petter Dass (1647–1707). His sermon hymns on the catechism were beloved long before they would be included in any hymnal. An equally gifted contemporary, Dorothea Engelbretsdatter (1634–1716), began to edify people with her many hymns, none of which were printed in official hymnals until the nineteenth century, when Magnus Brostrup Landstad (1802–80) included some in the first official Norwegian hymnal (1869). Iceland's Hallgrímur Pétursson (1614–74) shaped Icelandic piety from his time until today; his Fifty Passion Hymns as meditations, in the style of Baroque sermons, are still read on Icelandic radio during Lent.

Lutheran hymnody continued to develop in subsequent centuries. Jochen Klepper's (1903–42) hymns gained lasting importance in Germany. The 1960s brought new energy to Lutheran hymn writing. In Sweden, writers like Anders Frostenson (1906–2006) began writing hymns on contemporary issues without the theological terms and concepts of bygone days. Their audience was still the congregation, as in his "Your Love, O God, Is Broad as Beach and Meadow [Guds kärlek är som stranden och som gräset]." His colleague Britt G. Hallqvist (1914–97) extended his movement with many hymns for children and unbelievers. In Frostenson's spirit many new hymn writers emerged in Scandinavia. Svein Ellingsen (b. 1929) in Norway received a government stipend to write hymns. In Denmark, Lisbeth Smedegaard Andersen (b. 1934) is adding a new contemporary voice to the Danish hymnal. In the spirit of Frostensen, Finland's Anna-Mari Kaskinen

(b. 1958) is reshaping Finnish hymnody with her contemporary poetry set to music by the contemporary Finnish gospel musician Pekka Simonjoki (b. 1958).

When young Lutherans like John Ylvisaker (b. 1937), the Bob Dylan of American Lutheran folk hymnody, began their work in the mid-twentieth century, they were so immersed in the English tradition of hymnody that the notion of a hymn as a meditation on a text had been lost. Their hymns tended to be either paraphrases of biblical texts or songs of rejoicing.

Lutherans around the world are still creating hymns sung to their own music. In China, Xiao Min (b. 1970) has written over one thousand hymns. Her tunes and texts are in the vernacular, giving testimony to how her faith helps her live. Howard S. Olson (b. 1922), a Lutheran pastor from the Augustana Synod, has gathered an entire collection of native hymns in Tanzania by such writers as Bernard Kyamanywa (b. 1938), whose hymn "Christ Has Arisen, Alleluia," with its lively African tune, is typical of the collection. Latin American hymnody has also found its way into other languages and now enriches English Lutheran hymnody through translators such as Madeleine Forell Marshall and Gerhard M. Cartford.

At the root of most Lutheran hymnic movements is Luther's principle that the language of worship should be in the contemporary language and music of the people. That has tended to create a division between those at the forefront of the movement and those who would preserve the best of the tradition. Both urges, however, are deeply Lutheran and continue to move and grow where the Spirit leads.

See also Cruciger, Elisabeth; Crüger, Johann; Gerhardt, Paul; Grundtvig, Nikolai Frederik Severin; Kingo, Thomas Hansen; Literature, Music; Nicolai, Philipp; Rinckart, Martin; Sandell-Berg, Karolina Wilhelmina (Lina); Wallin, Johan Olof

Bibliography

Grindal, G. *Preaching from Home: The Stories of Seven Lutheran Women Hymn Writers.* Eerdmans, 2011; Watson, J. R., and E. Hornby, eds. *The Cambridge Dictionary of Hymnology.* https://hymnology.hymnsam.co.uk. Canterbury Press, 2013–.

GRACIA GRINDAL

Iceland

Iceland was settled by Norsemen beginning around 870. Some of them had been exposed to Christianity during prior sojourns in Scotland and Ireland, but considerable opposition to missionary efforts existed until around 1000, when priests sent by King Olaf Tryggvason of Norway were more favorably received by the Althing (*Alþingi*), the annual assembly of the commonwealth. Throughout the Middle Ages, there were two bishoprics: Skálholt in the south and Hólar in the north.

In 1523, after the breakup of the Union of Kalmar, Iceland became a dependency of the kingdom of Denmark-Norway. Thus it was primarily through Denmark that the Lutheran Reformation, or the "Change of Fashion" (*sidaskipti*), as Icelanders call it, came about. The first developments took place in the bishopric of Skálholt, where Oddur Gottskálksson and Gissur Einarsson, young priests who had encountered Lutheran teaching while studying abroad in Denmark and Germany, surreptitiously espoused the reform of theology and church practice. In 1541, the Danish king Christian III sent soldiers to Iceland to deport the old Catholic bishop Øgmundur Pálsson and persuade the Althing to approve a new Lutheran Church Ordinance. The king also appointed Gissur Einarsson as the new bishop of Skálholt in the following year. The northern part of Iceland remained Catholic, however, and in 1550 Bishop Jón Arason of Hólar sent a force to oust the Lutheran bishop of Skálholt. After Arason was captured and beheaded, the northerners too swore allegiance to the Danish king and accepted the appointment of a Lutheran bishop in Hólar.

Since the Lutheran Reformation was mostly imposed through governmental action, the process of changing the spiritual orientation of the people constituted a longer, final phase of the Reformation. A number of dedicated bishops led this, most notably Gudbrandur Thorláksson, who was bishop of Hólar from 1571 to 1627. He published the first complete Icelandic Bible in 1584, incorporating the earlier translation efforts of Oddur Gottskálksson. He also prepared a new hymnal in 1589 and a liturgical handbook, *Grallarin*, which remained in use for two hundred years.

The seventeenth and eighteenth centuries were difficult times in Iceland, due to numerous natural disasters and exploitative control by Denmark. The Danish kings diminished the power of the Althing and maintained a trade monopoly. The disastrous smallpox epidemic of 1707 and frequent volcanic eruptions also worsened living conditions. In the same period, many learned and devoted clergy worked to uplift the people. Hallgrímur Pétursson (1614–74), a second cousin of Gudbrandur Thorláksson, was a notable preacher and author of *Passíusálmar* (Passion hymns). These poetic meditations on the life of Christ have strongly shaped the spiritual lives of many Icelanders up to the present. The largest church in Iceland, built in Reykjavik in 1946–86, is named after him. Books containing the postil sermons of Jon Vídalín (1666–1720), bishop of Skálholt, were also owned and used for devotional purposes in most homes for many generations. The Pietist movement attracted strong support in Denmark in the early eighteenth century, especially during the reign of King Christian VI, and had a modest impact in Iceland, primarily through the influence of Ludvig Harboe, a Danish church inspector who worked there between 1741 and 1745. In general, however, Iceland did not experience major divisions within the church between Pietist and Orthodox Lutherans.

Notable changes in the modern era began with the merging of the dioceses of Skálholt and Hólar in 1801 and the transfer of episcopal administration to Reykjavik. The church established a seminary to train clergy in 1847 and then integrated it into the University of Iceland in 1911. Iceland did not become an independent sovereign state until 1918, but it was granted limited home rule by Denmark in 1874. At that time it created its own constitution, which made provisions for freedom of religion. The Lutheran Church was converted from an institution largely under the jurisdiction of the state into a national church with more control over its own internal affairs. In 1907 the church handed over most of its extensive property holdings to the state, and subsequently clergy were paid a salary instead of living off land rents. Tensions between theological conservatives and liberals during the nineteenth and twentieth centuries prompted the formation of two small Lutheran Free Churches, but the YMCA/YWCA, started in 1899, became the major agency of the more pietistic inner mission movement. In 1931 the Althing established a five-member national Church Council (*kirkjuráð*) to oversee the church. In 1957 this was replaced by a larger, more representative Church Assembly (*kirkjuþing*). In 1998 most power over ecclesiastical decisions was transferred from the Althing to the Assembly. The bishop annually assembles all pastors and theologians in a Pastoral Synod. The church is no longer so dominant a force in the social and political life of the people, but around 80 percent of Icelanders are registered as Lutherans. A third of the 150 pastors in the Evangelical Lutheran Church of Iceland are women, and in 2012 a woman, Agnes Sigurðardóttir, became the first woman chosen as bishop.

See also Denmark

Bibliography

Einarsson, S., ed. *Passíusálmar Hallgríms Péturssonar*. Mál og Menning, 1998; Fell, M. *And Some Fell into Good Soil: A History of Christianity in Iceland*. Lang, 1999; Fell, M., trans. *Whom Wind and Waves Obey: Selected Sermons of Bishop Jón Vídalín*. Lang, 1998; Hood, J. *Icelandic Church Saga*. SPCK, 1945; Karlsson, G. *The History of Iceland*. University of Minnesota Press, 2000; Lárusson, M. "The Church of Iceland." In *Scandinavian Churches*, ed. L. Hunter, 104–16. Augsburg, 1965; Pétursson, P. *Church and Social Change: A Study of the Secularization Process in Iceland, 1830–1930*. Plus Ultra, 1983.

Eric Lund

Iconoclasm

The rejection or destruction of religious images for spiritual or political reasons is called iconoclasm (image breaking). Iconoclasm is not limited to protests within Protestant circles, but is a form of revolutionary activity or "cleansing" discernable in the history, expansion, and preservation of numerous religious traditions, including Judaism, Christianity, and Islam. Among Christians, iconoclasm became an issue in the Byzantine Empire when Emperor Leo III published an edict in 726 describing all religious images as idols and ordering their immediate destruction. The resulting Iconoclastic Controversy animated the Greek Church into the ninth century, and contributed to the eventual separation of the Roman Church from the Greek Church. Iconoclasm also surfaced in the medieval protests of Cathars, Lollards, and Hussites, and in the missionary activity of Roman Catholics as they encountered the shrines of Aztecs and Incas in the Americas, and the temples of Buddhists in Asia. At its core, iconoclasm is an attack on the distinctive visual symbols of competing religious traditions and the specialists who represent and employ those symbols. By their attacks on symbolic materials with spiritual significance, iconoclasts also question the transcendent value of sacred objects altogether, a complexity captured by the Latin dictum *finitum non est capax infiniti* (the finite cannot convey the infinite).

In Reformation Europe, iconoclasm first arose in Wittenberg in connection with the teachings of Luther's colleague Andreas Bodenstein von Karlstadt, who publicly attacked the veneration of images in 1521 and published a pamphlet titled "On the Abolition of Images" in 1522. While Martin Luther was in protective custody at Wartburg Castle, Karlstadt gained control of the Wittenberg movement and called for the removal of all images from the local churches. Karlstadt's rationale was that carved and painted "idols" on the altars, as well as crucifixes, candles, holy water, salt, and other physical elements were not able to contain or objectify spiritual realities. In fact, Karlstadt argued, these idols were prohibited by the Decalogue and specifically banned in the expansion of the first commandment (Exod. 20:4), what later Reformed Christians counted as the second commandment. Karlstadt called for the immediate removal of images in places of community worship, a summons taken up in early 1522 by the preacher Gabriel Zwilling and a group of iconoclastic rebels, who overturned altars and participated in other acts of desecration.

In March 1522 Luther returned from Wartburg Castle and gave a different direction to the Wittenberg movement. He rejected the iconoclasts in a series of eight sermons delivered on successive days in early March known as the *Invocavit Sermons*. While not calling into question the faith of the other leaders, Luther encouraged his followers to be more loving toward the neighbor in their ecclesiastical reforms, emphasizing the core of the gospel message, the important law/gospel distinction, and the palpable needs of a community in transition. Demands by Karlstadt to destroy all images were rejected by Luther as a new form of works-righteousness. Instead, Luther appealed to the ancient ethical principle of adiaphora (undifferentiated matters): Christians should exercise their freedom about whether ceremonies or images are used in religious life. As long as neither the Bible nor the ruling authorities prohibited the use of a devotional image or object, it would be acceptable to use that image but not worship it. As they made decisions in such matters, Christians were bound to think of their neighbors' weak faith and to follow principles of good order in the community. In

the decades that followed, Luther and his followers continued to use images and material objects in worship and the churches, as well as in books, including the German translation of the Bible. Lutherans rejected the cult of the saints and remodeled church interiors to suit their needs, but they continued to utilize a central altar and decorative baptismal font, as well as devotional artwork, stained glass, crosses, vestments, liturgical books, candles, chalices, musical instruments, and other ceremonial objects. In addition, the Lutheran clergy developed an identifiable iconography for teaching Evangelical theology, promoting the catechism, and preparing confessional propaganda.

As the Evangelical movement diverged and spread to new regions and contexts, the Reformed churches made the most conspicuous use of iconoclasm as a means to challenge authority and press for religious change. In 1524 Zwingli and the Zurich authorities removed all images from churches under their control, both those associated with the cult of the saints and those tied to other aspects of traditional religious practice. The removal took place in an orderly way after the city magistrates decided that it was time to introduce Evangelical reforms and for a time also involved banning the use of pipe organs. Martin Bucer published the pamphlet *That Any Kind of Images May Not Be Permitted* in 1530 as part of the Evangelical reform of Strasbourg. Theologically, religious images were seen as breaking the "second" commandment and as worshiping matter, which could not contain the truly spiritual. Likewise John Calvin linked traditional devotional images with idolatry in his *Institutes of the Christian Religion* (1536–59), which powerfully shaped religious life in Geneva and from there in much of France, the Netherlands, England, Scotland, the German Reformed areas, and Puritan colonies in the Americas. Huguenot riots against Roman Catholic "idolatry" became a distinguishing feature of the French Wars of Religion (1562–98). Statues of Catholic saints were sometimes eviscerated with pikes or taken out into the street and shot, reflecting both the rage of Huguenot iconoclasts and a calculated attempt to redefine what was sacred. On the other hand, areas that accepted Wittenberg's form of Reformation, such as Scandinavia, left images intact.

Current research on iconoclasm has expanded into the lively arena of global Christianity and world religions, where religious competition is sometimes associated with attacks on images. In particular, the relationship between Christianity and other faiths and the role of iconoclasm in radical movements have been important topics of research with contemporary relevance.

See also Adiaphora; Bucer, Martin; Karlstadt, Andreas Bodenstein von; Zwingli, Ulrich

Bibliography

Aston, M. *England's Iconoclasts.* Vol. 1, *Laws against Images.* Oxford University Press, 1988; Besançon, A. *The Forbidden Image: An Intellectual History of Iconoclasm.* Trans. J. M. Todd. University of Chicago Press, 2009; Duffy, E. *The Stripping of the Altars: Traditional Religion in England, 1400–1580.* 2nd ed. Yale University Press, 2005; Eire, C. M. N. *War against the Idols: The Reformation of Worship from Erasmus to Calvin.* Cambridge University Press, 1986; Noyes, J. *The Politics of Iconoclasm: Religion, Violence and the Culture of Image-Breaking in Christianity and Islam.* I. B. Tauris, 2016.

MICHAEL J. HALVORSON

Igreja Evangélica de Confissão Luterana no Brasil (IECLB) (Evangelical Church of the Lutheran Confession in Brazil)

With approximately 670,000 members in 2014, Igreja Evangélica de Confissão Luterana no Brasil (IECLB) is the largest Lutheran Church body in Brazil. The IECLB officially came into being under this name in 1968 through the merger of four synods. Its beginnings, however, date from the nineteenth-century German immigration to Brazil. The immigrants formed congregations, which later gathered into four different synods: The Synod of Rio Grande do Sul (1886); the Evangelical Lutheran Synod of Santa Catarina, Paraná, and Other States (1905); the Evangelical Synod of Santa Catarina and Paraná (1911); and the Synod of

Central Brazil (1912). The Protestant synods recognized the Evangelical Church in Germany as their mother church, to which they felt related in terms of faith and history. They were of Lutheran, Reformed, and Union church traditions, with the exception of the Lutheran Synod, which identified itself as a confessional Lutheran synod.

The four synods united into a Synodical Federation on October 26, 1949. An earlier concentration on German language and culture gave way to a sense of responsibility for the Brazilian people and nation, its political, cultural, and economic life. In 1962 the designation Synodical Federation was replaced by the name Igreja Evangélica de Confissão Luterana no Brasil. The final official merger of the four synods into a church body occurred in 1968, when the church also adopted a national structure, with its headquarters in Porto Alegre, RS (Rio Grande do Sul).

In addition to many elementary and secondary schools, the IECLB maintains and operates three schools of theology. The largest of these is the Escola Superior de Teologia in São Leopoldo, RS. The IECLB ordains both men and women to its ministry. Social and educational activities have been promoted with the help of European aid organizations.

With the exception of the Lutheran Synod, the other three synods did not have a clear confessional statement, although the Augsburg Confession and Luther's Small Catechism were in use in these synods. It was only in 1997 that the IECLB for the first time officially adopted in its constitution the unaltered Augsburg Confession as its confessional foundation alongside Luther's Small Catechism. The IECLB has been ecumenically oriented since its beginnings. The Synodical Federation was accepted as a member of the LWF and of the WCC in 1950, and in 1958 it joined the Brazilian Evangelical Confederation. The IECLB is also a member of the Latin American Council of Churches and a charter member of the National Council of Christian Churches; it conducts theological dialogues with the Brazilian

Roman Catholic Church and the Evangelical Lutheran Church of Brazil.

See also Brakemeier, Gottfried; Brazil; Dohms, Hermann Gottlieb; Igreja Evangélica Luterana do Brasil (IELB) (Evangelical Lutheran Church of Brazil)

Bibliography
Dreher, M. N. *Kirche und Deutschtum in der Entwicklung der Evangelischen Kirche Lutherischen Bekenntnisses in Brasilien.* Vandenhoeck & Ruprecht, 1978; Prien, H.-J. *Evangelische Kirchwerdung in Brasilien.* G. Mohn, 1989.

PAULO WILLE BUSS

Igreja Evangélica Luterana do Brasil (IELB) (Evangelical Lutheran Church of Brazil)

With about 240,000 members in 2014, Igreja Evangélica Luterana do Brasil (IELB) is the second largest Lutheran Church in Brazil. Its beginnings go back to the German immigration to southern Brazil during the nineteenth century. Following a National Convention resolution of 1899, the Lutheran Church–Missouri Synod (LCMS) sent Rev. Christian J. Broders to Brazil in 1900 to verify the need of spiritual assistance of these immigrants and their descendants. Broders established the first LCMS congregation in Brazil that same year. More pastors were sent by the LCMS in later years. In 1903 the church initiated both a school for the training of pastors and teachers and a church periodical. In 1904 the mission became a district of the LCMS and remained as such until it became a partner church in 1980. Self-support was achieved in the year 2000.

Over the years the IELB extended its activities to all the states of the country, to neighboring countries, and to Portugal and Portuguese-speaking countries in Africa. The engagement of the church in educational activities resulted in the opening and maintenance of schools of all educational levels. In the area of social ministry, the IELB has been active in the care of orphans, elderly people, the poor, and people with special needs. Three lay organizations— the leagues of the youth, the women, and the laymen—have been mainly active in the areas of Christian education, missions, and the financial support of the church.

The IELB has been involved in theological dialogue and joint publications with the IECLB and is a member of the International Lutheran Council. The IELB defines itself as a confessional Lutheran Church and declares the Bible to be the only standard of its belief and practice. The Lutheran confessions, contained in the Book of Concord, are regarded as the correct interpretation of Holy Scripture.

See also Brazil; Igreja Evangélica de Confissão Luterana no Brasil (IECLB) (Evangelical Church of the Lutheran Confession in Brazil); Lutheran Church–Missouri Synod

Bibliography
Buss, P. W. *Um Grão de Mostarda.* Vol. 2. Concordia / Porto Alegre, 2006; Rehfeldt, M. *Um Grão de Mostarda.* Vol. 1. Concordia / Porto Alegre, 2003.

PAULO WILLE BUSS

Imperialism

Imperialism is the attempt of one country to establish economic and political control over additional territory beyond its own boundaries. Martin Luther lived and worked during the Holy Roman Empire, which, compared to today's nation-states, was a relatively loose confederation of territories extending from parts of France to Germany, Bohemia, the Netherlands, and parts of Italy, overseen by an emperor elected by the seven chief ecclesiastical and secular princes of the empire.

Luther's recommendations for religious reform ran into problems first with the church hierarchy of his day. But eventually he faced the combined weight of the church and the empire. At the Diet of Worms in 1521 he stood before Emperor Charles V and refused to recant his writings. Charles V, whose understanding of his job included defending the church (which had declared Luther a heretic), declared Luther an outlaw. By refusing to recant, Luther was, in effect, declining to acknowledge the authority of the Holy Roman Empire in matters of theology and church teaching. Though not opposed to the empire, he was placing limitations on its religious authority.

The only military action of which Luther approved was strictly defensive. This principle led him to oppose crusades. It also had implication for future empires, because extending control over new territory involves a nondefensive use of military force.

An unintended effect of Luther's Reformation was to strengthen the hand of local rulers over against the centralized power of the empire. In his *Address to the German Nobility*, Luther had already (in 1520) appealed to the princes of Germany for assistance with the reform of the church and reiterated the complaints previously voiced by others about sending to Rome money raised from indulgences in Germany. After the Diet of Worms in 1521, Elector Frederick the Wise of Saxony, who governed the portion of Germany in which Luther lived, protected Luther from the imperial decree by placing him in protective custody in Wartburg Castle. In 1530 it was Protestant principalities and imperial cities that signed the Augsburg Confession and presented it to the empire at the Diet of Augsburg. By 1555 the Peace of Augsburg made the religion of the prince the religion of the territory. And at the conclusion of the Thirty Years' War, the Peace of Westphalia in 1648 further weakened the empire. All of this had the effect of strengthening the authority of local rulers, rather than that of the empire.

Another unintended effect of Luther's Reformation was to arouse a new sense of German national identity. His writings and his translation of the Bible provided a more unified language (though still divided into German dialects of the lowlands and highlands). When he stood up to the theologians, the bishops in Germany (some of whom were Italian), the pope, and the emperor, he became a "national" hero of sorts. These were preliminary steps, and the territory that would become Germany was still highly fragmented into separately governed regions. At this point the growth of a national identity was a benign development. In the nineteenth century, as negotiated efforts proved unsuccessful, a rising German nationalism felt thwarted by the failure to achieve national unity. Bismarck managed to create the "second empire" (1871–1918) from the top down, but its supporters would again be disappointed by Germany's defeat in World War I. A more dangerous nationalism was then crafted by the Nazis, who proclaimed a "third empire (*Reich*)." Ultranationalistic and totalitarian, this third empire adopted a new (supposedly scientific) racial theory that barred Jews, the Roma people (Gypsies), and Slavs from full membership. Indeed, they were considered dangerous enough to be enslaved, forced to emigrate, or killed.

In Luther's day, the Holy Roman Empire could aim to govern all facets of life—social, political, economic, and religious—but it did not have the capacity to be totalitarian, in part because of the competing ruling interests within the empire. In lands directly controlled by a king (say, of France, England, or Spain [where Charles V ruled directly]), such control was less hampered although still responsible to a country's estates. This changed dramatically in the eighteenth century with the rise of absolutism and a concomitant development of state bureaucratic control and finally, in the twentieth century, with the use of new technology, which allowed for instant communication with masses of people and for far more monitoring and control of what people did or did not do. This capacity was available by the time of the Nazis, and they used it effectively. In addition to technology, an efficient bureaucracy was needed, a system that governs by establishing and implementing uniform policies. In the twentieth century this too was available. By rewriting governmental policies, the Nazis were able to control all facets of government in a way that would not have been possible in the more localized authority systems of the early sixteenth century—systems that were often built on personal loyalties rather than standardized policies.

Luther was only nine years old when Christopher Columbus brought back news of a New World. This opened the door for another transformation, in which empires became associated with colonialism. The intent to control did not change, but as control was extended beyond Europe to Africa, Asia, and the Americas, a relationship of dependency was created. The colony was a source of revenue and political influence in another part of the world. In most cases, a new line was drawn between "civilized" peoples and the "uncivilized" that affected life in the colonies. The decrees of Charles V were to some extent "universal" throughout the Holy Roman Empire, but modern colonial powers could and did treat people in their colonies differently from their own citizens. The "uncivilized" were often exploited in ways the Europeans were not, sometimes up to and including slavery. This created a dynamic of inequity quite different from the situation in the sixteenth century.

What role did religion have in supporting colonialism? In recent decades this question has been examined in some detail. Though Protestant missionaries were sometimes insufficiently sensitive to the indigenous culture and were linked by language and nationality with the colonial rulers, these studies have shown that the missionaries and the colonial rulers were often at odds. The missionaries typically worked among the less privileged. The colonial rulers opposed their presence because it threatened a lucrative trade with the local elites. And the missionaries were often very critical of the effects of colonial rule on the people with whom they worked.

While focusing on Lutherans, the story is complex, yet their missionary efforts were relatively immune to the influence of imperialism. Several factors contributed to this. In the nineteenth century, the countries with the largest numbers of Lutherans did not participate very actively in the quest for colonies. The Scandinavian countries had virtually no colonies, and those they did have were not sustained for very long. Under Bismarck (1871–90) Germany only halfheartedly participated in colonial projects. Not until quite late (1884)

did it join the quest for colonies. They were mostly commercial enterprises and relatively short-lived. Its three main colonies in Africa were lost in World War I, and German New Guinea was lost in World War II.

No Lutheran missionaries were sent out from Europe until 1705, when the Danish king, Frederik IV sent two German Pietists, Bartholomäus Ziegenbalg (1682–1719) and Heinrich Plütschau (1675–1752), to Tranquebar, a small Danish colony in southern India. Significantly, the missionaries were not themselves Danes. Once in India they endured several years of opposition from the Danish East India Company and its administrators, who did not want them to work with the Tamil people. Ziegenbalg was particularly successful at learning the Tamil language, understanding the Tamil people's culture, starting a Tamil congregation, organizing schools for both boys and girls, training Tamil evangelists and teachers, enhancing cross-cultural understanding, and establishing an indigenous Lutheran church. He benefited from examining the work of the Roman Catholics who had preceded him and stayed on good terms with the Muslims in Tranquebar.

It was not at all unusual for Lutheran missionaries from one country to serve in a colony governed by another. Even more often the missionaries came from more than one nation. In Ethiopia, for example, Lutheran missionaries were sent from Germany, Norway, Denmark, Iceland, and the United States. Lutheran missionaries in the French colony of Madagascar came from Norway and two Lutheran churches in the United States. And the source of personnel and support tended to shift. A mission started by church members in one European country, when cut off by war, would be adopted by a church or mission society from another country. When supported by mission societies from a nonruling country, the missionaries had little reason to see themselves as agents of a colonial government.

Those missions that developed into vibrant indigenous churches quickly learned to utilize native evangelists, who understood the culture and the people with whom they were working. This practice allowed the Western missionaries to concentrate on theological education, translating the Bible and worship materials, and organizing social services.

Missionaries often worked with the lower castes or with tribes without political influence in the nations where they were located. They developed schools and hospitals. The schools had the effect of producing indigenous leaders and empowering peoples who had previously suffered in resignation. Moreover, even before they became independent in the middle of the twentieth century, the indigenous churches adopted democratic practices and became training grounds for community leadership.

One wonders if there were any reasons that predominantly Lutheran countries did not, for the most part, foster imperialism or colonialism. Any full answer would be complex, depending on the country involved, the time in its history, and other specific circumstances, but some of the following may have played a role. Already mentioned was Luther's reluctance to allow the emperor to have control over the faith, a practice that continued in territorial churches, where the government's role was generally limited to maintaining order and securing finances for the churches. Another possible explanation is Luther's ambivalence about governmental power. On the one hand, governments are necessary to restrain evildoers and promote justice. On the other hand, governments often succumb to the sinfulness of humans, forgetting their primary purpose to serve the people and becoming self-serving instead. This is why Luther said that a prince in heaven is a "rare bird": the temptations are so great. Lutherans did not for the most part consider this world's flawed governments to be agents of God's kingdom. Also, societies have a way of falling victim to evil—that is, to the social forces that make it easier for an individual to do what is unjust and wrong than to do what is just and right. Governments are as liable to get swept up in these forces as are

individuals. As a result they are seldom wise enough to exercise control in a perfectly just manner, as they are called to do. Moreover, the centrality of the concept of Christian freedom is a significant factor for Lutherans. Believers are expected to be mature enough to make their own decisions about how to serve the neighbor. Also important is the nonhierarchical image of the church as a community centered on the actions of word and sacrament, where a uniformity of rites is not required (see, e.g., articles 7 and 15 of the Augsburg Confession). As a community of deliberation, a faith community seeks the best way to embody the gospel in a particular time and place. Its practices are more contextual and can be more readily indigenized than in some other expressions of Christianity.

By the early twentieth century, however, none of these countervailing forces was powerful enough to prevent a strong nationalism from developing in Germany that lent support to a totalitarian form of imperialism. Nor, during the Cold War, were they powerful enough to prevent the more subtle imperialism exhibited by nations on both sides of the East-West divide, as they sought to extend their international influence. The long-term effects of European colonialism remain significant both for Christianity and for humanity. They continue to provide fuel for some of the bloody conflicts between ethnic groups and adversarial religious groups in the Middle East, Africa, Asia, and elsewhere.

What those countervailing forces have managed to accomplish is to foster the growth of sometimes large, vibrant, growing Lutheran churches in Africa and Asia. These churches have been independent for the last half century or more. A few examples will suffice. According to the Lutheran World Federation, in 2013 each of the following non-European, non–North American countries had over 1 million Lutherans: 6.4 million in Ethiopia, 5.8 million in Tanzania, 5.8 million in Indonesia, 3.5 million in India, 3 million in Madagascar, 1.1 million in Namibia, and 1 million in Papua New

Guinea. Had they been more closely aligned with colonial rule, it is not at all clear that these churches would have flourished as they have in a postcolonial setting.

See also Holy Roman Empire; Mission and Evangelism; Slavery and Colonialism

Bibliography

Burgess, A., ed. *Lutheran Churches in the Third World*. Augsburg, 1970; Jeyaraj, D. *Bartholomäus Ziegenbalg: The Father of Modern Protestant Mission; An Indian Assessment*. Indian SPCK, 2006; Luther, M. "Temporal Authority: To What Extent It Should Be Obeyed." LW 45 (1962): 81–129; Luther, M. *To the Christian Nobility of the German Nation concerning the Reform of the Christian Estate*. LW 44 (1966): 115–217; Marius, R. *Martin Luther: The Christian between God and Death*. Harvard University Press, 1999; Porter, A. *Religion versus Empire? British Protestant Missionaries and Overseas Expansion, 1700–1914*. Manchester University Press, 2004; Rubenstein, R. "Bureaucratic Domination." In *The Cunning of History: Mass Death and the American Future*, chap. 2. Harper & Row, 1975.

DARRELL JODOCK

Independent Lutheran Organizations

Various incorporated or unincorporated, charitable or nonprofit or not-for-profit independent Lutheran organizations have been established—often but not exclusively in the United States, with varying duration—by those who identify themselves as Lutheran, to serve or benefit theology and church, education and research, missions and evangelism, humanitarian assistance and health care, and other causes and persons designated generally either as Lutheran or for Lutherans. This includes a number of mission societies and social institutions, many of which trace their roots to the early eighteenth century and August Hermann Francke's Foundations in Halle, Germany.

When Lutherans face serious issues that threaten their confessional or ecclesial identity, or when they seek to advance changes in relation to these or other cultural and social concerns, they often convene theologians, pastors, and church members regardless of synodical affiliation in free conferences, conventions, or the like. Following the example of confessional Lutherans in Germany in the 1840s, the Missouri Synod published *Lehre und Wehre* (*Doctrine and Defense*), seeking free conferences and hoping to rally Lutherans to counter Samuel Simon Schmucker's (1799–1873) anonymously issued *Definite Platform*, deemed an "Americanization" (and hence an adulteration) of the Lutheran Confessions. More broadly, its editor, C. F. W. Walther, also desired to unite the various Lutheran synods in America into one church faithful to the Book of Concord. Somewhat later a "free Lutheran diet" was held in 1877 in Philadelphia, attended especially by Lutherans from the East Coast. More recently, a series of Free Conferences on the Lutheran Confessions was held in reaction to Called to Common Mission (1999), the accord between the Evangelical Lutheran Church in America and the Episcopal Church USA. More regularly, the Luther Academy (USA) sponsors free conferences to foster Lutheran confessional identity and fidelity across Lutheran synods.

Similarly, various associations and societies exist to promote Lutheran Church studies and Luther studies. In 1853 the first *Gotteskastenverein* (Divine treasury association) was founded in Hannover, Germany, to support Lutheran émigrés. This movement grew, and in 1932 all the German *Gotteskastenvereine* were amalgamated to form the *Martin-Luther-Bund* (Martin Luther association), which today serves diaspora Lutherans in many parts of the world. Similarly, in 1918 the *Luther-Gesellschaft* (Luther society) was established to advance Luther studies. An International Congress for Luther Research is held every five years; its presentations are now published in the *Lutherjahrbuch*.

To maintain their biblical and confessional fidelity, Lutheran synods, particularly in the United States and Canada, rely or have relied on church-sponsored educational institutions, such as church schools, colleges, and seminaries, but not always. One exception is the Lutheran Bible Institute (LBI), begun in 1919 in St. Paul, Minnesota, and relocated in 1929 to Minneapolis; LBI's mission is to educate the laity for leadership in the church. Subsequently, LBI affiliates were established in Seattle (1944); Teaneck, New Jersey (1948); and Los Angeles (1951). Through various name changes, respectively, Trinity Lutheran College, Luther College of the Bible and Liberal Arts, and Lutheran Bible Institute in California, these institutions assumed independence from the Minneapolis LBI. The latter is today known as the Golden Valley Lutheran College/LBI-Minneapolis. Another endeavor is Valparaiso University in Valparaiso, Indiana. Originally a Methodist college founded in 1859, Valparaiso University was purchased in 1925 by the Lutheran University Association, a group of Missouri Synod pastors and laymen. Boasting a law school and various master's programs, Valparaiso is a highly ranked liberal arts school, esteemed by many for the architectural wonder of its Chapel of the Resurrection (1959).

Known now as Lutheran Hour Ministries, in 1917 a group of twelve men from the Missouri Synod formed the Lutheran Laymen's League (LLL) to raise funds for the church. In 1930 the LLL began a national, weekly radio broadcast, *The Lutheran Hour*, which went international in 1940 and today is the oldest continually broadcast Christ-centered radio program. By 1952 the LLL had expanded its repertoire by offering programs for television. In 1992 the now International LLL changed its name to Lutheran Hour Ministries, reflecting the popularity of its core broadcast program.

Taking to the air rather than the airwaves, by 1970 the Lutheran Association of Missionaries and Pilots (LAMP) was serving Lutherans in remote areas of northwestern Canada. Led by Pastor Les Stalke, LAMP recruited "lay missionaries" to relocate to northern regions and witness to the Lutheran faith. In time, LAMP greatly expanded its fleet of airplanes and missionary pilots to transport material assistance, vacation Bible school volunteers, and longer-term volunteers-in-ministry to assist and evangelize native peoples. A philosophical and subsequent legal fracas between the US and the Canadian portions of LAMP

nearly led to its dissolution. The US portion now operates as Lutheran Indian Ministries, and the Canadian portion retained the rights to LAMP's name and logo and has rebuilt a cadre of supporters in the United States.

Likewise, Lutheran Bible Translators (LBT) often use small aircraft to reach remote areas of the world. Founded in 1964 and funded solely by individuals, churches, and church organizations, LBT has missionaries and associate missionaries working on part or whole Bible translations and on other biblically related media. LBT seeks to make Scripture available and accessible in many native languages.

Under the banner Lutheran Services in America (LSA), perhaps most recognizable as Lutheran Social Services, over three hundred independent health and human service agencies provide services for addiction, the aged, child and family, disabled, emergency and disaster, housing and immigration, and physical and mental health throughout the United States. LSA's formal establishment in 1997 as a joint venture between the Evangelical Lutheran Church in America and the Lutheran Church–Missouri Synod does not detract from the independent nature of its constituent service providers.

Internationally, Lutheran World Relief (LWR), established in 1945 between the National Lutheran Council and the Missouri Synod, began as a chief member of the Council of Relief Agencies Licensed to Operate in Germany (CRALOG). Its work in Europe after World War II, assisting refugees and displaced persons both materially and spiritually, is now a global operation, serving wherever conflict and disaster lead to human hardship and deprivation. Collaborating with over one hundred local partners in thirty-five nations, LWR collects and distributes aid supplied by entities ranging from Lutheran ladies' groups to institutional church donors. Being a signatory to the International Red Cross/Red Crescent Code of Conduct, however, LWR cannot provide aid that may be considered to advance political or religious viewpoints.

See also Francke Foundations; Lutheran Church–Missouri Synod; Lutheran Social Services; Lutheran World Federation; Luther Congresses; Mission Societies and Academies

Bibliography

Anon. *Deutsch-evangelische Blätter* 23–24 (1898–99); Anon. *Deutsch-evangelische Blätter* 32 (Eugen Strien, 1907): 753–54; Anon. "Eine freie Konferenz." *Lehre und Wehre* 2 (Concordia, 1856): 84–90; Anon. *Lehre und Wehre* 44–45 (Concordia, 1898): 253; Anon. "Vorwort zu Jahrgang 1856." *Lehre und Wehre* 2 (Concordia, 1856): 1–5; Benne, R. *Quality with Soul: How Six Premier Colleges and Universities Keep with Their Religious Traditions.* Eerdmans, 2001; Jacobs, H. E., ed. *First Free Lutheran Diet in America.* J. F. Smith, 1878; Menacher, M. D. "Called to Common Mission—A Lutheran Proposal?" *LOGIA* 11 (Epiphany, 2002): 21–28; Nelson, C. E. *Lutheranism in North America 1914–1970.* Augsburg, 1972; Yates, P., and J. van Eijnatten, eds. *The Churches—The Dynamics of Religious Reform in Northern Europe 1780–1920.* Leuven University Press, 2010.

Mark D. Menacher

India

Lutherans account for about two million of approximately twenty-five million Christians in India and in 2012 represented the second largest concentration of Lutherans in Asia, after Indonesia. There are eleven autonomous Lutheran churches spread across the subcontinent and federated together as the United Evangelical Lutheran Churches in India (UELCI), all members of the Lutheran World Federation (LWF). The largest is the Andhra Evangelical Lutheran Church (800,000), followed by the Gossner Evangelical Lutheran Church (421,000) and the Jeyapore Evangelical Lutheran Church (175,000). In addition to the official members of the LWF, there are other newly formed independent Lutheran churches that have come into existence in recent years. It is estimated that about 85 percent of Indian Lutherans are Dalit and tribal converts brought to the faith through the work of various Lutheran mission societies and churches from Europe, Scandinavia, and the United States. Lutherans are scattered all over India, from the Himalayan region in the north to the southernmost tip of India, encompassing several racial, ethnic, caste, cultural, and linguistic groups.

Lutherans are therefore not a homogeneous group, and yet the shared Lutheran legacy and identity unite them.

The Christian presence in India predates the arrival of Lutheran/Protestants missions. The Syrian Christian tradition was planted in the Indian soil as early as the first century. Jesuit missionaries accompanying the Portuguese traders in the sixteenth century established churches by reconverting the Syrian Christians to Catholicism. The Lutheran/Protestant presence in India dates to the era of European colonialism, when Barthalomäus Ziegenbalg and Heinrich Plütschau, German Pietists from Halle, were ordained in Copenhagen and sent to India to preach to the "pagans" and "Moors." They landed in Tranquebar (the "City of Waves" on the eastern coast of South India) in 1706, under the sponsorship of King Fredrick IV of Denmark and the newly founded Society for the Promotion of Christian Knowledge in England (SPCK).

The Danish-Halle mission was the first organized, state-sponsored Lutheran/Protestant cross-cultural mission, coming nearly two centuries after the Lutheran Reformation. Ziegenbalg and Plütschau were not welcomed by the Danish trading establishment in India and experienced hostility and harassment. Ziegenbalg's work led to the establishment of the first Indian Lutheran church, called "Jerusalem," in Tranquebar in 1707. He wrote about the Hindu beliefs in *Genealogy of the Malabarian Gods* (1713), produced a Tamil translation of the New Testament (1715), translated Luther's Small Catechism and a service book, founded a seminary (1716), and recruited the first Indian pastor, Aaron (1698–1745), who was ordained in 1733 after serving fifteen years as a catechist.

The Tranquebar mission maintained close contact with the Church of England, demonstrating the ecumenical character of early Lutheran mission work. In other parts of India the Danish government and the Church of England sponsored other Christian missions through SPCK, SPG (Society for the

Propagation of the Gospel), Church Missionary Society, London Missionary Society, and the Basel Mission. When the Danish government sold their colony to England, some twenty thousand Lutherans converted to Anglicanism due to conflicts over caste within the church. The work of Ziegenbalg inspired other British evangelicals, like William Carey, to come to India under the auspices of the newly founded Baptist Missionary Society.

During the course of the nineteenth century, India had become a major center for missionaries from England, Germany, Scandinavia, and the United States. Missions bearing such names as Leipzig, Gossner, Danish, Hermannsburg, Schleswig-Holstein, Danish Pathan, Santal, Jeyapore, Church of Sweden, United Lutheran Church, the LCMS, and others had begun to form communities of converts to the Christian faith that eventually led to the formation of independent Lutheran churches in different regions of India. The Leipzig Evangelical Lutheran Mission established the Tamil Evangelical Lutheran Church (TELC) in 1919. The Danish Missionary Society, which also worked in the Tamil-speaking region, established the Arcot Lutheran Church in 1919. In north India, Johannes Gossner, a revivalist Catholic priest suspended from the church, later founded the Gossner Mission in 1836, sending mostly lay missionaries to Chotanagpur in eastern India. Their efforts led to mass conversions to Christianity at the turn of the twentieth century and resulted in the formation of the Gossner Evangelical Lutheran Church in 1919. The Jeyapur Evangelical Lutheran Church came into being through the work of Schleswig-Holstein Evangelical Lutheran Mission in 1928 among tribal and low-caste people in the state of Orissa. John C. F. Heyer (1793–1873) was the first American Lutheran missionary sent by the Ministerium of Pennsylvania to work in the Telugu-speaking region in South India. His efforts led to the formation of the Andhra Evangelical Lutheran Church (1927). The work of the German Hermannsburg Mission, later handed

over to what became the American Lutheran Church (1930) during the internment of German missionaries in 1914, resulted in the creation of the South Andhra Lutheran Church (1945). The Lutheran Church–Missouri Synod entered the India mission field when five missionaries who left the employ of Leipzig Mission in 1894 over doctrinal differences were recruited by the Missouri Synod. Their efforts eventually led to the founding of the India Evangelical Lutheran Church (1958).

The various Lutheran missions in India primarily worked among low-caste, Dalit, tribal, and marginalized communities to bring about social and spiritual transformation by establishing schools, health-care centers, hospitals, orphanages, boarding homes, vocational training centers, colleges, Bible schools, and seminaries. Indigenous leaders, pastors, catechists, evangelists, Bible women, and schoolteachers played significant roles in the formation of new congregations and were at the forefront of the missionary work. The mass conversions of Dalits to Christianity by joining Lutheran churches in Telugu-speaking regions in the later part of the nineteenth century were initiated by Dalits themselves, expressing their discontent against dominant castes.

With the proliferation of various Lutheran mission churches in India in the early twentieth century, the need was felt to foster Lutheran unity in order to overcome linguistic, ethnic, and regional differences. Early efforts included the formation of the All-India Lutheran Literature Society (1905), the All-India Lutheran Conference (1908), and the Lutheran National Missionary Society (1916). Under the leadership of Bishop Johannes Sandagren of TELC, a Swede, together with S. W. Sawarimuthu (TELC), Joel Lakra (Gossner Evangelical Lutheran Church), and many other indigenous leaders led the way in the formation of the Federation of Evangelical Lutheran Churches in India (FELCI) in 1926, without the member churches surrendering their identity and autonomy. An all-India Lutheran seminary, Gurukul, was established in

Madras (Chennai) as a symbol and instrument of Lutheran unity and cooperation in 1927 to train Indian pastors from various states of India. Rajah B. Manikam, the first elected Indian bishop (1956) of the TELC, was also the first promotional director of the FELCI. Under the auspices of FELCI Lutherans engaged in ecumenical conversations with the Church of South India (CSI), with a vision of forming a new church body to be called the Church of Christ in South India. Anticipating a potential merger of Lutherans with the CSI, Gurukul's academic programs were shifted to the United Theological College in Bengaluru and to the Serampore University, near Kolkata. But several nontheological factors, such as losing bilateral connections between the churches and their founding missions/churches overseas and the potential division of Lutherans between the South and the North of India, prevented the fruition of that vision. In 1975, the FELCI was renamed United Evangelical Lutheran Churches in India under the leadership of Kunchala Rajaratnam, a layman and economist, as the executive director. When the hopes of a union with CSI faded, Gurukul was revived as a national Lutheran Seminary. The UELCI together with Gurukul has been playing an active role in the transformation of the church in India, especially in empowering the marginalized communities, including women and Dalits, and in fostering cooperation with other Christian bodies for addressing religious, political, and economic issues of the country.

In this three-hundred-year history, Lutherans in India demographically represent a vibrant minority among the Christian minority in India. As the first Protestant mission to India, Lutheran contributions to the Indian church have been significant, especially in areas of Bible translation, national and regional theological education, printing and publishing Christian literature, education, disaster relief, medical missions, and promoting the rights of marginalized and Dalit communities. In India's postindependence era the Lutheran churches in India have emerged as autonomous and self-governing bodies while continuing to maintain their relationships with the founding missions or churches. Though Lutherans have chosen to retain their historical and denominational identity by not merging with other ecumenical denominations, they have nonetheless maintained full-communion relationships and collaborative engagements with all major Protestant denominations. Lutheran churches in India have been faithful to their received heritage and have diligently (often uncritically) preserved much of the Lutheran hymnody, catechisms, liturgy, and polity bequeathed to them by foreign missionaries. However, the relevance of the theological/confessional profile of Lutheranism, beyond being a denominational label in the religious and cultural context of India, remains insufficiently articulated by Indian Lutherans. In a country that is undergoing rapid economic transformation while grappling with the challenges of widespread poverty, economic injustice, and social discrimination, Indian Lutherans have understandably been far more concerned with addressing social, economic, political, and cultural issues affecting their witness than with articulating their theological identity. With the emergence of political Hinduism in recent decades with its overt opposition to Christianity, sporadic persecution of Christians, and promulgation of anticonversion laws in some states, Lutherans in India are challenged to articulate their theology, mission, and ministry in recognizably Indian and also distinctly Lutheran terms.

See also Aaron, S.; Heyer, Johann Friedrich Christian; Kugler, Anna Sara; Kumari Samuel, Prasanna; Manikam, Rajah Bushanam; Mission and Evangelism; Mission Societies and Academies; Petersen, Anne Marie; Rajaratnam, Kunchala; Schultze, Benjamin; Schwartz, Christian Friedrich; Ziegenbalg, Bartholomäus

Bibliography

Bachmann, E. T., and M. B. Bachmann. *Lutheran Churches in the World: A Handbook*. Augsburg, 1989; Christudas, D. *Tranquebar to Travancore*. ISPCK, 2008; Gross A., V. Kumardoss, et al., eds. *Halle and the Beginning of Protestant Christianity in India*. 3 vols. Franckesche Stiftungen, 2006; Jacob, J. *History of Tranquebar Mission, 1706–1981.*

Madras Publishing House, 1981; Jeyaraj, D. *Barth-tholomäus Ziegenbalg, the Father of Modern Protestant Mission: An Indian Assessment*. ISPCK, 2006; Swavely, C. H., ed. *The Lutheran Enterprise in India*. Federation of Evangelical Lutheran Churches in India, 1952; Webster, J. C. B. *Dalit Christians: A History*. Rev. ed. ISPCK, 2000; Yee, E., and J. P. Rajashekar, eds. *Abundant Harvest: Stories of Asian Lutherans*. Lutheran University Press, 2012.

J. Paul Rajashekar

Inner-Lutheran Ecumenism

Inner-Lutheran ecumenism is the nature and nurture of biblical, confessional, and practical agreement for what since the nineteenth century has been designated "altar and pulpit fellowship" among ecclesial bodies designating themselves as Lutheran.

Since the Reformation, inner-Lutheran ecclesial relations have been characterized by fidelity to the gospel (actual or perceived), constantly under pressure to accommodate ecclesial and secular philosophies, laws, traditions, and restrictions that obscure or undermine the teachings in the Augsburg Confession (CA) and later, for many churches, in the Book of Concord. Some trace the ambivalence or tension among Lutherans to the relationship between Luther and his closest colleague, Philip Melanchthon. Melanchthon's accommodating or even compromising humanist disposition, some say, contrasted and at times contradicted Luther's forthright, biblical positions. One support for this theory comes with Melanchthon's promotion of the CA, its Apology, and his *Treatise on the Power and Primacy of the Pope* at the expense of Luther's Smalcald Articles. After Luther's death (1546) and with the defeat of the Smalcaldic League by imperial forces (1547), hostilities in Germany between so-called Gnesio (genuine) Lutherans and Philippists developed, culminating in disagreements over the Lord's Supper in the 1570s. Encouraged by Lutheran princes and estates, such inner-Lutheran disagreements were formally resolved in favor of those Gnesio-Lutherans not associated with Matthias Flacius and open to Melanchthon's theological method through the Formula of Concord (1577) and the publication of the Book of Concord (1580).

By the seventeenth century, the resultant Lutheran Orthodoxy found in territorial and state churches in Europe began to be challenged doctrinally on many fronts. Considering the church to be either spiritually or practically deficient, or both, Lutheran Pietism sought to revitalize the universal priesthood of believers (now understood chiefly as the laity) through small group Bible study and charitable endeavors. Pietism's somewhat subjective tenor called for establishing "little churches within the church" and paradoxically relativized inner-confessional boundaries locally, regionally, and internationally. The Enlightenment, with its humanistic and rationalistic tenets, favored the philosophy and exercise of religion over the confines of confessional faith and doctrine. In reaction thereto, certain revivals of the eighteenth century emphasized inner, spiritual renewal through personal, religious experience and conversion, frequently opposed not only to the "dead letter" of doctrine but even sometimes to Scripture. The blurring or disregarding of biblical and confessional foundations and distinctions among Lutherans repeatedly reconfigured and rekindled the discordant tensions in alternative approaches to theology, ministry, and church.

In Prussia, King Friedrich Wilhelm III (r. 1797–1840) attempted to exploit confessional latitude to facilitate the unification of Lutheran and Reformed congregations in his lands. By first compelling his two court congregations to mark the three-hundredth anniversary of the Reformation by celebrating Communion together on October 31, 1817, the king later issued a common liturgical *Agenda* (service book), derived from German Lutheran, Anglican, and Swedish sources, to effect the union of these two confessions. Such unionizing trends in Europe and among Lutherans in America were vigorously resisted by both German Lutheran theologians (leading to a revival of confessional Lutheranism) and small groups of confessional Lutherans emigrating to America who provide the key to understanding inner-Lutheran ecumenism.

When Lutherans from Germany who were opposed to unionism, rationalism, and syncretism arrived in America, they continued to resist what they viewed as the adulteration of doctrine and practice in parts of the "Americanized" Lutheranism that they found there. Settling predominantly in Missouri, they gradually established doctrinal agreement with other like-minded German Lutherans from synods in Illinois, Minnesota, Ohio, and Wisconsin and with the Norwegian Synod to form the Synodical Conference in 1872. Although other Lutheran alliances with variously stringent Lutheran credentials already existed—the General Synod (1820), the General Synod South (1863), and the General Council (1867)—the Synodical Conference provided the backbone for biblical, confessional, and ecclesial fellowship stressing Luther's theology. In 1876 in Germany, the Saxon Free Church was founded and was accepted into fellowship by the Synodical Conference and its largest member church, the Missouri Synod. In 1917, putting aside the theological differences that had divided them, three Norwegian American Lutheran church bodies merged, forming what was later called the Evangelical Lutheran Church. In 1918 the aforementioned general Lutheran alliances merged to form the United Lutheran Church in America, a constituent member of the National Lutheran Council, which in turn helped form the Lutheran World Convention and its successor body, the Lutheran World Federation (LWF). Although the Synodical Conference resisted what they considered unionizing, ecumenical developments, relations within it eventually became strained. The Missouri Synod's relations with the American Lutheran Church and its stances on prayer, fellowship, scouting, and military chaplaincies gradually led the Wisconsin Evangelical Lutheran Synod (WELS) and the Evangelical Lutheran Synod (ELS) to withdraw from the Synodical Conference in 1963.

Today the WELS and the ELS are in fellowship internationally through the Confessional Evangelical Lutheran Conference (CELC), considered the successor to the Synodical Conference. The Missouri Synod relates ecumenically and internationally to its allied churches through the International Lutheran Council (ILC). In 2017 the LWF plans to celebrate the five-hundredth anniversary of the Reformation with the Roman Catholic Church.

See also Book of Concord; Formula of Concord; General Synod; General Synod South; International Lutheran Council; Lutheran Church–Missouri Synod; Lutheran World Federation; United Lutheran Church in America

Bibliography
Kolb, R., and T. Wengert, eds. *The Book of Concord: The Confessions of the Evangelical Lutheran Church.* Fortress, 2000; Kottje, R., and B. Moeller, eds. *Ökumenische Kirchengeschichte.* Vols. 2–3. Kaiser / Matthias-Grünewald, 1983; Oberman, H. A., ed. *Kirchen- und Theologiegeschichte in Quellen.* Vol. 3, *Die Kirche im Zeitalter der Reformation.* Neukirchener Verlag, 1985; Schuetze, A. W. *The Synodical Conference: Ecumenical Endeavor.* Northwestern Publishing, 2000; Teigen, E. T. "Ecumenism as Fellowship and Confession in the Evangelical Lutheran Synodical Conference of North America." *LOGIA* 12 (Eastertide 2003): 7–17; Wentz, A. R. *A Basic History of Lutheranism in America.* Muhlenberg, 1955.

MARK D. MENACHER

Inner Mission

The Inner Mission was an organization dedicated to coordinating social reform and welfare for Protestant churches in Germany. Already Martin Luther, Johannes Bugenhagen, and the developing Lutheran territorial churches emphasized poor relief, especially in the form of community chests. The foundations for the Inner Mission, however, were rooted in widespread concern over the "Social Question"—the social transformations of the nineteenth century brought about by the industrial revolution. Spikes in vagrancy, visible social immiseration, and diminishing church attendance led many to question traditional methods of church charity, which was linked to the structures of the regional churches (*Landeskirchen*). Drawing upon Pietist critiques of the *Landeskirchen*, religious reformers created voluntary institutions, such as foundling homes and "houses of salvation" (*Rettungshäusern*), which they saw as more efficient ways to solve social problems. By the 1840s, more than 1,500 Christian philanthropic societies existed in the German lands. They drew upon transnational models: city missions in Glasgow (founded 1826) and London (1835) as well as the Young Men Christian's Association (1844).

The Inner Mission was an attempt to consolidate these fragmented, local attempts into a more unified, coherent, and pan-German effort in the period before the political unification of Germany. At the Wittenberg Church Congress of 1848, Johann Hinrich Wichern founded the Central Committee for the Inner Mission, which coordinated and organized different philanthropic efforts throughout the German lands. Funded and supported by the Prussian King Friedrich Wilhelm IV, the leaders of the Inner Mission saw the social question as a religious and moral problem, and they targeted the German proletariat, hoping to win back those who had become socialists or revolutionaries. The founders also hoped to use the Inner Mission to foster German Protestant church unity and transcend the individual *Landeskirchen*. Inner Mission societies spread throughout the German-speaking territories, and in many areas they were integrated into the *Landeskirchen*.

Because of its close ties to Prussia, the Inner Mission was further institutionalized into state functions after German unification in 1871. By the late nineteenth century, the Inner Mission tackled a broad range of social issues: evangelism in urban areas (such as Scripture distribution and street evangelization); "moral" campaigns against alcohol, prostitution, and gambling; child welfare; prison reform; and hospital work for the poor. The Central Committee helped to coordinate the expanding philanthropic efforts nationally: it compiled statistics, organized conferences, and facilitated links and cooperation between the various individual institutions.

Yet its successes also engendered criticism. In the late nineteenth century, the Inner Mission garnered criticism from liberal Protestants, such as Friedrich Naumann, who wanted the Inner Mission to focus more on social rather than individual transformation. It also came under attack from conservatives like Adolf Stöcker, who hoped to mobilize the Inner Mission for partisan politics. Despite these criticisms, throughout the imperial period the Inner Mission remained the most important Protestant organization that organized discussions and debates surrounding the social question. During the First World War, the German state used the Inner Mission to centralize and regulate philanthropic efforts.

After the end of that war, the Inner Mission reorganized and tried to modernize its organizational structure by creating greater links between the local and central welfare societies. It retained its status as the principal health and welfare institution that organized the various organizations for Protestant churches. Along with its Catholic counterpart, the Catholic Caritas, the Inner Mission continued to see poverty and social evils as spiritual problems and to argue that welfare relief should remain in the hands of private, voluntary, religious organizations, a position that clashed with Progressive and Social Democrat visions over how to conduct charitable work.

Throughout the Weimar period (1919–33), the Inner Mission focused its efforts on trying to curb the "sexual revolution": the spread of birth control, declining birth rates, and the emergence of the "New Woman." The organization was also an early supporter of the eugenics movement. During the Nazi period, even though many individuals of the Inner Mission joined the Confessing Church and privately criticized the Nazi regime, the organization supported Nazi policies by carrying out thousands of sterilizations in asylums and hospitals affiliated with the institution.

After the war, the Inner Mission came under the auspices of the Evangelical Church in Germany (EKD), and in 1957 renamed itself the Innere Mission und Hilfswerk der EKD. In 1961 the German Democratic Republic founded its own Protestant Church welfare organization, the Diakonische Werk—Innere Mission und Hilfswerk der Evangelischen Kirchen in der DDR. In 1975 the Inner Mission in West Germany became the Diakonische Werk der EKD. In 1991 the two organizations of East and West Germany combined into the Diakonische Werk der Evangelischen Kirche in Deutschland, which still serves as the primary philanthropic and welfare agency for Protestant churches in Germany today.

See also Confessing Church; Deaconnesses; Pietism; Sieveking, Amalie Wilhelmina; Wichern, Johann Hinrich

Bibliography

Bigler, R. *The Politics of German Protestantism: The Rise of the Protestant Church Elite in Prussia, 1815–1848*. University of California Press, 1972; Dickinson, E. *The Politics of German Child Welfare from the Empire to the Federal Republic*. Harvard University Press, 1996; Euchner, W., et al. *Geschichte der sozialen Ideen in Deutschland*. VS Verlag für Sozialwissenschaften, 2000; Gerhardt, M. *Ein Jahrhundert Innere Mission: Die Geschichte des Central-Ausschusses für die Innere Mission der Deutschen Evanglischen Kirche*. C. Bertelsmann, 1948; Hong, Y.-S. *Welfare, Modernity, and the Weimar State, 1919–1933*. Princeton University Press, 1998; Shanahan, W. *German Protestants Face the Social Question*. University of Notre Dame Press, 1954.

ALBERT WU

International Lutheran Council

As a worldwide association of strongly confessional Lutheran church bodies, the International Lutheran Council (ILC) represents over 3.5 million baptized Lutherans worldwide. The ILC has its historical roots in a gathering of leaders from Lutheran churches around the world that did not join the Lutheran World Federation (LWF) when it was organized in 1947. Theologians and church leaders from Australia, Denmark, France, Germany, the United Kingdom, and the United States met in Uelzen, Germany, in 1952. At a third meeting in Cambridge, England, the name International Lutheran Theological Conference was given to this gathering of church leaders.

During the next three decades twelve additional conferences were held. Representatives from other confessional Lutheran churches in Argentina, Brazil, Canada, China, Ghana, Guatemala, Hong Kong, India, Japan, Korea, New Guinea, Nigeria, the Philippines, South Africa, Taiwan, and Venezuela joined this group. Dr. E. George Pearce from the Evangelical Lutheran Church in England was one of the most important leaders of this conference and served as its chairman from 1973 until his death in 1982. In 1975 the conference dropped the word "theological" from its name.

The ILC was formally organized in 1993 at the fifteenth meeting of the conference, in Antigua, Guatemala. A constitution was adopted that defines this new council as an association of Lutheran Church bodies "which proclaim the Gospel of Jesus Christ on the basis of an unconditional commitment to the Holy Scriptures as the inspired and infallible Word of God and to the Lutheran Confessions contained in the Book of Concord as the true and faithful exposition of the Word of God" (ILC Constitution). The president of the Lutheran Church–Canada, Edwin Lehman, was elected to serve as the first chairman of the council; Samuel Nafzger, the executive director of the Lutheran Church–Missouri Synod's Commission on Theology and Church Relations, served as its executive secretary from 1993 to 2010.

The ILC is expressly an association of churches, not a communion of churches (as is now the case for the LWF), and thus it does not carry out churchly functions. It exists for the purpose of sponsoring common study by authorized representatives of its member churches, focused on theological issues and concerns. It also aims to nurture and strengthen relationships among Lutheran churches unconditionally committed to the Scriptures and the Lutheran Confessions, to issue statements (when asked to do so) on contemporary questions confronting Christian church bodies today, and to work toward the closest possible joint expression of their faith and confession.

The ILC seeks to assist and strengthen its member churches in their confessional witness and mission, but it does not prescribe any course of action for its member churches.

Membership in the ILC does not require nor does it imply formally declared altar and pulpit fellowship (church fellowship) between each of its member bodies. But all members of the ILC are "pledged to exhibit mutual respect and fraternal regard for each other as fellow Christians and confessional Lutherans, and to foster, strengthen, and preserve confessional agreement which manifests itself at the altar and in the pulpit" (ILC Constitution). Its constitution recognizes two types of members: voting and associate.

In order to carry out its duties, the ILC is divided into five world areas: Africa, Asia, Europe, Latin America, and North America. An executive committee made up of the officers of the ILC (chairman and secretary), and one representative of each of its world areas, is responsible for implementing the council's objectives and providing supervision of the executive secretary. Member church bodies contribute financial support for the work of the council based on each church's baptized membership and on the GNP of the country in which each church exists. Meetings of the ILC take place on a three-year cycle: in the first year, regional meetings of member churches in each world area; in the second year, a world conference of the heads of each member church; in the third year, a conference of representatives from each member church's seminaries.

See also Lutheran Church–Missouri Synod; Lutheran World Federation

Bibliography

ILC Newsletter. Published four times each year as the council's official publication, in English and Spanish. http://www.ilc-online.org.

SAMUEL H. NAFZGER

Irbe, Kārlis

The first bishop of the Latvian Evangelical-Lutheran Church, Kārlis Irbe (1861–1934), studied theology at the University of Dorpat (Tartu), Estonia (1881–86), and established the first Latvian student corporation, Letonija (1882). Ordained in 1887, he served as pastor (1888–1905) and dean of Cēsis district (1902–5). After teaching (1905–9) and serving as director (1909–15) of the Maldonis secondary school, he became pastor of Latvian refugees at Kharkov, Ukraine (1915–17), and then founded the first Latvian Lutheran congregation in Moscow. Elected first president of the temporary consistory of the newly independent Latvian church in 1918, he returned to Latvia in 1920, participated in composing the church's constitution, and was elected bishop and president of the church in 1922. During his ministry the infrastructure of the church was restored; the Lutheran Hymnal (1922), agenda (1928), and church calendar (beginning 1927) were printed; and the theological institute (1923–37) and the church's secondary education program (1928–40) came into existence. Irbe strove to resolve tensions between German and Latvian church members and to establish good relationships between church and state. When the state interfered with ecclesiastical matters, Irbe protested, called an extraordinary synod, and resigned his office, then in his last years worked intensively with the church's youth department and foreign missions.

See also Latvia

GUNTIS KALME

Islam

Lutherans have responded to and engaged Islam throughout the history of the tradition, beginning with Martin Luther's writings on the Turks and continuing to contemporary interfaith dialogue. Since some of the largest and fastest-growing Lutheran congregations in the world are in Muslim-majority Indonesia and multifaith Africa, engagement with Muslims will become even more important in the future.

It is significant both for Lutheranism and for the overall development of Christian-Islamic relations that the high tide of the Ottoman Empire occurred at the same time as the Protestant

Reformation began. For Martin Luther and his fellow reformers, "the Turks" (generally equated with Islam) were of critical importance. Luther frequently mentioned them in his writings and dedicated several publications specifically to the theme of appropriate Christian responses to the Ottomans. While there were continuities with received medieval Christian understandings of Islam, the theological orientation of the Protestant reformers did cause important alterations in the history of Christian understandings of and responses to Islam. Martin Luther's contributions to these developments are therefore particularly significant.

The combination of Luther's frequent references to the Turks and the military threat to central Europe from the Ottoman Empire ensured that Lutheran thinkers would continue to engage Islam in their publications and sermons. As Ottoman power declined through the later seventeenth and eighteenth centuries, interest in Islam waned. Beginning around 1800 a new kind of engagement with Islam began to emerge within the Lutheran tradition. This key turning point saw considerable energy directed toward a serious historical-critical examination of Islam and limited engagement with living Muslims as a result of missions. These remained the dominant approaches in Lutheranism until after the two world wars. In the wake of postcolonialism, Christians have explored new approaches to Muslims. Since the 1980s, Lutherans in particular have made significant contributions to Christian-Islamic relations through active interfaith dialogue and cooperative activities. In the wake of the terrorist attacks on September 11, 2001, and the subsequent military actions by the United States and its allies, these endeavors have taken on added urgency.

Because Martin Luther directly engaged Islam in his writings, and because his works continued to be prominent within later Lutheranism, his positions and opinions about Islam carried considerable weight as a starting point for many later Lutheran treatments of the subject. Therefore any discussion of Lutheranism and Islam must begin with a summary of his central contributions, especially in three areas: (1) teachings about just war and crusades, (2) analysis of the overall nature of Islam and the Qur'an, and (3) understanding of the place of Islam in eschatology. Luther was both interested in Islam for its own sake and simultaneously utilized the trope of Islam to distinguish his theology from that of his Roman Catholic and Anabaptist opponents. Even though Luther did not systematically analyze Islam, the categories of understanding and vantage points that he established became paradigmatic for much of Protestantism.

In his pamphlets *On War against the Turk* (1529) and *Military Sermon against the Turks* (1530), Luther established his position concerning the appropriate Christian response to Islam. He strongly emphasized the absolute rejection of the crusade as a blasphemous confusion of the spiritual and the secular. Christians *as* Christian believers were not to lead or even participate in battle. Furthermore, ecclesiastical attempts at military leadership angered God. Clergy were to preach and pray, not to bear arms and fight. According to Luther, there is no *religious* justification for any military action—be it against false Christians, heretics, or even Turks. Spiritual enemies must be fought with spiritual weapons alone. No crusade or holy war is permissible. This represents a significant point of departure from the mainstream of medieval theology. Before Luther there had been critiques of crusaders (esp. in terms of morality), but never such a thoroughgoing theological critique of crusading. Since Pope Gregory the Great (ca. 540–604), many theologians argued that the coercion of those who hold false beliefs is an appropriate basis for just war.

Luther's criticism of crusade did not lead to a disavowal of violence against the Turks, however. The *Military Sermon* was written specifically to admonish the "fist" against the Ottomans. For Luther, the war against the Turks is his generation's example of a "good war." Fighting against the Turks is appropriate because it is the duty of legitimate rulers to defend society against the Turks, just as they would oppose all disturbers of the peace. If called on to give material or physical support to the military effort against the Turks, Christian subjects should give willingly.

As early as 1529, Luther lamented the fact that he had no accurate Latin translation of the Qur'an. About this time the Zurich reformer Theodor Bibliander initiated his study of Arabic with the intention of printing the Qur'an for the first time. By 1542 Bibliander had completed his edition, but a public debate in Basel concerning the danger that the Qur'an might be to Christians jeopardized the entire project. All printed copies were seized and the printer was jailed. Luther was instrumental in a concerted effort of support from several Protestant leaders across confessional lines, including Philip Melanchthon, to allow the printing to continue. Luther's published introduction to this first printed Qur'an emphasizes the need to have accurate knowledge of the beliefs of Muslims. This does not mean that Luther viewed Islam positively. He understood the Qur'an to be fundamentally a book of the law, not on a par with the Bible, but similar to the papal collections of canon law. Furthermore, these laws were not morally good or even neutral. For Luther, the Qur'an contained only human wisdom without God's Word and Spirit. Luther supported the publication of the Qur'an in Latin because he considered the public knowledge of the Qur'an to be the greatest weapon against Islam.

Luther understood Islam to be fundamentally a religion of works-righteousness. For Luther, Islam is so strongly stamped by "works" that every example of works-righteousness within or outside Christianity could be characterized as "Turkish." In sharp contrast to most medieval Christian writings on Islam, Luther deemphasized the person and biography of Muhammad. Lurid pseudo-biographies on Muhammad were available for anti-Muslim polemic, but in his main writings on the Turks,

Luther deliberately chose instead to focus on the Qur'an and its laws and doctrines. At times Luther did praise Muslims for their piety. According to him, the discipline of the Turks would shame any papist so much that none would remain in their faith if they spent just three days with the Turks. In the end, Luther's analysis of Islam was grounded in Christology: no matter how spiritual it looks, without Christ its adherents are lost. Like medieval critics, Luther often viewed Islam not so much as a separate religion but as a form of Arianism because of their denial of Christ's divinity.

Islam (at least insofar as it was represented by the Turkish invasion) was also central to Luther's eschatology. Comparing the contemporary condition of the world to Scripture, it was clear to Luther that he was living in the last days. Because the end of the world was near, the devil was raging with his two weapons: the antichrist (the papacy) and the Turks. Luther and his circle interpreted both Daniel and Revelation as prophecies that the Turks would be allowed dominion for a time but then would be destroyed. The most direct reference to the Turks in the Bible was found in Gog and Magog, understood by Luther to be the biblical designation for the Turks. This was such an important point for him that he published his translation of Ezek. 38–39 as a separate pamphlet, with an introduction that made clear the connection. According to Luther, Rev. 20 declared that after a thousand years the devil will be loosed to make war on the saints. He would gather Gog and Magog (identified in medieval tradition with the "red Jews" who, Luther claimed, were not Jews but the Turks) to besiege the city of God's people (for Luther, perhaps Vienna), but they would be destroyed by fire from heaven and cast into eternal damnation (20:7–10). Philip Melanchthon also identified the "Red Jews" with the Turks.

Despite Luther's eschatological hopes, Ottoman expansion threatened central Europe deep into the seventeenth century. This, in conjunction with the significant heritage of Luther's own writings on Islam, ensured that Lutherans continued to engage Islam, or at least continued to utilize their theoretical (mis)understandings of Islam in their theological writings. As a whole, these theologians followed Luther's christologically centered rejection of Islam and used it as an archetype of a religion of human works-righteousness. In his *Loci theologici*, for example, Martin Chemnitz (1522–86) mentioned Muhammad in direct relation to Arius, implying that the primary significance of Arius was his role in the development of Islam. Chemnitz asserted that since the Jews and Muslims do not pray in the name of Jesus, God would not hear their prayers. One typical example of an extensive seventeenth-century Lutheran theological treatment of Islam is found in Abraham Calov's important *Systema locorum theologicorum* (Wittenberg, begun 1655). Calov (1612–86) dedicated an entire section to the question, whether the religion of Muhammad is true? He did not attribute Islam's origin to Satan but identified it as a natural religion that did not worship the true God, or fundamentally any god at all, since it rejected the divinity of Christ.

Theologians of Lutheran Orthodoxy continued to see an important role for Islam in the eschaton. As the year 1666 approached, several Protestant tracts were published that specifically linked the Turks to the events of the books of Daniel and Revelation in a manner similar to Luther. As late as the eighteenth century, Luther's eschatological framework was still influential among some Protestants. As far away as North America, Jonathan Edwards's eschatology in relationship to Islam appears to be significantly influenced (indirectly) by Luther.

The Ottomans besieged Vienna again in 1683 and were once again unsuccessful. The retreat that ended this siege marked a significant reversal in power relations between the Islamic world and the West. As Ottoman power declined, so did the frequency with which Islam was mentioned in the writings of Lutheran theologians and pastors. However, a new phase in Lutheran engagement with Islam, centered on advanced scholarship, became evident beginning in the eighteenth century. One example of this new era of Lutheran scholarship on Islam is Christof Wilhelm Luedeke (1737–1805), the preacher for the Lutheran expatriate community in Ottoman Smyrna. His description of the "Turkish Empire" (published in Leipzig, 1787–89) has been recognized for its quality and evenhanded approach. Many Lutherans were prominent among the members of the Deutsche Morganländische Gesellschaft, the most prestigious European academic society dealing with the Islamic world. For example, Georg Heinrich August Ewald (1803–75), a prominent Lutheran thinker, was simultaneously one of the most prominent German orientalists of the nineteenth century. The more detached and religiously neutral perspective of these scholars is reflected in well-known Lutheran church histories such as Karl Heussi's *Compendium of Church History* (1st ed., 1908). Despite being a textbook on the history of Christianity, it contains short, relatively unbiased summaries of much of Islamic history.

Over the course of the nineteenth and early twentieth centuries, Lutheran missionaries served across the globe, although in Muslim-majority countries the largest indigenous Lutheran communities were those who were non-Muslim at conversion. Lutheran missionaries were sent to India as early as 1706, first by the Danish government in collaboration with the Halle Pietists. These missionaries were directed to the non-Muslim Tamil peoples. The same is true with one of the most successful Lutheran missions to any Muslim-majority country. In Indonesia beginning in the 1820s, there was great success among the non-Muslim Batak peoples. Significant Lutheran engagement with the Middle East began with the establishment of a joint diocese with Anglicans in 1841 in Jerusalem. As in other parts of the global activities of Lutheranism, the Lutherans of the bishopric of Jerusalem emphasized education and social ministry that went beyond Christians of the Levant and included Muslims as well.

Over the last fifty years, the Lutheran World Federation (LWF) has been carrying out inter-religious work and dialogue of many kinds, including with the Islamic world. While being careful not to neglect Christian witness and in distinction from the previous history of Lutheran-Muslim engagement, these endeavors have tried to move beyond a dialogue that goes no further than a comparison of abstract theological tenets of belief and a subsequent condemnation.

The most important formal activities in this regard began with the 1984 LWF Department for Theology series of studies "Theological Perspectives on Other Faiths." This was followed by a study program on Islam from 1992 to 2002 by the Department for Theology and Studies, and culminated in the Bangkok consultation in 1996 on theological perspectives on other faiths. Each of these endeavors produced published summaries of findings. In the wake of contemporary circumstances, and based on this prior work, in 2001 the LWF organized a new program specifically emphasizing conflict and peace in Christian-Muslim relations. This sustained and deep bifaith project centered on a series of case studies involving actual Christians and Muslims in Denmark, Indonesia, and Nigeria. The results of this study program, published as *Bridges instead of Walls*, is an example of the most sophisticated level of interfaith dialogue. Perhaps most important, it provides a nuanced understanding of the role of religion in Christian-Muslim conflict, making clear that although religion often gets used as a tool in conflict, the underlying causes are instead to be found in socioeconomic distress and group identity.

Over the last several decades Lutherans engaged with Islam have recognized the increasing problematic nature of "dialogue." These endeavors instead have emphasized "dialogue-in-action" (diapraxis), particularly the use of faith on both sides to ameliorate conflict. Interfaith activities have aimed at genuine conversation, genuine hospitality, and community building that can break down us-versus-them mentalities. This new approach has been articulated with the phrase "theology on the way."

Martin Luther's engagement with the Turks and Islam has been frequently mentioned in the course of contemporary interfaith meetings. In terms of Luther himself, most helpful is his interest in gaining accurate knowledge of Islam and his essential role in the publication of Bibliander's 1543 Qur'an. Theological discussion also explores how distinctly Lutheran themes relate to Islam, especially salvation by faith alone. In contemporary Lutheran engagement with Islam, Luther's opinions are generally understood to contain valuable aspects; yet it is acknowledged that much of what he said was a product of his historical context and must be rejected. This dual perspective of an appreciation of the valuable contributions from the tradition while at the same time moving beyond the past in the pursuit of peace and understanding has enabled Lutherans to be in a particularly good position to work with living Muslim communities who find themselves in the same situation. This, in combination with the dedication of LWF leadership to pursue active engagement with Islam, bodes well to meet the challenges in the future of Lutheran-Muslim engagement.

See also Lutheran World Federation; Middle East

Bibliography
Babinger, F. "Die Türkischen Studien in Europa bis zum Auftreten Josef von Hammer-Purgstalls." *Die Welt des Islams* 7 (1919): 103–29; Ehmann, J. *Luther, Türken, und Islam*. Gütersloher Verlagshaus, 2008; Francisco, A. *Martin Luther and Islam*. Brill, 2007; Luther, M. "Heerpredigt wider den Türken (Military Sermon against the Turks)." WA 30/2: 160–97; Luther, M. "On War against the Turk." LW 46:155–206; Luther, M. "Preface to Theodor Bibliander's Edition of the Koran" (1543). LW 60:286–94; Luther, M. "Preface to the Thirty-Eight and Thirty-Ninth Chapters of Ezekiel, on Gog." LW 59:277–84; Miller, G. "Luther's Views of the Jews and Turks." In *The Oxford Handbook of Martin Luther's Theology*, ed. R. Kolb, I. Dingel, and L. Batka, et al., 427–34. Oxford University Press, 2014; Miller, G. "Theodor Bibliander's *Machumetis*

saracenorum principis." *Islam and Christian-Muslim Relations* 24 (2013): 241–54; Rasmussen, L., ed. *Bridges instead of Walls.* Lutheran University Press, 2007.

GREGORY MILLER

Iwand, Hans Joachim

The Lutheran theologian and pastor Hans Joachim Iwand (1899–1960) was born in Breslau, Prussia, and educated at the University of Breslau under Erich Seeberg (1888–1945) and Rudolf Hermann (1887–1962). He wrote his first doctoral dissertation under Martin Schultze (1866–1943) at Königsberg (1921). In 1924 he wrote his second dissertation, published as *Rechtfertigungslehre und Christusglaube* (1930), which signaled his lifelong interests: Christology and Luther studies. Iwand obtained a position at Lutherheim, a seminary-like institution related to the University of Königsberg. His work continued there until the beginnings of the *Kirchenkampf* in 1933. Iwand's review of the first volume of Karl Barth's *Church Dogmatics*, titled *Jenseits vom Gesetz und Evangelium?*, pointed out important questions in the history of modern theological reflection on law and gospel. He was then dismissed from his position and left his family to teach briefly in Riga, Latvia, in 1934. His dismissal came from a denunciation by his own staff at Lutherheim that Iwand's wife was half Jewish. Soon afterward in 1935, Iwand directed a Confessing Church seminary. This seminary was located first in Blöstau, later in Jordanowo, Neumark (now Poland). After these seminaries were disbanded in 1937, he was called to be pastor of St. Marienkirche in Dortmund in 1938. He served this congregation until the end of the war, when he became a professor of systematic theology first at Göttingen and later at Bonn. In both positions Iwand lectured on a variety of topics, but especially Christology, while engaging in Christian-Jewish dialogue and ecumenical work between Reformed and Lutheran churches, and while pursuing common work with theologians in Eastern European countries. He died on May 2, 1960, at the beginning of a decade that would see a new groundswell of work on eschatology, reacting to the various lines of theology that were established in the 1920s, including the Luther Renaissance.

Iwand himself has proved important for a variety of these movements, especially insofar as they attend to Luther's theology of the bound will or the theology of the cross. Iwand's polemical but brief work "Wider den Missbrauch des *pro me* als Methodischer Prinzip" (Against the misuse of the *pro me* as a methodological principle) offers a criticism of existentialist and liberal theological appropriations of Luther. His work on nuclear disarmament, Jewish-Christian dialogue, and his various entries in the law/gospel debates of the early and middle twentieth century persist in importance. Continuing Rudolf Hermann and Karl Holl's (1866–1926) approach to Luther studies, Iwand's work on Luther easily moves from interpretation to constructive theological proposal. In many ways, he unites careful textual study with systematic theology in a way that is still exemplary.

See also Christology; Confessing Church; Gospels; Luther Renaissance; World Wars I and II

Bibliography

Iwand, H. *Nachgelassene Werke.* 6 vols. Ed. H. Gollwitzer, W. Kreck, K. Steck, and E. Wolf. Kaiser, 1962; Iwand, H. *Nachgelassene Werke: Neue Folge.* 5 vols. Ed. Hans-Joachim-Iwand-Stiftung. Gütersloher Verlagshaus, 1998–2004; Iwand, H. *Rechtfertigungslehre und Christusglaube: Eine Untersuchung zur Systematik der Rechfertigungslehre Luthers in ihren Anfangen.* 2nd ed. Kaiser, 1961; Iwand, H. *The Righteousness of Faith according to Luther.* Trans. R. Harrisville. Wipf & Stock, 2008; Iwand, H. *Um den rechten Glauben: Gesammelte Aufsätze.* Ed. K. Steck. Kaiser, 1959; Iwand, H. "Wider den Missbrach des *pro me* als methodisches Prinzip in der Theologie." In *Rechtfertigung als Grundbegriff evangelischer Theologie: Eine Textsammlung,* ed. G. Sauter, 274–79. Kaiser, 1989; Seim, J. *Hans Joachim Iwand: Eine Biographie.* Kaiser, 1999.

GREGORY WALTER

J

Jacobs, Henry Eyster

The influential historian, theologian, and church leader Henry Eyster Jacobs (1844–1932) served for much of his career at the Lutheran Theological Seminary at Philadelphia, in successive roles as professor, dean, and president. Jacobs graduated from two institutions of the General Synod, Pennsylvania College in 1862 (now Gettysburg College) and Gettysburg Seminary in 1865, but he eventually identified himself with the more conservative position that led to the founding of Philadelphia Seminary in 1864 and the formation of the General Council in 1867. He was licensed and then ordained by the Pittsburgh Synod in 1868 and served at both Thiel College and Pennsylvania College before his move to the Philadelphia Seminary.

Jacobs served as author, translator, or editor for a number of works, including *The Lutheran Movement in England* (1890), *A History of the Evangelical Lutheran Church in the United States* (1893), the *Lutheran Cyclopedia* (coeditor, 1899), the *Book of Concord* (1882), and numerous articles and essays in the popular church press.

Jacobs exerted an important moderating influence between the different factions within Eastern Lutheranism. Respected by all sides, he played a significant role in bringing the General Synod, General Council, and United Synod in the South together for work producing *The Common Service* (1888), the *Common Service Book with Hymnal* (1917), and in the movement culminating in the eventual reunification of all three bodies into the United Lutheran Church in America (ULCA) in 1918 on a common confessional basis.

See also General Council of the Evangelical Lutheran Church in North America; General Synod

Bibliography

Fisher, R. H. "Henry Eyster Jacobs." In *Witness at the Crossroads: Gettysburg Lutheran Seminary Servants in Public Life*, ed. F. K. Wentz, 99–111. Lutheran Theological Seminary at Gettysburg, 2001; Horn, Henry E., ed. *Memoirs of Henry Eyster Jacobs: Notes on a Life of a Churchman*. 3 vols. Church Management Service, 1974; Jacobs, H. E. Papers. Lutheran Archives Center of Philadelphia. Lutheran Theological Seminary of Philadelphia.

SUSAN WILDS MCARVER

Jammo, Daffa

Daffa Jammo (1910–2002) was an Ethiopian church leader. When a German mission station opened at Aira, he assisted and later helped to prepare a small Oromo-German dictionary as well as teaching material on catechisms of the Christian faith. In October 1933 Daffa went to Addis Ababa for two years of teacher training. He returned to Aira and was soon ordained as the first Ethiopian pastor in the Lutheran Church. During the Italian occupation, the Aira mission compound survived due to his supervision. He wrote twenty-seven books.

See also Ethiopia

Bibliography

Menberu, D. "Daffa Jammo (*Kes*) 1910 to 2002: Ethiopian Evangelical Church Mekane Yesus (EECMY) Ethiopia." In *Dictionary of African Christian Biography*. http://www.dacb.org/stories/ethiopia/daffa_jammo.html. Overseas Ministries Study Center, 2004.

FRIEDER LUDWIG

Japan

There are six major Lutheran church bodies and a number of smaller ones in Japan, totaling about thirty thousand members. The largest of them, the Japan Evangelical Lutheran Church (JELC), has about 140 congregations with around twenty thousand members. It has congregations throughout the nation. The Japan Lutheran Church (Nihon Ruteru Kyodan: NRK) has around thirty-five congregations in the Tokyo, Fukushima, Hokkaido, Niigata, and Okinawa areas, with around three thousand members. The Kinki Evangelical Lutheran Church has around thirty congregations in the Osaka, Wakayama, Nara, and Mie areas, with around twenty-five hundred members. The West Japan Evangelical Lutheran Church has around forty congregations in Osaka, Hyogo, Tottori, Shimane, Okayama, Hiroshima, and Chiba with three thousand members. The Japan Lutheran Brethren Church has around thirty congregations in the Akita, Miyagi, Aomori, Niigata, Kanagawa, and Saitama areas and has about nine hundred members. The Japan Fellowship Deaconry Evangelical Church has fifteen congregations in Osaka, Kobe, Ehime, and Tokyo and has about eight hundred members.

In 1892 the United Synod of the Evangelical Lutheran Church in the South (USA), now the ELCA, sent two Lutheran missionaries to the southern island of Kyushu. They began their mission activities and soon expanded to other parts of Kyushu Island, and even to the Tokyo area. In 1900 the Lutheran Evangelical Association in Finland (LEAF or SLEY [Suomen Luterilainen Evankeliumiyhdistys]) sent missionaries from Finland, then a Russian possession. They arrived in Hokkaido, the northernmost Japanese island, and initiated work there. World War II presented a severe test to all the religious bodies in Japan, including Christian churches. In 1941 the government forced all Protestant churches to merge into one denomination, the United Church of Christ in Japan. After the war, in 1947, the Lutherans withdrew from the United Church of Christ and reorganized to be a Lutheran church body. By 1963, the LEAF and the Augustana Synod (USA) decided to work with the Japan Evangelical Lutheran Church, and the Tokai Evangelical Lutheran Church joined the JELC.

Twelve Lutheran churches from Europe and America began their mission work in Japan between 1948 and 1954. The congregations that missionaries from the LCMS established became the foundation of the Japan Lutheran Church. Likewise, the West Japan Evangelical Lutheran Church was formed by the congregations that the Norwegian Lutheran Mission (NLM) established, and later the congregation that the Finnish Lutheran Mission (FLM) established joined the West Japan Evangelical Lutheran Church (WJELC). The Norwegian Mission Society (NMS) worked to form the Kinki Evangelical Lutheran Church, and the Evangelical Lutheran Free Church in Norway (ELFCN) had been working with it until recently. Likewise, the Lutheran Brethren Mission gave birth to the Japan Lutheran Brethren Church and the Fellowship Deaconry Mission to the Japan Fellowship Deaconry Church.

Major Lutheran churches had once jointly formed Seibunsha (Lutheran Publication Co.) and published Lutheran and Christian books and materials, including Luther's Works, the Book of Concord, and a common Lutheran hymnal. Most churches have sponsored the broadcasting of *The Lutheran Hour*. The churches maintain colleges, graduate schools, high schools, junior high schools, grade schools, kindergartens, nursery schools, homes for the elderly, camps, and Bible schools.

Some churches have been sending missionaries abroad, to such regions and countries as North and South America, Germany, Indonesia, and Hong Kong. The Japan Evangelical Lutheran Church and the Japan Lutheran Church sponsor a joint seminary in Tokyo; the West Japan Evangelical Lutheran Church and the Kinki Evangelical Lutheran Church jointly run a seminary in Kobe; and the Japan Lutheran Brethren Church has a seminary in Sendai. The Japan Evangelical Lutheran Church and the Kinki Evangelical Lutheran Church have association with the Lutheran World Federation. The Japan Lutheran Church is a member of the International Lutheran Council.

See also Kitamori, Kazoh; Nabetani, Gyoji; Tokuzen, Kazuyoshi

MAKITO MASAKI

Jenson, Robert W.

Born in 1930, Robert W. Jenson is a systematic theologian. After completing a dissertation on Karl Barth's doctrine of God at the University of Heidelberg under the supervision of Peter Brunner, Jenson spent his early career teaching theology at Luther College in Decorah, Iowa, and at Mansfield College, Oxford University. Then he served for two decades as professor of systematic theology at Lutheran Theological Seminary in Gettysburg, Pennsylvania. While later teaching in the religion department of St. Olaf College in Northfield, Minnesota, Jenson and Carl E. Braaten cofounded the Center for Catholic and Evangelical Theology and its journal *Pro Ecclesia*. Following his retirement from teaching, he accepted a position as senior scholar for research at the Center for Theological Inquiry, Princeton, New Jersey.

Jenson's sizeable literary output exhibits a distinct trajectory of development. An early phase (up to the early 1970s), marked by texts addressing issues fashionable during the period (Barth's theology, religion as a problem, theological language, etc.), was followed by two decades of general works on Lutheran theology, ecumenism, and various theological loci, culminating in a two-volume *Systematic Theology*. Jenson subsequently turned his attention to projects consisting of interpretations of texts, including two theological commentaries on Old Testament books (Song of Songs and Ezekiel) and a short monograph on the development of the canon and creeds in early Christianity.

Jenson's influence on contemporaneous Lutheran theology is difficult to calculate. His career-spanning appreciation for certain aspects of Barth's theology, commitment to theology's ecumenical responsibilities, "strong" ecclesiology and sacramental theology, and support for the so-called New Finnish interpretation of Luther put him closer to other confessional traditions than to certain streams within North American Lutheranism. Perhaps his most significant role has been as a foil, especially insofar as he has challenged Lutheran theology to take seriously the problems of time and history, not least in relation to ecclesiology and the doctrine of God.

Bibliography

Gunton, C. E., ed. *Trinity, Time, and Church: A Response to the Theology of Robert W. Jenson*. Eerdmans, 2000; Jenson, R. W. *Systematic Theology*. 2 vols. Oxford University Press, 1997–99; Jenson, R. W. *The Triune Identity: God according to the Gospel*. Fortress, 1982; Swain, S. R. *The God of the Gospel: Robert Jenson's Trinitarian Theology*. IVP Academic, 2013.

R. David Nelson

Jews

Luther's attitudes toward Jews and Judaism were important in his own time and continued to shape Lutheran opinion through the National Socialist era in Germany. The Nazis' propagandistic use of Luther's 1543 anti-Jewish polemics during the 1930s and 1940s raised questions about Luther's authority within the Lutheran tradition and whether Lutherans share a measure of responsibility for the Holocaust.

From his first series of Psalms lectures until his final "Admonition against the Jews," given from the pulpit in Eisleben shortly before his death in 1546, Luther referred to Jews frequently in his writings. Following Augustine's "Doctrine of Witness," he believed that their very existence in the Diaspora served as a proof for the truth of the Christian faith, since they continued to suffer the judgment of God for their rejection of Christ. Jews functioned as a trope within Luther's theology, with Jews exemplifying the opposite of the virtues that a faithful Christian should demonstrate. Instead of trusting in the grace of God, Jews sought to justify themselves through dutiful keeping of the law. Despite the loss of their homeland, kingship, temple, and temple priesthood fifteen hundred years earlier, Jews continued to assume that their covenant with God was still in effect. They hated Christ instead of loving and serving him. They mocked and blasphemed against him, just as their ancestors had done. They displayed arrogance and lovelessness toward non-Jews rather than loving their neighbors as themselves (Kaufmann 72).

At no time in his life did Luther have regular contact with his Jewish contemporaries. The only territory near Wittenberg where Jews lived was the county of Mansfeld. Although Luther visited Rome, Frankfurt am Main, and Worms, no reliable account survives that attests to contacts between him and Jews living in those large Jewish communities. The few encounters that he had with Jews served to confirm his previous opinions. When he met several rabbis in Wittenberg in 1526, Luther tried to convince them of the Christian interpretation of messianic prophecies in the Old Testament, but they rejected his assertions. As Luther recalled in a sermon that he gave on Jer. 23:6, "They did not stick to the text, but tried to escape from it" (WA 20:569.36–37). Decades later, in *On the Ineffable Name*, Luther wrote about the same conversation, "Despite my urging, they said that they must believe their rabbis and refused to allow me to offer any text" (WA 53:589.16–20). Luther's mention of a conversation with a "pious, baptized Jew," probably Bernhard Göppingen, in *That Jesus Christ Was Born a Jew* (LW 45:200) encouraged him in his belief that Jews could repent and believe in Christ "from the heart."

While Jews and Judaism played an important role in Luther's fundamental theology, he wrote only five books specifically related to Jews and Judaism, the so-called *Judenschriften*. In the first of these, *That Jesus Christ Was Born a Jew* (1523; LW 45:199–229), Luther decried the mistreatment of Jews, writing that Christians had treated Jews as "dogs, not human beings" (200). His criticism was less occasioned by humanitarian concern but rather was intended to contrast the old ungodly medieval church with the renewed church where the gospel was openly taught. Over the course of the book, Luther sketches out several conversionary arguments drawn from Old Testament prooftexts such as Gen. 3:15, and in the conclusion he appeals to Christians to treat Jews as their neighbors. He concludes: "If some of them should prove stiff-necked, what of it? After all, we ourselves are not all good Christians either" (229).

The other four *Judenschriften* were composed during the final decade of Luther's life, between 1538 and 1543, and are far more hostile in tone. By this time, Luther feared the influence of Jewish thought and biblical interpretation on Christian "Judaizers," whether Sabbatarian Anabaptists or Christian Hebraists (scholars dedicated to a close reading of Hebrew literature). In all of these writings Luther addressed Christian readers, both to "strengthen their faith" and to warn them of the dangers that "Jewish lies" posed for them. *Against the Sabbatarians* (1538) was the first instance since 1523 that Luther addressed Jews and Judaism in a public fashion, and he did so in the context of fighting Protestant heresy (LW 47:65–98). According to a letter that Luther received from Count Wolfgang Schlick of Falkenau, a group of Moravian Anabaptists were not only observing the Sabbath rather than Sunday, but they were also circumcising themselves, as if the Galatian heresy were being reborn in Luther's own time. Luther addressed the controversy by presenting a two-part argument for the Christian supersession of Jews as the chosen people of God. Luther asserted that for the past fifteen hundred years Jews had visibly suffered under the wrath of God, and that the Scriptures clearly taught that the law of Moses was valid only for a limited time and was no longer binding.

In late 1542, Luther received another letter from Count Wolfgang Schlick, this time with a dialogue between a Christian and a Jew, probably Sebastian Münster's *Messiahs of the Christians and the Jews* (1529; rev. ed., 1539), where the Jew sought to refute Christian interpretations of Old Testament prophecy. Luther wrote a three-part polemical response to what he perceived as the growing danger posed this time by Christian Hebraists, who not only reported Jewish interpretations of Scripture but also adopted, praised, and promulgated them. Luther spends most of *On the Jews and Their*

Lies (LW 47:137–306), the longest and most important of the this threefold response, attacking the religious claims of Judaism, and explaining a series of prooftexts such as Gen. 49:10 to demonstrate that Christianity has replaced Judaism as the only true faith. He also responds to some of the truth claims of Judaism, as he understood them from Antonius Margaritha's *Entire Jewish Faith* (1530). At the very end of the book, Luther offers "political" advice to Protestant rulers on how they have to act if they are to protect their subjects and lands from the dangers that he believes Jews pose through their usury, malice, blasphemies, and "lies" concerning the teaching of Scripture. Luther believed that exiling the Jews was the best policy option, but he also provided secular authorities with a shocking list of measures that they could impose on their Jewish subjects to limit the harm that they could cause. His advice included burning down synagogues, confiscating Jewish books, forbidding rabbis to teach, forbidding Jews to practice usury, and forcing them to perform manual labor (LW 47:268–72). Incongruously, Luther believed, even during the final years of his life, that Christians were to treat Jews kindly in their personal dealings. By contrast, rulers could and should show what he termed "sharp mercy" toward Jews (LW 47:268, 292). The political sphere and the realm of personal relations called for two very different ways of dealing with Jews.

The other two 1543 *Judenschriften* function as appendixes to *On the Jews and Their Lies*, though each work has its own particular argument. *On the Ineffable Name* (WA 53:579–648) focuses on two particular Jewish attacks on Jesus: *Toledot Yeshu*'s explanation of Jesus's miracles as acts of magic and Jewish criticisms of the Christian doctrine of the virgin birth (Isa. 7; Matt. 1). Luther employed his most vituperative, toxic invective in response to Jewish polemical attacks on the person and work of Christ. Even some of Luther's closest associates, such as Philip Melanchthon and Justus Jonas, were apparently shocked by the

intemperate violence of Luther's anti-Jewish rhetoric in this book. Yet in the conclusion to the book, Luther focuses his attention not on Jews and Judaism, but on Christian Hebraists, urging them to foreswear Jewish biblical interpretation. *On the Last Words of David* (LW 15:267–352) was also addressed to Christian Hebraists. In it Luther provides a model interpretation of 2 Sam. 23:1–7, highlighting the support that he believed it gave for the doctrine of the Trinity and the dual nature of Christ (human and divine). He asserts that any exposition of the passage that does not include these doctrines is Judaizing.

Reconciling Luther's more tolerant attitude toward Jews and Judaism of 1523 and his harsh, foul-mouthed, politically dangerous attacks on them in 1543 has been a concern not only for Luther biographers and Lutheran church historians but also for Jewish historians and scholars in many other fields because of their complicated reception history. Their immediate impact during Luther's own lifetime appears to have been somewhat limited. Landgrave Philip of Hesse, whose domain was home to a Jewish community, found the exegetical parts of *On the Jews and Their Lies* interesting, but he largely ignored the political advice Luther offered. While some Protestant princes changed their Jewish policies in small ways, only Prince George of Anhalt, Margrave Hans of Brandenburg-Küstrin, and Count Albrecht of Mansfeld expelled Jews from their lands.

Between Luther's death and the early eighteenth century, Lutheran theologians drew both from *That Jesus Christ Was Born a Jew* and from the 1543 polemics as they advised princes on Jewish policy, justified missionary outreach to Jews, and sought to refute Judaism as a religious error. The advice that the theological faculties of Jena and Frankfurt an der Oder gave the city fathers of Hamburg in 1611 is notable in that they drew on both the earlier and later Luther, yet both concluded that a Christian magistrate could tolerate the presence of a Jewish community. Lutheran

Orthodox thinkers were more inclined to follow the later Luther, while Pietists found the earlier Luther more congenial because (in their view) he supported missionary outreach to Jews and was concerned that Christians treat Jews humanely. Wallmann asserts that both German Pietists and Enlightenment theologians ignored Luther's later anti-Jewish polemics so that they were largely forgotten outside of scholarly circles (83–86). Among Lutherans outside of Germany, these writings were almost unknown until the 1930s. The first partial translations of *On the Jews and Their Lies* into Swedish (1934), Danish (1938), and English (1948), and a complete translation into Finnish (1939), were made by Nazi sympathizers.

The appropriation and use of Luther's 1543 polemics by the Nazis and the German Christians before the Nazi seizure of power and while Hitler ruled Germany have raised serious questions about Luther himself and his theological authority within the Lutheran tradition. Bishop Martin Sasse's exultant pamphlet *Weg mit Ihnen* (Away with them) celebrated the destruction of all of Germany's synagogues during Kristallnacht (which took place on the anniversary of Luther's birth) in 1938 as fulfilling Luther's demands for attacks on Judaism. During the Nuremberg trials Julius Streicher claimed that "Luther would very probably sit in my place in the defendant's dock" if he were still alive. This Nazi portrayal of Luther, however, was in its own way as selective as the Pietist appropriation of a Luther who rejected anti-Semitism, favored Jewish missions, and stressed the duty of Christians to treat Jews as neighbors.

Lutheran responses to Luther's anti-Jewish works since the Holocaust have taken several forms. Lutheran thinkers and church bodies in Germany and elsewhere have largely rejected Luther's 1543 *Judenschriften* as unchristian. Franklin Sherman, in his introduction to the first complete English translation of *On the Jews and Their Lies* (1971), stated flatly that publishing this book was not an endorsement of its "distorted views of the Jewish faith." It was printed in the Luther's Works series only to "make available the necessary documents for scholarly study of this aspect of Luther's thought, which has played so fateful a role in the development of anti-Semitism in Western culture" (LW 47:123). Addressing Luther's anti-Judaism throughout his corpus has proved to be a more divisive question. Traditionalist Lutheran bodies such as the Lutheran Church–Missouri Synod have argued that Scripture and the Lutheran confessions, not Luther's "personal writings and opinions," form the basis of Lutheran doctrine and practice. They deny any responsibility for the use of Luther's anti-Jewish writings during the Third Reich. The LCMS statement against anti-Semitism concludes that Lutherans should adopt this attitude toward the Jews: "We want to treat them with Christian love and pray for them, so that they might become converted and receive the Lord" (Resolution 3–09 [1983]). By contrast, the Evangelical Lutheran churches in Germany, and some Lutheran bodies elsewhere such as the Evangelical Lutheran Church in America, have officially stated that they partly share the guilt of the Holocaust because of Luther's anti-Semitic views and their propagandistic use by the Nazis. Discussion of these themes has been an important feature of the Lutheran-Jewish dialogue since the 1960s.

See also Holocaust

Bibliography

Brecht, M. *Martin Luther: The Preservation of the Church, 1532–1546*. Fortress, 1993; Burnett, S. G. "Dialogue of the Deaf: Hebrew Pedagogy and Anti-Jewish Polemic in Sebastian Münster's *Messiahs of the Christians and the Jews* (1529/39)." *ARG* 91 (2000): 168–90; Gritsch, E. *Martin—God's Court Jester: Luther in Retrospect*. Fortress, 1983; Hagen, K. "Luther's So-Called Judenschriften: A Genre Approach." *ARG* 90 (1999): 130–58; Kaufmann, T. "Luther and the Jews." In *Jews, Judaism and the Reformation in Sixteenth Century Germany*, ed. D. P. Bell and S. G. Burnett, 69–104. Brill, 2006; Missouri Synod–Lutheran Church. "To Clarify Position on Anti-Semitism." Resolution 3–9, July 1983. http://www.lcms.org/faqs/lcms views; Osten Sacken, P. von der. *Martin Luther und die Juden: Neu untersucht anhand von Anton Margarithas "Der gantz Jüdisch glaub" (1530/31)*. Kohlhammer, 2002; Schramm, B., and K. I. Stjerna, eds. *Martin Luther, the*

Bible, and the Jewish People: A Reader. Fortress, 2012; Schubert, A. "Fremde Sünde: Zur Theologie von Luthers späten Judenschriften." In Martin Luther: Biographie und Theologie, ed. D. Korsch and V. Leppin, 251–70. Mohr Siebeck, 2010; Sherman, F. Bridges: Documents of the Christian-Jewish Dialogue. 2 vols. Paulist Press, 2011–13; Wallmann, J. "The Reception of Luther's Writings on the Jews from the Reformation to the End of the Nineteenth Century." LQ 1 (1987): 72–97.

STEPHEN G. BURNETT

Ji Brothers

Won-Yong Ji (1924–2012) and Won-Sang Ji (1927–98) are brothers who contributed to the formation and development of the Lutheran Church in Korea (LCK).

Both were born in what is now North Korea. At age sixteen Won-Yong "by chance found a book on the great work of Martin Luther." The next year he was baptized at a Presbyterian church. Having graduated from Han-Kook Theological College and Seminary (1947), he went to the United States to study (1948). After studying at various universities there and Germany, he received his ThD degree at Concordia Seminary, St. Louis (1957). While studying there, he appealed to the Lutheran Church–Missouri Synod to initiate mission work in Korea. It sent three missionaries to Korea in 1958. He joined the mission team later in 1958 and served in Korea in 1958–68.

Won-Yong subsequently assumed positions as Asia Secretary of the Lutheran World Federation in Geneva (1968–75) and as a consultant to the Department of Missions of the Evangelical Lutheran Church in Bavaria, Germany (1975–78). In 1978 he was called to Concordia Seminary to teach, where he continued to teach even beyond his retirement in 1997. While at Concordia, he regularly returned to Korea for teaching, preaching, lecturing, and research. He was the first director of the Lutheran Theological Academy.

Won-Yong called himself a "lifelong student of Martin Luther." He was the general editor of Luther's Works–Korean Edition (12 vols.). He also translated the Book of Concord and Walther's Law and Gospel and authored numerous journal articles and several other books, including a history of Lutheranism in Korea. He received the "Best Publication Award" (1990) from the Association of Christian Publishers in Korea; a national honor of a Suk Ryu Jang medal (1972), and the "1996 Vision Award" from the Lutheran Society for Missiology.

Won-Sang graduated from Han-Kook Theological Seminary (1957). He studied also at Lutheran Seminary in Japan (1967). He was ordained and served as pastor at Immanuel Lutheran Church (1965–66) and Trinity Lutheran Church (1967–79). He became the first president of the LCK (1971), remaining in the position until 1993. He was the director of the Korea Bethel Series (1974–98) and chairman of the Luther University Board of Regents (1983–98).

Won-Sang's leadership reached far beyond his own church. A mediator and visionary for Christian unity and social service, he was involved in numerous ecumenical enterprises: Korean Bible Society (1965–98), Christian Broadcasting System (1985–93), Joint Hymnal Committee (1990–98), Love in Action blood donation campaign (1992–98), and Korea Christian Leaders' Association (1994–98), among others. He served on the Continuation Committee of the International Lutheran Conference (1975–84) and as an adviser on the LWF Council (1990–97).

He received a national honor of a Dong Baek Jang medal (1988), Presidential Prize for Love in Action blood donation (1992), Korea Red Cross Gold Prize for blood donation (1993), and US Military Chaplain Aaron and Hur Prize (1995).

See also Korea

Bibliography
Ji, W.-Y. By the Grace of God I Am What I Am. Lutheran Heritage Foundation, 2004; Ji, W.-Y. A History of Lutheranism in Korea: A Personal Account. Concordia Seminary Press, 1988.

JIN-SEOP EOM

Joachim II Hector

As elector of the Margraviate of Brandenburg in the Holy Roman Empire, Joachim II

Hector (1505–71) was a cautious advocate of the Evangelical faith who explicitly supported Lutheranism in his lands beginning in 1555. Joachim II was a prominent member of the Hohenzollern dynasty and the son of Elector Joachim I Nestor (r. 1499–1535) and Elizabeth of Denmark (1485–1555). Joachim II's father was a staunch defender of Roman Catholicism, but his mother was an adherent of Luther. When Luther's ideas circulated in the 1520s, Joachim I reacted guardedly and joined Emperor Charles V and others in suppressing the Evangelical movement. However, after Joachim I's death, Joachim II revealed an interest in Evangelical ideas and slowly introduced Lutheran reforms into his territory. The elector hoped to nurture Evangelical teaching quietly without changing traditional ceremonies, angering the emperor, or joining the militant Protestant Smalcaldic League.

When the Smalcald War began in 1546, Joachim II supported Charles V and the Roman Catholic alliance. After the military defeat of the Protestants, Joachim II's court theologian, Johann Agricola, helped draft the Augsburg Interim, and Joachim himself endorsed the so-called Leipzig Interim, which restored many traditional ceremonies eliminated in other Lutheran territories. However, the Peace of Augsburg (1555) allowed territorial rulers to choose the religion in their lands. Joachim II selected Lutheranism and worked for its full implementation. At Joachim II's death in 1571, his son, Elector John George (r. 1571–98), supported the Gnesio-Lutheran faction and sponsored negotiations leading to the Formula of Concord by sending Andreas Musculus to take part in drafting that document in its later stages.

See also Augsburg Interim; Holy Roman Empire; Leipzig Proposal (Interim); Peace of Augsburg; Smalcald War

Bibliography

Delius, W. "Die Kirchenpolitik des Kurfürsten Joachim II. von Brandenburg in den Jahren 1535–1541." *Jahrbuch für brandenburgische Kirchengeschichte* 40 (1965): 86–123; Nischan, B. *Prince, People, and Confession: The Second Reformation in Brandenburg.* University of Pennsylvania Press, 1994.

Michael J. Halvorson

Jonas, Justus

Eventually a friend and colleague of Luther at the University of Wittenberg and preacher in Halle, Coburg, and Eisfeld, Justus Jonas (1493–1555) was born Jodocus Koch in Nordhausen and began using the name Justus Jonas during his university studies at Erfurt, which began in 1506. After studying with the arts faculty in Erfurt, Jonas moved to Wittenberg in 1511 to begin his study of law. When he completed his legal studies in 1514, he moved back to Erfurt. There he was ordained a priest, received a doctorate in both law and theology, joined the cathedral chapter, and taught law at the university. While at the university in Erfurt, he helped reform its curriculum along humanist lines. Jonas was in regular contact with Erasmus and initially preferred his reform proposals to Luther's. At the Leipzig Debate between Luther and John Eck in 1519, however, Jonas was persuaded by Luther, and shortly thereafter he began to correspond with him. In 1521 Jonas accompanied Luther to the Diet of Worms, and soon thereafter, he became a professor at the University of Wittenberg and provost at the Wittenberg castle church. Just one year later, he was named dean of the theology faculty, a position he held for ten years. During his time in Wittenberg, he was also involved with writing new church orders for Ducal Saxony and the town of Zerbst. In 1541, Jonas moved to a preaching position in Halle, where he also wrote new church orders for the city in 1543. In 1546 the Saxon duke Moritz, a Lutheran prince in league with the Catholic Emperor Charles V in the Smalcald War, captured Halle, and Jonas fled. When he returned a few months later, Jonas exiled all remaining monks and nuns and suppressed Catholic practices. The ongoing Smalcald War led to another exile and return for Jonas. Finally Jonas was barred from preaching in Halle but allowed to teach Latin there. In 1550 he left

Halle to become court preacher in Coburg. In 1553 he became a superintendent in Eisfeld, where he died in 1555.

During his time in Wittenberg, Jonas forged deep friendships with both Luther and Melanchthon. His relationship with Melanchthon was somewhat strained by his opposition to the so-called Leipzig Interim that Melanchthon helped draft. For Luther, Jonas was a steadfast source of encouragement through his most arduous spiritual trials. Luther comforted Jonas at the death of Jonas's wife, and Jonas counseled Luther on his deathbed and preached his funeral sermon in Eisleben. Perhaps his most enduring contributions to the Reformation were his translations of both Luther's and Melanchthon's writings, which number more than thirty-five.

See also Erasmus of Rotterdam (Desiderius Erasmus Roterodamus); Leipzig Proposal (Interim); Melanchthon, Philip; Saxonies

Bibliography

Delius, W. *Lehre und Leben Justus Jonas, 1493–1555.* Bertelsmann, 1952; Lehmann, M. *Justus Jonas: Loyal Reformer.* Fortress, 1963; Pressel, T., *Justus Jonas.* Friderichs, 1862.

ANNA MARIE JOHNSON

Jüngel, Eberhard

For many years professor of systematic theology and director of the Evangelisches Stift (Evangelical [Lutheran] Foundation) at the University of Tübingen, Eberhard Jüngel (b. 1934) is regarded as one of the seminal European Protestant theologians since Karl Barth. His work extends into a number of areas, most notably systematic theology, New Testament interpretation, philosophy of religion, and ecumenism. Jüngel's theology is constructive and hermeneutical, especially notable for its rhetorical panache and depth of analysis.

Jüngel's early theology reflects the milieu of mid-twentieth-century thought at the intersection of critical university scholarship and Christian faith and practice. His dissertation *Paulus und Jesus*, supervised by Marburg New Testament scholar Ernst Fuchs, is a thoroughgoing exercise of the "New Hermeneutic"—shorthand for midcentury efforts, led by Fuchs, Jüngel, Zurich theologian Gerhard Ebeling, and others, to link the identity of Jesus of Nazareth to the Christ proclaimed by the church. Within the first decade of his career, Jüngel also wrote significant pieces on analogy, the doctrine of the Trinity (in dialogue with Barth), justification, and death—all prominent themes in academic Christian theology during the period. His best-known monograph, translated into English as *God as the Mystery of the World* (1976), finds him drawing on his breadth of expertise to answer the questions of how God can be known and heard in the world. Since the 1980s much of his work has been marked by his participation in multilateral ecumenical dialogues. His signal contribution in this area is the monograph *Justification*, published right around the signing of the Joint Declaration of the Doctrine of Justification and consisting of a formidable critique of that document. Since the turn of the millennium he has expanded his oeuvre with works in the areas of ecclesiology, sacramental theology, and the location of theology among the university disciplines.

See also Barth, Karl; Ebeling, Gerhard; Justification

Bibliography

Jüngel, E. *God as the Mystery of the World: On the Foundation of the Theology of the Crucified One in the Dispute between Theism and Atheism.* Bloomsbury, 2014; Jüngel, E. *Justification: The Heart of the Christian Faith.* Bloomsbury, 2014; Nelson, R. D., ed. *Indicative of Grace—Imperative of Freedom: Essays in Honour of Eberhard Jüngel in His 60th Year.* Bloomsbury, 2014; Nelson, R. D. *The Interruptive Word: Eberhard Jüngel on the Sacramental Structure of God's Relation ot the World.* Bloomsbury, 2014; Webster, J. B. *Eberhard Jüngel: An Introduction to His Theology.* Cambridge University Press, 1986.

R. DAVID NELSON

Jurisprudence

The Reformation was a theological movement that integrated legal issues into it and thus influenced modern institutions of public and private law, especially in the areas of education, marriage, and the relief of the poor. The Reformers were indebted to medieval and humanist legal teachings, but the Reformation "was not a revision or reversion of medieval legal thought but rather a skillful blend of Catholic and Evangelical, as well as canon and civil law doctrines and teachings" (Witte, *Law and Protestantism*, 184).

The Reformation did not produce a uniform jurisprudence. The Reformers used and developed legal science from different perspectives. In general, natural law continued to be the foundation on which key elements of judicial procedure rested in spite of the conviction that fallen humans were not capable of fully understanding or completely observing it. The principles of natural law were applied in the human conscience guided by faith and inspired by grace. Civil law was understood merely as a reflection of the will of the lawmaker. A general characteristic was also a reliance on the Decalogue and other biblical sources of legal doctrine. However, Roman law and portions of canon law were also used. Lutheranism's impact on the reception of Roman law in Germany was significant.

Martin Luther was not interested in jurisprudence as such, and his legal views were subservient to his theological doctrine. His doctrine of the two kingdoms, especially as expressed in *On Temporal Authority* (1523), explicated the idea that all legal endeavors belong to the civil government. Yet in his writings Luther treated many legal questions, as on marriage, usury, commerce, crime, property, and social welfare. After initial hesitation, he also saw the endorsement of Roman law as an important means of expressing support for imperial unity.

Other reformers—such as Philip Melanchthon, John Calvin, and especially the lawyers Johannes Oldendorp (ca. 1480–1567), Melchior Kling (1504–71), Hieronymus Baumgartner (1498–1565), and Johannes Scheidewein (1519–68)—valued jurisprudence. In slight contrast to Luther, Melanchthon supported the law of nature as politically relevant and thus related to the *usus politicus sive civilis* (civil use of the law). This law was to be entrusted to the pious territorial state in order to create peace and to reinforce the civil regiment with laws and arms. For Melanchthon, not only the divine law but also the civil law served both to make humans aware of their depravity and to impel them to grace. Oldendorp established an Evangelical order of law and civil society in the Protestant German states. He maintained the common good as the highest ideal of civil order. He also adopted the Aristotelian concepts of liberality and commutative justice as the "causes" of law. Later both concepts were fundamental to neo-Thomist legal thought (Berman 2004).

See also Law, Uses of the; Natural Theology; State; Two Realms

Bibliography

Berman, H. *Law and Revolution*. Vol. 2, *The Impact of the Protestant Reformation on the Western Legal Tradition*. Cambridge University Press, 2004; Estes, J. "Luther's Attitude toward the Legal Traditions of His Time." *Luther-Jahrbuch* 76 (2009): 77–110; Mäkinen, V., ed. *Lutheran Reformation and the Law*. Studies in Medieval and Reformation Traditions: History, Culture, Religion, Ideas 112. Brill, 2006; Pennington, K. "Politics in Western Jurisprudence." In *The Jurists' Philosophy of Law from Rome to the Seventeenth Century*, ed. A. Padovani and P. G. Stein, 157–211. A Treatise of Legal Philosophy and General Jurisprudence 7. Springer, 2007; Prodi, P. *Eine Geschichte der Gerechtigkeit: Vom Recht Gottes zum modernen Rechtsstaat*. Beck, 2003; Whitman, J. *The Legacy of Roman Law in the German Romantic Era: Historical Vision and Legal Change*. Princeton University Press, 1999; Witte, J., Jr. *Law and Protestantism: The Legal Teachings of the Lutheran Reformation*. Cambridge University Press, 2002; Witte, J., Jr. *The Reformation of Rights: Law, Religion, and Human Rights in Early Modern Calvinism*. Cambridge University Press, 2007.

VIRPI MÄKINEN

Justification

In the words of Valentin Löscher (1673–1749), Lutherans confess that justification is the article by which "the church stands or falls." Throughout the works of Luther and many other Evangelical reformers and in the Book of Concord, justification is presented as forensic: God evaluates sinners by means of Christ's alien, external righteousness, which offers a change of status before God, who evaluates, or "reckons," sinners to be righteous, not on the basis of their merit but instead because of the righteousness of Christ, the "mediator." For Luther, Melanchthon, and the Lutheran Confessions, the righteousness of faith does not depend on human works but instead on God's favorable regard and his "reckoning" on the basis of grace. Luther developed his views on justification in the context of late medieval Scholasticism, particularly the theology of Gabriel Biel (1420–96), who balanced God's initiative for salvation with human cooperation by insisting that "out of purely natural powers" (ex puris naturalibus) sinners could "do what is in them" (facere quod in se est). By doing their best they could produce works of "congruent merit," a worthiness or righteousness before God that is not intrinsically worthy, but nonetheless accepted by God as the basis for receiving God's grace. By contrast, Luther's intense study of and lectures on Paul and the Psalms (1513–21), supported by his reading of Augustine, led him to discover a passive righteousness, salvation through trusting God's word of promise of forgiveness, which imparted a new status and thereby a new nature, a "clean heart," for the believer. Such insights led Luther to an unthinkable move for the Scholastic theologians: distinguishing law from gospel. In this distinction, the law is not a manual that presents the steps to travel to God's grace and eventually to eternal life, but instead is a tormentor attacking any self-righteousness one seeks to offer God. The gospel is not "new law," as the Scholastics put it, but instead is a gift, the word of promise that assures terrified consciences of God's mercy given only to sinners, a word that awakens the dead to new life. Luther's discovery of a passive righteousness also allowed him to reframe his concept of active righteousness. Since trust alone sets the sinner right (where the old English term, "rightwises," is closest to Luther's meaning), righteousness can no longer be configured as works that merit righteousness before God. Instead, works take on a new meaning: God needs no works, but the neighbor does.

Luther's view of justification is grounded in the etymology of the German word recht-fertigen, "to justify" or "render righteous," meaning "to do justice to." In its medieval context, rechtfertigen means to inflict punishment "judicially" on the basis of a conviction and thus to execute the law's demands, or "to conduct a legal process as an activity of a judge," "to execute, to kill." From early on, Luther spoke of God's killing and making alive as he described justification, for he insisted that sinners must die (Rom. 6:23) and be resurrected to life in Christ. According to Luther, people are humanized by God's judgment that evaluates them as sinners. His insight is that outside of sheer trust in God's mercy, doing virtuous acts or loving deeds, so valued by late medieval piety and theology as a basis for earning merit, is tantamount to self-righteousness. Sin is thus reconfigured as not primarily misdeeds but instead as misplaced trust in one's own abilities and not complete trust in God's mercy in Christ.

Some scholars, beginning with Albrecht Ritschl and Karl Holl, disassociate Luther from a forensic approach to justification, fearing that it is implausible, a legal fiction, needing ethical or ontological supplementation or warrant. Of necessity, however, Luther's forensic approach conveys a specific effect since the justifying word is a verdict that simultaneously kills sinners and makes them alive. The justifying verdict is a performative word that does what it says and says what it does. Hence the attempt to pit a forensic approach, "being declared righteous," against an effective approach, "being made righteous," does not appropriately apply to Luther. Scholars who reject or criticize Luther's distinctively forensic approach to justification generally do not take Luther's view of language fully into account. He believed that words, especially God's Word, actually alter and create reality, that is, words can make the hearers, even ex nihilo (out of nothing), similar to God's creative

Word that originated and sustains the world. Justification by faith alone, in which God creates new creatures out of the nothingness of sin, parallels Luther's doctrine of creation, in which God creates and preserves all things out of nothingness. For Luther, Melanchthon, and the Lutheran confessions, however, faith in Christ alters not only the status but also the nature of believers: they receive "different, new, clean" hearts. God not only imputes a sinner's faith in Christ as righteousness, but such faith also embraces Christ, who through the Holy Spirit renews us within. For Luther, the article of justification describes how God remakes sinners to be people of faith. An "effective" dimension to justification is crucial for Luther. However, this effective dimension of justification, like the forensic dimension, is something human creatures passively undergo or receive. It takes the form or shape of death and resurrection—exactly what Christians (generally) first receive in the sacrament of holy baptism and in every visible and aural word of God thereafter.

In contrast to Scholastic theology, Luther's discovery was that there are two kinds of righteousness: active and passive. Before God (*coram deo*, "in the presence of God") individuals are rendered passive, suffer the death of the old creature, so that God might be allowed to be their God and to redeem them in Christ. Before the world (*coram mundo*), faith blossoms in good works, to help the neighbor and the world, similar to how good fruit flourishes on a good tree. Luther's teaching on justification is intertwined with a cluster of related themes: (1) an unfree or bound will before God, (2) distinguishing God's alien work of mortifying sinners from God's proper work of vivifying them, (3) God as hidden (*absconditus*) outside of Christ and as graciously offered in the proclaimed Word, (4) distinguishing Christ as gift (*sacramentum*) from Christ as example (*exemplum*), and finally (5) God's agency as mediated in word and sacrament.

Luther's view of justification for theology and wider culture did not always have the theological impact he might have hoped for. Instead, some of Luther's theological heirs welded the doctrine of justification by faith alone onto an anthropology inspired by philosophical concerns that maintained the free choice of the will, a position antithetical to Luther's position of the human before God. In essence, the Lutheran movement did not always maintain an anthropology compatible with Luther's view of justification—a serious weakness, given that Luther himself believed that justification by faith alone was definitive of humanity. While Melanchthon, author of the Augsburg Confession and the Apology of the Augsburg Confession, was a crucial collaborator and coworker with Luther, the later Melanchthon often seemed to imply that the will can passively assent to the divine call or actively reject it. Nevertheless, when faced with Andreas Osiander's denial of the forensic nature of justification by faith in favor of justification by the indwelling of Christ's righteous, divine nature, Melanchthon, his normal adversary Matthias Flacius, and many others rejected Osiander's position. This rejection is reflected in article 3 of the Formula of Concord. Orthodox dogmaticians such as Martin Chemnitz (1522–86) and Johann Gerhard (1582–1637) employed Scholastic categories to present Luther's faith but in so doing failed to construct a consistent approach of a passive role for the human *coram Deo*. Pietists such as Philipp Jakob Spener (1635–1705) tended to subordinate justification to sanctification as growth in godly behavior, while Enlightenment figures such as Immanuel Kant (1724–1804) asserted that freedom is not primarily liberation from sin but instead is experienced as autonomy, a rational exercise in choice when an agent implements the "categorical imperative"—acting on principles that have universal and necessary applicability.

In the nineteenth century, Albrecht Ritschl (1822–89) appropriated Luther's view of forgiveness within an ellipsis bounded by the twin points of forgiveness and ethical responsibilities; distinguishing Luther's view from Melanchthon's, Ritschl criticized Melanchthon's forensic approach. Nevertheless, especially as noticed by Theodosius Harnack (1817–89), Ritschl had overlooked basic elements of Luther's theology, such as God's wrath, judgment, the dialectical distinction between the law and the gospel, as well as Luther's more radical statements about sin and grace. Adolf von Harnack (1851–1930) revived a moralizing approach to Luther and claimed that for Luther justification is both "being righteous and becoming righteous." Similarly, Karl Holl (1866–1926) tended to situate Luther's work within an ethical framework. For Holl, Luther's is a "religion of conscience," one that included the element of "duty." Holl tended to blur the distinction between Luther's earlier pre-Protestant views and his later, more mature views. Thus Holl claimed, in agreement with Ritschl and Adolf von Harnack, that Luther made no distinction between being made righteous and being declared righteous and that Melanchthon was to blame for the forensic approach. Nineteenth- and early twentieth-century Luther studies tended to revamp Luther's view of justification in terms of Kantian approaches to ethics, accentuating human autonomy, the separation of metaphysics from ethics, and defining justification in the light of a "kingdom of ends," in which agents honor the autonomy of their peers. Gerhard Forde (1927–2005) argued that attempts to pit forensic against effective justification are unnecessary and inaccurate since for Luther the more forensic Luther's teaching becomes (esp. in preaching), the more "effective" it is. Reality is dependent on the Word, not vice versa.

A Finnish school of Luther studies, first developed by Tuomo Mannermaa (b. 1937) and growing out of conversations with Orthodox Christians, has aimed to present Luther's view of justification as properly divinization, or *theōsis*. In this perspective, a purely forensic view of justification falls short of the meaning of salvation for Luther, which Mannermaa regards as participation in God's very nature itself. For Mannermaa, when Luther speaks of grace as favor, Luther never disassociates or separates God's forgiveness from the gift of divine indwelling. Indeed, both *favor* (mercy) and *donum* (gift) form an inseparable unity in the person of Christ, who through faith is really, ontically present. Hence, in Mannermaa, the Lutheran Confessions' perspective of a forensic justification is fundamentally at odds with Luther himself. This school accentuates Luther's view of Christ as the "form" of faith in the Galatians lectures (1531). The difference between Luther and his Roman Catholic opponents is over whether it is love that establishes "formal righteousness" (the Roman Catholic position) or Christ himself, united with the believer through faith (Luther).

This view has been criticized by a number of scholars (M. Mattes, S. Paulson, W. Schumacher). The upshot of this critique is that throughout Luther's writings, especially the Galatians commentary (1535), Christ's atoning work in "salvation history" precedes faith. Indeed, because Christ is the object of faith (God's *favor*), he is present in faith as *donum* (gift). Hence, for Luther, salvation is based not on the indwelling Christ who deifies, but forensically on Christ who died for us. Indeed, Mannermaa's view leads to an unnecessary dilemma: *favor* is construed as objective while *donum* is somehow subjective. Instead, these critics argue, the truth is that this is a twofold objectivity. A spoken, "external word"—which is God's *favor* in the form of a gift, grounded both in the objectivity of the cross and also in the proclamation to sinners as a benefit that requires such distribution—imparts both death and life to its hearers. Just as God's will is an active Word ordering creation in Genesis, God's *favor* here is not God's own possession or essence but is precisely God's gift, applied to the unrighteous will (in that sinners are unrighteous). Only on account of this truly objective foundation of imputation as forgiveness for Jesus's sake is the gift (*donum*) of the present Christ preached and so given—not to the old creature as old, but to the new creature as the act of new creation itself. Undoubtedly Luther affirmed that the believer is united with Christ in faith. But it is equally clear that for Luther the Christian is justified on the basis of nothing else but Christ's imputed righteousness.

See also Anthropology; Biel, Gabriel; Finnish Interpretation of Luther; Forde, Gerhard; Harnack, Theodosius Andreas; Holl, Karl; Mannermaa, Tuomo; Sanctification; Ritschl, Albrecht

Bibliography

Ap IV; Bayer, O. *Living by Faith: Justification and Sanctification*. Trans. G. Bromiley. Eerdmans, 2003; CA 4; Ep/SD 3; Forde, G. *Justification by Faith: A Matter of Death and Life*. Fortress, 1982; Forde, G. *The Law-Gospel Debate*. Augsburg, 1969; Kolb, R., and C. Arand. *The Genius of Luther's Theology*. Baker Academic, 2008; Luther, M. *Lectures on Galatians* (1535). LW 26–27; Mannermaa, T. *Christ Present in Faith: Luther's View of Justification*. Trans. K. Stjerna. Fortress, 2005; Mattes, M. *The Role of Justification in Contemporary Theology*. Eerdmans, 2003; Paulson, S. *Lutheran Theology*. T&T Clark, 2011; Schumacher, W., *Who Do I Say That You Are? Anthropology and the Theology of Theosis in the Finnish School of Tuomo Mannermaa*. Wipf & Stock, 2010.

MARK C. MATTES

Just-War Theory

According to the Augsburg Confession, "It is right for Christians . . . to engage in just wars" (art. 16). In affirming the possibility of just war, Augsburg echoed the view of Luther, who stood squarely within the Christian just-war tradition, especially as espoused by Augustine, while also making distinctive contributions to it.

Legitimate political authority. According to Luther, the right to use lethal force is held by political authority. Political authority has been instituted by God to preserve peace, to protect the innocent, and to restrain and punish the wicked. The right to wage war is an extension of government's responsibility to administer justice. "What is just war," writes Luther in *Whether Soldiers, Too, Can Be Saved*, "but the punishment of evildoers and the maintenance of peace?" (LW 46:98). In conceiving war in judicial terms, Luther was following the tradition, but at the same time he reinterpreted government's task in light of his understanding of the two kingdoms. Political authority rules in the kingdom of earth, but not in the kingdom of God. In the kingdom of God, Christ rules without the sword and through the power of the Word. Thus, in the kingdom of God, Christians do not exercise self-defense; they suffer evil rather than resist it. The nature of the kingdom of God also implies limits on the scope of political authority, as became apparent when Luther considered the matter of just cause.

Just cause. Luther defined just cause more narrowly than others in the tradition. For example, against medieval Scholastic justification for crusades, Luther ruled out wars fought for religious causes. Government's only task, Luther believed, was to preserve peace and maintain justice. In *On War against the Turk*, Luther argued that one could not fight against the Ottomans in the name of Christ, "as though our people were an army of Christians against the Turk" (LW 46:165). Christians cannot wage war in Christ's name, because Christ teaches his disciples not to resist evil. Nor can the pope lead a "church army" against the Turks, "for the church ought not to strive or fight with the sword" (LW 46:168). According to Luther, only the Holy Roman emperor was justified in fighting the Turks. Even then, however, the emperor could not wage war as a "defender of the faith," but solely on the grounds that he was protecting his subjects. "The emperor's sword has nothing to do with the faith; it belongs to physical, worldly things" (LW 46:186). Luther thus rejected the idea of the crusade, parting ways with a significant portion of the Christian tradition.

In addition, Luther limited "just cause" to defense. In *Whether Soldiers, Too, Can Be Saved* Luther distinguished sharply between wars of desire and wars of defense (*Notkrieg*), stating baldly that "whoever starts a war is in the wrong" (LW 46:118). According to Karl Dietrich Erdmann, the limitation of just cause to defense was central to Luther's teaching on war (14). Many in the just-war tradition have held to a more expansive list of causes, one that includes things such as avenging injury, defending honor, and exacting retribution. Some, such as David D. Corey and J. Daryl Charles (94–95), have criticized "Luther's abandonment" of the traditional interpretation of just cause, because they believe it ruled out the possibility of military alliances as well as military interventions to help foreign neighbors. However, Luther did allow for defensive military alliances when considering the prospect of an attack on Protestant territories, while the question of humanitarian military interventions is one he never took up. In fact, Luther's definition of just cause would seem to align better than others in the tradition with the contemporary international legal framework established by the United Nations Charter.

Right intention. As a commonly recognized just-war criterion, right intention has both an objective aspect (war should be fought with the aim of establishing peace) and a subjective aspect (war should be fought without malice toward the enemy). Although Luther did not devote special attention to questions of right intention, both aspects of the criterion are present in his thought. Objectively, the purpose of war is to punish wrongdoing and to preserve peace. Subjectively, those who bear the sword perform a work of love. Although "slaying and robbing do not seem to be works of love," in fact they protect the good and preserve "wife and child, house and farm, property, and honor and peace" when performed as part of the soldier's office (LW 46:96). Soldiering is a legitimate vocation through which one serves the neighbor.

Ius in bello. Modern just-war theory devotes considerable attention to questions concerning right conduct in war (*ius in bello*), enunciating principles such as discrimination (to distinguish between combatants and civilians), the use of proportionate means, and so on. Luther never considered *in bello* questions in a notable way, although the horrors of war were well known and discussed by others of his day (see Erasmus's *Querela pacis*).

Political obedience and the right of resistance. In tone and tenor, Luther's political writings emphasize the duty of political obedience, something critics have seized on when charging that Luther taught absolute submission to political authority. The truth is that Luther established definite limits on the duty of obedience. His views on the right of resistance changed toward the end of his life, however, in ways that may not have been entirely consistent.

According to Luther, government's authority extends only over external things, such as life and property, and not over the soul. Thus government cannot command belief. In his treatise *Temporal Authority*, Luther goes so far as to say that government may not restrain heresy even for the sake of public order, since "heresy can never be restrained by force" (LW 45:114). In cases where government seeks to command the soul, Luther counsels noncooperation, or passive disobedience. Additionally, Luther argued that soldiers should not participate in wars they know to be unjust, thereby articulating a moral right of selective conscientious objection (LW 45:125–26; LW 46:130–31).

What Luther rejected was a right to resist even an unjust government with violence. Luther's view on this question was informed largely by his sense of government as a divine institution. Since the right to use force belongs to political authority, those who do not hold political office cannot employ force even if their cause is just. In the case of the Peasants' War, Luther recognized that the peasants had legitimate grievances, but held that those grievances did not justify rebellion. "We do not have the right to use the sword simply because the law and justice are on our side," he wrote in *Admonition to Peace*. "We must also have received power and authority from God" (LW 46:30). Luther's view on resistance was also shaped by his understanding of the two kingdoms or realms. Members of the kingdom of God are prepared to turn the other cheek and suffer evil. Since Christians have renounced the right of self-defense, they should suffer under tyranny rather than rebel against it.

Nevertheless, Luther did allow for the (very) limited possibility of tyrannicide. In *Whether Soldiers, Too, Can be Saved*, Luther says a king can rightly be deposed if he becomes insane. A madman is worse than a tyrant because he has lost all reason. By contrast, a tyrant retains his faculties so that one may hold out hope he will improve. Further, Luther believed tyranny to be so common that if deposing mere tyrants (as opposed to madmen) were permitted, tyrannicide would become routine (LW 46:105).

Luther also allows that the private use of force may sometimes be justified in exceptional cases, although his explanation for those exceptions is not always clear. In *An Open Letter on the Harsh Book against the Peasants*, Luther argues that when a rebel attacks the head of government, anyone who is able should pick up the sword to defend him. In this case, the private use of force is justified because the head is incapacitated and unable to issue the necessary command authorizing force (LW 46:80). More puzzling, perhaps, are Luther's views on exceptional cases of justified self-defense. Although Luther believes Christians generally should not exercise force on their own behalf, he allows for the rare possibility of self-defense in *Temporal Authority*. Luther considers the question, "Why may I not use the sword for myself . . . so long as it is my intention not to seek my own advantage but to punish evil?" He answers, "Such a miracle is not impossible, but very rare and hazardous." Only a "true Christian, filled with the Spirit," can perform the act of legitimate self-defense (LW 45:104). Previously, however, Luther had said that true Christians renounce self-defense, and he does not explain fully the reasons for the exception. In any case, he thinks it extraordinary for anyone to act devoid of selfish motives.

In the last decade of his life, Luther's position on armed resistance appears to have modified significantly. Worries that the Holy Roman emperor might move militarily against the Protestant princes in Germany were growing more acute. Although a number of jurists argued on constitutional grounds that the German princes could rightly defend themselves against an attack by the emperor, Luther had previously argued on theological grounds against the right to resist a superior. Thus Luther returned to the question of resistance in 1539, in the *Circular Disputation on Matthew 19:21*. In theses 31 and 32 Luther argues, "If a robber or thief wants to rob or use force against you, because you are a Christian, you must resist the evil, if you wish to be a pious citizen of this world. Because, just as the magistrate himself resists, whose member you are, so he commands that you resist, by virtue of the second table, which you are bound to obey" (WA 39/2:40.38–41.7). Luther appears to reason that resistance is authorized by virtue of the fact that the defender participates in the authority of the magistrate. The individual does not really act privately, but on behalf of public authority and in an emergency situation. From there Luther goes on in the disputation to argue that the pope is an illegitimate authority because he does not belong to any worldly estate. Therefore, if the pope seeks to impose his teachings with force, he can rightly be resisted—a conclusion seeming to imply that political authority is responsible for the care of religion. Unfortunately, *Circular Disputation on Matthew 19:21*, which has never been translated into English, is neither as well known nor as well studied as Luther's other political writings. Some of the arguments in the disputation appear strained. Yet they were anticipated, at least in part, by comments Luther made in *Temporal Authority* and *An Open Letter on the Harsh Book against the Peasants*. His arguments also may echo in the work of Justus Menius and Philip Melanchthon (*Von der Notwehr Unterricht* of 1547) and in the Magdeburg Confession of 1550, where such resistance is more fully explored.

See also Jurisprudence; Law Uses of the; State; Two Realms

Bibliography

Brecht, M. *Martin Luther: Shaping and Defining the Reformation*. Vols. 2–3. Trans. J. L. Schaaf. Fortress, 1990–99; Corey, D. D., and J. D. Charles. *The Just War Tradition: An Introduction*. ISI Books, 2012; Erdmann, K. D. *Luther über den gerechten und ungerechten Krieg*. Vandenhoeck & Ruprecht, 1984; Hermann, R. "Luthers Zirkulardisputation über Mt 19.21." *Luther-Jahrbuch* 23 (1941): 35–93.

H. David Baer

K

Kalnins, Harald

Harald Kalnins (1911–97) was a bishop in the Soviet Union and, after the fall of the Soviet Union in 1991, the first bishop of the reorganized Lutheran Church in Russia and other states.

Born in St. Petersburg to Latvian and German parents, Kalnins studied theology in Switzerland and then served the Lutheran Church in Latvia. With the outbreak of World War II, he was called to be chaplain to the Latvian units of the German Wehrmacht. He was imprisoned in Georgia but returned to Latvia after the war to serve as pastor at Jesus Church in Riga. In the 1960s, Kalnins received permission from the Soviet government to minister to German Lutherans in central Asia. He continued to visit Lutherans scattered throughout the USSR, and in 1980 the Soviets allowed him the title "Superintendent with the rights of a Bishop." From 1988 to 1994 he served as bishop of the Evangelical Lutheran Church of Russia and Other States (ELCROS).

See also Latvia; Russia

Matthew Heise

Kant, Immanuel

The nominally Lutheran philosopher Immanuel Kant (1724–1804) is the seminal thinker of Euro-American modernity. His "critical" philosophy fulfilled the aspiration, from the times of Descartes and Locke during the Wars of Religion, to found human knowledge on an indubitable ground that could liberate culture from the intractable and violent clash of dogmatic claims to revealed truth. In Kant, a new Platonic thesis of discontinuity between human perception and conception via Descartes was revitalized but turned against the possibility of knowledge, strictly speaking, of God. Kant's relation to the Lutheran theological tradition, especially Melanchthon's "theological philosophy" that came to Kant via Leibniz, was thus a vexed one (Hinlicky, *Paths*, 70–76).

In his *Conflict of the Faculties* (1798), Kant sharply rejected certain pretensions of the theological faculty representing Lutheran Orthodoxy, especially its ambition to leave the state-sanctioned ghetto of their ecclesiastical domain and trespass into the domain of philosophy, which is the tribunal of free and unfettered reason. In keeping with his critical restriction of rational understanding to the cognition of sensible phenomena, he argued that even if a revelation occurred, one could have no rational way of deciding whether it was true to the Infinite and thus true in comparison to other claims to revelation. In this way demolishing the rationality or reasonableness of the Christian (and any other) claim to theological truth, his *Religion within the Boundaries of Mere Reason* (1793) stigmatized the "ecclesiastical" form of faith as authoritarian and laid the ground for its replacement with the ethically free project of building on earth a Kingdom of Ends leading to Perpetual Peace.

Kant thus reduced (1) religion to morality and (2) replaced the church community with civil society by the (3) "critical" new Platonic move of dualizing into two spheres noumenal I-Thou relations of ethical freedom and phenomenal I-It relations of the causal nexus. With these steps, Kant's philosophy of religion inaugurated what Troeltsch later identified as the "neo-Protestant" project, although it was beset with its own inner contradictions in making Kant's philosophy a foundation for Christianity.

These themes from Kant indeed became the marching orders of nineteenth-century liberal

Lutheranism. That is especially clear in the theology of Albrecht Ritschl. Risto Saarinen, in a seminal study, argued that much Luther research from the nineteenth century superimposed the Kantian rejection of speculative metaphysics onto Luther. Christine Helmer has similarly shown that Luther's interest in the ontological or immanent Trinity does not abide the Kantian strictures against speculative metaphysics. These far-reaching contemporary criticisms of post-Kantian Luther research have now been refined and broadly substantiated by Theodor Dieter's study of the early Luther's (often positive) relationship to the Aristotelian tradition.

If Kant sought freedom from the dogmatism of Lutheran Orthodoxy, he held in even greater disdain Lutheran Pietism, which he regarded as pure "enthusiasm." In co-opting the term "enthusiasm," going back to Luther, Kant turned it against Pietism and Orthodoxy alike, indeed against Luther himself. In Kant's words from the Orientation essay: "Thus if it is disputed that reason deserves the right to speak first in matters concerning supersensible objects such as the existence of God and the future world, then a wide gate is opened to all enthusiasm, superstition and even atheism" (Kant 15). Kant took as "enthusiasm" *any* finite claim to knowledge of God; this is the "knowledge" he famously claimed to have destroyed in order to make room for faith. But "faith" here is taken as the ethically reasonable "postulates" of God, freedom, and immortality made by practical reason as it struggles with the disproportion of righteousness and happiness in human experience. Luther's own theology of the Spirit at work through the external Word is thus ruled out of bounds. Thus Kantianism claimed to have "fulfilled" or "completed" Luther's Reformation more consistently than Luther himself, albeit doing so against Luther's "dogmatic" intentions and "authoritarian" pretensions.

See also Enlightenment; Hamann, Johann Georg; Liberalism; Lutheran Orthodoxy; Philosophy; Pietism; Rationalism; Ritschl, Albrecht

Bibliography

Adkins, B., and P. Hinlicky. *Rethinking Philosophy and Theology with Deleuze: A New Cartography.* Bloomsbury Academic, 2013; Dieter, T. *Der junge Luther und Aristoteles: Eine historisch-systematische Untersuchung zum Verhältnis von Theologie und Philosophie.* De Gruyter, 2001; Frank, G. *Die Theologische Philosophie Philipp Melanchthons (1497–1560).* Benno, 1995; Helmer, C. *The Trinity and Martin Luther: A Study on the Relationship between Genre, Language and the Trinity in Luther's Works (1523–1546).* Von Zabern, 1999; Hinlicky, P. "An Irony of Enthusiasm." In *A Man for the Church: Honoring the Theology, Life, and Witness of Ralph Del Colle,* ed. M. R. Barnes, 302–15. Pickwick, 2012; Hinlicky, P. *Paths Not Taken: Theology from Luther through Leibniz.* Eerdmans, 2009; Kant, I. *Religion and Rational Theology.* Trans. A. Wood and G. Di Giovanni. Cambridge University Press, 2001; Lotz, D. *Luther and Ritschl: A Fresh Perspective on Albrecht Ritschl's Theology in the Light of His Luther Study.* Abingdon, 1974; Saarinen, R. *Gottes Wirken auf uns: Die transzendentale Deutung des Gegenwart-Christi-Motivs in der Lutherforschung.* Steiner, 1989; Troeltsch, E. *Religion in History.* Trans. J. L. Adams and W. Bense. Fortress, 1991.

PAUL R. HINLICKY

Karlstadt, Andreas Bodenstein von

As professor of theology in Wittenberg, Andreas Bodenstein von Karlstadt's (1486–1541) disagreements with Luther contributed to the division of the Evangelical movement in the early 1520s. Karlstadt took his name from the Franconian town of Karlstadt, where he was born into a prominent burgher family. He attended the universities of Erfurt and Cologne, where he learned the realist philosophy of Thomas Aquinas. In 1505 he moved to Wittenberg and studied with Johann von Staupitz, receiving his master of arts (1506) and then his doctorate in theology (1510); in 1510 he was also ordained as a priest. As archdeacon of the All Saints' Chapter in Wittenberg from 1511, he held one of the university's chairs in theology and so was first one of Luther's teachers (presiding at Luther's doctoral defense), then his colleague. After a six-month stay in Rome, he received his doctorate in law in 1516. He initially opposed Luther's developing theology, but after reading and then lecturing on Augustine, he became one of the most ardent supporters of Wittenberg's theological program. Although he defended Luther's understanding of law, grace, and works, his early writings show a somewhat different reading of Augustine and of German mysticism, leading him to emphasize the distinction between law and spirit in a way that contributed to his later disagreements with Luther.

Karlstadt played a key role in escalating the debate provoked by publication of Luther's Ninety-Five Theses. In May 1518 Karlstadt published an attack on John Eck's criticisms of the theses, which were being circulated in manuscript. In response Eck demanded a disputation with Karlstadt concerning grace and free will, which was held in Leipzig in the summer of 1519. Luther received permission to participate in this disputation only after his arrival in Leipzig, but his debate with Eck broadened the controversy to include the issue of papal authority. Eck added Karlstadt's name to *Exsurge domine*, the papal bull threatening Luther with excommunication in the summer of 1520. By that time Karlstadt was becoming one of the most prolific authors defending Wittenberg theology. He began to write almost exclusively in German in order to address a lay audience.

For his safety, the elector sent Karlstadt to Copenhagen in the spring of 1521, but he returned to Wittenberg within a few months. While Luther was hiding at Wartburg Castle, Karlstadt played a leading role in the movement to introduce practical reforms reflecting Wittenberg's theology. On Christmas Day 1521, he celebrated the first Evangelical Mass without donning the required vestments, omitting many of the prescribed gestures, and distributing both the bread and the wine directly to communicants. Over the next month he urged the removal of images from churches, helped draft a new liturgical ordinance for worship in Wittenberg, and married Anna von Mochau, a young woman from an impoverished local noble family. The leadership of the Evangelical movement divided over the pace and extent of reforms, however, especially in the face of the elector's opposition, causing Luther to return to Wittenberg in early March

1522. The sermons Luther preached after his return condemned the introduction of reforms for not having taken into account the weak, who did not yet understand the gospel's freedom. Karlstadt was blamed for the unrest that resulted from these reforms, and he was forbidden to preach and to publish, although he continued to lecture at the university. His growing alienation from his colleagues prompted him to leave Wittenberg in the summer of 1523 to become pastor of Orlamünde, a town near Jena whose parish provided some of the funds for Karlstadt's position as archdeacon. There he developed and spread an Evangelical theology that borrowed mystical concepts and terminology, emphasized the priority of the Holy Spirit in understanding God's Word, reinterpreted the sacraments as human acts, and rejected the belief that Christ's body and blood were physically present in the elements of the Lord's Supper. After attempting to recall Karlstadt to Wittenberg, Luther undertook a preaching tour in Thuringia in August 1524 to counter the influence of both Karlstadt and Thomas Müntzer. At a meeting with Karlstadt in Jena, Luther told Karlstadt to publish his views and promised to counter them with his own writings. Karlstadt sent several pamphlets to Basel, where they were published in 1524. His rejection of Christ's corporeal presence in the elements resonated with views that would also be promulgated by the Swiss reformers Ulrich Zwingli and Johannes Oecolampadius, and the pamphlets broke the unwritten taboo against challenging belief in Christ's corporeal presence in print. Before the fall of 1525 both Swiss reformers published their own attacks on Christ's corporeal presence, and the eucharistic controversy began in earnest.

Karlstadt was expelled from Electoral Saxony in September 1524. After traveling through Zurich, Basel, and Strasbourg, he went into hiding in Rothenburg ob der Tauber while seeking to have his banishment rescinded. He reemerged in the spring of 1525 as peasant armies began gathering in the region. Rejected by both the peasants and their opponents,

Karlstadt was forced to flee Rothenburg, and he and his family lived in secret with the newly married Luther, who was negotiating with the elector to allow Karlstadt's return to Saxony. After publishing pamphlets disavowing the peasant movement and presenting his view of the Lord's Supper as uncertain, Karlstadt was allowed to live in a small town near Wittenberg but was forbidden to teach, preach, or write. Despite pressure from the Wittenbergers, he did not change his understanding of the Lord's Supper, and he tried to contact others who shared his view. Threatened with imprisonment, he finally fled Saxony in early 1529 and spent several months as a wandering preacher in East Frisia, near the Dutch border. He asked to attend the Marburg Colloquy in October 1529, but Landgrave Philip of Hesse refused to invite him. In the spring of 1530 Karlstadt found refuge in Zurich, where he held a series of temporary positions, including a brief stint as pastor in the town of Altstätten in eastern Switzerland. In the summer of 1534 he was appointed professor of theology at the University of Basel; soon afterward he was also named pastor of Basel's Church of St. Peter. In 1536 he was part of the delegation that Basel sent to Strasbourg to hear Martin Bucer's justification of the Wittenberg Concord, which would be endorsed by Basel's church. In 1538 Karlstadt became embroiled in a conflict between Basel's professors and pastors over a reform of the university's statutes. This conflict was still unresolved when Karlstadt died of the plague on Christmas Eve 1541.

Luther's harsh criticism of Karlstadt in the two parts of *Wider die himmlischen Propheten* (*Against the Heavenly Prophets* [1524/25], LW 40:79–223) discredited Karlstadt's character as well as his theology. His ideas were adopted enthusiastically by Anabaptists and radical Sacramentarians, however, and the Swiss reformers may have used his arguments against Christ's real presence, although they did not acknowledge him as their source. Karlstadt's mystical theology influenced contemporary spiritualists such as Hans Denck and Caspar Schwenckfeld, and reprints of his works, without attribution of authorship, continued to circulate into the seventeenth century.

See also Lord's Supper; Wittenberg Unrest

Bibliography
Barge, H. *Andreas Bodenstein von Karlstadt.* 2 vols. Brandstetter, 1905; Bubenheimer, U. *Consonantia Theologiae et Iurisprudentiae: Andreas Bodenstein von Karlstadt als Theologe und Jurist zwischen Scholastik und Reformation.* Mohr, 1977; Burnett, A. N., ed. *The Eucharistic Pamphlets of Andreas Bodenstein von Karlstadt.* Truman State University Press, 2011; Burnett, A. N. *Karlstadt and the Origins of the Eucharistic Controversy.* Oxford University Press, 2011; Furcha, E. J., ed. *The Essential Carlstadt: Fifteen Tracts by Andreas Bodenstein (Carlstadt) from Karlstadt.* Herald Press, 1995; Kessler, M. *Das Karlstadt-Bild in der Forschung.* Mohr Siebeck, 2014; Pater, C. *Karlstadt as Father of the Baptist Movements: The Emergence of Lay Protestantism.* University of Toronto Press, 1984; Rupp, E. G. "Andrew Karlstadt: The Reformer as Puritan." In *Patterns of Reformation,* 49–153. Fortress, 1969; Sider, R. J. *Andreas Bodenstein von Karlstadt: The Development of His Thought, 1517–1525.* Brill, 1974; Sider, R. J., ed. *Karlstadt's Battle with Luther: Documents in a Liberal-Radical Debate.* Fortress, 1977; Zorzin, A. *Karlstadt als Flugschriftenautor.* Vandenhoeck & Ruprecht, 1990.

AMY NELSON BURNETT

Kavel, August Ludwig Christian
Pastor Kavel is hailed as the founder (*Gründer*) of Lutheranism in Australia. While serving as parish pastor of Klemzig in Brandenburg, August Ludwig Christian Kavel (1798–1860) came under the influence of the confessional theology of Johann Gottfried Scheibel and took his flock out of the Union Church in 1835. When persecution followed, Kavel petitioned Friedrich Wilhelm III for permission to emigrate, eventually leading his flock to the colony of South Australia in 1838 as the first wave of Old Lutherans (*Alt-Lutheraner*) to settle there. They found what they sought: religious freedom and a new life. However, Kavel soon encountered opposition on three major issues: his claim that his Apostolic Constitution for the fledgling church was the only one that accorded fully with the New Testament, his chiliastic beliefs, and his "Protestations" against certain statements in the Lutheran Confessions. In a fateful synod at Bethanien

in 1846, Kavel and his followers walked out, thereby precipitating a schism that took 120 years to heal. He continued to lead his congregations in a small synod that eventually became the Immanuel Synod. Kavel died in 1860, leaving behind a fragmented church, and his influence as a church leader diminished. Although his leadership was autocratic and divisive and his theological legacy is tarnished, he was without doubt a confessionalist, willing to act on his convictions.

See also Australia

Bibliography

Hebart, T. *The United Evangelical Lutheran Church in Australia (U.E.L.C.A.): Its History, Activities, and Characteristics, 1838–1938.* ET, ed. J. J. Stolz. Lutheran Book Depot, 1938. Reprint, Lutheran Publishing House, 1985; Leske, E. *For Faith and Freedom: The Story of Lutherans and Lutheranism in Australia, 1836–1996.* Rev. ed. Friends of Lutheran Archives, 2009.

DEAN ZWECK

Kenya

The history of Lutheranism in Kenya would have begun in 1844 had J. Ludwig Krapft and J. Rebmann started their missionary work in the name of the Lutheran church. The two German Lutherans were sent to Africa as missionaries by the Church Missionary Society (CMS), and their missionary efforts at the Kenyan coast led to the establishment and growth of the Anglican Church in Kenya and in other East African countries. Nevertheless the two missionaries, especially Krapft, indirectly contributed to the Lutheran missionary endeavors in Kenya by inspiring various Lutheran mission societies to come to the country.

The first Lutheran mission work in Kenya began in 1887, when the Neukirchener Mission Society, a German mission organization inspired by Krapft, started working in the coastal region. Yet this was a short-lived work, interrupted by World Wars I and II, and handed over to Methodists. In 1891 the Bavarian Evangelical Lutheran Mission started working in the eastern region, around Ukambani. In 1893 the work was taken over by the Leipzig Mission, also from Germany, but it too had to leave Kenya in 1914 because of World War I. It handed its work over to the African Inland Mission (AIM). Around the same time the Swedish Evangelical Mission (SEM) began efforts in the northeastern region, where it worked until 1935, when it was expelled by Somalia after the Kenya-Somali border was redrawn to make Jubaland part of Somalia. Around the same time, in 1939, Swedish Lutheran Mission (SLM) missionaries came to Nyanza, in the western part of Kenya, to start mission work, but this was delayed due to World War II. It is unfortunate that this early Lutheran mission work in Kenya disappeared, leaving almost no traces.

The unfavorable political atmosphere that frustrated the early attempts of the Lutheran work in Kenya did not entirely kill the spirit of mission to this land. In 1948 the SLM missionaries returned to the same area they previously visited in the western part of Kenya. The work began as a mission field of the SLM and transformed itself into a church body in 1959. However, the young church remained under the control of the mission organization until 1963, when it finally became an independent church body, the Evangelical Lutheran Church in Kenya (ELCK), with its own structures under local leadership. The ELCK membership is currently estimated at 120,000 Christians scattered throughout the country in four dioceses, with western and northwestern regions having the highest number.

In the mid-twentieth century other Lutheran work, distinct from ELCK, began in Kenya when some Tanzanian Lutherans working in Kenya started congregations, mainly along the coast and Nairobi. These congregations organized themselves into a synod of the Evangelical Lutheran Church in Tanzania. The synod elected its first Kenyan Bishop in July 1991 and transformed itself into an autonomous church body, Kenya Evangelical Lutheran Church (KELC), in February 1992. By 2011 the KELC had about 44,000 registered members in four districts and fifteen parishes in different parts of the country, with the highest concentration in Nairobi, the coast, and some parts of eastern region. In the early 1990s, these two Lutheran church bodies held unfruitful consultations on the possibility of merger into a single church body. However, this dream was not realized for both political and theological reasons. Politically, each church body seems to have feared losing its unique history and identity. Theologically, the two disagreed on a few doctrinal issues, including the ordination of women.

These differences notwithstanding, the two Lutheran churches in Kenya have worked closely in social programs. Besides carrying out their primary task of preaching the gospel of Jesus Christ, each of the two has contributed to the socioeconomic development of the country in one way or another, thus making impact on the lives of the people. This they have done in their own unique ways, often in collaboration with their mission partners and the umbrella bodies like the Lutheran World Federation (LWF) and its regional chapter, Lutheran Communion in Central and Eastern Africa (LUCCEA). Yet in terms of evangelism much remains to be done by the two churches to strengthen the presence of Lutheranism in Kenya.

Bibliography

Hildebrandt, J. *History of the Church in Africa: A Survey*. 3rd ed. African Christian Press, 1990; Imberg, R. *A Door Opened by the Lord: The History of the Evangelical Lutheran Church in Kenya*. Acme Press, 2008; Kenya Evangelical Lutheran Church. http://www.kelckenya.org.

JOSEPH T. OMOLO

Kepler, Johannes

The Lutheran theologian and mathematician Johannes Kepler (1571–1630) collaborated with Tycho Brahe (1546–1601) and other Catholic and Protestant scholars to make the heliocentric theories of Nicholas Copernicus (1473–1543) more accessible and anchored in the real world. Kepler trained at Tübingen and then accepted a position as a mathematics professor in Graz, where he lived for many years before moving to Prague to work with Brahe. Through these experiences he acquired the kind of technical proficiency in mathematics and physics needed to pursue the advanced study of astronomy; he also had the freedom to explore the theophilosophical implications of a Copernican system. One might describe him as a mathematical Platonist, who used geometry to better apprehend the structure of the universe and believed in a universal symmetry between material and spiritual worlds. He became widely known for pointing out that the distances of the six known planets from the sun corresponded to their positions relative to the sun, and to each other, if their spheres were inscribed within the "five Platonic solids": the cube, tetrahedron, octahedron, icosahedron, and dodecahedron (see his famous model in the *Mysterium Cosmographicum*). He was able to use this as evidence to support the popular assertion that nature is entirely predictable and follows mathematical laws put into place by a divine mathematician, or the Creator.

See also Brahe, Tycho; Natural Science

Bibliography

Field, J. V. *Kepler's Geometrical Cosmology*. University of Chicago Press, 1988; Jardine, N. *The Birth of History and Philosophy of Science: Kepler's "A Defense of Tycho against Ursus" with Essays on its Provenance and Significance*. Cambridge University Press, 1984; Stephenson, B. *The Music of the Heavens: Kepler's Harmonic Astronomy*. Princeton University Press, 1994.

KELLY J. WHITMER

Kierkegaard, Søren Aabye

Even though Søren Aabye Kierkegaard (1813–55), the great Danish philosopher of the nineteenth century, only lived to be forty-two years old, he greatly influenced Western religious and philosophical thinking from the late nineteenth century onward. With his numerous writings on faith, the nature of God, the church, and ethics, he became the seminal author of a new style of thinking that would later become known as "existentialism." Born as the seventh child of a wealthy businessman, Kierkegaard grew up in a pietistic yet intellectually stimulating household. Contrary to his father's wishes, he decided not to become a

Lutheran pastor, adopting instead a carefree, expensive lifestyle of a prodigal son and devoting himself fully to literature and philosophy. Kierkegaard wrestled deeply with religious ideas, however, and at the age of twenty-five he had a profound conversion experience, which resulted in his full dedication to the cause of Christian faith for the rest of his life. His thinking was deeply influenced by personal tragedy (his parents as well as five of his six siblings had died when he was still young), his complicated relationship with his father, and later his broken engagement with his fiancée, Regine Olsen. Since he wrote in Danish, he was only noticed at first by a handful of Danish intellectuals. It was not until the twentieth century that he became a well-known and widely read figure on the Western intellectual scene.

His writings can be divided into two time periods and six writing styles. The first time period is referred to as his "first authorship" (1843–46). This period was characterized by speculative philosophy, Romantic aestheticism, irony, and parody—written from the perspective of pseudonymous authors. These viewpoints of imaginary writers did not necessarily coincide with Kierkegaard's own positions: "If it should occur to anyone to want to quote a particular passage from the books, it is my wish, my prayer, that he will do me the kindness of citing the respective pseudonymous author's name, not mine" (*Unscientific Postscript*, 1:627). The second period consists of works mainly theological in nature written between 1847 and 1855, known as his "second authorship." These works contain a more direct communication of Kierkegaard's ideas in the form of reviews, discourses, and reflections. During the last months of his life, Kierkegaard carried out a relentless verbal attack on the state church in Denmark, which he judged as having departed from the path of genuine New Testament Christianity.

Kierkegaard rejected Hegelian deductive, abstract intellectualism, emphasizing instead a concrete, personal human individuality in its immediate existence. He did not accept the typical, modern epistemological concept of moral and religious knowledge, wherein philosophers focus on objective justification (evidence) for their beliefs. Truth is revealed in and through subjectivity, for, as Kierkegaard said provokingly, "Truth is subjectivity" (*Unscientific Postscript*, 1:189; §269). "The truth is a snare: you cannot get it without being caught yourself; you cannot get the truth by catching it yourself but only by its catching you" (*Journals and Papers*, 4:503; §4886).

The Kierkegaardian subjective self-examination, however, was not completely stripped of rationality in the sense of an intentional, intellectual self-reflection. Intellect is included in the process of knowing, though in itself it is not the guiding light, nor the driving motivational force, but a mere tool within a movement that is rooted much deeper in one's being (in terms of one's existential self-awareness). Having fulfilled the unconditional self-examination that leads the self to despair, reason has reached its limit and can go no further. The more "subjective" (internally reflective) one becomes, the more acutely present will be a sense of failure and alienation. Human failure and alienation on an existential level leads one to anxiety (relating to one's ethical reflection) and ultimately to despair (relating to one's religious reflection). Both anxiety and despair can be overcome solely in an encounter with the reality of God in a "leap of faith," that is, in a painful inner resolve to belong totally and unreservedly to God, who meets man in the divinely pronounced Word (*Logos*).

There is no redeeming system of religious thought nor a consecrated structure that would automatically lead people to this new, authentic (redeemed) existence. The Lutheran principle of *sola gratia* had, according to Kierkegaard, replaced the necessary "agony of soul" and served as a tranquilizer for maintaining a status quo within the "cultural Christianity" of a secularized Christendom. Kierkegaard wished to reintroduce passion into one's existence. He emphasized that, as a unity of the finite and the infinite, the human being is an individual, self-aware, creative, reflecting and self-reflecting, and yet contingent self that stands alone before God as the source and ultimate goal of each person's existence. Authentic existence of a subject is inseparable from an authentic experience of faith, which is stirred by Christ and is oriented toward following Christ—and, at the same time, is being born in acts of following. The subject of an individual, situated in a new existential state of authentic faith, perceives with inescapable urgency the ethical implications of this new state as natural expression and actualization of their being "in Christ" (Greek: *en Christō*).

Though Kierkegaard mentions Luther numerous times in his major works, most scholars argue that he did not have a profound knowledge of Luther's writings and theology. Kierkegaard seemed to know Luther only secondhand, with the possible exception of some of his sermons and the Table Talk, which he liked to read for his own personal devotion. He saw in Luther a pioneer in emphasizing subjectivity and the importance of an individual's experience of faith and appropriation of divine promises. While affirming Luther's emphasis on the necessity of good works in loving one's neighbor, as resulting from the justifying faith, after 1848 he criticized Luther for being "dialectically confused" (*Journals and Papers*, 3:80, §2467). According to Kierkegaard, Luther failed to embrace and apply the dialectical tension between law and gospel, following and receiving, example and gift. Nevertheless, Kierkegaard credited Luther for reforming the kind of medieval piety that lifted up the ascetic and contemplative life of religious orders, but blamed Luther for falling prey to the power of the princes, with grave social, political, and ecclesiastic consequences. In addition, nineteenth-century Christendom required new theological emphases; thus "Luther's true successor will come to resemble the exact opposite of Luther, because Luther came after the preposterous overstatement of asceticism, whereas he will come after the horrible fraud to which Luther's view gave birth"

(*Journals*, 3:82; §2518). While acknowledging some parts of Kierkegaard's criticism of Luther, some of his critique was based on a misreading and misunderstanding, and some of Kierkegaard's own original ideas have ambiguous (or even negative) implications for ethics. Nevertheless, the "positive existentialism" of Kierkegaard, with its ability to interweave the aspect of acute immanence of human self-awareness with the reality of transcendence—as both the anchor and goal of an individual's existence—carries great potential for contemporary philosophical, religious, and social-ethical discourse.

See also Denmark; Existentialism; Philosophy

Bibliography

Evans, S. C. "Faith as the Telos of Morality: A Reading of *Fear and Trembling*." In *International Kierkegaard Commentary*, ed. R. L. Perkins, 6:9–27. Mercer University Press, 1993; Evans, S. C. "Why Kierkegaard Still Matters—and Matters to Me." In *Why Kierkegaard Matters: A Festschrift in Honor of Robert L. Perkins*, ed. R. L. Perkins, M. A. Jolley, and E. L. Rowell, 21–32. Mercer University Press, 2010; Garff, J. *Søren Kierkegaard: A Biography*. Princeton University Press, 2005; Kierkegaard, S. *Concluding Unscientific Postscript to Philosophical Fragments*. Rev. ed. In *Kierkegaard's Writings*, vol. 1. Princeton University Press, 1997; Kierkegaard, S. *Kierkegaard's Writings*. 26 vols. Princeton University Press, 1978–2000; Kierkegaard, S. *Søren Kierkegaard's Journals and Papers*. Ed. and trans. H. V. Hong and E. H. Hong. 7 vols. Indiana University Press, 1967–78; Kirkpatrick, M. D. *Attacks on Christendom in a World Come of Age: Kierkegaard, Bonhoeffer, and the Question of a Religionless Christianity*. Pickwick, 2011; Lippitt, J., and G. Pattison, eds. *The Oxford Handbook of Kierkegaard*. Oxford University Press, 2013; Rae, M. "Kierkegaard, Barth, and Bonhoeffer: Conceptions of the Relation between Grace and Works." In *International Kierkegaard Commentary*, 21:143–67. Mercer University Press, 2002; Valčo, M. *Koncepcia subjektu a viery u S. Kierkegaarda a D. Bonhoeffera: etické implikácie* [*The concept of subject and faith in S. Kierkegaard and D. Bonhoeffer: Ethical implications*]. KUD Apokalipsa, 2016.

MICHAL VALČO

Kingo, Thomas Hansen

The Danish Lutheran pastor and bishop Thomas Hansen Kingo (December 15, 1634–October 14, 1703) was also a hymn writer. His grandfather was a weaver from Scotland who had immigrated to Denmark, where his family continued this trade. Kingo was fortunate

to receive a good education and showed aptitude for literature. Ordained in 1661, he served
several parishes, and in 1677 he was ordained
as bishop of Odense. He was elevated to the
rank of nobility in 1679 and was later granted
the degree of doctor of theology. Unlike many
Danish intellectuals of his day, he championed
hymn writing and literature in the Danish language and was a pioneer in writing hymns for
the Church of Denmark. His first hymnal, published in parts between 1673 and 1681, contained many of his own hymns. Commissioned
by the king of Denmark to develop hymnal
resources for the kingdom, he struggled to gain
approval for his projects, several of which were
rejected. Finally a committee was appointed
to finish the work, which it produced in 1699.
The resulting hymnal contained eighty-five
hymns by Kingo and was used by the church
of Denmark for over one hundred years. His
hymns have an important place in the worship
life of the Danish church and beyond Denmark
in wider Lutheranism.

See also Denmark; Hymnody; Music

Bibliography

Aaberg, J. C. *Hymns and Hymnwriters of Denmark*. Danish Evangelical Lutheran Church, 1945.

Mark A. Granquist

Kirchenordnungen

The Lutheran church ordinances (*Kirchenordnungen*) formed one of the most tangible expressions of the theological and ecclesiastical
innovations of the Protestant Reformation.
Enacted by both city governments and territories in the Holy Roman Empire and beyond, the ordinances addressed a wide array
of issues: liturgies and orders of worship,
brief doctrinal statements and catechisms,
descriptions of ecclesiastical hierarchies and
church offices, regulations for schools and universities, and instructions for pastoral care and
poor relief. These documents had their roots
in the numerous regulations of late medieval
cities (*Policeyordnungen*) and territorial decrees (*Landesordnungen*). A few, like the first
Prussian orders under bishops Georg Polentz

(Samland, 1524) and Erhard of Queiß (Pomesania, 1524) or the initial Hessian proposals
(*Reformatio ecclesiarum Hassiae*), drew on the
reform models of diocesan statutes (*Statuta
synodalia*).

The first explicitly Lutheran Church ordinances appeared in the early 1520s, when
towns like Wittenberg (1522), Leisnig (1523),
and Nuremberg (1524) sought to implement
new approaches to worship, strategies for
pastoral appointments, and community-
based models of poor relief. Following concessions made at the Diet of Speyer (1526),
the first territorial *Kirchenordnungen* were
introduced in the duchy of Braunschweig-
Lüneburg (1527) and in Electoral Saxony,
where Luther and Melanchthon worked with
Saxon councillors to draft the influential
Saxon *Unterricht der Visitatoren an die Pfar-
rherren* (Instructions by the parish visitors
for the pastors, 1528; LW 40:263–320), which
served as a model for several subsequent
Kirchenordnungen. Johannes Bugenhagen's
orders for the cities of Braunschweig (1528),
Hamburg (1529), and Lübeck (1531) also influenced a number of North German territories and Denmark. In southern Germany,
Andreas Osiander and Johannes Brenz collaborated on the widely disseminated Brandenburg (Ansbach)-Nuremberg church order
(1533). Brenz also drafted the Württemberg
order (1553/59), while Martin Bucer provided
orders for Strasbourg (1534), Hesse (1539),
and the failed effort at Cologne (1543). Dimensions of Lutheran confessionalization
are evident in the later sixteenth-century
Kirchenordnungen of Martin Chemnitz
(Braunschweig-Wolfenbüttel, 1569), Nikolaus Selnecker (Oldenburg, 1573), and Jakob
Andreae (Electoral Saxony, 1580).

The multifaceted *Kirchenordnungen* typically addressed elements of belief (*credenda*),
worship (*agenda*), and administration (*admin-
istranda*). Generally Lutheran reformers distinguished the occasional and even arbitrary
structuring of the church associated with a
Kirchenordnung (*ius humanum*) from the

divine legislative authority associated in the medieval church with canon law (*ius divinum*). The confessional dimensions of most Lutheran *Kirchenordnungen*, which emerged as doctrinal statements (*corpora doctrinae*), eventually yielded to the statements composing the Book of Concord. Regional patterns of worship, festival days, and even dialects were preserved in the numerous liturgical sections of the *Kirchenordnungen*, although the broad republication of Veit Dietrich's *Agenda-Büchlein* offered a pattern adopted by many cities and territories. Clerical regulations also received particular attention in these documents. The Lutheran office of superintendent (Latin equivalent of the Greek *episkopos*) first appeared in Johann Aepinus's order for Stralsund (1525), and Melanchthon and the North German pastor Jakob Runge attached his important outline for clerical examinations (*Examen ordinanden*) to the Mecklenburg order (1552). Matters of ecclesiastical discipline appeared in the numerous consistory orders, with significant patterns developed in Wittenberg and Württemberg. Along with reforming communal approaches to poor relief, most *Kirchenordnungen* addressed public education, especially establishing both Latin and vernacular schools in local parishes. Overall, the monumental collection of *Kirchenordnungen*, started by Emil Sehling in the early twentieth century and now nearly complete, testifies to their broad social and ecclesiastical impact.

See also Liturgy and Worship

Bibliography

Dingel, I., and A. Kohnle, eds. *Gute Ordnung: Ordnungsmodelle und Ordnungsvorstellungen in der Reformationszeit*. Evangelische Verlagsanstalt, 2014; Jaynes, J. "Church Ordinances." In *The Oxford Encyclopedia of the Reformation*, ed. H. Hillerbrand, 1:345–51. Oxford University Press, 1996; Sehling, E., et al., eds. *Die evangelischen Kirchenordnungen des XVI. Jahrhunderts*. 24 vols. Reisland, 1902–13, Mohr Siebeck, 1955–; Sprengler-Ruppenthal, A. *Gesammelte Aufsätze: Zu den Kirchenordnungen des 16. Jahrhunderts*. Mohr Siebeck, 2004; Witte, J. *Law and Protestantism: The Legal Teachings of the Lutheran Reformation*. Cambridge University Press, 2002.

JEFFREY JAYNES

Kitamori, Kazoh

The Japanese theologian, pastor, author, and professor Kazoh Kitamori (1916–98) was born in Kumamoto prefecture on Kyushu Island and baptized in a Lutheran Church while in high school. He entered Lutheran Theological Seminary in Tokyo in 1935 in order to study under the leading Luther scholar Shigehiko Satoh, who passed away in the very month Kitamori started his theological study. After graduation in 1938, he studied under Hajime Tanabe, a disciple of Kitaro Nishida, at Kyoto Imperial University, graduated in 1941, and continued there as an assistant until 1943, when he moved to the Eastern Japan Theological Seminary, later renamed Tokyo Union Theological Seminary. There he became professor in 1949 and taught systematic theology until his retirement in 1986. His PhD degree in literature came from Kyoto Imperial University in 1962.

After World War II, Kitamori did not join the reestablished Japan Lutheran Church but remained in the United Church of Christ in Japan, helping its re-formation in various ways, including drafting of a confession of faith in 1954, as he continued serving as a pastor for forty-six years.

Kitamori was a prolific author, leaving behind forty-two books and many articles in various areas, not restricted to theology. The theme of his major work *Kami no itami no shingaku* (*The Theology of the Pain of God*), published in 1946 and released in 1965 in English, was taken from the word appearing in the old translation of Jeremiah 31:20, describing the love of God who at the same time punishes and pardons sinners with a love that reveals God's inner struggle of painful suffering. Though the concept has drawn domestic and international attention and even was taken up by Jürgen Moltmann in his book of *The Crucified God* (1987), it has not necessarily been highly appreciated among professional theologians in Japan, although it certainly sparked vital and meaningful theological discussion among them. In 1992 Kitamori was commended for his distinguished merits and received the Achievement Award from Japan Christian Culture Association.

See also Japan

MAKITO MASAKI

Knubel, Frederick Hermann

As a Lutheran pastor in New York City, Frederick Hermann Knubel (1870–1945) worked for Lutheran unity through his service as the director of the first cooperative agency among Lutherans, the National Lutheran Commission for Soldiers' and Sailors' Welfare, founded in October 1917. Knubel had directed the General Synod's Inner Mission work, and his executive ability and theological acuity helped him navigate among contending Lutherans on the commission, who did not all recognize each other as orthodox but were forced to work together to get access to soldiers. He was elected first president of the United Lutheran Church in America in 1918 and until 1944 in that capacity led East Coast Lutheranism in the National Lutheran Council and led in articulating the principles of an ecumenical Lutheranism. The chief author with Charles Jacobs, professor at the Lutheran Theological Seminary at Philadelphia, of the paper "The Essentials of a Catholic Spirit" (1919, 1920), he stressed that Lutherans should meet each other without hostility, and in a gospel spirit accept the bona fide assurances of each church. Tests of orthodoxy beyond subscription to the Augsburg Confession were not Lutheran. He did not convince the more conservative Lutheran groups but did define the ULCA's approach for a generation and charted the path for Lutherans to follow in their merger efforts later in the century.

See also General Synod; United Lutheran Church in America

Bibliography
Bachman, E. T. *The United Lutheran Church in America, 1918–1962.* Fortress, 1997.

MARIA ERLING

Korea

The Lutheran Church in Korea (LCK), the only Lutheran Church in Korea, resulted from mission work initiated by the Lutheran Church–Missouri Synod (LCMS). Kurt E. Voss (1915–83), L. Paul Bartling (1931–2009), and Maynard Dorow (1929–) arrived in 1958 and formed the Korea Lutheran Mission (KLM). Won-Yong Ji (1924–2012), a Korean native, joined the team later that year.

KLM set a mission strategy that has shaped the history of the LCK. In the midst of church factions and schisms of Korean Protestantism following the Korean War (1950–53), KLM determined to be a contributing "plus" to the already-existing churches in Korea rather than simply adding another denomination competing with them. It focused on mass-media mission (later called the "A-approach") rather than traditional church planting (later called the "B-approach").

The Korea Lutheran Hour (since 1959), of which Won-Yong Ji was the founder and first director, is an A-approach par excellence in using electronic media. Its radio ministry covered all of South Korea, was beamed into North Korea, and was heard in northern China. As a follow-up to it, a Christian correspondence course began operation in 1960. LCK's publishing arm, *Concordia-sa* (since 1959), published numerous books of devotional and theological character, including Luther's Works–Korean Edition. The monthly magazine *New Life* appeared regularly (1961–80).

LCK's extensive Braille literature program has been welcomed by the blind. Likewise, its concern for the poor, the handicapped, and the disadvantaged has been expressed through its Diaconia program of Christian service. Its annual Wichern Service Prize is awarded to people who distinguish themselves in diaconal service.

Korea Bethel Series Bible study program, which LCK started in 1974, is a continuation of the A-approach and one of the most successful enterprises. Korea Bethel Series Life Dimension courses were added in 1980. The LCK has developed additional courses of its own: Salvation, Faith, and Worship. Between

403

1974 and 2014 some 470,000 individuals at 8,000 congregations have used this series as a tool for studying Scripture.

Under the B-approach, the first Lutheran worship service occurred in February 1959 at the Seoul YMCA and led to the establishment of Immanuel (now Tobong) Lutheran Church. St. John (now Wangshimni) Lutheran Church was formed in 1963, Trinity (now Joongang) in 1967, St. Luke (now Oksudong) in 1968, and Daejodong in 1970. With these five congregations LCK was officially organized as a national church in 1971 under the name of Han-Kuk Rutu-Kyo Sunkyo-Hoi (Korea Lutheran Mission Assembly) and became the Lutheran Church in Korea two years later. The first president elected was Won-Sang Ji (1927–98), Won-Yong Ji's younger brother.

LCK polity combines congregational and synodical elements. Its fifty congregations are spread over the peninsula, mostly in the capital and the surrounding satellite cities but even on Jeju Island in the south.

For years candidates for ministry had been trained at the Lutheran Theological Academy (established 1966), operated as a "house of studies" in cooperation with Yonsei University in Seoul. It eventually developed into Luther Theological University (LTU) on a campus in Yongin City and received full accreditation in 1997. Later added to the theology department were departments of social welfare, counseling, and speech-language pathology. The two years of the MDiv-level pastoral training program were replaced by three years of an accredited MDiv. Also, LTU offers MSW and MSLP degrees.

The LCK is a member of the Christian Council of Korea and, since 2011, of the National Council of Churches in Korea. It participates in various ecumenical enterprises: Korea Education Association, Christian Broadcasting System, Christian TV/CTS, Korean Bible Society, Korea Christian Service, the Joint Hymnal Committee, and other projects.

On an international level, it became a member church of the Lutheran World Federation in 1972. It is also a member of the International Lutheran Council since it was formally constituted in 1993. It hosted the ILC conferences in 1989 and 2009. It has a partnership with the LCMS and a close relationship with the Mission One World of the Evangelical Lutheran Church in Bavaria, Germany (ELCB). One German ELCB expatriate missionary has been serving with the LCK and LTU since 2000. In recent years the relationship between the LCK and the Japan Lutheran Church (NLK) has become closer. An LCK pastor has been serving with the NLK since 2013. The LCK is also sponsoring Lutheran mission work in Vietnam.

See also Ji Brothers

Bibliography

Ji, W.-Y. *A History of Lutheranism in Korea: A Personal Account*. Concordia Seminary, 1988.

JIN-SEOP EOM

Krauth, Charles Porterfield

As an American Lutheran theologian and educator, Charles Porterfield Krauth (1823–83) was a leading figure in the confessional revival among English-speaking Lutherans in the mid-nineteenth century. Born in Virginia, Krauth was the only son of Charles Philip Krauth, a respected pastor who served on the faculties of Gettysburg Seminary and Pennsylvania (later Gettysburg) College. The younger Krauth attended both institutions; after his seminary graduation in 1841, he began a pastoral career that took him to several parishes in Maryland, Virginia, and Pennsylvania.

During the 1850s, Krauth became a stanch opponent of Samuel Simon Schmucker's "American Lutheranism" program. Beginning in the 1840s, he had gradually taken a more confessional turn in his own thinking as a result of his study of patristic and Reformation writers. As early as 1849, in an essay published in the *Evangelical Review*, Krauth stressed the importance of the Lutheran confessional writings for Lutherans living "in the midst of sectarianism" in the United States.

The publication of Schmucker's anonymously issued *Definite Platform* in 1855 provoked the conservative Pittsburgh Synod to adopt what came to be known as the Pittsburgh Declaration. Written by Krauth, the document defended the Augsburg Confession against the "errors" alleged by Schmucker. Over the next few years, Krauth published a series of articles elucidating his view that the General Synod ought to affirm the "substantial correctness" of the Augsburg Confession. He remained conciliatory during this period, hoping to avoid a rupture in the General Synod by allowing for some latitude in how one understood the Augsburg Confession.

By 1865, however, Krauth had come to believe that a more precise confessional subscription was necessary for the unity of the church, and he now argued that all doctrinal articles in the Augsburg Confession are "articles of faith," and as such must be confessed "without reservation or ambiguity." At the same time political maneuverings within the General Synod led to the Ministerium of Pennsylvania's decision to establish a new seminary at Philadelphia, with Krauth as one of three faculty members. As tensions escalated, more confessionally minded synods met in 1866 and formed a new general body, the General Council of the Evangelical Lutheran Church in America. Krauth was a key figure in the organization of this new council, writing both the "Theses on Faith and Polity," which formed its doctrinal basis, and the constitution adopted by the new body. Krauth was an early president of the General Council, a position he held for ten years.

Krauth's magnum opus, published in 1871, was *The Conservative Reformation and Its Theology*. The book was not a systematic treatment of Lutheran theology, but a compilation of various essays he had written over the preceding two decades; nevertheless, it became the standard explication of the position of the confessional party among English-speaking Lutherans.

Krauth married his first wife, Susan Reynolds, in 1847; she died in 1853, and two years later he married Virginia Baker. In addition to his theological enterprises, he taught for several years at the University of Pennsylvania. His daughter, Harriet Krauth Spaeth, was deeply involved in the production of the *Church Book* and preserved his library as a gift to the Lutheran Theological Seminary at Philadelphia.

See also General Council of the Evangelical Lutheran Church in North America; General Synod; Inner-Lutheran Ecumenism; Ministerium of Pennsylvania; Schmucker, Samuel Simon; United Lutheran Church in America

Bibliography

Gustafson, D. A. *Lutherans in Crisis: The Question of Identity in the American Republic*. Augsburg Fortress, 1993; Krauth, C. P. *The Conservative Reformation and Its Theology*. Lippincott, 1871. Reprint, with new introduction, Concordia, 2007; Spaeth, A. *Charles Porterfield Krauth, D.D., LL.D.* Christian Literature Co., 1898.

RICHARD O. JOHNSON

Kretschmar, Georg

The second bishop of the revived Evangelical Lutheran Church of Russia and Other States (ELCROS) after the fall of the USSR was Georg Kretschmar (1925–2009). Born into the family of a Silesian pastor, Kretschmar served as a solider in the Ukraine during World War II. There he observed a Russian Orthodox service for the first time, something he would remember later as he engaged in ecumenical work. After theological study in Tübingen, Heidelberg, and Oxford, in 1955 Kretschmar became the youngest professor of theology in West Germany (University of Hamburg). In 1967 he left to teach at the University of Munich. In 1959 Kretschmar was invited by the Evangelical Lutheran Church of Germany to be a representative for an ecumenical dialogue with the Russian Orthodox Church. As a result, in 1963 he was assigned to lead the Lutheran World Federation's dialogue with Orthodox churches around the world. In 1989, Bishop Harald Kalnins requested that he become the rector of the first Lutheran seminary (Riga) established in the USSR since 1934. In 1994, after Kalnins left office, Kretschmar replaced him as bishop of ELCROS. He served in this capacity until 2005, when he retired to Munich.

See also Ecumenical Dialogues; Kalnins, Harald; Russia

MATTHEW HEISE

Krman, Daniel, Jr.

The Lutheran superintendent (bishop) Daniel Krman Jr. (1663–1740) was representative of late Lutheran Orthodoxy in Hungary. He studied in Breslau (Wroclaw; 1678–82), Leipzig (1682), and Wittenberg (1683), and served as pastor in western Slovakia (Turá Lúka, Myjava a Žilina). Krman sought to consolidate Lutheranism after the Counter-Reformation. During the anti-Hapsburg insurrection of Francis II Rákóczi, he was elected superintendent in 1707 at the synod in Ružomberok, which reaffirmed allegiance to the Book of Concord. The synod commissioned him to present a petition to the Swedish king Charles XII that sought aid for Lutherans in the Hungarian monarchy; his *Itinerarium* chronicled his journey to meet the king in Russia in 1709. The Peace of Satu-mare (1711) invalidated the decisions of the Synod of Ružomberok. Lutherans were subjected to increasingly severe restrictions until the Edict of Toleration of 1781. In 1731 Krman was imprisoned in Bratislava, where he died in 1740. Most of his works remained in manuscript. He cooperated with Matej Bel in preparing the so-called Halle Bible translation (1722), coedited the Lutheran hymnal of Vaclav Kleych (1717, 1722, 1727), and edited the first common Agenda for Lutherans in Slovakia (1734). His *Hungaria evangelica* and *Memorabilia* deal with the history of Lutheranism. A collection of his sermons, *Kniha života* (Book of life), was printed in 1704.

See also Hungary; Slovakia

Bibliography
Daniel, D. P. "Lutheranism in the Kingdom of Hungary." In *Lutheran Ecclesiastical Culture*, ed. R. Kolb, 455–522. Brill, 2008.

DAVID P. DANIEL

Kugappi, Aari

The bishop of the Evangelical Lutheran Church of Ingria in Russia from 1996, Aari Kugappi (b. 1953), was born in the village of Padozero in the Leningrad region of the USSR, but due to religious restrictions within Russia proper was confirmed in Narva, Estonia, in 1968. In 1974 he along with several believers began a Christian youth movement in the Ingrian region of Russia, resulting in the Soviet authorities granting permission in 1977 to reopen the Lutheran Church in Pushkin (Leningrad region). In 1980 Kugappi graduated from the Art and Industrial Academy in Leningrad. He continued gathering believers in the cemetery of his home village of Koltushi, where the Communists had burned down the Lutheran church building in the 1940s. Despite pressure from the Soviet secret police to inform on his parishioners, he refused. He was ordained as a deacon in 1990.

In 1992 he was ordained as the pastor of Koltushi's Lutheran Church. He was appointed as the vicar (deputy) of Leino Hassinen, a Finnish pastor who had become the Ingrian Lutheran Church's bishop. Hassinen handed over the bishop's crozier to Kugappi in 1996 so that a Russian-born bishop could oversee the believers in Ingria. Kugappi was honored as doctor of theology by Concordia Seminary (St. Louis) in 2006, the Finnish Order of Agricola in 2008, and the Order of the Estonian Cross (First Degree) in 2011.

See also Finland; Russia

OLAV PANCHU

Kugler, Anna Sarah

Anna Sarah Kugler (1856–1930) was born in Ardmore, Pennsylvania, and served as a medical missionary in India. She graduated from Friends' Central High School in Philadelphia and the Women's Medical School of Pennsylvania, earning an MD. Following an internship at Norristown State Hospital, she learned of opportunities to work among women in South India. Declining to send her as a medical missionary, the Women's Home and Foreign Missionary Society of the General Synod gave her a general charge. She arrived in Guntur, Andhra Pradesh, in 1883. Although her primary responsibility was teaching, in her first year she treated over four hundred female patients. In 1885 her assignment was shifted toward medical work. During a furlough in the United States, she did graduate study that prepared her to establish and manage a hospital. First she began a dispensary and then in 1897 opened the fifty-bed American Evangelical Lutheran Hospital. Local supporters included her missionary colleagues and Raja Rao Chinnamagari Satram. She also set up village dispensaries and raised funds for additional services at the hospital. Her book *Guntur Mission Hospital* combines autobiography and suggestions for how to conduct similar work. Twice she received the Kaisar-i-Hind Medal (1905, 1917). The hospital she founded was renamed in her honor: Kugler Hospital.

See also India

Bibliography

Kugler, A. S. *Guntur Mission Hospital, Guntur, India*. United Lutheran Church in America. Women's Missionary Society, 1928; Singh, M. C. "Women, Mission, and Medicine: Clara Swain, Anna Kugler, and Early Medical Endeavors in Colonial India." *International Bulletin of Missionary Research* 29 (2005): 128–33; Vethanayagamony, P. "St. Anna Sarah Kugler." *Lutheran Forum* 44 (Winter 2010): 40–49.

L. DeAne Lagerquist

Kuhr, Karl Otto

The first pastor sent to Brazil by the Lutheran Lord's Treasury (*Gotteskasten*) was Karl Otto Kuhr (1864–1938), who founded the Brazilian Lutheran Synod.

Kuhr studied theology in Neuendettelsau and went to the United States, where he served as pastor in the Ohio Synod. The Bavarian Lord's Treasury sent him to Brazil in 1897 to gather Lutheran German immigrants into congregations. Several additional Lutheran pastors were sent to help him in the next years, and together with them he founded a confessional Lutheran synod in 1905, the Evangelisch-lutherische Synode von Santa Catarina, Paraná und anderen Staaten von Südamerika, also known as Gotteskasten Synode. The synod accepted as its confessional basis the Holy Scriptures and the Lutheran confessions. Kuhr was elected as the synod's first president.

See also Igreja Evangélica de Confissão Luterana no Brasil (IECLB) (Evangelical Church of the Lutheran Confession in Brazil)

Bibliography

Fischer, J., and J. Christoph, eds. *Es begann am Rio dos Sinos*. Evangelisch-Lutherischen Mission, 1970; Prien, H.-J. *Evangelische Kirchwerdung in Brasilien*. G. Mohn, 1989.

Paulo Wille Buss

Kumari Samuel, Prasanna

Prasanna Kumari Samuel (1950–2006) was a theologian of the Andhra Evangelical Lutheran Church and professor of New Testament and Women's Studies at Gurukul Lutheran Theological College, Chennai. Her parents were evangelist and faith healer Sesharatnamma and her husband, Mulpuri Basavaiah. Kumari studied at the Hindustan Bible Institute, Chennai; United Theological College, Bengalaru; and Lutheran School of Theology in Chicago, which awarded her the PhD posthumously on the basis of her completed dissertation manuscript. She was survived by her husband Samuel W. Meshack and two daughters.

Her work with the Arcot Lutheran Church at Kalrayan Hills in Tamilnadu acquainted her more deeply with tribal communities and prepared her for a career in fighting against caste, class, and gender barriers. Kumari joined the Gurukul faculty in 1985 and was ordained in 1991, one of the first two Indian Lutheran women to be ordained. She served as executive secretary of the United Evangelical Lutheran Church in India (1992–98), a member of the LWF Council and chair of its program committee for theology and studies (1990–97), and a member of the Lutheran Orthodox dialogue (1986–92). Kumari was a candidate for the presidency of the LWF in 1997. She was vice president of the National Council of Churches in India at the time of her death. She established the Slum Women's Advancement Program, which creatively strove to elevate the status and activities of the poorest women in

Indian society. She founded the Church Women's Center to aid battered women and provide other diaconal services.

A prolific author, Kumari campaigned throughout her life for equal rights for women and men and for the Dalits of her land. She succeeded in winning approval of the Senate of Serampore College for including feminist theology in the Indian theological curriculum.

See also Gender: Men and Women; India

Bibliography

Meshack, S. W. *Mission with the Marginalized: Life and Witness of Rev. Dr. Prasanna K. Samuel*. Christava Sahitya Samthi, 2007; Schjorring, J. H., P. Kumari, et al., eds. *From Federation to Communion: The History of the Lutheran World Federation*. Fortress, 1997.

DAMODHER CHRISTUDAS

Kurds

Formal Lutheran mission work among the Kurdish people began soon after the Protestant International Conference on Foreign Missions in Edinburgh (known as the Edinburgh Conference) in 1910. Earlier work had begun in 1890 through the efforts of Rev. N. G. Malech, a Persian associate of Nestorian missionaries, working in the portions of Turkey, Iran, Iraq, and Syria populated by over twenty million Kurds. This distinct ethnic group traces its origins to the ancient Medes of Persia. Malech was successful in raising funds among Lutherans in America but was unable to sustain the effort of evangelizing among the largely Muslim population. When the Edinburgh Conference delegates suggested the need for a revitalized Lutheran effort among the Kurds, Rev. L. O. Fossum (1879–1920), an associate of Malech in the earlier mission, responded enthusiastically.

The new mission was named the Lutheran Orient Mission Society. In 1910, the year of its founding, the first issue of the mission's newspaper, *The Kurdistan Missionary*, was published. In 1911 the first missionaries were sent to the city of Soujbulak (present-day Mahabad): Rev. L. O. Fossum and Dr. E. Edman, a medical doctor. They forged a link between evangelism and medical work.

Small congregations began to grow alongside medical clinics. By 1912 the first congregation, Bethel Kurdish Evangelical Lutheran Church, was founded. A medical clinic and dispensary was built in Mahabad the same year, supported by Dr. Edman and two nurses, Augusta Gudhart and Meta von der Schulenburg.

The early years of the mission were challenged by war and deprivation. The mission in Soujbulak was destroyed in the war between Russia and Persia, 1912–16. Missionaries were forced to flee. After World War I, Fossum and his wife, Alma, returned to Kurdistan. Before his death in 1920 at the age of forty-one, Fossum produced a Kurdish alphabet; a grammar book; an English-Kurdish lexicon; and a translation of the New Testament, Luther's Small Catechism, and over a hundred hymns.

The mission grew slowly, with steady support from the Lutheran synods in the United States, despite challenges to funding and staffing during the Great Depression and World War II. Beginning in 1929, Rev. Henry Mueller began his ministry, following the example of L. O. Fossum and the French linguist and theologian George Barchimont. He emphasized evangelism coupled with humanitarian help, especially medical efforts. Dr. and Mrs. Richard Gardner, arriving in 1959, continued this approach despite the relocation of the church and hospital from Iraqi Kurdistan to Gorveh, Iran.

The work continued until the Iranian Revolution (1979) forced its closure. From 1980 to 1989 the Lutheran Orient Mission assisted with relief efforts in Bangladesh pending staff members returning to Kurdistan. In 1989 emergency relief work among the Kurds of Turkey began as a result of the First Gulf War. A period of collaboration with a longtime Middle East humanitarian worker and evangelist, Matthew Hand, marked the shift toward specific educational opportunities for girls, reconciliation among contending religious groups, and an increased emphasis on development work. The name of the organization was changed to Lutheran Mideast Development in 2007.

See also Islam; Middle East; Mission and Evangelism

Bibliography

Jensen, C. C. A. *God through the Shadows*. Lutheran Orient Mission Society, 1950; *The Kurdistan Missionary*. Assorted issues. Lutheran Orient Mission Society, 1911–56; Lutheran Orient Mission Archives. Evangelical Lutheran Church in America Region 3 Archives, 1896–2013.

PAUL A. DANIELS

Kuzmány, Karol

The Slovak professor of practical theology Karol Kuzmány (1806–66) was superintendent (bishop) and protagonist of "Patentalism." He studied theology at the University in Jena, with a particular interest in aesthetics and philosophy. He was a chaplain in Banská Bystrica in 1830 and then served as pastor in Zvolen and Banská Bystrica. Kuzmány coedited a new Lutheran hymnal, *Zpěvník evangelický*, designed to replace the traditional *Cithara Sanctorum* of Juraj Tranovsky. In 1849 he was named professor of practical theology at the theological faculty in Vienna. He published a *Practical Theology* that included extensive material on the legal status of Lutherans in Hungary.

Kuzmány supported the neo-absolutist politics of the court in Vienna after the revolutions of 1848. He contributed to the preparation of the imperial Protestant Patent (1859). Kuzmány considered the Patent an effective instrument that would improve the legal status of Lutherans in the Austro-Hungarian monarchy and inhibit the growing political and cultural Hungarian influence that threatened the status and practice of Slovak Lutherans. As a convinced "Patentalist" he actively opposed the group pleading for the self-governing sovereignty of the Lutheran Church in Hungary (so-called Autonomists). In 1860 Kuzmány was elected superintendent (bishop) of the newly created Prešporok (Bratislava) superintendency. He determinedly strove to safeguard the rights of Slovak Lutherans in Hungary.

See also Hungary; Slovakia

DAVID P. DANIEL

L

Laestadius, Lars Levi

Swedish Lutheran pastor and revival leader Lars Levi Laestadius (1800–1861) was born in northern Sweden, coming from a family of preachers. Through his mother he was connected to the Läsare, or Pietist "Readers." At Uppsala he studied theology and botany, then was ordained in 1825. Called to the northernmost parish in Sweden, Karesuanto, he ministered to the local Sami (Lapp) people and Finns. Early interest in botany resulted in several publications, but soon religious concerns took his attention. Several brushes with severe illness spiritually challenged him, but in 1844 his faith was restored by an encounter with a Sami woman, Maria. Laestadius was strongly concerned with the deep problems of his people and began a powerful revival in the area, preaching to the concerns of his people. This revival spread across northern Sweden and into Finland, where it took the greatest hold, marked by great emotion, lay preaching, and individuals' public absolution from sin. Laestadius published a periodical titled *The Voice of One Crying in the Wilderness*, but his lasting influence has come through collections of his sermons. In the last years of his ministry he struggled to keep this revival from spinning off into excess. His followers, mainly in Finland, are known as Laestadians, or Apostolic Lutherans.

See also Finland; Sweden

Bibliography

Saarnivaara, U. *They Lived in the Power of God: Lutheran Revival Leaders in Northern Europe*. Ambassador Publications, 2011.

MARK A. GRANQUIST

Latvia

In the aftermath of the bloody revolution of 1905 and the devastation of World War I, Latvia proclaimed its independence in 1918 and established it on the battlefield in 1919–20. Independence led to the emergence of a national Lutheran church in 1922; its first bishop was Kārlis Irbe and its first archbishop Teodors Grīnbergs (1932). Pastors were educated at the Faculty of Theology (1920) at the Latvian University in Riga, but without confessional orientation or a practical theology department. To provide balance, in 1923 the church itself founded the Theological Institute with a practical department and a more conservative theological orientation. In 1930 there were 163 pastors serving 272 congregations. Lutherans constituted 56 percent of the population. The church produced the weekly *Sunday Morning* (1920), a hymnal (1922), a choral book (1924), the monthly *The Way of Youth*, an annual calendar (1925), and an agenda (1928). It began its foreign mission in India.

The "Year of Horror" (1940) brought Soviet occupation with genocide (35,000 victims), deportation, and persecution of the church. Ten pastors were deported, several died in camps, and two were executed. The German invasion in June 1941 prevented a larger deportation planned for July. Germans regarded Latvia as an occupied country and controlled the church. Dean Pauls Rozenbergs protested German Jewish policy. Archbishop Teodors Grīnbergs requested that baptized Jews not be deported, with some success. In 1944 he was deported to Germany. Despite restrictions church life continued. In 1943 the theological faculty resumed work. From 1942 to 1944, thirty-three pastors were ordained.

The Soviet reoccupation began in 1944. Fearing genocide, 55 percent of the clergy and many laypeople fled to the West. Religious life was overseen by an officer of the Soviet secret police. The Church Supreme Board, led by Dean Kārlis Irbe, was deported in 1946. In 1948 the synod adopted a pro-Soviet constitution and elected Gustavs Tūrs as archbishop. In 1949 Soviet officials deported 42,149 people, many pastors among them. In 1949 confirmation classes were forbidden. Soviets took over church buildings, including the Riga cathedral. In 1954 a theological seminary was established. In 1961 the church still claimed 500,000 members (24 percent of the population), 214 congregations, 115 pastors, and 20 theological students. In 1963 the state drastically increased taxes on church buildings. After the deaths of archbishops Peteris Kleperis (1968) and Alberts Freijs (1968), Janis Matulis was elected in 1969. The Decree on Religious Associations (1975) limited church activities to services in church buildings. In 1986 Ēriks Mesters was elected archbishop. In 1987 there were 25,000 Lutherans in 202 congregations.

In 1987 active pastors formed the group Rebirth and Renewal, demanding self-government for the church, yet eliciting persecution. In 1989 members of this group were elected to the Consistory, and one of them, Karlis Gailītis, was elected archbishop. Perestroika was progressing; the government did not interfere. In 1990 the seminary became the faculty of theology. The Lutheran Church played the role of a spiritual leader in the regaining of Latvian sovereignty because in society it was rightly perceived as a persecuted and thus trustworthy bearer of spiritual values.

Archbishop Janis Vanags was elected in 1993. In 2016, 2 bishops, 15 deans, 136 pastors and assistant pastors, and 86 evangelists served in 292 congregations. The Diaconia Center was begun in 1994, Saint Gregor's School in 1995, and the Luther Academy for training of pastors in 1997.

See also Courland (Kurland); Grīnbergs, Teodors; Irbe, Kārlis; Livonia; Mancelius, Georgius; Rumba, Edgars; Turss, Gustavs (Tūrs)

Bibliography

Talonen, J. *Church under the Pressure of Stalinism.* Societas Historica Finlandiae Septentrionalis, 1997.

GUNTIS KALME

Law, Uses of the

Lutheran theological reflection concerning uses of the law represents an attempt to clarify the purpose and function of the law, especially in light of the doctrine of justification. The Lutheran discernment of law into distinct uses is a consequence of the discernment of God's Word as law and gospel, as well as the need to define each term accurately. Although there is general agreement among Lutherans regarding the law's first use (restrain the wicked and maintain order) and its second use (reveal sin, impel to Christ), differences exist concerning "the third use of the law" (as in article 6 of the Formula of Concord).

The discernment of the law's use is already implied in Luther's earliest negative formulations regarding the law. For instance, the Heidelberg Disputation begins with the claim that "the Law of God, the most salutary doctrine of life, cannot advance man on his way to righteousness, but rather hinders him" (LW 32:39). The question follows that, if the law cannot advance humans regarding righteousness before God (*coram Deo*, "in the presence of God"), then of what use is the law—especially for Christians?

As early as 1522, Luther preached about both a twofold use and a threefold use of the law. In these sermons, however, Luther's descriptions of the law's uses do not conform to the eventually preferred formulations. Similarly, in a 1525 sermon, "How Christians Should Regard Moses," Luther, while clearly distinguishing law and gospel, offered three "observations" of Moses, only one of which corresponds to the uses of the law familiar to later generations of Lutherans.

The 1531 Galatians lectures (published in 1535) are commonly cited as the source of Luther's developed thoughts regarding the law's uses. Commenting on Gal. 3:19 ("Why then the law?"), Luther explains that "one must know that there is a double use of the law. . . . The first understanding and use of the law is to restrain the wicked" (LW 26:308). Luther branded this the "civic use" of the law (elsewhere termed the "political use" or "temporal use"). This *usus politicus*—enforced by the state, preached and supported by the church—"has its own glory and reward in life here among humans, but not before God" (WA 39/1:441).

Continuing his commentary on Gal. 3:19, Luther clarifies: "The other use of the Law is the theological or spiritual one, which serves to increase transgressions. This is the primary purpose of the Law of Moses, that through it sin might grow and be multiplied, especially in the conscience" (LW 26:308–9). Citing Rom. 3:20, Luther explains how the law accuses, attacking the sinner's "presumption of righteousness"—a presumption that keeps "the proclamation of free grace and the forgiveness of sins" from entering the heart. Since it is the proclamation of the gospel that is ultimate, the law is consequently penultimate. For this reason, Luther emphasizes that the second use—the *usus theologicus*—is the chief usage for Christians, the "true and proper use of the Law" (LW 26:312). "Therefore we do not abolish the Law; but we show its true function and use, namely, that it is a most useful servant impelling us to Christ" (LW 26:314). In both of these uses, Luther clearly thinks of the law in God's hands, so that God uses the law to restrain evil and keep order (*usus civilis*) and drive to Christ (*usus theologicus*).

In later treatments of the subject, Luther favored the dialectical, or twofold, discernment of the law. For instance, in a 1537 commentary on John 1:17, Luther contends that "the Law serves to indicate the will of God and it leads us to a realization that we cannot keep it." In this way, "the Law was given to us for the revelation of sin . . . and impels us to cry, 'Lord Jesus Christ, help us and give us grace to enable us to fulfill the Law's demands!'" (LW 22:143). In the Smalcald Articles of 1536 (3.2), Luther also defines two uses of the law.

The notion that the law and its demands remain in force for all Christians is prevalent in Luther's writings, especially in his opposition to the antinomian position of Johann Agricola. Insofar as the believing saint is at the same time a sinner, the law and its consequences function to hold that sinner in check. However, as in the above commentary on John 1:17, it was also clear to Luther that a Christian can desire to fulfill the law out of humility and faith, rather than only out of fear of punishment.

This possibility of the Christian's positive orientation to the law—perhaps hinted at in the Augsburg Confession, articles 6 and 20—may have stimulated Lutheran (and, later, Reformed) impulses to define a third use of the law. In other words, if the law is used (1) to restrain "as the ropes or the chains prevent a lion or a bear from ravaging" (to use Luther's words in LW 26:308) and (2) to terrify consciences with the wrath of God in order to prepare them for the gospel, then it may also function (3) to guide regenerate believers in the "good fruits" that faith is bound to bring forth.

However, whether Luther himself held a sustained, formulaic doctrine of a *triplex usus legis* is disputed. Significantly, Werner Elert pointed out that the term's unique appearance in Luther's 1538 *Disputation against the Antinomians* was an interpolation by later transcribers. Elert's contention was based primarily on the fact that the term *triplex usus legis* appears in only two of the nine existing manuscripts of Luther's 1538 disputation and that none of the manuscripts dates before 1553. Most Lutherans interpret Elert's finding as definitive evidence that Luther did not teach a formal third use of the law.

On the other hand, it is beyond dispute that Melanchthon discerned the law in three distinct uses. Beginning in 1534, in the third edition of his commentary on Colossians, Melanchthon wrote of the three uses of the law in a formal sense—what Gerhard Ebeling described as the "Scholastic schema of the *triplex usus*." In the 1535 edition of his *Loci communes theologici*, Melanchthon, after describing the *usus politicus* and the *usus theologicus*, turned to a third use of the law. According to Melanchthon, this third use applies to Christians after regeneration: though they may desire to serve God freely and spontaneously, they still need to be guided and urged to advance in repentance, faith, and true good works. Melanchthon's third use appears to have been motivated, in part, by a desire to correct those who understood that Christ's commandments to his disciples were words of gospel. In other words, it can be argued that Melanchthon's introduction of the third use was borne of an attempt to distinguish Jesus's law of love from the promise of the gospel.

Influenced by the writings of Luther and Melanchthon, John Calvin (1509–64) adapted the threefold use of the law in his own theology, most notably in his *Institutes* (2.7.9–12). The Reformed expression of the law's three uses corresponds with, but is not identical to, the three uses outlined in the various editions of Melanchthon's *Loci*. Indeed, for Calvin the third use is the principal use for Christians, while Melanchthon, with Luther, maintained that the law's second use is the primary use.

At the core of Lutheran disputes regarding the law's third use is the proper interpretation of the claim that "the Law always accuses" (*Lex semper accusat*, as in, e.g., Ap 4.37). Some have interpreted the claim to mean that "the Law only accuses" (*Lex sola accusat*). A decade after Luther's death, debates regarding the third use of the law emerged among certain Gnesio-Lutherans. One such involved Andreas Poach (ca. 1515–85) and others arrayed against Martin Chemnitz (1522–86) and others who favored a third use of the law. Elsewhere, Andreas Musculus (1514–81) voiced a suspicion that although the third use of the law was purported to be a mere guide, it risked being construed as coercion or as an accusation for the believer as believer and, worse yet, as a means by which believers could present themselves as righteous before God. Musculus, using Luther's *Freedom of a Christian* (1520) as a guide, argued that true good works were done freely, spontaneously, and apart from the exhortations of an external guide.

After initial hesitation by the authors of the Formula of Concord, including Jakob Andreae (1528–90), Musculus's objections found their way into the Formula of Concord's article 6, "Concerning the Third Use of the Law." The Formula of Concord, Solid Declaration, art. 6 begins with a sentence naming the familiar and universally agreed-upon twofold use of the law. The next sentence states that the law "is also used when those who have been born anew . . . live and walk in the law" (SD 6.1, BC 587). Article 6 then describes the dispute "over this third and final use of the law," before continuing to "explain and settle this dispute definitively" (SD 6.2, BC 587).

Even though it does not use the phrase, article 6's explanation and settlement in the Solid Declaration hinge on an anthropology based on the fact that the believer is *simul iustus et peccator* (at the same time righteous and sinner). Insofar as sin adheres in the believer, the accusation and urging of the law are necessary and necessarily preached. However, insofar as believers do good works "apart from any admonition, exhortation, impulse, coercion, or compulsion" (SD 6.6, BC 588) but from a "free and merry spirit," they are "'no longer under the law but under grace,' as St. Paul says in Romans 8" (SD 6.17, BC 590). According to article 6, "the word 'law' has one single meaning, namely, the unchanging will of God, according to which human beings are to conduct themselves in this life." The Epitome concludes on a similar note, contending that "for both the repentant and the unrepentant, for the reborn and those not reborn, the law is and remains one single law" (Ep 6.7, BC 503). The only difference for believers is the question of how the law is obeyed: with or without coercion, with or without a willing spirit, "insofar as they are born anew."

Article 6 clearly and repeatedly elaborates that a single believer, as a result of being simultaneously saint and sinner, old self and new self, has two orientations toward the one law of God. Some interpreters of article 6 understand it to be arguing that the law can be used to guide believers in free and spontaneous good works without becoming an admonition or accusation. Others, however, insist that article 6 does not convincingly argue that both law and gospel inform good works freely done. Consequently, Lutherans continue to discuss whether article 6's affirmative theses clearly describe three, independent, formal uses of the law.

See also Antinomianism/Antinomian Controversies; Good Works; Justification; Law and Gospel

Bibliography

Arand, C. P., et al. "Chapter 9. The Majoristic and 'Antinomian' Controversies." In *The Lutheran Confessions: History and Theology of the Book of Concord*, 191–99. Fortress, 2012; "6. Concerning the Third Use of the Law." In *Formula of Concord; Book of Concord*, 502–3 (Epitome), 587–91 (Solid Declaration). Fortress, 2000; Ebeling, G. "On the Doctrine of the *Triplex Usus Legis* in the Theology of the Reformation." In *Word and Faith*, trans. J. Leitch, 62–78. Fortress, 1963; Elert, W. *Law and Gospel*. Trans. E. Schroeder. Fortress, 1967; Kolb, R., and J. Nestingen, eds. *Sources and Contexts of the Book of Concord*. Fortress, 2001; Lohse, B. "Law and Gospel." In *Martin Luther's Theology: Its Historical and Systematic Development*, trans. R. Harrisville, 267–76. Augsburg Fortress, 1995; Mattes, M. "Beyond the Impasse: Reexamining the Third Use of the Law." *Concordia Theological Quarterly* 69 (July/October 2005): 271–91; Melanchthon, P. *Loci communes 1543*. Trans. J. A. O. Preus. Concordia, 1992; Murray, S. *Law, Life, and the Living God: The Third Use of the Law in Modern American Lutheranism*. Concordia, 2002; Wengert, T. *Law and Gospel: Philip Melanchthon's Debate with John Agricola of Eisleben over Poenitentia*. Texts and Studies in Reformation and Post-Reformation Thought. Baker, 1997.

HANS WIERSMA

Law and Gospel

When God speaks, law and gospel are the two words uttered (authorized by Scripture) for proclamation to sinners. These two kinds of words establish two offices of preaching, each divine, while doing contradictory work: the law kills and the gospel gives life. In Scripture the distinction is made between utterances of curse and blessing, command and promise, letter and spirit, or judgment and forgiveness: for example, "The letter kills but the Spirit gives life" (2 Cor. 3:6b).

In describing the origin of his theological breakthrough in the 1545 preface to his Latin works, Luther associates it directly to the discovery and experience of the distinction between law and gospel. Decades later, the Solid Declaration of the Formula of Concord V (1577; *BC* 581) lauds it as "a special brilliant light" that must be guarded with care. Thus the two words are neither to be confused nor separated lest Christ's gift of forgiveness be obscured, and the troubled conscience be robbed of its true comfort. The law/gospel contrast is not a lens or interpretive tool through which a neutral subject views Scripture or the world. Instead, Lutherans view the distinction as a divine light that shines from without and reveals the truth of creator and creatures.

In the Apology of the Augsburg Confession (IV.5; *BC* 121), Melanchthon observes that all Scripture was properly divided into words of law and promise and accused the papal party of using only the law as the means for remitting sin. Justification by faith alone has two distinct offices of proclamation as its basis. When the distinction is made, the exclusive importance of justification by faith alone emerges; when the distinction is denied, the law necessarily substitutes for the gospel (by confusion [works righteousness] or separation [antinomianism]) as the remission of sins. Yet law and gospel also dare not be mixed. There is no synthesis, especially not by using grace as merely a means to fulfill the law, and thus law and gospel must both be preached.

Luther's rediscovery of the distinction between these two divine words arose in part because of the threat to the early church by Marcion (born ca. 110), who separated law and gospel (Old and New Testaments) into two gods: (1) the creator and alien god and (2) the true God as the Father of Christ. In opposition, Tertullian (160–220) seemed to argue for a synthesis of the two. Augustine (354–430) saw the limit to this hedge on the separation of law and gospel especially in his struggle with the Pelagians, who preached about the sufficiency of human nature to fulfill the law. Augustine's *The Spirit and the Letter* (see also *Christian Instruction*) uses 2 Cor. 3

to show that the law of works, which is divine and good, nevertheless does not help a person but kills if one lacks the gift of the Holy Spirit. Grace assists and aids in synthesizing law and grace, so that for Augustine letter/spirit becomes law/grace. The law causes flight from sin, and grace completes the journey. Grace, the gift of the person of the Spirit, is simply the law. Thus law ceases being an external thing concerning deeds and becomes internal, written on the heart when grasped in prayer. Although this distinction continued in an attenuated form in the Middle Ages, 2 Cor. 3:6 was more often used as a prooftext for the spiritual interpretations of texts over and above the literal.

Luther agreed with Augustine insofar as the law causes flight, but for him grace does not complete the law in sinners. Instead, it abruptly ends law and its accusation, so that Christians cannot use it to build a relationship with God and God's righteousness. Thus Luther substituted law/gospel for Augustine's law/grace (where grace simply gives the redeemed the power to fulfill God's righteous law). Luther turned Augustine's prayer for grace into proclamation of grace that gave exactly what it promised. Forgiveness comes not through the law (either at the beginning or end), but by a simple promise (called "gospel") on account of Christ's crucifixion.

Thus for Luther, all preaching and divine work depends upon this distinction between law and gospel, which became part and parcel of his Evangelical discovery. Law is everything that preaches something about sin and God's wrath, however and whenever that happens. The law has content (revealing human sin and God's wrath) as well as function (however and whenever it strikes the human heart, doing what Luther and Melanchthon call God's alien work). The gospel is a proclamation that points to and gives nothing but forgiveness in Christ—however and whenever that happens (doing what they call God's proper work).

For Luther, the preaching and experience of the law precedes that of the gospel as death precedes resurrection. One only understands the distinction of law and gospel there through experiencing it, that is, through genuine contrition ("affliction of the heart"), as Luther observes in the Smalcald Articles (III.2–4; BC 311–19). Even before sin, God threatened Adam with death and so with a law. In sin, God gives the law in the first place to curb sin by threat of punishment. In this, while restraining sinners outwardly, it ultimately failed to make people righteous inwardly. But second, the chief office of the law is to reveal original sin and the evil that comes from it. Thus, as Paul teaches (cf. Rom. 5:20), "sin becomes greater through the law." Curbing and revealing sin became the two "uses" of the law for Luther. This revelation, however, is not mere information but "the thunderbolt of God, by means of which he destroys both the open sinner and the false saint" (BC 312).

Only the gospel may then free sinners from sin, death, and devil. The gospel is the story of Jesus Christ, the Son of God, who became flesh and was crucified for our trespass, raised for our justification (Rom. 4:25), and established as Lord of a new realm whenever this is preached for the ungodly. The proper function of the gospel is to forgive sins in the form of a promise that functions differently than a command. The promise depends upon God's faithfulness and the power of God's Word to accomplish what it says and make sinners into believers, persons who trust in God. The extravagant richness of this grace comes in more than one way as proclamation, baptism, the holy Sacrament of the Altar, the power of the keys, and the mutual conversation and consolation of Christians.

This preaching of the two offices of God's Word became a source of struggle among Lutherans. Some separated the law completely from the gospel in various forms of antinomianism (e.g., Johann Agricola, 1494–1566) or confused the two by bringing the gospel under the law as God's true, eternal gift. The antinomian position could argue that there could be no contradiction in God or his words, since Aristotle taught that contraries cannot be parts of the same entity. This basic principle of reason necessarily rejected Luther's teaching of the contradiction in God between unpreached and preached God, between what law and gospel do regarding salvation and the distinction of wholly sinner and wholly saint (*simul iustus et peccator*) of the baptized. Instead, reason sought an overarching unity in the form of a gospel that included repentance and faith and denied the efficacy of the law in saving sinners.

Luther's distinction of law and gospel came in the disputation with the antinomians (1537–40) and centered on Rom. 10:4 ("Christ is the end of the law"). Agricola objected to Luther's assertion that the law kills because it cannot possibly be fulfilled and that the law must still be preached though it fails to lead to divine righteousness but only drives the sinner further from God. For Luther, Christ did not come to demand the obedience that the law requires of sinners; he came to give his own obedience to sinners. The eternal law of God is historicized in a surprising way by Christ's crucifixion and resurrection and the creation of a new kingdom. In light of the cross, the law is established as either "before Christ" or "after Christ." Before Christ, it accuses sinners, which is the law's proper work and is felt before its revelation. After Christ, law remains, but as fulfilled, and so eternally behind Christ. The eternal law depends only on faith, "to be fulfilled" in sinners or "as fulfilled" in the blessed—eternally in front of those in hell and eternally behind those in heaven.

But already in the Majoristic Controversy (1551–62) the understanding of a "third use" of the law for the redeemed, already proposed by Melanchthon in his Colossians commentary of 1534 and his *Loci communes* of 1535 and following works, was emerging into a central tenet of orthodox Lutheranism: the eternal law was a speculative necessity of God's essence that allowed some Lutheran preachers to avoid or subvert preaching a law that was impossible to fulfill. An old debate

between Jerome and Augustine was revived as theologians wondered what kind of God would demand impossible law. So the Eisenach Synod (1556), which condemned Majorists, asserted that while no sinner could actually and historically fulfill the law, in speculative theory (before sin) Adam must have been able to fulfill the law through works and thereby merit salvation. Otherwise God would contradict himself and deny essential goodness and trustworthiness. Martin Chemnitz (1522–86) began to teach the prior and ultimate unity of law and gospel, whose fulcrum was the substitutionary atonement of Christ. The eternal law required that the benefits won by Christ on the cross would perfectly satisfy the guilt and punishment that sinners owed to the law. In that way the law's eternality set the agenda for generations as a theological a priori that imagined a nonthreatening law existing before sin, to which humans could return through Christ.

In this line of thought the Luther scholar Theodosius Harnack (1817–89) proposed a difference between the *Amt* of the law (its accusing function following sin) and the *Wesen* of the law (its eternal being) that was to be the means of salvation before Adam's sin. He argued that God had an inner and absolute necessity for the sacrifice of his Son, since one can be redeemed from an accusing law only if the essence of the unpreached law has been satisfied a priori. Paul Althaus (1888–1966) repeated this speculation of a pre-sin and nonthreatening *Gebot* (command) that once gave Adam a free permission to obey, as opposed to the later, threatening *Gesetz* (law) that followed sin. But God's threat to sinless Adam is clear: "for in the day that you eat of it you shall die" (Gen. 2:17). Luther and Melanchthon's dictum remains: the law always accuses, and accusation means law.

Subsequent liberal historians, like Theodosius Harnack's son Adolf (1851–1930), tried to drive a wedge between Luther and Paul (and between Paul and Christ) on this distinction of law and gospel. Gerhard Ebeling (1912–2001), who, like Werner Elert before him, recovered the centrality of Luther's distinction between law and gospel, nevertheless carried on this contrast between Paul and Luther on law and gospel by saying Paul's distinction was salvation historical, the aeon of law ruling from Moses to Christ, followed temporally by a new positive historical entity called gospel, in which obedience shifts from Moses to Christ. Luther was viewed as taking the Pauline, historical distinction and making it existential. However close this description may fit Lutheran orthodoxy, it does not apply to Luther.

Likewise Ernst Troeltsch (1865–1923) and those who followed him (such as Wolfhart Pannenberg, 1928–2014) determined that Luther's law/gospel was a product not of the Bible but of medieval understandings of penance. For Paul, the problem of legalism was deemed circumcision and food; for Luther, it was pilgrimage and penance. They concluded that Luther reduced the distinction between law and gospel to the simple matter of absolution. Forgiveness and thus justification were no longer ways of being in a new historical era (Paul) but a daily, indefinitely repeated homiletical rubric (Luther) from which one never escaped or progressed.

Pietism actually helped C. F. W. Walther (1811–87) regain the significance of law-and-gospel proclamation by driving him first into prayer and inner struggle and away from the orthodox speculation. But only then, when he broke out of his own inner prayers and wrestlings to the external word and sacraments was he truly free from the law as in Thesis IX of *The Proper Distinction between Law and Gospel* (1897). Gerhard Forde (1927–2005), building on the work of Elert and Ebeling, recognized the crucial relation between law and atonement. In Lutheran Orthodoxy the law provided an eternal standard for the atonement by which God can be "bought off" from wrath. J. C. K. von Hoffmann's (1810–77) *Heilsgeschichte* replaced this eternal standard (and its substitutionary atonement) with a historical scheme of gospel that supersedes an epoch of law. Instead of these attempts, a return to proclamation of the two words of law and gospel was necessary. In the twentieth century, two recent possibilities emerged, one championed by Karl Barth (1886–1968), wherein true knowledge of the law is given only in the revelation of the gospel. In that case, law belongs properly to the new age of Christ and so is the form of the gospel. What precedes revelation of the gospel was merely a misunderstood law. The other, championed by Werner Elert among others, is the Lutheran response, in which law belongs to the old age. When the gospel is preached, God's use of the law actually comes to an end. The offices of law and gospel make two worlds, or ages, which overlap for the time being. The new age is not ordered by law but is freed from law by the gospel. Law and gospel do not form a process of development for the Christian, but law kills the old sinner and gospel raises up a new creature. The gospel is therefore the end of the law and establishes the law in its proper place in the old world (Rom. 3:31) until this world's end (begun in the gospel), when there is, eternally, no more law.

See also Antinomianism/Antinomian Controversies; Barth, Karl; Ebeling, Gerhard; Elert, Werner; Forde, Gerhard; Gospels; Iwand, Hans Joachim; Law, Uses of the

Bibliography

Althaus, P. *The Divine Command: A New Perspective on Law and Gospel*. Trans. F. Sherman. Fortress, 1966; Bayer, O. *Promissio*. Vandenhoeck & Ruprecht, 1971; Ebeling, G. "Reflexions on the Doctrine of the Law." In *Word and Faith*, 247–81. Fortress, 1963; Elert, W. *Law and Gospel*. Trans. E. H. Schroede. Fortress, 1967; Forde, G. *The Law-Gospel Debate*. Augsburg, 1969; Haikola, L. *Studien zu Luther und zum Luthertum*. Lundequistika Bokhandeln, 1958; Harnack, A. von. *The Constitution and Law of the Church in the First Three Centuries*. G. P. Putnam's Sons, 1910; Harnack, T. *Luthers Theologie*. Chr. Kaiser, 1927; Luther, M. *Answer to the Hyperchristian, Hyperspiritual, and Hyperlearned Book by Goat Emser* (1521). LW 39:143–228; Luther, M. Smalcald Articles. In *Book of Concord*. Ed. R. Kolb and T. J. Wengert. Fortress, 2000; Luther M. *Solus Decalogus est aeternus = Martin Luther's Complete Antinomian Theses and Disputations*. Ed. and trans. H. Sonntag. Lutheran Press, 2008; Pannenberg, W. *Systematic Theology*. Vol. 3. Trans. G. W. Bromiley. Eerdmans, 1998; Prenter, R. *Our Proclamation: Law and*

Gospel. Trans. J. H. G. Rasmussen. The Young People's Publishers, 1951; Preus, J. A. O. *The Second Martin.* St. Louis: Concordia, 1994; Walther, C. F. W. *The Proper Distinction between Law and Gospel.* St. Louis: Concordia, 1928; Wengert, T. J. *Law and Gospel: Philip Melanchthon's Debate with John Agricola of Eisleben over "Poenitentia."* Grand Rapids: Baker, 1997.

STEVEN D. PAULSON

Lectionary

The lectionary lists selected readings from the Old and New Testaments, especially appointed for the primary Sunday worship service but also for other services. Originally denoted in the margins of biblical manuscripts with *incipits* and *explicits* (the beginning and ending words), these were later listed in separate books (*comes*, meaning "Companion" to the Sacramentary), and then the full readings were printed, composing the actual lectionary. Readings were selected in accordance with the church year, following a yearly pattern, and lectionary selections were limited to the Gospel and the Epistle readings of the Mass. The first complete Western lectionaries date to the seventh century. A fairly standardized medieval lectionary, represented in the *Comes of Murbach*, was developed by Alcuin of York (eighth century). Luther and his colleague in Wittenberg found great value in preaching from the lectionary, while bemoaning the selection of Epistle texts that failed to reflect the Gospel. They developed a reading plan for Wittenberg in the *Deutsche Messe* following the *Comes* tradition, with alterations to the end of the church year. Yet they also encouraged a *lectio continua* (continual reading through books of Scripture) approach for certain weekday services (reading Matthew on Wednesdays at Vespers and John on Saturdays). Following Luther, the great majority of the Reformation church orders reflected the older *Comes* tradition with some modifications (Saxony, Hannover, Braunschweig, Margraviate of Brandenburg, the Scandinavian countries), a few encouraging a pattern of *lectio continua* (such as Riga, Brandenburg-Nuremberg, Poland). Eventually in Germany and Scandinavia the one-year series was augmented, especially in the nineteenth century, by preaching texts.

Currently three global directions exist in Lutheran lectionary development. North American Lutheranism has adopted some version of the new three-year series, the Revised Common Lectionary (based on the Second Vatican Council's *Ordo Lectionum Missae*). German Lutherans employ the one-year series of liturgical reading texts alongside a series of thematically linked preaching texts, resulting in six years of homiletical texts. The Scandinavian Lutheran churches follow a mixed economy with the Reformation-era series used alongside newer alternate series.

Bibliography

Bieritz, K.-H. "The Order of Readings and Sermon Texts for the German Lutheran Church." *Studia Liturgica* 21 (1991): 37–51; Kunze, G. "Die Lesungen." In *Leiturgia: Handbuch des evangelischen Gottesdienstes*, ed. K. F. Müller, 2:87–180. J. Stauda, 1955; Pfatteicher, P. *Commentary on the Lutheran Book of Worship: Lutheran Liturgy in Its Ecumenical Context.* Augsburg Fortress, 1990.

KENT J. BURRESON

Leibniz, Gottfried Wilhelm

The philosopher, mathematician, and polymath Gottfried Wilhelm Leibniz (1646–1716) was raised in the moderate Lutheranism of Georg Calixt. He was the final flower of the humanist project for a reformed Christendom through research and education that stemmed from Melanchthon. As one of Germany's great public Christian intellectuals, Leibniz resisted the mechanization of nature. He conceived the basic units of reality as "monads," not as "atoms," but his unfortunate terminology has the connation of a relationless, self-sufficient entity, though this characterization better fits the atoms of Hobbes against which Leibniz pitted his monads. For him, monad was certainly a principle of individuation; it denoted God's full and complete conception of each and every individual as each exists in God's "preestablished" and progressively unfolding harmony with all others in the best of all possible worlds. Thus Leibniz tried to affirm the entelechy of living organisms "all the way down" to the bottom and organized "all the way up" into ever greater harmonies: "The ultimate reason of things must be in a necessary substance in which the diversity of changes is only eminent, as in its source. This is what we call *God*. Since this substance is a sufficient reason for all this diversity, which is utterly interconnected, *there is only one God, and this God is sufficient*" (*The Monadology* §§38–99).

This is not Kant's Leibniz, least of all Voltaire's bitter caricature in the buffoon figure of Dr. Pangloss. He is not the rationalist philosopher who still tried to found natural science on a priori knowledge of essences. He is not the proto-idealist who made matter into the material of mind's dialectical self-realization. He is not the Platonist theologian who diminished divine omnipotence and freedom in order to save divine goodness and wisdom. In his own self-understanding Leibniz battles against new gnosticism, Cartesian dualism and voluntarism, and the determinisms of Hobbes and Spinoza. Recent scholarship locates him in the broad Augustinian tradition (Antognozza) as a major figure in the modernization "of a specifically Lutheran civilization" (Smith 111) by innovating "a method of social analysis founded on history" (Smith 104).

Leibniz frequently appealed to Melanchthon as an adherent of the Augsburg Confession (rather than a "Lutheran"). But he rediscovered the question of theodicy in Luther's brilliant but perplexing text *De servo arbitrio*. To a significant degree, he adopted from there Luther's *vita passiva*. As such, Leibniz retrieved themes from Luther to meet the challenge of totalizing naturalisms. But the Lutheran Orthodox accused Leibniz of syncretism (with Catholicism) by tackling the problem of the compatibility of divine sovereignty and human freedom, an effort that made Leibniz appeared Pelagian in their eyes. Pietists accused him of crypto-Spinozist determinism, ironically, for referring to Luther's, though not Zwingli's or Beza's, theology of divine election. Trying to sail between Scylla and Charybdis, Leibniz

was understood by few. On the whole, his was a path not taken.

See also Enlightenment; Kant, Immanuel; Philosophy

Bibliography

Antognazza, M. R. *Leibniz on the Trinity and the Incarnation: Reason and Revelation in the Seventeenth Century.* Trans. G. Parks. Yale University Press, 2007; Elert, W. *The Structure of Lutheranism.* Trans. W. A. Hansen. Concordia, 1962; Frank, G. *Die Vernunft des Gottesgedankens: Religionsphilosophische Studien zur frühen Neuzeit.* Frommann-Holzboog, 2003; Hinlicky, P. *Paths Not Taken: Fates of Theology from Luther through Leibniz.* Eerdmans, 2009; Leibniz, G. *The Monadology.* Trans. R. Latta. Clarendon, 1898; Reinhuber, T. *Kämpfender Glaube: Studien zu Luthers Bekenntnis am Ende von "De servo arbitrio."* De Gruyter, 2000; Smith, L. *Religion and the Rise of History: Martin Luther and the Cultural Revolution in Germany, 1760–1810.* Cascade, 2009.

PAUL R. HINLICKY

Leipzig Proposal (Interim)

The Leipzig Proposal was a draft prepared by the Electoral Saxon government in 1548 to accommodate the imperial insistence on conformity to the Augsburg Interim. After the promulgation of the Augsburg Interim in June 1548, the government of Electoral Saxony under Moritz, the newly imperially appointed successor to the imprisoned John Frederick, strove to formulate a policy that would both meet the Hapsburg demand for compliance with the imperial religious policy and heed the strong objections to it from both Melanchthon and his Wittenberg colleagues and from the nobles and town councils in his domains. Moritz believed he had received assurances from Emperor Charles V and his brother King Ferdinand that his support in the Smalcald War against the forces of the Smalcaldic League would ensure his not having to change Electoral Saxon religious teaching and practice, but the Hapsburg brothers remembered no such promise. Moritz appointed a committee consisting of secular counselors, prominent Roman Catholic leaders in the area around Saxony, and representatives of his clergy and his theological faculties from the University of Leipzig and newly acquired University of

Wittenberg; this committee was instructed to propose a plan for preserving the integrity of Lutheran theology while giving the appearance of the largest possible compliance with the imperial Interim. This document was to be presented to the Saxon diet for acceptance and implementation.

In August 1548, in the town of Pegau, this committee formulated a statement affirming justification by faith but omitting the word "alone," while asserting the necessity of the will's turning to the gospel, drawn by the Holy Spirit, in the process of coming to faith in the justifying work of Christ. These two factors undermined the document's integrity in the minds of many critics. In Meissen (July), Torgau (October), and Altencelle (November), the work on the proposal continued. In these meetings a series of compromises in matters of adiaphora (neutral matters neither commanded nor prohibited by Scripture) were framed to project the impression of acceptance of the imperial policy. These included treatments of confirmation, penance, extreme unction, ordination, and marriage in the same context with baptism and the Lord's Supper, conveying the idea (without expressly saying it) that these were all regarded as sacraments, as in the medieval church. Latin in the Mass was affirmed, including the use of "bells, lights, vessels, chanting, vestments, and ceremonies" that reintroduced medieval usage, along with the mandate to have the pericopes read in German as well. Abstinence from meat during Lent and on certain other days was commanded as an external ordinance of the empire. Melanchthon and his colleagues strove to make as few concessions as possible, but in general the document reflected Melanchthon's conviction, contained in article 15 of the Augsburg Confession, that these neutral matters should not be matters of dispute but rather opportunities to teach the biblical message.

In late December 1548 the Saxon diet meeting in Leipzig discussed the proposal and rejected it. The electoral government introduced many of its practices piecemeal where it thought opposition would not be strong. One of Luther's original disciples, Gabriel Zwilling, pastor in Torgau, and a few others were defrocked for their opposition to the local adoption of elements of the Leipzig Proposal.

Many of Melanchthon's disciples, including some of the most gifted, regarded this proposal as a betrayal of Luther and the entire Reformation of the church. Led by Matthias Flacius and others, these critics contended that in times of persecution nothing remains a neutral matter, emphasizing the significance of rites and usages for public confession of faith. Their criticism launched a series of controversies (beginning with the adiaphoristic controversy but also including controversies over original sin and free will, the Majoristic controversy, and several so-called antinomian controversies) that were not fully resolved until the Formula of Concord (1577).

See also Adiaphora; Antinomianism/Antinomian Controversies; Apology of the Augsburg Confession; Augsburg Interim; Charles V; Electors of Saxony; Flacius, Matthias Illyricus, and the Flacians; Major, Georg; Melanchthon, Philip; Original Sin; Smalcald War

Bibliography

Arand, C. P. "The Apology as a Backdrop for the Interim of 1548." In *Politik und Bekenntnis: Die Reaktionen auf das Interim von 1548*, ed. I. Dingel and G. Wartenberg, 211–27. Evangelische Verlagsanstalt, 2006; Arand, C. P., et al. *The Lutheran Confessions*. Fortress, 2012; Hase, H. C. von. *Die Gestalt der Kirche Luthers: Der casus confessionis im Kampf des Matthias Flacius gegen das Interim von 1548*. Vandenhoeck & Ruprecht, 1940; "The Leipzig Interim." In *Sources and Contexts of the Book of Concord*, ed. R. Kolb and J. A. Nestingen, 183–96. Fortress, 2001.

ROBERT KOLB

Lenski, Gerhard Emmanuel

The American Lutheran pastor and theologian Gerhard Emmanuel Lenski (1890–1978) was the son of R. C. H. Lenski, a biblical scholar and editor in the Joint Synod of Ohio. His sister, Lois, was a prolific writer for children. Lenski graduated from Capital University and its seminary and was ordained in 1914. He briefly served as an assistant pastor in Pennsylvania and as a navy chaplain in World War I. In 1920 he began a thirty-two-year ministry as pastor of Grace Lutheran Church in Washington, DC. From that influential pulpit he touched many government officials and their families.

Lenski earned a PhD in history at American University; his dissertation was later published as *Marriage in the Lutheran Church*. He also wrote several popular and devotional works, including a children's biography of Luther, *Stirring Scenes from the Life of Martin Luther*. He was a longtime columnist for the *Lutheran Standard*. A passionate advocate of Lutheran unity, he joined the faculty of the ULCA's new Pacific Lutheran Theological Seminary in 1952 and taught systematic theology there for six years; he also taught at Gettysburg Seminary in 1959–60. He married Christine Umhau in 1923; their son, Gerhard E. Lenski Jr., was a well-known sociologist of religion at the University of North Carolina.

See also American Lutheran Church (1930–60); Lenski, Richard Charles Henry

Bibliography

Lenski, G. Biographical File. ELCA Archives; Lenski, G. *Marriage in the Lutheran Church: A Historical Investigation*. Lutheran Book Concern, 1936; Lenski, G. *Stirring Scenes from the Life of Martin Luther: Retold for Growing Boys and Girls*. Lutheran Book Concern, 1935.

RICHARD O. JOHNSON

Lenski, Richard Charles Henry

The American Lutheran pastor, educator, and biblical scholar Richard Charles Henry Lenski (1864–1936) was born in Griefenberg, Pomerania. He emigrated to the United States in 1872 with his family, settling in Michigan. Lenski graduated from Capital University and its seminary and was ordained in 1887 by the Joint Synod of Ohio. He served parishes in Baltimore and in Ohio at Trenton, Springfield, and Anna before being called to teach at the synod's seminary in Columbus, Ohio, in 1911. He was dean of the seminary for many years; he also served as interim president of Capital University for a brief period, and as president of the synod's Western District for several terms.

He edited the Joint Synod's German publication, *Lutherische Kirchenseitung*, from 1904 to 1924. Lenski was the author of numerous books, the most significant of which was a multivolume commentary on the New Testament (some volumes published after his death). Considered a classic commentary from a conservative Lutheran perspective, Lenski's volumes are still in print today. He married Marietta Young in 1888; their son, Gerhard E. Lenski, was a well-known pastor in the American Lutheran Church. Following his wife's death in 1924, he married Helen Gruner.

See also American Lutheran Church (1930–60); Lenski, Gerhard Emmanuel

Bibliography

Lenski, R. C. H. Biographical File. ELCA Archives; Lenski, R. C. H. *Lenski's Commentary on the New Testament*. Augsburg, 2008.

RICHARD O. JOHNSON

Liberalism

A multifaceted theological movement, sometimes known as Protestant liberalism or neo-Protestantism, liberalism was dominant in the late nineteenth century through World War I in Europe, especially Germany, and in a slightly different form in the British Isles and North America. Liberalism, a pastiche of approaches and movements, can be narrowly associated with Albrecht Ritschl (1822–89), Adolf von Harnack (1851–1930), Ernst Troeltsch (1865–1923), and Rudolf Otto (1869–1937) in Germany and in a diffuse collection of theologians and ecclesial figures in the United States and Great Britain. In North America, liberalism lacked a centrally dominant figure, and many of its adherents were particularly aligned with what later historians have called the Social Gospel movement. Liberalism in Great Britain took far different forms from those in Germany and the United States in this period. After World War I, liberalism continued as a theological or ecclesial movement, especially as German and North American strands of liberalism underwent transformation in conjunction with other developments, including those that arose in response to liberalism.

The term merits clarification since it has been subject to polemical and apologetic use in theology. Owing to the diversity of approaches within liberalism, it can be wrongly identified with strategies of accommodation to the surrounding culture or to the prevailing scientific atmosphere. Though liberalism does practice theology as one human activity among many—ceding ground to practical philosophy, historical investigation, and natural science, especially as these domains are defined by neo-Kantians—it more properly employs a strategy of shielding those dimensions of Christianity that it sees either essential or pragmatically decisive and unique to the Christian community. This latter distinction is important since some liberal theologians reject any notion that there is some ahistorical or timeless essence to Christianity. Likewise, liberal theologians often have become identified with liberal political traditions, such as those associated with John Locke (1632–1704) or Immanuel Kant (1724–1804). However, liberal political philosophy marks off different theological traditions from those articulated in liberalism. Generally, any affinity between political and theological liberalisms arose from their antecedents in the rationalist theology of the various Enlightenment movements of Europe and North America.

Liberal theologians have often used historical study as the vehicle of their normative theological aims, ranging from attempts to show the ahistorical essence of Christianity to theories stressing the contingency of the entire Christian tradition. This draws them close to their antecedents in Enlightenment theology in both the Continent and in Great Britain, as well as showing their various debts to philosophical idealism. Liberal theologians have primarily written church history, history of dogma, ethics, and historical studies of Jesus. A special concern of German liberal theologians has been the study of Martin Luther for theological and ecclesial ends, and much

of the modern shape of Luther studies owes its contours to the liberalism of Ritschl, von Harnack, and Karl Holl (1866–1926). Further, in this regard, liberalism affected many important aspects of those who opposed it, especially in the emergence of dialectical theology, the Social Gospel movement, the reformulation of the role of the historical Jesus in normative theological inquiry, and other postliberal movements.

Liberalism's theological significance and its engagement with Martin Luther's theology are deeply related in German liberal Protestantism. With Albrecht Ritschl, liberalism began with a strong commitment to Christianity in its historical development, strong affinities with the resurgence of Kant's philosophy with Hermann Lotze (1817–81), and the study of Martin Luther. Ritschl undertook many historical studies of Christianity, in particular Protestant Pietism and the Reformation. He concluded that the Reformation and generations following either preserved Luther's Protestant insights or perpetuated Catholic elements also present in Luther. While Ritschl was no rationalist, he considered his search for this truly Protestant Luther decisive for identifying the truly normative dimensions of Christianity: freedom and morality. To his opponents, this meant that Ritschl was willing to weaken the normative strength of church dogma, creed, and confession in favor of his conception of freedom in Jesus. Ritschl's reading of Luther's *Freedom of a Christian* stimulated this orientation and elevated that treatise in a way that continues to this day. Although Ritschl did not follow the precision of his student Wilhelm Herrmann (1846–1922) in tying theology to the study of religion or in defining theology as a science, he drew an important distinction that marks liberalism in many of its forms: theology should exclude metaphysics. While many other kinds of modern theology, such as Ritschl's frequent sparring partner F. H. R. von Frank (1827–94) of the Erlangen school, drew sharp lines between philosophy, theology, and natural science, Ritschl did so in a way that decisively elevated the concept of revelation. Though liberalism would locate revelation in a variety of places, ranging from human experience to postulates of practical reason or authentic human existence, Ritschl set the basic pattern by creating a way for theologians to admit difference without abandoning what they thought God's revelation gave them. This means that liberalism has had a long legacy influencing many of its opponents, just as its contemporary advocates revive and modify its basic patterns established in the late nineteenth century.

See also Harnack, Adolf von; Holl, Karl; Ritschl, Albrecht; Semler, Johann Salomo; Troeltsch, Ernst

Bibliography

Harnack, A. von. *What Is Christianity?* Trans. T. Sanders. Fortress, 1986; Herrmann, W. *Die Religion im Verhältniss zum Welterkennen und zur Sittlichkeit*. M. Niemeyer, 1879; Ritschl, A. *Three Essays*. Trans. P. Hefner. Fortress, 1972; Troeltsch, E. *Writings on Theology and Religion*. Trans. and ed. R. Morgan and M. Pye. Westminster John Knox, 1990.

GREGORY WALTER

Liberation Theology and Marxism

Liberation theology centers on investigating the gospel's option for the poor, the marginal, and the oppressed, thus taking the side of the least among members of the human race. The poor are the socially insignificant, the invisible ones, and the social nonpersons. This option is primarily derived from God's own goodness. It is often referred to as being preferential, by attending first to the ones who need help the most. This also defines Christian discipleship: to follow Jesus by finding him among the poor and to see Jesus himself as one of the poor, finding God in the least expected places.

Poverty is no blissful state but an experience with suffering and death. Still, those are places for God's gracious presence and the promise of new life. Liberation theologians share with Lutherans a commitment to the power of the cross and resurrection, and they claim the hope of life arising from death.

Gustavo Gutiérrez, a Roman Catholic theologian, defines theology as a "critical reflection on praxis." The critical element is the analysis of the human condition using tools provided by the social sciences. Social analysis begins with experience, the confrontation with the human situation, which leads to the application of a "hermeneutics of suspicion" to structures of society. To apply suspicion means to ask the political question, pondering who actually benefits from the current socioeconomic and political conditions under which the majority of the population lives.

Liberation theology weighs the human condition from a faith perspective. For Gutiérrez, faith is always a "first act," while theological reflection is a "second act." Faith is a given, but theology takes time. Theological reflection is best done from the vantage point of committed Christians who are invested in the liberation of the poor. Therefore reflection is not an end in itself; it aims at the renewal or transformation of society through Christian praxis.

For liberation theologians, praxis is an encompassing concept that includes diverse instances of human activity, especially concerted efforts to change oppressive situations. Human beings engage the world by confronting the way things are and responding through transformative action. Liberation theologians agree with Marx that transformation of the world is more important than the need to understand it. To change the world, the materiality of life, human beings need action, not another theory of reality, either social or natural. This is the core of dialectical materialism: the world is not merely an object of contemplation but also the realm of action.

Theology commits itself to the process of liberation by making orthopraxis rather than orthodoxy the main focus of the Christian life. Theology cannot be done detached from actual life but by responding to people's clamor for life and the improvement of living conditions for the many. Faith cannot be reduced to right teaching alone.

Liberation theology has spread globally, especially across the two-thirds world. Theologies of liberation come under different names, with diversity of proponents and ecclesial contexts. This plurality has generated a complex relationship to Marxist sociology and philosophy in the last few decades. Early on, some liberation theologians embraced some form of Marxism, while others rejected any need to do so.

In the former group were those who basically agreed with Marx's critical view of society, and also of religion, in the form of a critique of oppression. Many believed that Marx's critique of political economy had merits that far surpassed its revolutionary shortcomings. But there were also those for whom the Christian tradition provided enough resources for the analysis of human dynamics, social, political, and otherwise. Gutiérrez has said that Marxism is a useful tool for the social analysis of the human condition, but that none of its more philosophical tenets—from its theory of revolutionary change to atheism—could be embraced by Christians.

Nonetheless, theologians have found in Marx a revealing dissection of society's illusory constructions, as in the critique of alienation. The abstraction of human nature from its own material reality is called alienation, which happens in both religion and politics. Individuals are alienated from real life by projecting themselves and their desires into a perfect realm and entity (what religion does) or into a perfect society and existence (what politics does). These are not exclusively problems of human consciousness, but consequences of the many divisions and conflicts in society.

Understanding the relation between ideology and domination is crucial for any theologian who cares about justice. In capitalism, a ruling class is also a society's ruling intellectual force: the material and intellectual means of production are in the same hands. This is the basic meaning of ideology. Moreover, by splitting manual and mental labor, individuals are alienated from themselves and from one another, creating the conditions for effective domination in society.

Theology can be ideological when used to legitimize injustice, thus becoming an instrument of subjugation instead of freedom. Luther himself denounced the dominant theology of his day; his was a critique of the church's and society's focus on power, riches, and works-righteousness. Already his Ninety-Five Theses called for giving to the poor rather than buying indulgences. Early Lutherans not only provided charity for the poor but also, in their own way (esp. through the establishment of community chests), showed some concern for the underlying causes of such poverty. In early Pietism (as in the Franckean institutions of Halle) and in the nineteenth century (as with the Inner Mission of German-speaking lands and the development of deaconesses in various places), Lutherans also showed concern for the poor but not always for the structures that caused poverty. Especially in India, Dalit theology among some of the Lutheran theologians has proved to be particularly important. In this way, certain strands of Lutheranism share liberation theology's desire to expose human infatuation with domination, wealth, self-sufficiency, and prestige.

See also Economic Issues: Capitalism and Socialism; Gender: Men and Women; Imperialism; Race/Minorities; Women's Movement

Bibliography

Altmann, W. *Luther and Liberation*. Fortress, 1992; Balibar, É. *The Philosophy of Marx*. Verso, 2014; Boff, L., and C. Boff. *Introducing Liberation Theology*. Orbis, 1987; Nickoloff, J. B., ed. *Gustavo Gutiérrez: Essential Writings*. Fortress, 1996; Miranda, J. P. *Marx and the Bible*. Orbis, 1974; Stumme, W., ed. *Christians and the Many Faces of Marxism*. Augsburg, 1984.

Nelson Rivera

Liberia

The Lutheran Church in Liberia (LCL) has tripled in size over the last twenty years. Its more than 71,000 members have been deeply affected by fourteen years of civil war (1989–2003). Trauma healing, peace building, and reconciliation are important dimensions of the work of LCL today.

Lutheran activities started in 1860 when Morris Officer and other missionaries were sent by antecedent bodies of the Lutheran

Church in America. David A. Day (1851–97), who arrived in 1874, was the first to survive for a longer period of time. He established a station inland from Monrovia, opened a school, and offered health services. Healthcare ministries became a special focus: in 1921 Phebe Hospital was opened; Curran Hospital followed in 1924. During the early period, Lutheran work concentrated among the Kpelle and Lona peoples in central and northwestern Liberia.

The LCL was organized in 1947, but the leaders of the sponsoring mission remained in control of finances and assignment of personnel. Only in 1965 did the church become fully autonomous. The first Liberian LCL president was Roland J. Payne (1920–94), elected in 1963. In 1971 he became bishop, nicknamed "the Jungle-Bishop" because of the rural focus of the church. Under his leadership the LCL started to grow more rapidly, and a lay training center and two literacy centers were established. Payne also led the LCL into membership in the LWF, the World Council of Churches, All Africa Conference of Churches, and the Liberian Council of Churches.

During the civil war (1989–2003), most of the LCL church buildings were looted or destroyed. Many LCL members found themselves displaced into other countries, and many of them moved to the United States, especially Minnesota. The Association of Liberian Lutherans in the Americas (ALLIA), founded in August 2011, held its first convention in August 2012 in Minneapolis. Many transnational interactions link Lutherans in the United States and Liberia. The LCL is also engaged in cross-border ministry and mentoring the new Lutheran Church in Guinea. For the war victims it offers the Trauma Healing and Reconciliation Program (THRP). The program has proved to be an invaluable tool for reconciliation between the victimizers and the victims of the civil war in Liberia. The LCL also provides counseling, testing, and support for individuals affected by HIV and AIDS. It is the only church institution in Liberia training counselors to work with HIV-positive persons. Another arm of the LCL is the Lutheran Development Service in Liberia, established in January 2002.

At the invitation of the son of a Mende chief, the LCMS began work in northwestern Liberia in 1978. Missionaries withdrew in 1990 at the outset of civil war; their work continues in the Evangelical Lutheran Church in Liberia Synod (ELCLS), with 18,000 members in 140 congregations, 6 of which have schools. The Evangelical Lutheran Church of Liberia, a smaller group with a background in Pentecostal churches, is now in fellowship with the LCMS.

Bibliography
Gbowee, L. *Mighty Be Our Powers: How Sisterhood, Prayer, and Sex Changed a Nation at War.* Beast Books, 2011; Ludwig, F. "Just Like Joseph in the Bible: The Liberian Christian Presence in Minnesota." In *African Christian Presence in the West*, ed. F. Ludwig and K. Asamoah-Gyadu, 357–80. African World, 2011; Payne, R. J. *A Miracle of God's Grace: A History of the Lutheran Church in Liberia.* Lutheran Church in Liberia, 2000.

FRIEDER LUDWIG

Lilje, Hanns

The Lutheran bishop and ecumenist Hanns Lilje (1899–1977) was born in Hannover. He studied history and theology in Göttingen and Leipzig, was ordained in 1924, and served the first three years of his ministry working with children and youth. From 1927 to 1935, he served as general secretary of the German Student Christian Movement. In 1933, Lilje joined with Martin Niemoeller (1892–1984) and Walter Künneth (1901–97) in organizing the Young Reformation Movement in opposition to the pro-Nazi Reich Bishop Ludwig Müller (1883–1945). Lilje and his colleagues in this movement called for a church that would be free to confess, unhampered by governmental control. In opposition to confessional Lutheran theologians such as Werner Elert (1885–1954), Paul Althaus (1888–1966), and Hermann Sasse (1895–1976), Lilje was a stalwart supporter of the Barmen Declaration. From 1935 to 1945, he worked as the general secretary of the Lutheran

World Convention. During this period Lilje actively engaged with others in the Confessing Church in opposition to National Socialism. This involvement would lead to his imprisonment for the duration of the war.

After the war, in 1947, Lilje became bishop of the Lutheran Church in Hannover, a position he held until his retirement in 1971. He was instrumental in the formation of the Lutheran World Federation in 1947 and was a member of its Executive Committee until 1970. From 1952 to 1957 Lilje served as its president. In 1948 he participated in the formation of the World Council of Churches.

Lilje was inspired by Martin Luther's life and teaching, and he sought to use Luther's theology as a foundation for public witness and ecumenical conversation. Lilje exercised wide influence in Lutheran church life in Germany and globally in the decades after the war. Known as a charismatic and courageous preacher, his sermons were marked by a strong emphasis on confidence and hope that Christians possess on account of Christ, countering the skepticism that colored the postwar period. Lilje's devotional commentary on the book of Revelation is reflective of this hope.

See also Barmen Confession; Confessing Church; Ecumenical Dialogues; German Christians (Deutsche Christen); Niemoeller, Martin; World Wars I and II

Bibliography
Lilje, H. *The Last Book of the Bible: The Meaning of the Revelation of St. John*. Trans. O. Wyon. Muhlenberg, 1957; Lilje, H. *The Valley of the Shadow*. Muhlenberg, 1950; Ulden, R. *Hanns Lilje: Bischof der Öffentlichkeit*. Lutherisches Verlagshaus, 1998.

JOHN T. PLESS

Lindbeck, George

Born in 1923 in China as a son of Lutheran missionaries, George Lindbeck became professor of theology at Yale Divinity School. Growing out of his work as a Lutheran ecumenist, Lindbeck, along with the late Hans Frei, helped found postliberal theology, which—in contrast to the individualist, rationalist, and foundationalist trends in theological liberalism—argues that theology should center on a narrative presentation of the Christian faith as regulative. This approach resists accommodation to secularism and seeks for theology to be faithful to the distinctive culture, grammar, and practices of faith. Appealing to Ludwig Wittgenstein's notion of "language games," in which communication is linked to practices that have their own distinctive grammar, Lindbeck has challenged the modern supposition of a common foundation for truth, such as Schleiermacher's "feeling of absolute dependence." Lindbeck built on Luther's conviction that it is an "external word" (*verbum externum*) through which God administers grace; thus he claimed that language shapes human life rather than an alleged "depth experience," as theological liberals maintain. Lindbeck has thus sought an alternative both to traditional orthodoxy, which views theology as informative propositions or truth claims about objective realities, and forms of theological liberalism, which see theology as nondiscursive symbols grounded in an existential orientation. In contrast, for Lindbeck, theological truth is found in how humans conform their behavior to the shape of life indicated by Scripture and tradition. Lindbeck's thinking thus offered a less defensive and more assertive and robust approach to Christian doctrine. Ecumenically, Lindbeck especially sought rapprochement between Lutherans and Roman Catholics, serving both as an observer at the Vatican II Council and as a member of the international Lutheran–Roman Catholic dialogue until 1987.

See also Ecumenical Dialogues; Theological Prolegomena

Bibliography
Lindbeck, G. *The Church in a Postliberal Age*. Ed. J. Buckley. Eerdmans, 2002; Lindbeck, G. *The Nature of Doctrine: Religion and Theology in a Postliberal Age*. Westminster, 1984.

MARK C. MATTES

Literature

The most valued literary genre in the Lutheran tradition is the hymn text. Martin Luther, while not a poet, had the poetic gifts to write both texts and tunes, several of which are unquestioned classics in the canon of hymnody. German hymnody from 1524 to 1675 gave the common people poetry that they could memorize and sing, cherishing its teaching and proclamation even if the Sunday sermon may have been far beyond their ken. Paul Gerhardt (1607–76) became the greatest literary talent of the German Lutheran movement. Hymn writers of the Lutheran movement in the other Lutheran lands were also, like Luther, pioneers in their respective literatures. Jiří Třanovský (1592–1637), known as Luther to the Slavs, wrote the collection *Cithara Sanctorum* (Lyre of the saints), published in 1636 in Czech, still the main corpus of Czech and Slovak hymnals. Thomas Hansen Kingo (1634–1703), the first great hymn writer in Denmark, established the poetic style and metrics of Danish as he was writing his hymns. His contemporary Dorothe Engelbretsdatter (1634–1716) in Bergen was the first woman in Norway to support herself by her hymns and poems. Magnus Brostrup Landstad (1802–80) in Norway wrote hymns that changed the language of worship in that country to a more authentic Norwegian, and Elias Blix (1836–1902), the more poetic hymn writer of northern Norway, established new Norwegian as a richly concrete poetic language still sung and recited among Norwegians. In Sweden, Jesper Svedberg (1653–1735), the compiler of the long-lived *Then Swenska Psalm-boken* (1694), cannot be ignored. His work as poet and scholar of the language profoundly influenced Swedish literature. Johan Ludvig Runeberg (1804–77), the national poet of Finland who wrote in Swedish, produced hymns that still live in the Finnish hymnal and literary canon. No greater Lutheran poet lived than Hallgrímur Pétursson (1614–74), the Baroque poet, whose fifty hymns on Christ's passion are still recited in Iceland during Lent on the radio and subjected to learned critique to this day.

Genres such as travel narratives and novels were beginning to develop after the Reformation. Lutherans may later have come to view such literature as somewhat suspect because it was not written in the language of theology and thus was ambiguous and unstable in its abstract meaning. However, during the Reformation Lutherans continued the medieval tradition of religious plays, but during Pietism the most passionate believers tended to shun literature and the theater because they dealt with fictional situations and frequently had to use unsavory characters and situations for the conflicts to be realistic. Lina Sandell (1832–1903), for example, would not attend operas for both of these reasons. While one could argue that most literature of the Lutheran lands—Germany, Denmark, Sweden, Finland, Norway, and Iceland—was always culturally Lutheran, it would not be true today, although deeply Lutheran structures may be beneath much of it. Petter Dass, pastor in northern Norway (1647–1707), wrote the first collection of poems on the far North—*Nordens trompet* (*The Trumpet of the North*)—and his hymns on Luther's catechism still charm with their colorful use of the local flora and fauna. One of the few novels of the Pietist Enlightenment period in Denmark was *Menoza* (1742–43) by Erik Pontoppidan (1698–1764), bishop of Bergen and later chancellor of the University of Copenhagen. A true bildungsroman, it describes the travels of a young Indian man to find the truth. He visits the Tranquebar Lutheran Mission, Mecca, Constantinople, Rome, Geneva, and Canterbury, and cannot find the truth until he arrives in Lutheran Denmark.

As national literatures developed through the eighteenth century into the nineteenth, people raised in Lutheran homes who were breaking away from their tradition contributed significantly, such as the internationally celebrated writers Henrik Ibsen and August Strindberg, both of whom were haunted by the Lutheran Pietism of their childhood.

In the modern era, Thomas Mann (1875–1955), raised in the Lutheran city of Lübeck, Germany, wrote perhaps the greatest of all modern novels on the rise and decline of a Lutheran family—*Buddenbrooks* (1901). Selma Lagerlöf (1858–1940), the first woman to win a Nobel Prize for Literature (1909), wrote her trilogy *Jerusalem*, featuring Swedish Pietists leaving for Jerusalem to be there when Jesus returned. It became a successful film in 1996. Most well known was her novel *Gösta Berling*, about an alcoholic Swedish priest, which was made into one of the first Swedish movies. The films of Ingmar Bergman (1918–2007), the Swedish pastor's son (*The Seventh Seal, Wild Strawberries, Through a Glass Darkly, Winter Light*, and *Fannie and Alexander*), all live in and around the Swedish Lutheranism that Bergman knew as a child. In America, the Pulitzer Prize–winning author Conrad Richter drew from German-American culture to write several novels about his Lutheran upbringing in Pennsylvania, including one about a Lutheran pastor, *A Simple, Honorable Man*. Ole Edvard Rølvaag's (1876–1931) *Giants in the Earth* is one of the most successful American novels of nineteenth-century immigration, featuring the struggles of the immigrant wife Beret to reconcile and live in the faith of her mothers and fathers on the barren South Dakota prairies: to survive there, she finds refuge in the hymns of the Dano-Norwegian hymnals of her day. Vilhelm Moberg's (1898–1973) novels on Swedish immigration became the basis for the popular films *The Emigrants* and *The New Land*. The greatest writer with Lutheran roots in the latter half of the twentieth century was John Updike (1932–2009), whose novels *Rabbit, Run; Rabbit Redux; Rabbit Is Rich*; and *Rabbit at Rest* are considered classics portraying middle-class America in the mid-twentieth century. Garrison Keillor's (b. 1942) radio program *A Prairie Home Companion* introduced more people around the world to upper midwestern American Lutherans than any other writer. While not himself a Lutheran, his portrayals of mythical small-town Lake Wobegon in Minnesota populated with Norwegian Lutherans and German Catholics drew huge audiences at the end of the twentieth century.

In China, although little literature by Christians has achieved notice, there are a good number of Chinese hymns by Christians from former Lutheran regions. Most notable is Xiao Min (b. 1970), the prolific and popular hymn writer from Henan province, who has written over one thousand hymns beloved by Chinese Christians.

See also Devotional Literature; Hymnody

GRACIA GRINDAL

Liturgy and Worship

Theology. The Reformation began in the renewal of liturgical practice. The Ninety-Five Theses (1517) focused on the abuse of ritual practice (indulgences, absolution, and preaching) and the theology that these practices reflected. Grace could not be purchased by throwing money in a coffer. Nothing a person might do could earn or buy a way around God's judgment. The first reforms, therefore, addressed practices of worship that reinforced an understanding of relationship to God based on works-righteousness.

Luther understood that ritual speaks as loud as the spoken word. Liturgical practice embodies theology. Rather than being fearful of traditional liturgical practice and relegating it or even eliminating it (as later generations did), Luther sought to renew worship in both word and sacrament, that is, in both word and rite, removing those aspects that obscured the gospel but keeping those things that enhanced it.

The focus of the majority of Luther's important treatises of the early Reformation period was proclamation in and through liturgical practice. The spate of tracts from 1519 (*A Sermon on Indulgences and Grace, On Penance, On Baptism, The Blessed Sacrament of the Holy and True Body of Christ and the Brotherhoods, A Meditation on Christ's Passion*) and *The Babylonian Captivity* of 1520 were theological treatises that reflected on liturgical practices. In these treatises, Luther shaped practice and theology into one coherent proclamation of the gospel.

For example, in the rite of baptism, Luther suggested that the infant or adult be fully immersed in the water. Through full immersion, participants could see that the whole person (mind and body) experienced the sacrament's purpose as dying and rising with Christ to new life. The practice of dunking in water—the symbolic gesture—was, for Luther, a visible sign of the proclamation of the gospel.

Attention to the sacrament of the altar (Holy Communion) was even more urgent. Perhaps there was no single practice of the medieval church that Luther opposed as vehemently as he did the sacrifice of the Mass. For Luther, the medieval Mass embodied a theology opposed to faith. The Mass was a work performed by the priest for the people. The people could watch and thereby receive the benefits of the unbloodied sacrifice of Christ by the priest, but rarely participate and then only in the eating of the bread, or they could pay for the sacrament to be "said," thereby reducing the time one or one's loved ones might spend in purgatory. The sacrament was a sacrifice directed toward God. Luther reversed the direction, not only of the sacrament but also of worship in general.

The sacrament was God's gift for the people, a benefit given to them and not a work that they needed to accomplish. Luther's entire Reformation insight is summarized in a simple liturgical practice: the priest (pastor) now speaks the gospel (the words of institution, "In the night in which he was betrayed, Our Lord Jesus took bread . . .") not to the high altar and upward toward God but rather facing the people and offering them both the bread and the wine. Sacrament is no longer understood as sacrifice but as gift or benefit. Worship is admonition and comfort: God breaking in to the assembly and opening a space for the Holy Spirit to create faith and leading to prayer and thanksgiving (Ap 24).

This dynamic was reflected in the CA, article 5 (Latin; *BC* 41) as follows: "So that we may obtain this faith, the ministry of teaching the gospel and administering the sacraments was instituted. For through the Word and the sacraments as through instruments the Holy Spirit is given, who effects faith where and when it pleases God in those who hear the gospel." The Holy Spirit works to create faith through both the teaching (preaching) and the administering (distributing, eating, drinking, and of course washing). The gospel is both preached and distributed, spoken and ritually enacted. As Philip Melanchthon reiterates in the Apology 13.5 (*BC* 219): "And God moves our hearts through the word and the rite at the same time so that they believe and receive faith. . . . For just as the Word enters through the ear in order to strike the heart, so also the rite enters through the eye in order to move the heart."

Luther's radical reversal of sacramental practice and theology was coupled with great reserve in his revisions of the Latin Mass. He hesitated to make any major reforms to the liturgical order of the Mass. In March 1522 he returned to Wittenberg from the Wartburg after hearing how more radical reformers, among them Andreas Karlstadt, were forcing liturgical reforms on the people. Luther reinstituted many practices of the medieval Mass, for example, allowing Communion in one kind out of concern that the weak in faith were not ready for these innovations. Liturgical reform needed to proceed with caution so that faith not be shaken and that the whole community be gradually shaped by proclamation in both word and sacrament.

In 1523 Luther produced the *Formula Missae* (Latin Mass) based on the medieval Mass and grounded in the liturgical year and its lectionary. He made no substantial change to the order of service except for the elimination of the offertory prayers and the prayers of the canon (spoken after the Sanctus), both of which in his opinion smacked of sacrifice or works-righteousness. In 1526 he produced the German Mass, which was a simplification of the *Formula Missae* and designed for the "uneducated." Rather than forcing German words into Latin chants, Luther used hymns with rhyme and meter that, he thought, matched the German way of singing.

Luther's comments in the Preface to the German Mass reveal his approach to worship in general and specifically to liturgical practice. A liturgical order is not to be a "rigid law" that is to be imposed in every context and on every community. The liturgical order translates the gospel, through word and sacrament, shaping the worshiping community into a gospel community. This translation may vary from place to place. The one constant is the grounding of the liturgy in word and sacrament, two activities where God has promised to be always present.

Luther was not opposed to innovation as long as it was in the service of the gospel, that is, as long as it continually proclaimed the Christ event for the gathered community. But even then innovation was to be rooted in the tradition. Luther noted favorably that there are many new experiments in worship but then also laments that some "have no more than an itch to produce something novel so that they might shine before others as leading lights, rather than being ordinary teachers" (Preface to the German Mass; LW 53:61).

Luther's insistence on worship in word and sacrament drew attention to the reality of worship as proclamation in both words and rites. The spoken word and the embodied word (or "visible Word," a phrase in Augustine often cited by Luther) are integral components through which God's promise is continually given to the faith community. The liturgical order in word and sacrament shapes both the mind and the body of believers. For Luther, the liturgical order is essential, for it "may make Christians out of us" (Preface to the German Mass; LW 53:62).

History. Even before Luther's German Mass of 1526, various liturgical orders (part of the *Kirchenordnung,* "church orders") were springing up in German cities influenced by the Reformation, most notably in Nuremberg (an initial liturgy was produced in 1524, subsequently revised several times by Andreas Osiander, and completed in 1533). These church orders regulated far more than simply liturgical practice. They also addressed questions of church administration and governance, congregational life, and schools.

Johannes Bugenhagen, Luther's pastor in Wittenberg, was an important contributor in the development and propagation of church orders (Braunschweig, 1528; Hamburg, 1529; Lübeck, 1531; Pomerania, 1535; Wolfenbüttel, 1543). Bugenhagen influenced the Wittenberg church order of 1533, produced by Justus Jonas, and he worked for two years in Denmark (1537–39) to establish a Danish (and Norwegian) church order, thus broadening the reach of liturgical reform. In collaboration with others, Philip Melanchthon also produced several important church orders, most notably for Cologne in 1543 (never enacted) and Mecklenburg in 1540 and 1552.

These church orders varied in structure and in practice. In *Christian Liturgy: Catholic and Evangelical,* Frank Senn notes (quoting Luther D. Reed) that the church orders could be classified into three groups: a central Saxon-Lutheran type, an ultra-conservative type, and a mediating or radical type. Medieval practices were more dominant in the ultra-conservative type, notably in Margraviate of Brandenburg; a reformed influence in Strasbourg and Geneva influenced the mediating or radical type in western and southern German lands, especially Württemberg (Senn 330–31).

In Sweden, Olavus Petri, who had been a student of Luther in Wittenberg in 1518–19, produced the Swedish Mass based on the *Formula Missae* and especially the Nuremberg church order. Perhaps influenced by the Nuremberg order, Petri created a public confession of sins at the beginning of the liturgical order. Luther does not have such a public confession either in the Formula Missae or in the German Mass, although certain comments make clear that such a public confession and absolution followed the sermon.

In the Lutheranism of the seventeenth century and beyond, Lutheran Orthodoxy and Pietism (later, the Enlightenment) influenced to some degree the shape of the liturgy, in which the Lord's Supper was celebrated less often, baptism became more of a naming ceremony and family ritual, and heavy emphasis was placed upon the sermon. Still, music and hymnody remained a fixture in most places. In Bach's Leipzig of the eighteenth century, the cantata became a fixture in the liturgy of the Word. As Lutheranism began to spread beyond Europe, these later practices also became part of Lutheran missions and influenced Lutheran worship to this day.

In North America, for example, Henry Melchior Mühlenberg (1711–87) produced a liturgical order that accommodated itself to the diversity of Lutheran traditions present in the colonies (around 1748). Mühlenberg recognized that he could not impose one particular style since the colonists were not only from much earlier Swedish immigration but also were German immigrants from western and southern regions who were suspicious of anything that might be too "papist" (such as chanting the prayers). Mühlenberg's liturgy, while following the order developed by Lutherans attached to the Hanoverian court in London, also follows Luther's admonition not to turn a liturgical order into a rigid law. Mühlenberg sought to adapt word and sacrament to the local context, though the celebration of the sacrament of Holy Communion was not regularly practiced.

Another example of liturgical reform in the American context comes from the late nineteenth century, when Edward T. Horn (1850–1915), along with colleagues at the seminary in Philadelphia (Mt. Airy), began working on a common service (1888, which eventually culminated in the Common Service of 1917). Horn had done extensive historical research into the development of the church orders in the German lands. He observed that new elements in the Lutheran service were (1) the reintroduction of the sermon, (2) the restoration of the general prayer, and (3) the insertion of an exhortation before Communion.

After ascertaining the contours of Lutheran worship, Horn then asked a contextual question: Does anything need to be added or taken away in the American context? Thus, Horn did not treat the liturgical orders as rigid laws. He realized that every age must ask what is edifying for the people. For example, Horn and his colleagues thought it wise to place a public confession of sins at the beginning of the service even though, as he states, this liturgical practice was not part of the majority of Lutheran church orders developed in the sixteenth century, although it does occur in Melanchthon's church order for Mecklenburg and in the Swedish Mass.

As of 1910, Luther D. Reed became secretary for the Joint Commission producing the materials for the Common Service of 1917. Immediately following World War II, in 1945, work began on a common liturgy and hymnal that became the monumental and highly influential *Service Book and Hymnal* (March 1958). Many representatives from numerous Lutheran church bodies worked on this liturgical order and hymnal, with Luther D. Reed taking on a leading role. Reed wrote the definitive commentary on the Common Service that served as a basis for the practice of Lutheran liturgical practice for several generations: *The Lutheran Liturgy* (1947).

With the Second Vatican Council (1962–65), the Roman Catholic Church now led the way in liturgical reform, particularly through its *Constitution on the Sacred Liturgy* (1963). The principles for reform identified in this document inspired and spurred on worship renewal in many Protestant denominations. Beginning in 1965, the Lutheran Church in America, the American Lutheran Church, and the Lutheran Church–Missouri Synod (LCMS) worked on producing a new service book, *Lutheran Book of Worship* (LBW), which was published in 1978 (though the Lutheran Church–Missouri Synod withdrew from the common project shortly before publication and released its own adaptation, *Lutheran Worship*, in 1982). More recently, the Evangelical Lutheran Church in America (ELCA) decided that it was necessary to produce a new worship book, due to changes in language patterns, the influx of new immigrants, the introduction of music from around the world, and a desire to underscore the theological rationale of the liturgical order. In 2006 the *Evangelical Lutheran Worship* (*ELW*) was published. Besides its sensitivity to language questions and the introduction of music from partner churches around the world, the *ELW* highlights the classic pattern of worship in word and sacrament, retrieving Luther's focus on the importance of worship as proclamation in both word and rite. In the same year, the LCMS published the *Lutheran Service Book*, understood as a blending of the best of *The Lutheran Hymnal* (1941) and *Lutheran Worship* and offering a variety of gospel-centered hymns from every age and many countries.

See also Hymnody; *Kirchenordnung*; Music; Prayer; Preaching

Bibliography

Lathrop, G. *Holy Things: A Liturgical Theology*. Fortress, 1998; Leaver, R. *Luther's Liturgical Music*. Eerdmans, 2007; Luther, M. *The German Mass*. Trans. D. Lange. In *The Annotated Luther*, vol. 3. Fortress, 2016; Luther, M. *An Order of Mass and Communion for the Church at Wittenberg*. LW 53; Senn, F. *Christian Liturgy: Catholic and Evangelical*. Augsburg Fortress, 1997; Wengert, T. *Centripetal Worship: The Evangelical Heart of Lutheran Worship*. Augsburg Fortress, 2007.

DIRK G. LANGE

Livonia

Livonia (1225–1561, today Latvia and Estonia) was located south of Scandinavia, on the eastern shores of the Baltic Sea, and was populated by Baltic and Finnic tribes, each speaking their respective languages. The name Livonia historically was applied to the territories that were progressively invaded by the Teutonic Order.

Livonia was the first country outside Germany to adopt the Reformation. Hussites had visited Riga fifty years before the Lutheran Reformation. Works of Erasmus were popular. Converted Catholic priests were important early supporters of the Reformation. From 1519 to 1521 the man who later was chaplain of St. Peter's at Riga, Andreas Knopken (also

Knöpken, Knopke, Knopius, Cnopha, 1468–1539), stayed in Treptow, Germany, where he succeeded Bugenhagen as the rector of the Latin school, studied Luther's teachings, read patristic and humanist writings, and corresponded with Erasmus. Knopken returned to Riga as a promoter of the Reformation with a letter of recommendation from Melanchthon to the city council.

Knopken found followers among the city councilors of Riga. A public debate was held in St. Peter's in June 1522. Knopken defended twenty-four theses that emphasized justification by faith and attacked medieval church practices. His commentary on Romans was published in 1524 at Wittenberg and was reprinted three times with Melanchthon's support and Bugenhagen's foreword. He wrote and translated many hymns into Low German; some were placed in the first Latvian hymnals. In October 1522 the city council, against the will of the archbishop, appointed Knopken as the archdeacon of St. Peter's. At St. James the city council placed another follower of Luther, Sylvester Tegetmeier (d. 1552) from Mecklenburg.

The city clerk Johannes Lohmüller (1483–1560) from Danzig, who was influenced by Luther's teaching as early as 1518, wrote Luther in August 1522 and in 1523, reporting on the progress of the Reformation in Riga and asking for a letter of encouragement. Luther replied in September 1523 with "To the Christians in Riga, Reval, and Dorpat." Luther wrote to Spalatin on February 1, 1524: "The Gospel has begun and spread in Livonia, especially around Riga successfully, whose letters and also an envoy I have just received. So amazing is Christ." To Konrad Durkop's response "on behalf of entire Christian Church in Riga," Luther sent *Exposition of Psalm 127 for the Christians of Riga and Livonia* and *A Christian Exhortation to the Livonians concerning Public Worship and Concord* in June 1525. Luther's support made Riga one of the leaders of the Reformation in Europe.

Lords and burghers supported the Reformation to free themselves from the Livonian Order (a branch of the Teutonic knights and an important local political force) and from the archbishop, while peasants were basically indifferent. Wolter von Plettenberg (ca. 1450–1535), the master of the Livonian Order, was too tolerant and Archbishop Jasper Linde (d. 1524) too old to resist the Reformation. In 1524 at a meeting in Reval, Burgomaster Koning of Riga declared that Riga "acquired the holy Gospel and will not leave it but will defend it with life and property." In March 1524 members of the merchant brotherhood "Blackheads" carried out an iconoclastic action, destroying their own altar in St. Peter's. Other iconoclastic attacks followed.

After Archbishop Linde's death, the Riga city council did not accept his successor, Johannes Blankenfeld (ca. 1471–1527), and offered the status of protector to Plettenberg. He guaranteed the freedom of religion to Lutheranism in 1525. In 1538 Riga joined the Smalcaldic League.

The Reformation gained the upper hand throughout Livonia, and in 1554 the Landtag of Wolmar pronounced freedom of religion, which in the context of two existing contesting denominations—Catholic and Lutheran—meant recognition of the Reformation's victory. In 1555 the Peace of Augsburg was signed by the representatives of the Livonian Order.

To unify the liturgy used in Lutheran services, Dr. Johan Briessman (1488–1549), a friend and pupil of Luther, was invited and became a pastor of the Riga cathedral and a superintendent (1527–31). He organized St. Peter's and cathedral schools. In 1528 the city council asked Luther's pupil Dutchman Jacob Battus to become its rector. In 1527 the city council asked Briessman to produce the Order of the Church, and in 1529 he came up with Brief Order of Church Service along with a statement on ceremonies (printed in Rostock, 1530). He used Königsberg's liturgy as a model. It was accepted in Revel and Dorpat also.

The first Latvians who accepted the Evangelical faith were the workers, who constituted one-third of the inhabitants of Riga. They became familiar with the Reformation through their guilds, which had altars in the churches, and their priests. A Latvian Lutheran congregation was established in Riga in 1524 at St. James. Notable preachers in Latvian included Nicolaus Ramm (1524–?), Lorenz von Scheden (1524–34), Johann Eck (1534–52), among others. Due to the lack of preaching in Latvian, the Reformation spread to the countryside slowly and gradually.

Latvian Lutheran texts were first mentioned in 1525 when the Lübeck Catholic council confiscated a large number of Lutheran missals in Latvian. The Reformation made a significant impact on education, schools, religious literature, and the production of Latvian literature. In 1537 Eck composed the Latvian church agenda (order). The first catechetical texts were translated, possibly by Ramm (ca. 1526), from the *Layen Bibel*. Ramm composed hymns and antiphons, Eck and Scheden translated Gospels and Epistles. Luther's entire Small Catechism was printed, perhaps as early as 1560 but certainly by 1586 (in Königsberg). Twenty-eight of Luther's hymns were accepted in the first Latvian hymnal, *Non-German Psalms*, in 1587. Burkard Waldis (1490–1556), a former Franciscan monk and a humanist, composed a play, *The Parable of the Prodigal Son* (performed February 17, 1527), one of the earliest and significant Reformation dramas.

The Reformation long remained primarily a movement of the Germans and Latvians in the large cities. It changed the religious and social situation of rural Latvians very little, and it did not lead to revolts as in Germany or Estonia. Latvian peasant religiosity generally remained the same—usually a syncretic mix between former paganism and formal Catholicism.

At the partition of Livonia in 1562, Courland and Semigallia went together with the Courland duke Gotthard Kettler's (1517–87) Lutheran Church, Vidzeme came under Sweden and remained Lutheran, but Latgallia was under Poland and re-Catholicized. After the Polish-Swedish War (1600–1629), a large part of Latvia, including Riga, came under Sweden, which ruled until the Great Northern War (1700–1721) with Russia, which invaded Latvia and ruled until 1917. In 1918 Latvia gained its independence. In 1922 the Latvian Lutheran Church was established.

See also Courland (Kurland); Estonia; Latvia; Mancelius, Georgius

Bibliography

Arbusow, L. *Die Einführung der Reformation in Liv-, Est- und Kurland.* Scientia, 1964; Hoerschelmann, D. *Andreas Knopken, Der Reformator Rigas: Ein Beitrag zur Kirchengeschichte Livlands.* Nabu, 2010; Packull, W. "Sylvester Tegetmeier, Father of Livonian Reformation: A Fragment of His Diary." *Journal of Baltic Studies* 16 (1986): 343–56; Plakans, A. *The Latvians: A Short History.* Hoover Institution Press, Stanford University, 1995; Puisans, T. *The Emerging Nation: The Path of Agonizing Development from Baltic Tribalism to Latvian Nationhood.* Riga Centre of Baltic-Nordic History and Political Studies, 1995; Stradiņš, J. "Martin Luther and the Impact of the Reformation on the History of Latvia—Dialogue between Christianity and Secularism in Latvia." *Annals of European Academy of Sciences and Arts* 15 (1996): 75; Wittram, R., ed. *Baltische Kirchengeschichte: Beiträge zur Geschichte der Missionierung und der Reformation, der evangelisch-lutherischen Landeskirchen und des Volkskirchentums in den baltischen Landen.* Vandenhoeck & Ruprecht, 1956.

GUNTIS KALME

Loehe, Wilhelm Konrad

Wilhelm Konrad Loehe (Löhe, 1808–72) was a Bavarian pastor and author known for his spiritual writings, liturgical scholarship, pastoral theology, and leadership in missionary and diaconal activity. Born into a pious merchant family in the village of Fürth, Loehe studied at the University of Erlangen, where he came under the influence of Christian Krafft (1784–1845), who countered the prevailing rationalism and affirmed his own Reformed confessional identity; that moved Loehe to affirm his own confessional Lutheran identity. Ordained in 1831, Loehe served as an assistant pastor in several congregations, where he experienced conflict with church officials, before being called to Neuendettelsau in 1837.

His young wife, Helene, died six years later. Never fully recovering from her death, Loehe devoted the remainder of his life to ministry in Neuendettelsau while also producing a constant stream of theological and devotional publications, establishing enduring institutions of mercy in his village, and directing missionary activities in North America. His ministry, often embroiled with controversy and held in suspicion by church authorities, had worldwide influence.

Responding to F. C. D. Wyneken's (1810–76) appeal for assistance in meeting the spiritual poverty of German immigrants in the North American Midwest, Loehe collected funds and sent "emergency helpers" (often called missioners) to assist the cause. In 1845 he sent colonists to the Saginaw Valley of Michigan, where they established Frankenmuth and made plans for missionary outreach to Chippewa Native Americans. Ultimately the men Loehe dispatched developed contacts with the Saxon immigrants in Missouri and were instrumental in the formation of the Fort Wayne Seminary and the Missouri Synod. Differences between Loehe and C. F. W. Walther (1811–87) over ecclesiology and the pastoral office strained this relationship, finally causing it to rupture in 1853. Those who sided with Loehe left Michigan and settled in eastern Iowa, where they established the Iowa Synod and with it Wartburg College and Seminary. Loehe remained a patron of the Iowa Synod, but after 1854 his efforts were mostly directed to the institutions in Neuendettelsau, especially the Deaconess House.

Clearly shaped by the Lutheran confessional awakening of his day as it was transmitted through Erlangen, Loehe saw the Lutheran Church as at the middle of Christendom, existing in its particularity between the Roman and the reformed churches. His untiring efforts led to a renewed appreciation of the Lord's Supper and the practice of individual confession and absolution as the focal point of pastoral care. His *Three Books about the Church* (1845) serves as the most accessible statement of his understanding of ecclesiology, pastoral care, liturgical life, and mission, demonstrating both his churchly focus and his eschatological perspective. Mission is the one church in motion, according to Loehe. He held that the doctrine of the Book of Concord is true but in need of further unfolding. For him all of Lutheran doctrine comes to its climax in the sacrament of the altar.

The diaconal and missionary organizations formed by Loehe have endured to the present day. His immediate successors extended his missionary work into New Guinea and Australia.

See also Deaconesses; Ohio/Buffalo/Iowa Synods

Bibliography

Blaufuß, D., ed. *Wilhelm Löhe: Theologie und Geschichte/ Theology and History.* Freidmund, 2013; Geiger, E. *Wilhelm Loehe, 1808–1872.* Concordia, 2010; Loehe, W. *Three Books about the Church.* 1845. Reprint, Fortress, 1969.

JOHN T. PLESS

Lord's Supper

For Luther and Lutheran theology, the doctrine of the Lord's Supper persistently received its orientation from the Reformation teaching of justification. As Luther notes, the Lord's Supper is the "sum and substance of the gospel" (*summa et compendium Evangelii*, WA 6:525.36). Thus controversy and confession of eucharistic theology and practice during the Reformation were not approached as isolated points of dogma but as constituent of the totality of Evangelical teaching.

Martin Luther's theological reflection on the Lord's Supper began with his ordination as a Mass priest in Erfurt in 1507. In preparation, Luther studied Gabriel Biel's commentary on the *Canon of the Mass* (1488), which mediated the late medieval theology and practice of the Eucharist. From this text Luther was taught that the priest, on behalf of the church, must in all purity present the body and blood of Christ (transubstantiated from the bread and wine) as a sacrifice to the living and true God. Such a priestly offering was conceived as a propitiation effective *ex opere operato* (by the performance of the rite), an intercession for the people, and a merit derived and applied from the merits of Christ's death on Calvary. For Luther, this interpretation of the eucharistic sacrifice became one of the most visible instantiations of Rome's fundamental misconception of the gospel.

In his earliest lectures (1513–18), Luther could speak about the Mass as a sacrifice, but focused primarily on it as a sacrifice of confession or of praise (*sacrificium confessionis . . . [aut] laudis*). Already, any language of the sacrament's efficacy privileged the Word and the preaching of the gospel (e.g., LW 25:123.67). Interacting with various strands of the exegetical and dogmatic tradition, Luther dwelled increasingly on the sacrament as a "testament" and "promise" (*testamentum . . . promissio*). The centrality of faith came to the fore in the indulgence controversy and in his debate with Cardinal Cajetan, when Luther stressed that the efficacy of the sacrament depended on faith (in the word of Christ) and that it was such faith rather than the sacrament per se that justified (LW 31:107, 261, 277–78).

All of these initial strands came together in his 1519 sermon "The Blessed Sacrament of the Holy and True Body of Christ" and then his *Treatise on the New Testament* in 1520. Together they would represent in broad strokes the Reformation's break with the prevalent medieval view. Already affirming only three of the seven Roman sacraments, Luther's sermon proposes a new sacramental definition that is inspired by but distinct from Augustine's definition. Luther held that a sacrament consists of a visible sign, the meaning of what is signified, and faith. In the Lord's Supper, the bread and wine—composed of many kernels and yet "one cake, one bread, one body, one drink"—point to the unity, love, and communion (*communio*) of the church as members of Christ's body. In this communion with Christ, Christians exchange sin for his righteousness and are united together in the forgiveness of sin even as they bear each other's burdens.

While Luther's sermon assumes the presence of Christ's "true natural body" and his "natural true blood," Luther places greater stress on the role of faith, "upon which everything depends." In one's earnest desire for the sacrament and firm belief that one receives what the sacrament signifies, a Christian participates in the spiritual body of Christ, in which Christ and the saints have all things in common. With such priority given to faith, Luther challenged the Scholastic notion of the sacrament as an *opus operatum*—an action that intrinsically offers grace without reference to the disposition or faith of the recipient. Thus "it is not enough that the sacrament be merely completed; . . . it must be used in faith" (LW 35:60, 63).

In his *Treatise on the New Testament*, Luther further develops the definition of the sacrament and its benefits on the basis of Christ's words of institution. The central and chief part of the sacrament, Christ's words, are his "testament," ratified by his death and offered as the promised gift of forgiveness and eternal life. Along with this promise is offered his body and blood "under the bread and wine" (LW 35:86), indicating Luther's increasing ambivalence toward the doctrine of transubstantiation. With Luther's emphasis on the sacrament as Christ's testament comes his explicit repudiation of the Mass as a propitiatory sacrifice, accusing the papal mass as that of a "tyrant" and the "antichrist" (LW 35:107). Thus, Luther says, in this sacrament "we learn that we do not offer Christ as a sacrifice but that Christ offers us" to God as our priest and mediator. Luther also raised the issue of Communion under both kinds (bread and wine), with laity receiving both the bread and cup. Since withholding the cup from the laity was a relatively recent tradition and not even universally practiced, Luther argued that it would be best if a council restore the cup to the people in order to conform the sacrament to Christ's original institution.

Luther's critique of the prevalent teaching and practice of the sacrament culminated in *The Babylonian Captivity of the Church* (1520). In this polemical treatise, Luther sets forth the distinctive characteristics already observed in earlier writings but now within the context of a definitive break with Rome. Luther identifies three "captivities of the Mass" by which the papacy imprisons the Christian church: the reservation of the cup for priests alone, the doctrine of transubstantiation, and the use of the Mass as a sacrifice and work to gain divine favor. All three areas of critique were aimed at the sacrament's pastoral implications for conscience, faith, and its relationship to the justifying promise of the gospel. Withholding the cup from the laity was regarded as an act of Roman tyranny, with no consistent or legitimate justification. The central problem with transubstantiation was its imposition as an article of faith rather than merely a human opinion, derived from Aristotle, about the nature of the sacrament. Rome's most egregious error, however, was regarded by Luther as the celebration of the Mass as a sacrifice, because it recast Christ's testament, which should be received as a divine gift, into a human work and merit.

While Luther's accent on faith and his rejection of the sacrifice of the Mass were broadly shared by other Protestant reformers, his continued profession of the bodily presence of Christ found resistance from those who viewed Christ as only spiritually present in the meal. By 1525 Luther began to publish against his opponents on the nature of Christ's presence in the sacrament, first against his former colleague at Wittenberg, Andreas von Karlstadt, and then against others: Cornelius Hoen, Ulrich Zwingli, and Johannes Oecolampadius. Tracts included *Against the Heavenly Prophets in the Matter of Images and Sacraments* (1525; LW 40:61–223); *The Sacrament of the Body and Blood of Christ—against the Fanatics* (1526; LW 36:329–61); *That These Words of Christ, "This is My Body," etc. Still Stand Firm against the Fanatics* (1527; LW 37:3–150); *Confession concerning Christ's Supper* (1528; LW 37:151–372). Luther dubbed his opponents *Schwärmgeister*, for not only did they hold to a symbolic interpretation of the words "This is my body"—an interpretation that he and his followers firmly rejected—but they also seemed strongly ambivalent toward the very possibility of spiritual benefits being communicated through physical means. Zwingli in particular, arguing on the basis of John 6:63, set forth that nothing creaturely could support faith. Such a position moved Luther's critique beyond the interpretation of individual biblical passages toward its deeper implications for the nature of salvation. Luther saw not only the presence of Christ in the Eucharist at stake, but at a more fundamental, christological level, the presence of God in Christ through his flesh, meaning the unity of the divine and human natures in the person of Jesus. Consequently, Luther and his heirs would develop further theological reflection on Christology and its eucharistic implications, relying heavily on the patristic tradition (this position was later reflected in the Book of Concord's "*Catalogue of Testimonies* [*Catalogus testimoniorum*] of 1580; in Martin Chemnitz, *Repetition of the Unadulterated Teaching about the True Presence of the Body and Blood of the Lord in the Supper* [*Repetitio sanae doctrinae de vera praesentia corporis et sanguinis Domini in Coena*], 1561; and in Martin Chemnitz, *Concerning the Two Natures in Christ, Their Hypostatic Union [and] the Communication of Attributes* [*De duabus naturis in Christo: De hypostatica earum unione; De communicatione idiomaticum*, 1561).

Though not entirely successful, subsequent efforts to come to a Protestant consensus on the Lord's Supper did produce some further doctrinal clarification. In particular, the Wittenberg Concord of 1536, agreed to by theologians of Strasbourg, Augsburg, and Wittenberg, favored Luther's earlier concept of *unio sacramentalis* (sacramental union) when speaking about the association of the sacramental elements *with* Christ's body and blood (see Luther, *Confession concerning Christ's Supper* [1528], LW 37:161–372). The signers of the Wittenberg Concord thus agreed

that "with the bread and wine the body and blood are truly and substantially present, offered, and received" (*cum pane et vino vere et substantialiter adesse, exhiberi et sumi corpus Christi et sanguinem*). Further, it was affirmed that the "unworthy" could also receive the body of Christ in the Supper (*manducatio indignorum*). What constituted an unworthy eating was left undefined, but Luther clearly understood the phrase to include the ungodly (*impiorum*) and those without faith, so that the presence of Christ in the sacrament rested on the power of the Word rather than in the hearts of those who commune.

Intra-Protestant and intra-Lutheran conflict over the Lord's Supper continued throughout the sixteenth and seventeenth centuries, as when Joachim Westphal attacked Calvin's apparent abandonment of the Wittenberg Concord by agreeing with the church in Zurich. Some of Philip Melanchthon's final comments on the Supper also placed his position concerning the real presence in doubt. Later, article 7 of the Formula of Concord clearly distinguished Lutheran doctrine from Rome on the one hand, and from Zurich and Geneva on the other. The Formula of Concord, written in direct reaction to so-called "Crypto-Calvinists" (or, better, Crypto-Philippists) who dominated Wittenberg's faculty in the 1570s, insisted that consensus on this doctrine ran through the Augsburg Confession of 1530, the Wittenberg Concord of 1536, and Luther's various writings on the matter. Focus on the mode of presence and reception was particularly important in the Formula of Concord: the oral reception of the sacrament was affirmed but distinguished from mere spiritual eating (i.e., by faith) on the one hand, and Capernaitic eating (natural, biological eating; see Jesus's discourse at Capernaum [John 6]) on the other hand. Instead, because of the *unio sacramentalis*, reception of Christ's body and blood is "supernatural" and "heavenly" eating, bringing "believers comfort and life," and bringing judgment to unbelievers. Thus it is the mouth that receives the sacrament, but faith alone receives the promise that such a sacrament is for forgiveness, life, and salvation. Article 8 of the Formula of Concord dealt with the christological issues connected to the eucharistic controversies.

As Lutheran theology and piety developed into the seventeenth and eighteenth centuries, the sacramental union became more deeply linked to the believer's mystical union with Christ (*unio mystica*). Participation in the benefits of the Lord's Supper was thus a participation in Christ himself. This gave further expression to an Evangelical bridal mysticism, which advanced an image of the Lord's Supper as the foretaste of the eschatological banquet, the marriage feast of the Lamb.

In the pastoral and political context of this period, admission to the Lord's Supper was increasingly a means for doctrinal and moral regulation. To this end, mandatory private confession in advance of Communion was not uncommon in Lutheran territories. Doctrinal and catechetical prerequisites for Communion were, in the case of Pietism, extended to include inner and moral renewal. At this time, definitions for a worthy reception of the Lord's Supper were subject to the political and confessional realities of early modern Europe, no longer centering on faith in the sacramental promises.

One such political reality, nineteenth-century Prussian hegemony, culminated in a Prussian union of churches. The state measures that forced Reformed and Lutheran churches into administrative, structural, and liturgical union raised to the fore the matter of Communion fellowship. Conflict over state coercion led some Lutherans to emigrate to Australia and the United States. In the United States, where broad denominational pluralism raised similar questions as in Germany, Lutheran sacramental theology continued to be shaped by the ecclesial implications of Communion fellowship. For many Lutheran immigrants, participation in the Lord's Supper was interpreted as a public act of confession and an ecclesiological mark of doctrinal agreement. This relationship of Communion fellowship to church fellowship continued to be debated throughout the twentieth century, conditioned by the effects of ecumenism alongside the various union movements among the European churches in the wake of the two world wars. Though the ecclesiological dimension of Communion fellowship is not a new element to sacramental theology (see Elert, *Eucharist and Church Fellowship in the First Four Centuries*, 1966), it persists as an unresolved issue in contemporary Lutheran thought. First in the twentieth century the Leuenberg Agreement between Reformed, Union, and Lutheran churches in Germany returned in broad terms to the confession of Christ's presence expressed in the Wittenberg Concord. Its terminology found its way into similar agreements between certain Reformed churches and the ELCA.

See also Christology; Ecumenical Dialogues; Formula of Concord; Justification; Sacraments; Wittenberg Circle, Parties within; Wittenberg Concord

Bibliography

Luther's Works: *The Babylonian Captivity of the Church* (1520). LW 36:5–126; *The Blessed Sacrament of the Holy and True Body of Christ and the Brotherhoods* (1519). LW 35:45–73; *The Sacrament of the Body and Blood of Christ—against the Fanatics* (1526). LW 36:329–61; *A Treatise on the New Testament, That Is, the Holy Mass* (1520). LW 35:75–111; **General Works:** Arand, C., R. Kolb, and J. Nestingen. "The Controversies over the Lord's Supper and Christology." In *The Lutheran Confessions: History and Theology of The Book of Concord,* 227–53. Fortress, 2012; Bizer, E. *Studien zur Geschichte des Abendmahlsstreits im 16. Jahrhundert.* Wissenschaftliche Buchgesellschaft, 1962; Burnett, A. N. *Karlstadt and the Origins of the Eucharistic Controversy: A Study in the Circulation of Ideas.* Oxford University Press, 2011; Elert, W. *Eucharist and Church Fellowship in the First Four Centuries.* Concordia, 1966; Hausammann, S. "Realpräsenz in Luthers Abendmahlslehre." In *Studien zur Geschichte und Theologie: Festschrift für Ernst Bizer,* ed. L. Abramowski, 157–73. Neukirchener Verlag, 1969; Hund, J. *Das Wort ward Fleisch: Eine systematisch-theologische Untersuchung zur Debatte um die Wittenberger Christologie und Abendmahlslehre in den Jahren 1567 bis 1574.* Vanderhoeck & Ruprecht, 2006; Jensen, G. "Luther and the Lord's Supper." In *The Oxford Handbook of Martin Luther's Theology,* ed. R. Kolb, I. Dingel, and L. Batka, 322–32. Oxford University Press, 2014; Sasse, H. *This Is My Body: Luther's Contention for the Real Presence in the Sacrament of the Altar.* Concordia, 2003.

ERIK HERRMANN

Löscher, Valentin Ernst

The theologian and opponent of Pietism, Valentin Ernst Löscher (1673–1749), was born in Sondershausen to Caspar Löscher and Cleophe Salome Sittig. He is considered one of the last representatives of Lutheran Orthodoxy. The Wittenberg-trained Löscher received a master's in philosophy in 1692 and doctorate in theology in 1700. Löscher lectured in philosophy at the universities in Jena and Wittenberg before becoming pastor in Jüterbog and superintendent in Delitzsch in 1698. After a two-year appointment as professor of theology at Wittenberg, Löscher moved to Dresden in 1709, where he became court preacher and superintendent. He remained there until his death in 1749. While in Jüterbog, he set forth the devotional program *Edle Andachts-Früchte* (Pure Fruits of Reflection; 1702), which reflected the recent Lutheran *Frömmigkeitsbewegung* (piety movement) and the integration of Theologia Mystica Orthodoxa (mystical, orthodox theology). His pastoral obligations led to the six-volume work *Evangelische Zehenden Gottgeheiligter Amts-Sorgen* (Evangelical tithes of divinely sanctified concerns from the office [of the ministry]). During his time as superintendent in Delitzsch, Löscher also used his pen to argue against attempts of Brandenberg-Prussia to effect unification between the Lutheran and Reformed churches. Beginning in 1701, Löscher edited the first theological periodical titled *Unschuldigen Nachrichten*. It addressed challenges to Lutheran Orthodoxy posed by competing confessions, religious radicals, and new forms of "atheistic" rationalism. It also printed many hitherto unknown documents from the Reformation. Though early in his career he had shown interest in Philipp Jakob Spener's church reform ideas, Löscher began using the periodical in 1705 to confront the advances of August Hermann Francke (1663–1727) and Halle Pietism, especially the ideas of Joachim Lange (1670–1744), Paul Anton (1661–1730), and Johann Anastasius Freylinghausen (1670–1739). The disputation with Pietism also resulted in Löscher's two-volume *Vollständiger Timotheus Verinus* (*The Complete Timothy Verinus*; 1718–22), which along with his periodical criticized Pietist views on justification and ecclesiology. Though critical of the Halle Pietists, Löscher hoped to establish common ground with them against rationalism while maintaining his theological convictions. This hope led him to an unsuccessful meeting with Francke in Merseburg in 1719. Löscher's attempts to protect a "pure" Lutheranism against the advances of Enlightenment rationalism and Pietism define his legacy.

See also Enlightenment; Lutheran Orthodoxy; Pietism

Bibliography
Baur, J., "Valentin Ernst Löschers Praenotiones theologicae: Die lutherische Spätorthodoxie im polemischen Diskurs mit den frühneuzeitlichen Heterodoxien." In *Heterodoxie in der Frühen Neuzeit*, ed. H. Laufhütte and M. Titzmann, 425–75. Frühe Neuzeit 117. Niemeyer, 2006; Loescher, V. *The Complete Timotheus Verinus*. Northwestern, 1998; Matthias, M., "Pietism and Protestant Orthodoxy." In *A Companion to German Pietism, 1660–1800*, ed. D. Shantz, 17–49. Brill, 2015; Petzoldt, K., *Der unterlegene Sieger: Valentin Ernst Löscher im absolutistischen Sachsen*. Evangelische Verlaganstalt, 2001.

PETER JAMES YODER

Lübeck

Lübeck was the leading city of the Hanseatic League, which became a bastion of Gnesio-Lutheran orthodoxy following the controversies over doctrine that divided Martin Luther's followers after his death in 1546. Located on the Trave River near the Baltic coast, Lübeck derived its pre-Reformation wealth and influence from its status as the capital city of the Hanseatic League, a network of mercantile cities in the Baltic and North Seas. Known as the "Queen of the Hansa," Lübeck's mercantile interests did much to shape the way the city experienced religious reform. While many city leaders initially viewed the new teaching with suspicion, Lübeck's magistrates proved particularly resistant to calls for church reform "from below"—from the artisans and craftsmen who made up the majority of the citizen population. Fearing disruption of the city's commercial lifeblood, the patrician city council avoided lasting concessions to Wittenberg-style reform until 1530, when increased anticlerical agitation combined with political and economic necessity to persuade them to embrace the Augsburg Confession. Political unrest plagued Lübeck during its first years as a Lutheran city; thereafter, however, magistrates and pastors successfully blended political conservatism with theological moderation to ensure that the city charted a middle course during the confessional age.

When Martin Luther's antagonist John Eck condemned the manner in which Lübeckers stripped the gold and silver ornaments from their churches in 1531, he was actually describing an act of public foreclosure rather than an iconoclastic riot. The date is significant: though reform-minded preachers proliferated in Lübeck from early 1522, it required repeated anticlerical agitation in late 1529—a phenomenon known as the "singing war" (Singekrieg) due to the burghers' strategy of protest—to bring the magistracy to terms concerning reform. Early the following year, the council and citizens' representatives agreed on two immediate measures: first, they would adopt an Evangelical church order based closely on the document that Wittenberg theologian Johannes Bugenhagen (1485–1558) had crafted for Hamburg in 1528–29; second, they would expropriate the treasures from Lübeck's churches—especially "idolatrous" furnishings containing gold, silver, and precious gems—which were duly melted down and used to fund military expeditions against the Danish and Dutch. Bugenhagen's church order stressed that these objects were being removed to preserve peace both at home and abroad—so that rulers and trading allies who remained loyal to Rome would not take offense—yet filling the city's coffers also played a major role in the council's change of heart between 1529 and 1530. Their attempt to limit the disruptive potential of reform was upset by an internal crisis caused by populist mayor Jürgen Wullenwever (1488–1537), whose attempts to buttress Lübeck's international influence caused a violent rift between guildsmen and the city council in 1533–34, led to military defeat in the Baltic in 1535, and culminated in Wullenwever's execution in 1537; he was condemned both for treasonous insurrection and on suspicion of being an Anabaptist. Meanwhile the old, aristocratic city council was restored to power. As later generations confronted Lübeck's decline as a commercial and political power, they responded by crafting an elaborate culture of rigorous Lutheranism in the city's churches, embodied in the long career of organist and composer Dietrich Buxtehude (1637–1707), who served there from 1668 until his death.

See also Bremen; Bugenhagen, Johannes; Hamburg

Bibliography

Cowan, A. *The Urban Patriciate: Lübeck and Venice, 1580–1700*. Böhlau, 1986; Dollinger, P. *The German Hansa*. Stanford University Press, 1964; Grassmann, A. *Lübeckische Geschichte*. 3rd ed. Schmidt-Römhild, 1997; Postel, R. "Hamburg und Lübeck im Zeitalter der Reformation." *Zeitschrift des Vereins für Lübeckische Geschichte und Altertumskunde* 59 (1979): 63–81.

JASON L. STRANDQUIST

Lundensian School

As developed by theologians at the University of Lund during the twentieth-century Swedish Luther Renaissance, the Lundensian School focused on developing a scientific method of theology they called "motif research." The Lundensians, as they came to be known, were led by Gustaf Aulén and Anders Nygren, but built on the previous work of Nathan Söderblom and Einar Billing at the University of Uppsala, who had turned to the study of Martin Luther as they developed a theological approach compatible with the new historical-critical method of biblical research.

The Lundensians continued these efforts to modernize theology so it could retain a place of relevance in the scientific era. First they rejected the previous reliance on philosophical and theological idealism along with speculative rationalism, viewing them as subjective and arbitrary and therefore unscientific. This likewise required a shift in the goal of theology. Aulén initially proposed that the task of theology rests in explaining the essential aspects of Christian faith for the present time without any attempt to assess validity or quality. He adopted a historical approach for achieving this purpose because only an objective investigation of previous expressions of Christianity could reveal its core elements. Aulén found Luther and the church fathers, especially Irenaeus, were the clearest in their presentation of these fundamentals. The results of Aulén's analysis were presented in his work *The Faith of the Christian Church*; the first of six editions appeared in Swedish in 1923 and in English in 1948.

Nygren built on Aulén's work, fully developing the method of motif research. Rather than a series of core elements, Nygren maintained that every religion has a *Grundmotiv*, or fundamental motif, which is the ultimate concept and driving force shaping all aspects of the religion. Motif research is the means by which one discovers and tests the validity of a *Grundmotiv*. Methodologically it is a refinement of Aulén's approach. Specifically, one begins the investigation by exploring primary sources to discover the *Grundmotiv*. Then one turns to secondary sources and seeks to test one's theory and address all possible objections. Nygren first discussed the method of motif research and applied it to Christianity in his work *Agape and Eros*, published in Swedish in 1930 and in English in 1939. Here he asserted that the *Grundmotiv* for Christianity must answer fundamental religious and ethical questions regarding divinity and goodness. Following his historical investigation, he concluded that Christianity's unique motif was agape, that is, spontaneous, self-sacrificing, creative love. As with Aulén, Nygren found the clearest expressions of this motif in the writings of Luther and Irenaeus as well as the Gospels and Pauline Letters.

Nygren's work was continued by his younger colleague Ragnar Bring, and to a limited extent by his student Gustaf Wingren. Wingren, however, ultimately rejected motif research because of its Kantian philosophical foundation and completely historicist perspective. While Wingren also drew heavily on historical research of Irenaeus and Luther, he ultimately turned toward a kerygmatic approach to theology firmly rooted in a doctrine of creation.

See also Aulén, Gustaf; Luther Interpretation and Reception; Nygren, Anders; Söderblom, Nathan; Sweden; Theological Prolegomena; Wingren, Gustaf

Bibliography

Anderson, M. *Gustaf Wingren and the Swedish Luther Renaissance*. Lang, 2006; Carlson, E. *The Reinterpretation of Luther*. Westminster, 1948; Erling, B. *Nature and History: A Study in Theological Methodology with Special Attention to the Method of Motif Research*. Gleerup, 1960; Ferré, N. *Swedish Contributions to Modern Theology: With Special Reference to Lundensian Thought*. Harper & Brothers, 1939; Lindroth, H. *Lutherrenässansen i nyare svensk teologi*. Svenska Kyrkans Diakonistyrelses Pokförlag, 1941.

MARY E. ANDERSON

Luther, Martin

Martin Luther (1483–1546), professor of Scripture at the University of Wittenberg, was born in Eisleben. Soon he moved with his family to Mansfeld, where his father, Hans, a master smelter in the copper mining industry, established their home and attained a respected position in the community. Luther's recollections of his parents and siblings are positive; it seems clear that his later religious crisis was not rooted in dysfunctional family relationships (Brecht 1:9). His recollections of his early education are far less positive, but he gained appreciation for music, classics, and the thorough grounding in Latin that facilitated his secondary education in Magdeburg and Eisenach, and then entrance to the University of Erfurt (1501). The educational program of this university, founded in 1389, was oriented by the *via moderna*, the "modern way" of Scholastic nominalist philosophy that valued experience and reason over speculative metaphysics (Oberman 113–19). Following his father's ambition that he become a lawyer, Luther completed his bachelor's and master's degrees in the arts and entered the school of law in the summer semester 1505. However, Luther soon radically changed course, vowing to become a monk when experiencing a narrow miss by lightning while returning to Erfurt after a visit home. Despite his father's strong disapproval, he entered the Erfurt house of the Observant Augustinian friars.

There Luther threw himself into self-mortification to gain God's favor: "I tortured myself with prayers, fastings, vigils, and freezing" (LW 24:24; see LW 54:339–40). A pastoral theology that promoted introspection on the basis of the church's translation of Eccl. 9:1 ("No one knows whether he is worthy of God's love or hate") and Luther's own rigorous self-examination only heightened his uncertainty regarding personal salvation. Toward the end of his life, Luther recollected: "We even concluded and taught that one had to be uncertain about God's mercy. Therefore the more I ran and the more I longed to come to Christ, the farther he withdrew from me" (LW 5:157; see LW 26:377–80). Luther's Reformation "breakthrough," as later historians have designated it, delivered him from "this monster of uncertainty. . . . The Gospel commands us to look, not at our own good deeds or perfection, but at God himself as he promises, and at Christ Himself, the Mediator. . . . This is the reason why our theology is certain: it snatches us away from ourselves and places us outside ourselves, so that we do not depend on our own strength, conscience, experience, person, or works but depend on that which is outside ourselves, that is, on the promise and truth of God, which cannot deceive" (LW 26:387).

Luther's confidence in God's promise grew from his meditative-exegetical biblical study initiated in the Augustinian cloister by his superior Johann von Staupitz (1465–1524). Staupitz, vicar general of the Augustinians in Germany and professor of theology at the new University of Wittenberg (established 1502), encouraged Luther to continue theological studies after his ordination in 1507. Luther received his doctorate in 1512 and replaced Staupitz at Wittenberg, beginning biblical lectures there in 1513. His lectures on the Psalms (1513–15), Romans (1515–16),

Galatians (1516–17), and Hebrews (1517–18) were informed by the linguistic tools provided by Renaissance humanists, a good library of commentaries, various translations, and, beginning in 1516, Erasmus's new edition of the Greek New Testament. Luther's intense biblical study led to his paradigm shift regarding the righteousness of God that exploded the late medieval understanding of Christianity and "changed the course of world history" (Hamm 31, 237, 255, 16). In contrast to the medieval piety of achievement, Luther asserted that salvation is received, not achieved, and that salvation is not the goal of life but life's foundation (Lindberg, *European Reformations*, 60–67; see LW 34:337).

Luther's breakthrough combined with his commitment to humanist educational ideals helped fuel a communal reform of the Scholastic curriculum in favor of the study of the Bible and the church fathers. In the spring of 1517, Luther wrote to his friend John Lang in Erfurt: "Our theology and St. Augustine are progressing well, and with God's help rule at our University. . . . Indeed no one can expect to have any students if he does not want to teach this theology, that is, lecture on the Bible or on St. Augustine or another teacher of ecclesiastical eminence" (LW 48:42). The new orientation led to a sharp critique of Scholastic theology and its basis in the Aristotelian emphasis on progress from vice to virtue (LW 31:12: "We do not become righteous by doing righteous deeds but, having been made righteous, we do righteous deeds"). His critique of the sacrament of penance and the related practice of indulgences soon followed with the Ninety-Five Theses (LW 31:25–33; Kolb, *Confessor*, 19–21). Whether or not the Ninety-Five Theses were posted on the Castle Church door in Wittenberg in addition to being mailed to Luther's superiors (the bishop of Brandenburg and archbishop of Mainz), they sparked an academic uproar. The Roman establishment realized that Luther's criticism of indulgences and their power undermined ecclesial, especially papal, authority. Pope Leo X's personal theologian, Sylvester Mazzolini Prierias (1456–1523), wrote to Luther: "He who says in regard to indulgences that the Roman Church cannot do what she has actually done is a heretic" (Lindberg, *Sourcebook*, 31). Prierias's tract formed the basis for the summons to Luther to appear in Rome within sixty days of its receipt. Both documents reached Wittenberg in August 1518, two months before his interview in October with the papal representative Cardinal Cajetan. The following June, while engaged in debate at Leipzig with John Eck (1486–1543), Luther stated that both the papacy and church councils could err. It was now publicly clear that, while Luther always gave some authority to conciliar and patristic statements, for Luther the sole final authority in matters of faith was Scripture. The threat of excommunication, *Exsurge Domini*, of 1520 was followed with the official papal bull of excommunication, *Decet Romanum Pontificem*, appearing on January 3, 1521. By then Luther had published four important reform-minded treatises. *On Good Works* in June 1520 (LW 44:21–114) demonstrates that faith alone produces obedience to God's will as expressed in the Ten Commandments. *To the Christian Nobility of the German Nation concerning the Improvement of the Christian Estate* in August 1520 (LW 44:115–217) argues for secular-led reform of the church when clerical authorities fail to reform. *The Babylonian Captivity of the Church* in October 1520 (LW 36:3–126) criticizes the Roman doctrine of the sacraments as an expression of papal tyranny that displaces the promise of God by ecclesial actions. *The Freedom of a Christian* in November 1520 (LW 31:327–77) proclaims that trust in God's promise in Christ liberates from the religiosity of self-achievement and for service to the neighbor.

The recently elected emperor, Charles V (r. 1519–56), had promised not to condemn anyone without a hearing, so Luther was cited to the Diet of Worms (1521) to retract his heresies. Luther's refusal to recant led to the imposition of the Edict of Worms, which placed Luther and his followers under imperial ban. On his return to Wittenberg, he was "kidnapped" (placed in protective custody) by plan of his prince, Frederick the Wise, taken to Wartburg Castle near Eisenach, and disguised as a knight. There from early May 1521 to March 1522, Luther continued his work. *Martin Luther's Judgment on Monastic Vows* (LW 44:243–400) denied that poverty, chastity, and obedience are divine counsels defining a higher form of Christian life; early parts of the *Church Postil* (model sermons for the assigned texts of the church year; see LW 52:75–76) provided meticulous exegesis of the appointed Sunday texts for Advent (in Latin) and Christmas to Epiphany (in German); and his translation of the New Testament into German on the basis of the Greek text (produced as a first draft in eleven weeks!) provided popular access to Scripture. With the aid of colleagues, the entire Bible appeared in German in 1534; improving biblical translations remained Luther's lifelong endeavor.

Meanwhile in Wittenberg, pressure mounted for the implementation of theological reform into social and ecclesial practice. Luther's faculty colleague and fellow priest Andreas Bodenstein von Karlstadt (1486–1541) celebrated Christmas Mass without vestments, in German, and distributed both bread and wine to communicants in their hands and without prior private confession. On January 19 he married; five days later he encouraged the town council's passage of religious and social legislation implementing a reform agenda. The resultant upheaval, including iconoclastic riots, prompted Luther's return to Wittenberg in March. In a series of sermons (LW 51:67–100) Luther did not disagree with the reform measures per se but criticized the mode of their implementation, which offended the weak in faith and thereby obscured the gospel. While Luther was criticized then and now for strategic temporizing, his fundamental point was that sermons based on "musts" and forced reform of the weak make the gospel of free grace into a new law. "Love, therefore, demands that you have compassion on the weak, as all the apostles had. . . . In short, I will preach it, teach it, write it, but I will constrain no one by force, for faith must come freely, without compulsion" (LW 51:74, 77). Luther consistently maintained his theology of the freedom of the gospel in one crisis after another. "We must see to it that we retain Christian freedom and do not force such laws and works on the Christian conscience, as if one through them were upright or a sinner" (*Against the Heavenly Prophets*, 1525; LW 40:83). In this spirit Luther more slowly reformed the liturgy, including lay participation and hymnody. Even his and Melanchthon's *Instruction by the Visitors for the Parish Pastors of Saxony* (1528) allowed Communion in one kind for weak consciences, a practice retained until 1538.

The theme of Christian freedom took a violent turn when preachers such as Thomas Müntzer (ca. 1491–1525) became involved in the Peasants' War (1524–26). Equating political, economic, and social rights with the gospel, they labeled opponents as the godless who had no right to live (Müntzer, *Sermon to the Princes*, 1524; in Lindberg, *Sourcebook*, 92). For Luther, issues of justice were matters for law and reason, not the gospel, and so in his *Admonition to Peace* (early May 1525; LW 46:3–43) he warned secular and ecclesial rulers that unless they amended their ways, they faced rebellion; he warned the peasants of false prophets who would make the gospel a new law and promote it by force; and he exhorted all sides to negotiate peacefully lest all Germany be destroyed. His plea went unheeded (in one instance, an attempt to preach directly against the rebels in Thuringia was met with contempt), and rebellion continued unabated, with huge loss of life, prompting Luther's *Against the Robbing and Murdering Hordes of Other Peasants* (1525; LW 46:45–55), which urged that the rebellion be put down by whatever means necessary. "For rebellion is not just simple murder; it is like a great fire, which attacks and devastates a whole land" (LW 46:50). In spite of Luther's harsh stance

toward rebellion and rebels, "the attraction of his ideas did not diminish among the populace in most places in the years following 1525" (Kolb, *Confessor*, 193).

The crisis of the uprising did not diminish Luther's own convictions either; on June 13, 1525, he married the escaped nun Katharina von Bora, he said, to please his father, spite the pope, make the angels laugh and the devils weep, and seal his testimony (WA BR 3:541, #900; 555, #911; 533, #892; WA TR 2:331, #2129a; LW 54:109). Clerical marriage contravened canon law and directly challenged episcopal and legal jurisdiction; even more scandalous was the marriage of monk and nun. Already in his *Address to the Christian Nobility* and even more harshly in his *Judgment on Monastic Vows*, Luther had criticized celibacy as the pope's law but not God's. The pope cannot command clerical celibacy any more than he can forbid "bowel movements" or "growing fat." The joy of his own marriage provided Luther experiences for theological reflection. The "Eden" of marriage was the location for vocation (God's callings to serve the neighbor in the world). Fathers washing smelly diapers may be ridiculed by fools, but "God with all his angels and creatures is smiling—not because the father is washing smelly diapers, but because he is doing so in Christian faith" (LW 45:40, published in 1523, before his marriage). The love of God is emphatically expressed by saying we are his children. "But you say: The sins which we daily do offend God; thus we are not holy. I answer: Mother-love is much stronger than the excrement and scabs of the child. So is God's love stronger than our filth" (WA TR 1:189, #437). Martin and Katharina had six children; to their great grief their daughter Elisabeth died in infancy in 1528, and in 1542 Magdalena died in Luther's arms at age thirteen (LW 54:430–32). Katharina nurtured and scolded Martin through more than twenty years of their event-filled marriage, while Luther remained convinced that God had blessed him with "my empress" and "my Moses"; "God came to my aid and gave me a wife" (LW 54:23; Lindberg, *European Reformations*, 92–98; Oberman 272–83).

Two internal crises in the reform movement particularly challenged Luther's conviction of the certainty of salvation based on God's Word of promise addressed to humanity from outside itself. The first came from the "Prince of the Humanists," Desiderius Erasmus (1467?–1536), with his tract *On the Freedom of the Will: A Diatribe or Discourse* (1524; LCC 17). Erasmus had long emphasized renewal of the church through moral reform; of course salvation was through the grace of God, but Erasmus found that Luther's assertion of the certainty of salvation through grace alone excluded human moral motivation contributing to salvation. Indeed, such assertions upset Erasmus: "So far am I from delighting in 'assertions' that I would readily take refuge in the opinion of the Skeptics" (LCC 17:37). For Luther, who called himself the assertor, the allowance of free will in the matter of salvation and Erasmus's apparent eagerness to join the skeptics only threw the burden of proof for salvation and theology itself back on the person. "For whatever work might be accomplished, there would always remain an anxious doubt whether it pleased God or whether he required something more, as the experience of all self-justifiers proves, and as I myself learned to my bitter cost through so many years. . . . Moreover, we are also certain and sure that we please God, not by the merit of our own working, but by the favor of his mercy promised to us" (LW 33:289). In short, "the Holy Spirit is no Skeptic, and it is not doubts or mere opinions that he has written on our hearts, but assertions more sure and certain than life itself and all experience" (LW 33:24; Oberman 211–25; Kolb, *Confessor*, 95–109).

The other major crisis was the long struggle concerning the Lord's Supper, beginning in Wittenberg with Luther's erstwhile colleague Karlstadt, and continuing in sharp exchanges with the Swiss reformers Ulrich (Huldrych) Zwingli (1484–1531) and Johannes Oecolampadius (1482–1531). All the reformers rejected the medieval doctrine of transubstantiation and the sacrifice of the Mass because they saw it as metaphysical speculation about how God communicates himself in the Lord's Supper and because it appeared to give priests power to confect Christ in the Mass. Salvation thus appeared as a human work dependent on a priestly class of Christians. The so-called Sacramentarians (a broad designation often employed by Lutherans for those who denied Christ's real presence in the Lord's Supper) such as Zwingli posited that the "is" in "This is my body" means "signify." So, just as a wedding ring signifies marriage but is not the relationship itself, when Jesus says, "This is my body," he means, "This signifies my body." The sacraments do not give faith but presume it; hence also the argument for believer's baptism against infant baptism. Baptism and the Lord's Supper are outer expressions of inner change, signs and symbols aiding the believer's recollection of God's grace and acts of the community confessing its faith. For Luther, this commemorative view of the Lord's Supper as a devotional exercise vitiated the gospel by making it depend on faith and personal piety. Thus in debates with both Sacramentarians and those he termed Anabaptists, Luther insisted on the centrality of Christ's promise. "My faith does not make baptism; rather, it receives baptism. [Baptism] . . . is not bound to our faith but to the Word" (LC in BC 463.53). The series of polemical exchanges between Luther and especially Zwingli and Oecolampadius led finally to a stormy colloquy at Marburg in 1529, where they parted ways (Lindberg, *Sourcebook*, 102–3, 113–18; Lindberg, *European Reformations*, 172–87).

Luther's polemics against anyone he perceived as undermining the promise of God were sharp-edged and at times ugly, no more so than in his attacks on Jews. While not strictly racist—the issue for Luther was not purity of blood, but attitudes toward Christ—his late writings, such as *On the Jews and Their Lies* (1543; LW 47:121–306), have had a sordid history in the modern world. Yet his correspondence and expressions of pastoral care also reveal a caring person with a sense of humor. A participant at the Leipzig Debate described the younger Luther as not only brilliant but also sociable, friendly, humorous, lively, and cheerful (Lindberg, *Sourcebook*, 32–33). Seen from the perspective of Luther's own theology, his own sinfulness and capitulation to a theology of glory caused him to treat Jews and others with anything but Christian love; faith alone enabled his love to be active for persons and society. His *Treatise on Good Works* (1520; LW 44:15–114) affirms that service to the neighbor flows from justification by grace alone. Thus, here and in his catechisms (1529; SC and LC in *BC*), still influential today, the Ten Commandments illustrate positive service to the neighbor. The twofold blessing of the Lord's Supper—"We partake of Christ and . . . permit all Christians to be partakers of us, in whatever way they and we are able . . . [to seek] the common good of all" (LW 35:67; cf. 53:84)—is the operative principle for Luther's social ethics as a form of worship in the world, the liturgy after the liturgy. Examples with continuing relevance include Luther's sustained attack on early capitalism (usury) as the source of marked income inequality, contributions to the development of tax-supported social welfare (the community chest), exhortation for public education and libraries. Faith active in love is not salvific but serves the common good through legislation guided by reason and equity (Lindberg, *European Reformations*, 108–29; Lindberg, *Sourcebook*, 68–84).

Through the latter half of his life, Luther was plagued by serious illnesses, especially heart disease and kidney stones, and yet continued his pastoral and professorial vocation, writing a variety of tracts (e.g., on prayer and on the nature of the church) and biblical commentaries (esp. on Galatians and Genesis). His last efforts involved mediating an inheritance dispute among the counts of Mansfeld, his first princes, whose massive castle stood overlooking Eisleben. There he succumbed to a heart attack on February 18, 1546, affirming with his last words his teaching and confidence in Christ. His body was returned to Wittenberg and is buried at the foot of the pulpit of the Castle Church.

Bibliography

Bayer, O. *Martin Luther's Theology: A Contemporary Interpretation*. Trans. T. H. Trapp. Eerdmans, 2008; Beutel, A. "Luther's Life." In *The Cambridge Companion to Martin Luther*, ed. D. K. McKim, 3–19. Cambridge University Press, 2003; Brecht, M. *Martin Luther*. 3 vols. Trans. J. L. Schaaf. Fortress, 1985–93; Gritsch, E. W. *The Wit of Martin Luther*. Fortress, 2006; Hamm, B. *The Early Luther: Stages in a Reformation Reorientation*. Trans. M. J. Lohrmann. Eerdmans, 2014; Kolb, R. *Luther and the Stories of God*. Baker Academic, 2012; Kolb, R. *Martin Luther: Confessor of the Faith*. Oxford University Press, 2009; Kolb, R., I. Dingel, and L. Batka, eds. *Oxford Handbook to Martin Luther's Theology*. Oxford University Press, 2014; Lindberg, C. *The European Reformations*. 2nd ed. Wiley-Blackwell, 2010; Lindberg, C. *The European Reformations Sourcebook*. 2nd ed. Wiley-Blackwell, 2014; Lindberg, C. "No Greater Service to God Than Christian Love: Insights from Martin Luther." In *Social Ministry in the Lutheran Tradition*, ed. F. R. McCurley, 50–68. Fortress, 2008; Oberman, H. A. *Luther: Man between God and the Devil*. Trans. E. Walliser-Schwarzbart. Yale University Press, 1989.

CARTER LINDBERG

Lutheran Church in America

The Lutheran Church in America (LCA) (1963–88) was an American Lutheran united church body, the result of the merger of the American Evangelical Lutheran Church (predominantly Danish-American), the Augustana Evangelical Lutheran Church (predominantly Swedish-American), the Finnish Evangelical Lutheran Church of America, and the United Lutheran Church in America (predominantly German-American). It began to function fully from the beginning of 1963 although the decision to form the LCA had officially been taken on June 28, 1962. Franklin Clark Fry was the LCA's first president, Melvin H. Lundeen the first secretary, and Edmund F. Wagner the first treasurer. At the outset, the LCA was the largest of the Lutheran church bodies in the United States, with a little more than 3.2 million members. As a body the LCA was divided into thirty synods, primarily organized on a geographical basis (defined by state lines), with the exception of the Finnish, Icelandic, and Slovak Zion Synods, which were organized on primarily a national or linguistic basis. Each synod was further divided into districts. Boards and commissions were a vital part of the LCA. Boards included those for American Missions, College Education and Church Vocations, Parish Education, Pensions, Publication (responsible for issuing the periodical *The Lutheran*), Social Ministry, Theological Education, and World Missions (sending missionaries to Argentina, British Guiana, China, Hong Kong, India, Japan, Liberia, Malaysia, Tanganyika [now Tanzania], and Uruguay). Commissions included those on Church Architecture, Church Papers, Evangelism, Press/Radio/Television, Stewardship, Worship, and Youth Activities. The official headquarters of the LCA were in New York City; for the most part, many of the boards and commissions met there as well, with the exception of Parish Education, Publication, Church Papers, and Youth Activities (in Philadelphia); Pensions (in Minneapolis); and American Missions (in Chicago). Constitutions were drafted for member synods of the LCA, as well as for churches within these synods. The highest legislative body of the LCA was the convention, which met biennially. It had an equal number of lay and clergy delegates. The executive council elected by the convention—consisting of the president, secretary, and treasurer along with fifteen clergy and fifteen laity who met periodically—was responsible for the operation of the LCA. Its publishing house was Fortress Press (a continuation of Muhlenberg Press of the ULCA). In 1962 the LCA consolidated four of its seminaries (as well as a fifth one in 1967) to form the Lutheran School of Theology at Chicago, though the attempt to consolidate the Gettysburg Seminary and the Lutheran Theological Seminary at Philadelphia did not materialize. LCA cut across traditional ethnic distinctions among Finnish, Danish, German, and Swedish Lutherans. Theologically, the LCA, while committed to the Lutheran Confessions, was the most progressive and ecumenically minded among the US Lutheran church bodies; its polity was somewhat more clerical and centralistic. The LCA also demonstrated a commitment to liturgy, as already observed among its predecessors. In 1988 the LCA along with the American Lutheran Church and the Association of Evangelical Lutheran Churches formed a new church body, the Evangelical Lutheran Church in America.

See also Augustana Synod; Danish-American Lutheranism; Finnish-American Lutheranism; United Lutheran Church in America

Bibliography

Gilbert, W. K. *Commitment to Unity: A History of the Lutheran Church in America*. Fortress, 1988; Knudsen, J. *The Formation of the Lutheran Church in America*. Fortress, 1978; Nichol, T. W. *All These Lutherans: Three Paths toward a New Lutheran Church*. Augsburg, 1986.

PETER VETHANAYAGAMONY

Lutheran Church–Missouri Synod

The Lutheran Church–Missouri Synod was organized in April 1847 in Chicago as *Die deutsche evangelisch-lutherische Synode von Missouri, Ohio und anderen Staaten* (The German Evangelical Lutheran Synod of Missouri, Ohio, and Other States). Congregations in the states of Illinois, Indiana, and Michigan were also represented among the charter members.

The organizers were pastors and congregations strongly committed to following the teachings of the Lutheran confessions found in the Book of Concord of 1580. Their roots lay in the confessional revival that had developed in the German territories in the early nineteenth century, largely in resistance of the efforts of Prussian king Friedrich Wilhelm III to bring Lutheran and Reformed churches into a united Protestant church. Opposition to this "unionism" was a hallmark of the synod's attitude toward relationships with other Lutherans, an attitude that called for complete agreement in doctrine and practice in order to embrace fellowship with other Lutheran bodies.

Pastor Carl Ferdinand Wilhelm Walther (1811–87) of St. Louis was chosen as the first president of the synod. He had become the leader of the Saxon Lutheran immigrants who had come to Missouri in 1838–39 as followers of Pastor (Bishop) Martin Stephan. Walther's publication *Der Lutheraner* had helped to bring the founding members of the synod together with the goal of founding a church body committed to confessional Lutheranism and dedicated to reaching out to the burgeoning German Lutheran immigrant population in the American Midwest. The experience of Walther and the Saxons with Martin Stephan's authoritarian leadership and his expulsion from the group for alleged sexual infidelity and misappropriation of funds led to the development of a church polity that balanced the roles of clergy and laity and emphasized the self-government of local congregations over against an advisory synodical organization.

The second president of the synod, serving from 1850 to 1864, was Friedrich Conrad Dietrich Wyneken (1810–76) of Fort Wayne, Indiana, whose stirring appeal for pastors to serve German immigrants to America had roused support in Germany for the training of missionary pastors for the New World. Pastor Wilhelm Loehe (Löhe, 1808–72) of Neuendettelsau, Bavaria, particularly responded to the call by sending several of the men who became charter members of the synod.

In its early years the major concerns of the synod, which have characterized the church body throughout its history, were missions and education. Its mission endeavors were directed at the large influx of Lutheran immigrants, but from its first meeting it also sought to bring the gospel to Native Americans in Michigan. The synod grew rapidly and by 1854 found it necessary to divide into districts in order to carry out its work more effectively. It quickly expanded beyond its original borders, founding congregations as far east as Boston and as far west as Missouri. These congregations needed pastors and teachers to serve them.

The synod's founders were determined, wherever possible, to establish parish schools in every congregation in order to train their children in the Holy Scriptures and the teachings of the Lutheran Church. Thus the training of pastors and teachers became one of the major undertakings of the new synod. Even before its organization, two theological seminaries had been established in congregations that joined the synod. One was in Perry County, Missouri, and the other in Fort Wayne, Indiana. These schools were turned over to the synod, and the Perry County school was moved to St. Louis, where Walther became its main professor and later president.

Over the years a system of preparatory schools was established at sites from coast to coast and in Canada, all dedicated to preparing students for entering the seminaries. In 1855 a school for training teachers was opened in Milwaukee; it was taken over by the synod in 1857 and transferred to Fort Wayne. Eventually it was moved to River Forest, Illinois. A second teachers college was opened in Seward, Nebraska, in 1894. By the late twentieth century the preparatory schools and teachers colleges had evolved into four-year colleges and universities with a broad range of degree programs to prepare students for a variety of church-work vocations as well as service in other vocations such as business, nursing, and so forth. The Concordia University System consists of ten campuses with many programs offered in branch locations and through online education.

The synod experienced phenomenal growth during its first decades. Walther succeeded Wyneken as president, serving a second stint between 1864 and 1878. At the same time he continued to serve as seminary president and professor, as pastor of Trinity congregation in St. Louis, as editor of *Der Lutheraner*, and also as editor of a theological journal, *Lehre und Wehre* (Doctrine and defense), for the continuing education of pastors.

Walther and the synod sought to establish relations with other Lutheran church bodies in the United States with whom agreement in doctrine and practice on the basis of the Lutheran confessions could be reached.

Discussions with older Lutheran synods in the East (that constituted the General Council) were not successful in this regard, but other Lutheran bodies in the Midwest were more in tune with Missouri's theological position. However, even relationships with groups that shared a strong confessional position, such as the Buffalo and Iowa synods, were not successfully established because of differences over issues of church authority and the place of the pastoral office in the church's life.

In 1872 the Evangelical Lutheran Synodical Conference of North America was organized with the Ohio Synod, the Wisconsin Synod, the Norwegian Synod, and several smaller groups joining with Missouri as members. The Synodical Conference established a mission program to reach African Americans in the South with the gospel, beginning in 1877, an effort that lasted into the 1960s, when the last of its congregations were integrated into the Missouri Synod.

The harmony of the Synodical Conference was disrupted in the 1880s with a dispute over the doctrine of predestination, which resulted in the withdrawal of the Ohio and Norwegian Synods. In the 1960s doctrinal disagreements with the Wisconsin Synod led to the eventual dissolution of the conference altogether.

The growth of the synod was steady throughout the nineteenth century and the first half of the twentieth century. From a membership of 345,000 in 1880, it climbed to 728,000 by 1900, 1,392,000 in 1940, and 2,383,000 in 1960. However, after reaching a high point of 2,886,207 in 1971, the membership has gradually declined to 2,196,788 in 2012.

From the synod's beginning some of its leaders recognized the need to be able to work with the English language in the American context and encouraged the training of pastors to use that language, yet the synod conducted its work largely in German until World War I. English-speaking congregations were organized, chiefly in the cities, in the late 1800s, but they were encouraged to form a separate English Missouri Synod. This body continued until 1911, when it was merged into the German synod as a nongeographical English District. The English Synod brought with it additional preparatory schools in Conover, North Carolina, and Winfield, Kansas, and an English-language publication, *The Lutheran Witness*, which continues to the present as the official publication of the synod.

World War I and the resultant antipathy toward all things German in many parts of the United States hastened the transition of the synod as a whole to the use of the English language. The word "German" was dropped from the synod's name, and the requirement that synodical conventions be conducted in the German language was removed from the synodical constitution. A new trilingual version of the Book of Concord (the so-called *Triglotta*) in Latin, German, and English was published. Nevertheless, many congregations continued to use German in their worship services for several more decades, even after the appearance of *The Lutheran Hymnal* in 1941.

From its beginning the Missouri Synod had recognized the responsibility of the church to proclaim the gospel throughout the world. Its founders were aware of German mission societies that were reaching out to Asia and Africa in the nineteenth century. Wilhelm Loehe (Löhe) had been a strong exponent of missions, sending a colony of Lutheran couples to Michigan in the 1840s to settle among Native Americans, with the express purpose of converting them to Christianity. But the idea of carrying on mission work in foreign countries was also on the synod's mind. In its early years the synod supported the work of the Leipzig and Hermannsburg mission societies.

Finally in 1893 the synod created a foreign mission board and directed that mission work should begin in Japan. Conditions in that country proved unfavorable at the time, but in 1894 two missionaries who had been affiliated with the Leipzig mission in India had resigned from that organization over doctrinal issues and were commissioned by the Missouri Synod to return to India. Over the years this work expanded into several areas and at various times included work among Muslims. Medical missions were also part of the mix. In 1958 the India Evangelical Lutheran Church (IELC) was organized.

In 1912 Pastor E. L. Arndt, a former professor in the synod's preparatory school in St. Paul, Minnesota, organized a China Mission Society, and in the following year he himself went to China. The synod took over this work in 1917 and continued there until 1952, when missionaries left the mainland because of the Communist revolution. The work among Chinese continued in Hong Kong and Taiwan, and in recent decades the synod has again been active on the mainland, where surviving remnants of the earlier work have been found.

Mission work also expanded into South America, beginning with Brazil and extending to other countries. The Synodical Conference work among African Americans in the South led to contacts with Christians in Nigeria who asked for Lutheran pastors to be trained for work in that country.

World War II brought many members of the synod in contact with people and places around the world in need of the gospel. Postwar relief efforts also meant sharing the gospel, and work was begun in the Philippines (1946), Japan (1948), New Guinea (1948), Korea (1958), and other areas. In the last decades of the twentieth century the synod extended its outreach efforts into many other areas of the world, including Eastern Europe, territories of the former Soviet Union, Africa, and Asia. Many of the mission fields have developed into autonomous partner church bodies, with local leadership trained and supported through the work of synodical seminaries. An International Lutheran Council serves to enable these church bodies to work together in theological education and disaster response.

World War II also brought members of the synod into closer contact with other Lutherans and other Christians in areas such as military chaplaincy, relief work, and theological discussions with German church leaders and professors. Such contacts introduced some divergent views regarding biblical interpretation and the meaning of the Lutheran confessions into the instruction at synodical schools. After increasing complaints an investigation was held into the theological views of the faculty at Concordia Seminary, St. Louis. In 1973 the synod in convention condemned the faculty's theological positions. The president of the seminary was subsequently removed from office, and the majority of the faculty and student body formed a Concordia Seminary in Exile (later Christ Seminary-Seminex), 1974–87. A number of congregations left the synod to form the Association of Evangelical Lutheran Churches. This group later combined with the American Lutheran Church and the Lutheran Church in America in 1987 to form the present Evangelical Lutheran Church in America.

The Concordia Seminary faculty was rebuilt, and the school continues to serve the synod in the preparation of pastors and deaconesses. It offers specialized programs in the areas of Hispanic ministry and the training of pastors to reach many of the growing African and Asian immigrant communities in the United States.

See also Pieper, Francis; Preus, Jacob; Prussian Union; Seminex and the Association of Evangelical Lutheran Churches; Walther, Carl Ferdinand Wilhelm

Bibliography

Baepler, W. A. *A Century of Grace: A History of the Missouri Synod, 1847–1947*. Concordia, 1947; Burkee, J. C. *Power, Politics, and the Missouri Synod*. Fortress, 2011; Meyer, C. S. *A Brief Historical Sketch of the Lutheran Church–Missouri Synod*. Concordia, 1963; Meyer, C. S., ed. *Moving Frontiers: Readings in the History of The Lutheran Church–Missouri Synod*. Concordia, 1964; Suelflow, A. R. *Heritage in Motion: Readings in the History of the Lutheran Church–Missouri Synod, 1962–1995*. Concordia, 1998; Todd, M. *Authority Vested*. Eerdmans, 2000.

MARVIN A. HUGGINS

Lutheran Council in the United States of America

A cooperative body of US Lutherans, the Lutheran Council in the United States of America (1967–88) is popularly known as LCUSA and was formed in 1967 by the American Lutheran Church (ALC), the Lutheran Church in America (LCA), the Lutheran Church–Missouri Synod (LCMS), and the Synod of (Slovak) Evangelical Lutheran Churches (SELC). The Association of Evangelical Lutheran Churches (AELC) joined in 1978, and the Latvian Evangelical Lutheran Church in America in 1982. The occasion for LCUSA's founding was the impending dissolution of the National Lutheran Council (NLC) as its eight churches moved toward mergers that would leave NLC with only two members. NLC leaders proposed a broader cooperative agency, hoping that LCMS, which had never joined NLC because of lack of doctrinal agreement, might be encouraged to take part. With the assurance that discussion of doctrinal matters would be central to the new agency, LCMS agreed to participate in the planning and ultimately joined the new council. LCUSA began operation on January 1, 1967, its member churches constituting some 95 percent of all US Lutherans. While NLC had eschewed theological and doctrinal discussion in favor of cooperative work in various fields, LCUSA placed theological matters at its center. Its constitution required that all member bodies participate in its Division of Theological Studies, while involvement in all other aspects of the council's cooperative work was optional. During its existence, LCUSA produced several significant theological studies; it functioned as the agency for Lutheran participation in some ecumenical conversations; it coordinated work among member churches in several areas of ministry; and it provided important resources in the areas of news reporting, public relations, and research. With the ALC, LCA, and AELC headed for merger in 1988, with the SELC having become a district of the LCMS in 1971, and with LCMS pulling back from engagement with other Lutherans, LCUSA was dissolved on December 31, 1987.

See also American Lutheran Church (1960–88); Evangelical Lutheran Church in America; Inter-Lutheran Ecumenism; Lutheran Church in America; Lutheran Church–Missouri Synod

Bibliography

Frost, N. *Golden Visions, Broken Dreams: A Short History of the Lutheran Council in the USA.* Lutheran Council in the USA, 1987; Wolf, R. *Documents of Lutheran Unity in America.* Fortress, 1966.

RICHARD O. JOHNSON

Lutheran Denominations in America, Minor

As of 2016 there were two major Lutheran denominations in the United States, the Evangelical Lutheran Church in America (3.8 million members) and the Lutheran Church–Missouri Synod (2.1 million), as well as a medium-sized denomination, the Wisconsin Evangelical Lutheran Synod (400,000). Besides these three, there are a number of other, smaller denominations, listed here in order of their founding. Many of these groups were founded as breakaway denominations, often in opposition to a merger or some other issue within an established denomination. This article only lists those minor Lutheran denominations still in independent operation as of 2016, and it is not a complete enumeration of all groups (membership figures rounded).

Church of the Lutheran Brethren (1900) was founded by Norwegian Lutherans who believed in a strict church discipline and the need for a conversion experience for members. Its headquarters, school, and seminary are in Fergus Falls, Minnesota (123 congregations, about 1,300 members).

Evangelical Lutheran Synod (1918) was founded by a group of pastors and laypeople from the Norwegian Synod unhappy about the theological agreement that led to the formation of the Norwegian Lutheran Church in America in 1917. Its headquarters, college, and seminary are in Mankato, Minnesota (130 congregations, 22,000 members).

Association of Free Lutheran Congregations (1963). When the Lutheran Free Church voted to join the merger that created the American Lutheran Church (1960–88), about one-sixth of the congregations decided not to join the new denomination. In 1963 they formed a new denomination, based on a congregational

451

polity, with headquarters, school, and seminary in Medicine Lake, Minnesota (210 congregations, 22,000 members).

American Association of Lutheran Churches (AALC, 1987) was formed by a group of pastors and congregations from the American Lutheran Church who held to biblical inerrancy and so did not want to join the newly formed Evangelical Lutheran Church in America. The AALC came into fellowship with the Lutheran Church–Missouri Synod, and the AALC seminary is now hosted by Concordia Theological Seminary, Fort Wayne, Indiana. The AALC headquarters is also in Fort Wayne (70 congregations, 20,000 members).

Lutheran Congregations in Mission for Christ (2001). This group was formed by pastors and congregations of the Evangelical Lutheran Church in America who were upset by theological and social liberalism in the ELCA. The trigger for this group's formation was the approval of an ecumenical relationship between the ELCA and the Episcopal Church in 1999, under an agreement known as Called to Common Mission. The LCMC does considers itself not as a synod or a denomination, but as a fellowship of Lutheran congregations, gathered for mission. It does allow women pastors. Its headquarters is in Canton, Michigan (770 congregations, 350,000 members).

North American Lutheran Church (2010). This denomination was formed by pastors and congregations of the Evangelical Lutheran Church in America who were in opposition to the decision of the ELCA in 2009 to allow partnered gay and lesbian persons to be pastors. The NALC follows a synodical polity, with a presiding bishop as its leader. It does allow women pastors. The denomination is headquartered in Hilliard, Ohio, and its seminary is partnered with Trinity School for Mission, Ambridge, Pennsylvania (400 congregations, 140,000 members).

There are a number of other even smaller Lutheran denominations in America; this is not a complete listing. Some of the smallest Lutheran denominations may consist of only a handful of pastors and congregations.

Bibliography
Granquist, M. *Lutherans in America: A New History.* Fortress, 2015; Wiederaenders, R., ed. *Historical Guide to Lutheran Church Bodies of North America.* Lutheran Historical Conference Publication No. 1. 2nd ed. Lutheran Historical Conference, 1998.

MARK A. GRANQUIST

Lutheran Education

Early Lutherans, starting with Martin Luther and Philip Melanchthon, gave considerable attention to the nature and function of education. They recognized that their theological reforms necessitated educational reforms as well, not only in universities but in other schools as well. Luther's *To the Councilmen of All Cities in Germany That They Establish and Maintain Christian Schools* (1524) (LW 45:347–78) urged civic leaders to support the establishment of Evangelical schools for the good of the church and state. The Small Catechism (1529), though not intended solely for schools, was taken up as an integral part of the curriculum and, as part of this goal, was also translated into Latin. Luther's *Sermon on Keeping Children in School* (1530) (LW 46:213–57) urged parents to spare no expense in the Christian training of their children. Other key figures in educational reform were Johannes Bugenhagen and Philip Melanchthon. Bugenhagen was active in establishing elementary schools throughout northern Germany and Denmark. He also authored many school orders, the most influential of which were the Braunschweig School Orders. Melanchthon, sometimes called the *Praeceptor Germaniae* (teacher of Germany), suggested many of the educational reforms contained in the 1528 Saxon Visitation Articles (LW 40:269–320) and was instrumental in the reform of institutions of higher learning and the establishment of Latin schools in important urban centers, especially Nuremberg (1526).

The pedagogical model that emerged combined the humanistic understanding of the liberal arts, with its emphasis on grammar, rhetoric, and logic, with Lutheran catechesis, in the hopes of producing faithful and pious Christians who would diligently exercise their vocations in the world and the church. At the same time, Lutheran territories and free cities in the Holy Roman Empire continued to establish new Latin schools and universities to train people for governmental and ecclesial positions. The work resulted in high rates of literacy within Evangelical territories and laid the groundwork for the modern concept of universal education. The Lutheran pedagogical model was copied by many other Protestant and Roman Catholic educators as they sought to effect educational reform in their own countries.

Lutheran education continued to flourish in the seventeenth century in Scandinavia and, despite the Thirty Years' War (1618–48), in German-speaking lands. However, in the latter half of the century, its nature began to change. Pietism, under the influence of pedagogues such as August Hermann Francke (1666–1727), introduced innovations such as schools for orphans and teacher seminaries aimed at standardizing levels of teacher training. At the same time and to some degree, they diminished the emphasis on catechetical training based on the Small Catechism. Rationalistic pedagogues, such as Johann Pestalozzi (1746–1827), introduced a more child-centered approach to education, but even more than the Pietists, they downplayed the confessional aspects of Lutheran schools.

The Lutheran Church has always understood education as an intrinsic part of its mission. As the Lutheran Church spread in North America, for example, Lutheran schools were established. The first was started in 1646 by Rev. Reorius Torkillus in Tinicum, Pennsylvania. Within a century, schools were established throughout Delaware, Pennsylvania, Georgia, Virginia, and Ohio. Most successful were the Ministerium of Pennsylvania's schools, with 240 of them at their peak in 1820.

The desire for a confessional school system free from the influence of rationalism and, to a lesser extent, Pietism was one motivation behind the decisions of many nineteenth-century confessional Lutherans to leave Germany. The largest and most influential movement in this regard was the Saxon immigration of 1838–39. Immediately after arriving in Missouri, the Lutherans, under the leadership of C. F. W. Walther, established a *Gymnasium* (the typical name for Latin schools) based on the classical education that they had experienced in Germany, but with a renewed emphasis on catechetical training. When the Evangelical Synod of Missouri, Ohio, and Other States was formed in 1847, its constitution required that every congregation provide for the Christian education of its children.

The largest Lutheran school system in North America remains that of the Lutheran Church–Missouri Synod. In 2014 it included 1,285 early childhood centers, 880 elementary schools, and 90 high schools. The Wisconsin Evangelical Lutheran Church, the Evangelical Lutheran Church in America, and the Evangelical Lutheran Synod also sponsor schools. While overall the number of elementary schools has declined in recent years, the number of early childhood education centers has increased markedly. In North America, at least forty-one universities and colleges maintain ties to Lutheran church bodies, and there are over a dozen seminaries.

Substantial Lutheran school systems also exist in Australia and South Africa. Lutheran schools are also proliferating in much of Africa, South America, and parts of Asia. In these areas, Lutheran schools are seen as an integral part of the church's mission and an indispensable tool in the catechetical process.

See also Bugenhagen, Johannes; Francke, August Hermann; Francke Foundations; Melanchthon, Philip; Theological Education; University of Wittenberg in the Sixteenth Century

Bibliography

Beck, W. H. *Lutheran Elementary Schools in the United States: A History of the Development of Parochial Schools and Synodical Educational Policies and Programs.* 2nd ed. Concordia, 1965; Korcok, T. *Lutheran Education: From Wittenberg to the Future.* Concordia, 2011.

THOMAS KORCOK

Lutheran Orthodoxy

Lutheran Orthodoxy refers to a movement of primarily academic theology produced in Germany, the Nordic countries, and Eastern Europe during the post-Reformation period. More than most terms of its kind, it is a literary construct. Lutheran theologians began referring to themselves and to their theology as "orthodox" toward the end of the sixteenth century in order to signal agreement with the early church (*consensus patrum*) and commitment to the Lutheran confessions, particularly with the Augsburg Confession *invariata* (1530) and the Formula of Concord (1577). They used it also to distinguish themselves from their opponents, ranging from other Lutherans to Roman Catholics, the Reformed, Socinians, "Enthusiasts," and so forth. Later generations, taking a cue from the Pietist historian and polemicist Gottfried Arnold (*Unparteyische Kirchen- und Ketzer Historie*, 1699–1700), used the term "orthodox" pejoratively to criticize a mode of academic theology allegedly detached from the world and from practical piety. Nineteenth-century historians began to use the term more broadly to designate a period of church history falling between the Reformation (ending around 1555) and the later period of Pietism (beginning in 1675) and the Enlightenment (often dated to begin among German-speaking Lutherans in 1740). Since the Reformed world saw an analogous phenomenon and speaks of "Reformed Orthodoxy," historians have at times referred to the two conjointly as "Old Protestant Orthodoxy" (*Altprotestantische Orthodoxie*).

Because Lutheran Orthodoxy can designate both a type of theology and a more general historical period, its precise beginning and end point can be difficult to assign. Lutheran Orthodox theology has a number of distinctive features, blending prominent commitments to the Lutheran confessions with biblical exegesis, an overt use of Aristotelian logic and metaphysics, and wide engagement with contemporaneous and historical authors. It strove to achieve an identifiable Lutheran consensus in teaching and to distinguish itself from doctrines and interpretations it deemed problematic or false. As a movement, it came into its own during and after the period of post-Reformation consolidation that led up to the Formula of Concord. Its dominance at university faculties began to wane during the late seventeenth century, as new philosophical approaches, the advance of empirical sciences, and the emergence of Pietism challenged many of its assumptions. Nonetheless, an identifiable Lutheran Orthodox theological voice remained active and potent throughout the eighteenth century and continued, in more local contexts, even longer.

As a period designation, Lutheran Orthodoxy fell into disuse during the late twentieth century as historians began to place less emphasis on the defining role of theology and ideas for historical eras. It has yielded to terms such as "confessionalization" or "confession-building." Such terms address an important development in the process of state formation in early modern Europe and describe the context within which theology operated. While rulers across Europe had begun to consolidate and centralize their powers much earlier, the unique political and religious settlement of the Peace of Augsburg (1555) afforded princes within the Holy Roman Empire new opportunities in that regard. Defined as custodians of their land's religious life, and thanks to the all-encompassing nature of religion in that period, they exercised increasing oversight over the churches of their territories as well as over schools, universities, and courts of law. Historians use the term "confessionalization" to emphasize the role played by confessional identity (e.g., Lutheran, Reformed, Roman Catholic) in that process. In such a view, early modern rulers consolidated their populaces by marginalizing members of other confessions, using the institutional instruments of their churches and schools to control public religious discourse and to exercise social discipline, and "otherizing" rival confessions, especially those associated with other states. In that model, the academic theology of Lutheran Orthodoxy, with its emphasis on confessional consensus and identifying opponents, lends a helping hand to confessionalization.

Others have observed, however, that academic theologians and church leaders often had agendas of their own and that these were at times divergent from, resistant to, and even openly critical of those of their princes. Furthermore, a rising number of microhistorical studies have shown that common people were even less in tune with the dictates of their rulers and often were disinclined to accept their moral and religious authority. In that sense, terms such as "confessionalization," "confession-building," and "confessional culture," while still useful, tend to take an overly optimistic view of the states' success and often fail to account for the dynamic and varied character of religious life during the period. Local cultures and "lower" cultures showed resistance to discipline "from above" and maintained a degree of independence, while many other cultural trends of the time were transconfessional and shaped the religiosity of early modern Europeans in ways that appear more similar than confessionally distinct. Recognition of both these factors (inner-confessional pluralism and transconfessional commonalities) have kept historiographic terminology in flux. Such observations are also changing perceptions of Lutheran Orthodoxy. Long viewed stereotypically as a closed and inward-looking structure, the movement is beginning to be understood on its own terms as something far more open and dynamic and with goals specific to the needs of its time. Lutheran Orthodoxy was a phenomenon focused primarily on theological discourse, more specifically on developing and regulating that discourse in ways that were faithful to its sources, engaged with contemporary interlocutors and challenges, and provided means for adjudicating and resolving religious disagreements.

In retrospect Lutheran Orthodoxy's theology appears to have been remarkably abstract. Its dogmatic textbooks, particularly the monumental works of Johann Gerhard (*Loci theologici*, 1625), Abraham Calov (*Systema locorum theologicorum*, 1655–77), and Johann Andreas Quenstedt (*Theologia didactico-polemica*, 1685), demonstrate a conceptual virtuosity and attention to detail seldom seen before or since in Christian history. The sheer volume of these works (over eight thousand pages in Calov's case) is staggering, particularly when one considers how much else their authors wrote. But was it "relevant"?

Lutheran Orthodoxy unfolded during a period of epochal global transformation. Some historians have referred to this as an age of "global crisis" (Parker), pointing to widespread war and agricultural crisis brought on by a Little Ice Age (Parker; Lehmann). Others emphasize the explosion of migratory movements, exploration, and trade, all of which brought about an unprecedented range of encounters between peoples, cultures, and religions. Perhaps astonishingly, hardly any of these global events left a mark on Lutheran Orthodox theology. Even the Thirty Years' War, a catastrophe that took place at their front door, scarcely registers in works of dogmatic theology. Such events often had a great impact on devotional writings of the same authors but do not overtly shape their dogmatic discourse.

Lutheran Orthodox theology derived its special character from a unique confluence of political, church-political, and intellectual circumstances. It was launched by a desire for inner-Lutheran consensus and "orthodoxy" during the highly contentious decades following Luther's death. A number of issues emanating from interpretations of Luther's doctrine of justification, as well as from a revival of the Lutheran-Reformed eucharistic controversy during the 1550s, pitted theologians and their followers against each other and led to the formation of polarized parties: Philippists, who claimed Philip Melanchthon's legacy, and Gnesio-Lutherans, avowing allegiance to Luther. A series of public controversies ensued: the Majoristic, second antinomian, synergistic, Osiandrian, adiaphorist, and others. Politicians intervened, both to encourage harmony and, as in the case of Saxon Elector August I during the 1570s, to root out "crypto-Calvinists" and other influences deemed dangerous. An arduous process of conciliation and inner-confessional consensus building, led most prominently by Tübingen theologian Jakob Andreae but also including Martin Chemnitz and David Chytraeus, led to the drafting of a new confessional statement, the Formula of Concord (1577). The Formula of Concord, along with earlier documents—such as the three ecumenical creeds, the Augsburg Confession, its Apology, Luther's Catechisms, and the Smalcald Articles—formed the Book of Concord (1580) and was adopted by many, though not all, of the Lutheran territorial churches. A foundation had been laid for theological consensus, and the next decade saw Lutheran university faculties adjust. Centers of Lutheran Orthodoxy emerged in Wittenberg, Leipzig, Tübingen, Rostock, Jena, Königsberg, Strasbourg, and Gießen, among others. Thanks in part to Andreae's efforts, an important new element was added to theological curricula: academic disputations. Though these had featured throughout medieval Scholasticism as well as during the Reformation (esp. at the University of Wittenberg starting in 1533), they were now reconfigured as a tool for intellectual conflict resolution and began to be held much more frequently. In keeping with the mood of the time, disputations on the articles of the Augsburg Confession were particularly common (Appold, *Orthodoxie*).

If the initial phase of Lutheran Orthodoxy emerged out of a need for inner-Lutheran consensus, that orientation quickly broadened. Important impulses came from without. No sooner had the ink on the Formula of Concord's subscriptions (encompassing about two-thirds of Lutheranism's churches in the Holy Roman Empire) dried than Lutherans found their attentions directed, once again, to their Roman Catholic competition. Catholic developments had never been far from their mind, and Martin Chemnitz's four-volume

Examen Concilii Tridentini (1565–73) testifies to their impact, but the 1580s saw something new: Robert Bellarmine's *De controversiis christianae fidei adversus hujus temporis haereticos* (1581–93), a sustained and comprehensive attack on Protestant theology and a defense of the papal church. Lutherans needed to find a response, and in doing so they gave renewed attention to their doctrines of justification, the church, and scriptural authority, and so on. Lutherans also began a serious re-examination of their theological methodology, rediscovering Aristotelian logic (already used by Melanchthon) and metaphysics in the process. Times were changing. While smaller-scale inner-Lutheran controversies continued throughout the seventeenth century, they now ceded center stage to Bellarmine and other Catholic interlocutors, particularly as the Counter-Reformation found its stride and the Jesuits turned the University of Ingolstadt into a Catholic anti-Wittenberg. Attempts by rulers to bring the two sides into direct conversation, such as at the Colloquy of Regensburg (1601), only sharpened the divide. Shorter works, some more polemical than others, abounded, as did a series of Lutheran dogmatic textbooks by Matthias Hafenreffer, Leonhard Hutter, and Ägidius Hunnius, among others. It would take until 1610, however, for someone to produce a large-scale work that addressed Bellarmine's critiques, absorbed the new methodologies, and developed a compelling synthesis of Orthodox Lutheran theology that distinguished it markedly from its Reformation predecessors. This work was Johann Gerhard's classic *Loci theologici*, whose nine volumes would not be complete until 1625. It remains perhaps the best-known work of its kind, republished several times and in print, in English translation, even today.

While Lutheran dogmatic theology traces its beginnings to Melanchthon's *Loci communes* of 1521, the seventeenth century brought significant changes to its structure and exposition (Appold, *Vocatio*). Interests in logical method received a transformational impetus by the reception of Italian neo-Aristotelian philosophy, particularly Giacomo Zabarella's *Opera logica* (1578). Zabarella's logic allowed first Reformed and then Lutheran theologians to conceive theology as a "practical" science, analogous to medicine in that it "applies" instruments of healing (i.e., the gospel) to a diseased (i.e., sinful) person. Drawing again on Zabarella, Lutherans developed their theologies "analytically," organized to specify first the science's goal, then its subject, and finally the means by which the subject is to be led to that goal. The results were called "systems," giving birth to the term "systematic theology." While Gerhard shows Zabarella's influence, and a number of Lutheran theologians proposed theological systems using the analytic method during the first half of the seventeenth century, it was Calov's *Systema locorum theologicorum* that presented the approach in its most mature and influential form. In such hands, theology was understood not as a science about God but more precisely as a science by which someone might lead others to God. The best way to do that, in the eyes of Abraham Calov, was to learn one's theological concepts as clearly as possible. Because they were always ultimately applied to concrete ministry, even the most abstract concepts were, in Calov's view, inherently "practical" (and relevant).

Methodology also helped address one of Lutheran Orthodoxy's central challenges: securing a reliable source of theological knowledge. That source was defined as revelation. Some revelation took place in nature and was therefore accessible to natural reason; interest in it fueled Lutheran Orthodoxy's abiding cooperation with natural science, including even astrology (still thought of by some as an exact science). Salvific content, however, was only available through scriptural revelation, and this became the primary focus of theologians' attention. Partly as a response to Catholic assertions that their understanding of scriptural authority was inadequate because it lacked an account of the church's authoritative

interpretation, Lutherans developed a doctrine of Scripture's verbal inspiration, clarity, sufficiency, efficacy, and normativity in theological discourse. The role of interpreters was less clearly defined, but in practice that task fell to academic theologians and their extensive biblical commentaries.

While the adoption of neo-Aristotelian methods gave Lutheran Orthodox theology a new look and definition, the new systems also moved beyond their Reformation predecessors substantively in many areas. These include Christology, eschatology, predestination, and ecclesiology. Some of its most notable developments came in the field of soteriology, and it described how the Holy Spirit enters a human subject. Called an *ordo salutis* (order of salvation) and based upon earlier work by Philip Melanchthon and Martin Chemnitz, this process included logical distinctions between calling, illumination, conversion, rebirth, and renewal. It culminated in mystical union, a close intimacy (but not fusion) between divine and human in the believer.

Dialogue and conflict with other Christians continued to occupy a central place in Lutheran Orthodoxy throughout the seventeenth century. Roman Catholics remained its most conspicuous opponents through the end of the Thirty Years' War in 1648, but they were not the only ones. Traditional conflicts with the Reformed, especially over the Lord's Supper, gained new urgency as the latter's influence spread, particularly in Hesse and Brandenburg, where formerly Lutheran dynasties became Reformed. The unitarian Socinians drew considerable attention as well, more heatedly after they were expelled from Poland and established themselves in Prussia. Religious colloquies sought to mediate between such tensions: the most momentous of these took place in the Prussian city of Thorn in 1645, where Catholics, Lutherans, Reformed, and Socinians were gathered by the king of Poland. The outcome was doubly detrimental. Not only did the intended rapprochement fail, but also a new rift emerged within Lutheranism. Georg

Calixt, theology professor at the moderately Lutheran University of Helmstedt, had come to Thorn with a proposal to effect interconfessional unity on the basis of the ancient ecumenical creeds (*consensus antiquitatis*), which all but the Socinians accepted. Virtually all the other Lutherans were appalled and accused Calixt of "crypto-papism" and "syncretism." The latter term stuck and lent its name to the ensuing "Syncretist Controversy," which pitted the Lutheran faculties of Wittenberg and Leipzig against Helmstedt and even resulted in an attempted new Lutheran confession, the *Consensus repetitus fidei vere lutheranae* (1655). That measure failed.

The rise of Pietism during the final decades of the seventeenth century coincided with Lutheran Orthodoxy's gradual decline. Whether these two phenomena are causally related remains unclear. Orthodox theologians had long cultivated a deep practical spirituality, evident in works such as Gerhard's *Meditationes sacrae* (1606), the many printed sermons of the period, its calls for social reform, and the profound hymnody and devotional literature of authors such as Paul Gerhardt, Christian Scriver, and Philipp Nicolai. Its academic theological discourse, though often technical and abstract, also remains notable for its pioneering work in homiletics, pastoral theology, and casuistry. Calls for reforming the church were especially conspicuous after the Thirty Years' War at faculties such as Rostock (Strom). Though Pietists such as August Hermann Francke had different theological emphases (e.g., on spiritual rebirth), there seems to be little inherent reason why the two movements would need to be opposed. The fact that they often were may have more to do with personalities and with an increasing vulnerability of Orthodoxy within the academy. Indeed, a more likely explanation for Lutheran Orthodoxy's decline could be linked to the rise of new philosophies and new ways of acquiring, securing, and disseminating knowledge. As these innovations influenced doctrines of scriptural authority and concepts of revelation, they struck at the core of Orthodoxy's assumptions. Neo-Aristotelian systems, no matter how learned, pious, and virtuosic, were losing their power to persuade.

See also Andreae, Jakob; Calov, Abraham; Chemnitz, Martin; Enlightenment; Gerhard, Johann; Löscher, Valentin Ernst; Luther Interpretation and Reception; Melanchthon, Philip; Pietism; Quenstedt, Johann Andreas

Bibliography

Appold, K. *Abraham Calov's Doctrine of Vocatio in Its Systematic Context*. Mohr Siebeck, 1998; Appold, K. *Orthodoxie als Konsensbildung: Das theologische Disputationswesen an der Universität Wittenberg zwischen 1570 und 1710*. Mohr Siebeck, 2004; Baur, J. *Lutherische Gestalten—heterodoxe Orthodoxien: Historisch-systematische Studien*. Mohr Siebeck, 2010; Greyerz, K. von, et al., eds. *Interkonfessionalität—Transkonfessionalität—binnenkonfessionelle Pluralität: Neue Forschungen zur Konfessionalisierungsthese*. Gütersloher Verlagshaus, 2003; Kaufmann, T. *Universität und lutherische Konfessionalisierung: Die Rostocker Theologieprofessoren und ihr Beitrag zur theologischen Bildung und kirchlichen Gestaltung im Herzogtum Mecklenburg zwischen 1550 und 1675*. Gütersloher Verlagshaus, 1997; Kolb, R. *Bound Choice, Election, and Wittenberg Theological Method: From Martin Luther to the Formula of Concord*. Eerdmans, 2005; Kolb, R., ed. *Lutheran Ecclesiastical Culture, 1550–1675*. Brill, 2008; Lehmann, H. *Das Zeitalter des Absolutismus: Gottesgnadentum und Kriegsnot*. Kohlhammer, 1980; Matthias, M. *Theologie und Konfession: Der Beitrag von Ägidius Hunnius (1550–1603) zur Entstehung einer lutherischen Religionskultur*. Evangelische Verlagsanstalt, 2004; Mayes, B. *Counsel and Conscience: Lutheran Casuistry and Moral Reasoning after the Reformation*. Vandenhock & Ruprecht, 2011; Parker, G. *Global Crisis: War, Climate Change and Catastrophe in the Seventeenth Century*. Yale University Press, 2013; Strom, J. *Orthodoxy and Reform: The Clergy in Seventeenth Century Rostock*. Mohr Siebeck, 1999; Wallmann, J. *Gesammelte Aufsätze*. 3 vols. Mohr Siebeck, 1995–2010.

KENNETH G. APPOLD

Lutheran Social Services

The term "Lutheran social services" refers both to a broad range of programs by which Lutherans have responded to ever-changing social needs and to specific Lutheran organizations in the United States. It typically denotes programs and services, rooted in the Lutheran ethos of serving one's neighbor, that respond to significant personal and social impairments of individuals and families that are unmet through other sources, especially those offered by the government and employers.

Social service has been integral to Christianity since the apostles appointed deacons to care for widows. When the Reformation closed monasteries, which had provided a variety of social services, Luther endorsed utilizing their liquidated assets to create a community fund, increased by regular donations from congregants and other means, to provide carefully administered support for the poor. When Luther also criticized recent economic changes for increasing hardship and poverty, he established a precedent that has often connected social criticism and social services.

In the early 1700s German Pietist August Hermann Francke established an orphanage at Halle that featured special vocational instruction. Medicines manufactured in the Halle pharmacy were distributed worldwide, including in connection with funding missions. In North America, Henry Melchior Mühlenberg dispensed them along with his spiritual care. In the late eighteenth and early nineteenth centuries, lacking effective publicity venues, local German Lutheran pastors, as part of their pastoral concern for the total well-being of their parishioners, often disseminated information to help prevent disease, promote health, and improve the quality of life.

Nineteenth-century German Lutherans responded to social needs stemming from accelerating industrialization, urbanization, and population growth. Complementing traditional governmental and church assistance were new voluntary associations that navigated between radical calls for social restructuring and traditional but inadequate church-dispensed charity. Such initiatives were often favored by German nobility and the emerging middle classes. In Kaiserswerth, Theodore Fliedner launched a Lutheran deaconess program and thereby provided communal and vocational opportunities for unmarried women, who learned nursing skills and spiritual nurture. Florence Nightingale credited her visit to Kaiserswerth as critical to her development in the field of nurs-

ing. Fliedner's program was soon emulated, notably by Wilhelm Loehe (Löhe) in Bavaria. Within decades Kaiserswerth deaconesses and their communal motherhouses established a global presence.

In Hamburg, Amelia Sieveking trained middle- and upper-class women volunteers in case analysis and spirituality to meet temporary difficulties of individuals and families caused by injury, illness, or death. Her local society was quickly replicated and developed into a network. Concurrently, Johan Heinrich Wichern gathered delinquent Hamburg youth into a home, called the Rough House, where they were rehabilitated, educated, and often trained as deacons to work with prisoners, alcoholics, and the homeless. In 1844 Fliedner initiated a deacon institute, and by the 1850s additional "brotherhouses" for deacons began appearing. Other social needs—such as child care, rehabilitation of prostitutes, homes for abused women, and railroad station ministries for stranded travelers—soon became part of the formal German *Innere Mission* (Inner Mission, i.e., mission within Germany), which Wichern helped launch with his famous 1848 speech. The Inner Mission coordinated the work of German Protestant charitable social ministry organizations in Germany until 1975, when it was renamed Diakonia.

Despite Germany's institution of health insurance and social security in the 1880s and significant emigrant outflows, unmet social needs remained large. Popular dissatisfaction with the middle-class church in the decades preceding World War I caused leading German theologians to examine the church's role in society, particularly its responsibility for a social order that minimized the need for special social services. Meanwhile at Bielefeld, Friedrich von Bodelschwingh's institutions served persons experiencing a variety of needs, especially developmental disabilities and spousal abuse.

Dramatic nineteenth-century growth of Lutheranism in North America evoked social ministries, primarily immigrant assistance at ports of entry, orphanages, and hospitals.

Kaiserswerth deaconesses helped William Passavant found the first American Lutheran hospital near Pittsburgh in 1849. LCMS German Americans began a hospital in St. Louis in 1858. By century's end, Swedish, Danish, German, and Norwegian hospitals also existed in Brooklyn, Minneapolis, St. Paul, Omaha, Milwaukee, and Chicago, often supported by new deaconess motherhouses. Notable was Norwegian Elizabeth Fedde's work in Brooklyn, where her legacy today is NYU Lutheran Family Health Centers. The motherhouse in Philadelphia, supported by philanthropist John D. Lankenau, offered multiple social services, which in 1902 led to the first Lutheran Inner Mission Society in America. By the early twentieth century, orphanages, hospitals, and homes for the elderly dotted the American Lutheran ethnic landscape, offering services in the language and religion of their beneficiaries.

Early in the new century, American Lutheran city missionaries began working in urban slums, preaching the gospel, and making agency referrals. Religious transformations were typically both the means and goals of these efforts. When leaders of charitable organizations began sharing concerns, insights, and collegial encouragement, they soon formed support organizations. Within the LCMS the Associated Lutheran Charities was formed in 1901. Its energies soon influenced the development of the Wheat Ridge association to care for persons with tuberculosis, the Bethesda home for persons with developmental disabilities, and a new deaconess organization.

The Lutheran Welfare Conference in America and the Lutheran Inner Mission Conference were founded in 1922 by Lutherans who later formed the Evangelical Lutheran Church in America (ELCA). The Depression of the 1930s caused lay Lutheran leaders to cross denominational lines, apply jointly for grants, and form consortiums.

By 1939 the National Lutheran Council both supported a network for Lutheran social agencies and established a refugee service, which resettled displaced persons following World War II. Continuing as Lutheran Immigration and Refugee Service (LIRS), it has become a major refugee agency in the United States. At the end of World War II, American Lutherans provided material assistance to Europe, particularly Germany, through Lutheran World Action, quickly renamed Lutheran World Relief (LWR). Some eighty thousand German deaconesses tirelessly assisted in distributing initially meager rations. With those needs met, LWR turned to global needs. Working with local partners, LWR provides disaster relief and sponsors long-term educational, agricultural, and sustainability projects in Asia, Africa, and Latin America. Quilts and "kits" assembled in the United States both provide relief materials and educate the makers and assemblers about LWR's work, which is supported by both the ELCA and the LCMS. The Orphan Grain Train, founded in Nebraska in 1992 by Lutherans, is a major collector and worldwide distributor of supplies to disaster and high-need locations.

In 1947 the DIAKONIA World Federation was formed with strong Lutheran participation to strengthen worldwide diaconal ministries based primarily in Europe and North America. In 1952, the Lutheran World Federation (LWF) brought the world Lutheran community into international service by creating Lutheran World Service. In 1959 a famine in India prompted the Evangelische Kirche in Deutschland (EKD, Evangelical Church in Germany) to launch a program called Brot für die Welt (BfdW, Bread for the World). The Evangelical Development Service (EDS) was created in Germany in 1970, when 2 percent of the church tax collected on behalf of EKD member churches was allocated to international relief projects. Diakonia (distinct from DIAKONIA) worked closely with EDS on international projects, often utilizing youth volunteers. In 2012, EDS, Diakonia, and BfdW merged to form Evangelical Work for Service and Development and emphasized development assistance, education, and disaster relief.

By the end of the twentieth century, welfare states in northern Europe had assumed responsibility for many social services, to which all citizens had access, a development attributed at least in part to the Lutheran ethos in these countries.

Within the United States, the 1960s witnessed major changes in Lutheran social services. The formation of the American Lutheran Church and the Lutheran Church in America prompted the consolidation of many individual Lutheran social ministry organizations (SMOs) into combined area and statewide agencies. By the 1970s, several dozen of these new entities had "Lutheran Social Services" or "Lutheran Family Services" in their name. When Medicare and Medicaid programs were added to Social Security in the late 1960s, they influenced the kinds and scope of Lutheran social services. As the federal government in 1972 shifted social programs to state governments through grants, Lutheran SMOs quickly partnered with states that provided substantial funding. Soon 60 percent of some Lutheran SMO budgets were funded by states.

The number of Lutheran hospitals in the United States peaked at about 170 in this period. Although rapidly increasing medical costs caused many Lutheran hospitals to close, merge, or restructure, new theological directions focused on emerging emphases of healing and holistic medicine. Agencies arranging for home placements supplanted orphanages. Federal entitlement programs enabled Lutheran elderly to join new Lutheran continuous-care retirement communities, which usually featured a range of social services. Homes for needy elderly remained, while new initiatives were launched to provide services and housing for the poor and needy seniors.

Governmental funding coupled with agency consolidations and program adjustments dictated increasingly sophisticated and professional services, including improved marketing and fund-raising techniques. Lutheran SMOs leveraged resources by drawing on multiple income streams: traditional donations but increasingly from cultivated donors partially incentivized by tax credits and tax deductions, governmental and private foundation grants, private and public partnerships, fees for services with sliding scales based on ability to pay, and voucher programs.

The 1996 Personal Responsibility and Work Opportunity Reconciliation Act in the United States, popularly known as Welfare-to-Work, both reduced the length of welfare eligibility and authorized governmental support for services provided by faith-based organizations in the new Charitable Choice program. While many previously excluded conservative religious groups welcomed this change, some Lutherans were ambivalent, sensing that the new federal guidelines could blunt an organization's prophetic voice and create overdependence on governmental funding. Nevertheless, Lutheran agencies effectively maintained their Lutheran identity and sense of mission.

To achieve greater efficiency, coordination, professionalization, and governmental advocacy, Lutheran Services in America (LSA) was organized in 1997, combining SMOs having "Lutheran Services" in their name with a broad array of agencies, especially those caring for the elderly. In 2015 LSA was among the twenty-five largest philanthropic organizations in the United States, with an aggregate annual budget of $21 billion, 250,000 employees, and 150,000 volunteers. Member agencies served one in every fifty Americans via 195 agencies for seniors, 103 for health care, 31 for immigration and refugee, and 105 for children, youth, and family services, as well as 22 economic empowerment programs, 55 housing and community development agencies, and 50 disability services. The more than 300 LSA member organizations are affiliated with either the ELCA or the LCMS or both.

Although virtually all American Lutheran social service organizations advocate politically for their programs, their scope of advocacy is limited by their 501(c)(3) tax-exempt status. However, the mission of some nonprofit organizations is primarily advocacy, as notably

461

is Bread for the World (distinct from the German organization, BfdW), originally organized by Lutherans, which lobbies proactively for specific legislation to ameliorate hunger domestically and globally. The Lutheran Office for Governmental Affairs in Washington, DC, a ministry of the ELCA, also engages in advocacy by supporting laws and programs that assist the disadvantaged.

These organizations and data do not, however, tell the full story of Lutheran social service, especially in the United States. Countless spontaneous initiatives have arisen to meet local, novel, or temporary needs, including food pantries, homeless housing, prison ministries, parish nurses, and child and elder day care. Most of these operate simply under the umbrella of local Lutheran congregations, invariably with meager budgets but with countless glad and compassionate volunteers.

See also Deaconesses; Fliedner, Theodore; Lutheran World Federation; Social Ministry, Community Chest, Poor Relief; Wichern, Johann Hinrich

Bibliography

Childs, J. *Joined at the Heart: What It Means to Be Lutheran in Social Ministry*. Lutheran Services in America, 2000; Kettunen, P., and K. Petersen. *Beyond Welfare State Models: Transnational Historical Perspectives on Social Policy*. Edward Elgar, 2011; Letts, H. C., ed. *Christian Social Responsibility: A Symposium in Three Volumes*. Muhlenberg, 1957; Lindberg, C. *Beyond Charity: Reformation Initiatives for the Poor*. Fortress, 1993; Lueking, F. D. *A Century of Caring: 1868–1968*. Board for Social Ministry in the Lutheran Church–Missouri Synod, 1968; McCurley, F. R., ed. *Social Ministry in the Lutheran Tradition*. Fortress, 2008; Uehling, C. T. *Hope and Healing: Lutheran Social Ministry Organizations Expressing the Compassion of Christ in American Life*. Lutheran Services in America, 1999.

JAMES W. ALBERS

Lutheran World Federation

The Lutheran World Federation (LWF) is a global body of 145 churches, which in 2016 comprised over seventy-two million people in ninety-eight countries. Thus the LWF embraces about 95 percent of the world's Lutherans. While the majority of these are still found in historic centers of Lutheran life in Germany, Scandinavia, and North America, the largest LWF member churches now include those in Tanzania, Ethiopia, Indonesia, and Madagascar.

In its current constitution, the LWF describes itself as "a communion of churches which confess the triune God, agree in the proclamation of the Word of God, and are united in pulpit and altar fellowship." This self-understanding has changed significantly since the first constitution's language of a "free association of Lutheran Churches." With only minor changes in expression, however, the LWF has continued to confess "the Holy Scriptures of the Old and New Testaments to be the only source and norm of its doctrine, life and service" and to "see in the three Ecumenical Creeds and in the Confessions of the Lutheran Church, especially in the unaltered Augsburg Confession and the Small Catechism of Martin Luther, a pure exposition of the Word of God."

Setting the Course. The LWF was formed in Lund, Sweden, in 1947. Its creation built on work of the Lutheran World Convention, an earlier effort toward international Lutheran collaboration formed after World War I, but the new body responded directly to the sharp disruptions of global Lutheran life from the Nazi period and World War II. Its first president was Swedish theologian Anders Nygren, with S. C. Michelfelder from the United States as the first executive secretary (soon changed to general secretary). The highest decision-making body was to be an assembly, ordinarily to meet every six years.

Directions set early have had lasting impact. Notably, the emphasis on humanitarian aid and care for displaced persons, urgent in the postwar context, helped heal and deepen ties of Lutheran unity while also establishing a lasting commitment to refugee relief. The LWF has been the largest faith-based partner of United Nations High Commissioner for Refugees (UNHCR), in 2015 providing assistance for more than 1.3 million refugees in more than thirty countries.

Ecumenically, as the World Council of Churches (WCC) was still itself in formation in 1947, the LWF immediately established close ties that led to long-term sharing of facilities at the Ecumenical Centre in Geneva, Switzerland. While there could be tension between attention to confessional identity and efforts toward Christian unity through conciliar bodies like the WCC, Lutheran churches have generally not seen these relationships as alternatives. The LWF has been among the most operationally active of the Christian family bodies; at the same time many of its member churches have also been prominent participants and supporters of the WCC.

One decision from the Lund beginnings, however, proved more open-ended and ambiguous. The constitutional description of the LWF as a "free association of Lutheran Churches" continues: "It shall not exercise churchly functions on its own authority, nor shall it have power to . . . limit the autonomy of any Member Church." According to historian Abdel Ross Wentz, the choice of "Federation" in place of the earlier "Convention" in the name had been made deliberately, "to indicate greater compactness and efficiency, to suggest permanence, to make possible wider areas of cooperation, and to insist upon the official participation of the churches without sacrifice of their sovereignty or autonomy." In all these ways, establishment of the LWF was "a turning point in the history of world Lutheranism" (1425). Yet the implications of life shared in the federation have required continued reflection and adjustment over the course of seventy years. Not for the first time, a consultation process called "Self-Understanding of the Lutheran Communion" was established to help prepare for the 2017 assembly.

From Federation to Communion. In its early years, the LWF engaged in multiple theological studies examining the significance of a world Lutheran body. Discussions with nonmember churches, notably the US-based Lutheran Church–Missouri Synod (which ultimately decided to pursue its international ties through the International Lutheran Council and is not an LWF member), raised questions of how mutual accountability could be exercised.

However, the struggle against apartheid most decisively moved the LWF toward an identity that was more than "a free association of churches." A crucial step was the 1977 decision of the Sixth Assembly at Dar es Salaam, which declared a *status confessionis* concerning apartheid, thus setting the stage for suspension (not expulsion) of two white South African churches at the next assembly, meeting in Budapest in 1984. Significant in itself, this process reflected changing engagement with social and ethical issues, in the LWF as well as in other Christian bodies, and brought to global prominence leaders like Bishop Manas Buthelezi from South Africa and Bishop Zephaniah Kameeta from what would become Namibia. For LWF identity, such an action seemed to many both necessary to meet the circumstances and at the same time "more" than a voluntary association of churches could properly do. These reflections helped lead to the decision at the Eighth Assembly in Curitiba, Brazil, to declare the LWF to be a "communion of churches," living in "pulpit and altar fellowship" with one another. As the LWF approached its fiftieth anniversary, its (1994–2010) General Secretary Ismael Noko reflected,

> The Lutheran churches over the years have grown together. They have cooperated in programs in proclamation and service and at the same time have acknowledged that the gift of communion with God in Christ calls for a life of interdependence among themselves. Pulpit and altar fellowship implies that the "federal" concept no longer adequately describes this global movement. . . . The concept of communion is not only biblically and theologically rooted; it also challenges Christians to live a life that is both rooted in and transcends current societal fragmentation marked by racism, nationalism, ethnicity, and gender oppression. (in Schjørring et al. xii)

To be sure, some theologians from LWF member churches object to this terminology and to the decisions made by the LWF as a communion of churches.

Thus the middle decades of the LWF's history led simultaneously to closer bonds among member churches and also to growing appreciation for multiple diversities among them and recognition of the contextual location of all theological reflections. How these are to be held together continues to be explored in the LWF, with reflections gathered around imagery from the Emmaus story in Luke 24, where the disciples, not yet seeing fully the risen Christ who joins them, engage in conversation as they journey together.

Ecumenical Engagements. The LWF's journey toward a more ecclesially defined identity—not as itself a church, but as a communion of churches—has always been entwined with its ecumenical activity. Cooperating with the Strasbourg Ecumenical Institute, it has focused ecumenical resources on sustained bilateral theological dialogues with other Christian families, notably including Anglicans, Orthodox, and Reformed. Two of these dialogue processes, with the Roman Catholic Church and the Mennonite World Conference, resulted in prominent, communion-defining actions.

In 1999 the LWF and the Catholic Church signed the Joint Declaration on the Doctrine of Justification in Augsburg, Germany. In this act they "declare together" that "a consensus in basic truths of the doctrine of justification exists between Lutherans and Catholics." While not uncontroversial, this role of the LWF as "signing partner" both reflected and strengthened its agency in advancing the communion.

Then, at the 2010 Eleventh Assembly in Stuttgart, Germany, the LWF asked for "forgiveness—from God and from our Mennonite sisters and brothers—for the harm that our forebears in the sixteenth century committed to Anabaptists, for forgetting or ignoring this persecution in the intervening centuries, and for all inappropriate, misleading, and hurtful portraits of Anabaptists and Mennonites made by Lutheran authors, in both popular and scholarly forms, to the present day."

In addition to its high ecumenical profile, the LWF has been engaged in interreligious dialogue since the mid-1960s. Beginning from the work of a consultation, "The Church and the Jewish People," the 1984 Assembly in Budapest received a statement, "Luther, Lutheranism, and Jews," which stated, "The sins of Luther's anti-Jewish remarks, the violence of his attacks on the Jews, must be acknowledged with deep distress. And all occasions for similar sin in the present or future must be removed from our churches."

In more recent times, multiple resources have been produced for Lutheran-Muslim relations and for engagement with religious pluralism more broadly, notably around questions of greed and economic justice. In addition to theological explorations, the LWF has engaged in collaborative humanitarian work with Muslim partners.

Present Activity and Challenges. By many measures, the daily work of the LWF is predominantly in diaconal and humanitarian activity, working with member churches and other partners. Its governance and activity are committed to draw from all the seven LWF "regions," three in Europe and the other four largely corresponding to continents. It also is committed to the inclusion of the voices of women and youth at all levels of its work. What after 2010 is called the "Communion Office" in Geneva is explicitly not considered "the LWF" but rather its center of coordination, oversight, and reflection. As do its companion and partner organizations, this center faces challenges of declining resources from its principal funders, primarily in the global north. At the same time, like other Christian expressions, it is strengthened and increasingly transformed by newer churches and by churches whose life and witness are carried out as challenged minorities in their contexts.

Claiming identity as a global communion intensified challenges of balancing autonomy and mutual accountability among member churches. For many years, movement toward closer communion relationships was encouraged on the basis of many dimensions of shared life in the LWF, parallel movements in other ecumenical families, and attention given to "communion" understandings of the church. With these commitments to relationship, the LWF continues to include, for example, both churches that have an episcopal polity and those that do not, both those who ordain women and those that do not. While the majority of member churches have come to a structure with episcopal ministry (all have a ministry of *episcopé*), and most ordain both women and men to all the ministries of the church (this latter practice is encouraged by actions of LWF assemblies), still agreement on these matters is not held necessary for sharing life in the Lutheran communion. Currently increased attention is demanded by issues concerning human sexuality and the family, on which member churches also have differences of practice and teaching. Beginning in the 1990s, frameworks and processes for discussion of these questions were provided by the LWF; their ability to avoid lasting rifts in the communion remains to be seen.

Five Hundred Years of Reformation. The year 2017 marks both a five-hundredth anniversary for the Lutheran movement and the seventieth anniversary of the LWF. Years before, the decision was made to locate the 2017 Twelfth Assembly not in Germany but in Namibia. Under the general theme of "liberated by God's grace," principles were articulated to guide the observance, principles recognizing that the Lutheran movement has become a "global citizen" and seeks to be "open to constant renewal" in responding to contemporary challenges. The third principle, ecumenical accountability and engagement, gained prominence as the inauguration of the anniversary year was planned for October 31, 2016. In a striking witness to what was called a movement "from conflict to communion," Pope Francis agreed to share with LWF leaders in the opening common prayer. The location, Lund Cathedral in Sweden, returns the LWF to its beginnings and thus provides a fitting image of the continuity and change in the global Lutheran communion.

See also Ecumenical Dialogues; Inner-Lutheran Ecumenism; Lutheran Social Services; Noko, Ishmael; Nygren, Anders

Bibliography

In addition to resources on the LWF website, http://www.lutheranworld.org, especially helpful is the **Fifty-Year Anniversary Volume:** Schjørring, J. H., P. Kumari, and N. A. Hjelm, eds. *From Federation to Communion: The History of the Lutheran World Federation.* Fortress, 1997; **Earlier Histories:** Nelson, E. C. *The Rise of World Lutheranism.* Fortress, 1982; Wentz, A. R. "Lutheran World Federation." In *The Encyclopedia of the Lutheran Church,* ed. J. Bodensieck, 1425–32. Augsburg, 1965.

KATHRYN L. JOHNSON

Luther Congresses

The International Congress for Luther Research is an academic forum for Luther and Reformation scholars, convening for a week every four to six years, and steered by a Continuation Committee of ten scholars, mostly theologians and church historians, representing German, Nordic, North American, and majority-world Luther research. The first Luther Congress was held in Aarhus, Denmark, in 1956 and was sponsored by the Lutheran World Federation (LWF); key figures in shaping the Congress as a symposium for free and serious Luther scholarship were Regin Prenter, chairman of the LWF Commission on Theology and professor in the faculty of theology at the University of Aarhus, and Vilmos Vajta, director of the LWF Department of Theology. Over the years LWF funding has been substantially reduced and is now exclusively aimed at enabling scholars from majority-world churches to participate. The twelve Congresses so far have been held in Denmark (Aarhus 1956; København [Copenhagen] 2002), Germany (Münster [West] 1960; Erfurt [East] 1983; Heidelberg 1997), Finland (Järvenpää 1966; Helsinki 2012), the United States (St. Louis 1971; St. Paul 1993), Sweden (Lund 1977), Norway (Oslo 1988), and Brazil (Canoas 2007). The Sixth Congress, held in Erfurt (1983) and commemorating the five-hundredth anniversary of Martin Luther's birth, was the largest conference (more than 250 invited participants). Each Luther Congress stands under an overarching theme and has a threefold program of main lectures, seminars, and short presentations, thus providing a nuanced overview of agendas and prospects of ongoing Luther research worldwide. The first five Congresses are documented in separately edited volumes. Since Erfurt 1983 the Congress papers have been published in the *Luther-Jahrbuch*. Recent themes have included "Luther after 1530: Theology, Church, and Politics" (2002), "Luther's Ethics in the Realms of Church, Household, Politics" (2007), and "Luther as Teacher and Reformer of the University" (2012). The thirteenth International Congress for Luther Research will meet in Luther's Wittenberg in 2017, celebrating the Reformation Jubilee under the title "1517. Luther between Tradition and Renewal."

See also Luther Interpretation and Reception

Bibliography

Lohse, B. *Martin Luther: Eine Einführung in sein Leben und Werk*. Beck, 1997; Schjørring, J. H., P. Kumari, and N. A. Hjelm, eds. *From Federation to Communion: The History of the Lutheran World Federation*. Fortress, 1997.

STEFFEN KJELDGAARD-PEDERSEN

Luther Interpretation and Reception

The thought and career of Martin Luther have attracted praise, criticism, careful analysis, and subjugation to a variety of agendas throughout the centuries since 1517. His initial followers experienced in Luther a larger-than-life personality, whose linguistic and rhetorical gifts and insights into Scripture and theology changed their perceptions of reality. Many repeated his insights without much reflection; others adapted his thought to their own backgrounds, situations, and predispositions. His students applied his thinking to their ever-changing circumstances in parish or university and bequeathed to seventeenth-century successors a manner of biblical interpretation and a body of public teaching that, while undergoing constant reappraisal and adjustment, remained at the core of the teaching

and practice of Lutheran churches into the eighteenth century.

Luther received immediate harsh criticism, both for his understanding of justification by faith alone, which Roman Catholic critics found impossible to fit into their understanding of theology, and for his rejection of papal governance of the church *de iure divino* (by divine right). They regarded both of these positions as destructive of order and discipline in church and society. The intent of some of their number to burn him as a heretic indicates the degree to which they saw his teaching and public stance of opposition to papal power as a menace to the structures of society. This criticism continued unabated in Roman Catholic circles into the twentieth century, when Joseph Lortz and others opened up a more appreciative appraisal of Luther for Roman Catholics.

Those who suspected that his view of the true presence of Christ's body and blood in the Lord's Supper retained aspects of medieval superstitious use of the material or physical elements also continued their criticism of his sacramental doctrine without focusing much on his understanding of the power actually effected in believers' lives through God's Word in sacramental as well as oral and written forms. His own colleague Andreas Bodenstein von Karlstadt broke with him on this issue, and it remained a significant dividing point between Luther's followers and other Protestants in subsequent centuries.

As rational accents in Lutheran "Orthodox" theology drifted toward what would be labeled the Enlightenment, Luther's strict understanding of salvation by grace through faith alone and the bound nature of human willing led some otherwise Orthodox theologians to promote the idea of an election to salvation "in view of faith." Leading Lutheran lay thinkers, such as Samuel Pufendorf, distinguished Lutheran thought from Calvinist theology by ignoring Luther's own teaching and forging a synergistic view of the relationship of God and human beings. Gradually an image of Luther emerged that deemphasized his teaching and reshaped him into a pioneer of "modern" individualistic thinking. At the same time as this stream of interpretation emerged around 1700, Pietists were forming their own vision of Luther, emphasizing his accentuation of Scripture and Bible reading as well as his teaching on the pious Christian life of prayer and new obedience and especially emphasizing the "younger Luther."

In the nineteenth century, German Lutherans found in the Wittenberg reformer a hero of national defiance to foreign influences, particularly in the wake of the disastrous Napoleonic Wars (1803–15). As efforts to form unions of Reformed and Lutheran churches progressed in several parts of Germany, in artwork and literature Luther appeared with his critics from the Reformed side (Ulrich Zwingli and John Calvin) as a harmonious team. Others revived a commitment to the Lutheran confessions and the specific aspects of Luther's theology that set it apart in the nineteenth century. They defended Luther's views against the liberal theology of Albrecht Ritschl and others. Leaders in this movement, such as Theodosius Harnack, built on fresh historical examination of the texts of his writings, furthered by the studies of Julius Köstlin and others, and aided by the publication of the imperial, or Weimar, edition of Luther's works, a model for scholarly editions of texts. These studies culminated in the developments labeled the "Luther Renaissance," led by Berlin professor Karl Holl. Its followers split into several groups, including those who tended to accent elements of Luther's thought that accorded with National Socialist thinking, and the "dialectical" theologians who used principles of Luther's theology to criticize National Socialist thought and policy. The first half of the twentieth century witnessed a search for the precise time of Luther's "tower experience," or "evangelical breakthrough" (often dated between 1512 and 1518), an effort now largely abandoned in favor of seeing a gradual maturing of his thought.

Marxist images of Luther, based on initial work by Friedrich Engels, became important through the desire of the government of the German Democratic Republic to use Luther as a cultural icon, but since the fall of European Communism that field of interest has largely disappeared. Recent decades have seen fresh investigation of the background and sources of Luther's thinking in both scholastic and monastic traditions, the social context in which his thought arose, as well as more extensive assessment of the nature of his impact on his own students and followers and on subsequent generations. For example, in Finland some theologians and historians have searched for ways to interpret Luther in the light of the commitments of ecumenical conversation partners, such as the Orthodox churches.

See also Finnish Interpretation of Luther; Holl, Karl; Luther Renaissance

Bibliography

Kolb, R. *Martin Luther as Prophet, Teacher, and Hero.* Baker, 1999; Mostert, W. "Luther, III. Wirkungsgeschichte." *TRE* 21 (1991): 567–94; Pelikan, J., ed. *Interpreters of Luther.* Fortress, 1968; Stayer, J. M. *Martin Luther, German Saviour: German Evangelical Theological Factions and the Interpretation of Luther, 1917–1933.* McGill-Queens University Press, 2000.

ROBERT KOLB

Luther Renaissance

A widespread scholarly movement interested in the theology of Martin Luther and sparked by the publication of the Weimar edition of Luther's Works (begun at the four-hundredth anniversary of Luther's birth in 1883), the Luther Renaissance was flourishing in the years following the fourth centenary of the Reformation in 1917. It was centered in Germany, particularly during the years of the Weimar Republic (1919–33), and continued in a somewhat weakened form well into the 1960s and beyond.

The Luther Renaissance was the product of the post–World War I wave of dogmatic or systematic theology in Protestant religious studies. However, it owed a major debt to the prewar period, in which church history was dominant. Both Albrecht Ritschl (1822–89) and Adolf von Harnack (1851–1930) sounded the theme that the Protestant Reformation rescued the church of Jesus and Paul from the deformations of Greek Orthodoxy and Roman Catholicism. The Reformation was the special German contribution to the history of Christianity. While Ritschl and von Harnack did not deny that Luther held to much that was inherited from the Greek and Latin churches, their concentration on Luther as the preeminent reformer emphasized the *new* elements he brought, which were focused in his doctrine of justification by faith alone. In 1904 Heinrich Denifle (1844–1905), a Catholic scholar, argued, on the basis of Luther's early theological lectures, that Luther was entirely conventional in his pre-Reformation teaching on justification and had later distorted the views of righteousness held by the medieval Scholastic doctors. This controversy contributed greatly to the Luther Renaissance.

Before 1906, when he received an appointment to the University of Berlin as a protégé of von Harnack, Karl Holl (1866–1926) was a church historian interested in the field of Greek patristics. At that time he began to write his own systematic theology on the topic of justification. From 1910 he began to study Luther's early theological lectures, the same ones denigrated as unoriginal by Denifle. Holl viewed Luther's doctrine of justification as connected tightly to regeneration, and he oriented it away from the individual's salvation to that of the community. In the same sense he gave Luther credit for a fuller perception of justification than Paul's understanding. Holl seems to have perceived justification as the center of God's severe, yet merciful, relation to humankind. His conception of theology was, in the tradition of his liberal theological forerunners, highly theocentric and had little explicit reference to Christ. It claimed Luther as a major link to Paul in the proclamation of true religion. (Augustine did not belong in this succession but was part of its Latin patristic deformation.) Holl even regarded his Luther

scholarship as part of Germany's "war effort." Unlike his liberal forerunners, who regarded the Reformation as Germany's contribution to the whole Protestant world, Holl saw it as a mark of the superiority of stern German "culture" to the frivolity of "Western civilization." When in defeat Germany was forced to adopt a Western parliamentary regime in which Catholics and Socialists played a prominent part, Holl contended that this was a betrayal of Germany's authentic Lutheran heritage. Holl was one of the first Luther scholars to make widespread use of the new critical Weimar edition (begun in 1883) of Luther's Works. He used this superior source collection to bolster the credentials of his major collection of essays on Luther that first appeared in 1921.

The Luther Renaissance was continued by Holl's brilliant student Emmanuel Hirsch (1886–1972) and Hirsch's student Erich Vogelsang (1904–45). One of Holl's more questionable contentions was that the spiritual tumults (*Anfechtungen*) in the monastery, about which Luther spoke openly in his later years, had occurred long before 1517 and had set the stage for his "discovery" of his distinctive theology of justification. Luther seemed to refer to this theological breakthrough in an autobiographical fragment of the preface to the first volume of his Latin works from 1545, the year before his death. Both Hirsch and Vogelsang concentrated on Luther's first lectures on the Psalms, 1513–15, and arrived at varying theories about which part of this lecture series documented Luther's "tower experience." Vogelsang was credited with solving the problem and at the same time was thought to have better integrated Christ into Luther's theology by identifying Luther's *Anfechtung* with those suffered by Christ on the cross. The basic contention of this phase of the Luther Renaissance was that Luther's theological discovery about justification "caused" the Reformation as its implications unfolded in Luther's mind and work. Hirsch joined the National Socialist Party in 1937, and both Hirsch and Vogelsang were members of the German Christian movement, through which Hitler tried to control the German Protestant churches. But Vogelsang's "solution" to the beginnings of Luther's theology continued to be widely accepted in Luther studies outside Germany. Heinrich Bornkamm (1901–78), another student of Holl but in the 1930s and 1940s a member of the Confessing Church, undertook an elaborate defense of the Vogelsang thesis in *Archiv für Reformationsgeschichte* in 1961 and 1962.

In retrospect the Luther Renaissance seems to have affected Luther studies in several respects. It insisted on a systematic, dogmatic presentation of a figure who was not a systematic theologian. It presumed that theology impelled historical events. It concentrated its work on the younger Luther instead of studying the mature and aging reformer, for whom ample source material is available.

See also Holl, Karl; Luther Interpretation and Reception; Luther's Breakthrough; Luther's Works

Bibliography

Assel, H. *Der andere Aufbruch: Die Lutherrenaissance; Ursprünge, Aporien und Wege.* Vandenhoeck & Ruprecht, 1993; Holl, K. *Gesammelte Aufsätze zur Kirchengeschichte.* Vol. 1, *Luther.* Mohr Siebeck, 1921; Stayer, J. M. *Martin Luther, German Saviour: German Evangelical Theological Factions and the Interpretation of Luther, 1917–1933.* McGill-Queen's University Press, 2000.

JAMES M. STAYER

Luther's Bible

Martin Luther's translation of the Bible is a classic in German as well as world literature. While exiled at the Wartburg, Luther produced his translation of the Greek New Testament into German in less than one hundred days. Drawing on the dialect of the Saxon court, yet sensitive to the common conversation of his students and Wittenberg parishioners' home and market experiences, Luther produced an incredibly successful translation, which spoke accurately and poetically in idiomatic, understandable German while respecting certain idiosyncracies of the Greek and (later for the Old Testament) Hebrew original.

After acquiring several lexical tools during a visit to Wittenberg in early December 1521, Luther used the newly revised (1519) Greek text by Erasmus along with a 1509 Latin Vulgate text. Luther also brought to the task significant linguistic skills and gifts: a sensitivity to the vernacular, a faith-filled commitment to the gospel, his exposure to the Bible as a friar and student of the original Greek and Hebrew, and a passionate desire to proclaim clearly the comforting promises of God fulfilled in Jesus Christ. The translation he brought with him back to Wittenberg in 1522 was then polished with, among other things, suggestions from Philip Melanchthon, Wittenberg's premier Greek scholar.

September 1522 saw the first edition of the New Testament in Wittenberg (thus the popular designation *Septembertestament*). Within three months a second edition (the *Dezembertestament*) appeared; throughout Luther's lifetime over twenty editions appeared in Wittenberg and almost a hundred (many without Luther's approval) by other printers, not uncommon in a world without copyright laws. In addition to the biblical text, Luther included his preface to the entire New Testament and to individual books, marginal glosses explaining important texts or giving cross-references, and Cranach woodcuts for the book of Revelation.

Collaboration with Philip Melanchthon and others continued as Luther and his team proceeded to translate the Old Testament. For the sake of time and cost, Luther determined to publish it in several installments. By mid-1523, the Pentateuch was available along with Luther's "Preface to the Old Testament." The following year, the books of Joshua through Esther were published. As Luther worked on the poetic and prophetic books, he struggled with making them speak the common German. The third part—Job, Psalms, Proverbs, and Ecclesiastes—appeared near the end of 1524.

Diversions of many kinds caused delay in completing the translation. Luther met with his "Bible colleagues" to explore troubling grammatical or historical details of the translation. He also lectured on several prophetic books and published their translations, completing the prophetic books in early 1532.

Convinced that the Bible was God's authoritative Word, Luther wanted to make sure that it was clear and understandable to the common folk. Although almost two dozen translations in both High German and Low German ("low" refers to the German lowlands of the north) were published before Luther's translation, most of them were slavishly literal translations—all from the (Latin) Vulgate and not the original languages. Luther's translation from the Greek, Hebrew, and Aramaic sought freshness and vibrancy. Explaining and defending his translation approach and method in 1530, Luther's treatise *On Translating: An Open Letter* (LW 35:175–202) provides several insights into his Bible. Recognizing that any translation is also an interpretation, Luther sought to articulate clearly the scriptural truths of God's gracious promises in the Old Testament and their fulfillment in Christ throughout the New Testament, in a way that was understandable and accessible. Avoiding academic and ecclesiastical Latin idioms, Luther wanted the biblical text to be heard in the language that common people used at home. At the same time, as recent work by Birgit Stolt has made clear, Luther also respected the peculiar sacral language of parts of the Bible, arguing in the same 1530 tract for the need not only to "look the [common] folk in the mouth" but also to preserve the peculiarities of the original texts.

The complete German Bible, including the Apocrypha, was finally published in Wittenberg in 1534; Luther continued to revise it until his death. The result was one of the foremost translations of the Bible, rivaling the Vulgate in its acceptance, and a standard for German literature for centuries. As both a literary achievement and a theological testimony, Luther's Bible remains a monumental legacy of Luther's life.

See also Bible Translations

Bibliography

Bluhm, H. *Luther Translator of Paul.* Lang, 1984; Bluhm, H. *Martin Luther: Creative Translator.* Concordia, 1965; Luther, M. *Word and Sacrament I.* LW 35. Fortress, 1960; Reu, J. M. *Luther's German Bible: An Historical Presentation Together with a Collection of Sources.* Lutheran Book Concern, 1934; Stolt, B. *"Laßt uns fröhlich springen!": Gefühlswelt und Gefühlsnavigierung in Luthers Reformationsarbeit.* Weidler, 2012.

Timothy Maschke

Luther's Breakthrough

The date and content of Luther's breakthrough to a Reformation theology has been a matter of debate in Luther studies at least since the late nineteenth century. The term "breakthrough" as well as other expressions such as "tower experience," "the reformatory turn," "inner turning point," and "rebirth" communicate that Luther "broke the mold" (Hamm 31) of late medieval Catholic doctrine. Several questions surround the term. What was the substance of this breakthrough? When did it occur? Was it a sudden event or a process? Was it really a breakthrough in the sense of shattering the regnant Scholastic system of theology, or only a personal, existential breakthrough for Luther due to his misunderstanding (productive or otherwise) of the tradition? Alternatively, was Luther's breakthrough a gradual development in continuity rather than in discontinuity with medieval Catholicism? Seminal studies from the last half-century (up to 1988) and devoted to these closely interwoven questions are collected in the volume by Lohse.

Luther's major testimony to his breakthrough is in his retrospective preface to the 1545 Latin edition of his writings (LW 34:323–38). He affirms that he "was once a monk and a most enthusiastic papist," willing even to murder "all who would take but a syllable from obedience to the pope, . . . [for I was] as one who, in dread of the last day, nevertheless from the depth of my heart wanted to be saved" (LW 34:328). Luther relates that he had lectured on the Psalms (1513–15), Romans (1515–16), Galatians (1516–17), and Hebrews (1517–18), yet his "extraordinary ardor for understanding Paul in the Epistle to the Romans" was blocked by the phrase "righteousness of God" (Rom. 1:17). "For I hated that word 'righteousness of God,' which, according to the use and custom of all the teachers, I had been taught to understand philosophically regarding the formal or active righteousness, as they called it, with which God is righteous and punishes the unrighteous sinner" (LW 34:336). Luther's received tradition presented him with a "gospel" in essence demanding that, no matter how much grace assisted the sinner, the burden of proof for salvation centered on human achievement. The tradition "had always understood [Paul and Augustine] to say that the Church distributes Christ's righteousness like the talents that can be increased by hard work and investment. Christ's justice does not make a man righteousness before God; it puts him in the position to become righteous. At the Last Judgment the righteous God will decide if the faithful have used and truly done justice to Christ's gift" (Oberman 152–53).

In 1545 Luther describes his breakthrough as a kind of paradigm shift, gained through intense meditative, exegetical struggle, to a new understanding of the righteousness of God. Righteousness before God is not achieved but received:

At last, by the mercy of God, meditating day and night, I gave heed to the context of the words, namely, "in it the righteousness of God is revealed, as it is written, 'He who through faith is righteous shall live.'" There I began to understand that the righteousness of God is that by which the righteous lives by a gift of God, namely, by faith. And this is the meaning: the righteousness of God is revealed by the gospel, namely, the passive righteousness with which merciful God justifies us by faith, as it is written, "He who through faith is righteous shall live." Here I felt that I was altogether born again and had entered paradise itself through open gates. There a totally other face of the entire Scripture showed itself to me.

Thereupon I ran through the Scriptures from memory. I also found in other terms an analogy, as the work of God, that is, what God does in us, the power of God, with which he makes us strong, the wisdom of God, with which he makes us wise, the strength of God, the salvation of God, the glory of God. (LW 34:337)

Luther relates a similar "breakthrough" in a 1518 letter to Staupitz regarding penance (LW 48:64–70; WA 1:525–27) and provides further retrospectives in his *Lectures on Genesis* (1542) and Table Talks (1531–32, 1538, 1542) and even making its way into Johannes Bugenhagen's lectures on Jonah. "I worked anxiously and diligently to understand the well-known statement in Romans 1:17. . . . I sought and knocked for a long time (cf. Matt. 7:7), for that expression 'the righteousness of God' stood in the way. . . . Finally, enlightened by the Holy Spirit, I weighed more carefully the passage in Habakkuk [2:4], where I read: 'The righteous shall live by his faith.' From this I concluded that life must come from faith. . . . And all Holy Scripture and heaven itself were opened to me" (*Lectures on Genesis*, LW 5:158). The Table Talk of 1532 provides the phrase "Tower Experience" for Luther's breakthrough.

The words "righteous" and "righteousness of God" struck my conscience like lightning. When I heard them I was exceedingly terrified. If God is righteous [I thought], he must punish. But when by God's grace I pondered, in the tower and heated room of this building [based upon recent archaeological findings, Luther's study was over the kitchen], over the words, "He who through faith is righteous shall live" [Rom. 1:17] . . . , I soon came to the conclusion . . . [that] salvation won't be our merit but God's mercy. My spirit was thereby cheered. For it's by the righteousness of God that we're justified and saved through Christ. . . . The Holy Spirit unveiled the Scriptures for me in this tower. (LW 54:193–94; cf. LW 54:308–9)

Since a variant of "heated room" may be "the privy" (the abbreviation "cl" in the text could mean either *claustrum* or *cloaca*; cf. WA TR 2, #1681), scholars wedded to psychoanalysis have had a field day with speculations on the relation of Luther's theological breakthrough and his "breakthrough" of frequent constipation (see, e.g., N. O. Brown, *Life against Death: The Psychoanalytical Meaning of History* [Vintage, 1959]; E. Erickson, *The*

Young Man Luther [Norton, 1958]; J. Osborne, *Luther* [Signet, 1961]). Yet such speculation, as Oberman (155) observes, misses the point: "The cloaca is not just a privy, it is the most degrading place for man and the Devil's favorite habitat. Medieval monks already knew this, but the Reformer knows even more now; it is right here that we have Christ, the mighty helper on our side. No spot is unholy for the Holy Ghost; this is the very place to express contempt for the adversary through trust in Christ." So, Luther declared, one of the devil's greatest assaults is trying to confuse us over active and passive justification. "But refuse to fall for this and say: 'Don't you know, Satan, that Christ was crucified, died, and raised again for poor sinners? I live in Christ's righteousness, not in my own righteousness. . . . That will send the Devil packing." And for good measure, Luther adds, "Go to hell, God is not wrathful as you say" (WA TR 1:66–67, #141).

The nature and dating of Luther's breakthrough have been controversial not only because the written sources are recollections from years after the "event," but also because (mainly German) systematic theologians have tended to posit the breakthrough as the point of rupture with medieval Catholic theology. Although earlier scholarship (esp. Karl Holl's) posited an early dating, until recently the scholarly trend, following Ernst Bizer (see Lohse 329), advocated a late date around 1518 when Luther's discovery of the "righteousness of God" impelled a definitive break with earlier theology. Brecht (221–37), for example, claims that it is not until Luther's lectures on Hebrews (1517–18) that he definitively moves from remnants of a medieval theology of humility that placed the burden of penance on the person who humbles self before God, acknowledging God's righteous judgment, and thereby gains the mercy of God. Thus Luther moves from seeing righteousness as self-accusation to righteousness as the righteousness of Christ that justifies the sinner through faith. Moving beyond questions and issues concerning penitential practices and indulgences, "Luther had broken through to the promising, merciful, liberating God, and in doing so he had shattered the system of works in the theology and piety of that time. Through the knowledge that God was not against him, but that he was united with him in Christ, he became inwardly free, strong, and victorious" (Brecht 237).

More recently, however, some scholars have viewed Luther's breakthrough less as an event than as a trajectory rooted in a medieval theology of piety that transformed tradition. Hamm (31), in particular, advances the thesis that "the Reformation's new and pioneering directions were set in motion already in the years from 1505 to 1511." Hamm's view of the "wide arc" of reformatory development "displaces the need to define [doctrinal or chronological] breakthroughs" (57). Both Hamm and Leppin note the importance of late medieval piety, especially the works of Tauler and Bernard, in Luther's gradual process toward a paradigm shift on justification.

Junghans notices that Luther was less interested in the chronology of his development than in relaying its substance. Thus it is difficult to ascertain where to place his new insight into justification in relation to his early lectures and writings. Luther's emphasis on his lengthy effort to overcome his difficulty in understanding Paul has given many readers the impression that his report of the discovery of the passive righteousness of God in Paul is a concluding experience in which the reformatory bursts forth. The interpreters who proceed with this view of Luther's discontinuity or rupture with the tradition have then described differently "the reformatory," partly employing precise formulations from Luther and partly using other concepts than Luther's in his 1545 preface. They arrive at the so-called late dating of the reformatory breakthrough because they can find the "reformatory" most specifically described first in Luther's expressions from the year 1518. Those who hold to Luther's wording, however, have no difficulty finding this discovery earlier.

The new understanding of the righteousness of God in Rom. 1:17 appears then only as one, even if a very significant, step on the way to a reformatory theology that Luther had begun already in his Erfurt period through his intensive study of Scripture. Oberman (173), a pioneer in arguing for Luther's medieval context, makes a similar point in his emphasis that already by the first Psalms lectures Luther had arrived at the basis of his developing turn to reform in his focus on the Word of God as key to understanding Scripture. In a number of stimulating and controversial writings, Leppin argues that recovering an understanding of Luther's continuity with the Middle Ages "can help produce a more nuanced theological conversation between different confessions . . . [and thus] seek to plumb the depths of common roots more comprehensively than can happen when the relationship between Martin Luther and the Middle Ages is depicted as a rupture" (384).

See also Holl, Karl; Luther Interpretation and Reception; Luther Renaissance

Bibliography

Bayer, O. *Martin Luther's Theology: A Contemporary Interpretation.* Trans. T. H. Trapp. Eerdmans, 2008; Bizer, E. *Fides ex auditu: Eine Untersuchung über die Entdeckung der Gerechtigkeit Gottes durch Martin Luther.* Neukirchen-Vluyn, 1958; Brecht, M. *Martin Luther: His Road to Reformation, 1483–1521.* Trans. J. L. Schaaf. Fortress, 1985; Hamm, B. *The Early Luther: Stages in a Reformation Reorientation.* Trans. M. Lohrmann. Eerdmans, 2014; Junghans, H. "Praefatio zu Martin Luther: OPERA OMNIA 1, Wittenberg 1545." In *Studienausgabe,* by M. Luther, 5:618–23. Evangelische Verlagsanstalt, 1992; Leppin, V. "Luther's Roots in Monastic-Mystical Piety" and "Luther's Transformation of Medieval Thought: Continuity and Discontinuity." In *The Oxford Handbook of Martin Luther's Theology,* ed. R. Kolb, I. Dingel, and L. Batka, 49–61 and 115–24. Oxford University Press, 2014; Leppin, V. "Martin Luther, Reconsidered for 2017." *LQ* 22 (2008): 373–86; Lienhard, M. "Une question controversée: La date et la nature de la percée Réformatrice de Luther." In *Martin Luther: Un temps, une vie, un message,* 384–94. Le Centurion / Labor et Fides, 1983; Lohrmann, M. "A Newly Discovered Report of Luther's Reformation Breakthrough from Johannes Bugenhagen's 1550 Jonah Commentary." *LQ* 22 (2008): 324–30; Lohse, B., ed. *Der Durchbruch der reformatorischen Erkenntnis bei Luther: Neuere Untersuchungen.* F. Steiner, 1988; Oberman,

H. A. *Luther: Man between God and the Devil.* Trans. E. Walliser-Schwarzbart. Yale University Press, 1989.

Carter Lindberg

Luther's Roman Catholic Opponents

The Roman Catholic response to Luther proved as diverse as the Reformation itself. Many humanists—Bernhard Adelmann, Vitus Bild, Erasmus of Rotterdam—expressed deep sympathy with Luther, even if ultimately they could not embrace the extent of his reforms or his theology. Italian Dominicans such as Sylvester Mazzolini (Prierias) and Thomas de Vio (Cajetan) stood more firmly against Luther from the outset, although, at least in the case of Cajetan, this was not without a degree of generosity and a desire for reconciliation. Still others—John Eck, Jerome Emser, and Johannes Cochlaeus—came to be known as Catholic "controversialists" for their often fierce polemic against Luther and his followers. With all variations of support and contestation, the Roman Catholic response to Luther was by no means a monolithic enterprise.

Luther's opponents, however, cannot be restricted to any specific group: humanists and Scholastics, Germans and Italians, Dominicans and Franciscans, and many others participated to greater or lesser degrees in the effort to oppose Luther. One of the first antagonists of Luther was the Dominican indulgence preacher Johann Tetzel (1465–1519), whose sale of indulgences in the Brandenburg region in some ways sparked Luther's composition of the Ninety-Five Theses. The two exchanged polemics, and in early 1518 Tetzel beseeched his fellow German Dominicans to petition Rome for Luther's excommunication. Archbishop Albert of Mainz, however, had already forwarded his own copy of the Ninety-Five Theses to Pope Leo X, who subsequently tried to silence Luther. In this effort, two Italian Dominicans took up the cause against Luther. Papal theologian Sylvester Prierias (1456–1527), who was given the task of refuting Luther, composed his *Dialogus* (June 1518) against Luther and thereby defended papal authority as "an infallible rule of faith." His fellow Dominican Thomas de Vio Cajetan (1469–1534), master general of the Dominican order, was sent by Pope Leo X to depose Luther in Augsburg in late 1518. He primarily interrogated Luther on the question of indulgences and the relationship between faith and sacramental absolution, though the list of objections would expand in the coming years.

On the German front, a professor of theology at Ingolstadt, John Eck (1486–1543), circulated his unpublished *Obelisci* (1517) against Luther's Ninety-Five Theses, and the two exchanged polemics before meeting at Leipzig in 1519. There, Eck opposed Luther primarily on issues of papal and ecclesial authority but also questioned his stance on free will, grace, and purgatory. Present at Leipzig was German humanist and professor of theology Jerome Emser (1477–1527), who also took issue with Luther's account of papal power. Emser continued to oppose Luther until the former's death in 1527, broaching such topics as the Mass, monastic vows, and Luther's translation of the Bible. The Universities of Leuven and Cologne censured Luther in 1519, decisions defended by Leuven theologian Jacob Latomus and Cologne inquisitor Jacob Hoogsträten, respectively. The following year a committee composed of at least Eck, Cajetan, and likely Prierias produced the papal bull *Exsurge Domine*, threatening Luther's excommunication. Eck promulgated this bull throughout the Holy Roman Empire, adding the names of other humanists he deemed suspect (B. Adelmann and W. Pirckheimer, among others). Luther responded by refuting the papal bull and burning it along with works of Eck, Emser, and a copy of canon law.

Roman opposition to Luther increased exponentially after this point. The year 1521 brought a condemnation from the theology faculty at Paris as well as the official bull of excommunication from Rome, *Decet Romanum Pontificem*. In England, Cardinal Thomas Wolsey (1472–1530) arranged a ceremony in which Luther's books were burned, and

Bishop John Fisher (1469–1535) preached and subsequently wrote against the "pernicious doctrine" of Luther. Even King Henry VIII of England (1491–1547) composed his *Defense of the Seven Sacraments* against Luther, earning him the title "Defender of the Faith" from Pope Leo X. In Germany, meanwhile, two Franciscans took up the pen. Thomas Murner (1475–1537) from Strasbourg, who first entered the debate in 1520 with a treatise on the papacy, published arguably his most famous satire in 1522, *On the Great German Fool*. Bavarian Franciscan Kaspar (or Caspar) Schatzgeyer (1463–1527) published a more irenic piece that same year, his *Scrutinium divinae scripturae*, which evidenced a systematic and biblical exposition of controversial doctrines as opposed to the more point-by-point polemic of the controversialists. Both Franciscans took a much more reserved stance on the extent of papal power than did their Dominican contemporaries, and Schatzgeyer's work was criticized by both Luther and the controversialists for being too conciliatory. Johannes Fabri (1478–1541), later bishop of Vienna, also wrote against Luther in his six-volume *Malleus haereticorum* of 1525. In 1524 the Dutch humanist Erasmus of Rotterdam (1467–1536), generally sympathetic with Luther's plea for reform, entered the doctrinal disputes with his famous defense of the freedom of the will, *De libero arbitrio diatribe* (*Discussion on Free Choice*), which Luther praised for attacking "the real issue, the essence of the matter in dispute" (LW 33:294), while nevertheless fiercely opposing Erasmus's method and conclusion as sophistry devoid of the Spirit. In 1527 Erasmus responded to Luther with his lengthier *Hyperaspistes* (*Treading on Snakes*). Not even this dispute, however, spared Erasmus the criticism of fellow Catholics such as the Sorbonne theologian Noel Beda, the Italian Cardinal Jerome Aleander, and the Spaniard Diego López de Zuñiga, who grouped Erasmus and his followers together with the Lutherans.

The following year John Eck released his most acclaimed work, the *Enchiridion* (1525)

against Luther, which would go through more than forty editions in the coming decades, including a German version in 1530. Eck begins this work by emphasizing the unity of the church in its corporeal and spousal nature: "Christ is no bigamist: there is one church" (Helfferich 51). His purpose was to expose Luther's protest as a heretical novelty in the vein of Wyclif and Hus, opposed to the unity of the church and thus opposed to the apostles, martyrs, and even Christ himself. "Why, then," Eck chided, "did God not send Luther in place of them all?" (Helfferich 55).

By far the most prolific opponent of Luther in the 1520s, however, was the German humanist Johannes Cochlaeus (1479–1552). During 1522–25, Cochlaeus wrote over seventeen pamphlets and books, most directed against Luther, and in 1524–25 he wrote two treatises to the German people, accusing Luther not only of heresy but also of treason. In 1529 Cochlaeus went further and compared Luther to the seven-headed dragon of the Apocalypse, and in the 1530s he composed a polemical biography of Luther published after the reformer's death. Aside from this more exaggerated polemic, Cochlaeus's style exhibited a fusion of humanism and Scholasticism in dealing with Luther and also with his colleague, Philip Melanchthon.

Following the signing of the Augsburg Confession in 1530, Cajetan composed treatises against the Lutherans defending the sacrificial nature of the Mass (1531) and the necessity of faith and works (1532). However, he also wrote a short piece titled *Guidelines for Concessions to the Lutherans*, wherein he distinguished between necessary matters of faith and mutable matters of religious practice, declaring in the latter category that the Lutherans may be permitted to follow the Greek custom of clerical marriage and also communion in both kinds (bread and wine). Similar attempts at concession were made in 1535 when papal nuncio Pietro Paolo Vergerio (1498–1565) met with Luther while seeking European support for an ecclesial council. Little came of this meeting,

other than Vergerio's eventual conversion to the Protestant cause.

Roman Catholic opposition to Luther broached all manner of topics—from political questions of treason, to vocational questions of monastic vows and the clerical state, devotional questions of the invocation of saints and the efficacy of indulgences, and matters of faith, grace, and the nature of the sacraments. However, it is noteworthy that from the start of "the Luther affair," a crucial question remained that of papal and ecclesial authority, a question that had plagued the church in the century leading up to Luther's birth. This long history evoked an instinctual response in so many of Luther's Roman opponents, who immediately pushed the debate from a question of indulgences to a question of the unity and apostolicity of the Roman Catholic Church, thereby pushing Luther to formulate a position he may have only reluctantly affirmed on his own.

See also Cajetan (Thomaso de Vio); Catholicism; Cochlaeus, Johannes; Eck, John; Emser, Jerome; Erasmus of Rotterdam (Desiderius Erasmus Roterodamus); Prierias, Sylvester; Tetzel, Johann

Bibliography

Bagchi, D. V. N. *Luther's Earliest Opponents: Catholic Controversialists, 1518–1525*. Fortress, 1991; Battles, F. L., trans. *Enchiridion of Commonplaces against Luther and Other Enemies of the Church* (1525). Baker, 1979; Fabisch, P., and E. Iserloh, eds. *Dokumente zur Causa Lutheri (1517–1521)*. 2 vols. CCath 41–42. Aschendorff, 1988–91; Fraenkel, P., ed. *Assertio septem sacramentorum adversus Martinum Lutherum*. Aschendorff, 1991; Helfferich, T., ed. and trans. *On the Freedom of a Christian with Related Texts*. Hackett, 2013; Hendrix, S. H. *Luther and the Papacy: Stages in a Reformation Conflict*. Fortress, 1981; Iserloh, E. *Der Kampf um die Messe in den ersten Jahren der Auseinandersetzung mit Luther*. Aschendorff, 1950; Posset, F. *Unser Martin: Martin Luther aus der Sicht katholischer Sympathisanten*. Aschendorf, 2015; Smolinsky, H. "Luther's Roman Catholic Critics." In *The Oxford Handbook of Martin Luther's Theology*, ed. R. Kolb, I. Dingel, and L. Batka, 502–10. Oxford University Press, 2014; Vandiver, E., R. Keen, and T. D. Frazel, eds. and trans. *Luther's Lives: Two Contemporary Accounts of Martin Luther*. Manchester University Press, 2003; Wicks, J., ed. and trans. *Cajetan Responds: A Reader in Reformation Controversy*. Wipf & Stock, 2011.

ERIC J. DEMEUSE

Luther's Works

Luther's writings, published and in manuscript, have experienced repeated editing and printing in collections, including those that aspired to offering readers the "complete" oeuvre.

The first "collected works" of a living author appeared in 1518, when the Basel printer Johannes Oporinus gathered Luther's Latin publications to that point and reprinted them. The jealousy of Oporinus's friend and employee Desiderius Erasmus and the condemnation of Luther in 1520 and 1521 by church and empire ended this project, although other printers produced small collections of Luther's works in the coming decades. In 1539, however, Elector John Frederick's mandate launched a much larger "Wittenberg" edition (1539–59), which produced twelve German volumes (the first in 1539) and seven Latin ones (beginning in 1545), in which the first volume of each series included prefaces by Luther. Gnesio-Lutheran criticism of later volumes of this edition led to the issuance of the "Jena" edition (1555–58), edited by the original editor of the Wittenberg edition, Luther's amanuensis Georg Rörer. Another Gnesio-Lutheran, and former amanuensis for Luther, Johann Aurifaber, edited the supplemental "Eisleben" edition (1564–65); an edition of Luther's letters (1565), and the reformer's Table Talk (Eisleben: Gaubisch, 1566).

A century later the Altenburg edition (1661/64) appeared, followed by a supplemental one-volume "Halle edition" (1702) and the "Leipzig edition" of 1729/34. Jena professor Johann Georg Walch recognized the need for updating Luther's sixteenth-century German and providing pastors with a German translation of the Latin works, publishing his twenty-three volumes in 1740–53, which included many supporting documents by other writers of the time. A. F. Hoppe and colleagues revised and updated this Walch edition for North American readers in the "St. Louis" edition (1880–1910).

By that time the first edition of Luther's works based on the developing critical standards of nineteenth-century editing appeared in the "Erlangen" edition (1826–57), revised in a second edition (Frankfurt am Main and Erlangen, 1862–85). Before its completion the imperial German government launched the "Weimar" edition, *D. Martin Luthers Werke* (1883–1993). It quickly became the standard critical edition of Luther's writings, published and unpublished. It includes seventy-three volumes of his works in all genres, twelve volumes of the work on the translation of the Bible into German, eighteen volumes of correspondence, and six volumes of Table Talk, along with supplemental aids to studying the reformer's works.

"Study" editions featuring selected works of Luther include the Braunschweig edition, edited by Georg Buchwald, Gustav Kawerau, and others (10 vols., 1889–92); the Clemen edition, edited by Otto Clemen (8 vols., 1912–33); the Munich edition, edited by H. H. Borcherdt and Georg Merz (13 vols., 1948–65); *Studienausgabe*, edited by Hans-Ulrich Delius (6 vols., 1979–99); *Lateinisch-Deutsche Studienausgabe*, edited by Wilfried Härle, Johannes Schilling, and Günther Wartenberg (3 vols., 2006–9); and *Deutsch-Deutsche Studienausgabe*, edited by Johannes Schilling (3 vols., 2012–16).

Multivolume "selected works" of Luther have appeared in several languages, including Japanese, Chinese, Korean, Spanish, Portuguese, and English. Henry Eyster Jacobs and colleagues at the Lutheran Theological Seminary in Philadelphia inaugurated the "Holman" or "Philadelphia" edition in 1915, producing six volumes through 1932. The primary English translation is found in the fifty-five volumes of *Luther's Works*, edited by Helmut T. Lehmann, Hilton C. Oswald, and Jaroslav Pelikan (1958–86). A twenty-volume supplement, published by Concordia, has begun to make additional materials available in English, edited by Christopher Boyd Brown (2009–). Access to Luther's printed sermons on the appointed lessons for Sundays and festivals will come in Concordia's supplement but is also possible through the reprint of the *Sermons of Martin Luther; The Church Postils*, edited by John Nicholas Lenker (1905–9; reprint, Baker, 1983–95); and freshly translated *Sermons of Martin Luther: The House Postils*, edited by Eugene F. A. Klug (Baker, 1996). Fortress Press began its six-volume *The Annotated Luther* in 2015, with Timothy J. Wengert, Kirsi Stjerna, Paul W. Robinson, Mary Jane Haemig, Hans J. Hillerbrand, and Euan K. Cameron serving as editors.

Bibliography

Kolb, R. *Martin Luther as Prophet, Teacher, and Hero*. Baker, 1999; Wolgast, E., and H. Volz. "Geschichte der Luther-Ausgaben vom 16. bis zum 19. Jahrhundert." WA 60:429–637.

ROBERT KOLB

M

Madagascar

The large island off the southeast coast of Africa, Madagascar, was a French colony from 1896 and was granted independence in 1960. The Malagasy Lutheran Church is one of the fastest growing Lutheran churches in the world. Madagascar was a major mission field of both the Norwegian and American Lutherans. In modern times, Madagascar has also been a leader in mission exchanges among African churches of the Southern Hemisphere.

A brief sixteenth-century Lazarist (Roman Catholic) mission to Madagascar was the first Christian mission. No other serious attempt was undertaken until the London Missionary Society (LMS) sent two couples in 1818. Within months, three of the four missionaries were dead from malaria. The sole survivor, David Jones, went to Mauritius, where he recovered and learned the Malagasy language. He returned to Madagascar in 1820 and began a very successful effort at evangelization. Madagascar was the first African country south of the Sahara to have the Bible translated into its own language. Shortly after this feat was accomplished in 1835, a new monarch, Queen Ranavalona I, expelled all missionaries and forbade Christianity. Intense persecution ensued for the next thirty years.

Upon her death (1861), Christian missions were again allowed. The recently created Norwegian Mission Society (NMS) sent two missionaries, John Engh (1833–1900) and Nils Nilsen (1834–1923), to Madagascar in 1866. Madagascar became the chief field of the NMS. After negotiations with the LMS, the NMS began work in the Vakinakaritra region, with the understanding that the NMS would concentrate its efforts to the south of the capital of Antananarivo, while the LMS worked

northward from the capital. A brief period of conflict between the LMS and the NMS ensued since LMS did not view Vakinakaritra as being sufficiently south of their own field and also because the NMS insisted on a representative in the capital. These disagreements were soon resolved, and the two missions worked amicably together.

The NMS's first station was at Betafo. The NMS concentrated their efforts equally on evangelization and education. Education was deemed important so believers could read and study the gospel in their own language. In 1874 the NMS opened work on the west coast, with centers in Tulear and Moronda, and on the east coast in 1888, with the base of operations located in Vaingandrano. A decision in 1887 resulted in mission work in the center of the island, extending south to the coast. The NMS missionary conference commissioned Peder Eilert Nilsen-Lund, from Ambato in the central highlands around Fianarantsoa, to make a momentous exploratory journey and recommend places for the society to establish new work. He has been called "the Livingstone of Madagascar." Nilsen Lund's route took him from the central highlands southwest to St. Augustine Bay, then across the semidesert of Mahafaly land and Androy, and finally to Fort Dauphin (now called Tolagnaro) on the southeast coast.

In the United States, Norwegian immigrants read the *Norske Misjonstidene* (Norwegian missionary times) and learned about the Madagascar work. When the Norwegian Conference decided to send out a missionary, they consulted with the NMS. It was decided that these American Lutherans would send their first foreign missionaries to Madagascar, serving with the NMS, but with all funds for their work coming from American congregations.

Georg Sverdrup, president of Augsburg College, Minneapolis, encouraged his students to form their own mission society. From this group came the first American missionaries to Madagascar, Jon Peder Hogstad and his wife, Oline Hogstad. They left for Madagascar in 1887. After language study in Ambato, the explorer Peder Nilsen-Lund led the Hogstads south to their new post in Fort Dauphin, arriving there in 1888. Two years later, Erick Hansen Tou and his wife, Elizabeth Tou, also from Augsburg College, arrived. They were assigned to Manasoa in southwest Madagascar, another station previously identified by Nilsen-Lund.

In 1892 the Norwegian-American Lutherans formed their own board of foreign missions to support their missionaries. The NMS graciously ceded the southern portion of the island to the Americans. Shortly thereafter, strife developed among the Americans who had just come together to form the United Norwegian Lutheran Church in America (UNLCA). The dispute was over whether Augsburg or St. Olaf was to be the preparatory school for the united seminary in St. Paul. St. Olaf won out, and shortly thereafter the "Friends of Augsburg" withdrew from the United Norwegian Lutheran Church. The "Friends of Augsburg" became the Lutheran Free Church (LFC) in 1897. Their field became the southwest quadrant of Madagascar, with the United Norwegian Lutheran Church (UNLC) working in the eastern portion of the island.

Despite strong British influence, thanks to LMS work, the French made Madagascar a colony in 1895. French colonial policy significantly hindered mission work, especially in the area of education. Fortunately the three Lutheran church bodies cooperated in the work in Madagascar. They joined forces in supporting one united theological seminary at Ivory, in Fianarantsoa. They also joined in supporting the formation of an indigenous, self-supporting, and self-governing Lutheran Church in Madagascar. In 1950 the three Norwegian fields, the Lutheran Board of

Mission (LFC), and the Evangelical Lutheran Church (the former UNLC) came together and formed a single Lutheran Church in Madagascar called Fiangonana Loterana Malagasy (FLM). The first president of FLM was Rakoto Andrianarijaona.

Today the church is growing rapidly. In 2014 the church had three million members. It comprises twenty-three regional synods, supports a school for the blind, a leprosarium, a printing house (Trano Printy Loterana), extensive medical work with seven hospitals and twenty-five dispensaries, as well as work in all of the *Toby* (revival centers) and a school to train nurses in Antsirabe. The FLM has development work and a vast educational system, with many schools spread throughout the island. Six regional seminaries funnel their top students to a master's program at the national seminary at Ivory, Fianarantsoa. Other students complete their studies for a diploma in theology at six regional seminaries.

Up until very recent times the only American Lutherans working in Madagascar were the ELCA and its predecessor bodies. The LCMS has initiated talks with two of the regional synods of the Malagasy Lutheran Church about receiving missionaries, and the LCMS has given a number of "mercy grants" in the areas of theological education, medical work, and development. Other Lutherans working in Madagascar in small numbers have been the French Church of the Augsburg Confession, the Paris Missionary Society, and the Danish Mission. A major factor in the expansive growth of the FLM is the revival movement called *Fifohazana* (the Awakening), a lively indigenous movement solidly embedded in the Lutheran Church.

See also *Fifohazana* Movement

Bibliography

Ditmanson, F. *In Foreign Fields*. Lutheran Board of Missions, 1927; Fuglestad, F., and J. Simensen, eds. *Norwegian Missions in African History*. Vol. 2, *Madagascar*. Norwegian University Press, 1986; Halvorson, A. *Madagascar: Footprint at the End of the World*. Augsburg, 1973. Hübsch, B., ed. *Madagascar et le Christianisme: Histoire oecuménique*. Karthala, 1993; Vigen, J. "A Historical and

Missiological Account of the Pioneer Missionaries of the American Lutheran Mission in Southeast Madagascar, 1887–1911: John P. and Oline Hogstad." ThD diss., Lutheran School of Theology, 1991. Copy, University Microfilms International, 1999.

JAMES B. VIGEN

Magdeburg

The North German city Magdeburg was an archbishopric in the Middle Ages. Magdeburg emerged in the ninth century as an important political and commercial city and became a bishopric in the late tenth century. Although technically subject to the archbishop, by the sixteenth century, when its archbishops included Albrecht of Mainz, the city council had established itself as a political force over against its clerical lord. The council therefore took action when priestly opposition to the preaching of Luther's message aroused unrest in the early 1520s. In 1524 the council invited Luther to leave his post in Wittenberg to lead the introduction of the Reformation in the city. He instead nominated his colleague and friend Nikolaus von Amsdorf, who successfully introduced Wittenberg reform and transformed the religious and social life of Magdeburg in the eighteen years he served as superintendent of the churches there, aided by other Wittenbergers, including Caspar Cruciger Sr. and Georg Major.

When the Smalcald War broke out, Magdeburg served as a firm supporter of the Smalcaldic League, of which it was a member. After the defeat of the league in 1548, the city attracted refugees from Wittenberg and other places occupied by or under threat from imperial forces. The city defied the imperial mandate to accept the Augsburg Interim, but in 1551 Elector Moritz of Saxony used military means to force Magdeburg into compromise. The incipient movement later labeled "Gnesio-Lutheran" (genuine Lutheran) formed in Magdeburg around 1550 under the leadership of Amsdorf, who returned to the city after being removed from his post as bishop of Naumburg and Zeitz; Nikolaus Gallus, former pastor in Regensburg; and Matthias Flacius Illyricus,

former Hebrew instructor in Wittenberg and the intellectual leader of the group. Gallus and others drafted the Magdeburg Confession of 1550, a classic statement of the vocation-based Wittenberg theory of the right to resist higher government powers. In the 1550s the Gnesio-Lutheran group in Magdeburg, led by Johannes Wigand and Matthaeus Judex, began implementation of Flacius's plan for a comprehensive church history, the *Magdeburg Centuries*. In the early 1560s strife between the Gnesio-Lutheran ecclesiastical superintendent Tilemann Hesshus and the city council over the return of Wigand to the city led to a weakening of the party's position there.

In 1566 the archbishopric fell to administration by the Hohenzollern family of Brandenburg, and with the exception of a period between 1632 and 1680, remained part of the Hohenzollern realm. In one of the worst atrocities of the Thirty Years' War, the Roman Catholic general Johann Tserclaes, count of Tilly, slaughtered many citizens in a bloodbath in the cathedral and burned most of the city. It never regained its earlier commercial status. It welcomed Huguenot refugees in the late seventeenth century.

See also Albrecht of Mainz; Amsdorf, Nikolaus von; Flacius, Matthias, and the Flacians; Smalcald War; Wittenberg Circle, Parties within

Bibliography
Rein, N. *The Chancery of God: Protestant Print, Polemic and Propaganda against the Empire, Magdeburg 1546–1551.* Ashgate, 2008.

ROBERT KOLB

Mahler, Carl Wilhelm Gustav

The first resident pastor and mission director of the Lutheran Church–Missouri Synod in South America was Carl Wilhelm Gustav Mahler (1870–1966). Born in Germany, Mahler began theological studies there and concluded them at Concordia Seminary, St. Louis, in 1893. In 1901 the Missouri Synod sent him to Brazil to serve as pastor and mission director for South America. Mahler opened a school and founded a congregation in Porto

Alegre, the state capital of Rio Grande do Sul. He became the first editor of a church periodical and was elected as the first president of the Brazilian District of the Missouri Synod (1904–10). He also served as instructor at Seminário Concórdia in Porto Alegre. Mahler returned to the United States in 1914, where he served several congregations as pastor and later became president of the Kansas District of the Missouri Synod (1932–39).

See also Brazil; Igreja Evangélica Luterana do Brasil (IELB) (Evangelical Lutheran Church of Brazil)

Bibliography

The Lutheran Witness 66 (June 17, 1947); Rehfeldt, M. *Um Grão de Mostarda*. Vol. 1. Concordia / Porto Alegre, 2003.

PAULO WILLE BUSS

Major, Georg

A Lutheran preacher and theologian at the University of Wittenberg, Georg Major (or Meier) (1502–74), was born in Nuremberg, where his father held a low-level position in that city's government. In 1511 he came to Wittenberg to sing in the boys' choir of the Castle Church and was thus present at the church on October 31, 1517. He matriculated at the University of Wittenberg in 1521, at the encouragement of Martin Luther and Philip Melanchthon. He received his bachelor of arts in 1522 and his master's degree in 1523. After his marriage in 1528, he was sent to Magdeburg to succeed Caspar Cruciger Sr. as rector of the Latin school. While there, he wrote a popular book on rhetoric (1535), based on Philip Melanchthon's work. In 1537 he returned to Wittenberg, was ordained by Luther, and became preacher at the Castle Church. In 1544, with Luther presiding, he received his doctorate in theology. In 1546 he represented Saxony at the second religious colloquy in Regensburg. During the Smalcald War he and his family fled Wittenberg, along with Philip Melanchthon and Katharina von Bora. In 1547 he received a call as court preacher in Merseburg for August of Saxony, brother of the newly named Elector Moritz. By 1548 he returned to Wittenberg as professor of theology. Once

there, he took part in negotiations between the Wittenberg theologians and the newly named Roman bishops of Merseburg and Naumburg, agreeing in principle to an early version of the so-called Leipzig Proposal (Interim), which permitted the reinstatement of certain medieval practices in Evangelical lands. At the same time, he authored several attacks on the Council of Trent. When attacks arose against the so-called adiaphorists and their Leipzig Interim, he assured critics that nothing had changed in Wittenberg. In his *Auslegung des Glaubens* (*Exposition of the [Apostles'] Creed*, 1550), he insisted (against Roman charges of antinomianism) that "no one can be saved *without* good works and that God will reward each person according to his works." This statement resulted in an attack by Nicholas von Amsdorf against Major. During his short stint as superintendent in Eisleben (1551–52), Major countered with an attack on von Amsdorf in which he insisted that he had always taught that good works were necessary for salvation (by which he meant the necessary result of salvation). With this, the so-called Majoristic controversy was born, and Major spent much of the rest of his career trying to prove his orthodoxy. Starting in 1555, Major embarked on what became his life's work: publishing commentaries on all the Pauline Epistles. In 1555 he published a *Vita Pauli* (*Life of Paul*) and in 1556 a rhetorical outline of Romans. By 1564 he had reached Philemon, then followed that with lectures on Hebrews in 1568. At the same time, he published German expositions of the Pauline corpus as well. He retired from teaching in 1571. Article 5 of the Formula of Concord addressed this controversy.

See also Amsdorf, Nikolaus von; Antinomianism/ Antinomian Controversies; Good Works; Leipzig Proposal (Interim); Wittenberg Circle, Parties within

Bibliography

Wengert, T. J. "Georg Major (1502–1574): Defender of the Wittenberg's Faith and Melanchthonian Exegete." In

Melanchthon in seinen Schülern, ed. H. Scheible, 129–56. Harrassowitz, 1997.

TIMOTHY J. WENGERT

Malawi

The Evangelical Lutheran Church in Malawi (ELCM), one of the fastest-growing churches in Africa, records a membership of more than 101,000 people. Laypeople who had become Lutherans abroad and returned to Malawi established the ELCM in 1982. The transnational connections continued to play an important role in the history of ELCM; in 1983 a Tanzanian pastor came as a visiting missionary, and in 1985 the Evangelical Lutheran Church in Zimbabwe sent a group to assist. A lecturer from Umpumulo Theological Seminary in South Africa came to provide leadership training, and in January 1987 the first three local pastors were ordained. In 1988 ELCM became a member of LWF and of the Christian Council of Malawi. In the following years, the Evangelische Missionswerk in Hermannsburg and the Lutheran Evangelical Association of Finland sent ecumenical coworkers. The headquarters of the church are in Lilongwe.

Bibliography

ELCM. "Brief Historical Background of Evangelical Lutheran Church in Malawi." http://elcm.weebly.com/about-us.html; Mijogra, H. B. P. "The Evangelical Lutheran Church in Malawi: Its Development." Chancellor College, n.d.

FRIEDER LUDWIG

Mancelius, Georgius

A seminal figure in the seventeenth-century cultural transformation of the eastern domains of the Baltic, Georgius Mancelius (1593–1654) was trained in method by some of the foremost contemporary Aristotelians in northern Europe. Yet his mind-set remained attuned to the culture of orality that characterized the region in which he had been raised. By providing segments of society that were deeply steeped in orality with their first taste of easily accessible written culture, Mancelius not only created a written idiom for the non-German-speaking segment of society, but by doing so,

underscored that the spread of literacy in the region could be furthered only if these written idioms retained the naturalness and spontaneity of oral culture.

Mancelius moved freely among a globalized academia, with Latin as its lingua franca; the world of commerce and cultural elites, which used changing standardized forms of German; and the communities that derived their sense of history and growth with the help of oral strategies. More than one hundred years after its inception, the Reformation had only marginally penetrated the segments of society in the Baltic that did not use German as their primary language of communication.

Born and raised in Courland, a Lutheran province in the multifarious Polish commonwealth, Mancelius, like many of his contemporaries from the Baltic, enrolled at the University of Rostock. Upon graduation, he returned to serve in Courland, only to be called by Swedish authorities in the newly formed provincial capital of Swedish Livonia, Dorpat/Tartu, to serve as church official, pastor, and professor of theology. He returned to Courland a decade later as confessor to the Duke of Courland.

During his tenure at Dorpat, Mancelius evolved into a leading facilitator of the policies of the Swedish statesman J. Skytte, whose goal was to create an infrastructure that would enable the central authorities in Stockholm to reach out to the disparate and culturally manifold corners of the empire. True to his Ramist convictions, Skytte envisioned Livonia as an experimental laboratory for new forms of education and administration, all for the purpose of creating a new societal model that embraced multiculturalism in the service of political integration. This required devising standardized written idioms and channels of communication.

Mancelius's *Lettische lang-gewünschte Postill* of more than a thousand pages can justifiably be regarded as the first major original prose text in Latvian. Its six editions well into the nineteenth century attest to its importance. His *Lettus, das ist Wortbuch*, a groundbreaking work in Latvian lexicography, enabled nonnative civil servants and church officials to reach broader spectrums of the Latvian-speaking population.

See also Courland (Kurland); Latvia; Livonia

Bibliography

Kreslins, J. *Dominus Narrabit in Scriptura Populorum: A Study of Early Seventeenth-Century Lutheran Teaching on Preaching and the "Lettische Lang-Gewunschte Postill."* Harrassowitz, 1992; Viiding, K. "Die lateinische Gelegenheitsdichtung von Georg Mancelius in Dorpat (1632–1638)." In *Classical Tradition from the Sixteenth Century to Nietzsche*, ed. J. Päll, I. Volt, and M. Steinrück, 45–85. Tartu University Press, 2010; Viiding, K. "Das Porträt eines liv- und kurländischen orthodoxen Theologen (Georgius Mancelius) anhand der ihm gewidmeten Geleit- und Begrüssungsgedichte." In *Orthodoxie und Poesie*, ed. U. Sträter, 37–46. Evangelische Verlagsanstalt, 2004.

JĀNIS KRĒSLIŅŠ

Manikam, Rajah Bushanam

The first national bishop of the Tamil Evangelical Lutheran Church was Rajah Bushanam Manikam (1897–1969), an ecumenist. Born in Cuddalore, Tamilnadu, Manikam received his BA (with honors) and MA degrees from Madras Christian College, Tambaram, in 1921 and 1923. In 1925 Columbia University awarded him a second MA, in psychology, and in 1929 a PhD. He obtained his bachelor of divinity (now master of divinity) degree from the Lutheran Theological Seminary at Philadelphia in 1929, where Theodore G. Tappert was his classmate. Returning to India, Manikam worked at Andhra Christian College, Guntur, for seven years. In 1937 he joined the National Christian Council of India, Burma, and Ceylon as a secretary and played a significant role in introducing religious education in schools and colleges. Serving as the joint East Asia Secretary of the World Council of Churches and the International Missionary Council, he encouraged Asian Christians to work on common concerns with Christians from other parts of the world. The Tamil Evangelical Lutheran Church elected him as its first national bishop in 1956; he remained in office until retirement in 1967. As the president and after his retirement as the promotional director of the Federation of Lutheran Churches in India, Manikam played a key role in the dialogue between the Church of South India and Lutheran churches, and in the merger talks of Gurukul Lutheran Theological College with the other ecumenical colleges through the "All India Lutheran Conference on Theological Education" a few weeks before his death. However, neither of these ecumenical programs could be sustained.

See also Ecumenical Dialogues; India

Bibliography

Diehl, C. G., and E. T. Bachmann. *Rajah Bushanam Manikam: A Biography*. Christian Literature Society, 1975; Manikam, R. B. *The Christian College and the Christian Community*. Diocesan Press, 1938.

SAMUEL W. MESHACK

Mannermaa, Tuomo

The Finnish ecumenical theologian Tuomo Mannermaa (1937–2015) was born on September 29, 1937, in Oulu, Finland. Mannermaa served as assistant professor of social ethics (1972–74), of systematic theology (1974–80), and thereafter as professor of ecumenical theology at the University of Helsinki. A proponent of the ordination of women (1988) in the Evangelical Lutheran Church of Finland and a fierce critic of the Leuenberg Agreement (1973), he is chiefly known as the father of the Finnish interpretation of Luther, known as the Finnish school of Mannermaa. He proposed a hermeneutical shift in the reading of Luther's doctrine of justification: criticizing nineteenth- and twentieth-century interpreters (Holl, Ritschl, Harnack) for their overreliance on German philosophy, rejecting Lutheran Orthodoxy's emphasis on forensic righteousness, and contrasting them to unfolding the centrality of effective righteousness in Luther's theology of salvation. With attention to the "real-ontic" indwelling of Christ in faith, Mannermaa insisted on the connection between love and faith in Luther's thought.

Mannermaa's provocative reexamination of the idea of theosis (Greek: *theōsis*), or divinization, in light of Luther's commentary on Galatians occurred in the context of ecumenical dialogues in the 1970s and 1980s on the issue of salvation (Bangkok 1973–74, Kiev 1977); he played a key role as a theological expert on the Lutheran side in the negotiations between the Orthodox Church of Russia and the Finnish Lutherans. Mannermaa mentored a generation of Luther scholars who have investigated further his premise that "oneness in faith" had a real-ontic quality for Luther and who further developed its possible contributions in contemporary ecumenical theology and relations.

Mannermaa's *A Little Book about God* was named the Christian book of the year in Finland in 2005; in 2007 he was the first recipient of the Cross of the Saint Henry.

See also Finland; Finnish Interpretation of Luther; Luther Interpretation and Reception

Bibliography

Mannermaa, T. *Christ Present in Faith: Luther's View of Justification.* Fortress, 2005; Mannermaa, T. *Der im Glauben gegenwärtige Christus: Rechtfertigung und Vergottung.* Lutherisches Verlagshaus, 1989; Mannermaa, T. *Two Kinds of Love: An Introduction to Luther's Religious World.* Fortress, 2010; Mannermaa, T. *Von Preussen nach Leuenberg: Hintergrund und Entwicklung der theologischen Methode der Leuenberger Konkordie.* Lutherisches Verlagshaus, 1981; Mannermaa, T., A. Ghiselli, and S. Peura, eds. *Thesaurus Lutheri: Auf der Suche nach neuen Paradigmen der Luther-Forschung.* Finnische Theologische Literaturgesellschaft, 1987.

KIRSI STJERNA

Marburg Colloquy

The theological discussion at the Marburg Castle on October 2–3, 1529, is called the Marburg Colloquy. The participants had been invited by Philip of Hesse in order to forge a common theological front among the Evangelical regions of the Holy Roman Empire and environs, especially on the issue of the Lord's Supper. A few months earlier, the Second Diet of Speyer had voted to enforce the 1521 Edict of Worms, upholding the ruling that Luther was a notorious heretic. In response, Philip of Hesse, along with five princes and the representatives of fourteen cities, formally protested, thus leading to the label of "protestants" (official litigants). The rulers of the Evangelical

territories realized, however, that their protest did not end the matter. They needed a united political front to protect their Evangelical territories, and discussion began on forming a defensive military alliance. They and their theological advisers insisted that such an alliance would need to be based on theological unity. Philip convinced the preeminent Evangelical theologians to gather. While Luther feared that more harm than good might result from such a meeting, he grudgingly agreed to attend. Before this meeting, however, he and other Lutherans formulated a confession of faith in the summer of 1529 (officially adopted later in Schwabach and hence called the Schwabach Articles) to outline their theological positions. Thus Luther and his colleagues came to Marburg with a clear agenda.

While Luther and Oecolampadius met privately (as did Melanchthon and Zwingli), on Friday, October 1, the formal colloquy did not begin until Saturday morning. Luther successfully requested that the colloquy be closed to the public and not recorded, despite Zwingli's wishes. Discussions focused on the main point of contention, the Lord's Supper. Zwingli, Luther, Oecolampadius, and others had disputed this matter publicly in various treatises published in the previous four years. While discussions were for the most part polite, nothing was said that had not already been thoroughly debated in their publications. Luther insisted on a literal reading of Christ's words "This is my body" and argued that Christ was bodily, and not just spiritually, present in the meal. While Zwingli and Oecolampadius argued that Christ could not be in the bread because he was at the right hand of God and because the words of institution could be understood figuratively (i.e., "This is like by body"), Luther countered that Christ's presence was not restricted to one place.

Although originally scheduled for eight days, the meetings were cut short because of an outbreak of an epidemic in Marburg. Thus the formal meetings concluded on Sunday evening, October 3, when Philip of Hesse decided that no agreement would be reached. However, Luther proposed a compromise statement that there was a substantial and essential presence of Christ's body in the meal. Luther's opponents rejected this proposal since it contradicted their reading of the biblical texts. The next morning, after a round of smaller, informal meetings, Philip of Hesse asked Luther to write up the agreement reached on the Triune God, original sin, salvation in Christ, faith, justification, baptism, good works, confession, and governing authorities. These articles were circulated among the participants, who (to the surprise of Luther and Philip Melanchthon) accepted fourteen of the fifteen points, disagreeing only on whether Christ's body is spiritually or actually present in the Lord's Supper. Nevertheless, the Marburg Articles were signed for the sake of solidarity (but not unity), by the Lutheran theologians Luther, Justus Jonas, Melanchthon, Andreas Osiander, Stephan Agricola, and Johannes Brenz; by the Swiss theologians Oecolampadius and Zwingli; and by the Strasbourg theologians Martin Bucer and Caspar Hedio. The single point of contention on the Supper, however, led to the presentation of separate confessions of faith at the Diet of Augsburg (1530): the Augsburg Confession, the Confession of the Four Cities (*Tetrapolitana*) drafted by Martin Bucer, and Ulrich Zwingli's personal confession. While the dogged determination of Bucer, aided by Melanchthon, led to agreement on the Lord's Supper in the Wittenberg Concord (1536), those sympathetic to Zwingli never did sign. In the generation after Luther's death, Lutherans fought among themselves on this same issue, later addressed in articles 7 and 8 of the Formula of Concord.

The failure to reach agreement on the bodily presence of Christ in the Lord's Supper at Marburg has haunted the Reformed and Lutheran theologians ever since. It scuttled the Reformed-Lutheran colloquy in Leipzig in 1631, meant to unite the Protestant forces in the Thirty Years' War. When Friedrich Wilhelm III imposed a union of the Lutheran and Reformed churches in his Prussian territories in 1817, some Lutherans, who protested this merger because of disagreement over the Lord's Supper, left Prussian-controlled territories and established a strong confessional Lutheranism in North America. One such group was the Lutheran Church–Missouri Synod (LCMS). When these Lutherans came to North America, they discovered that some of the established Lutherans (esp. from the General Synod) were open to a more Reformed view of the Lord's Supper, and tensions developed. The situation grew worse when Samuel Simon Schmucker proposed a new Americanized version of the Augsburg Confession, which many Lutherans thought had adopted, among other things, a view of the Lord's Supper that supported Zwingli's position at Marburg.

In 1973, with the signing of the Leuenberg Agreement, Lutheran and Reformed churches in Europe resolved the disputed article at Marburg. Agreement was made possible by focusing on the sacrament's effectiveness in doing what it promised, rather than the philosophical terminology of "real presence." This led to the 1998 Full Communion Agreement between three Reformed church bodies in the USA and the ELCA. However, some Lutherans, including the LCMS, accept neither the 1973 Leuenberg Agreement nor the 1998 Full Communion Agreement because language over Christ's bodily presence is still considered too imprecise. Nevertheless, for many Lutherans, the Lord's Supper controversy at Marburg has finally been resolved.

See also Colloquy; Lord's Supper; Melanchthon, Philip; Mömpelgaard/Montbéliard Colloquy; Oecolampadius, Johannes; Philip of Hesse; Schmucker, Samuel Simon; Wittenberg Concord; Zwingli, Ulrich

Bibliography

Andrews, J., and J. Burgess, eds. *An Invitation to Action: The Lutheran-Reformed Dialogue Series III, 1981–1983.* Fortress, 1984; Empie, P., and J. McCord, eds. *Marburg Revisited: A Re-examination of Lutheran and Reformed Traditions.* Augsburg, 1966; Hermelink, H. *Das Marburger Religionsgespräch, 1529–1929: Zum vierhundertjährigen Gedächtnis, Predigten, Reden, Ansprachen.* Koltz, 1930; Hunsinger, G. *The Eucharist and Ecumenism: Let Us Keep the Feast.* Cambridge University Press, 2008; Köhler, W.

Zwingli und Luther: Ihre Streit über das Abendmahl nach seinen politischen und religiösen Beziehungen. 2 vols. Bertelsmann, 1924/1953; Sasse, H. *This Is My Body: Luther's Contention for the Real Presence in the Sacrament of the Altar.* Augsburg, 1959.

Gordon A. Jensen

Marriage and Divorce

One notable change brought about in the sixteenth century was the shift in the theological doctrine on marriage and divorce introduced by Martin Luther and his followers and the subsequent change in legal and social rules governing both. These changes were to have profound implications for how marriage was conducted and who was allowed to marry: as one change, marriage was no longer considered a sacrament; as another change, all weddings and divorces were to be public. In addition, Luther argued that marriage was the only divinely ordained vocation for most men and women.

In *The Babylonian Captivity of the Church* (1520) Martin Luther broke with traditional church teachings, and even his own earlier doctrinal understanding of marriage, by asserting that marriage was not a sacrament, a statement he elaborated in *The Estate of Marriage* (1522; LW 45:11–49). He wrote that God expected most people to marry and discounted any elevated role for celibacy in salvation. While he first criticized canon law's restrictions on whom one could marry and insisted on using only biblical directives, by the 1530s Protestants reintroduced many but not all of the broader limitations. By the early 1520s Luther also developed a theological position supporting marriage as the chief form of sexual expression for everyone, including clergy, unless God had bestowed the extraordinary gift of celibacy on them. This led Luther and other reformers to argue for marriage for priests, monks, and nuns, and to call for the closure of convents and monasteries.

Luther's position on divorce was more complicated. In *The Babylonian Captivity of the Church* (1520), Luther stated that he "so detested divorce that [he] would rather allow bigamy than divorce." In *The Estate of Marriage* (1522), he acknowledged two valid reasons for divorce: abandonment and adultery; yet in at least one case he argued that spousal abuse was also valid grounds for divorce. Remarriage was sanctioned only for the innocent party, although he imagined that the perpetrator might marry in a far-off land. Luther's later stance on bigamy (esp. in the case of Landgrave Philip of Hesse) followed from his intent to avoid divorce in order to protect the integrity of marriage, an ambiguous position evident in his writings and recommendations to individuals seeking a divorce.

Sixteenth-century Lutheran theologians and commentators sectioned the world into three estates (*Stände*, "walks of life"): the ecclesiastical realm, temporal authority, and matrimonial estate (household). They argued that these, each with distinct duties and responsibilities, were interconnected and necessary for temporal order. Luther and his followers preached and wrote extensively on marriage because they argued that this first estate, created in paradise by God, was crucial to worldly and spiritual discipline. Thus they argued that the conduct of marriage must be improved for the sake of the temporal community and spiritual well-being. Responsibility for this was to be shared by church and temporal authorities, although the legal jurisdiction over marriage and divorce was to be a civil matter.

In the sixteenth and seventeenth centuries, theologians, jurists, and community leaders discussed this shift in numerous theological tracts, church ordinances, and legal opinions; they sought to establish greater oversight over marriage through new ordinances. Lutheran leaders also developed new procedures for conducting weddings, including parental consent, minimum age of marriage, and public ceremonies, and they established laws to prevent child marriages, secret marriages, bigamy, and incest. They argued that these changes were designed to create more stable marriages and public order. One outgrowth of connecting marriage to public order was the establishment of public marriage records in each parish. To publicize new expectations of marital relations, theologians described the ideal household, husband (*Hausvater*), and wife (*Hausmutter*) in sermons and in theological and popular tracts. To support these guidelines and to replace the now defunct episcopal courts, consistory courts and civil marriage courts were established after the 1530s to regulate disputes over weddings and to reconcile disorderly couples. Although Lutheran authorities discouraged divorce, men and women appealed to these courts in great numbers.

Luther's new understanding of marriage and divorce as a civil matter has contemporary ramifications. Local laws and synodical decisions still govern regulations and definitions of marriage and divorce in Lutheran churches throughout the world. Divorce remains allowable in some Lutheran synods only in the case of adultery and abandonment, whereas others recognize broader justifications. Synodical decisions on issues such as approaches to and regulation of same-sex marriage have caused significant controversy both within and between Lutheran churches.

See also Bora, Katharina von; Convents; Gender: Men and Women; Sexuality

Bibliography

Harrington, J. *Reordering Marriage and Society in Reformation Germany.* Cambridge University Press, 1995; Hendrix, S. "Luther on Marriage." *LQ* 19 (2000): 335–48; Plummer, M. E. *From Priest's Whore to Pastor's Wife: Clerical Marriage and the Process of Reform in the Early German Reformation.* Ashgate, 2012; Roper, L. *The Holy Household: Women and Morals in Reformation Augsburg.* Oxford University Press, 1989; Witte, J., Jr. *From Sacrament to Contract: Marriage, Religion, and Law in the Western Tradition.* 2nd ed. Westminster John Knox, 2012.

MARJORIE ELIZABETH PLUMMER

Marty, Martin Emil

The American Lutheran pastor and influential historian of Christianity Martin Emil Marty was born in 1928 at West Point, Nebraska. Marty received a PhD from the University of Chicago in 1956, served Lutheran (LCMS) congregations in the Chicago area for ten years, and then taught in the Divinity School of the University of Chicago from 1963 to 1998, advising 115 doctoral dissertations. A prolific author and commentator, author or editor of more than sixty influential books and over five thousand articles, chapters, or shorter pieces, he has served as columnist and senior editor of the *Christian Century* since 1956. Marty won a National Book Award for *Righteous Empire*, was honored with numerous other awards, including the National Humanities Medal, the Medal of the American Academy of Arts and Sciences, and eighty honorary doctorates. He served on several US presidential commissions and dozens of boards and organizations, including as president of the American Academy of Religion and the American Society of Church History. He was married to Elsa Schumacher (1951 until her death in 1981), then Harriet Myers (from 1982).

Bibliography

Marty, M. E. "Half a Life in Religious Studies: Confessions of an 'Historical Historian.'" In *The Craft of Religious Studies*, ed. J. R. Stone, 151–74. St. Martin's Press, 1998.

MARK A. GRANQUIST

Martyrdom and Persecution

Persecution, according to Luther's 1539 tract *On the Councils and Churches*, is the seventh and last "mark" or "holy possession" of the church. Christians "must endure every misfortune and persecution," and "they must be called heretics, knaves, devils, accursed, and the most harmful people on earth, so that even those who hang, drown, murder, torture, banish, and plague them do God a service." With these words Luther indicated that both the persecuted and persecutor serve the gospel in light of Christ's beatitude "Blessed are those when people persecute you for my sake" (WA 50:642; cf. LW 41:164–65).

Early in his career, Luther was both impressed by the "lives of the saints" and critical of "the nonsense and the lies" recorded in the medieval catalogs of confessors and martyrs (LW 48:17). As the threat of inquisitorial prosecution began to present itself to Luther, his correspondence began to reflect a martyr's sensibility. In May 1518 Luther wrote that he had nothing left to lose except for this "poor, worn body" already "exhausted by constant hardships"; therefore, his murderous enemies (acting in accordance with God's will) would only be depriving him of "an hour or two of life" (LW 48:69). By 1520, with the threat of an imperial summons imminent, Luther exclaimed, "Oh, that God would consider me worthy to be burned, torn to pieces, and expelled most disgracefully" for the sake of the Evangelical articles of faith (WA 7:588).

On July 1, 1523, two Augustinians, Johann van Esschen and Hendrik Voes, were burned at the stake in Brussels for supporting Luther's views. When Luther received the news, he reportedly responded, "I thought I would be the first one to be martyred by the Holy Gospel, but I am not worthy" (WA 12:74). Luther's public response came in the form of a ballad, Luther's first published hymn (LW 53:211–16), as well as a pastoral letter to the Christians in the Low Countries. In that letter Luther extolled "Saints Johann and Hendrik" for their bravery and faithfulness. He also congratulated the believers in the Low Countries that God had chosen them to be the first to suffer death for the sake of the newly reappeared gospel. At the same time, Luther reported that "up here [in Germany] we have not yet been considered worthy to become such a costly offering for Christ" (LW 42:78).

Luther's most developed martyrological writing came in the wake of the death of another Netherlander, Heinrich von Zütphen. In *The Burning of Brother Henry*, Luther distilled eyewitness reports into a detailed summary of Zütphen's death. He also wrote a letter of consolation to Zütphen's parishioners, wherein he explained that God permitted the deaths of Henry and others in order to "certify that [ours] is the right doctrine wherein the right Spirit is given . . . and by their martyrdom confirmed; just as the holy martyrs long ago died for the sake of the gospel and with

their blood sealed and certified it for us" (LW 32:265).

With such writings, Luther followed in the church's tradition of recording the lives and deaths of its martyrs. At the same time, Luther was not above emending the tradition in order to suit Evangelical commitments. That is, Luther knew that these new martyrs made no new contributions to the treasury of the merits of the saints. In addition, Luther made clear that the ability of these men to bear witness to the gospel unto death was purely an act and blessing of God, rather than a human good work.

On the other hand, Luther understood that the new martyrs contributed a number of things to the Evangelical movement. That is, although Luther may have rejected some aspects of the martyrological tradition, he was nevertheless happy to adapt other elements of the tradition to serve his purposes. First, for Luther, the martyrs confirmed God's approval of the Evangelical faith. Just as in the early church, the martyrs bore witness to the truth of Christianity, so now again, God was confirming the Lutheran confession as well. Second, just as in the early church, the new martyrs inspired surviving believers in their Evangelical faith, and drew new converts to the faith as well. Echoing Tertullian, Luther explained that the shed blood of Evangelical believers acted "as manure that fertilizes a field, making it lush and productive" (WA 52:602). Finally, the new martyrs exposed Luther's enemies as enemies of God. One feature of the tradition of Christian martyrdom is that true martyrs do not fight back nor curse their persecutors. In this way, Luther took pains to describe how the Evangelical martyrs went to their deaths in the manner of Christ: passively bearing their suffering and blessing their enemies all the while. For example, Luther was sure to explain how Brother Henry looked heavenward and prayed for his killers: "Forgive them, Father, for they know not what they do" (LW 32:285).

Luther himself lived a long life and died of natural causes. Worthiness for martyrdom continued to be a concern for Luther. For instance, in a 1539 sermon on Matthew 23:34 ("Therefore, I am sending you prophets. . . . Some of them you will kill and crucify" [NIV]), Luther waxed personal: "I would be honored to die ten times, even one hundred times, if God deemed me worthy of suffering for the sake of his Word" (WA 47:525). On the other hand, the Bible also gave examples such as Noah, a "martyr above all martyrs," forced to live hundreds of years among the unrighteous and the evil, whereas the "so-called martyrs . . . surmount all perils and temptations" and "overcome death in one hour" (LW 2:7).

After Luther's death, new collections of the stories of the church's martyrs, including the new Protestant martyrs, began to be published, several of which commemorated martyrs from Anabaptist traditions. Collections appeared in France, the Netherlands, and most famously in England, where in 1563 John Foxe first published his *Actes and Monuments of These Latter and Perillous Days* (*Book of Martyrs*). In the 1550s Ludwig Rabus, a Lutheran preacher and educator, published various volumes of *The History of the Saints*. Rabus's portrayals broadened the definition of "martyr" to include a large number of confessors of the faith who did not die a grisly death, Martin Luther among them. The tradition continues to the present, where various believers who died for the faith are remembered in Protestant church calendars, including Dietrich Bonhoeffer and Gudina Tumsa.

Bibliography

Akerboom, T. H. M., and M. A. M. E. Geilis. "'A New Song Shall Begin Here'. . . : The Martyrdom of Luther's Followers among Antwerp's Augustinians on July 1, 1523, and Luther's Response." In *More Than a Memory: The Discourse of Martyrdom and the Construction of Christian Identity in the History of Christianity*, ed. J. Leemans, 243–70. Annua Nuntia Lovaniensia 51. Peeters, 2005; Bagchi, D. "Luther and the Problem of Martyrdom." In *Martyrs and Martyrologies*, ed. D. Wood, 209–19. Blackwell, 1993; Christman, R. "'For He Is Coming': Revisiting Martin Luther's Reactions to the First Lutheran Executions." *Lutherjahrbuch* 82 (2015): 11–43; Duke, A. *Reformation and Revolt in the Low Countries*. 1990. Reprint, Hambledon, 2003; Gregory, B. *Salvation at Stake: Christian Martyrdom in Early Modern Europe*. Harvard University Press, 1999; Kolb, R. *For All the Saints: Changing Perceptions of Martyrdom and Sainthood in the Lutheran Reformation*. Mercer University Press, 1987; Kolb, R. "From Hymn to History of Dogma: Lutheran Martyrology in the Reformation Era." In *More Than a Memory: The Discourse of Martyrdom and the Construction of Christian Identity in the History of Christianity*, ed. J. Leemans, 295–311. Peeters, 2005; Kolb, R. "God's Gift of Martyrdom: The Early Reformation Understanding of Dying for the Faith." *Church History* 64 (1995): 399–411; Luther, M. *Letters of Spiritual Counsel*. Ed. and trans. T. Tappert. 1955. Reprint, Westminster John Knox, 2006; Wiersma, H. "The Burning of Brother Henry: The Story of a Lowlands Martyr as Chronicled by Jacob Probst and Martin Luther." In *Luther-Bulletin: Tijdschrift voor Interconfessioneel Lutheronderzoek* (2006): 50–60.

Hans Wiersma

Mathesius, Johannes

An influential student of Luther and model preacher, Johannes Mathesius (1504–65) was born in Rochlitz in Saxony and orphaned at an early age. He became a tutor in a noble family in Munich after studies at the University of Ingolstadt. Luther's *On Good Works* attracted him to Wittenberg in 1529; he returned three times for brief periods of study in the following thirteen years, boarding with the Luther family. His presence in the Black Cloister enabled him to record Luther's talk at table. After teaching in Altenburg in Saxony, he accepted a call to preach in Joachimsthal (Jáchymov) in Bohemia, a recently founded mining town, filled with miners who resettled there from Saxony and other points north. He rejected calls to other locations and constructed a Lutheran society in the town through his powerful preaching. He remained largely apart from the controversies of the 1550s that divided the Wittenberg circle; all sides appreciated and used his sermons. The pressure on Joachimsthal's Evangelical reform, coming from the Hapsburg government in Bohemia, commanded his attention and energy in the last two decades of his life.

Some five thousand of his sermons are extant, fifteen hundred in print, most having appeared posthumously. His preaching captured not only Luther's law/gospel hermeneutic but also much of his narrative style and command of effective rhetorical principles. His homiletical review of Luther's life, a response to Johann Cochlaeus's account of Luther's career, pioneered biographical writing of the reformer (1566). His *Postil* (1558, 1565) was second only to Luther's in popularity. His *Sarepta* (1562) used imagery from the miner's life to bring the gospel to his hearers and readers. He provided homiletical commentaries on Gen. 3:15 (1587), Ps. 130 (1565), Christ's life (1568), Christ's passion (1568, 1570, 1587), 1 and 2 Corinthians (1590), the flood (1587), and Jesus Sirach (1586), as well as collections of funeral sermons (1564), wedding sermons (1563, 1591), catechism sermons (1586), and sermons on the Table of Christian Callings (1561).

See also Hermann, Nikolaus; Wittenberg Circle, Parties within

Bibliography

Brown, C. B. *Singing the Gospel: Lutheran Hymns and the Success of the Reformation.* Harvard University Press, 2005; Loesche, G. *Johannes Mathesius.* Perthes, 1895.

ROBERT KOLB

Mau, Carl Henning, Jr.

The general secretary of the Lutheran World Federation from 1974 to 1985 was Carl Henning Mau Jr. (1922–95). He studied theology at the Lutheran Theological Seminary in Philadelphia. Ordained in 1946, Mau became a parish pastor in Portland, Oregon. He volunteered to assist in the rehabilitation of European Lutheran churches following World War II. From 1950 onward, he was an associate of Bishop Hanns Lilje. He became LWF assistant general secretary in 1964, leaving that post in 1972 to assume the position of general secretary of the US National Committee of the LWF.

In 1974 Mau was elected general secretary of the LWF, guiding the federation through critical general assemblies in Dar es Salaam, Tanganyika (now Tanzania) in 1957, and Budapest in 1984. He guided reorganization of the governing structures of the organization, led the LWF's criticism of apartheid, and promoted its efforts to bring the dependence of African churches on North American and

European leadership to an end. For the Budapest assembly, his negotiations with the Communist regime in Hungary to permit the first large Christian convention in a Soviet-dominated land typified his efforts to assist Lutheran churches in Soviet-dominated lands, including his sending aid to groups in Siberia. He promoted the concept of the Lutheran World Federation as a communion of churches.

See also Apartheid; Lutheran World Federation

ROBERT KOLB

Mecklenburg

As a region in northern Germany, during the latter half of the sixteenth century Mecklenburg became a Lutheran stronghold characterized by its commitment to Lutheran teaching and confessional unity within its borders. Its university in the port city of Rostock became an important champion of higher learning and exporter of Lutheran theology across the Baltic Sea.

During the sixteenth century it was customary for two dukes to share rule of a territory. At the time of the Reformation, Duke Albrecht VII held court in Güstrow, and his brother Duke Heinrich held court in Schwerin. The dukes were kept in check by a particularly well-organized and influential landed nobility who united in 1523 in order to protect their traditional sociopolitical claims. The relationship between the nobles and dukes influenced the reform effort in Mecklenburg significantly. Since the territorial church as an institution overlapped the traditional claims of the estates, they expected to be consulted by the dukes on matters of reform since they played an active role in the church's development. Owing to this arrangement, with progress dependent on agreement between sides, the Lutheran church in Mecklenburg developed slowly over the course of many years. Although Lutheran pastors gained permission from Duke Heinrich to preach in Mecklenburg during the early 1520s, the first official Lutheran church order was not issued until 1540, although regular visitations of the Lutheran churches began in

1534. Together the dukes and landed estates rejected the Augsburg Interim in 1549, and in 1552 they signed an updated church ordinance written by Philip Melanchthon. Mecklenburg committed itself to the Formula of Concord in 1580.

Beginning in the 1550s David Chytraeus, who quickly became Mecklenburg's leading theologian, worked to reform the University of Rostock, restructuring the curriculum to reflect the Lutheran identity of the territory. Under his direction enrollment increased and the university became an invaluable center of learning in northern Germany. It surpassed Wittenberg as the choice for students from across the Baltic Sea seeking Lutheran schooling. Its theology faculty, including Chytraeus, served as advisers to the dukes, church visitors, and members of the consistory and drafted numerous school and church orders for the territory.

Mecklenburg's long course of reform proved to be an advantage. Over many decades the Lutheran Church developed there in an atmosphere of cooperation and consensus, gradually but firmly taking root without the instability or violent rebellions experienced elsewhere in German lands. In 1620 the landed estates successfully countered an attempted second Calvinist Reformation. The confessional unity of Mecklenburg's church was maintained even as the territory fractured into separate duchies. The deep roots held even up until 1903, when non-Lutheran Protestants were finally permitted the right to worship publicly in the territory. Today Mecklenburg is part of the Evangelical Lutheran Church in Northern Germany, a result of the 2012 merger between the former Evangelical Lutheran Church of Mecklenburg, North Elbian Evangelical Lutheran Church, and Pomeranian Protestant Church.

See also Chytraeus, David

Bibliography

Miller, G. M. "The Lutheran State Church in Mecklenburg, 1549–1621." PhD diss., Yale University, 1998; Schmaltz, K. *Kirchengeschichte Mecklenburgs.* Vol. 2, *Reformation und Gegenreformation.* Bahn, 1936; Wieden, H. bei der, ed. *Menschen in der Kirche: 450 Jahre seit Einführung der Reformation in Mecklenburg.* Schmidt-Römhild, 2000.

TIMIOS COOK

Meier, Theophil

The Lutheran bishop who guided the Evangelical Lutheran Church of Russia during its first decades in the USSR was Theophil Meier (1865–1934). Born in what is now Latvia, Meier studied at Dorpat University and was ordained in 1890. He served parishes in Bessarabia and the Ukraine before moving to the Sts. Peter and Paul Lutheran Church in Moscow (1910–27). In the early 1920s, he worked closely with John Morehead of the National Lutheran Council in mitigating the famine in the Volga region. Named as bishop in 1924, he also negotiated with the government for opening a seminary and obtaining permission to hold the first General Synod in the Russian Lutheran church's history. He took mission trips to Siberia, writing about his experiences in *To Siberia in Service of the Evangelical Lutheran Church.* Meier also wrote *Luther's Heritage in Russia.* After his death in 1934, Sts. Peter and Paul was forcibly closed (1938).

See also Russia

MATTHEW HEISE

Melanchthon, Philip

As professor in the theology and arts faculties at the University of Wittenberg and Martin Luther's colleague (from 1518), Philip (Philipp) Melanchthon (1497–1560) was chief drafter of the Augsburg Confession and its Apology. He was born in Bretten to Georg Schwartzerdt, an armorer, and Barbara Reuter. After his father's death in 1508, Melanchthon studied at the Latin school in Pforzheim, living with a relative by marriage, Elizabeth Reuchlin. Her brother, the humanist Johannes Reuchlin, visited the school and gave Melanchthon a Greek grammar, inscribed with the Greek version of his name: *melan* (*Schwartz* = black) and *chthon* (*Erdt* = earth). He received a bachelor of arts from the University of Heidelberg in 1511 and his master of arts from Tübingen in 1514. There Melanchthon taught in the arts faculty and worked for a printer alongside Johannes Oecolampadius. On Reuchlin's recommendation, Melanchthon was called as professor of Greek at the University of Wittenberg and joined the faculty in August 1518, delivering an inaugural address on educational reform. Melanchthon became an avid supporter of Luther's cause and accompanied him to the Leipzig Debates in 1519. In addition to lecturing on Greek texts (including the New Testament), rhetoric, and logic (dialectics), Melanchthon received his bachelor of Bible under Luther's presidency on September 19, 1519. He then lectured on the content of the Latin Bible, including Romans, 1 and 2 Corinthians, and the Gospel of John. When published (by Luther without his permission), these annotations became best sellers. Instead of lecturing on Peter Lombard's *Sentences* (the standard medieval textbook), Melanchthon used Paul's Letter to the Romans as a template for constructing and lecturing on *loci communes* (commonplaces, general topics) in theology. He published these lectures (held before and after his marriage to Katharina Krapp in November 1520), with their chief topics (among others) of law, gospel, faith, and justification, under the title *Loci communes rerum theologicarum, seu hypotyposes theologicae* (General topics of theological matters, or theological outlines). The book went through at least seventeen printings in Latin and twelve in German. The lectures present the basic categories of Wittenberg's Evangelical theology over against medieval Scholasticism and contemporary Roman opponents. In 1535 Melanchthon produced a new and expanded Latin edition, edited substantially in 1543 (with additions in 1545 and 1548). In 1555 Melanchthon reworked the earlier German translation of Justus Jonas, adding a preface addressed to Anna Camerarius, his best friend Joachim's wife.

While Luther was at the Wartburg, Melanchthon supported the reform-minded faction of Wittenberg's faculty, including Nicholas von Amsdorf and Andreas Karlstadt, and was among the first laypersons to receive the Lord's Supper in both kinds (bread and wine) in September 1521. On Luther's return, Melanchthon helped publish Luther's translation of the New Testament into German. In 1523 Melanchthon was elected rector of the university and reformed the arts faculty along humanist and Reformation lines, adding to the required disputations regular declamations (formal speeches). In 1524 Melanchthon again took up lectures on the Bible in addition to his responsibilities in the arts faculty. After Elector John came into office and reconstituted the university in 1525, Melanchthon, like Luther, was given an extraordinary position and could lecture in both faculties, which he continued to do until his death. In 1527 he shepherded through the presses biblical lectures on Colossians in which he indirectly attacked Erasmus's understanding of free will. They were followed by commentaries on Proverbs (1529) and Romans (1529/30 and 1532). Around the same time, he produced new works on rhetoric and dialectics and began lecturing on Aristotle. In 1527, at Luther's urging, Melanchthon was elected chief theological member of a team of official visitors, empowered by the elector to examine the administrative and theological state of Saxony's churches. Melanchthon wrote Latin instructions for parish priests, which he and Luther published jointly in 1528 in a revised German version as *Instruction by the Visitors*. The revisions came about because of a theological disagreement between Melanchthon and Johannes Agricola over whether law or gospel caused true repentance. Melanchthon also wrote against the Peasants' Revolt and Anabaptists.

With Luther unable to travel safely outside Saxony, Melanchthon served as the elector's chief theologian at the 1530 Diet of Augsburg, becoming principal drafter of the Augsburg Confession. Prevented by the emperor from presenting its defense (Latin: *apologia*), Melanchthon published an expanded version of the Apology in May 1531 (revised September 1531). In 1533 he revised statutes for the theological faculty at Wittenberg, reinstituting the granting of theological doctorates. In the mid-1530s, Melanchthon functioned as the chief negotiator with some of the Roman party, with embassies from the English and French kings and with Martin Bucer (conferring on Luther's behalf to end the dispute with southern German and Swiss theologians over the Lord's Supper). In May 1536 these negotiations led to the Wittenberg Concord. Melanchthon also hardened his stance against Anabaptists and, with Luther, advocated the use of capital punishment against them for not only sedition but also blasphemy. In 1540–41, Melanchthon represented the Evangelical side in colloquies with the Roman party in Worms and Regensburg, for which he edited and published a new version of the Augsburg Confession (the so-called *Variata*). These talks reached tentative agreement on original sin and justification (rejected by Rome out of hand and criticized sharply by Luther and Bugenhagen) but faltered on the questions of transubstantiation and the authority of pope and councils.

Upon Luther's death in February 1546, Melanchthon was chief theologian for the Elector of Saxony John Frederick. Melanchthon's preface to the second volume of Luther's Latin works, published in June 1546 and republished separately with other documents pertaining to Luther's life and death, became the first important biographical sketch of this reformer. During the Smalcald War, Melanchthon fled Wittenberg with his family and Katharina von Bora. With the defeat and capture of Elector John Frederick, Wittenberg capitulated to his cousin, Duke Moritz, on whom the emperor bestowed the electoral title and lands. After some hesitation, Melanchthon helped reopen the University of Wittenberg and became Moritz's chief adviser during negotiations for the 1547–48 Diet of Augsburg, at which Charles V promulgated the Augsburg Interim, which Melanchthon attacked in print. After the removal of two Evangelical bishops installed by Luther (Nicholas von Amsdorf and Georg von Anhalt) and their replacement by theologians favorable to Rome, Melanchthon negotiated on behalf of the elector with these new bishops in order to protect Evangelical pastors and congregations while making some concessions to the Augsburg Interim. Rejected by the territorial Saxon diet in Leipzig in December 1548, this so-called Leipzig Proposal (Interim) became the flash point for objections to Melanchthon's theology and leadership by other Evangelicals, especially Matthias Flacius. Initial disagreements focused on adiaphora but later included objections to the freedom of the will and the Lord's Supper. In 1551 Melanchthon was to represent Electoral Saxony at the Council of Trent but never got beyond Nuremberg and drafted a "repetition" of the Augsburg Confession, the Saxon Confession, an official statement of Saxon teaching (along with the 1552 *Examination of Ordinands*), signed by many of Saxon's theologians and others.

The 1550s saw increased strife among adherents to the Augsburg Confession, sometimes centering on Melanchthon, but he continued to produce important works, including a history of the world (the *Chronicon Carionis*, which reached to Charlemagne and was completed by Melanchthon's son-in-law, Caspar Peucer), various works on Greek and Latin grammar, rhetoric and dialectics, biblical commentaries, refutations of his opponents, and as a final summary of his theology, the Bavarian Inquisition Articles (1558). He collected this final document, together with the Augsburg Confession (Variata), the Apology, the Saxon Confession, the *Examination*, and the *Loci communes*, into the *Corpus doctrinae* (Body of teaching, published shortly before his death in both Latin and German). In Saxony, it represented an official body of doctrine until replaced in 1580 by the Book of Concord.

Melanchthon's theology reflects chief aspects of Wittenberg's theology and the continuing influence of Luther. In the *Loci* of 1521, categories of justification by faith alone and the distinction between law and gospel play central roles. Influenced by correspondence with Luther from Wartburg Castle, Luther's sermons of March 1522, and Luther's tract *On Secular Authority*, Melanchthon developed a clearer distinction between human righteousness, valid for this world, and Christ's righteousness in the forgiveness of sins. This gave space for the humanities and human freedom in this world. Melanchthon combined two basic questions from dialectics ("What is a thing?" and "What are its effects?") with his understanding of law and gospel, thereby to define both what God's Word is (commands and promises) and also what it does to a person (terrify as law and comfort as gospel). In the 1530s, while retaining these basic premises, Melanchthon's own thought became more clearly differentiated (but not separate) from Luther's own. In 1539, both wrote treatises on the church and its authority. On the Lord's Supper, Melanchthon supported the Wittenberg Concord confessing Christ's presence *with* the bread and wine, but unlike Luther, he worried more about "bread worship" than about denying Christ's presence. In the late 1550s Melanchthon insisted on Christ's bodily ascension but held that through the communication of attributes Christ was with the church on earth. He even attacked his former student, Heidelberg professor Tilemann Hesshus, for hyperrealism regarding Christ's presence. Some of his students (including Peucer) spelled out clear differences to other Lutherans by insisting on a purely spiritual presence of Christ in the Supper. On free will, the 1536 *Loci* introduced three causes for salvation—the Word, the Holy Spirit, and the human will (where the latter was understood more as a material cause than anything else)—earning attacks in the 1550s from some Gnesio-Lutherans. In the so-called Leipzig Interim, Melanchthon argued that Christians had freedom to change practices (adiaphora), regardless of whether they were under persecution or not. On the necessity of good works for salvation (the Majoristic controversy), Melanchthon rejected arguments that good works were necessary for salvation while maintaining that they were indeed a necessary result of justification. He defended his understanding of forensic justification (God's declaration of forgiveness and righteousness for the sinner) against Andreas Osiander's insistence on the indwelling of Christ's divine righteousness in the believer.

The relation between Melanchthon and Martin Luther, already questioned by some during Luther's lifetime, sharpened during the 1550s over Melanchthon's faithfulness to Luther's legacy. While some scholars have depicted the relationship between these two as one of friendship marked by a series of crises and breaks, more recent work has argued that, with Luther's return from the Wartburg, they became two equally important colleagues in the shaping of the Wittenberg theological tradition, with lifelong respect for one another.

Melanchthon's reception by Lutherans has been marked by deep ambiguities. After his death, fights over the Lord's Supper at the University of Wittenberg in the 1570s intensified disagreement over his legacy. Some defended Melanchthon, especially his closest friend, Joachim Camerarius, who published a biography of Melanchthon in 1566. The authors of the Formula of Concord included former students (Nicholas Selnecker, David Chytraeus, and Martin Chemnitz), who distanced themselves from certain positions Melanchthon held but still employed his methods and categories. At the same time, other former students (e.g., Zacharias Ursinus and Christopher Pezel) became leaders among the Reformed. By the early seventeenth century Melanchthon's textbooks had fallen into disuse or even disrepute among Lutherans. In his "nonpartisan" history of the church published at the end of the seventeenth century, the radical Pietist Gottfried Arnold accused Melanchthon of completely neglecting the Bible. The first academic Melanchthon scholar, Theodor Strobel (1736–94), refuted this view and republished Camerarius's biography with extensive notes. In the mid-nineteenth century, the publication of Melanchthon's writings in the *Corpus Reformatorum* led to a renewed interest in his work. With the Luther Renaissance of the late nineteenth and early twentieth centuries, however, Melanchthon was sometimes depicted as a second-rate theologian. Karl Holl claimed that Melanchthon's doctrine of forensic justification undermined Luther's insight into justification's sanative nature. After World War II, the establishment of the Melanchthon Forschungsstelle in Heidelberg (dedicated to publishing Melanchthon's correspondence) and the work of its first director, Heinz Scheible—coupled with anniversary celebrations in 1960, 1997, and 2010—renewed interest in Melanchthon's contributions to Lutheranism.

See also Amsdorf, Nikolaus von; Apology of the Augsburg Confession; Augsburg Interim; Book of Concord; Electors of Saxony; Flacius, Matthias Illyricus, and the Flacians; Formula of Concord; Karlstadt, Andreas Bodenstein von; Leipzig Proposal (Interim); Luther Interpretation and Reception; Reuchlin, Johannes; Smalcald War; University of Wittenberg in the Sixteenth Century; Wittenberg Concord

Bibliography

Brettschneider, K., and H. Bindseil, eds. *Corpus Reformatorum*. 28 vols. Schwetschke, 1834–60; Preus, J. A. O., trans. *Loci communes, 1543*. Concordia, 1992; Satre, L., trans. *Loci communes theologici* (1521). In *Melanchthon and Bucer*, ed. W. Pauck. Westminster, 1969; Schieble, H. *Melanchthon: Eine Biographie*. Beck, 1997; Schieble, H., et al. *Melanchthons Briefwechsel*. 23+ vols. Frommann-Holzboog, 1977–; Wengert, T. *Human Freedom, Christian Righteousness: Philip Melanchthon's Exegetical Dispute with Erasmus of Rotterdam*. Oxford University Press, 1998; Wengert, T. *Philip Melanchthon, Speaker of the Reformation: Wittenberg's Other Reformer*. Ashgate, 2010; Wengert, T., et al. *Philip Melanchthon: Theologian in Classroom, Confession, and Controversy*. Vandenhoeck & Ruprecht, 2012.

Timothy J. Wengert

Methodism

The worldwide movement of Methodism originated with the evangelistic work of brothers John and Charles Wesley in eighteenth-century England. Response to their preaching led to the formation of religious societies beginning in 1739, first in Bristol and London, then elsewhere in rapidly industrializing England and Ireland. At first these societies were modeled after those of the Moravians, but soon they developed their own distinctive theology and practices. The Wesley brothers never intended emergent Methodism to become a separate denomination; they saw it as a reforming movement within, not an alternative to, the Church of England, on which it depended for priestly and sacramental services.

Methodism spread to North America as English and Irish immigrants brought their Methodist beliefs and practices with them. By the late 1760s Methodist societies existed in New York, Philadelphia, Baltimore, and surrounding regions. At the request of American Methodists, John Wesley began sending preachers from England to America in 1769, and Methodist work in the British colonies was more formally organized by 1773. As the tensions between England and the American colonies increased, leading to revolution, the Church of England ceased to exist in America, creating a sacramental crisis: there were no ordained ministers to provide the sacraments to American Methodists.

Failing to find another resolution to this crisis, in 1784 John Wesley took the irregular action of ordaining two of his lay preachers for service in America, and of "setting apart" Thomas Coke to be "general superintendent" of American Methodism, along with Francis Asbury (who had been in America since 1771). This led to the establishment of the Methodist Episcopal Church (MEC) in America, with Coke and Asbury as the first bishops. Beginning soon after John Wesley's death in 1791, the Methodists in Britain followed their American cousins by gradually forming a new church organization separate from the Church of England.

Flowing from a common origin, the Methodist movement thus divided into two broad streams, British and American, with many commonalties but some key differences. The growth and spread of Methodism in the nineteenth century was dramatic, especially in the rapidly expanding United States. By

1860 Methodists were the largest Christian denomination in North America. That growth did not come without friction. The fabric of American Methodism was repeatedly torn by schisms involving slavery and racial discrimination, polity, and governance, leading to the formation of a number of new church bodies. Attracted to the Holiness movement of the late nineteenth century, significant numbers of Methodists also withdrew to form a variety of new denominations, some of which provided the seedbed for Pentecostalism in the twentieth century. British Methodism suffered similar schisms over doctrine, polity, and practice, though not directly over racial issues. Some of these divisions were subsequently healed through mergers and reunions, eventually leading to the creation in the United Kingdom of the present Methodist Church in 1932 and in the United States of the present United Methodist Church (UMC) in 1968.

British and American Methodism shared common missional impulses. British Methodist missionaries established Methodism in India, southern Africa, the Caribbean, Canada, Australia, and New Zealand. American Methodist missionaries ventured into Latin and South America, Scandinavia and Germany, central and western Africa, and across the Pacific to Korea, Japan, China, and Southeast Asia, especially the Philippines. From the start, British Methodists tended to encourage the development of local autonomy in their missions, while American Methodists typically maintained more direct control. Both carried out their missionary work in the context of powerful European and American colonialism and were forced to cope with nationalism and decolonization after World War II. The churches outside the United Kingdom originating from British missionary activity have become autonomous or merged into United or Uniting Churches (as in Canada and Australia). The former American Methodist missions in Latin and South America, Korea, and parts of Africa are now autonomous, but the UMC continues to have significant and growing membership outside the United States, especially in the Philippines and sub-Saharan Africa.

The worldwide family of Wesleyan and Methodist churches now relate to each other through the World Methodist Council, which currently is made up of eighty Methodist, Wesleyan, and related Uniting and United Churches representing over 80.5 million people in 133 countries. Many of these denominations also maintain active bilateral and multilateral ecumenical dialogues with other Christian churches. One important example of the benefits of such ecumenical dialogues is the 2009 full communion agreement between the UMC and the ELCA, through which two churches formally recognize the ministry and mission of the other, the authenticity of each other's sacraments, and the full interchangeability of ordained ministers of both communions. Another example involves the World Methodist Council's 2006 acceptance of the Lutheran–Roman Catholic Joint Declaration on the Doctrine of Justification (1999).

See also Ecumenical Dialogues; Evangelical Lutheran Church in America; Wesley, John and Charles

Bibliography

Abraham, W., and J. Kirby, eds. *The Oxford Handbook of Methodist Studies*. Oxford University Press, 2011; Cracknell, K., and S. White, eds. *An Introduction to World Methodism*. Cambridge University Press, 2005; Gibson, W., et al., eds. *The Ashgate Research Companion to World Methodism*. Ashgate, 2013; Matthews, R. *Timetables of History for Students of Methodism*. Abingdon, 2007; Vickers, J. *Cambridge Companion to American Methodism*. Cambridge University Press, 2013; Yrigoyen, C., ed. *T&T Clark Companion to Methodism*. T&T Clark, 2010.

Rex D. Matthews

Mexico

American missionaries from the Lutheran Church–Missouri Synod, the Wisconsin Evangelical Lutheran Synod (WELS), and the American Lutheran Church (1930–60) introduced the Lutheran theological tradition in the predominantly Roman Catholic Mexico, building on earlier efforts among German immigrants. In 1936 Myrtle Nordin, a Lutheran from Minnesota, formed the Latin American (Lutheran) Mission (LAM) and began outreach among Spanish-speaking people in southern Texas and northern Mexico, which led to the founding of the Evangelical Lutheran Church of Mexico and membership in the Confessional Evangelical Lutheran Conference (CELC).

LCMS began mission work in 1940, working from bases in the southern United States and in Mexico. This led to the establishment of the Lutheran Synod of Mexico (SLM). In the 1960s it built the Lutheran Center; by 1968 the SLM became a sister church of the LCMS. In the early 1980s the LCMS withdrew during the debt crisis that struck Mexico, returning in 1987 with disaster relief and humanitarian work. In 2001, the SLM asked the LCMS to strengthen its partnership when representatives of the two churches met in Mexico City. Owing to a shortage of pastors, there is need for theological education leading to ordination, strengthening Lutheran identity, and building lay leadership. Currently the SLM shares altar and pulpit fellowship with the LCMS and is a member of the International Lutheran Council (ILC).

In 1969 native pastors David Orea Luna and David Chichia were received into fellowship by WELS and began mission work in Mexico City and Guadalajara. In 1970 the constitution of the Iglesia Evangélica Luterana Confesional (IELC) in Mexico was adopted. WELS pastors working in El Paso, Texas, periodically visited to instruct seminarians and counsel congregations and pastors. In 1993 the Mexican government legalized residency for foreign missionaries; Ernest Zimdars and Larry Schlomer became the first resident missionaries in Mexico. In 1995 a five-year plan was adopted to make the mission self-propagating, self-supporting, and self-governing. In 2005 Mexican Lutheran Seminary was established in Torreón.

In 1947 the American Lutheran Church began work in Mexico, building off the earlier work in south Texas that led to the formation of the Mexican Lutheran Church (MLC) in 1957. The MLC is in partnership with the Evangelical Lutheran Church in America and receives support from many ELCA congregations. In addition to working with Augsburg Lutheran Seminary, the ELCA-sponsored Young Adults in Global Mission (YAGM), based in Mexico City, supports the rights of children, migration, women's rights, community building, English as a second language instruction, and environmental education.

American Lutheran churches carried out missionary work among the poor, empowered indigenous leadership, and is expanding Lutheran influence in the region, but they have not found a way to combine their efforts.

See also Lutheran Church–Missouri Synod; Mission and Evangelism

Bibliography

http://www.celc.info/site/cpage.asp?sec_id=180010197&cpage_id=180031333; http://www.elca.Org/Our-Work/Global-Church/Global-Mission/Young-Adults-in-Global-Mission/Mexico#sthash.IAEW7fEL.dpuf; Jahnel, C. *The Lutheran Church in El Salvador*. Servicio Educativo Cristiano-LBCM, 2009; http://www.lutherancentral.com.

ORIN W. CUMMINGS

Meyfart, Johann Matthäus

The theologian, opponent of witch trials, and representative of the *Frommigkeitsbewegung* (piety movement) Johann Matthäus Meyfart (1590–1642) was born in Jena to theologian Michael Meyfart and Catharina Fiedler. He received his childhood education at the *Gymnasium* in Gotha before studying at the University of Jena, where he received his master of arts degree in 1611. He completed his theological studies in Wittenberg in 1614. Before becoming professor of theology in Erfurt in 1633, Meyfart taught at the gymnasium in Coburg and later was senior of the Erfurt Ministerium. The devastations of the Thirty Years' War influenced Meyfart's theological and devotional writings, which focused on Christ's imminent return and God's impending judgment. His trilogy, *Das himmlische Jerusalem* (1627), *Das höllische Sodoma*

(1630), and *Das jüngste Gericht* (1632) (The heavenly Jerusalem, The hellish Sodom, The last judgment), incorporates mystical-ascetic ideas common in his day with traditional eschatological expectations. As educator and representative of late European humanism, Meyfart produced works on rhetoric; as churchman and biblicist, he published sermons and tracts, writing against the witch trials of his time and criticizing the spiritual condition of the universities. His criticism of the state of the universities brought the praise of Johann Valentin Andreae, and the later Pietist Philipp Jakob Spener counted him as one of his theological predecessors. An indication of his influence on later Pietism can be seen in Gottfried Arnold's (positive) inclusion of him in his *Kirchen- und Ketzer-Historie.*

See also Arndt, Johann; Arnold, Gottfried; Lutheran Orthodoxy; Pietism

Bibliography

Hallier, C. *Johann Matthäus Meyfart: Ein Schriftsteller, Pädagoge und Theologe des 17. Jahrhunderts.* Reprint, Karl Wachholtz, 1982; Trunz, E. *Johann Matthäus Meyfart: Theologe und Schriftsteller in der Zeit des Dreißigjährigen Krieges.* Beck, 1987.

Peter James Yoder

Middle East

Lutheran awareness of the Middle East may be dated to Luther's extensive writings on the threat of the Turk and an appropriate Evangelical response to Muslims. In 1633 the first Lutheran missionary to the Middle East, Peter Heyling of Lübeck, arrived in Wadi Natrun, Egypt, to study Arabic and Syriac in order to share the gospel among, not Muslims, but Ethiopian Copts. In 1704 Arvid Gradin, a Swede, was sent to Constantinople, and from 1752 to 1783 Moravian missionaries went to Egypt: Friederich Wilhelm Hocker, Johanna Heinrich Danke, George Wieniger, and John Antes. All of these early efforts were directed toward Orthodox Christians and left no lasting tangible results.

Palestine became a focus of Lutheran attention during the 1800s. German and Scandinavian mission societies were created to evangelize Jews there, and Franz Delitzsch founded the Institutum Judaicum in Leipzig to prepare missionaries for this purpose. In 1849 John Nicolayson, a Danish Lutheran serving under Anglican orders through the London Jews' Society, succeeded in establishing Christ Church in Jerusalem to serve a small community of Jewish Christians. In 1845 the Anglo-Prussian bishopric in Jerusalem received a Lutheran bishop, Samuel Gobat, to oversee the work. He welcomed persons of Greek Orthodox tradition who in 1874 created another Protestant congregation in Jerusalem, St. Paul's Church. In 1898 the Lutheran Church of the Redeemer was built on the grounds of the crusading Knights Hospitaller that had been given to Kaiser Wilhelm I by the Ottoman sultan Abdülaziz I in 1869. A number of German-funded institutions grew up during the last half of the nineteenth century, including a settlement of three thousand millennial-thinking Württemberg migrants, a Brüderhaus of the German Pilgrims Mission who maintained themselves by their own work, an orphanage organized by Johann Ludwig Schneller and his wife after the Damascus massacres of 1860, the Talithi Kumi home for girls run by German deaconesses, and a hospice on the Mount of Olives.

Former students of these schools and institutions gradually established a church that in 1959 was recognized as independent and autonomous, now known as the Evangelical Lutheran Church in Jordan and the Holy Land (ELCJHL). This church of about three thousand members has six congregations in Jerusalem, Bethlehem, Ramallah, Beit Jala, Beit Sahour, and Amman. It hosts four schools for kindergarten through grade twelve, serving over three thousand students, and maintains other educational programs, including the Al-Mahaba Kindergarten on the Mount of Olives, the Martin Luther Community Development Center in old Jerusalem, and the Environmental Education Center in Beit Jala. Munib Younan has served as bishop since 1998.

Twentieth-century Lutherans in the Middle East have been attentive to ministry among

Muslims. In 1903 a Danish couple, Oluf Johannes and Marie Høyer, arrived in Yemen to share the gospel. The educational and medical ministries begun there were continued by the Danish Church Mission in Arabia until its departure in 1968. The Danish Mission to the Orient also maintained work in Syria from 1906 to 1927 and is considered significant in fostering Christian-Muslim relations.

In the mid-twentieth century several American Lutheran churches continued this attentiveness as they committed themselves to new Middle Eastern ministry. Carl Agerstrand led a Lutheran Church–Missouri Synod initiative in Lebanon in the 1950s that produced an orphanage, schools, two congregations, and a mass media ministry, the Middle East Lutheran Ministry (MELM). New emphases developed during the 1960s by Dennis Hilgendorf and John Stelling included ecumenical cooperation, attention to local culture, refugee ministry, and dialogue between Christians and Muslims. In 1962 the Lutheran Church in America and later the American Lutheran Church made ministry to Muslims a defining part of their new work in the Middle East. An approach developed by Bruce Schein specified a team of five, including an educator, a social worker, a pastor, an Islamicist, and a coordinator, who would develop a "conversation with Islam." Harold Vogelaar, called to the Islamicist position, began this conversation in Cairo. Several ministries developed there: pastoring St. Andrew's United Church of Cairo, caring for victims of conflict through St. Andrew's Refugee Services, and directing the graduate studies program at Evangelical Theological Seminary in Cairo. At the same time a Jerusalem-based staff focused on Palestinian refugee ministry and peacemaking in the aftermath of the Israeli-Palestinian wars.

Since 1948 the Lutheran World Federation has been caring for Palestinian refugees through its Jerusalem Project. This includes the Augusta Victoria Hospital with its specialized departments and mobile units, a vocational training program graduating thousands from centers in northern Jerusalem and Ramallah, and ministry to physical and social needs of refugees.

See also Islam; Kurds; Refugees

Bibliography

Grafton, D. *Piety, Politics, and Power: Lutherans Encountering Islam in the Middle East.* Pickwick, 2009; Hamilton, J. "Moravians in Moslem Lands during the Eighteenth Century." *The Moslem World* 10 (1920): 82–86; Kauffeldt, J. "Danes, Orientalism and the Modern Middle East: Perspectives from the Nordic Periphery." PhD diss., Florida State University, 2006; Öberg, I. "The Apologetic and Missiological Motifs in Luther's Work with Islam." In *Luther and World Mission: A Historical and Systematic Study*, trans. D. Apel, 428–91. Concordia, 2007; Younan, M. *Witnessing for Peace: In Jerusalem and the World.* Fortress, 2003.

MARK NYGARD

Migration

The movement of individuals and groups of people from one nation to another is migration: this involves emigration (leaving to escape difficult or dangerous conditions in their countries of origin) and immigration (entering another country to seek better economic and social conditions).

Such movements have always been a part of human history but have increased markedly since the sixteenth-century Reformation due to religious persecution, European exploration and colonization, advances in transportation, and more recently, globalization. Immigration has brought great advantages to many of those who have participated, but also brought about social and political conflicts within the countries affected. Lutheranism has dealt with the challenges of immigration almost from its beginnings. The migration of Germans from central Europe eastward began in the Middle Ages, and by the time of the Reformation there were significant German populations in Poland, Hungary, Transylvania, and the Baltic states. The new Protestant movement spread into these areas, and Lutheran congregations were thus established in parts of eastern Europe. At the same time, when faced with persecution, banished theologians and prominent leaders often sought shelter in

Saxony, Württemberg, and other friendlier venues. In the eighteenth century Germans were invited by Empress Catherine II, known as Catherine the Great, to settle in areas of southern Russia and Ukraine, especially in farming areas along the Volga. Lutheran congregations were formed in some of these communities; through internal migrations Lutherans also settled in areas of what is now Kazakhstan and Kyrgyzstan. Some of these Russian German Lutherans migrated to the United States and Canada in the nineteenth century.

Beginning in the seventeenth century several European Lutheran countries made sporadic efforts toward colonization, with a Swedish colony along the Delaware River in America, and a Danish colony in the Virgin Islands, but these efforts were limited. The major part of Lutheran immigration to North America during the eighteenth century was individual and economic, with European Lutherans (mainly Germans) settling in British North America. Since many of these immigrants were poor, a common practice was for individuals to indenture themselves for seven years of involuntary service, in return for the passage to North America. There were also some groups of Lutheran refugees who were resettled there, especially the Palatinates in New York and the Salzburgers in Georgia.

Although this immigration was disrupted in the late eighteenth and early nineteenth centuries by the American Revolution (1775–83) and the Napoleonic Wars (1803–15), the flow of immigrants to North America resumed in the nineteenth century, when millions of European Lutherans migrated across the Atlantic Ocean, mainly drawn by the availability of new farmland in the Midwest. It is difficult to know how many Lutherans left congregations in Europe for North America, but an estimate of between seven and ten million nominal Lutherans might be plausible. For the most part these immigrants were individuals and families; immigration of organized groups, such as the Saxons who came to Missouri in the 1830s, was an exception to the general pattern. Given American voluntary religious patterns, immigrants were left on their own to form Lutheran congregations and denominations in Canada and the United States. Gathering these Lutheran immigrants into congregations was by no means automatic; they were scattered, there were few Lutheran pastors and congregations, and some Lutherans decided to take advantage of American religious options to join other churches or no churches at all. Despite strenuous evangelistic efforts by American Lutheran leaders, only a fraction of the European Lutheran immigrants ever joined Lutheran congregations in North America. Still, the Lutheran congregations they formed were religiously and socially vital to the new ethnic communities and supported the waves of new immigrants in their assimilation to their new countries. Immigrant Lutherans formed not only congregations and denominations but also schools, colleges, and seminaries, as well as an array of social service agencies, such as hospitals, orphanages, and other institutions.

After World War I, immigration to North America was sharply curtailed by economic and political conditions. There were also smaller numbers of European Lutherans who migrated during the nineteenth century to other areas of the world, especially to southern Africa, parts of South America (esp. Argentina and Brazil), and Australia. These immigrants, primarily Germans but with some Scandinavians, also formed their own ethnic Lutheran congregations and denominations, paralleling the North American experience. Lutheran congregations in these areas generally limited their work to immigrants and, in contrast to some in South Africa, were not directly related to other mission work in these areas. In the first part of the twentieth century, Lutheran migration was more often the result of wars and social upheavals, with Lutheran refugees from Eastern Europe being resettled in Western Europe and North America as a result of World War II and the extension of

Communism. Lutheran churches were directly involved in refugee resettlement, and some Lutheran groups, such as those from the Baltic countries, formed their own Lutheran churches in exile.

Chinese Lutherans and Lutheran missionaries who left after the Communist takeover of China in 1949 established Chinese Lutheran congregations in Hong Kong and in other areas of Southeast Asia. As well, Lutheran mission activity in parts of Africa, Asia, and Latin America has resulted in a substantial membership increase in Lutheran churches on these continents. The late twentieth century saw a growing migration from those areas to Europe and North America, resulting in the formation of some new ethnic Lutheran congregations, especially in the United States. Though the flow of Lutherans from the Global South has not been a major development to this point, it will probably be an increasing factor in the twenty-first century. Migration and the flow of refugees around the world have been an increasing Lutheran concern during the late twentieth century, and agencies such as Lutheran World Relief and Lutheran Immigration and Refugee Service have been deeply involved in and well known for assisting dislocated populations. Though these efforts are generally humanitarian in nature, and not done specifically with Lutheran populations, some Lutheran congregations have been formed by refugees in North America, especially among Hmong and Lao people from Southeast Asia, and by Sudanese people from Africa. The rise of immigration and refugees, with the resulting social and political pressures, has also engaged Lutherans in the larger and often contentious debate over immigration policies and restrictions.

See also Lutheran Social Services; Refugees

Bibliography

Bachman, J. W. *Together in Hope: 50 Years of Lutheran World Relief*. Kirk House, 1995; Bachmann, E. T., and M. B. Bachmann. *Lutheran Churches in the World: A Handbook*. Augsburg, 1989; Granquist, M. *Lutherans in America: A New History*. Fortress, 2015; Solberg, R. W. *Open Doors: The Story of Lutherans Resettling Refugees*. Concordia, 1992.

MARK A. GRANQUIST

Ministerium of Pennsylvania

As the first Lutheran synod organized in North America, the Ministerium of Pennsylvania (1748–1962) became the model for many other Lutheran denominations. When Henry Melchior Mühlenberg arrived in Pennsylvania in 1742, as called by three congregations, he found a number of Lutheran congregations already meeting but few ordained pastors. On August 14–15, 1748, Mühlenberg called together all the local Lutheran pastors who had been sent out from Halle. At this initial meeting they examined and ordained John Nicolaus Kurtz, adopted a common liturgy based on the earlier Lutheran models derived from the common liturgies of the Christian West, consecrated the new church building of St. Michael's Church (the first German Lutheran Church in Germantown, then a suburb of Philadelphia), and promised to meet annually on a trial basis. While there were only five German pastors present, twenty-four laypersons attended, representing ten different congregations plus the provost for Swedish Lutherans, Pastor Johan Sandin. The usefulness of the organization proved itself, and by the next year another convention and ordination were held in Lancaster. By 1750 it was seen as desirable to have a presiding officer, or superintendent, who was to serve only for a one-year term; the office was renamed president in later documents. A treasury was established in 1804. During years 1755–59 no meetings were held, but they were resumed again in 1760 with the encouragement of Carl Magnus Wrangel, provost of the Swedish Mission. In 1762, in reaction to a split in St. Michael's Germantown, a model congregational constitution was written by Mühlenberg, Wrangel, and Brunnholtz, the pastor at St. Michael's, for that congregation. This document became the model for later Lutheran congregations, and included voting by the members for major expenditures and limited terms for council members (instead of lifetime tenure). Not until 1781 did the ministerium adopt a constitution for itself, and not until the second constitution, in 1792, did lay delegates to ministerium meetings receive a vote. In 1787 the handwritten liturgy of 1748 was finally printed, along with a common hymnbook of 718 hymns based on the Halle hymnal. The ministerium was divided into five conferences in 1783, and in 1786 the second synod was founded as the Ministerium of New York. The Ministerium of Pennsylvania now had congregations in New Jersey, Maryland, Virginia, and western Pennsylvania. In 1803 a program of traveling missionaries was begun, and pastors were sent to Ohio, Illinois, and eventually to Minnesota and Texas. John Christian Frederick Heyer was sent as the first foreign missionary to India in 1841. By its centennial, the Ministerium of Pennsylvania had grown to 222 congregations and 67 pastors. It initially supported Franklin College (from 1787) and had transferred its support to Pennsylvania (later Gettysburg) College by 1832. During the nineteenth-century debates about revivalism and the use of English in the General Synod, the ministerium espoused a strong confessional stance and the use of English and/or German. Having left the General Synod earlier, the ministerium eventually led a coalition of synods in 1867 to found the General Council on the basis of the unaltered Augsburg Confession. By 1898 the General Council counted 505 congregations and 337 pastors and had its own Muhlenberg College and a seminary in Philadelphia. The "Mother Synod" led the way to the merger of 1918, founding the United Lutheran Church in America, having produced the English language *Liturgy for the Use of the Evangelical Lutheran Church* (later called *Church Book*) of 1860 and contributing more than one-quarter of the members to the new body. In 1916 it elected Harvey A. Weller as its first full-time president. By 1948 it numbered 604 congregations and 534 pastors. In 1953 a realignment of congregations saw the synod become almost solely an eastern Pennsylvania geographic entity. Its New Jersey congregations

had formed a new synod there in 1950, and by the 1962 LCA merger it was renamed the Eastern Pennsylvania Synod. A few years later it was divided into the Northeastern and Southeastern Pennsylvania synods.

See also Francke Foundations; General Council; General Synod; Mühlenberg, Heinrich (Henry) Melchior; United Lutheran Church in America

Bibliography

Bachmann, E. T. *The United Lutheran Church in America, 1918–1962.* Fortress, 1997; Evangelical Lutheran Ministerium of Pennsylvania and the Adjacent States. *Documentary History of the Evangelical Lutheran Ministerium of Pennsylvania and Adjacent States.* Board of Publication of the General Council of the Evangelical Lutheran Church in North America, 1898; Handley, G. E. "The Ministerium of Pennsylvania from 1748." *LQ* 10 (1998): 362–83; Pfatteicher, H. E. *The Ministerium of Pennsylvania.* Ministerium Press, 1938; Pfatteicher, H. E. *The Ministerium of Pennsylvania Celebrates Its 200th Anniversary.* Muhlenberg, 1948.

KIM-ERIC WILLIAMS

Ministry

Ministry is the public, divine office or service to which Christians are called and ordered by the Word of the God who justifies sinners for the sake of Jesus Christ alone though faith. When Jesus started his earthly ministry, he called people to repent and to believe in the gospel because the kingdom of God was near (Matt. 4:17; Mark 1:15). He also called apostles and sent out the seventy with the same gospel. After his crucifixion and resurrection, Jesus Christ expanded his disciples' mission to include both Israel and the gentiles, baptizing them in the name of the Father and the Son and the Holy Spirit (Matt. 10:5–8; 28:19). Beginning in Jerusalem, repentance and the forgiveness of sins were to be preached in Jesus's name to all nations (Luke 24:45–47). Thus, from a Lutheran perspective, preaching this gospel is the highest apostolic office and the foundation for all other offices (LW 40:36).

The New Testament describes various offices within the early Christian community, using words such as *presbyteros* (elder), *diakonos* (servant; deacon), and *episkopos* (overseer; bishop) to define a host of responsibilities carried out by the leaders of these congregations and successors of the apostles. What began as relatively fluid terms became more fixed positions in later centuries. Fairly early in the church's development, the bishop of a locality came to represent that congregation in the wider world, to preside at baptisms and the Lord's Supper, and above all to preach by expounding the Hebrew Scriptures and the developing New Testament canon. This is reflected, for example, in Irenaeus's attack *Against Heresies*, including the gnostics: he holds that the rule of faith and the succession of teacher-bishops help guarantee pure teaching in the church.

The one term not initially used for such officeholders among Christians was *hiereus* (Latin: *sacerdos*; designation for Old Testament priests), a word that the New Testament reserves for Christ or, by extension, the entire body of Christians (1 Pet. 2:9 [*hierateuma* for priesthood]; Rev. 1:6) or, of course, for the Jewish priests in Jerusalem. Only in the third century did Christians begin to associate the word *hiereus* with the office of bishop and (later) priest. In Germanic, Romance, and Scandinavian languages, among others, the word *presbyteros* became the word (e.g., in English) "priest," and since there was no separate word for *hiereus* or *sacerdos*, the sacerdotal aspects of the Old Testament priesthood became associated with Christian priests. In the Middle Ages, with many of the traditional episcopal functions now performed by priests (with the exceptions of ordination and confirmation), the bishop's work became more and more associated with political rule and power, since the officeholders were often from noble households and the dioceses controlled vast tracts of land and the peasants who worked them. At the same time, as the Lord's Supper became more and more associated with private Masses, priests became sacerdotal functionaries offering up the unbloodied sacrifice of Christ's body and blood for the sake of the dead.

In the Late Middle Ages—as part of the struggle between conciliarists, who posited ultimate authority in the church to the church council, and curialists, who insisted on the ultimate authority of the bishop of Rome—theologians argued that the pope (or council) also had authority over secular powers. The crowning of the Holy Roman emperor by the pope (first occurring with Charlemagne in 800) was said to indicate such preeminence. From this perspective, there developed an understanding that the church consisted of two separate classes: a secular class or estate and the higher, spiritual one (priests, monks, nuns, and bishops).

Martin Luther was heir to these various strands in Christian thought. He began by asserting that God's Word propounds impossible things beyond human comprehension: the promise of forgiveness of sins. Upon this word of promise alone, faith in the true God is founded (WA 25:163.23–26), over against human idols of valuing money, honor, power, and favor more than God. Moreover, the validity and efficacy of God's Word is often paradoxically measured by the fallible reception of its hearers (WA 38:554.16–24). Therefore one should not measure the gospel by the crowd of those who hear it but by the small group that grasps it by faith; for God works in hidden, inconspicuous ways, always disregarded by the world (WA 12:509.13–15). For Luther, the subject matter of theology is "the accused and lost human being and the justifying God or Savior" (LW 12:311). Consequently, whoever "knows how to distinguish the gospel from the law may thank God and know that he is a theologian" (LW 26:115). For Lutherans, theology is for proclamation.

Human sin entails not only the desire to "be like God, knowing good and evil" (Gen. 3:5), but also accounts for the natural rebelliousness of humanity, which wants "to be God and God not to be God" (LW 31:10). One temporal manifestation of this occurs in "cooking and brewing the two realms in each other," that is, mixing governmental and ecclesiastical authority in such a way that the government thought it controlled the gospel and pastors thought they should rule the world, all of which for Luther was simply diabolical (LW 13:194), especially as experienced under the papacy (LW 22:258–59; 36:72–73). While under the threat of excommunication, Luther published *Address to the Christian Nobility of the German Nation* in August 1520 (LW 44:115–217), *The Babylonian Captivity of the Church* in October 1520 (LW 36:3–126), and *The Freedom of a Christian* in November 1520 (LW 31:327–77). In them, Luther attacked the foundations of the papacy and its understanding of the ministry while developing his own approach to the matter.

In the *Address to the Christian Nobility*, Luther insists that all Christians are of one and the same spiritual estate. Having one baptism, one gospel, and one faith, all Christians are equal (*gleich*). "In that sense, we are all consecrated priests through baptism [1 Pet. 2:9]" (LW 44:127). "For whatever has crawled out of [the waters of] baptism may boast to have been consecrated priest, bishop, and pope, although it is not fitting for everyone to exercise such office" (LW 44:129). Equality in sharing Christ's priesthood and thus becoming priests in Christ means that no one can thrust oneself or one's authority on the other priests without their consent. Furthermore, by dispelling the papal claim that ordination confers a sacramentally infused "indelible character," Luther both sets aside the division between clergy and laity and, equally important, distinguishes the pastoral office from the officeholder, declaring that anything dreamed to the contrary was "human, fictitious talk, and rules" (LW 44:129).

In the *Babylonian Captivity*, Luther attacked the traditional numeration of seven sacraments, reducing them to three (baptism, Lord's Supper, and penance, where the latter was simply a daily use of baptism). Regarding the "sacrament" of ordination, which in Luther's day was most often reduced to setting aside people especially to recite private Masses, Luther states, "The church of Christ knows nothing of this sacrament; it is an invention of the papal church," bearing no promise of grace

and no New Testament witness (LW 36:106–7). Stressing clarity of purpose and proclamation, Luther asserts the church's need to discern between the Word of God and human words. Luther interprets Augustine's famous line ("I would not have believed the gospel if the authority of the church had not moved me") to mean that the church's proclamation of the gospel does not raise the church above the gospel, because that would put the church above God (LW 36:107–8). Succinctly put, the priesthood is the ministry of the Word, "not of the law but [of] the gospel," and if ordination is anything at all within the priesthood of all Christians, then it is nothing but a rite (*ritum*) for calling and commending someone to the church's ministry. Regardless of such a call, however, "Whoever neither knows nor preaches the gospel is not only not a priest or bishop but is a sort of pest to the church, who under the false title of priest or bishop, being dressed in sheep's clothing, actually oppresses the gospel and acts like a wolf in the church" (LW 36:116). True ordination for Luther is "calling to and entrusting with the office of ministry" (LW 38:197; cf. 7:146–47).

In both *Concerning the Institution of the Ministry of the Church* (1523; LW 40:3–44) and *On the Councils and Churches* (1539; LW 41:3–178), Luther defines various ministrations of God's Word exercised and recognized within the common priesthood or holy Christian people. For Luther, "A priest is not so much a presbyter or minister; for the former is born, but the latter are made. . . . In short, all Christians are priests, and all priests are Christians" (LW 40:18–19; cf. 41:152; 38:187). Despite the sixteen-year interlude, Luther's seven marks of the church remained virtually unchanged in both treatises, with the first four—the ministry of the Word, baptism, the Lord's Supper, and the keys—being identical. (See also the Smalcald Articles 3.4 [*BC* 319].) For Luther, the "ministry of the Word is the highest office in the church; in short, it is unique and belongs to all who are Christians, not only by right but by command" (LW

40:23; cf. WA 41:187.17–31). For that reason, to baptize "is incomparably greater than to consecrate bread and wine, for it is the greatest office in the church, the proclamation of the Word of God. Thus, women, when they baptize, function legitimately in the priesthood, not as a private act, but as the public and ecclesiastical ministry which belongs only to the priesthood" (LW 40:23).

The remaining three characteristics in both treatises are variations on a theme. The former treatise (1523) lists these: fifth, self-sacrifice, praise, and thanksgiving; sixth, prayer, especially the Lord's Prayer; and seventh, judging doctrine (LW 40:28–34). Although Christian priests hold all these in common, "plainly, it is one thing to exercise a right publicly and another to use it in times of necessity. Publicly one may not exercise a right without consent of all (*universitas*) or of the church. In times of necessity one may use it in any way as one determines" (LW 40:34).

In the latter work (1539), the church as the Christian, holy people is recognized externally: fifth, by consecrating or calling ministers (*Diener* = servants) or having offices that it shall administer; sixth, by prayer, praise, and thanksgiving; and seventh, by the cross (LW 41:154–66). Regarding the apparent insertion of calling people to the public ministry, it should be recalled that Luther's purpose for writing the 1523 treatise was to advise the Bohemians on calling ministers without the masquerade of episcopal ordination, which Luther deemed to be unnecessary since it had no foundation in Christ (LW 40:20–21). In fact, such ordination is not only degrading theater before God, but it actually removes those so ordained from Christ's priesthood (LW 40:20). Luther's 1539 treatise clarified his position in 1523: he emphasizes that the Holy Spirit selects competent men and, apart from times of necessity (*Not*), excepts women (1 Cor. 14:34), children, and incompetent people from the public ministry (LW 41:154–55).

In this context, the Lutheran confessional witness falls into place. The Triune God (CA 1) addressed the sinful reality of fallen humanity (CA 2) when the Word of God took on human nature, suffered, was crucified, died, and was raised to forgive and reconcile sinners with God the Father through the faith (CA 3) by which sinners are justified apart from all human efforts (CA 4). "In order to obtain such faith God instituted the office of preaching [*Predigamt*; Latin version: *ministerium*], to provide the gospel and the sacraments, as through means, by which God grants the Holy Spirit who effects faith, where and when he wills, in those who hear the gospel" (CA 5). Through the pure proclamation or teaching of this gospel and its corresponding expression in the sacraments, the Holy Spirit calls, gathers, enlightens, and sanctifies all Christians in one, true faith in the one, true God, thereby uniting them as his church (CA 7; BC 42–43). With respect to the regulation of this office, no one shall teach publicly, preach, or administer the sacraments in God's church without a regular (German: *ordentlich*; Latin: *rite*) call (CA 14) because the priesthood of the holy Christian people deeply desire to ensure that the gospel and its articles of faith are purely proclaimed in word and sacrament. Lutherans have often been prepared to forego external ecclesial unity to maintain the gospel's purity (Ap 14 [BC 222–23]; WA 34/2:387.1–388.24). When understood as an office of the Word, the confessional documents even are willing to view ordination as a sacrament (Ap 13.7–12 [BC 220–21]). At the same time, when dealing with the outward, humanly regulated aspects of church life, Lutherans were willing, to different degrees, to accept the authority of bishops (CA 28), and Luther even went so far as to consecrate two bishops to traditional sees. Moreover, by often using the word "superintendent" to designate those charged with the oversight of congregations, the reformers were harking back to Augustine, who in lectures on the Psalms had suggested translating the Greek word *episkopos* into Latin as *superintendens*.

A complex of philosophical, legal, and socioeconomic dynamics and developments since the Reformation accounts for the variety, to say nothing of confusion and controversy, among Lutherans regarding the ministry. In the sixteenth century and beyond, for example, territorial and national churches maintained close relations with governmental authorities, which often had the final say in appointments to church offices and which often subscribed to confessional documents (including the Augsburg Confession and the Book of Concord). In areas governed by non-Lutherans, more independent traditions developed. Thus, in justifying the Saxon elector's authorization of church visitations, Luther compared his prince's action to Constantine's and later referred to princes as emergency bishops. In many cities, the city council functioned as the parish council, calling and removing pastors. In colonial America, some of Henry Melchior Mühlenberg's struggles within the developing Ministerium of Pennsylvania revolved around finding equivalent ways of establishing patronage for congregations in a society where the government no longer could be called on to intervene on the church's behalf.

Again, some churches view ordination sacramentally, and others prefer a more functional ordering. This difference became particularly important in the nineteenth century, especially in the United States, as pastors and churches struggled to come to terms with certain democratic principles and, in line with earlier arguments by certain Pietists, viewed the common priesthood of believers as directly informing church governance.

Some Lutheran churches have maintained or adopted an episcopal polity, and others reject it as a matter of principle. Some call and ordain women to the pastoral office, and others reject such practices as unbiblical. Wittingly or unwittingly, these variations at times reflect the mixing of the two kingdoms, the law with the gospel. Human efforts to create a purer church and ministry fall prey to a kind of works-righteousness and thus may be seen to compromise God's institution of the office of proclamation.

See also Priesthood of All Believers; Sacraments

Bibliography

Bekenntnisschriften der evangelisch-lutherischen Kirche. Vandenhoeck & Ruprecht, 1982; Forde, G. O. *Theology Is for Proclamation.* Fortress, 1990; Grane, L. *The Augsburg Confession—A Commentary.* Trans. J. H. Rasmussen. Augsburg, 1981; Kittelson, J. M., and H. Wiersma. "The Priesthood of Believers, the Office of Ministry and Ordination in the Works of Martin Luther." *Lutherjahrbuch* 71 (2004): 252–54; Kolden, M., and T. Nichol. *Called and Ordained: Lutheran Perspectives on the Office of the Ministry.* Fortress, 1990; Leppin, V. "Wie reformatorisch war die Reformation?" *Zeitschrift für Theologie und Kirche* 99 (2002): 162–76; Masaki, N. "Call and Ordination." *LOGIA* 23 (Reformation, 2014): 25–32; Maurer, W. *Historischer Kommentar zur Confessio Augustana.* 2 vols. Gütersloher Verlagshaus-G. Mohn, 1976; Menacher, M. D. "Ten Years after JDDJ the Ecumenical Pelagianism Continues." *LOGIA* 18 (Holy Trinity, 2009): 27–45; Wengert, T. J. *Priesthood, Pastors, Bishops: Public Ministry for the Reformation and Today.* Fortress, 2008.

MARK D. MENACHER

Mission and Evangelism

Martin Luther's understanding of God's Word as his conversation with his human creatures made an emphasis on giving witness to the gospel a natural part of the Wittenberg reformer's own cultivation of the faith and practice of his hearers and readers. Luther's own preaching urged the Wittenberg congregation to share God's Word with each other (esp. in the household) and with those who had not come to faith in Christ. Although he did not have opportunities to witness to many unbaptized people, Luther did strive to cultivate faith in the baptized of his era who had not come to faith through the piety of the medieval church; that was the purpose of all his reform efforts. He also recognized that the witness to those beyond the pale of Christendom was a part of the church's mission. Without a secular government engaged in overseas imperialist activities, such as the Spanish, French, and English were pursuing, Luther had no practical means of going beyond the borders of his German- and Latin-speaking worlds. Yet he urged Germans to learn the catechism well in case they were taken prisoner by the Turks, who were invading German territory at the time, so that they could give witness to their faith. He promoted the witness to Jewish neighbors when that was possible. In the 1529 edition of the *Personal Prayer Book*, Luther concluded the fifty woodcuts of the history of salvation with a depiction of the sending of the disciples two by two. Therefore, the criticism of his lack of a sense of the church's mission by the founder of modern missiology, Gustav Warneck, and by others may well be ill-informed and misplaced.

Among his students were some who totally ignored the wider mission of bringing the gospel to those outside the church, but others viewed the history of the church as a history of mission, such as Wittenberg professor and preacher Georg Major. Nikolaus Selnecker, one of the authors of the Formula of Concord, told merchants in his Leipzig congregation that, on their trips to the Levant to buy spices and other goods, they should witness to their faith to the Muslims they encountered there. Another author of the Formula, Jakob Andreae, preached thirty-three sermons on how the illiterate majority of his hearers could witness to Christ even if they could not use the Bible, as their literate neighbors could do. He sought to train them in the use of the catechism to testify to Christ's saving work in conversation with Roman Catholics, Sacramentarians, Anabaptists, and Schwenckfelders.

In the period of Orthodoxy, Swedish governmental efforts to include tribal peoples of northern Scandinavia in their empire, including the Samelats, brought missionaries to the area to bring natives to the Christian faith. John Campanius (1601–83) worked among the Lenape in the North American colony of New Sweden in the 1640s and translated Luther's Small Catechism as well as portions of the Bible into their Delaware language. The Danish government's attempts to plant trading stations along the West African coast in the 1660s also were accompanied by modest and ultimately unsuccessful mission efforts. Duke Jakob Ketteler of Courland founded colonies in the 1650s and 1660s in what is now Gambia and Trinidad and sent Lutheran missionaries to both. Their work ended when Courland had to surrender its colonies.

In 1652 the theological faculty in Wittenberg issued what has become an infamous memorandum in which it allegedly claimed that since the gospel had at one time spread to all peoples, according to widespread medieval legendary accounts, Christians no longer had any missionary obligations. In fact, the memorandum was not addressing the question of the necessity of Christian mission. It instead answered the queries of a nobleman who wished to convert to Roman Catholicism and who argued that the Lutherans were not the true church because they were not sending out foreign missionaries. Johann Gerhard of the University of Jena had already answered this argument, both by maintaining that the command to send missionaries to those outside the faith was not part of the essentials of the saving faith required by every individual Christian and that Lutherans were indeed engaged in "foreign" mission work, citing the activities of the Danish and Swedish governments. Also individual Germans were going from Lutheran churches to distant parts of the world, although such examples were few and far between. Lübeck native Peter Heyling launched an initiative of his own after studying law in the Netherlands. During his journey to Ethiopia he encountered interference from Roman Catholics working there but won success at the court of the emperor. He supervised a translation of the New Testament into Amharic and brought his Lutheran witness to the monophysite faith of the Ethiopians. Turks executed him on a trip north into the Sudan because he refused to reject Christ.

The first European missionaries to establish a mission and, hence, a "majority-world" church that endured came from the German Lutheran Pietist establishment at Halle under August Hermann Francke. He answered the request of King Frederick IV of Denmark for aid in founding a mission at his government's colony at Tranquebar, among the Tamils of southeast India. On July 9, 1706, two Halle missionaries, Bartholomäus Ziegenbalg and Heinrich Plütschau, landed in Tranquebar. Plütschau returned after five years to engage in mission education in Germany; Ziegenbalg's work until his death in 1719 provided a model for later missionaries. He learned Tamil and led translation of the Bible, Luther's Small Catechism, and other works into the native language. His ethnographic studies recorded vital materials about Tamil culture and Hindu practices for European audiences. His intervention on behalf of a native woman against oppressive measures by local Danish officials earned him time in the Danish jail in Tranquebar. Ziegenbalg and Plütschau initiated a flood of German Lutheran missionaries who worked throughout the eighteenth century and into the nineteenth in Lutheran missions and for Anglican mission societies. Without the support of the Danish king, the Norwegian pastor Hans Poulsen Egede and his wife, Gertrud Rask, raised funds to sponsor a mission to Greenland from 1721 onward. Disappointed in his hopes of finding descendants of Danish settlers there, they lived among the animistic Eskimos, learning their language and instructing them in the Christian faith. Moravian missionaries who arrived in the 1730s tried to frustrate their work because of their Orthodox Lutheran proclamation, but they persisted. Their son Paul completed an Inuit translation of the New Testament and with his brother continued preaching the gospel in Greenland.

Francke's establishment in Halle also sent missionaries to minister to German emigrants in Russia and North America. Heinrich Melchior Mühlenberg gathered scattered German settlers into congregations, renewed existing congregations, and organized the Ministerium of Pennsylvania in 1748.

In the nineteenth century, Lutherans in all the lands with established churches organized separate mission societies to carry on work overseas. Mission training centers—in Neuendettelsau (1841) under Wilhelm Loehe (Löhe, 1808–72); Hermannsburg (1848) under Louis (1808–65) and Theodor Harms (1819–85),

from whose followers came the Bleckmar Mission (1892); Steeden (1861) under Friedrich August Brunn (1819–95); Breklum (1876) under Christian Jensen (1839–1900); and Kropp (1882) under Johannes Paulsen (1847–1916)—sent pastors for German emigrants in North and South America and Australia, and for native peoples in several lands, including lands in eastern and southern Africa, Papua New Guinea, China, and India. Neuendettelsau and Hermannsburg sent groups of settlers to North America and Africa, respectively, as seedbeds for the gospel among local native peoples. Similar schools arose in the Nordic lands, such as the School of Mission and Theology of the Norwegian Mission Society in Stavangar (1843) and the mission training programs of Peter Fjellstedt in Uppsala (1846) and of his former colleague, Per August Ahlberg (ca. 1860), in Örebo, Sweden.

The Leipzig Mission (1836)—founded as a specifically Lutheran alternative to the Basel Mission (1815), which represented a mix of Lutheran and Reformed streams of thought, and as an alternative to other "Union" missions, such as that of the Rhineland (Barmen Mission, 1828) and the Gossner Mission in Berlin (1836)—also founded what became Lutheran churches. Only slowly, in the twentieth century, did some German territorial churches assume responsibility, often in coordination with mission societies, for work overseas.

In the Nordic countries mission societies were established during the course of the nineteenth century, many in connection with revival movements in these lands and others by the national churches themselves. These included the Danish Missionary Society (1821) of Bone Falk Ronne (1764–1833) and the Danish Sudan Mission (1904). The Santal Mission (1867) of Hans Peter Börresen (1825–1921) and L. O. Skrefsrud (1840–1910), former Gossner missionaries, brought together efforts of Baltic and Nordic churches. Norwegian societies include the Norwegian Mission Society (1842), the Norwegian Church Mission (1843), the Norwegian Mission to Israel (1844), the

Church of Norway Mission (1873) of Hans Paludan Smith Schreuder (1817–82), the Evangelical Lutheran Free Church Mission, the Norwegian Lutheran Mission (1891), and the Scandinavian Christian Missions to Buddhists (1920). Swedish missionary societies include the Swedish Evangelical Missionary Society (1856), the Church of Sweden Mission (1874), and the Missionary Society of True Friends of the Bible (1911). Finnish missions include the Finnish Evangelical Lutheran Mission (1859); the Lutheran Evangelical Association in Finland (1873), arising from the revival movement of Frederik Gabriel Hedberg (1811–93), and its Swedish-speaking sister society; Finnish Lutheran Mission; and Finnish Lutheran Overseas Mission.

Lutherans aided missionary activities sponsored by British societies not only in India but also in Africa. The Church Missionary Society sent Halle pastor Johann Ludwig Krapf to eastern Africa in 1837; encountering stiff opposition from Roman Catholics in the area, he ranged over a wider territory, including northeastern Africa and Palestine, translating Scripture into Swahili. In 1846 Johann Rebmann, another Halle missionary, joined him, and they began building the church in Tanganyika (now Tanzania). Among other exemplary nineteenth-century missionaries is Ludwig Ingwer Nommensen, sent by the Rhineland Mission Society to the island of Sumatra in the Dutch East Indies (Indonesia) in 1861. The churches that grew from his efforts in his more than half a century of ministry among the Batak peoples have taken the Augsburg Confession as the basis of their own confessions of faith. Nommensen translated Luther's Small Catechism and the New Testament into Batak. He launched teacher training of Bataks in 1875, extending this training program to pastoral candidates in 1882. A similar effort began in Madagascar in 1866 when the Norwegian Mission Society sent John Engh and Nils Nilsen there. Noteworthy are the contributions of Lars Dahle, who worked in Madagascar from 1870 to 1888,

translating the Bible into Malagasy and publishing ethnographic studies. European and North American missions have led to the establishment of particularly strong Lutheran churches in Indonesia, India, Papua New Guinea, Tanzania, South Africa, Ethiopia, Nigeria, and Brazil.

In the nineteenth century, German and Nordic Inner Mission efforts to reach those who had left peasant villages to find work in newly developing industrial areas met with varied levels of success but were often too little and too late. These efforts were not always specifically Lutheran in orientation but represented a pious Protestant worldview. Leaders in Inner Mission included Johann Hinrich Wichern (1808–81) and Friedrich von Bodelschwingh (1831–1910). Workers organizations, often Marxist in orientation, provided social support for factory workers and won many of them from any religious affiliation in the Lutheran lands of northern and central Europe.

Lutheran churches in North America were at first absorbed into establishing congregations among European immigrants, many of whom had not had strong connections with the church in their native lands. Although many from Lutheran lands in Europe turned to other or no churches in the United States and Canada, many had their associations with the Christian faith strengthened because Lutheran churches provided a cultural community in which they could feel at home. Early on, the Lutheran church bodies thought in terms of overseas missions; immigrant congregations began to celebrate mission festivals, depositing collected funds in accounts for future work or supporting outreach efforts in Africa and Asia by mission societies in the homelands. The North American Lutheran churches also lent aid to struggling immigrant congregations in Latin America and Australia.

North American Lutherans also recognized mission opportunities within their own countries. Jewish mission has come and gone on the agendas of these churches. Scandinavian Lutherans followed the example of the

Norwegian Mission to Israel in organizing the Zion Society for Israel in 1878. The LCMS efforts to reach Jewish people with the gospel began in 1883, those of the Iowa Synod in 1893, and of the Ohio Synod in 1896. The Iowa Synod's E. N. Heinmann, himself a convert from Judaism, conduced his mission among Israel from 1903 to 1920. Currently another convert, Steven Cohen, heads Apple of His Eye, working among Jewish people under the auspices of the LCMS. Outreach to Native Americans came with the Loehe (Löhe) settlers, whose work in the Saginaw Valley of Michigan was cut short by the US government's moving their Native American neighbors farther west, but missionaries followed to Wisconsin and Minnesota with some success. Iowa Synod work among the Crow began in 1856; missionary Moritz Braeuniger fell a martyr at the hands of the Oglala in 1859. In 1861 the mission spread to the Cheyenne and Arapaho. The WELS began its mission to the Apache in 1892. Norwegian Synod pastor T. L. Brevig initiated work among Eskimo tribes in Alaska in 1894. Currently the independent Lutheran Association of Missionaries and Pilots organization brings the gospel to remote Alaskan and Canadian native communities.

Attempts by Southern Lutherans to ordain African American pastors produced few results in the period following emancipation. African American pastors organized the Alpha Synod of Freedmen in 1889, but it lasted only two years. Organized outreach to the African American community in North America was begun by churches of the Synodical Conference in 1877 and by the Ohio Synod in 1915. The appeal of Rosa Young (1890–1971), an Alabama schoolteacher, for help in educating children in central Alabama was directed by Booker T. Washington to the Synodical Conference mission in 1916. From her work and leadership came Concordia College in Selma, Alabama, and many congregations.

Not only did American Lutheran denominations enter the mission fields at home and abroad, but independent missionary societies

also originated in North America. Gustaf Swenson began work among Puerto Ricans in 1898. The Independent China Mission Society brought chiefly Norwegian supporters together after 1890. The LCMS college professor Edward L. Arndt (1864–1929) and his family raised financing on their own through their Evangelical Lutheran Mission for China and began work there in 1912; it was subsequently adopted by the LCMS. The Lutheran Orient Mission initiated work in 1910 among the Kurds. The Sudan Mission, organized by the Norwegian-American layman A. L. Gunderson in 1923, has worked chiefly in Cameroon and the Central African Republic. The World Mission Prayer League, currently active in twenty countries, brings together the work of the American Board of the Santal Mission (1891), the South American Mission Prayer League (1937), and from 1945 the former Lutheran World Crusade. Lutheran Bible Translators (1964) has translation work going in fifteen countries at present and has completed translations of the New Testament into thirty-six languages.

In 1842 the Ministerium of Pennsylvania sent Johann Friedrich Christian Heyer (1793–1873), who had come from Germany to organize congregations among immigrants, to the eastern Indian coast. The Andhra Evangelical Lutheran Church there traces its origins back to Heyer's work, although other Lutheran church missions contributed to its growth. The General Synod sent missionaries to Liberia in 1860. The United Synod of the South entered Japan in 1892; the UELC did likewise in 1898. The LCMS began its overseas work by supporting Leipzig Mission missionaries in India in 1894 when they became dissatisfied with their mission's stance on the inspiration of Scripture. Several Lutheran synods, such as Iowa and Augustana and the ELC, moved quickly to replace German missionaries expelled from India, Papua New Guinea, and African lands occupied by French or British troops during World War I. After World War II, mission work, in part transferred from

China after the Communist revolution, in part begun from fresh roots, spread quickly and brought Lutheran churches to many lands previously without the Lutheran confession. Each mission involved the efforts and sacrifices of families, with wives and children bearing burdens and giving witness as they ministered to the spiritual and physical needs of local peoples.

Medical missions accompanied many mission efforts. Anna Sarah Kugler graduated from medical school in 1879 and became a General Synod missionary in Guntar, East India, in 1882. Missionary doctors and nurses introduced hospitals into cultures such as those of India. The sacrifices of these personnel brought physical healing and the gospel of Christ to many. Organized care for orphans was also introduced by many missions. Lutherans ardently promoted education through mission efforts, particularly at the primary and secondary levels. Lutherans pioneered in radio work, with *The Lutheran Hour* of the Concordia Old Testament professor Walter A. Maier, founded in 1930. From this broadcast evolved an international outreach mission, *Lutheran Hour Ministries*, with work currently in thirty-six countries. Lutheran Vespers, founded by Pastor Harry Gregerson in 1947, broadcast gospel messages weekly through 2009. *Radio Voice of the Gospel*, a project of the LWF, began bringing Christian witness to Africa from Addis Ababa in 1963 but was closed by the Ethiopian Communist revolutionary government in 1977.

Women's groups have promoted North American Lutheran mission efforts through prayer, education, and raising financial support. Lutheran churches in North America began to reach out to other European-Americans as well through witnessing, training, and programs that invited neighbors into congregations. These programs had some success in the 1950s and 1960s although participation and support for evangelistic outreach has lagged in many congregations.

From the time of Ziegenbalg and Plütschau, who built on an already lively tradition, Lutherans have been active in mission around the world as a logical outgrowth of Martin Luther's theology of the Word of God and his desire to bring the gospel to all people.

See also Francke Foundations; Loehe, Wilhelm Konrad; Mission Societies and Academies; Seamen's Missions; Sudan Mission; Ziegenbalg, Bartholomäus

Bibliography

Granquist, M. *Lutherans in America: A New History*. Fortress, 2015; Kolb, R. "Late Reformation Lutherans on Mission and Confession." *LQ* 20 (2006): 26–43; Laury, P. *A History of Lutheran Missions*. Pilger, 1899; Lueking, F. D. *Mission in the Making: The Missionary Enterprise among Missouri Synod Lutherans, 1846–1963*. Concordia, 1964; Scherer, J. *That the Gospel May Be Sincerely Preached throughout the World*. Kreuz, 1982; Swanson, S. H. *Foundation for Tomorrow: A Century of Progress in Augustana World Missions*. Board of World Missions, Augustana Lutheran Church, 1960; Wolf, L. B. *Missionary Heroes of the Lutheran Church*. Lutheran Publication Society, 1911; Zeilinger, G. *A Missionary Synod with a Mission, . . . 1854–1929*. Wartburg, 1929.

ROBERT KOLB

Mission Societies and Academies

The theological preparation of candidates for missionary work has been an important issue in the German Protestant missionary movement. In 1800 a first Missionsseminar (Mission seminary, for training missionaries) was founded in Berlin by Pastor Johannes Jänicke (1748–1827). It started with seven students, who were instructed in English, Latin, homiletics, and Bible knowledge. About one hundred students were trained in the forty-nine years of its existence; they worked for the Church Missionary Society and for the Netherlands Missionary Society. The most famous graduate was Karl Gützlaff (1803–51), who went to China.

The Basel Mission, founded in 1815, established its own mission seminary in 1816. In the early phases of its existence, some Dutch Reformed, British Anglican, and German Lutheran missionaries were also trained there. Most of the students had a family background in the skilled trades. Until it ended in 1956, the institute trained more than twenty-five hundred students.

The Barmer Mission Society started in 1818 as an association to help the Basel Mission. A mission school was opened with the intention to prepare students for further training in Basel. However, beginning in 1825 the school developed into a seminary of its own. The Mission Seminary in Barmen became the training institution of the Rhenish Mission, which succeeded the Barmer Mission Society in 1828. The seminary at Barmen continued until 1970.

Next in line were seminaries such as the Berlin Mission Society (to be distinguished from Jänicke's Seminary), which existed from 1829 to 1939, and the Hamburg Mission Seminary of the North German Mission Society (founded in 1819), which lasted from 1839 to 1849. It can be seen as a predecessor of the Hermannsburger Missionsseminar, founded in 1849. Since its founding, more than six hundred students have graduated from Hermannsburg.

The Mission Seminary in Neuendettelsau (Bavaria) was founded in 1853 and operated until 1985. More than eight hundred pastors and missionaries graduated in Neuendettelsau. Other mission seminaries existed in Breklum (1877–1931) and in Leipzig (1879–1949). Karl Graul, director of the Leipzig Mission from 1844 to 1860, had been in favor of a university-based academic training for missionaries, but it proved difficult to attract applicants with a university degree, and therefore the seminary was founded.

This points to one of the inherent tensions of these institutions: often mission seminaries were seen as insufficiently academic by university standards. Although a conference of mission seminaries' teachers was established in 1908, it remained challenging to guarantee the necessary academic qualifications. At the same time, supporters of mission tended to mistrust academic training, and mission societies were hesitant to invest in these educational institutions. Thus chronic underfunding was a continuous problem.

After World War II and during the processes of decolonization, the relationship between mission societies and the churches in Africa, Asia, and Latin America changed, and there were questions whether Germans training Germans in Germany for missionary work in the partner churches would still be an appropriate model; this also led to the gradual phasing out of the mission seminaries. Today there is increasing interest in researching the role of mission seminaries in training missionaries, the formation of those group identities and networks, and the social control they exercised.

See also Mission and Evangelism

Bibliography

Altena, T. *"Ein Häuflein Christen mitten in der Heidenwelt des dunklen Erdteils": Zum Selbst- und Fremdverständnis protestantischer Missionare im kolonialen Afrika 1884–1918.* Esp. 303–14. Waxmann, 2003; Gründler, W. "Das deutsche Missionsseminar." *Neue Allgemeine Missionszeitschrift* 6 (1931): 161–76; Kluge, H. *Die "allgemein missionarische" Ausbildung der Missionare: Referat auf der ersten Missionslehrer-Konferenz in Berlin den 6. und 7. Juli 1908.* Verlag der Missionsbuchhandlung, 1908; Reller, J., ed. *Ausbildung für Mission: Das Missionsseminar Hermannsburg von 1849 bis 2012.* LIT, 2015. Schlunk, M. "Missionsseminare und -institute." *RGG* 4:81–83. 2nd ed. Mohr, 1930.

FRIEDER LUDWIG

Mömpelgaard/Montbéliard Colloquy

The Mömpelgaard (French: Montbéliard) Colloquy is a dialogue between Lutheran representatives of the church of Württemberg and Calvinist representatives of the Genevan Reformation in 1586. Mömpelgaard/Montbéliard, a French duchy and enclave under the rule of the Dukes of Württemberg, officially belonged to the Lutheran confession of the faith but as a French-speaking territory had absorbed much of the Genevan Reformation. To resolve tensions within the duchy's churches, in part arising out of the definition of Wittenberg theology in the Formula of Concord (1577) and Book of Concord (1580), Duke Ludwig of Württemberg had his cousin, Friedrich, the Count of Mömpelgaard, organize a dialogue between (1) Johann Andreae and Lucas Osiander, representatives of the Württemberg court, and (2) Theodore Beza of Geneva and Abraham Musculus of Bern. The dialogue took place on March 21–26, 1586, and set in place the chief issues of difference between Lutheran and Reformed traditions for the future.

The doctrine of predestination had previously played a small role in Lutheran-Reformed controversy. At Mömpelgaard, agreement could not be reached on the predestination of the damned. Andreae held strictly to the law/gospel hermeneutic, which governed the treatment of the topic in the Formula of Concord, which he had helped write, in line with his statement on the subject in the Strasbourg Concord of 1563, which rejected double predestination. Beza cited Luther's *De servo arbitrio* in defense of his doctrine of double predestination, thus interpreting the Wittenberg reformer's statements outside the framework of the distinction of law and gospel.

Chief matters of controversy were the presence of Christ in the Lord's Supper and the related christological issues. Andreae argued for the standard Lutheran definitions embodied in the phrases "partaking [of Christ's body and blood] through the mouth" and "the partaking [of Christ's body and blood] by the ungodly" (who, by virtue of the promises in the words of institution, do receive Christ's body and blood but because of lack of faith receive no benefit from them). Beza argued for the spiritual presence of the person of Christ in the Supper and for partaking only by the faithful, even when they are unworthy. Beza further rejected the understanding of the communication of the attributes of Christ's divine and human natures in the manner of the Formula of Concord, arguing that the human nature by virtue of being human cannot be in more than one place at one time and, thus, after the ascension is at God's right hand. Andreae repeated the standard argument advanced by Luther that the right hand of God is not a place but a status (Dan. 7:13–14) and that because in the personal union of God and the human creature in Jesus, his humanity shares (but does not possess as its own) his divine characteristics, his body and blood in mysterious fashion can be in more than one place at one time.

Baptism and the use of images and various musical styles in churches also commanded the attention of the disputants. On the latter subject they found substantial agreement, although Andreae defended the use of organs, polyphony, and the graphic arts, while Beza preferred simplicity, the use of psalms, and as little decoration as possible in the churches. On baptism the differences became clear as the nature of baptism as a form of God's Word, which has re-creative power in its promise based on Christ's death and resurrection, was discussed. Beza's efforts to avoid any medieval "magical" power to the water prevented him from accepting Andreae's teaching of regeneration through the sacrament.

Publication of rumors regarding the colloquy detrimental to the Württemberg representatives led to their publishing their protocols of the colloquy despite an agreement that they would not be published. This provoked Beza's publication of his account of the exchanges. The ensuing public debate marked the further disintegration of the relationship between Reformed and Lutheran churches.

See also Baptism; Beza, Theodore; Calvinism as a Second Reformation; Christology; Colloquy; Formula of Concord; Lord's Supper; Predestination; Predestination (Election) Controversy

Bibliography
Raitt, J. *The Colloquy of Montbéliard.* Oxford University Press, 1993.

Robert Kolb

Monasteries, Evangelical

Martin Luther's treatise *The Judgment of Martin Luther on Monastic Vows* (1521; LW 44:243–400) encouraged the mass exodus from the medieval monastic orders that had already begun. Upon reading it, Prince Frederick the Wise sent Luther a fine piece of cloth for new clothes, suggesting that Luther could now take off his monk's habit and dress himself more stylishly, something that Luther did not do until 1524. For the most part, the history of the Reformation saw the transference of the "monastic" community to the "family" community.

The household was the new monastery, with father and mother as bishops. Nevertheless, a few monasteries, especially those for women, continued throughout this period in Lutheran territories. In the eighteenth century, the Moravian Church (Brüdergemeine) was founded by Count Nikolaus Ludwig von Zinzendorf (1700–1760), himself influenced by the Lutheran Pietism of Halle. This fellowship was primarily a movement rather than a tight-knit community, but especially at Herrnhut, Germany, and Bethlehem, Pennsylvania, it did keep alive a sense of community within the Reformation churches.

In 1935 Dietrich Bonhoeffer (1906–45) wrote, "The restoration of the church must surely depend on a new kind of monasticism, which has nothing in common with the old but a life of uncompromising discipleship, following Christ according to the Sermon on the Mount" (285). The early to mid-twentieth century saw the birth of a new kind of Evangelical monasticism: the Community of Grandchamp (Switzerland) and the Community of Taizé (France). The Community of Grandchamp, in Areuse, Switzerland, is an ecumenical community of women dedicated to furthering Christian unity. Their life and vision are shaped by this prayer for unity. The sisters come from several different Protestant traditions. They follow *the Rule of Taizé*.

Brother Roger founded Taizé in 1940. Without his realizing it directly, the Community of Taizé embodied a type of monasticism Bonhoeffer had called for: one grounded in the spirit of the Beatitudes (joy, simplicity, and mercy). Brother Roger's *Rule of Taizé* (1952–53) is considered one of the most visionary Gospel meditations of the twentieth century. The Community of Taizé is openly ecumenical and dedicated to reconciliation among Christians and all people. The brothers come from many different churches, including Roman Catholic. The community consists only of men who take the vows of poverty, obedience, and celibacy. The community's influence has spread throughout the world,

and young people gather in Taizé by the tens of thousands each year. The songs of Taizé are sung by Christians worldwide.

A different expression of community arose in Scotland. The Iona Community was founded by George MacLeod in 1938. He brought together unemployed skilled workers with seminarians in training to rebuild the old monastery on the island of Iona (west coast of Scotland) and to spiritually rebuild community in the life of the church. The Iona Community has become a witness to a deep spiritual life lived in a "community" that is dispersed around the world. Today, it is a popular place for spiritual retreats attracting a continual flow of pilgrims.

The Communities of Grandchamp and Taizé inspired the creation of many new Evangelical monasteries in the aftermath of World War II, most notably in Germany. The focus of these communities has been ecumenism and even more broadly reconciliation as the church sought to understand its failure to witness more publicly through the horrors of the first half of the twentieth century, especially in Germany. Several of these new evangelical communities, such as the Community of Imshausen (1955) or the Evangelical Sisterhood of Mary (Evangelische Marienschwesternschaft Darmstadt), are intentional communities (often for both men and women, singles or married couples). Other communities do not have a "core" group of persons residing in one place but members dispersed throughout the world (as the Iona Community). One such community is the Evangelical Michael Brotherhood (Evangelische Michaelsbruderschaft). The members are organized by regions, meeting occasionally for community time, and are dedicated to the deepening of spiritual life and the renewal and unity of the church. The Michael Brotherhood consists of both ordained leaders and laypersons. In North America, the Deaconess Community of the Evangelical Lutheran Church in America is a community of women devoted to a ministry of serving with love and prophetic diakonia.

See also Bonhoeffer, Dietrich; Convents; Deaconesses

Bibliography

Bonhoeffer, D. *London, 1933–1935*. Fortress, 2007; Bultmann, C., ed. *Luther und das monastische Erbe*. Mohr Siebeck, 2007; Clément, O. *Taizé: A Meaning to Life*. GIA Publications, 1997; Clifford, C., ed., *A Century of Prayer for Christian Unity*. Eerdmans, 2009; Muir, A. *Outside the Safe Place: An Oral History of the Early Years of the Iona Community*. Wild Goose, 2011; Oberman, H. A. "Martin Luther contra Medieval Monasticism: A Friar in the Lion's Den." In *Ad fontes Lutheri: Toward a Recovery of the Real Luther*, ed. T. Maschke et al., 183–213. Marquette University Press, 2001; Roger, Brother. *Parable of Community: Basic Texts of Taizé* [including the *Rule of Taizé*]. Mowbray, 1980.

DIRK G. LANGE

Moravian Church (Unitas Fratrum)

The Unitas Fratrum (Unity of the Brethren) is a global rather than American Protestant denomination organized into some two dozen provinces. The "Moravian" name is a misnomer since few members are ethnically Moravian. It is only called the Moravian Church in English-speaking lands. Over 90 percent of the members of the Unitas Fratrum today are African or Afro-Caribbean.

The Unitas Fratrum was founded in Bohemia by Gregory the Patriarch in 1457, during the Czech Reformation. Like the Waldensians, Gregory believed that Constantine had corrupted the church by making it part of the Roman Empire. Inspired by the writings of the pacifist Peter Chelcicky (Petr Chelčický, ca. 1390–ca. 1460), he formed a voluntary church dedicated to following Christ's teachings in the Sermon on the Mount. In 1467 the Brethren formalized their separation by establishing their own priesthood and consecrating their own bishop. Their worship services were entirely in the language of the people (either Czech or German), and they established schools to teach men and women to read the Bible. They strongly encouraged congregational singing and published their first hymnal in 1501.

The Brethren contacted Martin Luther shortly after his return to Wittenberg after the Diet of Worms. Luther arranged for the publication of their catechism and their confession of faith. The Brethren adopted Luther's doctrine that there are two sacraments rather than seven, and they stopped the practice of rebaptizing converts. However, the Brethren resisted Luther's teaching on justification by faith alone, insisting that faith must be completed in love. Bishop Luke of Prague defined six things as essential for salvation. Three things are God's actions: creation, redemption, and sanctification; the others are the human response in faith, love, and hope. Without love and hope, there is no faith, he said. After the Smalcald War, the Brethren cooled toward the Lutherans and gravitated more toward the Reformed church. In 1618 the Brethren participated in the Czech rebellion that launched the Thirty Years' War. When the Hapsburgs regained control of Bohemia and Moravia, they outlawed the Unitas Fratrum, and thousands of Brethren chose exile.

In 1722 several Protestants from Moravia sought refuge on the estate of Count Nikolaus von Zinzendorf in Saxony. They built the village of Herrnhut, and in 1727 they signed a Brotherly Agreement that made Herrnhut a unique religious community within the Lutheran parish of Berthelsdorf. Soon the Herrnhuters adopted several practices of the ancient Christian church, such as agape meals, the kiss of peace, and the Easter dawn vigil. They also started each day with a verse of Scripture chosen for that day. *Moravian Daily Texts*, or *Losungen* (watchwords), remains one of the most popular lay devotional guides for all Protestants in Germany. The Brüdergemeine (Community of Brethren) created by Zinzendorf in Herrnhut was not identical to the original Unitas Fratrum, but it shared so many features that the Moravians in Herrnhut considered 1727 as the renewal of the old church. Both the old and new Brethren instituted strict congregational discipline, allow women to give pastoral care to women, made music central to worship, and emphasized education. The identification with the old Unitas Fratrum was solidified in 1735 when Daniel Ernst Jablonski, one of the last two bishops of the Unitas Fratrum in Poland, ordained David Nitschmann of Herrnhut as a bishop of the Unitas Fratrum. Two years later Zinzendorf was made a bishop. The church adopted Zinzendorf's "Tropus" idea in the 1740s, which allowed members to hold joint membership in their national church and in the Unitas Fratrum. Thus he remained a Lutheran even though he was a Moravian bishop.

Zinzendorf was a Lutheran theologian, and the theology of the new Brethren was heavily influenced by Luther's doctrine of grace. Under his influence Moravian devotion focused primarily on the blood and wounds of Christ and the joy of salvation. In the eighteenth century Moravians wrote thousands of hymns and musical compositions. They also founded several religious settlements in Europe and America. Christiansfeld in Denmark is now a UNESCO world heritage site. The church also established many boarding schools, such as Fulneck in England, where Benjamin Henry LaTrobe studied, and Salem Academy and College in North Carolina, which claims to be the oldest women's school in the United States. Meanwhile in the English colonies of America, Zinzendorf had a sharp disagreement with Henry Melchior Mühlenberg, leader among American Lutheran pastors. Only in the 1990s did dialogue between Moravians and the ELCA lead to a "full communion" agreement.

The Moravians' greatest impact on Christian history was in the area of cross-cultural missions. They sent their first missionaries from Herrnhut in 1732 to the island of St. Thomas to preach to enslaved Africans. They pioneered methods that were later used to great success by English Baptists and Methodists, most notably the use of lay evangelists. They were the first church to ordain women, including women of African heritage, as deacons in the 1730s. By 1740 they had converts from Greenland to South Africa. In the nineteenth century hundreds of Lutheran missionaries were trained at the Moravian mission school in Kleinwelke, Germany. As part of their mission effort, the Moravians wrote the first grammars and dictionaries of Delaware, Tibetan, and several other languages. In 1957 the church was reorganized, and the former mission areas were granted authority over their own affairs. At that time The Ground of the Unity was adopted as the church's official statement of faith, yet it acknowledges the validity of the Augsburg Confession and other creeds of Christianity.

See also Zinzendorf, Nikolaus Ludwig von

Bibliography

Atwood, C. *Theology of the Czech Brethren from Hus to Comenius.* Pennsylvania State University Press, 2009; Comenius, J. A. *The Bequest of the Unity of the Brethren.* Trans. M. Spinka. National Union of Czechkoslovak Protestants in America, 1940; Crews, C. D. *Faith, Hope, and Love: A History of the Unitas Fratrum.* Moravian Archives, 2008; Crews, C. D., and R. Starbuck, eds. *Records of the Moravians among the Cherokees: Early Contact and the Establishment of the First Mission.* Cherokee Heritage Press, 2010; Hamilton, J. T., and K. Hamilton. *History of the Moravian Church: The Renewed Unitas Fratrum, 1722–1957.* Moravian Church in America, 1967; Sensbach, J. *Rebecca's Revival: Creating Black Christianity in the Atlantic World.* Harvard University Press, 2005; Wagner, W. *The Zinzendorf-Muhlenberg Encounter: A Controversy in Search of Understanding.* Moravian Historical Society, 2002; Wheeler, R. *To Live upon Hope: Mohicans and Missionaries in the Eighteenth-Century Northeast.* Cornell University Press, 2008.

Craig D. Atwood

Mörlin, Joachim

The German Lutheran theologian and pastor Joachim Mörlin (1514–71) was a defender of Lutheranism in the controversies among the second generation of the reformers. He was born in Wittenberg on April 6, 1514, the son of Jodok Mörlin, a professor of philosophy. In 1521 his father moved the family to Westhausen, near Coburg, but Joachim returned to Wittenberg in 1532, where he studied under Luther, Melanchthon, and Bugenhagen, earning the MA degree in 1536. In 1539 he became deacon in the city church at Wittenberg as well as Luther's substitute. In 1540 he received his doctorate in theology and, upon Luther's recommendation, was named superintendent in Arnstadt. Deposed in 1543 after disagreements with the Count of Schwarzburg, he was called in 1544 as superintendent to Göttingen, where he published his *Enchiridion*, or catechetical elaboration based on Luther's Small Catechism, one of the most frequently printed catechisms based on Luther's in the sixteenth century. Mörlin's tenure at Göttingen was cut short by the Augsburg Interim of 1548.

In 1550 he was called as cathedral preacher and inspector at Königsberg, where he soon came into conflict over the doctrine of justification with Andreas Osiander, a professor of theology there. Duke Albrecht of Prussia supported Osiander and, a few months after Osiander's death, forced Mörlin to leave. In 1553 he received a call to Braunschweig as superintendent, with his former associate in Königsberg, Martin Chemnitz, joining him as coadjutor there a year later. Mörlin and Chemnitz worked to deepen Braunschweig's commitment to the Lutheran Church and to strengthen its pastorate. Thus in 1563 all ministers in Braunschweig were required to subscribe to a *corpus doctrinae* (body of doctrine), a collection of Lutheran confessions of faith for the city, which differed in content from Philip Melanchthon's *Corpus Doctrinae* and also attempted to prevent the introduction of Reformed teaching there. Both Mörlin and Chemnitz played mediating roles in several inter-Lutheran disputes. In 1556 he was summoned to Bremen to settle a conflict between Johann Timann and Albrecht Hardenberg over the doctrine of the Lord's Supper. In 1557 he tried, without success, to bring resolution to the disputes between Melanchthon and Matthias Flacius through the Coswig Colloquy. In 1558 he sought to mediate between Flacius and Victorin Strigel over the doctrine of original sin, which eventually led to a break in Mörlin's friendship with Flacius.

In 1567 Duke Albrecht of Prussia, invited Mörlin to return to Königsberg to help resolve doctrinal division over Osiander that still lingered. Mörlin was disinclined to leave Braunschweig but was granted a leave of absence. He and Chemnitz both traveled to Königsberg, where they drafted the *Repetitio corporis doctrinae Christianae*, which rejected a number of controverted teachings (including that of Osiander) and brought confessional agreement to the territory. Having been coaxed back to Prussia, Mörlin became bishop of Samland in 1568. His efforts to address controversy and achieve doctrinal unity helped to consolidate Lutheranism in the generation after Luther's death. His work with Chemnitz in Braunschweig highlighted the need for agreement and introduced the means to achieve it. He died at Königsberg on May 29, 1571.

See also Chemnitz, Martin; Flacius, Matthias Illyricus, and the Flacians; Luther Interpretation and Reception; Melanchthon, Philip; Osiander, Andreas; Wittenberg Circle, Parties within

Bibliography

Diestelmann, J. *Joachim Mörlin: Luthers Kaplan—"Papst der Lutheraner."* Freimund, 2003; Kolb, R. "The Braunschweig Resolution: The *Corpus Doctrinae Prutenicum* of Joachim Mörlin and Martin Chemnitz as an Interpretation of Wittenberg Theology." In *Confessionalization in Europe, 1555–1700*, ed. J. M. Headly et al., 67–89. Ashgate, 2004.

GERHARD BODE

Morogoro, Lutheran Junior Seminary

The Lutheran Junior Seminary at Morogoro is a leading Lutheran school in Tanzania. At independence (1961), Christian churches were responsible for 60 percent of education in Tanganyika (Tanzania); the Lutheran Church was the second largest contributor. When the Leipzig Mission departed at the outbreak of World War I (1914), it had already established about a hundred schools with 8,500 students. Out of this developed the premier Lutheran secondary school at Ilboro in 1946. This school produced a number of government ministers for the first national cabinet, together with a significant number of church leaders.

As a result of the Tanzanian Education Act (1969), church schools were nationalized in January 1970. The churches appealed to the government for a way to educate their future leaders and were allowed to open junior seminaries, encompassing grades nine through twelve. Bishop Stefano Moshi and Evangelical Lutheran Church in Tanzania (ELCT) general secretary Joel Maeda planned in advance to open a Lutheran Junior Seminary (LJS). Pupils gathered for the first class in January 1969 at Kinampanda in the teachers training college. In early 1970 LJS moved to Vuga Bible Camp in the Usambara Mountains. Though classes were small and space limited, LJS was quickly recognized for its key role in training lay and pastoral leadership. Even the first three pastors who led LJS became bishops: Sebastian Kolowa, Northeastern Diocese; Stefano Msangi, Pare Diocese; and Dr. Hance Mwakabana, Eastern and Coastal Diocese.

When Joel Ngeiyamu became the executive secretary of the ELCT (1970), he established a board and organized departments as LJS began to grow. In 1975 LJS moved to a 120-acre plot in Morogoro, and 86 boys, chosen by qualifying exam, began the school year. In 1978 LJS became coed. An agriculture department was organized to help it become self-sustaining. In 1979 a leadership department was established for the purpose of training leaders and providing teachers for Christian education. This course produced many pastors, assistants to bishops, and even the Anglican bishop of Tanga. In 1980 the Swahili Language Training Center moved from Moshi to Morogoro; it trained more than two thousand expatriates from many countries and churches. A kindergarten was established and a program was developed for training kindergarten teachers by using the Montessori method. The LJS established an A-level (university preparatory) program in 1980, eliminating the need for qualified pupils to seek education elsewhere.

Joel Ngeiyamu hoped, through establishing LJS in Morogoro, to strengthen the church in that area. The original Lutheran Seminary, established in 1910 in the mountains overlooking LJS, was destroyed in World War I. British authorities removed the Lutheran Church from Morogoro in World War II, not allowing it to return until 1956. When LJS moved to Morogoro, only one Lutheran congregation existed; by 2015 there were eight. In 1999 the Morogoro Diocese established a Mission District centered at LJS, with pastors and students reaching out in evangelism. This resulted in the baptism of over twelve thousand new Christians from surrounding Muslim and Masai communities.

LJS continues to provide ELCT leadership. Alumnus Amani Mwenegoha became executive secretary (1987–2005), and many bishops are graduates. Currently LJS has about eight hundred students equally divided between secondary and A-levels. More than two thousand graduates are outstanding doctors, pastors, engineers, professors, lawyers, human rights advocates, and politicians.

See also Moshi, Stefano Ruben; Tanzania

Bibliography

Gustafson, M., ed. *Habari Zetu*. LJS Press, 1994; Lema, A. A. *The Lutheran Church's Contribution to Education in Kilimanjaro 1893–1933*. Tanzania Notes and Records, 1968; Maanga, G., ed. *Injili Kamili, Historia ya KKKT*. Moshi Lutheran Press, 2013.

HERBERT J. HAFERMANN

Mosheim, Johann Lorenz von

The church historian, educational reformer, and homiletician Johann Lorenz von Mosheim (1693–1755) taught at Kiel and Helmstedt, then in 1747 became chancellor at the recently established University of Göttingen, whose statutes mandating piety, irenicism, and freedom of teaching within confessional bounds had shaped the university's founding a decade earlier. Mosheim drew on critical historiography of the early Enlightenment to refute deism and revitalize Lutheranism. Using contextual interpretation, source criticism, and the ideal of "impartiality," he helped found ecclesiastical history as an autonomous discipline free from dogmatic premises, earning him a reputation as "the father of modern church history." His work, including the widely translated *Introduction to Ancient and Modern Church History* (1755), eschewed confessional polemics and treated the church as a diverse and changing human society in time.

A noted preacher, Mosheim also influenced contemporary homiletics, advocating clearly reasoned and practically oriented sermons designed to instruct the mind, move the will, and stir hearers toward ethical development.

See also Arnold, Gottfried; History

Bibliography

Fleischer, D. *Zwischen Tradition und Fortschritt: Der Strukturwandel der protestantischen Kirchengeschichtsschreibung im deutschsprachigen Diskurs der Aufklärung.* Spenner, 2006; Howard, T. A. *Protestant Theology and the Making of the Modern German University.* Oxford University Press, 2006; Mulsow, M., et al. *Johann Lorenz Mosheim (1693–1755): Theologie im Spannungsfeld von Philosophie, Philologie und Geschichte.* Harrassowitz, 1997.

ERIC CARLSSON

Moshi, Stefano Ruben

Stefano Ruben Moshi (1906–76) was a bishop at the forefront of the indigenization of the Lutheran Church in Tanzania. He was born May 6, 1906, at Mamba Kotela on the slopes of Mount Kilimanjaro. His father, Ruben, was an early evangelist and teacher for the Leipzig Mission and served as their indigenous representative at the Evangelical Ecumenical Council (1911) in Dar es Salaam. Stefano began his schooling at Gonja, in the Pare Mountains, where Ruben was teaching in a school established by the Leipzig Mission.

From Gonja the family returned to Kotela, where Stefano continued his education until 1922. After serving as a bush schoolteacher, assisting in primary education, he studied at Marangu Teachers College (MTC) from 1926 to 1929. During the next five years he taught there and carried on private studies with the University of London, from which in 1932 he received a Certificate in Education-Class 1. He also had privately been studying theology and later studied at Lwandai Theological Seminary. He was ordained on December 26, 1949.

In 1952 Stefano represented the entire Lutheran community of Tanganyika (Tanzania) at the Lutheran World Federation (LWF) assembly in Hannover. From there he went to the United States and studied for a semester at the Lutheran Bible Institute (Minneapolis), after which he visited Lutheran churches in the country. Returning to a leadership position at MTC, he was chosen in 1955 to be vice president and by 1958 to be president of the Lutheran Church of Northern Tanganyika (LCNT), the first Tanzanian head of a Lutheran church. The LCNT was then the largest Lutheran group in Tanganyika. He served as delegate to numerous church conferences, both nationally and internationally.

When the Evangelical Lutheran Church in Tanzania (ELCT) was formed in 1963, he was chosen to be its head. On Pentecost 1964 he was installed as bishop by Bishop Hanns Lilje of Hannover. He served (1963–70) on the executive committee of the LWF. In 1965 he was chosen as the first Tanzanian head of the Christian Council of Tanzania (CCT). In 1968 he was confirmed as the presiding bishop of the ELCT and in 1970 was awarded doctor of divinity degrees from Gustavus Adolphus College (St. Peter, Minnesota) and Concordia Seminary (St. Louis).

Active in the preparations for the LWF assembly in Dar es Salaam (1977), he was a vigorous leader in every respect until his death on August 16, 1976.

See also Morogoro, Lutheran Junior Seminary; Tanzania

Bibliography

Anderson, W. B. *The Church in East Africa, 1890–1974.* Central Tanganyika Press, 1977; Danielson, E. R. *Forty Years with Christ in Tanzania, 1928–68.* Lutheran Church in America, 1977; Maanga, G., ed. *Injili Kamili, Historia ya KKKT.* Moshi Lutheran Press, 2013.

HERBERT J. HAFERMANN

Mozambique

A former Portuguese colony, Mozambique became independent in 1975. Soon afterward, a seventeen-year civil war started, during which hundreds of thousands of people died and more than a million people fled the country. Lutheran World Services workers doing relief work in the country started the Evangelical Lutheran Church in Mozambique (ELCM) in

1989. In 1999 the ELCM became a member of the LWF. At the same time the church divided. Assisted by the LWF and the Lutheran Communion in Southern Africa (LUCSA), several reconciliation meetings were held between 2001 and 2003, and in August 2003 a new church council was elected. The ELCM has more than twelve thousand members.

The Igreja Evangélica Luterana do Brasil (IELB) began work in Mozambique in 2006 on foundations laid by social services established by the Lutheran Church of Canada. The church had fourteen congregations with twelve hundred members in 2015.

See also Igreja Evangélica Luterana do Brasil (IELB) (Evangelical Lutheran Church of Brazil)

Bibliography
The Evangelical Lutheran Church in Mozambique. *The Growth of a Young Church*. http://www.ielmlucsa.blogspot.de/2007/01/growth-of-young-church.html.

F R I E D E R   L U D W I G

Mühlenberg, Heinrich (Henry) Melchior

As a pastor and the founder of the Evangelical Lutheran Ministerium of Pennsylvania and Adjacent States (1748), Heinrich (Henry) Melchior Mühlenberg (1711–87) was a lifelong associate of Friedrich Michael Ziegenhagen, court chaplain in London, and Gotthilf August Francke, director of the Franckean Anstalt in Halle, Germany. Born in Einbeck, Hannover, on September 6, 1711, Mühlenberg was the seventh of nine children of a successful shoemaker, Nicolaus Melchior (ca. 1660–ca. 1723) and Anna Maria Kleinschmid (1675–1747). Following his father's death, Mühlenberg went to work to support the family but continued to study privately and learned to play the organ. With a scholarship from the city of Einbeck, he enrolled in the newly established University of Göttingen (1735), studying theology. The Pietist professor Joachim Oporin (1695–1753) became his mentor, and with his support Mühlenberg opened a charity school for poor children, an experience that provided him with valuable lessons in administration and social ministry. After Göttingen, Mühlenberg

traveled to Halle (1738) to study in its Mission Institute in preparation for missionary work in India. At Halle, he became acquainted with its influential director, the Pietist Gotthilf August Francke (1696–1769). Francke had Mühlenberg working in the orphanage and hospital. A year later (1739) Mühlenberg accepted a call to be the assistant pastor (deacon) in the village of Großhennersdorf. He was ordained by the Leipzig Consistory in St. Nicholas Church on August 19, 1739. He served under the senior pastor Johann Lucas Siese (1690–1743), attending to the parish as well as the orphanage that was maintained by Countess Henriette Sophie von Gersdorff (1686–1761), a Pietist and aunt to Count Nikolaus von Zinzendorf (1700–1760).

Financial reorganization of the parish in Großhennersdorf in 1741 prompted Mühlenberg to reconsider missionary service in India. On his thirtieth birthday (September 6, 1741), at a meeting with G. A. Francke to discuss options, Mühlenberg accepted a term call to three Lutheran congregations in the Delaware Valley of the colony of Pennsylvania. In preparation for his service in British North America, he traveled to London and spent two months in the home of the court chaplain Friedrich Michael Ziegenhagen (1694–1776). Mühlenberg set sail for North America, stopping in Charleston, South Carolina, and in Ebenezer to meet with Johann Martin Boltzius (1703–65) before arriving in Philadelphia on November 25, 1742.

Over the next thirty-four years Mühlenberg organized the Lutheran churches in colonial America into a network by creating a Lutheran (Pennsylvania) ministerium (1748); adopting a liturgy (1748); writing a congregational constitution that linked congregational leadership, clergy, and ministerium (1762); and editing a hymnal (1786). His commitment to social ministry is evident in his dispensing medicines imported from Halle (which, along with the sale of books, helped Halle support his ministry financially) and the wish to establish an orphanage, a home for retired clergy, as well as a seminary in Philadelphia as early as 1749. He initiated the construction of sanctuaries and schools, served congregations in the Delaware Valley, New York City (1751–52), and New Jersey (1758–59), and mediated a dispute among Lutherans in Ebenezer, Georgia (1774–75). He corresponded with many Lutheran settlements along the eastern seaboard. In terms of pastoral care, Mühlenberg followed Luther and worked to ease the troubled conscience. His vision of ministry was to establish a Lutheran church in America for the next generation by maintaining global connections with London and Halle and nurturing local partnerships with like-minded clergy, Michael Schlatter (German Reformed), Richard Peters and William Smith (Anglican), and Carolus Magnus von Wrangel (Swedish Lutheran). His relations with the Moravians and Ludwig, Count von Zinzendorf, were not nearly as charitable, sparking recriminations on both sides.

Mühlenberg retired from public ministry in July 1776 but continued to preach and administer the sacraments when asked. His last official act was to baptize a baby on September 29, 1787, two weeks before he died. He was awarded a doctor of divinity from the University of Pennsylvania in 1784. A loyal subject of the House of Hannover, which ruled Hannover, Germany, and Great Britain, he was grieved when the American colonies declared, fought for, and won their independence. Nevertheless, he took the oath of allegiance to the new country quietly in Montgomery County, Pennsylvania, on May 27, 1778, a few days before the legal deadline. His ministry is documented in his *Journals* and his extensive correspondence with colleagues in North America and his advisers in London and Halle.

Mühlenberg married Anna Maria Weiser (1727–1802), the daughter of the famous land developer Conrad Weiser (1696–1760), in April 1745. Together they had eleven children and saw seven reach adulthood. Although the three sons attended school in Halle and were ordained to the ministry, only the youngest, Gotthilf Heinrich (Henry) Ernest (1753–1815),

remained in the Lutheran pastorate, serving in New Jersey, Philadelphia, and Lancaster, Pennsylvania. He was also a renowned botanist, publishing several studies about America's flora and corresponding with American and European botanists and zoologists. The oldest son Johann (John) Peter Gabriel (1746–1807) left the ministry at the beginning of the conflict with Britain to serve in the Eighth Virginia Regiment and later the Continental Army. He fought in the Battles of Brandywine and Germantown and was with Washington's troops in Valley Forge in the winter of 1777. At the end of the war he entered politics. Friedrich (or Frederick) August (1750–1801) left the pastorate for a career in politics and was elected to the Continental Congress (1779) and the United States Congress (1789), becoming the first Speaker of the House of Representatives. Two daughters married Lutheran ministers: Eve Elizabeth (1748–1808) married Christopher Emanuel Schultze (1740–1809), and Margaret Henrietta (1751–1831) married John C. Kunze (1744–1807). The younger daughters did not. Maria Catharine (1755–1812) married Francis Swaine (1754–1820), a storekeeper in Trappe and sheriff of Montgomery County, while Maria Salome (1766–1827) married Matthias Richards (1758–1839), a prosperous saddler.

Mühlenberg died on October 7, 1787, and is buried in the cemetery of Augustus Lutheran Church in Trappe, Pennsylvania. His wife, who died in 1802, is buried next to him.

See also Boltzius, Johann Martin; Ebenezer Community; Francke, August Hermann; Francke, Gotthilf August; Francke Foundations; Pietism; Ziegenhagen, Friedrich Michael

Bibliography

Grabbe, H.-J. *Halle Pietism, Colonial North America, and the Young United States.* F. Steiner, 2008; Minardi, L. *Pastors and Patriots: The Muhlenberg Family of Pennsylvania.* Pennsylvania German Society, 2011; Mühlenberg, H. M. *The Correspondence.* Picton, 1993; Mühlenberg, H. M. *The Journals.* Lutheran Historical Society and Whipporwill Publications, 1982; Riforgiato, L. *Missionary of Moderation: Henry Melchior Muhlenberg and the Lutheran Church in English America.* Bucknell, 1980; Roeber, A. G. *Palatines, Liberty, and Property: German*

Lutherans in Colonial British America. Johns Hopkins University Press, 1993; Wellenreuther, H., et al., eds. *The Transatlantic World of Heinrich Melchior Mühlenberg in the Eighteenth Century*. Franckeschen Stiftungen, 2013.

KARL KRUEGER

Munk, Kaj

As a playwright, columnist, and pastor in the Evangelical Lutheran Church of Denmark, Kaj Munk (1898–1944) was assassinated by the Gestapo on January 4, 1944. Known as the "Poet-Pastor," Munk was a leading figure on the Scandinavian cultural scene in the 1930s and 1940s, due primarily to his successful plays that often focused on religious themes. Among the most famous was *The Word*, which, in Carl Theodor Dreyer's 1955 movie version, won the Golden Lion in Venice and the Golden Globe Award in the United States. The guiding theme of vocation and its implications, which emerged in his plays, paralleled the realities of his own life. In spite of his theatrical success as a playwright, his lifelong calling by 1924 was that of a parish pastor near the west coast of Jutland, far from the Copenhagen theaters and publishers.

Munk's theology is difficult to place. Although he disdained academic theology, he earned high scores in it. His primary teacher was the prominent liberal theologian Valdemar Ammundsen. Munk's own faith was anti-ideological and uncompromising. Similar to the emphasis on personal experience in his plays, he fervently sought a conversion experience but never felt he had one. He was heavily influenced by Pietism, but he also admired Catholicism. For instance, his play *Niels Ebbesen* depicts a Catholic priest as the best example of the Protestant perspective of the divine-human relation. His work on the role of suffering and martyrdom brings to mind that of Bonhoeffer. Politically, he opposed parliamentarism and democracy but praised heroism and the "strong man." In fact, he wrote admiringly about Hitler and Mussolini in the 1930s. The persecution of the Jews and World War II, however, made him one of the harshest critics of the Nazi regime, which led to his assassination. He saw it as the pastor's duty to address everything relevant for human life, including political issues, if no one else could. Inspired by N. F. S. Grundtvig (1783–1872), who was also his main character in the play *Egelykke*, he advocated for a necessary continuation of the Reformation. In spite of the fact that he held Luther as a historical figure in high regard, he was disinclined to give Luther a contemporary voice, as seen in his correspondence with the Luther scholar Niels Nøjgaard. Munk favored the doctrines of purgatory and private confession. In Munk's own version of the two-kingdoms doctrine, there are two "kings," of which Christ is unquestionably the higher (see Iversen 215–16). Although there has been some discussion over whether Munk deliberately sought martyrdom, he is now widely recognized as a genuine martyr, although more so outside of Denmark than in his own country.

See also Denmark; Literature; World Wars I and II

Bibliography

Dosenrode, S. *Christianity and Resistance in the 20th Century*. Brill, 2009; Iversen, H. R. "Rebellen og reformatoren: Kaj Munk og Luther." In *Lutherbilleder i dansk teologi 1800–2000*, ed. N. H. Gregersen, 203–19. Anis, 2012; Keigwin, R. P., trans. *Kaj Munk: Playwright, Priest and Patriot: Some Examples of His Work*. Free Danish Publishing, 1944; Munk, K. *Niels Ebbesen: Historical Drama in 5 Acts*. Trans. E. Voight and H. O. Miller. *The Scandinavian News*, September 1942–February 1943.

BO KRISTIAN HOLM

Müntzer, Thomas

The spiritualist reformer Thomas Müntzer (1489–1525) was a pastoral leader of peasant troops in the Peasants' War. The adversarial relation of Luther and Thomas Müntzer was dramatized but partially distorted by Müntzer's involvement in the German Peasants' War (1524–26) and Luther's opposition to that uprising. Müntzer was primarily a pastor and theologian who tried to establish a Reformation with its own territorial base and a different religious rationale from Luther's.

Müntzer matriculated at the University of Frankfurt an der Oder in the winter semester,

1512. There he received a Scholastic schooling, leading to his appointment to a minor prebend in Braunschweig in 1514–17. In 1517–18 he was present, but did not matriculate, at Wittenberg University, which at that time was undergoing a humanistic curriculum reform, to which Müntzer was exposed, likely under the influence of Andreas Karlstadt, Philip Melanchthon, and the humanist scholar Johannes Rhegius Aesticampianus. He would have considered himself a "biblical humanist," as is indicated by his statements at this time that the church had been in decline for three hundred years, since patristic theology was replaced by Scholastic theology, a point that Luther was also making at the time. Müntzer was certainly aware of Luther at Wittenberg and shortly afterward, when he probably attended the disputation between Luther and John Eck at Leipzig in 1519. In these years, before Luther's battle with the papacy dominated everything else, Wittenberg is more accurately regarded as a biblical humanist university, rather than a Protestant or Evangelical university. The German mystic Johannes Tauler was at this time an object of study by Luther, and in his lectures on Romans (1515–16) Luther began using Erasmus's annotations on the New Testament. To be sure, some Luther scholarship insists on distinguishing Luther's appropriation of Tauler and the "mystical" reception of Tauler by Karlstadt and Müntzer, nonetheless, it seems probable that Müntzer enriched his very important knowledge of Tauler in contacts with Karlstadt already in early 1519.

When the charge of St. Mary's church in Zwickau became vacant in May 1520, due to the leave of its biblical humanist pastor, Johannes Sylvius Egranus, Luther recommended Müntzer for the post. When Egranus returned in the autumn, Müntzer was reassigned to St. Catherine's Church. A quarrel developed between the two over the essence of biblical humanism that crystallized into Müntzer's distinctive theology. Egranus represented a radical version of Erasmus's biblical humanism—virtually a total superiority of the New Testament over the Old, an insistence that biblical inspiration by the Holy Spirit ceased after the time of the apostles, so that the application of biblical authority was a matter of textual study. Müntzer regarded this as an endorsement of the heresy of Marcion, which held that God revealed himself only in the New Testament. In his response, Müntzer declared that the revelation of the Holy Spirit was continuous—as he affirmed a little later in his Prague Epistle (or Manifesto, 1521): "Thomas Müntzer wants to pray to a speaking God, not a mute one." All parts of the Bible, Old and New Testaments, had to be respected in their integrity through *collatio locorum* (comparison of texts). God reveals himself in the "abyss of the soul" through human suffering, a suffering mirrored for the illiterate through animals' suffering in nature at the hands of human beings. God's will is fulfilling itself in the course of history through the building of a kingdom of Christ, foreshadowed by the proclamations of the Hussites and of Luther, and perfecting God's revelation through the patriarchs, prophets, and apostles of the Bible. Luther's theology was significantly at odds with Müntzer's. Luther did not reject the Old Testament, but he discovered believers in both Testaments and prioritized the New Testament as the fulfillment of God's promises, particularly as expressed in the Pauline Epistles and the Gospel of John. Luther did not believe in continuous, direct revelation to theologians but in the importance of study and exposition. He did not expect the creation of a kingdom of Christ on earth in history but looked forward to an imminent, suprahistorical judgment that would break in "like a thief in the night." He did not believe that God's grace was inevitably accessible through human suffering, but held that it was bestowed freely on sinners who were saved by the gift of faith.

The Zwickau council, perturbed by the quarrel between Müntzer and Egranus, discharged Müntzer in April 1521. From then until March 1523 Müntzer lived a wandering life. In Prague he hoped that the Utraquist heirs of Jan Hus would play their role in establishing the kingdom of Christ, but discovered that they were another group of Bible studiers who did not open themselves to the voice of the Spirit. During brief sojourns in Erfurt and Nordhausen, he encountered Luther's close friends Johannes Lang and Laurence Süsse, with whom he engaged in personal or theological quarrels, which certainly worsened Luther's impression of him. Meanwhile in Wittenberg, first Melanchthon, then Luther after his return from the Wartburg, encountered Nikolaus Storch and Markus Stübner, former Zwickau congregants of Müntzer, who transmitted garbled versions of Müntzer's belief about the continuous inspiration of the Spirit and his view about the historical undesirability of the introduction of infant baptism in late antiquity. Luther coined the term "Zwickau Prophets," which he used briefly in 1521–22, to describe these persons, whom he regarded as Müntzer's progeny.

In March 1523 Müntzer was installed in St. John's Church in Allstedt by the town council, acting on its own authority, although the post was formally under the patronage of Allstedt's sovereign lord, the Elector of Saxony. Allstedt was a territorial enclave surrounded by Catholic lands, most notably those of the Catholic Duke George of Saxony. Müntzer established cordial relations with Simon Haferitz, Allstedt's other pastor, as well as Hans Zeiss, the administrative representative of the Saxon elector in the enclave. Before the end of 1523 he instituted a German Evangelical Mass, as well as German liturgies for the great festivals of the church year. While the institution of these services was in itself a conservative approach to Reformation (later Luther introduced his own German Mass), Müntzer's scriptural translations in the liturgies mirrored his particular doctrinal standpoint about the arrival of faith through spiritual struggle. Difficulties began when villagers from surrounding Catholic regions flocked to Allstedt to attend Müntzer's services; their rulers forbade this, and the subjects were punished.

Müntzer denounced one of the neighboring rulers, Count Ernst von Mansfeld, from his pulpit. Eventually the Allstedt residents formed a "covenant" to defend themselves and their neighbors from persecution for the sake of the gospel.

Despite his awareness of doctrinal differences, Müntzer tried to establish amicable relations with Luther and Melanchthon but evaded their pressure to come to Wittenberg for theological discussions. The public break between Luther and Müntzer began when, in July 1524, Luther published his *Open Letter against the Rebellious Spirit in Allstedt*, addressed to the princes of Electoral Saxony, in which he took umbrage that Müntzer had "made a nest for himself in Allstedt, and thinks he can fight against me under my peace, shield, and protection." Virtually at the same time, on July 13, 1524, in the Allstedt Castle, Müntzer delivered a sermon to two bemused Electoral Saxon princes on Dan. 2, in which he asked them to protect the Reformation in Allstedt against its Catholic enemies, further threatening that, should his princes desert him, their power would be taken from them and handed over to the common people. In the next weeks things moved rapidly. The Electoral Saxon authorities dissolved the Allstedt "covenant," deprived Müntzer of access to a printing press, and assured themselves of the loyalty of Hans Zeiß and the Allstedt council.

Deprived of effective support, Müntzer fled Allstedt on the night of August 7–8, 1524, going to the free, imperial city of Mühlhausen in Thuringia, where a process of Reformation was proceeding under the leadership of the radical monk Heinrich Pfeiffer. In this period he secured the publication in Nuremberg of his two most important works: *Manifest Exposé of False Faith* and *A Highly Provoked Vindication, and a Refutation of the Unspiritual, Soft-Living Flesh in Wittenberg*. The first was the more substantial exposition of his theology, the second a bitter polemic against Luther. The course of Reformation did not run smoothly in Mühlhausen. In late September Müntzer and

Pfeiffer were expelled. By December, Pfeiffer was back, and in February 1525 Müntzer, after wanderings in southern Germany, became pastor of St. Mary's Church. The Mühlhausen Reformation was endangered from the outset. The imperial city had three princely protectors, Margrave Philip of Hesse (Lutheran), Elector Frederick of Saxony (Lutheran), and Duke George of Saxony (Catholic)—all invested in suppressing Müntzer's version of the Reformation. Naturally Müntzer regarded it as providential when the German Peasants' War spread to Thuringia in April 1525. Mühlhausen sent a small contingent of three hundred men under Müntzer's leadership to join the Thuringian peasant army of seven thousand at Frankenhausen. Müntzer became a sort of chaplain-strategist for the peasant army, which was destroyed by the combined forces of Hesse and Ducal Saxony on May 15, 1525. Müntzer was captured, fleeing the battlefield, and, following interrogation and torture, was executed on May 27, 1525. Ever afterward, even in his writings against the Turks, Luther regarded Müntzer as the epitome of rebelliousness, as did Philip Melanchthon.

See also Eschatology (Apocalypticism, Chiliasm, Millennialism, Millenarianism); Peasants' War

Bibliography

Bubenheimer, U. *Thomas Müntzer: Herkunft und Bildung*. Brill, 1989; Goertz, H.-J. *Thomas Müntzer: Apocalyptic Mystic and Revolutionary*. T&T Clark, 1993; Matheson, P., trans. and ed. *The Collected Works of Thomas Müntzer*. T&T Clark, 1988; Stayer, J. M. "Prophet, Apokalyptiker, Mystiker: Thomas Müntzer und die 'Kirche' der Patriarchen, Propheten und Apostel." In *Endzeiterwartung bei Thomas Müntzer und im frühen Luthertum*, ed. J. M. Stayer and H. Kühne, 5–25. Thomas-Müntzer-Gesellschaft, 2011.

JAMES M. STAYER

Musculus, Andreas

The German Lutheran theologian Andreas Musculus (1514–81) was one of the authors of the Formula of Concord. He studied at the University of Wittenberg and followed his brother-in-law Johann Agricola into the service of Elector Joachim II of Brandenburg, becoming pastor in Frankfurt an der Oder and a professor at its university. Although not personally associated with Gnesio-Lutherans to any great degree, he shared their positions and attitudes on many issues. Musculus opposed Andreas Osiander and later entered into controversy with his colleague Abdias Praetorius over Melanchthon's concept of the necessity of good works, interpreting "necessity" as "coercion" and insisting that the gospel motivates good works "from a free and merry spirit" (Solid Declaration 6.17 in *BC* 590). He preached the second use of the law with vigor and maintained, in line with Luther's *Freedom of a Christian*, that faith produces good works, thereby becoming unfairly accused of "antinomianism." His patristic studies and his imaginative work with literary genres, including pioneering examples of what became known as the "devil's book" (warnings against moral dereliction), made him an influential author in his day. His elector appointed him and his former student and colleague Christoph Körner as representatives to the negotiations that drafted the Formula of Concord, where he especially influenced the wording of article 6 of the Solid Declaration.

See also Agricola, Johann; Book of Concord; Formula of Concord; Good Works; Law, Uses of the

Bibliography

Kolb, R. "The Fathers in the Service of Lutheran Teaching: Andreas Musculus' Use of Patristic Sources." In *Auctoritas Patrum II*, ed. L. Grane et al., 105–23. Zabern, 1998.

ROBERT KOLB

Musculus, Wolfgang

The Reformed minister Wolfgang Musculus (1497–1563) was a theologian and biblical scholar in Strasbourg, Augsburg, and Bern. Born September 8, 1497, in the village of Dieuze, Lorraine, Musculus entered a nearby Benedictine monastery at age fifteen and was thereafter ordained to the Catholic priesthood and recruited to preach in several local parishes. In 1518 the young priest first encountered the writings of Martin Luther and began promulgating the reformer's message in his parish sermons and in the monastery, earning him the nickname "the Lutheran monk." In December 1527, Musculus renounced his monastic vows and departed for Strasbourg, accompanied by his fiancée, Margaretha Bart. Musculus was only in Strasbourg a brief time before the city minister Martin Bucer hired him as his personal secretary and appointed him to the rural parish of Dorlisheim. The following year, Musculus was transferred to the city cathedral, where he served as an assistant to Matthias Zell, studied Greek and Hebrew, and attended lessons in theology offered by Bucer and his colleague Wolfgang Capito. These formative experiences not only shaped Musculus as a preacher and churchman but also won him over to Bucer's brand of Protestantism.

In 1531 Musculus was appointed pastor of the Church of the Holy Cross in the city of Augsburg, a strategic Reformation outpost that had become unsettled by religious conflict between the followers of Luther and Zwingli, as well as Catholics and Anabaptists. During the next seventeen years, Musculus distinguished himself as a preacher, a lecturer on Scripture, and an astute theological guide, steering the city church's official theology between Lutheranism and Zwinglianism. In 1536 he represented the city as part of a delegation of southern German theologians at the Wittenberg Colloquy, where he met Luther and subscribed to the consensus on the thorny question of the sacraments (the Wittenberg Concord). He was also a delegate to theological colloquies held in Worms (1540) and Regensburg (1541) and aimed at achieving religious concord with Catholic opponents. At these theological colloquies, Musculus met and forged a warm relationship with Philip Melanchthon, with whom he maintained an extensive correspondence. Musculus's assessment of Luther, by contrast, became increasingly critical. Although Musculus paid due respect to Luther as a courageous reformer, he privately criticized the German theologian for his intransigence and arrogance, his explosive temper, and his lack of Christian charity toward theological opponents, especially the Swiss. For Musculus, Luther's harsh attacks on the so-called Sacramentarians—the term Luther used to impugn not only the followers of Zwingli but also southern German theologians such as Bucer—failed to appreciate the real theological differences between the parties. Musculus explained to Zurich minister Heinrich Bullinger in 1544 that his own sacramental theology was neither Zwingli's memorialism nor Luther's doctrine of real presence; rather, the Lord's Supper was a sacramental feast in which believers enjoyed spiritual communion with the true flesh and blood of Christ (Bodenmann 528–31).

When Augsburg's magistrates signed the Interim in the summer of 1548, Musculus and his family were forced to depart in search of a new home. Through the intercession of Bullinger and the Bernese minister Johann Haller, Musculus was appointed professor of Holy Scripture at the municipal secondary school in the Reformed city of Bern, a post he held until his death on August 30, 1563. Because of his Lorrainese dialect, Musculus preached only rarely in the city churches. Instead, he engaged in intense biblical scholarship and delivered academic lectures in Latin on theology and biblical exegesis. Many of these lectures subsequently appeared in print, including a popular theological textbook titled *Commonplaces of Sacred Theology* (1560), a refutation of the Council of Trent (1551), and eight highly regarded biblical commentaries. These writings demonstrate his theological erudition, his extensive knowledge of the Christian exegetical tradition, and his commitment to the moral interpretation of the biblical text. They also indicate that Musculus never abandoned his mediating position on the Lord's Supper: to the end of his life, he, like Bucer, was a partisan neither of Luther nor of Zwingli.

See also Bucer, Martin; Lord's Supper; Switzerland; Wittenberg Concord

Bibliography

Bodenmann, R. *Wolfgang Musculus (1497–1563): Destin d'un autodidacte lorrain au siècle des Réformes*. Droz,

2000; Dellsperger, R., R. Freudenberger, and W. Weber, eds. *Wolfgang Musculus und die oberdeutsche Reformation*. Akademie Verlag, 1997; Farmer, C. *The Gospel of John in the Sixteenth Century: The Johannine Exegesis of Wolfgang Musculus*. Oxford University Press, 1997.

SCOTT M. MANETSCH

Music

Martin Luther (1483–1546) gave expression to the musical mind of the church. He edited the Mass, excising references to sacrifice and works-righteousness (first in the 1523 Latin *Formula missae* and then in the 1526 German *Deutsche Messe*), while retaining the chanting in both versions and suggesting hymned versions of key liturgical material. In 1524, two musical books appeared. One contained chorales for the congregation, called the *Achtliederbuch* because of its eight chorales. The other contained motets for the choir based on chorales, *Geistliche Gesangbüchlein*, prepared by Luther's musical colleague Johann Walter (1496–1570).

Luther and his followers regarded music as a gift of God that proclaims the Word of God, celebrates Christ's battle over sin and death, and is in continuity with the music of the whole church. This perspective and cluster of books signaled that (1) the church's worship in its historic forms should be edited in each generation, not abandoned; (2) music in the church is tied to this worship; and (3) music in worship has both congregational and choral parts, related by alternation. A huge congregational and choral repertoire developed with chorales at its center. They were published in broadsheets and collected in hymnals; Valentin Bapst's hymnal of 1545 was the most careful collection in Luther's lifetime.

A chorale is a vernacular congregational hymn that stems from the sixteenth-century German Reformation, an invigorated continuation of the Germanic heritage of hymn singing among the people, stimulated by Gregorian chant and folk hymns called *Leisen* (after the refrain *Kyrie eleison*). Tunes were often variants of their originals. "Chorale" refers to both text and tune, though often to tune alone.

When referring only to the tune, textual associations remain in the tune names such as "Aus tiefer Not" (From depths of woe), "Ein feste Burg" (A mighty fortress), and "Nun danket alle Gott" (Now thank we all our God).

The word "chorale" is derived from the German word (borrowed from the Latin and Greek) *Choral*, meaning Gregorian chant (plainsong), or from *choraliter*—that is, in the manner of chant—as unison and unaccompanied. That is how chorales were sung at the Reformation and for more than a century and a half after it, although in 1586 Lucas Osiander published a book of harmonizations for the choir with the tune in the soprano voice. If the choir used such harmonizations with the congregation's unison line, four parts were heard. It was not until the eighteenth century, however, that the organ sometimes began to accompany the congregation's singing.

Luther wrote texts and tunes, like "From Heaven Above" and "A Mighty Fortress." He also wrote texts alone, such as "Savior of the Nations, Come" (based on a Latin hymn attributed to Ambrose of Milan) and "Christ Jesus Lay in Death's Strong Bands." Johann Walter, Luther's right-hand musical helper, perhaps with suggestions from Luther, supplied the tunes for the latter two. Others who wrote both texts and tunes include Nikolaus Hermann (1500–1561) for "Let All Together Praise Our God," Philipp Nicolai (1556–1608) for "Wake, Awake, for Night Is Flying" and "O Morning Star, How Fair and Bright" (called the "King" and "Queen" of the chorales), and Georg Neumark (1621–81) for "If You But Trust in God to Guide You."

Paul Gerhardt (1607–76), a pastor who lived through the Thirty Years' War, wrote approximately 130 texts that moved from the public ruggedness of sixteenth-century chorales to a more introspective smoothness of the Baroque era. As with Luther, the musician Johann Crüger (1598–1662) collaborated with him to compose the tunes. Crüger wrote at least seventy tunes, like the ones that go with Gerhard's "Awake, My

Heart, with Gladness," Johann Heermann's (1585–1647) "Ah, Holy Jesus," and Johann Franck's (1618–77) "Soul, Adorn Yourself with Gladness." Beginning in 1644 he edited *Praxis Pietatis Melica*, the most important hymn collection of the seventeenth century, which went through fifty expanding editions that continued long after his death.

Catherine Winkworth (1829–78), Robert Bridges (1844–1930), and August Crull (1846–1923) are among those who provided English translations for the German originals. But the chorale tradition's influence was not limited to Germany. A Danish hymnal was published in 1528, and Thomas Kingo (1634–1703) wrote Danish hymns. Olavus Petri (1493–1552) wrote Swedish hymns. His brother Laurentius Petri (1499–1573) edited Swedish hymnbooks. Martin Agricola (ca. 1510–57) edited Finnish worship books, and Jacob Finno (d. 1588) published a Finnish hymnal in 1583. An Icelandic hymnal was printed in 1589. The Slovak *Cithara Sanctorum* began its long history in 1636, named "Tranoscius" for Juraj Tranovsky (1592–1637), a pastor who compiled hymns and wrote both tunes and texts. Norwegian hymnody, first tied to Swedish and Danish alliances, came into its own in the nineteenth century when Magnus Brostrup Landstad (1802–80) was the most important hymn writer and Ludvig Mathias Lindeman (1812–87) the most important tune writer. The chorale's influence can be seen in English into the twentieth and twenty-first centuries. An example is "Now the Silence," by the pastor and poet Jaroslav Vajda (1919–2008) with its tune "Now" by the musician and composer Carl Schalk (b. 1929).

The German tradition took on a Pietist cast in the *Geistreiches Gesangbuch* (1704–, the "Halle Hymnal"). It was edited by the text and tune writer Johann Anastasius Freylinghausen (1670–1739). Editions continued after Freylinghausen's death and included fifteen hundred hymns and six hundred tunes. The *Vollständiges Marburger-Gesangbuch* (called the "Lutheran Marburg" to distinguish it from

its German Reformed counterpart) was published in 1757 and was one of the hymnals that immigrants brought to the United States and other countries around the world. The *Erbauliche Lieder-Sammlung* (1786), edited by Henry Mühlenberg (1711–87), the patriarch of Lutheranism in the United States, relied on it.

Sixteenth-century chorale tunes characteristically had irregular and somewhat dance-like rhythms ("rhythmic" tunes). By the time of J. S. Bach (1685–1750) the melodies had given way to regular successions of slower equal notes ("isometric" tunes). In the nineteenth century this musical stasis joined a loss of Lutheran liturgical and theological signatures through the influences of Pietism, rationalism, and, in the United States, revivalism. Extensive discussions and study throughout the century recovered and renewed what had been lost, so that the rhythmic chorale became a mark of confessional consciousness. Friedrich Layriz (1808–59), a German pastor and hymnologist, supplied four volumes of chorales in their original rhythmic versions. Nineteenth-century German immigrants to various countries sang in German. The more confessional ones recovered the rhythmic tunes, while the more unionizing ones continued to use the isometric forms. For example, Lutherans who had been in the United States and were accustomed to singing in English used the isometric versions, as in the *Church Book with Music* (1872) that Harriet Krauth Spaeth (1845–1925) prepared. However, when John Endlich (1845–92) supplied the music (1879) for its German translation (the *Kirchenbuch*, 1877), the chorale tunes were given in rhythmic forms. In Norway, Lindeman did not use the rhythmic forms, but he increased tempos, removed fermatas, and used dotted rhythms in the tunes he wrote. Landstad's hymnal and Lindeman's chorale book for it were published in Minneapolis in 1894 and 1899.

In the twentieth century chorales and the music they spawned received further impetus and renewal in line with the confessing church and its reaction to Adolf Hitler and Nazism. The neo-Renaissance choral and organ music of Hugo Distler (1908–42) is a prime example. Distler and other twentieth- and twenty-first-century composers were able to learn and renew their heritage with a long stream of examples from Johann Walter's music onward. This repertoire ran out the implications of the chorale in many different settings for choir and organ in a trajectory that led to the cantatas of J. S. Bach. Cantatas, which often utilized chorale tunes and their texts—Bach's remarkable harmonizations for the isometric versions of his time substituted for the rhythmic loss—were composed to proclaim the gospel in connection with the sermon, readings, and Hymn of the Day on each Sunday and feast day except penitential ones. Bach's four or five cantata cycles are at the center of his compositional output and the apex of this development, but Bach was not alone in writing cantatas. Johann Christoph Graupner (1683–1760) wrote over fourteen hundred of them, and Georg Philipp Telemann (1681–1767) wrote twelve cantata cycles.

This context stimulated other composing: settings of the passions, the Easter and Christmas narratives, psalms, and canticles; music for Vespers and the Ordinary and Proper of the Mass; hymn concertatos; chorale preludes, preludes, fugues, and other music for organ and keyboard; and orchestral pieces, which, like oratorios and J. S. Bach's *B Minor Mass*, extend outside worship.

A few more musicians may stand for all those not listed who have contributed to this repertoire, including countless anonymous ones: Hans Leo Hassler (1562–1612), Melchior Vulpius (1570–1617), Michael Praetorius (ca. 1571–1621), Heinrich Schütz (1585–1672), Samuel Scheidt (1587–1654), Heinrich Scheidemann (1596–1663), Dietrich Buxtehude (1637–1707), Johann Pachelbel (1653–1706), Wilhelm Friedemann Bach (1710–84), C. P. E. Bach (1714–88), Felix Mendelssohn (1809–47), Johannes Brahms (1833–97), Ernst Pepping (1901–81), Hugo Distler (1908–42), Jan Bender

(1909–94), Paul Manz (1919–2009), Richard Hillert (1923–2010), John Ferguson (b. 1941), and David Cherwien (b. 1957).

See also Bach, Johann Sebastian; Buxtehude, Dietrich; Crüger, Johann; Freylinghausen, Johann Anastasius; Gerhardt, Paul; Hermann, Nikolaus; Hymnody; Nicolai, Philipp; Petri, Olavus; Praetorius, Michael; Telemann, Georg Philipp

Bibliography
Blume, F. *Protestant Church Music*. Norton, 1974; Bunjes, P., and C. Schalk. "Chorale, Vocal Settings." In *Key Words in Church Music*, ed. C. Schalk, 115–21. Rev., enlarged ed. Concordia, 2004; Leaver, R. "Chorale." In *Canterbury Dictionary of Hymnology*, ed. J. R. Watson and E. Hornby, http://www.hymnology.co.uk/c/chorale. Canterbury Press, 2013–; Marshall, R. "Choral," "Choralbass," "Choralarbeitung," "Chorale," "Chorale cantata," "Chorale Concerto," "Chorale Fantasia," "Choral Fugue," "Chorale Mass," "Chorale Monody," "Chorale Motet," "Chorale Partita," "Chorale Prelude," "Chorale Ricercars," "Chorale Settings," and "Chorale Variations." In *The New Grove Dictionary of Music and Musicians*, ed. S. Sadie, 4:312–39. Macmillan, 1980; Schalk, C. "Chorale." In *Key Words in Church Music*, ed. C. Schalk, 109–14. Rev., enlarged ed. Concordia, 2004.

PAUL WESTERMEYER

Muss, Kurt

The Russian Lutheran martyr Kurt Muss (1896–1937) was born in St. Petersburg, attended St. Anne's Lutheran School, and studied theology at Dorpat University. In 1922 Muss was arrested on charges of espionage for assisting John Morehead and the National Lutheran Council with the distribution of food and clothing to Lutherans suffering from famine in southern Russia. Upon his release in 1926, he served as pastor of Jesus Christ Lutheran Church in Leningrad, the only Russian-speaking Lutheran congregation in the USSR. On December 17, 1929, he was again arrested for organizing Sunday school classes for youth in apartments scattered throughout the city. Muss was sentenced to a Gulag labor camp for ten years. In 1937, after being accused of propagating Christianity to fellow prisoners within the camp, he was sentenced to death and executed on October 4, 1937.

See also Russia

MATTHEW HEISE

Myconius, Friedrich

As pastor and reformer, Friedrich Myconius (1490–1546) helped implement the Reformation in Thuringia and Ducal Saxony. A Franciscan priest, Myconius became an early supporter of Luther's movement. In 1524 he accepted a call to Gotha to introduce reforms and oversee its city schools. He was involved in many broader aspects of the Reformation as well. He assisted Melanchthon with two church visitations, participated in several colloquies between religious parties to discuss theological differences, and was a signatory to Luther's Smalcald Articles. In 1538 Myconius was part of a Lutheran delegation to England to meet with King Henry VIII's theological advisers. After 1539 and the death of Duke George of Ducal Saxony, who had opposed the Reformation, Myconius was asked to help introduce the Reformation there. He worked in Annaberg and Leipzig for nine months before returning to Gotha due to declining health. When his health forced him to give up preaching, he turned his energies toward writing a history of the Reformation, *Historia reformationis vom Jahr Christi 1517 bis 1542* (History of the Reformation from the year of Christ 1517 until 1542).

See also Colloquy; Georg, Duke of Saxony; Henry VIII; Melanchthon, Philip; Saxonies

Bibliography

Myconius, F. *Geschichte der Reformation*. Ed. O. Clemen. Voigtländers, 1914; Ulbrich, H. *Friedrich Myconius, 1490–1546: Ein Lebensbild und neue Funde zum Briefwechsel des Reformators*. Osiander, 1962.

ANNA MARIE JOHNSON

Mystical Union

Mystical union (*unio mystica*) refers to the substantial union between Christ and believers. Such a union is received through the presence of the risen Christ in word and sacrament. Various interpretations of the doctrine and its relationship to the article of justification have caused conflict in the history of Lutheranism.

Although Martin Luther did not generally use the term "mystical union," the concept is firmly present in his Reformation-period writings (Elert 166–76). Among the early writings employing the concept, the treatise *On the Freedom of a Christian* (1520) stands out. In this work, Luther conceptualizes the relationship between Christ and believers as an exchange of realities ("happy exchange") mediated through faith. Christ gave the sinner life and righteousness and in return received sin and death (LW 31:351; WA 7:25–26). The language of exchange employed by Luther is both forensic and mystical-substantial.

Luther continued to develop this line of thought in the lectures on Galatians (1531) and the subsequent published *Commentary on Galatians* (1535). Here Luther sees Christ's death as a forensic and mystical unification with the person ("the person of all humanity") and sin of the whole of the human race (LW 26:281). Because Christ united himself with the identity and sin of the human race, he in turn suffers for its sin and renders satisfaction for it (LW 26:277–78). The unification of Christ with all of humanity's sin is the logical corollary of the believer's unity with Christ through faith. Throughout the commentary, Luther repeatedly emphasizes that justification is forensic (LW 26:132–33). Nevertheless, God's forensic act also finds its terminus in the effective reality of the sinner's mystical unification with Christ's person. Through faith and God's imputation, the believer subsequently becomes a single subject with Christ (LW 26:168).

The debate among Lutherans over the relationship between mystical union and forensic justification began shortly after Luther's death. Andreas Osiander (1498–1552) argued that the death of Christ according to his humanity only canceled sin's guilt; it did not bestow a positive status of righteousness before God (Vainio 99). Christ's humanity was only righteous according to "human righteousness" and not "divine righteousness" (Vainio 100). Positive righteousness before God could only be accomplished by the divinity of Christ mystically dwelling within believers (Arand, Kolb, Nestingen 218–19; Vainio 98–99).

Against this teaching, most other Lutherans (whether supporters of Melanchthon or opponents, such as Matthias Flacius or Joachim Mörlin) rallied around the teaching that Christ's total human-divine person and work forensically reconciled sinners to God (Arand, Kolb, Nestingen 219–20, 221–23). In particular, Flacius (1520–75) argued that as a unified divine-human person, Christ possessed both "active" and "passive" righteousness, which he gave to sinners in forensic justification (Schmid 354). Moreover, both Philippist and Gnesio-Lutherans agreed that sanctification and mystical union occurred subsequent to, and were an effect of, forensic justification (Wengert 70–78). For this reason, neither could serve as the basis of justification before God.

Ultimately this consensus found expression in the third article of the Formula of Concord (1577). The Concordists insisted that the total saving reality of Christ's person and work is imputed forensically to sinners through faith (SD 3.4; 3.9–21). Subsequently God renews sinners and mystically dwells within them (SD 3.54). Nevertheless, one does not possess a righteous status before God because of this mystical union or the good works that it produces (SD 3.39–41).

In the later theology of Lutheran Orthodoxy, the doctrine of mystical union remained important in the development of an elaborate *ordo salutis* (order of salvation; Schmid 407–9). Although there are some differences, the theologians of this era generally placed mystical union subsequent to justification in the manner of the Formula of Concord (Elert 160; Schmid 407–9, 481–86). Beginning in the nineteenth century, the so-called Repristination

theologians of German and American Lutheranism basically affirmed the doctrine as it was set down in the Formula of Concord and in the subsequent Lutheran Orthodox tradition (Hoenecke 385–94; Pieper 409–10). By contrast, existentialist Luther scholars such as Gerhard Ebeling (1912–2001) sidelined the doctrine since they believed that humans deal with God not with respect to substance but only with respect to relation.

The Finnish school of Luther interpretation provides a contemporary example of a significant development regarding the theology of mystical union. In recent decades, the Finns have argued that, for Luther, justification is either identical with or based on mystical union (Mannermaa 13–48). This conclusion has elicited criticism from scholars who have equated the Finnish interpretation with a revival of certain aspects of Osiander's teaching (Wengert 2–4).

See also Finnish Interpretation of Luther; Justification; Mannermaa, Tuomo; Osiander, Andreas

Bibliography

Arand, C., R. Kolb, and J. Nestingen. *The Lutheran Confessions: History and Theology of The Book of Concord.* Fortress, 2012; Elert, W. *The Structure of Lutheranism.* Trans. W. Hansen. Vol. 1. Concordia, 1962; Hoenecke, A. *Evangelical Lutheran Dogmatics.* Trans. J. Langebartels. Vol. 3. Northwestern, 2003; Mannermaa, T. *Christ Present in Faith: Luther's View of Justification.* Fortress, 2005; Pieper, F. *Christian Dogmatics.* Vol. 2. Concordia, 1960; Schmid, H. *The Doctrinal Theology of the Evangelical Lutheran Church.* Trans. C. Hay and H. Jacob. Augsburg, 1961; Vainio, O. *Justification and Participation in Christ: The Development of the Lutheran Doctrine of Justification from Luther to the Formula of Concord (1580).* Brill, 2008; Wengert, T. *Defending Faith: Lutheran Responses to Andreas Osiander's Doctrine of Justification, 1551–1559.* Mohr Siebeck, 2012.

JACK D. KILCREASE

N

Nabetani, Gyoji

The Japanese theologian, churchman, and writer Gyoji Nabetani (b. 1930) was born in the city of Kobe, Hyogo prefecture, in Japan. He studied at Keio Gijuku University, Kobe Lutheran Theological Seminary, received his MTh from Westminster Theological Seminary near Philadelphia in 1968, and his ThD from Concordia Seminary, St. Louis, in 1972. Nabetani served as the founding president of the West Japan Evangelical Lutheran Church, 1962–68. He served as the first Japanese president of Kobe Lutheran Theological Seminary, 1976–92.

Nabetani played a decisive role in founding the Japan Evangelical Theological Society, the Asia Theological Association/Japan, the Asia Graduate School of Theology/Japan, and the Kansai Mission Research Center. He wrote books on Old Testament hermeneutics, Isaiah, Psalms, Martin Luther, a biography of J. M. T. Winter and his daughter Maya (Danish missionaries to Japan), and his own biographical essay, along with translating and editing textbooks on Lutheran doctrine and ethics, Luther and Calvin, a history of theology in the modern age, Old Testament textual criticism, and many more for the use of seminarians.

See also Japan

MAKITO MASAKI

Namibia

In 1805, German missionaries in the employ of the London Missionary Society, among them the brothers Christian and Abraham Albrecht, began mission work in what is now Namibia. Early efforts suffered during tribal warfare that also aimed at the destruction of the mission. This work came under the jurisdiction of the Rhineland Mission when it entered the area in 1842.

The Rhineland Mission represented both Lutheran and Reformed confessions, but the church that evolved from its work followed the Lutheran tradition. In 1869 Finnish missionaries from the Evangelical Lutheran Mission entered the area that from 1884 was the German colony of Southwest Africa. The Rhineland Mission served as a refuge for some during the Herero-Nama War of Liberation (1863–70). The Rhineland Mission was not totally uncritical in its cooperation with the colonial government but largely supported its policies because the missionaries believed that only European governance could end tribal warfare and bring peace for the people. One result of this policy of cooperation was that racial discrimination infected the church. The colonial power's genocide against the Herero people in 1903–6 resulted in the deaths of thousands of Lutherans and the establishment of a German-speaking Lutheran church in the colony. Finnish work continued among the Ovambo in northern Namibia without the colonial connection and provided for a more harmonious cooperation between the populace and the missionaries, who were often called on to exercise political leadership when tribes became Christian because of the natural association of teacher and power in traditional thinking.

In 1915 the Union of South African forces completed the occupation of the German colony on its border. This placed the peoples of the area under the domination of a government that first informally and after 1948 formally embraced racial apartheid as its policy, resulting in a long, bitter struggle for native integrity and the independence of the former German colony from South African dominance, to which Lutherans contributed a great deal.

In 1954 the Finnish Mission formed the Evangelical Lutheran Ovambokokavango Church, now the Evangelical Lutheran Church in Namibia; it has more than 700,000 members. Leonard Auala became its first Namibian moderator in 1960 (bishop in 1963). His successor Kleopas Dumeni (bishop in 1978–2000) played a particularly important role in opposing the oppression of the apartheid system. In 1957 the Rhineland Mission became independent as the United Evangelical Lutheran Church South West Africa, now the Evangelical Lutheran Church in the Republic of Namibia; its membership exceeds 350,000. Following several missionary moderators, Paulus Gowaseb became its first African moderator in 1967, and J. L. de Vries its first African president in 1972. The two churches joined with the German-speaking Evangelical Lutheran Church to form the United Church Council of Namibia Evangelical Lutheran Churches and are working toward one national Lutheran church.

Lutherans played a prominent role in the struggle of the South West Africa Peoples Organization for independence and have provided significant governmental leadership since independence in 1990. They sponsor other educational institutions and have been deeply engaged in promoting the health of the population, particularly in combating HIV/Aids.

In 1963 the two African churches in Namibia established a joint seminary at Otjimbingwe, the Paulinum, which in 1997 moved to the capital city, Windhoek. More than half of Namibia's population of two million people belong to Lutheran churches.

See also Apartheid; South Africa

Bibliography
De Vries, J. L. *Mission and Colonialism in Namibia*. Ravan, 1978; Enquist, R. J. *Namibia: Land of Tears, Land of Promise*. Susquehanna University Press, 1990; Hellberg, C.-J. *Mission, Colonialism, and Liberation: The Lutheran Church in Namibia, 1840–1966*. New Namibia Books, 1997; Isaak, P. J., ed. *The Evangelical Lutheran Church in the Republic of Namibia in the Twenty-First Century*. Gamsberg Macmillan, 2000; Katjavivi, P., et al. *Church and Liberation in Namibia*. Pluto, 1989; McKittrick, M. *To Dwell Secure: Generation, Christianity, and Colonialism in Ovamboland*. Heinemann, 2000; Nambala, S. *History of the Church in Namibia*. Lutheran Quarterly, 1994.

ROBERT KOLB

Natural Science

The Lutheran Reformation was born in the medieval university, where the study of natural science was also fostered, and had close affinities with humanism, which also emphasized the arts and science. For nearly five centuries, Lutheran theologians have been fascinated with both natural science and doctrinal theology. The rigorous method of scientific inquiry, *Wissenschaft*, was borrowed for biblical interpretation early in the nineteenth century; and in largely Lutheran circles, historical-critical commitments to the truths within and surrounding the Bible became de rigueur. Lutheran spirituality consists primarily of understanding Holy Scripture (that is, standing under Holy Scripture) and the employment of scientific methods of interpretation to aid in honest understanding. But Lutheran understanding of the twofold righteousness (for this world and before God) allowed them from the beginning to use reason and science to understand the world around them, albeit usually employing Aristotelian categories.

Although it is not widely known, some early Lutherans supported what was later called the Copernican Revolution in natural science. While Nicolas Copernicus (1473–1543) was formulating what would become the heliocentric theory of the solar system, he was visited by a mathematics professor on the faculty at the University of Wittenberg, Georg Joachim de Porris, also known as Rheticus (1514–74). Rheticus brought Copernicus's handwritten manuscript *De revolutionibus orbium coelestium* back from Crakow (Kraków), Poland, to Wittenberg for printing in 1542. This was three years before Martin Luther passed away. Rheticus actually arranged for publication in Nuremburg, where the printing press was larger than the one in Wittenberg. The initial publication of the work that led to the

Copernican Revolution was published by the Lutherans, and it included an anonymous introduction by a Lutheran pastor, Andreas Osiander. Later astronomers with Lutheran ties include Tycho Brahe and Johannes Kepler.

What did Martin Luther think about Copernicus's idea? Luther's only recorded allusion to Copernicus is found in his Table Talk (LW 54:358–59, no. 4638), where he sarcastically describes a new astrologer "who wanted to prove that the earth moves and not the sky, the sun, and the moon. This would be as if somebody were riding on a cart or in a ship and imagined that he was standing still, while the earth and the trees were moving" (LW 54:358–59). We notice two items relevant to Luther's context. First, at this time the Copernican view had not yet become persuasive, so no good reason required either scientists or theologians to adopt heliocentrism. Second, this Table Talk entry is dated in 1539, for which we have only a copy made in 1553–54. This passage may have been a later interpolation into Luther's hand by an anti-Copernican, although this seems somewhat unlikely. Even more significant, Luther clearly distinguished between the sciences of astronomy and astrology, committing himself to the former and rejecting the latter. It is also worth noting that Luther's criticism was not theological but based upon human observation and argument.

In the twenty-first century the field of theology and science (sometimes called science and religion) is growing on nearly every continent. Lutheran theologians are leaders in a field that draws interest among other Christian, Muslim, Jewish, Buddhist, and Hindu thinkers. Of central concern is the picture painted of the natural world by scientists describing big-bang cosmology, quantum physical activity, biological evolution, genetic influence on heredity, stem-cell therapy, and the prospect of extraterrestrial intelligent life. Ecumenical centers for research that include a significant input from Lutheran scholars can be found in Heidelberg, Copenhagen, Berkeley, and Chicago.

See also Brahe, Tycho; Creation; Kepler, Johannes; Natural Theology

Bibliography

Dillenberger, J. *Protestant Thought and Natural Science: A Historical Interpretation*. Doubleday, 1960; Gingerich, O., and J. McLachlan. *Nicolaus Copernicus: Making the Earth a Planet*. Oxford University Press, 2005; Jackelén, A. *Time and Eternity: The Question of Time in Church, Science, and Theology*. Templeton Foundation Press, 2005; Pannenberg, W. *Toward a Theology of Nature: Essays on Science and Faith*. Ed. T. Peters. Westminster John Knox, 1993; Peters, T. *Anticipating Omega: Science, Faith, and Our Ultimate Universe*. Vandenhoeck & Ruprecht, 2006; Peterson, G. R. *Minding God: Theology and the Cognitive Sciences*. Fortress, 2003; Simmons, E. L. *The Entangled Trinity: Quantum Physics and Theology*. Fortress, 2014; Stenmark, L. *Religion, Science, and Democracy: A Disputational Friendship*. Lexington Books, 2013.

TED PETERS

Natural Theology

Natural theology is thinking about God apart from divine revelation. Early Christian theologians borrowed it from classical philosophy in order to achieve two goals. They wanted a theology that could (1) criticize different kinds of mythical and political theologies held by their non-Christian neighbors and (2) constructively establish the universal validity of the Christian faith by appealing to nature as a divine "book." Building on a Stoic idea, Paul claims in Rom. 1–2 that as created in the image of God, humans have a natural capacity for knowing God. With his theological predecessors, Luther shared the idea that all humans are born with a fundamental knowledge of God. But unlike the Thomists, Luther did not accentuate a philosophical distinction between nature and grace. In fact, the term *theologia naturalis* hardly played a role in the Reformation era. Instead, the Reformers were suspicious of a latent anthropological idealism in the medieval tradition. Luther was critical of the Scholastic teaching that humans possessed a natural capacity to utilize the intellect as a "higher" ability that divinely infused grace could then perfect in the process of salvation. In contrast, Luther did not build theology on an anthropology that regarded the intellect as more closely related to the divine than the body. Similar to Paul, he preferred a theological distinction between "spirit" and "flesh." For Luther, "spirit" meant human nature insofar as God's Spirit led it, and "flesh" meant human nature insofar as it lacked God's Spirit and was thus curved in upon itself (*incurvatus in se*).

In this perspective, natural knowledge about God is situated within the complex relationship between law and gospel. Both Luther and Melanchthon underscored the necessity to associate Christian faith with repentance, but they had slightly different nuances. Luther always regarded "natural" speculation about God as problematic, since it inevitably leads to doubt and despair. In his famous reply to Erasmus in *Bondage of the Will* (1525), he describes a hidden God (*Deus absconditus*) whose sheer majesty is dangerous to sinful humans, and whose will is revealed only in Scripture. But Luther's warning not to search for God outside biblical revelation did not prevent him from making constructive use of humanity's natural knowledge of the divine. For instance, even apart from revelation, humans are aware of God's existence, omnipotence, and omniscience. Additionally, Luther emphasized that the conscience is aware of certain ethical qualities, such as recognizing that God is the giver of all good things. The problem with this natural knowledge is that it guarantees no certainty about one's relation to God, a problem that can be resolved only through proclamation that properly distinguishes law from gospel (see, e.g., LC, Creed, par. 66; *BC* 440). Nevertheless, the question about natural theology bears not only on matters of theological prolegomena but specifically and acutely also on Luther's formulation of his Christology and the real presence of Christ in the Eucharist. He did not want to restrict the language about presence solely to biblical metaphors but instead shaped his insights in philosophical categories as well.

The Lutheran confessions continued this critical perspective on the limited human capacity for knowledge about God due to original sin. In the Apology of the Augsburg Confession, Melanchthon emphasized that apart from God's Word, humans are ignorant of God. God can be known only in his Word. Likewise, the Formula of Concord (SD 2) claims that the natural intellect (*humana ratio*) has "a dim spark of the knowledge that there is a God" and understands that there is a law, yet it emphasizes that human intellect is "weak, blind, and perverse." But one should notice that the confessors were keen to state the soteriological significance of these defects: human incapacity primarily concerns "divine promises and eternal salvation."

With Luther and the confessions, Melanchthon was suspicious of humanity's natural capacity to know God. In his 1521 *Loci communes*, Melanchthon pithily stated, "We adore the mysteries of the Godhead. That is better than to investigate them." Consequently, particularly in his exegetical writings, he would stress the loss of original justice due to sin. But even so he maintained a constructive use of natural reason in theology. Melanchthon saw God's existence proved through reason. In this way, he established the path for the scholarly relation between theology and philosophy for generations to come. In spite of the corruption caused by Adam's fall, natural knowledge (*notitiae naturalis*) formed an abiding structure within humanity. Through this internal structure within the mind, humanity can receive divine wisdom, particularly basic concepts of the law, such as punishment of evil and moral consciousness. But it also established other insights such as mathematical knowledge, natural order, and cause and effect. What remains outside human capacity is God's attitude toward the sinner, which is revealed only in the Scripture's proclamation of Christ.

Hence, for Melanchthon, there is, especially in matters of this world, an essential compatibility between the divine Spirit and the human spirit. Melanchthon suggested that some natural knowledge was innate and present at birth (*insita*), while other knowledge is acquired through experience of the created order (*acquisita*). Melanchthon's insights were due not only to his philosophical research, from which he concluded that the intellect (*mens*) held the most prominent place for natural communication with God, but were also reinforced by his exegetical research, particular in his *Commentary on Romans*. An important reason for Melanchthon's constructive use of natural theology lies partly in the creation's immanent traces (*vestigia*) of the Creator, and partly in the idea that the intelligent, finely tuned universe gives witness to a wise, masterful Architect.

In his lectures on Melanchthon's *Loci communes*, Martin Chemnitz follows Melanchthon in the distinction between innate and acquired knowledge, but links it more closely to the doctrine of justification. Chemnitz states that natural knowledge of God is either "nothing, imperfect, or feeble." There are three reasons for God to make himself known outside revelation: (1) for the sake of external discipline, (2) because God wants humans to seek him, and (3) to show that attempts to seek God are inadequate, even apart from revelation. Some of Melanchthon's disciples went even further and accorded the will a power in its ability to receive faith.

When metaphysics returned to the Lutheran university curriculum around 1600, it was necessary to clarify the relation between a constructive affirmation of a natural theology and a critical assessment of how far such knowledge could reach. When Daniel Hoffmann (1538–1611) attacked philosophy as "the mother of all heresies," other theologians responded by rejecting any theory of a "double truth." Instead, they claimed that revelation should build on the natural insights of metaphysics and thus gave metaphysics a propaedeutic function. Even so, Lutheran theologians were more concerned than their Tridentine Roman Catholic counterparts to distinguish between nature and grace. In opposition to Socinians, who identified reason and revelation, Lutheran theologians rejected a philosophical theology that did not distinguish

clearly (enough) between the two. Except for universities in Denmark and Sweden, most Lutheran universities did not adopt the method of Peter Ramus (1515–72), who wanted to situate both reason and revelation within a common logical system. Instead, following Melanchthon's lead, they opted for a version of Aristotelianism where logic had a purely instrumental function for theology. This limited metaphysical perspective served an important theological goal: to uphold the unique sacramental realism cherished by Lutherans, specifically that the thing (*res*) or real presence of Christ should not be subsumed or reduced to (mere) theory.

René Descartes (1596–1650) radicalized the theory of innate knowledge to the extent that humanity's relation to the external world was broken. In contrast, Lutherans claimed that there is a religious *habitus* (disposition), a condition of the soul present at birth, and which is not a result of human effort. But as a *habitus*, it is no innate idea, as Descartes claimed, but instead resulted from exposure to the external world. In part, it was an acquired knowledge. However, it was unclear whether this *habitus* was merely a disposition to know God or if this knowledge was gained at the time of birth. Johannes Musaeus (1613–81) claimed that children only had a "natural instinct" for divine knowledge; real knowledge did not come about until one had acquired experience.

The original Lutheran goal for natural theology was to balance the external "book of nature" with the internal "book of conscience." But this balancing act proved to be difficult. Theologians influenced by empiricism traced the beautiful, structured, and meaningful universe back to a Master Builder. For instance, William Paley (1743–1805) offered his famous watchmaker analogy in which just as a watch must have a watchmaker, so the world must have a God. But this appeal to the external world had its opponents too. In his *Dialogues concerning Natural Religion*, British philosopher David Hume (1711–76) rejected the possibility of deducing the existence of a deity from the existence of the world.

In that regard, Immanuel Kant (1724–1804) likewise agreed with Hume and rejected proofs of God's existence based on the "noumenal world" of the "things themselves." Kant claimed that human cognition, including alleged knowledge of God, is limited to the phenomenal world of appearance. In the *Critique of Pure Reason*, he conceded a natural—or rational—theology only insofar as it served the architectonic need to keep speculation about the unknowable noumenal realm at bay. Theology primarily is to serve moral theory, promising a rewarding afterlife for the immortal souls of the righteous. The natural world of things remained closed to religious knowledge.

Kant's philosophy echoed the spirit of the times (*Zeitgeist*). During the Enlightenment, there had been an increasing emphasis on internal anthropological categories for religion. The rational concept of "natural religion" replaced natural theology, which thereby lost revelation as its defining opposite. To be sure, Enlightenment theologians also preferred to speak of a "philosophy of religion" in distinction from natural theology, due to what they viewed as natural theology's inherent subjectivity in focusing on the conscience and the individual. But exclusion of the external world by using the term "natural religion" came at a high price, since Enlightenment theologians embraced a fundamental critique of both Scripture and dogma. Moreover, religious knowledge was considered a "positive" knowledge, a message, and not a mystical, sensual aspect of the world. The natural world had to be decoded as a text seen from the subjective perspective of the beholder. Additionally, the eclipse of natural theology correlated with the emergence of a bourgeois society: the social practices of the past were differentiated into the various functions of particular groups. Increasingly, with their "scientific" theology the religious professionals distanced themselves from the piety of the people.

In the nineteenth century, natural theology almost completely disappeared from Germany. For Schleiermacher (1768–1834), it deserved nothing but ridicule: "the malady of fragments put together from metaphysics and morality that one labels reasonable Christianity." Instead, he proposed the feeling of absolute dependence of the pious self as the characteristic trait of genuine spirituality. As one of its distinguishing traits, liberal theology consistently rejected natural theology. Albrecht Ritschl (1822–89), while influenced by Schleiermacher, criticized him for being too bound to metaphysical claims of the church, particularly the understanding of dogmatics as a treatment of church dogma. Ritschl wanted the justification of the individual to be at theology's core, which he developed solely on the basis of revelation. He suspected an evil intrusion of natural theology whenever there was a hint of knowledge of God independent of the Christian congregation because it would not be grounded in revelation.

However, the definitive break with natural theology came with Ritschl's pupils. Wilhelm Hermann (1846–1922) radicalized the innate structure of theology by claiming that the content of religion is subjective, a function of the soul itself. For Herrmann, Christ "happens" when the word "occurs" in the consciousness. There is a divide between the "core," the inner faith, and the "husk," the external medium. Adolf von Harnack (1851–1930) went so far as to say "without Christ I would have been an atheist."

Karl Barth (1886–1968), for all of his antipathy toward liberalism, continued this polemic against natural theology. He saw it as reason's opposition to the true theology of the word given in revelation. When his colleague Emil Brunner (1889–1966) claimed that in spite of sin there is a certain "point of contact" between God and humanity, Barth replied in 1934 with a book (in)famously titled *Nein!* (No!).

In spite of such modern efforts, natural theology cannot—and did not—disappear, although some theologians deemed the path unfruitful. Eberhard Jüngel (1934–), for example, claimed that by necessity natural theology would lead to a separation between the objective content of faith (*fides quae*) and personal belief (*fides qua*). However, Wolfhart Pannenberg (1928–2014) pointed out that the *Christian* use of the word "God" always implies a certain immediacy between humans and their Creator. He claimed that finite humans always understand themselves in light of an infinite being, even if that being is only vaguely conceived. For Pannenberg, this is a fundamental feature of humanity. Scandinavian theologies of creation (Løgstrup, Wingren) have also underlined the notion of structures or conditions of life that human beings hold in common, such as the confidence and trust of infants. Additionally, the Christian experience rests on a profound theological difference (from nonbelief or atheism) that reflects the eschatological difference between creation and redemption. Even if natural theology is a standing task for theology, one should be careful to underline the outcome as more preliminary than final.

See also Anthropology; Barth, Karl; Creation; Enlightenment; Jüngel, Eberhard; Kant, Immanuel; Melanchthon, Philip; Original Sin; Pannenberg, Wolfhart; Philosophy; Ritschl, Albrecht

Bibliography

Birkner, H.-J. "Natürliche Theologie und Offenbarungstheologie." In *Schleiermacher-Studien im Kontext*, ed. H. Fischer, 3–22. De Gruyter, 1996; Byrne, P. *Kant on God*. Ashgate, 2008; Elert, W. *Morphologie des Luthertums*. 2 vols. Beck, 1931–32; Frank, G. *Die theologische Philosophie Philipp Melanchthons (1497–1560)*. Benno, 1995; Friedrich, M. *Die Grenzen der Vernunft*. Vandenhoeck & Ruprecht, 2004; Schubert, A. *Das Ende der Sünde*. Vandenhoeck & Ruprecht, 2002; Sparn, W. "Natürliche Theologie." *TRE* 24:85–98; Sparn, W. "Die Schulphilosophie in den lutherischen Territorien." In *Grundriss der Geschichte der Philosophie: Die Philosophie des 17. Jahrhunderts*, ed. H. Holzhey and W. Schmidt-Biggemann, 4/1:475–587. Schwabe, 2001; Sparn, W. *Wiederkehr der Metaphysik*. Calwer, 1976; Wagner, F. "Das Problem der natürlichen Theologie bei Albrecht Ritschl." In *Gottes Reich und menschliche Freiheit: Ritschl-Kolloquium*, ed. J. Ringleben, 1–22. Vandenhoeck & Ruprecht, 1990; Weinhardt, J. *Wilhelm Herrmanns Stellung in der Ritschschen Schule*. Mohr Siebeck, 1996.

JOAR HAGA

Nesib, Onesimos

A native Oromo, Onesimos Nesib (ca. 1856–1931) was enslaved in 1869 and eventually brought to Massawa (in modern Eritrea), where he was freed and educated by the Swedish Evangelical Mission. He was baptized in 1872 and received his further education in Sweden. After his return to Massawa and some unsuccessful attempts to reach the Oromo region, he began with his translation work. With the help of Aster Ganno, he was able to translate the entire Bible. In 1904 Nesib at last returned to Welega and started to preach in the Oromo language. Despite some opposition from some Ethiopian Coptic priests, who saw to it that the emperor ban his preaching, after 1916 he was free to preach and distribute his translations until his death. A seminary of the Mekane Yesus Church in Ethiopia is named after him.

See also Ethiopia

Bibliography

Bulcha, M. "Onesimos Nasib's Pioneering Contributions to Oromo Writing." *Nordic Journal of African Studies* 4, no. 1 (1995): 36–59; Menberu, D. "Onesimus Nesib." In *Dictionary of African Christian Biography*. http://www.dacb.org/stories/ethiopia/onesimus_nesib.html. Overseas Ministries Study Center, 2005.

FRIEDER LUDWIG

Netherlands, The

Antwerp, during the Reformation era in the southern part of the Netherlands (part of Belgium from the 1830s), was the cradle of Dutch Lutheranism. Through trade and the travels of people like the artist Albrecht Dürer (1471–1528), but mainly through the Augustinian monastery (1513–22), there was a vivid connection between Wittenberg and Antwerp. Luther's writings circulated as early as 1518. They became part of the development of a broader Evangelical movement. But they were also the basis for a growing group that connected specifically with the Lutheran ideas and met in private homes. Lutheran services in a church building were only possible during a very short period, from September 1566 until

April 1567. This made Antwerp the first Lutheran congregation with the permission of the civil authorities in a non-Lutheran country. A congregation of about four thousand was served by six pastors, mostly orthodox Lutherans and six theological advisers, the most prominent being Matthias Flacius Illyricus (1520–75). Advisers and pastors authored the Antwerp Confession and the Antwerp Agenda. After the fall of Antwerp in 1585 to the Spanish troops and the imposition of Roman Catholic worship, most Lutherans left the city and moved to the northern part of the Netherlands, bringing with them these writings that formed the basis for the developing Lutheran congregations. The Lutherans from Antwerp also brought along their experience in how to maintain their Lutheran identity under a non-Lutheran authority and among other religious minorities.

In the German lands of the Roman Empire, the Peace of Augsburg (1555) established Lutheranism legally, according to the principle *cuius regio, eius religio* (whose realm, his religion), with the exception of imperial cities, such as Frankfurt and Augsburg, where both confessions worshiped openly. The Netherlands were organized differently. In the course of the Dutch Revolt (1555–1648) the political leadership in the northern provinces changed from Catholic to Reformed. As a result, the Reformed church became the public church, with the most legal rights and highest visibility. Other religious communities strived for and achieved—to a varying degree—representation in the public space. The basis for this was article 13 of the Union of Utrecht (1579), which guaranteed freedom of conscience.

The emerging Lutheran congregations were initially mostly formed by migrants from Antwerp, the German lands of the empire, and Scandinavia. The congregation in Amsterdam took the lead in organizational, financial, and theological respects. By 1660 Amsterdam had become a metropolis with an international trading network and 200,000 inhabitants—the third largest city in Europe, after Paris and London. The Lutheran congregation—with its social elite of merchants, traders, and representatives of German and Scandinavian courts—played an important part in that development. With almost 26,000 newly registered members between 1663 and 1700, it was the biggest Lutheran congregation in the world at that time. This gave Lutherans the leverage to negotiate a highly visible religious space, unlike other religious minorities such as the Arminians and Mennonites. Substantial regional differences existed in the Netherlands. This is reflected in the public appearance and status of the Lutheran congregations. While Lutherans in Amsterdam after 1633 could celebrate services in majestic, visible churches, their coreligionists in Frisia, for example, still came together in hidden churches (buildings that looked like houses on the outside but were clearly defined worship spaces in the inside).

The Lutheran community remained an independent church for more than four hundred years. In 2004, the year when Lutherans became a part of the Protestant Church in the Netherlands (Protestantse Kerk in Nederland), there were approximately twelve thousand Lutherans in the Netherlands.

Bibliography

Haefeli, E. *New Netherland and the Dutch Origins of American Religious Liberty*. University of Pennsylvania Press, 2012; Hiebsch, S. "The Coming of Age of the Lutheran Congregation in Early Modern Amsterdam." *Journal of Early Modern Christianity* 3, no. 1 (May 2016): 1–29; Kuijpers, E. "Poor, Illiterate and Superstitious? Social and Cultural Characteristics of the 'Noordse Natie' in the Amsterdam Lutheran Church in the Seventeenth Century." In *Dutch Light in the Norwegian Night*, ed. L. Sicking et al., 57–67. Verloren, 2004; Manen, K. G. van, ed. *Lutheranen in de Lage Landen: Geschiedenis van een godsdienstige minderheid (ca. 1520–2004)*. ET summary, 753–61. Boekencentrum, 2001; Spicer, A. "'Hic Coeli Porta Est, Hic Domus Ecce Dei': Lutheran Churches in the Dutch world, c. 1566–1719." In *Lutheran Churches in Early Modern Europe*, ed. A. Andrew, 445–82. Ashgate, 2012.

SABINE HIEBSCH

New Sweden

The American colony known as New Sweden (1638–55) began in 1638 when two ships from Sweden, the *Kalmar Nyckel* and the

Fogel Grip, arrived at what is now known as "The Rocks" in Wilmington, Delaware. These Swedes erected Fort Christina there and also named the river after their queen. They were the first of ten successful expeditions sent out to establish a colony between New Netherland (to the north) and Maryland (to the south). The expedition leader was the former governor of New Amsterdam, Peter Minuit, who had lost his position with the Dutch West India Company and picked the site on a tributary of the Delaware River in order to trade for furs with the Lenape. By the time of the third governor of New Sweden, Johan Printz (1643–53), the colony had become a royal venture with only Swedish investors. Unfortunately Sweden could not afford a colony while it was engaged in the Thirty Years' War and did not succeed in obtaining its own present boundaries until 1658, with the Peace of Roskilde. Sweden also lacked any overpopulation to provide immigrants, except for the "Forest Finns" who came to the Delaware in large numbers only at the end of the colony's existence, when it became clear that they could legally pursue slash-and-burn agriculture in New Sweden. The colony also lacked support from Queen Christina, who saw no need for it. When she abdicated and a new king, Karl X Gustaf, was crowned, he supported reinvigorating the venture, but it was already too late: the Dutch had decided to eliminate it because of competition with the Indian trade business.

Although some six hundred people had arrived in New Sweden over seventeen years, at the time of the Dutch invasion only three hundred were left. During this time Lutheran chaplains served the colony, first only at Fort Christina and then also at the newly built church (1646) at Fort New Gothenburg, Governor Printz's new capital on Tinicum Island (Essington, Pennsylvania). The first garrison chaplain was Pastor Torkil, whose name was sometimes Latinized to Reorus (the preacher) Torkillus. He arrived in 1641 on the second expedition and was the first Lutheran pastor to serve a call in America. He and his wife died two years later, and he was buried by his successor, the famed Swedish Lutheran missionary to Native Americans, Johan Campanius (1601–83). The six Lutheran pastors who served the colony provided a ministry of word and sacrament to the many people who had spread out in what came to be the states of Delaware, Pennsylvania, New Jersey, and Maryland. The colonists had generally good relations with the local Native Americans, and they traded, hunted, and assisted each other in a remarkable example of cultural harmony. When the colony was conquered by the Dutch in 1655, a new period began. New Sweden was given self-government by the Dutch as the "Swedish Nation," with its own militia, law court, and churches. Swedish remained the language of trade until the Quaker invasion of 1681. By 1693, when the famous letter was sent to the Swedish king asking for new priests, the inhabitants of the colony numbered about twelve hundred. The king and bishop Jesper Svedberg responded positively, and the church of Sweden renewed its mission on the Delaware with the arrival of three priests in 1697, one of whom was provost under the bishops of Sweden, authorized to ordain additional priests. They maintained cordial relations with the Pennsylvania Ministerium. The church of Sweden continued to send pastors to the area until the American Revolution, and the original two congregations eventually became eight. After the Revolution, these congregations became part of the Episcopalian Church.

See also Augustana Synod; Sweden

Bibliography

Craig, P. S. *The 1693 Census of the Swedes on the Delaware*. Swedish American Genealogist Publications, 1993; Craig, P. S., and K.-E. Williams, eds. *Colonial Records of Swedish Churches in Pennsylvania*. Vols. 1–6. Swedish Colonial Society, 2006–14; Dahlgren, S., and H. Norman. *The Rise and Fall of New Sweden, 1654–55*. Almqvist & Wiksell, 1988; Jacobsson, N. *Svenska öden vid Delaware 1638–1831*. Svenska Krykans Diakonistyrelses, 1938; Johnson, A. *The Swedish Settlements on the Delaware, 1638–1664*. 2 vols. University of Pennsylvania / D. Appleton, 1911.

KIM-ERIC WILLIAMS

Nicaragua

Lutheran work began in 1997 after Lutheran Church Canada (LCC, a partner church of the Lutheran Church–Missouri Synod) received an invitation to share the gospel there. The first missionary was a Nicaraguan refugee, Pastor Sandor Arguello. By January 2008, Iglesia Luterana Sinodo de Nicaragua (ILSN) was established. Its president is Marvin Donaire. Lutheran work has been a partnership between the LCMS, LCC, and the ILSN, with a commitment to a Lutheran presence and outreach in Central America, to provide leaders to assist with spiritual care, and to support new church plants.

Missionaries work with community members to identify people who are capable of serving in this capacity, and the LCC provides seminary instructors, including pastors, and especially faculty members of the Concordia Lutheran Theological Seminary, St. Catharines, Ontario, to train pastors and deaconesses. In March 2009 five pastoral candidates and nine deaconesses graduated from the in-service program. Mission work is carried out in evangelism, Christian education, medical and dental care, women's work, and outreach. Canadian Lutheran World Relief and the Concordia Lutheran Mission Society provide grants for educational programs.

The ILSN has twelve pastors, twenty-six deaconesses, twelve vicars, and thirteen deaconess interns. It has twenty-two congregations, four missions, two church plants in Honduras, two mission plants in Costa Rica, and a seminary. In 2008 the LCC approved formal altar and pulpit fellowship with the ILSN.

Bibliography

Jahnel, C. *The Lutheran Church in El Salvador*. Servicio Educativo Cristiano-LBCM, 2009; http://www.lutheran central.com; http://sdsynod.org/where-we-serve/globally /companion-synods/nicaragua/; http://www.lutheran church-canada.ca/missions.php?s=nicaragua.

ORIN W. CUMMINGS

Nicholas of Lyra

Born in Lyre, Normandy, Nicholas of Lyra (ca. 1270–1349) became the most famous late medieval exegete. He probably learned Hebrew at the Jewish center of learning in Évreux. Proficient in the Talmud, midrash, and the work of Rashi (Rabbi Solomon ben Isaac, 1045–1105), he was celebrated for his centering biblical interpretation in the literal text. He became a Franciscan in Verneuil (ca. 1300), relocated to Paris, and was Franciscan regent master at the University of Paris (1308–9). Due to his rank, he participated in the trials of the Knights Templar (1307) and the Beguine mystic Marguerite Porete (1310). A moderate Franciscan and friend of the French royal family, he served as Franciscan provincial of France from 1319 and Burgundy from 1324, during the conflict between the pope and the radical Franciscans over evangelical poverty.

The famous saying "If Lyra had not played the lyre, Luther would not have danced" is not entirely accurate, but it does reflect how the literal exegesis in Lyra's magnum opus, *The Literal Postil on the Whole Bible* (1322–31), influenced Luther. As the first biblical commentary to be printed in 1471–72 by Sweynheym and Pannartz in Rome and then reprinted with the Ordinary Gloss in 1495 in Strasbourg, it served in its numerous editions as the standard reference manual for biblical commentary in the late Middles Ages and early modern period and was readily available to Luther and Melanchthon and other reformers. By copying and redacting the Scholastic exegesis, especially of Thomas Aquinas, into his encyclopedic *Literal Postil*, Lyra made the medieval commentary tradition available alongside the standard early medieval ordinary gloss. Luther often began his exegesis by referencing Lyra, and he valued Lyra's critique of the Jewish commentators. Lyra's facility with the Jewish rabbinic interpretation provided Luther with a starting point, especially in his lectures on Genesis in 1536–45 (LW 1–6). In his preface to Ezekiel for the German translation of the Bible, Luther writes (LW 35:290): "One who would understand this building of the temple, altar, city, and land, which Ezekiel [40–48] describes, must take up Lyra with his figures and glosses; otherwise one will toil and labor in the matter in vain." Though he cited him, Luther did not always follow Lyra's lead, as he saw his literal readings and allegiance to Jewish interpretation in the Old Testament problematic for Christian interpretation. In the *Last Words of David* in 1543 (LW 15:269), he wrote, "Just consider that excellent Lyra. He is a good Hebraist and a fine Christian. What good work he produces when he, in accord with the New Testament, opposes the Jewish concept. But whenever he follows his Rabbi Solomon, how meaningless and unimpressive it sounds; it has neither hands nor feet, despite his good command of words and letters. Still he surpasses all the others, both old and new Hebraists, who follow the rabbis altogether too strictly." Luther appreciated Lyra's christocentric reading of the Scriptures but (given Luther's commitment to justification by faith alone) not Lyra's proposal that any commentator, Jewish or Christian, *rationally* should be able to find Christ in a literal reading of Old Testament texts. Luther was also not a follower of Lyra's famous double-literal sense adapted from Augustine and Aquinas and later used by Faber Stapulensis, in which Old Testament prophetic texts have one meaning for their context and a second, christological meaning. For Luther this was too cumbersome, and he "posits a single literal sense, which is at the same time *sensus grammaticus* and *sensus theologicus*" (Froehlich, *Sensing*, 42).

In his 1515 lectures on Romans, the young Luther objected to Lyra's interpretation of Rom. 1:17, "For in it [the gospel] the righteousness of God is revealed through faith for faith," as one moving from faith to faith, meaning from an unformed faith to a faith "formed" by love. Luther cites Nicholas as an authority and then rejects that interpretation (LW 25:152). A righteous person, he argues, cannot live by such an unformed faith (*fides informata*, the technical medieval term for faith in right doctrine not yet "formed" by the disposition of charity), nor can anyone believe by means of it (*Bible in Medieval Tradition*, 57). In a Table Talk he notes that while as a young scholar he loved the Gloss yet despised Lyra, but later learned his value for history (no. 116, in 1530; LW 54:14). Luther's second preface to the book of Revelation in 1530 demonstrates this turn toward history. In it he uses Lyra's literal/historical method and outline of history to explain the symbols of Revelation, but he only starts with Lyra and does not follow Lyra's insistence that one cannot identify contemporary historical events and figures within the church with the symbols and patterns of Revelation and that antichrist is not to be found in the church. Luther produces a new evangelical/historical genre of Apocalypse commentary (Krey and Krey). For Luther, Lyra is a key interpreter of the tradition, whom he reads, and then he draws his own conclusions by using his own genius and the wider tradition.

See also Bible Interpretation

Bibliography

Froehlich, K. *Sensing the Scriptures*. Eerdmans, 2014; Froehlich, K., and M. Gibson. *Biblia Latina cum Glossa Ordinaria: Introduction to the Facsimile Reprint of the Editio Princeps*, xvi–xxvi. Brepols, 1992; Krey, P., and L. Smith, eds. *Nicholas of Lyra: The Senses of Scripture*. Brill, 2000; Krey, P., and P. Krey. *Luther's Spirituality*, 48–56. Paulist Press, 2007; Levy, I., P. Krey, and T. Ryan, eds. *The Letter to the Romans*. In *The Bible in Medieval Tradition*, 50–58. Eerdmans, 2013; LW, vols. 1, 15, 25, 35, 54; Ocker C. "Scholastic Interpretation of the Bible." In *A History of Biblical Interpretation*, ed. A. Hauser and D. Watson, 2:266–67. Eerdmans, 2009.

PHILIP D. KREY

Nicolai, Philipp

The German pastor, polemical theologian, hymnist, and devotional writer Philipp Nicolai (1556–1608) was born in Mengeringhausen, a town in the county of Waldeck (now Hesse), where his father was a Lutheran pastor. He studied theology in Erfurt and Wittenberg (1576–79) and later received a doctorate from Wittenberg (1594). In 1583 he became pastor in Herdecke, where he faced opposition from the Catholic town council and was eventually driven out by Spanish mercenary troops. He was appointed court preacher to the counts of Waldeck in 1588 and served as pastor in Unna (Westphalia) from 1596 until 1601. Shortly after his arrival, Unna was devastated by the plague. To provide consolation to his parishioners he wrote *Mirror of the Joys of Eternal Life*. Published in 1599, this book also contained the two hymns for which he is most remembered: "Wachet auf, ruft uns die Stimme [Wake, awake for night is flying]" and "Wie schön leuchtet der Morgenstern [How brightly shines the morning star/O morning star, how fair and bright]." Nicolai moved to St. Katherine's Church in Hamburg in 1601 and served there until his death.

Nicolai was both a passionate defender of Lutheran doctrine and a contributor to the continuation of a more subjective, spiritual mode of theology, which also appeared in the writings of his contemporary Johann Arndt. Most of his writings were polemical in nature and especially critical of the Sacramentarians. He claimed that Calvinists turned God into a monster through their doctrine of double predestination and repeatedly denounced their denial of the bodily presence of Christ in and with the elements of the Lord's Supper. In his book *The History of the Kingdom of Christ* (1598), he portrayed the pope and Muhammad as the two antichrists but also rejoiced at the expansion of Christianity throughout the world. The strife of his day led him to expect the imminent arrival of the last judgment, and he speculated that it might happen in 1670.

The Mirror of Joys, by contrast, was free of polemics, focusing instead on a description of the eternal wedding that takes place between Christ and the Christian in the heavenly Jerusalem. Influenced by Augustine as well as Luther, Nicolai described the rest that the soul will find in a perfect bond of love with God and proposed that the indwelling of Christ could be experienced in this life as well as in the life to come. The spiritual wedding motif also appears in his hymn "Wachet auf," which is based on a parable in Matt. 25 and certain motifs from Revelation, and in "Wie schön leuchtet," a mystical bridal song based on Ps. 45. These hymns, often called the King and Queen of Chorales, have had an enduring place in Lutheran hymnody. They were incorporated into two of J. S. Bach's best-known cantatas (*BWV* 1 & 140) and into Felix Mendelssohn's oratorios *Elijah* (Opus 70) and *St. Paul* (36).

See also Hymnody; Music

Bibliography
Julian, J. *Dictionary of Hymnology*. Esp. 1:805–7. Rev. ed. J. Murray, 1907. Reprint, Kregel, 1985; Lindström, M. *Philipp Nicolais Verständnis des Christentums*. C. Bertelsmann, 1939; Stoeffler, E. *The Rise of Evangelical Pietism*. Esp. 197–200. Brill, 1965; Zeller, W. "Zum Verständnis Philipp Nicolais." In *Frömmigkeit in Hessen*, 67–79. Elwert, 1970.

ERIC LUND

Niemoeller, Martin

The German pastor and churchman Martin Niemoeller (Niemöller, 1892–1984) is known for his opposition to National Socialism. The son of a Lutheran pastor, he was born in Lippstadt, Westphalia. He entered the German Navy, where he served as an officer, eventually commanding a U-boat and being decorated with the Iron Cross for his accomplishments. After World War I, Niemoeller worked as a farmer before enrolling at the University of Münster in 1919, to pursue theological studies leading to ordination in 1924. After his ordination he worked with the Inner Mission in Westphalia until 1931, when he accepted a call to serve a congregation in Dalhem, a fashionable suburb of Berlin.

Early in his career, Niemoeller supported Hitler because he was convinced that National Socialism would restore Christian values to Germany. As he matured, he renounced this support and joined with others in opposing the party on theological grounds. In 1933 Niemoeller participated in the formation of the Pastors' Emergency League and the Young Reformation Movement, rejecting the "Aryan paragraphs" as contrary to Christian confession. He, like Bonhoeffer, opposed any compromise with National Socialism despite the fact that certain colleagues within the Confessing Church advocated a mediating position.

This created tension and caused some to hold Niemoeller suspect, but for others he became an icon of the church's resistance to the forces of Fascism. He was arrested in 1937, acquitted in 1938, but remained under custody as a "personal prisoner" of Hitler. In 1941 he was transferred to Dachau, where he was interred until 1945. Imprisoned with several priests, Niemoeller considered converting to Roman Catholicism.

After the war, Niemoeller addressed the question of the German people's guilt and his complicity in it with the Stuttgart Declaration of Guilt (1945) and Darmstadt Declaration (1947). From 1947 to 1964 he served as president of the territorial church in Hesse-Nassau, and in 1961 he was elected as one of the six presidents of the World Council of Churches. Niemoeller was a polemical figure during the Cold War, making trips to Communist countries, protesting nuclear armament, adopting a pacifist stance, and denouncing confessional differences as outdated and no longer church-divisive in light of the contemporary situation.

See also Bonhoeffer, Dietrich; Confessing Church; German Christians (Deutsche Christen); Holocaust; Thielicke, Helmut; World Wars I and II

Bibliography

Bentley, J. *Martin Niemoeller, 1882–1984.* Free Press, 1984; Locke, H. G., ed. *Exile in the Fatherland: Martin Niemoeller's Letters from Moabit Prison.* Eerdmans, 1986; Niemoeller, M. *From U-Boat to Pulpit.* Wilett, Clark, 1937; Schmidt, D. *Pastor Niemoeller.* Trans. L. Wilson. Doubleday, 1959; Scholder, K. *The Churches and the Third Reich.* Trans. J. Bowden. Vol. 1. Fortress, 1988.

JOHN T. PLESS

Nigeria

With approximately 174 million inhabitants, Nigeria is the most populous country in Africa and the seventh most populous country in the world. There are two Lutheran denominations. The Lutheran Church of Christ in Nigeria (LCCN, about 2.2 million members) has its headquarters in Numan (Adamawa State) and its stronghold in the Nigerian Middle Belt, especially in the cities of Yola, Kaduna, and

Jos. It became a member of the LWF in 1961. The Lutheran Church of Nigeria, with 148,000 members, is strongest in eastern Nigeria, particularly in the Qua Iboe region. It has close ties with the LCMS.

The origins of the LCCN can be traced back to the work of a Danish missionary, Dr. Niels Bronnum, who arrived in Numan on September 29, 1913. Maunde Chaugularam, a freed slave, was baptized in Numan in 1917. This resulted in an upsurge in the Lutheran Church. Chaugalaram remained a layperson; the first five Nigerian pastors were ordained in 1948. In 1956 the LCCN became independent. The first Nigerian to lead this church was Akila Todi, who in 1960 became president and in 1973 bishop. During this period the LCCN was able to establish congregations in almost all the cities in Nigeria. Discussions about the ordination of women and about dancing during worship, as well as accusations of ethnic favoritism, produced internal disagreements. Under Todi's successor, Windibiziri, the LCCN became strongly engaged in Christian-Muslim dialogue, vital in Nigeria. In 1993 the LCCN initiated the Association for Christian-Muslim Mutual Relations in Nigeria (ACMMRN). In 1997 women participated for the first time and gave papers on the rights of women in the society according to their religious traditions. Several conferences were held, and a dialogue center in Jos was established. In 2014, Archbishop Nemuel Babba led the LCCN to appeal to the violent Boko Haram group to come and dialogue instead of using arms.

The LCCN runs ten dispensaries and three maternity homes. Bronnum Lutheran Seminary and the interdenominational Theological College of Northern Nigeria in Bukuru are the major training institutions for pastors and church leaders. The LCCN also supports congregations in other African countries, for instance, in Sierra Leone.

The Lutheran Church of Nigeria (LCN) owes its existence to a large extent to the initiative of a Nigerian, Jonathan Udo Ekong (1881–1982). His forty-six years of ministry focused especially on the Ibibio people of southeastern Nigeria. Today the LCN operates schools, hospitals, and health-care centers as well as a seminary and a radio studio.

See also Islam

Bibliography

Bulala, D. *The Lutheran Church of Christ in Nigeria*. AD Printing, 2001; Gaiya, M. A. B. "Akila Todi." In *Dictionary of African Christian Biography*. http://www.dacb.org /stories/nigeria/todi_akila.html. Overseas Ministries Study Center, 2003; McGarvey, K. *Muslim and Christian Women in Dialogue: The Case of Northern Nigeria*. Lang, 2009; Nissen, M. *A Story of a Lutheran Church in Nigeria*. Numan, 1993; Rasmussen, L. *Bridges instead of Walls: Christian-Muslim Interaction in Denmark, Indonesia and Nigeria*. Lutheran University Press, 2007.

FRIEDER LUDWIG

Nihilism and Postmodernism

Both the terms "nihilism" and "postmodernism" assume complex and contradictory definitions. "Nihilism" can mean the denial of an intrinsic value to existence and aim at the leveling of all, which only death itself accomplishes (Kierkegaard). It can also denote a radical form of skepticism, entailing that nothing can be ultimately known but evanescent phenomena (Kant) or simulacra (Baudrillard) of things. Yet a confidence remains that a metaphysics of presence is unavoidable: even in the midst of death itself, affirmation persists even in pervasive negativity (Derrida). "*Postmodernism*" may equally range from an extreme fragmentation of all (Lyotard) to a holism of a cosmic neomystic harmony of all there is (Capra). No matter how these concepts are defined, the paroxysm they represent points simultaneously to contradictory characteristics, which are ascribed, in fact, to modernity as such. What they have in common is the realization of things falling to pieces in a perennial and ephemeral passing away, in utter continuous decadence; yet they also simultaneously reveal its twin side in the longing for the eternal and the whole (Baudelaire, Foucault, Giddens). Nihilism and postmodernity are names for this paroxysm of the late modern age's stratification; death and

life, fragmentation and integration, these are twins poles in the age of modernity.

The dawn of this age has been differently marked. Some date it as early as the eschatological vision of redemption and the law of love of the apostle Paul (Benjamin, Taubes, Badiou). Others look to Jesus himself with his apocalyptic urgency alongside outstanding ethical exigencies (Weiss, Schweitzer), which some regard as a paradox, if not a plain and illegitimate contradiction (Otto). Still others have argued in favor of Nicholas of Cusa as harbinger of modernity (Gadamer, Blumenberg). But there is also an argument, first advanced in the so-called Luther Renaissance of the early twentieth century but parallel to claims made in the Enlightenment, that presents Luther as the beacon of modernity. In this respect the proximity of Luther to Paul's own theology turns the query regarding the paroxysm of modernity into a postural question and not, primarily, a chronological issue. As a question of attitude, the ensuing paroxysm that modernity unleashes can be definitely recognized in Luther's radical view of the diastasis between faith and love; in the tension of being sinner and of being saint; between the bondage of the will and the human deliberate cooperation with God; flanked by an apocalyptic verve and love's required discipline; torn by the two regimes in which humans are inserted; being in the simultaneous exposure to being unconditionally molded before God by God's promise, and shaping one's calculated commitment in the world; being at once radically receptive in a *vita passiva* (passive life), and actively committed to love God's creatures; knowing God's end-time presence (*parousia*), and yet receiving it in the masks (*larvae*), that is, in the wrapping (*involucrum*) of this world and through the humbleness of representing it by finite means.

The very language of justification entails such paradox. This is the reason for Luther's seemingly hyperbolic language in which justification "destroys," "annihilates," "kills" all the presumptuousness of *vita activa* and *vita contemplativa*, which do not bring about any hope. However, hoping against any hope requires a commitment to Christian uncompromising love in its most meager, finite, and frail manifestations.

See also Kant, Immanuel; Kierkegaard, Søren Aabye; Philosophy

Bibliography

Badiou, A. *Saint Paul: The Foundation of Universalism.* Trans. R. Brassier. Stanford University Press, 2003; Blumenberg, H. *The Legitimacy of the Modern Age.* Trans. R. M. Wallace. MIT Press, 1985; Derrida, J. *The Gift of Death.* Trans. D. Wills. University of Chicago Press, 1995; Foucault, M. *The Foucault Reader.* Ed. P. Rabinow. Pantheon, 1984; Luther, M. *The Bondage of the Will.* In LW 33; Luther, M. *Confession concerning the Lord's Supper.* LW 37; Lyotard, J. *The Postmodern Condition: A Report on Knowledge.* Trans. G. Bennington and B. Massumi. University of Minnesota Press, 1984.

VITOR WESTHELLE

Ninety-Five Theses

The Ninety-Five Theses (LW 31:17–33), the later designation for Martin Luther's "Disputation on the Power and Efficacy of Indulgences," were written in Latin in late October 1517, sent on October 31, 1517, to the archbishop Albrecht of Mainz, and according to tradition, posted on the Castle Church door on the same day and distributed to other theologians for their written opinion. Despite the opening announcement, a public disputation was never held. Whether originally distributed in manuscript or printed form (no Wittenberg printing is extant), the Theses were printed in placard form in Leipzig and Nuremberg and in booklet form in Basel. Although a German translation was made in Nuremberg (though perhaps never printed), Luther viewed such a translation as inappropriate for a German-speaking readership, publishing instead his *Sermon on Indulgences and Grace*, which was reprinted over twenty times, making Luther overnight a best-selling author.

The Theses represent Luther's response to the sale of the so-called Peter's Indulgence. This plenary indulgence, proclaimed by Pope Leo X in 1516 to assist in building the basilica of Sts. Peter and Paul in Rome, was offered by Albrecht beginning in January 1517 and announced by the Dominican Johann Tetzel. Albrecht was raising money for this construction in Rome and to finance his own purchase of ecclesial office in the territories just to the west and north of Electoral Saxony (something Luther learned about only much later). The *Summary Instruction* issued by the archbishop's court theologians regulating such preaching promised the full remission of all satisfaction remaining for sin of the purchaser or of designated souls in purgatory, as well as certain other privileges.

Not the first in German territories to see problems with indulgences, Luther had already questioned them in his lectures on Romans (1515–16) and in a sermon delivered at the Castle Church in January 1517. In the Ninety-Five Theses he questions them based on an interpretation of Matt. 4:17 (cf. the Vulgate's *poenitentiam agite*, "Do penance") first proposed by Erasmus of Rotterdam's 1516 annotations on the Greek text. Luther expanded that text's meaning beyond the sacrament of penance to include the entire life of the Christian as one of continual penitence. His chief argument, introduced in thesis 5, concluded that, based on the history of penance and indulgences reflected in canon law, papal indulgences reached only as far as ecclesiastical penalties for sin and did not touch at all on God's punishments that brought the flesh under discipline and put the old creature to death. Attempts to avoid such divine penalties through indulgences ran contrary to true contrition (sorrow for sin out of love of God). On this basis, Luther rejected the claims of the indulgence preachers and the *Summary Instruction*; he insisted that teaching Christians to support the poor was a good work far superior to the purchase of indulgences. In an excursus on the treasures of the church (theses 56–68), he rejected the notion (derived from a decree of Clement VI) that such a treasury consisted of the merits of Christ and the saints. These merits worked the death of the old creature and the life of the new without indulgences since the true treasure of the church was the "gospel of the glory and grace of God." While still allowing preaching of indulgences to continue, he warned bishops and other church leaders against suppressing the gospel (theses 69–80), showed how indulgence preaching was raising unanswerable questions among the laity (theses 81–91), and closed by contrasting the false peace of indulgences to the preaching of the cross.

Upon their receipt, Archbishop Albrecht suspected false teaching and submitted them to his theology faculty in Mainz and to Rome. At the same time Johann Tetzel received a copy and attacked Luther's arguments in counter-theses composed by Konrad Wimpina, professor at the University of Frankfurt (an der Oder) and defended by Tetzel in a public disputation, for which he was awarded a doctorate in theology. The papal court's chief censor and theologian, Sylvester Prierias, composed a thoroughgoing refutation, published in the summer of 1518. In the spring of 1518 Luther produced a defense of his theses (the *Explanations* [LW 31:77–252]), which his local bishop, Jerome of Brandenburg, gave him permission to publish. At Luther's interview with Cardinal Cajetan (Thomas de Vio) in October 1518 (see LW 31:253–92), the explanation of thesis 7 (regarding the certainty of the priest's absolution) and thesis 58 (defining the treasure of the church) were debated. John Eck's handwritten refutation of the Theses (the so-called Obelisks) prompted Luther to publish this refutation with a response (the Asterisks). When the theology faculties of Louvain and Paris also condemned the Theses, Jacobus Latomus wrote a defense of Louvain's condemnation in 1519, which Luther answered in 1521 in *Against Latomus* (LW 32:133–260). By then the debate over indulgences had moved on to broader issues of theology, and Luther was excommunicated by the pope and condemned as an outlaw of the empire by the Diet of Worms. Though the Theses are sometimes used to represent Luther's work, most theologians today acknowledge that the Theses are

quite narrowly focused and show his developing theology, not his mature thought.

See also Albrecht of Mainz; Eck, John; Ninety-Five Theses, Posting of the; Prierias, Sylvester; Tetzel, Johann

Bibliography

Aland, K., ed. *Martin Luther's Ninety-Five Theses with the Pertinent Documents from the History of the Reformation.* Trans. P. J. Schroeder. Concordia, 1967; Bornkamm, H. *Thesen und Thesenanschlag Luthers.* Töpelmann, 1967; Brecht, M. *Martin Luther: His Road to Reformation, 1483–1521.* Trans. J. Schaaf. Esp. 175–237. Fortress, 1985; Iserloh, E. *The Theses Were Not Posted: Luther between Reform and Reformation.* Trans. J. Wicks. Beacon, 1968; Leppin, V., and T. Wengert, "Sources for and against the Posting of the Ninety-Five Theses." *Lutheran Quarterly* 29 (2015): 373–98; Ott, J., and M. Treu, eds. *Luthers Thesenanschlag—Faktum oder Fiktion.* Evangelische Verlagsanstalt, 2008.

TIMOTHY J. WENGERT

Ninety-Five Theses, Posting of the

From June 1546, when Philip Melanchthon first mentioned the posting of the Ninety-Five Theses in print in the preface to the second volume of Luther's Latin works, until the 1950s, no one questioned whether Martin Luther had posted his theses on the Castle Church door in Wittenberg on October 31, 1517. Such a posting of theses—a normal part of sixteenth-century university life—became over the centuries an iconic event, exemplified by the 1617 etching that depicts Luther, quill in hand, writing on the Castle Church door with a feather long enough to knock the tiara off the pope's head in Rome. Then in 1959 Hans Volz altered the received chronology and argued for a posting on November 1. In several publications appearing between 1961 and 1966, Erwin Iserloh, the Roman Catholic Reformation scholar from the University of Münster, suggested that the theses were not posted at all (ET in 1967). After initial skepticism if not downright antagonism, especially among Protestants, most scholars now admit that arguments may be made on both sides and that the most important event on October 31, 1517, was *not* the posting of the Theses but the mailing of them to Archbishop Albrecht of Mainz—the original cover letter in Luther's hand, dated October 31, 1517, rests in the Swedish royal archives. Albrecht's response (suspecting false teaching and sending them to his theologians in Mainz and to Rome) turned the Theses into a full-blown case. Thus most agree that Luther's Theses were not designed as a protest, that he showed the required deference to ecclesiastical authorities, and that he was genuinely surprised at how quickly the Theses were distributed.

Arguments against their posting include the fact that Melanchthon, who first mentioned the event in print, did not arrive in Wittenberg until August 1518 and was not an eyewitness. In later writings, in reminiscences from the Table Talk, and in letters from 1518, Luther stresses that he sent them to Albrecht and his immediate bishop, Jerome of Brandenburg. Thus, while it is certain that Luther had drafted his Ninety-Five Theses by October 31, it is not at all clear that he posted them. Added to this, theses for debate were only posted with the permission of the dean of the theological faculty and then affixed (with wax or paste) on all the church doors in Wittenberg by a university functionary, not by the professor himself. Another detail speaks against any posting: a reference to Luther's Theses in a November 11, 1517, letter to his friend in Erfurt, Johannes Lang, giving the title of the Theses, requesting written responses, and fixing no time or place for the disputation (which all agree never took place). In 1518, Luther insisted that the Theses were even kept from the electoral court's knowledge to avoid the appearance that it had encouraged Luther's attack on the archbishop. Christopher Scheurl, formerly a professor of law in Wittenberg living in Nuremberg, acknowledged receipt of the Theses in a letter from January 1518, and in a handwritten chronicle of the period written in 1528, he mentioned that Luther sent the Theses to scholars only in manuscript form (reading *bloslich geschriben* as "merely handwritten"). Some even explain away Luther's mention, in a letter to Bishop Jerome on February 13, 1518, that he issued a public invitation to debate.

Arguments in favor of the posting observe that Melanchthon had many opportunities to learn from Luther details of events from 1517. (Other supposed "inaccuracies" in Melanchthon's preface—for example, his dating of Luther's trip to Rome—were often questioned in the past but have now been substantiated.) Melanchthon's offhand remark assumes the normal function of university affairs regarding theses and not some sort of dramatic protest. Scheurl's account from 1528 even mentions that Luther had the right to publish such theses because he was in charge of the regular Friday disputations. Moreover, the phrase *bloslich geschriben* (modern German: *plötzlich*) means quickly written. Early accounts contain references not only to private correspondence with the bishops and with scholars but also to the public distribution of the Theses. While no printing from Wittenberg has survived (the town's only press was housed in the basement of the Augustinian friary where Luther lived), a recently discovered Wittenberg printing of other theses by Luther from 1517 shows that such a printing was possible. Moreover, reprints in Leipzig and Nuremberg use the very same single-sheet format, suggesting a single source. A handwritten note by Georg Rörer, which predates Melanchthon's preface, mentions that the Theses were posted on the doors of the churches (plural).

See also Ninety-Five Theses

Bibliography
See bibliography under Ninety-Five Theses.

TIMOTHY J. WENGERT

Noko, Ishmael

The general secretary of the Lutheran World Federation from 1994 to 2010 was Ishmael Noko, who was born on October 29, 1943, in the then-British colony of Southern Rhodesia (Zimbabwe). After studying theology at the University of South Africa, Pretoria, and the University of Zululand, he was ordained in

1972 and began studies at the Lutheran Theological Seminary, Saskatoon, Saskatchewan. McGill University in Montreal awarded him a PhD in 1977. The same year he assumed a professorship at the University of Botswana, becoming head of the Department of Theology and Religious Studies and later dean of the faculty of the humanities.

In 1982 he accepted a position with the Lutheran World Federation Department of World Service, working with refugees; in 1987 he became director of the LWF Department of Church Cooperation, and in 1990 director of the Department for Mission and Development. The LWF Council elected him general secretary in 1994, and he served in this office until 2010. Among the major accomplishments of his tenure was the conclusion of the Joint Declaration on the Doctrine of Justification with the Roman Catholic Church in 1999 and the formal apology of the LWF to the Mennonite World Conference in 2010.

See also Lutheran World Federation

Robert Kolb

Nommensen, Ludwig Ingwer

As one of the most illustrious missionaries in the modern missionary movement, Ludwig Ingwer Nommensen (1834–1918) has justifiably become known as "the apostle to the Bataks." He was a pioneer missionary among the Bataks of North Sumatra in Indonesia. In an impressive way he left the stamp of his gifted and unique personality on the Batak Church, for he was, more than anyone else, responsible for its growth and sound development.

Nommensen studied at the mission seminary of the Rhenish Missionary Society in Barmen, Germany, from 1857 to 1861. The mission seminary provided both theological education and missionary formation in the conservative Pietist and revivalist traditions that undergirded the nineteenth-century Protestant missionary movement. A strong emphasis was placed on developing an ability to communicate the Christian gospel and to seek conversion of non-Christian people overseas.

On December 24, 1861, he left for Sumatra, taking 142 days to reach it by ship. He lived among Bataks in northwestern Sumatra, though in the beginning some of them treated him suspiciously and even with hostility. However, he patiently treated the Bataks with gentleness, learned the Batak language, and spoke it fluently.

Nommensen did not compromise the gospel. He preached it and lived it; he taught it and defended it. He translated Luther's Small Catechism into the Batak language in 1874, as one of the important teaching materials for catechumens. His educational interests, concerns, and attention extended beyond the ecclesiastical sphere. He also employed his skills as a medical practitioner with unusual effectiveness. His homeopathic medicines and his sympathetic handling of the sick yielded fruit. Nommensen opened a school in August 1864. The number of schools grew rapidly as the number of teachers, missionaries, and local teachers significantly increased. By the beginning of the twentieth century, 300,000 people in North Tapanuli (a district on Sumatra) had access to over 200 schools. (By comparison, the 28 million people on Java had access to only 562 schools.) The first *Ephorus* (bishop) of the Batak Church, he still considered his primary work to be that of a missionary. He stayed in the mission field, moving from one place to another.

Nommensen remained vigorous and active into old age, carrying out his work with zest and joy. The lines he had once written still applied to him: "The Lord grants joy for work with its blessings, and indeed we know that joy in our vocation flows from joy in the Lord, and strength is derived from this joy." At the time of his death, the Batak Church had grown to 40 mission stations and around 480 branch stations, a total of 520 Christian congregations with almost 180,000 members. Approximately 510 schools enrolled 30,655 children. Serving in the Batak Church were 13 missionary deaconesses, 34 native pastors, 19 evangelists, 789 teachers, and 2,241 elders. Today the Batak Church numbers around four million.

See also Batak Church; Batak Confession

Bibliography

Aritonang, J. S. *Mission Schools in Batakland (Indonesia), 1861–1940.* Brill, 1994; Aritonang, J. S., and K. Steenbrink, eds. *A History of Christianity in Indonesia.* Brill, 2008; Hasselgren, J. *Rural Batak, Kings in Medan: The Development of Toba Batak Ethno-religious Identity in Medan, Indonesia, 1912–1965.* Uppsala University, 2000; Lehman, M. E. *A Biographical Study of Ingwer Ludwig Nommensen (1834–1918).* Mellen, 1996; Pasaribu, P. M. *Dr. Ingwer Ludwid Nommensen: Apostel di Tanah Batak.* Universitas HKBP Nommensen, 2005. 2nd ed., 2007.

VICTOR TINAMBUNAN

Norway

Monks and priests from the British Isles came as missionaries to the western coast of Norway in the ninth and tenth centuries. Missionaries from the diocese of Hamburg/Bremen brought the Christian message to Norway at the same time. Christianization achieved a breakthrough with the Christian kings beginning at the end of the tenth century. Olav Tryggvason (r. 995–1000) was baptized during a Viking raid in England. When he came to Moster in the western part of Norway in 995, he ordered a Christian worship service to be held. On his initiative the first churches were built. The process of Christianization gained momentum during the reign of Olav Haraldsson from 1015 to 1030. He tried to organize his kingdom under Christian law. After his death in a battle at Stiklestad in 1030, his body was transferred to the city of Nidaros (Trondheim); he was canonized and became the saint of Norway. The medieval cathedral of Nidaros was built in his memory. Subsequent kings continued to replace heathen traditions with Christian worship and customs. People slowly changed from Norse religion to Christianity. The Norwegian archdiocese of Nidaros was created in 1152. By the end of the twelfth century the archdiocese included bishoprics in Norway, Iceland, Greenland, the Isle of Man, the Orkney Islands, Shetland, the Faroe Islands, and the Hebrides.

Beginning at the end of the thirteenth century, Norway experienced a history of decline politically and economically. The church was weakened. The country lost more than one-third of its population from the plague in 1349–50. Through the Nordic Union (the so-called Kalmar Union) from the end of the fourteenth century, Norway lost its independence and came under Danish rule for more than four hundred years (until 1814).

The Reformation was introduced in Denmark/Norway by a decree of King Christian III in 1537. He declared Lutheran doctrine to be the official religion in his twin kingdom. The Roman Catholic archbishop of Nidaros, Olav Engelbrektsson, was forced to leave the country. Catholic priests were forcefully evicted or left to adapt to the new church order. Monastic orders were suppressed. The Crown took over church property. New bishops, called superintendents, were appointed by the king. But the transition to the Reformation among the people did not come easily. It took time until the church obtained qualified Lutheran pastors and people became familiar with the Lutheran worship service and learned to listen to the sermon and join the singing. Some historians claim that it took almost a hundred years before ordinary members of the parishes understood the main content of the Lutheran faith. In the year 1660 absolute monarchy was introduced, and Christian V's Norwegian law of 1687 declared that the confessional basis of the church consists of the three ancient creeds, the Augsburg Confession, and the Small Catechism of Martin Luther. The king was bound to the Lutheran confession and had supreme legislative and administrative authority in church matters. He appointed the clergy.

In the eighteenth century Pietism brought renewal for the Norwegian church. King Christian VI, who ruled from 1730 to 1746, was influenced by German Pietism and made confirmation instruction obligatory for all youth. The reform required a new catechism. Eric Pontoppidan (1698–1764) was appointed to write an explanation of Luther's Small Catechism, which was published in 1737 under the title *Truth to Godliness*. It was approved by the king and was authorized reading for all preparing for confirmation in Denmark and Norway. When the elementary schools were established in 1739, this catechism was used as an introduction to the Lutheran faith and remained in Norwegian elementary schools and confirmation instruction until the last decades of the nineteenth century. A rich harvest of deeply Evangelical hymns, together with the sermons and the genuinely Lutheran liturgy, also contributed to put a Lutheran mark on the piety of the people.

Influenced by this Pietist heritage, the lay preacher Hans Nielsen Hauge (1771–1814) inspired a revival movement that renewed the church and parish life around 1800, with positive effects for generations to come. Hauge traveled on foot around the country with his revivalist message and at the same time encouraged people to start businesses. He emphasized the priesthood of all believers and the necessity of personal conversion. At that time it was forbidden for laypeople to preach the gospel without permission from the local pastor. Hauge was taken to court and put in prison for ten years for violating this law. Influences from the Haugean movement reduced the distance between laity and clergy and were of great importance for the rise of several missionary organizations that worked abroad and at home.

From the middle of the nineteenth century, the voluntary Christian missionary organizations served as a revivalist dimension in the Norwegian church structure. But the influence of a more experiential (as opposed to intellectual) theology, coming from Germany in the second half of the nineteenth century, contributed to a certain renewal among the clergy. Around the turn to the twentieth century a rather sharp theological conflict arose between confessionally oriented clergy and laity on the one hand and those who were influenced by liberal theology on the other.

As an upshot of the Napoleonic Wars, Norwegian ties with Denmark were severed in 1814, and Norway entered into union with Sweden until 1905. The Norwegian Constitution of 1814 (*Grunnloven*) established a high degree of political independence but retained the strict status of state church for the church of Norway. Jews, Jesuits, and monastic orders were forbidden to enter the country. The constitution confirmed that the Evangelical Lutheran Church remained the "public religion of the state," and that the king was bound to confess the Lutheran faith. Upholding the tradition of absolute monarchy, the Norwegian Constitution affirmed that the king order all public worship.

During the German occupation (1940–45) the small National Union Party (Nasjonal Samling) under the Nazi leadership of Vidkun Quisling (1887–1945) took over the church functions of the king and the control of the state's Church Department. The bishop of Oslo, Eivind Berggrav (1884–1959), took the initiative to create a church front within the resistance movement and succeeded in establishing the Christian Consultative Council (Kristent Samråd), consisting of members from central Lutheran branches of the Norwegian Church. Quisling wanted to use the church in his plan of Nazification, and he let the Church Department take ideological and political decisions that the church could not accept. The church resistance started with sharp protests against the occupying power's violation of justice, law, and conscience. Due to Nazi interference in church affairs, the seven bishops resigned from their official state positions in February 1942. At Easter 1942 more than 92 percent of the pastors laid down the state functions of their office on the basis of a confessional declaration called the Foundation of the Church (*Kirkens Grunn*). As far as possible the pastors—by referring to their call and ordination—continued their pastoral duties in the parishes. After the resignation of the clergy the Norwegian Church was independent of the state from 1942 to 1945. The relatively few members and sympathizers of the National Union Party were loyal to the small number of pastors remaining in the state church. When the occupation came to an end, the clergy took up the entire responsibility of their offices, again within the framework of the constitutional state church.

Since the second half of the nineteenth century, a reform movement within the church of Norway has been trying to develop a more independent relationship to the state. But it has been a long and difficult process, dependent on political acceptance from the Norwegian Parliament, which only in 1920 granted the establishment of Parish Councils, and in 1933 passed regulations for each diocese to elect a diocesan council. In the postwar period (from 1945) there was not enough political will to give the church a real new order with more self-determination. But in 1969 the parliament decided to let the church form a central Church Council (Kirkerådet) to foster initiatives, inspire the parishes, and coordinate the ongoing work in the dioceses. Some years later, in 1984, the Church Assembly (Kirkemøtet) was established. The assembly, acting as a general synod, is the highest authority in the church and is composed of the representatives of the dioceses and a few more extra representatives, currently totaling 115. The Church Council, which has fifteen members, is the executive body of the Church Assembly. In 1992 the Assembly decided to establish a council for church life among the Sami people, the Sami Church Council (Samisk Kirkeråd), answerable to the Church Assembly. The responsibility for international and ecumenical affairs is taken care of by the Ecumenical Council (Mellomkirkelig Råd). The church of Norway is a member of the Lutheran World Federation and of the World Council of Churches. The Norwegian Church Abroad (Sjømannskirken) is an independent church organization serving Norwegians abroad through over thirty churches and sixteen mobile centers in thirty countries. Immigrants from Norway have had significant influence in Lutheran churches in the United States. From 1825 until now about 800,000 Norwegians have settled in the United States.

Norway has three theological faculties, educating people for ministry in the church and for religious teaching in schools, colleges, and universities: The Theological Faculty, University of Oslo; MF Norwegian School of Theology, Oslo; and School of Mission and Theology, Stavanger. Other universities and colleges have programs for religious and Christian studies qualifying students for teaching religion in Norwegian schools and for missionary work at home and abroad.

In 2012 the Norwegian Constitution was revised, changing the relationship between state and church. A central paragraph states that the values of the kingdom of Norway are based on the Christian and humanistic heritage. The Evangelical Lutheran Church is no longer defined as the public religion of the state. A new paragraph asserts that "the Church of Norway—an Evangelical Lutheran church—remains Norway's People's Church [Norges Folkekirke]." The government still provides funding for the church according to number of members as it does with other faith-based communities. The local activity of the church is mainly financed by the municipalities. Since 1997 Diocesan Councils have appointed parish pastors and, according to the constitutional amendment in 2012, they are also responsible for appointing the deans for a number of parishes. The process of appointing bishops is now handed over to the Church Council. The king is no longer the constitutional head of the church, but he is obliged to profess himself a Lutheran. The church is still regulated by the church law (Kirkeloven), passed by parliament. Clergy are still state employees, and the central and regional church administrations are part of the state administration of church affairs. At present a legal process is under way aimed at establishing a legal basis for the Church of Norway as an independent autonomous church.

The Church of Norway has an episcopal-synodical structure with eleven dioceses. In 2011 the church—which still was a state church—appointed a twelfth bishop to be the leading bishop (*preces*) and moderator of the Bishop's Meeting (Bispemøtet). Of a population of 5,109,056 (as of January 1, 2014), 75.2 percent of the Norwegians are members of the Church of Norway. The church has 1,280 parishes and a hundred deaneries. Compared with the other Nordic Lutheran churches, Norway has the highest ratio of parishioners to pastors, with three thousand persons per pastor. As a result of considerable immigration of non-Lutherans and of withdrawal from the church, infant baptism has fallen from 96.8 percent of the population in 1960 to 62.0 percent in 2013, while the proportion of confirmands has decreased from 93 percent in 1960 to 63.6 percent in 2013.

Alongside the Church of Norway, two or three small Lutheran churches exist. The oldest is the Evangelical Lutheran Free Church (Frikirken), founded in 1877. It has about eighty congregations and more than twenty thousand members. Those who are baptized and confess the Christian faith have voting rights. Adapting to international principles of religious freedom, Norway today allows a variety of religious groups. More than 120,000 Norwegian citizens are Muslims. The Roman Catholic Church counts about 120,000 and has recently had the greatest increase in church membership, partly due to a growing number of immigrants from Poland.

See also Hauge, Hans Nielsen; Norwegian-American Lutheranism

Bibliography

Aarflot, A. "The Church, Christian Life and Religions in Norway." In *Norway*, ed. K. Ødegaard. The New Millennium Series. Carol Nord ehf, 2003; Aarflot, A. "Norwegen." In *Evangelische Kirchenlexikon*, vol. 3. Vandenhoeck & Ruprecht, 1992; Austad, T. *Kirkelig motstand: Dokumenter fra den norske kirkekamp under okkupasjonen 1940–45 med innledninger og kommentarer*. Høyskoleforlaget, 2005; Hassing, A. *Church Resistance to Nazism in Norway 1940–1945*. University of Washington Press, 2014; Montgomery, I. "Norway." In *Religion Past and Present: Encyclopedia of Theology*, vol. 9. Brill, 2011; Montgomery, I. "Norwegen." *TRE* 24:643–59. De Gruyter, 1994; Oftestad, B. T., J. Schumacher, and T. Rasmussen. *Norsk kirkehistorie*. Universitetsforlaget, 2010.

TORLEIV AUSTAD

Norwegian-American Lutheranism

In the century between 1825 and 1925, when immigration was heaviest, one-third of Norway's population came to the United States. This period overlapped with Norway's post-Napoleonic union with Sweden, which ended in 1905. A growing sense of national identity followed adoption of the Norwegian Constitution in 1814, yet this also was a time of economic hardship that made American opportunities attractive. Norwegians left behind a strong state-supported church that had been deeply influenced by Pietist awakenings associated with Hans N. Hauge and Gisle Johnson. In the United States a high percentage of these 800,000 newcomers associated themselves with Lutheran congregations, many in rural areas of the upper Midwest. Released from the unifying constraints of the Norwegian Church, they formed more than a dozen church bodies distinguished by significant, if subtle, differences in their appropriation of their common religious tradition and their adaptation to American religious freedom.

Many immigrants carried with them copies of the Bible, the Small Catechism as interpreted by Erik Pontoppidan, and Johann Arndt's *True Christianity*. Early congregations were established in rural Wisconsin, near Madison. Beginning in the 1830s lay preachers traveled to serve these pioneers. Both Elling Eilsen and C. L. Clausen were ordained in 1843, on the basis of their gifts rather than their training. The next year a university-trained, state-church-authorized pastor, J. W. Dietrichson, arrived. Shortly thereafter the Pietist party organized as the Eielson's Synod (1846), and those in sympathy with the state church formed the Norwegian Evangelical Lutheran Church of America (1853, the so-called Norwegian Synod). Other congregations and their pastors crossed ethnic borders and affiliated with the Synod of Northern Illinois (1851).

Norwegians followed the general westward settlement patterns of the time. Many benefitted from the Homestead Act as they expanded into Iowa, across Minnesota, and throughout the Dakotas. Smaller numbers settled in other states, including Texas. They also formed urban communities in Brooklyn and Seattle. Local congregations met their spiritual and social needs. Even without a resident pastor, people gathered for worship, which could be an all-day affair. The lay *klokker* provided liturgical leadership, sometimes combined with responsibility for the building. In some congregations a pastor in a long black robe and a starched white ruff presided over a ritual imported from Norway, but other groups rejected such formality in favor of something more akin to Pietist conventicle meetings. Norwegian was the primary language for worship into the twentieth century, until the transition to English accelerated during and after World War I.

In contrast to Norway, churches in the United States received no government support, and church membership was entirely voluntary. Thus immigrants learned to pay pastors, finance buildings, and support charitable institutions and schools. Women's organizations—both local and federated—supplemented regular budgets and provided members with opportunities for study and conviviality. Congregations and individuals organized orphanages, old people's homes, and hospitals. Deaconesses staffed hospitals in Brooklyn, Chicago, and Minneapolis. Children attended public schools and special religious instruction, usually in the summer and often in Norwegian.

Theological debate, synodical realignments, and institution building continued through the late nineteenth and early twentieth centuries. Colleges and seminaries did both educational and symbolic work, training leaders and fostering group identity. They also became subjects of controversy. Disagreement about slavery ended the Norwegian Synod's educational alliance with the Missouri Synod and prompted the founding of Luther College in 1861. Debates about justification and election, in the 1870s and 1880s, were carried

on in church publications and in a series of "free conferences." In 1890 the Norwegian Augustana Synod (1870), the Conference of the Norwegian-Danish Evangelical Lutheran Church of America (1870), and the Anti-Missourian Brotherhood (1887) consolidated in the United Norwegian Lutheran Church of America (UNLCA). The Friends of Augsburg (College) withdrew from that body in response to conflicts over pastoral education and the status of congregations; they formed the Lutheran Free Church (1897, LFC). In 1917 the Norwegian Synod, the Hauge Synod (1853), and the UNLCA gathered nearly all Norwegian-American Lutherans into the Norwegian Lutheran Church in America, later called the Evangelical Lutheran Church (ELC).

The ELC was one constituent of the American Lutheran Church in America (1960); the LFC joined three years later. Outside of the Evangelical Lutheran Church in America (1988), congregations founded by Norwegian-Americans are members of the Lutheran Brethren (1890), the Evangelical Lutheran Synod (1917), and the Association of Free Lutheran Congregations (1962).

See also American Lutheran Church (1960–88); Norway

Bibliography

Lagerquist, L. D. *In America the Men Milk the Cows: Factors of Gender, Ethnicity, and Religion in the Americanization of Norwegian-American Women.* Carlson, 1991; Nelson, E. C., and E. L. Fevold. *The Lutheran Church among Norwegian-Americans: A History of the Evangelical Lutheran Church.* 2 vols. Augsburg, 1960; Nichol, T. W., ed. *Crossings: Norwegian-American Lutheranism as a Transatlantic Tradition.* Norwegian American Historical Association, 2003; Preus, H. A. *Vivacious Daughter: Seven Lectures on the Religious Situation among Norwegians in America.* Trans. and ed. T. W. Nichol. Norwegian American Historical Association, 1990; Rølvaag, O. E. *Concerning Our Heritage.* Trans. and ed. S. Zempel. Norwegian American Historical Association, 1998.

L. DeAne Lagerquist

Nuremberg

As a leading city of the Lutheran Reformation, Nuremberg was the first imperial city to adopt the new faith. It played a crucial role in the promotion and institutionalization of the Lutheran Reformation, especially in southern Germany. The seeds of the Evangelical movement in Nuremberg were sown in the late 1510s when Johann von Staupitz, head of the Augustinians in the Holy Roman Empire, visited the city and was warmly received by a circle of humanists who included some of Nuremberg's leading lights: Lazarus Spengler (city council secretary), Christoph Scheurl (legal counsel to the city council), Albrecht Dürer (artist), and several prominent members of the patrician council that governed Nuremberg. In 1517 Wenceslaus Linck, who replaced von Staupitz, moved to Nuremberg from Wittenberg and further promoted Luther's teaching among these Evangelical humanists, one of whom, Kaspar Nützel, translated the Ninety-Five Theses into German (although it is unclear whether this translation was ever published). Spengler wrote the first lay defense for Luther, the popular *Apology . . . [for] Luther's Teaching* (1519), which caused him to be named on the papal bull that threatened Luther with excommunication. (Spengler's name was later removed from the official list of heretics.) The Evangelical movement received further encouragement from the appointment of reform-minded clergy to the city's leading churches in the early 1520s, among them Andreas Osiander (an accomplished Hebraist whose later position on justification, formulated when he was professor in Königsberg, was attacked by many other Lutherans). Experimentation with new Evangelical liturgies then took place, as did further lay pamphleteering for Luther, including the famous poem "Wittenberg Nightingale" by the Nuremberg shoemaker-poet Hans Sachs. Popular protests against the traditional faith occurred, especially when the imperial estates and papal representatives were in town, but the city council did not officially adopt the Reformation until 1525, when it judged that Evangelical theologians had bested Catholic theologians at the local Colloquy on Religion. The late-medieval Mass was then abolished, and the reform of the city's religious

life began in earnest, which culminated in the 1533 Brandenburg-Nuremberg Church Ordinance. Authored by Osiander and Johannes Brenz (pastor in Schwäbisch-Hall and adviser to the Duke of Brandenburg-Ansbach), it became one of the most influential guides for worship and belief in Lutheran lands. Veit Dietrich, a former student in Wittenberg, helped to promote the Evangelical cause in Nuremberg when he was appointed as a preacher in 1535. The 1530s witnessed an important debate in Nuremberg over the imposition of an Evangelical rite of private confession and also saw the city council try to plant the Evangelical faith more firmly in the city even as it sought to maintain cordial relations with the emperor. Nuremberg signed the Augsburg Confession but refused to join the Smalcaldic League. At the conclusion of the Smalcald War of 1546–47, Nuremberg was forced to accept the Augsburg Interim, although many Evangelical pastors and preachers remained. Lutheranism was fully reestablished in the city after the Peace of Augsburg and a purging of the leaders loyal to Osiander in 1555. Military defeats in the early 1550s harbingered an end to Nuremberg's golden age as a leading city of the empire.

See also Brenz, Johannes; Dietrich, Veit; Osiander, Andreas; Sachs, Hans

Bibliography

Pfeiffer, G. *Nürnberg: Geschichte einer europäischen Stadt.* Beck, 1971; Rittgers, R. K. *The Reformation of the Keys: Confession, Conscience, and Authority in Sixteenth-Century Germany.* Harvard University Press, 2004; Seebaß, G. "The Reformation in Nürnberg." In *The Social History of the Reformation*, ed. L. P. Buck and J. W. Zophy, 17–40. Ohio State University Press, 1972; Strauss, G., *Nuremberg in the Sixteenth Century: City Politics and Life between Middle Ages and Modern Times.* John Wiley & Sons, 1966; Vogler, G., "Imperial City Nuremberg, 1524–1525: The Reform Movement in Transition." In *The German People and the Reformation*, ed. R. P. Hsia, 33–49. Cornell University Press, 1988.

RONALD K. RITTGERS

Nygren, Anders

Born into a pastor's family in the conservative diocese of Gothenburg, Sweden, the childhood experience of Anders Nygren (1890–1978) was infused with the intensely church-focused clericalism of Henrik Schartau. But in his theological studies and work as a professor, Nygren looked beyond the realm of devotion and worship and made Lutheran theology relevant to the challenge facing the church on an international stage and to the needs of a scientific age. Primarily a theologian deeply committed to rigorous methodology, Nygren chose to define Christianity as essentially a faith oriented toward a way of loving quite distinct from other religious and secular frameworks. To define proper Christianity and to highlight the application of his method to other ways of life and even other belief systems, Nygren identified the motif that characterized each kind of religious impulse or orientation and described how each had been manifest in Christian history and experience. *Agape*, self-giving love, was the motif that defined what was characteristic of Christian faith, while other motifs—*nomos* as law abiding, and *eros* as striving—certainly also present within Christian traditions, denoted other theological tendencies, often entirely other faith systems. Nygren's approach was more sophisticated than a simple assigning of categories—Jewish religion is law/nomos oriented, while Christianity is love/agape oriented—but the heuristic device of assigning a characteristic motif to different faith systems provided a way for modern theology to engage with theological pluralism and secularism without limiting itself to parochial or confessional boundaries.

Nygren, Gustaf Aulén, Gustaf Wingren, and Ragnar Bring brought Lund's theological ferment, with its characteristic of fully using Luther as a theological resource, to a wider readership after World War II, assisted by interpreters who translated their findings into German and English.

Early in his career Nygren embraced the ecumenical movement as a theologian and as a bishop. Two milestone ecumenical events occurred in Lund, where he was bishop: the founding meeting of the Lutheran World Federation in 1947, and the Faith and Order meeting of the World Council of Churches in 1952. As the first president of the Lutheran World Federation, Bishop Nygren worked intensely to refashion the ties that bound together these various Lutheran church bodies throughout the world. His wife, Irmgard, was German, and the estrangement among Lutherans because of World War II was something he experienced personally. He proposed that Lutherans go "Forward to Luther" as a way to invigorate a modern, forward-looking Lutheranism that did not seek to repristinate sixteenth-century theology, but instead press ahead with other Lutherans to realize the vision for the church that Luther had also seen but had not fully realized. The Lutheran World Federation took this theological trajectory to heart, recognizing that going forward to Luther was not an exercise in nostalgia or sentiment, but instead an effort to take responsibility for the future witness to the gospel. The confidence in its own identity as a Lutheran communion of churches served to foster an ecumenical future for the Lutheran World Federation.

See also Aulén, Gustaf; Ecumenical Dialogues; Lundensian School; Lutheran World Federation; Wingren, Gustaf

Bibliography

Erling, B. *Nature and History*. Gleerup, 1960; Hall, T. *Anders Nygren*. Word, 1978; Kegley, C. W. *The Philosophy and Theology of Anders Nygren*. Southern Illinois University Press, 1970; Nygren, A. *Agape and Eros*. Westminster, 1953.

MARIA ERLING

O

Ockham, William of

The exact year of the birth for William of Ockham (or Occam, ca. 1288–1347) is not known. His ordination as a subdeacon in London in 1306 is the first dated event in his life. Assuming that he had reached the canonical age of eighteen for this ordination, which is likely, his birth can be placed around 1288. He was born in the village of Ockham on Surrey; nothing is known of his background or family. It is unclear whether he grew up speaking French or English. He became a Franciscan at an early age, but because there was no Franciscan convent near his home, he probably received his prior education from a local parish priest. As a Franciscan, he studied grammar and philosophy at Greyfriars (a common term in England for Franciscans) in London; this might have been his home convent. From London, Ockham went to Oxford to pursue the baccalaureate in theology. Beginning in 1317, he lectured there on Lombard's *Sentences*, which was standard practice for students in the higher faculty of theology. By 1321 he had been appointed lecturer in philosophy in one of the Franciscan convents, probably London, while he waited to be chosen by the order to proceed toward the doctorate in theology. Between 1321 and 1324 Ockham composed several works on philosophy and theology, including disputations, commentaries on Aristotle's works, a textbook of logic (*Summae logicae*) that proved to be his main philosophical work, a treatise on predestination and future contingents, and two treatises on the Eucharist (*Tractatus de quantitate* and *De corpore Christi*). The latter came in response to philosophical attacks from John Lutterell, a former chancellor of Oxford University. These attacks involved topics such as Ockham's teaching on universals and his understanding of transubstantiation. As the opposition mounted, Ockham found himself summoned to Avignon, where the popes resided at the time, to face charges of teaching heresy. He left England for Avignon around May 1324.

Ockham's teaching had become controversial in the first place because of his philosophical stance on universals and in the second place because of how he discussed theology in light of this position. Simply put, Ockham taught that individual entities had real existence as opposed to deriving their existence from a form or universal, as scholars like Thomas Aquinas and Duns Scotus before him had maintained. It is tempting to see this as a result of the famous Ockham's razor—"Plurality is not to be posited without necessity" is one way that he himself put it—yet this principle of parsimony is not the only or even the main reason Ockham attacked realist ontology. Rather, he considered his opponents' arguments to be incoherent or to be conducive to making statements that were false. In any case, his position on universals had profound implications for understanding cognition. Human knowledge, according to Ockham, comes from an understanding of individual things rather than resulting from apprehending the universal in some way, either in or apart from the thing itself. Ockham rejected a real existence for the universals, explaining instead that human beings created terms—that is, universals—as concepts rather than entities, from the observation of individual things. Thus humanity, according to Ockham, is not an overarching entity with a real existence above and apart from actual human beings but an idea that is used to describe that which is common to all people. Ockham's understanding of individuality and existence also meant that the entire created order could be thought of as contingent rather than necessary. It was the product of God's will in choosing to create this world rather than another and not the product of God's intellect in creating a world that reflects his being at every step.

As a result of this philosophical position, Ockham's theological explanations departed from those of his predecessors on some key points, such as the idea of merit and reward in justification. Ockham insisted that the merit acquired by good works in a state of sin was not in itself worthy of reward, that is, that these things stood in an absolute and real relationship (*meritum de condigno*). Instead, he explained their relationship as the contingent product of God's decision (*meritum de congruo*). Only in a state of grace could a person merit grace *de condigno*. Similarly, Ockham's philosophy appeared to threaten the idea of transubstantiation as the mode of Christ's eucharistic presence, which had been official church doctrine for a little over a century when he wrote. Ockham did not reject transubstantiation but did emphasize that it had to be understood as a mysterious exercise of God's power that did not follow the rules of nature with regard to substances, a position echoed by Pierre D'Ailly, whom Luther would later cite. In this case, the idea did not really achieve its purpose of providing a rational explanation for the Eucharist. Ockham was particularly concerned with the difficulty of separating quantity and substance. He and others questioned whether the accidents of bread without the substance of bread could be considered worthy of receiving the body of Christ.

The summons to Avignon marked a dramatic turning point in Ockham's career. All but one member of the committee appointed to investigate his teaching were philosophical realists and thus hostile to his philosophical stance, so condemnation seemed to be the likely outcome. Yet as usual the wheels of justice ground very slowly in Avignon, and Ockham spent four years there. Since he would

have spent very little of that time in his defense, he had a chance to immerse himself in a world of scholarship. Numerous Franciscans made their way to and through Avignon at the time, many of them involved in the controversy over apostolic poverty. Michael of Cesena, the minister general of the Franciscans, was among them, arriving in December 1327. Michael had been summoned by the pope to answer for his opposition to papal decrees allowing the Franciscans to own property. Michael and many other Franciscans opposed these decrees, believing that Francis's rule obligated them to observe absolute poverty in imitation of Christ and the apostles. Michael won Ockham over to this cause during their time together. Seeing that neither of their cases was likely to have a positive outcome, they fled Avignon on May 26, 1328, along with some other Franciscans. Leaving without permission brought a papal sentence of excommunication. Eventually reaching Pisa, they joined the entourage of the Holy Roman emperor Louis IV (Ludwig the Bavarian). Louis was in the midst of his own conflict with Pope John XXII, having declared him deposed in Rome and installing an antipope there. Ockham was one of a number of antipapal apologists who accompanied Louis to his court in Munich in 1329.

In Munich, Ockham turned his pen against Pope John XXII and began the political phase of his career. He accused the pope of heresy with regard to the beatific vision (John had stated that the souls of the departed would not experience it until after the day of judgment, which undercut the entire cult of the saints) and also with regard to his opposition to the absolute poverty of the Spiritual Franciscans. The latter topic led him to consider the nature of papal authority and what recourse the church might have in correcting a papal decision. Four treatises that resulted from this consideration—*The Work of Ninety Days*, *Letter to the Friars Minor*, *Dialogue*, and *Eight Questions on the Power of the Pope*—contained some ideas that would prove influential for discussing authority in the church and for political theory more generally. As a result, Ockham has been credited as aiding in the development of the conciliar theory of church government, democratic government in general, and the theory of natural rights.

When Ockham died the night of April 9–10, 1347, it was by no means clear that he had founded an influential school of philosophical thought. His philosophy and theology were used by later theologians to undergird the theological approach known as the *via moderna*, while his political writings received attention as part of the conciliar movement of the late fourteenth and early fifteenth centuries. Ockham's influence diminished as a result of the Thomist revival of the sixteenth century, which culminated in the theological formulations of the Council of Trent.

Luther often referred to Ockham negatively, usually as part of a list of theologians whose positions on a particular point he rejected. Though Luther rejected Ockhamist formulations concerning justification, he perpetuated other ideas prominent in Ockham, such as the contingency of creation and the absolute freedom of God to do as he wills. Luther spoke of Ockham as his master on several occasions (e.g., LW 34:27; WA 39/2:160, 420). His language was sometimes ironic, but it also reflected a convention of philosophers and theologians trained in the nominalist tradition as he had been. Gabriel Biel, for example, used the same phrase.

See also Biel, Gabriel; Philosophy; Scholasticism, Late Medieval; Thomas Aquinas

Bibliography

Adams, M. M. *William Ockham.* 2 vols. 2nd, rev. ed. University of Notre Dame Press, 1989; Burr, D. *The Spiritual Franciscans: From Protest to Persecution in the Century after Saint Francis.* Pennsylvania State University Press, 2001; Leff, G. *William of Ockham: The Metamorphosis of Scholastic Discourse.* Manchester University Press, 1975; Leppin, V. "Occam, William of." In *RPP*, s.v. "Occam." 4th ed. Brill, 2007–13; McGrade, A. S. *The Political Thought of William of Ockham: Personal and Institutional Principles.* Cambridge University Press, 1974; Miethke, J. *Ockhams Weg zur Sozialphilosophie.* De Gruyter, 1969; Spade, P. V., ed. *The Cambridge Companion to Ockham.* Esp. 17–30, "The Academic and Intellectual Worlds of Ockham," by W. J. Courtenay. Cambridge University Press, 1999; Tierney, B. *The Idea of Natural Rights: Studies on Natural Rights, Natural Law, and Church Law, 1150–1625.* Scholars Press, 1997; William of Ockham. *A Letter to the Friars Minor and Other Writings.* Ed. J. Kilcullen and A. S. McGrade. Cambridge University Press, 1995.

PAUL W. ROBINSON

Oecolampadius, Johannes

As humanist theologian and early supporter of Luther in Basel, Johannes Oecolampadius (1482–1531) became one of the most influential opponents of Luther's understanding of the Lord's Supper. He was born Johannes Husschin in Weinsberg in southwestern Germany and adopted the Graecized form of his family name as a young man. Oecolampadius received his bachelor's (1501) and master's (1503) degrees in Heidelberg, where he associated with the humanist circle around Jakob Wimpfeling. He began studying law in Bologna but soon returned to Heidelberg to study theology. His further education was interspersed with positions as tutor to the sons of the Palatine elector (1506–8) and as preacher in Weinsburg (1510–13); he also studied briefly in Tübingen, where he became friends with Philip Melanchthon and Johannes Brenz. In 1515 Oecolampadius moved to Basel, where he assisted Erasmus in the preparation of the annotations for and text of the Greek New Testament. He returned to Weinsberg as preacher in 1516, but in early 1518 he accepted a position overseeing cases of penance for the bishop of Basel. After receiving his doctorate in theology in Basel later that year, he became cathedral preacher in Augsburg. There he was involved with the humanist circle that supported Luther, and he acquired a reputation for learned piety through his Latin translations of works by several Greek church fathers. He resigned his preaching post to enter a monastery near Augsburg in 1520, but his Evangelical sympathies caused conflict, and in 1522 he fled the monastery to avoid arrest for heresy.

After serving briefly as castle chaplain for Franz von Sickingen, Oecolampadius moved to Basel, where he became a leading figure in the

Evangelical movement. He became provisional pastor of St. Martin's Church in 1523; two years later the position was made permanent. He was also appointed professor of theology in 1523 and began lectures on the Bible that he gave regularly for the rest of his life, even after the university closed temporarily in 1529. Oecolampadius was one of the earliest reformers to use the Hebrew text and rabbinical exegesis in his lectures on the Old Testament. His commentaries on 1 John and Isaiah, published in 1524 and 1525, were welcomed by the Wittenbergers, and his lectures on all but two of the remaining Old Testament prophets were published over the next decade, some of them posthumously. He also published Latin translations of works by Cyril, Chrysostom, and Theophylact.

As Basel's censor, Oecolampadius approved the printing of Andreas Karlstadt's eucharistic pamphlets in the fall of 1524, although he prevented publication of a pamphlet against infant baptism. He worked closely with Ulrich Zwingli to promote a symbolic understanding of the Lord's Supper, and his ideas strongly influenced the Zurich reformer. Oecolampadius's 1525 *De genuina verborum domini, Hoc est corpus meum, iuxta vetutissimos authores, expositione liber* (Genuine exposition of the Lord's words, "This is my body," according to the most ancient authorities) included extensive citations from the church fathers, and it was attacked by Lutherans and Catholics alike. Oecolampadius responded in print to Luther's criticisms in 1526, a year before Zwingli first addressed Luther directly. Luther wrote his two eucharistic works of 1527 and 1528 against both Oecolampadius and Zwingli. A careful comparison of their works suggests that Luther considered Oecolampadius the more dangerous opponent. The two debated the Lord's Supper on the first day of the Marburg Colloquy in 1529, with no significant results. Oecolampadius's last major contribution to the eucharistic controversy was *Quid de Eucharistia veteres senserint* (What the fathers thought about the

Eucharist, 1530), a dialogue repeating his assertion that the church fathers taught a symbolic view of the Lord's Supper.

In the fall of 1525 Oecolampadius introduced a Reformed Lord's Supper service in Basel that differed from that of Zurich; the liturgy became known through its publication the following year. Because Zwingli could not safely leave Zurich, Oecolampadius was the chief Evangelical opponent of John Eck at the Disputation of Baden, held May–June 1526. In January 1528 he participated in the Disputation of Bern, which led to the Reformation of that city. After an iconoclastic riot in early 1529 that resulted in Basel's official adoption of the Reformation, Oecolampadius was chosen as cathedral pastor and so head of the city's church. In that capacity he helped draft a church ordinance for the city, provided advice for the reorganization of the city's school system, including its university, and advocated the introduction of church discipline by pastors and lay elders. His ideas concerning church discipline would influence Martin Bucer and, through him, John Calvin. Oecolampadius also worked to counter the spread of Anabaptists in Basel's territory, and the confession he delivered at a synod of the Basel clergy was the basis for the city's official confession of faith adopted in 1534. In 1531 Oecolampadius was invited to Ulm to reform that city's church together with Bucer and Ambrosius Blarer. He died on November 23, 1531, after a short illness.

See also Lord's Supper; Marburg Colloquy; Switzerland; Zwingli, Ulrich

Bibliography

Burnett, A. N. "Oekolampads Anteil am frühen Abendmahlsstreit." In *Basel als Zentrum des geistigen Austauschs in der frühen Reformation*, ed. C. Christ-von Wedel, S. Grosse, and B. Hamm, 215–31. Mohr Siebeck, 2014; Burnett, A. N. *Teaching the Reformation: Ministers and Their Message in Basel, 1529–1629*. Oxford University Press, 2006; Fudge, T. R. "Icarus of Basel? Oecolampadius and the Early Swiss Reformation." *Journal of Religious History* 21 (1997): 268–84; Kuhr, O. *"Die Macht des Bannes und der Buße": Kirchenzucht und Erneuerung der Kirche bei Johannes Oekolampad (1482–1531)*. Lang, 1999; Poythress, D. *Reformer of Basel*. Reformation

Heritage Books, 2011; Rupp, E. G. "Johannes Oecolampadius: The Reformer as Scholar." In *Patterns of Reformation*, 3–46. Fortress, 1969; Staehelin, E., ed. *Briefe und Akten zum Leben Oekolampads, zum vierhundertjährigen Jubiläum der Basler Reformation*. 2 vols. Heinsius, 1927–34; Staehelin, E. *Das theologische Lebenswerk Johannes Oekolampads*. Heinsius, 1939.

AMY NELSON BURNETT

Oetinger, Friedrich Christoph

Theologian, pastor, and complex figure of Württemberg Pietism, Friedrich Christoph Oetinger's (1702–82) eclectic mind drew from rabbinic, patristic, Catholic, mystical, theosophist, cabalistic, Lutheran, and Pietist traditions. Born on May 2, 1702, in Göppingen, the son of a town clerk, he attained the master of arts degree at Tübingen in 1725, followed by theological studies. Study of Leibniz and Wolff left him doubting and confused. Through reading Jacob Böhme, Oetinger discovered "a living knowledge of God" as a creative life force in the world. Oetinger's first book promoted the works of Böhme: *Good Reasons to Read the Writings of Jakob Böhme* (1731). Due to Bengel's influence, Oetinger was also committed to the basic themes of biblical theology. Reluctant to assume a church position, Oetinger pursued nine years of academic travel and independent study, including visits with Zinzendorf in Herrnhut. He also served in a variety of tutoring positions. In 1738, at Bengel's encouragement, he became pastor in Hirsau, a community near Calw, and married Christiana Linsenmann. In later years Oetinger authored many works, including hymns, prayers, the *Weinsberg Sermons*, and an autobiography, while continuing his alchemical studies. Despite Oetinger's theosophical tendencies, his basic convictions and intentions remained in accord with the Lutheran tradition, from which he never separated himself.

See also Bengel, Johann Albrecht; Böhme, Jacob; Pietism; Württemberg

Bibliography

Oetinger, F. C. *Genealogie der reellen Gedancken eines Gottes-Gelehrten: Eine Selbstbiographie*. Ed. D. Ising.

Evangelische Verlagsanstalt, 2010; Weyer-Menkhoff, M. "Friedrich Christoph Oetinger." In *The Pietist Theologians*, ed. C. Lindberg. Blackwell, 2010.

DOUGLAS H. SHANTZ

Ohio/Buffalo/Iowa Synods

Three nineteenth-century German-speaking church bodies in America ultimately merged to form the American Lutheran Church (ALC) in 1930. The earliest of these was the Evangelical Lutheran Joint Synod of Ohio and Other States, founded in 1818 as the result of missionary work of the Ministerium of Pennsylvania in the Ohio Valley. Strongly influenced by German immigration, it grew increasingly conservative doctrinally as it reinforced the strict confessionalism of some German theologians and of many nineteenth-century immigrants. The Joint Synod was the largest of the bodies forming the ALC, with some 284,000 members in 1,034 congregations.

The Buffalo Synod, organized in 1845, was guided by J. A. A. Grabau, leader of a group of Lutherans who left Prussia in 1839 in opposition to the Prussian Union. Firmly pledged to the Lutheran confessions, the synod adopted Grabau's hierarchical view of the ministry; this kept it from closer fellowship with other strongly confessional German groups such as the Saxon immigrants who formed the Missouri Synod. Centered as it was in Upstate New York, the Buffalo Synod never grew significantly; at the time of the 1930 merger, it numbered about ten thousand members in fifty-one congregations.

The Evangelical Lutheran Synod of Iowa and Other States was the result of missionary pastors sent by Wilhelm Loehe (Löhe) of Neuendettelsau, Bavaria. While Loehe's pastors originally affiliated with the Missouri Synod, differences over the doctrines of church and ministry led to a separation of some of them, who formed the Iowa Synod in 1854. One of its characteristics was a belief in "open questions"—doctrinal matters that are not settled definitively by Scripture and confessions, which thus remain open for discussion.

The Iowa Synod also incorporated the First Evangelical Synod of Texas, organized in 1851 but affiliated with Iowa in 1895. At the time of the 1930 merger, the Iowa Synod consisted of about 212,000 members in 915 congregations.

Sharing both German heritage and language and a staunchly confessional doctrinal basis, the three synods moved in and out of relationships with each other and with other Lutheran groups through the nineteenth and early twentieth centuries. Both Ohio and Iowa were involved in the early discussions that led to the formation of the General Council in 1867, but neither ultimately joined (though Iowa maintained very cordial relationships with the council throughout its existence). Ohio, always seeking closer relationships with the Missouri Synod, joined with Missouri and other conservative bodies in forming the Synodical Conference in 1872, but withdrew ten years later in the controversy over predestination. Common opposition to the Missouri Synod led to increasing conversations between Iowa and Ohio. Iowa's separation from the General Council, as the latter body became part of the United Lutheran Church in America in 1918, removed the last obstacle to altar and pulpit fellowship between the two synods, and discussion almost immediately began about organic union. The Buffalo Synod, which had previously stayed mostly to itself, asked to join in the discussions in 1925, and the three synods united as the American Lutheran Church in 1930.

See also American Lutheran Church (1930–60)

Bibliography

Deindoerfer, J. *Geschichte der Evangel.-luth. Synode von Iowa und anderen Staaten*. Wartburg, 1897; Lang, R. C. "The History of the Buffalo Synod up to 1866." BD thesis, Wartburg Theological Seminary, 1949; Meuser, F. W. *The Formation of the American Lutheran Church*. Wartburg, 1958; Sheatsley, C. V. *History of the Evangelical Lutheran Joint Synod of Ohio and Other States*. Lutheran Book Concern, 1913.

RICHARD O. JOHNSON

Oldendorp, Johannes

Much of the early life and career of the jurist and reformer Johannes Oldendorp (ca. 1490–1567) is unclear. Born in Hamburg, Oldendorp began the first phase of his studies in Rostock in 1504. He studied law in Bologna, leaving by 1515. A year later he was in Greifswald, receiving his doctorate "in iure caesareo" in 1518. Beginning in 1520 he was professor of law at the University of Frankfurt an der Oder, and in 1521 he became professor in Greifswald. In 1526 he was called to Rostock at the behest of the Duke of Mecklenburg, where he became syndic of the city council and advocate of the Reformation. In 1534 he made his way secretly to Lübeck, where he advised the burgomaster Jürgen Wullenwever, becoming caught up in Wullenwever's disastrous involvement in the Danish Count's Feud over royal succession. In 1536 he left Lübeck, presumably for Hamburg, where he continued his academic pursuits. In 1538 he appeared in Cologne during the time that Hermann von Wied was archbishop, eventually becoming professor of law. He followed a call to Marburg in 1540, and after a brief stint again in Cologne, from which he was expelled, he returned to the University of Marburg in 1542 for the remainder of his career. There he reformed the legal curriculum and became counselor to Philip of Hesse. Oldendorp published at least fifty-six legal tracts, including three in German. He was a pivotal figure in developing a distinctively Lutheran approach to jurisprudence on the basis of humanist principles. Long neglected in the literature, he received his due in the scholarship of Harold Berman.

Bibliography

Berman, H. *Faith and Order: The Reconciliation of Law and Religion*. Scholars Press, 1993; Berman, H. *Law and Revolution*. Vol. 2, *The Impact of the Protestant Reformations on the Western Legal Tradition*. Harvard University Press, 2003; Witte, J. *Law and Protestantism: The Legal Teachings of the Lutheran Reformation*. Cambridge University Press, 2002.

SABINE PETTKE

Ordass, Lajos

Born as Lajos Wolf in the Hungarian part of Austro-Hungary, Lajos Ordass (1901–78) at age eleven had the chance to attend a Saxon boarding school in Hermannstadt (Sibiu, Romania), but his father refused, saying, "Ich lass' aus dir keinen Pangerman machen" (I'll not let them make a pan-German out of you). Love of Hungary and the Lutheran Church would characterize Lajos's adult life. In 1944 he changed his name to Ordass, the Hungarian equivalent of Wolf, to protest the German occupation of Hungary. In 1945 he was elected bishop in Hungary's Lutheran Church; in 1947 and 1957 he was elected vice president of the LWF. Because Ordass refused to consent to the nationalization of Hungary's church schools, he was arrested in 1947 and sentenced to two years in prison. During the 1956 Hungarian Revolution, he returned to his bishop's office, but he was removed again in 1958. The years until his death were spent in relative isolation. His memoirs, *Nagy idők kis tükre* (Large times in a small mirror), were smuggled out of Hungary in the 1970s and, to the consternation of the church leadership at the time, later published in Vienna. In 1990 Ordass was rehabilitated posthumously by the Hungarian state.

See also Hungary

Bibliography

Baer, H. D. *The Struggle of Hungarian Lutherans under Communism.* Texas University Press, 2006; Terray, L. G. *He Could Not Do Otherwise: Bishop Lajos Ordass, 1901–1978.* Eerdmans, 1997.

H. David Baer

Original Sin

It should come as no surprise, in the light of Luther's broader theological concerns, that his account of original sin was theocentric and closely tied to the doctrine of justification by faith. Throughout his career, it was not Luther's observation of human corruption—ample though his opportunities were to see it in others, as well as in himself—but the extremity of God dying on the cross that led him to a profound doctrine of original sin. To suggest that original sin could be simply erased even by so great a thing as baptism, or that it could be overcome by diligent human effort,

was an insult to the crucified Christ. Thus in time Luther came to differentiate himself from Scholastic accounts that left natural human powers unimpaired, original sin itself only a stain on an otherwise intact humanity, and concupiscence the mere "tinder of sin" (*fomes concupiscentiae*) rather than sin itself.

Quite the contrary, Luther strongly emphasized that the inclination toward sin was a matter of human culpability. True, the *guilt* of original sin was no longer imputed after baptism, because of faith, but the *power* of sin or its "material element" (as Melanchthon put it in the Apology in 1530, employing medieval terminology to defend Luther) remained and had to be battled. Already in his Romans lectures of 1515–16, Luther painted a vivid description of the human malady, affecting the entire human being: "It is not only a lack of a certain quality in the will, nor even only a lack of light in the mind or of power in the memory, but particularly it is a total lack of uprightness and of the power of all the faculties both of body and soul and of the whole inner and outer man. On top of all this, it is a propensity toward evil. It is a nausea toward the good, a loathing of light and wisdom, and a delight in error and darkness, a flight from and an abomination of all good works, a pursuit of evil" (LW 25:299). This view of original sin, interrelated with Luther's interpretations of free will and justification by faith, lay at the heart of many disputations and controversies in his early career, especially in the Heidelberg Disputation (1518), the Leipzig Debate with Eck (1519), and his exchanges with Latomus (1521) and Erasmus (1525). Causing especial outrage was his repeated contention that even our good works are sinful if not performed in faith.

In the early 1530s Luther proffered more detailed accounts of original sin in exegetical rather than controversial contexts. His exposition of Ps. 51 insisted that one must look at "the root of wickedness or sin," because without so doing one cannot understand grace (LW 12:304). Sin is not in the first place sins—that is, individual evil thoughts, words, or actions—but "all that is born of father and mother, before a man is old enough to say, do, or think anything" (LW 12:307). He calls Augustine to his defense in the contention that original sin is no longer imputed, yet remains in the believer. It is the seed or mass from which all human life takes its form that is corrupt, and therefore all that comes from it inherits the corruption. (Here, the German term *Erbsünde*, "inherited sin," captures this more clearly than the English equivalent "original sin.") "So we are not sinners because we commit this or that sin, but we commit them because we are sinners first" (LW 12:34; cf. Matt. 7:17). The one who is righteous by faith fights constantly with the remnants of sin within. Thus "both statements are true: 'No Christian has sin'; and 'Every Christian has sin'" (LW 12:328). The theocentric foundation of the doctrine shows itself here again: "We must avoid minimizing these remnants of sin. If you minimize them, you also minimize Him who cleanses them and the gift of cleansing—the Holy Spirit" (LW 12:331). The same theocentrism is evident in Luther's assertion that original sin cannot be known via philosophical knowledge of the human person, which thinks in terms of powers and capacities. It requires revelation through the illumination of the Holy Spirit. "This is the most difficult teaching of this psalm, yes, of all Scripture or theology; without it, it is impossible to understand Scripture correctly" (LW 12:351).

In his Genesis lectures, beginning in 1535, Luther exposited the biblical account of the fall. In some detail he recounted the many great powers and capacities of the human person *before* the fall—all the more to magnify the horror of the loss that resulted from it. Certainly the "most serious loss" was that the human "will turned away from God," but the others were by no means insignificant (LW 1:141). At the heart of the story for Luther was human doubt in God's Word. The serpent didn't need to make Eve break any commandment but the first, since once that was broken, all the others

would follow in its wake. Satan preached, just like God preached, but with a false word, to try "to induce Eve's mind to reach the conclusion that God is not consistent" (LW 1:153). As soon as she came to that conclusion, she sinned, even before biting into the forbidden fruit, for disbelief always precedes sinful acts.

That was bad enough, but the attempted cover-up that followed was even worse, in Luther's estimation. Neither Eve nor Adam would take responsibility for their unbelief and consequent misdeeds. This illustrated for Luther how one sin begets another with ever-spiraling consequences. "Unless God immediately provides a cure and calls the sinners back, they flee endlessly from God and, by excusing their sin with lies, heap sin upon sin until they arrive at blasphemy and despair. Thus sin by its own gravitation always draws with it another sin and brings on eternal destruction, till finally the sinful persons would rather accuse God than acknowledge their own sin" (LW 1:175, pluralized). For this reason Luther refused again, as he had already done in *The Bondage of the Will* (1525), to speculate as to why God allowed sin to happen in the first place. Such questions ultimately seek to blame God for personal human evil. Luther identified this as not merely a human sin but as also a demonic sin, "because the devil everlastingly hates, accuses, and damns God but exonerates himself" (LW 1:179).

At about the same time, Luther drafted the Smalcald Articles, assuming them to be his theological last will and testament (due to illness). The same major points were made as before: "Sin comes from that one human being, Adam, through whose disobedience all people became sinners and subject to death and the devil. This is called the original sin [*Erbsünde*], or the chief sin. The fruits of this sin are the subsequent evil works" (SA 3.1.1–2; *BC* 310). "This inherited sin has caused such a deep, evil corruption of nature that reason does not comprehend it; rather, it must be believed on the basis of the revelation in the Scriptures" (SA 3.1.4; *BC* 311). After an enumeration of Scholastic errors, Luther concludes, "We cannot tolerate these purely pagan teachings, because, if these teachings were right, then Christ has died in vain" (SA 3.1.11; *BC* 311).

Melanchthon had dealt with original sin in much the same way in two other documents that also found their way into the Book of Concord: the Augsburg Confession and the Apology (both 1530). Article 2 of the former announces, "It is taught among us that since the fall of Adam, all human beings who are born in the natural way are conceived and born in sin. . . . This same innate disease and original sin [*Erbsünde*] is truly sin and condemns to God's eternal wrath all who are not in turn born anew through baptism and the Holy Spirit. Rejected, then, are the Pelagians and others who do not regard original sin as sin in order to make human nature righteous through natural powers, thus insulting the suffering and merit of Christ" (CA 2.1–3; *BC* 36, 38, German text). Article 19 adds, "Although almighty God has created and preserves all of nature, nevertheless the perverted will causes sin in all those who are evil and despise God. This, then, is the will of the devil and of all the ungodly" (CA 19; *BC* 52, German text).

Apology 2.3 maintains the new Evangelical definition of concupiscence as "not only its acts or fruits, but [also] the continual tendency of our nature" (*BC* 112), "a disease because human nature is born corrupt and faulty," which involves "being ignorant of God, despising God, lacking fear and confidence in God, hating the judgment of God, fleeing this judging God, being angry with God, despairing of his grace, and placing confidence in temporal things" (Ap 2.6, 8; *BC* 113). Melanchthon also stresses the totality of the corruption, especially of the supposedly "unimpaired" natural powers: "Concupiscence is not simply a corruption of the physical constitution, but a perverse turning toward carnal things in the higher powers" (Ap 2.25; *BC* 115). He concludes: "We cannot know the magnitude of Christ's grace unless we first recognize our malady" (Ap 2.33; *BC* 117).

Original sin became a topic of intense controversy within the Lutheran party in the generations following Luther's death, though in part due to deliberate overstatements to illustrate a point (a technique not unknown to Luther himself) and misunderstandings between competing claimants for authentic Lutheranism. Matthias Flacius Illyricus was at the center of these debates, especially at the University of Jena, for his apparent contention that sin was not merely an "accident" but the "substance" of the human person—if one were to insist on using Aristotelian terms. However, the terms themselves distorted the discussion, thereby causing the controversy. His opponent, Viktorin Strigel, argued on the contrary that original sin is an "accident," not part of the human essence but rather a quality external to the created substance of the human being. For him, Flacius's position made God the creator of evil. For Flacius, Strigel's position smacked of the Pelagian tendencies in late-medieval theology.

The matter was taken up in the Formula of Concord (1577), in the very first article, where the question concerned whether original sin *is* the person or is rather the *corruption* of the person. The formulators perceived two errors that had to be rejected equally: the Manichaean error, which destroyed the doctrine of creation by making the person nothing but sin and undercut the hope of the resurrection, and the Pelagian error, which underestimated the gravity of human corruption and consequently the magnitude of Christ's redemption. To the first error, the Epitome states, "We believe, teach, and confess that there is a difference between original sin and human nature—not only as God originally created it pure, holy, and without sin, but also as we have it now after the fall." To the second, it states, "The damage is so indescribable that it cannot be recognized by our reason but only from God's Word" (Ep 1.2, 3; *BC* 488). Both the Epitome and the Solid Declaration warn against using imprecise or arcane terminology that might confuse the laity, and the latter commends preaching against both errors so that "people will better recognize and praise all the more the benefits of the Lord Christ and his precious merit, as well as the gracious work of the Holy Spirit" (SD 1.3; *BC* 532). While these statements were acceptable to most Lutheran theologians, some followers of Flacius refused to subscribe to the Formula because of this article.

Altogether, the first century of Lutheranism advocated a lively preaching of the total corruption of the human being due to original sin, not for the purpose of browbeating those already suffering under its domain but to stir up faith in the salvation freely offered in Christ Jesus.

See also Anthropology; Flacius, Illyricus, and the Flacians; Formula of Concord; Free Will; Justification; Melanchthon, Philip; Strigel, Viktorin

Bibliography

Book of Concord: Apology to the Augsburg Confession (1530); Augsburg Confession (1530); Formula of Concord (1577); Smalcald Articles (1536); **Debates:** The Heidelberg Disputation (1518). LW 31:37–70; The Leipzig Debate (1519). LW 31:309–25; **Luther, M.:** *Against Latomus* (1521). LW 32:135–260; *The Bondage of the Will* (1525). LW 33; "Lecture on Psalm 51" (1532). LW 12:303–401; *Lectures on Genesis, Chapters 1–5* (1535–36). LW 1; *Lectures on Romans* (1515–16). LW 25; Wengert, T. J. *A Formula for Parish Practice.* Eerdmans, 2006.

SARAH HINLICKY WILSON

Orphanages

Lutheran care for orphans, rooted in Luther's advocacy of social welfare through the "Common Chest" ordinances that included provision for orphans and poor children, developed into institutional orphanages throughout the world on the model of the Halle orphanage complex founded by August Hermann Francke (1663–1727).

Francke, under the aegis of Pietism, created an orphanage in marked contrast to the often inhumane institutional conditions of his time that housed and worked poor children. The orphanage was to be a spiritual "nursery" (*Pflanzgarten*) in which teachers would form the young for the improvement of the world, through study of the Bible and

Luther's catechisms as well as practical trades. The Halle orphanage bloomed beyond an orphanage in a narrow sense, attracting many students who were not orphans. It became financially self-sufficient through its many successful enterprises: printshop and bookseller, pharmacy, teacher training, agricultural production, and the like. Halle's promotion of Christian improvement of society through religious, social, and educational reforms spread throughout the world through its publication programs, its ministerial graduates, missionaries, and observers such as George Frederick Handel (1685–1759), whose admiration of Halle impelled his significant support for the London Foundling Hospital, including an annual benefit concert of his *Messiah*. One of the first orphanages in America was established in 1737 on the Halle model, in the settlement of Salzburger refugees in Georgia led by Johann Martin Boltzius (1703–65) and Israel Christian Gronau (1714–45).

The Enlightenment and the industrial revolution sparked increased attention to issues of child welfare. Living conditions degenerated, and the number of neglected and abandoned children soared in urban industrial areas. In 1833 Hamburg, Johann Hinrich Wichern (1808–81) began a rescue home, the Rauhe Haus, for destitute, delinquent boys. He developed the family principle to replace large institutions and emphasized education and vocational training. Wichern's theological-social concerns led to city missions, and in 1848 to the Inner Mission movement. Modern Lutheran diaconal movements and organizations developed from this as well as the work of Theodor Fliedner (1800–1864) in Kaiserswerth, Wilhelm Loehe (Löhe, 1808–72) in Neuendettelsau, and others also in America, such as William A. Passavant (1821–94), who was instrumental in establishing orphanages in Pennsylvania, New York, and Massachusetts.

Institutional orphanages remained significant forms of social ministry under the impact of immigration and the wars of the modern era. Yet, after World War II, Lutheran leaders of social ministry in Europe and North America began to raise questions concerning the institutional mentality of orphanages and to promote alternatives of foster care, adoption, and residential programs for youth. Today Lutheran churches throughout the world work in concert with the Lutheran World Federation, Lutheran World Relief, and Church World Service in a plurality of ministries that address the plight of youth affected by poverty, disasters, armed conflicts, and AIDS. Lutheran contributions to care of children continue to reflect Luther's conviction that "there is no greater service of God than Christian love which helps and serves the neighbor, as Christ himself will judge and testify at the Last Day, Matthew 25[:31–46]" (LW 45:172).

See also Deaconesses; Fliedner, Theodore; Francke, August Hermann; Francke Foundations; Loehe, Wilhelm Konrad; Lutheran Social Services; Passavant, William Alfred; Social Ministry, Community Chest, Poor Relief; Wichern, Johann Hinrich

Bibliography

Beyreuther, E. *Geschichte der Diakonie und Inneren Mission in der Neuzeit.* Christliche Zeitschriftenverlag, 1983; Lindberg, C. *Beyond Charity: Reformation Initiatives for the Poor.* Fortress, 1993; McCurley, F. R., ed. *Social Ministry in the Lutheran Tradition.* Fortress, 2008; Shantz, D. H. *An Introduction to German Pietism: Protestant Renewal at the Dawn of Modern Europe.* Johns Hopkins University Press, 2013; Veltmann, C., and J. Birkenmeyer, eds. *Kinder, Krätze, Karitas: Waisenhäuser in der Frühen Neuzeit.* Verlag der Franckeschen Stiftungen zu Halle, 2009.

CARTER LINDBERG

Osiander, Andreas

A Lutheran pastor in Nuremberg and professor of theology in Königsberg, Andreas Osiander (1498–1552) was ordained in 1520 after studies at the University of Ingolstadt. He served as a tutor in Hebrew at an Augustinian friary in Nuremberg before being called as pastor in the same city to the church of St. Lorenz in 1522, where he immediately professed allegiance to the Reformation. With other important Nurembergers (including Albrecht Dürer) he introduced the Reformation in 1525, when he also married. With Johannes Brenz, he was the author of the influential 1533 church order for Nuremberg and Brandenburg-Ansbach. Noted for his preaching skills and his knowledge of Hebrew, he participated in many of the important events of the early Reformation (1529: Colloquy at Marburg; 1530: Diet of Augsburg; 1537: signer of the Smalcald Articles). With the defeat of the Smalcaldic League in 1547 by imperial forces, Osiander left Nuremberg for the duchy of Prussia, becoming professor of theology at the University of Königsberg (established 1544) and adviser to Duke Albrecht of Prussia, the last head of the Teutonic Knights, who had secularized his realm in favor of the Reformation. Osiander served in that position until his death in 1552.

In addition to polemical tracts against such figures as Jerome Emser and Ulrich Zwingli and various sermons, Osiander's writings included a revision of the Vulgate according to the Hebrew text (1523), the *Katechismus oder Kinderpredigten* (Catechism or children's sermons, 1533), a harmony of the Gospels printed in parallel columns (1537), and the 1543 anonymous preface for Copernicus's *De revolutionibus orbium coelestium* (On the movements of the celestial spheres), which proposed a heliocentric universe. The *Kinderpredigten* expanded the topics of Luther's Small Catechism to include an explanation of the office of the keys, which later generations then regularly appended to Luther's work. In the 1530s a dispute over the efficacy of the general, public absolution broke out between Osiander and Veit Dietrich, pastor at St. Sebald's and a former student of Luther and Melanchthon at Wittenberg, in which the Wittenberg faculty sided with Dietrich and insisted (against Osiander) that such a general absolution should be retained.

Osiander is most well known for the dispute, now called the Osiandrian controversy, which broke out between him and (among others) Joachim Mörlin, head pastor at the central church in Königsberg, over the nature of justification by faith. In a formal disputation at the university in 1550, Osiander argued that while redemption took place through

Christ's suffering on the cross, this did not constitute the believer's righteousness before God. Instead, the believer was justified by the indwelling of Christ's divine nature, which made a person essentially righteous before God. He attacked the notion that a believer's righteousness was constituted by the declaration of forgiveness (imputed righteousness). When Duke Albrecht sent Osiander's chief writing, *Von dem Einigen Mitler Jhesu Christo und Rechtfertigung des Glaubens Bekantnus* (Confession concerning the one mediator Jesus Christ and justification by faith, 1551), to other Lutheran churches for their opinions, it was roundly condemned by all of them with the lone exception of the church in Württemberg, then led by Johannes Brenz, who, while not accepting Osiander's basic premises, tried to bring his position more in line with standard interpretations of imputation. In the midst of this controversy, Osiander died, leaving behind only a relatively small number of supporters in Königsberg and Nuremberg, most of whom later lost their positions, especially with the return to Königsberg in 1566 of Joachim Mörlin, whom the duke had banished in 1553. Osiander's *Kinderpredigten* and the church order for Nuremberg, however, enjoyed continued popularity and influence throughout the sixteenth century.

See also Brenz, Johannes; Justification; Mörlin, Joachim; Nuremberg; Wittenberg Circle, Parties within

Bibliography

Bachmann, C. *Die Selbstherrlichkeit Gottes: Studien zur Theologie des Nürnberger Reformators Andreas Osiander.* Neukirchener Verlag, 1996; Osiander, A. *Gesamtausgabe.* 10 vols. Ed. G. Müller and G. Seebaß. G. Mohn, 1975–97; Wengert, T. J. *Defending Faith: Lutheran Responses to Andreas Osiander's Doctrine of Justification, 1551–1559.* Mohr Siebeck, 2012.

TIMOTHY J. WENGERT

P

Palatinate, The

The Palatinate (*die Pfalz*) secured its elevated stature among German states in the fourteenth century when its prince, the Count Palatine (*Comes palatinus*), was named one of the seven electors of the Holy Roman Empire. The Wittelsbach dynasty controlled the territory, which in the early sixteenth century included both a principality in northern Bavaria (*Oberpfalz*) and several holdings along the Rhine and Neckar rivers (*Unterpfalz*), including Heidelberg. At the beginning of the Lutheran Reformation, Elector Ludwig V (d. 1544) ruled the principal territory in the Rhineland, while his brother Frederick II administered the Upper Palatinate; two other brothers were bishops in neighboring Speyer and Worms.

Martin Luther's impressive showing during the Heidelberg Disputation (1518) won support from the academics, including Johannes Brenz and Martin Bucer. Although Elector Ludwig refused to enforce the Edict of Worms against Luther (1521), turmoil in the region during the Knights' Revolt and Peasants' War kept him firmly within the imperial camp, resisting reform, although the Palatine court asked Philip Melanchthon (whose father had been the court's armorer) for an opinion of the peasantry's demands. After Ludwig's death, Frederick II introduced the first Lutheran reforms and church order in the region, but was almost immediately forced to accept the terms of the Augsburg Interim (1548). Elector Ottheinrich's subsequent reign saw the first real implementation of Lutheran territorial reform, drawing on the model of Württemberg.

Wittelsbach control of the territory expired with Ottheinrich (d. 1559), replaced by the house of Pfalz-Simmern and the new elector, Frederick III. Frederick relied on the Reformed theologian Kaspar Olevianus to draft a church order for the territory that featured the decidedly Reformed Heidelberg Catechism (1563), primarily the work of the theologian Zacharias Ursinus (an erstwhile student of Melanchthon). Lutheran and Catholic critics insisted that Frederick had violated the agreements of the Peace of Augsburg (1555), but Elector Frederick countered that the *Variata* version of the Augsburg Confession allowed for the understanding of the Lord's Supper contained in his territory's confession. His successor, Ludwig, moved decisively in Wittenberg's direction, subscribing to the Book of Concord (1580). The leading role of the Palatinate in the world of international Calvinism resumed later in the sixteenth century, under the leadership of Regent Johann Casimir and Elector Frederick IV (r. 1583–1610). Prince Christian von Anhalt, ruler of the Upper Palatinate in the early seventeenth century, brokered Palatine leadership for the Protestant Union and arranged for the marriage of Elector Frederick V to Elizabeth Stuart, daughter of England's James I (= James VI in Scotland).

Frederick V's (the Winter King) misguided decision to accept the Bohemian Crown in 1618 served as a catalyst for the Thirty Years' War and resulted in the temporary loss of the electoral dignity to Bavaria. Although the electorate was reestablished with the Peace of Westphalia (1648), the Palatinate played a minor political role during the balance of the seventeenth century. French military incursions in the region, especially under Louis XIV, drove many Protestants from the territory, with Palatine Lutheran and Reformed immigrants flocking to the middle colonies of colonial North America in the early eighteenth century.

See also Thirty Years' War

Bibliography

Bierma, L., ed. *An Introduction to the Heidelberg Cate-chism: Sources, History, and Theology.* Baker Academic, 2005; Kohnle, A. *Kleine Geschichte der Kurpfalz: Land an Rhein und Neckar.* Kleine Buch Verlag, 2014; Otterness, P. *Becoming German: The 1709 Palatine Migration to New York.* Cornell University Press, 2004; Press, V. *Calvinismus und Territorialstaat: Regierung und Zentralbehörden der Kurpfalz 1559–1619.* Klett, 1970.

JEFFREY JAYNES

Pannenberg, Wolfhart

Longtime professor of systematic theology at the University of Munich and author of several of the key publications of twentieth-century Lutheran theology, Wolfhart Pannenberg (1928–2014) took a doctorate at Heidelberg under Edmund Schlink on Dun Scotus's concept of predestination. Following a *Habilitationsschrift* on the doctrine of revelation and the idea of analogy, he turned his attention to the problem of historical consciousness and became the de facto leader of the so-called Revelation as History cadre, the members of which produced several significant publications in the 1960s. Pannenberg's own work in this context proved decisive for his subsequent career. Convinced by several key insights from Hegel and Troeltsch, Pannenberg argues that God reveals himself, albeit indirectly, through the unfolding course of history. Theology and faith thus have vested interests in historical research. This basic methodological supposition lies behind Pannenberg's most significant early work, *Jesus—God and Man*, during the course of which he labors to construct a Christology from the ground up, by establishing the Christian confession of the lordship of Christ in the life and events of Jesus of Nazareth.

In his work in the 1970s and 1980s, a subtle but significant shift in Pannenberg's theology can be detected: the exclusive focus on history as a problem for theology is replaced by a concern for the theological significance of "reality," or the "cosmos." Concomitantly, the texts during this period reflect an appreciation for the methods and discoveries of modern science. Two publications in particular— *Theology and the Philosophy of Science* (1973) and *Anthropology in Theological Perspective* (1983)—stand as classic examples of theology undertaken in rigorous engagement with the natural sciences. The encyclopedic and wide-ranging three-volume *Systematic Theology* (1988–93) draws together Pannenberg's interests in the historical and scientific disciplines with his attentiveness to the history and problems of Christian dogmatics.

Pannenberg seems little interested in developing Lutheran dogmatic theology per se, and his work only modestly engages with Luther's works and the Lutheran confessions. But he remains influential as a Lutheran theologian who addresses head-on the challenges of post-Enlightenment developments in reason and religion. He was also very active in German ecumenical discussions with Rome.

See also Christology; Eschatology (Apocalypticism, Chiliasm, Millennialism, Millenarianism); Natural Science; Philosophy

Bibliography

Bradshaw, T. *Pannenberg: A Guide for the Perplexed.* T&T Clark, 2009; Grenz, S. J. *Reason for Hope: The Systematic Theology of Wolfhart Pannenberg.* 2nd ed. Eerdmans, 2005; Pannenberg, W. *Jesus—God and Man.* 2nd ed. Westminster, 1977; Pannenberg, W. *Systematic Theology.* 3 vols. Eerdmans, 1991–97; Wenz, G. *An Introduction to Wolfhart Pannenberg's Systematic Theology.* Vandenhoeck & Ruprecht, 2012.

R. DAVID NELSON

Papacy

With the exception of his insights into the nature of justification, no aspect of Martin Luther's thought has had a broader and more lasting impact than his rejection of papal authority. Over a period of a little more than three years beginning in 1517, Luther first questioned the limits of papal authority, then the papacy's claim that it was the divinely instituted spiritual head of the church, then its position as the church's humanly ordained pinnacle—all before finally rejecting it as the embodiment of the antichrist and addressing the practical implications of this conviction. The motivation for his persistent struggle against the papacy may be found in an effort to free himself and the consciences of the faithful from spiritual tyranny, coupled with an increasing certitude that Scripture alone must be the sole foundation of authority in the church. In his later life, Luther considered his opposition to the papacy to be his greatest work, a sentiment to which his friend and colleague Philip Melanchthon attested in the epitaph found on the last image of the reformer produced during his lifetime: "Doctor Martin Luther. Alive I was your plague, O pope, Dead I shall destroy you" (Oberman 329).

Although later in life Luther referred to his earlier self as an "archpapist," it appears that his feelings toward the institution before the indulgence controversy (1517) were ambivalent. In fact, Luther spent little time reading authors critical of papal power, made surprisingly few references to it, and generally appears to have accepted the necessity of a visible church, with a hierarchy and a head established by God. It is perhaps noteworthy, however, that even in his early years Luther never interpreted the "rock" referred in Matt. 16:18, the passage upon which the papal party based its claims of the institution's divine origins, as Peter but rather took it to mean Scripture, Christ, or faith—interpretations not uncommon during this period.

It was in the debate sparked by the Ninety-Five Theses that Luther first became embroiled in fundamental questions regarding papal power, the infallibility of councils, and the right to admonish the church on scriptural grounds. The Late Middle Ages had seen a major expansion in the indulgence trade, increasingly considered the prerogative of the pope in large part due to Sixtus IV's bull of 1476 that had extended their efficacy to include souls in purgatory. When, in the spring of 1517, the indulgence preacher and Dominican monk Johannes Tetzel (d. 1519) became active in the Brandenburg territories near Wittenberg, some of the townsfolk crossed the border to buy them. It was not long before Luther began hearing about Tetzel's claims regarding their powers, and he was appalled.

His response, articulated in the Ninety-Five Theses, was an attempt not merely to rein in overzealous indulgence preachers, but also to stress the necessity of true repentance and to clarify the limited value of indulgences—a point to which Luther referred in thesis 49: "Christians are to be taught that papal indulgences are useful only if they do not put their trust in them, but very harmful if they lose their fear of God because of them" (Luther, Ninety-Five Theses, 29–30). This was no assault on papal authority, but a severe limiting of papal authority regarding indulgences' efficacy.

In the following months, all who responded to the Ninety-Five Theses construed them as a direct attack on papal power, best exemplified by the curial theologian Sylvester Prierias. In his *Dialogue concerning the Power of the Pope against the Presumptuous Positions of Martin Luther*, he forcefully asserted the papacy's supreme power to make dogmatic decisions. So vigorous were such responses as to be conspicuous, for none of the earlier debates surrounding indulgences had focused on the issue of papal authority. It seems likely that their increasing distribution had heighted the papacy's uncertainty about them, and far from shaking Luther's assurance in his positions, such reactions strengthened his conviction that papal power was limited (Moeller 108).

Luther's interview with Cardinal Cajetan at Augsburg in December 1518 drove him from a more moderate position. Conducted in response to a papal summons, the encounter was a formal step in the legal process against Luther and his followers that should have taken place in Rome had not papal and imperial politics intervened. Cajetan, a convinced defender of papal authority and a champion of indulgences, placed the issue of the pope's authority in the foreground. What surprised Luther was that the legate's claims—particularly that Clement VI's papal bull *Unigenitus* was indisputable—were made without any reference to the Scriptures. Promulgated in 1343, that bull had defined the church's conception of the "treasury of merits" and the pope's power over it, key components in its doctrine of indulgences. In response, Luther asserted the authority of Scripture against one document of church law, a contested one at that. This was an important moment because from it Luther concluded that the church stood against the Scriptures, and he later wrote that at this point he really began to fight against the papacy. That same December, in a letter to his friend Wenceslaus Linck, he first raised the suspicion that the antichrist alluded to in 2 Thess. 2:4 might be in control of the curia, that is, the papal court.

Not until the Leipzig Disputation of July 1519 did Luther begin to declare his opinions more openly. In preparation for the debate, his opponent, John Eck, professor of theology at Ingolstadt, had composed twelve propositions to debate with Karlstadt. Luther, who realized that many of Eck's points were aimed directly at him, countered by publishing thirteen propositions, the last of which questioned papal authority since 1100. In his own preparations for the disputation, Luther undertook a thorough investigation of canon law and church history, concluding that in many cases laws had been made without regard for Scripture and that the papacy had assumed its current form only rather recently. When it appeared that the debate might not materialize, Luther penned the treatise *Luther's Explanation of Proposition Thirteen concerning the Power of the Pope* (WA 2:180–240), in which he included a comprehensive exegesis of Matt. 16:16–19, the scriptural verses upon which the papacy had established its claims of primacy as a divine right. Again Luther argued that when Christ said, "You are Peter, and on this rock I will build my church" (Matt. 16:18), he had not meant that the church would be established on the person of Peter, but on the confession of faith that Peter had given. Thus the power of the keys belonged to the community of believers, not to the pope, whom Scripture did not mention at all. Luther still conceded that the pope was the head of the Western church by human right and therefore enjoyed the authority given him by God that all earthly rulers had, but his power did not rest on the foundation of divine right.

During the disputation itself Eck invoked *Unam Sanctam*, the 1302 bull of Pope Boniface VIII, considered to be the medieval church's most extreme articulation of papal power, which included the claim that subordination to the Roman pontiff was essential to salvation. When Luther responded by affirming relevant positions of Jan Hus, who had been condemned as a heretic by the Council of Constance (1415), Eck accused Luther of dishonoring a legitimate church council. As a result, Luther was forced to recognize that not only was the pope fallible, but also that all authority outside of the Scriptures, including church councils, could err, although he still stopped short of completely rejecting the papacy or publicly identifying the pope as the antichrist.

For a while things stood at an impasse. Then in February 1520 Luther read Lorenzo Valla's treatise *On the Donation of Constantine*, a text that exposed as fraudulent the legal document purporting to transfer authority over the Western Roman Empire from the emperor Constantine to Pope Sylvester as the former departed Rome for his newly established capital of Constantinople. In response, Luther wrote to his friend Georg Spalatin that he could scarcely doubt that the pope was the antichrist. Publicly, however, in his treatise *On the Papacy in Rome, against the Most Celebrated Romanist in Leipzig* (June 1520), Luther still accorded respect for the pope on the same level with obedience to other authorities, but added to his views on papal authority a rejection of the notion that the pope could proclaim new articles of faith or brand those not under his obedience as heretics. On June 15, 1520, the bull *Exsurge Domine* appeared, threatening Luther with excommunication. It included the assertion that the pope's judgment was infallible because Christ had promised that he would remain with his disciples until the end of the world. Luther was unmoved.

At the urging of the former and present heads of Luther's order in Saxony, Johann von Staupitz and Wenzeslaus Linck, Luther made one last personal appeal directly to Pope Leo X in November 1520, in an open letter appended to his treatise *The Freedom of a Christian*. Here he retained the distinction between the office of the papacy and the person of the pope, continuing to demonstrate respect for the temporal authority of the papacy while railing against the papal curia. Nonetheless, on December 10, 1520, he burned a copy of the papal bull and canon law, telling his students the next day that they could not be saved unless they opposed the papal kingdom with their whole hearts. By this act he completely rejected papal claims of authority. From that time on, Luther considered the pope a fictitious creation of this world, a fabrication (Hendrix 119). As a result, when his excommunication was made official on January 3, 1521, in the bull *Decet Romanum Pontificem*, Luther experienced it as a liberating event, one that confirmed for him that the pope worked against Christ, that the papacy set itself up against the Scriptures. For Luther, the matter had been concluded.

Once he had definitively rejected the papacy as the antichrist, he began to publicize his conviction and to address its implications for Christian ethics and ecclesiology. Already in 1521, Lucas Cranach's famous pamphlet *Passional of Christ and the Antichrist* was published in Wittenberg, consisting of a series of woodcuts with facing-page images in which the actions of Christ and the pope as antichrist were depicted in sharp contrast. Certainly Luther, along with Melanchthon, had a hand in its production. By the time of the Diet of Worms in the spring of 1521, it is clear that Luther had understood the implications of his position as he asserted that the laws of the pope and the doctrines of men have vexed and flayed the consciences of the faithful. Already in his treatise *The Freedom of a Christian*, Luther had begun the process of demonstrating how the faithful should be taught to act without the yoke of papal law; he did so by establishing an ethic of Christian love, motivated by gratitude toward God and based on the example of Christ.

For the rest of his life, Luther continued to attack the institution of the papacy. During the 1530s he developed the notion that the holy Christian church can exist very well without a symbolic head, because such a person serves no Christian office: Christ fulfills this role. In 1545, just a year before his death, Luther published what was perhaps his coarsest and most polemical work on the matter, *Against the Roman Papacy, an Institution of the Devil*, in which he summed up his view of the papacy: "He who wants to hear God speak should read the Holy Scripture. He who wants to hear the Devil speak should read the pope's decretals and bulls" (*Against the Roman Papacy*, LW 41:332).

Luther's realization that the papacy's legal argument for temporal authority was based on the fraudulent Donation of Constantine and his historical judgment that the early church had survived without anything resembling a pope helped convince him that the papacy was an illegitimate institution. But his rejection of it ultimately rested on theological grounds. The Scriptures held no justification for a divinely instituted human head of the church. By assuming that role, the papacy had usurped Christ's lordship. Furthermore, the papacy had insisted on human cooperation with God's grace in the process of salvation and instituted a variety of unbiblical and unchristian concepts, laws, and practices to facilitate and encourage this belief, at the same time failing to execute properly the obligations of preaching the word and administering the sacraments. Reliance for salvation on something other than Christ was, for Luther, tantamount to idolatry, evidence that the pope was the antichrist sent by the devil into the heart of the church. Luther's response was a rigorous, unrelenting, and lifelong antipapalism that went beyond that of other mainstream reformers.

In the following centuries, Luther's position was often followed without question.

Twentieth-century Lutheran-Catholic dialogue on the theology of salvation has resulted in the consensus of the Joint Declaration on the Doctrine of Justification (1999) and deepened conversations about the nature of authority in the church and especially in the papacy. But despite discussions between the two sides over the "special apostolic ministry" of the bishop of Rome, the rift begun by Luther over the role and legitimacy of the papacy has yet to be overcome.

See also Cajetan (Thomaso de Vio); Catholicism; Eck, John; Luther's Roman Catholic Opponents; Ninety-Five Theses; Prierias, Sylvester; *Treatise on the Power and Primacy of the Pope*

Bibliography

Bäumer, R. *Martin Luther und der Pabst*. Aschendorff, 1971; Hendrix, S. *Luther and the Papacy: Stages in a Reformation Conflict*. Fortress, 1981; Luther, M. *Against the Roman Papacy, an Institution of the Devil* (1545). LW 41:257–376; Luther, M. Ninety-Five Theses (1517). LW 31:17–33; Luther, M. *On the Papacy in Rome, against the Most Celebrated Romanist in Leipzig* (1520). LW 39:49–104; Luther, M. Proceedings at Augsburg (1518). LW 31:253–92; Moeller, B. "Luther und das Papsttum." In *Luther Handbuch*, ed. A. Beutel, 10–15. 2nd ed. Mohr Siebeck, 2010; Oberman, H. *Luther: Man between God and the Devil*. Yale University Press, 1989; Russell, W. "Martin Luther's Understanding of the Pope as the Antichrist." *ARG* 85 (1994): 32–44; Whitford, D. "The Papal Antichrist: Martin Luther and the Underappreciated Influence of Lorenzo Valla." *RQ* 61 (2008): 26–52.

ROBERT J. CHRISTMAN

Papua New Guinea

In less than 130 years, Lutheranism in the country now known as Papua New Guinea has grown from a slow start to number well over one million people. Lutheran mission began on July 12, 1886, when Johann Flierl, a Neuendettelsau missionary who had served among Aboriginal people in Australia, landed at Finschhafen on the northeastern coast of New Guinea, which at that time had just been annexed as Kaiser-Wilhelmsland. The beginnings were not promising, partly because the people were ambivalent about the German colonial presence. It was thirteen years before the first baptism occurred. The real breakthrough came with the realization that evangelism in the

Melanesian context does not work if conversion isolates new Christians from their people and culture. Over the years a mission strategy was developed, particularly through the work of Christian Keysser (Keyser/Kaiser), with two constant factors. First, when missionaries and their helpers went into new areas, they would persuade village leaders and the whole community to agree communally to receive evangelists, whose task then was to live among the people and catechize them in preparation for baptism. The second key factor in evangelization was that the newly baptized were called on to take the good news to those who had not yet heard it. Initially that meant sending young evangelists to people in the next valley, and later it meant sending them far away, even to the remotest areas of the highlands. From the very beginning Lutheranism in New Guinea was a grassroots movement, and this has been one of its enduring strengths.

The work of the Neuendettlesau and Rhenish missions began to flourish, and the gospel spread rapidly as new congregations sprang up along the coast and in the mountainous hinterland. The gospel ran its course despite the negative impact of two world wars. World War I saw New Guinea pass from German to Australian hands, and as a result the mission, now cut off from Germany, was all but orphaned. Calls to Lutheran churches in the United States and Australia were heard, and in the ensuing period a mission organization was formed, Lutheran Mission New Guinea (LMNG), which was supported by sending churches and mission societies from three continents. Far more serious was the disruption caused by the Japanese invasion during World War II and the long Allied campaign to repel it. Niuginian evangelists and elders continued to work faithfully, and congregations survived and even grew.

After the war there was a massive mission effort to rebuild what had been lost and also to open new mission fields in the Highlands, an area that had only just begun to have contact with the outside world. Other Lutherans came into the picture during this period, some to work with LMNG and others to establish their own missions. The Australian Lutheran Mission (ALM) looked after the work on Siassi Island and began a new field in Menyamya on the mainland. Entering the field in 1948, the Lutheran Church–Missouri Synod (LCMS), with assistance from ALM, pioneered the work among the large Enga language group in the Highlands.

As the work grew, so did the recognition that it was high time to make the big move from mission organization to indigenous church. The Evangelical Lutheran Church of New Guinea (ELCONG, later ELC-PNG) was established in 1956, with LMNG continuing as a supporting organization. The need for indigenous pastors to serve in the fledgling church was addressed by the establishment of three seminaries, two vernacular and one English. The first indigenous bishop, Zurewec Zurenuoc, was consecrated in 1971. Similarly, the LCMS mission transitioned to become Wabag Lutheran Church, later renamed Gutnius Lutheran Church (GLC), which has its own seminary.

Today the ELC-PNG is said to have about 900,000 members while the GLC accounts for a further 150,000. Both churches are founded on a clear confessional basis. Representatives of all the Lutheran churches and missions in PNG worked collaboratively for nine years to produce a confessional statement of faith that takes into account both worldwide and local theological issues. *Tok Bilip bilong Yumi* (A statement of faith) was published in 1972 and is used today in all the Lutheran seminaries.

From the beginning there has been a strong emphasis on education, medical work, and helping the people in development. A particular strength of the church is *wok meri* (women's work). Lutheranism is flourishing still in Papua New Guinea even in the face of various problems.

See also Australia; Flierl, Johann; Mission and Evangelism

Bibliography

Committee on Theology and Inter-Church Relations. Tok Bilip bilong Yumi / A Statement of Faith. Kristen, 1972; Frehrichs, A. and S. *Anutu Conquers in New Guinea.* Rev. ed. Augsburg, 1969; Fugmann, G., ed. *The Birth of an Indigenous Church: Letters, Reports and Documents of Lutheran Christians of Papua New Guinea.* Melanesian Institute, 1986; Keysser, C. *A People Reborn.* Trans. A. Allin and J. Kuder. William Carey Library, 1980; Pilhofer, D. G. *Die Geschichte der Neuendettelsauer Mission in Neuguinea.* 3 vols. Freimund, 1961–63; Wagner, H., and H. Reiner, eds. *The Lutheran Church in Papua New Guinea: The First Hundred Years, 1886–1986.* Lutheran Publishing House, 1986.

Dean Zweck

Passavant, William Alfred

Born in Zelienople, Pennsylvania, William Alfred Passavant (1821–94) became a Lutheran pastor, editor, and founder of social service agencies. He studied at Gettysburg Lutheran Seminary and was ordained in 1843. He was a pastor and also served as editor of a number of publications, including the *Lutheran Observer* and the *Missionary* (eventually *The Lutheran*). While a pastor in Pittsburgh, he helped form the Pittsburgh Synod, and later he was instrumental in founding the General Council in 1867.

Passavant was a tireless home missionary and made many journeys around the United States to assist newly arrived Lutheran immigrants. His largest contribution was as the founder of Lutheran hospitals in Pittsburgh, Chicago, and Milwaukee, and of orphanages in New York, Philadelphia, and Boston. For the hospitals Passavant was instrumental in establishing the first communities of Lutheran deaconesses in the United States, following models from Germany. Some of these deaconesses served the troops during the Civil War. Passavant also assisted in the founding of Thiel College in 1870 and the Lutheran Theological Seminary, Maywood, Illinois. He was constantly traveling throughout his career, especially in raising funds for the operation of the institutions he helped to form. Passavant was one of the outstanding leaders of American Lutheranism in the nineteenth century.

See also Deaconesses; General Council of the Evangelical Lutheran Church in North America; Lutheran Social Services; Orphanages

Bibliography

Gerberding, G. H. *The Life and Letters of W. A. Passavant.* The Young Lutheran Co., 1906.

Mark A. Granquist

Patristics

The Discipline of Patristics. In modern parlance, "patristics" or "patrology" means the academic study of the history of the early church, especially of those writers who are considered orthodox teachers, and thus (using a much older term) "fathers" (*patres*), with particular focus on their writings and theology. The boundary between the patristic era and the Middle Ages is placed at various times, as early as the end of the fifth century or as late as the eighth century. In the eleventh and twelfth centuries, awareness of disunity in the fathers' teachings led to efforts by the Italian Benedictine Gratian and the French theologian Peter Lombard at harmonizing the entire Latin patristic witness. Their works remained in use as law and theology textbooks until Luther's time. In the fifteenth century, new translations began to be made of Greek patristic writings into Latin, making them accessible to educated people. Such translations together with compilations of the Latin fathers continued throughout the Reformation era, made by notable patristic editors such as Desiderius Erasmus. Programs suggested to theology students for reading the fathers differed among Lutheran theologians, though Augustine and Bernard of Clairvaux usually were most highly recommended. Later the Cappadocians gained in importance. Textual criticism of the fathers' writings and the identification of pseudonymous works, carried on already by Erasmus, gained momentum through the sixteenth and seventeenth centuries, as Roman Catholic and Reformation theologians demanded a critical appreciation of the fathers. Lutherans tended to be more interested in the content of ancient sources than their authorship, as several citations in the Augsburg Confession indicate.

Patristic Authority. Luther learned his theology not only from Scripture but also from the early church fathers. He treasured the fathers as saints and witnesses to the church's faith in Christ (LW 60:328–29). Yet the fathers' authority is below Scripture: "It will not do to frame articles of faith from the works and words of the holy Fathers. . . . The rule is: The Word of God shall establish articles of faith, and no one else, not even an angel" (SA 2.2.15; cf. Gal. 1:8). If the Scriptures are a spring, the fathers are streams flowing away from the spring (LW 41:26–27). Their authority is secondary to Scripture, since they themselves point to Scripture as the only completely reliable source of truth; the fathers and councils contain only a part of Christian doctrine, not all of it, and sometimes the fathers and councils disagree with one another. In Luther's estimation, Augustine holds a place far above the other early church fathers (LW 41:27; 59:288; 60:44; cf. CA 27.35). Luther recognized only four "principal councils" of the early church—Nicaea (325), Constantinople (381), Ephesus (431), and Chalcedon (451)—and stated that the latter two had not been well understood before his time (LW 41:121). With few exceptions, Luther's view of scriptural and patristic authority is shared by all other Reformation theologians. Yet this must not be allowed to disguise the spectrum of approaches to patristic authority among Lutherans in and after the Reformation.

Philip Melanchthon viewed the fathers' authority similarly to Luther. He valued the fathers as witnesses to the truth (*testes veritatis*) and thus placed them beneath the authority of Scripture. He could criticize the fathers, yet he also thought Scripture should not be interpreted without respecting the ancient church's exegetical tradition. More than Luther, he emphasized the importance of hearing the fathers' voices, while agreeing with Luther on their limited authority for theology.

Later Lutherans combined the two sides— critique of and high esteem for the fathers—in varying degrees. Patristic study and theological use of the fathers flourished especially from the late Reformation until the beginning of the Enlightenment. From the mid-1500s through about 1640 many Lutheran patristic theologies were written, in which the doctrines taught by Luther and his heirs were shown to be in harmony with the fathers. Writers of these works included Matthias Flacius Illyricus, Urbanus Rhegius, Erasmus Sarcerius, Michael Neander, Heinrich Eckhard, Hermann Empsychovius, Martin Chemnitz, Johann Gerhard, and others.

In his effort to overcome the rift resulting from the Reformation, Georg Calixt (1586–1656) turned to the patristic era to find a second doctrinal principle besides Holy Scripture. Starting with Vincent of Lérins's (d. ca. 445) threefold criterion for religious truth—universality, antiquity, and consent—Calixt excluded universality as no longer knowable and formulated the other two as the "consensus of antiquity." Abraham Calov and other Orthodox Lutheran theologians of the later seventeenth century rejected Calixt's proposals as "syncretism." The traditionalism in theology begun by Calixt did not take permanent hold in Lutheranism; its proponents often left Lutheranism for other confessions. Among Enlightenment theologians in the latter half of the eighteenth century, the fathers lost their authority; the early church no longer supplied arguments for polemics and examples for dogmatics. Nevertheless, the study and knowledge of the fathers continued among various Lutheran groups of the nineteenth century and was never fully extinguished. A critical edition of the Greek fathers, for example, was being published at the turn of the twentieth century in Germany. In Sweden, the work of Gustaf Aulén on the atonement, for example, used the church fathers extensively. English-speaking Lutherans also made rich use of patristic texts in their original languages and in translations of the fathers into English.

See also Augustine of Hippo; Authority; Bernard, Abbot of Clairvaux; Calixt, George; History; Melanchthon, Philip

Bibliography

Backus, I., "Patristics." In *The Oxford Encyclopedia of the Reformation*, ed. H. Hillerbrand, 3:223–27. Oxford University Press, 1996; Bergjan, S.-P. "Die Beschäftigung mit der Alten Kirche an deutschen Universitäten in den Umbrüchen der Aufklärung." In *Zwischen Altertumswissenschaft und Theologie*, ed. C. Markschies and J. van Oort, 31–61. Peeters, 2002; Bergjan, S.-P., and K. Pollmann, eds. *Patristic Tradition and Intellectual Paradigms in the Seventeenth Century.* Mohr Siebeck, 2010; Fraenkel, P. *Testimonia Patrum: The Function of the Patristic Argument in the Theology of Philip Melanchthon.* E. Droz, 1961; Hägglund, B. "Verständnis und Autorität der altkirchlichen Tradition in der lutherischen Theologie der Reformationszeit." In *Oecumenica, 1971–72: Tradition in Lutheranism and Anglicanism*, ed. E. Gassmann and V. Vajta, 34–62. Augsburg, 1972; Hendrix, S. "Deparentifying the Fathers." In *Auctoritas Patrum*, ed. L. Grane et al., 1:55–68. Von Zabern, 1993; Herrmann, E. "Luther's Absorption of Medieval Biblical Interpretation and His Use of the Church Fathers." In *The Oxford Handbook of Martin Luther's Theology*, ed. R. Kolb, I. Dingel, and L. Batka, 71–90. Oxford University Press, 2014; Mayes, B. "Lumina, Non Numina: Patristic Authority according to Lutheran Arch-Theologian Johann Gerhard." In *Church and School in Early Modern Protestantism*, ed. J. J. Ballor, D. S. Sytsma, and J. Zuidema, 457–70. Brill, 2013.

BENJAMIN T. G. MAYES

Paul

The apostle Paul (ca. 10 CE–ca. 64) was a Greek-speaking Jewish biblical theologian of the tribe of Benjamin (Phil. 3:5), from Tarsus in Cilicia (Acts 21:39), who initially opposed the Jesus movement; he was known as Saul within the Aramaic-speaking community (Acts 13:9; 26:14). In the midst of his persecution of the early church, Saul/Paul experienced the risen Christ on the "road to Damascus" (Acts 9:3). In this life-changing encounter, Paul experienced a call and a commission by God to become an apostle to the gentiles (Gal. 1:1; 2:2).

Paul's writings are a major presence in the New Testament canon. By tradition, fourteen of the twenty-seven books of the New Testament are attributed to the apostle Paul or, according to critical scholarship, to his "school." Of these, the authorship of Hebrews was generally disputed by the early church in the West (Heen and Krey xviii), as well as by Renaissance interpreters including (on occasion)

Luther. Modern critical scholarship has been able to agree that seven of the remaining works are secure in terms of their Pauline authorship. In canonical order they are Romans, 1 and 2 Corinthians, Galatians, Philippians, 1 Thessalonians, and Philemon. Of the remaining, Colossians is held by many scholars to have been penned by Paul. The authorship of Ephesians, 2 Thessalonians, and the "Pastorals" (Titus, 1 and 2 Timothy), however, are variously questioned. Three letters that carried the name of Paul were rejected by the early church in the extended process of canonization: *Letter of Paul to the Laodiceans* (found in some Latin manuscripts until the end of the Middle Ages and well received by some Lutherans), *Letter to the Alexandrians*, and *Third Corinthians*, a part of an apocryphal *Acts of Paul* (Krodel 1737). Though Paul also plays a major role in the narrative of the canonical Acts of the Apostles, modern scholars who participate in the quest for the historical Paul have largely agreed to base their reconstructions on the seven "undisputed" epistles, supplemented by a critical-historical readings of Acts and the deutero-Pauline materials. If one, however, has determined that the historical Paul wrote all thirteen letters (or fourteen if one includes Hebrews), then a somewhat different Paul emerges, in terms of theology as well as the chronology of his life.

There are significant autobiographical passages written by Paul in the New Testament (e.g., 2 Cor. 11:16–12; Gal. 1:13–2:14; Phil. 3:4–8). In fact, more is known about Paul than any other figure from the period of the early church, with the exception of Jesus. Paul was well trained in the Torah (Jewish law), understood both as Scripture and as halakah (Oral Torah: the ongoing debates on Jewish rules and practices to be observed). Paul affiliated himself with the diverse Pharisaic movement (Phil. 3:5), which enjoyed a range of interpretive perspectives from Hillel to Shammai. The pre-Damascus Paul was probably more oriented toward the rigorist house of Shammai than that of the more pastoral house of

Hillel, even though Acts 22:3 has Paul as a student of Gamaliel, the grandson of Hillel. Hillel was known for a version of the Golden Rule: "That which is hateful to you, do not do to your neighbor: This is the whole Torah (law); the rest is commentary" (Babylonian Talmud, Shabbat 31a). Acts also reports that Paul was a citizen of Tarsus (21:39) and the Roman Empire (22:27–28), rarities for Jews in antiquity. It is on the basis of this citizenship that Paul in Acts appeals for a hearing before the Roman emperor after his arrest in Jerusalem around the year 59 (Acts 25:10; 26:32). At the end of Acts, Paul has been under house arrest in Rome for two years (28:16, 30). Noncanonical Christian tradition indicates that Paul was martyred in Rome (1 Clem. 5.5–7), perhaps during the persecutions that occurred under Nero in 64 CE.

Paul never knew or participated in the ministry of the historical Jesus. Shortly after the crucifixion, when Paul did encounter the *kerygma* (proclamation) of the early church, he perceived it as blasphemous and became a violent persecutor of the church. One might ask what it was about the early Christian message that was so offensive to Paul that he sought vigorously to eliminate it as an expression of faith in the God of Israel. A variety of possible answers exists to this question. One that Paul himself alludes to is found in Gal. 3:13, where he quotes Deut. 21:22–23: "When someone is convicted of a crime punishable by death and is executed, and you hang him on a tree, his corpse must not remain all night upon the tree; you shall bury him that same day, for *anyone hung on a tree is under God's curse*" (emphasis added). The pre-Damascus Paul was revolted by the claim that Jesus—who was hung on a tree to die—was the Messiah of Israel. How could he be? Scripture itself says that Jesus came "under God's curse" on the cross. Desiring to protect the righteousness of Israel (and with a clear prooftext of Scripture to support his zeal), Paul went after those who proclaimed Jesus to be God's Christ. In the midst of this campaign against what Paul took to be the church's blasphemy, he encountered the risen Christ. This event turned Paul's understanding of God (and religion) upside down. Rather than finding himself "justified" by God for his "zeal for the law," as Phinehas had (Num. 25; cf. Ps. 106:30–31), Paul discovered that he had become, unwittingly, God's enemy. In other words, Paul discovered that his pious, biblically informed understanding of righteousness did not reflect God's understanding of righteousness. God's righteousness—surprisingly, counterintuitively—had been revealed, once and for all, in the scandal, even the blasphemy, of a crucified messiah. God's Christ *was* hung on a tree. The intimate knowledge of this apocalyptic reversal, where the "curse" of the law was transformed into an expression of God's "righteousness," lies at the heart of all of Paul's subsequent theology. After the cross, everything—even the Holy Scriptures of Israel and its teaching (Torah/*nomos*)—needed to be interpreted in light of the new revelation of God's righteousness in Christ, crucified and risen. Remarkably, on the cross, God revealed that the force of the indictment of God's holy law had been reversed. The curse of the law had fallen on God's holy righteous one (Christ) with the result that the *un*righteous—including the persecutor Paul— in an extraordinary display of God's mercy, might be redeemed from the power of sin and made righteous for Christ's sake (2 Cor. 5:21; Gal. 3:13).

A primary metaphor Paul uses to describe the Christ event, especially in Galatians and Romans, is "justification": In Christ, God makes "just/righteous" precisely that which is in fundamental rebellion against God. In doing so, the depth of human bondage to sin is revealed, while the power of both sin and death is destroyed, making a new relationship with God and creation possible. In getting at the multifaceted effects of the Christ event, Paul will use a variety of other metaphors in addition to "justification." They include "salvation," "reconciliation," "expiation," "redemption," "freedom," "new creation," "sanctification," "glorification," and "pardon." For Paul the "means" by which such effects come into a fallen world is always the obedience of Christ (Phil. 2:8). The "agency" through which these are made real is through one's trust (*pistis*) that in Christ, God's attack on sin as well as God's mercy have been revealed.

Paul's occasional letters written to early Christian communities (ca. 48–58 CE) became recognized almost immediately as theologically significant and were eventually canonized as part of Scripture. Paul's writings, because they often proceed at a high level of critical thinking, present various challenges to understanding. This was true even in the early church (2 Pet. 3:16), and in the early Western (Latin) church, Paul's Letters were largely neglected until the second half of the fourth century (Froehlich 285). In the early Reformation, Galatians and Romans, the Pauline Letters that most discuss the related topics of "works of the law" and "justification," became foundational to Lutheran theology. While Luther lectured on Romans, Galatians, and Hebrews in 1515–18, Galatians became the primary text for Luther's grounding in Paul (Hultgren 233), and Melanchthon came to focus on the text of Romans (publishing five separate commentaries on the book), which in his *Loci communes* of 1521 he called a "compendium of Christian doctrine" (2.7.25). In addition, Paul's letters to the Corinthian community contained expositions of what came to be known as the "theology of the cross" (1 Cor. 1:18–31; Cousar) and an understanding of the atonement described as the "happy exchange" (2 Cor. 5:21); both are central to the Reformation's understanding of the Christ event. Luther himself relates his theological breakthrough on the basis of a close reading of *dikaiosynē theou* ("the justice/righteousness of/from God" in Rom. 1:16–17 ("Preface to the Latin Readings, 1545," LW 34:336–37). Of the fourteen pages of index of biblical citations in the English translation of the Book of Concord, five of them list Pauline texts (Kolb and Wengert 669–74).

From the 1960s, a growing movement in biblical studies that falls under the rubric of the "New Perspective on Paul" has taken issue with what scholars trained in New Testament studies (rather than the Reformation period) characterized as Luther's reading of Paul (Stendahl 1976; Sanders 1977; Dunn 2005; Wright 2009). In this school, both the anti-Judaism of the later Luther as well as his understanding of Jewish law (torah/halakah) was disputed. "Justification," rather than being the keystone of Christian doctrine as Luther had characterized it (LW 26:26, 120, 283), was a time-conditioned strategy by which the apostle to the gentiles argued for the inclusion of gentiles into Israel without circumcision or other observances of "ceremonial" Jewish law, a position similar to arguments found in Jerome and Erasmus. In this revisionist school, "the Lutheran" understanding both of Judaism (characterized as a "works-righteous" religion analogous to Luther's experience of late medieval Roman Catholicism) and of Jewish law (the basis of Luther's understanding of Jewish "legalism") takes on a pejorative edge. While much good has come from the New Perspective on Paul, including an intolerance for Christian anti-Semitism in New Testament biblical studies and a renewed appreciation for the diversity of Second Temple Judaism, it can be argued that the New Perspective (1) stays with popular characterizations of the Lutheran understanding of justification and faith and therefore does not truly understand how Luther or Melanchthon themselves understood either, and (2) does not fully appreciate the extent to which the post-Damascus Paul comes to view Torah (understood as Scripture as well as halakah, Oral Torah) in very different ways than he did before his call/conversion to Christ (Westerholm; Heen).

See also Bible Interpretation; Justification; Scripture

Bibliography

Cousar, C. B. *A Theology of the Cross: The Death of Jesus in the Pauline Letters.* Fortress, 1990; Dunn, J. D. G. *The New Perspective on Paul: Collected Essays.* Mohr Siebeck, 2005; Froehlich, K. "Which Paul? Observations on the Image of the Apostle in the History of Exegesis." In *New Perspectives on Historical Theology*, ed. B. Nassif, 279–99. Eerdmans, 1996; Heen, E. M. "A Lutheran Response to the New Perspective on Paul." *LQ* 24 (2010): 263–91; Heen, E. M., and P. Krey. *Hebrews.* Ancient Christian Commentary on Scripture. InterVarsity, 2005; Hultgren, A. J. "Luther on Galatians." *Word & World* 20 (2000): 232–38; Kolb, R., and T. Wengert, eds. *The Book of Concord.* Fortress, 2000; Krodel, G. "New Testament Canon." In *The Encyclopedia of the Lutheran Church*, ed. J. Bodensieck, 3:1732–43. Augsburg, 1965; Sanders, E. P. *Paul and Palestinian Judaism: A Comparison of Patterns of Religion.* Fortress, 1977; Stendahl, K. *Paul among Jews and Gentiles.* Fortress, 1976; Westerholm, S. *Perspectives Old and New on Paul: The "Lutheran" Paul and His Critics.* Eerdmans, 2004; Wright, N. T. *Justification: God's Plan and Paul's Vision.* IVP Academic, 2009; Zetterholm, M. *Approaches to Paul: A Student's Guide to Recent Scholarship.* Fortress, 2009.

ERIK M. HEEN

Paulssen, Bertha

The German-American teacher and social worker Bertha Paulssen (1891–1973) was born in Leipzig on January 15, 1891. She attended university at Göttingen and Leipzig and received her doctorate in psychology from the latter in 1917. Paulssen began a career in social services in northern Germany, working with the Inner Mission and the Lutheran churches to pioneer work among women, youth, and families. She also taught and lectured on these subjects throughout Germany. With the rise of Hitler, Paulssen left Germany, first to go to England, and then in 1936 to America. In 1944, after shorter teaching terms at various Lutheran colleges and at the Lutheran Deaconess Motherhouse in Philadelphia, she was called to be professor of Christian sociology and psychology at Gettysburg Lutheran Theological Seminary. Paulssen was the first woman faculty member to be tenured at a Lutheran seminary in North America and was important in the shaping and development of social ministry organizations among American Lutherans. She was also influential in wider Protestant circles, lecturing at Union Seminary (New York) and Princeton Seminary. Retired from Gettysburg Seminary in 1963, she remained active in her field for a number of years until her death in 1973.

See also Lutheran Social Services; Social Ministry, Community Chest, Poor Relief

Bibliography

Wentz, A. R. *Gettysburg Lutheran Theological Seminary.* Vol. 1, *History, 1826–1965.* Esp. 439–40. Evangelical Press, 1965.

MARK A. GRANQUIST

Peace of Augsburg

As a constitutional edict in the Holy Roman Empire, the Peace of Augsburg (1555) legally guaranteed the coexistence of two religious confessions in the Holy Roman Empire: Roman Catholicism and adherence to the Augsburg Confession.

The Peace of Augsburg (signed September 1555) culminated over thirty years of political, religious, and legal deliberation and military struggle in the German lands that took place in response to Evangelical reforms and changes to the imperial constitution. The edict reformulated the relationship between the emperor and the empire, further defined the legal rights of the imperial estates (individuals or entities entitled to vote in the empire), and secured the legal existence of Roman Catholicism and Lutheranism into the modern era.

The Edict of Worms (1521) outlawed Martin Luther and condemned his teachings. However, in 1526 the Diet of Speyer gave the Evangelical princes some maneuvering room: they could use their own judgment on religious issues as long as they understood that they were "accountable before God and his Imperial Majesty." Although the pope and the emperor continued to pressure the estates to remain under papal obedience, Evangelical reform gained momentum at the next Diet of Speyer (1529). There, a number of the estates entered a formal "protest" confessing their faith against the renewed decision of the Diet to enforce the Edict of Worms (and thus rescind the temporizing decision of 1526). Similarly, at the Diet of Augsburg (1530), Evangelicals defended Luther's teaching and presented the Augsburg Confession. By the next year the Smalcald League was formed. With negotiations at

Regensburg in 1541 and 1546 having broken down, an Evangelical defensive alliance, the Smalcaldic League (including especially Elector John Frederick and Landgrave Philip of Hesse), took steps to defend the Evangelical cause militarily, resulting in the Smalcald War (1546–47), a confrontation that pitted the League and imperial forces (including some Evangelicals, notably Duke Moritz of Saxony) against one another in the heart of the empire, leading to the defeat of the League. A subsequent Revolt of the Princes (led by Moritz) in the early 1550s led to the Treaty of Passau (1552).

In February 1555 the imperial estates gathered at the Diet of Augsburg to resolve the political and religious controversy that had divided the Empire. Emperor Charles V remained in the Netherlands, exhausted from decades of war and his inability to defend and reinstate Roman Catholicism. His brother, Ferdinand, Archduke of Austria and the future emperor (r. 1556–64), convened negotiations with the imperial estates. Fears about war with the Ottomans permeated the diet, and legal representatives from both sides worked to find a compromise that would keep the peace and preserve the rights of the imperial estates. The negotiators based their work on the language of recent agreements, especially the Treaty of Passau (1552).

At the final recess of the diet, a formal edict was promulgated that became known as the Peace of Augsburg. Its terms stipulated that each prince within the empire should determine the religion in his territory, provided that the religion was either Roman Catholicism or that of the Augsburg Confession. (This legal right was soon explained as *ius reformandi*, the right to reform.) The edict prohibited the religion of other groups, including Zwinglians, Calvinists, Anabaptists, and other sects. The prince was free to choose one of the two approved faiths. However, individual subjects were *not* legally free to choose: they were required to follow the religion of their sovereign. (Those who had an objection to the chosen religion were given the right to emigrate.) Lesser nobles with the standing of imperial knight were also allowed to choose either faith. In an effort to emphasize the superior standing of the princes, the right to reform was denied to urban magistrates, which created resentment and further protests in the free, imperial cities. However, in the cities where both confessions were active (such as Augsburg), the rights of each group were to be honored. Roman Catholic ecclesiastical jurisdiction over the Lutheran lands was suspended for the terms of the peace, but if a Roman Catholic bishop or officeholder converted to the Augsburg Confession, the ecclesiastical territory that they controlled was to remain Roman Catholic, in the possession of the imperial church. (This later corollary was issued separately by Ferdinand and remained highly controversial.)

The Peace of Augsburg was the most important imperial edict passed between 1356 and 1648. The settlement maintained an uneasy peace between Roman Catholics and Lutherans in an era that was known for its destructive religious wars. The agreement's most famous slogan, "whose the rule, his the religion" (*cuius regio, eius religio*), was devised by the jurist Joachim Stephani in 1582 to encapsulate the landmark decision. Although it was designed as a temporary solution, the Peace of Augsburg, though interrupted by the Thirty Years' War (1618–48), was confirmed with few changes by the Peace of Westphalia in 1648, which ended the Thirty Years' War. It stayed in force until the dissolution of the Holy Roman Empire in 1806.

See also Augsburg Confession; Augsburg Interim; Electors of Saxony; Holy Roman Empire; Smalcald War; Thirty Years' War

Bibliography

Brady, T. A., Jr. *German Histories in the Age of Reformations, 1400–1650.* Cambridge University Press, 2009; Brady, T. A., Jr., E. Cameron, and H. Cohn. "The Politics of Religion: The Peace of Augsburg 1555." *Germany History* 24 (2006): 85–105; Buschmann, A., ed. *Kaiser und Reich: Verfassungsgeschichte des Heiligen Römischen Reiches Deutscher Nation vom Beginn des 12. Jahrhunderts bis zum Jahre 1806 in Dokumenten.* 2nd ed. Nomos, 1994; Graf, G., G. Wartenberg, and C. Winter, eds. *Der Augsburger Religionsfrieden: Seine Rezeption in den Territorien des Reiches.* Evangelische Verlagsanstalt, 2006; Whaley, J. *Germany and the Holy Roman Empire.* Vol. 1. Oxford University Press, 2012.

MICHAEL J. HALVORSON

Peasants' War

A series of conflicts of peasants and, sometimes, artisans and workers from the towns with governmental authorities in 1524–26 is called the Peasants' War. In the years that Günther Franz dominated the historiography of the German Peasants' War, following his classic monograph of 1933, it was "obvious" that the popular outbreaks that occurred in 1525 had no coherent program and were not connected to the Reformation. When Peter Blickle became the leader of the historical interest in the Peasants' War around the 1975 anniversary, it was accepted that the Twelve Articles were the "conceptual glue" that gave coherence to the various uprisings and that they were linked to the Reformation. While Blickle's paradigm has not been totally rejected in the past forty years, there has been growing skepticism about its two propositions. While the outbreaks of 1524–26 were too disparate to conceptualize all of them on the model of Upper Swabia and while many leaders of the revolt were sympathetic to the Reformation (which they conceived in various ways), it is by no means clear that the rank and file thought of themselves as fighting for the Reformation. Moreover, far from all of the leaders of the peasant bands were primarily interested in religion.

Leading up to 1525, Martin Luther was constantly contending with the external enemies of his Reformation, as well as associates who resisted his leadership. In 1523 he wrote *On Temporal Authority*, in which he delineated the proper spheres of the Christian church and the temporal rulers, as a protest against the Catholic champion Duke George of Saxony, who was trying to ban the circulation and sale of Luther's writings and his translations of the Bible. But Luther had all sorts of adversaries among his fellow reformers. In July 1523 he wrote his *Open Letter to the Princes of Saxony against the Rebellious Spirit*, denouncing Thomas Müntzer, who had established a competing version of the Reformation in the Electoral Saxon enclave of Allstedt and was rallying his followers for self-defense against neighboring Catholic authorities.

A major step in the beginning of the uprisings of 1525 was the assemblage of three peasant bands at Memmingen in Upper Swabia in March 1525. On March 20 they endorsed the Twelve Articles of the Common Peasantry, now thought to have been authored by Christoph Schappler, the Swiss-born Memmingen pastor. Schappler was close to Ulrich Zwingli and attended one of the disputations of 1523 that launched the Zurich Reformation. The Twelve Articles were intended to articulate "divine justice," which supposedly transcended local custom, and thus provided a legitimation for the subjects of various lordships to band together. Following a prologue, which defended the Reformation against accusations of being the source of disorder, articles 1–2 and 12 provided a religious framework for the peasant demands: each parish claimed the right to choose and dismiss its pastors and also to retain its tithes for local use. The last article set up the Bible as the authority for all the others and promised to withdraw any demand not in harmony with Scripture. Article 3 rejected serfdom; since Christ died for people in all estates, it was unseemly for Christians to hold each other as property. Articles 4–5 and 10 protested against the peasants not having free access to the common resources of the village, forests, waterways, and meadows. Articles 6–9 and 11 criticized labor services, rents, and dues, as well as legal penalties that the band members regarded as untraditional, unjust, and infringing on their livelihood.

In the course of April 1525 uprisings in villages and market towns spread over much of southwest Germany. Particularly since the Twelve Articles claimed the authority of the Reformation, Luther responded to this claim. In late April he published *Appeal for Peace:*

A Response to the Twelve Articles. He took the characteristic pastor's tack of denouncing both sides. In the first section addressed to the princes and landlords, he said they were receiving a punishment from God for abusing their subjects. But in the second section, directed to the rebels, he dismissed the rebels' overall claim to have a divine mandate, rejected some articles outright, and said that others were not matters that concerned him as a pastor. Specifically, while he endorsed the parishes' demand to choose their own pastors, he denounced article 2 on tithes as robbery of the landlords, to whom the tithes belonged, and article 3 against serfdom, since there was slaveholding in the Bible: Abraham, for instance, was a slaveholder.

Meanwhile the peasant uprisings continued to spread toward Luther's own region, involving Thomas Müntzer, who had become a leading pastor in Mühlhausen in Thuringia. Moreover, they were marked by notorious brutality, which to Luther belied their claims to be a godly undertaking. The lynch-mob execution at Weinsberg of the Count of Helfenstein, the Austrian governor of Württemberg, on April 16, 1525, was the direct provocation for Luther's *Against the Murderous, Thieving Peasant Hordes*, published on May 6, in which he called for the princes to put the peasants down like rabid dogs: "Stab, strike, strangle, whenever you have the chance!" He went on to make the notorious assertion that in these strange times a prince battling the peasants could more easily gain heaven by killing rebels than another prince could gain heaven through prayer. Luther, of course, was referring to his previous writing of 1523 in which he described the prince's God-given task as the preservation of temporal order. Hence, in slaying rebellious peasants the prince was carrying out his God-given vocation. Notably, at the same time, Luther's dying protector, Elector Frederick the Wise of Saxony, was advising his successor, Duke John, to seek a conciliatory settlement with the rebels. In July Luther published still another pamphlet about the Peasants' War, his *Open Letter on the Harsh Booklet against the Peasants*. By this time virtually all of the uprisings had been suppressed, almost all of them by Catholic authorities who thought of themselves as striking a blow for the old faith (with the single exception of Philip of Hesse, who joined with Luther's enemy, Duke George of Saxony, in defeating the Thuringian peasant band, encouraged by Thomas Müntzer, at Frankenhausen on May 15). Luther insisted that he had struck exactly the right tone in the harsh pamphlet of May and added that anyone who criticized him could properly be suspected of sympathizing with the rebels.

It has sometimes been contended that as the result of his pamphlets against the Peasants' War, Luther lost the adherence of the popular masses in southern Germany, many of whom returned to Catholicism. This is probably not the case. Luther demonstrated a genuine political and social position in 1525 that in 1531 aided in creating the Smalcaldic League, a pro-Reformation confederacy of princes and towns, and facilitated his continuing spiritual authority among his fellow reformers from the early 1530s to his death in 1546. However, in those years the success of the German Reformation was primarily centered in the nobility and townspeople, and only from these centers to the countryside, where the (often) town-bred and increasingly university-educated Lutheran pastors became instruments of both the gospel and "social discipline."

See also Just-War Theory; Müntzer, Thomas; Two Realms

Bibliography

Blickle, P. *The Revolution of 1525: The German Peasants' War from a New Perspective*. Johns Hopkins University Press, 1981; Franz, G. *Der deutsche Bauernkrieg*. 1st ed. of 12. Oldenburg, 1933; Stayer, J. M. "The Dream of a Just Society." In *Reformation Christianity*, ed. P. Matheson, 190–211. Fortress, 2007.

JAMES M. STAYER

Pelikan, Jaroslav

The American historian of Christian doctrine Jaroslav Pelikan (1923–2006) was the son of Slovak immigrants to the United States and was raised in Chicago. His father and grandfather were leading Lutheran pastors in the Slovak Synod. Pelikan learned the Christian faith through Luther's Small Catechism, Lutheran chorales (in Czech translation), traditions of Slavic piety, and books from his father's library. A precocious child and talented pianist, he attended the Lutheran Church–Missouri Synod's junior college in Fort Wayne (1936–42) and then received a bachelor of divinity from Concordia Seminary, St. Louis, and a PhD from the University of Chicago, both in the same year (1946), when he was twenty-two. From childhood on he acquired expertise in multiple languages, which allowed him to master primary sources in the history of Christianity. His description of his doctoral adviser's vocation applies equally to his own career: He strove to keep "theologians historically aware and historians theologically responsible." He taught at Valparaiso University (1946–49), Concordia Seminary, St. Louis (1949–53), the University of Chicago (1953–62), and Yale University (1962–96). He also delivered innumerable public lectures (e.g., the Jefferson Lecture [1983] and the Gifford Lectures [1992–93]) and served as the president of the American Academy of Arts and Sciences (1994–97) and of the American Academy of Political and Social Science (2000–2001). The author of nearly forty books and the editor of over a dozen multivolume reference works, he wrote extensively on themes relating to the arts and humanities: classical culture, the history of Rome, Dante, Bach, Goethe's *Faust*, the "idea of the university," constitutional law, rhetoric, icons, Jesus, and Mary, to name just a few. Although he came to be widely regarded as the world's foremost virtuoso on the entire history of Christianity, his initial research focused on Luther and the Reformation. His doctoral dissertation, which he wrote under the direction of Wilhelm Pauck, examines "The [First] Bohemian Confession" of 1535 and Luther's preface to it. Other early works analyze continuities and discontinuities between Luther's thought and later developments in Protestant theology and philosophy, the "catholic substance and Protestant principle" (to cite Tillich) in Luther's theology, and Luther's ambiguous views toward ecclesial institutions. Pelikan interpreted the church of the Augsburg Confession as a confessional movement within Western Catholicism and not as a separate denomination. He reflected this "evangelical catholic" perspective in his pre–Vatican II book, *The Riddle of Roman Catholicism*, which traces the development of the Roman church and offers a balanced theological critique of it in the interests of furthering ecumenical understanding. (The book's publication coincided with Kennedy's presidential campaign.) As editor of the American edition of Luther's Works (1955–86), for which he wrote the companion volume on Luther's exegesis and also translated and annotated thirteen of the other volumes, Pelikan exerted a powerful influence on the appropriation of Luther's ideas among English speakers. His magnum opus, the five-volume *The Christian Tradition*, is the most significant history of the development of Christian doctrine to be written since Adolf von Harnack's *History of Dogma*. The fourth and largest volume in that project interprets Luther's teaching of the gospel against the background of doctrinal pluralism in late medieval Europe and in relation to doctrinal developments in other churches (e.g., at Trent, among the Reformed, and by Radical Reformers). Pelikan also coedited four large tomes of Christian creedal documents and wrote their companion volume. In 2004 he was given the Kluge Prize for his monumental achievements in the human sciences. Although a Lutheran for most of his life, he was received into the Orthodox Church in 1998.

See also Luther's Works

Bibliography

Hotchkiss, V., and P. Henry. *Orthodoxy and Western Culture: A Collection of Essays Honoring Jaroslav Pelikan on His Eightieth Birthday*. St. Vladimir's Seminary Press, 2005; Pelikan, J. *The Christian Tradition: The Development of Christian Doctrine*. 5 vols. University of Chicago Press, 1971–89; Pelikan, J. *Creeds and Confessions of Faith in the Christian Tradition*. 4 vols. and CD-ROM. Yale University Press, 2003; Pelikan, J. *The Melody of Theology: A Philosophical Dictionary*. Harvard University Press, 1988.

Matthew L. Becker

Penance, Penitence, Repentance

All three of the English terms "penance," "penitence," and "repentance" stem from the Latin *poenitentia* (German: *Buße*), which in the medieval tradition could mean inward sorrow for sin, external acts to demonstrate this sorrow (and atone for the penalty of sin), and the sacrament of penance itself. The later Middle Ages showed considerable interest in trying to explain how these three aspects of *poenitentia* were related. Central to these efforts was the attempt to define sorrow for sin. Late medieval theologians made a distinction between perfect sorrow for sin (contrition) and imperfect sorrow for sin (attrition). Contrition was sorrow for sin out of love of God; attrition sorrow for sin out of fear of punishment. Some held that contrition rendered the sacrament of penance unnecessary or at least secondary, reasoning that God would behold such true inward penitence and reward it directly with forgiveness of sin and that priests thus acted as Levitical priests in determining whether penitence was real. However, most believed that contrition was quite rare and that confessors, by virtue of their possession of the power of the keys, could transform attrition into contrition when they pronounced absolution in the sacrament of penance. Assigned penances were thought to help foster greater sorrow for sin and also to serve to satisfy any remaining penalty for sin.

The early sixteenth century saw an important challenge to the sacrament of penance that was related to differing meanings of *poenitentia*. In his annotations on the Latin New Testament, which accompanied his *Novum Instrumentum*, the first printed Greek New Testament, Erasmus famously challenged the traditional interpretation of Matt. 4:17 ("Repent, for the kingdom of heaven has come near"), which had been taken as a scriptural warrant for the sacrament of penance. Rather than translating the verse as "do penance," Erasmus rendered it "be penitent," thus placing the emphasis on inward contrition rather than external participation in a churchly rite.

Luther had great sympathy for the contritionist position and for Erasmus's interpretation of Matt. 4:17. He thought that God required true sorrow for sin from human beings, which was a major cause of his *Anfechtungen* [attacks], for he could never believe that he could achieve this perfect sorrow through his own efforts. A central tenet of his new Evangelical soteriology was that contrition, like salvation itself, was a gift of divine grace worked through God's word of law. (In viewing this as a gift, Luther was following his spiritual mentor, Johann von Staupitz, who had similarly taught that God both required contrition and gave it as a gift to those who asked for it.) But Luther still placed great emphasis on the necessity of contrition, for he believed that such an emphasis confronted sinners with their spiritual impotence and also exposed the superficiality of much of the popular piety of his day. Luther was a preacher of penitence even as he was a preacher of grace. In fact, one could say that the Reformation began with a call to true repentance, both inward and outward. Theses 1–3 of the famous Ninety-Five Theses read as follows: "1. When our Lord and Master Jesus Christ said, 'Repent' [Matt. 4:17], he willed the entire life of believers to be one of repentance. 2. This word cannot be understood as referring to the sacrament of penance, that is, confession and satisfaction, as administered by the clergy. 3. Yet it does not mean solely inner repentance; such inner repentance is worthless unless it produces various outward mortifications of the flesh" (LW 31:25).

One of Luther's major objections to indulgences was that they typically functioned to relieve Christians of the ongoing need for true inward and outward penitence. His belief in the priority of grace in the Christian life did not cause Luther to downplay or diminish the importance of repentance. Quite the opposite:

he stressed time and again the necessity of repentance, even as he insisted that repentance was effected in the Christian by the law and grace. Luther's law/gospel dialectic assumes the importance of repentance in the Christian life, for the central function of the law is to convict of sin and thus to produce repentance. The fact that Luther placed the Ten Commandments at the beginning of his Small Catechism was indicative of his belief that the Christian life began with law-induced sorrow for sin and repentance.

Luther's Evangelical soteriology thus had radical implications for his reception of the traditional (Western) understanding of repentance. He stressed the importance of contrition but insisted that it was a gift of grace (the work of the Holy Spirit, using the law to convict sinners), thus freeing Christians of the need (and ability) to produce sorrow for sin of their own accord or even in cooperation with divine grace. While continuing to stress the necessity of lifelong repentance, he rejected penances, believing that Christ's death on the cross had rendered full satisfaction for sin, leaving no remaining penalty or punishment for which sinners needed to atone. Penances and the penitential piety they inspired had no place in Luther's Evangelical Christianity. Luther also rejected the sacrament of penance as practiced in the medieval church, arguing that it had no biblical foundation and that it was a source of untold anxiety for sensitive consciences (like his own) that had sought in vain for comfort in the confessional. He thought the traditional sacrament had become a form of works-righteousness, owing to its requirement that penitents confess all their mortal sins and perform all the works of satisfaction that their confessors assigned to them in order to receive forgiveness. Luther also thought the power of the keys belonged to the whole church, not just to ordained clergy. However, he did highly value private confession and absolution, seeing them as the best way to apply the gospel to the troubled conscience, and soon he developed a new Evangelical version of the traditional rite that became a prominent feature of early modern Lutheran pastoral care and piety. It required repentance for sin, as graciously worked by God through the law, along with confession of one's sinfulness, but it included no requirement of full confession of all sins and allowed no penances or works of satisfaction for the penalty of sin.

Lutherans debated the relationship between law, gospel, and repentance throughout the sixteenth century in what were later called antinomian controversies. Repentance also became an important theme in early modern Lutheran culture. Reformation scholars have argued that the stress on repentance in Lutheranism grew ever stronger as the sixteenth century wore on. Fear that the Evangelical message was not changing people and society for the better but rather giving people license to sin, coupled with Lutheran military defeats and a continuing fascination with prognostication and portents signaling the end times—all contributed to an increased emphasis on repentance in the face of impending divine wrath.

Movements of spiritual renewal in early modern Lutheranism also placed a premium on repentance. Johann Arndt's famous *True Christianity* opens in the following way:

Dear Christian reader, that the holy Gospel is subjected, in our time, to a great and shameful abuse is fully proved by the impenitent life of the ungodly who praise Christ and his word with their mouths and yet lead an unchristian life that is like that of persons who dwell in heathendom, not in the Christian world. Such ungodly conduct gave me cause to write this book to show simple readers wherein true Christianity consists, namely, in the exhibition of a true, living faith, active in genuine godliness and the fruits of righteousness. . . . [I also wished to show] how true repentance must proceed from the innermost sources of the heart; how the heart, mind, and affections must be changed, so that we might be conformed to Christ and his holy Gospel.

Philipp Jakob Spener (1635–1705) sounded much the same message in his influential *Pia Desideria*, where he interpreted the natural disasters and generally lamentable moral condition of Lutheran lands as a divine summons to repentance. Pietists made a distinction between a "first repentance" and a "second repentance," the former referring to repentance at conversion to faith and the latter referring to daily repentance in the life of a Christian. Some commentators have seen this distinction as a betrayal of Luther's emphasis of lifelong repentance grounded in baptism.

In the modern period Dietrich Bonhoeffer (1906–45) sought to dissuade the Lutherans of his day from their reliance on "cheap grace" and urged them instead to embrace "costly grace," in which true repentance and faith in God's mercy were experienced, not simply acknowledged. In *The Cost of Discipleship*, he writes,

Cheap grace means grace as a doctrine, a principle, a system. It means forgiveness of sins proclaimed as a general truth, the love of God taught as the Christian "conception" of God. An intellectual assent to that idea is held to be of itself sufficient to secure remission of sins. The Church which holds the correct doctrine of grace has, it is supposed, *ipso facto* a part in that grace. In that Church the world finds a cheap covering for its sins; no contrition is required, still less any real desire to be delivered from sin. Cheap grace therefore amounts to a denial of the living Word of God, in fact, a denial of the Incarnation of the Word of God. (p. 35)

In the current situation there are efforts to apply Bonhoeffer's notion of costly grace to Lutheran liturgical life, as liturgists seek to recover an emphasis on sin and repentance in worship, in the face of the contemporary predilection for worship oriented as entertainment and therapeutics.

See also Anthropology; Antinominanism/Antinomian Controversies; Arndt, Johann; Bonhoeffer, Dietrich; Confession (Private) and the Confessional; Justification; Ninety-Five Theses; Original Sin; Sacraments; Spener, Philipp Jakob

Bibliography
Arndt, J. *True Christianity*. Trans. P. Erb. Paulist Press, 1979; Bonhoeffer, D. *The Cost of Discipleship*. Trans.

R. H. Fuller. Macmillan, 1963; Leppin, V. "'Omnen vitam fidelium penitentiam esse voluit'—Zur Aufnahme myst-ischer Traditionen in Luthers erster Ablaßthese." *ARG* 93 (2002): 7–25; Lualdi, K. J., and A. T. Thayer, eds. *Penitence in the Age of Reformations.* Ashgate, 2000; Luther, M., *Disputatio pro declaratione virtutis indul-gentiarum/Ninety-Five Theses* (1517). WA 1:233–38. LW 31:17–33; Luther, M. *Ein Sermon von Ablaß und Gnade* (1518). WA 1:243–46; Luther, M., *Ein Sermon von dem Sakrament der Buße* (1519). WA 2:713–23; Rittgers, R. K. *The Reformation of the Keys: Confession, Conscience, and Authority in Sixteenth-Century Germany.* Harvard University Press, 2004; Soergel, P. M. *Miracles and the Protestant Imagination: The Evangelical Wonder Book in Reformation Germany.* Oxford University Press, 2012; Spener, P. J. *Pia Desideria.* Trans. T. G. Tappert. Fortress, 1964; Sundberg, W. *Worship as Repentance: Lutheran Li-turgical Traditions and Catholic Consensus.* Eerdmans, 2012; Tentler, T. N. *Sin and Confession on the Eve of the Reformation.* Princeton University Press, 1977.

RONALD K. RITTGERS

Pentecostal/Charismatic Christianity

A sense of exhilaration from direct experience of the Holy Spirit characterizes the Pentecostal movement, which first arose out of Holiness churches in the United States around 1900. In the 1970s a neo-Pentecostal movement emerged in established mainline churches in the United States and Canada, originating in the Episco-pal congregation of St. Mark, in Van Nuys, California. Soon afterward neo-Pentecostal, or charismatic, renewal movements touched Roman Catholic and Lutheran churches as well. The three Lutheran church bodies, The American Lutheran Church (TALC, 1960–), the Lutheran Church in America (LCA, 1962–88), and the Lutheran Church–Missouri Synod (LCMS) experienced a degree of disruption and renewal. Church conventions requested studies, conducted by panels of selected experts who examined the sociological, psychological, theological, and historical dimensions of the phenomenon. Lutheran charismatics were consulted in the process of these investigations. The churches proceeded with caution, endorsing the spiritual strength that came to congregations, but warning against dilution of traditional Lutheran teaching that God's gift of salvation comes through means, word, and sacraments, and not through immediate experience.

Congregational disputes over interpretation of Scripture, faith healing, and worship led to denominational studies. The LCA issued a 1962 study on faith healing, citing a physician who encouraged productive relationships be-tween pastors and doctors. A focus on speak-ing in tongues, however, became the more prevalent way in which Lutherans encountered the Pentecostal/charismatic movement. When a seminary professor at Luther Seminary in St. Paul (later: Luther Northwestern) became involved in the movement, that aroused the theological suspicions of the major Lutheran denominations.

In 1972 the LCMS Commission on Theology and Church Relations produced *The Charis-matic Movement and Lutheran Theology.* It was cautious and critical in three major areas: the movement's baptismal theology, disruptive spiritual pride, and neglect of Christ's role in the doctrine of atonement. These concerns surfaced in the LCA pamphlet *The Charis-matic Movement in the LCA: A Pastoral Per-spective* (1974), which sought to help pastors understand rather than antagonize those in the movement. In their investigations officials in TALC, as well as the Lutheran Council in the United States of America (LCUSA), requested clarification of teachings on baptism.

Larry Christenson, a pastor at Trinity Lu-theran Church in San Pedro, California, was consulted by all the denominational commis-sions. He began publishing after lecturing at Wartburg Seminary's Luther Academy on speaking in tongues. *Speaking in Tongues and Its Significance for the Church* (1968) estab-lished Christenson as spokesperson and pub-licist for the Lutheran charismatic movement. His book in 1970 titled *The Christian Family* drew from his Trinity Lutheran Church's Bible study work (in San Pedro), and this aligned the Lutheran charismatic movement with the evangelical right in its views of gender roles and marriage. Most Lutheran charismatics sought to refresh and renew the Lutheran Church rather than to leave it. They took steps to adapt their message, consolidate leadership, and adopt Lutheran theological emphases and language, specifically the understanding of baptism. They aimed to build a separate but not separatist network.

Annual Holy Spirit conferences began in 1972 and later were developed as Lutheran Charismatic Renewal Services in Minneapolis and associated with North Heights Lutheran Church in Roseville, Minnesota. Annual conferences continued until 2014. Charismatic renewal work resulted also in a seminary program, The Master's Institute, tied to Regent University, a Pentecostal university at Virginia Beach, Virginia. These stronger ties to Pentecostal institutions provided an alternative to the Lutheran educational system, and North Heights Lutheran Church has become an independent Lutheran congregation.

Lutheran churches worldwide have experienced charismatic movements, and these in part are connected with the rapid growth of Lutheran churches in Madagascar, Ethiopia, and Tanzania. Those Lutheran churches have a friendlier attitude toward charismatic movements. Pentecostalism's impact on Lutheran churches resulted in official dialogues between representatives of the Lutheran World Federation and Pentecostal churches that met between 2006 and 2010. The dialogue report stressed the diversity of responses to Pentecostalism within the Lutheran churches. Pentecostal and Lutheran participants told each other their histories and identified issues that stood in the way of closer relationships. The critical report of the Lutheran Church–Missouri Synod from 1972, even though the LCMS is not a member of the Lutheran World Federation, served as the framework for presenting the traditionalist view, which was challenged because it presumed the notion of cessationism, a view that the Holy Spirit's bestowal of spiritual gifts ceased at the end of the apostolic age. Once this presumption is challenged, new avenues for appreciating the Pentecostal movement are present. The traditional Lutheran restriction of the ways or means of grace to two media, word and sacrament, could perhaps be addressed by

using alternative language, the dialogue suggests. How Christ "encounters" the believer might be helpful, because it can also include experiences beneficial to the believer, but not necessarily classified dogmatically as a means of salvation.

The Lutheran encounter with Pentecostalism has been important for individuals and congregations as they adapt their theological tradition to be of use to the needs of the church in a variety of cultural contexts. These challenges have been welcomed by some Lutheran churches in the world as opportunities that deepen spiritual strength in their congregations. Because Pentecostal churches do not have equivalent international structures, the identification of dialogue partners is difficult, and the agreements achieved may not reach very far into the communities. Pentecostal churches and movements are very diverse culturally and theologically, so that dialogues started with some Pentecostal churches would not apply to many others. Lutherans who have been involved in the charismatic movement within the established churches, however, can provide important interpretive services to help fellow Lutherans understand and appreciate the benefits of charismatic renewal in the congregation and in personal experience.

Bibliography

Christenson, L. *Charismatic Renewal among Lutherans: A Pastoral and Theological Perspective*. Lutheran Charismatic Renewal Services, Bethany Fellowship, 1976; http://www.strasbourginstitute.org/wp-content/uploads /2016/07/Guide-to-Pentecostal-Movements-for-Lutherans .pdf.

MARIA ERLING

Peru

The first Lutherans were among the German immigrants who founded a congregation in Lima in 1897, founded again in 1950 as the Evangelical Lutheran Church in Perú (Iglesia Evangélica Luterana en el Perú, IELP), and recognized by the LWF. In the 1960s IEL-P launched a diaconal project assisting children, Casa Belén, and invited pastors from the Lutheran Church of America to do mission among its families. This mission expanded, leading to the founding of congregations, and eventually to the formation of the Peruvian Lutheran Evangelical Church in 1986. In 2015 procedural aspects with church governance and contention in the church caused ten of its congregations to secede and form the Lutheran Church of Perú, which also belongs to the LWF.

The work of the Norsk Luthersk Misjonssamband (Norwegian Lutheran Mission, NLM) in the area of Arequipa since 1978 resulted in the founding of the Evangelical Lutheran Church-Perú (Iglesia Evangélica Luterana-Perú, IEL-P) in 1995. The Swedish Evangelisk Luthersk Mission and the WMPL established mission work together in the area of Chiclayo, resulting in the formation of the Evangelical Lutheran Church of Chiclayo (Iglesia Evangélica Luterana de Chiclayo, IELCH) in 2007. The NLM also created the seminary and professional school Andean Lutheran Theological Seminary (Seminario Teológico Luterano Andino, SETELA), which cooperates with IEL-P, IELCH, the Christian Evangelical Lutheran Church of Bolivia, and the Lutheran Bible Institute of Ecuador. Both the LCMS and the Evangelical Lutheran Synod are currently doing mission in Peru.

Bibliography

Cruz, J. M. *The Histories of the Latin American Church: A Handbook*. Esp. 475–512. Fortress, 2014; http://www.elmbv .se/index.php?option=com_content&view=category&layout=blog&id=38&Itemid=59; http://els.org/worldoutreach/world-outreach-peru; http://www.ev-kirche-peru .org/wp/; http://www.ielp.org/index.php/; http://ilc-online .org/members/latin-america/peru/; http://www.lcms.org /peru; https://www.lutheranworld.org/country/peru; http:// www.nlm.no/nlm/internasjonalt/soer-amerika/nlm-i-soer -amerika; http://www.setela.net/; Theodore, E., and M. B. Bachmann. *Lutheran Churches in the World: A Handbook*. Esp. 523–27. Augsburg, 1989.

ANDRÉS ROBERTO ALBERTSEN

Petersen, Anne Marie

As a Danish Lutheran missionary to South India and founder of the Porto Novo Mission, Anne Marie Petersen (1878–1951) was a supporter of Indian nationalism and a close friend of Mahatma Gandhi. Born in 1878 in Roskilde, Denmark, and trained as a teacher by 1909, she left for India as a missionary of the Loventhal Mission at Vellore. After the death of Edward Loventhal (1871/72–1914), the founder of the mission, in 1919 she joined the Danish Missionary Society (DMS), which she served as schoolteacher. In protest against the DMS hesitance in appointing qualified Indians as missionaries on equal footing with Western missionaries, she left the DMS in 1920 and founded the Porto Novo Mission in 1921, which tried to establish an Indian church led and shaped by Indians.

The Grundtvigian tradition in which she was raised led her to conclude that Indian Christianity had to be rooted in Indian spiritual traditions and culture. The Indians were to create an Indian theology and an Indian church, enriched with their own cultural and philosophical traditions, independent of Western doctrines and attitudes. Her lenience toward developing an indigenous Christianity naturally led her to be closely connected to the Indian Christians, like Sadhu Sundar Singh and Venkel Chakkarai, who strove to establish an Indian Christian theology. She never denied the importance of baptism, but realizing the complications it caused for some Indians, she did not insist on baptism to such an extent that most of her supporters in Denmark accused her of denying the doctrine of baptism and not remaining faithful to Grundtvigian tradition.

Petersen enjoyed the lasting friendship of Mahatma Gandhi (1869–1948), the champion of Indian nationalism and father of independent India, after her first visit to Gandhi's Sabarmati *ashram*. She was instrumental in the meeting of Gandhi and Sadhu Sundar Singh (1889–1929), a well-known Indian Christian mystic. Her identification with the struggle of Indians for independence made her scandalous both in Denmark and India; British officials denied her a visa to enter India, and the Danish committee that supported her mission work dissolved in 1926.

The school Petersen established in Porto Novo (Parangipettai), Tamil Nadu, became popular because Gandhi laid its foundation. It still serves under the name Seva Mandir (the temple of service). Her aim was to establish a national Christian school for girls based on the model used by the Danish Folk High School and the living and working conditions in Gandhi's *ashram*. She passed away in 1951, leaving the work in the hands of her able Indian sisters.

See also India

Bibliography

Hansen, B. S. *Dependency and Identity: Problems of Cultural Encounter as a Consequence of the Danish Mission in South India between the Two World Wars.* World Heritage Press, 1998; Larsen, T. E. *Anne Marie Petersen—a Danish Woman in South India: A Missionary Story 1909–1951.* Lutheran Heritage Archives, 2000.

PETER VETHANAYAGAMONY

Petersen, Johanna Eleonora

Née von Merlau, Johanna Eleonora Petersen (1644–1724) was the most important female author of early German Pietism. Descended from lower nobility, she came into contact with early Pietism in Frankfurt am Main around 1675 and became friends with Johann Jakob Schütz and Philipp Jakob Spener. William Penn and Anna Maria van Schurmann belonged to her circle of correspondents. She married Johann Wilhelm Petersen in 1680 and had one son, who did not follow the Pietist orientation of his parents. Between 1689 and 1719, she published fifteen titles, most of which dealt with the exegesis of the Bible. As did her husband, she developed first a millenarian system that she then expanded into expectation of the *apokatastasis* (see Acts 3:21). The topics treated by the two Petersens were similar, but their manner of argumentation and style differed noticeably. While Johanna Petersen described the visionary experiences that induced her to engage Holy Scripture, she cannot be characterized as a visionary or mystic; the interpretation of biblical texts constitutes the main focus of her work. Her autobiographical memoirs continue to find great interest,

and she has been the subject of intense study within women's and gender studies.

See also Eschatology (Apocalypticism, Chiliasm, Millennialism, Millennarianism); Gender: Men and Women; Petersen, Johann Wilhelm; Pietism

Bibliography

Albrecht, R. *Johanna Eleonora Petersen: Theologische Schriftstellerin des frühen Pietismus.* Vandenhoeck & Ruprecht, 2005; Albrecht, R. "Johanna Eleonora Petersen in the Context of Women's and Gender Studies." In *Pietism in Germany and North America 1680–1820,* ed. J. Strom et al., 71–84. Ashgate, 2009; Becker-Cantarino, B., ed. *The Life of Lady Johanna Eleonora Petersen, Written by Herself.* University of Chicago Press, 2005; Petersen (née von Merlau), J. E. *Leben, von ihr selbst mit eigener Hand aufgesetzet: Autobiographie.* Ed. P. Guglielmetti. Evangelische Verlagsanstalt, 2003.

RUTH ALBRECHT

Petersen, Johann Wilhelm

Pietist theologian, author, and poet Johann Wilhelm Petersen (1649–1727) was born in Osnabrück after his family came from Lübeck. Following his theological studies, Petersen became a Lutheran pastor and superintendent in Hannover, Eutin, and Lüneburg. He married Johanna Eleonora von Merlau in 1680. Following dismissal from his ecclesial position, he and his wife lived as estate owners and independent theological authors in Brandenburg-Prussia. Petersen defended millenarian ideas and the *apokatastasis* (restoration of the original state of humanity and creation; Acts 3:21) in countless books, especially polemical tracts. In addition, he composed hymns and poems. Contesting fundamental tenets of Lutheran thought, he is reckoned among the most influential representatives of radical Pietism. Alongside other distinctive elements of his eschatological thought, Petersen maintained an effective (as opposed to forensic) doctrine of justification. He further made a case for the continuation of divine revelation that did not cease with the completion of canonical Scripture. He and his wife both wrote an autobiography. From the over two hundred titles that he printed, his three-volume collection on the *apokatastasis* stands out. His extant and extensive correspondence would afford many insights into the network of both Petersens, but little has been published. Aside from Pietists, Petersen corresponded with leading scholars, including Gottfried Wilhelm Leibniz.

See also Eschatology (Apocalypticism, Chiliasm, Millennialism, Millennarianism); Petersen, Johanna Eleonora; Pietism

Bibliography

Matthias, M. J. W., and J. E. Petersen. *Eine Biographie bis zur Amtsenthebung Petersens im Jahre 1692*; Vandenhoeck & Ruprecht, 1993; Petersen, J. W. *Das Leben Jo. Wilhelmi Petersen*. Author, at the expense of good friends, 1717; Petersen, J. W. *Mystērion Apokatastaseōs Pantōn*. 3 vols. Author, 1700–1710.

RUTH ALBRECHT

Petri (Nericus), Laurentius

The Swedish reformer and archbishop Laurentius Petri (1499–1573) was born in 1499 in Őrebro, Sweden, the son of a blacksmith, and first named Lars Persson; his older brother was the reformer Olavus Petri. The additional surname Nericus is based on the province where he was born, Närke (distinguishing him from his successor archbishop, Laurentius Petri Gothus). Laurentius attended the University of Wittenberg, where he was strongly influenced by Martin Luther and Philip Melanchthon. Returning to Sweden in 1527, Laurentius gained attention from King Gustavus Vasa, who appointed him professor at Uppsala University. In 1531 the king decided to fill the position of archbishop of Uppsala, the head of the Swedish Church (vacant since 1521), and Laurentius was elected and consecrated to the position, which he held until his death in 1573. Also in 1531 Laurentius married the daughter of a cousin of the king. Laurentius defended the church's traditional rights, carefully navigating around the king's attempts to gain the power and wealth of the Church of Sweden. In 1539 Laurentius was forced to concur with the death sentence against his brother Olavus, though the sentence was later commuted. With his brother, Laurentius produced a Swedish translation of the Bible in 1541. Laurentius's primary achievement during his long tenure as archbishop was firmly guiding the transition of the Church of Sweden to Lutheranism, which was codified by the adoption of his Evangelical Liturgy and Church Order in 1571. He died on October 27, 1573.

See also Petri, Olavus; Sweden; Vasa, Gustav

Bibliography

Yelverton, E. E. *An Archbishop of the Reformation, Laurentius Petri, Archbishop of Uppsala, 1531–73*. Augsburg, 1959.

MARK A. GRANQUIST

Petri, Olavus

Born on January 6, 1493, in Őrebro, Sweden, Olavus (or Olaus) Petri (d. 1552), was a Swedish theologian and reformer. In 1516 Olavus left for Germany, where after a brief stay at Leipzig he went on to the University of Wittenberg, where he received his master's degree in 1518. Strongly influenced by Luther, Olavus returned to Sweden, where he eventually became a teacher at the Cathedral School in Stockholm. Through friends he gained favor with the new king, Gustavus Vasa, who appointed him as city clerk in Stockholm in 1524. Married in 1525, Olavus began to advocate the new Reformation ideals; he began to preach in Swedish, helped translate the New Testament into Swedish, and edited the first vernacular hymnal in 1526. He also introduced the first Swedish liturgy in 1529 and became an important adviser to the king, serving as chancellor (1531–33). Resisting the king's increasing confiscation of power from the church, Olavus was tried and convicted of treason in 1539, but the death sentence was commuted. Olavus was appointed senior priest at the cathedral in Stockholm, where he continued to promote reforms within the Swedish church, which by the time of his death on April 19, 1552, had become thoroughly Lutheran. His younger brother Laurentius Petri served as archbishop of the Church of Sweden (1531–73).

See also Petri (Nericus), Laurentius; Sweden; Vasa, Gustav

Bibliography

Bergendoff, C. *Olavus Petri and the Ecclesiastical Transformation in Sweden, 1521–1552: A Study in the Swedish Reformation*. Macmillan, 1928.

MARK A. GRANQUIST

Peucer, Caspar

Melanchthon's son-in-law, professor of medicine, and leader of Wittenberg crypto-Philippism was Caspar Peucer (1525–1602), who was born in Bautzen in the Oberlausitz, came to Wittenberg in 1540, and lived in Melanchthon's home. He eventually married Magdelena Melanchthon; they lived with or next to her parents and cared for Melanchthon in his later years.

Peucer joined the Wittenberg arts faculty in 1548, teaching astronomy (which included astrology) and mathematics, also aiding Melanchthon in editing and continuing the survey of human history, the *Chronicon Carionis*. In 1554 Elector August named him professor of medicine.

The elector also named Peucer his court physician in Dresden in 1563, and he became the elector's trusted adviser and baptismal sponsor of one of the elector's children. His continuing exercise of his medical professorship in Wittenberg maintained his influence there. Together with a new member of the theological faculty, Christoph Pezel, who had never met Luther and heard Melanchthon lecture for only one semester, he promoted a spiritualizing view of the Lord's Supper, supported also by some colleagues at the university and in the Saxon Ministerium. Although Peucer thought he was strengthening and defending his father-in-law's position, his thoroughgoing Aristotelianism did not permit him to understand "presence" in the way in which Luther viewed the presence of Christ's body and blood in the Lord's Supper. When Elector August and his wife, Anna, discovered that Peucer, Pezel, and their party were promoting these spiritualizing positions, they felt betrayed because of the secret nature of their assertion of their ideas and because their position threatened to violate the status of Saxony under the religious Peace of Augsburg. Thus this party is called crypto-Philippist or (less accurately) crypto-Calvinist. Peucer was jailed (1574–86) for this betrayal. After his release, he served as physician and counselor for the princes of Anhalt.

See also Lord's Supper; Melanchthon, Philip; Saxony; Wittenberg Circle, Parties within

Bibliography
Wartenberg, G., and H.-P. Hasse, eds. *Caspar Peucer (1525–1602)*. Evangelische Verlagsanstalt, 2004.

ROBERT KOLB

Pfeffinger, Johann

The German Lutheran pastor and theologian Johann Pfeffinger (1493–1573) was a reformer in Leipzig and involved in the synergistic controversy. Born in Wasserburg am Inn on December 27, 1493, he was ordained at Reichenhall in 1518. Pfeffinger was priest at Saalfelden in 1519 before becoming preacher at Passau in 1521. There he learned of Luther and his reforming work. In 1523 he fled to Wittenberg, where he studied for four years. He was called to serve the parish at Sonnenwalde in 1527, where he was married. In 1530 he was called to Eicha, and, within a year and a half, to Belgern.

Upon the death of Duke George of Saxony, Pfeffinger was sent to help introduce the Lutheran Reformation in Leipzig, where in 1540 he was called as pastor of the Saint Nicolai Church and superintendent. In 1541 he became theological adviser to Moritz, Duke of Saxony. He began lecturing in theology at the university and in autumn 1543 received the doctorate in theology. As a trusted adviser to Moritz of Saxony, in 1548 he participated in the deliberations concerning the Leipzig Interim. As a convinced follower of Philip Melanchthon, his published theses of 1555 asserted his own understanding of Melanchthon's teaching on free will and thereby initiated the Synergistic Controversy, especially with Nikolaus von Amsdorf. He wrote on ethics and pastoral care and engaged in polemics. Pfeffinger died in Leipzig on January 1, 1573.

See also Synergistic Controversy; Wittenberg Circle, Parties within

Bibliography
Peterson, L. D. "Johann Pfeffinger's Treatises of 1550 in Defense of Adiaphora: 'High Church' Lutheranism and Confessionalization in Albertine Saxony." In *Confessionalization in Europe, 1555–1700*, ed. J. M. Headley, H. J. Hillerbrand, and A. J. Papalas, 91–105. Ashgate, 2004;

Seifert, F. *Johann Pfeffinger: Der erste lutherische Pastor zu St. Nikolai und Superintendent in Leipzig.* Pöschel & Trepte, 1888.

GERHARD BODE

Philip of Hesse

As the landgrave of Hesse in the Holy Roman Empire, Philip (Philipp) of Hesse (1504–67) was a key political and military supporter of Luther and Protestant efforts to form defensive alliances in the German lands, including the Smalcaldic League (1531). His commitment to the Evangelical side was hastened by a chance encounter with Philip Melanchthon, as the latter made his way back to Wittenberg after visiting his family. Philip of Hesse often took a middle path in intra-Protestant confessional disputes and worked to bring the competing factions together. He sponsored the Marburg Colloquy (1529) and numerous theological dialogues in the 1530s and 1540s. Landgrave Philip also developed an early theory of resistance to political authority, which would become a foundation of Lutheran opposition to Catholic imperial forces in Magdeburg. His bigamous second marriage to Margarethe von der Saale (1522–66) created a political and religious dilemma for Philip's supporters, including Luther, Melanchthon, and Bucer, who were criticized for supporting or at least not preventing the landgrave's marital union. Philip of Hesse commanded many of the northern troops in the Smalcaldic League until the alliance's defeat in 1547. As a result of his leadership role in the Smalcald Wars and his personal rebellion against the emperor, the landgrave was imprisoned from 1547 to 1552. After his release, he resumed his conciliatory activities, participating in pan-Protestant talks and also negotiations leading to the Peace of Augsburg (1555).

See also Holy Roman Empire; Marburg Colloquy; Peace of Augsburg; Smalcald War

Bibliography

Brady, T. A., Jr. *German Histories in the Age of Reformations, 1400–1650.* Cambridge University Press, 2009; Hillerbrand, H. J. *Landgrave Philipp of Hesse, 1504–1567: Religion and Politics in the Reformation.* Foundation for Reformation Research, 1967; Whitford, D. M. *A Reformation Life: The European Reformation through the Eyes of Philipp of Hesse.* Praeger, 2015.

MICHAEL J. HALVORSON

Philippists. *See* Wittenberg Circle, Parties within

Philosophy

Philosophy is rational, critical thinking that focuses on questions such as the nature of truth, reality (metaphysics), reason (logic), goodness (ethics), and beauty and art (aesthetics). It originated in ancient Greece as an attempt to offer a scientific explanation of the origin and structure of the cosmos in contrast to mythological views. While a minority of Christian thinkers reject philosophy in its entirety as a threat to faith, most have in varying degrees sought to understand its relation to faith. Luther devoted no single treatise to the relation between philosophy and theology, but in addition to the Heidelberg Disputation of 1518, he clarified his views in several late disputations and other writings. In general, Luther shared the medieval view that philosophy is a "handmaid," or auxiliary discipline, to theology. However, given Luther's consistent opposition to speculation about God as a way for sinners to overcome their rebellion against God, he rejected philosophy's claim to offer a comprehensive explanation of reality, when that included God. Additionally, his view of justification by faith made him critical of employing an Aristotelian view of human nature, since he saw Aristotle's focus on human potential as finally incompatible with any fundamental receptivity before God. For Luther, philosophical concepts need to be "bathed" before they can be employed in theology. That is, they must be interpreted primarily through and accepted only on the basis of the grammar of faith found in the Scriptures.

The medieval legacy of situating the relationship between philosophy and theology was shaped by several figures. Augustine (354–430) appropriated aspects of Neoplatonism in order to clarify his view of the Christian life as a grace-enabled pilgrimage from earthly to heavenly things. After the European rediscovery of Aristotle's works in the High Middle Ages, realist thinkers such as Thomas Aquinas (1225–74) worked hard to accommodate Christian Neoplatonism with Aristotle's metaphysics, ethics, and logic. Aquinas's view reinforces the conviction that grace assists sinful creatures in their journey toward their ultimate fulfillment in heaven. Nominalist thinkers such as William of Ockham (ca. 1287–1347) challenged certain Platonic assumptions embedded in Augustinianism, which claimed that the reality of universals is properly immaterial and transcends earthly instantiations. They proposed instead that universals were simply generalizations about properties shared by particular things.

Luther was trained in nominalist views of language analysis, signification, and disputation, and he appreciated these aids for clear thinking. Provided that such tools honored the primary grammar of faith, they were useful for theology. Even so, conflict dominates Luther's understanding of the relation between philosophy and theology. He conceded that philosophical inquiry was beneficial in penultimate matters pertaining to earthly affairs, but he claimed that it could give no certainty with respect to ultimate or divine matters. In other words, philosophy cannot dictate the substance of faith. At best, it offers an analysis of words and arguments that can help order, analyze, and reflect on the content of faith. For example, with respect to Aristotle's fourfold view of causality, Luther said that philosophy can know something of the material (the matter of which something is made) and formal (the shape in which something is made) causes, but nothing with respect to the efficient (the maker of something) and final (the purpose of something) causes. For knowledge of the last two, believers need recourse to biblical authority, which alone reveals the nature of God and humankind's purpose.

That philosophy and theology are intertwined in irresoluble conflict is guaranteed by various theological moves that Luther makes in his attempt to secure the gospel as a word of promise. First, Luther's distinction between the accusing, death-dealing law and the life-giving, comforting gospel cannot be metaphysically systematized. Second, the opposition between God's frightful hiddenness as "unpreached" and God's merciful goodness as "preached" is likewise not capable of being transcended by an overarching metaphysical scheme. Such conflict arising out of God's transcendent and threatening boundlessness and God's merciful goodness unveiled in the preaching of Jesus's cross and resurrection cannot be hushed by theory but only by the proclamation of the gospel. Third, Luther's conviction that God's promise comes sacramentally embodied through tangible, physical, and contingent means, such as water (baptism) or bread and wine (Lord's Supper), undermines a transcendental perspective of metaphysics. Fourth, in Neoplatonic assumptions of medieval Augustinianism, the Christian pilgrimage toward union with God is motivated by a desire for ultimate fulfillment in God. In contrast, for Luther, humanity's predicament is not that it is turned toward the earth and need redirection toward heaven but instead that sinners are curved in on themselves. A desire for ultimate *self*-fulfillment in God is not awakened but instead extinguished by grace. Thereby freed of such egocentrism, we can love God for God's own sake and our neighbors as ourselves, and thus do not love based on how God or others could secure our ultimate self-fulfillment. Fifth, because God is not re-creating new beings out of old but only creates out of nothing, the death of the old being is required. Luther thus rejects any philosophical assumption of a continuously existing self. The only continuity that exists between the sinner and the new person in faith is God's Word. Finally, Luther's theology, of sinners in need of justification and the God who justifies, allots no neutral space for philosophy to do its work. Since philosophy is a product of rebellious humans, it is vulnerable to being sinners' self-justification by means of either thinking (metaphysics) or doing (ethics).

Luther's coworker Philip Melanchthon maintained this sense of conflict. Melanchthon argued that philosophy is useful for scientific inquiry, civil governance, and living well in this world. He had high regard for Aristotle's logic, physics, and ethics (lecturing on them throughout his career) but, like Luther, low regard for Aristotle's metaphysics, singling out Aristotle's view of God as "prime mover" as unable to represent God's love. While he appreciated both Plato and Aristotle, Melanchthon found certain statements in Plato more agreeable for theology, especially the supposition that nature is the product of an eternal mind and not chance. He likewise affirmed the Platonic supposition that humans possess "innate ideas" and not all scientific knowledge is the result of empirical investigation.

The challenge for Lutheranism as a movement has been to balance a healthy use of philosophy with Luther's understanding of the conflict between it and theology. Building on the logical rigor of the disputations that Luther sponsored late in his career and Melanchthon's systematic approach to the presentation of doctrine, Orthodox Lutheran theologians such as Martin Chemnitz (1522–86), Johann Gerhard (1582–1637), and their disciples retrieved a scholastic method for doing theology, indebted to Aristotelian logic, but whose content sought to preserve Evangelical teaching. Following their work, leading Lutheran voices sought instead a greater accommodation with philosophy, especially as more secular modes of thinking developed. With the rise of modern secularism, Europeans and North Americans wished to carve out a sphere for human creativity independent from God. Many factors led to secularism, but two important ones were (1) burgeoning capitalism, in which people increasingly sought to define themselves by purchased goods, and (2) the quest to establish a nonreligious foundation for society as a response to the political violence of the Wars of Religion. Blaming political violence on confessional differences instead of the intolerance of absolute despots, early modern philosophers sought a nonconfessional foundation for society by means of a natural theology.

Representative of nascent modernity, René Descartes (1596–1650) sought to ground truth no longer in religious authority but instead in the self as a "thinking thing." Desiring certainty in ultimate matters, as had Luther, Descartes nevertheless departed from Luther in that he dispensed with Scripture as a basis for such security. Instead, he posited reason alone as the foundation for all truth, since reason can secure the fact of one's existence on the basis of the indubitable claim that "I think," which then serves as the basis to infer all other knowledge. Descartes's thinking did not tolerate Luther's appreciation for the senses (in his affirmation of an "embodied word") nor Luther's insistence on the death of the old being through the law's accusations. Building on the Cartesian view of reason's capacity to structure all reality, Gottfried Wilhelm Leibniz (1646–1716) sought a transparency between faith and sight by means of a comprehensive metaphysics centered on monads (basic units of reality), each possessing a mental dimension and operating within a preestablished harmony under God as the highest monad. Leibniz's endeavors are difficult to square with Luther's conviction that God is hidden in nature and the cross.

Eschewing Leibniz's metaphysical transparency, Immanuel Kant (1724–1804) argued that reality, the "noumenal," was unobtainable to the human mind, since it can know only how it constructs the world "phenomenally" by providing the conditions for experiencing the world, such as space and time. Access to the world is not through metaphysics but only ethics, by means of the categorical imperative, which unconditionally commands how a rationally free human being ought to behave. For Kant, God is tantamount to a regulative idea, the transcendental assumption of the human longing for the unity of all knowledge. In contrast to the opinion of Albrecht Ritschl

(1822–89) and others who sought to appropriate Kant's thought into their theology, Kant's rejection of metaphysics is different from Luther's antispeculative view of God. Though skeptical of a comprehensive metaphysical inquiry, Luther along with all medieval thinkers believed that God was a metaphysical reality, indeed the most real of all realities. Similarly, Kant's approach reduces the gospel to ethics: for Luther and Melanchthon, this is a breach of the law/gospel distinction.

Noting the inconsistencies in Kant's claim to know the conditions for experience without knowing reality, Georg W. F. Hegel (1770–1831) commandeered Luther's christological conviction that the "finite is capable of conveying the infinite" in order to express his view that reality itself is in an ever-evolving process of establishing its own subjectivity by transcending all of its instantiations that inadequately attempt to convey it. Religion, for Hegel, possesses the true content of this ultimate subjectivity but fails to do it in its true form, which can only be obtained in philosophy, where Spirit (*Geist*) thinks by means of human philosophical inquiry. Again, if Kant seeks to obviate the law-gospel distinction through a comprehensive ethics, Hegel does so through a comprehensive metaphysics.

Comparable to Hegel's quest for a comprehensive metaphysics, a small cohort of twentieth-century Lutherans appealed to the empiricist-influenced "process metaphysics" of Alfred North Whitehead (1861–1947) in order to understand God's reality. This view sees God not as the sole ultimate reality but instead as only the moral absolute within the wider metaphysical absolute of "creativity," the process that constitutes the cosmos. While process metaphysics could be employed to highlight Luther's understanding of God's pathos, it is hard to square with Luther's affirmation of God's omnipotence.

Informed by the Lutheran proclivity for paradox, the existentialist Søren Kierkegaard (1813–55) attacked Hegel in order to affirm truth as "subjectivity," grounded in the individual self, and not a metaphysical system. Although appropriated by many twentieth-century Lutheran theologians, Kierkegaard fails to convey Luther's grounding of experience in the Word and not vice versa. In the twentieth century, another theologian influenced by existentialism was Gerhard Ebeling (1912–2001), who stressed the disconnect between theology and philosophy in Luther's thought and centered human experience in the Word. Different from Ebeling, Oswald Bayer (b. 1939) appeals to J. L. Austin's (1911–60) "speech-act" theory and aspects of Ludwig Wittgenstein's (1889–1951) cultural-linguistic approach to philosophy in order to interpret Luther's law and gospel distinction as two different, irreconcilable speech acts. This offers a performative and not merely descriptive view of language. Thereby language alters reality and does not merely describe reality or direct human behavior. Bayer also appeals to Johann Georg Hamann's (1730–88) appropriation of Luther's view of the sacraments as "embodied words" in order to appreciate the role of the senses in knowledge. Additionally, in Hamann's reading of Luther, reason is affirmed as a gift from God conveyed linguistically and culturally, but it is not a foundation of reality. Hence all knowledge is conveyed through culture, history, and language. Finnish scholar Tuomo Mannermaa (1937–2015) seeks to draw out ontological implications of Luther's thinking by appealing to Luther's presentation of Christ as the "form" of faith. Mannermaa posits a "real-ontic" union between Christ and believers. While the Mannermaa school helpfully aims to situate Luther in his late medieval context, it reverses the rapport between God's favor and gift. For Luther, the gift of Christ's unity with sinners is a result of God's merciful favor to them.

Luther left little room for philosophy as a transcendental enterprise, one that encompasses all knowledge and reality. At every point, philosophy is accountable to the grammar of faith. Though some criticize Lutheranism's inability to establish a constructive philosophical system, the fact that Lutherans continue to criticize philosophy's role in theology means that they need not justify a philosophical system as part of their confessional witness. One must recognize, however, that while for Lutherans philosophy and theology are in conflict, that does not entail that philosophy can be summarily dismissed. Theology appreciates philosophy's ability to clarify doctrine through rigorous thinking, its contribution to scientific inquiry, and its ability to offer ethical reflection for human flourishing.

See also Augustine of Hippo; Chemnitz, Martin; Ebeling, Gerhard; Hamann, Johann Georg; Hegel, Georg Wilhelm Friedrich; Justification; Kant, Immanuel; Kierkegaard, Søren Aabye; Leibniz, Gottfried Wilhelm; Mannermaa, Tuomo; Melanchthon, Philip; Natural Theology; Ockham, William of; Thomas Aquinas

Bibliography

Luther's Works: *The Disputation concerning Man* (1536). LW 34:137–44; *The Disputation concerning the Passage: "The Word Was Made Flesh"* (1539). LW 38:237–77; "The Law of Identical Predication." In *Confession concerning Christ's Supper* (1528). LW 37:294–303. **General Works:** Bayer, O. *Theology the Lutheran Way.* Eerdmans, 2007; Bielfeldt, D., M. Mattox, and P. Hinlicky. *The Substance of the Faith: Luther's Doctrinal Theology for Today.* Fortress, 2008; Dieter, T. *Der junge Luther und Aristoteles: Eine historisch-systematische Untersuchung zum Verhältnis von Theologie und Philosophie.* De Gruyter, 2001; Dragseth, J. H., ed. *The Devil's Whore: Reason and Philosophy in the Lutheran Tradition.* Fortress, 2011; Ebeling, G. *Luther: An Introduction to His Thought.* Fortress, 1972; Gerrish, B. *Grace and Reason: A Study in the Theology of Martin Luther.* Clarendon, 1962; Haga, J. *Was There a Lutheran Metaphysics? The Interpretation of* Communicatio Idiomatum *in Early Modern Lutheranism.* Vandenhoeck & Ruprecht, 2012; Hinlicky, P. *Paths Not Taken: Fates of Theology from Luther through Leibniz.* Eerdmans, 2009; Sponheim, P. *Faith and Process: The Significance of Process Thought for Christian Faith.* Augsburg, 1979; Vainio, O. *Engaging Luther: A (New) Theological Assessment.* Cascade, 2010; White, G. *Luther as Nominalist: A Study of the Logical Methods Used in Martin Luther's Disputations in the Light of Their Medieval Background.* Luther-Agricola-Society, 1994.

MARK C. MATTES

Pieper, Francis

In addition to serving as professor and president of Concordia Seminary, St. Louis, Missouri, Francis (Franz) Pieper (1852–1931) was also president of the Lutheran Church–Missouri Synod. He was born in a small town in the Prussian province of Pomerania where his father was the town mayor. Pieper attended the preparatory schools (*Gymnasia*) at Köslin and Kolberg, completing his studies in 1870. In that year he came to America with his widowed mother and several brothers and settled in Watertown, Wisconsin, where he enrolled in the ministerial preparatory school of the Wisconsin Synod. He next attended Concordia Seminary in St. Louis, where the Wisconsin Synod sent its students before it had a seminary of its own. After completing his studies in 1875, he served congregations at Centerville and Manitowoc, Wisconsin.

In 1878 Pieper was elected by the Missouri Synod to fill a new professorship at the St. Louis seminary, in which he would work under President C. F. W. Walther with the idea that he would become Walther's successor. In addition to his teaching duties, he quickly began to produce editorials and theological articles for the synod's official publication, *Der Lutheraner*, and its theological journal, *Lehre und Wehre*. In 1880 a controversy broke out among the Lutheran synods of the Evangelical Lutheran Synodical Conference over the doctrine of predestination, or election to salvation. Pieper became heavily involved in publishing articles in defense of the Missouri Synod's position in the controversy. The year 1880 also saw the publication of his first book, a treatise on the Augsburg Confession in observance of the 350th anniversary of its presentation. He became a frequent presenter of doctrinal essays at conventions of the synod and its districts throughout his career. These essays were widely distributed and read throughout the synod, giving Pieper a paramount position in the development and maintenance of its theological positions. The culmination of his literary output was the publication of his three-volume *Christliche Dogmatik* (*Christian Dogmatics*), the first volume of which appeared in 1917, the year of the 400th Reformation Jubilee. The entire work was completed in 1924.

This work became the standard theological textbook in the Missouri Synod's seminaries, continuing into the twenty-first century after its translation into English in the 1950s. Throughout his career Pieper was actively involved in various boards and committees of the synod, and in 1899 the synod elected him as its president, a position he held until 1911.

See also Lutheran Church–Missouri Synod; Repristination Theology; Walther, Carl Ferdinand Wilhelm

Bibliography

Graebner, T. *Dr. Francis Pieper: A Biographical Sketch.* Concordia, 1931.

MARVIN A. HUGGINS

Piepkorn, Arthur Carl

The Lutheran pastor, military chaplain, and professor of theology Arthur Carl Piepkorn (1907–73) had graduated from the LCMS college in Milwaukee (1925) and its flagship seminary, Concordia, St. Louis (1928), before earning a PhD in oriental languages at the University of Chicago (1932). There he discovered the catholicity of the Lutheran confessions. He later described himself first as a Christian, second as a Western catholic Christian, and third as a Western catholic Christian in the Church of the Augsburg Confession in America. Thus, he viewed the Lutheran Church as a "confessing movement" within the Western catholic church. He was among the first Americans to prefer Nathan Söderblom's descriptive label "evangelical catholic," in place of the more sectarian-sounding "Lutheran." He held that the Roman Catholic Church, which was formally defined at the Council of Trent, did not have a monopoly on catholic tradition. In his view, the Church of the Augsburg Confession was an ecumenical church that sought to be "the reconciling center of Christendom." After completing his doctorate, he wanted to serve as a missionary to China, something he had long desired to do, but this was impossible, due to the financial crisis of the Great Depression. So he served as a pastor to a congregation in Minnesota and then to one in Ohio. Between 1936 and 1940 Piepkorn was a reserve army chaplain. During World War II he went on active duty and rapidly advanced in rank. Eventually he served on the personal staff of General Eisenhower and became the senior military chaplain in postwar Europe. Afterward he was the commandant of the US Army Chaplain School (1948–50) and the president of the Army's Chaplain Board (1950–51).

In 1951 Piepkorn accepted a teaching position at his alma mater, Concordia Seminary, St. Louis, where he taught confessional and ecumenical theology. During these years he published in a variety of journals (e.g., *Una Sancta*). Primarily an essayist, he wrote on a wide range of topics, including liturgical renewal, sacramental theology, the proper interpretation of the Lutheran confessions, biblical authority, comparative symbolics, and church and ministry. He interpreted the Lutheran confessions not as denominational documents but as "a catholic interpretation of the prophetic and apostolic writings of the Old and New Testaments." Piepkorn was the leading Lutheran participant in the North American Lutheran–Roman Catholic dialogue from its inception in 1965 until his death. In these meetings he addressed such matters as baptism, the Eucharist, ordination, the church, and Mary the mother of God. His magnum opus, *Profiles in Belief*, examines the public teachings of all of the principal Christian church bodies in North America. As a member of the so-called faculty majority at Concordia, St. Louis, Piepkorn's teaching was condemned by the 1973 LCMS Convention (led by Jacob A. O. Preus) as "false doctrine which cannot be tolerated in the church of God." A few days before Piepkorn's death, the seminary's board reassigned him against his will to a nonteaching position and offered him "honorable retirement," which he refused. His life and writings have continued to exert influence on those within and beyond the church of the Augsburg Confession who share his concern for evangelical catholicity.

See also Ecumenical Dialogues; Lutheran Church–Missouri Synod; Seminex and the Association of Evangelical Lutheran Churches

Bibliography

Piepkorn, A. C. *Profiles in Belief*, 4 vols. in 3. Harper & Row, 1977–79; Plekon, M. P., and W. S. Wiecher, eds. *The Church: Selected Writings of Arthur Carl Piepkorn*. American Lutheran Publicity Bureau, 1993; Secker, P. J., ed. *The Sacred Scriptures and the Lutheran Confessions: Selected Writings of Arthur Carl Piepkorn*. CEC Press, 2007.

MATTHEW L. BECKER

Pietism

As the most important reform movement within German Protestantism after the Reformation, the Pietist movement stressed religious experience and active participation of the laity. It fostered church reform, instituted new patterns of biblical devotion, and encouraged organized missionary work. Among its distinctive characteristics were emphases on regeneration, conversion, and conventicles, and an openness to millenarian ideas. Pietism remained, however, theologically heterogeneous. Pietists emerged most visibly in Germany, but the movement influenced Lutheran churches from Eastern Europe to Scandinavia to North America.

The definition of Pietism remains contested. Some scholars such as Stoeffler see Pietism as part of a much broader Protestant renewal movement of the early modern period encompassing English Puritanism and the Dutch *Nadere Reformatie*, where others, especially Wallmann, conceive of Pietism in narrower terms, centered, though not exclusively, on its original association in German Lutheranism and figures like Philipp Jakob Spener and August Hermann Francke. The chronological scope of Pietism as a movement, even within Germany, has also been vigorously debated. The most recent scholarship has reached no consensus on these issues, but in general Stoeffler's capacious understanding of Pietism has not prevailed. Scholars see both Lutheran and Reformed expressions of German Pietism and increasingly emphasize the role of radical Pietists who challenged and influenced more moderate, church Pietists, who nonetheless remained committed to the confessions of the territorial churches.

The origins of Pietism can be traced to a new form of piety that emerged around the turn of the sixteenth century to the seventeenth. Some scholars have traced this to a crisis of piety, in which some Lutherans perceived a disjuncture between doctrine and piety; others locate this in a series of crises faced by German Protestants at the time, including crop failure, climate change, epidemics, and political instability. Some devotional writers, such as Philipp Nicolai (1556–1608), sought to comfort his readers amid the suffering and trouble in the world by pointing toward the joys of salvation. Others, such as Johann Arndt (1555–1621), focused on the disparity of nominal Christians who heard sermons and observed the church's sacraments and rituals, yet nonetheless appeared to deny true Christianity with their lack of repentance and immoral lives. Arndt's *True Christianity* (1605–10) became one of the great devotional works of Lutheranism.

Themes of piety and reform were widespread in seventeenth-century Lutheranism. The caricature of a sclerotic Lutheran Orthodoxy in much popular work is contradicted by the profound concern for piety evinced by major figures of Lutheran Orthodoxy, such as Johann Gerhard. Concern for reform permeated much of Lutheran Orthodoxy, including proposals for more effective church discipline, better schools, rigorous religious observance, and the improvement of clerical formation. These reforms tended to be focused, however, on top-down approaches. In practice, they often foundered on resistance from the civil authorities, although some rulers, such as Duke Ernst the Pious of Saxe-Gotha, earnestly sought religious reform.

As a socially tangible movement, Pietism first emerged in Lutheranism in Frankfurt am Main under the leadership of Philipp Jakob Spener. Two laymen approached him in 1670 about pious gatherings outside of regular worship. In a world where freedom of assembly was not a guaranteed right, these conventicles, which came to be known as *collegia pietatis*, allowed laity under Spener's supervision to come together in his parsonage to sing, pray, read Scripture, and discuss devotional works. Spener came to understand these conventicles in terms of the early apostolic meetings (1 Cor. 14) and developed the distinctive notion of the *ecclesiola in ecclesia* (little church within the church), in which the gathered pious would become the center of reform that would eventually permeate the larger church.

In 1675 Spener also published his famous programmatic *Pia Desideria* (*Heartfelt Desire*) as a foreword to a new edition of Johann Arndt's sermons. Spener's proposals became the chief programmatic document of the early Pietist movement. Although his criticisms of contemporary Christianity overlapped with those of many Lutherans in the seventeenth century, the *Pia Desideria* also marked a departure both for its prognosis and the proposed remedies for reform. Spener articulated an optimistic vision of the in-breaking of better times for Christianity, a vision that had millenarian overtones. Furthermore his reforms, especially the practice of *collegia pietatis* (conventicles) and his emphasis on the lay encounter with the entire Bible, set his proposals apart from those of earlier German Lutherans.

The initial response to the *Pia Desideria* was strong, though not without some criticism. Conventicles, the participation of women in *collegia pietatis*, and the expectation of the conversion of the Jews provoked controversy. The lines between Pietist and Orthodox parties were, however, not easily fixed. In the first Pietist theological controversy, Georg Konrad Dilfeld, a follower of the Lutheran theologian Georg Calixt, criticized Spener for arguing that the theological enterprise was not a purely intellectual endeavor. Embracing the role of faith and the illumination of the Holy Spirit in theology and drawing on Luther and the confessions, Spener, in fact, emerged in the public dispute as the more "orthodox" Lutheran of the two.

During much of the 1680s, the Pietist movement was not especially controversial. Some

conventicle movements arose briefly outside of Frankfurt but then subsided, in part because of separatist tendencies. Where conventicles or *collegia pietatis* continued, they were tightly restricted. However, in the late 1680s the Pietist movement took on a new and more divisive character in Germany. In Leipzig, one of the centers of this new form of Pietism, August Hermann Francke had established a *collegium philobiblicum* for the academic study of the Bible in 1686. After a visit to Leipzig in 1687, Spener urged Francke and his colleagues to focus on more devotional issues related to the Bible. Gradually the *collegium* turned in a more Pietist direction. Later that same year, Francke's conversion in Lüneburg shaped him and the emerging Pietist movement in profound ways. Attendance at the *collegium* grew, and other colloquia and conventicles developed in the city, drawing many laypeople to them. The theology faculty, who had initially encouraged the *collegium philobiblicum*, now became alarmed at the religious fervor that gripped many of the students and townspeople in Leipzig. The Saxon authorities ordered an investigation. Francke defended himself in an apology (1689), and the jurist Christian Thomasius entered the fray on the side of the Pietists. Francke left under duress in 1689, and the following year Thomasius was expelled and conventicles in Leipzig were prohibited.

Controversies surrounding Pietism were by no means limited to Leipzig. Across cities in Middle and North Germany, Pietist disturbances broke out in the early 1690s. Some were connected to ecstatic experiences in conventicles and others to the emergence of Pietist visionaries and prophets. Moderate Pietists such as Spener viewed the excesses critically, but the extraordinary events deepened the divide between Pietist and Orthodox Lutherans. The polemical exchange of pamphlets that appeared on both sides became the most vigorous within German Lutheranism since the early Reformation. At issue were questions of religious enthusiasm, millenarianism, conventicles, the common priesthood, and perfectionism.

Most civil authorities in German territories and cities viewed the movement with suspicion and sought to suppress it. In many cases clerical advocates of Pietism lost their positions, not only young pastors such as Francke, who was dismissed in Erfurt, but also more prominent figures such as the superintendents Johann Wilhelm Petersen in Lüneburg or Bartholomäus Meyer (1644–1714) in Wolfenbüttel. However, in the territories of Brandenburg-Prussia, Pietists were able to find a measure of tolerance and often explicit support. The ruling Hohenzollerns were Reformed, and they saw support for Pietists as one means of reshaping traditional Lutheranism. In 1691 Spener became a leading church prelate in Berlin and an influential advocate in Brandenburg-Prussia. He was instrumental in seeing that many Pietists and Pietist sympathizers would find appointments at the academy in Halle, which became a full university in 1694.

Dismissed from his pastoral position in Erfurt, Francke was appointed professor in Halle in 1692. He also held a clerical appointment in Glaucha, just outside the walls of the city. In Halle, Francke's views moderated, and he distanced himself from the more radical Pietist visionaries and prophets. The university also became strongly Pietist in orientation, making Halle the intellectual center of Pietism. In 1695 Francke founded the famous orphanage in Halle. The Francke Foundations, as the orphanage, schools, and related enterprises have become known, grew into the largest Pietist institution in Germany. Alongside pedagogical and charitable work, the foundations had a large-scale printing house, produced pharmaceuticals, and, in cooperation with the Danish Crown, initiated the first Protestant mission to India. Halle Pietists were instrumental in sending Heinrich Melchior Mühlenberg to Pennsylvania, thereby shaping Lutheranism in North America.

Pietism also flourished in other parts of Brandenburg-Prussia. In Berlin, Spener and his allies exercised considerable influence. The theology faculty in Königsberg became increasingly pro-Pietist in the early 1700s, and clerical appointments in the territorial churches of Brandenburg-Prussia often favored graduates of Halle and Königsberg. In other territories, Pietists had less success. In Electoral Saxony the universities of Leipzig and Wittenberg were decidedly anti-Pietist, and the Dresden superintendent Valentin Ernst Löscher (1673–1749) became one of Pietism's most capable opponents. In other territories, such as Hessen-Darmstadt and Württemberg, the reception of Pietism was more mixed.

The division between church Pietists and radical Pietists was often blurry. Johanna Eleonora Petersen and her husband, Johann Wilhelm Petersen, were both closely allied with Spener and the early Pietist movement in Frankfurt. They moved in increasingly radical directions, particularly after J. W. Petersen was dismissed in 1692 and came to espouse positions on millenarianism, prophecy, and the *apokatastasis pantōn* (Acts 3:21) that church Pietists would not espouse. Others like Gottfried Arnold, the author of the famous *Impartial History of the Church and Heresy* (1699/1700), a thoroughgoing attack on Lutheran Orthodoxy, had an especially radical phase rejecting all church structures, embracing theosophy, and advocating celibacy as a spiritual discipline before he married and accepted a clerical position in the Lutheran Church. Scholars debate the extent to which Arnold truly moderated his views, but his external conformity illustrates the permeable boundaries between radical and church Pietists.

Some radicals never reconciled themselves to the confessional churches. One of Arnold's followers, Johann Conrad Dippel (1673–1734), became an implacable foe of established Christianity. Ernst Christoph Hochmann von Hohenau (1670–1721) rejected formal church structures but encouraged loose association among conventicle movements. Most separatist groups were short lived, such as the notorious Mother Eve Society of Eva von Buttlar

(1670–1721), whose bizarre communal practices scandalized Germany. One of the most enduring were the New Baptists (Dunker), many of whom emigrated to Pennsylvania, where their descendants formed Brethren churches that continue today.

After 1740 support for Pietism waned in many parts of Germany. The intellectual vitality of the early movement faltered, and its political fortunes changed, especially in Brandenburg-Prussia, where Friedrich II (1712–82) disdained Pietists. The University of Halle itself became one of the leading centers of the Enlightenment in Germany. Pietism flourished, however, in Württemberg, led by figures such as the biblical scholar and millennial thinker Johann Albrecht Bengel and his student Friedrich Christoph Oetinger. In 1743 Württemberg authorized conventicle gatherings in the Lutheran Church, thereby institutionalizing a key Pietist practice. To this day, Pietist influence continues in Württemberg.

The Moravians represent another long-lasting expression of Pietism. Emerging in the 1720s among refugees on Nikolaus Ludwig von Zinzendorf's estate, the movement had unmistakable Pietist influences but also differentiated itself from other Pietists. Under Zinzendorf's influence, Moravians developed their own distinctive emphases on the theology of the cross, ecumenism, missions, and communal life. Though relatively small in numbers, the geographic reach of the Moravians was extraordinary; into the twenty-first century it remains a global denomination.

Scholars disagree on the extent to which Pietism is a useful label beyond the eighteenth century. There is no question that Pietist impulses continue well into the nineteenth and twentieth centuries in the *Erweckungsbewegung*, the inner mission, mission societies, and biblical piety, among German as well as Scandinavian and North American Lutherans. Pietism remained, nonetheless, heterogeneous theologically, and figures as diverse as Hans Nielsen Hauge or Friedrich Schleiermacher could claim Pietist influences.

In many twentieth-century expressions of Lutheranism, Pietism retained pejorative connotations, especially among confessional and neo-Orthodox Lutherans, but there is no question that Pietism shaped, both positively and negatively, the identity and practice of modern Lutheranism.

See also Arndt, Johann; Bible Translations; Conventicles; Francke, August Hermann; Francke Foundations; Hauge, Hans Nilsen; Löscher, Valentin Ernst; Mission Societies and Academies; Moravian Church (Unitas Fratrum); Petersen, Johanna Eleonora; Pontoppidan, Erik Ludvigsen; Spener, Philipp Jakob; Tolstadius, Erik; Zinzendorf, Nikolaus Ludwig von

Bibliography

Erb, P. *Pietists: Selected Writings.* Paulist Press, 1983; Lehmann, H. "Perspektiven für die Pietismusforschung." *Theologische Rundschau* 77 (2012): 226–40; Lehmann, H., and J. Strom. "Pietism." In *The Oxford Handbook of Early Modern Theology, 1600–1800,* ed. U. Lehner et al. Oxford University Press, 2016, http://www.oxfordhandbooks.com/view/10.1093/oxfordhb/9780199937943.001.0001/oxfordhb-9780199937943-e-31; Lindberg, C. *The Pietist Theologians.* Blackwell, 2004; Schneider, H. *German Radical Pietism.* Scarecrow, 2007; Shantz, D. *Companion to German Pietism, 1660–1800.* Brill, 2014; Shantz, D. *An Introduction to German Pietism.* Johns Hopkins University Press, 2013; Strom, J. "Problems and Promises of Pietism Research." *Church History* 71 (2002): 536–54; Wallmann, J. *Der Pietismus.* Vandenhoeck & Ruprecht, 2005; Ward, W. R. *Protestant Evangelical Awakening.* Cambridge University Press, 1992.

JONATHAN STROM

Poland

Poland, like other countries of the region, lies on the border between Western and Eastern Christianity. Its ruler was baptized in the Western tradition in 966. On the eve of the Reformation, Poland's parish system was still weaker than in Western Europe. In 1385 and 1569, the kingdom of Poland and the Grand Duchy of Lithuania sealed unions. The Polish-Lithuanian state, officially called the Commonwealth of Both Nations (*Rzeczpospolita Obojga Narodów*) after 1569, reached dimensions of 867,000 square kilometers and constituted the largest country in Europe. Its population was multiethnic and multiconfessional. The commonwealth ended when it was partitioned between Protestant Prussia, Catholic Austria, and Orthodox Russia at the end of the eighteenth century (1772–95). A Polish Republic emerged again after World War I (1918) as a much smaller country (over 388,000 km²); it still had a multiconfessional population, 3 percent of which was Protestant. After World War II (1945), Polish borders moved again; the Communist Republic of Poland sought to become homogeneous in both ethnic and religious senses. However, despite Communist attempts, it did not become a secular country but remained predominantly Roman Catholic. Today the Evangelical Church of the Augsburg Confession has over seventy thousand adherents, about 0.2 percent of the population of Poland.

Poles first encountered the Reformation directly after the publication of Martin Luther's Ninety-Five Theses (1517). Three groups demonstrated major interest in Luther's message: the German-speaking population of larger cities, the humanists and intellectuals from the milieu of the university in Cracow (Kraków), and the Catholic clergy.

At the dawn of the Reformation, the image of Martin Luther was mostly negative. His name became a term for all kinds of heresy, just as all kinds of Protestant sympathies were stigmatized as Lutheranism. In 1521 a papal nuncio tried to burn Luther's books and images. Some Polish humanists followed the controversy between Luther and Erasmus of Rotterdam very closely and reprinted the polemics of both authors in Cracow, clearly taking Erasmus's side. Soon the German anti-Lutheran polemics written by Johann Cochlaeus, John Eck, Georg Witzel, and Cardinal Cajetan (Tommaso de Vio) were brought to Poland and were even dedicated to the Polish king. Among the Polish anti-Protestants, the most active were Martin Dobrogost, Andrzej Krzycki (Andreas Cricius), Walenty Wróbel, and Jan Dantyszek (Ioannes Dantiscus).

Before publication of the anti-Protestant edict forbidding studies in Wittenberg (1535), Luther met some Polish students. Jan Dantyszek, ambassador of the Polish king in the Holy Roman Empire, visited Luther in Wittenberg. However, Luther did not establish strong connections to Poland. Philip Melanchthon developed closer relations with Poles. He wrote over twenty letters to his Polish friends and cultivated friendships with the leaders and intellectuals of what became the Reformed church, like Jan Łaski (Johannes à Lasco) and Andrzej Frycz Moderzewski (Andreas Fricius Modrevius). Between 1530 and 1535, Melanchthon received several invitations to settle in Poland and to join the university in Cracow.

Polish kings remained neutral or hostile toward the Reformation. Sigismund I of the Jagiellon dynasty (r. 1506–48) intervened in Danzig (Gdańsk) in 1526 to prevent the city from officially turning Lutheran. In 1520–44, the king issued a series of anti-Protestant edicts. He forbade importing and publishing Luther's works, preaching Lutheran theology, and enrolling at universities and schools that supported the Reformation. These edicts hindered citizens and noblemen from converting but were rarely used to prosecute the offenders. However, the confessional position of the king's court was not unequivocal. Some members of the court were notorious for their sympathies toward Protestantism. In international politics, the king loyally supported his vassal, Lutheran prince Albrecht of Prussia. Finally his son and successor, Sigismund August (r. 1548–72), showed an inclination toward the new theology.

When Sigismund August became king, confessional matters changed. Protestant churches started acting as ecclesiastical organizations. Lutherans, Calvinists, and the Bohemian Brethren developed three independent territorial organizations. All organizations held synods and church visitations. Twenty years after the first invitations, in 1557, leaders of the Protestant movement again invited Melanchthon to organize a Protestant church in one province of the country. The Lutheran churches already had an ecclesiastical organization in the west-central province of Poland, known as Greater Poland. At a synod in 1558 the churches of that province officially accepted the Augsburg Confession. By 1560 the Lutherans in Greater Poland had about sixty churches and thirty pastors, who elected their first superintendent, Johann Caper. In 1565 Erasmus Gliczner became the second superintendent and, until his death in 1604, had a strong impact on the consolidation of the organization.

Soon the churches were preparing their translations of the Bible. The first Polish translation of the entire Protestant Bible was published in 1563 by the Calvinists. The first Lutheran full translation was published in cooperation with the Reformed churches in Danzig in 1632 (Biblia Gdańska). However, some partial translations were printed earlier, such as the New Testament translated by Stanisław Murzynowski (1528–53), edited by Jan Seklucjan (d. 1578), and published in Königsberg in 1551.

By the middle of the sixteenth century, Protestantism reached the nobility; it became a mass movement as well as a political power. Confessional matters were discussed during assemblies (Sejm), and in 1555, 1562/63, and 1570 the nobility tried to submit Protestant confessions to the king. Sigismund August, suspected of Protestant sympathies, allegedly read Calvin's works privately. In 1557, in the wake of the imperial Peace of Augsburg (1555), he recognized and confirmed for the Royal Prussian Cities (Danzig, Elbing, and Thorn) the right to celebrate Communion in both kinds (bread and wine). After the king's death (1572), during the process of the election of a successor, the nobility prepared an agreement restricting religious persecution. This document, called the Confederation of Warsaw, was proclaimed by the nobility in April 1573 and later confirmed by kings as a part of the conditions of their election. The document guaranteed followers of all confessions an equal right to live and practice their religions peacefully in Poland.

At the turn of the sixteenth century, the number of the Lutheran parishes escalated to about 150. Periodically in the seventeenth and eighteenth centuries, the number of Lutherans in Greater Poland rose due to migration from the German territories. However, not all Lutheran parishes in Greater Poland joined the existing ecclesiastical organization. People complained that some German-speaking pastors of Greater Poland were reluctant to meet at the synods. Apart from the Lutheran organization in Greater Poland, some independent Lutheran parishes were active in other parts of the commonwealth. Three Pomeranian cities—Danzig (Gdańsk), Elbing (Elbląg), and Thorn (Toruń)—were the strongest centers of Lutheranism. However, Lutheran parishes existed in many other cities such as Vilnius, in the duchy of Lithuania. Furthermore, a Lutheran parish was opened in the small, neighboring town of Węgrów for Lutherans who lived in Warsaw.

The synods in Greater Poland made constant efforts to produce a uniform liturgy, prepare a common church order, administer education, and publish a new translation of the Augsburg Confession. However, in the second half of the seventeenth century, they had to face the growing pressure of Catholic bishops supported by secular authority and the ascendant Jesuit order. The pressure of Catholic monarchs and bishops, who sought to limit the rights previously guaranteed to Lutherans, encouraged the Lutherans to cooperate on a regional level with the Reformed churches. Both confessions organized some general synods in Royal Prussia, and they sealed a short-lasting Church Union in Sielce in Mazovia (1777).

At the end of the Polish Republic, about 115 Lutheran congregations still survived. After the partitions of Poland (1772–95), they were incorporated into the structure of the Lutheran Church of Prussia. Today's Evangelical Church of the Augsburg Confession (Kościół Ewangelicko-Augsburski w Polsce) was established by the decree of the president of Poland in 1936. Its existence was confirmed after World War II in 1946, and again after the fall of Communism in 1994. According to Lutheran World Federation statistics, in 2013 there were approximately seventy thousand members in 133 congregations scattered around the country. It educates its clergy at the Christian Academy of Theology in Warsaw (Chrześcijańska Akademia Teologiczna).

Bibliography

Kłaczkow, J., ed. *Kościoły luterańskie na ziemiach polskich (XVI–XX w.).* 3 vols. Uniwersytet Mikołaja Kopernika, 2012; Kneifel, E. *Geschichte der Evanglisch-Augsburgischen Kirche in Polen.* Self-published, 1964; Kriegseisen, W. *Ewangelicy polscy i litewscy w epoce saskiej (1696–1763).* Semper, 1996; Lutheran World Federation, https://www.lutheranworld.org/sites/default/files/LWI-Statistics-2013-EN.pdf; Schramm, G. *Der polnische Adel und die Reformation 1548–1607.* F. Steiner, 1965.

Maciej Ptaszyński

Pomerania

The duchy of Pomerania ruled by the House of Greifen belonged to Lutheran territories of the Holy Roman Empire on the Baltic Sea. The territories were almost exclusively German speaking; in the eastern parts of the duchy (in the vicinity of Stolp and Kolberg) lived some Poles and Kashubians who spoke their own languages. On the eve of the Reformation, the Pomeranian territories were parts of three different dioceses: Kammin, Schwerin, and Roskilde. After the Thirty Years' War (1618–48), the duchy ended its history as an independent political and ecclesiastical entity and was divided between Brandenburg and Sweden. In 1637 Bogislaw XIV, the last of the Greifen line, died without any successor.

The Reformation reached Pomeranian cities very early. In 1522, Stettin asked Martin Luther for a Protestant preacher, and Luther sent Paul vom Rode (von Rode or Rhoda, 1489–1563). Meanwhile, Evangelical preachers (Johann Amandus, Jakob Hogensee, Christian Kelehut, Johann Kureke, and Peter Suawe) visited main cities such as Stolp, Kolberg, Köslin, and Stralsund. This led to much tension with Catholic priests and secular authorities. In Stralsund, the conflicts almost devolved into iconoclastic controversies (*Stralsunder Kirchensturm*, 1525). Following these events, Stralsund, as the first city in northern Germany, accepted the church order (*Kirchenordnung*), written by Johannes Aepinus, later superintendent in Hamburg.

In many respects, the process of establishing the Reformation in Pomerania followed the pattern of Lutheran Saxony. The Reformation was officially introduced by the Dukes of Pomerania after the diet in Treptow 1534–35. The dukes implemented the church order written by Johannes Bugenhagen (a native of Pomerania) and, following Bugenhagen's instructions, started the first church visitation. In 1563/69, the second church order was prepared by superintendent Jakob Runge (1527–95) with assistance from Philip Melanchthon; it was accepted by all church authorities. Runge's church order systematically describes the ecclesiastical institutions that emerged after 1535 or that were being established. As its confessional basis, the church chose the Corpus Doctrinae Misnicum, prepared by Philip Melanchthon and printed in Wittenberg in 1560. The Augsburg Confession (Variata and Invariata) was a part of later printings of the Corpus Doctrinae Misnicum, along with the Apology and Melanchthon's *Loci communes*.

The superintendents, as officials of the princes, led the church administration. The church was divided into three main provinces, with superintendencies in Greifswald, Stettin, and Kolberg. The dukes and superintendents established the first consistories in Greifswald (1556), Kolberg (1558), and Stettin (1561). The city of Stralsund appointed its own city superintendent and a consistory to restrain ducal power over the city. Between 1541 and 1593, synods of entire provinces and districts met regularly. After ferocious disputes on christological matters sparked by earlier eucharistic controversies, the dukes refused to convene further synods.

The strongest theological controversies broke out between ducal superintendents Johannes Knipstro and Jakob Runge on the one hand, and city pastors and superintendents of Stralsund, Johannes Freder and Jakob Kruse, on the other. In the second half of the sixteenth century, the Pomeranian synods spoke out against the teachings of Andreas Osiander, Matthias Flacius, and John Calvin. Although Pomerania considered itself to be orthodox in its Lutheranism, Pomeranian theologians avoided participation in the preparation of the Book of Concord. The importance of the legacy of Melanchthon was one of the main reasons for the refusal to sign the Torgau Book (1576). The Pomeranian church never officially signed the Book of Concord; however, an allegiance to the Formula of Concord was obligatory for students in the Faculty of Theology at the University of Greifswald after 1623.

See also Bugenhagen, Johannes

Bibliography
Heyden, H. *Kirchengeschichte Pommerns*. 2nd ed. 2 vols. Fischer & Schmidt, 1957.

Maciej Ptaszyński

Pontoppidan, Erik Ludvigsen

The theologian and writer Erik Ludvigsen Pontoppidan (1698–1764) was a propagator of Pietism in Denmark/Norway. Born in Aarhus, he traveled widely in Europe, married three times, and was father of ten. Among his professional titles are preceptor for Duke Frederick Carl of Holstein-Plön, court preacher, professor of theology, and codirector of the royal orphanage in Copenhagen, which was based on inspiration from the Francke Foundations. He was member of the newly founded Royal Danish Academy of Sciences and Letters, bishop in Bergen (1747–48), and prochancellor of the University in Copenhagen (1755–64). Known as the "northern Fénelon," Pontoppidan was a prolific writer engaged in geography, economics, and church history. In the preface to his first topographical work, *Theatrum Daniae* (1730), he explains his effort to map earthly territory as an exercise for describing the heavenly geography in the afterlife, a statement typical of his Pietist attitude toward work. In the tradition of Montesquieu's *Lettres persanes* (1721), he wrote the novel *Menoza* (1742) about, as indicated

in the subtitle, "An Asian Prince who traveled the world in search of Christians but without finding them." His *Truth unto Godliness* (1737) was an influential explanation of Luther's Small Catechism. Much in the spirit of August Hermann Francke and Gotthilf August Francke, Pontoppidan strove to improve and cultivate the teaching estate in society. His insistence that God elects *intuitu fidei* (in view of faith) led to struggles among American Norwegian Lutherans in the late nineteenth century.

See also Francke, August Hermann; Francke, Gotthilf August; Norway; Norwegian-American Lutheranism; Pietism

Bibliography
Cyranka, D. "Blinde Flecken? Das Verhältnis von Halle und Tranquebar im Spiegel von Pontoppidans *Menoza-Roman*." In *Beiträge zum Ersten Internationalen Kongress für Pietismusforschung 2001*, 795–811. Hallesche Forschungen 17/2. Max Niemeyer, 2005; Neiiendam, M. *Erik Pontoppidan: Studier og Bidrag til Pietismens Historie*. 2 vols. G. E. C. Gads, 1930–33; Olson, J. B. "Erik Ludvigsen Pontoppidan and the American Influence of His Catechism." In *The Lutheran Historical Conference: Essays and Reports 1990 of the Fifteenth Biennial Meeting, Lutheranism and Pietism*, 20–39. Augsburg Fortress, 1992.

Kristian Mejrup

Praetorius, Michael

The cantor, composer, and author Michael Praetorius (1571–1621) was born in Creuzburg, son of Pastor Michael Schultheiss (Praetorius is the Latin form of the family name). The father had studied theology with Luther and Melanchthon in Wittenberg and taught at the Latin school in Torgau, where he was a colleague of Johann Walter, Luther's friend and musical collaborator. Praetorius studied at the University in Frankfurt an der Oder, and in 1586 he served as organist at the university church. Without much formal musical training, he became organist in Wolfenbüttel in 1595, then added an appointment as Kapellmeister in Groningen in 1604. Praetorius traveled widely in Germany during the years 1613–16; he conducted in many of the leading cities and associated with other leading musicians. His publications include the *Musae*

Sioniae (1605–10), *Leiturgodia* (1607, 1611) and the *Syntagma musicum* (1614–20). The *Musae Sioniae* was published in nine parts, containing over twelve hundred chorale settings ranging from simple four-voice pieces with the chorale tune in the soprano (cantional style) to eight or more voice settings in the Italian polychoral style; many were intended to be sung in alternation, with the congregation singing in unison and unaccompanied. *Leiturgodia* contains settings of the texts of the Latin mass, and the three-volume *Syntagma musicum* includes a treatise on church music and an encyclopedia of musical instruments. Praetorius's works are performed in their original languages and translations to this day, including his setting of "Es ist ein Ros' entsprungen" (Lo, How a Rose E'er Blooming) for Christmas. He succeeded in keeping the tradition of the Lutheran chorale alive by using it as the basis for compositions in the increasingly popular emerging Italian styles; his work sets the stage for further developments through the music of J. S. Bach.

See also Bach, Johann Sebastian; Hymnody; Music

Bibliography
Schalk, C. "Michael Praetorius." *Music in Early Lutheranism*. Concordia Academic Press, 2001.

MICHAEL E. KRENTZ

Prayer

Especially in the Large Catechism, Martin Luther taught that God commands Christians to pray, promises to hear them, and even provides the words to pray. Luther saw prayer as an integral fruit of the Spirit in the Christian life. He consistently advocated that prayer be frequent, bold, honest, and forthright. Luther's approach to prayer centered on the same law-promise dynamic that shaped his theology. Prayer's starting place is not the human being but rather God: God has spoken, in both command and promise, and has invited, encouraged, and shaped the believer's response. The structure of Luther's catechisms reflects this: He placed first the commandments, a confession of how God

wants us to live, and understood the second commandment to include the positive admonition to "call upon, pray to, and praise" God in every time of need. The Apostles' Creed, a confession of what God does for us, follows. Prayer, in the form of the Lord's Prayer, then comes as a response to God's command and promise. Just as God creates and redeems humans "without any merit or worthiness" on our part, so also God promises to hear prayer, regardless of our worthiness.

Luther insisted that medieval prayer books and practices had conveyed many false ideas about prayer. At least five aspects of medieval prayer practices needed reform. Medieval Christians (1) were encouraged to pray to the Virgin Mary and the saints, (2) were taught that God would hear them only if they were worthy to be heard, (3) considered prayer a good work and therefore (4) encouraged repetition (whether or not faith was present) as helpful in building up this good work, and (5) thought prayer to be primarily a work for clerics. Over against this Luther then asserted that we pray to God because God has commanded it, has promised mercifully to hear us, and is capable of hearing, something no saint can claim. God hears our prayer despite our unworthiness. Prayer is not a good work but rather honest communication of the believer's heartfelt needs to God. Christians should not mindlessly repeat prayers but instead boldly and persistently present their needs to God. All should pray, not just clerics.

Furthermore, Luther saw prayer as essential in the Christian's battle against unbelief and faithless conduct. The circumstances of our lives drive us to pray. As he wrote in his Large Catechism, "We are in such a situation that no one can keep the Ten Commandments perfectly, even though [they have] begun to believe. Besides, the devil, along with the world and our flesh, resists them with all his power." So Luther thought it necessary "to call upon God incessantly" and ask "that he may give, preserve, and increase in us faith and the fulfillment of the Ten Commandments and remove all that stands in our way and hinders us in this regard."

Luther centered his reflections on prayer in the Lord's Prayer. He expressed his high opinion of that prayer already in *An Exposition of the Lord's Prayer for Simple Laymen* (1519): "Since our Lord is the author of this prayer, it is without a doubt the most sublime, the loftiest, and the most excellent. If he, the good and faithful Teacher, had known a better one, he would surely have taught us that too" (LW 42:21).

In addition, Luther recommended the use of catechetical elements to structure prayers and shape content. In 1535, in a tract dedicated to his barber, who had asked him about prayer, Luther reported his own prayer practice and gave concrete advice on what should precede prayer and be contained in prayer. He reported that he said "the Ten Commandments, the Creed, and . . . some words of Christ or of Paul, or some psalms" before reciting the Lord's Prayer (LW 43:193–94) and then going back over the individual petitions in more detail. Luther focused on the three chief parts of the catechism—Ten Commandments, Apostles' Creed, and Lord's Prayer—to shape prayers. He described how he used the Ten Commandments to shape prayer: "I divide each commandment into four parts. . . . That is, I think of each commandment as, first, instruction, which is really what it is intended to be, and consider what the Lord God demands of me so earnestly. Second, I turn it into a thanksgiving; third, a confession; and fourth, a prayer" (LW 43:200). Luther included similar advice for praying the Apostles' Creed and the Lord's Prayer. He also cautioned against too many words: "Take care, however, not to undertake all of this or so much that one becomes weary in spirit. Likewise, a good prayer should not be lengthy or drawn out, but frequent and ardent" (LW 43:209).

Often Luther cited biblical examples to teach both form and content of prayer and to remind his listeners that God does indeed answer. Commenting on Lot's request while fleeing Sodom (Gen. 19:17–22), Luther taught how to structure a prayer. The three parts of Lot's petition showed "all the requirements of a good prayer."

> The first requirement of a good prayer is that it give thanks to God and recall in the heart and in words the benefits you have received from God. . . . In the rules of rhetoric this is called gaining goodwill, which is best brought about by praise and giving thanks. In the second place, there is either the complaint or the mention of the need. . . . In the third place, Lot states what he wants granted to him; . . . he enlarges on this request in an excellent manner by giving particulars. (LW 3:288–89)

Many other biblical examples appealed to Luther. In *On War against the Turk* (1529), he wrote:

> In exhorting to prayer we must also introduce words and examples from the Scriptures which show how strong and mighty a man's prayer has sometimes been; for example, Elijah's prayer which St. James praises [Jas. 5:17]; the prayers of Elisha and other prophets; of kings David, Solomon, Asa, Jehoshaphat, Jesias, Hezekiah, etc.; the story of how God promised Abraham that he would spare the land of Sodom and Gomorrah for the sake of five righteous men. For the prayer of a righteous man can do much if it be persistent, St. James says in his Epistle [Jas. 5:16]. (LW 46:173–74)

Luther believed Christians should pray at all times and particularly in all times of need. He encouraged a forthright statement of needs and requests. In his Small Catechism his explanation of the fourth petition, "Give us today our daily bread," gives a glimpse of the things for which believers may pray, for "daily bread" means "everything included in the necessities and nourishment for our bodies, such as food, drink, clothing, shoes, house, farm, fields, livestock, money, property, an upright spouse, upright children, upright members of the household, upright and faithful rulers, good government, good weather, peace, health, decency, honor, good friends, faithful neighbors, and the like" (*BC* 357). Luther thought prayer in times of distress to be absolutely essential and a necessary exercise of faith. Instead of running away from the God who seems to have forgotten the believer and/or is allowing awful things to happen, Luther urged that all should turn toward this God in distress. God wants to hear prayer, so much so that he sends events into believers' lives that drive them to pray. Luther explained in his commentary on Ps. 118:

> Let everyone know most assuredly and not doubt that God does not send him this distress to destroy him. . . . He wants to drive him to pray, to implore, to fight, to exercise his faith, to learn another aspect of God's person than before, to accustom himself to do battle even with the devil and with sin, and by the grace of God to be victorious. Without this experience we could never learn the meaning of faith, the Word, Spirit, grace, sin, death, or the devil. (LW 14:60)

While Luther encouraged persistent prayer, he warned against mindless repetition. In his lectures on 1 John (1527) Luther complained, "In the past . . . we did not know how to pray but knew only how to chatter and to read prayers. God pays no attention to this" (LW 30:324).

Prayer may include contradicting God and boldly asking God to change his revealed will, Luther believed. Such forthright petitions contrasted sharply with what Luther termed "murmuring." "It is murmuring, however, when we have been offended by a perplexing situation and ask God why He does this or that in such a manner. . . . We must not be inquirers into the wherefore and say to God: 'Wherefore art Thou doing this in such a manner?' We must obey His will; and if anything in His actions offends us, we must pray" (LW 3:291). While allowing for lament and honest expressions of the believer's situation, Luther pointed his listeners away from speculating about God's purposes and rather encouraged them into active interaction with God that may include boldly asking God to change his will.

Set times and habits of prayer could be helpful to the Christian, according to Luther. His Small Catechism lays out the practices of morning and evening prayers as well as prayers before and after meals. He advised his barber that prayer ought to be "the first business of the morning and the last at night" (LW 43:193).

Luther discussed prayer in connection with many themes. Prayer (*Oratio*) was the first of the three steps (*Oratio, Meditatio, Tentatio*) in studying the Bible (*Preface to German Writings*, LW 34:285–87). Luther advised to "straightway despair of your reason and understanding" and instead "kneel down . . . and pray to God with real humility and earnestness, that he through his dear Son may give you his Holy Spirit, who will enlighten you, lead you, and give you understanding." In *An Order of Mass and Communion for the Church at Wittenberg* (1523), Luther commented on the prayers used in worship. While firmly rejecting the canon of the Mass, Luther translated, used, adapted, and wrote many collects and prayers for worship. Prayer is one of the seven signs of the church, Luther declares in *On the Councils and the Church* (1539): "The holy Christian people are externally recognized by prayer, public praise, and thanksgiving to God" (LW 41:164).

Luther made comments on prayer in many contexts: sermons, lectures and commentaries on books of the Bible (such as Jonah and Genesis), his *Personal Prayer Book* (1522), his catechisms (1529), "A Simple Way to Pray" (1535) written for his barber, letters, and even polemical pieces such as *On War against the Turk* (1529). Printing statistics indicate that his works on prayer were popular. For example, Luther's *Personal Prayer Book* was printed seventeen times between 1522 and 1525 and at least forty-four times by the end of the century.

In the Lutheran confessional writings, prayer is most prominent in Luther's catechisms, but other writings also discuss prayer. The Augsburg Confession (1530) and the Apology of the Augsburg Confession (1531) specifically reject prayer to the saints (art. 21) as do the Smalcald Articles (1537, part 2, art. 2), on the grounds that Scripture does not teach or command such prayer. The Solid Declaration (1577, art. 2) discusses with approval "prayers . . . for divine instruction, illumination, and sanctification" (SD 2.15; BC 546).

Lutheran theologians continued to use catechisms, prayer books, sermons, and hymns to teach prayer. One of the most popular and persistent prayer books in Lutheran practice was Johann Habermann's (1516–90) *Betbüchlein*, first published in 1567 and reprinted numerous times in many languages in the following centuries. Its first part offers eight prayers for each day, including morning and evening prayers, a thanksgiving, two petitions, two intercessions, and a prayer for protection. The second part contains twenty-six prayers, including some to be used by people in various estates, such as pastor, parishioner, ruler, subject, husband, mother, child, maid, young man or woman, widow and widower, and some for particular situations such as in times of storm, sickness, and before and after the Lord's Supper. Johann Arndt's (1555–1621) *Paradiß-Gärtlein* (The garden of paradise), first published in 1612, was an enduring and influential Lutheran prayer book. Lutheran Pietism cultivated the practice of prayer within groups centered on the study of Scripture and among individuals in personal devotion. Pietism believed the best prayer was inner and heartfelt. Ole Hallesby's (1870–1961) prayer book (1927) in this tradition is one of the most prominent in recent centuries.

Bibliography

Luther's Works: *Appeal for Prayer against the Turks* (1541). LW 43:219–41; *The Collects.* LW 53:127–46; *An Exposition of the Lord's Prayer for Simple Laymen* (1519). LW 42:19–81; *On Rogationtide Prayer and Procession* (1519). LW 42:87–93; *An Order of Mass and Communion for the Church at Wittenberg* (1523). LW 53:15–40; *Personal Prayer Book* (1522). LW 43:11–45; *A Simple Way to Pray* (1535). LW 43:193–211; The Small Catechism and The Large Catechism. In *The Book of Concord: The Confessions of the Evangelical Lutheran Church*, ed. R. Kolb and T. J. Wengert, 345–480. Fortress, 2000; **General Works:** Bayer, O. "Promise and Prayer." In *Martin Luther's Theology: A Contemporary Interpretation*, 346–54. Eerdmans, 2008; Brown, C. B. "Devotional Life in Hymns, Liturgy, Music, and Prayer." In *Lutheran Ecclesiastical Culture, 1550–1675*, 205–58. Brill, 2008; Ebeling, G. "Beten als Wahrnehmen der Wirklichkeit des Menschen, wie Luther es lehrte und lebte." *Lutherjahrbuch* 66 (1999): 151–66; Haemig, M. J. "Jehoshaphat and His Prayer among Sixteenth-Century Lutherans." *Church History* 73 (2004): 522–35; Haemig, M. J. "Prayer as Talking Back to God in Luther's Genesis Lectures." *LQ*, NS 23 (2009): 270–95; Koch, T. *Johann Habermanns "Betbüchlein" im Zusammenhang seiner Theologie.* Mohr Siebeck, 2001; Lehmann, M. *Luther and Prayer.* Northwestern, 1985; Peters, A. *Commentary on Luther's Catechism: Lord's Prayer.* Concordia, 2011; Schulz, F. *Die Gebete Luthers: Edition, Bibliographie und Wirkungsgeschichte.* G. Mohn, 1976; Wengert, T. J. "Luther on Prayer in the Large Catechism." In *The Pastoral Luther: Essays on Martin Luther's Practical Theology*, ed. T. J. Wengert, 171–97. Eerdmans, 2009.

MARY JANE HAEMIG

Preaching

As Martin Luther matured in his preaching practice and understanding, he established a theology of preaching that has become a hallmark of Lutheran practice and tradition. It is characterized by a sensitivity to law and gospel, a focus on a theology of the cross, and a sacramental understanding of preaching as the conveyer of the living presence of Christ. He also brought changes to the practice of preaching, his innovation extending not only to a theological understanding of the purpose and power of preaching but also to sermon design and style. Although, by his own admission, he came to preaching reluctantly, through encouragement by his mentor, Johann von Staupitz, Luther began to realize his role as a Bible scholar to be primarily that of a preacher. It became a central place where he worked out his theology and showed his care for God's people.

Luther and his Wittenberg colleagues had ample opportunity to practice their homiletical craft. The Wittenberg congregation heard three sermons each Sunday (early morning Epistle sermons, midmorning Gospel sermons, and afternoon sermons on the Old Testament or the catechism). Each weekday presented further preaching obligations, with the preaching staff working continuously through books of the Bible (at Vespers, Matthew on Wednesdays, and John on Saturdays). In addition, Luther preached during his travels, in his home for family and friends, and on occasions such as funerals, baptisms, and weddings; he delivered classroom expository lectures on the books of the Bible that were to some extent sermonic in nature. Though Luther was only one among several preachers in Wittenberg, he preached an estimated four thousand sermons or more between the beginning of his preaching career in 1510 and his last sermon, given three days before his death in 1546. His preaching corpus also includes several books known as postils, containing material that today would be called homiletical aids.

We have access to Luther's sermons by virtue of notes taken by his students and friends. While Luther preached exclusively in German, this collection of sermon transcriptions, twenty-three hundred in number, was written in a mixture of German and Latin by his literate auditors. These notes reveal how Luther in his earliest preaching moved from the Scholastic methods he had been taught to a preaching style that was less academic and more accessible to his lay audiences.

Early in his career, Luther subscribed to the hermeneutical method popular in the medieval church, the Quadriga. It was a fourfold method of interpreting Scripture that allowed the exegete to escape the literal for the spiritual, that is, for the doctrinal, moral, and eschatological senses of the text. For the Roman church, preaching typically had the function of explaining doctrine or pointing to the sacraments of penance or the Eucharist. Preaching was understood to serve the sacraments, especially the sacrament of penance. Already in his biblical lectures Luther moved away from the Quadriga and also developed his own approach to preaching, based in part on an expository approach found in the church fathers. Emphasizing the literal sense of Scripture, he came to view the purposes of preaching to be conveying the promises of God, glorifying Christ, and proclaiming the good news of his life, death, and resurrection. Luther's goal was to use Scripture to teach and exhort his listeners to deeper faith.

Contrary to the Scholastic style of preaching of his day, wherein a theme was subdivided and examined, developing into points and sub-points, Luther settled on an expository form of preaching (*auslegende Predigt*), which laid out, often word by word, the meaning of the text, similar in some ways to ancient patristic forms. Eschewing theoretical and scholarly language, Luther preached in a simple manner, speaking heart to heart in a way that even the common, illiterate people in his audience could grasp. He aimed his preaching at shopkeepers, farmers, milkmaids, and common laborers rather than simply at the many scholars who were part of the Wittenberg congregation.

Luther's sermon preparation began with the study of Scripture; on Sundays or feast days this was a lectionary text. From there he sought the heart (*Sinnmitte*) or kernel (*Kern*) of the text, which he then developed into an outline (*Konzept*) that he would loosely follow in the pulpit. Although he was well trained in rhetoric and used many rhetorical tropes, he avoided the rigid structure and artistry of classical grandiloquence, fearing that such devices would obscure the message of the sermon or draw attention to the preacher. Yet he frequently used two techniques. He would employ antithesis to build tensions in his sermons between propositions, for example, between law and gospel, sin and grace, or God and evil. He also employed the use of improvised dialogue to enliven the biblical narratives that were so much a part of Luther's preaching.

In the pulpit, Luther was known to be articulate yet plainspoken, impassioned, humorous, and affective. Because preaching was, for him, a battle for souls, his preaching was powerful and persuasive. His prepared *Konzept* allowed Luther to stay near the center of his preaching intention, yet was used so loosely that his sermons were delivered with daring disarray. Luther's preaching was idiosyncratic, yet deeply founded on theological commitments that guided his practice and set forth a theological tradition for Lutheran preaching that is largely still in place. His first commitment was to the Scriptures.

Because the purpose of preaching is to proclaim Christ, Luther sought Christ in all of Scripture for the sake of faith. The Old Testament was interpreted in light of the messianic fulfillment. The Psalms were understood to reflect Christ's voice and the voice of the believer in Christ. And the entire New Testament was a source for proclaiming the passion and resurrection of Jesus for the contemporary hearer. Whether preaching on the Law, the Prophets, the Epistles, or the Gospels, Luther proclaimed the promise of God's love and salvation in Christ. Following the apostle Paul, Luther proclaimed a theology of the cross, emphasizing that Christ's power is made manifest in weakness and his glory is seen most tellingly on the cross.

Closely tied to his focus on Christ was Luther's understanding that in preaching, the living Word of Christ is heard. When the preacher speaks, it is God's own voice making Christ known. So strongly is this etched into the tradition of Lutheran preaching that Bonhoeffer would later say that when the preacher speaks, it is as if Christ himself were walking among the people in the congregation. With Luther, he believed in a kind of "real presence" of Christ in proclamation.

The most central theological commitment for Lutheran preachers has come from Luther's own belief that every sermon needed to contain the law and the gospel. For people who are *simul iustus et peccator* (simultaneously righteous and sinner), the Holy Spirit uses the law to lead them to know their need of the gospel, terrify them, put the old creature to death and to turn them to Christ for forgiveness and salvation. This remains a key commitment for preaching that lies within the Lutheran tradition.

Later Lutheran preachers did not always follow Luther's example, although preachers like Joachim Mörlin of the Reformation's second generation understood the centrality of the proclamation "for you." Many preachers, however, were also influenced by Philip Melanchthon's writings on preaching. Some, such as Georg Major, professor at Wittenberg and preacher at the Castle Church, used *loci communes* (commonplaces) to identify the main themes of a sermon. The central thrust of preaching the gospel, to provide comfort to the terrified conscience, was still preserved, especially in the unique history of Lutheran funeral sermons. In later centuries, the Orthodox preacher's concern for right doctrine and the Pietist's concern for moving the heart toward regeneration often obscured Luther's insights. Nevertheless, through the unbroken publication of Luther's postils, commentaries of the appointed Sunday and festival texts, Lutheran preachers had access to Luther's homiletical work. With the Luther Renaissance and a renewed interest in Luther's rhetoric, scholars have once again discovered Luther's contributions to preaching.

See also Bible Interpretation; Law and Gospel; Theology of the Cross; Word of God

Bibliography

Edwards, O. C., Jr. *A History of Preaching.* Abingdon, 2004; Gritsch, E. W., and R. W. Jenson. *Lutheranism: The Theological Movement and Its Confessional Writings.* Fortress, 1976; Kittelson, J. M. *Luther the Reformer: The Story of the Man and His Career.* Augsburg, 1986; Leroux, N. R. *Luther's Rhetoric: Strategies and Style from the Invocavit Sermons.* Concordia, 2002; Marius, R. *Martin Luther: The Christian between God and Death.* Harvard University Press, 1999; Meuser, F. W. *Luther the Preacher.* Augsburg, 1983; Old, H. O. *The Reading and Preaching of the Scriptures in the Worship of Christian Church: The Age of the Reformation.* Vol. 4. Eerdmans, 2002; O'Malley, J. W. "Luther the Preacher." In *The Martin Luther Quincentennial,* ed. G. Dünnhaupt, 3–16. Wayne State University Press for Michigan Germanic Studies, 1985.

CLAYTON J. SCHMIT

Predestination

Martin Luther (1483–1546) and the Evangelical Lutheran confessions (1580) hold the doctrine of justification to be the *praecipuus locus* (chief topic), the heart and lifeblood of the Christian faith. Indeed, the divine word of absolution, imparting free forgiveness of sin on account of Jesus Christ, *is* "the very voice of the gospel" (Ap 11.2). It is an effective word (*verbum efficax*) that "brings not the shadow of eternal things but the eternal blessings themselves" (Ap 7; 8.15). Therefore Lutherans treat predestination not as an isolated doctrine but in direct relation to justification by faith alone.

Luther treats predestination in *De servo arbitrio* (1525), in the context of his debate with Erasmus over free choice. There Luther describes the God who "has not bound himself by his word, but has kept himself free over all things," the God who "neither deplores death nor takes away death, but works life, death, and all in all." Luther's distinction between God hidden (*Deus absconditus*) and God revealed (*Deus revelatus*), between God in his word (*Deus indutus*) and God outside of it (*Deus exutus*), "between the word of God and God himself"—such distinction has sometimes been misinterpreted as a speculative concept alien to and inconsistent with Luther's *theologia crucis*. For Karl Holl (1866–1926) the distinction concerned only finite humanity's epistemological limits. For Albrecht Ritschl (1822–89) it was a nominalist carryover from medieval Scholasticism; for John Dillenberger (1918–2008), a psychological extension of Luther's own anguished conscience; for Reinhold Seeberg (1859–1935), merely ontological; for Karl Barth (1886–1968), dualistic; for Werner Elert (1885–1954), logical; and for Paul Althaus (1888–1966), a mere inference. But for Luther, God preached and God not-preached was a necessary theological assertion demanded by the proclamation of the gospel itself. It distinguished the activity of God—first outside of his word, in himself (*in se*), and only then within his word, "for you" (*pro te*). According to Luther, it is truly God himself who is God for us. However, this identification is not a universal and self-evident principle but is true only within the particular setting of proclamation, so that there is no rule for the correspondence of the economic to the immanent Trinity. Nor is God's alien work of wrath and judgment (*opus alienum*) always and everywhere

configured within the necessary, preliminary movement toward God's proper work of mercy and grace (*opus proprium*). Instead, Luther begins with the one God whose two words of law and gospel ground faith in the concrete, external, and divinely instituted means of grace. Through the word of the law, hearers are taught to flee *from* God as he is hidden and to flee *to* God as he is revealed. It is therefore the selfsame God from whom (fear) and to whom (love and trust) the sinner flees. Since this God, who alone is true, is "completely one and completely simple," he is never partially present in his promises, but through them bestows all that he is and has wholly and completely. If one has the revealed God in his promise, then one also has the hidden God together with the God who has been revealed. Consequently, the wrath of God is not merely epistemological but is a reality that must either overtake human creatures or be overcome. But how can God's wrath be overcome? Where can one find a gracious God? Neither a person's choice nor the church's dogmatic decree would suffice. It is in the absolving word alone that the hidden God becomes the God revealed "for me"—not by "correspondence" but by contradiction: killing and making alive, wounding and healing, destroying the old world and bringing forth a new creation. God is God, and the sinner cannot have it otherwise. The sinner's one hope is that God would come up against God; that God would be so for the sinner in his promise that he would be against himself in his judgment. The silent being of God is conquered only in his becoming spoken.

Though it may sound counterintuitive, Luther's *Lectures on Genesis* (ca. 1540) describe predestination as the one true pastoral care of souls (*Seelsorge*). When preached to the troubled conscience, it announces the evangelical will of God, which cannot be thwarted. The distinguishing feature of Luther's doctrine is that faith's certainty is found not in the internal awareness of the one who hears, but in the external word (*externum verbum*) of the God who speaks (*Deus dicit*)—the God whose promises do not deceive (see Num. 23:19; Titus 1:2; Heb. 6:18). Where faith takes leave of God's promise, however, there the question must inevitably arise: "Am I one of the elect?" But the sinner is not asked to examine what one has ("Do you have faith?") or has done ("Do you have works?"), but only to consider what God has done unto oneself: "Have you been baptized? Have you received the absolving word of forgiveness? Have you partaken of the flesh and blood of your Lord Jesus Christ in the Supper?" Thus proclamation is election itself. Faith therefore trusts not in election as such, but in the promise that elects. "Listen to the incarnate Son," writes Luther, "and predestination will present itself of its own accord." Predestination is what proclamation does.

Philip Melanchthon (1497–1560) used a mediating approach to explain this Evangelical teaching: "Everywhere I speak as if [*quasi*] predestination followed our faith and works." He experimented with "three causes" of justification (the Holy Spirit, the Word, and the human will) in light of charges of Manichaeism by Roman opponents who suspected Stoicism in Calvin's writings, and because of his concern for theodicy and the need to defend God's goodness in the face of evil. This planted the seed for later Lutherans to suggest that predestination is always *intuitu fidei* (in view of faith).

Nikolaus von Amsdorf (1483–1565) charged Melanchthon's approach with leading to synergism in such Scholastic distinctions as that between relative necessity (*necessitas consequentis*) and absolute necessity (*necessitas consequentiae*), terms that Luther used in *The Bondage of the Will*, or between God's antecedent will (*voluntas antecedens*) and consequent will (*voluntas consequens*). Instead, Amsdorf asserted that God elects and hardens (as in the case of Pharaoh) on the basis of his will, which is entirely one and simple. Whether God will have mercy on any single person depends, in turn, on receiving the divine word of promise. However, in his attempt to preserve the monergistic working of God in justification, Amsdorf's warning opened

the temptation to speculate abstractly about "double predestination" apart from and prior to proclamation. Johannes Brenz (1499–1570) imagined that election took place "before the creation of the world" in the "secret, divine chancellery." Proclamation then merely revealed an eternal decision.

In the wake of seven sermons published by Cyriacus Spangenberg in 1567, the doctrine of predestination briefly became a matter of public controversy in Saxony. Spangenberg affirmed the unmerited favor of God as the sole cause of justification; thus he denied any contribution of the human will in receiving God's favor. When the faculty of Wittenberg rejected Spangenberg's teaching in favor of their own appropriation of Melanchthon's categories, Martin Chemnitz's (1522–86) defense became the basis for an article in the Formula of Concord on predestination.

Chemnitz proposed a synthesis of Melanchthon and Luther. Predestination gives sweet comfort to the Christian since justification is by faith alone. Only through the proper distinction of law and gospel can this be known. To the law pertains damnation, whose singular cause and origin is the sinner's willful rejection of divine mercy. To the gospel pertains election, which gives faith, with its blessed consolation in the forgiveness of sins. With Luther, Chemnitz concluded that faith does not properly trust in election, but in the electing promise. With Melanchthon, Chemnitz concluded that God is the cause of all that is good, while God merely has foreknowledge (*praescentia*) of what is evil. The mark of Chemnitz is easily discernible in the eleventh article of the Formula of Concord. Here the confessional Lutheran writers sought to address what they perceived would become a dividing issue in the future of the Evangelical church: the causal relationship between election and justifying faith. "Am I one of the elect because I have faith? Or do I have faith because I am one of the elect?" Against the Calvinists, who defined election as the unmediated (*nude*) determination of the divine will to save some and to damn others, the formulators taught "that the entire teaching of God's intention, counsel, will, and preordination concerning our redemption, calling, justification, and salvation must be taken as a unity" (FC SD 11.13–14). Christian certainty is never acquired independently of grace, but is always communicated through the divinely ordained means of grace. The act of election in word and sacrament does not merely include God's foreknowledge, according to which God foresees the salvation of the elect, but is itself the cause that "creates, effects, aids, and promotes our salvation" (FC SD 11.8). Predestination is what happens when "the Holy Spirit creates true faith through the hearing of the Word" (FC SD 11.69). As with Luther, predestination is what proclamation does, God electing with the word of his promise "as with a net, through which the elect are snatched out of the jaws of the devil" (FC SD 11.76).

The Orthodox Lutheran dogmaticians of the seventeenth and early eighteenth centuries sought to safeguard this threefold unity between Christ's atoning work, the means of grace that flow from his pierced side, and the faith that the Holy Spirit creates through them. Yet a clear departure came with the phrase *intuitu fidei*. Aegidius Hunnius (1550–1603) first used the phrase in his debate with Samuel Huber (1547–1624), while trying to find a middle way between Calvinism and synergism. He intended to preserve the connection between election and church proclamation. Johann Gerhard (1582–1637) understood *intuitu fidei* to mean that God justifies sinners in view of the faith he himself creates in them—and this always through the ordained means of grace. Faith neither causes nor contributes to election; yet it is also true to say that election occurs neither apart from faith, nor on account of faith, but through faith. Such faith neither compels nor incites the promise of God, but purely and passively receives it. Despite all of this, Gerhard transposed election from the locus of justification and subsumed it under the broader locus on creation and providence.

For that reason Gerhard was closer to Calvinism than to Luther when treating election and reprobation as parallel decrees in God. Conceived as an act in eternity, election is subsumed under the eternal law prior to and outside the proclamation of the gospel. Later, with Abraham Calov (1612–86), Johannes Andreas Quenstedt (1617–88), Johannes Baier (1647–95), and David Hollatz (1648–1713), synergism caught up predestination in an endless causal nexus.

In America, the debate over the causal connection between election and justifying faith continued, producing a split among Lutherans. C. F. W. Walther (1811–87) insisted against his former student F. A. Schmidt (1837–1928) that election was unto faith, and not in view of it. According to Walther, predestination was, properly taught, "the most consolatory of all doctrines." Schmidt accused Walther of leaving no place for human agency and thus of propounding a subtle form of Calvinist determinism. The ensuing confrontation resulted in a fractured Synodical Conference. It also resulted in a distinction between two "forms" of election among Norwegians in the 1880 controversy on election: one form by the preached word, the other by Pontoppidan's (1698–1764) version of *intuitu fidei*.

Werner Elert (1885–1954) sought to recapture the existential dynamic of Luther's doctrine. Gustaf Wingren (1910–2000) reclaimed the link between election and preaching. Gerhard Forde (1927–2005) recognized that the problem of the unpreached God is not his evident absence (atheism), but his inescapable presence (antitheism). What possible remedy is there for sinners who find themselves confronted by this wrathful God? The only solution to the absolute is actual absolution. Theology either drives to the electing act of proclamation, or it surrenders itself to speculation and the endless attempt to include some human cause of justification. God, in the fullness of time, actually arrives at his (pre)destination: "You." Oswald Bayer (b. 1939) has recognized that the terrifying incomprehensibility of God

(*Deus absconditus*) is not to be treated in a way that logically parallels the God who reveals himself (*Deus revelatus*). The line of causal thinking that extends from Melanchthon to the present-day controversies over election was predestined to fail precisely because it turns the ear away from the contingent and historical event of proclamation, in which the promise of Jesus Christ is actually given, to a timeless situation that is not our own. That would be an imaginary time when the law did not accuse before sin, and before a preacher was needed in place and time. But this is not possible, and ultimately unnecessary, since predestination is what proclamation does, the unthwartable promise of election—God in his words for you rather than God outside his words in himself.

See also Bayer, Oswald; Chemnitz, Martin; Elert, Werner; Forde, Gerhard; Free Will; Justification; Law and Gospel; Norwegian-American Lutheranism; Predestination (Election) Controversy

Bibliography

Luther's Works: *De servo arbitrio* (1525). LW 33; *Lectures on Genesis: Chapters 26–30* (ca. 1543). LW 5:42–50. **General Works:** Arand, C., R. Kolb, and J. Nestingen, eds. *The Lutheran Confessions: History and Theology of the Book of Concord*. Fortress, 2012; Bayer, O. *Martin Luther's Theology*. Eerdmans, 2008; Chemnitz, M. *Loci Theologici*. Trans. J. A. O. Preus. Vol. 2. Concordia, 1989; Chemnitz, M. *Ministry, Word, and Sacraments: An Enchiridion*. Trans. L. Poellot. Concordia, 1981; Elert, W. *The Structure of Lutheranism*. Concordia, 1962; Forde, G. *Theology Is for Proclamation*. Fortress, 1990; Gerhard, J. *Theological Commonplaces*. Vol. 10. Concordia, 2013. Vol. 26. Concordia, 2011; Melanchthon, P. *The Chief Theological Topics: Loci Praecipui Theologici 1559*. Trans. J. A. O. Preus. 2nd ed. Concordia, 2010; Melanchthon, P. *Commonplaces: Loci communes 1521*. Trans. C. Preus. Concordia, 2014; Melanchthon, P. *Loci communes 1543*. Trans. J. A. O. Preus. Concordia, 1992; Thuesen, P. J. *Predestination: The American Career of a Contentious Doctrine*. Oxford, 2009; Wingren, G. *The Living Word*. Muhlenberg, 1960.

STEVEN D. PAULSON AND D. JEROME KLOTZ

Predestination (Election) Controversy

A series of theological disputes among conservative American Lutherans during the latter part of the nineteenth century came to be called the Predestination (Election) Controversy. Traditionally, Lutheran theology has seen this doctrine as of lesser importance; though article 11 of the Formula of Concord (1577) addresses the topic, it is mainly concerned with differentiating the Lutheran position from that of the Calvinists. In the late nineteenth century, strictly confessional Lutherans in America formed a number of different denominations, including the Missouri Synod, the Iowa Synod, and Ohio Synod among the Germans, as well as the closely allied Norwegian Synod. In 1872 some of these groups were generally allied in the formation of a cooperative body, the Synodical Conference. Ongoing theological discussions among these different groups ranged over many fine points of confessional Lutheran theology.

In 1877 Henry Allwardt and Frederick Stellhorn of Missouri and Frederick Schmidt of the Norwegian Synod accused the leading theologian of the Missouri Synod, C. F. W. Walther, of teaching a Calvinist version of predestination. This was a very serious charge, especially given the confessional Lutheran antipathy toward Calvinism, and Walther opened a heated debate with his opponents, which quickly also involved theologians of the Iowa and Ohio Synods. The dispute has been characterized in this way: "The man who believes in Christ and his atoning merit is . . . predestined to be saved. But shall we say that God's predestination is the cause of his faith and his salvation, or shall we say that his faith is the cause of his predestination? The Missourians took the first alternative, . . . [insisting] that a man cannot believe in Christ unless God causes him to do so. . . . [Missouri's opponents] took the second alternative, and insisted that God elects man to salvation 'in view of his faith' in the merits of Christ" (Wentz 206). Walther's opponents charged him with determinism and fatalism, along with Calvinism. Walther and his supporter charged these critics with a position on predestination that was synergistic and semi-Pelagian. This theological battle raged on into the 1880s and was joined by other confessional Lutheran theologians, including Sigmund and Gottfried Fritschel of the Iowa

Synod and Matthias Loy of the Ohio Synod, who also opposed Walther. Allwardt and Stellhorn, the original Missouri critics of Walther, left that synod and joined the Ohio Synod. Increasingly this battle became a struggle between the various German-American confessional Lutheran denominations, and strained relations between these synods, resulting in the departure of the Ohio Synod from the Synodical Conference in 1882, and likewise the Norwegian Synod in 1883. This dispute cemented a long-running antipathy between the Missouri Synod, the largest of these denominations, and the Ohio and Iowa Synods.

The second phase of this theological struggle shifted to the congregations of Norwegian-American Lutheranism in the 1880s. Many of the leaders of the confessional Norwegian Synod were closely allied with Walther and the Missouri Synod, but this relationship was not shared by others within the Norwegian Synod, especially Frederick Schmidt and a number of other pastors and lay leaders of the synod. Within the Norwegian Synod about two-thirds seemed to support Missouri's position (the "first form"), while another one-third supported the opponents' position (the "second form"). Unlike with the German-American denominations, this debate within the Norwegian Synod quickly filtered down into the congregations and caused a large number of congregations to adopt one position or the other, or often to split into competing factions. In 1884 the majority tried to make the Missouri position official for the Norwegian Synod (An Accounting), which drove the minority to issue their own document (The Confession). The minority group moved swiftly to form a group known as the Anti-Missouri Brotherhood; it set up a treasury and institutions separate from the Norwegian Synod to support "second form" pastors and seminarians. In 1886–87 this Anti-Missouri group separated from the Norwegian Synod, and in 1890, along with other Norwegian-American Lutheran denominations, formed the United Norwegian Lutheran Church (UNLC). The

antipathy between the UNLC and the Norwegian Synod lingered for a generation, until in 1912 the parties reached a carefully ambiguous resolution, the Madison Agreement (*Opjør*), which stated that, within parameters, both first and second form positions were confessionally Lutheran. This allowed the unification of the Norwegian-American denominations in 1917, although a minority of the Norwegian Synod split off in protest at this point to form the Evangelical Lutheran Synod (the "Little Norwegian Synod") in 1918. Echoes of the Predestination Controversy continued to reverberate among American Lutherans well into the twentieth century.

See also Fritschel, Sigmund and Gottfried; Lutheran Church–Missouri Synod; Norwegian-American Lutheranism; Pontoppidan, Erik Ludvigsen; Predestination; Walther, Carl Ferdinand Wilhelm

Bibliography

Granquist, M. *Lutherans in America: A New History.* Fortress, 2015; Nelson, E. C., and E. Fevold. *The Lutheran Church among the Norwegian Americans.* 2 vols. Augsburg, 1960; Tappert, T., ed. *Lutheran Confession Theology in America, 1840–1880.* Oxford University Press, 1972; Wentz, A. R. *A Basic History of Lutheranism in America.* Rev. ed. Fortress, 1964.

Mark A. Granquist

Preus, Jacob

The American Lutheran professor, seminary president, church president, and translator Jacob ("Jack") A. O. Preus II (1920–94) was born in St. Paul, Minnesota, as the elder son of Jacob ("Jake") A. O. Preus, a two-term Republican governor of that state and an unsuccessful candidate for the United States Senate. After his second term, Jake Preus moved the family to Chicago, where he sold insurance and later helped to found the Lutheran Brotherhood Insurance Company. Jake's sons, Jack and Robert, attended Luther Seminary, St. Paul, an institution of the Evangelical Lutheran Church (ELC), which formed from the merger of several Norwegian synods (1917). Jack Preus graduated in 1945, briefly served an ELC congregation, and then completed a PhD in classics from the University of Minnesota

(1951). He soon left the ELC to join the Evangelical Lutheran Synod (ELS, "the Little Norwegian Synod"), established by conservatives who declined to join the ELC. Like his brother, who had left Luther Seminary to complete his studies at the ELS seminary in Mankato, Minnesota, Jack Preus favored the ELS's perceived stricter orthodoxy. He joined the ELS in 1947, but not before publicly accusing Luther Seminary of harboring teachers of false doctrine.

While working on his PhD, he taught classics and religion at the ELS junior college in Mankato and then served six years as a pastor to several ELS congregations. Throughout that decade he publicly criticized the alleged heresies of non-ELS churches. In 1955 he and his brother were instrumental in leading the ELS to break fellowship with the LCMS, which they accused of tolerating doctrinal errors. Ironically, Robert joined the LCMS in 1957, when he accepted an appointment to its flagship seminary, Concordia, St. Louis, and Jack did so a year later, when he accepted a position at the Synod's "practical" seminary in Springfield, Illinois. A few years later Jack was elected president of that school.

During the 1960s the Preus brothers aligned themselves with LCMS conservatives who attacked various professors, especially at Concordia Seminary, St. Louis, for failing to teach in harmony with "orthodox Lutheran doctrine," such as the complete inerrancy of Scripture. After conservative politicking, especially by Herman Otten (*Christian News*), Jack Preus was unexpectedly elected president of the LCMS at its 1969 convention. His investigations of the majority of Concordia's faculty and its newly elected president, John Tietjen, launched a decade of turmoil within the synod. Preus authorized "A Statement of Scriptural and Confessional Principles," which the 1973 LCMS convention narrowly elevated to near-confessional status. That document was later used as a standard by which the faculty majority's teaching was condemned as "false doctrine which cannot be tolerated in the church of God." Forty-five of fifty professors

were eventually forced out of their positions (they continued as a "seminary-in-exile" or Christ Seminary-Seminex) and were replaced by conservatives. Eventually the ongoing conflict led some pastors and congregations who opposed Preus to leave the Missouri Synod and form the Association of Evangelical Lutheran Churches (1976). Preus himself served as president of the LCMS until 1981. In addition to translating several books by Martin Chemnitz and writing a biography of him, he translated Melanchthon's 1543 *Loci communes*.

See also Lutheran Church–Missouri Synod; Seminex and the Association of Evangelical Lutheran Churches

Bibliography
Adams, J. E. *Preus of Missouri and the Great Lutheran Civil War*. Harper & Row, 1977; Burkee, J. C. *Power, Politics, and the Missouri Synod: A Conflict That Changed American Christianity*. Fortress, 2011.

MATTHEW L. BECKER

Prierias, Sylvester

The Italian Dominican Sylvester Prierias (1456–1527), a professor of theology, carried the title Master of the Sacred Palace and was an early opponent of Luther. Born Sylvester Mazzolini from the Italian village of Prierio, he entered the Dominican order in 1471, where he studied under the famous Thomist Pietro da Bergamo. Prierias became a renowned preacher and lecturer, eventually being appointed regent master at the University of Bologna and vicar general of the Dominican Congregation of Lombardy; later he received a number of clerical offices from Inquisitor of Milan to prior in Cremona and Venice. A prolific writer during these periods, Prierias was eventually called to Rome in 1515 to serve as chair of theology at the Sapienza and Master of the Sacred Palace (the pope's leading theologian), an office that he held until his death.

Until this appointment, Prierias had maintained a relatively high reputation outside of Italy and even in Germany. This, however, was to change when in 1516 Prierias opposed the German humanist Johannes Reuchlin (1455–1522). Luther later criticized Prierias for his position against the famous Hebraist. In May of 1518 the juridical process against Luther commenced in Rome, with Prierias composing his *Dialogus* in response to Luther's Ninety-Five Theses. The *Dialogus*, written in three days and published in June of 1518, articulates five points in which Luther erred, most pertaining to ecclesiology and the power of the pope. Therein, Prierias refers to papal authority as an "infallible rule of faith," reflecting the late medieval "curialist" (as opposed to "conciliar") view of papal authority, finally dogmatized at the First Vatican Council in 1870. This position, however, won him little support in Germany; even Erasmus criticized what he saw as Prierias's mishandling of the Luther affair. For the next two years, Prierias and Luther exchanged tracts, with Prierias composing his *Replica* in November of 1518 and his *Errata et argumenta* in March of 1520, both in response to direct retorts from Luther. During this time, Prierias served on the consistories assembled to deal with the Luther affair. It is likely that he served on the committee that issued *Exsurge Domine*, threatening Luther's excommunication, though it is unknown whether he contributed to *Decet Romanum*, which formally excommunicated Luther. After 1520 Prierias seems to vanish from the Luther scene, instead focusing his attention on other matters in Italy. However, one writing, the *Consilium super reformatione ecclesiae*, written for Pope Adrian VI in 1522 and attributed to a Dominican theologian, arguably belongs to the hand of Prierias. This document later informed theologians at the Council of Trent. After 1524 little information remains of Prierias's activities. In the middle of 1527 he died, the cause unknown.

See also Luther's Roman Catholic Opponents; Reuchlin, Johannes

Bibliography

Fabisch, P., and E. Iserloh, eds. *Dokumente zur Causa Lutheri (1517–1521)*. Vol. 1. CCath 41. Aschendorff, 1988–91; Scionti, J. N. "Sylvester Prierias and His Opposition to Martin Luther." PhD diss., Brown University, 1967; Tavuzzi, M. M. *Prierias: The Life and Works of Silvestro Mazzolini da Priero, 1456–1527.* Duke University Press, 1997; Wicks, J. "Roman Reactions to Luther: The First Year, 1518." *Catholic Historical Review* 69 (1983): 521–62.

Eric J. DeMeuse

Priesthood of All Believers

Although Martin Luther did not use this phrase exactly, he certainly expounded on the meaning of the text in 1 Pet. 2:9: "You are a chosen people, a royal priesthood, a holy nation, God's special possession" (NIV). His understanding of it followed from a number of his key insights: (1) All believers (clergy and lay) are made priests by baptism into Christ their high priest and not by clerical vows. (2) Christians can approach God and Christ directly, without the intervention of priests and saints. That makes them "free lords of all, subject to none." (3) All Christians can pray for and care for each other, not simply rely on priests to do so. (4) All Christians have important callings (vocations) given by God, not just the clergy. (5) A Christian can read the Scriptures directly. Luther translated the Bible into German so laypeople could read the sacred texts. Yet they do so in conversation with other Christians in the church, especially with pastors and scholars. After all, it is "priesthood of all *believers*," not "priesthood of *a believer*."

This first set of meanings apply to the Christian standing before God (*coram Deo*, in God's presence). Luther also offered a set of meanings for our lives in relation to other human beings in the world (*coram mundo*). Believers are priests to their fellow human beings as Christ is priest to them: by mediating the love of God to the neighbor through one's callings or vocations. Thus believers are "servant of all, subject to all." So they are priests in a double fashion, before God and before other human beings.

These understandings had a powerful effect on Western religious and social life. They united clergy and laity into the single body of Christ, activating the laity to take more responsibility for their own spiritual lives; they indicated that lay vocations are just as pleasing to God as clerical vocations; and they opened the Scriptures to millions of devout readers. These insights also gave great dignity to lay callings—marriage, work, citizenship, life in the church—since the laity are as important in conveying God's love as the clergy. This gave religious and moral seriousness to ordinary life in the world, but without undermining the callings of pastors and teachers in the church.

There have been many distortions of Luther's teaching on the priesthood of all believers. One is that everyone can read the Bible on their own and come to true conclusions themselves. This was far from Luther's meaning, which called for a corporate reading of the Bible by the whole church. Proper interpretation relied on scholarly study, right theological interpretation, immersion in the life of the church, and a faithful heart and mind. It was a work of the whole body of Christ, not that of a sole Christian coming to one's own conclusions.

A second distortion obliterates the distinctions between clergy and lay, generally denying any special role for the clergy. But neither was that the teaching of Luther, who in *The Babylonian Captivity of the Church* and the *Address to Christian Nobility* argued that the church sets aside trained people for the special function of preaching the word and administrating the sacraments. "There are indeed priests whom we call ministers. They are chosen from among us and . . . do everything in our name. That is a priesthood that is nothing else than a ministry."

In modern Lutheranism the "priesthood of all believers" is not always strongly emphasized, perhaps because of the individualistic twist that has been given it among some religious groups. But, given the right interpretation, it still contains important meanings.

See also Baptism; Bible Interpretation; Confession (Private) and the Confessional; Ministry; Prayer; Word of God

Bibliography

Nagel, N. "Luther and the Priesthood of All Believers." *Concordia Theological Monthly* 61 (October 1997): 283–84; Wengert, T. *Priesthood, Pastors, Bishops: Public Ministry for the Reformation and Today.* Fortress, 2008.

ROBERT BENNE

Printing in Sixteenth-Century Lutheranism

The invention of printing with moveable type by Johannes Gutenberg in Mainz in the mid-fifteenth century, about forty years before Martin Luther was born, has been called a media revolution. The new technique permanently changed the way learned books were produced, and it created new possibilities of reaching broader audiences. By 1500, about twenty-seven thousand different book titles had been printed, but most were modeled after medieval manuscripts. Only at the beginning of the sixteenth century did the new medium unfold its revolutionary potential and become a mass medium, especially through the mass printing of pamphlets and booklets. While the Ninety-Five Theses were published only three or four times in limited quantities and in Latin, Luther's subsequent German work *Sermon on Indulgences and Grace* (1518) was the first best-selling title by a living author (reprinted more than twenty times) and turned Martin Luther's protest against indulgences into a media event. The medium of printing had found its message. "It was probably first and foremost this 'explosion in production' of printed matter increasingly related more or less directly to the person and concerns of Luther—an explosion which is borne out by the statistical data which has led to the overall interpretation of the Wittenberg Reformation as a media event" (Nieden).

Different factors played a role in this outburst: better printing techniques and cheaper paper made simple prints of one page to four folios—resulting in up to thirty-two pages—affordable for almost everyone, and print runs of more than a thousand copies could be produced within days. Although the average rate of literacy has been estimated at only 5 percent of the total population, in the cities it may have reached 25 percent. The distribution of the new Reformation ideas was not based only on print. Printed matter was integrated into an oral culture where printed texts were read aloud in public places and distributed by traveling news agents. The Evangelical message was preached, sung, learned by heart, and multiplied by the joint reading of texts. Scholars have estimated that a total of ten thousand different books, pamphlets, and broadsheets were printed within the years 1518–30, with a presumed average print run of a thousand copies. This comes to a total of a million prints, or at least one copy for every person with reading ability in the German-speaking lands. A use of vernacular language indicates the emergence of new groups of readers during the early years of the Reformation: While in the fifteenth century the vast majority of texts were printed in Latin, the vernacular became prominent in the first decades of the sixteenth century, especially after 1520. Luther himself wrote in both Latin and German. In 1520 he wrote such popular texts as the *Treatise on Good Works* and *Address to Christian Nobility* in German and even produced the *Freedom of a Christian* in both German and Latin.

Not only had the readership broadened but also the authorship had changed: Reformation booklets and pamphlets were written by learned scholars as well as authors from other ranks of society, including artisans and women. Other Wittenberg scholars, including Andreas Karlstadt, Philip Melanchthon, and Johannes Bugenhagen, published their own works. On the other side, their opponents wrote against them. Together they established what has been called the "Reformation public": a vivid public discussion of religious topics via printing. As early as 1520, Luther had become a best-selling author. His tract *An den christlichen Adel* (Address to Christian nobility) was first printed in four thousand copies, which were torn out of the hands of the booksellers within a few days. His writings were sold not only in Germany but also in many other European countries like Italy, France, Scandinavia, and the Netherlands.

This remained so even after he was banned in 1521, but then some of Luther's writings appeared pseudonymously or anonymously. Among Luther's most popular works were his catechisms (1529), his translation of the New Testament and Bible (1522/34), and his commentary on Sunday texts (the so-called postils of 1522 and following).

After the turmoil of the Peasants' War in 1525–26 and the Diet of Augsburg in 1530, the printing of polemical pamphlets and booklets decreased somewhat, in part because publishers found new ways to increase their own print runs. The printing of polemical tracts saw a new increase after 1548 with the Augsburg Interim and the so-called post-Interim debates among the Protestant theologians, which continued for the next three decades. Scholars have recently emphasized that the shaping of Lutheran theology and the Lutheran confession of faith especially after Luther's death in 1546 took place in public debates conducted in print, which constituted a specific "culture of conflict." The settlement of some of these debates in the Formula of Concord of 1577 became in 1580 the founding document for Lutheran churches all over Europe when the Formula was printed and bound together with other basic texts in the Book of Concord, itself based on earlier collections (called *corpus doctrinae*) from 1560 and later.

But the role of printing for the Lutheran Reformation consisted not only in its use as a mass medium for propagating the new message, for religious polemics, and for shaping the theology; devotional books—including catechisms, hymnals, postils and other sermon collections, and above all Bible translations—played an even more important role and saw higher print runs and numbers of editions. Beginning with the "September testament," Luther's new German translation of the New Testament was first published in September 1522 and continued as a joint work of Wittenberg theologians until Luther's death; the complete Bible edition appeared in 1534 and was printed in hundreds of editions. It became overwhelmingly important for public reading in worship and private devotion and influenced the development of the modern German language. Printed songbooks for domestic as well as congregational use changed the way of singing within the church. Luther's Small Catechism became the basic schoolbook for elementary schools, and printed sermons on the occasion of weddings or funerals turned into a typical Lutheran genre of the late sixteenth and seventeenth centuries. One can say without exaggeration that the Lutheran confessional culture of the sixteenth century was dominated by the printed word. The importance of print for spreading the Lutheran movement and establishing Lutheran churches can hardly be overestimated.

See also Bible Translations; Luther's Bible

Bibliography

Dingel, I. "Pruning the Vines, Plowing Up the Vineyard: The Sixteenth-Century Culture of Controversy between Disputation and Polemic." In *The Reformation as Christianization*, ed. A. M. Johnson and J. A. Maxfield, 397–408. Mohr Siebeck, 2012; Edwards, M. U., Jr. *Printing, Propaganda, and Martin Luther*. University of California Press, 1994; Moeller, B. *Luther-Rezeption: Kirchenhistorische Aufsätze zur Reformationsgeschichte*. Ed. J. Schilling. Vandenhoeck & Ruprecht, 2001; Nieden, M. "The Wittenberg Reformation as a Media Event." In *EGO: European History Online*. Leibniz Institute of European History (IEG), 2012. http://ieg-ego.eu/en/threads/european-media/european-media-events/marcel-nieden-the-wittenberg-reformation-as-a-media-event; Pettegree, A. *Brand Luther: 1517, Printing, and the Making of the Reformation*. Pelican, 2015; Würgler, A. *Medien in der Frühen Neuzeit*. Oldenbourg, 2009.

HENNING P. JÜRGENS

Prophecy

As a professor of Old Testament, Luther took seriously scriptural passages indicating how ancient Israel struggled in establishing a criterion for distinguishing the true prophet from the false. Throughout the Genesis lectures, he frequently criticized accounts of voices and visions and preferred *prisca theologia*: that the promise of the Messiah had been handed down from Adam to the present through preaching. Prophecy for Luther had little, if anything, to do with religious hallucination; for him,

prophecy is preaching the promise of God to a particular people. Although on occasion Luther did admit that the Holy Spirit could work outside of the means of grace, for him this was rare, bordering on the impossible, and always subject to the Word of God.

Drawing on Rom. 1:2–4, he regarded prophecy as the Spirit's preaching of the gospel that God spoke once and for all in raising Jesus from the dead (Prenter 111–12). This word from God tells a messianic story that constitutes a recognizable event (LW 40:358); it comes as news from outside the self to unite with the self and so to transform the existing self. The "prophetic" word is news that is truly good: "the pure gospel, the noble and precious treasure of our salvation. This gift evokes faith and a good conscience in the inner man," as Luther wrote against hallucination *redivivus* in the "heavenly prophets" of his time (LW 40:139; cf. SA 322–33).

Since the gospel's news of Christ's coming in mercy is not known innately, "outwardly [God] deals with us through the oral word of the gospel and the material signs" of baptism and the Lord's Supper. "Inwardly he deals with us through the Holy Spirit, faith, and other gifts. . . . The inward experience follows and is effected by the outward. . . . Observe carefully . . . this order, for everything depends on it" (LW 40:146). The sequence is essential; it reflects the narrative structure of this new birth by which true prophecy is recognized and distinguished from imposters. If believers "tear down the bridge . . . by which the Spirit might come," we end up teaching "not how the Spirit comes to you but how you come to the Spirit" (LW 40:146). Then they give heed to some other spirit than the Spirit who led Jesus in obedience to his Father's will for the disobedient.

Luther tests the spirits (1 John 4:1–2) by the external Word: just such disputation constitutes theology's essence and how its preaching is prophetic. Dietrich Bonhoeffer's "Bethel Confession" (Hinlicky, *Verbum Externum*) announced at the outset: "Only through the

Holy Spirit do we hear the word of God from the Bible. But this Spirit itself comes to us only through the word of the Scriptures in their entirety, and therefore can never, except by 'enthusiasm' (*Schwärmerei*), be separated from this word" (*Berlin*, 365). This back-and-forth between the Word from the Scriptures and the Spirit's contemporary preaching and persuading to faith in it explicitly grounded Luther's external Word in trinitarian theology (*Berlin*, 382–83; Hinlicky, "Theological Circle").

As the Holy Spirit is the Spirit "who spoke by the prophets" and in the fullness of time *told forth* the crucified Jesus as the Christ, the Son of God, the Holy Spirit *is* the Spirit of the Word, even as the Word incarnate declares the Spirit's work for believers to receive the gift of faith (John 16). In this dynamic version of the Augustinian rule that "the external works of the Trinity are indivisible," genuine prophecy is discerned, yet precisely not as new revelation apart from the Word incarnate, which would be in Luther's words *enthusiasmus*, worship of the god within.

See also Scripture; Word of God

Bibliography

Bonhoeffer, D. *Berlin, 1932–1933*. Dietrich Bonhoeffer Works 12. Ed. L. Rasmussen. Fortress, 2009; Hinlicky, P. R. "The Theological Circle" section of "Luther's Antidocetism in the *Disputatio de divinitate et humanitate Christi* (1540)." In *Creator est creatura: Luthers Christologie als Lehre von der Idiomenkommunikation*, ed. O. Bayer and B. Gleede, 169–77. De Gruyter, 2007; Hinlicky, P. R. "*Verbum Externum*: Dietrich Bonhoeffer's Bethel Confession." In *International Bonhoeffer Interpretations*, ed. R. Wüstenberg, 189–215. Lang, 2012; Prenter, R. *Spiritus Creator*. Trans. J. M. Jensen. Muhlenberg, 1953.

PAUL R. HINLICKY

Prussia

Prussia was located on the Baltic Sea, between Pomerania, Poland, Lithuania, and the Duchy of Moscow. It was a bulwark of Lutheranism in Eastern Europe. In the thirteenth century, the region was conquered by Knights of the Teutonic Order. After wars against the Kingdom of Poland, in 1466 Prussia was divided into two parts: one controlled by the Polish king,

and the other belonging to the Order. In 1525 the Grand Master of the Teutonic Knights, Albrecht von Hohenzollern (1490–1568), secularized the order in Prussia, converted to Lutheranism, and as a "duke in Prussia" swore allegiance to the King of Poland. Prussia was then officially divided into Royal Prussia, a part of the Polish monarchy, and Ducal Prussia, a vassal of the Polish king. The Lutheran Reformation was introduced in both regions: in Ducal Prussia, officially by Duke Albrecht, and in Royal Prussia, unofficially, though with tacit agreement from city councils.

Ducal Prussia became the first Protestant Duchy in Europe. In the course of political struggle with the Order of the Teutonic Knights, the Duchy was outlawed by the emperor (1532), however, without any further consequences. Since Albrecht Friedrich, the son and successor of Duke Albrecht, showed some signs of mental disorder by 1572, his cousin, Georg Friedrich of Brandenburg-Kulmbach, was appointed regent (1578). Consequently the regency over Prussia came to the line of the Hohenzollern family, which ruled in Brandenburg as margraves and electors in the Empire. Finally Johann Sigismund of Brandenburg-Kulmbach became elector of Brandenburg (1608) and duke in Prussia (1611). In 1657 the Duchy of Prussia gained sovereignty. In 1701 the elector of Brandenburg, Friedrich Wilhelm, was crowned in Königsberg as the "King of Prussia."

Albrecht von Hohenzollern met Martin Luther and Andreas Osiander (1498–1552) in 1523. After initial meetings, Luther sent Johannes Briesmann (1488–1549) and Paul Speratus (1484–1551) to Königsberg, where the preachers gained the support of the bishops, Georg of Polentz (1478–1550) and Erhard von Queis (1490–1529). As a result, both bishops introduced some elements of the Protestant Reformation in their dioceses. When Albrecht officially introduced the Reformation, the majority of the knights were already acquainted with Lutheran teaching. The first church order (Kirchenordnung) (1525) was prepared by

Georg von Polentz, Erhard von Queis, Johann Poliander, Briesmann, and Speratus. Further church orders were published in 1544 and 1558.

Shortly after 1526 the bishops started the first church visitation, and in 1527 they printed the first hymnbook. Due to their location, preachers had to serve believers in several languages and used interpreters. In Konigsberg, Luther's catechisms, New Testament, and confessions were printed in Polish. Furthermore, in 1579–80, the first Lithuanian translation of the Bible by Jonas Bretkūnas (Johannes Bretke) was published there.

As both the bishops of Pomesania and Semigallia officially turned Lutheran, they maintained their offices but abandoned their secular power. In 1566 the duke appointed new bishops: Joachim Mörlin (1514–71) and Georg Venediger (1519–74), followed by Tilemann Heshusius (1527–88) and Johann Wigand (1523–87). After opening a university in Konigsberg in 1544, Prussia became a center of Lutheran orthodoxy. The university hosted many students from Poland, Lithuania, the German Empire, Sweden, and Denmark. Shortly after its founding, the university witnessed serious theological controversy over the doctrine of justification, provoked by its new professor, Andreas Osiander, previously a pastor in Nuremberg. In 1577 controversy developed between two Protestant bishops, Heshusius and Wigand, concerning the person of Christ related to continuing controversies over the Lord's Supper among Lutherans. Finally, in 1578, the duchy accepted the Formula of Concord.

The conversion of Johann Sigismund (1613), duke in Prussia and elector of Brandenburg, to Calvinism dramatically changed the situation in the duchy. In response, the Prussian and Brandenburg nobility obtained a guarantee of their right to remain Lutheran, so Johann Sigismund explicitly broke with the rule *cuius regio eius religio* and created a biconfessional state, although his subjects were overwhelmingly Lutheran.

In Royal Prussia, the first Protestant preachers were already active in 1522. On July 13,

1522, Jakob Hegge held a fiery sermon in Danzig (Gdańsk). At his side worked Paul Kerlin, Johann Bonholt, Matthias Bienwald, Jakob Müller, Ambrosius Hitfeld, and two preachers known only as Michael and Antonius. In 1523 iconoclastic riots occurred. After further riots in January 1525, the city council decided to introduce the Reformation. Monasteries and convents were closed and "all opponents of the Gospel" were asked to leave the city. The city council asked Martin Luther for preachers. He sent Arnold Warwick (Burenius) and Michael Meurer (Galliculus, Hänlein).

Between 1523 and 1525 similar conflicts erupted between city magistrates and citizens in Elbing, Thorn, and other cities in Royal Prussia. The Polish king, after proclaiming some anti-Protestant edicts, decided to proceed with military intervention. In April 1526 he came to Danzig, imprisoned over forty citizens, and condemned thirteen to death. Many Protestant preachers escaped from Danzig and settled either in the Duchy of Prussia or in the Duchy of Pomerania.

After this intervention, the Reformation returned to its previous clandestine and unofficial character. Protestant preachers like Pankratius Klemme (1474–1546), Ambrosius Feierabend (1490–1543), and Johannes Glaser (Hyalinus) were active in Danzig, Elbing, and Thorn. Additionally, cities in Royal Prussia hosted some refugees: Anabaptists from the Netherlands, the Bohemian Brethren, and Scottish Presbyterians.

In 1557 Danzig, Thorn, and Elbing received privileges from the Polish king that guaranteed freedom of religion. The city councils introduced Lutheranism officially and took control over city churches. However, Roman Catholics were still present in the cities, and the power of the bishops remained uncontested. Gradually the number of Calvinists rose among the city councils in Danzig. In 1602 the city council appointed Bartholomäus Keckermann, famous Reformed philosopher and theologian, rector at the city high school. At this time the Reformed members of the city council were involved in a series of conflicts with Lutheran pastors. Throughout the seventeenth century, the major cities of Royal Prussia remained multiconfessional to some extent.

See also Prussian Union

Bibliography

Kneifel, E. *Geschichte der Evanglisch = Augsburgischen Kirche in Polen*. Roth bei Nürnberg, 1964; Müller, M G. *Zweite Reformation und städtische Autonomie im Königlichen Preußen: Danzig, Elbing und Thorn in der Epoche der Konfessionalisierung (1557–1660)*. Akademie Verlag, 1997; Zieger, A. *Das religiöse und kirchliche Leben in Preußen und Kurland im Spiegel der evangelischen Kirchenordnungen des 16. Jahrhunderts*. Böhlau, 1967.

MACIEJ PTASZYŃSKI

Prussian Union

With its capital in Berlin, early modern Prussia was made up of the Baltic kingdom of Prussia and the principality of Brandenburg, an influential state within the Holy Roman Empire. Although both Prussia and Brandenburg had long ties to the Lutheran Reformation, Reformed Protestantism also carried significant influence in Prussia. This began with the conversion of Brandenburg's ruling family to Calvinism in 1613 (most subjects remained Lutheran) and continued with Prussia's welcome of French Huguenot exiles after 1685. Other factors contributing to the eventual unification of Lutheran and Reformed Protestants in Brandenburg-Prussia included administrative expediency, Enlightenment ideals of rationalism and tolerance, and Halle Pietism, which often emphasized action and piety rather than doctrinal precision.

In a narrow sense, the Prussian Union refers to the September 27, 1817, declaration by King Friedrich Wilhelm III of Brandenburg-Prussia that Lutheran and Reformed churches in his realm would be joined into a single Protestant body. More generally, the Prussian Union describes the church body that developed over the next century, namely, the Evangelical Church in Royal Prussian Lands, which was for a time the largest Protestant church in the world. On the political level, the Prussian Union provided a pragmatic response to the religious diversity within the kingdom: by the early 1800s, Prussia had expanded west to the Rhine and east into Poland, thereby conquering territories whose citizens were predominantly Reformed and Roman Catholic. Further complicating religious institutional life, the Napoleonic Wars of the early 1800s had disrupted previous church administration systems, making a reorganization of church governance politically possible and desirable following the Congress of Vienna (1814–15).

This unification process, however, took decades to implement and met with steady opposition. Claus Harms, pastor in Kiel, famously published Ninety-Five Theses for Reformation Day, 1817, opposing the kind of religious rationalism exemplified by the Prussian Union. Nevertheless Harms lived in Schleswig-Holstein, which was not then a part of Prussia. Within Prussia, an order for worship (*Agenda*) published in 1822 came highly recommended by the official church but was not required for use in all congregations; a later *Agenda* of 1834 became mandatory, raising the stakes for those who opposed the new liturgy. Consequences of this stronger policy included religious emigration to Australia and the United States, the birth of new confessional movements like Old Lutheranism, and the push to establish free churches not affiliated with the state.

The Prussian Union left many lasting marks. First, the Prussian Union clearly viewed religion as a servant of the monarchy, so that churches became tools for advancing, rather than challenging, the nationalist movements of the nineteenth and early twentieth centuries. Second, though the Prussian monarchy came to an end after World War I, many present-day German church bodies (*Landeskirchen*) have remained union churches, ecumenically open and embracing a variety of Protestant perspectives. Third, the protests generated by the Prussian Union led many Reformed and Lutheran communities to reclaim their Reformation roots more intentionally. Among Lutherans in the United States, for instance, this impulse motivated church leaders like J. A. A.

Grabau, C. F. W. Walther, and Wilhelm Loehe (leaders of the Buffalo, Missouri, and Iowa Synods, respectively). Then and now, the Prussian Union has raised important questions of Christian unity, connections between church and state, and the value of unique Reformation legacies.

See also Harms, Claus; Loehe, Wilhelm; Lutheran Church–Missouri Synod; Prussia

Bibliography

Holborn, H. *A History of Modern Germany*. Vol. 2, *1648–1840*. Princeton University Press, 1964; Rogge, J. "Evangelische Kirche der Union." *TRE* 10:677–83. De Gruyter, 1982; Thadden, R. von. "Preußen II." *TRE* 27:364–76. De Gruyter, 1997.

Martin J. Lohrmann

Pufendorf, Samuel

Samuel Pufendorf (1632–94) was a jurist, historian, and a founding father of modern secular natural law. Born in Saxony, he was appointed professor of law in Heidelberg in 1661. After moving to Sweden in 1670, he was first professor at Lund, and then in 1677 he became secretary of state, councilor, and royal historiographer to King Karl XI in Stockholm. From 1688 until his death he was employed at the court in Berlin to write the history of the elector Friedrich William of Brandenburg.

Pufendorf became especially famous for his work *De Jure Naturae et Gentium* (Of the law of nature and nations, 1672), which involved him in disputes with Lutheran Orthodoxy—for example, with Valentin Alberti in Leipzig, a proponent of a Christian natural law founded on the Decalogue. Pufendorf conceptualized society based on the principle of sociality and ascribed the formation of state to a secular fiction of an original social contract. Nevertheless, he remained a faithful Protestant. Against the background of a resurgent papacy and Catholic sovereigns, he aimed for a reformation of theology that would reconcile Lutherans and Calvinists. Searching for essential articles for salvation, Pufendorf conceived a system of federal theology in his *Jus Feciale Divinum Sive de Consensu et Dissensu Protestantium* (The divine feudal law, or, covenant with mankind, represented, 1695), describing the true religion as a covenant between God and humans.

Bibliography

Döring, D. *Samuel Pufendorf in der Welt des 17.* Jahrhunderts. Klostermann 2012; Pufendorf, S. *The Divine Feudal Law, Or Covenants with Mankind, Represented* [1695], Liberty Fund 2002; The Whole Duty of Man [1673], Liberty Fund 2003.

Martin Kühnel

Q

Quenstedt, Johann Andreas

The Lutheran theologian Johann Andreas Quenstedt (1617–88) was a professor in Wittenberg and a prolific author of dogmatic texts and other theological materials. He was a nephew of Jena theologian Johann Gerhard. Quenstedt left his native Quedlinburg to study at the nearby University of Helmstedt rather than in Jena, because of the death of his uncle as he began his studies. In Helmstedt he sat at the feet of Georg Calixt (1637–44). After a brief period of private study and preaching in Quedlinburg, he renewed theological study in Wittenberg with Wilhelm Leyser and taught liberal arts courses at the university. In 1649 he began teaching theology in Wittenberg and became a professor of theology in 1660. He also served as dean of the Castle Church.

Quenstedt's broad interests are reflected in his publications, which include historical works, an important pastoral theology, his *Ethica pastorum* (1678), and dogmatic works, above all his massive *Theologia didactico-polemica* (1685), a harvest of a century of Lutheran theological work. His strong defense of the tradition of Lutheran Orthodoxy was joined with an irenic spirit and admonitions to colleagues that they defend the faith with gentleness and respect.

See also Calixt, Georg; Gerhard, Johann; Lutheran Orthodoxy

Bibliography

Preus, R. D. *The Theology of Post-Reformation Lutheranism*. 2 vols. Concordia, 1970–72.

ROBERT KOLB

R

Race/Minorities

With respect to matters of justice, Christians are inconsistent: sometimes they speak out against oppression, but all too often they tolerate it (Barndt 29). When it comes to racial injustice, especially among blacks and whites in cultures shaped by slavery or colonization, Martin Luther and his theological heirs, like others, have a mixed track record.

With many Europeans, Luther was concerned about the threat of Turkish expansion into Europe. This heightened his awareness of Islam, with its Arabic roots, and thus, indirectly (since "race" as a conceptual category arose later in Western thought), matters of race. Luther acknowledged that the "Saracens" were a great people but that they, like the Jews, were spiritually bankrupt. "The Saracens . . . boast of Ishmael, and they do not see that their pride was reduced to nothing by his excommunication. Like the Jews, they want to have the glory from their ancestors, but not the spirit of their ancestors" (LW 4:71). Commenting on Ps. 79, Luther continued his negative spin on Muslims, maintaining that the Saracens are among those who foment derision among Christians (LW 11:92). Additionally, Luther wondered how non-Christians like the Turks, Saracens, and others would interpret the significance of the Diet of Worms (LW 32:129), whose decisions he viewed as a betrayal of the gospel. Finally, Luther also could tie his concern about Islam to matters of color. As Luther reported, the church father "Jerome writes that he chastened and chastised his flesh with fasting until his skin became wrinkled and as black as coal, yes, as black as the skin of a Moor" (LW 22:226). Luther identified the land of the Moors as surrounding Israel and Judah to the south (LW 35:274).

Influence of Pietism and the Enlightenment on Race Matters. Early Lutheran missionaries to North America, for example, also encountered Native Americans and black slaves and sought to convert non-Christians to the Christian faith. Already by 1637, the Church of Sweden sent Johan Campanius (1601–83) as a missionary to Native Americans (Wolf 5). Another colonial pastor, Jacob Fabritius (d. 1696), baptized a black man named Emanuel on Palm Sunday 1669. He had black members in his congregations in Albany, New York City, and northern New Jersey (Nelson 76). Likewise, Justus Falckner, the first Lutheran pastor to be ordained in North America, ministered to racially diverse people in the Hudson River valley as he continued the work of Fabritius (Bente 25).

The rise of both Pietism and the Enlightenment in Germany and later in North America was to significantly influence Lutheran attitudes about race. An example is found in a young Ghanaian, Anton Wilhelm Amo (ca. 1703–ca. 1759), whose baptism was sponsored by Duke Anton Ulrich von Wolfenbüttel and his first son, Wilhelm, after both of whom he was named (Sephocle 187). He received an outstanding university education and encountered Enlightenment ideals as embodied in Leibniz and his students. He became the first black in Germany to earn a doctorate, writing a 1733 Wittenberg dissertation titled "Dissertatio inauguralis de jure Maurorum in Europa" (Inaugural dissertation on the rights of Moors [Africans] in [eighteenth-century] Europe) (1729). He taught at Wittenberg until 1735, and at Halle University until 1739. In 1740 he moved to Jena, but left in 1746 to return to Ghana.

The American Experience. Not only the Enlightenment but also Pietism, as centered at

Halle University and embodied in the teaching of Augustus Hermann Francke, were instrumental in shaping matters of racial justice. Transplanted to North America, Francke's theology led to the formation of the only Lutheran body in the United States to oppose slavery publicly, the Franckean Synod.

Colonial missionary Henry Melchior Mühlenberg (1711–87) was a product of Halle. When Mühlenberg first arrived in Charleston, South Carolina, in 1742, he reported, "A pair of black heathen, who are sold as slaves to the white Christian people, came on board our ship. I questioned them concerning various matters, but they knew nothing of the true God, nor of him whom he sent" (Mühlenberg 1). He observed that the city's population was predominantly black, with a ratio of fifteen to one. He also criticized the faulty logic that if the Christian religion was shared with blacks, then they would kill all whites and make themselves masters of Carolina (Mühlenberg 1). Upon arrival in Charleston he noticed that the ship taking him and immigrants from Salzburg to Savannah had on board a young runaway female slave. He asked her to whom she belonged, since he knew that harboring a runaway slave could bring arrest to all on board (Mühlenberg 2). Mühlenberg reflected, "I wonder if it will not produce severe judgments if people who pretend to be Christians use their fellow creatures, who have been redeemed along with themselves, as mere body slaves and do not concern themselves about their souls. This the future will show" (Mühlenberg 2).

Mühlenberg's father-in-law, Conrad Weiser, served as an Indian agent, a negotiator with several Indian tribes. In travels with Weiser, Mühlenberg encountered scattered Lutherans who chose to have their households baptized and catechized, without any distinction based on race or status (Nelson 74).

Unfortunately, the progressive thinking of Halle alumni in North America was interrupted when William C. Berkenmeyer replaced Fabritius as pastor in New York, Albany, and northern New Jersey, after the death of Fabritius. Berkenmeyer, a graduate of Hamburg and follower of Lutheran Orthodoxy, owned two Negro slaves and "inserted in the church constitution of 1735 a provision that baptism does not dissolve the tie of obedience" (Nelson 74). His death in 1751 permitted the more revivalistic, ecumenical, and justice-minded Halle Pietism to reassert itself in North America (Kuenning 45).

John Bachman (d. 1874) was emblematic of North American ambiguity about racial matters. Trained by clergy in America who had attended Halle, this New Yorker had been raised in a slaveholding household prior to New York State emancipation. An educated naturalist, he believed that all humans had a vocation to develop scientific inquiry in themselves and others. He helped establish the Lutheran Theological Southern Seminary and Newbury College, and served as the president of the Synod of the South during the Civil War.

Called to St. John Lutheran, Charleston, South Carolina, he nurtured leadership within the congregation and stimulated the generosity of the congregation as they opened their membership to Negroes as early as 1816. He sent two free Negroes, Jehu Jones and Daniel Alexander Payne, to the North for ordination or for further training to serve free Negroes. Jones was to be sent to West Africa for mission work. But with little financial support and difficulties in moving his family northward to Philadelphia, he started the first Lutheran church to service Negro members, St. Paul Lutheran, in 1834 in Philadelphia. Payne (later a leader in the African Methodist Episcopal Church) was to be trained as an educator for Negroes in the North after his work in Charleston had been outlawed. Bachman also ordained and sent a third member of his congregation, Boston J. Drayton, directly to Liberia to be a missionary in 1845. In spite of these efforts toward racial equality, Bachman was a slaveholder, illustrating the ability to support free Negroes while still supporting slavery (Bost 403).

The Franckean Synod, whose constitution forbade its pastors and members from holding slaves, ordained Daniel Alexander Payne, who had studied at Gettysburg. Payne was licensed by synod president John D. Lawyer a few days before their initial meeting in May 1837. The synod assumed the credit for the gradual alteration of other Lutheran church-body stances on slavery, since they sent out almost yearly challenges to the maintenance of slavery. They also noticed that the pace of change was slow (Stange 7).

The Danish West Indies / United States Virgin Islands. Beginning in 1666, Denmark provided pastoral leadership for the Danish citizens who were staffing the Danish West Indies Company. Unfortunately, the Danes had been a part of the slave trade as early as 1659. Johnson reports that when possible, a pastor was placed on such slave ships traveling from Africa to the Americas (Johnson 37). Recorded baptisms of Negro slaves are listed in 1713 and 1718 (Larsen 33). Among the slaves, house servants and skilled craftsmen tended to learn to speak Danish and become freedmen long before general emancipation. Field laborers constituted 90 percent of the slave population. All slaves outnumbered whites by a ratio of eight to one (Larsen 59).

Aware of the slaves' needs, the Moravian church began mission work in the Danish West Indies in the 1730s (Larsen 63). Lutherans undertook specific missionary work with West Indies Negroes in 1757, with an emphasis on rigorous catechesis as a way to determine the effectiveness of their teaching. In contrast to Moravian mission work, this method proved to be ineffective (Larsen 79). Even so, translations of Luther's Small Catechism, a spelling book, a hymnal, and a grammar in Creole were undertaken.

Slaves under Danish rule received their freedom on July 3, 1848: after rioting, Governor Peter von Scholten (1784–1854) emancipated the slaves (Larsen 188). With the six-day riot quelled, von Scholten left the island and returned to Denmark to be tried and condemned for dereliction of duty (Larsen 191).

Denmark sold the Virgin Islands to the United States in 1916–17, and the Lutheran congregations at that time were welcomed into the United Lutheran Church in America (Minutes 12).

The Alpha Synod. After the Civil War, some Southern congregations still had the remnants of black ministries. In North Carolina, Thomas Frye, a former slave of George Washington, had in 1868 been licensed to preach by the Tennessee Synod; it is likely that he was the first black preacher in the Carolinas. Due to his advanced age he preached for only three months (Drewes 7). Michael Coble of Alamance County, North Carolina, was licensed to preach in 1868. In a year he was leading two congregations and two Sunday schools. David Koonts, Samuel Holt, and Michael Coble were examined and licensed to preach in 1876. Along with Nathan Clapp, they became the core of the Alpha Evangelical Lutheran Synod of Freedmen in America, organized on May 8, 1889. Koontz served as president, Phifer as secretary, and Holt as treasurer of this first and only black Lutheran synod within the continental United States. They served in Concord, Charlotte, Elon College, Gibsonville, and Lexington, all in North Carolina, ministering to 180 souls in three buildings. Koontz and Phifer could read and write. With limited support ($25) coming from the North Carolina Synod, the pastors sought assistance from the Synodical Conference (Johnson 145).

More Recent Developments. The twentieth century in America found the three major Lutheran bodies (and their predecessors)—The American Lutheran Church, the Lutheran Church–Missouri Synod, and the Lutheran Church in America—working in different constituencies in the United States and having different responses to repressive laws affecting nonwhites. Lutherans tended to reflect the overriding attitudes of their neighbors with respect to ministry to nonwhites. The church schools of the South reflected separate educational systems. The churches of the North were mission outreach posts to racially defined neighborhoods. The church attempted to address migration to the industrial North and

West during the two world wars and the Depression. A critical point of change came with the Supreme Court decision of *Brown v. Board of Education*. The American Lutheran Church questioned the continuation of separate mission boards and raised the issue of a ministry housed in the National Lutheran Council. To expose its youth to the efforts to help blacks achieve full equality, the ALC invited Martin Luther King Jr. to address its Luther League Convention in 1961. The Lutheran Church–Missouri Synod absorbed all black ministry congregations of the Synodical Conference. The eight years leading to the formation of the Lutheran Church in America found the constituting document focused on an integrated church, especially with the attempt to set goals for inclusion of minorities at all levels of the church's endeavors.

During their ministry, Lutherans have exhibited ambivalent attitudes toward matters of race, but there has been a general progression toward increased recognition of equality, consistently tempered by local social attitudes. Even so, Johnson well summarizes the core of the church's mission with respect to race: "As one goes about the business of 'making disciples of all nations,' the message concerning Jesus Christ is not an ethnic ideology nor is the church to become an ethnic enclave. Luther and the Reformers understood that" (Johnson, 262).

See also American Civil War; Apartheid; Enlightenment; General Synod South; Mühlenberg, Heinrich (Henry) Melchior; Pietism; Slavery and Colonialism

Bibliography

Barndt, J. *Becoming an Anti-Racist Church*. Fortress, 2011; Bente, F. *American Lutheranism*. Concordia, 1919; Bost, R. "The Reverend John Bachman and the Development of Southern Lutheranism." PhD diss., Yale University, 1963. University Microfilms, 1963; Drewes, C. *Half a Century of Lutheranism among our Colored People, a Jubilee Book*. Concordia, 1927; Johnson, J. *Black Christians: The Untold Lutheran Story*. Concordia, 1991; Kuenning, P. *The Rise and Fall of American Lutheran Pietism: The Rejection of an Activist Heritage*. Mercer University Press, 1988; Larsen, J. *Virgin Islands Story*. Fortress, 1950; Luther, M. Luther's Works. Trans. J. Pelikan, H. C. Oswald, and H. T. Lehmann. Vols. 4, 11, 22, 32, 35. Fortress/Concordia, 1955–86; "Minutes of the Thirty-Sixth Convention of the General Council of the Evangelical Lutheran Church in North America, Held in Zion Lutheran Church, Witherspoon Hall, and Holy Communion Church, Philadelphia, PA." In *Minutes of the Thirty-Sixth Convention of the General Council*, 12, 32, 95–103. General Council Publication Board, 1917; Mühlenberg, H. M. *The Notebook of a Colonial Clergyman*, ed. T. Tappert and J. Doberstein. 2nd ed. Fortress, 1998; Nelson, E. *The Lutherans in North America*. Fortress, 1975; Sephocle, M. "Special Issue: The Image of Africa in German Society." *Journal of Black Studies*, December 1992, 182–87; Stange, D. *Radicalism for Humanity: A Study of Lutheran Abolitionism*. Olive Slave, 1970; Wolf, L. B. *Missionary Heroes of the Lutheran Church*. Fortress, 1911.

RICHARD N. STEWART

Rajaratnam, Kunchala

A charismatic Indian leader, institution builder, and lay theologian, Kunchala Rajaratnam (1920–2010) was an ardent supporter of oppressed and marginalized people. He was born August 6, 1920, and received his early education at Tirupathi, Andhra Pradesh, then earned his BA (with honors) at Madras Christian College, MA from the Madras University, and PhD from the London School of Economics. His twenty-two years of teaching in several universities and Christian colleges in India and visiting professorships around the world challenged him to establish a Centre for Research on the New International Economic Order, focusing on action-research and training in new approaches to development education leading to the PhD and MPhil degrees and pioneering several socioeconomic programs for empowering weaker and oppressed communities. As the master of the Serampore College Council, the only Christian theological university in India, he inaugurated new thrusts in theological education relevant to the context, having become the director of Gurukul Lutheran Theological College (Chennai) (1985–2009) and using it as his research center.

While serving as the executive secretary of the United Evangelical Lutheran Churches in India and the president of the National Council of Churches in India nationally, and while involved in the Lutheran World Federation and the World Council of Churches in the international arena, Rajaratnam challenged existing forms of ministries, seeking new forms for faithful witnessing of the church in society. The Academy of Indian Ecumenical Theology and Church Administration awarded him an honorary doctorate of divinity, recognizing his contributions in striving to break the dichotomy between sacred and secular, while remaining faithful to his confessional faith in ecumenical context.

See also India

Bibliography

Meshack, S. W., ed. *Dalit Liberation: A New Paradigm for the Mission in India; Contributions of Dr. K. Rajartnam.* Academy of Ecumenical Indian Theology and Church Administration, 2014; Sonawane, E., and E. Andrews, eds. *Living the Faith: Memorabilia of an Ecumenist Dr. K. Rajaratnam.* ISPCK, 2005.

Samuel W. Meshack

Rationalism

Rationalism is an approach to knowledge that elevates reason over other means of attaining truth, such as sense experience, tradition, or revelation. With roots stretching back to antiquity, modern rationalist philosophy—led by René Descartes, Baruch Spinoza, and Gottfried Wilhelm Leibniz—began in the seventeenth century as a response to skepticism. Earlier sources of rationalism in theology came from corners of the so-called Radical Reformation, notably Socinianism, which subjected Scripture and doctrine to the light of natural reason. Although some proponents affirmed special revelation as a source of truths above reason, rationalism became linked to anti-supernaturalism and fostered both deism and modern atheism. Thus the term came to connote a critical stance toward revealed religion more generally.

Optimism about humans' rational faculties stood in tension with Luther's and Orthodoxy's dim view of fallen reason's ability to grasp truth about ultimate matters apart from faith and revelation. Nevertheless, rationalism decisively shaped Lutheran theology in the eighteenth century, most directly through the philosophy of Christian Wolff (1679–1754), which came to dominate Protestant university curricula in Germany. Wolff posited a simple harmony of reason and revelation and developed a reason-based ethics centered on ideas of perfection and happiness. These themes were taken up by neology, the liberal theology of the later Enlightenment, which affirmed special revelation in principle but rejected doctrines, such as original sin and Christ's substitutionary atonement, that were seen to conflict with the dictates of reason and morality. A more radical wing of Wolffianism came to reject special revelation altogether. For example, Hermann Samuel Reimarus's work, published posthumously in the 1770s, demythologized Old Testament texts and depicted the Gospels as pious frauds, thereby instigating the modern quest for the historical Jesus. In their apologetic responses to rationalist critiques of the Bible, Lutheran divines refocused theology on problems of history, biblical hermeneutics, and religious experience, while also bequeathing to liberal Protestantism a growing skepticism about the supernatural.

Immanuel Kant's critique of pure reason's ability to know the noumenal world effectively ended rationalism in philosophy. His *Religion within the Boundaries of Mere Reason* (1792–93), however, extracted from Christian doctrine a core of teachings that would promote ethical development and gave new impetus to theological rationalism in a Lutheran mode. Weimar pastor Johann Friedrich Röhr found a wide audience for his *Letters on Rationalism* (1813), depicting Jesus as a teacher of moral perfectibility; theologians Hermann E. G. Paulus (1761–1851) and Julius A. L. Wegscheider (1771–1849), among others, labored to preserve the New Testament by uncovering its presumed moral and rational kernel. Autonomous reason would continue to function as a controlling principle within liberal Protestantism, eliciting critical responses from supernaturalists, neo-Pietists, and existentialists, and instigating the twentieth century's neo-orthodox revolution with its insistence on the primacy of faith.

See also Enlightenment; Kant, Immanuel; Leibniz, Gottfried Wilhelm; Liberalism; Natural Theology; Philosophy

Bibliography

Beutel, A. *Kirchengeschichte im Zeitalter der Aufklärung.* Vandenhoeck & Ruprecht, 2009; Dragseth, J. H., ed. *The Devil's Whore: Reason and Philosophy in the Lutheran Tradition.* Fortress, 2011; Graf, F. W., ed. *Profile des Neuzeitlichen Protestantismus.* Vol. 1, *Aufklärung, Idealismus, Vormärz.* Gütersloher Verlagshaus, 1990.

Eric Carlsson

Reformation and Luther Jubilees, Anniversaries

Special commemorations of Luther's life, death, and reforming activities connected to the Wittenberg movement have served to define anew the significance of the reformer and his reform throughout Lutheran history. Sixteenth-century followers of Luther noticed his birth and death dates; his student Cyriacus Spangenberg preached a series of sermons over twelve years on those dates, and others occasionally observed these anniversaries in order to take special note of his stand against Rome and/or the Sacramentarians. These observances accentuated elements of his teaching, particularly on justification by faith and the sacramental forms of God's Word.

Celebrating anniversaries of the posting of the Ninety-Five Theses in 1517 emerged as the focal point of such festive commemorations in the 1610s as the war clouds of the Thirty Years' War (1618–48) overshadowed the German empire with ever-stronger Roman Catholic threats of military force to eradicate Evangelical churches. Reformed officials under Elector Frederick V of the Palatinate and the Heidelberg theological faculty led efforts to use the one-hundredth anniversary of the posting of the Ninety-Five Theses as a rallying point for all Protestants in the empire against the Roman Catholic menace in 1617. Lutherans, particularly in Saxony, who had formulated only modest plans for the observance, finally made more of the commemoration as well. Sermons of the time emphasized the problems that Luther had addressed in his call for reform and the teachings on which his reform centered. Special services on October 31, 1617, and following days acclaimed Luther's epoch-changing contributions to the church and society.

A mixture of voices took note of the two-hundredth anniversary of the Ninety-Five Theses in 1717. Landgrave Ernst Ludwig of Hesse-Darmstadt rallied Lutheran princes to remember their identity as followers of Luther, though governmental concern not to disturb the peace of the empire tended to dampen anti–Roman Catholic polemic in this anniversary year. Ernst Salomon Cyprian, a counselor at the court in Gotha, led a publication campaign to reinforce memory and identity among Lutherans through the observance of the Ninety-Five Theses anniversary. Many pastors throughout Lutheran lands conducted special celebratory services on and around October 31. Universities also used the occasion to highlight their own history as Evangelical centers of learning and to focus on elements of Luther's teaching. At the same time Pietist emphasis on the principle of "Scripture alone" and Enlightenment focus on Luther as a symbol of casting off medieval ways and of individual freedom also affected public perceptions of the Wittenberg reformer. Gotthold Ephraim Lessing called for taking refuge in Luther's spirit—that is, in conscience and reason—rather than in Luther's writings, which imposed the yoke of tradition.

In 1817 the Enlightenment views of Luther remained prominent, expressed often in sermons promoting the values of the rising bourgeois civic leadership, but were joined by two new agendas. Kiel professor of theology Claus Harms published his own Ninety-Five Theses calling for a return to the theology of the Reformation and a fresh renewal of Luther's focus on Jesus Christ and justification by faith. Harms's theses provided an important impetus for the confessional revival of subsequent decades. The desire of the Hohenzollern monarchy of the kingdom of Prussia to unite the Reformed church, to which the family had adhered since 1618, with the majority Lutheran Church in its domains came to partial fruition with the introduction of the union of the two confessions. In addition, in the wake of the Napoleonic Wars, German national longing championed Luther as the hero of German resistance to foreign domination, whether Italian or French.

By 1917 commemorations of the Reformation had gone international. Within Germany, Luther served as one more rallying point for a nation engaged in a bloody war. In the United States the anniversary became the occasional for celebrating Luther's thought and for bringing together church bodies within the Lutheran family, uniting most Norwegian Lutherans in the Evangelical Lutheran Church and, in 1918, bringing together the General Synod, the General Council, and the Synod of the South.

Other Luther anniversaries won new recognition in the late nineteenth and early twentieth centuries. In 1883, celebrations of his birthday in churches, schools, and society took place in European Lutheran lands as well as in the Americas and Australia. The new imperial or Weimar edition of Luther's Works was launched, pioneering modern editorial standards in what became over a century of work, producing one hundred volumes of Luther texts and aids for their use. The infant second German empire also used the occasion to portray Luther as a model German and applaud his contributions to the German language and literary tradition. Also anniversaries of Luther's death occasioned more modest observances of aspects of his teaching and career.

The jubilee years of the Augsburg Confession occasioned some festive observances as well. In 1730 the mission of Barthomäus Ziegenbalg and Heinrich Plütschau that had taken the Augsburg Confession to India received mention, along with other praise designed to solidify Lutheran or more general Protestant identity. In 1830 the Augsburg Confession's anniversary strengthened the growing confessional revival among Lutherans while also giving occasion for more general acknowledgment of the Reformation's role in laying the groundwork for other elements of modern society. The study of such anniversaries focus renewed attention on the matter, but generally tells far more about the time of the celebration than it does about the Reformation and Martin Luther.

See also Prussian Union

Bibliography

Cordes, H. *Hilaria evangelica academic: Das Reformationsjubiläum von 1717 an den deutschen lutherischen Universitäten*. Vandenhoeck & Ruprecht, 2006; Kolb, R. *Martin Luther as Prophet, Teacher, and Hero*. Baker, 1999; Lehmann, H. *Luthergedächtnis 1817 bis 2017*. Vandenhoeck & Ruprecht, 2012; Lehmann, H. *Martin Luther in the American Imagination*. Fink, 1988; Mostert, W. "Luther, III. Wirkungsgeschichte." *TRE* 21:567–94. De Gruyter, 1991; Schönstädt, H.-J. *Antichrist, Weltheilsgeschehen und Gottes Werkzeug: Römische Kirche, Reformation und Luther im Spiegel des Reformationsjubiläums 1617*. Steiner, 1978.

ROBERT KOLB

Refugees

Because of its own refugee heritage and its embrace of the biblical and theological grounds for "welcoming the stranger," the Lutheran Church has often exercised a special engagement with refugees. The Old Testament presents the story of a refugee people, the people of Israel who fled from Egypt. At the center of the New Testament is the story of a refugee family, the Holy Family, who had to seek refuge in Egypt. Jesus was a refugee. In Reformation times Martin Luther had to be spirited away and given sanctuary at the Wartburg, and Philip Melanchthon, Katharina Luther, and their families were refugees during the Smalcald War. More recently, at the close of World War II, one out of every six Lutherans in the world was a refugee or displaced person. A major purpose for establishing the Lutheran World Federation (LWF) in 1947 was to carry out diaconal services on their behalf. The first resolution of the First Assembly of the LWF dealt with refugees.

For Christians, the call to respond positively to the needs of migrants, refugees, and those fleeing persecution is not ideologically based but biblically mandated. The exodus from slavery to freedom became the linchpin of Hebrew identity. The laws of Israel's God demand preferential treatment for the stranger, the alien, the poor, and the defenseless. "You shall also love the stranger, for you were strangers in the land of Egypt" (Deut. 10:19). The foundational experience in the history of Christian people is the Christ event: the incarnation, life, teaching, suffering, death, and resurrection of Jesus of Nazareth, who shared the passion for justice and concern for the stranger found in the Hebrew Bible. Jesus's story is the story of welcome, of inclusion, of hospitality, of service both to citizens and to the strangers in their midst, particularly those considered outsiders (see Matt. 25:31–45).

Lutherans continue to actively carry out service with refugees through the LWF, the global communion of 145 churches in the Lutheran tradition, and through the many Lutheran service organizations, congregations, and individuals who reach out a hand of welcome to those who have been displaced. In 2015 the LWF assisted more than two million forcibly displaced persons, making it the largest faith-based partner of the United Nations High Commissioner for Refugees and UNHCR's fourth-largest NGO partner overall. In the United States the National Lutheran Council pursued active resettlement of refugees following World Wars I and II. By 1949 the council organized the Lutheran Resettlement Service, later Lutheran Immigrant and Refugee Service (LIRS), with LCMS participation from 1954 onward.

Today, Lutherans around the world are committed to promoting human rights, peace, and reconciliation; alleviating human suffering; and addressing the root causes of social, economic, and gender injustice. Service in the world is integral to Lutheran identity, freed by grace to love and serve the neighbor.

See also Lutheran Social Services; Lutheran World Federation; Middle East; Migration

Bibliography
Bouman, S. P., and R. Deffenbaugh. *They Are Us: Lutherans and Immigration*. Augsburg Fortress, 2009; Marty, M. *When Faiths Collide*. Oxford University Press, 2005; Schjørring, J. H., P. Kumari, and N. A. Hjelm, eds. *From Federation to Communion: The History of the Lutheran World Federation*. Fortress, 1997; Solberg, R. W. *Open Doors: The Story of Lutherans Resettling Refugees*. Concordia, 1992.

RALSTON DEFFENBAUGH

Regensburg Colloquy

The 1541 Regensburg Colloquy was part of a series of theological discussions ordered by Holy Roman emperor Charles V, held in conjunction with an imperial diet that same year. The colloquy brought together Roman Catholic and Protestant theologians to mediate the theological differences that divided German imperial territories. This was the final attempt by Emperor Charles V to unite his German territories politically by reconciling their theological differences.

Theological issues raised by Martin Luther and other reformers had split imperial German territories into those who agreed with Luther's Reformation writings and those who held with papal authority and the Roman Catholic Church. Charles V sought the united support of these territories to defend his realm from Turkish military advances. After a church council, first called by Pope Paul III in 1536, was delayed, Charles V called for a series of colloquies to mediate these theological differences. Following preliminary discussions at Haguenau and Worms, terms for the colloquy at Regensburg were set. Discussion would focus on theological articles secretly drafted by Johannes Gropper, a Roman Catholic, and Martin Bucer, a Protestant. Written in private meetings conducted by the emperor's first minister, Nicolas de Granvelle, the twenty-three articles mediating disputed teachings were termed the Regensburg Book.

Charles V wanted Protestant and Roman Catholic theologians to develop and agree on a statement of doctrine and practice that could be presented for consideration at the full imperial diet. That statement would then serve as the foundation for reuniting German territories. Although the pope was not pleased that the emperor was hosting theological discussions, he sent his papal legate, Cardinal Contarini, to Regensburg.

Charles V appointed six collocutors: John Eck, Johannes Gropper, and Julius Pflug to represent the Roman Catholics; and Philip Melanchthon, Martin Bucer, and Johann Pistorius for the Protestants. These six collocutors would be joined by six lay witnesses. Discussions were private, but after each day's session, information was shared with the various delegations at the diet. Key topics agreed to at earlier diets, including such doctrines as the Trinity, the two natures of Christ, and the creeds, were not included in the discussions.

Early in the discussions, agreement was quickly reached on the first four articles, dealing with the human condition before the fall, freedom of the will, the cause of sin, and original sin. With these four articles as a framework, the fifth article, with compromise language on justification, was addressed, defining the believer's righteousness as both extrinsic (the proclaimed forgiveness of God) and intrinsic (the righteous works of love). Although not specifically stated, the article considered justification to be conveyed by means of the church through the authority granted by Christ and vested in the papacy. When this became explicit, Melanchthon objected, but over his objection the compromise language was approved.

As discussion in Regensburg proceeded to new topics, news of the agreement on justification reached both the Saxon elector John Frederick and Rome. When John Frederick heard details of the agreement, he wrote to Luther and Johannes Bugenhagen, and, in a joint reply, they rejected the Regensburg article on justification. Melanchthon, in response, was hopeful that the imperial diet itself would improve the language. In Rome, the papal consistory gave a rather ambiguous decision that the article was not approved, but neither was it rejected. Thus it was soon clear that the article

on justification would never be received into the churches of either the Protestants or the Roman Catholics. As discussions at Regensburg continued, the two sides were deeply divided over authority in the church, interpretation of Scripture, and the sacraments of the Lord's Supper and private confession.

After Charles V received the book from the collocutors, modified with changes agreed on and notes on remaining differences, he exerted his imperial authority and demanded that Contarini, as papal legate, tolerate some differences for the sake of unity. Contarini refused. When Charles V in turn demanded toleration from the Protestants, John Frederick's Saxon delegation refused as well. The diet ended with the Regensburg Recess of 1541, which replaced the 1530 Augsburg Recess. In the 1541 recess, the Protestants were allowed to interpret the Regensburg articles as they had been proposed. Court proceedings, lawsuits, and imperial bans against members of the Smalcaldic League were suspended, pending the appointment of a new imperial court. John Frederick promised at least temporary military support for Charles V to move against the Turks. In the recess, Charles V also agreed to support the German Catholic League, but he would not allow himself to be obligated politically in any war that league might begin against the Protestants.

Following the end of the 1541 diet, the pope called for the long-awaited general church council, which eventually convened at Trent in 1545. A second colloquy in Regensburg in 1546 also met with failure.

See also Bible Interpretation; Bucer, Martin; Charles V; Colloquy; Eck, John; Justification; Lord's Supper; Melanchthon, Philip

Bibliography

Ganzer, K., and K.-H. zur Mühlen, eds. *Akten der deutschen Reichsreligionsgespräche im 16. Jahrhundert.* Vol. 3, *Das Regensburger Religionsgespräch (1541).* Vandenhoeck & Ruprecht, 2007; Hequet, S. *The 1541 Colloquy at Regensburg: In Pursuit of Church Unity.* VDM, 2005; Lexutt, A. *Rechtfertigung im Gespräch: Das Rechtfertigungsverständnis von Hagenau, Worms und Regensburg 1540/41.* Vandenhoeck & Ruprecht,

1996; Matheson, P. *Cardinal Contarini at Regensburg*. Clarendon, 1972; Ziegler, D. J., ed. *Great Debates of the Reformation*. Random House, 1969.

SUZANNE S. HEQUET

Repristination Theology

Repristination theology is a term used to describe a theological method that sought to preserve Christian doctrine from rationalistic dilution and subjective reformulation by trying to replicate both the content and form of seventeenth-century Lutheran Orthodoxy. The terminology was often used in contrast with Neo-Lutherans of the nineteenth century (i.e., Erlangen theology), who sought to critically appropriate Lutheran categories for addressing challenges raised by the theology of Friedrich Schleiermacher (1768–1834) and the emerging "scientific" approach to the study of the Scriptures. Names most often associated with repristination theology are Carl Paul Caspari (1814–92), Friedrich Adolf Philip (1809–82), and Ernst Wilhelm Hengstenberg (1802–69) in Germany, plus the German-American dogmaticians Francis Pieper (1852–1931) and Adolf Hoenecke (1835–1908). Repristination theology was marked by a commitment to the inerrancy of the Holy Scriptures and the vicarious atonement of Christ. While others used the phrase "repristination theology" as a term of derision, it was taken as an emblem of honor by the theologians who wanted to assert and demonstrate their fidelity to the Scriptures as the Word of God, the Lutheran confessions as the correct exposition of the Scriptures, and theologians of Lutheran Orthodoxy as unsurpassed standards of doctrinal precision. The repristination theologians were suspicious of novelty in theology, rejecting these innovations as "neology" that would corrupt sound doctrine.

See also Erlangen; Hengstenberg, Ernst Wilhelm; Liberalism; Lutheran Orthodoxy; Pieper, Francis; Rationalism

Bibliography
Hoenecke, A. *Evangelical-Lutheran Dogmatics*. 4 vols. Northwestern, 2009; Pieper, F. *Christian Dogmatics*. 3 vols. Concordia, 1950.

JOHN T. PLESS

Reu, Johann Michael

Born on November 16, 1869, in Diebach, Bavaria, Johann Michael Reu (1869–1943) was educated at the Lutheran missionary institutions in Neuendettelsau, Bavaria. In 1889 Reu came to the United States, where he was ordained to serve as a pastor to German Lutheran immigrants. Ten years later, he joined the faculty of Wartburg Theological Seminary in Dubuque, Iowa, which had been founded by other Neuendettelsau missionaries in 1854.

Reu remained on the faculty of Wartburg Theological Seminary until his death on October 14, 1943, becoming one of the most prolific and influential Lutheran theologians in the United States. A leader in the movement toward Lutheran unity, Reu helped to form the American Lutheran Church (1930–60) and served as that body's delegate to the Lutheran World Convention, predecessor organization to the Lutheran World Federation.

In addition to his numerous contributions to the causes of Lutheran unity and vitality, Reu helped the American Lutheran Church to articulate an understanding of the Bible that affirmed its Reformation authority as the written Word of God while avoiding fundamentalist ascriptions of textual inerrancy. In this way, Reu championed the Reformation principle of *sola scriptura* for twentieth-century contexts and applications among Lutherans in the United States.

See also American Lutheran Church (1930–60); Scripture

Bibliography
Johnston, P. I., ed. *Anthology of the Theological Writings of J. Michael Reu*. Mellen, 1997; Meuser, F. W. *The Formation of the American Lutheran Church: A Case Study in Christian Unity*. Wartburg, 1958.

PAUL A. BAGLYOS

Reuchlin, Johannes

A prominent lawyer, jurist, and court functionary in Württemberg, Johannes Reuchlin's (1454/55–1522) passion was humanist scholarship. He pioneered Hebrew learning in Germany, writing an important Hebrew grammar and encouraging Philip Melanchthon, whose grandmother was related to Reuchlin through marriage, to continue his studies of Greek and Hebrew. Reuchlin studied at Freiburg im Breisgau, Paris, and then at the University of Basel, where he received his BA (1474) and MA (1477). He then studied law at Orléans, Poitiers, and Tübingen, where he received his doctor of law degree (1484–85). From 1482 to 1496, Reuchlin served in the court of Eberhard im Bart (the Bearded) of Württemberg. After a period of political exile in Heidelberg (1496–98), Reuchlin served as a member of the Swabian League tribunal from 1502 until his retirement in 1512/13. He moved to Stuttgart and devoted himself to his scholarly interests. Reuchlin briefly taught Greek and Hebrew at Ingolstadt (1520–21) and at Tübingen (1521–22) before his death on June 30, 1522.

Initially known for his expertise in Greek, Reuchlin met Pico Della Mirandola on a diplomatic mission to Florence in 1490, and the latter convinced him to pursue kabbalistic studies. Reuchlin lived in Rome from 1498 to 1500 and hired Obadiah Sforno to teach him Hebrew. Reuchlin went on to write a number of Hebraica books including *The Wonder-Working Word* (1494), *Rudiments of Hebrew* (1506), and *The Art of Kabbalah* (1517).

Reuchlin became embroiled in lengthy controversy with Johannes Pfefferkorn and his Dominican supporters at the University of Cologne over Hebrew learning. In July 1510, Emperor Maximilian I invited Reuchlin to serve on a commission that would advise him whether to allow Pfefferkorn's campaign to confiscate Jewish books to go forward. Reuchlin opposed it on both legal and pragmatic grounds in the legal opinion he submitted. Pfefferkorn responded by publishing *Handspiegel* (1511), a pamphlet attacking both Jews and Reuchlin, which stopped just short of accusing Reuchlin of heresy. Reuchlin responded by writing *Augenspiegel* (1511), in which he defended his own learning and honor, and also published his legal brief in defense of Jewish books. For the next nine years Reuchlin

endured a series of trials in Mainz, Speyer, and Rome, which inspired other humanists to defend him as a proponent of humanist learning. Although not directly involved in the dispute, Luther and others in his circle expressed their support for Reuchlin.

Reuchlin's main influence on the Wittenberg Reformation came through his relation with Philip Melanchthon. Reuchlin encouraged Melanchthon's study of Greek and Hebrew and introduced him to his formidable network of fellow humanists in Heidelberg, Tübingen, and elsewhere. Following Reuchlin's recommendation, Elector Frederick the Wise appointed Melanchthon as professor of Greek at Wittenberg in August 1518. Reuchlin quickly came to disapprove of Luther and of Melanchthon's support for him. In December 1519 he tried to convince Melanchthon to leave Wittenberg and accept a position at the University of Ingolstadt, an offer that Melanchthon rejected. In 1521 Reuchlin apparently asked Melanchthon to stop corresponding with him and later disinherited him.

Reuchlin's Hebrew learning also had an impact on the Wittenberg Reformation through his Hebrew grammar and dictionary, *The Rudiments of Hebrew* (1506). This textbook was an important piece of scholarship, containing not only an intermediate-level Hebrew grammar, but also a Hebrew-Latin glossary. From its appearance until the mid-1520s, it was the most substantial Latin-language work of its kind available for Christian students of Hebrew. Both Luther and Melanchthon owned copies of the book, and Luther used it in his Hebrew-related scholarship until the very end of his career, when he lectured on Genesis. Already before the Reformation, Luther also used Reuchlin's Latin rendering of the penitential Psalms to produce his own translation into German, one of his very first publishing ventures.

Reuchlin also had an impact on Hebrew learning at Wittenberg through two of his Hebrew students, Melanchthon and Johannes Forster. While Melanchthon was best known for his Greek scholarship, he played an important role in supporting Hebrew studies at Wittenberg as well. Between 1518 and 1521, Johannes Boeschenstein, Matthaeus Adrianus, and Bernhard Göppingen briefly taught Hebrew at the University of Wittenberg. After each of them left the university, Melanchthon was obliged (against his will) to teach Hebrew in their place. Only in 1521, when Matthaeus Goldhahn (Aurogallus) was hired, could he give up Hebrew teaching entirely. Melanchthon remained involved in Hebrew study, however, because he and Goldhahn worked closely with Luther first in translating the Old Testament from Hebrew into German and then in revising the translation. In 1549 Johannes Forster, who had studied Hebrew with Reuchlin at Ingolstadt, joined the Wittenberg faculty, teaching Hebrew from 1549 until his death in 1556.

See also Humanism and the Reformation; Melanchthon, Philip

Bibliography

Brecht, M. *Martin Luther: His Road to Reformation, 1483–1521.* Fortress, 1985; Burnett, S. G. "Reassessing the 'Basel-Wittenberg Conflict': Dimensions of the Reformation-Era Discussion of Hebrew Scholarship." In *Hebraica Veritas? Christian Hebraists and the Study of Judaism in Early Modern Europe,* ed. A. P. Coudert and J. S. Shoulson, 181–201. University of Pennsylvania Press, 2004; Price, D. H. *Johannes Reuchlin and the Campaign to Destroy Jewish Books.* Oxford University Press, 2011; Scheible, H. "Johannes Reuchlin of Pforzheim." In *Contemporaries of Erasmus,* ed. P. G. Bietenholz and T. B. Deutscher, 3:145–50. University of Toronto Press, 1987; Scheible, H. "Reuchlins Einfluss auf Melanchthon." In *Reuchlin und die Juden,* ed. A. Herzig and J. H. Schoeps, 123–49. Thorbecke, 1993.

Stephen G. Burnett

Reusch, Richard Gustavovich

The pioneering Lutheran missionary Richard Gustavovich Reusch (1891–1975) was born on October 31, 1891, into the home of a devout Lutheran schoolteacher and deacon in the Volga River German colony. When his father moved to the Caucasus, Richard was sent to live with the Terek Cossacks. He learned to appreciate the diversity of his Sunni and Shia Muslim and Russian Orthodox compatriots when he

became part of the Imperial Cadet Corps in 1904. Reusch pledged allegiance to Czar Nicholas II as a second lieutenant and served until July 1911. He graduated from Tartu University (Estonia) in 1916 with a theological degree while at the same time teaching Arabic. On Easter Sunday 1917 he was ordained, in the same year as the Bolshevik Revolution was breaking out. The new pastor joined forces with loyal subjects of the czar, and they forced the Bolsheviks out of Estonia and Latvia.

In 1921 he completed his master's degree at Tartu and was accepted by the Leipzig Mission to serve in their Kilimanjaro Mission. He entered Tanganyika (now Tanzania) in 1923, using his imperial Russian passport endorsed by the Russian embassy in Copenhagen (which was not yet under Bolshevik control). In 1929, disturbed by Islamic inroads, he traveled disguised as a Circassian dervish. His dervish pilgrimage ended in Sanaa (Yemen), where he came to understand better the reason for the upsurge of Islam in Tanganyika. He returned to his pastoral duties and continued his efforts to unite the Leipzig Mission the Augustana Synod Mission. In 1927 he married Elvida Bonander, a nurse from Augustana.

Eventually in 1937 he opened the Augustana training school at Kinampanda in the Singida area. In 1940 he was elected president of the Mission Churches Federation, a united Protestant group (not including the Anglicans) that intended to foster an indigenous unified African church. From this time on he tirelessly visited the federation churches throughout the Tanganyika. In 1940 he also opened a Lutheran seminary at Machame on Kilimanjaro. He served as president of the newly formed Lutheran Church of Northern Tanganyika (1942–46).

During a furlough in 1947, he received an honorary doctorate in theology from and taught at Gustavus Adolphus College (St. Peter, Minnesota). He also became a US citizen. Returning to Tanganyika, he poured his energies into his work among the Masai people. When his efforts to establish an independent Masai mission were rejected by both the Americans and authorities in the church in Tanganyika, Reusch dejectedly returned to the United States in 1954 and taught at Gustavus Adolphus until he retired in 1961. He continued to advocate for work among the Masai. In 1967 he accepted a parish call to Stacy, Minnesota, and revived an ailing parish. He died in 1975.

Reusch was an epic bridge builder in multiple respects. Joining the efforts of the Leipzig Mission with the American missions, he was instrumental in the formation of a viable Lutheran church in Tanganyika. Sir Edward Twining, the last colonial governor of Tanganyika, paid tribute to Reusch in 1954: "In the thirty years or so that Dr. Reusch has been in Tanganyika, he has gained for himself the position of being one of the outstanding personalities in the territory. He still has the élan of a former Cavalry Officer of the Imperial Russian Cossacks, but underneath is the Lutheran missionary with a blend of sincerity and robust common sense" (quoted in Johnson, *Presentation*).

See also Tanzania

Bibliography

Bernander, G. *Lutheran Wartime Assistance to Tanzanian Churches 1940–45*. Gleerup, 1968; Danielson, E. R. *Forty Years with Christ in Tanzania, 1928–68*. Lutheran Church in America, 1977; Johnson, D. *Loyalty: A Biography of Richard Gustavovich Reusch*. Sun Ray Printing, 2008; Johnson, D. "Rev. Dr. Richard Gustavovich Reusch (1891–1975)." http://augustanaheritage.org/Dan_Johnson _Presentation_on_Reusch.pdf.

HERBERT J. HAFERMANN

Revelation

Luther never treats revelation apart from Christ or the Scriptures. For him, revelation is not so much opposed to "reason"—as if human reason and divine revelation were parallel, analogous, and possibly competing structures of knowledge—as it is opposed to sin's distortion of reason. Revelation is what comes in spite of human reason, not in addition to reason.

Luther grants that the sinful person can know something of God by the power of reason. Even the gentiles can deduce that there is a Creator and the basic content of the natural law (cf. Rom. 1). But, as Luther explains in sermons on the Gospel of John (1537), this is only "legal knowledge" of God and not yet "true knowledge of Him" (LW 22:151). True or "evangelical knowledge" of God is knowledge of the gospel: "the depth of divine wisdom and of the divine purpose, the profundity of God's grace and mercy, and what eternal life is like" (LW 22:152–53). Such knowledge can only come from the Son of God, "for He comes from the Father, and He knows the truth. . . . He who is in the divine essence descends from heaven to us and becomes man. Who else could have revealed God to us?" (LW 22:156). "To know God from the Law with His back turned to us is a left-handed knowledge of Him. Therefore walk around God and behold His true countenance and His real plan. God is seen properly only in Christ" (LW 22:157). Without Christ, God remains hidden. Thus revelation is a function of Christology, or more properly of the Trinity, as Luther had already outlined in the Large Catechism (1529): "We could never come to recognize the Father's favor and grace were it not for the Lord Christ, who is a mirror of the Father's heart. Apart from him we see nothing but an angry and terrible judge. But neither could we know anything of Christ, had it not been revealed by the Holy Spirit" (LC, Creed, par. 65 in *BC* 440).

This in turn raises a key question: How does the Holy Spirit inform us about Christ? For Luther, the answer is always God's Word, especially Holy Scripture, by which means the Spirit bears authoritative witness to the Son's revelation in history of the just and merciful Father. Scripture is the means, not the end, though it is an indispensable and irreplaceable means. Thus Scripture was the basis for Luther's critique of medieval church practice and theology, which had elevated certain human traditions in contradiction to the Scriptures; and it was equally the basis of his even more scathing critique of the Zwickau prophets,

Karlstadt, and other spiritualists who, in Luther's view, jettisoned the Bible altogether in favor of alleged private revelations from the Spirit. Luther characterizes and then criticizes their stance in *Against the Heavenly Prophets* (1525), where the trinitarian basis is again foundational: "Others are to learn outwardly by their word, which they call an external witness. But they themselves are better and superior to the apostles, and pretend to learn inwardly in their spirit without an external Word and without means, though this possibility was not given to the apostles, but alone to the only Son, Jesus Christ. Thus you see how this devil, as I said already, disregards the external Word and does not wish to have it as a forerunner to the Spirit" (LW 40:195). Luther sees in this also an effort at self-justification, basing salvific knowledge of God on an internal and personal work rather than on the reception of God's public and freely offered works.

Whether of the Roman or of the spiritualist kind, Luther anticipates that extrascriptural "revelations" will prove their falsity by making a new law out of what is a matter of freedom, acting in violence, and refusing to engage in fair debate; in fact, refusing to participate in the structures of human reason. In each controversy, Luther employed the skills of human reason—linguistic study, logic, literary analysis, historical inquiry—in his exposition of the Scriptures, in order to demonstrate the self-defeating incoherence of his opponents' positions. Reason overreaches itself when it indulges in metaphysical speculations about God's nature and human agency apart from what has been revealed in Christ and the Scriptures. But within its own domain—namely, this world—Luther can argue that "reason is the most important and the highest in rank among all things and, in comparison with other things of this life, the best and something divine" (Thesis 4, *The Disputation concerning Man* [1536], LW 34:137).

The revelation given in Christ does not, however, answer every question or allay every objection. Luther maintains that what Christ has done and taught for our salvation is absolutely true and reliable; nevertheless, within this vale of tears and within our own natural and sinful limitations, difficulties persist, most pointedly regarding that "which looks so very like injustice in God" (*Bondage of the Will*, LW 33:291). Luther commends trust in the righteousness of God, who has given us the light of grace in addition to the light of nature, in anticipation of the light of glory, "when the light of the Word and of faith comes to an end, and reality itself and the Divine Majesty are revealed in their own light[.] Do you not think that the light of glory will then with the greatest of ease be able to solve the problem that is insoluble in the light of the Word or of grace, seeing that the light of grace has so easily solved the problem that was insoluble in the light of nature?" (LW 33:292).

See also Bible Interpretation; Christology; Scripture; Theology of the Cross; Word of God

Bibliography

Luther, M. *Against the Heavenly Prophets in the Matter of Images and Sacraments* (1525). LW 40:73–223; Luther, M. *The Bondage of the Will*. LW 33; Luther, M. *The Disputation concerning Man* (1536). LW 34:133–44; Luther, M. Large Catechism. In *The Book of Concord*, ed. R. Kolb and T. J. Wengert, 379–480. Fortress, 2000; Luther, M. *Sermons on the Gospel of St. John, Chapters 1–4* (1537). LW 22.

SARAH HINLICKY WILSON

Revivals, *Erweckungsbewegung*

The term *Erweckungsbewegung* (religious awakening) is often used to describe the emergence of renewed Christian life in nineteenth-century Germany in reaction to both widespread religious indifference and the theological rationalism of the Enlightenment. As part of an international Protestant renewal movement, it ran parallel to and was interconnected with the Swiss, French, and Dutch *Réveil*, British evangelicalism, the Scandinavian revivals, and the Second Great Awakening in the United States. Although several German revivals took place earlier, and while some of its leaders exerted their greatest influence only later, its height is usually associated with the *Vormärz* era between Napoleon's final defeat in 1815, which convinced many of God's providential role in history, and the revolutions of 1848. Some scholars prefer to use the plural *Erweckungsbewegungen* to indicate the diversity of the movement.

The Moravian diaspora and the missionary-minded Deutsche Christentumsgesellschaft in Basel prepared the way for the *Erweckungsbewegung*. There were often powerful preachers or pastors (like L. Hofacker in Stuttgart, G. D. Krummacher in Elberfeld, and J. C. Blumhardt in Möttlingen) at the center of local revivals, or university professors (including C. Krafft in Erlangen and A. Tholuck in Halle) whose teaching and pastoral care had a lasting impact on their students; occasionally also pious nobility (e.g., A. von Thadden in Trieglaff, Baron H. E. von Kottwitz in Berlin, Countess F. von Reden in Buchwald). The centers of the *Erweckungsbewegung* included Württemberg, Pomerania, Berlin, Siegerland, the Wuppertal region, Bremen, Hamburg, Minden-Ravensberg, Saxony, and Franconia, whereas other areas such as the Palatinate, Thuringia, Braunschweig, Oldenburg, and Mecklenburg were left relatively untouched. Although the revivals had a significant impact on the church and sometimes even the social life of a particular region, its adherents remained a small percentage of the total population.

While some free churches did spring from the revivals, the German *Erweckungsbewegung* of the first half of the nineteenth century took place primarily inside the established (often Lutheran) territorial churches. Revivalist preachers emphasized the Bible as God's Word and the need for a personal experience of the Christian life, insisting on such Reformation tenets as human depravity, the divinity of Christ, and reconciliation through his substitutionary death. Politically, the German *Erweckungsbewegung* condemned the French Revolution as ungodly and supported the late-Romantic ideal of a godly Christian prince who lovingly ruled his people as the head of a family. After 1830, the year of the tricentennial celebration of the Augsburg Confession, part of the *Erweckungsbewegung* took on a decidedly confessional, mostly neo-Lutheran, stance (e.g., L. Harms, E. W. Hengstenberg, W. Löhe). In Silesia, "Old Lutherans" led by J. G. Scheibel split from the state church in protest against the imposition of the Prussian Union, and some emigrated to the United States or Australia. Other revivals, like those in Württemberg and the Lower Rhine region, were marked by significant continuity with earlier Pietism.

An essential characteristic of the *Erweckungsbewegung* was its Christian activism expressed both by private charitable work, leading to the *Innere Mission*, and world missions. Inspired by the British example, various revivalist groups (led, for example, by Friedrich Bodelschwingh, Theodore Fliedner, Amalie Sieveking, or Johann Hinrich Wichern) established orphanages, deaconess motherhouses, temperance societies, prison ministries, Sunday schools, mission societies, mission seminaries, Bible societies, tract societies, youth clubs, and other initiatives. In such networks, Christians from all layers of society met and worked together. They also produced widely circulated periodicals and other Christian literature. In so doing, they believed they were serving and building the kingdom of God—a concept central to their acute sense of history and eschatology.

See also Bodelschwingh, Friedrich (the Elder) and Friedrich (the Younger) von; Erlangen; Fliedner, Theodore; Grundtvig, Nikolai Frederik Severin; Harms, Claus; Hauge, Hans Nielson; Hengstenberg, Ernst Wilhelm; Inner Mission; Laestadius, Lars Levi; Loehe, Wilhelm Konrad; Mission Societies and Academies; Moravian Church (Unitas Fratrum); Pietism; Prussian Union; Rosenius, Carl Olof; Sieveking, Amalie Wilhelmina; Spitta, Karl Johann Philipp; Wichern, Johann Hinrich

Bibliography

Benrath, G. A., "Die Erweckung innerhalb der deutschen Landeskirchen 1815–1888: Ein Überblick." In *Geschichte des Pietismus*, vol. 3, *Der Pietismus im neunzehnten und zwanzigsten Jahrhundert*, ed. U. Gäbler, 150–271. Vandenhoeck & Ruprecht, 2000; Beyreuther, E. *Die*

Erweckungsbewegung. 2nd ed. Vandenhoeck & Ruprecht, 1977; Crowner, D., and G. Christianson, ed. and trans. *The Spirituality of the German Awakening: Texts by August Tholuck, Theodor Fliedner, Johann Hinrich Wichern, and Friedrich von Bodelschwingh*. Paulist Press, 2003; Gäbler, U. *"Auferstehungszeit": Erweckungsprediger des 19. Jahrhunderts; Sechs Porträts*. Beck, 1991; Ising, D. *Johann Christoph Blumhardt, Life and Work: A New Biography*. Cascade, 2009; Railton, N. *No North Sea: The Anglo-German Evangelical Network in the Middle of the Nineteenth Century*. Brill, 2000; Schnurr, J. C. *Weltreiche und Wahrheitszeugen: Geschichtsbilder der protestantischen Erweckungsbewegung in Deutschland 1815 bis 1848*. Vandenhoeck & Ruprecht, 2011.

Jan Carsten Schnurr

Rhegius, Urbanus

The Lutheran reformer in Augsburg and Lower Saxony Urbanus Rhegius (1489–1541) was born in Langenargen on Lake Constance, the son of a priest and a concubine. He studied the arts and theology at Freiburg, Ingolstadt, and Basel. At Freiburg he met the theologian John Eck, later a prominent opponent of the Reformation. When Eck left to take a professorial post in Ingolstadt, Rhegius followed him there. Rhegius was ordained in 1519, and in 1520 he was named cathedral preacher in Augsburg. In that capacity he read the papal bull against Luther from the pulpit in 1520, although he did not take steps to enforce it. By 1521 Rhegius was convinced that Luther's theology was a faithful statement of catholic doctrine. When he began endorsing Luther's ideas from the pulpit in 1521, he was asked to leave, and he retired to Tirol. He was invited to return in 1523 by the Augsburg town council, which asked him to lead the Church of St. Anne and to help institute reforms. In 1524 he married, and in 1525 he led the first Evangelical celebration of the Lord's Supper in Augsburg. From his position in Augsburg, Rhegius became involved in several intra-Evangelical debates. In 1524–25 he tried to distance the Evangelical movement from revolutionary movements, especially the Peasants' Revolt. In 1527–28 Rhegius was involved in opposing the Anabaptists. Throughout the late 1520s he also participated in the ongoing debate between Zwingli and Luther over the Lord's Supper. Rhegius sought to maintain unity between the two reformers, and his own views of the Eucharist at this time reflect his attempt to moderate each of them. While in Augsburg, Rhegius authored several pamphlets on Evangelical theology, piety, and polemics. His treatise *Seelenärtzney für die Gesunden und Kranken zu disen gefärlichen Zeyten* (Soul medicine for the healthy and the sick in these dangerous times) was reprinted 121 times in the sixteenth and seventeenth centuries. At the Diet of Augsburg (1530), Rhegius was an active member of the Lutheran party. While attending the diet, Duke Ernst of Lüneburg (a signer of the Augsburg Confession) invited him to become Superintendent of Lüneburg and to help institute the Reformation there. Rhegius held this position from 1531 until his death in 1541. During this time he traveled with Duke Ernst to several meetings of the Smalcaldic League, including the meeting in 1537 when Luther's Smalcald Articles and Melanchthon's *Treatise on the Power and Primacy of the Pope* were circulated, to which Rhegius subscribed. While in Lüneburg, he penned exegetical works, catechisms, and two church orders (for Lüneburg in 1531 and Hannover in 1536). A homiletical handbook, which summarized basic Lutheran doctrine, explained Reformation controversies, and outlined implications for piety, was printed in 1535. In all of his writings, Rhegius emphasized the teaching of justification by faith and its significance for Christian life.

See also Augsburg; Eck, John; Marburg Colloquy; Melanchthon, Philip; Saxonies; Smalcald Articles; *Treatise on the Power and Primacy of the Pope*; Zwingli, Ulrich

Bibliography

Hampton, D. "Urbanus Rhegius and the Spread of the German Reformation." PhD diss., Ohio State University, 1973; Hendrix, S., ed. and trans. *Preaching the Reformation: The Homiletical Handbook of Urbanus Rhegius*. Marquette University Press, 2003; Liebmann, M. *Urbanus Rhegius und die Anfänge der Reformation*. Aschendorff, 1980; Rittgers, R. "Christianization through Consolation: Urbanus Rhegius's *Soul-Medicine for the Healthy and the Sick in These Dangerous Times* (1529)." In *The*

Reformation as Christianization, ed. A. Johnson and J. A. Maxfield, 322–45. Mohr Siebeck, 2012; Zschoch, H. *Reformatorische Existenz und Konfessionelle Identität: Urbanus Rhegius als evangelischer Theologe in den Jahren 1520 bis 1530*. Mohr Siebeck, 1995.

ANNA MARIE JOHNSON

Rheticus, Georg Joachim

The Lutheran physician Georg Joachim Rheticus (1514–74) was also a mathematician and an astronomer. As Nicholas Copernicus's "only student," Rheticus played a crucial role in helping his mentor publish the groundbreaking cosmological treatise *De revolutionibus orbium coelestium* (*On the Revolutions of Heavenly Spheres*), which generated an entirely new way of thinking about the structure of the universe. Rheticus is often referred to as the "first Copernican," and several scholars have even argued that without his urging, Copernicus may not have published the work he was doing to prove that the universe was heliocentric, not geocentric. Rheticus's father was an Austrian physician who was executed on charges of sorcery and theft when his son was only fourteen. Thanks to the support of a family friend, Rheticus was able to continue his studies and ended up at the University of Wittenberg in the 1530s, where he became an ally of Philip Melanchthon (1497–1560). From here he went on to work closely with Copernicus before becoming a professor and teacher of mathematics in Wittenberg in 1541—and at the University of Leipzig the following year. Rheticus spent the rest of his career as a mathematician-astronomer, also an instrument and mapmaker, in the service of a variety of patrons, including King Sigismund Augustus II (1520–72) of Poland, Holy Roman Emperor Maximilian II (1527–76), and Duke Albrecht of Prussia (1490–1568).

See also Melanchthon, Philip; Natural Science; University of Wittenberg in the Sixteenth Century

Bibliography

Burmeister, K. H. *Georg Joachim Rhetikus, 1514–1574*. Guido Pressler, 1967; Danielson, D. *The First Copernican: Georg Joachim Rheticus and the Rise of the Copernican Revolution*. Walker & Co., 2006; Westfall, R. *The Copernican Question: Prognostication, Skepticism, and Celestial Order*. University of California Press, 2011.

KELLY J. WHITMER

Rhetoric

Training in writing and delivering public addresses and, later, in analyzing the speeches and writings of others is called rhetoric. This discipline originated in the Greek city-states and became the principal form of higher education throughout the ancient world, especially as mediated to the Latin-speaking West through Cicero. The whole of rhetoric includes a breadth of concerns, despite frequent tendencies in history to reduce it to style and delivery. In the Middle Ages and the Renaissance the liberal arts course consisted in three verbal arts (the *Trivium*: grammar, dialectic, rhetoric), which prepared pupils to study four mathematical arts (the *Quadrivium*: arithmetic, geometry, music, and astronomy). The *Trivium*'s arts overlap: both grammar and rhetoric taught the rhetorical figures; mid-sixteenth-century curricular revisions modified the disciplinary domains among the *Trivium*'s arts.

Cultural change, both civic and religious, prompted specialization in the practice of rhetoric, as demonstrated in the medieval proliferation of manuals for preaching and letter writing. Rhetoric and the Renaissance are inextricably linked. Rhetoric appealed to the humanists because it trained pupils to use the full resources of the ancient languages and because it offered a genuinely classical view of the nature of language and its effective use in the world. The predominant rhetorical manuals of the Renaissance derived from Cicero (*On Invention*) and Quintilian (*Institutio oratoria*). Until the Renaissance, Cicero's *On Invention* and the pseudo-Ciceronian *Rhetorica ad Herennium* had dominated instruction in rhetoric. The latter work covered the whole of rhetoric: the three genres established by Aristotle, the five skills the orator must master, and the six parts of an oration. It was the five skills (invention, arrangement, style, memory, delivery) that were fully restored in the Renaissance.

Luther had training in the *Trivium* arts even before matriculating at the University of Erfurt, which had strong humanist leanings just prior to his arrival. At Wittenberg, Luther praised Philip Melanchthon's inaugural lecture in 1518, which championed language study (Greek and Hebrew) and stressed a reinvigorated *Trivium*, thus bolstering curricular proposals outlined in Nikolaus Marschalk's inaugural address as the first rector of the University of Wittenberg (1503). Melanchthon's rival for the Greek chair in Wittenberg, Peter Schade (Mosellanus) of Leipzig, published one rhetoric textbook; Melanchthon eventually wrote six textbooks on rhetoric and dialectic, emphasizing the connections between the two arts. Melanchthon was also the first to analyze the rhetorical structure of Paul's Letter to the Romans (1522), a type of analysis carried on by his students, including Caspar Cruciger Sr. and Georg Major, who published commentaries on the entire Pauline corpus.

Luther's Table Talk contains reflections on rhetoric and dialectic including his famous, if traditional, summary of the relation of rhetoric and logic: "Dialectic teaches [*docet*]; rhetoric motivates [*movet*]" (WA TR 2:259, #1906B). Luther was familiar with Aristotle's linking of rhetoric as counterpart (*antistrophos*) of dialectic (*Rhetoric* 1.1.1). However, Luther emphasized more often the Word proclaimed than a preacher's artistry. Clearly Luther valued both, however, as in his 1537 Table Talk verse: "*Res et verba Philippus, . . . res sine verbis Lutherus*" (Philip commands subject matter and the words, Luther the subject matter but not the words) (WA TR 3:460.39). The *De servo arbitrio* (1525), in which Luther surpasses Erasmus in classical allusions and references, demonstrates that Luther could indeed excel at rhetorical eloquence. His grasp of the classics found expression in his final written words, citing Cicero's *Epistles* and calling the Scriptures "this divine Aeneid" (WA TR 5:318; LW 54:476).

Knowledge of classical authors notwithstanding, the eloquence of the biblical writers provided Luther his best models for imitation; he also recommended Augustine as a model (*On Christian Doctrine*, a work praised by Luther and Spalatin). Luther named the Holy Spirit's eloquence that of a rhetor.

Contemporary scholars have noticed Luther's knowledge of rhetoric through his incorporation of its precepts across numerous genres: Stolt's many studies show Luther's rhetorical virtuosity; Nembach demonstrates Luther's esteem for Quintilian; Dockhorn perceives compatibility between Luther's concept of faith (*Glauben*) and rhetoric's notion of conviction (*pistis*); Junghans displayed Luther's recognition of various rhetorical devices the psalmists used (documented in the first Psalms lectures); O'Malley argues that Luther's preaching shows definite influence of the *Trivium* and labels him a Christian grammarian.

Luther's followers made their own contributions to rhetorical theory and used rhetoric to propagate the gospel. They established *Lateinschulen* (*gymnasia*), wrote preaching manuals (Melanchthon, after 1529; Veit Dietrich, after 1529; Hyperius, 1553) and handbooks of figures and tropes (Susenbrotus, 1540). Bach's *Passions* employed rhetorical structure, and other Baroque musicians developed systems of musical-rhetorical devices. Surely contemporary scholars will profit from the above (and other) studies and produce additional evidence of rhetoric in the writings of Luther and Lutherans.

See also Humanism and the Reformation; Melanchthon, Philip; Preaching

Bibliography

Dockhorn, K. "Rhetorica movet." In *Rhetorik*, ed. H. Schanze, 17–42. Athenaion, 1974; Junghans, H. *Der junge Luther und die Humanisten*. Böhlau, 1984; Leroux, N. *Luther's Rhetoric: Strategies and Style from the Invocavit Sermons*. Concordia, 2002; Mack, P. *A History of Renaissance Rhetoric, 1380–1620*. Oxford University Press, 2013; Nembach, U. *Predigt des Evangeliums*. Neukirchener Verlag, 1972; O'Malley, J. "Luther the Preacher." *Michigan Germanic Studies* 10 (1984): 3–16; Stolt, B. *Martin Luthers Rhetorik des Herzens*. Mohr Siebeck, 2000; Stolt, B. *Studien zur Luthers Freiheitstraktat*. Almquist & Wiksell, 1969.

Neil Leroux

Rinckart, Martin

The pastor, poet, and musician Martin Rinckart (or Rinkhart; 1586–1649) was born in Eilenburg, near Leipzig; his father was a poor coppersmith. Rinckart became a scholarship student and chorister at the St. Thomas school, Leipzig, in 1601; beginning in 1602 he studied theology at Leipzig University. In 1610 Rinckart became the head of the gymnasium and cantor of the St. Nicholas Church in Eisleben. He served as deacon in Erdeborn beginning in 1613 and archdeacon in Eilenburg from 1617 until his death. In 1617, for the centenary of the Reformation, Rinckart wrote seven dramas on Luther and the Reformation. Recognized as poet laureate, he authored sixty-six hymns during the period of the Thirty Years' War, a time of famine, plundering (the Swedes twice surrounded the city), and plague. In 1637 Rinckart was the only pastor in Eilenburg when plague struck the city. He conducted forty to fifty funerals per day, and altogether eight thousand people died in a two-year period, including Rinckart's first wife, Catherine. Today Rinckart is known for his hymn "Nun danket alle Gott," translated by Catherine Winkworth as "Now Thank We All Our God." The hymn was first printed in Rinckart's 1636 *Jesu Herz-Büchlein*. Johann Crüger paired the text with its familiar tune in the 1647 edition of his hymnal, *Praxis pietatis melica*. "Nun danket alle Gott" was sung at the celebration of the Peace of Westphalia in 1648. Found in many hymnbooks, it is now a celebratory song for state and civic occasions, often called the "German Te Deum."

See also Hymnody; Literature; Music

Bibliography

Julian, J. "Rinkart, Martin." In *A Dictionary of Hymnology*, 902–3. Dover Publications, 1957; Watson, J. R. "Martin Rinckart." In *The Canterbury Dictionary of Hymnology*, ed. J. R. Watson and E. Hornby, http://www.hymnology.co.uk/m/martin-rinckart. Canterbury Press, 2013–; Westermeyer, P. *Hymnal Companion to Evangelical Lutheran Worship*. Esp. 724–25. Augsburg Fortress, 2010.

Michael E. Krentz

Ritschl, Albrecht

As professor at the University of Bonn (1846–64) and at Göttingen (1864–89), Albrecht Ritschl (1822–89) was one of the most influential theological teachers during the second half of the nineteenth century, inspiring others, such as Adolf von Harnack, Wilhelm Herrmann, Karl Holl, Walter Rauschenbusch, and Ernst Troeltsch, to go beyond his own accomplishments. His father, a Protestant bishop in Pomerania fromin 1827 to 1854, was an advocate of the Prussian Union between Lutherans and Calvinists. Unlike the Confessionalists of his day, Ritschl retained his father's pro-Union sympathies.

At first deeply influenced by F. C. Baur, in 1856–57 Ritschl broke with Baur's framework for interpreting the early church. He retained Baur's emphasis on examining the whole panorama of biblical and church history in order to understand Christian teachings. But he moved away from the idealism of Schelling and Hegel toward a more sociological-historical approach, taking seriously the particularities of each context in which the faith was expressed. He charted the path followed by theology from the 1860s and continuing at least into the 1960s.

Ritschl gave a good deal of attention to studying the Bible. When compared with Baur and others, his views were rather conservative. He accepted an earlier dating of the New Testament books and identified an underlying consensus among the apostolic authors, even when working in differing social contexts (e.g., Jewish or gentile). The Bible was to be understood from within the community of faith, and its message was normative for Christianity.

Most exciting to Ritschl's younger contemporaries was his emphasis on Martin Luther, at a time when few studied Luther directly. Ritschl thought the experiential dynamism of the early Luther had been obscured by the Scholastic categories reintroduced as Luther defended his theology and further obscured by Philip Melanchthon and Lutheran Orthodoxy. He appealed to the young Luther to inspire ongoing reform. In so doing, Ritschl contributed significantly to the emerging Luther Renaissance and to skepticism regarding Melanchthon's contributions.

Ritschl also tried to develop a more dynamic and personal concept of God as "loving will," eschewing the abstractions of what he called "metaphysics" and what later came to be known as "classical theism." For Ritschl "all genuine knowledge of God is based solely on his self-revelation in Christ" (Lotz 42).

In ways not typical of his day, he insisted on the centrality of justification by grace through faith. This emphasis, as well as his emphasis on community, put him at odds with the rationalists or Enlightenment theologians. Reflecting the methods of historical theology, his magnum opus (The Christian Doctrine of Justification and Reconciliation, 1870–74; revised during the 1880s) has three volumes, one on the historical development of the doctrine, the second on its biblical grounding, and the third on its "positive development," or constructive proposals.

Ritschl also tried to spell out a Christian ethic that overcame the bifurcation between faith and life. For this he drew on a second Reformation idea: vocation. Though he shared with Pietism an emphasis on finding a way of life suitable for a person of faith, he objected to what he considered Pietism's world-renouncing orientation. This he associated with medieval piety rather than the community involvement advocated by Martin Luther.

For Ritschl, a movement is best understood by examining its original purposes. Once these purposes are understood, the historian can assess subsequent developments, distinguishing between continuities and distortions. Thus, he claimed, the core of Christianity can be identified by a historical examination of Jesus and the apostles, and Protestantism can be understood by examining Luther and Calvin, who had authority because of their insight into the biblical message.

Ritschl gave voice to the anxiety of his day that human freedom was threatened by a machinelike scientific image of the world and an increasingly industrialized society. People seemed to be but cogs in a machine. While not opposing science, he understood religion to provide support for persons over against this threat and viewed religion as a matter not just of passive belief but also of participation. His thinking was deeply influenced by Luther's treatise Freedom of a Christian.

One difficulty for studying Ritschl is that many of his insights are buried in his historical writings. The only publication that comes close to summarizing his thought is Instruction in the Christian Religion (1875) (Hefner 220–91), but this summary is too tame to convey anything of the excitement with which his ideas were greeted. The third volume of Justification and Reconciliation discusses only one part of Christian theology and is not well understood apart from his historical and biblical studies. A second difficulty has been the dismissal of Ritschl by neo-orthodox theologians, especially Karl Barth. This dismissal has obscured Ritschl's influence on early twentieth-century theology and the deep and important continuities linking Ritschl and Barth.

See also Barth, Karl; Baur, Ferdinand Christian; History; Holl, Karl; Liberalism; Luther Interpretation and Reception

Bibliography

Hefner, P., ed. Albrecht Ritschl: Three Essays. Fortress, 1972; Jodock, D., ed. Ritschl in Retrospect: History, Community, and Science. Fortress, 1995; Lotz, D. Ritschl and Luther: A Fresh Perspective on Albrecht Ritschl's Theology in the Light of His Luther Study. Abingdon, 1974; Ritschl, A. [The Christian Doctrine of Justification and Reconciliation. Vol. 1,] A Critical History of the Christian Doctrine of Justification and Reconciliation. Trans. J. S. Black. Edmiston & Douglas, 1872. Vol. 2 [no ET published]. Vol. 3, The Positive Development of the Doctrine. ET ed. H. R. Mackintosh and A. B. Macaulay. T&T Clark, 1900.

DARRELL JODOCK

Rosenius, Carl Olof

Born to a Swedish pastor and his wife in Nysätra, Norrland, Sweden, Carl Olof Rosenius (1816–68) eventually studied at the teachers school in Umeå and the gymnasium in Härnösand. The piety he knew as a youth put great value on Martin Luther's works, especially on justification, alongside the songbooks of the Moravian Swedes, *Sions Sånger* and *Sions nya sånger*. In 1830 Rosenius experienced a spiritual crisis that was resolved after he read Erik Pontoppidan's *Mirror of Faith*. He enrolled at the University of Uppsala in 1836 to study for the ministry, but had to withdraw for reasons of poverty and his disapproval of the theology, especially the biblical-historical criticism he found there. In 1839–40 he became an assistant to the Methodist preacher George Scott, who served the English in Stockholm. Scott helped Rosenius with his questions on the authority of Scripture, and soon Rosenius began preaching for him at the Bethlehem Church in the city. Scott helped Rosenius found the magazine *Pietisten*, published by Evangeliska Fosterlandsstiftelsen (National Evangelical Publisher) founded in 1856, and where Rosenius worked until his death. His theology centered on God's Word and a strong sense for Martin Luther's theology of justification: a sinner is saved by God's grace alone. For that he received the moniker "Little Luther." His magazine and devotional writings were mostly read in Sweden, yet much of it was translated into over thirty languages. Readers still treasure his devotional writings, *Believer Free from the Law* and *A Faithful Guide to Peace with God* (both appearing first as columns in *Pietisten*), and a few beloved hymns. His personality was larger than life: August Strindberg, Rosenius's contemporary and Sweden's greatest dramatist, said Rosenius "beamed with heavenly gladness." His preaching and writing, along with Lina Sandell's hymns, changed Sweden in their day. He died in Stockholm on February 24, 1868.

See also Pietism; Sweden

Bibliography

Arden, G. E. *Four Northern Lights*. Augsburg, 1964; Rosenius, C. O. *A Faithful Guide to Peace with God*. Augsburg, 1923; Rosenius, C. O. *Romans: A Devotional Commentary*. Covenant, 1978.

GRACIA GRINDAL

Rotermund, Wilhelm

The Brazilian Lutheran pastor who founded the Riograndian Synod (RS) was Wilhelm Rotermund (1843–1925). He was born in Germany, where he studied theology. After working as a private tutor, pastor, and school inspector, Rotermund was appointed secretary of the Committee for German Protestants in Southern Brazil in 1873. He earned a doctorate at Jena and was sent to Brazil by the Supreme Church Council of Berlin, becoming pastor of the Evangelical Church in São Leopoldo, RS, in 1875. Rotermund published textbooks for schoolwork, a calendar for the Germans in Brazil, and a periodical defending the Evangelical church against its opponents. He founded the Riograndian Synod in 1886 and was its president in 1886–94 and 1909–19.

See also Brazil; Igreja Evangélica de Confissão Luterana no Brasil (IECLB) (Evangelical Church of the Lutheran Confession in Brazil)

Bibliography

Dreher, M. N. *Kirche und Deutschtum in der Entwicklung der Evangelischen Kirche Lutherischen Bekenntnisses in Brasilien*. Vandenhoeck & Ruprecht, 1978; Prien, H.-J. *Evangelische Kirchwerdung in Brasilien*. G. Mohn, 1989.

PAULO WILLE BUSS

Rudbeckius, Johannes

A native of Sweden, Johannes Rudbeckius (April 3, 1581–August 8, 1646), became a Swedish Lutheran bishop and university professor. Building on his early education in Sweden, he received a master's degree from the University of Wittenberg in 1603. After returning to Sweden, he taught Hebrew and theology at Uppsala University and also served as rector. King Gustavus Adolphus appointed him to be his chaplain and court preacher, and he followed the king on his extensive campaigns and travels. During this time he was also deeply involved in a new translation of the Bible into Swedish, which became known as the Gustavus Adolphus Bible. In 1619 Rudbeckius was appointed bishop of Västernås, which he served for twenty-six years and where he had his greatest impact. As the leading Swedish bishop of his age, Rudbeckius worked tirelessly to improve conditions within his diocese, especially founding schools at all levels (including for girls in 1632 and for pastors), as well social service institutions. In 1627 the king appointed him as episcopal visitor to Estonia, where he helped institute many fundamental changes. Rudbeckius was a strong advocate for the Church of Sweden and came into conflict with the king and his chancellor, Axel Oxenstierna, over the power of the bishops and the church. After the king's death in 1632, the chancellor blocked him from being appointed archbishop, and he remained as bishop in Västernås until his death.

See also Sweden

MARK A. GRANQUIST

Rumba, Edgars

The Latvian pastor, theologian, polyglot, and martyr Edgars Rumba (1904–43) studied theology in Riga and Uppsala. As vicar in Jelgava (1927–28), he made a profound impression on the future Latvian church leader Roberts Feldmanis, becoming his father confessor. Ordained in 1929, Rumba taught in a Lutheran high school (1929–33) and at the Rīga Teacher's Institute (1934–36), at the same time exercising pastoral duties at the Swedish congregation in Riga (1931–41): Riga Christ's congregation (1932–39), Riga's university church (1936–41), and Mežapark's Gustavus Adolphus congregation (1941). He lectured at the Riga Faculty of Theology (1933–36, 1939–40) and was a member of the editorial board for the *Latvian Conversational Dictionary*. Among his publications were (in Latvian) *Archbishop Nathan Söderblom* (1936), *Christ and the Parish* (1937), *The Task of Preaching and Its Preparation* (1939), and *The Church and the Office in Ecumenical-Lutheran Understanding* (1939). He actively promoted ecumenical relationships and served in various administrative posts in the church, including leadership of foreign missions (1931–36) and as a member of Latvian church's board of directors. He edited two journals, *The Road of the Youth*

(1931–35) and *Foreign Missions* (1936–37), and published hymns in periodicals and in *The Supplement of the Lutheran Hymnal* (1938).

Rumba and his family were arrested on May 14, 1941, in the first Soviet deportation of Latvians. The family was separated; he was deported to Reshoti, Irkutsk region, Siberia, where he secretly served as pastor and eventually died of hunger. Recently his collected works have been published (in Latvian), *Beyond Prejudices: Denials and Illusions* (1994), and his poetry, *Today I Will Not Come Home* (2013).

See also Feldmanis, Roberts Emīls; Latvia

GUNTIS KALME

Russia

Lutheran skilled tradesmen began arriving in the Russian Empire in appreciable numbers during the reign of Ivan the Terrible (r. 1547–84). Ivan at first reacted favorably to Lutheranism and in 1576 allowed the first Lutheran church (St. Michael's) to be built in Moscow. Eventually Ivan decided that Martin Luther was a heretic who minimized the necessity of good works. Lutherans were subsequently often subjected to periods of persecution throughout their history in Russia, despite their contributions to society in the commercial, governmental, and educational spheres.

The position of Lutherans improved in the eighteenth century under the influence of sympathetic czars, including Peter the Great (r. 1689–1725) and Catherine the Great (r. 1762–96). In 1702, Peter the Great issued a historic decree giving ethnic minorities freedom of religion. In the process, he marginalized the state Orthodox Church by forming a Holy Synod to regulate religious affairs. Under the direction of the Holy Synod, weddings were now allowed between people of different faiths without the stipulation that the one party had to convert to Orthodoxy. Bell towers of Lutheran churches, banned under previous czars, were once again allowed. In 1723 the Holy Synod even permitted the translation and printing of Luther's Small Catechism into Russian.

Upon her accession to power, Catherine the Great, who was born into a Lutheran German noble family but converted to Russian Orthodoxy, continued Peter's favorable treatment of the Lutherans. In a manifesto issued on July 22, 1763, she invited Germans to settle the Volga River region and practice their faith freely. The government provided assistance in building churches and allowed Germans to bring along their own pastors, the majority being Lutheran. They were, however, still forbidden to convert Orthodox believers to Lutheranism. Czar Alexander I (r. 1801–25) continued his grandmother's policy, inviting Germans, most of whom were Lutherans, to settle the Black Sea region in what is today the Ukraine. Although German was the dominant language among Lutherans, by the nineteenth century the Lutheran Church was becoming multiethnic. More than 70 percent of its parishioners were German, followed in statistical order by Finns, Estonians, Latvians, Swedes, Lithuanians, Poles, and a surprising number of Armenians. On December 28, 1832, the Lutheran Church became more closely linked to the state when Nicholas I (r. 1825–55) signed into law a church constitution that made him titular head of the Russian Lutheran Church in theory if not in practice.

During the nineteenth century, the Lutheran Church became renowned in Russia for its charitable institutions. St. Petersburg led the way as its largest congregation, St. Peter's, established the first home for orphans in 1821. Lutherans not only assisted the most vulnerable in society but also preached their faith. Hospitals, homes for widows, and various associations to help the unemployed or provide aid for the poor were established. Lutheran schools became so respected in society that even ethnic Russians enrolled, including the future famous musician Modest Mussorgsky. Lutheran pastors often founded these schools; the most famous founder was Pastor Heinrich Dieckhoff of Moscow.

The outbreak of World War I in 1914 initiated a time of trial, with the loyalty of ethnic Germans considered suspect by the government. Eighty-four Lutheran pastors suffered varying forms of persecution (including imprisonment), and thirty of them were exiled to Siberia. Despite the Lutheran Church's trials, on the eve of the Bolshevik Revolution in 1917 there were still 3,674,000 Lutherans and 1,828 churches and prayerhouses throughout Russia.

The coming of the Bolshevik Revolution proved to be a tragedy for all Christians. A governmental decree issued on January 23, 1918, called for a separation of church from state and school from church. The decree severed Lutheran churches from the substantial properties and charitable institutions developed throughout their 350-year existence in Russia. Religion classes were forbidden, forcing the closure of approximately 1,300 Lutheran church schools and affecting the spiritual education of 100,000 children.

With the Baltic states now independent from the Soviet Union, the Lutheran Church lost its seminary in Dorpat, Estonia, as well as many pastors of foreign origin, who fled to more hospitable countries. After the initial phase of persecution, however, a window of opportunity appeared for the Lutheran Church. In 1924 a Lutheran Church Synod was allowed in Moscow for the first time in history. Likewise, a seminary was permitted to open its doors in 1925, holding classes in St. Anne's Lutheran Church in St. Petersburg.

These positive steps led many Lutherans to believe that they might be able to withstand the growing influence of atheism in the USSR, but those hopes were dashed when Joseph Stalin won the struggle for political power. The persecution of the church intensified when Stalin issued a decree on April 8, 1929, banning Christian education within the churches and permitting only divine worship. Some pastors tried to thwart the law but were soon arrested. In autumn 1929, the workweek was altered with the result that Sunday was no longer a universal day of rest for laborers. These assaults on the church drastically reduced the number of active parishioners and pastors.

The future prospects of the church dwindled even further when the seminary was forced to close in 1934 due to the arrests and forced military service of the remaining students. On Christmas Eve 1937 the last remaining church, St. Peter's in Leningrad, was closed.

While the official Lutheran Church was dead, parishioners secretly kept alive the faith in their homes and communities. In the 1970s permission was given to restore congregations in Russian territory, first in Petrozavodsk and then in Pushkin. One year before the fall of the Soviet Union, a law allowing freedom of conscience was passed, and upon the demise of the Communist state (USSR) in 1991, Lutheran churches began to reopen throughout the country.

Today there are three major Lutheran church bodies operating in Russia. The largest church is the Evangelical Lutheran Church of Russia and Other States (ELCROS), the second is the Evangelical Lutheran Church of Ingria, and the third is the Siberian Evangelical Lutheran Church. The first is a member of the LWF. The second a member of both the LWF and the ILC. The third a member of the ILC.

See also Dieckhoff, Heinrich Wilhelm; Gregorius, Johann Gottfried; Kretschmar, Georg; Kugappi, Aari; Meier, Theophil; Muss, Kurt; Volga Germans

MATTHEW HEISE

Sachs, Hans

As Nuremberg shoemaker, poet, and lay propagandist for the Lutheran Reformation, Hans Sachs (1494–1576) hailed from an artisan home but attended Latin school, after which he apprenticed as a shoemaker. A fellow artisan introduced him to master-singing, a method of composing and performing verse and melody that was popular among artisans in many German cities. He married in 1519 and had seven children, none of whom survived him; and, upon the death of his first wife, he remarried in 1561. Sachs had an astonishing literary career, producing over six thousand texts. The majority were master songs, but some were comedies, tragedies, Lenten carnival plays, fables, farces, prose dialogues, and poems, all of which had a strong moralistic content.

Deeply sympathetic to Luther, Sachs used his literary talent to author pamphlets that conveyed the Evangelical message to his fellow artisans. The most popular of these pamphlets was *The Wittenberg Nightingale* (1523). (Richard Wagner later drew on it in his opera *Die Meistersinger von Nürnberg*, 1868.) In 1527 the pro-Luther but conservative Nuremberg city council placed him under a temporary publication ban for his harsh verses against the papacy. Sachs remained a committed Lutheran but lamented the lack of wholesale societal reform that he hoped the Reformation would bring to his city.

See also Literature; Nuremberg

Bibliography

Bernstein, E., *Hans Sachs*. Reinbeck, 1993; Keller, A. V., and E. Goetze, eds. *Hans Sachs Werke*. 26 vols. Litterarischen Verein, 1870–1908. Reprint, Olms, 1964–82; Russell, P. A. *Lay Theology in the Reformation: Popular Pamphleteers in Southwest Germany, 1521–1525*. Esp. 165–84. Cambridge University Press, 1986.

RONALD K. RITTGERS

Sacraments

"Sacrament" comes from a Latin term for a pledge or military oath of allegiance that became in ecclesiastical Latin something to be kept sacred. In the Latin Vulgate, Jerome translated the Greek *mystērion* as *sacramentum*, leading to its use to designate baptism and especially the Lord's Supper. Peter Lombard's identification of seven sacraments in the *Sentences* (baptism, the Eucharist, penance, ordination, marriage, confirmation, and last rites) became standard in the Middle Ages. Luther, who criticized the medieval sacramental system in *The Babylonian Captivity of the Church* (1520), saw sacraments as the external means that God established to promise and deliver the benefits of Christ's redeeming work to sinners.

Luther confessed that God deals with humanity externally through the verbal words of the proclaimed gospel. These dominical words attached to water, bread, and wine become (using Augustine's designation) visible words and give what they promise. Yet Luther does not begin with an overarching and generic definition of "sacrament" and then proceed to enumerate specific "sacraments." His starting point, instead, are the words of Jesus, which institute or establish the sacraments. This approach can be seen both in the Small Catechism, intended for the instruction of children and the laity, and in his longer theological treatises.

Luther the reformer continues to use the traditional sacramental language of the church even while critiquing the medieval abuses. His teaching on the sacraments is anchored in his confidence that Christ alone is the Lord who has accomplished the salvation of sinners by his death and resurrection and now delivers the fruits of that work in these means that he has instituted. Luther understands baptism, the word of absolution, and the Lord's Supper to be the most concentrated form of the gospel because they deliver what they promise, the forgiveness of sins. He continues to use the Augustinian language of "sign" in reference to baptism and the Lord's Supper, but these "signs" are far from mere symbols pointing to realities located within the believer or in the heavenly realm; the signs themselves carry and deliver what they promise. In a similar way in the 1521 edition of the *Loci communes*, Philip Melanchthon identifies signs with miracles.

While the confession of the sacraments and their right use would occupy Luther for his entire career, his 1520 treatise *The Babylonian Captivity of the Church* set the stage. Here Luther denies that there are seven sacraments, listing at this point three: baptism, penance, and the Lord's Supper. These three have "been subjected to miserable captivity by the Roman curia, and the church has been robbed of all her liberty" (LW 36:18). Luther focuses on the Sacrament of the Altar (Eucharist), declaring that it is held captive in three ways: the withholding of the chalice from the laity, the teaching of transubstantiation, and the understanding of the Mass as sacrifice. As he did in an earlier writing, *Treatise on the New Testament, That Is, the Holy Mass* (1519), Luther accents the character of the Lord's Supper as a testament, a word entailing both the incarnation and the atonement. In these early writings he argues for a clear distinction between the testament of Christ and the prayers of the congregation. Luther's liturgical reforms reflect his convictions of the promissory nature of the Lord's Supper and faith's reception of what God bestows in the sacrament. The sacraments are not the work of the priest but of the Triune God.

Luther's battle for the sacraments, especially the Lord's Supper, was fought on two fronts. In addition to his multifaceted polemic against papal doctrine and practice, he also engaged the so-called Sacramentarians,

represented by Ulrich Zwingli (1484–1531) and Johannes Oecolampadius (1482–1531). This controversy, begun in 1524, culminated at the Marburg Colloquy in October 1529, where Luther decisively rejected a spiritualistic understanding of Christ's presence in the Lord's Supper. Leading up to this event, Luther produced several significant treatises, especially *That These Words of Christ, "This is My Body," etc., Still Stand Firm against the Fanatics* (1527) and the *Confession of Christ's Supper* (1528), making the case for an understanding of the Lord's Supper based on the words Christ used to institute the sacrament; he was adamant not to depart from the clear meaning of the words of Jesus, "This is my body. . . . This is my blood." After the Colloquy of Marburg (1529), the discussions continued with Martin Bucer and other southern Germans over the nature of Christ's presence in the sacrament of the Lord's Supper, leading to the Wittenberg Concord of 1536. Aspects of these controversies, fueled by the emergence of Calvinism, continued after Luther's death and did not reach decisive conclusion until 1577, when article 7 of the Formula of Concord confessed, using exegetical arguments and careful distinctions, that Christ's true body and blood are given with bread and wine, to be consumed by all who eat and drink.

There was less of a battle over baptism with Rome than over the Lord's Supper. Rome had retained the baptism of infants but had narrowed the scope of baptism's efficacy to a cleansing from original sin and initiation into the church's sacramental life of grace. Luther insisted that baptism washes away all sin, delivers the entire Christ with all his gifts, and bestows the Holy Spirit, who regenerates sinners in this sacrament. For Luther, the Christian life is a continual return to baptism in repentance and faith. Penance, Luther wrote in the Large Catechism, is no "second plank" once the ship of baptism has been splintered in the stormy seas of actual sin, as Jerome had argued; instead, it is a return to baptism, which forever remains intact (LC, Baptism, 77–82 in *BC* 466).

Even as Luther was doing battle with the Sacramentarians over the Lord's Supper, he was also writing against Anabaptists, who rejected the baptism of infants, especially in *On Rebaptism* (1528; LW 40:225–62) and the Large Catechism (1529). Luther held together the divine Word with the water; the two are inseparable because God has joined them. Faith clings to the promise that God has placed in the water. The Radical Reformers, Luther asserts, despise the water and in doing so they despise the Word itself. In large part, Luther's exposition of baptism in both of the catechisms is polemically directed against the Anabaptists even as he seeks to pastorally demonstrate the Evangelical significance of baptism for the consolation of terrified consciences. It is in the externality of baptism that Luther sees the comfort of God's unfailing promise of the Spirit's regenerating work and the bestowal of the forgiveness of sins. This theme is carried forward in Luther's treatment of both baptism and the Lord's Supper in his Genesis lectures of 1535–45, and it is given liturgical expression in his revised baptismal rite of 1526.

Luther was able to speak of penance—that is, absolution—as a "third sacrament," although he did not see it as independent of baptism. Luther argued that private confession is to be retained in the church for the sake of absolution, and he was frustrated when Christian freedom was used as an excuse to set it aside. In 1531 Luther inserted a brief order for confession into his earlier version of the Small Catechism, along with catechetical questions for confession and directions on how confession is to be made. Locating this material between baptism and the Sacrament of the Altar, Luther anchored confession and absolution in baptism since they anticipate a salutary eating and drinking in the Lord's Supper. Article 11 of the Augsburg Confession asserts that private absolution is retained without the enumeration of sins, linking it to repentance in article 12.

Article 13 of the Augsburg Confession demonstrates the Wittenberg reformers' concern for the Evangelical use of the sacraments against Zwinglian and Roman positions. The sacraments are not only signs or marks of the profession of faith among human beings, as Zwingli and others held, but also "signs and testimonies of God's will toward us" (CA 13.1 in *BC* 47) through which the promise is extended. Rejected is the teaching that the sacraments are rituals that justify by performance (*ex opere operato*) rather than by faith in the promise that they bestow. In the Apology 13.7–12 (*BC* 220–21), Melanchthon makes arguments for why ordination could under certain circumstances also be considered a sacrament.

Theologians of the period of Lutheran Orthodoxy, following the lead of Martin Chemnitz, would engage in a spirited defense of the doctrine of the sacraments against the decrees of the Council of Trent on one side and those of the heirs of Calvin on the other side, even as the hymns and devotional writings of the period reflect a vital appreciation for their benefits in the lives of believers. Pietism and rationalism, each in its own way, posed critical challenges to the Lutheran understanding of the sacraments as divinely instituted means of grace. Out of both Pietism and rationalism, new questions emerged regarding the objectivity of the sacraments and the place of faith in subjectively appropriating their benefits. The Confessional Revival of the nineteenth century witnessed a renewed and often vigorous reclaiming of the sacraments in doctrinal theology, catechesis, churchly piety, and liturgical life.

In the twentieth century Lutherans had to address the challenges of Karl Barth regarding the practice of baptizing infants, and of New Testament exegetes who questioned whether the words instituting baptism and the Lord's Supper came from Jesus himself or were the product of the early Christian community. Such critical exegesis of the New Testament along with ecumenical and liturgical movements caused Lutheran theologians and churches to reassess historic teachings and practice. Some hailed these movements as broadening traditional Lutheran understandings of the sacraments, leading to ecumenical achievements—such as the Arnoldshain Theses (1957), the Leuenberg Agreement (1977), and *Baptism, Eucharist and Ministry* produced by the World Council of Churches in 1982—and giving birth to numerous new hymnals with sacramental practices previously not seen in the Lutheran tradition. Others feared a loss in both the substance of the unique Lutheran confession of the sacraments and the introduction of liturgical forms and practices alien to the tradition. The place of the sacraments in contemporary Lutheran theologies and practices remains a matter of contention, as can be seen in debates over worship, the purpose of the sacraments, the relation of the ordained ministry to the administration of the sacraments, and questions relating to church fellowship and so-called eucharistic hospitality.

See also Baptism; Lord's Supper; Ministry; Penance, Penitence, Repentance

Bibliography

Forde, G. "Preaching the Sacraments." In *The Preached God: Proclamation in Word and Sacrament*, ed. M. Mattes and S. Paulson, 89–115. Eerdmans, 2007; Jensen, G. "Luther and the Lord's Supper." In *The Oxford Handbook of Martin Luther's Theology*, ed. R. Kolb, I. Dingel, and L. Batka, 322–32. Oxford, 2014; Olson, O. K. *Reclaiming the Lutheran Liturgical Heritage*. Reclaim Resources, 2007; Paulson, S. "What Is Essential to Lutheran Worship?" *Word & World* 26 (Spring 2006): 149–61; Peters, A. *Commentary on Luther's Catechisms: Baptism and the Lord's Supper*. Trans. T. Trapp. Concordia, 2012; Reu, J. M. *Two Treatises on the Means of Grace*. Augsburg, 1952; Sasse, H. *This Is My Body: Luther's Contention for the Real Presence in the Sacrament of the Altar*. Augsburg, 1959; Sasse. H. *We Confess the Sacraments*. Trans. N. Nagel. Concordia, 1985; Schlink. E. *The Doctrine of Baptism*. Trans. H. Bouman. Concordia, 1972; Wisløff, C. *The Gift of Communion*. Trans. J. Shaw. Augsburg, 1964.

JOHN T. PLESS

Salvation

As a key soteriological term of comprehensive character and historically variable metaphors, "salvation" comprehends everything the Christian faith proclaims and teaches concerning God's activity in and through Jesus Christ

for humankind and the world (Seils 622–24). Luther succinctly described salvation when discussing baptism in his catechisms: "To be saved, as everyone well knows, is nothing else than to be delivered from sin, death, and the devil, to enter into Christ's kingdom, and to live with him forever" (*BC* 459.25; 359.5–8). Yet, as Luther's voluminous writings illustrate, he could never say enough concerning salvation. Throughout his career he interpreted, expounded, preached, and sang salvation as the essence of theology. "The proper subject of theology is humankind guilty of sin and condemned, and God the Justifier and Savior of the human sinner. . . . The issue here is the future and eternal life; the God who justifies, repairs, and makes alive; and humans, who fell from righteousness and life into sin and eternal death" (LW 12:311, alt.; Bayer, *Theology*, 17–21).

The focal point of Luther's understanding of salvation is justification: this is not what the sinner achieves but what the sinner receives. "God does not want to redeem us through our own, but through external righteousness and wisdom; not through one that comes from us and grows in us, but through one that comes to us from the outside. . . . Therefore, we must be taught a righteousness that comes completely from the outside and is foreign" (LW 25:136). Luther "undid the entire traditional understanding of salvation and its historical religious logic of gift and giving back. In place of the two-way medieval Catholic path of gradual cooperation between God and humanity that leads to salvation, there entered the new theme that God alone is effective. . . . In total passivity, as absolute beneficiaries, they—the poor and the pitiful—receive a heaven, a salvation, and a blessedness that have been prepared for them by God alone" (Hamm 257; cf. Bayer, *Theology*, 24).

Luther's unconditional theocentric soteriology provided certainty of salvation. "The Gospel commands us to look, not at our own good deeds or perfection but at God Himself as He promises, and at Christ Himself, the Mediator. . . . This is the reason why our theology is certain: it snatches us away from ourselves and places us outside ourselves, so that we do not depend on our own strength, conscience, experience, person, or works but depend on that which is outside ourselves, that is, on the promise and truth of God which cannot deceive" (LW 26:387; see also LW 35:88; Lienhard 388: "Luther's Christology is from the beginning, soteriology").

In the Formula of Concord and in the Lutheran Orthodoxy that arose with it, Lutherans continued to stress the centrality of salvation (see Solid Declaration, art. 3, on justification). With the Enlightenment and idealism, however, Lutheran theology once again became increasingly anthropocentric. "Salvation" focused on emulation of Jesus's God-consciousness and ethics. For liberal theologians such as Adolf von Harnack (1851–1930) and Ernst Troeltsch (1865–1923), the significance of Jesus was his proclamation of God's kingdom of love. The shock of World War I and the initiation of the Luther Renaissance by Karl Holl (1866–1926) contributed to the rise of dialectical theology (God's "no" to sin and "yes" to redemption). Theologians such as Paul Tillich (1886–1965), Rudolf Bultmann (1884–1976), and Gerhard Ebeling (1912–2001), among others, found resources in Luther's theology for contemporary proclamation, as have some recent expressions of Latin American liberation theology (e.g., Walter Altman, *Luther and Liberation: A Latin American Perspective* [Fortress, 1992]). Ecumenical reflections on Luther's understanding of salvation include the focus on theosis (Greek: *theōsis*) advanced by the Finnish school of Luther research spearheaded by Tuomo Mannermaa, and the controversial Joint Declaration on the Doctrine of Justification developed in Lutheran-Catholic ecumenical dialogue.

See also Atonement; Baptism; Bultmann, Rudolf (Karl); Ebeling, Gerhard; Good Works; Holl, Karl; Justification; Sanctification

Bibliography

Bayer, O. *Theologie*. Gütersloher Verlagshaus, 1994. Partial ET as *Theology the Lutheran Way*. Trans. J. G. Silcock and M. C. Mattes. Eerdmans, 2007; Frey, J., S. Krauter, and H. Lichtenberger, eds. *Heil und Geschichte: Die Geschichtsbezogenheit des Heils und das Problem der Heilsgeschichte in der biblischen Tradition und in der theologischen Deutung*. Mohr Siebeck, 2009; Hamm, B. *The Early Luther: Stages in a Reformation Reorientation*. Trans. M. J. Lohrmann. Eerdmans, 2014; Lienhard, M. *Luther: Witness to Jesus Christ: Stages and Themes of the Reformer's Christology*. Trans. E. H. Robertson. Augsburg, 1982; Sattler, D., and V. Leppin, eds. *Heil für Alle? Ökumenische Reflexionen*. Herder / Vandenhoeck & Ruprecht, 2012; Seils, M. "Heil und Erlösung: IV. Dogmatisch." *TRE* 14:622–37.

CARTER LINDBERG

Sanctification

In medieval theology, sanctification was not a separate category in theological systems. For Martin Luther, sanctification is God making sinners holy. In the Large Catechism, Luther speaks of the Holy Spirit applying the treasure of salvation to sinners by the preaching of the word so that to sanctify "is nothing else than to bring us to the Lord Christ to receive this blessing, which we could not obtain by ourselves." Luther distinguished Christian sanctification as an alien and passive holiness: God is working sanctification in sinners, not sinners working it in themselves. Here, and already in the Heidelberg Disputation (1518), Luther fought against Aristotelian teaching that people become just by doing just things. In order to become holy, people must despair of themselves, even of their best works, and trust in the forgiveness of Christ. God works holiness in sinners by his word, which "sanctifies everything it touches" (LW 41:149), and through which the Holy Spirit creates faith, which grabs hold of Christ and his righteousness. The Holy Spirit works through the preaching of the word, the sacraments, and the absolution to give us the treasures of Christ's death and resurrection. In contrast to typical notions of human progress, Luther viewed sanctification not as the improvement or rehabilitation of the sinner, but as God putting the old, sinful creature to death and raising the new creature to life in Christ (LW 12:384).

In theological discourse, sanctification has been controversial as it relates to justification, the teaching that sinners are forgiven and receive righteousness through faith in Christ alone. Within Luther's lifetime, among both his Roman Catholic opponents and his Wittenberg colleagues, there was a concern that justification was not sufficient in itself to save a sinner and that sanctification supplied what was lacking. The Roman authors of the Augsburg Interim allowed that people are justified by faith, but suggested that justified persons are subsequently sanctified, understood as an outpouring of God's love into their hearts, and that without such love, their righteousness would be incomplete.

In Wittenberg, reformers began to distinguish between forensic and effective justification, especially in light of the Osiandrian controversy. The Lutheran understanding of justification has always been forensic in character (i.e., imputed): God reckons as righteous the one who has faith in Christ. The term "forensic" has been helpful in stating that we are righteous not in ourselves but for Christ's sake, as Melanchthon used it in the first edition of the Apology: "'Justify' is used in a judicial [forensic] way to mean 'to absolve a guilty man and pronounce him righteous,' and to do so on account of someone else's righteousness, namely, Christ's, which is communicated to us through faith" (Ap 4.305, in Tappert, 154). We are righteous because God has declared us to be so (cf. Ap 4 in *BC* 165). The judicial language, however, could be misinterpreted to imply that our righteousness is merely a legal fiction—the indulgent judge winking at the guilty party, who remains guilty—and so theologians distinguished between forensic justification and effective justification, on the assumption that the former left sinners intact, whereas the latter made them righteous in ways that could be measured by the law.

Andreas Osiander (1498–1552) tried to stress justification's effectiveness over against its forensic nature by positing that faith is a mystical union of indwelling between sinners and Christ's divine nature, such that Christ's love flooded into believers and then spilled out from them. This approach was widely rejected by other Lutherans, so that the Formula of Concord defended a forensic understanding and countered that our righteousness consists in God's forgiveness—without our past, present, or future worthiness, such as Christ's love spilling from us. The Formula, using a phrase coined by Philip Melanchthon in the 1530s, directs attention to the *particulae exclusivae*, the exclusive terms in which Paul separates Christ's justifying of sinners apart from the merits of the justified. At the same time, the Formula insists that faith is active and that there can be no true faith that does not result in good works.

In its efforts to describe the effectiveness of justification, Lutheran Orthodoxy took a cue from Philip Melanchthon and David Chytraeus, who had spoken of three aspects of saving faith (*notitia*, *assensus*, *fiducia*), from which they developed their own *ordo salutis*, with steps such as calling, illumination, repentance, regeneration, justification, and sanctification. Lutheran Pietism, insofar as it was a reaction against the perceived dryness of Orthodoxy, spoke of the ways in which faith must be lived and not merely taught and insisted that Christians not overly rely on the saving power of their baptism while continuing to live unholy lives. Thus teachers of both Lutheran Orthodoxy and Pietism directed attention first to the inner workings and then to the outer work of the regenerated sinner, which does not square well with faith that gives sinners ears for Christ alone.

Indeed, for those who wanted to treat sanctification as a separate step that supplements something lacking in a supposedly ineffective justification, sanctification ends up being measured according to the law. *The Lutheran Cyclopedia* of 1899 stated as much unapologetically: "The standard of sanctification is the law of God." Regin Prenter (1907–90) pointed to this problem in his study of Luther's writings on the Holy Spirit, *Spiritus Creator* (230–31).

The problem with measuring sanctification according to the law is twofold. First, according to Scripture, sanctification comes by faith, and even though faith itself can be commanded in the law, as it is in the first commandment, Christian faith does not come from obedience to the law but from the working of the Holy Spirit through the Word, even breaking the will of the sinner who recoils from the law. The law can command, but it cannot give. Luther uses the term *spontanea sanctificatio* (spontaneous sanctification) in his lectures on Isaiah to designate the kingdom of Christ, where the Christian acts not out of compulsion but willingly (LW 16:29).

The apostle Paul points out the second problem with measuring sanctification according to the law: Christ has become our sanctification (1 Cor. 1:30), and Christ has died. The law no longer has authority over one who has died (Rom. 7:1–6), which means the law has no authority over our sanctification. While it is true that the Holy Spirit extracts truly good, empirical works from Christians, and while those works can be seen and judged according to the law, their true standard, what makes them holy, is not their conformity to the commandments, but that God is the one who works and extracts them.

Such an understanding of sanctification is antinomian only in the sense that the new life of believers is lived with the law behind them as an accomplished fact, since Christ has fulfilled the law and freed us from the law's judgment. On the other hand, it is not antinomian in the sense of Johann Agricola (1499–1566), who maintained that the law is to be heard in the courthouse and not the church. Christians continue to preach the law against the flesh, which clings. Luther even spoke of the importance of the law in relation to sanctification in *On the Councils and the Church*: "We need the Decalogue . . . to discern how far the Holy Spirit has advanced us in his work of sanctification and by how much we still fall short of the goal, lest we become secure and imagine that we have now done all that is required" (LW 41:166). The precision of his language here is to be observed. The law can reveal how much good the Holy Spirit has done, and how much the sinner has fallen short. Thus the law gives praise to God and condemns the person as a sinner. In regard to one's own work, the law is not intended as a helper, but as a humbler. The law cannot aid one's own contribution to sanctification, but only reveal what progress God has made and where the sinner has failed. Luther's comments elsewhere about the hiddenness of the Christian life are to safeguard against the idea that sanctification is entirely observable and measurable by the law. The sheep will say to Christ, "When did we see you hungry and feed you?" So Christians are unaware of the full extent to which God is drawing real fruit from them.

Christians preach about the regenerated life because there is no true distinction between forensic and effective justification. Justification by faith is always effective because it is the Holy Spirit who works faith, and the Holy Spirit's working of faith is never less than the death of sinners and a new creation, as Christ indicates in his conversation with Nicodemus in John 3. Justification and sanctification are the bearing in of God on sinners, and so sinners are no longer in charge of their salvation or holiness. This awareness of God's sovereign working must be kept in mind as one reads Luther in *On the Councils and the Church*, where he chastises preachers who want to discuss redemption but not sanctification. The sinner has come under the working of God, and so it makes no sense for Christians to say that they want to be redeemed and yet continue in sin. The old Adam and Eve are no longer in charge. Christ is ruling over his people by the Holy Spirit.

Justification and sanctification are of the same cloth, and a person must be careful not to make too great a distinction between the two. The notion of a momentary justification followed by a progress in sanctification is foreign to Scripture. Acts 26:18 speaks of being sanctified by faith. Paul speaks of sanctification as a completed event alongside justification (1 Cor. 6:11), and Heb. 10:14 speaks of the sanctified as already perfected. Gerhard Forde (1927–2005) described sanctification as getting used to one's justification. One must never treat progress in sanctification as though one gradually needed less and less of Christ's forgiveness.

The extent to which sanctification has been equated almost exclusively with good works is responsible for some of the confusion. One finds comments in Luther connecting the two, but Luther continually returns to the theme of the sanctifying power of God's Word and Holy Spirit, a theme that Osiander's opponents and the authors of the Formula of Concord also pick up on. In the Large Catechism, Luther's definition points to sanctification as the Spirit's work of bringing sinners to Christ for salvation. Because this is the Spirit's complete and radical new creation, love of God and neighbor spontaneously happen, as Luther already stressed in *Freedom of a Christian*. That the Word and Spirit enliven and yield fruit is a given with Luther, but in Luther one does not sense the same preoccupation found in other writers who defend the honor of the Word and Spirit by inventorying their fruit. Where Luther does speak about the good works associated with sanctification, he insists that they are the fruit of holiness, not the building blocks.

The fruit that the Holy Spirit extracts from believers is despised by the world, and so Christians must be cautious about trusting visible evidence of the Spirit's working. Luther often contrasted the spiritual disciplines and pomp of Rome to the daily work of parents caring for their children or (in the LC, Ten Commandments 145; *BC* 406) a maidservant making beds in the household. Rome's external religious practices might seem more attractive, yet it was the work of parents or children that was sanctified by God's Word. When Lutherans speak of the fruit of sanctification, they often turn to discussion of vocation and particularly the estates of church, household, and political and economic life. Involvement in these walks of life does not give life to the Christian, but the

opposite. God spends his Christians, depleting them as they give themselves in service to their neighbor. The exhausted mother who has tended a sick child all night and cries, "I'm spent, I have nothing left to give!" is feeling God's work in using her for the benefit of her children. In this way, God sanctifies Christians according to both the first and second tables of the law. The Holy Spirit sanctifies us according to the first table by the preaching of the Word and faith, and, according to the second table, by teaching us to honor father and mother, raise Christian children, and so forth. Here Lutheran teaching can allow for progress in sanctification: as the Christian is further and further spent, God mortifies the flesh until it is completely subdued in death. Meanwhile, the whole time, Christians qua Christians are already perfectly sanctified in faith and will see their sanctification with their own eyes when Christ returns in glory.

See also Good Works; Justification; Law, Uses of the; Osiander, Andreas

Bibliography
Luther's Works: Large and Small Catechisms (1529); *On the Councils and the Church* (1539). LW 41; *Sermons on Isaiah* (1528–29). LW 16–17. WA 31/2.21; *Solus Decalogus est Aeternus: Martin Luther's Complete Antinomian Theses and Disputations.* Ed. and trans. H. Sonntag. Lutheran Press, 2008; *Treatise on Good Works* (1520). LW 44; **General Works:** Bayer, O. *Living by Faith.* Eerdmans, 2003; *The Book of Concord.* Ed. T. Tappert. Fortress, 1959; Elert, W. *The Structure of Lutheranism.* Concordia, 1962; Forde, G. "Forensic Justification and the Christian Life: Triumph or Tragedy?" In *A More Radical Gospel.* Eerdmans, 2004; Forde, G. "The Lutheran View of Sanctification." In *The Preached God.* Eerdmans, 2007; Köberle, A. *The Quest for Holiness.* Trans. J. Mattes. Ballast, 1999; Kolb, R. "Models of the Christian Life in Luther's Genesis Sermons and Lectures." *Lutherjahrbuch* 76 (2009): 193–220; Lindberg, C. *The Pietist Theologians.* Blackwell, 2005; Mannermaa, T. *Two Kinds of Love.* Trans. K. Stjerna. Fortress, 2010; Prenter, R. *Spiritus Creator.* Trans. J. Jensen. Muhlenberg, 1953; Wingren, G. *Luther on Vocation.* Trans. C. Rasmussen. Muhlenberg, 1957.

PAUL KOCH AND STEVEN D. PAULSON

Sandell-Berg, Karolina Wilhelmina (Lina)

As the daughter of a Lutheran pastor in Fröderyd, Småland, Sweden, Karolina Wilhelmina Sandell-Berg (1832–1903) began writing hymns as a young teenager. Her father was part of the Rosenius revival and knew many other pastors who shared his piety and concern for the spiritual life of Sweden. These pastors noticed that, while Sandell was still a teenager, her poetic gifts could help the revival. Not long after writing her most famous hymn, "Children of the Heavenly Father," when she was about sixteen, she began sending her hymns to the spiritual magazines of the time. For a while she did not take credit for the hymns, but as her hymns appeared in various publications, they would be signed L. S. Some years after the death of her father in 1858, when she was about thirty, she was asked to come to Stockholm to work in the publishing house of the revival (Evangeliska Fosterlandsstiftelsen [EFS]) alongside Carl Olof Rosenius.

From the first, Oscar Ahnfelt, (1813–82) the Swedish evangelical troubadour, set her texts to melodies that made them much beloved. She spent the rest of her life writing hymns, translating hymns from English and American evangelicals into Swedish, writing Sunday school materials and edifying children's literature—all this making her one of the founders of children's literature in Sweden. After a persistent courtship, in 1867 she finally married Oscar Berg, a wealthy evangelical who was working to improve social conditions for the poor and also a strong supporter of foreign missions. The marriage, to her surprise, turned out to be happy, although early on they suffered the loss of a stillborn child, something she never mentioned. Together they were a force for Evangelical renewal throughout Sweden. To their surprise and sorrow, Berg had to go to debtors' prison because of bad note he had cosigned for a relative. Although he finally was able to pay it back, the experience shamed both Sandell and Berg. She continued writing her hymns and Sunday school materials, but toward the end of the century, it became known that she was failing. She died in 1903. Thousands of grateful Swedes attended her funeral. Her home in Fröderyd remains a place of pilgrimage for people from around the world who come to see the birthplace of their favorite hymn writer.

See also Hymnody; Music

GRACIA GRINDAL

Sasse, Hermann

The German-Australian theologian and churchman Hermann Sasse (1895–1976) is known for his early involvement in the struggle against National Socialism and for his strong commitment to the Lutheran Confessions for contemporary church life and ecumenical witness.

Educated at Berlin with Karl Holl, Adolf von Harnack, Reinhold Seeberg, and Adolf Deissmann as his teachers, Sasse completed a postdoctoral year (1925–26) at Hartford Seminary in the United States. There he encountered Wilhelm Loehe's *Three Books about the Church*, which prompted him to become a confessional Lutheran. He was called to the faculty at Erlangen in 1933, a position he held until 1948. Sasse collaborated with Dietrich Bonhoeffer, Georg Merz, Wilhelm Vischer, and Friedrich von Bodelschwingh in the drafting of the Bethel Confession of 1933. In spite of such collaboration, he refused to sign the Barmen Declaration of 1934 on confessional grounds because he saw it as a unionistic document. Sasse's protest against unionizing tendencies within German Lutheranism came to head in 1948, when he resigned his membership in the Bavarian Church. The next year he received a call to teach at Immanuel Seminary in North Adelaide, Australia, where he served for the remainder of his life.

Staunchly Lutheran, Sasse was tirelessly involved in ecumenical discussion throughout his career, including service on official delegations such as that of the Lausanne Conference in 1927 and numerous personal contacts in the Roman Catholic and Reformed churches. Sasse was instrumental in the merger of the two Lutheran bodies in Australia into the Lutheran Church of Australia in 1966. He made several visits to the United States, where he had ties to a wide range of theologians in all major Lutheran bodies.

Sasse's theological contributions fall into four major categories: the nature of confession, the doctrine of the Holy Scriptures, the Lord's Supper, and ecclesiology, particularly church fellowship. His first major work, *Was heißt lutherisch?*, was translated by Theodore Tappert in 1938 under the title *Here We Stand*; it became a standard text on Lutheran identity in American seminaries at midcentury. Another important work, *This Is My Body*, served as a historical-theological exposition of Luther's doctrine of the Lord's Supper. Sasse sought to forge a path between historical-critical reductions of Holy Scripture on the one hand and mechanical theories of verbal inspiration built on Aristotelian categories on the other. Although he never finished the intended book on this topic, numerous essays and letters reflect his struggle to articulate a doctrine of Scripture that embraces the Bible as both divine and human.

A significant influence in global Lutheranism of the later period of Sasse's life would be his "Letters to Lutheran Pastors," written on historical, dogmatic, and contemporary issues. These circular letters, often sent out in mimeographed form, were published in a number of venues in Australia, Europe, and North America; they served to strengthen and sharpen theological discussion among Lutherans as they engaged current challenges.

Bibliography

Pless, J. T. "Hermann Sasse (1895–1976)." In *Twentieth-Century Lutheran Theologians*, ed. M. C. Mattes, 155–77. Vandenhoeck & Ruprecht; Sasse, H. *Here We Stand*. Trans. T. Tappert. Harper & Brothers, 1938; Sasse, H. *Letters to Lutheran Pastors*. Ed. M. C. Harrison. 3 vols. Concordia, 2013–14; Sasse, H. *The Lonely Way*. Ed. M. C. Harrison. 2 vols. Concordia, 2002; Sasse, H. *This Is My Body: Luther's Contention for the Real Presence in the Sacrament of the Altar*. Augsburg, 1959.

JOHN T. PLESS

Saxonies

The historiographic term "Saxonies" refers to territories of the Holy Roman Empire under the rule of the House of Wettin since the fifteenth century, which formed the most important sovereign entity in the Holy Roman Empire after the Hapsburg holdings, centered in Austria. The name is derived from the duchy of Saxe-Wittenberg, to which the Saxon electoral dignity was bound. The territorial dichotomy was regulated by the Partition of Leipzig (1485). Ernest (1441–86), the founder of the Ernestine line, was allotted the lands around Wittenberg—thereby procuring the title of elector—and areas in southern Osterland, central Thuringia, Vogtland, and in the Franconian area surrounding Coburg. Ernest's younger brother Albert (1443–1500), founder of the Albertine line, ruled over larger areas in Saxony, Meissen, northern Osterland, and northern Thuringia. In the wake of the Reformation, differing religious policies intensified the continual rivalry between the two dynasties.

After the publication of Luther's Ninety-Five Theses (1517), the University of Wittenberg, founded by Ernestine Frederick in 1502 to rival the older University of Leipzig under Albertine control, became the center of an Evangelical movement that spread throughout the empire. Elector Frederick III (1463–1525) provided Luther the freedom to propagate his theology. Philip Melanchthon systematized the new teachings and initiated curricular reforms necessary to educate Evangelical pastors and teachers. Liturgical reforms were introduced, in part tumultuously, by individual preachers. Radical theologians, including Andreas Karlstadt (ca. 1486–1541) and Thomas Müntzer (ca. 1489–1525), were especially active in Thuringia, where in 1525 a series of peasant revolts arose in the name of religious and social reform. To subdue these upheavals, Elector John (1468–1532), an early supporter of the Evangelical cause, joined forces with Luther's staunch opponent Duke Georg of Saxony (1471–1539).

John, Frederick's brother, and after him John's son John Frederick I (1503–54), systematically introduced the Reformation into Ernestine Saxony through several administrative acts. The emerging territorial church became a model for other Protestant areas. After Duke Georg's death in 1539, his brother Henry (1473–1541) initiated a restructuring of the church in Albertine Saxony with direct support from Elector John Frederick. The consolidation of this transformation continued under the next generation of princes.

In the aftermath of John Frederick's defeat in the Smalcald War (1546/47) the Albertine Duke Moritz (1521–53), as ally of the victorious emperor Charles V, gained significant portions of the Ernestine territory, including Wittenberg, and thereby the electoral title. With Melanchthon as the leading theologian, Duke Moritz continued reform through the Universities of Leipzig and Wittenberg, with confessional subscription later based on Melanchthon's *Corpus doctrinae Christianae* of 1560. In spite of substantial territorial losses, the Ernestine princes endeavored to further assume their forerunner role as Protestant princes by founding the rival University of Jena and pursuing a rigorous policy of confessional consolidation in their territorial church, on the basis of a strict interpretation of Luther's teachings. Instrumental in this process were the issuing of new ordination oaths and confessional documents that were later compiled with older testimonies of Christian and Lutheran faith in the so-called *Corpus doctrinae Thuringicum* (1570), publishing a complete edition of Luther's works (1555–58), conducting visitations, and promoting polemical campaigns to distinguish themselves from other Protestants, sometimes accusing the church in Albertine Saxony of adulterating Lutheran teachings. Rivalry at this level began with the controversy over the Augsburg Interim (1548). The inner-Wettin Colloquy of Altenburg (1569) intensified rather than settled the differences. Only after the Albertine elector Augustus (1526–86) assumed the guardianship over the Ernestine territories in 1573 could both Saxonies be drawn together confessionally under the Formula of Concord (1577) and the Book of Concord (1580).

See also Electors of Saxony; Georg, Duke of Saxony; Holy Roman Empire

Bibliography

Gehrt, D. *Ernestinische Konfessionspolitik: Bekenntnisbildung, Herrschaftskonsolidierung und dynastische Identitätsstiftung vom Augsburger Interim 1548 bis zur Konkordienformel 1577*. Evangelische Verlagsanstalt, 2011; Herrmann, R. *Thüringische Kirchengeschichte*. Vol. 2. Frommann, 1947; Junghans, H., ed. *Das Jahrhundert der Reformation in Sachsen*. 2nd ed. Evangelische Verlagsanstalt, 2005.

Daniel Gehrt

Schlieper, Ernesto Theophilo

The Brazilian Lutheran pastor and theologian Ernesto Theophilo Schlieper (1909–69) was also president of the Evangelical Church of the Lutheran Confession in Brazil. Born in Brazil, Schlieper studied theology in Germany. In Bonn he met Karl Barth, whose theology left a lifelong impression on Schlieper's thinking. An emphasis on the Word of God then replaced his earlier accent on German language and culture, and he joined the Confessing Church. Schlieper served several Brazilian congregations as pastor, taught at the pretheological institute, and also served as rector and professor of practical theology at the School of Theology of the Riograndian Synod from 1960 to 1966. He was elected president of the Synodical Federation and, in 1968, the first president of the Igreja Evangélica de Confissão Luterana no Brasil (IECLB), which he helped to found. He envisioned a church historically shaped by Martin Luther's Reformation but where Calvin's theology would also have its place. Schlieper was influential in moving his church out of ethnic isolation into a more integrated place in the Brazilian context and into ecumenical cooperation with other churches and organizations. He himself served as a member in committees of the Lutheran World Federation and of the World Council of Churches.

See also Barth, Karl; Brazil; Confessing Church; Igreja Evangélica de Confissão Luterana no Brasil (IECLB) (Evangelical Church of the Lutheran Confession in Brazil)

Bibliography

Hoffmann, A., et al. *Vertentes da identidade confessional da IECLB*. Sinodo Rio dos Sinos, 2001; Schlieper, D. E. T. *Testemunho Evangélico na América Latina*. Ed. J. Fischer. Sinodal, 1974.

PAULO WILLE BUSS

Schlink, Edmund

The German Lutheran pastor, theologian, and ecumenist Edmund Schlink (1903–84) was born in Darmstadt, where his father taught aeronautics. Schlink was raised in an atmosphere of Moravian Pietism. Interested in literature, philosophy, and music, he completed a doctorate in psychology at the University of Marburg (1927). After suffering a crisis of faith, he pursued a doctorate in theology at the University of Münster (1931). His dissertation, directed by Karl Barth, analyzed the problem of "natural religion." A second dissertation, completed at Giessen (1934), explored the question, "What are human beings in the light of Christian preaching?" This issue would remain central in his thinking. As a pastor in Hesse, he opposed the intrusion of Nazism into the church and joined the Confessing Church. He drew on the Lutheran confessions as the authoritative witness to church doctrine and found in them the means for theological resistance. From within this situation, he wrote his first major work, *The Theology of the Lutheran Confessions*. While it largely ignores the historical contexts of the individual documents, it does offer a synthetic summary of their principal theological themes. The book underscores the need to distinguish law and gospel properly in the articulation of *all* articles of faith. Its central chapters, on law and gospel, initially written separately as a Lutheran interpretation of the Barmen Declaration, reveal Schlink's respectful criticism of Barth's theology. For Schlink, every essential doctrine of the faith cannot be fully articulated independently of the law/gospel distinction, that is, independently of faith in the gospel. Schlink often returned to this crucial theme, most notably in his *Ecumenical Dogmatics*. For him the Lutheran confessions do not support a sectarian denominationalism; rather, they provide the basic motivation for seeking church unity. Toward this end he taught dogmatic theology at Heidelberg for almost thirty years (1946–71). There he established an ecumenical institute, the first of its kind in Germany, and he encouraged interdisciplinary research, convinced that theology must be in critical dialogue with all other university disciplines.

For nearly four decades Schlink was also active in the World Council of Churches, especially its Commission on Faith and Order. He helped to found the first working group of Protestant and Catholic theologians in the world and to establish two important ecumenical journals (*Ökumenische Rundschau* and *Kerygma und Dogma*). In all of these settings he articulated new approaches to such issues as altar fellowship, the eschatological dimension of Christian unity, ecumenical methodology, and conciliarity. Not only did he seek ecumenical dialogue with Eastern Orthodox theologians; he also served as an official Lutheran-Protestant observer at the Second Vatican Council. His widely read analysis of that event stressed the need for all churches to undergo what he termed a "Copernican Revolution," to see themselves as all revolving around Christ, their center. His study of baptism helped to pave the way for the WCC document Baptism, Eucharist and Ministry. Convinced that the goal of complete organic church unity in Christ could only be achieved *theologically*, he offered his massive *Ecumenical Dogmatics* (completed one year before he died) as a further resource for overcoming divisions within Christendom.

See also Barmen Confession; Barth, Karl; Confessing Church; Ecumenical Dialogues

Bibliography

Becker, M. "Edmund Schlink (1903–1945)." In *Twentieth-Century Lutheran Theologians*, ed. M. Mattes, 195–222. Vandenhoeck & Ruprecht, 2013; Schlink, E. *Schriften zu Ökumene und Bekenntnis*. 2nd ed. 5 vols. Vandenhoeck & Ruprecht, 2004–10. ET, *Ecumenical and Confessional Writings*. Ed. and trans. M. L. Becker and H. Spalteholz. Vandenhoeck & Ruprecht, forthcoming; Skibbe, E. *A*

Quiet Reformer: An Introduction to Edmund Schlink's Life and Ecumenical Theology. Kirk House, 1999.

MATTHEW L. BECKER

Schmucker, Samuel Simon

The American Lutheran theologian Samuel Simon Schmucker (1799–1873) was the primary architect of the so-called American Lutheranism movement. Born in Hagerstown, Maryland, he was the son of John George Schmucker, a prominent Lutheran pastor and president of the Ministerium of Pennsylvania, who had been strongly influenced by German Pietism. At an early age the younger Schmucker determined to follow his father's vocation; he entered the University of Pennsylvania in 1814, while at the same time reading theology with Justus H. C. Helmuth. He continued his studies at Princeton Theological Seminary, where his theology was shaped by the Puritan sympathies of the staunchly Presbyterian faculty, as well as by the revivalism that was popular among American Protestants of the period. His Princeton experience also gave him an ecumenical outlook and sympathy unusual among Lutheran pastors of that era. Schmucker was ordained by the Ministerium of Pennsylvania in 1821 and accepted a call to serve several congregations around Haymarket, Virginia. He was an active supporter of the newly formed General Synod and continued his enthusiasm even after the Ministerium of Pennsylvania withdrew in 1823. His young wife, Elenora Geiger, had recently died, but Schmucker threw himself into what he would later call "a desperate effort to sustain the General Synod." He wrote letters and twisted arms to be sure that at least token representation from several synods would be present at the 1823 meeting of the synod. Schmucker's energetic work probably saved the General Synod from dissolution.

While Schmucker was still at Princeton, he became convinced that Lutherans in America needed three things: a textbook of theology in the English language, a theological seminary, and a college. While serving the churches in Haymarket, he began work on an English translation of Storr and Flatt's *Lehrbuch der christlichen Dogmatik*, published in Stuttgart. He published his work in 1826 as *An Elementary Course in Biblical Theology*.

Meanwhile, Schmucker worked to persuade the General Synod to establish what became the Gettysburg Theological Seminary, and in 1826 he was inaugurated as its first professor. He served as the seminary's primary theological faculty member until his retirement in 1864; during those decades, Gettysburg was the primary training institution for Lutheran pastors in America. Recognizing that few of his theological students had the benefit of a college education, Schmucker asked the seminary board of directors to establish a "classical school" that would prepare students for study at the seminary. They agreed and delegated Schmucker to take the lead. The new institution, which would become Gettysburg College, opened in 1827 with Schmucker as its first president. In 1834 he published *Elements of Popular Theology*, the first work on systematic theology to be written by an American Lutheran. It went through nine editions and for the next several years was the primary textbook for those training to be Lutheran ministers in America. For several decades he was easily the preeminent theologian among American Lutherans, especially in the eastern United States. In addition to his theological influence, he took a major role in preparing constitutions, liturgies, and hymnals for General Synod congregations, thus shaping the ecclesial life of Lutherans in the antebellum period.

As Schmucker wrote in the preface to *Elements*, he intended to provide a resource that "united in a portable form the primary aspects of Christian Doctrine and Practice, . . . sustaining at the same time some relation to the Lutheran Church" (iii). Much of the work was organized as a kind of commentary on the first twenty-one articles of the CA. But one can already see the theological trajectory that would lead Schmucker into serious controversy. He was convinced that "orthodox Christians" (meaning Protestants, excluding Catholics and Unitarians) held certain "fundamental doctrines of Scripture" in common, and that those doctrines were really the heart of Christian teaching. As a Lutheran, he believed that the Augsburg Confession was "substantially correct" in its presentation of these fundamental doctrines. Yet his approach allowed a theological latitude quite out of harmony with classical Lutheranism. He outlined, for example, a continuum of possible understandings of the Eucharist, ranging from a strictly memorialist view to a conviction of the "real presence of Christ." He admitted that these views could be found among Lutherans in America, but then argued that debates over the mode of Christ's presence were "unprofitable," that Scripture is not clear on the matter, and that Lutherans should be "left to follow the dictates of their own conscience, having none to molest them or make them afraid" (*Elements*, 255).

In 1840 he delivered an address to the Synod of West Pennsylvania, subsequently published in 1851 with several other writings as *The American Lutheran Church, Historically, Doctrinally, and Practically Delineated*. In this discourse he listed seven ways in which American Lutheranism had "improved" the church of the Reformation. The improvements included rejection of the authority of the church fathers, refusing to insist on the real presence of Christ in the Eucharist, the abandonment of private confession, and the refusal "to bind her ministers to the minutiae of any human creed" (67).

In the 1850s Schmucker's latitudinarian theological approach led to a serious rift among Lutherans affiliated with his beloved General Synod. Concerned by the increasing immigration of Lutherans who had been influenced by the rising tide of confessionalism in Germany, he began to advocate for a Lutheranism more suited to the spirit of American Protestantism. In 1855 he wrote a document, published anonymously, titled *Definite Platform, Doctrinal and Disciplinarian, for Evangelical Lutheran District Synods*, in which he argued for an "American Lutheranism" that would adapt Lutheran doctrine to the dominant Reformed Protestantism of the United States. As a part of this "platform," Schmucker proposed an "American recension of the Augsburg Confession" that would eliminate what he took to be five errors in the premier doctrinal statement of the Lutheran Reformation: the doctrines of the real presence of Christ in the Eucharist and of baptismal regeneration (despite being doctrines held by Henry Melchior Mühlenberg); the Augsburg Confession's retention of private confession and the "ceremonies of the Mass"; and its denial of the "divine obligation of the Christian Sabbath."

Schmucker's critics—including both confessionally strict recent immigrants and the more conservative Lutherans in the General Synod—accused him of eviscerating Lutheranism of many of its key doctrines, but he continued to write and speak in support of his "American Lutheranism." His advocacy of his *Definite Platform* threw the General Synod into turmoil. A rival seminary was founded in Philadelphia in 1864, and in 1867 the more confessional party withdrew from the General Synod and formed the General Council of the Evangelical Lutheran Church in America. Schmucker and "American Lutheranism" were largely discredited, and even his sympizers within the General Synod moved steadily away from his doctrinal positions.

Beyond his significance to American Lutheranism, Schmucker's passion for interchurch cooperation was expressed in a variety of ways. His 1838 *Fraternal Appeal to the American Churches, with a Plan for Catholic Union, on Apostolic Principles* called for a kind of federation of American Protestants that foreshadowed both the conciliar movements and full communion agreements of the twentieth century. Schmucker was an active participant and leader in several of the Protestant agencies that are sometimes called the Evangelical Empire, including the American Bible Society, the American Tract Society, the American

Sunday School Union, and the American Board of Commissioners for Foreign Missions. He was also involved in antislavery, temperance, and Sabbath observance societies. He was one of the founders of the American branch of the Evangelical Alliance in 1867.

After his retirement Schmucker continued to write; his several dozen books and pamphlets made him one of the most prolific of American Lutheran writers in the nineteenth century. Despite widespread criticism of his theological program, Schmucker was an irenic and tolerant man, personally well regarded even by his opponents. His many positive contributions to Lutheranism in America have been widely acknowledged.

Schmucker was married three times. After his first wife's death, which left him with one infant child, he married Mary Catherine Steenbergen, who was the mother of his other twelve children. After her death in 1848, he married Esther M. Wagner. One of his sons, Beale Melanchthon Schmucker, was a prominent theologian and liturgical scholar in the General Council, whose work was in many ways a repudiation of his father's legacy.

See also American Lutheranism Controversy; Evangelical Lutheran Church in America; General Synod; Krauth, Charles Porterfield; Ministerium of Pennsylvania

Bibliography
Ferm, V. *The Crisis in American Lutheran Theology.* Century, 1927; Gustafson, D. A. *Lutherans in Crisis: The Question of Identity in the American Republic.* Augsburg Fortress, 1993; Schmucker, S. S. *The American Lutheran Church, Historically, Doctrinally, and Practically Delineated.* Harbaugh & Butler, 1851; Schmucker, S. S. *Elements of Popular Theology.* Leavitt, Lord, 1834; Wentz, A. R. *Pioneer in Christian Unity: Samuel Simon Schmucker.* Fortress, 1967.

RICHARD O. JOHNSON

Scholasticism, Late Medieval

Scholasticism—derived from *scholasticus* (scholar)—is the term used to identify both the method and content of formal education in the High and Late Middle Ages. During this time of late medieval Scholasticism (ca. 1300–ca. 1500), teaching and learning at the

higher levels migrated almost entirely from the monasteries and cathedral schools to the universities, and Paris became the most important of these for the study of theology. The Scholastic method was based on Aristotle's logic and involved the understanding of language and proper divisions or distinctions of the subject matter. The actual subject was an authoritative text. In the case of theology, this was usually the Bible or Lombard's *Sentences* (a collection of citations from the fathers around important theological issues); for canon law, it was Gratian's *Decretum* (a collection of the legal decrees of councils, popes, and theologians). Teachers offered students their commentary on the text in the form of glosses, expositions, and explanations of the words and ideas presented in or related to the text under discussion. Students honed their craft through "disputations" (debates), in which they demonstrated their ability to recall and employ the proper definitions and divisions of the subject matter.

Though conflicts between scholars and the formation of different schools of thought had been endemic to the Scholastic enterprise, the Late Middle Ages saw significant expansion and hardening of such divisions. First, the followers of Thomas Aquinas, whose systematic synthesis of theology and philosophy in the thirteenth century marks the apogee of Scholastic theology for some historians and philosophers, came under attack for alleged Aristotelian error. Beginning in 1277, certain tenets of Aristotelianism were condemned by ecclesiastical authorities in Paris and Oxford. Though Aquinas was not named in these condemnations, a number of scholars drew their own conclusions and named some of his ideas as heretical. Second, the mendicant orders were increasingly opposed to each other theologically, in part because the Dominicans tended to champion Aquinas as one of their own while the Franciscans followed what they saw as an older, Augustinian tradition. Third, the condemnations prompted new directions in theological thought, resulting eventually in what came to be called the *via moderna* (the modern way), whose practitioners generally followed William of Ockham. Other approaches, particularly those of Aquinas and John Duns Scotus, were referred to as the *via antiqua* (the ancient way). The conflict between these two *viae* was especially keen in German universities.

Ockham departed from the philosophical tradition in general, and the Thomist tradition in particular, by rejecting any sort of real existence for universals, that is, the Platonic forms that were said to structure reality. For example, for Ockham *being* was individual and did not result from a form that exists in some relation to God as the ultimate source of being. The human mind simply recognized the common traits of those things that are said to exist, and the concept of *being* was understood to apply to them. In Ockham's thought the universals or forms are, therefore, simply concepts or ways of speaking. The term applied to his thought, "nominalism," derives from the Latin *nomen* (name) and reflects this idea. (In spite of the name, Ockham's was not the more radical nominalism espoused by Roscelin in the eleventh century. For Ockham the universals were not merely names but are truly universal ideas: *conceptualism* might be a more accurate label.)

As Ockham applied his insights, he weakened the link between knowledge of the world and knowledge of God. For Aquinas, because being continued to exist in relation to God, the human mind could reason from the created order back to God, who created it, even though this ability to reason in this manner was imperfect since the fall. For Ockham, this sort of knowledge of God was not possible and, in addition, was not desirable because it subjected God to the necessity of creating a world that would perfectly reflect his nature. Ockham understood the created order to be entirely contingent and believed that God could have created any one of an infinite number of worlds. To believe anything else, he claimed, limited God's power. In defending his thought, Ockham relied on a distinction that already existed in Scholastic thought, that between God's *potentia absoluta* (absolute power) and *potentia ordinata* (ordered power). God's absolute power means that he could create whatever he willed; his ordered power means that he chose to create the world that is and that he remains faithful to the design he ordained.

Ockham's influence was felt through his writings in spite of his excommunication. Although he had not worked out his ideas in every area of theology, his successors did. The result was a system that was called semi-Pelagian by the sixteenth-century reformers as well as by its opponents in the fourteenth and fifteenth centuries. Nominalist theologians built on the idea of God's ordered power to posit a covenant made by God with his human creatures that would enable them to cooperate in their salvation. Human works could not by their own merit earn God's grace, but within the covenant God said he would reward human efforts as if they had merited grace. This semi-merit (*meritum de congruo*) enabled human creatures to progress toward salvation by gaining enough grace to be rewarded for their efforts with a merit worthy of eternal life (*meritum de condigno*). God would reward with grace those people who put forth their best effort (*facere quod in se est* or, in its complete form, *facientibus quod in se est, Deus non denegat gratiam* [to those who do what is in them, God will not deny grace]). The attraction of this understanding of salvation was that human beings are not helpless before God but can help themselves toward salvation by their own efforts, unaided at first by God's grace except as it was present in the giving of the law and the bestowing of free will. Yet this understanding created profound uncertainty for some, since there was no fixed standard by which to judge what a person's best effort might be.

Ockham's contemporaries, such as Meister Eckhart (d. ca. 1328) in Germany and Thomas Bradwardine (d. 1349) in England, had dissented from similar ideas. Eckhart focused on a Neoplatonic return to God unhindered by the clutter of human works. Bradwardine upheld the Augustinian idea of absolute predestination and thus of the sovereign grace of God. Other English scholars, too, rejected Ockham's theories. Yet his approach as elaborated by nominalist theologians gained ground in other European universities. In fact, in spite of restrictions placed on the study of Ockham's writings in 1339, the University of Paris became a bastion of nominalism. Two of its leading lights—Pierre d'Ailly, who served as chancellor at the university from 1389 to 1395, and Jean Gerson, who succeeded his friend and mentor d'Ailly as chancellor and served until 1418—played significant roles in the conciliar response to the papal schism and influenced efforts at church reform. Many of their works were in print by the late fifteenth century and were read by Luther.

In the Holy Roman Empire, too, nominalism took root. Both Albert of Saxony (d. 1390), who become the first rector of the University of Vienna, and Marsilius of Inghen (d. 1396), who served as rector at Heidelberg, studied under the nominalist John Buridan at Paris. One of the most articulate German nominalists, Gabriel Biel (d. 1495), imbibed his nominalism at Erfurt, whose faculty had been greatly influenced by Ockhamist thought.

Luther's theological study was, in addition to his humanist grounding in the arts faculty, entirely Scholastic and profoundly nominalist in its orientation. His teachers at Erfurt, Bartholomeus Arnoldi and Jodocus Truttvetter, were nominalists. He also studied the works of Gabriel Biel, both his commentary on Lombard's *Sentences* and his *Exposition of the Canon of the Mass*. As a result, Luther's theology retained many characteristics of nominalism, such as an emphasis on God's absolute power. Yet when it came to working out his understanding of justification, Luther frequently rejected the teaching of nominalist theologians by name—for example, Biel and d'Ailly. Many of his early opponents were also

nominalist in their orientation. In many of his works, Luther attacked Scholastic theology in general, rejecting its method as impiously rooted in human reason rather than in God's revelation. As Luther's theology took hold and the Reformation ran its course, Scholastic theology in the Roman church underwent renewal and renovation as well. Nominalism had largely disappeared by the time of the Council of Trent, and the Catholic intellectual landscape came under the sway of a Thomist revival, one of whose principal architects was Luther's interlocutor at Augsburg in 1518 and opponent: Cardinal Cajetan. Nevertheless, later Protestant orthodox theologians often referred back to the works of medieval theologians in constructing their own Scholastic arguments.

See also Biel, Gabriel; Cajetan (Thomaso de Vio); Church; Economic Life and Lutheranism; Ockham, William of; Philosophy; Theological Prolegomena; Thomas Aquinas

Bibliography

Asselt, W. J. van, and E. Dekker. *Reformation and Scholasticism: An Ecumenical Enterprise.* Baker Academic, 2001; Colish, M. L. *Remapping Scholasticism.* Pontifical Institute of Medieval Studies, 2000; Knowles, D. *The Evolutions of Medieval Thought.* 2nd ed. Longman, 1988; Luscombe, D. *Medieval Thought.* Oxford University Press, 1997; Oberman, H. A. *The Harvest of Medieval Theology: Gabriel Biel and Late Medieval Nominalism.* Harvard University Press, 1963; Overfield, J. H. *Humanism and Scholasticism in Late Medieval Germany.* Princeton University Press, 1985. (Review by F. Oakley in *RQ* 40:91–93); Rashdall, H. *The Universities of Europe in the Middle Ages.* Ed. F. M. Powicke and A. B. Emden. Oxford University Press, 1951; Rummel, E., ed. *Biblical Humanism and Scholasticism in the Age of Erasmus.* Brill, 2008.

PAUL W. ROBINSON

Schultze, Benjamin

The German Lutheran missionary to India named Benjamin Schultze (1689–1760) was a linguist, ecumenist, and founder of the English Mission in Chennai (Madras). He arrived at Tranquebar six months after the demise of Bartholomaus Ziegenbalg (1682–1719) and became the third primate of the mission. For the next seven years Schultze stabilized the struggling mission and steered it to new heights amid internal disputes among the missionaries, indifference of local colonial authorities, and continuing tension within the Mission Collegium in Copenhagen. He expanded evangelistic efforts far beyond the borders of the Tranquebar colony to the hitherto untouched British territories. By 1717 he had completed the Tamil Bible translation began by Ziegenbalg and compiled and translated over one hundred German hymns into Tamil.

Schultze's most unique contribution was the establishment of the English Mission. After being convinced of the strategic position of Chennai about two hundred miles north of the remotely located Tranquebar, and the importance of engaging the British in evangelistic effort if the whole of India was to be Christianized, Schultze envisioned and worked diligently to create a cooperative mission of the Anglicans and Lutherans (1728). In spite of opposition from the Mission Collegium in Copenhagen and caginess on the part of the Halle leadership, Schultze was able to establish the English Mission in Madras under the supervision of and with the fiscal support of the SPCK, an Anglican missionary society. Though the circumstances and reasons for moving to Chennai from Tranquebar triggered controversies in Europe, the move opened up a new epoch in Lutheran-Anglican ecumenical relationships as well as Halle-London cooperative endeavors that lasted for more than a century. The Anglican missionary societies appointed Lutheran missionaries in spite of their concern about the irregularity of Lutheran ordinations, and the Lutherans continued to supply missionaries in spite of their concern for the integrity of the Lutheran confessional heritage.

Schulze pioneered Protestant Christian missionary work among the Telugu-speaking people and the Urudu-speaking Muslims in Chennai and its neighborhood. He was the first European to have studied Telugu and Dakkhini. Through his work the study of these languages was introduced to Europe. Among his significant works in Telugu are the translation of the Bible and Luther's Small Catechism; a Telugu Grammar; a polyglot dictionary in English, Telugu, Tamil, and Latin; and the bilingual book on Madras. Among his works in Dakkhini, the *Grammatica Hindostanica* is exceptional. This book became the basis for the development of grammar books in Hindustani, a reliable source for understanding the development of Dakkhini and Hindustani and the way Dakkhini was spoken in the Madras region under the influence of Tamil and Telugu. Schultze continued his work of translation and of publishing his works even after he left Madras in 1743. His printing of Tamil, Telugu, and Hindustani literature after his return to Halle stands as a witness to the commitment he had for the church in India. In Halle he continued to teach English and Indian languages and promoted the cause of mission in India till his death in 1760. It was his initiative that led Christian Frederick Schwartz to learn Tamil and thereby help Schultze in the printing of the Tamil Bible in Halle, and later to go as a missionary to India. Though Schultze's leadership style contributed to conflicts and the noncooperation of his colleagues, he was certainly a visionary leader willing to break the boundaries, so that something good could come out of it for the mission. His observations on India's culture remain a treasure trove of data.

See also Francke Foundations; India; Ziegenbalg, Bartholomäus

Bibliography

Vethanayagamony, P. *It Began in Madras: The Eighteenth-Century Lutheran-Anglican Ecumenical Ventures in Mission and Benjamin Schultze*. ISPCK, 2010.

PETER VETHANAYAGAMONY

Schütz, Heinrich

The composer and musician Heinrich Schütz (1585–1672) was born in Köstritz. In 1599 he moved with his family to Weissenfels, went to Marburg in 1608 to study law, and from 1609 to 1612 studied music with Giovanni Gabrieli in Venice. In 1613 Schütz was named second court organist in Moritz; in 1617 he went to

Dresden as Kapellmeister for the rest of his life, yet with leaves in 1628–29 to study in Venice with Monteverdi; and in 1633–35, in 1637, and in 1642–45 to work in Copenhagen.

Contemporaneous with the prolific composer, organist, and theorist Michael Praetorius (ca. 1571–1621), Schütz was the finest German composer of the seventeenth century and the finest Lutheran church musician before J. S. Bach. Extremely adept at setting German texts, he integrated Italian and German styles, old and new, and wrote for large and small groups as the Thirty Years' War required. His music includes Italian madrigals; polychoral and simple Psalm settings; Latin motets; settings of Latin and German biblical texts; a German *Exequien* anticipating Brahms's *German Requiem*; the seven words of Christ on the cross; and Christmas, resurrection, and passion histories. His setting of the *St. Matthew's Passion*, written in his eighties, is one of the church's treasures.

See also Bach, Johann Sebastian; Music; Praetorius, Michael

Bibliography

Johnston, G. ed. *A Heinrich Schütz Reader.* Oxford University Press, 2013; Moser, H. J. *Heinrich Schütz.* Trans. C. Pfatteicher. Concordia, 1959; Smallman, B. *Schütz.* Oxford University Press, 2000.

PAUL WESTERMEYER

Schwartz, Christian Friedrich

An eminent German Lutheran missionary to South India, Christian Friedrich Schwartz (1726–98) is celebrated as "Prince of Tranquebar Mission." For forty-eight years he served uninterruptedly in three towns, Tranquebar, Trichy, and Tanjore. Born in Sonnenberg, Prussia (now Poland), and trained in Halle, Schwartz learned Tamil at Halle from Benjamin Schultze (1689–1760) and assisted in Schultze's translation projects. On Schultze's recommendation he was sent to India. His fluency in several Indian and European languages as well as his caring and engaging personality made him a renowned preacher, mentor, diplomat, and guardian of princes.

Schwartz's first twelve years of ministry were carried out in Tranquebar, caring for the existing congregations and establishing schools in several congregations after the pattern of the Francke Foundations. Through the assistance of Indian "helpers," mission was extended to Trichy, Tanjore, and Tirunelveli. His favorite method was sending the Indian evangelists and catechists two by two into villages. In 1762 at Trichy, his pastoral care to the victims of a powder magazine explosion, regardless of the victims' religion, as well as his work as a military chaplain for British troops in 1764, found him permanently stationed in Trichy as a missionary, financed by the SPCK (Society for Promoting Christian Knowledge). In 1768 he was also appointed as a British military chaplain, although he continued his ministry as a fully ordained Lutheran pastor and staunch ecumenist. Noteworthy is his involvement in politics. Schwartz became an ally of King Tulasi after he helped the citizens of Tanjore in 1773 following a famine created by political unrest; after this, from 1778 to 1798, his ministry was based there. Although the king never converted to Christianity, Schwartz developed a trusting relationship with him, which would serve him well later in life. Shortly before his death the king committed to Schwarz the education of his adopted son and successor Serfoji. In 1779 the British authorities invited him to go on a peace mission to Hyder Ali, the Muslim ruler of Mysore. His knowledge of Urudu and Persian and the trust Ali had for Schwartz enabled him to undertake this peace mission. Although the war could not be averted, he was well received by Ali. Even though the British government further pressed him into service as a peacemaker, Schwartz never neglected his evangelical work. He had the distinction of identifying and equipping young Indians who became builders of the indigenous church. Three Christians he mentored—Raya Clarinda, Sathiyanathan Pillai, and Sundaradam David—were instrumental in laying the foundation of the most influential Christian community of Tirunelveli. He also has the honor of mentoring the first Christian poet and hymnodist, Vedanyaga Sastri. Schwartz also introduced education reform, combining Christian literature and Enlightenment sciences in Indian schools, which were very successful. He died in Tanjore in 1798.

See also Francke Foundations; India; Schultze, Benjamin

Bibliography

Gohdes, C. B. *Schwartz, The Apostle to India*. Lutheran Book Concern, 1927; Lamb, G. H. *Memoir of Christian Frederick Schwartz*. Christian Literature Society, 1948; Pearson, H. *Memoirs of the Life and Correspondence of the Rev. Christian Frederick Schwartz*. 3rd ed. 2 vols. Appleton, 1835.

PETER VETHANAYAGAMONY

Schwenckfeld, Caspar von

The German reformer, spiritualist, and author Caspar (or Kaspar) von Schwenckfeld (1489–1561) was born into a noble family in the duchy of Liegnitz, Silesia, in the village of Ossig (hence also, Schwenckfeld von Ossig). After studies in Cologne between 1505 and 1507 and in Frankfurt an der Oder, he served the ducal court of Liegnitz from 1510 onward. Through reading Luther's works he became a follower of the Wittenberg Reformation. Schwenckfeld's active involvement in the reform movement contributed to Duke Frederick I's embracing of Protestantism in 1523. Although initially an admirer of Luther's theology, Schwenckfeld began theologically to drift from mainstream Lutheranism. By 1525 he had developed a spiritual interpretation of the Lord's Supper, which was supported by the humanist Valentin Krautwald, claiming that believers should nourish themselves with the spiritual body, the heavenly flesh of Christ, and he stopped receiving the sacrament. That year he met Luther in Wittenberg and presented his theses on the Lord's Supper, opposing Luther's understanding of the real presence of Christ in the elements. Luther considered Schwenckfeld's views heretical, even writing several sermons on the Lord's Supper as a way to counter false teaching. As the polemics surrounding Schwenckfeld grew after he developed controversial positions on a variety of theological subjects, including the role and interpretation of the Bible and infant baptism, so did his following grow. When Emperor Ferdinand I demanded the suppression of Protestantism in the duchy of Liegnitz, Schwenckfeld left his native land on April 19, 1529, and went to Strasbourg, where for two years he lived in the house of Wolfgang Capito. He remained in Strasbourg until August 1534, when he left due to theological disagreements with Martin Bucer. From then on, Schwenckfeld lived a life of exile, fleeing persecution several times. He stayed in many different locations in the western and southern territories of the Holy Roman Empire of the German Nation, mostly in free imperial cities such as Augsburg, Esslingen, Kempten, Kaufbeuren, and Ulm, where he found favor with Mayor Bernhard Besserer, or on the estates of nobles, sometimes incognito. During the 1540s Schwenckfeld spent much of his time expanding and writing down his theology, and in the 1550s he became involved in the theological and particularly Sacramentarian controversies that evolved following Luther's death and the defeat of the Smalcaldic League. On December 10, 1561, he died in Ulm in the house of the patrician family Streicher.

By offering original views on Word and Spirit, the church, baptism, and the Lord's Supper, Schwenckfeld was preaching a middle way, in which he attempted to bring together the Lutherans and Roman Catholics. He rejected the stances of the Augsburg Confession on predestination, free will, and infant baptism. In March 1540 Melanchthon and twelve other Evangelical theologians condemned Schwenckfeld's Christology at a meeting in Schmalkalden, dubbing it Eutychian because in their opinion Schwenckfeld denied the true humanity of Christ. Between 1553 and 1559 Schwenckfeld engaged in a written debate with the Lutheran theologian Matthias Flacius Illyricus over the role of the Bible and the preached Word. Particularly Schwenckfeld's book *On the Holy Scriptures*, published in 1551, stirred unrest among Lutherans. In it,

Schwenckfeld argued for a spiritual interpretation of the Scriptures and called for a distinction between the internal and external words, the former being the word of the Spirit, the latter spoken by the preacher. He claimed that the Bible had become a new pope on paper for Protestants and that a church ceremony such as the Lord's Supper does nothing for Christians. Over the course of the following years, Flacius wrote nine books against Schwenckfeld, the first one being *On the Holy Scripture and Its Effect*, with a preface and conclusion by Nikolaus Gallus, Lutheran superintendent of Regensburg, who also opposed Schwenckfeld.

By introducing his ideas into the theological polemics among the second generation of reformers, Schwenckfeld essentially sealed his own fate as a heretic. His ideas, however, survived among his adherents in southern Germany and in Silesia, from where many fled to Count Nikolaus Ludwig von Zinzendorf's estate in Herrnhut from persecution in 1726. The Schwenkfelder Church emerged from the descendants of Schwenckfeldians who immigrated to Pennsylvania in the first half of the eighteenth century and was established as a denomination in 1909; it has survived into the twenty-first century with a handful of congregations in and around Philadelphia.

See also Flacius, Matthias Illyricus, and the Flacians; Lord's Supper

Bibliography

Corpus Schwenckfeldianorum. Ed. C. D. Hartranft, E. E. S. Johnson, and S. G. Schultz. Vols. 1–14, Breitkopf & Härtel, 1907–13. Vols. 15–19, Board of Publication of the Schwenckfelder Church, 1959–61; Keller, R. *Der Schlüssel zur Schrift: Die Lehre vom Wort Gottes bei Matthias Flacius Illyricus.* Esp. 25–92, chap. 1, "Die Kontroverse mit Caspar von Schwenckfeld." Arbeiten zur Geschichte und Theologie des Luthertums, Neue Folge 15. Lutherisches Verlagshaus, 1984; McLaughlin, R. E. *Caspar Schwenckfeld, Reluctant Radical: His Life to 1540.* Yale University Press, 1986; Mielke, H.-P. *Kirche im Geheimen: Orthodoxes und liberales Schwenkfeldertum in Süddeutschland und seine Auswirkung auf Geistesgeschichte und politisches Handeln in der Spätrenaissance.* 2 vols. Traugott Bautz, 2012; Weigelt, H. *Von Schlesien nach Amerika: Die Geschichte des Schwenckfeldertums.* Neue Forschungen zur Schlesischen Geschichte 14. Böhlau, 2007.

Luka Ilić

Scripture

The Lutheran Reformation inherited the late medieval church's understanding that the Christian Scripture of the Old and the New Testaments is the foundation for all theology and church practice. What separated the Lutherans from the Roman Catholics was the manner in which Scripture was thought to be authoritative in the life of the church and the role and method of the Roman magisterium in constructing doctrine from it. One way the subsequent Lutheran tradition expressed this perceived difference was that the Lutheran confessions were normed by Scripture (*norma normata*) so that Scripture was "the norming norm" (*norma normans*) rather than vice versa—that church tradition normed Scripture, the perceived position of Rome. Luther's reported words at the Diet of Worms epitomizes the Reformation's prioritizing of "Scripture" over church "tradition" in resolving theological disputes: "Unless I am convinced by the testimony of the Scriptures or by clear reason [*convictus testimoniis Scripturae aut ratione evidente*] (for I do not trust either in the pope or in councils alone, since it is well known that they have often erred and contradicted themselves), I am bound by the Scriptures I have quoted, and my conscience is captive to the Word of God. I cannot and I will not retract anything, since it is neither safe nor right to go against conscience" (LW 32:112). This commitment is referred to by subsequent Lutherans as the *sola scriptura* (Scripture alone) principle of the Reformation. In fact, as David Steinmetz points out, "*Sola scriptura* generally meant *prima scriptura*, Scripture as the final source and norm by which all theological sources and arguments are to be judged, not Scripture as the sole source of theological wisdom" (Steinmetz, 1997:245). The Reformers were guided in their interpretations of the Scriptures by the ecumenical councils' articulations of the doctrines of the Trinity and the person of Christ and had no quarrel with Rome over them (SA 1:1). The early Reformers also drank deeply from the patristic well of scriptural interpretation. Given the centrality of Scripture to the Reformation cause, it is perhaps curious that no distinct article on the role of the Bible in theological discourse is found in the Augsburg Confession, the Apology, the Catechisms, the Smalcald Articles, or even any edition of Philip Melanchthon's systematic presentation of theology, the *Loci communes*. "This silence of the Confessions on this point," observes Edmund Schlink, "amounts to a doctrinal declaration. . . . The absence of such an article in the Augsburg Confession is not to be construed as an evasion of the controversial problem of the relation between Scripture and tradition. Rather, it reflects the genuinely Lutheran urgency of coming to grips at once with the *viva vox evangelii* [the living voice of the gospel] itself" (Schlink 1–2).

Luther's close reading of Scripture was the basis for his criticism of the medieval Quadriga, the practice of scriptural interpretation by means of delineating four senses of Scripture, one literal and three "spiritual": allegorical, moral, and anagogical. While Luther retained a robust sense of the literal meaning of Scripture, the uses of the other three senses of Scripture were diminished. In particular, it was the allegorical sense that Luther found most problematic. In medieval practice, the biblical text was clarified by a spiritual reading (allegory) that cohered with a doctrinal system and thus transcended (i.e., was "outside") of the biblical text. The allegorical sense of Scripture, then, was thought to teach the *credenda*, the basic articles of belief (Steinmetz, "Divided," 248). Obscurities in biblical texts were often reconciled to the church's theology by means of allegory. Luther, however, posited that Scripture should interpret itself (*scriptura sacra sui ipsius interpres*; WA 7:97; Wood 161). This can be understood in two senses. First, that "one passage of Scripture must be clarified by other passages of Scripture" (LW 37:177), a principle that Luther shared with the early church: "The holy fathers explained Scripture by taking the clear, lucid passages

and with them shed light on obscure and doubtful passages" (cited in Wood 162). For Luther the content of the Bible, as it is for anyone who has firsthand knowledge of the Scriptures, was anything but straightforward and unproblematic. Luther held, rather, that the Bible is "a very complicated book, . . . full of antinomies and tensions" (Steinmetz, 1999: 472). One way of negotiating the Bible's complex terrain (rather than resorting to a dogmatic use of allegory), then, is to allow the clear passages to interpret those that are obscure and problematic. In the generations that followed Luther, this notion of *loci classici* (classic passages) evolved into a system of *dicta probantia* (prooftexts) within the more propositional ethos of Lutheran Scholasticism. This method came to have its own "prooftext" in Rom. 12:6, which in the Greek speaks of the "analogy of faith" (*analogian tēs pisteōs*).

Scriptura sui ipsius interpres also means that Luther relied on the church's long practice of typological interpretation, where Old Testament types (e.g., Adam) are held to be fulfilled in New Testament antitypes (e.g., Christ, as the second Adam; see Rom. 5:14). Rather than allegory's doctrinal escape from the text to a "higher" spiritual reality that lies outside of it, typology's orientation is chronological and stays within the world of biblical text. The interpretive relationship between type and antitype is reciprocal, as is the nature of promise and fulfillment. For example, the New Testament understanding of Christ informs one's understanding of Adam, and one's understanding of Adam informs one's understanding of the person and work of Christ. In so thinking, Luther, like patristic and medieval exegetes, was following the lead of the New Testament theologians themselves (e.g., 1 Cor. 10:1–6; 1 Pet. 3:21). Through his commitment to a typological reading of Scripture, Luther understood that its chief content, in both Testaments, is "Christ." In effect, Luther claimed that the literal sense of Scripture was Christ in that the Old Testament prophetic sense *literally* (i.e., typologically) pointed to Christ. Luther's literal understanding of Scripture was, then, "big-bellied" (Steinmetz, "Divided," 249), in that it included an aspect of what the church had understood to be the spiritual sense of Scripture (i.e., typology but not allegory). In fact, Luther held that the literal sense of Old Testament texts might have two referents, one in the Old Testament's present (Adam as the literal-historical referent) and one in the future (Christ as the literal-prophetic referent). Luther's literal understanding of Scripture, then, is very different from modern hermeneutical notions of literal that are often based in the Scottish philosophy of common sense (commonsense realism). Luther's understanding was more akin to Nicolas of Lyra's "double-literal" sense.

The Lutheran Reformation also occurred within the context of Renaissance humanism. It participated in a variety of ways in its movement *ad fontes* (back to the sources). Johannes Reuchlin's work on the Hebrew text of the penitential Psalms and Erasmus's publication of the Greek text of the New Testament in 1516 with his annotations correcting the standard Latin version helped to encourage the study of the original languages of the biblical text so that when Luther translated the Bible into German he worked from Hebrew and Greek texts rather than relying solely on the Vulgate, the standard Latin translation that constituted the canon of the Roman church, or on the Greek Septuagint. Since its beginning, the Reformation scriptural impulse has been to ground exegesis and vernacular translations in the deep study of Hebrew and Greek (LW 45:363). At the same time, second-generation Wittenberg theologians, such as Georg Major, began to focus on the authority of the Scriptures over against their opponents' claims to papal and conciliar authority.

In the period of Lutheran Orthodoxy that followed the first generations of Lutheran scholars, biblical theology reclaimed aspects of the Aristotelian method that Luther eschewed but that Melanchthon and others supported. Scriptures' attributes were delineated under such topics as authority, perfection, sufficiency, perspicuity, and efficacy. Thereby Scripture, as the divine Word of God, was understood as true in all its expressions. In certain circles (e.g., Johannes Andreas Quenstedt, 1617–88), the notion of the inerrancy of the biblical text naturally evolved—not only in matters that pertain to salvation, but even in all areas of knowledge. This claim of factual inerrancy in all matters was to play a problematic role as the church moved increasingly into the modern era, especially as historical-critical approaches to the biblical texts were adopted and as the distance between the world of the Bible and the world described by modern science became issues. Some Lutheran church bodies accepted historical criticism as an appropriate tool of biblical study. Others rejected it as contrary to the Lutheran understanding of the Word of God (Reumann).

Beginning in the nineteenth century various attempts were made to counter a creeping biblicism that merged a commonsense understanding of the literal sense of Scripture with the inerrancy of Lutheran Scholasticism. The distinction between the material principle (justification) and the formal principle (Scripture) of the Reformation was articulated by some to suggest that Lutherans emphasized the material principle over the formal principle in ways that set them apart from other Protestants (Heen). Other theologians used an analogy based in the Chalcedonian understanding of the two natures of Christ to suggest that the Bible is both truly human and truly divine (Jacobs 27, 147). Others recovered the Orthodox distinction between "inspiration" and "revelation" to suggest that while all biblical text is "inspired," not all text equally reveals that which is unknown of God and God's intent for humanity (Jacobs 27). Others, following the lead of J. C. K. von Hoffmann (1810–77), sometimes referred to as the mediating "Erlangen" school, located the revelation of God in the "history of salvation" (*Heilsgeschichte*) to which the Bible witnesses. More recently the "literary" turn in biblical studies has been appropriated to suggest that "story" or "narrative" is the primary method of God's communication with humanity (Hans Frei, George Lindbeck). The precise manner in which Scripture is the efficacious Word of God continues to be discussed within larger Lutheranism. One way of thinking about the intra-Lutheran differences suggests that some church bodies tend to return to Luther and the early Reformation for their hermeneutical inspiration while others are more naturally based in the propositional codifications of the seventeenth-century Lutheran Scholasticism (Sittler).

See also Bible Interpretation; Bible Translations; Law and Gospel; Luther's Bible; Word of God

Bibliography

Frei, H. W. *The Eclipse of the Biblical Narrative: A Study in Eighteenth and Nineteenth Century Hermeneutics*. Yale University Press, 1974; Heen, E. M. "The Distinction 'Material/Formal Principles' and Its Use in American Lutheran Theology." *LQ* 17 (2003): 329–54; Jacobs, H. E. *Elements of Religion*. Board of Publication of the General Council of the Evangelical Lutheran Church in North America, 1898; Lindbeck, G. A. *The Nature of Doctrine: Religion and Theology in a Postliberal Age*. Westminster, 1984; Reumann, J. *Studies in Lutheran Hermeneutics*. Fortress, 1978; Schlink, E. *Theology of the Lutheran Confessions*. Trans. P. F. Koehneke and H. J. A. Bouman. Fortress, 1961; Sittler, J. *The Doctrine of the Word in the Structure of Lutheran Theology*. Board of Publication of the United Lutheran Church in America, 1948; Steinmetz, D. C. "Divided by a Common Past: The Reshaping of the Christian Exegetical Tradition in the Sixteenth Century." *Journal of Medieval and Early Modern Studies* 27 (1997): 245–64; Steinmetz, D. C. "The Intellectual Appeal of the Reformation." *Theology Today* 57 (2001): 459–72; Wood, A. S. "Luther and the Interpretation of Scripture." In *Captive to the Word*, 159–68. Paternoster, 1969.

ERIK M. HEEN

Scriver, Christian

The theologian and hymn writer Christian Scriver (1629–93) was a mediating figure between Orthodoxy and Pietism. Born in Rendsburg, Scriver studied in Rostock, a center of a reforming theology in the mid-seventeenth century. Rising to prominence as a preacher in Stendal, Scriver became senior pastor in Magdeburg in 1667. Through his reputation in the pulpit and publications, he became one of the best-known preachers in Germany.

Encouraged by Philipp Jakob Spener, Scriver followed a call to Quedlinburg as court preacher amid the Pietist controversies in 1690. Scriver was sympathetic to many of the reform aims of moderate Pietists like Spener, but his popular style of preaching and writing differed from the plain style that most Pietists favored. Scriver relied heavily on emblems and *Realien* to structure and illustrate his sermons and tracts. Telemann set a number of Scriver's hymns to music. His best-known work, *Seelen-Schatz*, 1675–92 (Treasure of the soul), was a multivolume collection of sermons that was reprinted and translated frequently. His 1667 folksy collection, *Gottholds vierhundert zufällige Andachten* (Gotthold's emblems), found widespread distribution, including several nineteenth-century editions in Britain and North America.

See also Hymnody; Lutheran Orthodoxy; Music; Pietism; Spener, Philipp Jakob

Bibliography

Lund, E. ed. *Seventeenth Century Lutheran Meditations and Hymns*. Paulist Press, 2011; Müller, H. *Seelsorge und Tröstung: Christian Scriver (1629–1693): Erbauungsschriftsteller und Seelsorger*. Hartmut Spenner, 2005; Scriver, C. *Gotthold's Emblems*. T&T Clark, 1857.

JONATHAN STROM

Seamen's Missions

Lutheran Seamen's Missions are characteristic of Nordic and German churches. The father of the Nordic Seamen's Mission was J. C. H. Storjohann, a Norwegian pastor, who during his studies in Scotland became acquainted with British Missions to seafarers. He served as the first Norwegian seamen's chaplain in London. He founded the Norwegian Seamen's Mission in 1864 in Bergen and, at his imitative, the Danish Seaman's Church in Foreign Harbors (1867), the Finnish Seamen's Mission (1875), and Swedish Seamen's Mission (1876) were started. The German Seamen's Mission was founded in 1898; its background was in the German Inner Mission.

The Nordic and German Seamen's Missions were organized on the model of missionary societies, which collected their financial support from voluntary contributions. Today they receive support from church and governmental funds.

The Seamen's Missions were influenced by the earlier British ministry to seafarers, which was primarily interested in providing church services and pastoral care for seafarers and tried to help them stay away from drinking and other temptations in seaports. Nordic and German Missions added to this agenda many social services and the possibility of communicating with their home country and families in their own language. In addition to regular worship and pastoral care, chaplains visited seafarers on board ships (in hospitals and jails too), wrote letters for seamen and forwarded their mail, and arranged sports activities and sightseeing tours. The Seamen's Missions have club rooms with newspapers and books, access to TV, fax, and internet. The Finnish Missions have saunas.

Seafarers no longer spend much time in seaports. Seamen's Missions now direct their attention more to others, such as migrant workers, tourists, au pairs (esp. in London), truck drivers (in mainland Europe), and so forth. The Scandinavian Seamen's Missions are integrated into the diaspora work of their churches. Their present names indicate this. The Norwegian Seamen's Church is called The Norwegian Church Abroad. It has over thirty congregations around the world. Church of Sweden Abroad has about forty-five congregations, most of them in Western Europe. The first was established in Paris in 1626, the second a century later in London. The Church of Sweden Abroad is under the episcopal oversight of the bishop of Visby in Gotland. Danish Seamen's Church and Church Abroad has fifty-three seamen's and overseas churches around the world, the earliest established in 1698 in London. The Finnish Seamen's Mission and the Finnish Church Abroad are separate organizations, yet they cooperate closely.

The Lutheran Seamen's Missions belong to the ecumenical International Christian Maritime Association (ICMA), founded in 1969.

See also Mission and Evangelism; Mission Societies and Academies

Bibliography

Kortrey, B. "Seafarers and International House: An Evolution of Service." In *Essays and Reports of the Lutheran Historical Conference* 18 (1998); 339–46; Mauk, D. *The Colony That Rose from the Sea: Norwegian Maritime Migration and Community in Brooklyn, 1850–1910.* Norwegian-American Historical Association, 1997.

SIMO HEININEN

Seckendorff, Veit Ludwig von

The jurist Veit Ludwig von Seckendorff (1626–92) was chancellor of Saxe-Zeitz, founding chancellor of the University of Halle, scholar of the Reformation, and supporter of Pietists. Born into a family of old nobility in Franconia, his youth and education were determined by the Thirty Years' War. The most important influence on Seckendorff was Duke Ernst of Saxe-Gotha, "the Pious" (1602–75), and Seckendorff became an official in the church of Saxe-Gotha. Later, when he was chancellor of Saxe-Zeitz, the Jesuit Louis Maimbourg published the *Histoire du Lutheranisme* in 1680. Alarmed by this eloquent defamation of the Reformation, Seckendorff spent ten years collecting sources on Luther and the Reformation to refute it. This first scholarly history of the Reformation contained nearly all sources of Luther's work then available. Widely used by historians in the following centuries, it even contained sources that have subsequently been lost or destroyed. Seckendorff became a friend of Philipp Jakob Spener in 1682 and acted in defense of Pietists until the end of his life. His last public task was to mediate between Orthodox Lutheran pastors of Halle/Saale and the Pietist August Hermann Francke (1663–1727), who had been nominated as professor at the newly founded university.

See also Arnold, Gottfried; Francke, August Hermann; History; Spener, Philipp Jakob

Bibliography

Seckendorff, V. L. von. *Commentarius historicus et Apologeticus de Lutheranismo.* 1688. Gleditsch, 1692; Spitz, L. W. "Veit Ludwig von Seckendorff an Orthodox Defender of Pietists." *Concordia Theological Monthly* 16

(1945): 744–57; Strauch, S. *Veit Ludwig von Seckendorff (1626–1692).* LIT, 2005.

SOLVEIG STRAUCH

Selnecker, Nikolaus

The German Lutheran theologian and hymn writer Nikolaus Selnecker (1530–92) was also involved in the drafting of the Formula of Concord. Born in Hersbruck, December 5, 1530, Selnecker early demonstrated musical ability. In 1549 he began studying at Wittenberg, becoming close to Melanchthon, Eber, and Bugenhagen. Appointed court preacher at Dresden in 1558, he was involved in the disputes between the Philippists and Gnesio-Lutherans. Selnecker was dismissed from his Dresden office in 1564, likely because of his criticisms of the nobility and his theological views. In 1565 he was called to a theological professorship at Jena but was released after two years to go to Leipzig as professor and superintendent.

As pastor of the St. Thomas Church at Leipzig, he also helped develop its choir. At this time he received his theological doctorate from Wittenberg. Between 1570 and 1574 he worked with Martin Chemnitz and Jakob Andreae to continue the reforms in Braunschweig-Wolfenbüttel. Gradually coming to reject the crypto-Philippist positions on the Lord's Supper, he became a key figure among the Lutherans who drafted the Formula of Concord in 1577 and was one of its chief defenders. After Elector August's death in 1586, Selnecker was deposed from his Leipzig positions and became ecclesiastical superintendent in Hildesheim. He died shortly after his return to Leipzig, on May 24, 1592. Selnecker composed more than 120 hymn texts and many hymn tunes. His other writings include exegetical, historical, doctrinal, and devotional works.

See also Book of Concord; Formula of Concord; Hymnody; Music; Wittenberg Circle, Parties within

Bibliography

Jungkuntz, T. R. "Nikolaus Selnecker—The Weather Vane?" In *Formulators of the Formula of Concord,* 89–109. Concordia, 1977; Klän, W. "Der 'vierte Mann': Auf den Spuren von Nikolaus Selneckers (1530–1592)." *Lutherische Theologie und Kirche* 17 (1993): 145–74; Kolb, R. "The Doctrine of Christ in Nikolaus Selnecker's Interpretation of Psalms 8, 22, and 110." In *Biblical Interpretation in the Era of the Reformation*, ed. R. A. Muller and J. L. Thompson, 313–32. Eerdmans, 1996; Kolb, R. "Pastoral Practice in the Funeral Sermons of Nikolaus Selnecker (1530–1592)." *LQ* (2014): 22–48.

GERHARD BODE

Seminex and the Association of Evangelical Lutheran Churches

The American Lutheran seminary called Seminex was related to the Association of Evangelical Lutheran Churches from 1973 to 1987. In the 1950s and 1960s, some elements within the Lutheran Church–Missouri Synod began to adopt moderating theological positions and sought to move the synod toward closer relations with other American Lutheran denominations. Moderates were evident among the faculty at Concordia Seminary in St. Louis, Missouri, but were opposed by an organized conservative bloc within the synod. In 1969 the conservatives helped elect a strongly conservative synodical president, J. A. O. Preus, who began to move against moderates in positions of power within the denomination, especially seminary president John Tietjen. Preus instigated an investigation of the theological positions of the seminary and its faculty and began to appoint his own partisans to the seminary's Board of Control. After consolidating his position in 1973 by winning reelection, early in 1974 Preus removed Tietjen as seminary president. On February 19, 1974, forty-five (of fifty) seminary professors and the vast majority of students literally walked out of the grounds of Concordia Seminary and then reconstituted themselves as Christ Seminary in Exile, or Seminex.

Moderates within the Missouri Synod had already in 1973 formed their own group, Evangelical Lutherans in Mission (ELIM), which sought to support this new institution. As the conservatives gained more power in the synod and as Preus began to move against synodical district presidents perceived as being moderates, a number of the moderate group within the synod decided it was necessary to form their own separate denomination, the Association of Evangelical Lutheran Churches (AELC), in 1976. Although the moderate group within the Missouri Synod was quite sizeable, organizers of the AELC were disappointed in the lower numbers of moderates who actually left Missouri to join the new denomination; leaving Missouri was logistically and emotionally difficult for many. The new AELC faced a number of difficult issues, chief among them was that the denomination was top-heavy with pastors and professors and did not have enough positions to employ them all. A number of these persons had to leave the AELC to find positions within other American Lutheran denominations.

Seminex continued its independent existence for several years in St. Louis but by the early 1980s was unable to continue, and its remaining students and professors were distributed among several other American Lutheran seminaries, especially the Lutheran School of Theology at Chicago. Out of the shadow of the Missouri Synod, the AELC adopted more liberal positions and practices, including the ordination of women to the ordained ministry. The AELC also elected Rev. Will Herzfeld as one of its presidents, making him the first African American Lutheran to head an American Lutheran denomination. The continuing instability of the AELC led it to reach out to two other large American Lutheran denominations, the American Lutheran Church and the Lutheran Church in America, to explore merger negotiations, which resulted in the formation of the Evangelical Lutheran Church in America in 1988. In 1987 the AELC consisted of 100,000 members in 267 congregations.

See also Evangelical Lutheran Church in America; Lutheran Church–Missouri Synod; Preus, Jacob

Bibliography

Adams, J. E. *Preus of Missouri and the Great Lutheran Civil War*. Harper & Row, 1977; Burkee, J. *Power, Politics, and the Missouri Synod*. Fortress, 2011; Danker, F. W. *No Room in the Brotherhood: The Preus-Otten Purge of Missouri*. Clayton Publishing, 1977; Marquart, K. E. *Anatomy of an Explosion: A Theological Analysis of the Missouri Synod Conflict*. Concordia Theological Seminary Press, 1977; Tietjen, J. *Memoirs in Exile: Confessional Hope and Institutional Conflict*. Augsburg Fortress, 1990; Todd, M. *Authority Vested: A Story of Identity and Change in the Lutheran Church–Missouri Synod*. Eerdmans, 2000; Zimmerman, P. *A Seminary in Crisis: The Inside Story of the Preus Fact Finding Committee*. Concordia, 2007.

MARK A. GRANQUIST

Semler, Johann Salomo

As a leader of the German Enlightenment, Johann Salomo Semler (1725–91) has been called the founder of neo-Protestantism and historical-critical theology and the most influential theologian of the eighteenth century. His critical approach to Scripture and tradition paved the way for liberal theology (*theologia liberalis*, a term Semler coined). His corpus of over 250 works ranges from demonology to Rosicrucianism but centers on biblical interpretation, the history of church and dogma, theological method, and their implications for contemporary religious life.

Reared in a Lutheran pastor's home, Semler moved in Pietist circles in his native Thuringia and as a student at the University of Halle, where, under the mentorship of Siegmund Jacob Baumgarten, he also encountered biblical and historical scholarship of the early Enlightenment. Semler later polemicized against "enthusiasm" but kept an emphasis on the moral-experiential dimensions of faith over against specific dogmatic formulations. In 1753 he was appointed to Halle's theological faculty, a post he held until his death.

The central problem in Semler's work concerns the relationship between the presumed essence of a universal, morally oriented Christianity and the diverse outward manifestations of the Christian religion over time. Semler deployed what he viewed as Luther's distinction between the Bible and the Word of God, insisting that unfettered historical criticism of the former would not harm the latter. His *Treatise on the Free Investigation of the Canon* (1771–75) argued that the biblical canon was merely a historical designation without inner unity or inherent authority for contemporary

Christians. It was up to the pious and enlightened modern reader to separate the kernel of inward moral religion proclaimed by Jesus from the husk of the outmoded Jewish thought forms to which he had accommodated himself. Semler appealed to the theory of divine accommodation, too, to defend the essential historicity of the Gospel accounts against the deist attacks of H. S. Reimarus.

Semler's later work developed a conceptual distinction between inner, personal *Religion* and *Theologie*, which comprised scholarly endeavors to articulate Christian teaching in the language of the day. Academic theology was a progressive enterprise that required freedom of inquiry. Semler further distinguished between state-sanctioned "public" religion (with its particular doctrines, rites, and institutions) and "private" religion, meaning the pious individual's ethically oriented construal of the faith. Both were necessary, and on the grounds that it preserved public order, Semler defended Prussia's 1788 edict requiring clergy to adhere to the basic sense of the Protestant symbolical books. He came to hold, however, that the Christian religion itself was perfectible, and he looked to a future in which confessional divisions would dissolve and Christianity would become a universal religion of love embracing all humankind.

See also Eighteenth Century; Enlightenment; Liberalism; Rationalism

Bibliography

Fleischer, D. *Zwischen Tradition und Fortschritt: Der Strukturwandel der protestantischen Kirchengeschichtsschreibung im deutschsprachigen Diskurs der Aufklärung.* Spenner, 2006; Hornig, G. *Johann Salomo Semler: Studien zu Leben und Werk der Hallenser Aufklärungstheologen.* Niemeyer, 1996; Reill, P. H. *The German Enlightenment and the Rise of Historicism.* University of California Press, 1975; Schröter, M. *Aufklärung durch Historisierung: Johann Salomo Semlers Hermeneutik des Christentums.* De Gruyter, 2012.

ERIC CARLSSON

Servetus, Michael

A founder of early modern antitrinitarianism, a physician and polymath, was Michael Servetus (1509/11–1553). Born in Villanueva (Aragon), in his youth Servetus served the future confessor of Emperor Charles V, Juan de Quintana, who sent him to study law in 1528–29 in Toulouse. Interested in a deeper understanding of the Bible, Servetus traveled to Basel in 1530, where he was a guest of Johannes Oecolampadius. During his subsequent stay in Strasbourg, Servetus became acquainted with Martin Bucer and Wolfgang Capito. During this period he wrote his influential works *De Trinitatis erroribus libri septem* (Seven books on the errors of the Trinity) and *Dialogorum de Trinitate libri duo* (Two books of dialogues on the Trinity), published in 1531 and 1532, respectively. In these works, Servetus developed a modalistic understanding of God, in which he assumed that the one God of the Bible had over the course of time revealed himself in different figures and that the Nicene dogma of the Trinity had not come from the Bible but from the tradition of Platonic thought. In spite of the fact that the councils of Strasbourg and Basel banned the sale of Servetus's books, they circulated widely and during the course of the sixteenth century led to a critical reappraisal of the dogmas of the early church, particularly among Italian dissenters. Acquainted with these early publications of Servetus, Philip Melanchthon, in later editions of his *Loci communes* (1535–59), refuted Servetus's critique of dogma and laid greater emphasis on the traditional doctrine of the Trinity.

After moving to France in 1532, Servetus worked under the assumed name Michel de Villeneuve (Villanovanus) since the Inquisition had initiated investigations against him. Cooperating closely with the printer brothers Melchior and Gaspard Trechsel in Lyons, he prepared two editions of Ptolemy's *Geography* (1535, 1541) and a new edition of the Latin Bible translation of the Italian scholar Santes Pagninus (1542), and later he published a seven-volume edition of a glossed Bible (1545). After concluding his study of medicine in Paris, during which he studied alongside the famous anatomist Andreas Vesalius under Johannes

Winter (Guinther) of Andernach, he entered the service of his benefactor Pierre Palmier, the archbishop of Vienna, in 1541–43. In Vienna, Servetus served as a physician. In 1545 he began corresponding with John Calvin, the reformer of Geneva. He wrote about thirty letters to Calvin, mostly antitrinitarian in content. In 1545–46 he also began writing his last great work, *Restitutio christianismi* (The restoration of Christianity), in which he tried to synthesize a dualistic worldview, a rejection of the doctrine of original sin, and Neoplatonic concepts of *Logos* in a somewhat idiosyncratic way. Its publication in 1553 by Balthazar Arnoullet and Guillaume Guéroult in Vienna resulted in Inquisitional proceedings, which Servetus escaped by fleeing. So he traveled to Geneva, where he was arrested. Servetus was tried for heresy under Calvin's aegis and burned at the stake on October 27, 1553. That event, while widely praised in Protestant circles at the time (including by Philip Melanchthon), in later centuries led to a depiction of Calvin as reactionary and intolerant.

See also Anabaptists/Spiritualists; Antitrinitarians; God and Trinity

Bibliography

Bainton, R. H. *Hunted Heretic: The Life and Death of Michael Servetus, 1511–1553*. Beacon, 1953. Blackstone edition, 2005; Friedman. J. *Michael Servetus: A Case Study in Total Heresy*. Droz, 1978; Hillar, M. *The Case of Michael Servetus (1511–1553): The Turning Point in the Struggle for Freedom of Conscience*. Mellen, 1997; Plath, U. *Der Fall Servet und die Kontroverse um die Freiheit des Gewissens: Castellio, Calvin und Basel 1552–1556*. Alcorde, 2014.

KĘSTUTIS DAUGIRDAS

Sewushane, Martinus

Martinus Sewushane (1838–1924) was one of very few black Lutheran evangelists in South Africa. He was ordained as a missionary by the Berlin Mission Society (BMS) in 1885. Sewushane seceded from the BMS as a protest to its paternalistic attitudes and with Johannes Winter established the independent Bapedi Lutheran Church in South Africa in 1890, thus forming one of the first indigenous Lutheran churches in South Africa.

See also South Africa

Bibliography

Heyden, U. van der. *Martinus Sewushan: Nationalhelfer, Missionar und Widersacher der Berliner Missionsgesellschaft im Süden Afrikas*. Erlanger Verlag für Mission und Ökumene, 2004; Malunga, F. "Schism and Secession: The Founding of the Bapedi Lutheran Church, 1890–1898." *Historia* 48 (2003): 48–65.

FRIEDER LUDWIG

Sexuality

Christianity's complicated view of sexuality has had a manifold effect in the lives of men and women in the Christian tradition. By depending on the Bible's predominantly male imagery for God and imbibing, from some forms of Platonism, a peculiar mistrust of the body, ancient Christianity offered quite different views of sexuality in comparison to the preceding and competing Jewish and Greco-Roman traditions. Many of these views passed into the medieval tradition as well. The Reformation, in contrast, introduced a more positive perspective on human sexuality and marriage, as evidenced in the significant reform of clergy marriage.

In early Christian experience, body, human relations, sexual love, and pleasure were viewed with significant ambivalence. Early followers of Jesus, living in what they perceived was the eve of the end of times, pointed to the celibate lifestyle in comparison to marriage, which seemed futile in the prospect of the kingdom of God's fruition. Early church fathers, some of them married themselves, preferred the ascetic celibate lifestyle over domestic and sexual relations, which they feared would distract Christians from prayer and love of God. Augustine of Hippo's discomfort with his own sexual desires, combined with his teaching on original sin as inherited through sexual act (found also in Tertullian), not only led him to choose an ascetic lifestyle, but also came to shape the ensuing Christian tradition's conflicted teaching of sexuality.

In the Middle Ages, "proper" sexual relations came more and more under the control of the institution of marriage, now considered a sacrament, even if deemed inferior to the celibate lifestyle of the monastics. Clerical celibacy, institutionalized in the Middle Ages, only further elevated sexual abstinence; such a "spiritual" lifestyle could be sought after also in marriage. At the same time, prostitution in medieval society allowed an organized, even if shunned, outlet for (supposedly) single men. (Houses of prostitution were closed with the Reformation, and sex workers were forced outside the city walls.) The medieval church had special stipulations regarding the sexual transgressions of its clergy. Medieval peniten- tial materials were also concerned with the sexual experiences of their parishioners.

For women in particular, virginity persisted as an ideal within European cultures; premari- tal transgressions could jeopardize a woman's future and marriage potential, tarnish her reputation, and lead to severe punishments. Sexual "purity" was particularly esteemed in women, whose female sex/sexuality was poorly understood by the men who were in positions of control as fathers, husbands, and male clergy and who set the rules and ideals. It is impossible to measure the degree to which rape and incest were common, although some laws against such behavior existed. The fre- quently occurring witch hunts and heresy trials were often sexually charged, as the devil was feared to find an especially vulnerable victim in sexually insatiable women whose "wandering uterus" posed a threat to all.

In the sixteenth century, human sexuality received positive attention. A God-created good, even if tainted with original sin, human sexuality was recognized as a normal force best practiced in a marriage. Luther wrote that be- cause only few people had a special, divine gift of celibacy,

> it [one's sexual nature] is more than a com- mand, namely, a divine ordinance [*werck*] which it is not our prerogative to hinder or ignore. Rather it is just as necessary as the fact that I am a man, and more necessary than sleeping and waking, eating and drinking, and emptying the bowels and bladder. It is a nature

and disposition just as innate as the organs involved in it. Therefore, just as God does not command anyone to be a man or a woman but creates them the way they have to be, so God does not command them to multiply but creates them so that they have to multiply. And whenever people try to resist this, it remains ir- resistible nonetheless and goes its way through fornication, adultery, and secret sins, for this is a matter of nature and not of choice. (*Estate of Marriage*, LW 45:18)

Even before he married (in 1525), Luther sought to demolish many of the impediments the church had set for potential married couples (from bad eyesight to "wrong faith" to being a godparent). The inability or unwillingness to participate in the conjugal life of marriage he considered a reason not to marry or even to divorce. Proper sexual relations belonged to a monogamous marriage, protected by secular laws, and beginning with a public promise of faithfulness and intercourse. With the Genesis narratives, Luther taught that human beings were created of the same flesh in two sexes for the sake of offspring, companionship, and spousal love, which was to resemble divine love, and that such unions were to channel grace and support men and women in their respective vocations. To be sure, Luther's views were oriented toward heterosexual relations. Because of changes in attitudes on the issues in the Western world, some Lutherans today argue that sexual and spousal relations are no longer limited to heterosexual partnerships.

With vast differences between different traditions around the globe, the Lutheran churches continue to debate values regarding sexuality, which some argue is best done in light of modern sciences and contemporary experiences, and others argue on the basis of scriptural prohibitions and admonitions. In this situation, major changes have already oc- curred with movements of women's liberation, increased access to birth control, and efforts to end the sexual discrimination of various types. Globally speaking, heterosexual and (often) male voices are balanced with the experiences of women and people with different sexual orientations, and with those who wish to marry and those who prefer a single life. Theologically and in practice, Lutherans from different cultural contexts continue to address the many distorted expressions of sexuality in an overly sexualized culture where sex sells, sexuality is "secularized," and sexual crimes against women and children in particular threaten to tarnish the very aspects of life that Luther considered one of God's most precious gifts to humankind.

See also Creation; Gender: Men and Women; Marriage and Divorce; Women's Movement

Bibliography

Crawford, K. *European Sexualities, 1400–1800*. Cambridge University Press, 2007; D'Emilio, J., and E. B. Freedman. *Intimate Matters: A History of Sexuality in America*. University of Chicago Press, 1988. 3rd ed., 2012; Licata, S., and R. Petersen, eds. *Historical Perspectives on Homosexuality*. Haworth, 1981; Luther, M. *The Estate of Marriage* (1522). LW 45:13–49; Luther, M. *Judgment on Monastic Vows* (1521). LW 44:251–400, esp. 243; Roper, L. *Oedipus and the Devil: Witchcraft, Sexuality and Religion in Early Modern Europe*. Routledge, 1994. Reprint, 1995; Stjerna, K. "Luther on Marriage, for Gay and Straight." *Seminary Ridge Review* 16, no. 2 (Spring 2014): 64–85. Reprint as "Luther on Marriage: Considerations in Light of Contemporary Concerns." In *Theologie im Spannungsfeld von Kirche und Politik/Theology in Engagement with Church and Politics*, ed. C. Nessan, M. Heesch, and T. Kothmann, 409–26. Glaube und Denken: Jahrbuch der Karl-Heim-Gesellschaft 31, Sonderband. Lang, 2014; Trumbach, R. *Sex and the Gender Revolution*. University of Chicago Press, 1998; Wiesner-Hanks, M. *Christianity and Sexuality in the Early Modern World: Regulating Desire, Reforming Practice*. Routledge, 2000.

KIRSI STJERNA

Sierra Leone

Sierra Leone has been called "the Morning Star of Africa" by the mission historian Andrew Walls. In the early nineteenth century, especially Freetown became the home of freed slaves, and it was here that the first mass movement to Christianity in modern Africa took place. The Anglican Church Missionary Society played an important role, but its first missionaries were German Lutherans: Melchior Renner and Peter Hartwig arrived from Jänicke's mission seminary in Berlin in 1804;

soon they were joined by others. Thus Lutherans contributed to the success of Anglicanism.

The modern Evangelical Lutheran Church of Sierra Leone (ELCSL) dates back to 1988; it was founded by a Sierra Leonean who became Lutheran while living in the United States. Soon connections to the ELCA and the LCCN (Lutheran Church of Christ in Nigeria) were established. In 1990 ELCSL became a member of the LWF. It records 4,500 members. The women are organized in the Lutheran Women's Organization, which engages in various developmental activities.

Bibliography

"Evangelical Lutheran Church in Sierra Leone." http://elcsl.weebly.com/.

FRIEDER LUDWIG

Sieveking, Amalie Wilhelmina

Born in Hamburg, Amelia Wilhelmina Sieveking (1794–1859) pioneered in social service ministry and new roles for women. Despite early rationalistic tutoring, a religious awakening created a deeply personal faith, which provided a strong sense of independent judgment and discernment. Unmarried and from an elite Hamburg family, she long contemplated creating a Protestant sisterhood. Demonstrating nursing leadership in the 1831 Hamburg cholera epidemic enabled her to launch the Female Association for the Care of the Poor and Sick in 1832. Her association focused on careful assessments of persons and families with needs that, if carefully met through fiscal, personal, and spiritual support, could relieve them during temporary duress and return them to self-sufficiency. Her middle- and upper-class women visitors gained a purposefulness beyond their homes and introduced them to larger social issues and associational functioning. While such involvement of women was pioneering and in the long term advanced the cause of women's rights, the association's focus on individual needs rather than social reform was politically conservative and fulfilling traditional Christian obligations to the poor. She conducted a school for girls, maintained extensive correspondence, and was an adviser to many, including the queens of Denmark and Prussia. Her association, religiously oriented but independent of direct church control, became widely emulated.

See also Inner Mission; Lutheran Social Services; Revivals, *Erweckungsbewegung*; Women's Movement

Bibliography

Poel, E. *Life of Amelia Wilhelmina Sieveking*. Ed. and trans. C. Winkworth with S***. Longman, Green, Longman, Roberts & Green, 1863; Prelinger, C. M. *Charity, Challenge, and Change: Religious Dimensions of the Mid-Nineteenth-Century Women's Movement in Germany*. Greenwood, 1987; Sieveking, A. W. *The Principles of Charitable Work-Love, Truth, and Order—As Set Forth in the Writings of A. W. Sieveking*. Compiled and translated by S***. 1863. https://babel.hathitrust.org/cgi/pt?id=njp.3210 1066955723;view=1up;seq=6. Reprint, Nabu, 2010.

JAMES W. ALBERS

Slavery and Colonialism

European nations with Lutheran state churches or with strong Lutheran churches were not very prominent in the slave trade, due in large part to political and economic reasons. The organization of a transatlantic slave-trade network was difficult for smaller nations such as Sweden, Courland, and Brandenburg, and their efforts were short lived. A Swedish African Company, founded in 1647 in Stade, was dismantled after ten years; the enterprise established by Duke James of Courland lasted only from 1651 to 1661. The Brandenburg Africa Company, founded in 1682, established a small West African colony in today's Ghana, but its settlements were soon taken over by the Dutch. The Danes participated over a longer period, but their slave trade was not particularly profitable, and at the recommendation of the Great Negro Trade Commission in 1791, Denmark was the first European country to abolish the slave trade.

In contrast to some other Protestant denominations, there were no Lutheran pressure groups advocating for abolition of the slave trade, and for a long time Lutheran churches tended to tolerate or to legitimize this trade with human beings. There were, however,

some exceptions: Franz Daniel Pastorius (1651–1719), a German Lutheran immigrant to Pennsylvania, helped to prepare the first antislavery petition in British America, in 1688. The Salzburg Lutheran refugees who began settling in Georgia in the 1730s initially also opposed slavery. Later, however, they began to accept the practice, especially after Samuel Urlsperger (1685–1772) advised them: "If you take slaves in faith, and with the intent of conducting them to Christ, the action will not be a sin, but it may prove a benediction." Urlsperger, a pastor in Augsburg, had close links to the Salzburgers since they passed through southern Germany. He was also connected to the Dänisch-Hallesche Missiongesellschaft and wrote a book about the first Lutheran missionary to India, Bartholomäus Ziegenbalg (1682–1719). During a brief stay at the Cape in South Africa, Ziegenbalg had criticized European slaveholders "for using their slaves so hard, and denying them the benefit of baptism" (11). The remark indicates that while Ziegenbalg did not challenge the system of slavery as such, he advocated better treatment of the slaves. The Moravians, too, cannot be seen as early abolitionists, but as missionaries in the Caribbean they had intense interactions with slaves. In the congregations they treated them as brothers and sisters, and sometimes there was intermarriage. Indirectly this challenged the system of slavery.

After the abolition of international slave trade by most European nations in the first quarter of the nineteenth century—Britain followed Denmark in 1807, the United States in 1808, and after the Congress of Vienna in 1814 other foreign powers started to adopt a similar policy—the task was to combat the system of slavery itself. In the United States, the head of the General Synod, Samuel Schmucker (1799–1873), was a persistent and outspoken opponent of slavery. Schmucker argued that the Hebrew word ʿebed, used in the Old Testament and sometimes translated "slave," actually means "servant"; he argued that slavery as an institution is opposed to the "very character and nature of God." But Lutherans were not united on this; in 1835, the South Carolina Synod condemned abolitionists' demands as "unjustifiable interference with our domestic institutions." The General Synod split along regional lines, and in 1863 Lutherans formed the separate Evangelical Lutheran Church in the South.

In the Danish West Indies, the Lutheran Church directed slave education. In 1847 King Christian VIII of Denmark promised full emancipation in 1859, but due to slave protests led by Moses Gottlieb, an emancipation proclamation was issued already in 1848. Some German theologians, such as the church historian August Neander (1789–1850), supported the abolitionists' cause, but it was only in the 1880s that there was an organized antislavery movement with Friedrich Fabri (1824–91), inspector of the Rhenish Mission since 1857, playing a leading role in it. In 1887 Fabri also became a member of the board of directors of the German Colonial Association. Both activities were closely connected; Fabri defended Germany's expansion as a mechanism to end slavery. Thus the suppression of one unjust system, slavery, was used to legitimate another system, colonialism.

The Berlin Congo Conference of 1884–85 is an important landmark in the wholesale partition of Africa between European nations. Togo, the Cameroons, German East Africa (including today Burundi, Rwanda, and the mainland of what is now Tanzania), and German West Africa (today Namibia) became German "protectorates." In addition, Germany also acquired two colonies in the Pacific: German New Guinea and German Samoa.

The relationship between mission and colonialism was complex. Since many Protestant mission societies had taken up their work before the 1880s, there could be tensions and power struggles. Missionaries tended to disagree when the colonial administration cooperated with Muslims. Some of them also protested against the colonial troops' brutal suppression of revolts such as Maji-Maji in East Africa (1905–7) or the Herero-Nama uprising in Namibia (1904–8). In general, however, missionaries cooperated with colonial governments. They contributed by providing services especially in the educational and health-care sectors. To justify the colonial system, they employed Lutheran concepts such as the two-kingdoms doctrine or the orders of creation.

After Germany lost its colonies during World War I, indigenous church leaders took over more responsibilities; and following World War II, African Lutherans started to challenge European domination. The first All Africa Lutheran Conference in Marangu in 1955 also emphasized theological independence and recommended a *confessio Africana*. A critical reflection on the use and misuse of Lutheran theology to legitimize unjust systems and human rights violations started especially since the Umpumulo Conference in South Africa in 1967.

See also Apartheid; Mission and Evangelism; Race/ Minorities

Bibliography

Chapman, R. M. "Just Enough? Lutherans, Slavery, and the Struggle for Racial Justice." *Trinity* 71 (2008): 16–20; Duchrow, U., and W. Huber, eds. *Die Ambivalenz der Zweireichelehre in lutherischen Kirchen des 20. Jahrhunderts.* Gütersloher Verlagshaus, 1976; Eltis, D., and S. L. Engerman, eds. *The Cambridge World History of Slavery.* Vol. 3. Cambridge University Press, 2012; Gründer, H. *Christliche Mission und deutscher Imperialismus.* Schöningh, 1982; Kistner, W. "Der Hintergrund des Umpumulo Memorandums von 1967." In *Zwei Reiche und Regimente: Ideologie oder Evangelische Orientierung? Internationale Fall- und Hintergrundstudien zur Theologie und Praxis lutherischer Kirchen im 20. Jahrhundert,* ed. U. Duchrow, 161–88. Gütersloher Verlagshaus Mohn, 1977; Kuenning, P. *The Rise and Fall of American Lutheran Pietism.* Mercer University Press, 1988; Kunter, K., and J. H. Schjorring, eds. *Changing Relations between Churches in Europe and Africa.* Harrassowitz, 2008; Ziegenbalg, B. *Propagation of the Gospel in the East.* Downing, 1711.

FRIEDER LUDWIG

Slovak Confessions of the Faith

Confessio Pentapolitana (1549), Confessio Heptapolitana (1559), Confessio Scepusiana

(1569)—these three confessions were prepared by Lutherans of northern Hungary (Slovakia) during the sixteenth century. Each confession was prepared for submission to ecclesiastical and royal authorities, to defend Lutherans from the charge of heresy. Brief and moderate in language, they reflect the theology of the Augsburg Confession (1530) and local circumstances.

The Pentapolita, the confession of the five free royal towns of eastern Slovakia, responds to the Hungarian law of 1548 banning Anabaptists and other religious innovators from the kingdom. Compiled by Leonhard Stöckel, it was presented to representatives of the king and the bishop of Eger, Anton Verančič.

Ten years later clergy of the seven mining cities of central Slovakia (Montana) adopted the Confessio Montana, or Heptapolitana, compiled by Ulrich Cubicularius, to present to the archbishop of Esztergom, Nicholas Oláh. Based on the Pentapolitana, it expanded the discussion of the true church but omitted a discussion of free will.

The Confessio Scepusiana (1569) was prepared by Valentin Megander and Cyriacus Obsopaeus for twenty-four towns in Spiš and Šariš counties for presentation to visitors sent by the bishop of Oradea, George Bornemisza. It emphasized a proper vocation for clerical office, defined the nature of good works, and tolerated the veneration of the saints.

See also Slovakia

Bibliography

Daniel, D. P. "The Acceptance of the Formula of Concord in Slovakia." *ARG* 70 (1979): 260–77; Daniel, D. P. "Lutheranism in the Kingdom of Hungary." In *Lutheran Ecclesiastical Culture*, ed. R. Kolb, 455–522. Brill, 2008.

DAVID P. DANIEL

Slovakia

The Lutheran Reformation first entered the Carpathian-Danubian region during the early 1520s. However, advocates of ecclesiastical reform in the kingdom of Hungary, including what is now modern Slovakia, started to define their particular theological and ecclesiastical identity only after the defeat of the Hungarian king at the battle of Mohacs (1526), the subsequent occupation of the Danubian basin by the Turks, and the presentation of the Augsburg Confession (1530). Between 1540 and 1570 the Wittenberg reform movement grew. The first synods of Seniorats (regional association of pastors) were held, schools were established or reorganized, and confessions of faith (Pentapolitana, 1549; Montana, 1559; Scepusiana, 1569) were prepared. Following the Peace of Augsburg in 1555, Lutherans in northern Hungary, roughly modern-day Slovakia, defended their right to exist and defined their theological stance as Helvetic Reformed; Philippist influences increased in the kingdom, especially among the Magyars. In a score of publications and in a dozen synods and colloquies, the differences between the Lutheran and the Reformed in Hungary were delineated. During the thirty years between the appearance of the Book of Concord (1580) and its adoption at the synods of Žilina (1610), Spišské Podhradie (1614), and Prievidza (1620), Lutherans consolidated their theological norms and their ecclesial structures. They obtained a legal recognition of their right to exist by the Treaty of Vienna (1606) and the laws adopted by the diet (parliament) of 1608, supported by some of the region's leading noble families, including the Thurzo, Nadasdy, and Revay families.

While non-Catholics far outnumbered the politically influential Roman Catholics at the end of the sixteenth century, during the seventeenth century the Hapsburg monarchs allied with post-Tridentine Catholicism to halt and then reverse the spread of the reform movements. Baroque Catholicism was persistent and persuasive, supported by royal grants of land and high positions in the state to Catholic nobles and ecclesiastics. Many families that formerly had supported the Reformation movements were persuaded to return to Roman Catholicism. On the other hand, emigrants from Bohemia and Moravia bolstered the number of Slavic Lutherans. The hymn and prayer books of Juraj Tranovsky and the

Czech translation of the Bible prepared by the Unitas Fratrum in Kralice became treasures of Slovak devotional literature. The Treaty of Linz (1645) granted the right to choose one's faith even to the peasantry. No one was to be forced to convert.

After the Thirty Years' War (1648), the Austrian Hapsburgs sought to realize their ideal of one monarch and one faith also in Hungary. Leopold I, who ascended the throne in 1657, was determined to exterminate Protestantism in his lands. He supported the most violent manifestations of the Counter-Reformation. Protestants were accused of treason; nearly eight hundred churches and almost all Protestant schools were confiscated. The majority of Protestant pastors and teachers were forced from office or into exile. Scores were imprisoned; two dozen were sold as galley slaves. During the "tragic decade" (1670–80) Protestantism was prohibited in Hapsburg Hungary. But internal and external pressures forced the Hapsburgs to accept the decisions of the Diet of Sopron (1681) that designated a few places for Protestant worship. However, even this privilege was subsequently limited by royal edicts after the expulsion of the Turks from Hungary.

During the last noble revolt that attempted to constrain royal power, the Synod of Ruzomberok (1707) reorganized Lutheran congregations into four districts and worried about the influence of Pietism in their ranks. But in 1715 decisions of religious matters were reserved to the monarch. The superintendencies (bishoprics) of the Lutherans were abolished only to be revived and defined by royal authority in 1734. For much of the eighteenth century, bureaucratic regulations, legal discrimination, and the restriction of the civic rights and economic opportunities of non-Catholics reduced the number of Protestants in Hungary more drastically than during the era of the forced conversions of the seventeenth century. The activity of Protestant pastors was severely circumscribed and subjected to the oversight and supervision of Roman Catholic ecclesiastics. Nevertheless, about 120 Lutheran churches continued to exist in 1780 in what is the territory of modern Slovakia.

The Edict of Toleration proclaimed by Joseph II in 1781 enabled a resurgence of Lutheranism in Slovakia. Although the Lutheran churches did not gain legal parity with Roman Catholics until after 1848, the edict restored the civil rights of the Lutherans, who now were able to worship publicly. During the next three decades Lutherans established about 150 new congregations. But they also had to confront ethnic and confessional-theological rivalries during the so-called era of national awakening.

Slovak Lutherans contributed significantly to the development of the Slovak language and literature. During the revolutions of 1848 they tended to support the Hapsburg cause against those Magyar Lutherans and Reformed who wished to create a Magyar state with a single Protestant church. After the suppression of the revolution, the Compromise of 1867 gave the Hungarians an opportunity to achieve their aims. Regulations required the use of Hungarian as the primary language in education, in public discourse, and even in the administration of the churches. Earlier attempts to effect a merger of the Lutheran and Reformed churches were renewed. Opposition revived long-dormant theological tensions. Religious and national aims fused and collided on the eve of World War I, which led to the collapse of the kingdom of Hungary and the creation of Czechoslovakia.

Slovak Lutherans supported the creation of this new state. In 1922 they adopted a new constitution for the Slovak Lutheran Church. Theological and national tensions remained between Czechophils and Slovak nationalists, and among Slovaks, Hungarians, and Germans. These tensions intensified during World War II. Many Lutheran leaders and laymen resisted the state controlled by the Fascists and Roman Catholics and the attempts to force them to accept membership in the Hlinka Guard or Hlinka Youth. Many were active in the resistance, helped Jews circumvent arrest or transportation to concentration camps in Germany, and participated in the Slovak National Uprising in 1944. At the same time, during the war, a separate German Lutheran Church in the Slovak Republic was established.

After the war many Germans and Magyars left the country, voluntarily or as part of an exchange of population. The postwar window for ecclesiastical renewal quickly closed when a Communist-dominated government was established in February 1948. The government subsequently abolished many religious societies, diaconal organizations, and church institutions; it imprisoned or strictly controlled pastors, teachers, and members of the church. Nevertheless, congregations continued to function, and contacts with world Christian organizations were maintained.

In the quarter century since the "Velvet Revolution" of 1989, the Evangelical (Lutheran) Church of the Augsburg Confession, with 320 congregations in fourteen Seniorats and two districts, has sought to revive, rehabilitate, and renew itself in an independent Slovak state. By adopting a new constitution in 1993 and issuing a new agenda and revisions of other liturgical and educational materials, this Lutheran Church seeks to foster congregational life, religious and theological education, and diaconal work among its 326,250 members, the nearly 6 percent of the population of Slovakia who consider themselves Lutherans.

See also Czech Republic; Hungary; Kuzmány, Karol; Slovak Confessions of Faith

Bibliography

Daniel, D. P. "Lutheranism in the Kingdom of Hungary." In *Lutheran Ecclesiastical Culture, 1550–1675*, ed. R. Kolb, 455–507. Brill, 2008; Daniel, D. P. "The Reformation and the Creation of National Intelligentsias in the Kingdom of Hungary." In *The First Millennium of Hungary in Europe*, ed. K. Papp, J. Barta, et al., 455–507. Debrecen University Press, 2002; Kusendová, D, and M. Benža, eds. *Historický atlas Evanjelickej cirkvi a. v. na Slovensku*. Tranoscius, 2011; Mannova, E., ed. *A Concise History of Slovakia*. Academic Electronic Press, 2004; Schwarz, K., and P. Svorc, eds. *Die Reformation und ihre Wirkungsgeschichte in der Slowakei: Kirchen- und konfessionsgeschichtliche Beiträge*. Evangelischer Presseverband, 1996; Uhorskai, P., and J. Alberty, eds. *Evanjelici v dejinách slovenskej kultúry*. Tranoscius, 2002; Veselý, D. *Dejiny krest'anstva a reformácie na Slovensku*. Tranoscius, 2004.

DAVID P. DANIEL

Smalcald Articles

As one of three documents in the Book of Concord by Martin Luther, the Smalcald Articles distinctively articulate the Evangelical-Lutheran doctrinal program. Luther's emphasis on "the first and chief article" (SA 2.1) gets to the core: only Christ justifies sinners through God's grace alone, and this message, revealed only by God's Word, is received by faith alone (such faith itself is engendered by God's grace). Written in late 1536, then revised, expanded, and published in 1538, the Smalcald Articles acknowledge agreement with some doctrines of the Roman opponents, offer critique of the differences, and prioritize doctrine.

The specific catalyst for the SA was the directive by Saxon elector John Frederick on December 11, 1536, for Luther to pen a document that could serve a twofold purpose. First, the prince wanted a "theological testament" from the aging reformer, a retrospective to summarize and clarify his life's work. Second, the prince wanted Luther's evaluation of the pope's call for a May 1537 general council of bishops, in part to respond to the issues raised by the Lutheran Reformation. (The council finally began in 1545 in Trent.) John Frederick was to meet with the Smalcaldic League (a defensive alliance of Protestants) in February 1537, at Smalcald, Hesse (now Thuringia), and this document was to inform the league's deliberations.

In late December, a group of colleagues (Nikolaus von Amsdorf, Johann Agricola, Johannes Bugenhagen, Caspar Cruciger Sr., Justus Jonas, Philip Melanchthon, and Georg Spalatin) gathered at the ailing Luther's home to discuss a draft and offer revisions, eventually subscribing the clean copy made by Spalatin (who delivered their work to John Frederick on January 3). Although John Frederick took the manuscript with him to Smalcald, the princes neither discussed nor adopted it, in part due to

Melanchthon's intervention. A debilitating illness kept Luther from extensive participation in the proceedings. The assembly reaffirmed adherence to the Augsburg Confession (directing Melanchthon to write an addendum on the papacy, a topic unexplored in the Augsburg Confession). Melanchthon wrote what would become *Treatise on the Power and Primacy of the Pope* (1537) at Smalcald. By the time the Book of Concord was published in 1580, this addendum to the Augsburg Confession had become mistakenly attached to the Smalcald Articles, due to early printings of them together.

At Smalcald, however, the attending theologians subscribed the Smalcald Articles as an expression of their individual adherence to Luther's doctrine. By the summer of 1538, Luther made more revisions, added the preface, and published it. The document then made its way toward its present confessional status through its role in the intra-Lutheran confessional controversies of mid-sixteenth-century Germany (e.g., its inclusion in various *corpora doctrinae*). Favored by Gnesio-Lutheran parties, the Smalcald Articles were an established doctrinal benchmark by 1580, when the confessors published the Book of Concord.

The Smalcald Articles have a threefold structure. Part 1 summarizes traditional trinitarian and christological doctrine. Because "both sides confess" these ecumenical convictions, Roman Catholic and Lutheran Christians belong to the one, holy, Christian, and apostolic church. This trinitarian foundation serves as a basis for the discussion of contentious issues to follow.

Part 2 opens with the article on justification, describing the office and work of Jesus Christ. Luther draws heavily from Scripture to distinguish between the law as God's righteous demand and the gospel as God's gracious gift. No "work, law, or merit" can earn God's grace. Rather, "faith alone justifies" believers. Luther then criticizes three major aspects of his opponents' practices through this gospel lens: the Mass (2.2), monasticism (2.3), and the papacy (2.4). The Mass, tied to the priest's power to offer the body and blood of Christ for sins, leads believers away from God's saving work in Christ. For Luther, God's Word, together with the bread and wine, makes the Lord's Supper a sacrament, a means of grace, eliminating not only the sacrifice of the Mass but also related topics (purgatory, prayers for the dead, pilgrimages, fraternities, relics, indulgences, and invocation of saints). Monasticism is not a higher vocation or surer path to heaven than are other Christian callings. The papacy, as an important human institution, is not divinely instituted as head of the church. Therefore to require submission to the pope as a precondition for salvation violates the gospel.

Part 3 offers to "discuss the following matters or articles with learned, reasonable people." Here Luther implements his law/gospel methodology as he moves from topics such as sin, law, and repentance to the gospel, the sacraments, and the church. Yet at the outset he cautions, "The pope and his kingdom do not value these things very much" (SA 3; *BC* 310).

Although the Smalcald Articles rank among the lesser known Lutheran confessions, Luther counted them as his testament of faith: "These are the articles on which I must stand and on which I intend to stand, God willing, until my death. I can neither change nor concede anything in them. If anyone desires to do so, it is on that person's conscience" (SA 3.15.3; *BC* 326). As new issues arose among Lutherans after Luther's death, the Smalcald Articles were reprinted with new prefaces aimed at providing Luther's answers to controversies over adiaphora, justification, the Lord's Supper, and the like. Included in several Gnesio-Lutheran bodies of doctrine (*corpora doctrinae*), it then made its way into the Book of Concord.

See also Book of Concord

Bibliography

Arand, C. P., et al., eds. *The Lutheran Confessions: History and Theology of the Book of Concord.* Fortress, 2012; Führer, W. *Die Schmalkaldischen Artikel.* Mohr

Siebeck, 2011; Gassmann, G., and S. Hendrix. *Fortress Introduction to the Lutheran Confessions.* Fortress, 1999; Huffman, G. S., ed. *The Lutheran Confessions: A Digital Anthology.* Fortress, 2011; Meuser, F., and S. Schneider. *Interpreting Luther's Legacy.* Augsburg, 1969; Russell, W. R. *Luther's Theological Testament: The Schmalkald Articles.* Fortress, 1995.

WILLIAM R. RUSSELL

Smalcald War

A military conflict in the Holy Roman Empire between the forces of the Smalcaldic League and Holy Roman emperor Charles V (July 1546–April 1547) is called the Smalcald War. The Smalcaldic League was founded in December 1530 in the Thuringian town of Schmalkalden. The founding members of the league were Elector John of Saxony, Landgrave Philip of Hesse, the princes of Anhalt-Bernburg and Mansfeld-Hinterort, and certain cities. In the coming years this included Lübeck, Magdeburg, Bremen, Strasbourg, Ulm, Memmingen, Constance, Biberach, Lindau, and Isny, along with Esslingen, Braunschweig, Goslar, Einbeck, Göttingen, Frankfurt am Main, Kempten, Hamburg, and Hannover. Princes who later joined the league included the dukes of Pomerania and Württemberg, the count of Pfalz-Zweibrücken, and two princes from Anhalt-Dessau. The purpose of the league was to defend these Evangelical (Lutheran) territories against the actions of the emperor, the imperial diet, other princes of the empire, and the imperial chamber court. This was necessary because ecclesiastical changes flowing from the Reformation were deemed illegal in the empire, eliciting a formal "*protestatio*" (legal appeal) of five Evangelical princes and the representatives of fourteen free, imperial cities at the Diet of Speyer (1529) to the Imperial Chamber Court. After the Diet of Augsburg (1530), the Augsburg Confession became the core doctrinal statement of the league, and the group organized into districts, raised taxes, and established a military council. In the years between 1532 (the year an armistice went into effect) and 1541, when the imperial diet did not meet, the general assembly of the league served as the equivalent of a Protestant diet.

The biggest gains of the league were political, not military. Between 1530 and 1555, Protestant leaders pressed for the right of reform (*ius reformandi*) in their territories. This right was specifically prohibited by the Imperial Chamber Court, but members of the league continued to encourage Evangelical teaching in their respective lands. In 1541 Charles V softened his stance against the league and tried to encourage religious agreement among the opposing factions. In particular, Charles V hoped to secure military support from the Protestant leaders for his wars against the Ottomans and the French. However, the failure of the colloquies of Worms (1540) and Regensburg (1541, 1546) made clear that there could be no theological resolution to the dispute. The league had protected the infant Evangelical movement for sixteen years, but the time for the empire's first religious war had arrived.

The intense period of military conflict known as the Smalcald War took place between July 1546 and April 1547, in part spurred by earlier action by the Smalcaldic League against Duke Henry of Braunschweig-Wolfenbüttel, who (they claimed) had been guilty of aggression against Evangelicals. The league was represented on the field by the forces of Elector John Frederick of Saxony and Landgrave Philip of Hesse. Emperor Charles V commanded the imperial forces, and he was supported by General Fernando Álvarez de Toledo, a veteran of the Italian Wars. Charles was also supported by a contingent of Paul III's papal armies and troops from the Netherlands, under the command of Maximilian of Egmont. The war is often depicted as one of the first "modern" military conflicts in the empire, as it contested trained foot soldiers with pikes and harquebuses, mounted cavalry, and mobile cannon squads employing the newest artillery. Although the Protestant forces were outnumbered, they were presented with a narrow opportunity for victory at the outset of the war. In September 1546, the league began a spectacular bombardment of the emperor's forces near Ingolstadt. When the smoke cleared, however, they were unwilling to commit their full resources to press their advantage. After an initial stalemate assisted by a wet winter near the banks of the Danube River, additional troops arrived to support the imperial army, including the emperor's brother, Archduke Ferdinand of Austria, and Duke Moritz of Saxony, the second cousin of Elector John Frederick, who, although Evangelical, was not a part of the Smalcaldic League and hoped by supporting the emperor to use the war to wrest the electorship from his cousin. The emperor's bolstered forces were victorious over the Protestants at the Battle of Mühlberg on Easter Day (April 25, 1547). After the decisive defeat, the league was disbanded; John Frederick and Philip lost their territories, were imprisoned and were (briefly) under sentence of death. Duke Moritz was rewarded with the title of elector and considerable territory held by John Frederick.

With the defeat of the league, Charles V, at an imperial diet in Augsburg, imposed a provisional religious settlement on the empire known as the Augsburg Interim (1548) in an attempt to resolve the religious schism. The agreement, which allowed married priests and communion in both bread and wine, was designed to restore the church unity largely along Roman Catholic lines and reestablish peace until a general council of the church could fully adjudicate the religious controversy. It was opposed by many Evangelical princes, including Elector Moritz, who had assumed (given his support for the emperor) that his territories would be exempt from any such changes. Despite their weakened political and military situation, however, members of the League developed a number of responses. Where Spanish troops were near, Lutheran pastors (such as Martin Bucer and Johannes Brenz) fled. In electoral Saxony and elsewhere, compromise was sought with newly installed Roman Catholic bishops. But many Lutheran leaders (esp. those in the northern cities) pressed forward

with their support of Evangelical reforms. They were able to do this in part because of the empire's distributed system of governance, which allowed the princes and imperial cities to manage their own affairs within certain limits. Although the Smalcaldic League did not fully realize its goals of insuring the religious safety of its members and the free course of their teaching, the league lasted long enough to allow the Evangelical cause to grow and become widespread. Emperor Charles V won the Smalcald War and dictated his terms via the Augsburg Interim, but his victory was short-lived (ending with the Revolt of the Princes and the Truce of Passau [1552] and Peace of Augsburg [1555]) and did not succeed in stamping out the Evangelical movement. With the exception of Constance, which the Hapsburgs annexed, all other cities where the Augsburg Interim was directly imposed returned to the Evangelical fold after the Peace of Augsburg.

See also Augsburg Interim; Charles V; Electors of Saxony; Holy Roman Empire; Peace of Augsburg; Philip of Hesse; Regensburg Colloquy; Smalcald Articles; Thirty Years' War

Bibliography

Brady, T. A., Jr. *German Histories in the Age of Reformations, 1400–1650*. Cambridge University Press, 2009; Brady, T. A., Jr. "Phases and Strategies of the Schmalkaldic League: A Perspective after 450 Years." *Archive for Reformation History* 74 (1983): 162–82; Nexon, D. H. *The Struggle for Power in Early Modern Europe: Religious Conflict, Dynastic Empires, and International Change*. Princeton University Press, 2009; Oman, C. *A History of the Art of War in the Sixteenth Century*. Stackpole, 1999.

MICHAEL J. HALVORSON

Social Ministry, Community Chest, Poor Relief

Luther's paradigm shift on justification introduced a new social ethic that facilitated the rationalization and secularization of social welfare, which continues into the development of the modern welfare state. Salvation by grace alone apart from works cut the nerve of the medieval ideology of poverty that fatalistically presented poverty and wealth as God's plan, saw the poor as an opportunity for meritorious works by the rich, and emphasized voluntary poverty as part of a higher state of the Christian life. By despiritualizing poverty, Luther and his colleagues revealed poverty as a social as well as a personal evil to be combated for the sake of the common good. By 1522 the Wittenberg Town Council, influenced by Luther's arguments, established a "common chest" ordinance for poor relief. Funded by ecclesiastical endowments, offerings, and taxes, the ordinance prohibited begging; provided interest-free loans, support for poor orphans and children of the poor, dowries for poor women, and the refinance of high-interest loans for burdened citizens; supported education and vocational training of poor children; and later even paid for medical services for the impoverished. The common chest was soon emulated in cities and towns wherever the Reformation took root. Luther's colleague Johannes Bugenhagen promoted these in church ordinances in the northern German areas; other colleagues initiated such programs elsewhere in the Holy Roman Empire. The incipient conception of the welfare state understood the reception of support not as charity but as a social right that contributed to the common good. Luther also recognized the systemic injustice of the capitalism of his day and called for government regulation of banks and businesses and the elimination of usury.

Reformation contributions to social welfare continued in Pietism and the Awakening through the social and economic upheavals of the Thirty Years' War (1618–48), urban developments, and the rise of industrialization. Institutions for the poor, orphans, ill, elderly, and vocational training were established in Frankfurt (1679), Berlin (1702), and other places through the influence of the Pietist leader Philipp Jakob Spener (1635–1705). August Hermann Francke (1663–1727) differed from Spener (who emphasized state responsibility for social welfare) when he established the famous Halle institutions, including its orphanage, as private concerns. Spener and Francke, as well as other Pietist leaders, viewed education as crucial for fighting poverty; they understood poverty in terms of the larger social context rather than as individual failings.

Lutherans of the Awakening and Inner Mission movements of the nineteenth century, especially in German-speaking lands, strove to respond to challenges of industrialization and worker alienation from a church seen as allied with industry and government ("throne and altar" ideology). Johann Hinrich Wichern (1808–81) developed a male diaconate from the Hamburg House of Rescue he established for street gangs. His call to the church to influence government and society through social services, what he called "Inner Mission," was endorsed at the 1848 Wittenberg Kirchentag, with the mandate that Wichern form the Central Committee for the Inner Mission. Like Luther and Spener, Wichern realized that mass poverty was not the sum of individual failings but a sickness of the whole society. He called for government redress of the systemic injustices of economic and political structures and also advocated self-help associations such as trade unions. So many Lutheran pastors and social reformers echoed this call that by the 1890s this "Christian Socialism" was denounced by Kaiser Wilhelm II; pastors were told to stick with preaching and pastoral care and to avoid addressing political and social problems. Yet the realization that poverty was not a moral defect but a consequence of economic contexts continued to spur reformers toward the goal of social welfare. Venues for this included not only the diaconal movements but also associations such as the Evangelical Social Congress long led by Adolf von Harnack (1851–1920).

Implementation of these goals has been most successful in Germany and the Nordic countries, especially following World War II. These developments were not without controversy; nevertheless, recent studies argue that Lutheran motifs such as vocation and the two realms informed public discourse leading to these welfare states. In contrast, the American ideology of limited government, private property, and individual freedom becoming ascendant over communitarian values has restricted Lutheran social contributions to the realm of philanthropic organizations. Nonetheless, the fundamental Lutheran diaconal motif of faith active in love manifests itself through Lutheran Services in America, one of the largest health and human services networks in the country. In addition, the Evangelical Lutheran Church in America supports international outreach in disaster relief and health programs, as well as the Lutheran World Federation's programs of service and advocacy for human rights, justice, and peace. The Lutheran Church–Missouri Synod has similar programs. In worldwide Lutheranism, the work of Lutheran World Relief and the support of hospitals and other social service agencies may be found in a variety of national Lutheran churches.

See also Bugenhagen, Johannes; Economic Issues: Capitalism and Socialism; Francke, August Hermann; Francke Foundations; Inner Mission; Justification; Lutheran Social Services; Orphanages; Seamen's Missions; Spener, Philipp Jakob; Twofold Righteousness; Two Realms; Wichern, Johann Hinrich

Bibliography

Lindberg, C. *Beyond Charity: Reformation Initiatives for the Poor*. Fortress, 1993; Lindberg, C. "Luther on Wall Street and Welfare." *Logia: A Journal of Lutheran Theology* 23, no. 4 (2014): 7–12; Lorentzen, T. *Johannes Bugenhagen als Reformator der öffentlichen Fürsorge*. Mohr Siebeck, 2008; McCurley, F. R., ed. *Social Ministry in the Lutheran Tradition*. Fortress, 2008; Naumann, I., and P. Markkola, eds. "Lutheranism and the Nordic Welfare States." *Journal of Church and State* 56 (2014): 1–150; Raunio, A. "Luther's Social Theology in the Contemporary World." In *The Global Luther: A Theologian for Modern Times*, ed. C. Helmer, 210–27. Fortress, 2009; Sachsse, C., and F. Tennstedt. *Geschichte der Armenfürsorge in Deutschland: Vom Spätmittelalter bis zum 1. Weltkrieg*. Kohlhammer, 1980; Torvend, S. *Luther and the Hungry Poor: Gathered Fragments*. Fortress, 2008; Wee, P. "Reclaiming Luther's Forgotten Economic Reforms for Today." *Lutheran Forum* 48 (2014): 52–56.

CARTER LINDBERG

Söderblom, Nathan

As theological professor, archbishop of Uppsala, and ecumenical pioneer, a more extroverted church leader can hardly be imagined than Nathan Söderblom (1866–1931). Son of a pastor in the northern part of Sweden, in Hälsingland, he developed into a worldwide church leader at home with Christian leaders from Istanbul to Rock Island, Illinois. Söderblom made lively contacts wherever he went, creating an ecumenical legacy for the Church of Sweden. His wide-ranging influence emerged when he was still a student during his first international trip, a visit to America in 1890, where he attended Dwight W. Moody's conference in Northfield, Massachusetts, and imbibed the organizational enthusiasm of the YMCA and the world of enlightened denominational Protestantism at Yale Divinity School. Back at the University in Uppsala, he established a reputation for superb oratory in 1893, giving a speech calling on Sweden to expect a new epoch of greatness, in line with the fame of the Swedish Protestant king Gustavus Adolphus. The convivial spirit of Christian student life in universities cultivated through the World Student Christian Federation, with its regular conferences and programs of discussion and Bible study, together with Sweden's Young Church movement and the Nordic Student gatherings, where Söderblom was an early leader, gave him confidence that these relationships could be built further, into a network of goodwill through the churches.

Söderblom produced a major work in the field of world religions, *Origin of Belief in God* (1914), which analyzed fieldwork conducted in the life of what were then called primitive societies in order to detect through their rituals and belief systems the progression of belief through the ages, a method that purported to show the evolutionary trend toward monotheism. Söderblom's characteristic emphasis on personal religion, however, led him to emphasize continuities through the ages and not to dismiss the religious importance of primitive religion. His research on world religions made him suspect to more traditional Lutherans, giving him a reputation for tolerance and liberality. When he later joined the theological faculty at the University in Uppsala in 1898, his closest friends were in the arts and sciences, not the theological faculty. Söderblom's lectures were well attended, as was his preaching in the nearby Holy Trinity parish, where the university's "Nicodemus" characters—those embarrassed about their Christian convictions, or filled with questions—came to hear him. His welcome to them was legendary, and so was the hospitality extended to students during musical evenings in the home he shared with Anna and their large family.

Nathan Söderblom became archbishop of the Church of Sweden in 1914, and his ecumenical leadership began in earnest. Theological dogmatism hampered cooperative work, especially among Lutheran churches; to circumvent this, Söderblom gave his mature attention to the Life and Work conferences and especially tried to broaden the participation through the Universal Christian Conference on Life and Work that he hosted in Stockholm and Uppsala in 1925. This important avenue for practical, diaconal work by the churches formed one of the strong pillars supporting the later work of the World Council of Churches.

Plagued by ill health throughout his career, he was able to mask his painful symptoms so that few were prepared for his death when in 1931 Söderblom gave the Gifford Lectures—his last public performance. These lectures were published posthumously in 1932 as *The Living God*, bringing especially to English readers his exceptionally passionate portrayal of the way Christians, in the heights and depths of their experience, are promised an encounter with an active, loving God.

See also Ecumenical Dialogues; Lundensian School; Sweden

Bibliography

Ferré, N. F. S. *Swedish Contributions to Modern Theology.* Harper & Row, 1967; Söderblom, N. *The Nature of Revelation.* Oxford University Press, 1933; Sundkler, B. *Nathan Söderblom: His Life and Work.* Gleerup, 1968.

MARIA ERLING

South Africa

Lutherans represent less than 2 percent of the South African population. The largest organization is the Evangelical Lutheran Church of Southern Africa (ELCSA), constituted in 1975, with approximately 580,000 members. The United Evangelical Lutheran Church in Southern Africa (UELCSA), established in 1964, includes mainly churches from a German background and has about 16,000 members. The Moravian Church in South Africa, also a member of the Lutheran Communion in Southern Africa (LUCSA), has about 50,000 members. The Free Evangelical Lutheran Synod in South Africa (FELSiSA) and the Lutheran Church in Southern Africa (LCSA), both affiliated with the International Lutheran Council, have together about 23,000 members. There are other bodies such as the Lutheran Bapedi Church, founded in 1880, but altogether the number of Lutherans is not more than 750,000 out of a total of 53 million inhabitants.

In 1774 German Lutherans erected their own church in Cape Town. Formal mission work among the Khoikhoi had begun in 1737 with the Moravian Georg Schmidt. In the nineteenth century, several mission societies followed. The Rhenish Mission started in Cape Colony in 1829, the Berlin Missionary Society in 1834 (Orange River, later Cape Colony, Natal, Transvaal), the Norwegian Mission Society in 1844 (Natal), the Hermannsburg Mission in 1854 (Natal, Western Transvaal), and the Church of Sweden Mission in 1876. After a conflict with the Norwegian Mission Society in 1873, the Schreuder Mission was founded and later came under the administrative oversight of the Norwegian Evangelical Lutheran Church in America. In the Hermannsburg Mission there was also a split when in 1893 three congregations seceded under the supervision of the Bleckmar Mission.

In missionary efforts, Africans played a key role. After Georg Schmidt returned to Europe in 1744, Vehettge Lena Tikhuie continued to conduct prayer meetings and Bible instructions every evening. The Hermannsburg Mission among the Tswana was prepared by David Mokgatla Modibane (ca. 1814–74). Johannes Dinkwanyane (d. 1876), a half brother of the Pedi king, assisted the Berlin Mission in the

Transvaal but in 1873 established a separate Christian community. Timotheus Sello (d. 1894) and Martinus Sewushane (ca. 1830–1929) were the first two Africans ordained as Lutheran pastors, in 1885. Sewushane established the independent Bapedi Lutheran Church in 1890. Paulina Dlamini (1856–1942) preached and taught in northern Zululand; she was described as a female apostle.

Missionaries were divided by different national backgrounds and different understandings of Lutheranism. The German concept of *Volkskirche*, which aimed to plant specifically national churches, contributed to the emergence of a patchwork of distinct Lutheran churches. It could also be used to support the apartheid system of racial segregation, which was enforced beginning in 1948 until 1994.

Considerable efforts to overcome the denominational divisions were made in the twentieth century. In January 1910, the Norwegian, Swedish, and Berlin Mission Societies established the Cooperating Lutheran Mission (CLM). In 1953 the Council of Churches on Lutheran Foundation in South Africa (CCLF) was founded, which also included the American Lutheran Mission (Schreuder Mission) and the Hermannsburg, Moravian, Rhenish, and Finnish Missionary Societies. In 1966 a Lutheran federation came into being.

The ELCSA was founded in December 1975 at Rustenburg, including "black Africans," "Coloreds," and Indians. Since the UELCSA did not join the ELCSA and was also hesitant to reject apartheid, the ELCSA in 1988–89 withdrew from the federation. In 1984 two UELCSA churches were suspended by the LWF assembly meeting in Budapest. Their attitude toward apartheid was declared a *status confessionis*. Upon evidence of a changed attitude, they were restored to LWF membership in 1990; they also became members of the Lutheran Communion in Southern Africa (LUCSA) in 1991. But even after 1994 the question of the churches' historic involvement in the development of an unjust system remains crucial. At the same time, the Lutheran churches are facing many new challenges in the new South Africa.

See also Apartheid; Botswana; Dlamini, Paulina; Namibia; Noko, Ishamel; Race/Minorities; Sewushane, Martinus; Tikhuie, Vehettge Lena

Bibliography

Chidester, D. *Religions of South Africa.* Routledge, 1992; Klän, W., et al., eds. *Mission und Apartheid: Ein unentrinnbares Erbe und seine Aufarbeitung durch lutherische Kirchen im südlichen Afrika.* Edition Ruprecht, 2013; Lessing, H., et al., eds. *The German Protestant Church in Colonial Southern Africa: The Impact of Overseas Work from the Beginnings until the 1920s.* Harrassowitz, 2012; Scriba, B., and G. Lislerud. "Lutheran Missions and Churches in South Africa." In *Christianity in South Africa: A Political, Social, and Cultural History*, ed. R. Elphick and R. Davenport, 173–94. University of California Press, 1997; Wilkinson, P. *Church Clothes: Land, Mission, and the End of Apartheid in South Africa.* Maisonneuve, 2004.

FRIEDER LUDWIG

Spain

With few exceptions, Luther and the Lutheran tradition have been interpreted in Spain's history as archetypes of Protestant heresy. News of Luther arrived in Spain soon after the publication of the Ninety-Five Theses via the Basel publisher Froben. Juan Manual (d. 1543), then imperial ambassador in Rome, reported the curia's great fear of Luther's criticisms based on the German's great intellect and trenchancy. In matters concerning the corruption of morals, numerous Spanish humanists and reform-minded clergy were sympathetic, but the ecclesiastical officials were chary of Luther's acute critique of papal authority. What came to be the standard Roman opinions formed after the publication of the papal bulls *Exsurge domine* (June 1520) and *Decet Romanum Pontificem* (January 1521): Luther was a dangerous heresiarch with diabolical aspirations to corrupt Spanish territory.

Luther caused a sensation among Charles V's entourage at Worms: they rushed to behold the rough monk who threatened all Christendom. As the attending imperial secretary Alfonso Valdés (1490–1532, brother of humanist Juan [see below] and later an irenic interlocutor with Melanchthon at the Diet of Augsburg in

1530) lamented, a dispute that should have remained a "quibble among monks" had become a bold attack on the papacy. Spain's Inquisition banned Luther's works the same month (April 1521), and Charles V ordered the burning of them in May, laws that were only sporadically implemented; exemplars continued to reach Spain's enthusiastic readers from Antwerp, then Spanish territory.

Many among Spain's intelligentsia were as ripe for reform as colleagues in Luther's Germany, especially those associated with the University at Alcalá. Patronized by the cardinal Francisco Jiménez de Cisneros (1436–1517), the magnum opus of this humanist powerhouse was the Complutensian Polyglot Bible (1516), a parallel edition in six languages of the complete biblical text, made possible by the stupendous erudition of its converso contributors (Jews forced to adopt Christianity). Many of Spain's reformers who were later exiled were educated in Alcalá.

Luther earned varied judgments from Spanish luminaries. Juan Ginés de Sepúlveda (1490–1573) slandered the ex-monk's character, propagating what would later become clichés about Luther's greed, lasciviousness, and ignorance of church tradition. Dominican Francisco de Vitoria (1483–1546) argued with more discipline against Luther's teachings on justification by faith without works, though without profound engagement. In his *Spiritual Exercises* (1522), Ignatius of Loyola (1491–1556) seemed to oppose Luther directly by calling Christians to "work with love." Spanish humanists in general sympathized with Luther's calls for reform but worried that his bombast would scuttle their reforming efforts.

From the 1520s marginal religious groups, though unconnected with Luther, began to suffer repression as *luteranos*. The mystical *alumrado*s, many of whom were intellectuals of Jewish heritage such as Juan de Vergara (1492–1557), came under increasing suspicion after 1529 for praying and studying Scripture outside the structures of the church, as well as for their conviction of human perfectibility.

Later in Seville and Valladolid, house conventicles, excited by ideas about justification by faith that they had learned from preachers such as Constantino Ponce de la Fuente (1502–60, sometime personal chaplain to Charles V) met privately to deepen their faith and study banned books—suspicious activities that eventually brought them to judgment and burning at an auto-da-fé in 1558 for the crime of "Lutheranism." Even conventional figures like Bartolomé Carranza (1503–76, occasional confessor of both Charles V and Queen Mary of England) were not above suspicion. Despite identifying Luther as the source of all heresy in his earlier work, the tone of this Dominican's later writings led to a long and famous trial before the Inquisition, with Lutheranism as a major accusation; though acquitted of heresy after eight years of confinement, Carranza was deprived of almost all his responsibilities. Students of Erasmus and the reformers alike were tainted.

This repression fomented a generation of exiles. Among others were Juan Perez de Pineda (1500–1567, disciple of the above-mentioned Ponce de la Fuente), who published from Geneva Spanish translations of the Bible, Luther, and Calvin; Francisco de Enzinas (1518–52), who studied Greek with Melanchthon in Wittenberg, then offered his Castilian New Testament to compatriot Charles V in Brussels in 1543; and humanist Juan Valdés (1509–41), who influenced the Roman Catholic reforming *spirituali* (Jacopo Sadoleto [1477–1547], Gasparo Contarini [1483–1542], and Reginald Pole [1500–1558]), as well as Peter Martyr Vermigli, and drew on both Luther and Melanchthon in his books, safe from the Inquisition in Naples.

From the second half of the sixteenth century, Luther became the foil to a pantheon of Iberian heroes who would compensate for his damage to Christendom. This was particularly prevalent in Spanish America, which by geographic isolation and quarantine from the contagion of Jews, Muslims, and Protestants, became the locus for the Spanish clergy's implementation of Counter-Reformation orthodoxy. Writing from Mexico at the end of the sixteenth century, Franciscan friar Gerónimo de Mendieta (1528?–1604) saw Luther's advent eclipsed by Mexico's conqueror Hernán Cortes, both born (so he thought) in the same year: while the one was destined to drive millions from the fold in the Old World, the other would replace them with even more in the New World. In sermons and images throughout Peru and Mexico, one finds reference to Luther as the archheretic; frequent motifs picture Luther, Calvin, and other Protestant leaders being crushed by the cart of the triumphant church or drowning beside the ship of the church. In Mexico, the Virgin of Guadalupe was seen as an antidote to Luther's toxin, a role also performed in seventeenth-century Spain by Teresa of Avila (1515–82).

At the very same time, ironically, a catechism by the above-mentioned Ponce de la Fuente, already condemned as "Lutheran" in Spain for its suspicious emphasis on justification by faith, lived a second life in Mexico under the supposedly safe authorship of Franciscan bishop Juan Zúmarraga (1468–1548), later influencing the Jesuit catechisms of Brazil and Goa. Though not directly drawing from Luther or Lutheran sources, suspicious Reformation ideas continued to circulate despite prohibition.

After the reforms of Charles's son Phillip II, there is little record of engagement with the Lutheran tradition save for occasional trials, mostly of foreign Protestant merchants suspected of importing heretical literature or proselytizing. Slander of Luther by repeating the details in Cochlaeus's biography is scattered through literature and drama. However, certain revolutionary governments in Spanish America invited significant numbers of German Lutheran colonists, whom they hoped would help industrialize and modernize their still-feudal territories with hard work and technical know-how.

The nineteenth century saw the end of the Inquisition, and with its demise came efforts to reappropriate silenced voices. In hopes of fomenting religious change, Luis Usóz y Río gathered important writings (never printed earlier) of Spain's forgotten reformers into the twenty-four-volume *Reformistas Antiguas Españoles* (1874–1904), which Benjamin Wiffen published from London and Strasbourg. Roman Catholicism was the only legal religion under the dictatorship of Francisco Franco (1892–1975), and since the establishment of religious freedom in 1978 a handful of Protestant churches have been established. Lutheran churches remain marginal at best, though interest in Luther is stronger than this would suggest, with a significant biography by Ricardo Garcia-Villoslada published in the 1970s, many serious engagements at the quincentenary of Luther's birth, and more recently a best-selling historical novel by Miguel Delibes (*El hereje*, 1999) illustrating the Reformation's turbulent reception in Spain during the mid-sixteenth century.

See also Charles V; Cochlaeus, Johannes; Erasmus of Rotterdam (Desiderius Erasmus Roterodamus); Holy Roman Empire; Humanism and the Reformation

Bibliography

Andrés Martin, M. "La Imagen de Lutero en España hasta 1559." In *Lutero y Reforma: Simposio de la Universidad de Extremadura sobre Martín Lutero*, ed. J. B. Zimmermann et al., 55–85. Universidad de Extremadura, 1985; Bataillon, M. *Érasme et l'Espagne*. New ed. Droz, 1991; Gaztambide, J. G. "La Imagen de Lutero en España: Su evolución histórica." *Scripta Theologica* 15 (1983): 469–528; Idigoras, T. *Melanchthon y Carranza*. Centro de Estudios Orientales y Ecuménicos Juan XXIII, Universidad Pontificia, 1979; Mayer, M. *Lutero en el Paraíso*. Fondo de Cultura Económico, 2005; Nesvig, M. "Heretical Plagues and Censorship Cordons: Colonial Mexico and the Transatlantic Book Trade." *Church History* 75 (2006): 1–37; Nieto, J. *El Renacimiento y la otra España*. Droz, 1997; Thomas, W. *Los protestantes y la Inquisición en España en tiempos de Reforma y Contrarreforma*. Leuven University Press, 2001; Usoz y Río, R., B. Wiffen, and E. Boehmer, eds. *La Biblioteca de Reformados Antiguos Españoles*. 24 vols. Bently, Wilson & Fley / Trübner, 1874–1904. Frankling, 1952–; Vilar, J.-B. "La formación de una biblioteca de libros prohibidos en la España isabelina: Luis Usoz y Río, importador clandestino de libros protestantes (1841–1850)." *Bulletin Hispanique* 96 (1994): 397–416.

ANDREW L. WILSON

Spalatin, Georg

As private secretary, confessor, and court preacher for Elector Frederick III, Georg

Spalatin (1484–1545) was an intermediary between Frederick and Luther. Born Georg Burckhardt in the town of Spalt in Franconia, Spalatin received a thoroughly humanist education in his studies at Latin school in Nuremburg and later at the University of Erfurt. He received an MA at the University of Wittenberg in 1503, after which he studied law there. It was during his time at the University of Wittenberg that he began using the humanist name of Spalatinus. Shortly after his ordination to the priesthood in 1508, he began tutoring Elector Frederick's nephew, Duke John Frederick, in Torgau. In 1511 he moved into the Wittenberg Castle to tutor two other nephews of Frederick's, and in 1514 he began to tutor Frederick's son. In 1516 Spalatin became Frederick's private secretary, in 1518 he became Frederick's confessor, and in 1522 Frederick made Spalatin his court preacher.

By his own account, Spalatin maintained his ties with the papacy until 1523. Nonetheless, as one charged with oversight of the University of Wittenberg, he was instrumental in securing Frederick's early protection of Luther. During Luther's stay at the Wartburg in 1520–21, all of Luther's correspondence and manuscripts passed through Spalatin's hands. He had the dual challenge of prodding a reluctant Frederick to support Luther's movement while also buffering Luther's irascibility. He succeeded in retaining Frederick's support for Luther, but he was not able to persuade Frederick to initiate widespread reforms in the churches of his land. After Frederick's death in 1525, Spalatin left the court to become a parish pastor in Altenburg. He remained active in the ongoing events of the Reformation, attending meetings of Evangelical princes and participating in negotiations between Evangelicals and papal representatives. Frederick's successor, Elector John, asked Spalatin to help with parish visitations (1527–29) in Electoral Saxony. Spalatin also accompanied John as a theological adviser to the Diet of Augsburg in 1530. When Elector John died in 1532, his successor, John Frederick, continued to call

on Spalatin for assistance with negotiations and visitations. Most notably, Spalatin helped carry out visitations in Ducal Saxony when it became Evangelical in 1539. Spalatin was also asked to manage the University of Wittenberg library beginning in 1536. Throughout his career, Spalatin was a humanist and historian. He translated both Erasmus and Petrarch into German and collected historical material about the Saxon court. From this material he composed a biography of Frederick III and a three-volume *Saxon Chronicle*. Spalatin died on January 16, 1545, in Altenburg.

See also Augsburg Confession; Electors of Saxony; Erasmus of Rotterdam (Desiderius Erasmus Roterodamus); Humanism and the Reformation; Saxonies

Bibliography

Höss, I. *Georg Spalatin, 1484–1545: Ein Leben in der Zeit des Humanismus und der Reformation*. Böhlau, 1956; Spitz, L. *The Religious Renaissance of the German Humanists*. Harvard University Press, 1963; Weide, C., ed. *Georg Spalatins Briefwechsel: Studien zu Überlieferung und Bestand (1505–1525)*. Evangelische Verlagsanstalt, 2014.

ANNA MARIE JOHNSON

Spangenberg, August Gottlieb

The theologian and missionary August Gottlieb Spangenberg (1704–92) was a close collaborator with Nikolaus Ludwig von Zinzendorf. Spangenberg studied Lutheran theology at the University of Jena, where he was involved in a Pietist student group. After his ordination he was appointed to head the orphanage in Halle in 1731, but concerns over his ties to Zinzendorf led to his dismissal in 1733. Spangenberg accepted an invitation to move to Herrnhut, and in 1734 he was sent to inspect the Moravian mission on St. Thomas. Next he negotiated with the trustees of the Georgia colony to secure an exemption for Moravian missionaries from swearing oaths and bearing arms. While in Savannah, Spangenberg established a close relationship with John Wesley, and he played a key role in Wesley's turn to Evangelical Christianity. In 1744 he was consecrated a bishop and assumed leadership of the Bethlehem commune in Pennsylvania. He was also overseer of the extensive Moravian evangelism among Native Americans and German-speaking settlers. In the 1750s Spangenberg made the plans for the Wachovia settlement in North Carolina. He was recalled to Europe in 1762 and served on the governing council of the Brüdergemeine. He wrote two important apologetic works after Zinzendorf's death: *Leben Zinzendorfs* (8 vols.) and *Idea Fidei Fratrum*. The latter book tried to demonstrate that the doctrine of the Moravians was in line with orthodox Lutheran teaching.

See also Moravian Church (Unitas Fratrum); Zinzendorf, Nikolaus Ludwig von

Bibliography

Atwood, C. "Apologizing for the Moravians: Spangenberg's *Idea Fidei Fratrum*." *Journal of Moravian History* 8 (2010): 53–88; Reichel, G. *August Gottlieb Spangenberg*. Mohr, 1906; Spangenberg, A. G. *An Exposition of Christian Doctrine, as Taught in the Protestant Church of the United Brethren, or, Unitas Fratrum*. Trans. and ed. B. LaTrobe. 3rd English ed. Moravian Church, 1959.

CRAIG D. ATWOOD

Spangenberg, Johann and Cyriacus

Like several of Luther's early followers, Johann Spangenberg (1484–1550) came out of the humanistic circle formed by Conrad Mutianus Rufus at the University of Erfurt. As pastor in Nordhausen beginning in 1527, he cultivated reform in Wittenberg style and promoted the education of children. In 1546 he became superintendent of the churches in the county of Mansfeld. His literary efforts provided key support for the integration of Luther's thought into pastoral practice among the reformer's followers. They include his *Margarita theologica* (*Theological Pearls*); an introduction to biblical teaching for advanced students, formatted as questions and answers and shaped by Melanchthon's *Loci communes*; as well as catechetical materials, numerous aids to preaching, and devotional literature.

Cyriacus (or Cyriakus) Spangenberg (1528–1604), son of Johann, lived with the Luther family during his initial studies in Wittenberg. He dedicated his life to defending his interpretation of Luther's teaching while celebrating

his person, as in a decade-long series of sermons on the reformer preached on anniversaries of his birth and death. As pastor in Mansfeld, Cyriacus worked together closely with fellow Gnesio-Lutherans in the county ministerium and attacked foes of Luther's teaching from Roman Catholic, Reformed, and divergent Wittenberg orientations. His support of Matthias Flacius's doctrine of original sin led to his exile from Mansfeld in 1574. His last thirty years were spent in various places, as pastor or as private scholar. His prodigious scholarship produced a homiletical commentary of Pauline Epistles in eight folio volumes, a commentary in chart form on the first eighteen books of the Old Testament, editions of his own and his father's funeral sermons, catechetical sermons, a collection of wedding sermons, and numerous other devotional and polemical works. He also composed chronicles of Mansfeld, Henneberg, Holstein, and the bishopric of Verden. Using the loci method, he produced weighty treatises on several topics, including the nobility and music. His adherence to Luther's teaching, combined with his use of Melanchthonian humanistic tools and methods, made him one of the most significant intellectual figures of his age.

See also Flacius, Matthias, and the Flacians; Humanism and the Reformation; Wittenberg Circle, Parties within

Bibliography

Kolb, R. *Martin Luther as Prophet, Teacher, and Hero*. Baker, 1999; Rembe, H. *Der Briefwechsel des M. Cyriacus Spangenberg*. 2 vols. Naumann, 1887–88; Spangenberg, J. *A Booklet of Comfort for the Sick, and On the Christian Knight*. Ed. and trans. R. Kolb. Marquette University Press, 2007.

ROBERT KOLB

Spener, Philipp Jakob

The leader of the early Pietist movement, Philipp Jakob Spener (1635–1705), was one of the most influential Lutheran theologians of the seventeenth century. Born in Rappoltsweiler, Alsace, Spener pursued philosophical and theological studies at Strasbourg and Basel, followed by an academic tour to Switzerland

and France. As companion and teacher of two young noblemen, he stayed for some time in Württemberg. He received a call as professor of history in Tübingen, but he returned to Strasbourg in 1663 to become a preacher without pastoral duties, where he completed his doctoral thesis. In 1666 he was appointed senior pastor of the ministerium in Frankfurt am Main. Prompted by several pious men in his parish in 1670, Spener initiated the first private meeting to study devotional books and the Bible (*collegium pietatis*) in his study.

In 1675 he wrote his important preface to a collection of sermons by Johann Arndt. Several months later he published this preface as a separate booklet with the title *Pia Desideria, or Heartfelt Desire for a God-Pleasing Reform of the True Evangelical [i.e., Lutheran] Church*. This tract became the foundational text of Pietism, the most important religious movement among Lutherans after the Reformation. After describing the defects of the church in his times and demonstrating that things could get better, Spener submitted six proposals for the improvement of the church. The first was to further disseminate the Word of God. The second was to form groups of Christians under the leadership of a pastor in order to read the Bible and provide mutual spiritual support, thus realizing the priesthood of all believers (understood as the laity). And finally, Spener made some proposals to improve the theological studies and the education of future pastors. These proposals were widely discussed and met, by and large, with approval. Conventicles began in several cities. In his own town of Frankfurt, however, other *collegia pietatis* soon began and competed with Spener's. A more critical attitude toward the official church developed among them, and when members of these groups separated from the Lutheran Church, Spener wrote an essay called *Der Klagen über das verdorbene Christenthum mißbrauch und rechter gebrauch* (The correct and incorrect usage of complaints concerning the corruption of Christendom), published in 1685. Appointed senior court preacher of the

Saxon Elector Johann Georg III in Dresden in 1686, he established contact with several pious students in Leipzig, who met to read the Bible for mutual edification in their personal faith. One of these, August Hermann Francke, later founded the Halle orphanage, which became the starting point and center for the worldwide spread of Pietism. Spener stayed only a few years in Dresden. After a serious conflict with the elector in the spring of 1689, he was appointed provost at the Nicolas Church in Berlin in 1691. Because of his close connections with influential people in the court of the Elector of Brandenburg, he helped shape the foundation of the University of Halle to become the first "Pietist" university. Alongside this, his most important work in this period was to describe and defend themes that arose in concert with the Pietist movement: the sanctification of true Christians and the possibility of moral perfection, the spiritual priesthood of all believers, millenarian hopes, and questions concerning the "true church."

Spener wrote many books, often in reaction to tracts by opponents. In his final years Spener composed his *Theologische Bedencken* (Theological reflections, 1700–1702), a four-volume work with texts taken from his extensive correspondence, giving advice on theological, moral, and other questions and describing his role in the Pietist movement. These *Bedencken* were completed after his death with the additional *Letzte theologische Bedencken* (1711) and *Consilia et judicia theologica Latina* (1709), each in three volumes. Besides these publications, the greatest part of his oeuvre consists of compilations of sermons, in which he explains his doctrine. He always considered himself to be an orthodox Lutheran and sought to defend his teaching, using arguments made by theologians of his own time as well as Martin Luther. He was able to do this because, as one of the day's foremost experts on the writings of Luther, he had compiled a Bible commentary using only texts by Luther; unfortunately this work was never published. In his apocalyptic expectations he went beyond the Augsburg Confession (art. 17), expecting "better conditions in the church," supported by the as yet unfulfilled biblical promises regarding Israel, the final fall of Roman Catholicism, which he (like Luther) regarded as the whore of Babylon (see Rev. 17–18). Many, even those critical of Pietism, have later recognized Spener as a fundamentally orthodox Lutheran. It is correct to label him the "father" of Pietism, at least of Lutheran Pietism in its narrower sense. Due to his engagement, Pietism became not only a devotional but also a social movement.

See also Conventicles; Francke, August Hermann; Hildebrand, Carl (Baron von Canstein); Lutheran Orthodoxy; Pietism

Bibliography

Spener, P. J. *Briefe aus der Dresdner Zeit.* Mohr Siebeck, 2003–; Spener, P. J. *Briefe aus der Frankfurter Zeit.* Mohr Siebeck, 1992–; Spener, P. J. *Pia Desideria.* Fortress, 1964; Spener, P. J. *Schriften.* Reprint. Olms, 1979–; "Spener, Philipp Jakob." *RGG* 7 (2004): 1564–66; Wallmann, J. *Philipp Jakob Spener und die Anfänge des Pietismus.* Mohr Siebeck, 1986.

KLAUS VOM ORDE

Spitta, Karl Johann Philipp

The German Lutheran pastor, theologian, and hymn writer Karl Johann Philipp Spitta (1801–59) was born in Hannover to a family of Huguenot background. He studied in Göttingen under a rationalistic faculty. Following a serious illness, he experienced a spiritual awakening after reading tracts by F. A. Tholuck (1799–1877). As a result of this renewal, he delved deeper into study of the Bible and Luther's works. Upon ordination, he served in various capacities in Hannover: first as an assistant pastor at Sudwalde; second as a chaplain to prisoners in the garrison of Hamelin for two years (until military authorities had him dismissed on charges of Pietism and mysticism); and finally as a parish pastor in Wechold. In 1837 he married Joanna Mary Magdalene Hotzen; they became the parents of Friedrich (1852–1924), a professor of New Testament and practical theology in Strasbourg, and Philip Julius August (1841–94), a

biographer of J. S. Bach and leading musicologist at the University of Berlin.

Karl Spitta is best known for his hymns, which reflect a warm and intimate piety and were widely used among awakening circles in Germany. His *Psalter und Harfe* passed through no less than fifty-five editions by 1889, making him perhaps the greatest German hymnist of his century. In the twentieth century, English versions of several of his hymns appeared in Lutheran hymnals in the United States, including "We Are the Lord's" (*TLH* 453; *LBW* 399) and "O Happy Home, Where Thou Art Loved Most Dearly" (*TLH* 626).

See also Hymnody

Bibliography

Polack, W. G. *The Handbook to the Lutheran Hymnal.* Esp. 582–83. Concordia, 1942.

JOHN T. PLESS

State

One of the main protests of the Lutheran Reformation concerned the relationship of the Roman Catholic Church to the governments of the time, the Holy Roman Empire, and individual territories within it. Luther believed that the Roman Catholic Church had enmeshed itself too deeply in political affairs, partly because it had not accurately delineated the specific roles of church and government. For Luther, the church's mission was to proclaim the gospel and administer the sacraments; the government's role was to maintain order and justice. The former had only the power of the Word, but the latter wielded coercive power. This distinction later led to the Lutheran doctrine of the two ways: God reigns in the world, through the law enforced by the governments and through the gospel proclaimed by the church. In Luther's view, the Roman Catholic Church had usurped the role of political authority.

Already in 1520 in his *Address to the Christian Nobility of the German Nation,* Luther attacked the "three walls of the Romanists," one of which was the claim that the secular authorities had no jurisdiction over the church and that, on the contrary, the spiritual authorities had jurisdiction over the secular. Luther argued that both church and temporal government are on equal footing before God; they differ rather in function, the state enforcing the law and the church proclaiming the gospel. After the break with Rome, Luther further encouraged the laity (the princes and city councils) to take responsibility for reforming, supporting, and protecting the church and its leaders, since the Roman Catholic hierarchy could no longer do so. At first he looked on this as a provisional matter, but it gained permanence as Luther and others recognized the legitimate role of government in the temporal affairs affecting the church. Sometimes it led them to confuse the government's power with the church's gospel. This later made the church in certain realms dependent on political power, especially in the nineteenth century, turning certain German and Scandinavian churches into state or folk churches. Being dependent on the state sometimes made it difficult for the churches to resist the state's incursion into church affairs or to criticize the secular government for not attending to its own God-given duties.

In his *Temporal Authority: To What Extent It Should Be Obeyed* (1523), Luther cited Rom. 13:1–2 as the scriptural basis for the legitimacy of the government. It is a "godly estate" established after the fall for "the punishment of the wicked and the protection of the upright" (LW 45:86). However, following 1 Pet. 2:13–14, Luther teaches that secular authority is beholden to the law of God, and if it governs contrary to God's will, Christians are to obey God instead (Acts 5:29). He also exhorts the princes to rule with justice and concern for the poor.

In his catechisms, Luther locates the proper Christian attitude toward all governing authorities under the commandment "Honor your father and mother" (Exod. 20:12). Like parents and household heads, secular rulers possess an "office" to help parents and enact good laws; they must keep order and justice and therefore should be honored and obeyed.

Luther seemed to reinforce a powerful role for secular authority when the Peasants' Revolt (1524–26) threatened to destroy not only civil peace but also the Reformation of the church. While chastising peasants for their rebellion and the nobility for their unjust treatment of the peasants in *An Admonition to Peace*, Luther finally turned his anger toward what he viewed as the peasants' anarchy in his *Against the Thieving, Murderous Horde of Peasants*, in which he used what even some of his contemporaries viewed as intemperate language to encourage the nobility to put down the revolt. The nobles, who were already mercilessly putting down the revolt, helped for some observers to reinforce Luther's reputation for siding with the powerful. At the same time other reformers, including Philip Melanchthon and Johannes Brenz, had also taken positions against the rebellion.

Nevertheless, Luther also initially cautioned princes regarding rebellion against their own overlords. After being convinced by the Saxon courts' lawyers in 1531 that the Elector of Saxony was an equal to Charles V—and only then—could he and Philip Melanchthon agree to a defensive alliance against the latter. In the 1530s they could argue that Evangelical princes possessed a *cura religionis* (care for religion) that included extirpating blasphemous teachings from their realms. In the wake of the Smalcald War of 1547, Philip Melanchthon also encouraged an active defensive war against the emperor, a position that paralleled the Magdeburg Confession of 1550. Much of this understanding of resistance was lost on later Lutherans, who often equated Luther's early attitude with unquestioning obedience to secular authorities.

This developing view of Lutheran history led later commentators to charge that Lutheranism had consistently had a sorry record of quietism in the presence of the state's power. For instance, in his magisterial *The Social Teachings of the Christian Church*, Ernst Troeltsch makes the following points: "The yielding spirit of its wholly interior spirituality adapted itself to the dominant authority of the day. This passivity involved the habit of falling back on whatever power happens to be dominant at the time." He argued that from the very beginning it has, unlike Calvinism and Catholicism, lacked a "capacity to penetrate the political, legal, and economic movements of Western nations." "Its tendency is to alleviate but not re-create" (574–75). In relation to the state, Troeltsch argued, Lutherans were persistently passive.

H. Richard Niebuhr imbibed Troeltsch's teaching fully. Though he correctly understood many aspects of Lutheranism in his account in *Christ and Culture*, he followed Troeltsch in an assessment of Lutheranism's relation to the public square. He saw Lutheranism as essentially dualistic, tempted toward both antinomianism in personal ethics and quietism in social and political ethics. Its profound grasp of the wonder and transcendence of God's grace in Christ made it indifferent to the relative distinctions that are so important in earthly life, especially to the political task of governing. So it adapted to whatever is, preferring order over the chaos that might accompany constructive change (186–89).

H. Richard Niebuhr's more politically active brother, Reinhold, followed both Troeltsch and his brother in their assessment, as in *The Nature and Destiny of Man*:

> By thus transposing an "inner ethic of spontaneous love" into a private one, and making the "outer" or "earthly" ethic authoritative for government, Luther achieves a curiously perverse social morality. He places a perfectionist private ethic in juxtaposition to a realistic, not to say, cynical, official ethic. . . . This has led to an absolute distinction between the "heavenly" or "spiritual" kingdom and the "earthly" one, which destroys the tension between the final demands of God upon the conscience, and all the relative possibilities of realizing the good in history. (194–95)

In spite of the efforts of American Lutheran scholars such as George Forell and William Lazareth and European scholars such as

Gustaf Wingren and Heinrich Bornkamm to show that Lutheranism was not and need not be quietistic and dualistic, the Troeltschian/Niebuhrian analysis continues to wield influence. The verdict is often that Lutheranism has blindly followed the state. Moreover, Lutheranism's historical record sometimes seems to bear witness to its bad reputation. Luther and his cohorts carried out a Reformation of the church without touching the medieval understanding of society. For example, Lutheranism in Germany in the 1930s remained—except for the relatively small Confessing Church—quiescent amid the rise of Nazism. There are also the recent cases of perceived Lutheran quietism in the face of authoritarian and unjust governments in Soviet satellite countries, Chile, and South Africa.

More recent scholarship, however, has begun to correct this view. Indeed, the condemnation heaped on Lutheranism by the Troeltsch/Niebuhr analysis has been sharply revised by John Witte, a Reformed scholar trained in both theology and law. His book *Law and Protestantism* argues that early Lutheranism was a species of "constructive Protestantism." It built a Lutheran version of Christendom. After the upheavals of the first years of the Reformation, Lutheran theologians cooperated with Lutheran secular authorities, especially jurists, to rebuild a new society out of the chaos of the old. Lutheran theologians, employing the doctrine of the two realms, worked hand in hand with secular agents to reform law, politics, and society.

Witte also analyzes how Melanchthon worked with the great Lutheran jurists Eisermann and Oldendorp to shape a Lutheran society. They all began their work "with a basic understanding of Luther's two-kingdoms framework. While Luther tended to emphasize the distinctions between the two kingdoms, Lutheran jurists tended to emphasize their cooperation" (Witte 168). For example, Witte argues that Melanchthon and the jurists tended more than Luther to view the Bible as an essential source of earthly law and to apply the three uses of the law to the governance of the earthly kingdom. In short, they built bridges between the two kingdoms (170). Witte concludes the book with the claim that "a good deal of our modern Western law of marriage, education, and social welfare, for example, still bears the unmistakable marks of Lutheran Reformation theology" (295).

Later history also indicates that Lutheranism was never congenitally quiescent in its relation to the state. The Norwegian Lutheran Church resisted the Nazis during the 1940s. Lutherans in East Germany protested their nation's nuclear policy and were instrumental in bringing the Communist regime down peacefully in 1989. In the United States, the Lutheran Church in America developed social statements regarding government policies. The Lutheran Church–Missouri Synod has had a long history of resisting incursions on its religious freedom. The Evangelical Lutheran Church in America also has supported advocacy efforts of a more liberal bent. It can safely be said that American Lutheranism is no longer uncritical and passive in relation to the state. The same may be said of worldwide Lutheranism, where resistance to the apartheid regime among some Lutherans in South Africa is a case in point.

See also Confessing Church; Peasants' War; Troeltsch, Ernst; Two Realms; World Wars I and II

Bibliography

Lazareth, W. *Christians in Society: Luther, the Bible, and Social Ethics*. Fortress, 2001; Niebuhr, H. Richard. *Christ and Culture*. Harper & Row, 1951; Niebuhr, Reinhold. *The Nature and Destiny of Man*. 2 vols. Scribners, 1943; Stumme, J., and R. Tuttle, eds. *Church and State: Lutheran Perspectives*. Fortress, 2003; Troeltsch, E. *The Social Teachings of the Christian Church*. 2 vols. Harper & Brothers, 1960; Witte, J. *Law and Protestantism*. Cambridge University Press, 2002.

ROBERT BENNE

Staupitz, Johann von

As provincial vicar general of the Reformed congregation of the Order of Augustinian Eremites in Saxony, Johann von Staupitz (1460/69–1524) was Luther's superior as he entered the Augustinian order. Staupitz came from a Saxon noble family with close connections to the court of the Saxon electors. After studying in Leipzig, Cologne, and Tübingen, where he engaged the theology of Gabriel Biel shortly after Biel's death, Staupitz left his second position as a prior in Munich to found the theological faculty in Wittenberg in 1502, when Frederick the Wise established the university there. His preaching made him popular in educated circles, especially in Nuremberg, where a *Sodalitas Staupitziana* (Staupitzian sodality) brought together pious citizens interested in learning, particularly in the trend of humanistic interest in ancient sources. His views on predestination, arising out of the Augustinian tradition, emphasized God's grace and placed sinners totally in the hands of the merciful God, who in Jesus Christ sacrificed himself for their sin. With this message, as Luther's father confessor, he consoled the troubled friar under his supervision.

The burden of his duties in the monastic order led Staupitz to seek a successor for the theological professorship in Wittenberg. Against Luther's will, Staupitz mandated that he pursue a doctorate in theology, expediting his chosen heir's course through the curriculum, so that by October 1512 Luther was awarded the degree and stood ready to assume Staupitz's university duties as a lecturer on the Bible. Staupitz stood by his disciple in the controversy following the publication of the Ninety-Five Theses and tried to mediate between him and Cardinal Cajetan in Augsburg in 1518. When their talks led nowhere, Staupitz formally released Luther from his vows, an action that protected Luther from additional charges in that regard. In 1520 Staupitz left his office in the Augustinian order to become preacher and adviser at the court of the archbishop of Salzburg. In 1521 he transferred to the Benedictine order and became abbot in Salzburg. Even though Staupitz did not support aspects of Luther's call for reform, his love for Luther is evident in their last correspondence.

See also Augustinianism; Luther, Martin; University of Wittenberg in the Sixteenth Century

Bibliography

Steinmetz, D. C. *Luther and Staupitz.* Duke University Press, 1980; Steinmetz, D. C. *Misericordia Dei: The Theology of Johannes von Staupitz.* Brill, 1968.

ROBERT KOLB

Stöckel, Leonard

The humanist pedagogue and theologian Leonard Stöckel (1510–60) was honored in his lifetime as the *Praeceptor Hungariae* (teacher of Hungary). After early schooling in Bardejov and Kosice, Stöckel enrolled in the Albertine secondary school in Breslau (Wroclow) in 1526. He began studies at Wittenberg in 1530 and was acquainted with Luther and especially close to Melanchthon, with whom he carried on a lifelong correspondence. He taught in Eisleben from 1534 to 1536 but returned to Wittenberg until 1539, when he was called home to become the director of the Bardejov Latin school.

Stöckel's humanist principles were reflected in the administrative and curricular rules (*Leges scholae Bartphensis*) for the school, which attracted students from throughout Hungary. He prepared the Šariš articles in 1540 to regulate church life in Bardejov, Prešov, and Sabinov, and in 1549 he compiled the Confessio Pentapolitana. Stöckel joined with Michael Radasinus, the city pastor of Bardejov, to combat the influence of Anabaptism and Zwinglianism in northeastern Hungary. He prepared a catechism, at least one school drama (*Susanna*), a treatise on music, and annotations to the *Loci communes* of Melanchthon that were published with the *Loci* in Basel in 1561. His homiletical handbook, the *Formulae tractandarum sacrarum concionum*, and a collection of sermons for the church year, the *Postilla*, also were published after his death.

See also Hungary

Bibliography

Daniel, D. P. "Lutheranism in the Kingdom of Hungary." In *Lutheran Ecclesiastical Culture,* ed. R. Kolb, 455–507. Brill, 2008.

DAVID P. DANIEL

Strasbourg

With roughly twenty-two thousand inhabitants, Strasbourg was one of the largest and most influential of the southern German imperial cities subject directly to the emperor. Throughout the sixteenth century it was a major printing center, and most of Luther's vernacular works were reprinted there in the early years of the Reformation. The Evangelical movement took root through the preaching of Matthaeus Zell, who was joined in 1522–23 by Caspar Hedio, Wolfgang Capito, and Martin Bucer. Under pressure from the populace, Strasbourg's city council, long at loggerheads with their absentee bishop, allowed liturgical reforms and gradually extended its control over the clergy and church. The city was Evangelical according to most measures by the spring of 1525, although the Mass was not abolished until 1529, and four convents for women continued to exist throughout the sixteenth century. The city's reformers sided with Ulrich Zwingli at the beginning of the eucharistic controversy, but they also tried to win Luther's support by downplaying the disagreement over the Lord's Supper. Luther rejected their pleas for toleration in *That These Words of Christ, "This Is My Body," Still Stand Firm against the Fanatics* (1527). Strasbourg's political leaders saw alliance with the Swiss as the best guarantee of safety against the Catholic emperor, and in 1530 the city signed a mutual defense treaty with Zurich, Basel, and Bern.

Although Capito was the most influential figure during the 1520s, Bucer emerged as leader of Strasbourg's church in the early 1530s; he worked closely with the city's most prominent statesman, Jacob Sturm. Zwingli and Oecolampadius's deaths in 1531 and Zurich's defeat in the Second Kappeler War spelled the end of Strasbourg's alliance with the Swiss. The Wittenberg theologians, however, insisted on religious agreement as the basis for political alliance. As a result the Strasbourg council supported Bucer's efforts to end the controversy over the Lord's Supper. As an alternative to the Augsburg Confession, Bucer wrote the Tetrapolitan Confession (1530) for the Strasbourg church; it was also endorsed by Constance, Memmingen, and Lindau. Strasbourg joined the Smalcaldic League in 1532, accepting the Augsburg Confession along with the Tetrapolitana, and it regarded the 1536 Wittenberg Concord as the key to interpreting the Augsburg Confession on the Lord's Supper and Baptism. Strasbourg was also home to a number of Anabaptist groups, and in 1533 a synod was held to counter their influence. This led to the 1534 ordinance that institutionalized the city's church. In 1539 a reorganization of the city's school system led to the creation of an academy directed by Johann Sturm. This school became a model for other Latin schools in Germany and Switzerland.

Strasbourg was forced to accept the Augsburg Interim after the defeat of the Smalcaldic League in 1547. Bucer was exiled, and celebration of the Mass was restored in four of the city's churches. Bucer's successor, Johannes Marbach (1521–81), who received his doctorate in theology under Luther, led the successful effort to end the Mass after the Peace of Augsburg (1555). During Marbach's long tenure the church moved in a decisively Lutheran direction, which led to conflict with those still loyal to Bucer among the pastors and academy faculty. A controversy between clergy and professors over predestination and the Lord's Supper in 1563 contributed to the sharpening of confessional differences throughout the empire. Strasbourg's council tried to remain on good terms with both its German Lutheran and Swiss Reformed neighbors, however, and it refused to endorse the Formula of Concord in 1577 despite its pastors' urging. Marbach's successor, Johannes Pappus (1549–1610), was even more committed to bringing the church into the Lutheran fold, and he was aided by generational change within the council. In 1598 the city adopted a new church ordinance that included acceptance of the Formula of Concord, paving the way for Lutheran Orthodoxy. Its staunch Lutheranism continued well into the seventeenth century, where one of the

academy's later graduates was the founder of German pietism, Philipp Jakob Spener.

See also Augsburg Confession; Augsburg Interim; Bucer, Martin; Peace of Augsburg; Smalcald War; Wittenberg Concord

Bibliography

Abray, L. J. *The People's Reformation: Magistrates, Clergy, and Commons in Strasbourg, 1500–1598.* Cornell University Press, 1985; Brady, T. A., Jr. *Protestant Politics: Jacob Sturm (1489–1553) and the German Reformation.* Humanities Press, 1995; Brady, T. A., Jr. *Ruling Class, Regime and Reformation at Strasbourg 1520–1555.* Brill, 1978; Chrisman, M. U. *Lay Culture, Learned Culture: Books and Social Change in Strasbourg, 1480–1599.* 2 vols. Yale University Press, 1982; Chrisman, M. U. *Strasbourg and the Reform: A Study in the Process of Change.* Yale University Press, 1967; Edwards, M. U. *Printing, Propaganda, and Martin Luther.* University of California Press, 1994; Kittelson, J. M. *Toward an Established Church: Strasbourg from 1500 to the Dawn of the Seventeenth Century.* Von Zabern, 2000; Leonard, A. *Nails in the Wall: Catholic Nuns in Reformation Germany.* University of Chicago Press, 2005.

AMY NELSON BURNETT

Strigel, Viktorin

Viktorin Strigel (1524–69) is the German Lutheran theologian whose position on the role of the human will in conversion represented the Philippist position in the debate over the issue. Born at Kaufbeuren on December 26, 1524, Strigel was educated at Freiburg im Breisgau (1538–42) and Wittenberg (1542–44), where he was strongly influenced by Melanchthon. In 1549 he was called to establish the ducal Saxon academy in Jena with the famous poet Johann Stigel. His teaching at Jena drew him into theological controversy, with Strigel supporting Melanchthon's teaching on free will. In 1558 the Jena school became a university and added Matthias Flacius, who opposed other Wittenberg theologians, to its faculty. Arrested for refusing to teach according to the Gnesio-Lutheran Confutation Book, the official statement of faith for ducal Saxony, in 1560 Strigel was allowed to debate Flacius. At the resulting Weimar Disputation, Strigel argued that the Holy Spirit initiates conversion by means of the Word, whereupon the human will cooperates with God's grace in salvation. In rejecting

Strigel's arguments, Flacius used terminology that led to his dismissal from Jena. In 1562 Strigel left Jena for Leipzig, where he was appointed professor but came under suspicion of Calvinist views on the Lord's Supper. In 1567 he left Leipzig for a professorship in ethics in Heidelberg (a Reformed stronghold), where he died on June 26, 1569.

See also Anthropology; Flacius, Matthias Illyricus, and the Flacians; Free Will; Original Sin

Bibliography

Koch, E. "Viktorin Strigel (1524–1569): Von Jena nach Heidelberg." In *Melanchthon in seinen Schülern*, ed. H. Scheible, 391–404. Harrassowitz, 1997; Kolb, R. "Die Theologische Pilgerschaft von Viktorin Strigel: Vom 'Gnesiolutherischen' Hoftheologe zum 'Calvinistischen' Professor." In *Calvinismus in den Auseinandersetzungen des frühen konfessionellen Zeitalters*, ed. V. Leppin et al., 79–96. Vandenhoeck & Ruprecht, 2013.

GERHARD BODE

Sudan Mission

The Sudan Mission (SM) was an independent Lutheran mission agency that worked in Cameroon and that part of French Equatorial Africa that eventually became the Central African Republic from 1918 through 1951. It is to be distinguished from the Sudan Interior Mission (SIM), active from 1893, and the British-based Sudan United Mission (SUM), established in 1904, both multidenominational agencies that eventually focused on work in Nigeria, though the SUM maintained some stations as far east as Sudan. All three missions were part of an urgent awareness, voiced at the missionary conference in Edinburgh (1910), that virtually no Christian witness existed for tens of millions of sub-Saharan Africans.

Adolphus Gunderson spent four years in Nigeria with the SIM before returning to the United States to seek Lutheran support for a similar effort in Cameroon. He established such a mission independently when his own American church body, the newly founded Norwegian Evangelical Lutheran Church (NELC), found itself unable to commit to a new mission effort at the time. The first SM board president was J. A. O. Stub, president of Lutheran Brotherhood of America and executive secretary of the National Lutheran Commission; board members included such St. Olaf College faculty members as H. M. Thompson and Edward W. Schmidt. Gunderson traveled over 25,000 miles, gave more than 350 lectures, and passed out 31,000 tracts to raise prayer and financial support for the new venture. By 1922 that support was sufficient for four persons to go abroad for French study—Adolphus, his wife Marie, and two Lutheran deaconesses, Olette Berntsen and Anne Olsen. By 1923 they had made the fifty-five-day trek from the Cameroonian coast to Ngaoundere in the interior. By 1927 they had begun a broad base of evangelistic, educational, medical, and industrial ministries among Gbaya people in Mboula, where they started work, and in neighboring Binako, between Ngaoundere and Meiganga. The work grew rapidly; the Gundersons returned to the United States permanently in 1935 to take over fund-raising and recruitment. The 1937 annual report suggests that there were twenty missionary personnel and records the decision to enter into Poli, a new geographical and linguistic area north of Ngaoundere. By 1949 the mission employed thirty-one missionaries from five different Lutheran synods, including six ordained pastors, five registered nurses, a number of teachers, and various other lay workers. Work had expanded to Meiganga, Garoua Boulai, and Poli in Cameroun, and Baboua and Abba in French Equatorial Africa. Four years later it included the massive territory of Rey Bouba east from Tchollire.

In 1951, the year Gunderson died, the annual SM missionary conference decided to ask the Evangelical Lutheran Church (ELC, formerly the NELC) to take responsibility for the mission work that the Sudan Mission had been doing and to consider it one of the mission fields of the church. The request was accepted, and from 1953 former SM work was included in the budget of the Board of Foreign Missions of the ELC. That ended SM's corporate existence in the United States but not in Cameroon. Property registered in the name of SM under the colonial government remained that way into the independence era, and only a late century extensive investment of time and money by the ELCA was able to transfer SM lands, churches, schools, hospitals, radio stations, and the like into the name of the fruit of its labors, Église Évangelique Luthérienne du Cameroun (EELC).

See also Cameroon; Gunderson, Adolphus; Nigeria

Bibliography
Christiansen, R. *For the Heart of Africa*. Augsburg, 1956; Trobisch, I. *On Our Way Rejoicing!* Harper & Row, 1964.

MARK NYGARD

Sunday and Sabbatarianism

Since the first century the Christian practice has been to gather the community for worship on the first day of the week, Sunday. Because of its historical connections with Judaism, Christianity has long wrestled with the question of the Old Testament commands to observe a Sabbath that includes prohibitions on work and other activities. Since Sunday is the Christian Sabbath, some Christians thought that the Old Testament rules should therefore be transferred to Sunday. When Christianity became widespread in the Mediterranean and Europe, Sunday became the official day of rest. In the Middle Ages, Thomas Aquinas separated the moral and the ritual aspects of the Sabbath, keeping the divine requirement for Sunday worship, but not the rest of traditional Jewish Sabbath laws; this stance became known as semi-Sabbatarianism. Martin Luther and other reformers attacked this idea, as did the Augsburg Confession (art. 28), which held that the laws of the Jewish Sabbath had been eliminated by the New Testament. Nevertheless, Luther strongly urged the proper maintenance of rest and worship on Sundays, only not on a legal basis. For him, proclaiming the Word of God made any day holy. In the seventeenth century the idea of semi-Sabbatarianism came back into Lutheranism through the Orthodox theologians, especially Johann Gerhard,

and the issue of the nature of the Sabbath has continued to be an open question among Lutherans, and in the wider culture. Strict observance of the Sunday Sabbath, especially prohibitions on work and activities other than worship, were revived by the Reformed theologians after Calvin, especially through the influence of Theodore Beza.

In England the strict observance of the Sunday Sabbath was adopted by many Puritans, and its influence was spread by them to the Anglo-American religious world, including the United States. Not only did they encourage such a strict understanding of the Christian Sabbath; the Puritans and their descendants also worked to enact these Sabbath requirements into civil law. In nineteenth- and twentieth-century America these Sabbath restrictions and other moral laws derived from Christianity (known as blue laws) were common and widespread. American Lutherans encountered this religious ethos and often embraced it, although many of them had reservations about the wisdom of putting these moral proscriptions into civil law. The Missouri Synod and the Iowa Synod disputed this issue, with Missouri arguing that such laws were the improper mixing of church and state, while Iowa contented that such issues were "open questions" on which Christians could disagree. At the same time, theologians of the General Council (esp. Henry Eyster Jacobs) argued that such rules for Sabbath keeping ran contrary to Luther's teaching. In the twentieth century, many of these legal enforcements of Christian Sabbatarianism have been removed, and Sunday has become, for many, just another day. It has been difficult for Lutherans to argue for a reverent observance of Sunday Christian worship apart from some form of Sabbatarianism, as the culture invades its traditional space. In reaction, some Lutheran congregations have developed alternate worship services on Saturdays or weeknights, while others wish to continue to hold to the traditional Sunday worship patterns.

See also Law, Uses of the

Bibliography
Thomas, W. "Sabbaterianism" and "Sunday." In *The Encyclopedia of the Lutheran Church*, ed. J. Bodensieck, 3:2089–90 and 2277–80. Augsburg, 1965.

Mark A. Granquist

Suriname

The Evangelical Lutheran Church in Suriname (ELKS), established in 1975, has its roots in the Lutheran community in Paramaribo, Suriname, founded in 1743, the oldest Lutheran church in Latin America and the Caribbean.

In 1740 a small group of Lutheran plantation owners on the east coast of South America sent a letter to the Lutheran Consistory in Amsterdam, requesting to establish a Lutheran church. In 1741 they received a positive response from the consistory, which attached several limitations to the charter, including that the church could not attract the notice of the Dutch Reformed Church. Immediately the Lutherans began to plan a worship space, call a pastor, and set up other facilities. In 1742 the Rev. Johannes Pfaff came to Suriname from the Netherlands at the request of the Lutheran community, to serve as the first Lutheran pastor in the territory of Dutch Guyana. When the "Maarten Luther Kerk" was consecrated in 1747, a permanent Lutheran presence was established.

For the next 230 years, pastors were sent from the Netherlands to serve the community in Paramaribo. Although it was organized for Lutheran colonizers and landowners, in its early years the church permitted slaves from Africa to observe worship services. The transition from a predominantly ethnically European congregation to an ethnically African congregation came shortly after the 1863 emancipation, when former slaves began attending worship regularly and having their children baptized and confirmed.

Throughout its history Martin Luther Church continued to receive pastors and funding from the Netherlands. In 1962 the Lutheran community joined with the Dutch Reformed Church in Suriname to begin worship services in two new locations, Bethlehem Church, in Zorg en Hoop, an area of Paramaribo, and Saint Paul's Church, in the community of Lelydorp. This was a significant act because Lutherans were finally beginning to recognize the need to reach out and do mission work outside of the historical Martin Luther Church and their own community. They were shifting from being a receiving church to becoming a church in mission. In 1997 a new Lutheran church, Community of Hope, was established on the outlying area of Paramaribo.

Finally in 1974 the first Surinamer, Rev. Leo H. King, was ordained into ministry. His ordination led the way for several other Surinamers to study theology in the Netherlands and in Jamaica and receive their ordination in the ELKS during the late 1980s and 1990s.

In 1940 a block of houses was built for elderly members of the Lutheran Church. In 1964 the Lutheran Church joined other Protestant churches in Suriname to cofound the Deacons Hospital. Soon afterward, the Lutheran Church became a charter member of the Christian Council of Churches. In 1975 it recognized the need to be a self-governing body, and the name of the congregation was changed from Martin Luther Community to the Evangelical Lutheran Church in Suriname. Each of these actions demonstrated that the church was growing in stature and significance in the wider community. While remaining a small Lutheran Church of about two thousand members in a country of 500,000 people, the Lutheran presence is being felt even stronger in its mission and ministry in Suriname and South America.

Bibliography
Gerding, P. I. *On the Way to Greater Heights*. Evangelical Lutheran Church in Suriname, 2002.

Kevin L. Jacobson

Sweden

Sweden is the largest of the three Scandinavian kingdoms in northern Europe, with a population of about ten million people. Historically it has been a strong Lutheran country since the sixteenth-century Protestant Reformation.

The Church of Sweden is officially Lutheran and now numbers 6.4 million members, although regular participation in church life is very low. The Church of Sweden is divided into thirteen dioceses, with the archbishop of Uppsala as the head of the church. Swedish Lutherans have been very active in world missions and continue to maintain important ties with Lutheran churches in the Global South through membership in the Lutheran World Federation. Some very small conservative Lutheran groups have recently broken away from the Church of Sweden.

Sweden was one of the last European countries to become Christian. Though St. Ansgar began a mission to the Swedes in the ninth century, Christianity did not take general hold in the country until the twelfth century. The foundation of the archbishopric of Uppsala in 1164 signaled the recognition of the Church of Sweden, and the institutions of the medieval Roman church were established slowly. Monasteries and convents were formed, especially the community founded by St. Bridget in Vadstena, but the institutions of the medieval church were not widespread.

After a period of union with the other Scandinavian kingdoms, in 1523 Sweden again became independent under King Gustav Vasa. During the 1520s Protestant ideas came into the country through Germany, principally through the Swedish preacher Olavus Petri, who had studied in Germany with Luther and Melanchthon. With the support of the king, Petri began to introduce the elements of the Protestant Reformation into Sweden, married in 1525, and introduced a Swedish New Testament in 1526. In 1524 Gustav Vasa broke formal ties between Sweden and the papacy, and he began the process of reforming the Swedish church along Evangelical lines. The transformation of the church did not, however, mean a rupture with its medieval past, as the Church of Sweden maintained an episcopal structure and continuity with the succession of bishops. Although the Church of Sweden has continued to maintain this succession, they have officially stated that this succession is an important historical pattern but not constitutive of the essence of the church itself.

The long process of reforming the Church of Sweden along Protestant theological lines was carried out under the long term of Laurentius Petri (Olavus Petri's brother) as archbishop of Uppsala, 1531–73. As the church became more Lutheran, it was also increasingly tied to the royal government and became officially a part of the state. Laurentius Petri's influence peaked with the adoption of his Church Order of 1571, which defined the life and liturgy of the Church of Sweden along Lutheran lines. Though subsequent kings were either Calvinist or Roman Catholic in sympathy, the Church of Sweden had become solidly Lutheran and resisted royal pressures in either direction. In 1593 a church convocation at Uppsala formally adopted the Augsburg Confession as its doctrinal standard, a major turning point in the development of the Church of Sweden.

When King Sigismund was dethroned in 1599 for his attempts to reestablish Roman Catholicism in Sweden, the throne passed back to a Lutheran line of the royal family, most notably Gustavus Adolphus (r. 1611–32). His military intervention in the Thirty Years' War in 1628 and victory at the Battle of Lützen in 1632 saved the Protestant cause in Germany, though he was killed during that battle. The seventeenth century saw the influence of the "great bishops" such as Johannes Rudbeckius and Laurentius Gothus, who wielded significant influence; pastors and bishops formed one of the four houses of Swedish Parliament. Lutheranism was made the official religion in the constitution of 1634, and no other religious options were allowed; this stance was reaffirmed and strengthened by the adoption of a new church law in 1686. The Book of Concord was also recognized during this time as a "further explanation" of the Evangelical faith. The introduction of a new church hymnbook in 1695, led by Jesper Svedberg, had a strong impact on church life for centuries to come. A rigorous pattern of pastoral visitation and examination of Swedish citizens was a prominent aspect of Swedish Lutheran life during seventeenth-century Orthodoxy. This was also the height of Sweden as an imperial power in the Baltic, and Lutheranism was similarly strengthened in Swedish territories such as Finland, Estonia, and Latvia.

During the eighteenth century, Protestant Pietism came into Sweden, beginning with returning prisoners of war who had been converted in their camps. Pietism, especially that of the Moravians (in Sweden known as Herrnhutism), came to have a significant impact on many in Sweden, especially in the regions of Skane, Västergötland, and Norrland. These awakenings often involved gatherings of local believers to read Lutheran devotional literature, including works by Luther, Johannes Arndt, and others, and to sing Moravian hymns; the awakened were known as the Readers (*läsare*). Their implicit and explicit criticisms of the official Church of Sweden led to a strong response, and in 1726 the parliament passed the Conventicle Act, prohibiting worship and religious meetings without the presence of a pastor. During this period the Enlightenment and religious rationalism also took root among significant portions of the Lutheran clergy and university faculties and made inroads into the parishes. Catechisms and liturgies along these lines were introduced into the church. In this spirit, Anglican and Calvinist settlers in Sweden were allowed their own private worship, an Edict of Toleration was passed in 1781, and even Jews were allowed limited residence in the country. One prominent example of this Enlightenment influence was the scientist and mystic Emanuel Swedenborg (1688–1772). The Pietists, the "Old Readers," quietly continued many of their meetings and activities, often aided by sympathetic local pastors or governmental officials, although such activities were still illegal.

In the nineteenth century waves of religious revival swept through Sweden. In the South, Pastor Henrik Schartau (1757–1825) led an influential revival movement that remained within the Church of Sweden. In the North a movement often known as the New Readers (*läsare*) took root, and more activity challenged the official church; there were separatist elements within this movement, especially the followers of Eric Jansson, many of whom immigrated to America. In Stockholm an English Methodist missionary George Scott gained a great following from 1830 to 1842. After his departure from Sweden, this work was taken over by his lay associate, Carl Olof Rosenius (1816–68), who came to define the new awakening in Sweden through his preaching and his editing of the influential publication *Pietisten*. Rosenius strongly wished to keep this new revival movement within the Church of Sweden, and in 1856 he founded the National Evangelical Foundation (NEF, Evangelisk Fosterlands Stiftelsen) to support the Lutheran awakening. In some areas the NEF set up separate chapels, while in other areas it worked within the local parishes. The awakening movement strongly supported religious reform and revivals within Sweden, the temperance movement, and the establishment of mission societies to address religious causes at home and around the world. Independent mission schools were also developed as means of training leaders, and colporteurs were commissioned to distribute religious literature around the country. Another important element of the revivals was the revival hymns, some out of the Anglo-American gospel tradition, but many others by beloved hymn writers and composers such as Oskar Ahnfelt and Karolina Sandell-Berg. This period of religious revival greatly strengthened Protestant Christianity within Sweden.

Some elements of the Church of Sweden worked strongly against these revivals and temperance, but the tide was against them, and the Conventicle Act of 1726 was officially repealed in 1858. After 1860, separatist elements within Sweden moved toward forming their own independent and non-Lutheran congregations. Baptist congregations began in 1848 and Methodist congregations in 1868; the Pentecostal movement took root in Sweden after 1900. After the death of Rosenius in 1868, the leadership of the NEF fell to the Lutheran pastor Paul Peter Waldenström, who came into conflict with official Lutheranism, especially with his "Sermon on the Atonement" of 1872, where he challenged aspects of Lutheran theology and confessional authority in favor of the primacy of the Bible alone. Waldenström and one faction of the NEF withdrew to form the Swedish Mission Covenant (sometimes called the Mission Friends), who founded independent chapels around the country; however, many within the Covenant (including Waldenström) did not officially withdraw from the Church of Sweden.

Toward the end of the nineteenth century movements arose toward democratic political reform and the growth of the labor movement. The leaders of these were often alienated from the church and from religious life. Such events are often seen as one root of modern Swedish secularism and forced the Church of Sweden to be on the defensive. Toward the beginning of the twentieth century, stirrings of new life within the Church of Sweden came through the leadership of theologian Einar Billing and Bishops J. A. Eklund and Manfred Björkquist. The Young Church movement (ungkyrkorörelsen) in the early twentieth century was a key catalyst for religious reform and renewal of the parishes, especially with its view of the church as a folk church within Swedish society. Under the leadership of Archbishop Nathan Söderblom (1866–1931), the Church of Sweden became a leader within world Lutheranism and also reached out for closer relations with the Anglican Communion. The Church of Sweden was also internationally known in the twentieth century for its prominent theologians, especially Ragnar Bring, Gustaf Aulén, Anders Nygren, and Gustaf Wingren, notably for their contribution to the revival of Luther studies (the Luther Renaissance).

During the twentieth century Sweden developed its signature "middle way" between capitalism and communism, a democratic and socialistic welfare state that influenced the life of all Swedes. As Sweden became increasingly secular and liberal, the Church of Sweden has struggled to demonstrate the relevance of the church and of Christianity to the Swedish people. The Church of Sweden has continued to move in a determinedly liberal direction, beginning with the ordination of women as pastors in 1958 and the adoption of other socially liberal positions. It has also moved toward being more democratic and has allowed locally elected lay councils a large degree of power. The Church of Sweden itself was formally disestablished and severed from the state in 2000, although the state still functions to collect the church tax that supports the church. As a society, Sweden is highly secularized, and a majority of Swedes consider themselves either atheists or agnostics. Polls in the early twenty-first century consistantly show that less than 20 percent of the people have traditional theistic beliefs. Official membership in the Church of Sweden was at about 65 percent of the population in 2014, but this has been declining, down from 82 percent in 2000. Regular church attendance is in the low single digits, and the percentage of baptisms, confirmations, church weddings, and funerals are dropping as well. Swedes continue to be willing to financially support the Church of Sweden, perhaps as an important part of their culture and history, but many of them do not find it personally important, even for the various life-cycle rituals.

See also Augustana Synod; Aulén, Gustaf; Gustavus Adolphus; Lutheran Orthodoxy; Luther Renaissance; Moravian Church (Unitas Fratrum); Nygren, Anders; Petri (Nericus), Laurentius; Petri, Olavus; Pietism; Rosenius, Carl Olof; Rudbeckius, Johannes; Sandell-Berg, Karolina Wihelmina (Lina); Söderblom, Nathan; Vasa, Gustav; Wallin, Johan Olof; Wingren, Gustaf

Bibliography

Bergendoff, C. *Olavus Petri and the Ecclesiastical Transformation in Sweden.* Macmillan, 1928; Brilioth, Y., and H. Holmquist. *Handbok i svensk kyrkohistoria.* Svenska Kyrkans Diakonistyrelses, 1948; Hunter, L. S., ed. *Scandinavian Churches.* Augsburg, 1965; Murray, R. *A Brief History of the Church of Sweden: Origins and Modern Structures.* 2nd ed. Verbum, 1969; Österlin, L. *The Churches of Northern Europe in Profile.* Canterbury, 1995; Ryman, B., et al., eds. *Nordic Folk Churches: A Contemporary History*. Eerdmans, 2005; Yelverton, E. *An Archbishop of the Reformation: Laurentius Petri Nericius*. Augsburg, 1959.

MARK A. GRANQUIST

Switzerland

The early Swiss Reformation can be characterized as a blending of Erasmian and Lutheran elements within the specific political context of the Swiss Confederation. The Zurich Reformation led by Ulrich Zwingli was the most influential model for reform, while Zwingli's successor, Heinrich Bullinger, gave enduring shape to Zurich's church and became one of the most influential theologians in Europe during his long tenure in office.

The Swiss Confederation was a strikingly diverse group at the beginning of the sixteenth century. Its thirteen full members included both mountainous rural cantons and prosperous cities. In rotation they jointly ruled several smaller areas known as Mandated Territories. The confederation's members were also allied with other independent areas, such as Geneva and Graubünden (Grisons), that are part of modern Switzerland. Although French was spoken along the western edge and Italian in the South and East, the dominant language was German, and Swiss humanists had close ties to their counterparts in the Holy Roman Empire.

Erasmus settled in Basel in 1514 and published his edition of the Greek New Testament two years later. His presence in Switzerland encouraged the development of a network of younger humanists inspired by Erasmus's ideal of a Christianity renewed through educational reform. Several of these men, including Johannes Oecolampadius in Basel and Wolfgang Capito in Strasbourg, would become later reformers. Basel was a major printing center, and beginning with the Ninety-Five Theses, its printers quickly reprinted the works of Luther, Philip Melanchthon, and Andreas Karlstadt, as well as Luther's German New Testament, thus helping to spread early Wittenberg theology. The Swiss humanists initially saw Luther as promoting Erasmian educational and devotional reforms, and they eagerly read his early works. Luther's excommunication forced them to choose between remaining loyal to Rome, like Erasmus himself, or embracing the authority of Scripture alone and rejecting papal authority. Only gradually did these radical Erasmian reformers come to understand and endorse Luther's theology of justification.

Ulrich Zwingli's preaching helped introduce humanist/Evangelical ideas in Zurich from 1519 onward. Popular movements more strongly influenced by Luther emerged in Basel, Bern, Schaffhausen, and St. Gallen. The earliest Evangelical disturbances in all these cities in 1522–23 challenged the Lenten fast, clerical celibacy, and the veneration of relics; individual priests also used German while baptizing babies. These movements had broad popular support, but they did not win the upper hand in most cities due to a combination of effective resistance by the Catholic clergy, the lack of forceful Evangelical leaders, and the unwillingness of city governments to break decisively with Rome. In Zurich, however, Catholic opposition was relatively weak, and Zwingli had the full support of Zurich's government. As a result, that city took the lead in introducing reforms. After a public disputation with representatives of the bishop of Constance in January 1523, the Zurich Council endorsed Zwingli's preaching. The disputation helped make Zwingli's ideas better known outside Zurich, not only to those who attended the disputation but also through the subsequent publication of the disputation's acts and Zwingli's *Exposition of the 67 Articles*. A second disputation in October concerning images and the Mass was attended by over nine hundred people, many from outside Zurich. Over the next year traditional practices and ecclesiastical institutions were dismantled in the city, culminating in the abolition of the Mass and its replacement with a simplified celebration of the Lord's Supper for Easter 1525.

By this time the Evangelical movement in Zurich had divided. Zwingli's most radical supporters rejected the reformer's identification of church and civic community, and in January 1525 they adopted adult baptism and began to celebrate the Lord's Supper in private houses. The Anabaptists ("rebaptizers," a name given them by those who upheld the validity of infant baptism) were expelled from Zurich, which gave them opportunity to spread their views and win adherents in other areas of the Swiss Confederation that were already open to the Evangelical message and in southern parts of Germany. Anabaptist teachings spread at the same time that the unrest of the Peasants' War reached Switzerland, contributing to debates concerning serfdom and the payment of tithes. The governments of Zurich and Basel were able to reach negotiated settlements with the peasants in their territories, thereby preventing the bloodshed associated with the Peasants' War in Germany. Disappointed in their hopes for reforming society at large and faced with growing diversity of practice, Anabaptist leaders gathered at Schleitheim in Schaffhausen's territory in February 1527 and adopted seven articles that outlined their separation from the world. Despite the execution of many of their leaders in both Catholic and Protestant areas, the Anabaptists managed to survive, especially in rural areas and border regions where they could avoid the attention of the authorities.

The Swiss reformers also broke with Luther over the issue of the Lord's Supper. Karlstadt's treatises on the Lord's Supper, published in Basel in the fall of 1524, attacked the belief that Christ's body and blood were corporally present in the bread and wine of the sacrament. By this time both Zwingli and Oecolampadius had also rejected belief in Christ's bodily presence, and in the spring and summer of 1525 they also published treatises defending their position. The controversy expanded rapidly, with Strasbourg joining Basel and Zurich in arguing for a symbolic understanding of the Lord's Supper. Luther contributed two major treatises to the debate in 1527 and 1528; in them he portrayed the controversy

as motivated by Satan and renounced fellowship with the Swiss. A colloquy between the Lutherans and the Swiss at Marburg in the fall of 1529 did not bring agreement but did put a provisional end to the public polemics.

The introduction of Evangelical reforms had larger political consequences for Zurich, which was isolated within the Swiss Confederation. The five inner cantons (Lucerne, Uri, Schwyz, Unterwalden, and Zug) remained firmly committed to Rome. Basel, Schaffhausen, and Bern had Evangelical sympathies but officially remained neutral and so could do little to support Zurich. In 1525 John Eck repeated an earlier offer to hold a disputation with Zwingli. The Catholic cantons accepted this offer, and a disputation was held in conjunction with a diet of the confederation's members in Baden in May–June 1526. Zurich would not let Zwingli attend out of fear for his safety, and so Oecolampadius was Eck's main opponent. The debate was seen as a victory for the Catholics, and in its wake nine of the thirteen cantons in the Swiss Confederation condemned Zwingli as a heretic and called for the enforcement of the Edict of Worms.

Zwingli tried to repair the damage caused by the Baden disputation with his publications, but a more effective counter was the disputation held in Bern in January 1528. The Bern Council invited theologians from Switzerland and southern Germany to attend the disputation, and a few days after its conclusion the city voted to reform its church. That decision emboldened the Evangelical party in Basel, and in February 1529 an outbreak of iconoclasm led to that city's official adoption of reform. Schaffhausen officially reformed its church in September 1529. The decisions were not so clear-cut in other areas: Appenzell split into Catholic and Protestant halves, while in Glarus and Graubünden individual communities were given the right to adopt the new faith or remain loyal to Rome.

Tensions within the Swiss Confederation increased through 1527–28 as both Catholic and Reformed cantons formed political alliances with coreligionists both within and outside of the confederation. In June 1529 Zurich threatened war with the Catholic cantons, but battle was avoided by the First Peace of Kappel. Conflicts continued, however, and in the fall of 1531 war broke out again. On October 11, Zurich was decisively defeated by its Catholic opponents, and Zwingli, who was serving as chaplain, was killed in battle. Two weeks later a Catholic army decisively defeated the army of Zurich's Reformed allies. The war was ended by the Second Peace of Kappel, which recognized the right of the Reformed churches to exist but reestablished Catholicism in some places. It also favored the position of Catholics in the Mandated Territories, which prevented the further spread of Protestantism within the Swiss Confederation. When Oecolampadius died in November after a short illness, the Reformed churches had no prominent theologians to replace its two most significant leaders.

Zurich chose the young Heinrich Bullinger (1504–75) as Zwingli's successor. Bullinger faced two challenges. The first was to preserve the achievements of the Zurich Reformation despite the city's political defeat. Under his leadership, the church gained a governing structure through the synod, the semiannual meetings of all pastors in the city and its rural parishes. Zurich's educational system was reorganized, and the church's wealth was used to create an academy for the education of future pastors and to fund stipends supporting those students. The liturgy for the church's various forms of public worship was standardized, and Leo Jud wrote shorter and longer catechisms for the religious instruction of children and adults.

Bullinger's second challenge was to defend the reputation of Zwingli and the Zurich church. Luther saw the deaths of Zwingli and Oecolampadius as God's judgment. In his publications he denounced Zwingli as a heretic, and he refused fellowship with the Zurich church unless it renounced Zwingli's

teachings, especially on the Lord's Supper. This Bullinger would not do. At first he was cautiously supportive of Martin Bucer's concord efforts, but he gradually turned against Bucer. In 1538 Zurich used its dominance, especially in the eastern part of the Confederation, to bring an effective end to further negotiations concerning the Lord's Supper. Protected from the Catholic emperor by their membership in the Swiss Confederation, these areas did not feel any pressure to reach agreement with the Lutherans.

Bucer had more success along the western edge of the Swiss Confederation, however. Under the leadership of Oswald Myconius, the Basel church endorsed Bucer's understanding of the Lord's Supper. From 1537 a Buceran party dominated Bern's church, although they were challenged by a faction loyal to Zurich. Bern's conquest of the Vaud in 1536 led to the introduction of the Reformation in this Francophone territory and encouraged the independent city-republic of Geneva to abolish the Mass as well. Geneva's two reformers, Guillaume Farel and John Calvin, were expelled in 1538 for defending the church's independence from the magistrate. Calvin spent the next three years in Strasbourg, and when he returned to Geneva in 1541, his theology was influenced by Bucer. Through the 1540s the relationship between Geneva and Bern would be strained as each side sought to influence the churches in the territory of Vaud. These tensions also affected Calvin's ties with Bullinger, who associated Calvin with Bucer.

Zurich remained the dominant influence in eastern Switzerland through the 1540s, and its influence grew at the end of the decade. The defeat of the Smalcaldic League led to Bucer's exile from Strasbourg and the end of his influence in Switzerland. In Bern, the Zwinglian faction gained the upper hand, and the Bucerean pastors were expelled. In order to improve his standing with Bern, Calvin sought to strengthen his ties with Zurich. The result was the 1549 Consensus Tigurinus, which set forth a common understanding of the Lord's

Supper in terms unacceptable to the Lutherans. Although Zurich and Geneva continued to disagree on other issues, such as the relation between church and state, the Consensus Tigurinus provided a basis for unity, especially in the wake of renewed attacks by Lutheran theologians, and it would be accepted by most of the other Swiss Reformed churches. Their unity would be reinforced by their acceptance of the Second Helvetic Confession in 1566. Basel maintained its Buceran course into the 1570s, but increasing doctrinal controversy led to a more clearly Reformed identity in that city by the 1580s.

Bullinger's growing international reputation and his long tenure in office gave the Zurich church much greater prestige through the third quarter of the sixteenth century than it had during Zwingli's time. Calvin's successor in Geneva, Theodore Beza, maintained close ties with Bullinger and then with Bullinger's successor, Rudolph Gwalther. By the end of the sixteenth century the Swiss Reformation was fully institutionalized within the separate but allied Swiss Reformed Churches.

See also Anabaptists/Spiritualists; Bullinger, Heinrich; Calvin, John; Geneva; Marburg Colloquy; Oecolampadius, Johannes; Zurich; Zwingli, Ulrich

Bibliography

Backus, I. "The Disputations of Baden, 1526, and Berne, 1528: Neutralizing the Early Church." *Studies in Reformed Theology and History* 1 (1993): 1–130; Bruening, M. W. *Calvinism's First Battleground: Conflict and Reform in the Pays de Vaud, 1528–1559.* Springer, 2005; Burnett, A. N. *Teaching the Reformation: Ministers and Their Message in Basel, 1529–1629.* Oxford University Press, 2006; Burnett, A. N., and E. Campi. *A Companion to the Swiss Reformation.* Brill, 2016; Campi, E. *Shifting Patterns of Reformed Tradition.* Vandenhoeck & Ruprecht, 2014; Gordon, B. *The Swiss Reformation.* Palgrave, 2002; Head, R. C. "A Divided Switzerland in Reformation Europe." In *A Concise History of Switzerland,* ed. C. H. Church and R. C. Head, 73–103. Cambridge University Press, 2013; Locher, G. W. *Die Zwinglische Reformation im Rahmen der europäischen Kirchengeschichte.* Vandenhoeck & Ruprecht, 1979; Snyder, C. A. "The Birth and Evolution of Swiss Anabaptism (1520–1530)." *Mennonite Quarterly Review* 80 (2006): 501–645. https://peacetheology.files.wordpress.com/2013/02/snydere2809422birth-and-evolution-of-swiss-anabaptism22.pdf.

AMY NELSON BURNETT

Synergistic Controversy

A doctrinal dispute in the late 1550s among Lutheran theologians seeking to clarify Luther's understanding of the role of the human will in conversion is termed the synergistic controversy. The Philippists and Gnesio-Lutherans debated the question of the role of the human will in coming to faith, but also the related questions of original sin, predestination, the work of the Holy Spirit, and the nature of saving faith. The issue was addressed by article 2, On Free Will, of the Formula of Concord (1577). Luther's teaching of justification by grace through faith alone was central to his Reformation message and led to the closer definition of other aspects of Lutheran doctrine being articulated in the sixteenth century. The role of the human will in conversion, faith, and salvation was no exception. In his 1521 *Loci communes*, Melanchthon had maintained a teaching on free will drawn from his Pauline exegesis and consistent with Luther's own. In his *On the Bondage of the Will* (1525; better translated as *On Bound Choice*), Luther asserted that the unregenerated human will was able to conform to civil laws, but because of its bondage to sin, it could neither fulfill God's law nor respond to the gospel. God's unconditional grace alone justifies sinners.

While Melanchthon continued to stress the human will's inability to obtain faith, despite its freedom in matters of this life (CA 18), he also tried to address other theological concerns, especially Lutheran opponents' charge of Manichaeism. In the 1530s he set out to identify more precisely the human role or responsibility in conversion. In the second edition of the *Loci communes* (1535), he began to teach that conversion involves three cooperating factors: (1) the Holy Spirit, or the effective cause; (2) God's Word, the instrumental cause; and (3) the human will not resisting but assenting to God's Word, which is the material cause on which the Spirit and Word work. In other words, the human will cannot, on its own, come to God, but it does have the power to assent to God's graceful action in conversion.

Already in 1536 Nikolaus von Amsdorf voiced his criticism of Melanchthon's related views of contingency but not his use of this Aristotelian framework. Melanchthon continued to hold this position, and in a revision of the third edition of the *Loci communes* (from 1548), he explained that the free choice in the human is the ability to apply oneself toward grace. This view had also found expression in the so-called Leipzig Interim (1548). Later Melanchthon and others argued that humans, in a small and weak way, have a cooperative role once the Spirit and the Word move them. His concern was acknowledging that the will becomes a factor in conversion only as a result of the action of the Holy Spirit on it through the Word. This, he thought, would preserve the notion that the Holy Spirit works effectively through the means of grace, unlike certain Reformed thinkers. He also wanted to hold human beings accountable for their own sinful actions and to prevent the assumption that God is responsible for evil. His anthropological teaching recognized that what it means to be God's human creation is not diminished or excluded from God's work of bringing sinners to repentance, faith, and salvation.

One of Melanchthon's students who supported and further developed his position was Johann Pfeffinger, who assisted Melanchthon in drafting and defending the Leipzig Interim. In 1555 Pfeffinger expanded on Melanchthon's teaching on conversion, arguing that with their own powers human beings are able to assent to God's Word, grasp its promise, and not resist the Holy Spirit. Pfeffinger, like Melanchthon, believed that the human will, along with the Word and the Spirit, is the third factor in conversion. Pfeffinger's *Five Questions concerning the Freedom of the Will* (1555) was a restatement of Melanchthon's position, yet went beyond Melanchthon, asserting that one difference between the elect and those not elected to salvation was found in the role of the human will. Those rejecting God's grace are not elected, while those who accept his grace are elected to salvation. Pfeffinger maintained that the human

will was corrupted by sin but not entirely powerless. Weak as it may be, the human will's assent to God's grace plays a key role in conversion. This the Gnesio-Lutherans rejected.

In 1558 Nikolaus von Amsdorf criticized Pfeffinger's position in his *Public Confession of the Pure Teaching of the Gospel and Confutation of Present Day Fanatics*, attributing to him the claim that humans are able by their own natural powers to assent to God's Word, and marking the public start of the controversy. The Jena professor Matthias Flacius soon joined Amsdorf in his refutation of Pfeffinger's view. Flacius asserted Luther's position that the human will remains completely passive in the unregenerate person and has no contribution to make in conversion to saving faith in Christ. Not only is the sinful human will unable to respond to God's grace, but it also is resistant and even hostile to God. Only God can transform the human will and bring a person to faith.

In 1558 Duke Johann Friedrich of Ernestine Saxony decided to address a number of controverted teachings that were disrupting the Lutheran churches. Since no resolution had been found to the conflicts over adiaphora, justification by faith, the Lord's Supper, and good works, he sought yet another approach to finding harmony. Amsdorf and Flacius proposed a confession of faith for the territory that would include the refutation of errors, among them synergism. The duke agreed, and the final product appeared in early 1559 and was known as the Book of Confutation. It was to be the official doctrinal position of the land, and all pastors and professors were to subscribe to it. Jena professor Viktorin Strigel, who, like Pfeffinger, had maintained that the unconverted person had a latent ability to cooperate with God's grace in conversion, refused to sign and was imprisoned. In an effort to convince Strigel of his error, Flacius proposed a disputation between the two, which was held at Weimar in 1560. The debate became deadlocked over the first topic, namely, the question of the role of the human will in conversion. No resolution was found, and the controversy continued. Flacius did not help his cause by trying to articulate scriptural teaching by means of Aristotelian concepts. He later argued that humans cannot turn themselves to God in conversion because of original sin, which, he asserted, is the very substance or essence of the unregenerate human creature. This sparked its own controversy, which the Lutherans later addressed, and led to Flacius's dismissal from Jena.

Although the arguments over the role of the human will in conversion were redirected into another conflict over original sin, the controverted questions about free will remained an issue. Eventually the Formula of Concord (art. 2) focused on a key point of dispute: What are the powers of the human will after the fall into sin with regard to spiritual matters? Are human beings able, by their own abilities, to respond favorably toward God's grace and to come to accept that grace offered by the Holy Spirit in God's Word? This article, drafted in large part by David Chytraeus and Martin Chemnitz (both of whom had lectured on Melanchthon's *Loci*), answered that the human will has no active role to play in conversion and faith but is able to be converted by God through the Spirit and the Word. After the fall into sin, human reason cannot see and understand spiritual matters by its own powers. The human will is not only turned away from God but has also become God's enemy, so that it desires and wills only evil and what is opposed to God. Nevertheless, the Holy Spirit does not convert unregenerate humans without means but uses the preaching and hearing of God's Word to this end. Faith comes by the hearing of God's Word. It is God's will that all hear his Word and come to faith. The conversion of sinful human beings, then, is accomplished solely by the grace and power of the Holy Spirit. Humans have no free will in conversion. All that leads to faith and salvation is ascribed to God's grace, so that no one might boast before God.

The Formula condemned those teachings about human free will that it held contradicted the Scriptures. It rejected the "semi-Pelagian"

teaching that humans by their own powers can initiate their conversion to faith, but they cannot complete it without the working of the Holy Spirit. And, while affirming that the human will is completely passive in conversion, the Formula affirmed that the Holy Spirit through the Word converts a person, whose will is then renewed solely by God's power and activity and becomes an instrument and means of the Holy Spirit, in that the will not only receives grace but also cooperates with the Spirit in the works that follow. The Formula, insisting that the teaching about three causes had only served to confuse students, clarified that the Spirit and the Word (as the Spirit's instrument) are the only two causative factors of conversion. Human beings must hear God's Word, yet cannot believe and accept it by their own powers, but solely by the grace and operation of God the Holy Spirit.

In resolving the controversy, the Formula took seriously the chief concerns of both sides. It recognized the Philippist assertion that the human will is not completely passive in conversion, and at the same time it affirmed the Gnesio-Lutheran argument that the will can only resist God until the Spirit has converted it to faith in the gospel. It also emphasized the commitment of both groups to the Holy Spirit's effective use of the means of grace in salvation. Its rejection of the Flacian position led this party to reject the Formula.

See also Chemnitz, Martin; Chytraeus, David; Flacius, Matthias Illyricus, and the Flacians; Formula of Concord; Free Will; Melanchthon, Philip; Pfeffinger, Johann

Bibliography

Arand, C. P. *The Lutheran Confessions*. Fortress, 2012; Green, L. C. "The Three Causes of Conversion in Philipp Melanchthon, Martin Chemnitz, David Chytraeus, and 'the Formula of Concord.'" *Lutherjahrbuch* 47 (1980): 89–114; Mühlenberg, E. "*Synergia* and Justification by Faith." In *Discord, Dialogue, and Concord: Studies in the Lutheran Reformation's Formula of Concord*, ed. L. W. Spitz and W. Lohff, 15–37. Fortress, 1977; Preus, R. D., and W. H. Rosin, eds. *A Contemporary Look at the Formula of Concord*. Concordia, 1978; Wengert, T. J. *A Formula for Parish Practice*. Eerdmans, 2006.

GERHARD BODE

Taiwan

Lutheran mission work in Taiwan began in the early 1950s after foreign mission societies were expelled from mainland China in 1949. The initial target of outreach work in Mandarin included General Chiang Kai-shek's soldiers, military dependents, and refugees who had fled the mainland, rather than indigenous people. Hoping to return to the mainland soon, little consideration was given to contextualizing the gospel within indigenous culture. Such an approach had a long-lasting impact. Despite mission societies' membership in the Lutheran Church of China in the mainland (except the LCMS mission), initial attempts to form one common Lutheran Church failed: cooperation between the various missions fell apart during the 1950s. This failure bore the fruit of fragmentation as American, Norwegian, and Finnish mission societies founded six separate Lutheran church bodies throughout the 1950s and 1960s. While these churches established a loose federation (the Chinese Lutheran Churches Association in Taiwan) in 1979, meaningful cooperation is still minimal, and the fragmentation of Taiwan Lutheranism continues to be a formidable challenge.

The Taiwan Lutheran Church (TLC) was established in 1954 by seven American and Scandinavian missions. The Lutheran Church of the Republic of China (LCROC) was established in 1956 by the Norwegian Lutheran Mission (NLM). The Chinese Lutheran Brethren Church (CLBC) was established in 1956 by the American Church of the Lutheran Brethren (CLB). The China Evangelical Lutheran Church (CELC) was established in 1966 by the Lutheran Church–Missouri Synod (LCMS). The China Lutheran Gospel Church (CLGC) was established in 1973 by the Norwegian

Evangelical Lutheran Free Church (NELFC). The Lutheran Church of Taiwan (LCT) was established in 1974 by the Finnish Missionary Society (FMS). Specialized emphases of each include the following: cell groups, leadership training, and evangelism (TLC); social ministry, Christian broadcasting, and Christian schools (CELC); theological education (LCROC); Hakka minority ministry (CLBC); rural ministry (LCT); and medical mission (CLGC). Total Lutheran church membership stands around twenty-five thousand.

During and after the process of becoming independent from their founding missions, these churches established their own governance structures, forms of ministry, and ecumenical relationships. This thirty-year phase from the mid-1960s to the mid-1990s resulted in the establishment of many new congregations, student ministries, media ministries, schools, medical clinics/hospitals, and preaching stations. The LCROC and LCT joined the Lutheran World Federation (LWF), while the TLC holds dual membership in the LWF and WCC.

After initial attempts at theological education in Kaoshiung, Taichung, and Chiayi ended unsuccessfully, the CLB, NLM, NELFC, and FMS founded China Lutheran Seminary (CLS) in Hsinchu on January 30, 1966. In 1989 all but the CELC signed the "Agreement to Build an Expanded Chinese Lutheran Theological Seminary." In 1995 all six Lutheran churches signed the "Agreement to Continue Supporting the Chinese Lutheran Theological Seminary." After fifty years, CLS continues to offer training in classic Lutheran theology and an MTh program in Luther studies, and it serves as the only existing platform of cooperation for all six Lutheran synods. As the only Mandarin-speaking Lutheran seminary in the world, CLS serves not only all six Lutheran churches, but also the broader Taiwanese church.

Beginning in the mid-1990s, the leadership of TLC, led by Rev. Peter Yang, began to leave behind the confessional, liturgical Lutheran tradition in favor of theological influences from the United States, South Korea, and Singapore. These included charismatic/Pentecostal styles, cell groups, and church growth emphases; embracing the "praise and worship" movement in place of the liturgy; and valuing methods and strategies over classic Lutheran theology. Many Lutheran churches minimized sacramental theology, emphasizing the unmediated experience of the Holy Spirit. Doctrine came to be seen as an obstacle to church growth and vitality; practical leadership development became more important than theological fidelity to the Lutheran tradition. While this trend was most evident in the TLC, in the past twenty years it has penetrated all Lutheran churches.

On the eve of the Reformation's five-hundredth anniversary, Lutheranism in Taiwan is at a crossroads. It faces questions regarding its ability not merely to preserve the Reformation gospel of justification by grace but also to bring that gospel to engage ever-deeper dimensions of Chinese culture. Theological training and formation have emerged as indispensable resources and must be brought to bear on the question of whether the Lutheran movement can transcend differences of style, method, and preference, remaining faithful to its confessional heritage while being boldly creative in mission. The challenges of contextualizing the gospel (without becoming subsumed by the surrounding evangelical context) and of continuing to reform (while overcoming fragmentation) remain.

See also China

Bibliography

Hsiao, Andrew. *A Brief History of the Chinese Lutheran Church*. Hong Kong: Taosheng Publishing House, 1999; Steensland, Gustav. *Cultivation of Christian Leadership in a Confucian Context: A Study of the Preparation of Pastors for Ministry in the Taiwan Lutheran Church 1948–87*.

School of Mission and Theology Dissertation Series, vol. 4. Stavanger, 2005; Yu, Thomas. "Taiwan: Its Vision and Challenges." Unpublished paper presented at the Consultation on the Development of Joint Lutheran Theological Education in Taiwan, April 20–21, 1990, Taipei.

Jukka A. Kääriäinen

Tanzania

Tanzania came into existence on April 22, 1964, with the union of Tanganyika and Zanzibar. After a brief interlude of Portuguese presence, by the nineteenth century the island of Zanzibar (including Pemba) and much of the coastal area was under the control of Omani sultans. As a result of the Berlin Conference of November 1884, Anglo-German Agreements of 1886 and 1890 established the British Protectorate of Zanzibar and German East Africa, which included most of the up-country area together with Burundi and Rwanda. The Treaty of Versailles (1919) gave the Rwanda/Burundi area as a mandate to Belgium and the rest of the mainland area to the British as Tanganyika Territory. In 1946 this area came under the Trusteeship of the United Nations. Tanganyika became independent in 1961 and on December 9, 1962, became a republic. Soon after a revolution on Zanzibar against the Omani sultan in January 1964, the United Republic of Tanzania came into being.

Lutheran activity began when two Lutheran missionaries serving the Church Mission Society came from Rabai area in Kenya to establish contacts in Tanzania. Johann Krapf from Württemberg visited Sultan Kimweri at Vuga in the Usambara Mountains in 1848, promising to return. In 1848 his compatriot Johann Rebmann visited Mangi Mankinga at Machame, on the southern slopes of Kilimanjaro. The names of these places were remembered in mission-minded circles in Germany when Krapf inspired Ludwig Harms to found the Hermannsburg Mission. German colonial possession renewed interest in these areas.

The history of the Lutheran Church in Tanzania began modestly in Dar es Salaam with the arrival of Pastor Johann Jacob Greiner, sent by the Evangelical Mission Society in

Berlin, on July 2, 1887. From this simple beginning in the Islamic milieu of Dar es Salaam has sprung the Evangelical Lutheran Church in Tanzania (ELCT). Greiner began his work at Immanuelskap, located near the presidential mansion of present Tanzania, in Dar es Salaam. By 1892 he moved to Kisarawe, twenty miles up in the hills, in Zaramo country. Here he began work among the Islamic people together with a community of freed slaves who had been committed to his care. At about the same time Alexander Merensky led a group of Berlin missionaries from South Africa across Lake Nyassa to begin work in Manow, in the Mbeya area that later became known as Konde. German Moravians began to arrive in the same area, led by Traugott Bachmann, who later become noted for his efforts at indigenizing the church.

German missionaries quickly divided the area around Mbeya between Moravians and Lutherans. Lutherans of the Leipzig Mission and the Roman Catholic Holy Ghost Fathers in the Kilimanjaro area worked out a peaceful division in the 1890s. The areas were divided into chiefdoms separated by rivers alternating across the base of the mountain. The Catholics began at Kilema in the East at the Kenya border, with the Lutherans ending at Machame in the West. This resulted in a mostly friendly rivalry between the missions that led the Kilimanjaro area to become the most prosperous part of the country, with a proliferation of schools and medical facilities.

Leipzig missionaries came to the Moshi area in August 1893. After a short time the Anglican CMS missionaries at Old Moshi left the Lutherans in charge of the Protestant work there and moved to Kenya. Lutheran work was centered at Nkwarungo in the Machame area, and from there mission work extended west to Meru and Arusha areas and south to the Pare area.

In 1890 August Kraemer of the Bethel Mission began work in Tanga among the Digo people in the northeast. More Bethel missionaries arrived and began work in the Usambara

Mountains by 1891. By 1905 Bethel missionary Ernst Johannsen left his first station in the Usambaras and crossed the country, intending to establish a mission in Rwanda. When he returned from his visit, the German colonial administrator persuaded him to settle in Bukoba in 1910. Here he connected with the nascent Protestant community started by Isaya Kibira and Andrea Kajerero, who had been influenced by the revival in Uganda. With the beginning of a Lutheran Church in Bukoba, much of the initial area of the Lutheran Church was in place, and from this area it expanded into other parts.

In 1911 the first Evangelical Ecumenical Council was held in Dar es Salaam. Lutherans were represented by delegations from the Berlin, Bethel, and Leipzig Missions, with a Tanzanian representative in each group. The Moravians sent missionaries from their fields of Rungwe and Tabora, and one Anglican missionary represented the CMS. The next meeting was scheduled but never materialized because of the outbreak of World War I (1914). A result of the first conference was the formation of a teachers training college in the area named Schlesien, in the mountains overlooking Morogoro. It was staffed by Lutherans and by the end of 1913 had Lutheran, Moravian, and Anglican students. By 1915 fourteen teacher trainees graduated, but soon afterward the school was destroyed as battles raged across the country. By 1920 the victorious British had deported the Lutheran missionaries, with the exception of several who claimed Estonian and Alsatian citizenship.

The Iowa Synod, at the request of the Leipzig Mission, sent Pastor A. C. Zeilinger to the Leipzig field to explore the area. As a result, the Augustana Synod agreed to adopt the Leipzig field and soon concentrated on the newly developed area of Singida. By 1923 the Leipzig Mission was also permitted to send some missionaries, among whom was Richard Reusch, who continued to play a leadership role in the church. From this time, Augustana assumed financial responsibility and began sending missionaries who later played a leadership role, including Pastors George Anderson and Elmer Danielson. By 1926 the Marangu Teachers Training College was reopened and continued to provide teachers and leaders for the ever-growing Lutheran Church.

The Great Depression and World War II resulted in great changes in mission outreach. German missionaries were removed at the outbreak of World War II (1939). After the war several Scandinavian and American mission agencies sent personnel to staff the existing Lutheran institutions. While these were stop-gap measures, a vibrant indigenous Lutheran Church began to grow rapidly under leaders trained locally as well as in common institutions such as Marangu Teachers Training College and Lwandai Theological Training Center (later moved to its permanent location at Makumira in 1955).

By 1937 Lutherans formed a Mission Church Federation. This led to the formation of the Federation of Lutheran Churches, in which half of the delegates were Tanzanians. While the missions still maintained their own council, by 1939 the indigenous churches assumed the administration of the Lwandai Theological Training Center, the Vuga Press, and the Bumbuli Medical Training Center.

Tanzanian delegates to the All African Lutheran Conference at Marangu in 1955 precipitated a change in leadership structures to include the possibility of bishops. Some churches consecrated bishops in "apostolic succession" (received from the Swedish church); other churches (e.g., the Lutheran Church in Northern Tanganyika) installed bishops according to the customs of Germany. Others retained superintendents or presidents as leaders.

In 1962 the seven regional Lutheran churches met to draw up the constitution of the ELCT. This new church came into existence in Dar es Salaam, uniting the Lutheran churches of Iraqw (Mbulu), Northern Tanganyika, Buhaya, Ubena-Konde, Uzaramo-Uluguru, Usambara-Digo, and Iramba-Turu. From its inception this was a mission church, reaching

out across its borders. Part of the impetus came from the hundreds of thousands of refugees from newly emerging neighboring countries who were ministered to by the Lutheran World Federation and surrounding Lutheran churches. Thus, the first mission reached out to eastern Kenya in 1967, giving rise to the Kenya Evangelical Lutheran Church. In 1968 the work extended to Kalemie in Zaire (now the Democratic Republic of the Congo) resulting in five dioceses. Mission work in Malawi, Mozambique, and Zambia followed in quick succession, resulting in Lutheran churches. By 1991 outreach to Uganda and Burundi began. After the Rwandan massacre, thousands of refugees returned to Rwanda in the 1990s, resulting in the formation of a vibrant Lutheran Church there.

Other major events include the formation of the Lutheran Junior Seminary (now at Morogoro). In 1977 the ELCT hosted the Lutheran World Federation meeting in Dar es Salaam. Tanzanian bishop Josiah Kibira was chosen president. Makumira Theological College, the premier Lutheran theological training center in Africa, led a movement in the 1980s to form Lutheran universities in Tanzania. Kilimanjaro Christian Medical Center in Moshi is an outstanding Lutheran hospital, and other medical centers have been upgraded. With changes in the national education policy since the 1990s, ELCT dioceses are establishing new junior seminaries together with good quality secondary schools, as well as a new Lutheran Teachers Training college in Mbeya. *Radio Voice of the Gospel* continues from Tanzania even after the Ethiopian revolution closed its headquarters. The ELCT continues to serve as a center for renewal and evangelical outreach throughout Tanzania and the world. By 2015 the ELCT had over 6,340,000 members and 1,104 congregations, with over 2,000 pastors. For eight years the bishop of Dar es Salaam, Dr. Alex Malasusa, was the much-appreciated head (Swahili: *mkuu*) of the ELCT, succeeded in 2016 by the bishop of the Northern District, Dr. Fredrick Shoo. The entire country is divided into twenty-four dioceses, each headed by a bishop, together with three mission areas of Tabora, Kigoma, and Zanzibar.

See also Greiner, Johann Jakob; Morogoro, Lutheran Junior Seminary; Moshi, Stefano Ruben; Reusch, Richard Gustavovich

Bibliography

Anderson, W. B. *The Church in East Africa, 1890–1974.* Central Tanganyika Press, 1977; Bernander, G. *Lutheran Wartime Assistance to Tanzanian Churches 1940–1945.* Gleerup, 1968; Danielson, E. R. *Forty Years with Christ in Tanzania, 1928–68.* Lutheran Church in America, 1977; Johnson, D. *Loyalty: A Biography of Richard Gustavovich Reusch.* Sun Ray Printing, 2008; Kretzmann, P. *John Ludwig Krapf: The Explorer-Missionary of Northeastern Africa.* Book Concern, ca. 1918 (now online at: https://archive .org/stream/johnludwigkrapfe00kretiala/johnludwig krapfe00kretiala_djvu.txt; Maanga, G. S. "The Evangelical Lutheran Church in Tanzania, 1963–2013." *LQ*, NS 28 (2014): 179–93; Maanga, G. S., ed. *Injili Kamili: Historia ya KKKT.* Moshi Lutheran Press, 2013; Sahlberg, C. E. *From Krapf to Rugambwa.* Evangel Publishing House, 1986; Sicard, S. von. *The Lutheran Church on the Coast of Tanzania 1887–1914.* Gleerup, 1970.

HERBERT J. HAFERMANN

Tappert, Theodore Gerhardt

The American Lutheran teacher, historian, and editor Theodore Gerhardt Tappert (1904–73) was the son of a Lutheran pastor. A Connecticut native, he graduated from Wagner College and the Lutheran Theological Seminary at Philadelphia (LTSP); he also held a master's degree from Columbia University. Ordained in 1930 by the Ministerium of Pennsylvania, he served briefly as assistant pastor at Trinity Church, Staten Island, New York, before beginning a forty-two-year career as professor of church history at LTSP. He edited several Lutheran journals, including *Lutheran Church Quarterly* (1938–39), *Lutheran World Review* (1948–50), and *Lutheran Quarterly* (1953–65). Perhaps his most significant service to the church was as general editor of Fortress Press's 1959 edition of the *Book of Concord*, the standard English edition for four decades, for which he translated the Augsburg Confession, Apology, and Luther's Small Catechism. Tappert was also coeditor and translator (with J. W. Doberstein) of the three-volume English edition of the *Journals of Henry Melchior Muhlenberg*, and the author of *Lutheran Confessional Theology in America, 1840–1880*, as well as numerous other books and articles. In addition to his editorial and scholarly work, he served on numerous commissions and boards for the ULCA and the LCA. He married Helen Louise Carson in 1937.

See also Book of Concord; United Lutheran Church in America

Bibliography

Tappert, T. G. Biographical File. ELCA Archives; Tappert, T. G. *The Book of Concord.* Fortress, 1959; Tappert, T. G. *Lutheran Confessional Theology in America, 1840–1880.* Oxford University Press, 1972.

RICHARD O. JOHNSON

Tausen, Hans

The foremost theological voice in the reception of Lutheran teaching in Denmark was Hans Tausen (ca. 1494–1561). Born in Birkende, Tausen became a Johannite monk and was exposed to biblical humanism during studies in Rostock, Copenhagen, and Leuven. In 1523 he moved to Wittenberg, where he came under the influence of Luther. When he returned to Denmark, to a monastery in Viborg, he was imprisoned because of his Evangelical preaching. Popular support led to his release, and with the assistance of Jørgen Sadolin he established a strong Lutheran community in Viborg. In 1526 he left his order and married Sadolin's sister, Dorothea. King Frederik I rescued Tausen from episcopal opposition by making him a royal chaplain. In 1529 he became pastor of St. Nicholas Church in Copenhagen. During the civil war that followed the king's death in 1533, Bishop Rønnow charged him with blasphemy, but again popular support prevailed and the verdict was reversed. Tausen played a leading role in the final transition to a Danish territorial church under Christian III and served as bishop in Ribe from 1542 until his death in 1561. His most influential writings were his Danish translation of the Pentateuch (1535) and his postil sermons (1539).

See also Denmark

Bibliography

Bugge, K. ed. *Tro og Tale—Studier over Hans Tausens Postil*. Gads, 1963; Dreyer, R. "An Apologia for Luther—The Myth of the Danish Luther: Danish Reformer Hans Tausen and 'A short Answer' (1528/29)." In *The Myth of the Reformation*, ed. P. Opitz, 211–32. Vandenhoeck & Ruprecht, 2013; Dunkley, E. H. *The Reformation in Denmark*. Esp. 114–31. SPCK, 1948; Lausten, M. S. *A Church History of Denmark*. Ashgate, 2002.

ERIC LUND

Telemann, Georg Philipp

Music critics of the time regarded the German composer Georg Philipp Telemann (1681–1767) to be Germany's leading composer, not Johann Sebastian Bach (1685–1750) or George Frederick Handel (1685–1759). Telemann wrote prodigious quantities of music, including cantatas, oratorios, passions, operas, orchestral suites, concertos, chamber music, and keyboard works. His 1730 *Fast allgemeines evangelisch-musicalisches Lieder-Buch* (Very general Evangelical musical songbook), an organ accompaniment book for the Lutheran hymnal, is unique because of its inclusion of melodic and harmonic variants. Best known today for his secular instrumental music, Telemann himself considered his work for the church, as composer and practicing musician, to have been his primary occupation. Born in Magdeburg, Telemann enrolled at Leipzig University as a law student, but his musical interests prevailed. After holding music positions in Leipzig, Sorau, Eisenach, and Frankfurt, Telemann became musical director of Hamburg's five main churches, where he provided two cantatas for each Sunday and a new Lenten passion each year, in addition to other music. He still found time to direct the opera and the *collegium musicum*. In 1722 Telemann applied for and was offered the position of cantor at the Thomas Church in Leipzig. When the Hamburg council did not answer his petition to be released, he successfully leveraged the offer to get a raise in Hamburg and stayed in the Hanseatic city. J. S. Bach was subsequently appointed to the position at Leipzig. Telemann was a leader in establishing the so-called mixed musical style, one that unites the German contrapuntal style with French, Italian, and Polish styles.

See also Bach, Johann Sebastian; Music; Schütz, Heinrich

Bibliography

Hirschmann, W., C. Lange, and W. Hobohm, eds. *Auf der gezeigten Spur: Beiträge zur Telemannforschung*. Ziethen, 1994; Lange, C., and B. Reipsch, eds. *Telemann und die Kirchenmusik*. Olms, 2011; Neubacher, J. *Georg Philipp Telemanns Hamburger Kirchenmusik und ihre Aufführungsbedingungen (1721–1767)*. Olms, 2009; Poetzsch-Seban, U. *Die Kirchenmusik von Georg Philipp Telemann und Erdmann Neumeister: Zur Geschichte der protestantischen Kirchenkantate in der ersten Hälfte des 18. Jahrhunderts*. Ortus, 2006.

DIANNE M. MCMULLEN

Temperance and Prohibition

Temperance is an idea and program for moderating or eliminating the personal use of items such as alcohol, tobacco, and illicit drugs, and is particularly associated with such movements in the United States. Prohibition was the legal ban on the production and consumption of alcoholic beverages that was in force in the United States between 1919 and 1933. Beginning in the late eighteenth century, religious and social reformers identified the use of alcohol, drugs, and tobacco as a widespread and destructive epidemic in the Western world and sought to organize efforts to counter such habits. Although the initial approach was simply to urge limits on their use, increasingly in the nineteenth century there was a move toward total abstinence from such substances, especially alcohol. Voluntary organizations to spread the message of temperance were initially formed in the early nineteenth century in the United States, Canada, and England, and eventually spread to other parts of Europe as well, especially the Scandinavian countries. Although this movement was originally focused on individual abstinence, it quickly moved toward urging legislative actions to restrict or even prohibit the manufacture and sale of alcohol. After the end of the American Civil War in 1865, the Temperance movement became widespread in America, with the Protestant denominations leading the way. Increasingly this movement sought to eliminate the consumption of alcohol in the United States on the state or federal level, which culminated in the complete ban on alcohol (Prohibition) on a national level with the Eighteenth Amendment to the US Constitution in 1919. Prohibition was difficult to enforce, increasingly unpopular, and repealed in 1933, but various state and local legal restrictions on alcohol consumption continued to exist. As American Lutherans moved into the world of English-speaking Protestantism, they generally adopted these attitudes toward alcohol, and many Lutheran denominations, especially those of Scandinavian origins, were strongly supportive of temperance and prohibition. Some of the German-American denominations, however, especially the Missouri Synod, were not in favor of the push toward total abstinence from alcohol and officially opposed the adoption of Prohibition as an improper mixing of church and state. Though legal prohibition on alcohol was repealed, many Lutheran congregations and organizations, especially those with Scandinavian-American roots, continued to prohibit the consumption of alcohol on their premises. Many Lutherans have also been supportive of the efforts of groups such as Alcoholics Anonymous and Narcotics Anonymous, who work with those whose lives are severely affected by alcohol and drug addiction.

Bibliography

Rorabaugh, W. J. *The Alcoholic Republic: An American Tradition*. Oxford University Press, 1979.

MARK A. GRANQUIST

Ten Commandments

In the medieval church, the Decalogue had been subsumed under and overshadowed by catalogs of virtues and vices, assembled both to bring the faithful to the knowledge of sin for the sacrament of penance and to guide Christian conduct. It was only in the thirteenth century that the Ten Commandments were specifically utilized as preparation for the sacrament of penance. Early on, Luther accents the place of the Decalogue in bringing Christians to a recognition and confession of sin, first preaching on the Decalogue in 1516 (published in Latin in 1518). In his 1522 *Personal Prayer Book*, Luther gives examples of how each commandment is broken and fulfilled. The language of Luther's 1524 hymn "These Are the Holy Ten Commands" (LW 53:277–79) is a doxological interpretation of the Decalogue even as it anticipates the vocabulary Luther will use in the Small Catechism. Six years after writing the catechisms, Luther demonstrated how the Ten Commandments formed the platform for prayer in his 1535 *A Simple Way to Pray*.

Luther's catechetical use of the Decalogue is reflective of his understanding of both the Old Testament and the nature of the law. In his 1525 treatise *How Christians Should Regard Moses*, the reformer argues that the Ten Commandments as such do not pertain to Christians in that they were given to Israel at Sinai. It is only insofar as the Decalogue is coherent with the New Testament and natural law that it is binding on believers. Luther understands the Ten Commandments as reflecting the divine law written into creation and discernible to the conscience.

The numbering of the Ten Commandments was disputed in the pre-Reformation church. Luther followed the Western tradition of including the prohibition of graven images under the first commandment, while John Calvin and the Reformed tradition followed the Hebrew Bible and the rabbis in making the prohibition of images a distinct commandment and combining the two commandments on coveting.

Departing from the traditional catechetical ordering of the Lord's Prayer, Apostles' Creed, and Ten Commandments, Luther places the Decalogue at the beginning of the Small Catechism because the law precedes the gospel, revealing the human creature's incapacity to fear, love, and trust in the Creator above all things. The priority of the first commandment is determinative for Luther's interpretation of the whole Decalogue. He sees it as "the chief source and fountainhead that permeates all others; again to it they all return and upon it they all depend, so that end and beginning are completely linked and bound together" (LC, Ten Commandments, par. 329). Luther demonstrates this by placing the epilogue to the first commandment (see Exod. 20:5–6; Deut. 5:9–10) as the conclusion to the Decalogue itself in the Small Catechism. The explanation of each commandment begins with "we should fear and love God so that," thus providing a linkage back to the first commandment.

According to Luther, the first commandment is universal. He omits the biblical prologue (Exod. 20:2) from his citation of the first commandment in the Small Catechism to demonstrate that this divine word is addressed not only to ancient Israelites but also to all of humanity. In the same vein, the reformer relocates the significance of the third commandment from ritual observance of the Old Testament Sabbath to hearing and keeping the Word of God, which sanctifies the day. "For the Word of God is the true holy object" (LC par. 91). The ceremonial aspect of the commandment is fulfilled in Christ and is no longer binding on the Christian conscience.

For Luther, the Ten Commandments and the first article of the Apostles' Creed interpenetrate each other in that the Creator uses the law to order human life in creation, so that it is guarded and defended from evil. Lutheran theology rejects any suggestion that the keeping of the commandments leads to salvation. Rather the commandments demonstrate the will of God for his human creatures as they live lives trusting in him for every good and devoting themselves to the good works he has commanded for the sake of the neighbor. The commandments stand guard against self-chosen good works, directing the believer to the life of love lived according to the will of the Creator.

While Luther's treatment of the Decalogue in the Small Catechism is concise in his focus on what God both prohibits and requires, his exposition of the commandments in the Large Catechism is more didactic as he works to apply each commandment to the daily life of the believer, providing concrete instruction for the Christian's life of repentance, faith, and good works. For Luther, the double commandment of love of God and of neighbor (Matt. 22:37–39) is embodied in the first and second tables of the law.

Debates regarding the nature of the law and particularly the place of its "third use" (as a guide for Christians) began already in the sixteenth century, in the later phases of the so-called antinomian controversies. (See Formula of Concord, art. 6.) Similar debates in the twentieth century have influenced the understanding of the commandments among contemporary Lutherans as has the so-called biblical theology movement following the impulses of Karl Barth (1886–1968). Recent interest in a retrieval of natural law theory has prompted some Lutheran theologians to probe more carefully the connection between natural law and the Decalogue. Perceived antinomian tendencies in modern Lutheranism as well as charges of ethical relativism have sparked both disputation over the place of the Ten Commandments and renewed emphasis on their usage in the Christian life.

See also Antinomianism/Antinomian Controversies; Catechisms; Law, Uses of the; Law and Gospel

Bibliography

Baker, R. *Natural Law: A Lutheran Reappraisal*. Concordia, 2011; Bornkamm, H. *Luther and the Old Testament*. Trans. E. Gritsch, and R. Fortress, 1969; Bouman, W. "The Concept of 'Law' in the Lutheran Tradition." *Word & World* 3 (Fall 1983): 413–22; Braaten, C. E., and C. R. Seitz. *I Am the Lord Your God: Christian Reflections on the Ten Commandments*. Eerdmans, 2005; Elert, W. *The Christian Ethos*. Trans. C. J. Schinder. Fortress, 1957; Engelbrecht, E. *Friends of the Law: Luther's Use of the Law for the Christian Life*. Concordia, 2011; Girgensohn, H. *Teaching Luther's Catechism*. Trans. J. Doberstein. Vol. 1. Muhlenberg, 1959; Peters, A. *Commentary on Luther's Catechisms: Ten Commandments*. Trans. H. Sonntag. Concordia, 2009.

JOHN T. PLESS

Tetzel, Johann

The Dominican friar Johann Tetzel (1465–1519), a preacher of indulgences in Germany, was an early opponent of Luther. Born in Saxony, Johann Tetzel began his studies at the University of Leipzig in 1482, entering the Dominican order shortly thereafter. In 1509 Cardinal Cajetan, master general of the Dominicans, appointed Tetzel as inquisitor of Poland, and later as inquisitor for Saxony. By that time Tetzel had acquired relative renown for his preaching of indulgences, a fame that in 1516 earned him an appointment by Cardinal Archbishop Albrecht of Mainz as subcommissioner of indulgences. In early 1517 Tetzel traveled through territories associated with that archbishop (Eisleben, Halle, and Zerbst) and preached a plenary indulgence, the proceeds of which would support the rebuilding of St. Peter's Basilica in Rome. It was Tetzel's stop in Jüterbog, a small town twenty-six miles (43 km) northeast of Wittenberg, that seems to have solidified Luther's criticisms of Tetzel's preaching and led to the eventual composition of the Ninety-Five Theses in October of that year. Luther was appalled by what he deemed to be Tetzel's overstatement of indulgences' power and efficacy and of the power claimed by the pope to grant them. Among others, thesis 27, in which Luther criticizes those who preach the ditty "As soon as the money clinks into the money chest, the soul flies out of purgatory," is usually considered to be aimed at Tetzel, though the phrase is not found in the Dominican's writings and in fact was also associated with the promulgation of the Jubilee Indulgence in 1503. Tetzel was the first to respond to the Ninety-Five Theses in his defense of countertheses, written by Konrad Wimpina, at the University of Frankfurt an der Oder, for which Tetzel received a doctorate in theology.

Luther followed up his Ninety-Five Theses with *A Sermon on Indulgences and Grace.* Published in early 1518, this pamphlet further criticizes exaggerations in Tetzel's preaching and the Wimpina theses. Tetzel responded to Luther with his *Vorlegung.* Earlier that year at a meeting of Dominicans, Tetzel heavily criticized Luther and encouraged his fellow Dominicans to petition Rome for Luther's excommunication. In May of 1518, arguably at the behest of these German Dominicans, the Roman juridical process against Luther commenced, though Tetzel would not live to see its culmination. The subject of libelous rumors of unchastity and embezzlement, Tetzel eventually withdrew to the monastery at Leipzig in late 1518, dying there the following year. Luther reportedly wrote a (no longer extant) letter of consolation to the ailing Tetzel and assured him that he (Tetzel) was not the cause of the indulgence controversy.

See also Luther's Roman Catholic Opponents; Ninety-Five Theses

Bibiography

Fabisch, P., and E. Iserloh, eds. *Dokumente zur Causa Lutheri (1517–1521).* Vol. 1. CCath 41. Aschendorff, 1988–91; Pastor, L. *The History of the Popes from the Close of the Middle Ages.* Vol. 7. Herder, 1908; Paulus, N. *Johann Tetzel, der Ablaßprediger.* Kirchheim, 1899; Wicks, J. "Roman Reactions to Luther: The First Year, 1518." *Catholic Historical Review* 69 (1983): 521–62.

Eric J. DeMeuse

Thailand

Compared to most Lutheran churches in Asia, the history of Lutheranism in Thailand is rather recent. Though Karl Gutzlaf, a German Lutheran, visited Thailand in 1828, the actual Lutheran mission enterprise in Thailand did not begin until the late 1960s, when Thailand first received Lutheran missionaries from the Marburger Mission. Not long after that, the ELCA's predecessor, the LCA, also initiated work. Both worked with the Church of Christ in Thailand, an indigenous ecumenical church body.

With the arrival of Emil K. Aasheim and Neil Peder Kjetsaa of the Norwegian Mission Society (NMS) in 1976, the NMS began its work in Thailand. Since these first two missionaries were transferred from Taiwan and Hong Kong, respectively, they were able to connect with the Chinese leadership of the Church of Christ in Thailand. However, after missionaries of the Finnish Evangelical Lutheran Mission (FELM) arrived in 1978, the

NMS and FELM reached an agreement to form Lutheran Mission in Thailand (LMT) with the objective of establishing one Lutheran church body in Thailand. Work among national Thais was difficult. After three years it was possible to hold the first baptism in the LMT. A series of consultations on cooperation between the Lutheran Mission in Thailand and LCMS missionaries led to an initial partnership for producing literature, including Luther's Small and Large Catechisms and the Augsburg Confession in Thai.

The ministry of the LMT continued with the goal of establishing the Evangelical Lutheran Church in Thailand (ELCT), formed in 1994. Banjob Kusawadee was the first bishop of ELCT. Despite slow growth and faced with the challenges of self-support, the ELCT was able to continue its ministries through around forty congregations and satellites. It reached tribal people in the northern and northeastern parts of the country. Its diaconal ministries among marginalized people were well received. Established before the ELCT, Luther Seminary in Thailand has been a key instrument in equipping national Lutherans in lay training, evangelism, and ministerial formation. The ELCT became a member of the LWF in 1995. The church continued its partnership with churches from Norway, Finland, Hong Kong, Japan, Singapore, Germany, and Australia. The church has around forty-five hundred members.

The goal of a single Lutheran Church did not materialize. The unsuccessful dialogue on the cooperation with the LMT had led the LCMS to develop its work into the Journey into Light organization in 1991. Its ministry includes radio programs, literature publication, congregational ministries, ministry to students, and so forth. Since the failure of the LMT and LCMS dialogue, other mission agencies also have come to work in Thailand, including the WELS mission, which focuses its work among tribal people in northern Thailand. More congregations were organized as they are moving toward establishing the Lutheran Evangelical Church in Thailand (LECT). The Norwegian Church Abroad and the Evangelical Lutheran Church in Canada also worked in Thailand.

Bibliography

Aageson, J., and A. Jacobson, eds. *The Future of Lutheranism in a Global Context*. Augsburg Fortress, 2007; Yee, E., and P. Rajashekar, eds. *Abundant Harvest: Stories of Asian Lutherans*. Lutheran University Press, 2006.

PONGSAK LIMTHONGVIRATN

Theological Education

Theological education is primarily, though not solely, concerned with the development of educated leaders for Christian communities. In the Lutheran context this has meant the organization of institutions and programs to educate candidates for the ministry and, to facilitate this, the development of professional theological teachers and scholars for such education. Lutheranism as a movement was born in a university setting, led by scholars such as Luther and Philip Melanchthon, and has always aspired to a high degree of theological training for its leaders, even if this has not always been achieved.

In the early church, leaders were often trained as "apprentices," tutored by local bishops or senior clergy, though some catechetical schools, such as in Alexandria or Rome, were established for a time. In the Middle Ages, this pattern of theological education continued. Schools were developed in monasteries or around the cathedrals. Eventually universities (derived from a Latin term for guilds) arose in Italy and especially in Paris, France, in the latter with faculties of theology. But the great majority of Christian clergy received at best a limited education, and many of them were essentially illiterate. Priests received whatever education they could get from other local priests or monasteries, which rarely went beyond rote memorization.

Luther's reform movement in the sixteenth century focused on the proclamation of the Word of God, and as such required theologically educated pastors, as well as lay Christians who were literate enough to read the Bible and to teach the catechism to their children. One of the major complaints of the reformers was the shocking theological ignorance and illiteracy of most priests and people, and they urged the development of schools to produce competent theological leaders. As Protestant churches were established in the Lutheran territories of Germany and Scandinavia through the middle of the sixteenth century, increased theological education for pastors became the standard. The goal was to have all pastors provided with a theological education in the Protestant universities, although this was not always possible, mainly because not all candidates had the basic education to prepare them for university. Still, the level of theological education was much improved over previous centuries.

The theological faculties at the universities in Protestant areas became an important part of the Lutheran tradition. Not only were they responsible for the theological education of pastors and teachers; they also came to operate, along with other clerical leaders, as the theological "magisterium" for the churches. The theological faculties worked to develop theological judgments on contested issues and to defend the Lutheran cause from attacks by other Christian traditions. Thus the sixteenth-century Roman Catholic Counter-Reformation also developed first-rate schools and universities across Europe. These institutions, established in part to counter the rise of Protestantism, sometimes put Protestant educational institutions on the defensive, needing to meet the challenge of their Roman Catholic rivals. Universities were developed in many of the German territories and in the Scandinavian kingdoms to provide theological education for pastors and teachers in those territories. Some of these universities also attracted Lutheran candidates from minority Lutheran populations in eastern and southern Europe. These universities were, to begin with, confessionally specific (Lutheran or Reformed), although there were some that eventually had parallel Protestant faculties and, much later, even parallel Protestant and Roman Catholic faculties.

By the seventeenth century, theological education focused on apologetics and dogmatics, in a period commonly known as the age of Orthodoxy, although many practical materials were also produced. Theologians most often lectured on systematic and exegetical themes. Indeed, the concern was to formulate correct doctrine, developed through academic disputation. Although later critics often called this a period of "sterile" doctrine, the sermons and other devotional literature produced have called this into question. Many theologians also produced a rich treasury of pastoral and devotional classics, as well as deeply spiritual poems and hymns.

In German-speaking lands, the Thirty Years' War, from 1618 to 1648, shook all aspects of life: the population was reduced by warfare, hunger, and disease to one-half or one-third of its previous numbers. At various times many schools and universities were damaged or destroyed, and the theological education of pastors and teachers was often disrupted. The hard-won gains in theological education from the previous century were reversed; yet at the level of university training, the integrity of the system remained relatively stable.

In the late seventeenth century the rise of Pietism brought about some shift in theological education away from dogmatics and apologetics. Pietist leaders, such as Philipp Jakob Spener in his *Pia Desideria*, pushed for ministerial candidates who were above all pious and believing, and insisted that their theological education be centered on the study of the Bible and on practical training for ministerial careers. In Germany, Pietism was centered on the newly established University of Halle (founded in 1694), which, through the work of August Hermann Francke, embodied this new vision of theological education, and which also began to train missionaries for the spread of the gospel. It became normal for ministerial candidates to graduate from one of the universities, although in many territories church officials also insisted on additional training and examinations in the arts of practical ministry.

In the eighteenth century many faculties of the European universities came under the influence of the Enlightenment, with its stress on the use of reason in theology, also moving away from confessional dogmatics and apologetics. This new approach viewed theology as a "scientific" discipline, apart from confessional specificity. The European theological faculties were divided over this new approach: some embraced it while others tried to maintain the traditional confessional grounding for theological education. The growing trend toward religious rationalism and naturalism sparked countertrends in the later eighteenth century and especially in the nineteenth, when a neo-confessional revival sought to recover traditional Lutheran approaches to theology. The result was mixed. As a reaction against a perceived movement toward theological liberalism, a number of "free" Lutheran theological schools were established in Germany and the Nordic lands to provide an alternative university education for ministerial candidates.

While European Lutheran churches have generally maintained the requirement of theological study at the university level for their ministerial candidates, many have also developed additional experiences in theological education for them before ordination. Many churches require candidates to study at a pastoral seminary (for a year or more) beyond their university study, as well as a pastoral internship before they are ordained. Starting in the nineteenth century, Lutherans also began missionary training schools, principally for theological education for those seeking to serve as missionaries and theological leaders in areas outside the European churches themselves. The presence of Lutherans in some areas of eastern Europe resulted both in the establishment of theological schools and, beginning already during the Reformation, in the sending of ministerial candidates to German or Baltic lands for study.

Lutheran immigration to North America began in the eighteenth century, with a flow of Germans (and some Danes and Swedes) to the new areas that would become the United States and Canada. This migration was often not organized, so that groups of Lutherans would eventually develop and form congregations, but often without pastoral leadership. The earliest Lutheran pastors in North America were sent from Europe to minister to these congregations, but there was a chronic shortage of pastors and many clerical imposters. Relying on European-educated pastors in North America was not always possible, especially during and after the Revolutionary War, so Lutherans were forced to improvise to provide for ministerial education. They relied on an apprenticeship model of theological education, where candidates for ministry would learn theology and practical ministerial skills from an established pastor. Once the candidate was deemed ready, he would undergo an examination by the local Lutheran synod and, if acceptable, would be ordained.

With the growth of American Lutheranism this process proved to be inadequate, and by the beginning of the nineteenth century these Lutherans began to form their own seminaries, self-standing educational institutions for theological education. The European model of theological education through established universities was not possible in the United States. Instead, seminaries most resembled the European mission schools. Although they aspired to the academic standards of the European system, the pressing need for pastors and the poor educational background of many ministerial candidates meant that their theological education was uneven at best. Many seminaries were forced to open academies to prepare students with remedial instruction, and a number of these schools would eventually become their own colleges. The transition to the use of English called for development of theological and educational resources in that new language. Most groups of immigrant Lutherans formed their own denominations and seminaries, so that the number of Lutheran seminaries in America multiplied. Lutheran pastors were also sent from European seminaries and mission schools, such as Neuendettelsau, Brekkum, and Hermannsburg in Germany, and Alhberg and Fjellstedt in Sweden.

In the twentieth century, American Lutheran seminaries were strengthened and became more professional. The general requirement was that students would have an undergraduate degree, and eventually the seminary degree (which traditionally was called a bachelor of divinity) was renamed a master's degree, with three years of academic study and (after World War II) a one-year practical internship as a norm. As the various Lutheran denominations merged, there were corresponding mergers of seminaries, reducing the overall number. As of 2016, there are about twenty Lutheran seminaries in North America, although some of them are the institutions of very small Lutheran denominations. The twenty-first century has seen the establishment of a few independent Lutheran seminaries that offer theological training through distance education. Many established Lutheran seminaries have also developed forms of distance theological education.

European Lutherans also immigrated to Africa, Australia, and Latin America, and formed church bodies there. Their experience in theological education and the development of pastors has largely paralleled the North American situation, where the supply of European pastors was inadequate and there was a need for local options. In Latin America the eventual transition from the European languages to Spanish or Portuguese also reinforced this need. Seminaries were formed in Australia, Brazil, and Argentina; elsewhere in Latin America and the Caribbean Lutheran pastors were educated in pan-Protestant seminaries.

With the great expansion of Lutheran missions in the last two centuries, there was a widespread and urgent need for theological education for the new Lutheran churches in the Global South. The immediate need was to train Christians to become teachers, catechists, and evangelists so as to spread the gospel in the local languages, and missionaries quickly set up such schools within their territories. Some of the earliest of these were in India and China, soon joined by schools in Africa and the rest of Asia. The initial need for basic theological education was soon expanded, and eventually the schools began to educate pastors and other church leaders, who would take over the leadership of the church bodies with the transition to independence. The rapid growth of Lutheranism in the Global South, especially in Africa, has strained the resources of these theological seminaries as they attempt to educate enough pastors and leaders for their burgeoning congregations.

See also Apologetics; Education; University of Wittenberg in the Sixteenth Century

Bibliography

Appold, K. G. "Academic Life and Teaching in Post-Reformation Germany." In *Lutheran Ecclesiastical Culture, 1550–1675*, ed. R. Kolb, 65–115. Brill, 2008; Appold, K. G. *Orthodoxie als Konsensbildung: Das theologische Disputationswesen an der Universität Wittenbeg zwischen 1570 und 1710*. Mohr Siebeck, 2004; Cherry, C. *Hurrying toward Zion: Universities, Divinity Schools, and American Protestantism*. Indiana University Press, 1995; Dingel, I., and G. Wartenberg, eds. *Die theologische Fakultät Wittenberg 1502 bis 1602*. Evangelische Verlagsanstalt, 2002; Gonzáles, J. *The History of Theological Education*. Abingdon, 2015; Hall, S. G., and Martin Brecht. "Theologiestudium." *TRE* 33 (2007): 349–59; Howard, T. A. *Protestant Theology and the Making of the Modern German University*. Oxford University Press, 2009; Jorgenson, C. S., et al. "Theological Schools." In *The Encyclopedia of the Lutheran Church*, ed. J. Bodensieck, 3:2341–84. Augsburg, 1965; Miller, G. T. *Piety and Profession: American Protestant Theological Education, 1870–1970*. Eerdmans, 2007.

MARK A. GRANQUIST

Theological Prolegomena

The term "prolegomena" comes from the Greek *prolegomenon*, which derives from *prolegein* (*pro* + *legein*), meaning "to say beforehand." Accordingly, theological prolegomena say what theology is about: its nature, scope, and task. Prolegomena typically address the relationship between the natural and revealed knowledge of God and the boundary between theology and philosophy generally (Pannenberg 25–48). Theological prolegomena deal with epistemological, ontological, semantic, and methodological issues. What can be known about God, and how is it best known? What is the being of God, and how can humans properly know and speak about this being? What is meant by language about God, and how does it apply to God? What procedures should be employed in knowing and speaking of God?

Although Martin Luther did not write explicit theological prolegomena, his late medieval philosophical education, combined with the developing humanist thought, did sensitize him to semantic, ontological, and epistemological concerns and to the task of drawing the proper boundary between philosophy and theology (White 297–99). He knew Aristotle well, especially as he was interpreted through Luther's late medieval nominalist professors Jodocus Truttvetter and Bartholomaus Arnold von Usingen. In his many disputations Luther showed considerable analytical skill in identifying the proper meaning of theological terms while manifesting concern always for the proper *modus loquendi theologus* (theological manner of speaking) (Grane 146–51). In his 1518 Heidelberg Disputation, Luther decried those who would misuse Aristotle for theological purposes, arguing instead that a correct understanding of Aristotle displays the radical difference of the theological and philosophical realms, a discontinuity that Luther contended was the appropriate context for understanding God's action in word and sacrament (Dieter 431–631).

Lutheran theologians are divided as to whether Lutheran theology should have prolegomena. Some believe that enunciating prolegomena is entirely misguided. Steven Paulson declares, "There are no prolegomena to Lutheran theology except the *foolishness* of preaching" (62). More subtly, Robert Jenson denies theological prolegomena as "axioms and warrants needed to set specifically theological cognition in motion," and instead

conceives it simply as an "advanced description of the enterprise" (3). Rejecting "the Enlightenment's elevation of the Greek element of our thinking to be unilateral judge of the whole," Jenson declares that Greek philosophy is "simply the theology of the historically particular Olympian-Parmenidean religion, later shared with the wider Mediterranean cultic world" (9–10).

To reject theological prolegomena on these grounds is problematic, however, since the philosophical trajectory beginning as "Olympian-Parmenidean religion" has become highly developed and deeply integrated with mathematics and logic, the natural and social sciences, and Western ideas about truth generally. Accordingly, it is difficult to detach theological claims and their evaluation from the assumptions, presuppositions, canons, and language constituting Western rationality generally. Moreover, although Lutheran theology may not need prolegomena to establish conditions for properly engaging in theological reflection, prolegomena nonetheless are often employed in advancing theology's relevance for our contemporary situation.

Many Lutheran theologians believe it fruitful to engage in theological prolegomena. Robert D. Preus (1924–95) maintained that prolegomena properly "lay the ground rules for a theologian in constructing a Christian dogmatics" by establishing "a substructure and starting point for the work of presenting Christian doctrine in the church" (73). David Lumpp adds that theological prolegomena articulate a theology's purpose or agenda, its theme or core doctrinal assertions, its authority or criteria, and its theological method (21). Echoing arguments already found in all editions of Philip Melanchthon's *Loci communes theologici*, Lumpp insists that since every discipline has a purpose, a starting point, rules of proceeding, and a set of core assertions, it is difficult to see how theology as a discipline can escape theological prolegomena. The question is whether the prolegomena will be explicit or remain implicit.

Many important Lutheran dogmaticians clearly believed that explicit prolegomena are useful in doing theology effectively. Pannenberg (28) provides the following list of theological prolegomena: (1) the concept of theology, (2) the notion of the Christian religion as the general object of theology, (3) Scripture as the guiding principle of theology, (4) the articles of faith, and (5) the use of reason.

Johann Gerhard (1582–1637) engages in a theological prolegomenon when carefully distinguishing between teaching drawn from God's Word, which instructs in true faith—theology abstractly considered—and the divine disposition (Latin: *habitus*) conferred by the Holy Spirit to the believer, making the acquired knowledge the desire of the heart—theology concretely considered. About this Robert Scharlemann wrote: "The two are interdependent. Nothing can really be concretely effective if it is not objectively true; and everything which is objectively true (that is, drawn from Scripture) has the latent power of being concretely effective" (27–28). In an age when the authority and perspicuity of Scripture have been deeply challenged, preaching and teaching without explicit prolegomena risks separating the concrete effectiveness of the gospel message from its objective truth.

Seventeenth-century dogmatics generally operated with the principles of the *principium cognoscendi*, knowledge of divine things grounded in Scripture, and the *principium essendi*, the being of God grounding all things, including knowledge (Muller). Epistemological and ontological issues remain crucial in articulating Lutheran theological prolegomena today.

Contemporary cultural and intellectual ethos may relegate talk of God to the realm of subjective feeling and value, and also assume that "to be real is to have causal powers" (Kim 348). The idealism of the nineteenth century sanctioned religious reverence for the ideas of goodness, beauty, and historical progress, but in the West the horrors of the twentieth century, and its concomitant intellectual movements, have produced impatience with theology and religion generally. People want to know what the church *does* that is not done better by secular institutions. What does theological discourse mean or do that cannot be meant or done by other kinds of discourse? Ought theological discourse be eliminated in favor of language referring to real objects, states of affairs, properties, or events in the world? Should it be retained even though it is reducible to other discourses either logically or ontologically? Or might such language refer to a sui generis divine realm?

For many today, explicit theological prolegomena must operate to bring to awareness the dominant intellectual and cultural trajectory, which assumes that God is not and cannot be a causally relevant entity. The Enlightenment has bequeathed to the present these three philosophical default presuppositions:

- The term "God" does not refer to a being that exists apart from human awareness, perception, conception, and language. Whatever is meant by the term "God," it does not denote a being that exists on its own apart from human being (presupposition of theological irrealism).
- Since there is no divine being existing apart from human being, talk about God actually does other linguistic "work" than referring to this being (presupposition of semantic irrealism).
- Since the physical universe is causally closed, there is no action on events and entities in the universe not explicable in terms of the actions of other physical events and entities within the universe. Talk of God thus connects to human value, not to nature in itself (presupposition of divine causal isolation).

Scripture and the Lutheran confessions do not directly engage these three presuppositions because none of the three had yet been generally posed. Educated people in the West today, however, are likely to be drawn to all three. Since reading the Lutheran confessions with irrealist presuppositions may distort the meaning of the texts, theological prolegomena become necessary in order to interpret the texts in ways consonant with their original context. The following three principles constitute a counterpoint to contemporary irrealist assumptions; each acts as an interpretive control on whole classes of theological statements:

- *Theological realism.* God exists apart from human awareness, perception, conception, and language. This assertion is compatible with the statement that the contour of the divine cannot be known. Theological realism does not assert knowledge of the *quiddity* (whatness) of God, but merely acknowledges the *existence* of a divine Other, not merely a phenomenological experience of human beings.
- *Semantic realism.* While language cannot describe the divine aseity (see preceding principle), it nonetheless refers to the divine entity and to divine properties, events, and states of affairs. A prolegomenon addressing this issue offers an interpretation of the terms and predicates of theological statements in ways that recall their interpretation in the sixteenth century.
- *Theophysical causation.* While theologians may not be able to specify the "causal joint" by which the divine interacts in the world as Creator, Redeemer, and Sanctifier, these prolegomena explicitly assert the possibility of causal connectedness. If the causal closure of the physical holds, then divine action is precluded. Without theophysical causation, it is argued, there simply is no way that God qua God can actually save human beings. (One could deny theophysical causation and cogently hold that the idea of God has causal power.)

The question of Lutheran theological prolegomena connects to the issue of whether a point of contact between God and the world aids in gospel proclamation and hearing. Insofar as gospel empowerment connects to its truth, some theologians contend that theological prolegomena are entirely appropriate.

A Savior without causal power clearly cannot save.

See also Apologetics; Enlightenment; Lutheran Orthodoxy; Natural Theology; Philosophy

Bibliography

Dieter, T. *Der junge Luther und Aristoteles: Eine historisch-sytematische Untersuchung zum Verhältnis von Theologie und Philosophie.* De Gruyter, 2001; Grane, L. *Modus Loquendi Theologicus: Luthers Kampf um die Erneuerung der Theologie (1515–1518).* Brill, 1975; Jenson, R. *Systematic Theology.* Vol. 1, *The Triune God.* Oxford University Press, 1977; Kim, J. *Supervenience and Mind: Selected Philosophical Essays.* Cambridge University Press, 1993; Lumpp, D. *First Things First: A Primer in Lutheran Theological Prolegomena.* Concordia Seminary Press, 2012; Muller, R. *Dictionary of Latin and Greek Theological Terms: Drawn Principally from Protestant Scholastic Theology.* Baker, 1985; Pannenberg, W. *Systematic Theology.* Trans. G. Bromiley. Vol. 1. Eerdmans, 1988; Paulson, S. *Lutheran Theology.* T&T Clark, 2011; Preus, R. *The Theology of Post-Reformation Lutheranism.* Concordia, 1970; Scharlemann, R. *Thomas Aquinas and John Gerhard.* Yale University Press, 1964; White, G. *Luther as Nominalist: A Study of the Logical Methods Used in Martin Luther's Disputations in the Light of Their Medieval Background.* Luther-Agricola-Society, 1994.

DENNIS BIELFELDT

Theology of the Cross

Luther first expounded a theology of the cross (*theologia crucis*), which advocates that God's revelation comes under the appearance of the opposite, when he was called by his mentor Johann Staupitz, the vicar of the German Congregation of Augustinian Eremites, to explain his new approach to theology in Heidelberg. This followed only months after the beginning of the indulgence controversy, in which Luther, on behalf of the spiritual and temporal well-being of common people, protested the sale of indulgences and in the process challenged Albrecht of Mainz and the chief indulgence commissioner, John Tetzel, to change the shape of such preaching. Luther prepared twenty-eight theological and twelve philosophical theses for disputation of the Augustinians meeting in Heidelberg on April 26, 1518. The resulting Heidelberg Disputation, presenting Luther's theology of the cross, provides not only a research program opposed to the Scholastic theology of the day (what

Luther terms a "theology of glory" [*theologia gloriae*]), but also a template for his further research and an outlook in which the Christian life is not something that we do but instead is something that is done to us. The Christian life is less about our progress in holiness and more about God's work of making us to be people of faith. The theology of the cross also occurs in the *Explanations of the Ninety-Five Theses* (LW 31:225), a far more widely distributed tract, published in the summer of 1518.

At its core the Heidelberg Disputation is an assault on the late medieval view of salvation taught by Gabriel Biel and others, which affirmed that God does not withhold his grace from those who do what they are capable of doing. Luther challenges Biel's view head-on in thesis 16: "The person who believes that he can obtain grace by doing what is in him adds sin to sin so that he becomes doubly guilty." Late medieval nominalists, like Biel, taught that God has established a covenant (*pactum*) with humanity, in which God has agreed to give his saving grace to those who do their best. Luther's position contradicted Biel's view of this covenant with humanity as based on human cooperation and merit.

Luther calls this a "theology of glory" because it focuses on the Christian life as an agenda that human beings fulfill. In contrast, the theology of the cross is God's program to unbelieving sinners who ultimately must despair of themselves (thesis 18). To remake such sinners into people of faith, God destroys one's most treasured defenses and the convictions that sustain human self-righteousness before God. Hence, God reveals himself, but only paradoxically, as concealed in the cross: God's wisdom is granted in foolishness, his power in weakness, his glory in lowliness, and his life in the death of his Son (cf. 1 Cor. 1:18–25). Luther describes his theses as "theological paradoxes," carefully designed to "attack and vex Scholastic theology." In a word, the flip side of God's gracious generosity is the painful exposure of human powerlessness and impotence, an experience that human beings want neither to admit nor to endure. The roots of this paradoxical language in Luther come from Johannes Tauler (ca. 1300–1361) and the anonymous devotional treatise *Theologia Deutsch*, which Luther had edited only the year before. But the radicality of this approach was unique to Luther.

Luther's theological approach was based on his study of Scripture as augmented by his studies in humanism and Augustine. When Moses requested to see God's own glory, God granted Moses nothing other than God's own backside (*posteriora Dei*; Exod. 33:18–23), for no one can see God's glory and live. Similarly, following Paul in Rom. 1:20–32, knowledge of God on the basis of God's works in nature does not catapult us into the inner workings of divine mystery, but instead condemns us as self-centered, as failing to give God his proper due.

The theological theses move from a discussion about God's law (thesis 1) to one of God's love (thesis 28). The overall outline of the theses examines (1) the nature and worth of human works over against the question of sin (theses 1–12), (2) the impotence of human free will to avoid sin (theses 13–18), (3) the divide between the theologian of the cross and the theologian of glory (theses 19–24), and (4) God's love in Christ as a creative act that brings believers into being (theses 22–28). In contrast to the *pactum* theology, Luther contended that sinners misunderstand the role of human works and God's work. In human estimation, human works are splendid and good (thesis 3), while God's works, grounded in Christ's suffering and death, are deformed and bad (thesis 4). But Luther asserts that, in truth, human works are "mortal sins" (thesis 3), while God's works are "immortal merits" (thesis 4). Thus it is clear for Luther that appearance and reality do not correspond with respect to human potential. In light of God's work, one's identity is not based on actualizing one's potential before God (*coram deo*, "in God's presence"), but on God's claiming the sinner, the ugly, the despised, even (especially) what is nothing. The paradox of

God's love, in contrast to human love and virtue, is that God loves the unlovable, is attracted to what is ugly, and desires the worthless. Thus thesis 28 reads: "The love of God does not find, but creates, that which is pleasing to it. The love of man comes into being through that which is pleasing to it."

Luther thus unmasks a theology of glory as driving a wedge between appearance and reality. God's law appears to be a means to advancement but in reality threatens the pilgrim (*viator*) (thesis 1). Human works appear attractive but in reality are mortal sins (thesis 3). The works of God appear unattractive but in reality are eternal merits (thesis 4). The will appears to be free and potent but in reality produces only mortal sin (thesis 13). It appears that if God gives humans such directives as are enshrined in the law, then this must entail that humans are able to fulfill them. In reality, the law proves to be undoable in thought, word, and deed. It thwarts sinners. Hence righteousness in the presence of God is something that people cannot obtain by doing righteous deeds. Instead, the righteousness that saves is something that people receive through the advocacy of a defender, Jesus Christ.

Thesis 28 states that God's love creates that which is pleasing to God and thus implies a "passive righteousness" *coram deo*. In contrast to the Aristotelian-inspired Scholastic views of righteousness, in which right deeds lead to righteous habits and thus ultimately produce a righteous character, Luther contends that righteousness before God is passive. While such reasoning about an active righteousness is appropriate, beneficial, and necessary in civil matters, Luther claimed that it had no bearing on one's standing before God. Scholars debate as to when Luther's Evangelical breakthrough happened. While it is possible that a fully developed view of what the later Reformation tradition would term forensic justification is not present in the Heidelberg Disputation, there can be no question that Luther's argument here is a crucial step on the way to this insight.

Pastorally speaking, Luther knew that humans run from their crosses. In fact, however, suffering and pain are the way by which God breaks down self-centeredness so that humans can actually rely on God for their lives and well-being. The correlate of a theology of the cross is not one of glory, but instead of resurrection. It is because God raises the dead that people of faith can be confident in entrusting their lives into God's care. As the Scholastics taught, there is a sense in which people of faith are properly ordered to the divine, but it is not the path of exercising virtues that deifies them. Rather, God's alien work (*opus alienum*) of putting to death through the law breaks down human defenses such that people can live by sheer trust in God, thereby come to trust God as their only good, and be restored to this creation as created good.

Challenging the theology of glory makes sense within a schema of merit. Luther claims that genuine faith must endure being contradicted by both reason and experience and so fix its sight on the word of promise (a point made especially strongly in the *Explanations of the Ninety-Five Theses*). The paradoxical upshot is that God is mighty in human weakness, imparts life even in its destruction, and grants grace by judgment. For Luther, God imposes suffering on sinners in order to dislodge them from their own self-trust and let them live from trust in God: to flee from God (as wrath) to God (as mercy).

Only in the twentieth century has Luther's theology of the cross begun to be fully articulated by Lutherans and others. This is due in part to the renewal in Luther studies begun in the late nineteenth century but also especially to the study of Walter von Loewenich. Post-Reformation Lutheran theology separated Luther's theology of the cross from his theology of the Word and in the process lost the theology of the cross. Philosophers, such as G. W. F. Hegel (1770–1831), transformed the theology of the cross into a metaphysic, what Oswald Bayer calls a "natural theology of the cross," which on the basis of Jesus's crucifixion in history sees God's being as a process unfolding itself in the history of the cosmos and human suffering, but with the goal of God's own self-realization and ultimate human enlightenment. In various degrees this Hegelian perspective has been appropriated by contemporary theologians such as Jürgen Moltmann (b. 1926), Eberhard Jüngel (b. 1934), Wolfhart Pannenberg (1928–2014), and Robert Jenson (b. 1930) as a theodicy. Yet having dealt with tremendous loss due to the two world wars, genocides, and environmental destruction on a massive scale, some theologians (Gerhard Forde, Oswald Bayer, Douglas John Hall) have returned to a theology of the cross in recognition of God's judgment on human pride but also in confident trust in God's life-giving Word of promise and renewal.

See also Atonement; Biel, Gabriel; Christology; Forde, Gerhard; Free Will; Justification; Late Medieval Nominalism; Law and Gospel; Luther's Breakthrough; Predestination; Twofold Righteousness

Bibliography

Forde, G. *On Being a Theologian of the Cross: Reflections on Luther's Heidelberg Disputation, 1518*. Eerdmans, 1997; Kolb, R. *Martin Luther: Confessor of the Faith*. Oxford University Press, 2009; Lienhard, M. *Luther: Witness to Jesus Christ*. Trans. E. Robertson. Augsburg, 1982; Loewenich, W. von. *Luther's Theology of the Cross*. Trans. H. Bouman. Augsburg, 1976; Luther, M. LW 31:37–70; 31:225; McGrath, A. *Luther's Theology of the Cross*. Blackwell, 1985; Prenter, R. *Luther's Theology of the Cross*. Fortress, 1971; Sasse, H. *Briefe an lutherische Pastoren* 18 (October 1951). ET as "Luther's Theology of the Cross," trans. A. J. Koelpin, 10 pages. http://www.wls essays.net/bitstream/handle/123456789/1986/SasseCross .pdf?sequence=1&isAllowed=y.

MARK C. MATTES

Thielicke, Helmut

The German systematic theologian, ethicist, and apologist Helmut Thielicke (1908–86) was also a popular preacher. Born in Wuppertal, Thielicke's childhood was marked by sickness and deprivation associated with World War I. Illness would also interrupt his studies at Greifswald, where he came under the influence of the New Testament exegete Julius Schniewind (1883–1948) and the Luther scholar Rudolf Herrmann (1887–1962). Schniewind especially would leave a lasting imprint on Thielicke as both a theologian and a preacher. From Greifswald, Thielicke continued his studies at Bonn, where he had his initial contact with Karl Barth (1886–1968) in 1932. He successfully completed his habilitation at Erlangen with Paul Althaus (1888–1966). In 1936–40 Thielicke was on the faculty at Heidelberg until dismissed for his opposition to the Nazi Party.

Unable to secure another teaching position, Thielicke served in the army for a short time and then, as part of the Confessing Church, was a pastor in Ravensburg and theological adviser to Bishop Theophil Wurm (1868–1953) in Stuttgart. During this period, as Thielicke faced the devastation of war, he wrote *Death and Life*. After the war, Thielicke was called to Tübingen as professor of systematic theology. In 1954 Thielicke moved to Hamburg, where he became instrumental in founding the theological faculty at the university. Thielicke remained in Hamburg for the rest of his life, and here (as in Stuttgart) he also achieved fame as a preacher. Worn down by the student revolt of 1968, Thielicke retired from the faculty. In his retirement, Thielicke engaged in apologetics, most notably his Faith Information Project, which sought to engage religious questions of young people. He lectured internationally in the United States, South America, Africa, Australia, and Asia, also writing extensively on these experiences.

As a systematic theologian, Thielicke sought to address contemporary culture by "actualizing" rather than "accommodating" the biblical message. Fundamental for Thielicke's methodology was the distinction between "Cartesian" and "non-Cartesian" theologies. Thielicke maintained that "Cartesian" approaches were essentially anthropocentric, focusing on the person being addressed rather than the content of the message. Non-Cartesian approaches are essentially conservative in that they insist on the integrity of the message and endeavor to actualize it in proclamation. Thielicke champions and demonstrates the non-Cartesian approach in his three-volume dogmatics, *The*

Christian Faith, in apologetic pieces written against Rudolf Bultmann (1884–1976), and in his sermons.

A major achievement was Thielicke's *Theological Ethics*. Here Thielicke seeks to articulate an evangelical ethics that is also eschatological in that the believer lives on "the borderline," in an existence where there is both continuity and discontinuity between the old and new aeons.

Thielicke recognized that theology serves proclamation, and this is demonstrated in his own preaching. Thoughtful, exegetically informed, and warmly evangelical, Thielicke's sermon series on the early chapters of Genesis, the Apostles' Creed, the Lord's Prayer, the Sermon on the Mount, and the parables were widely read and cited. Thielicke demonstrated that intellectual rigor and the life of faith need not be divorced. His work in homiletics, especially his study of Charles Spurgeon, sought to assist preachers in engaging their hearers with the biblical text in a way that was vibrant and relevant.

See also Apologetics; Confessing Church; Preaching

Bibliography

Pless, J. "Helmut Thielicke." In *Twentieth-Century Lutheran Theologians*, ed. M. Mattes. Vandenhoeck & Ruprecht, 2013; Thielicke, H. *The Evangelical Faith*. Trans. G. Bromiley. 3 vols. Eerdmans, 1974; Thielicke, H. *Notes from a Wayfarer*. Trans. D. Law. Paragon House, 1995; Thielicke, H. *Theological Ethics*. Trans. W. Lazareth. Fortress, 1966; Thielicke, H. *The Waiting Father: Sermons on the Parables of Jesus*. Trans. J. Doberstein. Harper & Row, 1959.

JOHN T. PLESS

Thirty Years' War

A prolonged period of political and military conflict in central Europe (1618–48), the Thirty Years' War killed at least five million people and left an enduring mark on European politics, society, and religion. The Thirty Years' War has been depicted as the culmination of a century of "religious wars" in Europe, which began with conflicts between Roman Catholics and Protestants in the Holy Roman Empire (HRE) and intensified in France's Wars of Religion (1562–98) and the Dutch Revolt (1568–1609). Although the ostensible cause of the Thirty Years' War was ongoing theological and jurisdictional conflicts among rival confessions (esp. the unresolved question of Reformed Christians' status in the empire), the quarrel was intensified by Hapsburg attempts to consolidate and assert control, by unresolved questions about the empire's constitution, and by a shift in the balance of power among European states. The war was fought mostly within the HRE but involved armies, alliances, and personalities from neighboring Bohemia, Denmark, Sweden, Spain, the Netherlands, northern Italy, and France. It was thus a Europe-wide conflict, fought with weapons, strategies, and warfare casualties unknown in the Middle Ages. The negotiations and settlement that concluded the war (the Treaty of Westphalia, 1648) reaffirmed the language tolerating adherents of the Augsburg Confession expressed in the Peace of Augsburg (1555), strengthened the empire's constitution, and established a new theoretical basis for international relations.

Causes. When Holy Roman Emperor Charles V abdicated in 1556, the powerful Hapsburg dynasty split into Spanish and Austrian lines. Charles V's son, Philip II, ruled Spain, the Netherlands, and Spanish possessions in the New World; Charles V's brother, Ferdinand, ruled Austria, Hungary, and Bohemia and was elected Holy Roman emperor. The Hapsburgs remained the dominant political family in central Europe, but the region was a swirling amalgamation of political and religious affiliations. In the HRE, the Peace of Augsburg stipulated that each prince should determine the religion in his own territory, as long as the prince selected one of the two approved faiths—Roman Catholicism or Lutheranism based on the Augsburg Confession. In the second half of the sixteenth century, Jesuit missionaries and other advocates for Roman Catholicism worked to reevangelize areas that had adopted Protestant reforms. A new generation of princes also embraced the Reformed faith (Calvinism), introducing Reformed doctrines and worship into the Palatinate (1561–76, 1583–1623) and Brandenburg (1613). As a result of these developments, the Lutherans were weakened politically in the HRE, despite a productive period of peacemaking related to the conciliatory Formula of Concord (1577). To protect Protestant interests, a group of Lutheran and Reformed rulers met in 1608 near Nördlingen to found the Protestant Union, a defensive league designed to protect Protestant lands from the emperor and others who would threaten the public peace. In Munich in 1609, a large number of southern German Catholic princes assembled to form the Catholic League, which pledged a similar purpose.

Although Lutheran, Roman Catholic, and Reformed leaders were preparing for military confrontation, a broader European war was still not inevitable. The Peace of Augsburg had kept the peace in the HRE for over fifty years, and most leaders still looked to the emperor and the constitution to resolve tensions and abate religious hostilities. The chief causes of the wider military conflict were related to the Hapsburg dynasty's ambition to crush regional rivals, dominate the empire's structures, and reestablish Roman Catholicism. The slide toward war began toward the end of the reign of Emperor Rudolf II (r. 1576–1612), who showed increasing signs of mental illness and struggled with his brother Matthias (r. 1612–19) over control of Bohemia, Hungary, Moravia, and the Austrian lands. Matthias eventually set his brother aside and then moved to increase his control over the bureaucratic institutions of the empire. When Matthias promoted his cousin and heir, the future Ferdinand II (r. 1619–37), to be king of Bohemia in 1617, the maneuver proved inflammatory. Ferdinand was a committed Catholic who hoped to severely restrict the rights of Protestants in Bohemia. When several hundred Protestant representatives assembled in Prague in May 1618 and threw two prominent Catholic officials out a window, this defiant act of defenestration led to a wider rebellion of

Protestants in Bohemia. The revolt was seen by the Hapsburgs as a threat to their authority and the discretion of a king to determine the religion in his territory. However, the Bohemian Protestants moved forward and boldly elected Frederick V, the Elector of the Palatinate and a Calvinist, to be the new king of Bohemia. The Protestants also issued a general call to all enemies of the Hapsburg dynasty to fight along with the Bohemians in their holy cause. The regional conflict quickly drew in partisans from both sides and plunged the empire into political and military crisis.

Phases of the War. The war can be divided into three main phases. The first phase of the war (1618–30) is characterized by Catholic imperial victories and an unwillingness of all Protestants (esp. the Elector of Saxony) to join in the fray. Unfortunately for the Protestants, the new king of Bohemia, Frederick V, was quickly defeated in 1620 by Johann Tserclaes, Count of Tilly, at the Battle of White Mountain near Prague. This defeat earned Frederick V the nickname "the Winter King," as he effectively ruled Bohemia only during the winter of 1619–20. Ferdinand II then became Holy Roman emperor and reestablished himself as the king of Bohemia, where he instituted Catholic rule and worship. In 1625 King Christian IV of Denmark entered the war in support of the Protestant side, but he was defeated by Tilly's Catholic League and the forces of Albrecht von Wallenstein, an accomplished Bohemian general who joined in support of the emperor. In 1629 the emperor issued the Edict of Restitution, which demanded that Protestants return all properties that had been taken from Catholics in the HRE since the Treaty of Passau in 1552. In addition, the edict prohibited the Reformed religion in the empire, which had been growing as an alternative to Lutheranism.

The second phase of the war (1630–35) was marked by a number of Protestant victories and the emergence of a Protestant military champion, King Gustavus Adolphus of Sweden. In 1630 Emperor Ferdinand dismissed

Wallenstein and curtailed his army. Gustavus Adolphus then brought a large army into the empire and defeated Tilly's imperial army at Breitenfeld in September 1631. Gustavus Adolphus marched into southern Germany, led the Protestants to a string of victories, yet was mortally wounded near Leipzig at the Battle of Lützen (November 1632). Sweden remained in the war until its conclusion, supported by the Dutch, but the Protestant side had lost the initiative. In September 1634 the Catholic imperial army defeated the combined Protestant forces decisively at the Battle of Nördlingen.

In the third phase of the war (1635–48), both sides appeared to be weary and disorganized, but the fighting continued when France directly entered the conflict in 1635, declaring war on the Spanish Hapsburgs. Although France was predominantly Catholic, the French supported the Protestant cause because they feared growing Hapsburg dominance in Europe. This phase of the war was the most destructive in the German lands, as Protestant and Catholic forces swept back and forth through the empire, destroying buildings, plundering the population, and spreading terror, disease, and death. In 1643 some of the parties initiated peace negotiations, which carried on for five years. Finally diplomats met in the Westphalian cities of Münster and Osnabrück and produced a comprehensive settlement known as the Peace of Westphalia (1648). By June 1650 the conflict was finally over, and the last surviving armies had been demobilized and compensated.

The peace settlement reinforced the multireligious composition of the HRE as stipulated by the Peace of Augsburg. The Reformed faith (Calvinism) was also added to the list of officially accepted confessions. The most important change in religion was that the normative date of the settlement was set as 1624. Any conversions or reinstatements that happened before that date were considered to be valid; any that came after 1624 were allowed for the territorial rulers, but the common people were not required to convert to match the religion of the prince. European rulers were forced to recognize the sovereignty of other states over the long term, which curtailed Hapsburg dreams of territorial dominance. A small selection of territories and principalities also changed hands in the empire, especially where there were long-standing border disputes. One of the war's most important legacies was the adoption of the conference system of resolving disputes and managing diplomatic relations; it became a distinctive feature of future peacemaking processes. Within the HRE, the imperial constitution was strengthened, and the characteristic distributed system of governance was preserved, remaining intact until the dissolution of the empire in 1806 as a consequence of the Napoleonic Wars.

See also Holy Roman Empire; Peace of Augsburg; Smalcald War

Bibliography

Asbach, O., and P. Schröder. *The Ashgate Research Companion to the Thirty Years' War*. Ashgate, 2014; Asbach, O., and P. Schröder. *War, the State and International Law in Seventeenth-Century Europe*. Ashgate, 2010; Asch, R. G. *The Thirty Years War: The Holy Roman Empire and Europe, 1618–48*. St. Martin's Press, 1997; Brady, T. A., Jr. *German Histories in the Age of Reformations, 1400–1650*. Cambridge University Press, 2009; Burkhardt, J. *Der Dreißigjährige Krieg*. Suhrkamp, 1992; Evans, R. J. W., M. Schaich, and P. H. Wilson, eds. *The Holy Roman Empire, 1495–1806*. Oxford University Press, 2011; Medick, H., and B. Marschke. *Experiencing the Thirty Years War: A Brief History with Documents*. Bedford / St. Martin's, 2013; Whaley, J. *Germany and the Holy Roman Empire*. Vol. 1. Oxford University Press, 2012; Wilson, P. H. *The Holy Roman Empire, 1495–1806*. 2nd ed. Palgrave Macmillan, 2011; Wilson, P. H. *The Thirty Years War: Europe's Tragedy*. Belknap Press of Harvard University Press, 2009.

MICHAEL J. HALVORSON

Thomas Aquinas

Thomas Aquinas (1224/25–1274) proved to be the most influential of the medieval theologians and for many scholars represents the high point of Scholastic theology. As such, his relation to Luther and Lutheranism took on a new importance in the twentieth century, especially as Roman Catholic scholars reappraised Luther's theological contributions.

Thomas was born in the Aquino family castle of Roccasecca in late 1224 or early 1225. Although his ancestors had been Counts of Aquino, by the time of his birth his family ranked among the lower nobility. Thomas was the youngest of four boys born to Landulf and his second wife, Theodora. As the youngest son, Thomas was marked for a career in the church and was presented to the monks at the Benedictine abbey of Monte Cassino at about age five to begin his education. Though this made him an oblate—that is, a child given by his parents to a monastery—he seems not to have taken solemn vows as a Benedictine. Thomas left the abbey in 1239 as a result of new hostilities between the pope and Emperor Frederick II. In that fall he entered the university founded by Frederick at Naples in 1224 to continue his education in the liberal arts. Here for the first time he encountered the natural philosophy of Aristotle.

Thomas also encountered the relatively new Order of Preachers, the Dominicans, resident in Naples since 1227. The Dominicans were a mendicant order, not tied to a single monastery for their residence or income like traditional monks: they often moved about and, originally at least, lived by begging. These friars, as they were called, dedicated their lives to preaching. Because study was essential to the task, they both developed their own schools and worked in conjunction with established universities. Young Thomas was attracted to the mixture of preaching activity, study, and contemplation that their way of life represented. He received the Dominican habit in Naples and was assigned to further his studies in Paris. On his way there, in the company of the head of the Dominican order, he was abducted by a group of soldiers led by his brother Reginald. His family had planned for him to eventually become abbot of Monte Cassino, a position of power and influence that would not be open to him if he remained a Dominican, so they hoped to persuade him to abandon the order. Numerous legends that may or may not be based on fact surround subsequent events,

including his brothers' tempting him with a prostitute. What is clear is that he was confined to the family home for about a year while his parents and siblings tried to dissuade him from his chosen path. Eventually he was allowed to resume his journey to Paris.

Thomas arrived in Paris in 1245. There he may have studied with Albert the Great, another Dominican, but certainly studied with him after Albert was sent to Cologne in 1248 to organize a *studium generale* (a school that operated like a university but did not grant degrees, although at this time a university might also be referred to as a *studium generale*). Albert was known for the depth and breadth of his knowledge. Studying with him, Thomas became immersed in Aristotelian philosophy in the context of the patristic tradition. He also continued his career as a scholar, serving as *cursor biblicus*, a junior scholar whose job was to familiarize beginners with biblical content. In 1252 Thomas was sent back to Paris to become a master in theology. As part of his study, he lectured on the principal theological textbook of the day, Peter Lombard's *Sentences*, and participated in formal theological debates called disputations. At this time the religious orders had begun to establish their own chairs in theology at the university; the Dominicans, for example, had two. This created tension between them and the secular masters, those teachers of theology who were not members of religious orders. Treatises were written against the mendicants, classes were suspended, and friars were even physically assaulted. In September 1255, shortly before Thomas was to occupy the second Dominican chair in theology, King Louis IX had to send royal archers to protect the friars and their priory. In spite of the opposition to his appointment resulting from this conflict, Thomas became a master of theology in the spring of 1256. For the next three years he fulfilled his duties as master by lecturing, holding and participating in disputations, and preaching.

Thomas left Paris for Italy in 1259. First, in all likelihood, he went to his home convent in Naples and then to Orvieto, where he was assigned to be lector, one who gave lectures on Scripture, at the Dominican priory. Pope Urban IV arrived in Orvieto in 1262, and he and Thomas became friends. At Urban's request Thomas wrote his commentary on the four Gospels (*Catena aurea* [*The Golden Chain*], composed mostly of citations of the ancient fathers) and *Against the Errors of the Greeks*. In addition, one of his most significant works, the *Summa contra gentiles* (literally, A summary [of the faith] against the gentiles, though *summa* could also have the meaning of *compendium*), was completed at this time. Begun shortly before he left Paris in 1259, this work did not result directly from his lectures but was written for Dominicans in Spain to aid them in their encounters with Islam. For this apologetic task, Thomas focused on arguments concerning those doctrines that, according to his system, were accessible to human reason and did not rely on revelation alone.

In 1265 Thomas was sent to Rome to open a *studium* for the Roman province of his order. It was here that he began the work for which he is most well known, the *Summa theologiae* (Summary of theology). The *Summa* was meant to be an introduction to theology for beginners in the subject. In it Thomas meant to provide a systematic overview without unnecessary elaboration or repetition, thus correcting what he saw as deficiencies in other theological textbooks. He divided the topic into two parts: God and the human being's movement toward God. These topics were spread across three books, with God the sole subject of the first, and Christ and the sacraments as the subjects of the third. The second book represented the greatest departure from Lombard's order in the way it described the human return to God through the virtues. Essentially Thomas brought Aristotelian order and content to the topics of Peter Lombard's *Sentences*. Though Thomas wrote numerous other works alongside the *Summa*, this monumental undertaking occupied him for the rest of his life and remained unfinished at his death.

While Thomas was teaching in Rome, another attack was launched on the mendicants at the University of Paris. In 1268 Thomas was recalled to Paris to occupy the Dominican chair for foreigners, probably because of his presumed ability to refute the charges of the secular masters. For the next four years he immersed himself in scholarly activity, lecturing and writing extensively, as well as debating. He employed a staff of secretaries to aid him in the production of manuscripts and is said to have dictated to three or four of them at a time, each on a different subject. By the end of 1271, the attack on the mendicants had spent itself for the moment, and Thomas was free to return to Italy the next year.

In these same years another controversy had arisen involving Parisian masters in the arts faculty, especially Siger of Brabant, who followed Averroes (Ibn Rushd), a twelfth-century Muslim interpreter of Aristotle. The controversy involved the nature of the soul. Averroes taught that the human soul was not immortal. Instead, he ascribed immortality to the "possible intellect" that was one for all humankind. Although Thomas had written against Siger, his own ideas became suspect when the bishop of Paris condemned thirteen propositions of the Averroists in 1270. Thomas, using Aristotle, had taught that the soul was the substantial form of the body, meaning that a human person could not be said to exist without a body. Although this was quite different from ascribing immortality to a single human intellect, it also differed from the typical Scholastic approach that described multiple forms of the body in an effort to identify one that was immortal apart from the body. This Platonic division between soul and body was unacceptable to Thomas, who instead grounded his thinking concerning human immortality in the resurrection of the body. Nevertheless, opposition arose to Thomas's reliance on Aristotle, and his immediate theological legacy was placed in jeopardy by this condemnation and a second one pronounced posthumously in 1277.

From Paris, Thomas traveled to Naples, where he established a theological *studium* for the Dominican Roman province. There he taught and wrote as usual until December 6, 1273. During Mass something profoundly changed Thomas, and subsequently he no longer wrote or dictated anything. When questioned by a companion, he responded in part, "All I have written seems like straw to me." The experience has been described by scholars as a breakdown, a medical event, a mystical experience, or some combination of these. Three months later, on March 7, 1274, Thomas died at Fossanova on his way to the Second Council of Lyons, having struck his head (against a fallen tree) during the journey.

Immediately following his death, Thomas's disciples were forced to defend his legacy against charges of heresy. Although Thomas was canonized in 1323, he remained only one of many theological voices until the sixteenth century. A revival of his thought, in which Cardinal Cajetan played a key role, eventually led to the dominance of Thomist theology in the doctrinal formulations of the Council of Trent.

Luther's knowledge of Aquinas has been the subject of much debate. While it is true that Luther was trained by nominalist theologians at Erfurt, there is evidence that he read at least parts of both the *Summa contra gentiles* and the *Summa theologiae* and that his understanding of Thomas was comparable to that of other Scholastic theologians, with the exception, of course, of the Thomist experts. He also would have been exposed to Thomas's arguments in some sections of Gabriel Biel's work. Yet Thomas was simply not as much part of Luther's conversation as were the nominalists. What Luther seemed to object to most in Thomas was his growing influence and the fact that his disciples now regarded him as a nearly infallible teacher. In the twentieth century, Roman Catholic Luther research was aided by a hypothesis of Josef Lortz, who argued that if Luther had known Thomas's theology more thoroughly, the sixteenth-century break

in the church may not have occurred. Although now widely disputed, it gave new impulse to careful reading of Luther's theology among Roman Catholic scholars.

See also Biel, Gabriel; Catholicism; Luther Renaissance; Ockham, William of; Philosophy; Scholasticism, Late Medieval

Bibliography

Janz, D. R. *Luther on Thomas Aquinas: The Angelic Doctor in the Thought of the Reformer.* Steiner, 1989; Kretzmann, N., and E. Stump, eds. *The Cambridge Companion to Aquinas.* Cambridge University Press, 1993; Pesch, O. H. *Die Theologie der Rechtfertigung bei Martin Luther und Thomas von Aquin: Versuch eines systematisch-theologischen Dialogs.* Matthias-Grünewald-Verlag, 1967; Torrell, J.-P. *Saint Thomas Aquinas.* Vol. 1, *The Person and His Work.* Trans. R. Royal. Catholic University of America Press, 1996; Turner, D. *Thomas Aquinas: A Portrait.* Yale University Press, 2013; Weisheipel, J. A. *Friar Thomas d'Aquino: His Life, Thought, and Works.* Blackwell, 1974.

PAUL W. ROBINSON AND DANIEL RICHES

Thomasius, Christian

The jurist and philosopher Christian Thomasius (1655–1728) was a protagonist of the early Enlightenment in Germany. After studies in his hometown Leipzig and Frankfurt an der Oder, he worked as a private lecturer in Leipzig beginning in 1679–80. Early on, he was involved in numerous controversies with the academic establishment and representatives of Lutheran Orthodoxy, but the most significant conflicts came over his vindication, following Pufendorf, of natural law based on natural reason and not on revelation, his assertion for freedom of religion as an individual right, his insistence on a religiously neutral state as a guarantor for peace and welfare, and eventually his role as a legal counsel for the Pietist August Hermann Francke in a heresy inquest (1689). Repeatedly charged with heterodoxy and atheism, Thomasius fled from Saxony to Halle an der Saale, in the electorate of Brandenburg (1690), becoming initiator and professor of a new university (officially founded in 1694), which rose to the center of Enlightenment and Pietism. Continuously Thomasius struggled for the separation of state and church and against the influence of theologians on secular authority. For this reason, he conceded to the sovereign the right to regulate all external matters of church as an instrument to ensure religious freedom for individuals and external peace, leading in turn to further quarrels with the now-established Pietists in Halle.

See also Enlightenment; Lutheran Orthodoxy; Pietism

Bibliography

Hunter, I. *The Secularisation of the Confessional State: The Political Thought of Christian Thomasius.* Cambridge University Press, 2011; Kühnel, M. *Das politische Denken von Christian Thomasius: Staat, Gesellschaft, Bürger.* Duncker & Humblot, 2001; Thomasius, C. *Essays on Church, State, and Politics.* Liberty Fund, 2007.

MARTIN KÜHNEL

Three Estates

Sometimes referred to as the three hierarchies or orders of church (*ecclesia*), household (*oeconomia*), and state (*politia*), this triad is found in the medieval tradition as a way of delineating stations or structures of life that human beings occupy within an ordered community. In this ordered community, human beings have the responsibility to discharge particular social duties. This tripartite ordering was characteristic of medieval interpretations of Aristotelian ethics. Luther used these categories in confessing God's creative work in establishing the places where human life is preserved and defining Christian callings in the world. The three estates are instituted by God and are upheld by his word of law in order to curb the effects of sin and to allow humanity to flourish. In contrast to the monastic notion that the superior form of the spiritual life is an ascetic withdrawal from the earthly and temporal, Luther understood the place of the Christian life to be in the world in these "three fundamental forms of life" (Bayer, *Theology*, 122). In his lecture on Ps. 111 (1530), Luther said, "These three divine stations continue and remain throughout all kingdoms, as wide as the world and to the end of the world" (LW 13:369). Luther also wrote of the three estates in his treatise *On the Councils and the Church* (1539), where he identified these three "hierarchies" as "ordained by God," saying that "we need no more; indeed, we have enough to do in living aright and resisting the devil in these three" (LW 41:177). Here the reformer again uses these three God-ordained estates as a polemic against "the self-chosen works" (Col. 2:23) of religious orders.

The most succinct treatment of the three estates in Luther comes in the summary of his teaching in the final section of the *Confession concerning Christ's Supper* (1528). Here he declares that "the holy orders and true religious institutions are these three: the office of priest, the estate of marriage, the civil government" (LW 37:364). Faith is not bound to any particular order or estate and is found in all three estates, but none of them provides a path to righteousness before God; instead, they are the concrete locations where faith is active in love for the well-being of the neighbor. "Above these three institutions and orders is the common order of Christian love, in which one serves not only the three orders but also serves every needy person in general with all kinds of benevolent deeds, such as feeding the hungry, giving drink to the thirsty, forgiving enemies, praying for all men on earth, suffering all kinds of evil on earth, etc. Behold, all of these are called good and holy works. However, none of these orders is a means of salvation. There remains only one way above them all, viz., faith in Jesus Christ" (LW 37:365). For Luther, these estates were "holy orders" for they were sanctified by God's Word. Every human being, according to Luther, lives in all three estates because everyone is bound by obligations to God and the neighbor. By faith the Christian recognizes that these estates are created by God and are works of his providential care for the good of his creation. In Luther's view, God is hidden behind the masks (Latin: *larvae*) of those who fill various stations in the estates, using them as instruments for his ongoing work on behalf of human beings.

The first estate established in creation is the church, the place of God's speaking and human beings' answering. Just as the first commandment is fundamental and universal, so human beings are created to worship their Creator and cannot escape this demand even when the response is unbelief or idolatry. In his Genesis lectures, Luther spoke of the establishment of a church "without walls" (LW 1:103) preceding both the household and state. After the fall, the church as an order of creation remains, but it is corrupted by unbelief, which is false worship. Rather than clinging to the promise of grace and blessing, human beings exchange the truth of God for the lie and worship "the creature instead of the Creator" (see Rom. 1:25).

Household, the second estate, is inclusive not only of the biological family members but also of all those who live and work under the same roof, a situation typical of Luther's predominantly rural society. Marriage is at the center of this estate, for it is through this union that God creates and nurtures new human life. This is the place where daily bread is given and received. Living before the Industrial Revolution, where daily work is generally separated from the home, Luther saw work in the context of the family and for the good of these people who are the nearest neighbors.

If the second estate produces life, the third estate protects, guards, and defends life. The third estate, the political order, was founded on the household for the reformer since "all other authority flows and spreads out from the authority of the parents" (LC, Ten Commandments, par. 141). After the fall there is a necessity to this estate, in Luther's thinking, for it functions as a coercive means to prevent human society from collapsing into complete chaos and corruption: "There was no government of the state before sin for there was no need of it. Civil government is a remedy required by our corrupted nature. It is necessary to be held in check by our corrupted nature. It is necessary that lust be held in check by the bonds of the laws and by penalties" (LW

1:104). Government, according to Luther, was established in creation out of the household, but the state is established after the fall.

The three estates were articulated in the Small Catechism as the *Haustafel* (previously translated as "table of duties" or, more recently, as "household chart of Bible passages") where Luther provides a catalogue of biblical texts "for all kinds of holy orders" (SC, "The Household Chart," 1; *BC* 365–67) modeled after Jean Gerson's *Tractate concerning the Way of Life for All the Faithful*. Here Luther makes use of the term "holy orders," which was traditionally used in reference to monastic orders, but now applying it to the various callings or "walks of life" within the three estates. The reformer intended that these scriptural verses would serve to admonish Christians to faithfulness in their particular offices in the church, the civil community, and the household. In language reminiscent of the *Confession concerning Christ's Supper* written in the previous year, Luther concludes this section of the Small Catechism with texts from Rom. 13:9, which calls for one to love the neighbor as the self, and 1 Tim. 2:1, which urges prayers for all people.

Luther's teaching on the three estates is reflected in article 16 of the Augsburg Confession, on civil affairs. Here orderly government, laws, and good order are confessed as being "created and instituted by God" (CA 16.2; *BC* 48), and therefore Christians may without sin exercise political authority; serve in secular offices, including that of soldier and executioner; engage in economic undertakings; and be married. Directed against the Anabaptists and the monastic life, article 16 affirms that these orders are instituted by God and acceptable and necessary arenas for Christian vocation. Further, article 16 asserts that "the gospel does not overthrow secular government, public order, and marriage but instead intends that a person keep all this as a true order of God and demonstrate in these walks of life Christian love and true good works according to each person's calling" (CA 16.5–6; *BC* 48,

50). Christian perfection is found not in the forsaking of life within the worldly estates but in the fear of and faith in God lived out in a life of love. On this basis, CA 28 distinguishes proper episcopal authority from that of secular princes.

In the late nineteenth century, some German Lutheran theologians proposed a fourth estate: the nation. As a result, numerous twentieth-century theologians have worked with Luther's understanding of the estates, often against the backdrop of National Socialism and World War II. Werner Elert (1885–1954) saw the estates in the context of "nomological existence," binding creature to Creator, in opposition to notions of human autonomy. Elert's colleague at Erlangen, Paul Althaus (1888–1966), saw the estates, which he reduced again to three after the debacle of Nazism, as a fundamental aspect of Luther's ethical thought, as the divine command is made concrete in these orders. Helmut Thielicke (1908–86) developed the three estates as the places of "borderline existence," where believers live in the overlap of the new aeon with the old aeon. The Swedish theologian Gustaf Wingren (1910–2000) pioneered a renewed appreciation for Luther's doctrine of vocation with life in the three estates in view. William Lazareth (1928–2008) attempted to show the relevance of Luther's theology of the three estates for a contemporary Lutheran ethic where faith is active in love especially in the political realm. Dietrich Bonhoeffer (1906–45) also took up the three estates but preferred to speak of them in terms of "mandates" rather than "orders" since he thought that mandate was less static and more indicative of a divinely imposed responsibility. Critics have argued that Luther's understanding of the three estates is too static and given to a preservation of the status quo, leading to an identification of the Christian ethic with cultural conservatism.

In contemporary theology, Oswald Bayer is especially significant for demonstrating the interplay between the teaching of the two governments and the three estates, noting that neither may be set aside at the expense of the other. In each of the three estates, Bayer understands God's instituting word joined to the earthly element thereby establishing church, household, and government as the location for God's creative and providential work. Bayer also observes that the radical discipleship demanded by the first commandment does not reduce to an ethic contrary to the estates but is lived out within the estates.

See also Creation; Law, Uses of; Marriage and Divorce; Two Realms; Wingren, Gustaf

Bibliography

Alfsvåg, K. "Christians in Society: Luther's Teaching on the Two Kingdoms and the Three Estates Today." *Logia* 14 (Reformation 2005): 15–19; Althaus, P. *The Ethics of Martin Luther*. Trans. R. Schultz. Fortress, 1972; Bayer, O. *Freedom in Response: Lutheran Ethics; Sources and Controversies*. Trans. J. Cayser. Oxford University Press, 2007; Bayer, O. *Martin Luther's Theology: A Contemporary Interpretation*. Trans. T. Trapp. Eerdmans, 2008; Elert, W. *The Christian Ethos*. Trans. C. J. Schindler. Fortress, 1957; Lazareth, W. *Christians in Society: Luther, the Bible, and Social Ethics*. Fortress, 2001; Peters, A. *Commentary on Luther's Catechisms: Confession and the Christian Life*. Trans. T. Trapp. Concordia, 2013; Thielicke, H. *Theological Ethics*. Trans. W. Lazareth. 2 vols. Fortress, 1966; Wingren, G. *Luther on Vocation*. Trans. C. Rasmussen. Muhlenberg, 1957.

JOHN T. PLESS

Tikhuie, Vehettge Lena

A Khoisan woman, Vehettge Lena Tikhuie (d. ca. 1800) was one of the best students of Wilhelm Schmidt, a Moravian missionary who worked in South Africa from 1737 to 1744. She was baptized in 1742 and named Magdalena. When Schmidt returned to Germany, she continued to hold Bible lessons and prayer meetings under the pear tree that Schmidt had planted. When three Moravian missionaries arrived in 1792, she was having others read passages from the Dutch New Testament that Schmidt had given her. She supported them in their work. As one of the earliest indigenous church leaders, she became a living legend. She died around 1800.

Bibliography

Krüger, B. *The Pear Tree Blossoms: A History of the Moravian Mission Stations in South Africa, 1737–1869.*

Genadental, 1966; Millard, J. A. *Malihambe: Let the Word Spread*. Unisa, 1999.

FRIEDER LUDWIG

Tillich, Paul J.

Born in Starzeddel, Germany, Paul J. Tillich (1886–1965) earned degrees in both philosophy and theology, writing two theses on Schelling. His work focused on constructing a theology of culture, relating religion to the arts, history, literature, politics, psychoanalysis, and sociology. Tillich was dismissed from his professorship at the University of Frankfurt for speaking out publicly against Hitler's anti-Jewish policies. Then he immigrated to the United States and held teaching positions at Union Theological Seminary in New York, Harvard University, and the University of Chicago.

No single label can adequately characterize his thought. He has been called an apologetic, existentialist, dialectical, and even a neo-orthodox theologian. Each label contains a kernel of truth. As an apologetic theologian, Tillich used philosophy to formulate the questions to be answered by theology. He found the categories of Heidegger's existentialism useful to describe the conditions of human existence addressed by the gospel. He said that the rise of existentialism is the good fortune of Christian theology because it reveals the "sickness unto death" that the gospel promises to heal. As a dialectical theologian, Tillich applied the "law of contrasts" he found in Luther's theology to hold in tension contrasting concepts, such as the hidden and revealed nature of God, the wrath and the love of God, the strange work of God (*opus alienum*) and his proper work (*opus proprium*), the kingdom of the left hand of God and of the right hand. In terms of neo-orthodoxy, Tillich rejected the liberal theology of German Protestantism à la Schleiermacher, Ritschl, and von Harnack to reappropriate the classical doctrine of the Trinity and Christology of patristic Christianity. But underlying all such descriptors is Tillich's ecclesial self-understanding as a Lutheran theologian. As a student of Martin Kähler, Tillich was deeply influenced by the way Kähler organized his entire system around the doctrine of justification. Specifically, Kähler reformulated the doctrine of justification through faith alone by using the idea of acceptance, widely used in psychotherapy in what is sometimes termed a method of correlation. Faith is the acceptance of one's acceptance in spite of being unacceptable before God.

Tillich then used this "method of correlation" to construct his own theological system. Every part correlates answers given in biblical revelation to the existential questions of doubt, meaning, and truth. Like Luther's, his theology was radically christocentric. For Luther, *was Christum treibet* (what conveys Christ) is the criterion of all theological truth; for Tillich, the center and criterion of Christian theology is the manifestation of the "New Being in Jesus as the Christ." Tillich retrieved the patristic idea of the *Logos* to affirm both the universality of God's revelation in the world religions and its finality in the incarnation of God in Jesus Christ.

The chief criticism of Tillich's theology given from his contemporaries is the way he translated the religious symbols of the Bible and Christianity into the Neoplatonic and idealist categories of mystical ontology. For Tillich, "Being itself" is the prime nonsymbolic definition of God. God is the ground and meaning of being. Expressing the Christian faith in such ontological terms, critics claim, does not enhance the practices of prayer and proclamation. To counter such criticism, Tillich rightly claimed that some of the greatest theologians of the Christian tradition, including Origen, Augustine, and Aquinas, used metaphysics to interpret the Bible.

See also Apologetics; Barth, Karl; Existentialism

Bibliography
Tillich, P. *The Courage to Be*. Yale University Press, 1952; Tillich, P. *Dynamics of Faith*. Harper & Row, 1957; Tillich, P. *The Protestant Era*. University of Chicago Press, 1948; Tillich, P. *Systematic Theology*. 3 vols. University of Chicago Press, 1951; Tillich, P. *Theology of Culture*. Oxford University Press, 1959.

CARL E. BRAATEN

Tokuzen, Kazuyoshi

The theologian, Reformation historian, and Lutheran pastor Kazuyoshi Tokuzen (b. 1932) served as professor at Japan Lutheran College and Seminary. Born in Tokyo, Dr. Tokuzen was educated in the University of Tokyo's faculty of engineering and entered the Rikkyo University theology department as a doctoral student. He transferred to Japan Lutheran Seminary in 1956 and graduated from there in 1957. He was called to Lutheran congregations in Chiba, studied further at Hamburg University and Heidelberg University, and then in 1964 joined the faculty of what is now Japan Lutheran College and Seminary, where he has served as a professor since 1972.

Tokuzen became the founding director of the Luther Research Center in 1985. He has taught at Aoyama Gakuin University, Tokyo Woman's Christian University, Keio Gijuku University, Rikkyo University, Kokugakuin University, Tokyo Union Theological Seminary, and seminaries in Taiwan, India, the United States, and Germany. Tokuzen was granted an honorary doctorate in theology from Wartburg Lutheran Seminary. Active in promoting ecumenical relationships in Japan, he was elected to be the vice president of the National Christian Council in Japan in 1994, and then the president in 1997. He was honored by this council with an Ecumenical Achievement Award and also by Japan Christian Culture Association with a Japan Christian Achievement Award in 2014.

See also Japan; Luther's Works

MAKITO MASAKI

Tolstadius, Erik

The Swedish Lutheran pastor and conservative Pietist Erik Tolstadius (February 21, 1693–July 28, 1759) was born into a clerical family. He attended Uppsala University and was ordained a priest in 1719. For a time he was house chaplain for several noble families, but in 1723 he was appointed to Skeppesholm, a minor congregation on the outskirts of Stockholm. Tolstadius had been influenced by the Pietist movement, and in early 1723 he preached a strong sermon about "wicked and false priests," which was seen as an attack on the established church. Though brought before the consistory, he was let off with a warning. His revival preaching attracted crowds of people, and his work with conventicles kept him under suspicion. When German radical Pietist Johan Conrad Dippel came to Stockholm in 1726, Tolstadius defended him, even when Dippel was expelled for heretical teachings. Tolstadius was accused of errors similar to those of Dippel and was only cleared of these charges in 1731. In 1734 he again came under investigation on a charge of being a Calvinist and a radical, but again he managed to escape conviction. Tolstadius attracted a popular following because of his strong Pietist preaching and was referred to as the "Swedish Francke" for his charitable and educational works. He did not write books during his lifetime, but his sermons were collected and printed after his death.

See also Pietism; Sweden

MARK A. GRANQUIST

Tradition

Luther took a characteristically nuanced view of tradition, or more precisely *human traditions*. Insofar as they were proclaimed to be necessary for salvation or even for good standing in the church, Luther denounced them relentlessly. He frequently invoked the fact that if even the law of Moses, given by God on Mount Sinai, could not justify, how much less could human traditions do so, given their lack of scriptural foundation or dominical command.

He urged courage, therefore, in rejecting the false requirements of human traditions, as in his treatise *That a Christian Assembly or Congregation Has the Right and Power* (1523), where he exhorted the appointment of Evangelical preachers in defiance of the bishops: "One should not care at all about human statutes, law, old precedent, usage, custom, etc., even if they were instituted by pope or emperor, prince or bishop, if one half or the whole world accepted them, or if they lasted one year or a thousand years. . . . This matter must be dealt with according to Scripture and God's word; for God's word and human teaching inevitably oppose each other when the latter tries to rule the soul" (LW 39:306). Human traditions carry no ecclesiological weight in themselves. "If you are troubled and anxious as to whether or not you are truly a church of God, I would say to you, that a church is not known by customs but by the Word" (*Concerning the Ministry* [1523], LW 40:41).

Luther thus had no use for those who thought that the observance of human traditions was necessary for salvation: "Anyone who teaches or urges either the Law of God or human traditions as something necessary for righteousness in the sight of God does nothing other than give birth to slaves" (*Lectures on Galatians* [1531/35], LW 26:443). But he was equally disdainful of those who thought that the *rejection* of human traditions was necessary for salvation. To do so would mean rejecting many things that are useful and good for church and perhaps, in the end, even the necessary things themselves. Already in *The Freedom of a Christian* (1520), he observed: "There are very many who, when they hear of this freedom of faith, immediately turn it into an occasion for the flesh and think that now all things are allowed them. They want to show that they are free men and Christians only by despising and finding fault with ceremonies, traditions, and human laws; as if they were Christians because on stated days they do not fast or eat meat when others fast" (LW 31:372). Later, criticizing those Anabaptists who insisted on discarding everything inherited from the papacy, he wrote,

> The whole thing is nonsense. Christ himself came upon the errors of scribes and Pharisees among the Jewish people, but he did not on that account reject everything they had and thought (Matt. 23[:3]). We on our part confess that there is much that is Christian and good under the papacy; indeed everything that is Christian and good is to be found there and

has come to us from this source. For instance we confess that in the papal church there are the truly holy Scriptures, true baptism, the true sacrament of the altar, the true keys to the forgiveness of sins, the true office of ministry, the true catechism in the form of the Lord's Prayer, the Ten Commandments, and the articles of the creed. (*Concerning Rebaptism* [1528], LW 40:231–32)

Luther's proposal for navigating between the Scylla of retaining everything as necessary for salvation and the Charybdis of rejecting everything as unnecessary and even inimical to salvation was already evident in his Invocavit sermons, preached upon his return to Wittenberg from the Wartburg in 1522. Sharply denouncing the sudden rush under Karlstadt's leadership to remove images from the church building and the canon of the Mass from the Communion liturgy, Luther announced: "Therefore all those have erred who have helped and consented to abolish the mass; not that it was not a good thing, but that it was not done in an orderly way. You say it was right according to the Scriptures. I agree, but what becomes of order? For it was done in wantonness, with no regard for proper order and with offense to your neighbor" (LW 51:73). Regardless of whether the issue is retaining or eliminating, "do not make a 'must' out of what is 'free,' as you have done, so that you may not be called to account for those who were led astray by your loveless exercise of liberty" (LW 51:74).

Luther revisited the issue of freedom over against human traditions set in the context of love for the neighbor in *On the Councils and the Church* (1539). He asked how Peter could assert that salvation comes by faith in Christ alone while James required adherence to certain aspects of the Mosaic law in Acts 15. His explanation: "So these two articles, that of St. Peter and that of St. James, are contradictory and yet they are not. St. Peter's deals with faith, St. James's with love. St. Peter's article tolerates no law; it eats blood, strangled meat, meat sacrificed to idols, and the devil in the bargain, without paying much attention, for it feels responsible to God alone and not to man, and does nothing but believe in the gracious God. But St. James's article lives and eats with man; it also directs everything to St. Peter's article, carefully warding off any obstacle that might obstruct the way" (LW 41:77). How much more, then, does this principle apply to the traditions of the church—even festival dates that were once the subject of intense controversy.

> We therefore have and must have the power and freedom to observe Easter when we choose; and even if we made Friday into Sunday, or vice versa, it would still be right, as long as it were done unanimously by the rulers and the Christians. . . . Days or seasons are not to be lords over Christians, but rather Christians are lords over days and seasons, free to fix them as they will or as seems convenient to them. For Christ made all things free when he abolished Moses [= the Law]. However, we will let things remain as they now are, since no peril, error, sin, or heresy is involved, and we are averse to changing anything needlessly or at our own personal whim, out of consideration for others who observe Easter at the same time as we do. (LW 41:67)

Concern for the weak brother or sister, and the fact that many good things did pass down through the ages alongside the bad, leads Luther to a final principle: human traditions are innocent until proved guilty. Unless a tradition is clearly contrary to Scripture, interferes with the development of faith, or is understood wrongly to be mandatory, its precedence has a certain weight that cannot be lightly dismissed. Ceremonies and practices are, indeed, necessary in general—even if none of them is necessary in particular—for training in the faith, and one must proceed with caution rather than recklessly changing everything all the time.

Thus, in his first *Order of Mass and Communion for the Church at Wittenberg* in 1523, Luther wrote of his desire for a peaceful removal of the canon of the Mass, such that he "used neither authority nor pressure. Nor did I make any innovations. For I have been hesitant and fearful, partly because of the weak in faith, who cannot suddenly exchange an old and accustomed order of worship for a new and unusual one, and more so because of the fickle and fastidious spirits who rush in like unclean swine without faith or reason" (LW 53:19). He saw no need to get rid of the service altogether—after all, the Communion of bread and wine came from Christ and the apostles themselves—but only to purify it. He retained the Kyrie, introits, Bible readings (only changing them to the vernacular), Gloria, graduals, alleluias, creed, Sanctus, Agnus Dei, and distribution hymn. He expressed a certain skepticism about "vestments, vessels, candles, and palls, of organs and all the music, and of images" but was willing to tolerate them for the time being (LW 53:22). Only the canon absolutely had to be removed. But even as he advocated local development of appropriate rites, he added, "Let us approve each other's rites lest schisms and sects should result from this diversity in rites. . . . For external rites, even though we cannot do without them—just as we cannot do without food or drink—do not commend us to God" (LW 53:31).

The same principles are invoked in the German Mass of 1526. On the one hand, "while the exercise of this freedom is up to everyone's conscience and must not be cramped or forbidden, nevertheless, we must make sure that freedom shall be and remain a servant of love and of our fellow-man" (LW 53:61). On the other hand, "this or any other order shall be so used that whenever it becomes an abuse, it shall be straightaway abolished and replaced by another. . . . No order is, therefore, valid in itself—as the popish orders were held to be until now. But the validity, value, power, and virtue of any order is in its proper use" (LW 53:90).

Melanchthon neatly captures Luther's nuance in article 15 of the Augsburg Confession (1530):

Concerning church regulations made by human beings, it is taught to keep those that may be kept without sin and that serve to maintain peace and good order in the church, such as specific celebrations, festivals, etc. However, people are also instructed not to burden consciences with them as if such things were necessary for salvation. Moreover, it is taught that all rules and traditions made by human beings for the purpose of appeasing God and of earning grace are contrary to the gospel and the teaching concerning faith in Christ. That is why monastic vows and other traditions concerning distinctions of foods, days, and the like, through which people imagine they can earn grace and make satisfaction for sin, are good for nothing and contrary to the gospel. (CA 15 in *BC* 48, German text)

Detailed application of these principles appears later in the CA regarding "abuses that have been corrected," including Communion in both kinds, clerical marriage, the Mass, confession, the distinction of foods, and monastic vows. The concluding article, 28, pleads with the leadership of the church not to abuse its power by imposing human traditions on the faithful as if they were necessary for salvation.

In the wake of the Smalcald War and the resultant Augsburg Interim, Lutherans again debated matters involving tradition, in this case whether traditions done away with could be reintroduced to the church for the sake of peace and the preservation of Evangelical churches or whether persecution turned such matters of adiaphora (such as chasubles or prayers for the hours) into issues requiring resistance. While reaffirming the reality of adiaphora and tradition and the fact that they were not per se church-dividing issues, the Formula of Concord insisted that in times of persecution resistance was mandatory. During Luther's lifetime all of the foregoing discussion had presumed a situation of political and ecclesiastical freedom. As soon as human traditions are enforced by coercion, the case has to be referred to the principles of adiaphora, mandata, and *damnabilia*.

See also Adiaphora; Law, Uses of; Papacy

Bibliography

Luther's Works: *Concerning Rebaptism* (1528). LW 40:225–62; *Concerning the Ministry* (1523). LW 40:3–44; *Eight Sermons at Wittenberg* (1522). LW 51:67–100; *The Freedom of a Christian* (1520). LW 31:327–77; *The German Mass and Order of Service* (1526). LW 53:51–90; *Lectures on Galatians* (1531/35). LW 26; *On the Councils and the Church* (1539). LW 41:3–178; *An Order of Mass and Communion for the Church at Wittenberg* (1523). LW 53:15–40; *That a Christian Assembly or Congregation Has the Right and Power to Judge All Teaching and to Call, Appoint, and Dismiss Teachers, Established and Proven by Scripture* (1523). LW 39:305–14. **Other Work:** Melanchthon, P., ed. The Augsburg Confession (1530). BC 30–105.

Sᴀʀᴀʜ Hɪɴʟɪᴄᴋʏ Wɪʟꜱᴏɴ

Treatise on the Power and Primacy of the Pope

In 1537 Philip Melanchthon composed *Treatise on the Power and Primacy of the Pope* for the Smalcaldic League as a supplement to the Augsburg Confession, which lacked an article on papal primacy. Pope Paul III's calling of an ecumenical council in 1536 and his invitation issued to German Evangelical princes to send participants to the council demanded a response from the governments of the Smalcaldic League. Although Elector John Frederick of Saxony proposed that the Smalcald Articles (as they were later dubbed), which he commissioned Martin Luther to write, serve as the League's agenda at the council, his fellow princes rejected the idea at a meeting of the League in Smalcald in February 1537. They instead decided to present the Augsburg Confession as their basis for negotiation at the council, but they also recognized that the doctrine of the papacy needed to be discussed. Because Luther, though in attendance at the meeting, became too ill to write such a document and perhaps because the princes feared Luther's harsh judgment, they charged Philip Melanchthon with the task. Melanchthon reported that he had not shied away from a clear confrontation with papal teaching on the pope's authority and exercise of that authority in the treatise that he produced.

His document rejected the papal claim to superiority by divine right over all bishops and pastors of the church, the papal assertion of its divine right to confer and transfer secular authority, and the papacy's dictum that it is necessary for salvation to believe in papal supremacy in the church and society. Melanchthon's argument against these claims emerged on the basis of careful exegetical review of a number of Bible passages and extensive historical argument, based on citations from the ancient councils, ancient church fathers, and examples of noncentralized governance in the early church. The treatise accentuates biblical authority and defines ecclesiastical power in terms of Christ's command to the church to retain and forgive sins. The office of the word depends on God's Word as given in Scripture. Melanchthon came to the conclusion that all Christians should abandon and curse the pope and his minions as the realm of the antichrist. A brief repetition of the argument of article 28 of the Augsburg Confession regarding the power and jurisdiction of the bishops concluded Melanchthon's treatise.

The signatures of thirty-two theologians present or represented at Smalcald affirmed Melanchthon's statement. The actual meeting of the council did not begin until December 1545, and no Evangelicals attended it in its first series of sessions (1545–47). The *Treatise on the Power and Primacy of the Pope* first appeared in print in 1540, appended to another document, and a German translation was published in 1541. It was appended to Luther's Smalcald Articles in some later printings, and by 1577 its authorship and its Latin original had disappeared from public consciousness. Thus it was viewed into the twentieth century as an appendix to the Smalcald Articles. Nikolaus Selnecker translated the German version into Latin for the 1580 Latin version of the Book of Concord because he did not know of its origin, a confusion corrected in the 1584 authorized Latin edition.

See also Augsburg Confession; Book of Concord; Melanchthon, Philip; Papacy; Smalcald Articles

Bibliography

Arand, C. P., et al. *The Lutheran Confessions*. Esp. 153–57. Fortress, 2012; Hendrix, S. H. *Luther and the Papacy*. Fortress, 1981.

ROBERT KOLB

Troeltsch, Ernst

The German Protestant professor of systematic theology, philosophy, and the history of religion and culture Ernst Troeltsch (1865–1923) was born near Augsburg into a middle-class family; his father was a well-regarded physician. Ernst began his study of theology at nearby Erlangen University (1884–85), whose theology faculty was required to teach in accord with the Lutheran confessions. Troeltsch left after one year since he considered the faculty's perspective too parochial and incompatible with scientific knowledge, historical-critical methodology, and modern culture. From an early age he desired to reconcile liberal Protestant piety, shaped by Kant and Schleiermacher, with the principal values of the Enlightenment, which had become dominant in Europe since the eighteenth century. To pursue this goal he continued his studies at Berlin (1885–86) and finally at Göttingen (1886–88), where he was influenced especially by Albrecht Ritschl. After passing his initial exams (at Erlangen), Troeltsch served one year as an assistant pastor in Munich (1888–89). Then he returned to Göttingen, where he completed his exams and wrote a dissertation on the relationship between reason and revelation in Johann Gerhard and Philip Melanchthon. Already in this work Troeltsch defended the thesis that the theology of Luther and early Protestantism thoroughly reflected a medieval worldview. Not only did Luther address a church-dominated "Christian civilization," but he also focused on the premodern question, "How can I become certain of my salvation?" By contrast, modernity is marked by religious pluralism, doubts about the reality of God, and crises of human meaning. During the twenty years that Troeltsch taught theology and ethics at Heidelberg (1894–1915), he criticized Ritschlians for being insufficiently historical, prone to modernizing Luther's medieval ideas, and inattentive to modern scholarly theories of religion. He also stressed the differences between Lutheranism—which he thought was inherently authoritarian, culturally conservative, and politically quietistic—and Calvinism, which he considered to be more progressive. His friendship with Max Weber certainly contributed to his view that Calvinism, not Lutheranism, was the principal religious influence on the rise of liberal cultural values, modern science, and capitalism. Troeltsch thus emphasized the cultural gap between the age of Luther and the modern world, a position he developed further in his classic study *The Social Teachings of the Christian Churches*. From 1915 until his death he served on the philosophy faculty at Berlin, a position created especially for him, since conservative Lutherans protested his initial appointment to the theology faculty there. At Berlin, Troeltsch lectured on the philosophy of religion, the social sciences, and Christianity, which he continued to interpret historically and sociologically and not dogmatically. In his principal writings, some unfinished at his death, he sought to show the persisting cultural importance of Christianity and its abiding religious and ethical norms (at least for Europeans), all couched within a historicist perspective, wherein all cultural values (including religious ones) are relative. For Troeltsch, Christian faith reassures the individual believer under threat from modern dehumanizing and depersonalizing economic and political forces. Alongside Harnack, he is remembered as the most significant liberal Protestant theologian of the past century, whose criticisms of Lutheranism were passed on in English-speaking realms through the work of Reformed thinkers such as the Niebuhrs.

See also Enlightenment; Liberalism; Luther Interpretation and Reception; Ritschl, Albrecht; State; Two Realms

Bibliography

BBKL 12:497–562; Drescher, H. *Ernst Troeltsch: His Life and Work*. Fortress, 1993; "Ernst Troeltsch" in *ER* 14:9364–67; "Ernst Troeltsch" in *RPP* 13:115–18; Troeltsch, E. *Protestantism and Progress: The Significance of Protestantism for the Rise of the Modern World*. Fortress, 1986; Troeltsch, E. *Religion in History*. Fortress, 1991; Troeltsch, E. *The Social Teaching of the Christian Churches*. 2 vols. Westminster John Knox, 1992.

MATTHEW L. BECKER

Tumsa, Gudina

Gudina Tumsa (1929–79) was general secretary of the Ethiopian Evangelical Church Mekane Yesus in 1966–79 and first chair of the Council for the Cooperation of Churches in Ethiopia, formed in 1976. He was an active participant in the Lutheran World Federation and the World Council of Churches. Born in 1929 in the Oromo village of Bodji, Western Wollega, the son of poor farmers, he converted to Christianity at age ten and was ordained at twenty-one. He was the first Ethiopian pastor of the Nekemte congregation. In 1955–58 he studied nursing at the Swedish Missionary School in Nedjo. He earned a bachelor of divinity (now called a master of divinity) degree from Luther Seminary, St. Paul, Minnesota, after studying there from 1963 to 1966.

Gudina Tumsa was a committed pastor and a gifted theological leader, who spoke for and to his church. His theological education equipped him to be heard by, and sometimes to challenge, non-African church leaders. While tirelessly proclaiming Christ, he advocated for ministry to the whole person, the church's independence from overseas control, and its independence from the revolutionary government that began in 1974. Especially after 1977, this government regarded his leadership and influence with suspicion. He refused to do its bidding or endorse its Marxism. Imprisoned and released twice, he refused to flee, even though he had been granted refuge in Tanzania. In July 1979 he was abducted and murdered (though not until 1992 did anyone know his fate). Because he refused asylum, was martyred, and was influenced by Bonhoeffer, he has often been called "the Bonhoeffer of Africa."

See also Ethiopia

Bibliography

Ecumenical Challenges. Vol. 3 of Journal of Gudina Tumsa Forum. Lutheran University Press, 2014; Eide, Ø. *Revolution & Religion in Ethiopia, . . . 1974–85.* Ohio University Press, 2000; *Emerging Theological Praxis.* Vol. 2 of Journal of Gudina Tumsa Forum. Lutheran University Press, 2012.

DARRELL JODOCK

Turss, Gustavs (Tūrs)

The Latvian church leader Gustavs (Tūrs) Turss (1890–1973) studied law (1910–18) and later theology at Dorpat (Tartu), Estonia, and was ordained into the ministry of the Latvian Lutheran Church in 1920. He served as pastor and teacher in thirteen parishes (1920–46). Soviet authorities had him appointed acting archbishop and president of the church's board of directors; in 1948 he was elected archbishop as the first Latvian church leader under the Soviet occupation and under the constitution of the church, accepted by the synod in 1948. In 1954 he founded a program for theological education, participated in the creation of a new hymnal (1954–57), led the work of the New Testament emendation committee (1957–61), and instituted the printing of a church calendar. The University of Leipzig awarded him an honorary doctorate in 1959. By developing relationships with foreign churches, he was able secretly to inform them of the conditions of the church life under the Soviet occupation. Although sharply criticized for his accommodation of Soviet occupation authorities, Turss strove to withstand the massive attack of the USSR Communist regime and the Soviet secret police. He was forced to retire in 1968.

See also Latvia; Livonia

Bibliography

Talonen, J. *Church under the Pressure of Stalinism.* Pohjois-Suomen Historiallinen Yhdistys, 1997.

GUNTIS KALME

Twofold Righteousness

Luther's distinction of "two kinds of righteousness," or "twofold righteousness," served as a foundation of his understanding of what it means to be human. It presumed that God's righteousness is his loving, merciful disposition that expresses itself in the unconditioned creation of human creatures and the unconditioned restoration of their humanity after they had become sinners.

Throughout most of Christian history, theologians defined the righteousness of believers—their identity and integrity as people of God—in terms of human performance of God's law. Even teachers of the church who emphasized divine grace as the exclusive cause of salvation (Augustine) or as the "prevenient" or initial, causative impetus in rescuing sinners from their sinfulness (Aquinas) evaluated the human being in terms of fulfilling God's entire law. A combination of forgiveness and human action made sinners righteous in God's sight and the sight of others.

In contrast, Luther distinguished human righteousness or identity in relationship to God from that which makes human beings righteous, living out their identities, in relationship to God's other creatures. Luther's distinction runs parallel to Jesus's description of human creatures in Matt. 22:37–39: they trust God completely and love their neighbors as themselves. Luther began developing this view of humanity in 1518, in the treatise *On Three Kinds of Righteousness*, in which he contrasted three kinds of sin: (1) criminal, (2) essential or original, and (3) sinful acts committed by Christians. Corresponding to these, Luther posited (1) civil righteousness, deeds performed apart from faith in Christ but conforming outwardly to God's law; (2) essential righteousness, an unconditionally given gift from God, which takes form in human trust in him; and (3) the righteousness of deeds that flow from faith in conformity with God's law. Because he lived in a world of baptized people, his 1519 treatise *On Two Kinds of Righteousness* (LW 31:297–306) treated only the second and third kinds. He labeled the second (the core identity of a person) as "alien" righteousness; he called the third kind (deeds flowing from faith) as "proper" righteousness. These terms are inadequate translations of the

Latin. "Alien" righteousness (*iustitia aliena*) is the identity bestowed from the outside by someone else. "Proper" righteousness (*iustitia propria*) is the active living out of the core identity by the person who has been made righteous by another. Luther also used similar categories in *Freedom of a Christian* (1520).

In his Galatian lectures of 1531 (LW 26:7) Luther claims that the distinction of the two-fold righteousness constitutes "our theology." By this time he had adopted the designations "passive" righteousness and "active" righteousness for these two aspects of humanity. Like the creation of Adam and Eve and like the gift of life from parents, the gift of life as God's child takes place without any condition or contribution from the human being. God creates "out of nothing" a relationship in which he promises to be faithful and bestows the gift of trust. This trust determines human personhood, as Luther explained in his Large Catechism (explanation of the first commandment, in BC 386–90). Like all parents, God then expects his children to behave according to the new identity he has fashioned for them, as outlined in his law. Carrying out God's purposes through their own actions, God's children perform active righteousness. It does not contribute to their standing in God's sight but rather fulfills his expectations for the creatures he designed to praise him and to love and serve other creatures.

In Luther's and Melanchthon's usage, God's law commands trust in the first commandment, but trust always comes as a gift. Thus, in the relationship of believers with God, their being the person God re-created them to be is always a gift. Luther defined "gospel" as the word of promise, based on Christ's death and resurrection, which creates the trust and determines the essential personhood of individual believers as new creatures in Christ. This gospel motivates the active righteousness of both the vertical and horizontal dimensions. In the horizontal dimension the motive power of the gospel produces new obedience, the good works that bring God's love to others. In the

vertical dimension, the same gospel moves the believer to "call upon [God] in every trouble, pray, praise, and give thanks" (SC, second commandment, BC 352).

In the Apology of the Augsburg Confession, Philip Melanchthon develops his discussion of justification out of this distinction, labeling the two aspects "the righteousness of faith" and "the righteousness of the law" or "of reason." The latter embraces human activity that is possible apart from faith; the righteousness of faith receives forgiveness of sins and bestows righteousness through the Holy Spirit's gift of new birth in Christ (Ap 4:21–47).

In his *Examination of the Council of Trent* (1565), Martin Chemnitz labels the distinction between the two kinds of righteousness "the chief controversy between the papalists and us": "whether the regenerate are justified by that newness which the Holy Spirit works in them and by the good works which follow from that renewal" or whether Abraham and all believers still are righteous before God because of his unconditioned grace and mercy. Chemnitz viewed human creatures as completely dependent on God for being God's children, without any admixture of merit from their own performance at any point (481–83).

Because this anthropological distinction did not win a place in the "topical" tradition of Lutheran dogmatics, it fell into disuse as a category of systematic theology but remained implicit in repetitions of the Wittenberg doctrine of justification by faith. Its revival in the twentieth century contributes much to the Lutheran witness in an age in which the meaning of being human has claimed a central spot in ecumenical dialogue and missiological thinking.

See also Anthropology; Creation; Good Works; Justification; Original Sin; Salvation; Two Realms

Bibliography

Chemnitz, M. *Examination of the Council of Trent.* Part 1. Trans. F. Kramer. Concordia, 1971; Kolb, R. "Luther on the Two Kinds of Righteousness: Reflections on His Two-Dimensional Definition of Humanity at the Heart of His Theology." *LQ* 13 (1999): 449–66; Kolb, R., and C. P. Arand. *The Genius of Luther's Theology: A Wittenberg*

Way of Thinking for the Contemporary Church. Baker Academic, 2008.

Robert Kolb

Two Realms

Luther's term *zwei Reiche* (two kingdoms/realms) has wrought confusion within and outside Lutheran circles because, unaware that he was formulating terminology to be used for centuries, he was not careful in his use of the phrase.

Luther employed the phrase in at least three different ways. Rarely did he use it in a manner similar to certain medieval interpretations of Augustine's two cities, for secular government and church. Much more frequently his usage contrasted the rule of God and the rule of Satan as their respective "kingdoms." He also used the term "two kingdoms" for the two dimensions of human life, built into human nature by God: the realm of the "vertical" relationship with God (he called it the "heavenly" kingdom, later dubbed "the kingdom of the right hand") and the realm of the "horizontal" relationships with other creatures (the "temporal" or "earthly" kingdom, "the kingdom of the left hand"). Some recent scholarship has used the word "realm" for the latter distinction, while applying the term "kingdom" to the conflicting reigns of God and Satan. Failure to recognize this distinction has sometimes led to the equation of the temporal realm with Satan's kingdom, contrary to Luther's teaching. He held that God and Satan are in a life-and-death conflict on the battlefields of both realms or dimensions of human life.

The vertical relationship of human life is established by God's gift of passive righteousness, made concrete in faith or trust in God through the work of Christ and by the power of the Holy Spirit. In this dimension of life, believers express their faith through active obedience in prayer and praise of God, motivated by the gospel to perform the acts God has planned as demonstrations of trust in him. In the horizontal realm of human life, believers, alongside those outside the faith, seek the good of society through obedience to God's plan for his creation. Although both believers and those outside the faith seek that good, believers are motivated by the passive righteousness of faith, acting out the identity of God's children in deeds of love and service.

Following medieval social theory, Luther taught that God has structured the horizontal realm in three *Stände*, traditionally translated as "estates," better translated as "walks of life": the structural forms of the church (*ecclesia*); society, particularly those in leadership positions (*politia*); and the household (*oeconomia*). In his Table (Household Chart) of Christian Callings (in SC), Luther recognized what has become much clearer since the Industrial Revolution: within the *oeconomia*, family life and economic activities should be distinguished. Medieval theory held that within each *Stände* individuals have *Ämter*, usually translated "offices," that is, the responsibilities to carry out the purposes of each walk of life. Luther did not develop terminology distinguishing the role or position of responsibility from the functions that carry out the responsibility but discussed both with the term *Amt* (plural: *Ämter*).

Medieval thinkers assigned each individual to one walk of life, but Luther came to see that every person has responsibilities in all of them. He also transformed the medieval usage of the concept of calling, *Beruf* or *vocatio*, from a designation for sacred responsibilities held by priests, monks, and nuns to a designation for the Christian exercise of responsibilities in all walks of life. Every person exercises these responsibilities, but believers experience them as special callings from God.

Luther placed all human institutional activity into the horizontal realm. The household and the church are walks of life in which the realm of the right hand—the proclamation and instruction of the gospel—take place, but both are also social forms within the realm of the left hand.

Distinct from Luther's usage of the concepts of "kingdom" and "realm" in these senses is his understanding of the biblical terminology of Christ's rule, reign, or kingdom. Because none of these concepts became dogmatic topics in the Lutheran systematizing of biblical teaching, his heirs followed biblical usage in their preaching but did not speak of the "kingdom of Christ" as a formal dogmatic topic. Luther's catechetical teaching remained, however. In his explanation to the second petition, Luther states that Christ rules "whenever our heavenly Father gives us his Holy Spirit, so that through his grace we believe his holy Word and live godly lives here in time and hereafter in eternity" (SC, Lord's Prayer 8, *BC* 357).

The distinction of the two realms found no place in the topical structure of seventeenth-century Lutheran dogmatics, but elements of it influenced public teaching into the nineteenth century, when some used it to free secular governments from strict adherence to Christian standards of conduct. It was also revived in more faithful form in thinking on the callings of Christians in the horizontal realm, above all in Nordic circles. Dietrich Bonhoeffer used this framework in his ethics; Robert Benne has applied it to North American public life. This distinction provides a valuable framework to support Luther's understanding of salvation by grace through faith in Christ and for ethical thinking.

See also Creation; Law, Uses of; Law and Gospel; State; Three Estates; Twofold Righteousness; Vocation

Bibliography

Benne, R. *The Paradoxical Vision: A Public Theology for the Twenty-First Century*. Fortress, 1995; Bonhoeffer, D. *Ethics*. SCM, 1955; Cranz, F. E. *An Essay on the Development of Luther's Thought on Justice, Law, and Society*. Harvard University Press, 1959; Heckel, J. *Lex Caritatis: A Juristic Disquisition on Law in the Theology of Martin Luther*. Trans. G. Krodel. Eerdmans, 2010; Kolb, R., I. Dingel, and L. Batka, eds. *Oxford Handbook of Martin Luther's Theology*. Articles by R. Kolb (168–84), J. Strohl (365–69), and E. Wolgast (397–413). Oxford University Press, 2014; Wingren, G. *Luther on Vocation*. Trans. C. C. Rasmussen. Muhlenberg, 1957.

ROBERT KOLB

Tyndale, William

The English Evangelical reformer and Bible translator William Tyndale (ca. 1494–1536) was born in Gloucestershire and educated at Oxford (BA, 1512; MA, 1515). His initially Erasmian reformist proclivities first became evident upon his return to Gloucestershire and brief employment as tutor in the manor of Sir John Walsh, for whom he translated Erasmus's *Enchiridion Militis Christiani* (ET, *Handbook of the Christian Soldier*). Further inspired by Erasmus, who in the preface to his own 1516 edition of the New Testament expressed support for vernacular translations of Scripture, and encouraged by Walsh, Tyndale sought the London bishop Cuthbert Tunstall's permission to produce a translation of the Bible into English. Though himself of humanist sympathies, Tunstall, maintaining the official antipathy engendered through the previous century by heretical Wycliffite translations, denied the request. Securing financial support among London's merchants, however, Tyndale embarked for Germany, visiting Wittenberg in 1524 and settling in Cologne the following year. Here the publication of his now-translated New Testament was begun, though the project's discovery forced him to flee to Worms, where the first complete edition was printed in 1526. Official hostility provoked by the popularity of copies smuggled into England again prompted Tyndale's flight, to Antwerp, where for nearly a decade he engaged in (but never completed) a translation of the Old Testament, a revision of a second (1534) New Testament edition, and the production of various theological and polemical works such as *The Parable of the Wicked Mammon* (1528), *The Obedience of a Christian Man* (1528), *The Practice of Prelates* (1530), and *An Answer unto Sir Thomas More* (1531). When his identity was betrayed in 1535, he was arrested and imprisoned outside Brussels. He was condemned for heresy in August of 1536; in early October of that year he was executed by hanging, and his body was burned.

Tyndale's theological debt to Luther is evident not only in his biblical translation, which included preface and prologues clearly dependent on Luther's, but also in his subsequent treatises and commentaries. *The Parable* reproduces and expands on Luther's 1522 sermon on the unjust steward, and his exposition of the Sermon on the Mount (1533) similarly follows Luther's own of the previous year. Tyndale's adoption of Luther was never without adaptation, however. By 1530 he had clearly rejected Luther's eucharistic theology, favoring instead that of reformers Ulrich Zwingli and Johannes Oecolampadius. And even while consistently advocating justification by grace through faith, his emphasis on regenerate obedience was occasionally articulated in a manner suggesting that salvation was conditional on such obedience. His most enduring legacy, though, is unquestionably his New Testament translation, which not only introduced terminology that would remain central in Anglophone theology (e.g., atonement), but which would also become the urtext for subsequent English Bibles, including that of Miles Coverdale (1535), which reproduced the whole of Tyndale's New Testament, and the much more influential Authorized "King James" Version (1611), which retained some 90 percent of his vocabulary and syntax.

See also Bible Translations; England; Henry VIII

Bibliography

Daniell, D., ed. *Tyndale's New Testament*. Yale University Press, 1996; Daniell, D. *William Tyndale: A Biography*. Yale University Press, 1994; Trueman, C. *Luther's Legacy: Salvation and English Reformers, 1525–1556*. Oxford University Press, 1994; Walter, H., ed. *Works of William Tyndale*. Reprint in 2 vols. Banner of Truth, 2010; Werrell, R. *The Theology of William Tyndale*. James Clarke, 2006.

KOREY D. MAAS

U

United Lutheran Church in America

As an American Lutheran church body, the United Lutheran Church in America (ULCA, 1918–62) formed in 1918 by the merger of three Lutheran groups embodying the Mühlenberg tradition and located predominantly in the eastern United States. The first general church body in the United States was the Evangelical Lutheran General Synod in the United States (General Synod), formed in 1820 by synods who traced their history to the missionary work of Henry Melchior Mühlenberg and others in the eighteenth century. The American Civil War resulted in the separation of Southern synods, who formed the General Synod of the Evangelical Lutheran Church in the Confederate States (later "in the South," popularly known as the General Synod South) in 1863. Theological disputes within the General Synod over the meaning of the Lutheran confessions for Lutheran identity led to a schism in 1866, when the departing synods, including the Pennsylvania Ministerium (founded in 1748), formed the General Council of the Evangelical Lutheran Church in North America (General Council).

In the late nineteenth century, a number of free conferences and joint projects (esp. the development of a common liturgy and hymnal) nudged the three groups toward conversations about reunion. The final catalyst for this merger was the celebration of the quadricentennial of the Reformation in 1917; as the date approached, these bodies formed a joint committee to plan a celebration, and spurred on by lay members of this committee, a proposal emerged to reunite the three groups. It came to fruition in November 1918, when delegates from the constituent groups formally constituted the ULCA. The new church existed until 1962, when it became part of the merger that formed the Lutheran Church in America (LCA). At its founding, the ULCA was made up of forty-five constituent synods with some thirty-seven hundred congregations. With a baptized membership of over a million—nearly two-thirds of them in the middle Atlantic states—the church soon became the largest Lutheran body in the United States and remained so throughout its existence.

The rapidity with which the merger was consummated led to some administrative challenges; there was, for example, considerable geographical overlap among its constituent synods. The ULCA fostered a series of synodical mergers, particularly in its first decade. There were also a few new synods organized over the years, and two previously independent synods (the Slovak Zion Synod and the Icelandic Synod) became a part of the ULCA; at the end of its existence in 1962, the ULCA was composed of thirty-two synods. The ULCA also struggled to some degree with the burden of inheriting from the predecessor churches a dozen seminaries, with a thirteenth established shortly after the merger. Since the seminaries were controlled by the synods, it was difficult to force mergers or closings, and there were still ten seminaries in operation when the church became part of the LCA in 1962. The church also operated fourteen colleges.

In the course its forty-two years, the church was led by only two presidents, both of whom were widely respected in inter-Lutheran and ecumenical circles. Frederick H. Knubel, elected the first president in 1918, led the ULCA in its developmental years into close cooperation with other Lutherans through the National Lutheran Council and the Lutheran World Conventions. Under his presidency, the new church developed its home and foreign missions programs. It kept an open door to ecumenical relationships, with a consultative relationship with the Federal Council of Churches and active participation in a number of other interchurch societies and conferences. Upon Knubel's retirement in 1944, Franklin Clark Fry was elected president. He led the ULCA into even more interaction with other churches, including membership in the National Council of Churches, the World Council of Churches, and the Lutheran World Federation; Fry himself was a prime mover in the beginnings of each of those organizations. He was often called "Mr. Protestant" and was featured on the cover of *Time* magazine in 1958. His ministry brought the ULCA firmly into the limelight as a major player in American Protestantism.

Following the lead of some other American Protestant groups, the ULCA established a Department of Social Action, pushing the church into greater awareness of and concern for societal issues. Generally regarded as the most theologically liberal of the Lutheran Church bodies, the ULCA was often criticized by the more conservative midwestern Lutheran church bodies; nonetheless, it was committed to the Scriptures, the ecumenical creeds, and the unaltered Augsburg Confession as its doctrinal basis; its constitution (rather naively) contained a standing invitation to other Lutheran churches agreeing with that basis to unite with them. It was also the most Americanized Lutheran body, having roots going back to the colonial era; while it continued to have some work in German, by its later years only a few of its congregations conducted services in German. In terms of its polity, the ULCA was the most centralized of American Lutheran bodies, with considerable authority being granted to synods and to the national church. The ULCA operated the United Lutheran Publication House in Philadelphia, which published under the imprint Muhlenberg Press. The official organ of the church was a magazine known as *The Lutheran*. In 1962 the ULCA joined with the Augustana Evangelical Lutheran Church, the American Evangelical Lutheran Church, and the Suomi Synod to form the Lutheran Church in America. The ULCA was the largest of the four bodies, bringing into the merger some 4,540 congregations with 2.5 million baptized members.

See also Fry, Franklin Clark; General Council of the Evangelical Lutheran Church in North America; General Synod; General Synod South; Lutheran Church in America

Bibliography

Bachmann, E. T. *The United Lutheran Church in America, 1918–1962*. Fortress, 1997; Flessner, D. A., et al. "Lutheran Church in America: The United Lutheran Church in America." In *The Encyclopedia of the Lutheran Church*, ed. J. Bodensieck, 2:1375–407. Augsburg, 1965; Wentz, A. R. *A Basic History of Lutheranism in America*. Fortress, 1964.

RICHARD O. JOHNSON

United States of America

The first known presence of Lutherans in North America dates from 1619, with a Danish expedition to find the fabled Northwest Passage to Asia. There were subsequent colonizing efforts by the Scandinavian kingdoms, with a Swedish colony on the Delaware after 1638 and a similar Danish colony on the Virgin Islands after 1672; in both colonies Lutheran congregations were established. The seventeenth-century Dutch settlement of New Netherlands contained a number of Lutherans, and though discouraged by the Dutch authorities, they founded a Lutheran parish there from 1649, which is the oldest continual Lutheran congregation in the United States. But the majority of Lutherans who came to British North America were German immigrants who began arriving in the late seventeenth century and settled in the middle colonies of Pennsylvania, Maryland, and New Jersey. Groups of Lutheran refugees were settled in New York and Georgia and later Virginia. Since this immigration consisted primarily of individuals and families, the formation of Lutheran congregations proceeded slowly, impeded by the poverty of the people and the lack of Lutheran clergy willing to settle in North America. This need for pastors sometimes meant that congregations often had to rely on failed or fraudulent clergy from Europe, which caused a great deal of trouble.

Such often chaotic situations began to be addressed in 1742, when the Pietist Halle Institution sent Pastor Henry Melchior Mühlenberg to Pennsylvania. Although he was called to only three congregations in Philadelphia, through his personal presence he became the acknowledged leader of Lutherans in the middle colonies. Lutheran pastors gathered to form the Ministerium of Pennsylvania in 1748, in order to ensure a supply of pastors, to help to resolve disputes, and to defend Lutheran congregations from the inroads of clerical imposters and other religious groups, such as the Moravians. Though there were other Lutheran leaders in America at the time, most Lutherans soon recognized Mühlenberg as the key leader. In colonial America, Lutherans developed a network of German-speaking congregations that stretched from New York to Georgia, with outlying congregations in Nova Scotia and Maine. By 1790 there were perhaps twenty-five thousand Lutheran congregational members in North America. Though they were mostly German speaking, American Lutherans could not avoid the divisions of the American Revolution (1775–83). Many tried to remain neutral in the struggle, while others sided with the American revolutionaries, with some Lutherans serving in prominent positions in the American armed forces. Still others wished to remain loyal to the British king, who was also a German prince, and after the war left the new United States for Canada. British policy had been to keep settlers on the eastern side of the Appalachian Mountains, but after the end of the war, Americans were free to move into the new western lands of the Ohio River valley. Lutherans joined this movement into the frontier, which caused major problems for American Lutheran leaders. The continuing shortage of pastors meant that gathering in the scattered Lutherans was a constant problem, while established eastern congregations were depleted by this migration. Traveling Lutheran pastors occasionally visited Lutheran families on the frontier, and slowly Lutheran congregations were formed in the new western states. Because of the distance, new regional Lutheran synods were formed in New York, Ohio, Maryland, Virginia, and the South.

After the Revolutionary War, American Lutherans also battled over a transition to the use of the English language. Many in the younger generations championed this change, but older leaders sought to maintain the use of German. This struggle was intense but brief: the inevitable transition occurred through the first decades of the nineteenth century. American Lutherans learned to worship and do theology in English, and in doing so many moved in the religious directions of their English-speaking Protestant neighbors. The dispersion of Lutherans and the development of regional synods also pushed them to consider a national structure for all American Lutherans, another controversial development. The first such structure, the General Synod, was formed in 1820, and although it did not represent all American Lutherans, it did establish the first American Lutheran seminary at Gettysburg, Pennsylvania, in 1826. In America, the early nineteenth century was a time of great religious fervor and expansion among all Protestants, as religious revivalism and evangelism expanded throughout the country. Having made the transition to English, American Lutherans became involved in this religious renewal, which called into question aspects of Lutheran theology and practice, and by extension raised issues of the authority of the Lutheran confessional documents. Wishing to become more deeply involved with their Protestant neighbors, some Lutherans sought to distance themselves from some of the distinctive confessional ideas of traditional Lutheranism. This American Lutheranism became a center of dispute over a proposed "American Edition" of the Augsburg Confession in the 1850s. Some American Lutherans resisted this and urged instead a renewal of the distinctive elements of traditional Lutheran confessional theology within their synods, in line with a growing confessional revival in Germany. The resulting confessional conflict was also complicated by the increasingly bitter American struggle over slavery and its abolition, which began to create tensions between Northern and Southern Lutherans. While only a few of the Northern Lutheran synods actually adopted statements supporting abolition, with the coming of the Civil War (1861–65) the Southern Lutherans formed their own General Synod South. Northern Lutherans split over confessional issues in 1867, with the formation of a new General Council to rival the General Synod.

Large-scale immigration from Europe began again after 1840, and by World War I as many as thirty million people had immigrated to North America. Millions of new Lutherans, mainly Germans and Scandinavians, settled in the United States and began to form their own congregations and synods. These groups wanted to use their native languages, and some were deeply suspicious of the already established, English-speaking Lutherans. These new immigrants pushed farther into the central midwestern region of the United States, and began the further expansion of organized Lutheran denominations in the country; by 1900 there were at least a dozen major groups, with many other smaller ones. Differences in languages between the immigrants was one cause, but often there was a splintering even within linguistic groups over Lutheran theology and practice, reflecting issues brought with them from Europe. German, Swedish, Norwegian, Danish, Finnish, Slovak, and Icelandic denominations were formed, and many grew rapidly, especially the German-language Missouri Synod. By the end of the nineteenth century, American Lutherans, when added together, had grown to be the third largest Protestant communion in the United States. The lives of these new immigrants often centered on their Lutheran congregations, which provided them not only familiar religious services in their ethnic languages but also social and cultural worlds, and helped the transition to American life. The immigrants had to establish and maintain these congregations themselves (a major transition from the European situation, where many churches depended upon some form of governmental support), and these congregations and denominations were key to their ethnic culture. This being said, only a fraction of immigrants from Lutheran countries actually joined Lutheran congregations in the United States.

There were never enough pastors and congregations to serve the far-flung immigrant communities, and some new arrivals exercised their new religious freedom to join other denominations or to forego organized religion altogether. During the nineteenth century, despite these difficulties, American Lutherans developed an extensive network of institutions, not only congregations and synods but also schools, colleges, and seminaries, along with hospitals, orphanages, and other social-service institutions. Women were prominent in supporting the local congregations and other institutions through their own organized mission societies. Lutherans also developed a rich written culture, with publication houses that produced periodicals and books by the thousands. Even though the task of gathering in the Lutherans in America taxed these denominations to the limits of their resources, some American Lutherans looked beyond their ethnic borders and longed to join the Protestant mission movement around the world. For some, this meant outreach to domestic populations, such as African Americans and Native Americans. Others longed to do mission work overseas in Asia, Africa, and South America, or to organize mission societies to support these endeavors.

Much of this religious culture was developed within the ethnic community of American Lutheranism, but in the twentieth century cultural forces and political events drove Lutherans into the American religious mainstream. World War I (1914–18) was key, as antiforeign attitudes accelerated the linguistic transition to English (esp. of German speakers), assisted by the virtual cessation of further immigration. As they began to work in English, there was less need for separate, ethnically specific denominations, and a prolonged process of merger and consolidation began, a trend that would define American Lutheranism in the twentieth century. Many American Lutherans also began to work together through pan-Lutheran organizations, such as the National Lutheran Council and the Synodical Conference, and took prominent roles within the world Lutheran communion. The expansion of American Lutheranism was temporarily impeded by the Great Depression (1929–41), which financially constricted many of its institutions. The events of World War II (1941–45) also diverted American Lutheran attention, but they participated fully in the postwar expansion and the baby boom. This expansion, especially into new suburban areas and into the American South and West, challenged Lutherans to provide enough new congregations and facilities to meet the need. The swell pushed American Lutheranism to its numerical heights, which numbered over nine million members by the 1960s.

Merger activities also culminated at this time, with the formation of two large American Lutheran denominations, the American Lutheran Church (ALC) in 1960 and the Lutheran Church in America (1962). With the existing Lutheran Church–Missouri Synod (LCMS), these three denominations represented over 95 percent of all Lutherans in America. During this period Canadian congregations formed their own separate Canadian Lutheran denominations. During the postwar period most American Lutheran groups had fully moved into the American cultural mainstream, and especially into the American Protestant mainstream, but just as that mainstream itself began its long decline. The political, social, and cultural tensions of the 1960s rocked the nation and caused deep concerns and divisions within American Lutheranism. One result was the decision to ordain women as Lutheran pastors,

adopted by the ALC and LCA in the 1970s, but not by the LCMS. The LCMS was racked by internal divisions during this time, as a new conservative regime took over control of the synod, dividing the denomination and splitting its flagship seminary in St. Louis. In 1976 a group of moderate pastors and congregations left and formed a new denomination, the Association of Evangelical Lutheran Churches (AELC). As theological and social division widened in the 1980s between the LCMS and the ALC, LCA, and AELC, the latter three entered into further merger negotiations, which resulted in the formation of the Evangelical Lutheran Church in America (ELCA) in 1988. The new ELCA contained about two-thirds of American Lutherans, while the LCMS contained most of the remaining third, with the conservative Wisconsin Evangelical Lutheran Synod (400,000 members) as the largest of a number of other much smaller denominations. American Lutheranism in the late twentieth century was not immune from the general decline of mainline American Protestantism and the rise of conservative evangelical Protestantism, and by 2015 the number of American Lutherans declined to about seven million. While the LCMS has seen a slow loss in membership, the ELCA has experienced a much steeper decline, substantially caused by divisive controversies over ministry, ecumenism, and sexuality, including the decision in 2009 to ordain gay and lesbian pastors in committed relationships. Out of these controversies, those departing the ELCA have formed two new American Lutheran denominations, the Lutheran Congregations in Mission for Christ (2001) and the North American Lutheran Church (2010), which together represent about half a million American Lutherans, this being the largest American Lutheran schism since the 1860s. In the twenty-first century American Lutheranism faces some serious issues but has a strong tradition and many assets with which to meet them.

See also American Lutheran Church (1930–60); American Lutheran Church (1960–88); General

Council of the Evangelical Lutheran Church in North America; General Synod; General Synod South; Lutheran Church in America; Lutheran Church–Missouri Synod; Lutheran Denominations in America, Minor; Lutheran Social Services; Ministerium of Pennsylvania; Race/Minorities; United Lutheran Church in America; Wisconsin Evangelical Lutheran Synod

Bibliography

Granquist, M. *Lutherans in America: A New History.* Fortress, 2015; Lagerquist, D. *The Lutherans.* Denominations in America 9. Greenwood, 1999; Nelson, E. C., ed. *The Lutherans in North America.* Fortress, 1975; Wiederaenders, R., ed. *Historical Guide to Lutheran Church Bodies of North America.* Lutheran Historical Conference Publication 1. 2nd ed. Lutheran Historical Conference, 1998; Wolf, R. C. *Documents of Lutheran Unity in America.* Fortress, 1966.

MARK A. GRANQUIST

Universidade Luterana do Brasil (ULBRA)

The Universidade Luterana do Brasil (Lutheran University of Brazil, ULBRA), the largest Lutheran university in Latin America, was founded by the Evangelical Lutheran São Paulo congregation of Canoas, a congregation of the Igreja Evangélica Luterana do Brasil (IELB). By 2014 ULBRA's educational system comprised seventeen elementary and high schools, including one school for the deaf and several dozen undergraduate and graduate fields. The first step of this system was the 1969 founding of Colégio Cristo Redentor (Christ the Redeemer School) by the São Paulo congregation under the leadership of Pastor Ruben Eugen Becker. In 1972 the congregation founded the Faculdades Canoenses, offering college undergraduate courses. In 1981 classes began to be held at the new university campus under construction in the city of Canoas, RS; in 1988 the institution was granted university status. During the next eight years, ten more campuses were created and operated by ULBRA, five in the state of Rio Grande do Sul and the other five in the states of Rondônia, Pará, Amazonas, Tocantins, and Goiás. Since 2006 the university has also offered distance education courses. Pastor Becker continued as rector of the university until 2009, when Pastor Marcos Ziemer was elected to that position.

Through an agreement between the university and the IELB, the future pastors of the IELB have received most of their training at the university since 1995. By 2014 more than 160,000 students had graduated from one of the programs offered by ULBRA.

See also Brazil; Igreja Evangélica Luterana do Brasil (IELB) (Evangelical Lutheran Church of Brazil)

PAULO WILLE BUSS

University of Wittenberg in the Sixteenth Century

When the territory of the Wettins was divided between the brothers Albert and Ernest in 1485, Ernest received the electoral title and the duchy of Saxony-Wittenberg (Ernestine Saxony), but Saxony's historic University of Leipzig (founded 1409) lay within the territory under the rule of Albert (Albertine Saxony). The University of Wittenberg was thus founded, by imperial privilege dated July 6, 1502, as part of the plan of Elector Frederick III ("the Wise," r. 1486–1525) to give prominence to the city of Wittenberg as the elector's residence. It was named Leucorea, the Greek equivalent of Wittenberg, "White Mountain." It was officially dedicated by a papal representative on January 17, 1503, having started classes on October 18, 1502.

From its founding this university was open to the movement of humanism, though the various schools of Scholastic thought (realism, or the *via antiqua*; nominalism, or the *via moderna*; and Scotism) were dominant in the faculty of theology. Martin Luther first came to the Leucorea in 1508–9, during which time he lectured on moral philosophy and continued his theological studies, receiving the degrees of *baccalaureus biblicus* and *baccalaureus sententiarius* (bachelor of Bible and bachelor of the Sentences [of Peter Lombard]). In 1511 he transferred permanently to the Augustinian monastery at Wittenberg (founded in 1504). Luther's mentor Johann von Staupitz, who had been involved as consultant in the founding of the university, urged him to take up doctoral studies in theology, and eventually Luther assumed Staupitz's chair in theology at the university. Luther developed as a theologian and lived out his vocation as professor, pastor, and reformer in the context of Wittenberg and its university, which as a result became the center of the German Evangelical movement and of the Lutheran Reformation.

Luther developed his Evangelical theology not in isolation but in the collegial atmosphere of this university and through the influence (both positive and negative) of others. The reform movement developed first in the context of curricular reform at the university, shaped by humanist principles. Luther wrote in May 1517, "Our theology and St. Augustine are progressing well, and with God's help rule at our University. Aristotle is gradually falling from his throne. . . . It is amazing how the lectures on the *Sentences* are disdained" (LW 48:42). Yet early curricular reforms focused not so much on Luther's new theology or removing the Scholastic and Aristotelian curriculum but rather on a humanist program that supplemented Scholasticism and focused on languages and literature. The brilliant young humanist Philip Melanchthon was called to teach Greek at the university in 1518 and was instrumental in these reforms. As the controversy over indulgences developed into a reform movement, from 1518 to 1522 the colleagues (including Melanchthon and Andreas Karlstadt) and students at the university played critical roles both in the Evangelical movement and in this (humanist) curricular reform. Upon Luther's return from the Wartburg in March 1522, when he again took a prominent role in the reform movement, the University of Wittenberg became its intellectual center. Luther and his colleagues taught, published, coordinated reforms elsewhere, and translated the Bible into German. Eventually curricular reforms (in 1524 of the arts faculty and in 1533 of the theology faculty, both written by Melanchthon) also bore the stamp of the new theology. By 1535 the university had become the de facto ecclesiastical center of

the Lutheran movement in Germany as ordinations to the pastoral office were conducted at the university. Regular declamations were introduced into the arts faculty in the 1520s. Likewise formal disputations (a now-reformed inheritance of Scholasticism) were resumed in 1533 for the granting of doctoral degrees in theology, medicine, and law and continued in the granting of the degree of master of arts in the arts faculty.

After Luther's death, the defeat of the Lutheran Smalcaldic League by imperial forces in 1547 led to the transfer of the electoral title and of Wittenberg to the Albertine Duke Moritz of Saxony, who was determined to make the university central to his (short-lived) policy of cooperating with the emperor. While the defeated Duke John Frederick established a new *Hochschule* in Jena, Melanchthon's decision to remain in Wittenberg both preserved Wittenberg University's central role in the Reformation in Saxony and contributed to the controversy over the so-called Leipzig Interim, which led to the development of various parties (often named Gnesio-Lutheran and Philippist) in a period of Lutheran discord. Despite increasing enrollments in the later years of Melanchthon's leadership and the university's acceptance of the Formula of Concord in 1581, the school's influence as the dominant center of the Lutheran Reformation began to decline after Melanchthon's death in 1560. Repeated charges of "crypto-Philippism" in the 1570s and eventually "crypto-Calvinism" were laid against the university's faculty of theology. Calvinism in the university had its heyday under Elector Christian I (r. 1586–91) but was repudiated in later reigns, and by the end of the sixteenth century the university became a leading center of Lutheran Orthodoxy. Among the important figures were Polycarp Leyser, Agidius Hunnius, and Leonhard Hutter.

See also Electors of Saxony; Humanism and the Reformation; Leipzig Proposal (Interim); Lutheran Orthodoxy; Melanchthon, Philip; Wittenberg Circle, Parties within

Bibliography

Kruse, J.-M. *Universitätstheologie und Kirchenreform: Die Anfänge der Reformation in Wittenberg 1516–1522.* Von Zabern, 2002; Rosin, R. "The Reformation, Humanism, and Education: The Wittenberg Model for Reform." *Concordia Journal* 16 (1990): 301–18; Scheible, H. "Die Philosophische Fakultät der Universität Wittenberg von der Gründung bis zur Vertreibung der Philippisten." *ARG* 98 (2007): 7–44; Wengert, T. "Higher Education and Vocation: The University of Wittenberg (1517–1533) between Renaissance and Reform." In *The Lutheran Doctrine of Vocation*, ed. J. Maxfield, 1–21. Vol. 11 of *The Pieper Lectures*. Concordia Historical Institute and Luther Academy, 2008.

JOHN A. MAXFIELD

V

Valla, Lorenzo

Italian humanist Lorenzo Valla (1405/7–1457) is most famous in Lutheran circles for his treatise *De falso credita et ementita Constantini donatione* (The falsely believed and forged donation of Constantine). Born into a family of jurists and church officials around 1405 to 1407 in Piacenza, Valla studied in Rome, mastering rhetoric and Greek in addition to classical Latin style. Seeking employment in northern Italy, he became professor of rhetoric at the University of Pavia in 1431. There he published *De voluptate* (*On Desire*, also known as *De vero bono* [On the true good]). After the municipal jurists forced him to leave in 1433 for criticizing the great jurist Bartolo de Sassoferrato for not understanding Roman law correctly, Valla's life reveals a pattern of such conflict. He once wrote that he was often criticized "because I never fail to select someone to chastise." His subsequent travels eventually took him to Florence, where he met some of the great humanist scholars. At the same time he sought to return to Rome, preferably through employment in the court of Pope Eugene IV. In 1435, having failed to gain a position in the papal court, he entered the service of King Alfonso V of Aragon, whom he served as secretary at his court in Naples until 1447. During this period Valla produced several important works. In addition to a history of Alfonso's reign, they included *De libero arbitrio* (On free will) and *Dialecticae disputationes* (Dialectical disputations, 1439), in which Valla argued for the place of rhetoric over philosophy. This was followed by *De professione religiosorum* (The profession of the religious) and his work on the *Donation of Constantine* (1440). In that same year he completed the *Elegantiae linguae Latinae* (The elegances of the Latin language), which

he had begun in Pavia. He added *Annotationes in Novum Testamentum* (Annotations on the New Testament) in 1444, where he criticized the standard Latin translation (the Vulgate) on the basis of the Greek text. At the same time, Valla faced an inquiry by the Inquisition in Naples and was threatened with another in Rome. Ultimately he was cleared, perhaps as a result of King Alfonso V's intervention. Valla's continued conflict with other scholars and with church officials, in addition to the criticisms he had leveled against the pope in the *Donation*, meant that his further requests for a position at the papal court continued to fall on deaf ears. However, when Pope Nicholas V succeeded Eugene IV, Valla received a secretarial position. Other appointments followed. Appointed professor of rhetoric at the university in 1450, he was named apostolic secretary and made a canon of St. John Lateran by Pope Calixtus III in 1455. His works from this period continued to target other scholars, including Poggio Bracciolini, a humanist who had become famous for discovering classical Latin manuscripts in monastic libraries. Even Valla's final work, a speech in praise of Thomas Aquinas, aroused controversy by insisting that his successors had misunderstood Thomas. Valla died on August 1, 1457.

Though as a humanist Valla concerned himself with language, the religious focus of many of his writings is clear and has been increasingly emphasized in recent scholarship. His famous work on the *Donation*, for example, was on its face a critical approach to the text of the document in terms of its language and content, demonstrating beyond doubt that it was a much later forgery. Yet Valla's work was also a critique of the institutional church that frequently defended itself with that text. The speeches inserted into the mouth of the

Donation's purported recipient, Pope Sylvester, contrasted with and highlighted the misplaced priorities of the papacy in Valla's own day. It is not surprising that the *Donation*, which Luther read in the sixteenth-century edition produced by Ulrich von Hutten, influenced Reformation arguments against the papacy, including Luther's own. Luther, however, had used and valued Valla's works, such as the *Annotations* and *Dialectical Disputations*, throughout his career, leading him to remark on one occasion, "Valla pleases me. He is a good author and a good Christian; I read him most avidly" (WA TR 5:333 #5729).

See also Humanism and the Reformation; Papacy

Bibliography
Lindhardt, J. "Valla and Luther on the Free Will." In *Widerspruch: Luthers Auseinandersetzung mit Erasmus von Rotterdam*, ed. K. Kopperi, 46–53. Luther-Agricola-Gesellschaft, 1997; Valla, L. *On the Donation of Constantine*. Trans. G. W. Bowersock. Harvard University Press, 2007; Whitford, D. M. "The Papal Antichrist: Martin Luther and the Underappreciated Influence of Lorenzo Valla." *RQ* 61 (2008): 26–52; Wright, W. J. *Martin Luther's Understanding of God's Two Kingdoms: A Response to the Challenge of Skepticism*. Baker Academic, 2010.

PAUL W. ROBINSON

Vasa, Gustav

King of Sweden from 1523 to 1560, Gustav Vasa (1496–1560) was a resolute leader who expelled the Danes, reformed the Swedish church, and changed the monarchy from an elected to a hereditary office. During the early years of Vasa's reign, Sweden went through a gradual process of adopting Lutheran reforms. The movement began in 1523 with the introduction of Evangelical preaching. Vasa appointed Laurentius Andreae and Olavus Petri to important positions in Stockholm, where they advocated Evangelical ideas and translated the New Testament into Swedish. In 1527 the Swedish church became a national church, with King Vasa as its supreme head. In the 1530s and 1540s, Vasa encouraged church leaders to reform the liturgy, reduce the power of bishops, end clerical celibacy, and introduce other ecclesiastical reforms. However, Vasa was not personally involved in many of the decisions; he controlled the church but was not especially interested in matters of doctrine. Vasa skillfully supervised the state-building process in early modern Sweden and used the country's new Lutheran faith as a way of solidifying his own power base and building a united and independent nation.

See also Petri (Nericus), Laurentius; Petri, Olavus; Sweden

Bibliography
Roberts, M. *The Early Vasas: A History of Sweden, 1523–1611*. Cambridge University Press, 1986.

MICHAEL J. HALVORSON

Venezuela

In 1529 Charles V of Spain, deeply in debt, turned the administration of Venezuela over to the Welser Banking House of Augsburg. There is, however, no evidence to substantiate the claim that Lutheran congregations were established in Venezuela during the twenty-year Welser regime. What Lutheran influence entered colonial Venezuela came in the form of tracts, Bibles, catechisms, and hymnbooks hidden in bolts of cloth and smuggled into the Spanish colonies to avoid confiscation by agents of the Inquisition. In 1671 four Venezuelan priests were arrested, imprisoned, and accused of being Lutheran heretics. Three of these priests were Canary Islanders and one, Juan de Frias, a Venezuelan by birth. Refusing to recant, all four priests were burned at the stake in Cartagena on May 30, 1688.

After Venezuelan independence (1811) and the end of the Inquisition, some Lutheran settlers came to the new republic. The spiritual needs of the immigrants were served by the chaplains of German and Scandinavian ships frequenting the port of La Guaira. Services were conducted in German or one of the Scandinavian languages. From 1894 to 1930, German-speaking pastors from Europe were sent to serve the Lutherans in Caracas. The end of World War II brought to Venezuela a huge influx of Lutherans from the war-ravaged countries of Europe. Their coming to Venezuela led to the establishment of two Lutheran church bodies.

Responding to requests from listeners to the *Spanish Lutheran Hour*, German-speaking refugees, and English-speaking Lutherans working in the oil industry, missionaries affiliated with the Lutheran Church–Missouri Synod helped organize the Lutheran Church of Venezuela (Iglesia Luterana de Venezuela, ILV) in 1951. The ILV saw as its mission the evangelization of native Venezuelans and the establishment of congregations and schools that reflected the language and culture of people of Venezuela. Congregations were established in Caracas, Maturín, Ciudad Guayana, and the rural areas of the states of Monagas and Bolivar. More recently new mission congregations have been planted in Maracay, Valencia, Barcelona, Barinas, and Barquisimeto. Church workers are being prepared through Juan de Frias Theological Institute, established in 1970.

Under the auspices of the LWF, a multilanguage congregation was established in Caracas in 1952, as were congregations in Maracaibo, Valencia, Barquisimeto, and Turén. Together these congregations formed the Lutheran Church in Venezuela. As the descendants of the European immigrants have become more integrated into Venezuelan life and culture, Spanish has become the primary language employed in most of the congregations. More recently, missionaries from Finland have worked with the Lutheran Church in Venezuela in a number of evangelistic and humanitarian projects.

RUDOLPH BLANK

Vilmar, August Friedrich Christian

The German theologian August Friedrich Christian Vilmar was born on November 21, 1800, in Solz (Kurhessen) and died on July 30, 1868, in Marburg. A committed rationalist during his student years at Marburg, Vilmar had a change of heart through personal awakening and study of the church fathers; also important was the three-hundredth anniversary of the Augsburg Confession. He held various posts, including representative to the Kurhessen Assembly and, most important, professor of theology at Marburg. As spiritual leader of the Hessian Lutheran Church during the middle decades of the nineteenth century, Vilmar is remembered as a controversial figure in the history of modern German theology. He earned this criticism by engaging in fierce conservative polemics throughout his ecclesiastical career. Vilmar was the implacable foe of radicalism in theology. His most influential work is *The Theology of Facts versus the Theology of Rhetoric* (1856). There he asks: "Is the discipline of theology intended for the body of Christ or the university? Does it serve proclamation and discipleship or an academic career? These are the crucial questions." Vilmar calls theology that obeys the church "the theology of facts"; theology that conforms to the university he dubbed "the theology of rhetoric." Between these two ways of doing theology is fixed a chasm that cannot be crossed.

Bibliography

Vilmar, A. F. C. *The Theology of Facts versus the Theology of Rhetoric* (1856). Trans. R. Harrisville. Introduced by W. Sundberg. Lutheran Legacy Press, 2008.

WALTER SUNDBERG

Vocation

Although Luther never wrote an extended general treatise on Christian vocation in the world, what he says about it revolutionized Christian self-understanding and action in this world. Luther's teaching about vocation may equal his view of justification by faith in its significance.

Luther speaks of vocation in two ways. One is the "spiritual" calling to cast oneself into the arms of God's mercy. This is the shared call to faith, to become a Christian, and to receive baptism. This is vocation as gospel *coram Deo* (before God). Though all Christians share this calling, they live out their faith in a life of love through and in their own distinctive callings. This is vocation as law *coram hominibus* (before human beings). These callings include the varied social stations or spheres occupied by individual Christians. Each human life is providentially situated. This includes one's location in domestic life and work, neighborhood, social status, citizenship, and more. Developed from the apostle Paul's words in 1 Cor. 7:20, Luther says Christians should remain in the calling (Greek: *klēsis*; German: *Beruf*) they occupied when they were called (to become a Christian). Luther identifies social location, or *Stand* (walk of life), a Christian occupies as *Beruf* (Latin: *vocatio*), a calling from God through which to serve one's neighbors.

Luther developed his doctrine of vocation in a polemic with contemporary Roman Catholic and, to a lesser degree, Anabaptist views of vocation. As a former priest and Augustinian monk, Luther had intimate knowledge of vocation in his Catholic context. This context restricted vocation to the "spiritual" vocations of being a priest or living under a vow as a monk, friar, or nun. The latter form of the spiritual life involved going beyond the commandments to live according to the "counsels of perfection," summed up in the vows of poverty, chastity, and obedience. By taking these vows, entering these callings, and excelling in "good works," one would experience a second baptism (removing all guilt and punishment for sins committed up until then) and enter "a state of perfection": although by no means perfect, the good works had more worth and the sins less effect on the soul. These modes of life were thought to be religiously superior to mundane lives in marriage and family, work, and politics.

Luther turned this approach to vocation on its head. He rejected the separation of the counsels of perfection and the commandments. He taught that Christians serve God, not by isolating themselves in convents and monasteries, but by meeting the needs of neighbors in and through their many callings. All Christians, by virtue of their baptism into Christ, share Christ's priesthood, and they live out that priesthood as parents, husbands, wives, children, farmers, judges, citizens, domestic servants, rulers, and any other station in life they occupy. By obeying God in these and other roles, Christians do holy work that is precious to God, namely, loving the neighbor. Some walks of life are sinful and cannot be a calling. Among these, Luther lists "robbery, usury, public women, and, as they are at present, the pope, cardinals, bishops, priests, monks, and nuns" (*Church Postil*, 249). Monastics are "idlers, who, like locusts, caterpillars, and beetles devour everyone else's substance. . . . But they in their turn neither serve nor show charity or do good to anyone" (*Judgment of Martin Luther on Monastic Vows* [1521], LW 44:335).

Luther rejected the religious works so highly praised by the late medieval church, including donating money for ornate cathedrals, engaging in ceremonies, chanting, and singing vigils and Masses. He says, "Do you think that God will permit himself to be paid with the sound of bells, the smoke of candles, the glitter of gold and such fancies?" God has commanded none of this, and none of it benefits one's neighbors. Instead one should follow Christ's example. "If you see your neighbor going astray, sinning, or suffering in body or soul, you are to leave everything else and at once help him in every way in your power" (*Church Postil*, 146).

In his reflection on Anna, widow and prophetess who prayed night and day in the temple (Luke 2:36–38), Luther observes that she must have been a widow without any children or parents: "otherwise she would not have served God but the devil by not departing from the temple and neglecting her duty of managing her household according to the will of God" (*Church Postil*, 281). He says that God "cannot bear to see anyone neglect the duties of his calling or station in life in order to imitate the works of the saints" and that if a married woman were to follow Anna's example and therefore forsake duties to husband, children, and parents to "go on a pilgrimage, to pray, fast, and go to church," she would "tempt God, confound the matrimonial estate," and "desert her own calling." This would be like "walking on one's ears, putting a veil over one's feet and a boot on one's head, and turning all things upside down." Luther recommends praying and fasting but warns, "You must not thereby be kept from or neglect the duties of your calling and station" (*Church Postil*, 281; see also *Address to the Christian Nobility*, LW 44:170–71).

Luther's view of vocation is deeply shaped by his doctrine of the two kingdoms or realms. The heavenly or spiritual kingdom is God's redemptive activity, bringing about forgiveness of sins and eternal life. It is the place for faith and not works. Here one stands before God on the basis of God's mercy alone. Here one's soul or conscience either sinfully strives to justify oneself by good works or, despairing of that, instead trusts in God's promises revealed in Jesus Christ. God also works as Creator and Judge in the temporal or earthly kingdom. This divine administration aims at earthly peace, justice, and the unfolding of God's good creation. This is the realm of one's vocations in daily life. Life here is governed by reason; the Bible is primarily about matters pertaining to the spiritual kingdom and is only indirectly relevant to complex decisions in most earthly matters.

Following medieval social theory, Luther thought that in the earthly kingdom we relate to others in three "estates" (*Stände*; "walks of life"). These express God's continuing creative activity and so are not static but dynamic. Nonbelievers unknowingly serve God in these places. But believers perceive their social places through faith as vocations from God (*Beruf*). The most basic estate is the household. In Luther's day this included home and economic life, parents and children and servants. Two other estates grew out of the first: temporal authority and church. The temporal power is concerned with justice, common goods, defense of innocents, and punishing evildoers.

This authority, as part of the temporal realm, uses coercion, even to the point of lethal force, to punish evildoers and protect innocent life. At this point Luther argues against the pacifist Anabaptist reformers, who denied that Christians could be soldiers, hangmen, princes, or any occupation requiring coercion against evildoers. Luther taught that Jesus's directives to turn the other cheek, not to resist evildoers, and to give to anyone who wants to borrow from you (Matt. 5:38–42) did not apply to official actions involving uses of the sword. They applied to individual Christians and to motivation, but not to people acting in their callings as prince, judge, or hangman. Officials are "masks" of God's justice as they in their official activity protect innocent life. Luther says that if the community lacks "hangmen, constables, judges, lords, or princes, and you find you are qualified," Christians should offer their services. Luther demands that all use of coercion be directed, not to selfish purposes, but to the protection of others. "In what concerns you and yours, you govern yourself by the gospel and suffer injustice toward yourself as a true Christian; in what concerns the person or property of others, you govern yourself according to love and tolerate no injustice toward your neighbor" (*Temporal Authority*, LW 45:95–96).

Marriage, household, economy, and temporal authority all deal with created, earthly things and so are shared by believers and nonbelievers alike. In these areas faith may shape motivation, but for the most part actions here should be guided by practical wisdom. Having faith, for example, will not lead to a distinctively Christian judicial system or to a greater ability to apply laws to complex cases. Nor will faith provide unique approaches to complex decisions in marriage and family life; here, too, practical wisdom sheds as much light or more light than the Bible. Thus Luther says that a Christian may marry "a Turk, a Jew, or a heretic" because "marriage is an outward, bodily thing, like any other worldly undertaking. Just as I may eat, drink, sleep, walk, ride with, buy from, speak to, and deal with a heathen, Jew, Turk, or heretic, so I may also marry and continue in wedlock with him" (*Estate of Marriage*, LW 45:25).

The third estate is the church. Here believers join together for worship, praise, and fellowship. Insofar as churches need offices, rules, and external structures, they are part of the temporal realm. Official church membership includes wheat and chaff, believers and nonbelievers. Like Augustine, Luther thought that only God truly knows who is a true believer. Nevertheless, the external marks of preaching the gospel and the sacraments define where such believers assemble, despite unbelievers in their midst.

Several theological ideas are central to Luther's understandings of calling. First is the doctrine of justification by faith alone. The works of love undertaken in and through one's callings do not cause salvation; rather, they are the result of receiving God's salvation through faith. Faith trusts the promises of God given in Jesus Christ, that God is full of mercy and eager to give new spiritual life to all who believe the good news about God in Christ. Yet faith and the salvation it bestows are gifts of God's grace worked by the Holy Spirit through the Word of God. They are received and not achieved through human works that earn a right relation with God. Faith in Christ brings about a new identity, one that no longer strives to earn God's favor through good works but rather spontaneously expresses love for God by loving one's neighbors. Though believers do good works in and through their callings, these works are the result, not the cause, of God's grace.

A second theological idea is the doctrine of creation and providence. Creation is unfinished, and God continues to nourish what is being created and to bring all things to their appointed purposes. Parents and members of the household, aptitudes and senses of priority, time in history, citizenship, and all facets of the human beings' socially situated lives—all these have been shaped by God's providence and continuing creation. These are not solely the result of chance, fate, or human freedom; they are shaped by God's will and providence. Faith alone reveals the human situation in creation and brings a profound religious sensibility to daily life and its opportunities for service to God and others. Because God's creative activity specifically situates our lives in relation to creation and our neighbors, discerning God's will is a creative, responsive process for believers. There are no easy rules or formulas to determine what we are called to do in each case.

Third is the incarnation. Luther had a profound realization that Jesus Christ, incarnate in the flesh, is also incarnate in human need and that in serving others through their callings, believers are serving Christ. Luther advises fathers to look on the tedious tasks of early child care through the eyes of faith, and so to imagine that they are holding the baby Jesus in their hands while they are changing dirty diapers (*The Estate of Marriage*, LW 45:41). A central biblical passage supporting Luther's approach is the parable of the final judgment, in which the king returns to judge the nations and separate the sheep from the goats. He will put the sheep at his right hand, bless them, and welcome them to inherit the kingdom prepared for them from the foundation of the world. The basis for doing so is giving Christ food, drink, welcome, clothing, and visitation in prison. The opposite is true for the goats at the king's left hand.

In addition to seeing Christ incarnate in the needs of the neighbor, Luther perceived Christ in the actions of those helping others in and through their callings. When people feed the hungry and support the lonely, they are being Christ for their neighbors. Christ is present in acts of justice, love, and mercy. When acting in their callings, agents become "masks of God," for ultimately God is acting through both the needs of neighbors and the authority of those who hold social power.

There are conservative elements in Luther's view of vocation. His beliefs that God appoints rulers and that Christians should be subject to them (Rom. 13:1–3), and his fear of individuals becoming their own judges caused him to reject rebellion against unjust rulers. His acceptance of a medieval hierarchy and his distrust for restless coveting of positions held by others cause him often to counsel Christians to stay in their callings and to obey those in authority.

But there are also socially reformist tendencies in his view of calling. In one's callings one should always look first to obedience to God's commandments (*Church Postil*, 244; Large Catechism, Ten Commandments, par. 116 in *BC* 402). He supported what today is called civil disobedience, when temporal powers demand that people disobey God's commandments. Luther's appeal to the calling of the German nobility is revolutionary in its attack on the Roman Catholic Church and in Luther's attempt to strip temporal powers from the Catholic church. Luther did not "submit" to papal authority or quietly endure the penalties imposed by the pope. Based on his own calling as a pastor and theologian, he wrote and spoke in ways nothing short of revolutionary and in ways that advanced far-reaching political and social change. When criticizing parents for forbidding their children to marry, Luther limits parental authority and advises children to disobey parents. Since marriage is a divine ordinance, willed by God and structured into the very fabric of creation, it is contrary to God's will to forbid one's child from entering into the callings of marriage and family. Parents contradicting these bounds "are to be regarded as if they were not parents at all, or were dead; their child is free to become engaged and to marry whomsoever he fancies" (*That Parents Should neither Hinder nor Compel*, LW 45:390).

In this, and in other ways, Luther's view of vocation has had profound influence. Though later Lutherans drew from the more conservative aspects of Luther's view, the socially and spiritually transformative strands are indeed present and ripe for harvest.

See also Creation; Good Works; Household, Children, Parents; Law, Uses of; Law and Gospel; Marriage and Divorce; State; Twofold Righteousness; Two Realms

Bibliography

Althaus, P. *The Ethics of Martin Luther*. Foreword and trans. R. C. Schultz. Esp. chaps. 3–4, 6. Fortress, 1972; Barth, K. *Church Dogmatics*. Vol. 3/4, *The Doctrine of Creation*. Ed. G. W. Bromiley and T. F. Torrance. Trans. G. W. Bromiley. Esp. chap. 12, §56.2. T&T Clark, 1961; Billing, E. *Our Calling*. Trans. C. Bergendoff. Fortress, 1964; Heiges, D. R. *The Christian Calling*. Esp. chap. 3. Fortress, 1958; Luther, M. *The Christian in Society*. Vol. 1. Ed. J. Atkinson. LW 44. Fortress, 1966; Luther, M. *The Christian in Society*. Vol. 2. Ed. W. I. Brandt. LW 45. Fortress, 1962; Luther, M. *Luther's Church Postil*. Vol. 1, *Gospels: Advent, Christmas and Epiphany Sermons*. In vol. 10 of *The Precious and Sacred Writings of Martin Luther*. Ed. J. N. Lenker. Lutherans in All Lands, 1903; Schuurman, D. J. *Vocation: Discerning Our Callings in Life*. Eerdmans, 2004; Troeltsch, E. *The Social Teaching of the Christian Churches*. Vol. 2. Trans. O. Wyon. Esp. chap. 3, §§1–2. Harper & Row, 1960; Wingren, G. *Luther on Vocation*. Trans C. C. Rasmussen. Muhlenberg, 1957.

DOUGLAS J. SCHUURMAN

Volga Germans

On July 22, 1763, Russian empress Catherine the Great, herself a German princess, issued a decree granting free transportation, land, and freedom of religion to German settlers. Upon arrival in the Volga region, the Germans proceeded to build fifty-nine Lutheran, thirty-three Catholic, and twenty-three Reformed churches. On October 25, 1819, the Evangelical Lutheran Consistory of the Volga was formed in Saratov, naming Dr. Ignatius Aurelius Fessler as bishop and superintendent. By the middle of the nineteenth century, the Volga consistory oversaw 120 schools with 32,706 students and 147 teachers. On the eve of the Bolshevik Revolution in 1917, there were 1,249,000 Lutherans in Russia with approximately 425,000 living in the Volga region. For example, St. Mary's Lutheran Church in Saratov numbered 16,400 parishioners.

In September–October 1941, fears of the invading German army uniting with ethnic Germans in Russia caused the Soviet government to deport 446,480 Volga Germans to central Asia (primarily Kazakhstan) and Siberia. With the fall of the USSR in 1991, it was decided that the Volga German Autonomous Soviet Socialist Republic (formed in 1924, dissolved in 1941) would not be restored. Many Volga Germans took advantage of the new freedoms in the new Russian Republic and immigrated to Germany.

See also Russia

Bibliography

German, A. A., et al. *Istorija nemcev Rossii*. MNSK, 2007; Licenberger, O. *Deutsche evangelische Siedlungen an der Wolga*. HFDR, 2013.

OLAV PANCHU

W

Walch, Johann Georg

As professor in Jena, 1718–75, and author of nearly three hundred works, Johann Georg Walch (1693–1775) is best known for his German dictionary of philosophy (1726), a ten-volume history of the Lutheran Church (1724–39), and a twenty-four-volume edition of Luther's works (1739–53), which was the basis for the later St. Louis edition. (1880–1910).

Walch's principal contributions were in philosophy, where he was influenced by Christian Wolff (1679–1754) and Christian Thomasius (1655–1728), and in church history, where his more balanced and moderate approach helped pave the way for Enlightenment historiography. Walch's attention to detail and terminological exactitude, first evident in his dictionary of philosophy, are constant throughout his work. Although sympathetic to many Pietist concerns, Walch's theological views were typical of late Lutheran Orthodoxy. He became a vehement critic of the Moravian Church and its founder, Count Nikolaus Ludwig von Zinzendorf. Walch's professorship at the University of Jena spanned fifty-eight years, the longest tenure of any professor there to date.

Bibliography

MacDonald, G. *Johann Georg Walchs Darstellung und Beurteilung des Grafen Nikolaus Ludwig von Zinzendorf und der Herrnhuter Brüdergemeine*. Unitas Fratrum Beiheft 25. Herrnhuter Verlag, 2015; Walch, J. G. *Doktor Martin Luthers Sämtliche Schriften*. 24 vols. Gebauer, 1739–53; Walch, J. G. *Historische und theologische Einleitung in die Religions-Streitigkeiten der Evangelisch-Lutherischen Kirchen*. Jena, 1730–39. Reprint, 1972–85; Walch, J. G. *Philosophisches Lexicon*. Leipzig, 1726. Reprint, 2001.

GERALD MACDONALD

Wallin, Johan Olof

The Swedish pastor and hymn writer Johan Olof Wallin (1779–1839) was born in Stora Tuna, Sweden, to a poor soldier and his wife, as one of nine children. Wallin distinguished himself at his studies. Ordained in 1806, he became lector at the military school in Karlberg and pastor in Solna. In 1812 Wallin began serving as pastor of Adolf Fredrik Church in Stockholm, and in 1815 he became a member of parliament, while serving as dean of the cathedral in Vasterås; from 1818 to 1821 he served as head pastor in the Storkyrkoförsamligen in Stockholm and became archbishop of Sweden in 1837, but suddenly died before he moved to Uppsala to take up residence in the office. He published his poems early and received several prizes for them from the Swedish Academy. While his topics ranged from secular to religious and he is still considered a great Swedish poet, especially for his final poem, "Angel of Death" (Dödens ängel), he is most remembered for his hymns. By 1812 he had worked on two trial hymn collections, preparing for the first official Swedish hymnal since 1696, which he compiled and edited. including many revisions of older hymns, and nearly 130 of his own. He completed the manuscript in 1816, even rearranging the traditional order of hymns in the hymnal. In 1819 the hymnal—in every sense Wallin's hymnal, as it became known—was approved by the king. A man of the Enlightenment but no deist, his hymns were admired for their skillful poetic style, yet Swedish Pietists frowned on the influence of the Enlightenment in Wallin's work. While Wallin's hymns do not appear in English translation in *Evangelical Lutheran Worship*, several were published in the *Lutheran Book of Worship*. The most well-known hymn is "All Hail to You, O Blessed Morn" (Var Hälsad. Sköna Morgon Stund), without which a Swedish Christmas morning service (Julotta) is not complete.

See also Hymnody; Sweden

GRACIA GRINDAL

Walther, Carl Ferdinand Wilhelm

The American Lutheran theologian and denominational leader Carl Ferdinand Wilhelm Walther (October 24, 1811–May 7, 1887) was born into a clerical family. He was ordained in 1837 but was dismayed by the prevailing religious rationalism in Germany. In 1839 he immigrated to the United States with a group of strictly confessional Saxon Lutherans led by their bishop, Martin Stephan, who settled in Missouri. After Stephan was removed from leadership of the group, the young Walther took charge of the community, gave it a more congregational polity, and remained in control of the group the rest of his life. In 1841 he became pastor of Trinity Lutheran Church in St. Louis, as well as other congregations in the area, which he served until his death. Already in 1839 Walther participated in founding a log-cabin "college," which eventually moved to St. Louis and became Concordia Seminary; he served as professor of theology and president (1854–87) and was strongly influential through his training of generations of pastors.

In 1847 he was instrumental in gathering other confessional Lutheran leaders to form the German Evangelical Lutheran Synod of Missouri, Ohio, and Other States (popularly known as the Missouri Synod), and he served as president of the synod from 1847 to 1850 and again from 1864 to 1878. After organizing a series of free theological conferences, Walther helped form the Synodical Conference in 1872, which attempted to bring into fellowship all the strictly confessional Lutheran denominations in North America. This plan was seriously disrupted by the conflicts of the predestination controversy of the 1870s and 1880s, where Walther was accused by others of having a Calvinist doctrine of predestination. Walther engaged in a strong theological debate with his critics over the issue, which saw a number of the other synods moving away from the influence of Missouri, but which also clarified the internal position of Missouri over the issue. Walther was a strong theological partisan for a strict reading of the Lutheran confessions and often strongly criticized what he saw as the inadequate confessional positions of the other American Lutheran denominations.

Before and during the Civil War, Walther took a controversial, somewhat mediating position on the question of slavery, seeing it not as a sin, but as a "moral evil" in punishment for sin; he also opposed the abolitionist movement. Beyond his control of the Missouri Synod and its seminary, Walther had a wide influence through his multifaceted journalistic and theological activities. Already in 1844 he founded an influential and widely circulated religious periodical, *Der Lutheraner*, which he edited until his death in 1887. In 1854 he also founded and edited the synod's theological journal, *Lehre und Wehre*, and served as its editor until 1864. Beyond these activities he wrote and published a significant number of theological books and pamphlets, the most enduring being *The Proper Distinction between Law and Gospel*, a transcription of a lecture series from 1884–85, which was not collected in book form until 1897. Walther was a distinctive and influential theologian and church leader who molded the Missouri Synod into a leading American Lutheran denomination and who had an important influence far beyond its borders.

See also Law and Gospel; Lutheran Church–Missouri Synod; Predestination (Election) Controversy

Bibliography

Meyer, C. S., ed. *The Letters of C. F. W. Walther: A Selection*. Fortress, 1969; Spitz, L. W., Jr. *The Life of C. F. W. Walther*. Concordia, 1961; Sueflow, A. *Servant of the Word: The Life and Ministry of C. F. W. Walther*. Concordia, 2000; Walther, C. F. W. *Walther's Works*. 7 vols. to 2017. Concordia, 2010–.

MARK A. GRANQUIST

Wellhausen, Julius

The text and literary critic, exegete, and translator, Julius Wellhausen (1844–1918) abandoned Lutheran Orthodoxy while a student at Göttingen. After licentiate promotion and habilitation in Old Testament at Göttingen, he was called in 1872 as ordinarius (full professor) to Greifswald. There he wrote two epoch-making works in Old Testament history: *Die Composition des Hexateuchs* (1876/77; composition of the Hexateuch) and *Geschichte Israels*, vol. 1 (1878; history of Israel), later titled *Prolegomena zur Geschichte Israels*. In 1894 followed *Israelitische und jüdische Geschichte* (Israelite and Jewish History). In 1882 he resigned his chair in Evangelical-Lutheran theology, unable to bridge the gulf between academia and the church. Called to the philosophical faculty of Halle, he taught as an extraordinarius for Semitic languages and Islamic studies. In 1885 he answered the call to Marburg, and seven years later to Oriental studies at Göttingen.

Using the Graf-Kuenen literary-critical method, Wellhausen deconstructed the supposed origin of Old Testament tradition in Mosaic law for the sake of a late dating of the Pentateuch. According to his scheme, early Israelite religion was natural and free from law. Subsequently its festivals were cut off from nature and given new dates. Finally a religion emerged in which festivals were fixed on precise days of the calendar year. This scheme is most clearly illustrated in Wellhausen's treatment of sacrifice. Worship, he wrote, arose out of the midst of ordinary life. This conception later gave way before the advancing culture, and with it came into prominence the one universal occasion, sin, and the one universal purpose, propitiation. Transplanted from its natural soil, worship was thus deprived of its natural nourishment, a move for which Deuteronomy paved the way. In sum, the law succeeded the prophets.

Analogously, Wellhausen deconstructed the early history of Christianity and Islam in terms of a history of decline. Tracing the succession of the Gospels from Mark to John as a continuous Christianizing and ecclesiasticizing of the figure of Jesus, Wellhausen concluded that "Jesus was not a Christian but a Jew. He did not proclaim a new faith, but taught to do the will of God." Though abandoning hope in historical reconstruction of the life of Jesus, Wellhausen nevertheless described Christianity as beginning with Jesus's resurrection, a faith resulting from the impact the historical Jesus had on his disciples during his lifetime.

Wellhausen's research reflected a decided subjective element. His debt to the German philosophical movement of Romanticism is clearly detectable in his affinity for the pure and simple, for early Israelite or Islamic religion, and for what Jesus taught unadorned by dogma. It is present in his conviction that what followed in each case was a decline. Just as Israelite religion had declined from good origins to theocracy and legalism, so what Jesus taught gave way to "the stinking corpse . . . called the orthodox or even the liberal German Protestant church." Wellhausen's personal stance toward Jesus resulted in his omitting to apply to Jesus the same rigorous method he had applied to Judaism and Islam. Wellhausen was convinced that a paradigmatic life makes greater impact on religious history than concepts or rules.

Wellhausen's influence continues to the present. He held to the two-source theory of the Synoptics but gave priority to Mark. He engaged in source analysis and pioneered in researching the Gospels' Aramaic background. His view of John's Gospel as reflecting a complicated prehistory anticipated modern scholarship. His concentration on the one gospel of Jesus as the crucified and risen Christ would have its imitators for more than a century. When twentieth-century scholarship engaged in researching preliterary tradition, Wellhausen in 1905 had already supplied its moniker: "form criticism." Last, mention needs to be made of Wellhausen's anti-Semitism, his "modest contribution to the 'final solution' of the Jewish problem under the Third Reich," a generation after his death (Blenkinsopp, 20).

See also Bible Interpretation; Germany since 1870; Liberalism

Bibliography

Betz, H. D. "Wellhausen's Dictum 'Jesus Was Not a Christian, but a Jew' in Light of Present Scholarship." *Studia*

Theologica 45 (1991): 83–110; Blenkinsopp, J. *Prophecy and Canon.* University of Notre Dame Center for the Study of Judaism and Christianity in Antiquity 3. University of Notre Dame Press, 1977; Dahl, N. "Wellhausen on the New Testament." *Semeia* 25 (1983): 89–110; Levenson, J. D. *The Hebrew Bible, the Old Testament, and Historical Criticism: Jews and Christians in Biblical Studies.* John Knox, 1993; Smend, J. D. *Julius Wellhausen: Ein Bahnbrecher in drei Disziplinen.* Carl Friedrich von Siemens Stiftung, 2004; "Wellhausen." *RGG* 6:1594. Mohr, 1962; "Wellhausen." *RGG* 8:1835–36. Mohr Siebeck, 2005; "Wellhausen." *RPP* 13:447–52.

ROY A. HARRISVILLE

Welz, Justinian von

The early Lutheran missionary, ascetic, and church critic Justinian von Welz (1621–68?) was born in Styria to noble, Protestant parents. During the turmoil of the Thirty Years' War, his family sought religious refuge in Saxony in 1628. Welz studied law in Leiden and published several tracts in Holland in the early 1640s criticizing tyranny and the Spanish monarchy. He returned to Germany, but little is known about his life until the early 1660s, when he began publishing a series of titles advocating an ascetic form of Christianity, church reform, and mission to non-Christian peoples. Welz called for the formation of a society, the Jesus-liebenden Gesellschaft (Jesus-loving society), dedicated to mission and the reform of Christianity. Aided by the lawyer and spiritualist Johann Georg Gichtel (1638–1710), Welz sought the support of the Corpus Evangelicorum in Regensburg in 1663–64 for the establishment of such a society. His ideas found only tepid support in Regensburg, and prominent Lutheran clergy opposed his plans. Welz left Regensburg for Holland, where he joined other Lutheran dissidents, including Friedrich Breckling (1629–1711). Ordained there, Welz traveled to Suriname as a missionary in 1666. Nothing is known of his work there, and Breckling reported that he lived as a hermit, dying in 1667 or 1668. Welz's ideas of mission, the formation of mission societies, and especially the ongoing task of the Great Commission were innovative in Germany at the time and would become commonplace only in eighteenth-century Lutheranism.

See also Mission and Evangelism; Suriname

Bibliography

Laubach, F., ed. *Justinian von Welz: Ein Österreicher als Vordenker und Pionier der Weltmission; Seine Schriften.* Brockhaus, 1989; Scherer, J., ed. and trans. *Justinian Welz: Essays by an Early Prophet of Mission.* Eerdmans, 1969; Schnabel, W. W. "Justinian oder Wie man zum Schwärmer wird." In *Heterodoxie in der Frühen Neuzeit,* ed. H. Laufhütte and M. Titzmann, 337–411. Niemeyer, 2006.

JONATHAN STROM

Wesley, John and Charles

The founders of the Methodist movement were raised in an Anglican rectory. John Wesley (1703–91) and his brother Charles (1707–88) were descendants of Puritan ministers, and their parents, Samuel Wesley and Susanna Annesley Wesley, were both nurtured in Nonconformist households. Conforming to the Church of England prior to marriage, they raised their children as devout Anglicans yet never lost the Puritan moral rigor and spiritual seriousness of their upbringing.

Both Wesley brothers studied at Christ Church, Oxford. John received his BA degree in 1724, was elected Fellow of Lincoln College in 1726, and completed his MA degree in 1727. Charles received his BA in 1730 and his MA in 1733. At Oxford, the Wesley brothers became the nucleus of a group that gradually transformed into a religious society seeking to replicate the practices of primitive Christianity. This earned the group disparaging names such as "the Holy Club" and "the Methodists."

In 1735 John and Charles each accepted appointments as missionaries in the newly established colony of Georgia in North America. The most important result of a generally disappointing experience was their exposure to a form of German Pietism through their acquaintance with the Moravians. Soon after returning to London in early 1738, they came under the influence of the Moravian Peter Böhler and corresponded with Count Nikolaus Ludwig von Zinzendorf. On May 21, 1738, while reading Luther's commentary on

Galatians, Charles had a profound religious experience. During a Moravian society meeting on Aldersgate Street three days later, while someone was reading from Luther's preface to Romans (cf. LW 35:365–80), John felt his heart "strangely warmed."

The Wesleys (esp. John) soon came to have increasingly serious doubts about what they perceived as the "quietism" and "antinomianism" of the English Moravians and broke connection with them in 1740, but the influence of Pietism on the life and theology of both brothers is unmistakable. One lasting result was the subsequent emphasis in their preaching and teaching on the doctrine of justification by faith alone, which they came to regard as the beginning point of subsequent growth in grace through the process of sanctification, moving toward the goal of Christian perfection, understood as embodiment of the Great Commandment about love of God and neighbor.

In 1739, at the urging of George Whitefield, John Wesley became involved in an evangelistic revival around Bristol and then enlisted his brother Charles. Their itinerant preaching led to the emergence of religious societies, first in Bristol and London, then elsewhere throughout England and Ireland. This marked the beginning of Methodism, of which John was the organizational manager and theological mentor for five decades, traveling an estimated 250,000 miles by horse or carriage and preaching more than 40,000 sermons. Charles contributed his poetic genius to the movement, writing (by most estimates) over nine thousand hymns and poems, including such hymns as "O for a Thousand Tongues to Sing," "Hark! The Herald Angels Sing," and "Love Divine, All Loves Excelling." The Wesley brothers shared what were perceived as Arminian theological commitments to doctrines of unlimited atonement, universal prevenient grace, and conditional election; this put them into sharp conflict with the dominant Calvinism of their day, especially concerning the doctrine of predestination, which they fiercely opposed.

John Wesley's personal life suffered as a consequence of his tireless leadership of the Methodist movement. In 1751 he married Mary "Molly" Vazeille, the well-to-do widow of a London merchant, but their marriage was unhappy. She soon grew resentful of his ceaseless travels and financial expenditures in support of Methodist work and jealous of his extensive and intimate correspondence with female Methodists; they separated in 1758. Charles had a much happier family life; in April 1749 he married Sarah "Sally" Gwynne, and by 1756 he had ceased itinerating to help raise their children, creating tension with John.

In 1784, prompted by the sacramental crisis brought on by the American Revolution, John Wesley took several actions to make it possible for the Methodists in America to form a new church, including the ordination of some of his lay preachers. This created a breach between the brothers that was never fully healed. Charles insisted that John's actions meant the separation of the Methodists from the Church of England, but John refused to acknowledge this. When Charles died in 1788, at age eighty-one, he was by his request buried in the graveyard of his parish church in London, St. Marylebone, but when John died three years later, at age eighty-seven, he was laid to rest behind what is now known as Wesley's Chapel on City Road, London.

John and Charles Wesley are commemorated together in the ELCA Calendar of Saints on March 2 as "renewers of the church." The Wesleys and their movement were already known to Lutherans in the English American colonies. In 1780, Henry Melchior Mühlenberg notes in his *Journals* (3:297) that he had approvingly read John Wesley's *Conferences*. He also attended sermons by George Whitefield, an erstwhile ally of the Wesleys, complimenting much of his message but disagreeing on the question of baptismal regeneration. John's reported last words aptly summed up the life and work of both brothers: "The best of all is, God is with us."

See also Methodism; Moravian Church (Unitas Fratrum); Zinzendorf, Nikolaus Ludwig von

Bibliography

Heitzenrater, R. *John Wesley and the People Called Methodists*. 2nd ed. Abingdon, 2013; Lloyd, G. *Charles Wesley and the Struggle for Methodist Identity*. Oxford University Press, 2007; Maddox, R., and J. Vickers, eds. *The Cambridge Companion to John Wesley*. Cambridge University Press, 2009; Rack, H. *Reasonable Enthusiast: John Wesley and the Rise of Methodism*. 3rd ed. Epworth, 2002; Tyson, J. *Assist Me to Proclaim: The Life and Hymns of Charles Wesley*. Eerdmans, 2008.

REX D. MATTHEWS

Westphal, Joachim

As a German Lutheran pastor and theologian, Joachim Westphal (1510–74) became one of the leading polemicists in the second controversy over the Lord's Supper among Lutherans in the mid-sixteenth century. Born in Hamburg in 1510, Westphal studied with Luther and Melanchthon at Wittenberg beginning in 1529 and received his master of arts degree in 1532. After teaching at the Hamburg academy for two years, in 1534 he returned to Wittenberg and in 1537 began to lecture on philology. In 1541 he was called to serve as pastor in Hamburg. In 1562 he was named acting superintendent, and in 1571 he was elected to the post. Westphal engaged in several doctrinal controversies of the time, including debates in Hamburg over Christ's descent into hell and disputes over the so-called Leipzig Interim (1548) and the adiaphoristic controversy.

In 1552, alarmed at the rapid spread of Calvin's teaching on Christ's presence in the Lord's Supper and the Genevan's agreement with the Zurich church (in the Consensus Tigurinus of 1549), Westphal wrote several works opposing him. Calvin countered Westphal's critique. A six-year controversy between the two ensued, with supporters lining up on each side. The effect was to widen the breach between the Lutherans and the Reformed. Westphal's arguments were important in the Lutheran affirmations of Christ's bodily presence in the Lord's Supper. He died in Hamburg, January 16, 1574.

See also Calvin, John; Lord's Supper; Switzerland; Wittenberg Circle, Parties within

Bibliography

Janse, W. "Joachim Westphal's Sacramentology." *LQ* 22 (2008): 137–60; Schade, H. von. *Joachim Westphal und Peter Braubach*. Wittig, 1981; Tylenda, J. "The Calvin-Westphal Exchange: The Genesis of Calvin's Treatises against Westphal." *Calvin Theological Journal* 9 (1974): 182–209.

GERHARD BODE

Wichern, Johann Hinrich

The prominent social reformer Johann Hinrich Wichern (1808–81) was founder of the Rough House (*das Rauhe Haus*) in Hamburg and the Protestant Inner Mission. Born in Hamburg to a modest middle-class family, Wichern studied theology at Göttingen and Berlin, where he came under the influence of the church theologian August Neander. In Berlin he joined a circle of awakened Pietists, including Baron Hans von Kottwitz and the theologian August Tholuck. After finishing his studies, Wichern returned to Hamburg and founded *Rauhes Haus*, a home for abandoned children, whose daily lives were organized along strict pietistic principles. German Pietists saw the organization as a model for addressing the myriad social issues caused by industrialization. Through his popular newsletter, the *Fliegende Blätter*, Wichern came to be known as the most influential social reformer of his day. At the Wittenberg Church Congress of 1848, Wichern delivered a speech on Luther's grave—later called the "Protestant Manifesto"—in response to the revolutions of 1848. Wichern called for a new approach to Protestant social work, arguing that individual conversion and social charity provided the key to stemming revolutionary fervor. In 1849 Wichern helped form the Central Committee for the Inner Mission, which had pan-German ambitions to coordinate charitable organizations throughout the German lands. He was further appointed to the Prussian Ministry of Internal Affairs to oversee poor relief and prison reform. Later, he was appointed to the Supreme Ecclesiastical Council of the Evangelical State Church in Prussia. In 1871 he retired to Hamburg, where he spent his last years. Throughout his life, Wichern argued for the use of voluntary religious organizations, as opposed to the established *Landeskirchen*, as a way to rejuvenate Protestant piety. He was also a major proponent of a pan-German "people's Church" (*Volkskirche*).

See also Fliedner, Theodore; Inner Mission; Pietism; Sieveking, Amalie Wilhelmina; Vocation

Bibliography

Crowner, D., and G. Christianson. *Spirituality of the German Awakening*. Paulist Press, 2003; Gerhardt, M. *Johann Hinrich Wichern: Ein Lebensbild*. 3 vols. Agentur des Rauhen Hauses, 1927–31; Oldenburg, F. *Johann Hinrich Wichern: Sein Leben und Wirken*. Agentur des Rauhen Hauses / Mauke, 1882; Wichern, J. H. *Sämtliche Werke*. Ed. P. Meinhold and G. Brakelmann. 10 vols. Lutherisches Verlagshaus, 1958–88.

ALBERT WU

Wigand, Johann

As a key figure in the controversies among the second generation of Lutherans in the sixteenth century, Johann Wigand (1523–87) worked to reach agreement in the Formula of Concord (1577). Born in Mansfeld in 1523, Wigand studied at Wittenberg from 1538 to 1541. After teaching at the Saint Lorenz school in Nuremberg for three years, he returned to Wittenberg in 1544. He was called as pastor to Mansfeld in 1546, and then to Magdeburg in 1553, where he also was superintendent. With colleagues Matthäus Judex and Matthias Flacius, he played a key role in defending Luther's teaching in the adiaphoristic, the Majoristic, and synergistic controversies and in producing the *Magdeburg Centuries*, a groundbreaking critical study of ecclesiastical history. In 1560 he was called as professor of theology at Jena but along with Flacius was dismissed the following year because of his opposition to the ducal government. Wigand returned to Magdeburg until being called to Wismar to serve as superintendent. In 1568 he returned to Jena, where he engaged in debate with Flacius over original sin. On the death of the Saxon duke Johann Wilhelm in 1573, Wigand lost his position in Jena. He became professor of theology at Königsberg, and in 1575, bishop of Pomesania. To this office he added the bishopric of Samland in 1577, holding both positions until his death at Liebemühl on October 21, 1587.

See also Adiaphora; Flacius, Matthias Illyricus, and the Flacians; Good Works; History; Major, Georg; Wittenberg Circle, Parties within

Bibliography

Diener, R. "Johann Wigand, 1523–1587." In *Shapers of Religious Traditions in Germany, Switzerland, and Poland, 1560–1600*, ed. J. Raitt, 19–38. Yale University Press, 1981; Kolb, R. "The Advance of Dialectic in Lutheran Theology: The Role of Johannes Wigand, 1523–1587." In *Regnum, Religio et Ratio: Essays Presented to Robert M. Kingdon*, ed. J. Friedman, 93–102. Sixteenth Century Journal Publishers, 1987.

GERHARD BODE

Wingren, Gustaf

Swedish theologian Gustaf Wingren (1910–2000) was the younger son in the large family of a tanner; his mother died when he was a young boy. Nevertheless, he received a classical education, partly because he had lost two fingers on his right hand and would not have been suited for a craft. His teachers recognized his aptitude for study, and he then entered theological studies but continued to use his working-class background as a lens through which to challenge the prevailing cultured assumptions of the role of theological study in Sweden, Europe, and America. Upon assuming the chair in theology at Lund, the combative Wingren attacked his predecessor Anders Nygren's theological position. This very public confrontation—along with further challenges made by Wingren against Karl Barth, Rudolf Bultmann, and Paul Tillich, as well as other theologians in Sweden—had the result of polarizing and sidelining Lundensian theology.

For Wingren, theology was a discipline that should interpret the Bible for the people, making the living connection between their working lives and God's ongoing care for creation and for them. His own constructive theological efforts embraced creation and dismissed any theology that focused only on how to be saved from it. He is best known among Lutherans in English-speaking churches for his work based on his dissertation, *Luther on Vocation*, in which he examines Luther's view of the kingdom of Christ and Satan on the backdrop of the reformer's insights into daily life and callings. His several other books return to the theme of law, creation, and the Christian's calling through different lenses, from the role of the sermon to his attack on theologians for their neglect of their call to be a prophetic, biblically confident interpreter of the moment.

Wingren was a theologian who opposed otherworldly preoccupations in theology as well as its cultural refinement and captivity, and his critical perspective launched him into a career marked by ongoing dispute with systems of theology aloof from ordinary concerns in church, workplace, and home. It was also marked by personal challenges directed at other theologians, colleagues, and former colleagues, so that Wingren's legacy as a theologian was not always the constructive one that his incisive critique might have created; he is remembered in Sweden primarily as a combative figure. The biography by Bengt Kristensson Uggla features not only his attacks on the high-church theology but also his personal break with the church when he set aside his clergy status in protest over the way that the church had mishandled the issue of women's ordination by creating the conscience clause. Later he divorced his wife, marrying a far left political leader, moving even further away from the social milieu of the Church of Sweden and the University of Lund.

See also Ludensian School; Nygren, Anders; Sweden; Vocation

Bibliography

Anderson, M. E. *Gustaf Wingren and the Swedish Luther Renaissance*. Lang, 2006; Uggla, B. K. *Gustaf Wingren: Människan och teologin*. Brutus Östlings bokförlag Symposion, 2010; Wingren, G. *Luther on Vocation*. Muhlenberg, 1957; Wingren, G. *Theology in Conflict*. Muhlenberg, 1958.

MARIA ERLING

Wisconsin Evangelical Lutheran Synod

The Wisconsin Evangelical Lutheran Synod (WELS) developed amid the vast migration of German immigrants to the upper Midwest of the United States, from the early 1840s to the outbreak of World War I. Founded in 1850 by Milwaukee pastor Johannes Muehlhaeuser (1803–67) and four other Lutheran pastors, the German Evangelical Ministerium of Wisconsin originally practiced a "mild" form of confessionalism during much of its first two decades. But under the leadership of theological professor Adolf Hoenecke (1835–1908) and Pastor Johannes Bading (1824–1913), the synod moved toward a more rigidly confessional stance beginning in the 1860s. The Wisconsin Synod formed a federation with Lutheran synods in Minnesota and Michigan in 1892, and the Nebraska Synod was added in 1904. Then in 1917 these synods amalgamated to become the Joint Evangelical Lutheran Synod of Wisconsin and Other States, which adopted the name Wisconsin Evangelical Lutheran Synod in 1959.

After initially relying on German mission societies to provide pastors for the many growing congregations in Milwaukee and the Wisconsin countryside, the synod established its own seminary in Watertown in 1863 and a preseminary college in 1865, initially called Northwestern University. The seminary was closed in 1870 but reopened in 1878 in Milwaukee, then in 1893 relocated to Wauwatosa, a western suburb of Milwaukee. The twentieth century saw the flowering of what has been called "the Wauwatosa Theology," associated with Professors John Philipp Koehler (1859–1951), August Pieper (1857–1946), and John Schaller (1859–1920). This triumvirate, with John P. Meyer (1873–1964) replacing Schaller in 1920, urged direct study of Scripture and the historical disciplines as an antidote to the mechanical repetition of theological deductions inherited from the Lutheran fathers. In 1904 this seminary faculty began publication of *Theologische Quartalschrift*, today called *Wisconsin Lutheran Quarterly*.

In 1872 the Wisconsin Synod was one of six midwestern synods that established the Evangelical Lutheran Synodical Conference of North America, and for more than ninety years the Wisconsin Synod enjoyed church fellowship with the Lutheran Church–Missouri Synod (LCMS). Beginning in the 1930s, however, disagreements chiefly over the teaching and practice of church fellowship led Wisconsin to declare a break in fellowship with the LCMS in 1961 and to discontinue membership in the Synodical Conference in 1963.

The requirement of complete doctrinal unity as a basis for church fellowship has precluded WELS participation in larger twentieth-century Lutheran mergers, such as the United Lutheran Church in America (1918), the American Lutheran Church (1930), The American Lutheran Church (1960), the Lutheran Church in America (1962), and the Evangelical Lutheran Church in America (1988). Church fellowship disputes also led to an exodus of pastors and congregations in the 1950s and 1960s, many of whom formed the Church of the Lutheran Confession (CLC) in 1960. The WELS remains in doctrinal fellowship with the Evangelical Lutheran Synod (ELS), known in the past as the "Little Norwegian Synod." The WELS and the ELS are partners with seventeen other Lutheran bodies around the world in the Confessional Evangelical Lutheran Conference (CELC), founded in 1993.

The WELS maintains two preparatory high schools, Luther Preparatory School in Watertown, Wisconsin, and Michigan Lutheran Seminary in Saginaw, Michigan; one undergraduate college for education and preseminary studies, Martin Luther College in New Ulm, Minnesota; and Wisconsin Lutheran Seminary, located since 1929 in Mequon, Wisconsin. Martin Luther College was formed in 1995 as a result of the amalgamation of Northwestern College, Watertown, Wisconsin, and Dr. Martin Luther College, New Ulm, Minnesota. Federations of individuals and congregations support Wisconsin Lutheran College in Milwaukee and maintain twenty-four regional Lutheran high schools. *Forward in Christ*, formerly *The Northwestern Lutheran*, is the synod's monthly news magazine.

The process of acculturation to American life, already under way early in the twentieth century, was greatly accelerated by World War I and its aftermath. Organized originally to maintain and reclaim German immigrants for the faith, the WELS now conducts neighborhood canvasses and has planted new congregations in many metropolitan areas of the United States, particularly where historically Lutheranism has been underrepresented. The year 2015 saw WELS congregations in 48 of the 50 states, 4 provinces in Canada, and 3 locations in the West Indies. Synodical statistics for 2012 show 380,728 baptized members in 1,278 congregations, served by 1,394 pastors. Congregations maintain 319 elementary schools with a total enrollment of 24,254 students in kindergarten through eighth grade, served by more than 1,800 teachers, and an additional 400 congregations offer early childhood education. The numerical strength of the WELS remains in Wisconsin, Minnesota, and Michigan, with a significant representation of congregations in Arizona, California, Texas, Florida, and other parts of the Great Lakes and northern plains regions.

Since 1893 the Wisconsin Synod has conducted missionary work among the Apache Indians in Arizona. Since World War II the WELS has initiated mission work on every populated continent, beginning with work in Japan and Africa in the 1950s. As of 2013, WELS world missions were serving more than eighty thousand baptized Christians in twenty-three fields, including Cameroon, Malawi, Nigeria, and Zambia; Indonesia, Thailand, and Japan; Chinese-speaking peoples in east Asia, Albania, Bulgaria, and Russia; Brazil, Colombia, Cuba, the Dominican Republic, and Mexico; and India, Nepal, and Pakistan. The synod continues to provide humanitarian aid throughout the world.

See also Lutheran Church–Missouri Synod

Bibliography

Braun, M. E. *A Tale of Two Synods: Events That Led to the Split between Wisconsin and Missouri*. Northwestern, 2003; Brenner, J. M., and P. M. Prange. *Jars of Clay: A History of Wisconsin Lutheran Seminary, 1863–2013*. Wisconsin Lutheran Seminary Press, 2013; Brug, J. F. *WELS and Other Lutherans*. 2nd ed. Northwestern, 2009; Fredrich, E. C. *The Wisconsin Synod Lutherans: A History of the Single Synod, Federation, and Merger*. Northwestern, 1992; Koehler, J. P. *The History of the Wisconsin Synod*. Faith-Life, 1970; Sauer, T. A., H. R. Johne, and E. H. Wendland, eds. *To Every Nation, Tribe, Language, and People: A Century of WELS World Missions*. Northwestern, 1992; Schuetze, A. W. *The Synodical Conference: Ecumenical Endeavor*. Northwestern, 2000.

MARK E. BRAUN

Witchcraft and Magic

In many regions of Europe and the Americas between 1450 and 1750, there was widespread belief in the reality of witchcraft. Over this period it is estimated that some fifty thousand people, mostly women, were executed for this crime. Witches were believed to cause a great deal of harm through their spells; however, the crime was seen by authorities as principally a spiritual one in which witches abandoned their faith in God and formed a pact (either implicitly or explicitly) with the devil. Many believed that at night they would fly to large gatherings and there engage in grotesque rituals mocking the Christian faith. Beliefs about the nature of witchcraft varied considerably by region, and there was vigorous debate among scholars and theologians about its reality. By and large, however, there was a general agreement about its fundamental character, concentrating on the combination of harmful magic and the satanic pact. It is recognized today that both Catholic and Protestant churches viewed witchcraft as a real threat. Differences in the number of people tried and executed generally varied much more along social, regional, political, and legal lines than along confessional lines. However, in the era of state building, where confessional loyalties were sometimes tied to political motives, accusations of witchcraft were at times used to reinforce political ends.

Lutheran jurisdictions were among those that experienced witch hunts involving large numbers of victims. In southwest Germany there were large trials in Lutheran territories— for example, in Wiesenstieg in 1562–63 and in Esslingen a century later in 1662–66. In Lower Saxony, Duke Heinrich Julius of Braunschweig-Wolfenbüttel executed dozens of suspected witches, particularly during the years 1590–94. Smaller trials involving only a single defendant or a small number of suspects occurred across the Lutheran lands of the Holy Roman Empire. Some Lutheran jurisdictions, such as Rothenburg ob der Tauber, however, avoided convictions despite pressure from the population. In Sweden, central authorities discouraged witch trials until a major panic broke out in 1668 in Dalarna, which spread rapidly in the northern provinces in the 1670s. In the 1590s and early 1600s ordinances condemning witchcraft were passed in Denmark and Norway. Particularly important was a decree of 1617, in which the "right" witches were defined as those who had attached themselves to the devil or who consorted with him. Lutheran clergy played a role in large witch hunts in Jutland and in Finnmark, where ministers took part in questioning the suspect outside the courtroom in the pretrial and trial phase, as well as preparing the accused persons before their deaths. In Denmark-Norway, scholars identify a strong connection between witch hunting, state building, and religious conformity, especially under Christian IV.

Luther's first writings on magic and witchcraft are found in his earliest published work, a set of sermons on the Decalogue given in Wittenberg in 1516–17 and first published in Latin in 1518. The first half of the sermon on the first commandment is taken up with a long discussion of the varieties of magic and witchcraft. Luther condemned all forms of magic, singling out particularly the many forms of popular superstition common in his day. For him these were all direct violations of the first commandment because, as he explained in later writings, those who practice any form of magic reject the command to look for all comfort and relief, both temporal and eternal, through faith in God. It followed that the spiritual crime is the same whether the magic is intended for harm or for healing. In later expositions of the Ten Commandments, witchcraft comes to be associated with the second commandment, on taking God's name in vain. On the questions of the reality of witches' flight and whether witches could transform themselves into animals, Luther was largely skeptical, taking most of the stories of such things to be merely illusions created by the devil to fool innocent Christians.

Luther's concern was with faith in the gospel of Christ and not with the extermination of witches. For this reason he focused on local and popular magical superstitions rather than on witchcraft in a full sense, a focus that became characteristic of Protestant demonologists. In his pastoral concerns, Luther warned against those who blamed their misfortunes on witches rather than looking within themselves for the origins of God's punishment. A zeal for persecuting suspects, he argued, served only the devil's ends. However, this did not absolve the secular courts from their duty to carry out proper punishment. Indeed, Luther himself could be fulsome in condemning sorcerers. In a weakly authenticated excerpt from Johann Aurifaber's Table Talk (WA TR 6:222, no. 6836), he is recorded as saying, "Just as all sins are a turning away from God's works, so that God is horribly enraged and offended, so magic, because of its abomination, may be fairly called a *crimen laesae majestatis divinae* [a crime against the divine majesty]." Despite this, Luther did not believe that all witches deserved death, and opponents of the trials frequently cited him.

Luther's sometimes ambivalent stance on the proper response to witchcraft produced conflicting attitudes among Lutheran pastors and theologians. There were those, such as Abraham Saur and Paulus Frisius, who took Luther's harshest pronouncements against witches to heart, associated it with public blasphemy (a crime that Luther and Philip Melanchthon had argued in the 1530s should be punished by authorities), and insisted on the full application of the law. It was the insistence on enforcing Mosaic law that underscored Lutheran condemnations of witchcraft and could lead to the large persecutions. Others, however, urged caution in prosecuting witches. The Stuttgart superintendent Johannes Brenz (1499–1570) and the Danish theologian Nils Hemmingsen (1513–1600) both emphasized that people's suffering produced by witches comes from God, with the witch being merely the vehicle through which God's punishment is directed. Hemmingsen's treatises reached even the periphery of Denmark-Norway and were used in the churches there, as were the works of other Danish theologians, like Hemmingsen's follower Jesper Brochmand (1585–1652) and Poul Andersen Medelby (1557–1662). At the extreme end of those casting doubt on the witch trials, the Rhineland physician Johann Weyer (1515–88) argued that most of the accused were melancholic old women, on whom the devil preyed in a manner akin to those possessed. In the seventeenth century other critics of the witch trials focused on the widespread use of torture to extract confessions. The Lutheran theologian Johann Matthäus Meyfart (1590–1642) compared torture to the worst suffering brought about by the devil and argued that the confessions obtained through it were no more reliable than the ranting of a melancholic.

In sum, both Luther himself and the pastors and theologians who followed him played some part in the persecution of those suspected of witchcraft, although attitudes varied by person and by place. What distinguishes Lutheran theological attitudes was a focus on popular superstitions rather than demonic hordes, and a strongly providentialist interpretation of the crime, regarding it in terms of the Christian's duty to see all things as deriving only from God.

Bibliography

Clark, S. *Thinking with Demons: The Idea of Witchcraft in Early Modern Europe*. Oxford University Press, 1997;

Haustein, J. "Martin Luther als Gegner des Hexenwahns." In *Vom Unfug des Hexen-Processes: Gegner der Hexenforschung von Johann Weyer bis Friedrich Spee*, ed. H. Lehmann and O. Ulbricht, 35–51. Harrassowitz, 1992; Haustein, J. *Martin Luthers Stellung zum Zauber- und Hexenwesen*. Kohlhammer, 1990; Henningsen, A., et al., eds. *Early Modern Witchcraft: Centres and Peripheries*. Clarendon, 1993; Kauertz, C. *Wissenschaft und Hexenglaube: Die Diskussion des Zauber- und Hexenwesens an der Universität Helmstedt (1576–1626)*. Verlag für Regionalgeschichte, 2001; Luther, M. *Decem Praecepta Wittenbergensi predicata populo* (1518). WA 1:398–521; Midelfort, E. H. C. *Witch Hunting in Southwestern Germany, 1562–1684: The Social and Intellectual Foundations*. Stanford University Press, 1972; Rowlands, A. *Witchcraft Narratives in Germany: Rothenburg, 1561–1652*. Manchester University Press, 2003; Willumsen, L. H. *Witches of the North: Scotland and Finnmark*. Brill, 2013.

PETER A. MORTON

Wittenberg, City of

The city most closely associated with Luther, and his home from 1511 to 1546, Wittenberg was (with Torgau) one of the administrative centers of the electorate of Saxony. In addition to being a residence for Electoral Saxony's rulers, it was home to their university, founded in 1502. Wittenberg's population was about twenty-five hundred at the time of Luther's arrival, but it almost doubled during his lifetime. For almost sixty years, beginning in the 1520s, Wittenberg's university had the largest enrollment of any in German-speaking lands. Though never more than a small city, Wittenberg wielded considerable influence on Lutheran church life, theology, politics, and publishing in the sixteenth and seventeenth centuries.

As birthplace of the Reformation movement, Wittenberg was seen by many as a model for Evangelical reform in church and society. Its reorganization of church life and social welfare helped establish patterns for Lutheran reform elsewhere. After Luther's death, the city—and particularly its university—continued to be a center of influence for Lutheran theology and church life through the seventeenth century. Wittenberg's importance waned in the eighteenth century, together with the fortunes of its Saxon rulers. The merging of its university into the newer university in Halle in 1817 spelled the end of Wittenberg's cultural significance except as a site for the veneration of Luther's memory.

Wittenberg became part of the kingdom of Prussia in 1815. While the Prussian kings positioned themselves as the leading dynasty in the German lands, royal patronage of the historic Luther sites influenced the Protestant German nationalism that culminated in the German Empire of 1871. Though a relative backwater in terms of economic importance (home only to a number of chemical plants and fertilizer factories), Wittenberg's historical resonance kept it as an important site for church meetings and political rallies through the period of the Third Reich. Reflecting this symbolic importance, the city's official name was changed in the 1930s to Lutherstadt Wittenberg.

In the postwar era of the German Democratic Republic, Wittenberg continued to have significance as a tourist site, attracting visitors from the West. The five hundredth anniversary of Luther's birth in 1983 saw an unprecedented number of Western visitors, encouraged by the Communist regime. Since German reunification in 1989, Wittenberg's historic buildings have been extensively renovated, and it now is a UNESCO world heritage site. In 2017 the five hundredth anniversary of the Reformation again put Wittenberg in the center of German and international attention and made it the site of large popular gatherings and mass worship events.

In Luther's day Wittenberg was a fortified city stretched out along the north side of the Elbe River, at the point of an important bridge. First mentioned in 1180, Wittenberg only became significant as a princely residence in the late fifteenth century. The Elbe connected Wittenberg to Torgau and Dresden in the southeast, and to the northwest, to Magdeburg, Hamburg, and the North Sea. In Luther's time, the Elbe was an important source of food, and the fishers' guild was prominent. Marking this, a salmon appears on the city's coat of arms.

From the ducal castle (and the Castle Church) at the west end, to the university quarter and Augustinian monastery (now the Luther museum) at the east end, the city is about a kilometer long. The city's fortification walls were demolished in the nineteenth century, and a greenbelt park was created around the old city, neatly separating the footprint of Luther's city from the new city and its suburbs. Wittenberg has one main street running from east to west. In the center, the market square, town hall, and main city church create open space that in Luther's time included a cemetery around the city church.

Until the Reformation, the city of Wittenberg was under the ecclesiastical authority of the bishop of Brandenburg and the archbishop of Magdeburg. It had a parish church in the city center, dedicated to St. Mary (with its dependent Corpus Christi cemetery chapel), and the newer Castle Church, a collegiate church dedicated on January 17, 1503, to All Saints, which served both as ducal chapel and university church. In addition, the Franciscan monastery and the Augustinian monastery each had chapels of their own (dedicated to St. Barbara and the Holy Spirit, respectively), and the Hospital Brothers of St. Anthony maintained a small chapel (dedicated to Mary and St. Anthony) at the west end of the city. During the reform of the city in the 1520s, the monasteries were dissolved, and all but the two main churches were closed, but archaeological remains continue to be discovered.

See also Saxonies; University of Wittenberg in the Sixteenth Century

Bibliography

Junghans, H. *Wittenberg als Lutherstadt*. Union-Verlag, 1982; Krentz, N. *Ritualwandel und Deutungshoheit: Die frühe Reformation in der Residenzstadt Wittenberg (1500–1533)*. Mohr Siebeck, 2014.

R. Guy Erwin

Wittenberg Circle

The group that formed around Martin Luther and his colleagues, the Wittenberg circle, determined to carry his call for reform across the German lands and much of northern and eastern Europe in the period from 1520 to 1580.

No significant intellectual, social, or political movement attains institutional organization and remains a force over a long period solely on the ideas and organizational abilities of a single person. Such movements are set in motion by a team supporting and supplementing the contributions of a charismatic leader. Such a team formed around Martin Luther, a circle of theologians and laity, who carried and refined Luther's call for reform to the broader public and created the Reformation, which found its center and foundation in his thought.

The Lutheran Reformation was carried out by this circle centered in Wittenberg but not exclusively concentrated there. Its university faculty gave able and extensive leadership to this circle throughout the sixteenth century, especially in the first generation of the movement. It included fellow faculty members Philip Melanchthon, Johannes Bugenhagen, Justus Jonas, Caspar Cruciger Sr., and also Nikolaus von Amsdorf, who left Wittenberg in the 1520s to head reform in Magdeburg, as well as jurists and courtiers, including Georg Spalatin. Also, the wives of the reformers, most notably Katharina von Bora and Elisabeth Cruciger, played active roles in the discussion of theology and piety. Wittenberg printers, especially Johannes Rhau and Hans Lufft, and the artist Lucas Cranach with his workshop, helped spread Wittenberg theology. Courtiers at the Electoral Saxon court, among them Gregor von Brück and Christian Beyer, played strong supporting roles. Significant contributions came also from contemporaries who led Wittenberg-style reform in other places, including Antonius Corvinus as advisers to governments in Hesse and Braunschweig-Calenberg, Johann Spangenberg in Nordhausen, Urbanus Rhegius in Augsburg and Braunschweig-Lüneburg, and Johannes Brenz in Swabia. Lay supporters, such as Argula von Grumbach and Katharina Zell, along with princes and political officials, also aided in the propagation and cultivation of Wittenberg theology and church life.

In addition, hundreds of students who imbibed the teaching of Luther and his colleagues can be reckoned as members of the circle, propagating its thinking and way of life in German lands, the monarchies of Denmark-Norway-Iceland and Sweden-Finland, Hungary, Poland, and in the Baltic lands. Representative are those who remained in Wittenberg, notably Georg Major and Paul Eber, and those who preached and taught in other places, including Joachim Mörlin, Johann Pfeffinger, Matthias Flacius, Nikolaus Gallus, Joachim Westphal, Johannes Wigand, and many others.

Two elements define the Wittenberg circle: (1) participation in major events, such as the introduction of reform or its public confession (e.g., in the Augsburg Confession and Smalcald Articles); and (2) a common theological method based on the distinction of law and gospel and a common theological anthropology, expressed in the distinctions of the twofold righteousness of the human creature and life in the two realms of relationship with God and relationships with other creatures.

The boundaries of the circle were somewhat fluid. Early adherents found significant differences to separate them from Luther, as exemplified by Johannes Oecolampadius and Andreas Bodenstein von Karlstadt. Later, Johann Agricola (a student of Luther already in 1515) and Andreas Osiander came to be excluded from the circle when, in the case of Osiander, despite his years of active support for Wittenberg reform, others found his doctrine of justification corresponded little to Luther's teaching. Especially after Luther's death, conflict over the proper definition of certain elements of Wittenberg theology and practice caused controversy, but participants in those disputes all counted themselves as the true followers of Luther and Melanchthon and shared the core of Wittenberg thinking, centered on justification by grace through faith in Christ.

The Wittenberg circle ceased to exist as the generation of those who had studied under Luther and Melanchthon or who had been contemporaries of those students died out in the 1570s and 1580s. The Book of Concord of 1580 marks a certain maturing within the Wittenberg circle, as well as the demarcation from those whose doctrines of the Lord's Supper and Christology led them to support Calvinist thought.

See also Amsdorf, Nikolaus von; Bugenhagen, Johannes; Cruciger, Caspar, Sr.; Jonas, Justus; Major, Georg; Melanchthon, Philip; Wittenberg Circle, Parties within

Bibliography

Dingel, I., ed. *Justus Jonas (1493–1555) und seine Bedeutung für die Wittenberger Reformation.* Evangelische Verlagsanstalt, 2009; Dingel, I., and G. Wartenberg, eds. *Georg Major (1502–1574): Ein Theologe der Wittenberger Reformation.* Evangelische Verlagsanstalt, 2005; Junghans, H. "Die Ausbreitung der Reformation von 1517 bis 1539." In *Das Jahrhundert der Reformation in Sachsen*, ed. H. Junghans, 33–65. Evangelische Verlagsanstalt, 1989; Kolb, R. "Luther's and Melanchthon's Students: The Wittenberg Circle and the Development of Its Theology to 1600." *Religion Compass* 3 (2009): 471–87; Leder, H.-G. "Luthers Beziehungen zu seinen Wittenberger Freunden." In *Leben und Werk Martins Luthers von 1526 bis 1546*, ed. H. Junghans, 1:601–12 and 2:863–70. Evangelische Verlagsanstalt, 1983; Wengert, T. J. "The Wittenberg Circle." In *The Oxford Handbook of Martin Luther's Theology*, ed. R. Kolb, I. Dingel, and L. Batka, 491–502. Oxford University Press, 2014.

ROBERT KOLB

Wittenberg Circle, Parties within

During the 1550s the circle of students and other adherents of Martin Luther and Philip Melanchthon developed into two groups, each claiming to represent their mentors' legacy. From the end of the eighteenth century, scholars have labeled them "Gnesio-Lutherans" and "Philippists." These terms, however, were not used in this sense during the groups' existence in the second half of the sixteenth century.

In the wake of the Smalcald War and the Augsburg Interim (rejected by the entire Wittenberg circle), the Electoral Saxon government under Elector Moritz drafted Philip Melanchthon and his Wittenberg colleagues, along with other Lutheran theologians in his lands, as part of a committee to formulate a proposal for fending off an anticipated invasion by the armies of Charles V and any subsequent suppression of the Lutheran Church in Moritz's lands. This "Leipzig Proposal," dubbed the "Leipzig Interim" by its critics, was viewed by some in the Wittenberg circle as a betrayal of Luther and the gospel as well as an act of bad faith by their beloved preceptor, Melanchthon, for its embrace of medieval customs that had been laid aside with the Reformation and that still carried associations with medieval religion. Melanchthon and his supporters in turn reacted to the received criticism with deep-felt disappointment and resentment, seeing those attacks as a betrayal forged in bad faith. Acrimony and recriminations from both sides, some present before Luther's death, fueled the divisive bitterness. Such a process of adjustment and refinement of definition and direction has parallels in all such movements in which ideas and institutions experience reform, but in this case the process took place in circumstances that elicited deep mistrust.

The depth of the division between the two groups should not be exaggerated. All sought to repeat and represent the theology that they had learned from their Wittenberg professors and that reflected the spirit of the Augsburg Confession. All demonstrated that Melanchthon's methods and thought, along with Luther's teaching, had shaped their own thinking. Some issues attracted support for a position from both parties, particularly regarding original sin and the use of the law in the Christian life. All in both groups opposed Andreas Osiander's teaching on justification. Both groups made significant contributions to disciplines outside theology. Some individuals changed sides. A majority of Wittenberg students and adherents did not take part in the public disputes between the two. At the same time, some important Evangelical theologians, especially Johannes Brenz and the church in Württemberg, were not often directly party to these disputes and were neither Gnesio-Lutherans nor Philippists. The Gnesio-Lutherans formed around Matthias Flacius and others in Magdeburg in 1549–50 and found agreement from others across the German lands. The Philippists formed around Melanchthon and

his Electoral Saxon colleagues in opposition to their critics.

In four areas of ecclesiastical life the two parties showed significant differences. First, the Gnesio-Lutherans tended to interpret Luther's theology in a fashion that departed more radically from medieval expressions than did the Philippists. This arose largely out of differing emphases in how the different parties distinguished God's total responsibility for all things from human responsibility for all things in the individual's sphere of accountability. For instance, some Gnesio-Lutherans joined Flacius in echoing Luther's radical expressions concerning original sin, defining it as the essence or substance of fallen human beings, who were judged to be "in the image of Satan." Nikolaus von Amsdorf repeated Luther's dictum that "good works are detrimental to salvation" when trusted for salvation. Most Gnesio-Lutherans rejected this language, but all joined Amsdorf and Flacius in rejecting the Philippist Georg Major when he contended that "good works are necessary for salvation." They also rejected formulations framed by Johann Pfeffinger, Viktorin Strigel, and Melanchthon that seemed to imply some role for the human will in coming to faith. Some Gnesio-Lutherans rejected Melanchthon's concept of the third use of the law, holding that it implied coercion in the sanctified life or some degree of merit in the Christian's performance of good works. Other Gnesio-Lutherans defended his "third use of the law."

Second, Gnesio-Lutherans were more radical in their rejection of medieval polity and practice than were the initial Philippists (although later Philippists also turned toward a radical rejection of many medieval practices). Melanchthon and some other Philippists tried to hold out hope of Roman Catholic acceptance of Lutheran obedience to a papal system that was recognized as existing only by human right or law rather than divine right. The Philippists put more effort initially into negotiations with the papal representatives than did their Gnesio-Lutheran counterparts.

The latter more often worked for simplification of liturgical and other rituals, including at least one unsuccessful attempt to pull altars away from the wall in order to permit pastors to proclaim the words of institution to the congregation and make it clear that there is no magical formula being repeated in the consecration. Philippists, such as Prince Georg von Anhalt, favored retaining as much of the medieval liturgy and other customs as possible.

Third, although both groups expected secular rulers to support the church, the Gnesio-Lutherans insisted more forcefully that decisions regarding doctrine and ecclesiastical policy be made by the church's own leadership and without governmental interference. The Philippists were more likely to submit to governmental policies and permit the secular administration to play a larger role in the church. The dispute over the Leipzig Proposal of 1548 illustrates these positions: the Philippists cooperating with Elector Moritz's government in shaping a policy of compromise; the Gnesio-Lutheran critics resolute in their resistance to aiding secular government in such efforts. In 1550 the Gnesio-Lutherans in Magdeburg, which was resisting an imperially ordered siege conducted by Duke Moritz, composed a confession that articulated the Wittenberg doctrine of resistance to oppressive governmental authority (in part taught by Melanchthon since the 1520s but especially in his reworking of Justus Menius's *Instruction on Defensive War* [*Von der Notwehr Unterricht*]), which justified the city's use of armed force against imperial power. Gnesio-Lutheran pastors earned exile through their sharp criticism of municipal councils and princely courts: examples are Simon Musaeus, exiled eight times for criticizing doctrinal decisions by rulers, yet also for attacking one town council for oppressing peasants on lands surrounding the town; and Tilemann Hesshus, exiled six times for calling on members of the merchant class in two towns to repent of moral deviations, for defending the integrity of the church's governing power over its own affairs,

and over doctrinal issues. Duke Johann Friedrich of Saxony directly and indirectly drove out Flacius, Musaeus, Johann Wigand, Matthaeus Judex, and other Gnesio-Lutherans, whom he had previously supported, because of their resistance to his orders. Particularly the reorganization of his consistory with more power assigned to his court and his exercise of press censorship over theologians' publications led to the decisive break between the prince and his theologians. Philippists tried to avoid offending their secular rulers, for example, trying to hide deviations from Elector August's views (esp. on the Lord's Supper) in Electoral Saxony in the 1570s—an attempt that, once discovered, resulted in imprisonment and banishment and led to their being called crypto-Philippists or crypto-Calvinists.

Fourth, their attitudes toward secular government were reflected in the general tone of their church-leadership style as well. Gnesio-Lutherans confessed their faith publicly with radical abandon and contended adamantly for theologically detailed statements in public teaching. Philippists sought shelter to minimize the storms of public controversy and establish peace in the public life of the church. In the controversy over the adiaphora of the Leipzig Proposal, the Gnesio-Lutherans argued that "in a time when clear confession of the faith is demanded, nothing is an adiaphoron," whereas the Philippists embraced Melanchthon's principle, formulated already in the 1530s, that concessions in practice could be tolerated if the gospel of justification by grace through faith in Christ remained intact. This attitude caused a significant split among the Gnesio-Lutherans when disciples of Flacius were separated from others over their defense of the definition of original sin as the substance of fallen sinners, and divided among themselves over the question of whether the corpse remains substantially in original sin until the last day and the resurrection. Philippists suppressed differences, for instance, over the Lord's Supper in the early 1570s. In one letter to the Danish king in 1558, Georg Major denied ever having taught that good works are necessary for salvation, although he occasionally seemed to use the phrase after that.

Such differences between the two groups were reflected in general throughout the period, also in the ways in which each sought the restoration of harmony within the Wittenberg circle. Soon after the outbreak of the controversy in 1549–50, efforts were made both by theologians and by leading Lutheran princes to restore unity in the common confession of the faith. First, Gnesio-Lutherans tended to favor the leadership of theologians in that process; Philippists sought princely leadership, fearing that a conclave of theologians would only produce more controversy. Although both sides made occasional efforts to involve the other kind of leadership in their plans, this pattern held to a large extent throughout the period. Second, the Gnesio-Lutherans believed that only detailed positive expositions of the disputed doctrines could truly solve the disputes; the Philippists favored brief, general statements of the core of the doctrine under discussion. Third, the Philippists sometimes favored *amnestia* (cf. Greek: *amnēstia*, amnesty), a "forgetting" of the formulations to be rejected and silence regarding the expressions of what was defined as false teaching; the Gnesio-Lutherans sought explicit condemnations of false teachings and false teachers.

Both groups produced a range of theological works, including polemical tracts: their members remained active across the range of disciplines. Matthias Flacius pioneered work in biblical hermeneutics, church history, and biblical exegesis. Johann Wigand and Matthaeus Judex composed the *Magdeburg Centuries*, a project conceived and organized by Flacius. Wigand made more modest contributions in botany. Both groups produced significant historical works; the Gnesio-Lutheran Cyriacus Spangenberg and the Philippist Caspar Peucer composed chronicles of note, the latter completing what his father-in-law, Philip Melanchthon, had begun. Neo-Latin poetry came from both groups as well. Wittenberg faculty members furthered astronomical studies, and some of them advanced astrological theorizing, as had Melanchthon, a practice that earned them attacks from a few Gnesio-Lutherans.

The evolution of these groups during their three-decades-long history followed two distinct paths. Most Gnesio-Lutherans continued to hold positions that they or their comrades had maintained in the 1550s into the 1570s; the core of their group consisted of their positions on doctrinal issues and related practices. Only the division over original sin altered the Gnesio-Lutheran landscape. Joachim Westphal of Hamburg added the issue of the Lord's Supper to the agenda of controversy, with support from fellow Lower Saxon Gnesio-Lutherans, including Joachim Mörlin and Martin Chemnitz of Braunschweig. The Gnesio-Lutherans united behind their strict adherence to Luther's formulation of the doctrine of the Lord's Supper.

In contrast, the Philippists underwent a significant change in at least one aspect of their doctrinal orientation around 1570: the group did remain centered at the University of Wittenberg and in Electoral Saxony. The nature of this group as focused on Melanchthon's person and Electoral Saxon politics became clear in this shift. In the political milieu created by the controversies between the groups, the Philippists maintained a certain stability of association despite rising tensions among them over the characterization of the presence of Christ in the Lord's Supper, which replaced the adiaphora of the Leipzig Proposal and the issues related to the role of human capability in salvation as the defining doctrinal issue for the group.

The conservative liturgical stance and affinity for medieval forms and practices exhibited in the Leipzig Proposal and by Georg von Anhalt and others, in 1548–55, gave way to an ever-increasing distancing from all things Roman as the Wittenberg theologians and their allies moved in the direction of a spiritualizing definition of the presence of Christ's body and blood in the Lord's Supper. This shift was anticipated in the late 1550s with the increased influence of Caspar Peucer, professor of medicine and Melanchthon's son-in-law, over the views of his father-in-law on the possibilities of defining "presence" in Aristotelian categories, the tools of his medical trade. Paul Eber, Wittenberg's leading theologian at Melanchthon's death in 1560, retreated from a more spiritualizing definition of Christ's presence in the Lord's Supper in 1561 after being admonished by Elector August of Saxony. When Eber died in 1569, theological leadership of the Wittenberg theological faculty fell to Christoph Pezel, who had never experienced Luther and had spent but one semester in Wittenberg during Melanchthon's life. He had studied at Jena under Viktorin Strigel, who moved to Heidelberg, as his affinity for John Calvin's understanding of Christ's presence became evident in the mid-1560s. Pezel and Peucer worked together after Pezel joined the Wittenberg faculty in 1567. Their spiritualizing definition of Christ's presence earned them and their supporters the designation "crypto-Calvinist." In fact, they were developing certain ideas in Melanchthon's writings in directions other than those found by other Melanchthon students, including Martin Chemnitz and David Chytraeus, who found the preceptor largely in agreement with Luther, or Paul Crell and Johannes Bugenhagen the Younger, who dismissed Peucer's and Pezel's distancing Melanchthon from Luther and held to a position on the Lord's Supper that extracted elements from both Luther's and Melanchthon's teaching.

Within the Electoral Saxon ecclesiastical establishment a sharp rift developed, largely kept out of public view, but nonetheless serious enough to generate maneuverings between the supporters of Peucer and Pezel, and those gathered around Major and his son-in-law Crell, the court preacher Georg Listhenius, and others. When Elector August and his wife, Anna of Denmark, discovered that the Peucer party had been intentionally but surreptitiously moving Electoral Saxon public doctrine toward its spiritualizing views, the ducal couple regarded those actions as a personal betrayal and a threat to the welfare of the electorate, since its legality under the Religious Peace of Augsburg could be questioned if their position could be shown to be contrary to the Augsburg Confession. Four "crypto-Philippists" were imprisoned; several others went into exile. The moderate Philippists slowly moved toward accommodation with the Gnesio-Lutherans as Jakob Andreae, Martin Chemnitz, and Nikolaus Selnecker, one of the Philippists' own number (who had gotten to know Andreae and Chemnitz in their team effort to introduce the Reformation into the duchy of Braunschweig-Wolfenbüttel, 1568–70) together with David Chytraeus, Andreas Musculus, and Christoph Körner composed the Formula of Concord.

The Flacian Gnesio-Lutherans, who rejected the Formula, died out by the early seventeenth century, having been driven largely into exile in Hapsburg lands. Many of the "crypto-Philippists" did drift into Calvinist churches. The majority of Gnesio-Lutherans and Philippists found their way together through the Concordist formulation of agreement in the Formula of Concord. In it Chemnitz, Andreae, and Chytraeus sought to honor the concerns of both sides insofar as they believed they reflected biblical teaching. These groups dissolved into the developing post-1580 theology and institutions of the Lutheran Church.

See also Adiaphora; Amsdorf, Nikolaus von; Antinomianism/Antinomian Controversies; Flacius, Matthias Illyricus, and the Flacians; Formula of Concord; Good Works; Justification; Lord's Supper; Major, Georg; Melanchthon, Philip; Original Sin; Osiander, Andreas; Peucer, Caspar; Pfeffinger, Johann; Strigel, Johann; Wittenberg Circle

Bibliography

Dingel, I. *Concordia controversa: Die öffentlichen Diskussionen um das lutherische Konkordienwerk am Ende des 16. Jahrhunderts.* Gütersloher Verlagshaus, 1996; Gensichen, H. W. *We Condemn: How Luther and Sixteenth Century Lutheranism Condemned False Doctrine.* Trans. H. Bouman. Concordia, 1967; Hund, J. *Das Wort ward Fleisch: Eine systematisch-theologische Untersuchung zur Debatte um die Wittenberger Christologie und Abendmahlslehre.*

Vandenhoeck & Ruprecht, 2006; Kolb, R. *Luther's Heirs Define His Legacy*. Variorum, 1996; Wengert, T. J. *Defending Faith*. Mohr Siebeck, 2013; Wenz, G. *Theologie der Bekenntnisschriften der evangelisch-lutherischen Kirche*. Vol. 2. De Gruyter, 1998.

ROBERT KOLB

Wittenberg Concord

The agreement reached in Wittenberg on May 29, 1536, the Wittenberg Concord, was between the Wittenberg and southern German theologians on the doctrinal issues of the Lord's Supper, baptism, and absolution, issues that had caused division among them for over ten years. The two groups of theologians were originally scheduled to meet in Eisenach, but the meeting was moved to Grimma, and finally to Wittenberg because of Luther's poor health. The agreement was made possible primarily because of the tireless work of Martin Bucer of Strasbourg, who with Philip Melanchthon worked out a formula on the most contentious issue, the Lord's Supper, which was acceptable to both sides. The very public disputes over the Lord's Supper in the 1520s, which the Marburg Colloquy (1529) had failed to resolve, meant that the Evangelical territories and their theologians were unable to present a united front to Emperor Charles V at the Diet of Augsburg (1530). During the diet, Bucer met with Melanchthon in Augsburg and Luther at the Coburg Castle, and these encounters led to further conversation. Aided by Melanchthon's growing friendship with Bucer (the former had at first refused to meet with him at Augsburg), along with Bucer's further clarifications of his position on the Lord's Supper, led in December 1534 to a seminal meeting in Kassel, where the basic principles of an agreement were reached. Before this meeting Bucer had met with reform-minded theologians from throughout southern Germany and Switzerland, drumming up support for some form of concord. Bucer's Constance Articles (1534), approved only weeks before the Kassel negotiations, paved the way for southern German support. Luther cautiously agreed with the formulation that had been reached

at Kassel, even though he worried that the agreement could backfire on the Evangelicals and cause irreparable damage to the cause of unity. While the Swiss reformers rejected Bucer's formulations as not doing justice to Zwingli's position on the Lord's Supper, Bucer continued to work to bring the Swiss and southern Germans into agreement with the Wittenberg theologians; with the encouragement of Elector John Frederick of Saxony and Landgrave Philip of Hesse, parties finally came together in Wittenberg. Following a week of negotiations, the Wittenberg Concord was signed on May 29, 1536. The Concord, drafted by Melanchthon, had articles on the Lord's Supper (1–3), baptism (4), and absolution (5). It was signed by southern German theologians such as Wolfgang Musculus (of Augsburg), Wolfgang Capito, and Bucer (of Strasbourg), plus the Wittenberg theologians Luther, Jonas, Cruciger, Bugenhagen, Melanchthon, Menius, Myconius, Rhegius, Spalatin, Melander, and others. However, the southern Germans rejected an article on the role of civil authorities in religious affairs, which the Wittenberg theologians all signed.

Regarding the Lord's Supper, the Concord states that Christ is truly and substantially present with the bread (*cum pane*) and wine, compromise wording first proposed by Bucer that satisfied Luther and his colleagues. They also agreed that the sacrament is efficacious for both the worthy (*pii*) and unworthy (*indigni*). For Luther, these two categories included everyone, while Bucer added a third category, the ungodly (*impii*), who, while offered Christ's body and blood, received only bread and wine in the meal. The article on baptism approved of infant baptism, insisting that it granted the child the forgiveness of sins, the gift of the Spirit, and salvation. This article, like the one on the Lord's Supper, also provided a response to the fiasco a year earlier in Münster, where militant Anabaptists seized the city, intent on establishing a new Jerusalem, before Roman Catholic and Protestant forces regained the city. The article on absolution encouraged private absolution in the churches for pastoral reasons, even though a complete enumeration of all sins, demanded by the Fourth Lateran Council (1215), was no longer required.

The impact of the Wittenberg Concord was somewhat muted by the fact that the reform-minded Smalcaldic League had, in December of 1535, made the signing of the Augsburg Confession an expectation of all its members, including those in southern Germany. Thus the civil authorities already had the theological basis for their alliance. However, a definitive opinion on the influence of civil authorities in religious affairs, which the civil authorities needed from the gathering at Wittenberg, failed to materialize.

While some territories, especially all of the Protestant parts of the Swiss confederation, had struggles with accepting the Wittenberg Concord, it was officially adopted in many of the Evangelical territories. However, because it was not accepted in all Protestant territories, it had a somewhat limited impact, although it did limit polemic among Evangelicals on the Lord's Supper until the 1550s, when Lutheran theologians (notably Joachim Westphal) attacked John Calvin for having abandoned the Concord by signing an agreement with the church in Zurich. When the Concord was signed, the English delegation in Wittenberg also ultimately failed to convince the newly formed Church of England to adopt a similar concord. The Concord's wording "with the bread and wine" somewhat influenced Luther's wording on the Lord's Supper in the Smalcald Articles, and it was used in the Altered Augsburg Confession (Variata) of 1540 and 1542 to reword the article on the Lord's Supper. Nevertheless, the Wittenberg Concord was also extensively quoted in article 7, on the Lord's Supper, in the Solid Declaration (1577; SD 7.13–16; *BC* 595–96). However, the Concord was unable to bridge the gap between Lutheran and Reformed theologians in later dialogues and colloquies, such as at Mömpelgard (Montbéliard) (1586) and Leipzig (1631).

The Wittenberg Concord is often overlooked in Lutheran history. However, it introduced an important component to later intra-Lutheran and ecumenical discussion by the way it produced consensus on important matters, even when the parties involved understood the meaning of the agreement in different ways. This method is termed "differentiated consensus" in the Joint Declaration on the Doctrine of Justification.

The Leuenberg Agreement (1973), between the Lutheran and Reformed Churches of Europe and the 1998 Full Communion Agreement between three Reformed church bodies and the Evangelical Lutheran Church in America, both of which consciously used the language of the Concord, brought together some of the theological traditions that the Wittenberg Concord had tried, with various amounts of success, to bring together in the sixteenth century.

See also Augsburg Confession; Bucer, Martin; Colloquy; Formula of Concord; Lord's Supper; Melanchthon, Philip; Musculus, Wolfgang; Strasbourg

Bibliography

Bizer, E. *Studien zur Geschichte des Abendmahlsstreits im 16. Jahrhundert*. Wissenschaftliche Buchgesellschaft, 1940. Reprint, 1962; Jensen, G. "Luther and Bucer on the Lord's Supper." *LQ* 27 (2013): 167–87; Köhler, W. *Zwingli und Luther: Ihre Streit über das Abendmahl nach seinen politischen und religiösen Beziehungen*. 2 vols. Bertelsmann, 1924. Reprint, 1953; Sasse, H. *This Is My Body: Luther's Contention for the Real Presence in the Sacrament of the Altar*. Augsburg, 1959.

GORDON A. JENSEN

Wittenberg Unrest

The turmoil in Wittenberg that began in the fall of 1521 during Luther's absence, the Wittenberg Unrest, was brought to an end by his return to the city in March 1522. Older accounts of this unrest stress the threat of violence and political disorder and Karlstadt's leading role in the movement. In contrast, more recent studies place the disturbances in the broader context of the relationships between elector, city council, and university; downplay the actual extent of the violence; point to the agreement among Luther's supporters through most of this period; and suggest that Karlstadt was made the scapegoat as a way to deflect blame from both the elector and Luther.

After the Diet of Worms in April 1521, Luther went into hiding at the Wartburg, and leadership of the Evangelical movement in Wittenberg continued among his colleagues at the university, the most prominent of whom was Andreas Bodenstein von Karlstadt but included also Philip Melanchthon, Justus Jonas, and Nikolaus von Amsdorf. At the end of September, Melanchthon and some of his students, all laymen, received Communion in both kinds in the parish church. A week later the Augustinian Gabriel Zwilling gave a sermon attacking private Masses, Communion in one kind, and the veneration of the consecrated host. Soon thereafter several of his fellow Augustinians refused to celebrate Mass in the traditional way, and some left their friary entirely. At the university, disputations were held to defend veneration of the host and Communion in both kinds. Criticism of host veneration was quickly suppressed, but a university commission advocated the abolition of private Masses and supported Communion in both kinds, although the canons of the All Saints chapter resisted any type of reform. Mixed groups of students and townspeople also interrupted worship with verbal abuse and stone throwing, although these altercations did not differ significantly from earlier cases of conflict between the city, the university, and the church. Luther secretly returned to Wittenberg in early December and expressed his satisfaction with developments. In his *Sincere Admonition to All Christians to Guard against Insurrection and Rebellion* (LW 45:57–74), however, he stated that his followers should focus on preaching and not rebel against the authorities.

Throughout the autumn, Karlstadt acted as a moderating influence on those calling for immediate reform, and challenges to traditional practices were limited to the university and the clergy. The situation changed significantly at the end of the year, however, with a series of innovations that directly involved the laity. In December a group of citizens petitioned the city council to abolish all private Masses and allow Communion in both kinds. In response, Karlstadt celebrated a simplified "Evangelical Mass" on Christmas Day without donning the required vestments, omitting many of the prescribed gestures, and replacing the silent canon of the Mass with Christ's words instituting the sacrament, spoken aloud in German. He also administered the sacrament by placing both the bread and the cup in the hands of the lay recipients, many of whom had not first made sacramental confession. This service was repeated a week later, drawing a substantial crowd. Karlstadt, together with Zwilling, now became the most prominent spokesmen for the immediate introduction of practical reforms. In sermons and pamphlets, he urged that images be removed from the city's churches, and he was the first Wittenberg priest to marry. A committee of reform-minded university professors and city council members drafted an ordinance, issued on January 24, 1522, that prescribed a new liturgy incorporating Karlstadt's reforms, provided for the removal of images from the city's churches, and abolished begging—a measure aimed especially against mendicant friars. In introducing these changes, the reformers went against the express command of Elector Frederick. Concerned about disunity among the clergy and growing unrest in the city, Frederick had decreed in mid-December that there were to be no innovations until all involved were united behind the changes. Negotiations between the reforming party, the conservative canons of the All Saints' Foundation, and the elector's representative failed to win support for even limited innovations, however. By February the reforming party was dividing between those who defended the changes as according with God's Word and those who felt that the innovations should be rolled back in order to obey the elector and to prevent scandal to the weak.

Luther was kept informed of developments in Wittenberg by letter. In early March, in part because of requests from parishioners, he returned to the city to resume his pastoral work and thereby to reassert control over the movement. On March 9, 1522, he began a weeklong series of sermons, published as *Eight Sermons at Wittenberg*, better known as the Invocavit sermons because the first one was preached on Invocavit Sunday (the first Sunday in Lent). Luther criticized efforts to reform the Mass without the elector's permission and condemned those who argued that Scripture required such reforms without taking account of the offense caused to the weak. With one minor exception, Luther did not mention anyone by name, but his criticisms were clearly aimed at Karlstadt and Zwilling. Karlstadt justified his own position in a pamphlet against the Mass, but he was not allowed to publish the pamphlet, nor was he allowed to preach. He remained in Wittenberg for another year and continued to lecture at the university, but he began to distance himself from the rest of the theology faculty.

In the summer of 1523 Karlstadt left Wittenberg for Orlamünde. The disagreements between Luther and Karlstadt that emerged in the spring of 1522 influenced their published exchange over the Lord's Supper in 1524–25.

See also Karlstadt, Andreas Bodenstein von

Bibliography

Bubenheimer, U. "Luthers Stellung zum Aufruhr in Wittenberg 1520–1522 und die frühreformatorischen Wurzeln des landesherrlichen Kirchenregiments." *Zeitschrift der Savigny-Stiftung für Rechtsgeschichte*, kanonistische Abteilung 71 (1985): 147–214; Burnett, A. N. *Karlstadt and the Origins of the Eucharistic Controversy: A Study in the Circulation of Ideas.* Oxford University Press, 2011; Krentz, N. "Auf den Spuren der Erinnerung: Wie die 'Wittenberger Bewegung' zu einem Ereignis wurde." *Zeitschrift für historische Forschung* 36 (2009): 563–95; Krentz, N. *Ritualwandel und Deutungshoheit: Die frühe Reformation in der Residenzstadt Wittenberg (1500–1533).* Mohr Siebeck, 2014; Oehmig, S. "Die Wittenberger Bewegung 1521/22 und ihre Folgen im Lichte alter und neuer Fragestellungen." In *700 Jahre Wittenberg: Stadt, Universität, Reformation*, ed. S. Oehmig, 97–130. Böhlau, 1995; Preus, J. S. *Carlstadt's Ordinaciones and Luther's Liberty: A Study of the Wittenberg Movement, 1521–22.* Harvard University Press, 1974; Sider, R. J. *Andreas Bodenstein von Karlstadt: The Development of His Thought, 1517–1525.*

Brill, 1974; Simon, W. "Karlstadt neben Luther: Ihre theologische Differenz im Kontext der 'Wittenberger Unruhen' 1521/22." In *Frömmigkeit—Theologie—Frömmigkeitstheologie*, ed. G. Litz et al., 317–34. Brill, 2005.

AMY NELSON BURNETT

Women's Movement

Although Luther's theology and sixteenth-century reforms had the potential to raise the social and religious status of women in this world, the immediate effects of Luther's insight and Reformation agenda were mixed at best: this potential is only gradually being realized. If the reformers understood that before God women and men are both equally sinners who are saved by divine grace and thus equally members of the priesthood of all believers, nonetheless their conformity to the social norms of their age limited the application of this gospel freedom in women's lives both inside and outside the church. The implications of the priesthood of all believers had religious significance but was at the same time restricted in this world by the Lutheran teaching about the orders of creation. On the one hand, the spiritual worth of family life was recognized, and girls were given basic education in support of their own piety and in expectation that they would influence their own children. On the other hand, most women's ministry was restricted to the domestic arena. To be sure, some women exercised a kind of public ministry as wives of pastors, with Katharina von Bora (Luther's wife, 1499–1552) and Katherina Schützin Zell as models. The early hymn writer Elisabeth Cruciger (née von Meseritz) had few if any imitators. Argula von Grumbach (1492–1568) was one of a small number of noblewomen who became patrons of reform. Opportunity for further study, greater leadership, and most alternatives to marriage, however, disappeared with the reformers' general rejection of monastic life. In the nineteenth century women's religious activities among Lutherans expanded somewhat. Pietism, particularly in Scandinavia, allowed for female lay preachers and used hymns written by women. In Germany, the office of deaconess was revived in the 1840s by Theodore Flieder (1800–1864) and gave women access to both medical and educational ministry. Among American Lutherans several groups of deaconesses provided services and expanded the scope of their ministry beyond those communities. Elizabeth Fedde's (1850–1921) leadership with Norwegian-American deaconesses in New York and Minneapolis is representative. Several communities of deaconesses worked among American Lutherans beyond their ethnoreligious group. In the United States members of local and federated women's organizations gathered for study, worship, and companionship as well as to aid the church. Notable leaders of national federations included Emmy Carlsson Evald (1857–1947), president of the Augustana Synod Women's Missionary Society, and Katherine Lehmann (1876–1960), president of the women's organization first of the Ohio Synod and then of the American Lutheran Church formed in 1930. As foreign missions grew, women's organizations provided material and spiritual support; in addition to the wives of missionaries, single women such as Anna Kugler (1863–1930) served in various religious, educational, and medical capacities. By the early twentieth century, Lutheran women brought their professional skills to responsibilities in the church, notably in higher education and social service.

The second wave of American and European feminism, in the mid-twentieth century, renewed attention to the reformers' legacy for women: its failures and its possibilities. Ordaining women as pastors was a major issue, along with women's full participation in the church and women's status in the larger society. Among Lutherans, the Church of Sweden led the way on ordination in 1960. The practice has also exposed disagreements about biblical interpretation among Lutherans worldwide. For example, in America, while the Lutheran Church–Missouri Synod and the Wisconsin Evangelical Lutheran Synod do not ordain women as pastors, the Lutheran Church in

America and the American Lutheran Church, predecessors to the Evangelical Lutheran Church in America (ELCA), began to ordain women in 1970: Elizabeth Platz and Barbara Andrews (1935–78). In Europe, early female bishops include Maria Jepsen (Germany, 1992), Rosemarie Köhn (Norway, 1993), Lise-Lotte Rebel (Denmark, 1995), and Irja Askola (Finland, 2010). In the United States, April Ulring Larson was the first woman elected bishop of the ELCA in 1992. Meanwhile in many congregations laywomen assumed greater responsibilities, although this was somewhat tempered in the more conservative synods. Lutheran women's organizations were challenged to recognize and adapt to women's changing lives. Those preparing new worship books, especially in English-speaking lands in the 1970s, worked to make liturgy and hymns more inclusive, particularly regarding references to humanity. This effort continues and has expanded to address images of God as informed by ongoing theological debate.

Catechetical instruction has long equipped Lutheran girls and women for theological reflection; however, until the late twentieth century few women had the training to participate in the more formal enterprise. In recent decades this has changed, in the United States and around the world. By the late twentieth century women were contributing to the full range of theological activity, including ecumenical dialogues, internal consultations, and theological education. Their work reexamines and expands Lutheran theology. Offering critique and building on its foundation, they recover its liberating potential for women's lives. They also provide fresh insight about classic concerns such as Christology and justification, along with addressing contemporary issues such as ecological crisis and economic justice.

See also Gender: Men and Women; Household, Children, Parents

Bibliography

Erling, M., and S. McArver. "Americanization of American Lutheranism: Democratization of Authority and the Ordination of Women; A Case Study [in 2 parts]." In

Sources of Authority in the Church: Lutheran Traditions in North American Contexts, ed. D. Brondos, 22–56. Lutheran University Press, 2012; Grindal, G. "Women in the Evangelical Lutheran Church in America." In *Religious Institutions and Women's Leadership: New Roles inside the Mainstream*, ed. C. Wessinger, 180–210. University of South Carolina Press, 1996; Lagerquist, L. D. *From Our Mothers Arms: A History of Women in the American Lutheran Church*. Augsburg, 1987; Stjerna, K. *Women and the Reformation*. Wiley-Blackwell, 2008; Streufert, M. J., ed. *Transformative Lutheran Theologies: Feminist, Womanist, and Mujerista Perspectives*. Fortress, 2010.

L. DeAne Lagerquist

Word of God

In the Lutheran tradition the expression "Word of God" signifies a variety of related semantic domains that arise out of close readings of the biblical narrative and are, in turn, shaped by the trinitarian and christological confessions of the church catholic. Paradigmatically, God speaks and (1) "calls into existence the things that do not exist" and (2) "gives life to the dead" (Rom. 4:17). Thus the term "Word of God" describes the way in which God creates (Gen. 1:1; Heb. 11:3), sustains all things (Gen. 1:3; Matt. 4:4; Heb. 1:3; 1 John 1:1), and gives new life to that which is either spiritually (John 5:24) or physically (John 11:43; 1 Cor. 15:22) dead. Humans, created in the image of God (Gen. 1:26–27), are invited by the "living," "active" (Heb. 4:12), and "enduring" (1 Pet. 1:23–25) Word into a particular communicative relationship in which the identity of God, characterized by love for the world (John 3:16) and mercy for humanity (Luke 1:54), is revealed. The same Word (*Logos*) that spoke the cosmos into being and promised to be faithful and merciful to the people of God (Acts 26:6; Rom. 4:13–25; Gal. 3:14) became incarnate in Jesus of Nazareth (John 1:1–4, 14; Heb. 1:1–4). "In the beginning" God speaks, and the cosmos itself is created through the *Logos*. In the Word incarnate (Jesus Christ), God speaks again in a way that reveals God's love for a world held captive by sin and death, defeats evil, and establishes renewed and reconciled relations with humanity and wider creation (Rom. 8:20–22).

The apostolic proclamation of the living Word of God, based in the crucified and risen Jesus Christ, is "the power of God for salvation to everyone who has faith" (Rom. 1:16), through which the old Adam is put to death and life is created anew (Rom. 5:18). This incarnate Word continues to be effective through the power of the Holy Spirit in the church's kerygma (proclamation; Greek: *kērygma*) "in Jesus' name" (Acts 4:30; 19:13; 1 Cor. 6:11) of what God has effected in the birth, ministry, death, and resurrection/exaltation of Jesus (Acts 6:7; Rom. 10:8–17), as well as in the efficacious presence of the Word in the sacraments of baptism (John 15:3; Eph. 1:13; 5:26) and the Lord's Supper. In the "visible words" of the sacraments, the real presence of Christ makes true his promise of the forgiveness of sin as the external Word is proclaimed over the elements of water, wine, and bread (Matt. 26:28; Luke 24:47) and "attaches to itself that 'visible' reality that stands out there over against our subjectivity" (Jenson 3). The inscripturated Word (Bible), too, is "God-breathed" (*theopneustos*) and "useful for teaching, for reproof, for correction, and for training in righteousness" (2 Tim. 3:16). As the Son proceeds from the Father, so the Spirit proceeds from God's Word (John 14:16; 15:26), indicating the inseparability of the Word from the Father and the Spirit in the mystery of the Triune God. The classic statement of the binding of the Word to the Spirit, in particular, is the Smalcald Articles (1537), where Luther states, "It must be firmly maintained that God gives no one his Spirit or grace apart from the external word which goes before" (SC 3.8.3). As J. Silcock points out, "Luther knows that God is present everywhere in the universe through the Spirit, but God does not want me to look for him everywhere. 'Seek him rather where the Word is, and there you will lay hold of him in the right way'" (LW 36:342; Silcock 298).

Verbum Efficax. The primary observation that unites the various understandings of the Word of God is that when God speaks, things happen. Luther, in describing this performative speech act of the Word, called it a *Thettel-Wort*, distinguishing it from another kind of "word" labeled in the German-speaking medieval world a "*Heissel-Wort*." D. Steinmetz explains the difference:

> A *Heissel-Wort* is a word used to affix a name to something that already exists—a wall, a book, a window. All of these things existed before they were called by their respective *Heissel-Wörter*. Calling is a way of fastening a label to something already there. But a *Thettel-Wort* is an altogether different kind of word. . . . A *Thettel-Wort* is a deed-word, a word which, once uttered, brings into existence a thing that did not exist before and could never have existed apart from that spoken word. For Luther, the instrument by which God creates and redeems the world is his *Thettel-Wort*. (167–68)

O. Bayer provides an example of such a performative speech act in the declaration of absolution: "I absolve you of your sins!" Bayer observes, "The sentence 'I absolve you of your sins!' is not a judgment that merely states what is true already. It does not assume that an inner, divine, proper absolution or justification has already taken place. Rather, the absolution is seen as a speech act that first constitutes, brings about, a state of affairs, by creating a relationship between the one in whose name it is spoken and the one to whom it is spoken and who believes in the promise. Such a speech act establishes communication, liberates and gives certainly. Luther calls it '*verbum efficax*,' an active and effective word" (129–30). Luther often quotes Isa. 55:11 as epitomizing the deed-word character of God's speech: "So shall my word be that goes out from my mouth; it shall not return to me empty, but it shall accomplish that which I purpose, and succeed in the thing for which I sent it." God's spoken *Thettel-Wort*, according to Luther, *always* accomplishes its purpose, "albeit sometimes more darkly and at other times more clearly" (LW 7:138).

Given Luther's understanding of the effective power of the spoken Word, there is a sense that, for Luther, God desires the Word to be proclaimed in living speech: "The mouth of Paul, of the apostles and preachers, is called the mouth of God. Therefore God consoles us that although our word is persecuted and resisted, it will nevertheless achieve results, because it is the Word of the mouth of God" (LW 17:258). This understanding of the Word of God as a *Thettel-Wort* is the basis of the much-quoted saying from Luther that the church is a "mouth house" and not a "pen house," an aphorism that comes from his interpretation of the Gospel for the first Sunday of Advent published in his postil in 1522. In the sermon Luther expands on a philologically suspect etymology of the place-name "Bethphage" in Matt. 21:1:

> The word "Bethphage" . . . means, as some say, "mouth-house," for St. Paul says in Romans 1:2, that the gospel was promised afore in the Holy Scriptures, but was not preached orally and publicly until Christ came and sent out his apostles. Therefore the church is a mouth-house, a not a pen-house, for since Christ's advent that gospel is preached orally which before was hidden in written books. It is the way of the gospel and of the New Testament that it is to be preached and discussed orally with a living voice. Christ himself wrote nothing, nor did he give command to write, but to preach orally. Thus the apostles were not sent out until Christ came to his mouth-house, that is, until the time had come to preach orally and to bring the Gospel from dead writing and pen-work to the living voice and mouth. From this time the church is rightly called Bethpage, since she has and hears the living voice of the Gospel. (trans. Lenker 44)

Law and Gospel: The Threefold Word. Though Luther at times had a tendency to privilege the proclaimed Word of God over its other forms, one should note that this was not meant to eclipse either the written Word, which also contains God's clear promises (e.g., Matt. 28:20; Bayer 129, 131) and is fully God's Word, or the sacramental Word, in which Christ, by the power of the Holy Spirit, is also truly, efficaciously present. Luther was, after all, a professional biblical scholar who worked tirelessly both to translate the Scriptures into German and to expound in detail on both the Old and New Testament canon. He was an exegete and priest as well as a preacher. "There is for Luther, one means of grace. And that one means of grace is the Word of God in all its complexity" (Steinmetz 169).

The subsequent Lutheran theological tradition understood, then, the Word of God, in addition to its christological meaning, as active in three forms: (1) oral proclamation experienced through the office of preaching as well as the "mutual conversation and consolation of brothers and sisters" (SA 4; BC 319), (2) the visible Word of the sacraments of baptism and the Lord's Supper, and (3) the written Word of Scripture. In all three forms, the *scopus* (goal/heart) of the Word is understood to be the justification of the sinner by God's gift of the forgiveness of sin in Christ, experienced through trust in the promises of God as revealed through God's own speech. Although later Orthodox Lutheran theologians of the seventeenth century often concentrated their efforts on understanding the reliability and inspiration of the Bible as the Word of God, neither they nor their successors ever lost this multiform approach.

The Word of God experienced as a *verbum efficax* in its threefold expressions (oral, sacramental, written) is further described by Lutherans in terms of the dialectic of law and gospel. In this expression (law/gospel) the law, itself a plurisignificant term in Lutheran theology, refers to the second use of the law (*usus theologicus*), rather than the first use (*usus politicus*). The second use of the law is tied up with the "grace of new life" in comparison to the "grace of preservation" characteristic of the first usage (Bayer 106). In this second "theological" use, the function of the law is to reveal sin: "to reduce to nothing [the] things that are" (1 Cor. 1:28), so that the gospel might create new life. The word of God, then, both kills the old Adam and gives birth to the new Adam. In this dialectic, the law, experienced as God's "alien" work, is not an end in itself,

but functions to drive one to Christ. The grace experienced in the gospel is understood as an expression of God's "proper" work. That is, the mercy experienced by one's justification by grace through faith reveals God's true identity. Though this law/gospel distinction is, at one level, a simple one, *God's* use of the law as well as the experience of new life by means of the Word of God spoken in Christ is not. It is, in fact, often difficult to distinguish between the alien and the proper work of God. As Luther declares, "This art, namely, the proper distinction between law and gospel, . . . is easy to learn as far as the words are concerned. But when it comes to experiencing it and putting it to the test in our heart and life, it is a high and difficult art and we cannot begin to understand it" (Bayer 73). Both the depth of our sinfulness and our inability to believe in the promises of God make the working of the law and the gospel a constant in the life of Christ. Since one is *simul iustus et peccator* (simultaneously saint and sinner); one is also *semper est in motu et initio* (always in motion and at the beginning; LW 10:53) in one's repentance (*metanoia*). Is there, then, any progress from the constant work of the Word of God experienced as law and gospel on the sinner? As J. Silcock states, "Christians progress by continually going back to their baptism and reappropriating its promise every day anew. . . . Therefore, progress in the Christian life remains hidden. It is marked not by an increasing absence of sin but rather by a deeper awareness of sin and the sufficiency of God's grace" (Silcock 304–5).

See also Bible Interpretation; Justification; Law, Uses of the; Law and Gospel; Preaching; Sacraments; Scripture

Bibliography

Bayer, O. *Theology the Lutheran Way*. Ed. and trans. J. G. Silcock and M. C. Mattes. Eerdmans, 2007; Bouman, W. "Bible as Word of God." In *The Encyclopedia of the Lutheran Church*, ed. J. Bodensieck, 1:229–36. Augsburg, 1965; Jenson, R. W. *Visible Words: The Interpretation and Practice of Christian Sacraments*. Fortress, 1978; Lenker, J. N., ed. and trans. *Luther's Church Postil Gospels: Advent, Christmas, and Epiphany Sermons*. Vol. 1. Lutherans in All Lands, 1905; Silcock, J. G. "Luther on the Holy Spirit and His Use of God's Word." In *The Oxford Handbook of*

Martin Luther's Theology, ed. R. Kolb, I. Dingel, and L. Batka, 294–309. Oxford University Press, 2014; Steinmetz, D. C. "Luther, the Reformers, and the Bible." In *Living Tradition of the Bible: Scripture in Jewish, Christian, and Muslim Practice*, ed. J. E. Bowley, 163–76. Chalice, 1999.

ERIK M. HEEN

World Wars I and II

The two world wars of the twentieth century had significant and sometimes tragic effects on Lutherans in both Europe and America and on Lutheran missions throughout the world. During World War I, Lutherans in Germany were widely supportive of the kaiser and the war. Church leaders were willing agents for prowar propaganda; the official "Call to the German People" issued by Kaiser Wilhelm was written by a prominent Lutheran scholar, Adolf von Harnack.

One result of the war was the separation of the Lutheran Church from organic involvement with the German state. There was also a loss of mission opportunities in colonies formerly under German control. Before the United States' entry into the war, Lutherans in America, especially those of German heritage, were generally opposed to US involvement and supportive of Germany; this was particularly true of more recent immigrants, who often still had family in the "old country." When America declared war on Germany, many Lutherans were shocked. This astonishment only deepened as an anti-German sentiment swept America. Some Lutheran groups, notably the Missouri Synod, were still very German in their life and culture; they worshiped in German, conducted their meetings in German, and sponsored parochial schools where German was the language of instruction. All of these things immediately came under suspicion. There were reports of churches being painted yellow (for cowardice), of pastors being tarred and feathered. In some areas, laws were passed forbidding the use of German in public assemblies. Accusations were made that the kaiser was the Lutherans' "pope" and that students in German Lutheran schools began their day by singing "*Deutschland über alles.*"

Scandinavian-American Lutherans were often also attacked since the anti-German partisans were unable to distinguish between European groups. This prejudice led to a rapid increase in the acculturation of the immigrant synods; worship and teaching in German and other European languages declined as these Lutherans tried to demonstrate their Americanism. Many congregations began displaying the American flag in their places of worship. Most of the Lutheran synods quickly supported the war effort through encouraging the purchase of war bonds and other patriotic acts. The war also stimulated cooperation among various Lutheran synods as it became necessary to work together to provide ministry to men in the armed services. The result was the National Lutheran Commission for Soldiers' and Sailors' Welfare, in which most Lutheran synods took part; the Missouri Synod, however, organized its own Army and Navy Board. After the war, American Lutherans dedicated themselves to providing relief and assistance to a devastated Europe. The experience with the Lutheran Commission emboldened them to form the National Lutheran Council to coordinate this work; this agency included most of the synods (though again the Missouri Synod and its Synodical Conference partners stayed out) and became an important catalyst toward greater Lutheran unity.

As World War II approached, significantly different factors were at play, both in Europe and in America. The German church went through a tumultuous time under Hitler. The new regime was hostile to the church and tried to bring it under the control of the Reich by establishing the *Reichskirche*, uniting the various territorial churches under a bishop appointed by Hitler. In this, Hitler was supported by the so-called German Christians, who generally endorsed the entire Nazi philosophy and platform. In reaction to this arose the Confessing Church, which produced the famous Barmen Declaration in 1934. One of the leaders of this movement, Martin Niemoeller, was arrested in 1937 and was held at the Dachau concentration camp until liberation by the allies in 1945; another leader was Dietrich Bonhoeffer, a young theologian who was hanged by the Nazis in the waning days of the war. After the Allied victory, leaders of the Confessing Church established a new Council of the Evangelical Church in Germany; one of its first actions was approval of the Stuttgart Declaration, a confession of the church's guilt in not opposing Nazism more courageously. The Lutheran Church was persecuted by the Nazis elsewhere in Europe, notably in Norway, where Bishop Eivind Berggrav was one of the leaders of resistance to the Nazi puppet regime. The Danish church was also active in organizing resistance to the occupying German forces.

As events heated up in Europe, many American Lutherans (esp. in the Missouri Synod) were anxious about a possible repeat of the anti-German hysteria of 1917–18; yet while there were a few instances of hostility toward German Lutherans, it was much less widespread than during the earlier war. Some American Lutherans were supportive of Hitler during the 1930s and opposed to US involvement in Europe. A complicating factor was a tendency, particularly in the Missouri Synod, toward anti-Semitism; there was also an increasing fear of communism, which led some to defend Hitler as bulwark against the Russians. Missouri Synod periodicals remained mostly uncritical of the Nazis through the 1930s, while the publications of several other Lutheran groups gradually shifted against Hitler. This is not to say there was no pro-Nazi sentiment among other Lutheran groups; in one widely publicized case at the end of the war, a ULCA pastor who had emigrated from Germany was convicted of being an agent of the Germans. After the 1941 attack on Pearl Harbor, US Lutherans fairly unanimously and enthusiastically supported the war effort. The National Lutheran Council coordinated American efforts to assist the "orphaned missions": German Lutheran work in foreign fields cut off from support from Germany under

Hitler. The council also assumed responsibility for recruiting Lutheran chaplains. When the conflict was over, Lutherans threw themselves wholeheartedly into postwar European reconstruction. The National Lutheran Council also took the lead in this, drawing on its experience after World War I. Once again this increased cooperation helped to spur the cause of Lutheran unity; Synodical Conference churches did not join the council's effort, but a measure of cooperation in this work was attained. The partnership of American and European churches in meeting the postwar needs was one factor that encouraged the founding of the Lutheran World Federation in 1947.

See also Barmen Confession; Bonhoeffer, Dietrich; Confessing Church; German Christians (Deutsche Christen); Lutheran World Federation; Niemoeller, Martin

Bibliography

Gritsch, E. W. *A History of Lutheranism*. 2nd ed. Fortress, 2010; Nelson, E. C. *Lutheranism in North America, 1914–1970*. Augsburg, 1970; Scholder, K. *The Churches and the Third Reich*. Fortress, 1988.

RICHARD O. JOHNSON

Württemberg

The duchy of Württemberg was the largest principality in southwestern Germany. Its adherence to the Reformation smoothed the way for many of the imperial cities and smaller principalities in the region to do the same. During the years 1519–34 Württemberg was governed by regents for Archduke Ferdinand of Austria, who had acquired the duchy after its hereditary ruler, Duke Ulrich, had been driven into exile for various crimes. During his exile Ulrich adopted the Evangelical faith (1523–24), and in 1534 he was restored to his duchy by an army led by Landgrave Philip of Hesse. The terms of the treaty of restoration permitted Ulrich to foster Lutheranism but forbade the toleration of Zwinglianism. But Ulrich, who had ties to both parties, initially entrusted the Reformation of the duchy jointly to the Zwinglian-leaning Ambrosius Blarer and the Lutheran Erhard Schnepf. After patching together a compromise formula on the real presence, Blarer and Schnepf set to work appointing suitable Protestants as pastors.

The confessional balance, however, soon began to tip in favor of Lutheranism. In 1535 Ulrich summoned the Lutheran reformer Johannes Brenz to help with the organization of his fledgling church. The addition of Brenz's catechism to the church order of 1536, together with Brenz's reorganization of the University of Tübingen in 1537–38, placed the duchy on a firmly Lutheran footing. In 1538 Blarer left the duke's service, taking the last trace of Zwinglian influence with him.

During the 1540s, Ulrich and his advisers succeeded in establishing a stable system of church government based, as Brenz had recommended in 1535, on periodic visitations, the results of which were examined and dealt with by a central body of "visitation counselors." In 1548 the future of Lutheranism in Württemberg, but not the duke's control of ecclesiastical affairs, was seriously threatened by the imposition of the Augsburg Interim. The duke turned his visitation counselors into a "council for the administration of church business," which was charged with the difficult task of implementing (and where possible undermining) the reintroduction of Catholicism into the duchy. When the Interim was lifted (1552), the council for the administration of church business, reorganized and renamed the consistory, became the central organ of church governance. The task of restoring the local and intermediate levels of administration fell to Ulrich's successor, Duke Christopher (r. 1550–68), and to Brenz, whom Christopher had retained as his principal theological adviser. Their work of reorganization reached its culmination in the Great Church Order of 1559. According to this order, the duke's responsibility for the care of the church was administered by a hierarchy of competent theologians and clergymen under the "supreme superintendence" of Brenz and his successors as provost of the Stuttgart Collegiate Church. In 1565 Duke Christopher and the territorial diet reached an agreement that enshrined the Lutheran faith in the constitution of Württemberg as well as in the church polity that Christopher and Brenz had established, an agreement that remained in force until the dissolution of the Holy Roman Empire in 1806. After Brenz's death in 1570, theological leadership fell to Jakob Andreae, whose work on the Formula of Concord paved the way for Württemberg's acceptance of the Book of Concord.

See also Andreae, Jakob; Brenz, Johannes

Bibliography

Brecht, M., and H. Ehmer. *Südwestdeutsche Reformationsgeschichte: Zur Einführung der Reformation im Herzogtum Württemberg 1534.* Calwer, 1984; Estes, J. M. *Godly Magistrates and Church Order: Johannes Brenz and the Establishment of the Lutheran Territorial Church in Germany 1524–1559.* Centre for Reformation and Renaissance Studies, 2001.

JAMES M. ESTES

Wyclif, John

As an English philosopher and theologian, John Wyclif's (ca. 1330–84) thought and works both precipitated the native Lollard movement and greatly influenced the Bohemian reformist and martyr Jan Hus. Born in Yorkshire and educated at Oxford, where he would teach until 1381, Wyclif was also employed in the 1370s as an adviser to the Crown. In this capacity, and in the context of England's expensive war with France, Wyclif controversially defended the prerogative of the Crown to suspend payments to Rome and to confiscate church properties. More controversially, this practical advice was given theoretical support in complementary treatises explicating his theory of dominion. True dominion, Wyclif held, belonged to God alone by right and was possessed by humans only by divine grant. Crucially, such was understood as a "dominion of grace"; it was therefore forfeited by one in a state of mortal sin. Further, Wyclif conceived of civil dominion as a result of the fall into sin and thereby tainted by sin. Thus, while now necessary, the exercise of temporal authority was to be shunned by the church and its clergy. The civil magistracy could therefore justifiably seize temporal power and possessions held by clergy, especially if a cleric were understood to be in a state of mortal sin. A series of papal bulls condemned the views expressed in *On Civil Dominion* (1376), and Wyclif was summoned to London for examinations in 1377 and 1378, though both concluded without immediate consequences.

From 1378 and in part prompted by the scandal of the papal schism of that year, Wyclif became increasingly critical of contemporary doctrine and practice. In addition to questioning indulgences, pilgrimages, and the veneration of saints, he articulated a definition of the true church consisting only of the predestined (*On the Church*, 1378), sharply critiqued the institution of the papacy (*On the Power of the Pope*, 1379), and began explicitly to reject the doctrine of transubstantiation (*On the Eucharist*, 1380). Though without naming him, the previously supportive Oxford University condemned Wyclif's eucharistic doctrine in early 1381. The political patronage that had protected him through the examinations of the previous decade was fatally compromised the same year when his name was invoked by the leaders of a large-scale peasant uprising. The following May the Blackfriars Synod condemned twenty-four propositions drawn from his works, and a ban on his writings was quickly announced. Again, however, Wyclif himself was never formally condemned; he was instead allowed to retire to the Lutterworth rectory previously granted to him by the Crown, where he died naturally on December 31, 1384.

Wyclif's influence remained very much alive, however, most immediately among those already before his death being called Lollards. These popularizers of Wyclif not only continued his critiques of popular piety, sacramental theology, and clerical immorality; they also realized Wyclif's advocacy for vernacular Scripture, compiling the English "Wycliffite Bible." (Though the translation was sometimes attributed to Wyclif himself even before the century's close, his direct involvement is unlikely.) The early popularity of Lollardy prompted parliamentary legislation making heresy punishable by death via burning in 1401, and in 1409 an ecclesiastical prohibition on vernacular Bible translations in England was established. Influential support for Lollardy eventually dissolved, however, in the same manner as it had for Wyclif. Backlash following a failed 1414 rebellion led by known Wycliffite John Oldcastle drove Lollardy underground, though without completely eradicating it. When Luther's writings and Tyndale's New Testament began entering England in the 1520s, surviving Lollard networks were among their early distributors.

Ironically, Wyclif's theology enjoyed a more lasting influence on the other side of Europe, where it was championed by Jan Hus and his followers in Bohemia. Imported by students returning from Oxford, by 1400 Wyclif's works appear to have been well known in Bohemia, where he would come to be known as the "evangelical doctor." Wyclif's philosophical realism was especially embraced by the Bohemian minority in the University of Prague, which remained dominated by German proponents of nominalism. Hus more explicitly appropriated and popularized his theology, apart from Wyclif's eucharistic views. He frequently quoted the Englishman, even reproducing large sections of Wyclif's works in his own. It was the concordance of Hus's theology with Wyclif's that finally led to Wyclif's formal condemnation three decades after his death. As prelude to Hus's condemnation at the Council of Constance (1415), Wyclif was first declared a heretic by the same council. Accordingly, in 1428 his body was exhumed and burned. There seems to be little indication that Luther knew Wyclif's work directly, but insofar as the English theologian influenced Hus, Luther had indirect access to his work, although on the question of the Eucharist, Luther and Wyclif held widely divergent views. Only in later historiography are Wyclif and Hus (sometimes along with Savanarola) named as precursors of the Reformation.

See also England; Hus, Jan; Scholasticism, Late Medieval; Tyndale, William

Bibliography

Evans, G. R. *John Wyclif: Myth and Reality*. IVP Academic, 2006; Hudson, A. *Selections from English Wycliffite Writings*. University of Toronto Press, 1997; Hudson, A. *Studies in the Transmission of Wyclif's Writings*. Ashgate, 2008; Kenny, A. *Wyclif in His Times*. Oxford University Press, 1986; Lahey, S. E. *John Wyclif*. Oxford University Press, 2008; Rex, R. *The Lollards*. Palgrave Macmillan, 2002; Wyclif, J. *Latin Works*. 36 vols. Wyclif Society, 1883–1922; Wyclif, J. *On the Truth of Holy Scripture*. Ed. I. C. Levy. Western Michigan University, 2001.

Korey D. Maas

Y

Youth Work

Lutherans' concern for the education of its youth began already during the Reformation, where catechisms like Luther's helped to instruct them in the basics of the faith. Work with orphans became a particular emphasis of the Franckean Institutions at Halle, which flourished in the eighteenth century, and similar work sprang up in other Lutheran areas as well. In the nineteenth century, in part as a response to the Industrial Revolution, attempts were made in German-speaking lands and elsewhere to provide special care for youth. This includes the *Rauhes Haus* of Wichern. Lutheran churches in the majority world have fostered many youth organizations and educational opportunities, from which many of their leaders receive initial training.

Organized youth work in the United States has its roots in C. F. W. Walther's congregation, Trinity Lutheran Church in St. Louis, where the Jünglingsverein (young men's society) was organized in 1848. The concept of societies dedicated to the spiritual needs of young people spread, though these groups were sponsored by congregations and generally focused on what today are called young adults. The late nineteenth century saw the beginnings of nationally organized youth groups in many denominations. The Society of Christian Endeavor, an interdenominational Protestant group, was founded in 1881 and attracted some Lutheran youth societies; many Lutherans viewed it as a threat to maintaining a distinct Lutheran identity, and this encouraged the establishment of specifically Lutheran youth organizations. The Walther League was organized by Missouri Synod members in 1893, but its growth was slow. It was only after World War I, when the Missouri Synod was going through a rapid period of Americanization (including a growing use of English in teaching and worship), that the Walther League became a significant force within the synod. A catalyst for further Americanization, the Walther League published several periodicals (including the *Walther League Messenger*); many of its adult leaders (such as Walter A. Maier and O. P. Kretzmann) went on to become prominent figures in the Missouri Synod.

Youth work among the "Mühlenberg tradition" Lutherans had its roots in a Young People's Religious Society formed in 1875 by Junius Remensnyder, a pastor from Lewiston, Pennsylvania, who was affiliated with the General Synod. The Luther League of America was organized in 1895, when some four hundred delegates gathered in Pittsburgh, Pennsylvania. It was established as an intersynodical association, and local groups from all synods were welcome to participate. The Luther League of America became a unifying force among eastern Lutherans, functioning as the official youth organization of the United Lutheran Church in America when it was formed in 1918. The group published the *Luther League Review* and held biennial national conventions. Most synods in the ULCA also had a Luther League structure with significant programs on a regional level. The various synods that did not participate in the ULCA gradually developed their own youth organizations—sometimes called Luther League (esp. in congregations), but with no organic connection to the ULCA group. The Augustana Synod Luther League was organized in 1910 (and after the ULCA merger, it did in fact maintain close ties with the Luther League of America). The Norwegian Evangelical Lutheran Church in America, founded in 1917, established its Young People's

Luther League in 1919. The American Lutheran Church, organized in 1930, formed its own Luther League, bringing together the youth organizations of its three predecessor bodies.

In the 1960s many synods of American Lutheranism merged into two churches, The American Lutheran Church (1960) and the Lutheran Church in America (1962), each with its own Luther League organization. The 1960s found Lutheran youth fully engaged in the social and political turmoil of the era, and this sometimes caused controversy within their churches. Martin Luther King Jr. was a speaker at the 1961 convention of the ALC's Luther League, while folk singer Pete Seeger (suspected by some of Communist sympathies) was part of the program of the Walther League's national convention in 1965; Seeger also spoke at the 1970 Luther League convention, along with antiwar senator George McGovern. An attempt was made at an intersynodical All Lutheran Youth Gathering in 1973, but it turned out to be a onetime event. Perhaps in part because the national organizations were taking up increasingly controversial subjects, and in part simply because of changing youth culture, the LCA's Luther League of America was disbanded in 1968, and the Walther League followed in 1977. This did not mean, of course, that these churches abandoned youth ministry, but that ministry became more focused in congregations than in a national organization. In contrast, the ALC's Luther League continued until the formation of the Evangelical Lutheran Church in 1987. At that time it went out of existence in favor of the ELCA's new Lutheran Youth Organization. This group focused on leadership development and conceived of itself as offering a "youth voice" within the church; it was ultimately disbanded in 2012. Both the ELCA and the LCMS continued to sponsor mass "youth gatherings"; the 2013 LCMS youth gathering brought together some twenty-five thousand youth, while the 2015

ELCA gathering was attended by over thirty thousand. Alternative programs also grew up as a kind of counterpoint to the "official" youth programs, such as Lutheran Youth Encounter (founded in 1965 as an intersynodical ministry) and Higher Things (begun around 2000 with a Missouri Synod constituency). Throughout the twentieth century, many Lutheran churches of the two-thirds world have used youth organizations for evangelism and the identification of future pastoral leaders.

See also Francke Foundations; Household, Children, Parents; Lutheran Education; Wichern, Johann Hinrich

Bibliography

Conrad, L., Jr. "Youth Organizations." In *The Encyclopedia of the Lutheran Church*, ed. J. Bodensieck, 3:2547–55. Augsburg, 1965; Jackson, M. J. "Luther League." In *Encyclopedia of Christian Education*, ed. G. T. Kurian and M. A. Lamport, 765–67. Rowman & Littlefield, 2015; Pahl, J. *Hopes and Dreams of All: The International Walther League and Lutheran Youth in American Culture, 1893–1993*. Wheat Ridge Ministries, 1993; Senter, M. H., III. *When God Shows Up: A History of Protestant Youth Ministry in America*. Baker Academic, 2010.

RICHARD O. JOHNSON

Yu, Thomas (Yu Qi-bing)

The Chinese churchman and leader of Lutheranism in Taiwan named Thomas Yu (Yu Qi-bing) was born July 6, 1941. He studied at National Taiwan University (BA, 1968), Luther Seminary in St. Paul (MDiv, 1973), and Boston University (ThD, 1984). Yu's doctoral thesis integrated a theology of the cross within the Chinese ecclesial context. Ordained in the Taiwan Lutheran Church (TLC, 1975), he later served as TLC president (1990–93). After teaching at Lutheran Theological Seminary, Hong Kong (1984–88), Yu returned to Taiwan, to China Lutheran Seminary (CLS). As CLS president (1993–2014), Yu's achievements include anchoring the seminary's Lutheran identity, strengthening its Lutheran and ecumenical relationships, obtaining Asia Theological Association accreditation, and completing a major capital campaign. A respected church statesman, beloved teacher, preacher, and counselor, Yu has written and taught extensively in the areas of pastoral care and counseling, worship, homiletics, filial piety, and ancestor veneration. As he retired from CLS's presidency, his articles and sermons were published as *Cross, Life, Ministry*.

See also Taiwan

Bibliography
Yu, T. *Cross, Life, Ministry*. CLS Press, 2014.

JUKKA A. KÄÄRIÄINEN

Z

Zambia

The Evangelical Lutheran Church in Zambia was established in 1983 and officially registered with the government in 1986. It records fifty-six hundred members in thirty congregations and is affiliated with the LWF, the LUCSA, and the Christian Council of Zambia.

Another Lutheran denomination is the Lutheran Church of Central Africa (LCCA), which is working not only in Zambia but also in Malawi. Ministers of the LCCA are trained in the Lutheran Seminary in Lusaka. The LCCA was started in Lusaka in 1953 by missionaries of the Wisconsin Evangelical Lutheran missionaries. It is linked to the Confessional Evangelical Lutheran Conference and has more than eleven thousand members.

FRIEDER LUDWIG

Ziegenbalg, Bartholomäus

Born in Pulsnitz, Saxony, Bartholomäus Ziegenbalg (1682–1719), missionary to India, admired the Pietist teachings of August Hermann Francke in Halle an der Saale, Germany, and became the first Lutheran missionary sent as part of the Danish-Halle Tranquebar Mission. His arrival in Tranquebar on the southeastern coast of India in July 1706 marked the beginning of an indigenous Tamil Lutheran community there. Shaped by Pietism, Ziegenbalg's life and legacy reveal key principles of mission including personal evangelism and the reading of the Bible in the vernacular. Ziegenbalg translated the New Testament into Tamil and had it printed (1714–15). His letters, reports, and writings, as in *Malabarian Heathenism* (1711) and *Genealogy of the Malabarian Gods* (1713), also reveal his conviction that missionaries must understand the religious, historical, and economic contexts of the people. He knew that those who embraced Christianity faced social ostracism and economic hardships. Therefore he organized schools, orphanages, and small-scale lending to support new Christians and strengthen the nascent community. Ziegenbalg recognized the temporary role of European missionaries and established a theological seminary (1716) for training Tamil Christian leaders to pastor local congregations. His marriage with Maria Dorothea Salzmann opened the way for noncelibate missionaries to India. He opposed caste distinctions, founded the first mechanized printing press in Tranquebar, and became the patriarch of Tamil Protestant Christianity.

See also Aaron, S.; Denmark; Fabricius, Johann Philipp; Franke Foundations; India; Mission and Evangelism; Schultze, Benjamin; Schwartz, Christian Friedrich

Bibliography

Jeyaraj, D. *Bartholomäus Ziegenbalg, The Father of Modern Protestant Mission: An Indian Assessment.* ISPCK, 2006; Singh, B. *The First Protestant Missionary to India: Bartholomaeus Ziegenbalg (1683–1719).* Oxford University Press, 1999.

DANIEL JEYARAJ

Ziegenhagen, Friedrich Michael

As a Lutheran clergyman at the English royal court, Friedrich Michael Ziegenhagen (1694–1776) was a key figure in the worldwide operations of Halle Pietism. Born in Pomerania, Ziegenhagen studied at Halle and Jena. In 1722 he was named chaplain of the German Lutheran Court Chapel in London, serving until his death under the Hanoverian kings George I, George II, and George III.

Ziegenhagen not only functioned as pastor and theologian, but his prestigious position and location in the metropolis of London also provided favorable conditions for his independent engagement on behalf of Halle Pietist ventures worldwide. Ziegenhagen worked within a transnational and multiconfessional network and became a member of the influential Society for Promoting Christian Knowledge (SPCK), which supported many of Halle's activities. Amid confessional tensions between Halle and England, Ziegenhagen played an important mediating role. He sought pragmatic solutions to conflicts in the joint Lutheran-Anglican mission to India. He looked after missionaries traveling through London, corresponded with them, and pursued financial support for their work. He cooperated with the SPCK in other areas as well. Ziegenhagen was the first to tell the English public about the expulsion of the Salzburger Protestants, and his work on behalf of the exiles who immigrated to Georgia became indispensable. Especially for Germans seeking to immigrate to British North America, he became a natural contact partner, a role he also played for Lutheran congregations in Pennsylvania prior to and after Henrich Melchior Mühlenberg's arrival. He even provided Mühlenberg with official letters authorizing his call to the congregations there.

See also England; Francke Foundations; India; Mühlenberg, Heinrich (Henry) Melchior; Pietism; Ziegenbalg, Bartholomäus

Bibliography

Brunner, D. L. *Halle Pietists in England*. Vandenhoeck & Ruprecht, 1993; Jetter-Staib, C. *Halle, England und das Reich Gottes Weltweit—Friedrich Michael Ziegenhagen (1694–1776)*. Verlag der Franckeschen Stiftungen Halle, 2013; Threinen, N. J. "Friedrich Michael Ziegenhagen." *Lutheran Theological Review* 22 (2000): 56–94.

CHRISTINA JETTER-STAIB

Zimbabwe

Lutheranism has its traditional stronghold in the rural regions of southern Zimbabwe, but today the membership is also increasing in Bulawayo, Harare, and other urban centers. The Evangelical Lutheran Church in Zimbabwe (ELCZ) reported 242,000 members in 2013. Women, who constitute the majority, have had a significant impact: already in the 1930s, they established a volunteer organization, Vashandiri, which focuses on adult education, theological training, and secular themes such as child care. The ELCZ is a member of the WCC, the LWF, the Fellowship of Evangelical Lutheran Churches in Southern Africa, and the Council of Churches in Zimbabwe.

Lutheranism entered today's Zimbabwe in 1903, when missionaries from the Church of Sweden in Natal moved into what was called Southern Rhodesia. It was agreed with the London Missionary Society and other societies that had already started missionary work that the Church of Sweden would concentrate its activity among the Ndebele people in the southwestern part of the country. The church became independent in 1962. According to Bhebe, the war that led to majority rule had an impact on theological thinking, where black Lutheran clergy in the rural areas supported the guerrillas. After the war, they supported the new government; yet especially the western dioceses suffered from repression in the 1980s. The Christian Council of Zimbabwe started to confront the Mugabe regime under the presidency of Bishop Ambrose Moyo (ELCZ).

Bibliography

Bhebe, N. *The Zapu and Zanu Guerrilla Warfare and the Evangelical Lutheran Church in Zimbabwe*. Mambo, 1999; Söderstrom, H. *God Gave Growth: History of the Lutheran Church in Zimbabwe 1903–1980*. Swedish Institute of Missionary Research, 1984.

FRIEDER LUDWIG

Zinzendorf, Nikolaus Ludwig von

The nobleman and theologian Count Nikolaus Ludwig von Zinzendorf (1700–1760) was founder of the Brüdergemeine (renewed Moravians). Zinzendorf was one of the most provocative and controversial Lutheran luminaries of the eighteenth century. Deeply influenced by the Pietist movement and the Philadelphian movement of Jane Leade, Zinzendorf dedicated himself to global evangelism and ecumenism. He was also the founder of the Brüdergemeine, an ecumenical organization that welcomed Moravian Brethren, Lutherans, Reformed, Anglicans, Mennonites, and radical Pietists.

Zinzendorf was educated at the Pedagogium of the Franckean Institutes in Halle and studied law at the University of Wittenberg. He was largely self-taught in Lutheran theology and church history. His ecumenical work began in earnest with a tour of Western Europe in 1719, during which he visited Dutch Jews and Mennonites and became friends with the primate of the Catholic Church in France. He formed a secret society called the Order of the Grain of the Mustard, which included leaders in different churches who were dedicated to global evangelism.

In 1721 he married Countess Erdmuth Dorothea von Reuss and purchased the estate of Berthelsdorf. The Brüdergemeine began when Protestant refugees from Moravia built the village of Herrnhut on his estate. In 1727 Zinzendorf's Brotherly Agreement allowed the Moravian Brethren to govern their own spiritual affairs while officially remaining in the Lutheran parish of Berthelsdorf. A revival in August of that year generated publicity about the unique religious life of Herrnhut, and the movement spread to other regions in Europe. The Herrnhuters affirmed the Augsburg Confession, but they also developed liturgical innovations modeled on the worship and piety of Christians in the apostolic age, including agape meals, foot washing, and addressing one another as "Brother" and "Sister." Zinzendorf hoped to legitimate his work by securing ordination in the Lutheran Church, which he did in Stralslund in 1734, but his relationship with Halle grew increasingly strained as the Brüdergemeine expanded. In 1732 the Herrnhuters sent their first missionaries to non-European peoples. They established work with enslaved Africans on the island of St. Thomas in 1732 and in Greenland in 1735. Zinzendorf instructed missionaries to respect other cultures and preach in the language of the people rather than forcing European languages and culture on them.

The Saxon government banished Zinzendorf for disturbing the religious peace. For nearly twenty years he lived as a sojourner, changing residence every few years. He made two transatlantic journeys to inspect Moravian missions. The first was to St. Thomas in 1739 and the second to Pennsylvania from late 1741 to early 1743. During that latter visit he lived for several weeks in a Delaware tribal village. While in Pennsylvania, Zinzendorf attempted to implement a bold ecumenical venture that would bring together all German-speaking Protestants in an ecumenical synod called the Church of God in the Spirit. Rather than healing church divisions, his efforts accelerated the formation of ecclesiastic organizations for the Lutherans and German Reformed in America.

In the 1740s Zinzendorf published German and English versions of his sermons. Zinzendorf proposed a rethinking of Lutheran doctrine based on what he called "Religion of the Heart," which was existential rather than rationalistic. He also argued that the Hallensians, Methodists, and deists were Pelagian rather than Pauline in their view of law and grace. His most popular hymn "The Savior's Blood and Righteousness" (or "Jesus, Thy Blood and Righteousness") is his artistic expression of Luther's idea of the alien righteousness of Christ. Thousands were inspired by Zinzendorf's sermons and hymns on Christ as the crucified God, but their devotion to the wounds of Christ, especially his side wound, was often ridiculed in the public forum. Even more controversial was Zinzendorf's insistence that the most appropriate name for the Holy Spirit was "Mother." His claim that sexual intercourse (within marriage) should be an act of religious devotion was also ridiculed by opponents who accused him of antinomianism and immorality. Dozens of volumes of anti-Zinzendorfiana were published during his lifetime, and there were also anti-Moravian riots in England and America in the 1740s.

In 1749 Zinzendorf persuaded the British Parliament to recognize the Unitas Fratrum as an episcopal church whose members were exempt from swearing oaths and bearing arms. His plans to make London his permanent headquarters faltered after a financial crisis in 1753 nearly bankrupted him and the church. Zinzendorf returned to Germany, where he died in 1760. At the time of his death he had followers from Germany to North America, Greenland to India. There was a revival of interest in his theology among Lutherans in the twentieth century.

See also Moravian Church (Unitas Fratrum)

Bibliography
Atwood, C. *Community of the Cross: Moravian Piety in Colonial Bethlehem*. Pennsylvania State University Press, 2005; Freeman, A. *An Ecumenical Theology of the Heart: The Theology of Count Nicholas Ludwig von Zinzendorf*. Moravian Church, 1998; Meyer, D. *Bibliographisches Handbuch zur Zinzendorf-Forschung*. C. Blech, 1987; Meyer, D., and P. Peucker, eds. *Graf ohne Grenzen: Leben und Werk von Nikolaus Ludwig Graf von Zinzendorf*. Unitätsarchiv in Herrnhut, 2000; Weinlick, J. R. *Count Zinzendorf*. Abingdon, 1956. Reprint, Moravian Church, 1989; Zinzendorf, N. L. von. *A Collection of Sermons from Zinzendorf's Pennsylvania Journey. 1741–42*. Ed. C. Atwood. Trans. J. T. Weber. Moravian Church, 2002; Zinzendorf, N. L. von. *Hauptschriften in sechs Bänden*. Ed. E. Beyreuther and G. Meyer. Olms, 1962–65.

CRAIG D. ATWOOD

Zurich

In the 1520s the Swiss city of Zurich was a leading center of the Reformation, second only to Wittenberg and equal to Strasbourg in influence. Ulrich Zwingli had arrived in Zurich in 1519. At Easter 1525 the new Reformation order was established, with the formal abolition of the Mass, the culmination of a process that had lasted two years, during which time the city had adopted the teachings of Zwingli. The influence of Luther in the city was, nevertheless, enormous. In nearby Basel, Luther's works had been published in vast numbers, and many of the talented churchmen assembled by Zwingli in Zurich during the 1520s came from German lands and had embraced Wittenberg's gospel after hearing Luther's message.

The relationship between Luther and Zurich was, however, dominated by the German reformer's conflict with Zwingli and his successors, especially over the Lord's Supper. During the 1520s the polemic was fierce, with the Zurich reformers classed by Luther as an undifferentiated group of "fanatics." The designation caused great offense among the Swiss, who argued that Luther wanted to assert his authority over the whole reform movement and would brook no dissent. For Luther, however, despite their expressed desire for unity, the Swiss were minions of the devil.

The issues on which the Zurichers and Luther differed were significant. As followers of Erasmus, the biblical exegetes in Zurich emphasized philology, an emphasis grounded in their commitment (shared with Wittenberg) to the Hebrew and Greek original texts. During the 1520s the Zurich church leaders worked on a new translation of the Bible into the vernacular, but until the task was completed in the 1530s, the Zurich church continued to rely on Luther's translation. The differences between the two translations, often evident from the marginal comments, demonstrated the different emphases in reading the Bible. The theological emphasis of the Zurichers constructed the continuity of the Old Testament in the New through God's various covenants. They did not adopt as central Luther's distinction between law (God's word of judgment) and gospel (God's word of forgiveness).

The difference in reading Scripture led to the most significant debate between Zurich and Luther over the Lord's Supper and the understanding of the words of institution. At the heart of the matter was the "is" in Christ's statement, "This *is* my body." Zwingli read the passage to mean, "This *signifies* my body," a position that Luther rejected. They also disagreed on Christ's ascension to the right hand of God. Zwingli was eager for agreement, despite the polemic on both sides, for he envisaged a Protestant union that would extend from the Rhine to the Baltic Sea. For that hope to be realized, agreement on the sacrament was needed. But while the Marburg Colloquy of

1529, held under the aegis of Landgrave Philip of Hesse, revealed to each side the strengths and conviction of the other, agreement proved elusive.

The struggle between Zurich and Wittenberg over the Lord's Supper dogged the Reformation movement during its first decade. In the South German cities, Zwingli's influence was extensive because of the attractiveness of his teaching on the Lord's Supper and the relative political power of the canton. Traditional connections between the German imperial cities and the Swiss aided the spread of Swiss theology. Zwingli's death, in 1531 during the Second War of Kappel, greatly diminished the influence of the Swiss Reformed churches. Under Zwingli's successor, Heinrich Bullinger, relations did not improve with Luther or the other Wittenberg theologians, and the sticking point remained the Lord's Supper. With the Wittenberg Concord of 1536, Swiss theological influence in the German Empire lessened. The Swiss, principally Zurich, were isolated as Bullinger turned his attention to rebuilding the ministry of his church.

Under Bullinger, however, the Zurich church would reemerge in the 1540s as a leading voice of the European Reformation. This transformation had begun before Luther's death in 1546. Disagreement continued to the end, however, with Luther roundly rejecting a 1543 gift of the Zurich Latin Bible, sent by the printer Froschauer. Zurich and Wittenberg would not be reconciled, though Philip Melanchthon remained in correspondence with Bullinger. Zurich gained new standing when Bullinger and John Calvin forged an agreement in 1549, the Zurich Consensus, but their alliance did not end hostility with Lutherans.

See also Bullinger, Heinrich; Marburg Colloquy; Switzerland; Wittenberg Concord; Zwingli, Ulrich

Bibliography

Gordon, B. *The Swiss Reformation*. Manchester University Press, 2002; Potter, G. R. *Zwingli*. Cambridge University Press, 1976; Wandel, L. P. *The Eucharist in the Reformation*. Cambridge University Press, 2006.

BRUCE GORDON

Zwingli, Ulrich

As pastor and reformer in Zurich, Ulrich (Huldrych/Huldreich) Zwingli (1484–1531) was one of Luther's chief opponents in the eucharistic controversy and a founding figure for both the Reformed and Anabaptist traditions. Zwingli came from a family of prosperous peasants and local officials in the village of Wildhaus in Toggenburg, an area in eastern Switzerland subject to the abbey of St. Gallen. He attended schools in Basel and Bern, then studied at the universities in Vienna and Basel, both early centers of humanism. Zwingli received his master's degree in arts in Basel in 1506. Unlike Luther, who was trained as a nominalist, Zwingli followed the *via antiqua*, the realist philosophy of Thomas Aquinas, which taught a necessary connection between perceptions of the world and of the reality, including God, that lay beyond it. Zwingli studied theology for only one semester before becoming parish pastor in Glarus in the summer of 1506. Over the next ten years, he continued his humanistic literary pursuits and his independent study of Scholastic theology, including the works of Thomas Aquinas and John Duns Scotus. In the fall of 1515, he accompanied the Glarus contingent of Swiss mercenaries to Italy, where he witnessed their crushing defeat in the Battle of Marignano. This turned Zwingli against mercenary service, and in his later preaching he would denounce the hiring of mercenaries by foreign powers. In 1516 Zwingli became the priest responsible for the pastoral care of visitors to the abbey and pilgrimage church of Einsiedeln, where he continued his independent studies. Spurred by his encounter with Erasmus, Zwingli added the Bible and the church fathers to his earlier interests in humanist and classical authors. Particularly important for Zwingli's development was the Neoplatonic distinction between body and spirit that he found in both Renaissance philosophers and in Erasmus.

Zwingli's sermons brought him to the attention of the canons of the Great Minster (Grossmünster) in Zurich, and in December

1518 he was elected to a position that combined preaching with pastoral care of the Great Minster's clergy. With his first sermon on January 1, 1519, Zwingli broke with the medieval practice of following the traditional lectionary and began to preach on the Gospel of Matthew in the form of a running commentary. His sermons over the next few years reflected a deeper reading of Augustine and of Luther's works, combined with an Erasmian emphasis on the Scripture text and on criticism of ecclesiastical abuses. In March 1522 he attended a gathering in which others deliberately broke the Lenten fast by eating pieces of sausage. His sermon defending the fast-breakers was published soon afterward and contributed to the Evangelical ferment in the city. Efforts by the bishop of Constance to muzzle dissent led to a public disputation in Zurich on January 29, 1523; as a result of the disputation, the Zurich Council endorsed Zwingli's preaching. Zwingli wrote a summary of his teaching in the form of Sixty-Seven Articles for the disputation, and the following summer he published *Auslegen und Gründe der Schlussreden* (Analysis and reasons for the articles), which spread his ideas to a wider audience. Disagreement over the pace of introducing practical reforms in Zurich led to a second disputation in October. Zwingli's acceptance of the Zurich Council's right to control the timing and degree of reforms disillusioned some of his more radical followers, who eventually broke with him over the issue of infant baptism. A disputation in January 1525 failed to resolve the issue, and on January 21 the radicals performed their first adult baptisms. Over the next two years Zwingli wrote three treatises against the Anabaptists. At the heart of their disagreement was Zwingli's view that the political and religious communities were joined as one Christian body (*corpus Christianum*); he rejected the voluntary church of the Anabaptists.

Zwingli's dispute with the Anabaptists was made more difficult by the fact that they shared his belief that the sacraments did not convey grace but instead entailed an act of confession made by believers. This had implications for his understanding of the Lord's Supper. By the summer of 1524 Zwingli had abandoned belief in Christ's real presence in the Eucharist and adopted the suggestion of Cornelis Hoen that Christ's words of institution mean "This signifies my body." When Karlstadt's eucharistic pamphlets were published that fall, Zwingli felt compelled to distinguish his own understanding of the sacrament from that of Karlstadt; he did so in his short *Ad Matthaeum Alberum de Coena Dominica Epistola* (Letter to Matthew Alber concerning the Lord's Supper) and in a section of his much longer *De Vera et Falsa Religione Commentarius* (Commentary on true and false religion), a presentation of Evangelical teaching addressed to the king of France. Over the next two years Zwingli published several shorter works elaborating his understanding of the Lord's Supper. The Zurich Council replaced the Mass with a Reformed Lord's Supper at Easter in 1525; publication of the liturgy helped advertise this change. Zwingli's most dangerous opponents were the Catholic theologians who pressured the diet (*Tagsatzung*) of Swiss cantons to condemn Zwingli as a heretic and force Zurich to abandon its religious innovations. John Eck challenged Zwingli to a disputation, which was held in Baden in May–June 1526, but Zwingli did not attend out of fear for his safety; in his place Johannes Oecolampadius defended a symbolic understanding of the Eucharist. In the spring of 1527 Zwingli published two works addressed to Luther: *Amica Exegesis* (Friendly exegesis) and *Früntlich verglimpfung vnd ableynung* (Friendly moderation and defense). The publication of these treatises coincided with Luther's first direct attack on Zwingli and Oecolampadius (*That These Words 'This Is My Body' . . . Still Stand Firm against the Fanatics*; LW 37:3–150) in 1527, and Luther responded to these treatises in his *Confession concerning Christ's Supper* (1528; LW 37:151–372). Luther and Zwingli met for the only time at the Marburg Colloquy in 1529.

After three days of fruitless debate over the sacrament, the two sides accepted fifteen articles, fourteen of which stated positions shared by both parties. The fifteenth article rejected the Catholic understanding of the Mass but acknowledged Evangelical disagreement over the correct understanding of the Lord's Supper. Zwingli prepared his personal confession of faith (*Ratio Fidei* [An account of the faith]) to be presented to the emperor at the Diet of Augsburg (1530); he restated his positions in the confession he wrote for the King of France a year later (*Expositio Fidei* [A short and clear exposition of the faith]). Luther regarded these confessions as a retreat from what had been agreed on at Marburg, which contributed to the vehemence with which he condemned Zwingli in his *Brief Confession concerning the Holy Sacrament* (1544; LW 38:279–319).

In 1525 Zwingli and his colleagues began holding the "Prophecy," daily lectures interpreting and explaining the text of the Bible in the original languages, which were intended as remedial education for the city's clergy. Zwingli's exegetical work would be published as commentaries both during his lifetime and posthumously. These lectures also contributed to the Zurich Bible, a translation published in 1529. The Prophecy itself would eventually be institutionalized within the Carolinum, the highest level of the city's Latin school system.

Zwingli also pushed for the spread of Evangelical teachings outside of Zurich. In January 1528 he was one of several reformers invited to participate in a disputation in Bern. The theses debated reflected Zwingli's theology and resulted in that city's official adoption of the Reformation. This increased tensions with the five Catholic cantons of central Switzerland, and armed conflict (the First Kappel War) was only narrowly averted in 1529. The spread of Evangelical preachers into territories governed jointly with the Catholics exacerbated the situation, and Zwingli urged war against the Catholic cantons. A food blockade enforced by Zurich led the Catholic cantons to declare war against the city and its Evangelical allies. On October 11, 1531, the Zurich army was defeated by a much larger army from the Catholic cantons. A significant number of Zurich's political and religious leaders were killed, including Zwingli, who was serving as a chaplain with the Zurich army. The defeat led to a popular backlash against the pastors' political influence in Zurich. Zwingli's successor, Heinrich Bullinger (1501–75), bore much of the responsibility for stabilizing the church in the aftermath of Zwingli's death and for defending Zwingli's memory and theology during his long tenure in office.

See also Bullinger, Heinrich; Marburg Colloquy; Oecolampadius, Johannes; Switzerland; Zurich

Bibliography

Bolliger, D. *Infiniti Contemplatio: Grundzüge der Scotus- und Scotismusrezeption im Werk Huldrych Zwinglis: Mit ausführlicher Edition bisher unpublizierter Annotationes Zwinglis*. Brill, 2003; Bromiley, G. W., ed. *Zwingli and Bullinger: Selected Translations with Introductions and Notes*. Westminster, 1953; Furcha, E. J., ed. *Huldrych Zwingli, 1484–1531: A Legacy of Radical Reform; Papers from the 1984 International Zwingli Symposium*. McGill University, 1985; Furcha, E. J., and H. W. Pipkin, eds. *Huldrych Zwingli: Writings*. 2 vols. Pickwick, 1984; Gäbler, U. *Huldrych Zwingli: His Life and Work*. Fortress, 1986; Jackson, S. M., et al., eds. *The Latin Works and the Correspondence of Huldreich Zwingli: Together with Selections from His German Works*. 3 vols. Putnam's Sons, 1912–29; Locher, G. W. *Zwingli's Thought: New Perspectives*. Brill, 1981; Potter, G. R. *Zwingli*. Cambridge University Press, 1976; Stephens, W. P. *The Theology of Huldrych Zwingli*. Clarendon, 1986; Zwingli, U. *Huldreich Zwinglis sämtliche Werke*. Ed. E. Egli et al. CR 88–108. Heinsius / TVZ, 1905–91.

Amy Nelson Burnett

List of Entries

Name Index

Greiffenberg, Catharina Regina von, 240

Greiner, Johann Jakob, **304–5**, 720–21

Gribaldi, Matteo, 29

Griesbach, J. J., 212, 222

Grīnbergs, Teodors, **305**, 410

Gritsch, Eric, 334

Gronau, Israel Christian, 95, 200, 566

Gronenberg, Johann, 90

Gropper, Johann, 55

Gropper, Johannes, 107, 123, 636

Großgebauer, Theophil, 28, 169

Grotius, Hugo, 115

Grumbach, Argula von, 275, **305**, 787, 796

Grundmann, Walter, 286

Grundtvig, Nikolai F. S., xxi, 82, 184, 190, 193, **306**, 351, 522

Gruner, Helen, 421

Grynaeus, Simon, 174

Gudhart, Augusta, 408

Guéroult, Guillaume, 681

Gunderson, Adolphus L., **307–8**, 510, 707

Gunderson, Marie, 308, 706

Gussick, Robert, 216, 307, 340

Gustaf, Karl X, 540

Gutenberg, Johannes, 621

Gutiérrez, Gustavo, 423, 424

Güttel, Caspar, 27

Gützlaff, Karl Friedrich August, 139, 511, 727

Gwynne, Sarah, 779

Habermann, Johann, 188, 192, 611

Haeckel, Ernst, 203

Hafenreffer, Matthew, 322

Haferitz, Simon, 524

Haller, Johann, 526

Hallesby, Ole, 193, 611

Hamann, Johann Georg, 81, 212, 296, **311–12**, 597

Hambré, Jonas, 263

Hamilton, Patrick, 5, **313**

Hamm, Heinrich, 27

Hammarskjöld, Dag, **313–14**

Handel, George Frederick, 566, 724

Hans of Brandenburg-Küstrin (margrave), 380

Haraldsson, Olva, 550

Harboe, Ludvig, 353

Hardenberg, Albert, 104, 137, 517

Harms, Claus, 193, **314**, 626, 634

Harms, Louis, 508

Harms, Ludwig, **314**, 720

Harms, Theodor, 508

Harnack, Adolf von, **314–16**
  and Hermann Sasse, 661
  Jesus Christ, 537

justification, 252, 388
  and Karl Holl, 330
  liberalism, 421, 422
  and Luther, 252, 388, 416, 468, 585
  and Paul Tillich, 747
  social service, 692
  and Word War I, 801

Harnack, Theodosius Andreas, **316–17**, 388, 416, 467

Harran, M., 168

Hartmann, Nicolai, 199

Hartwig, Peter, 683

Hasenburg, Zbyněk von, 348–49

Hasselquist, T. N., 56

Hätzer, Ludwig, 90

Hauge, Alfred, 317

Hauge, Hans Nielsen, 166, 193, **317–18**, 551, 553, 603

Hauswig, Katharina von, 98

Hedberg, Fredrik Gabriel, 250, 251, 509

Hedio, Caspar, 107, 705

Heerbrand, Jakob, 150

Heermann, Johann, 193, 231, 351

Hefner, Philip, 179, 239

Hegel, Georg Wilhelm Friedrich, 81, 95, 214, 295–96, 311, **318–20**, 327, 339, 399, 570, 597, 647, 736

Hegge, Jakob, 625

Heidegger, Martin, 111, 241, 747

Heim, Karl, 5, 37, 178, **320–21**

Heinmann, E. N., 510

Heinrich, Duke, 490

Helding, Michael, 55

Helgesen, Poul, 188, 189

Helmer, Christine, 394

Helmuth, Justus H. C., 665

Hemmingsen, Niels, 189, **322–23**, 785

Hengstenberg, Ernst Wilhelm, **323**

Henry, Duke, 214, 283, 663, 690

Henry II, 261

Henry VIII, 5, 76–77, 113, 174, 175, 215, 218, 219, **323–24**, 329, 474, 530

Henry of Uppsala, 248

Herakleides, Jakobos Basilikos, 196

Herder, Johann Gottfried, 312

Heresbach, Konrad, 123

Hermann, Nikolaus, 188, 324

Hermann, Rudolf, 330, 375, 737

Hermann of Schildesche, 60

Herrgott, Hans, 90

Herrmann, Wilhelm, 422, 537

Herzfeld, Will, 679

Hess, Tobias, 20

Hesshus, Gottfried, 325

Hesshus, Heinrich, 325

Hesshus, Tilemann, 85, 257, **324–25**, 480, 494, 625, 790

Hessus, Eobanus, 201

Heubach, Joachim, 200

Heussi, Karl, 373

Heyer, John Christian Frederick, 279, 325, 364, 502, 510

Heyling, Peter, 234, 498, 507

Hilary of Poitiers, 89

Hildebrand, Carl, 91, **326**

Hilgendorf, Dennis, 499

Hirsch, Emanuel, 286, 330–31, 468

Hitler, Adolf, 6, 78, 215, 229, 290, 331–32, 381, 518, 543, 580, 801

Hobbes, Thomas, 418, 419

Hodnefield, Olava, 140

Hodža, Michal Miloslav, 348

Hoederkamp, Robert, 216

Hoen, Cornelius, 436

Hoenecke, Adolf, 782

Hoffman, Melchior, 231, **328–29**

Hoffmann, Daniel, 536

Hoffmann, Johannes C. K. von, 49–50, 228, **327–28**, 417, 675

Hogstad, Jon Peder, 479

Hogstad, Oline, 479

Hohenau, Ernst Christoph Hochmann von, 602

Holbein, Hans, the Younger, **329**

Holberg, Ludvig, 190, **329–30**

Hölderlin, Friedrich, 218

Holl, Karl, **330–31**
  Anabaptists, 17
  and Hans Iwand, 375
  and Hermann Sasse, 661
  justification, 386, 388
  liberalism, 422
  and Luther, 142, 375, 386, 388, 422
  Luther Renaissance, xxi, 291, 467, 468
  and Paul Althaus, 5
  and Philip Melanchthon, 495
  predestination, 614
  salvation, 656

Hollatz, David, 35, 616

Hollazius, David, 322

Holt, Samuel, 631

Honterus, Johannes, **341**, 345

Hoogsträten, Jacob, 474

Hooper, John, 119

Hopf, Friedrich Wilhelm, 33

Hoppe, A. F., 476

Horn, Edward T., 431

Hotzen, Joanna Mary Magdalene, 701

Høyer, Marie, 499

Huber, Samuel, 616

Hubmaier, Balthasar, 52

Hume, David, 536

Hunnius, Aegidius, 616

Hunnius, Nikolaus, 30

Subject Index

Note: A boldface number directs readers to an article dedicated to the subject.

Act of Six Articles, 5, 77, 219, 324
Act of Supremacy, 215–16
Act of Uniformity, 216, 220
Adam, 204, 275, 416, 564, 565, 623, 674, 800
Address to the Christian Nobility (Luther), 67, 358, 504, 701
adiaphora, **1–2**, 40, 256, 355
Adventist tradition, 209
African Independent Churches, 248
African National Congress (ANC), 32
Against Hanswurst (Luther), 147
Against the Antinomians, 3
Against the Heavenly Prophets: Concerning Images and the Sacraments (Luther), 45, 146, 642
Against the Murderous, Thieving Peasant Hordes (Luther), 583
Allstedt, 524
Alpha Synod, 8
Altenburg Colloquy, 152
Altona Confession, **6–7**
American Association of Lutheran Churches (AALC), 452
American Civil War, **7–9**, 279
American Evangelical Lutheran Church (AELC), 183, 184, 235
American Indian Movement, 94
American Lutheran Church
  1930–60, **9–10**, 561, 638
  1960–88, **10–11**, 451, 763–64, 807
American Lutheran Church, The (TALC), 10, 11, 164, 183
American Lutheran Church in America, 554
American Lutheran Conference, 10, 57
American Lutheranism, **11–14**, 404–5, 446–47, **451–52**, 500, 617–18, 665, 666, 730–31, 760–64, 801, 802
American Revolution, 123–24, 201
Anabaptists, **14–18**
  and Andreas Karlstadt, 396
  ecumenism, 209
  and Johannes Brenz, 105
  Kingdom of Münster, 15, 16
  and Luther, 27, 66, 445, 655, 749

Lutheran World Federation, 464
  and Martin Bucer, 107, 163
  and Melchior Hoffmann, 328–29
  and Philip Melanchthon, 493
  punishment, 66, 105
  Swiss, 714
  tradition, 748
  and Ulrich Zwingli, 814
Anglicanism. *See* Church of England
Angola, **21**
Annotations (Erasmus), 224
anniversaries, 634–35
Ansbach Memorandum (Ansbacher Ratschlag), 5, **21**
anthropology, theological, **21–24**
anti-Catholicism, 132. *See also* Roman Catholicism
Anti-Conventicle Act, 166
antinomian controversies, 3, **25–29**, 412, 415–16
Anti-racist Program (WCC), 32
anti-Semitism, 285–86, 291, 332, 381, 777, 802
antitrinitarianism, **29–30**, 123, 680–81
Antwerp, 538–39
apartheid, **30–34**, 463, 695
apocrypha, **34–35**
apologetics, **36–38**
Apology of the Augsburg Confession, **38–40**, 162, 565
Apostles' Creed, 129–30, 146, 179, 180, 225, 315, 330
Apostolicum dispute, 315
Appeal for Peace: A Response to the Twelve Articles (Luther), 583
architecture, **40–41**
Argentina, **42**
Arminianism, 120, 220
ars moriendi, 186, 187
art, 44–46, 172–74. *See also* images
Aryan clause/paragraph, 5, 21, 156, 285, 332, 543
Association of Evangelical Churches, 11
Association of Evangelical Communities of Santa Catarina and Paraná, 103
Association of Evangelical Lutheran Churches (AELC), 678–79, 764
Association of Free Lutheran Congregations, 451–52

astrology, **46–47**, 534
astronomy, 100–101, 534
Athanasian Creed, 179, 180
atonement, **48–51**, 328, 388
Augsburg, **52–53**
Augsburg Confession (CA), xxiii, **53–55**
  adiaphora, 1–2
  American Lutheranism, 11, 12, 13, 14
  Anabaptists, 16–17
  anniversary, 635
  authority, 66–67
  baptism, 74
  Brazil, 356
  and Charles V, 136, 213
  civil affairs, 745
  confession (of faith), 161, 405
  confession (rite), 158
  ecclesiology, 147
  ecumenism, 206
  and Elizabeth I, 220
  faith, 299
  free will, 270
  Lord's Supper, 152
  other confessions, 79
  Peace of Augsburg, 580
  Philip Melanchthon, 16, 366, 492
  Pittsburgh Declaration, 405
  Reformed tradition, 262
  revised, 75
  sacraments, 655
  sin, 563
  Smalcaldic League, 690
  subscribers, 182
  Wittenberg Concord, 794
  works, 299
  See also Apology of the Augsburg Confession
Augsburg Interim, 55, 803
  and Charles V, 2, 52
  and Elector Moritz, 214
  and Jakob Andreae, 18
  and Joachim II, 3, 383
  and Johann Agricola, 3
  and Johannes Brenz, 105–6
  and Johannes Bugenhagen, 108, 109
  and Leipzig Proposal, 419
  and Magdeburg, 480
  and Martin Bucer, 108
  and Matthias Flacius, 256